THE OXFORD HANDBOOK OF

THE PHILOSOPHY OF CONSCIOUSNESS

The Oxford Handbook of the Philosophy of Consciousness provides the most comprehensive overview of current philosophical research on consciousness. Featuring contributions from some of the most prominent experts in the field, it explores the wide range of types of consciousness there may be, the many psychological phenomena with which consciousness interacts, and the various views concerning the ultimate relationship between consciousness and physical reality. It is an essential and authoritative resource for anyone working in philosophy of mind or interested in states of consciousness.

THE OXFORD HANDBOOK OF

THE PHILOSOPHY OF CONSCIOUSNESS

Edited by
URIAH KRIEGEL

Great Clarendon Street, Oxford, OX2 6DP,
United Kingdom

Oxford University Press is a department of the University of Oxford.
It furthers the University's objective of excellence in research, scholarship,
and education by publishing worldwide. Oxford is a registered trade mark of
Oxford University Press in the UK and in certain other countries

© the several contributors 2020

The moral rights of the authors have been asserted

First published 2020
First published in paperback 2023

All rights reserved. No part of this publication may be reproduced, stored in
a retrieval system, or transmitted, in any form or by any means, without the
prior permission in writing of Oxford University Press, or as expressly permitted
by law, by licence or under terms agreed with the appropriate reprographics
rights organization. Enquiries concerning reproduction outside the scope of the
above should be sent to the Rights Department, Oxford University Press, at the
address above

You must not circulate this work in any other form
and you must impose this same condition on any acquirer

Published in the United States of America by Oxford University Press
198 Madison Avenue, New York, NY 10016, United States of America

British Library Cataloguing in Publication Data
Data available

Library of Congress Cataloging in Publication Data
Data available

ISBN 978–0–19–874967–7 (Hbk.)
ISBN 978–0–19–889965–5 (Pbk.)

Links to third party websites are provided by Oxford in good faith and
for information only. Oxford disclaims any responsibility for the materials
contained in any third party website referenced in this work.

The manufacturer's authorised representative in the EU for product safety is
Oxford University Press España S.A. of El Parque Empresarial San Fernando de Henares,
Avenida de Castilla, 2 – 28830 Madrid (www.oup.es/en or product.safety@oup.com).
OUP España S.A. also acts as importer into Spain of products made by the manufacturer.

Contents

List of Contributors	ix
Introduction: What is the Philosophy of Consciousness? URIAH KRIEGEL	1
1. The Problem of Consciousness DAVID PAPINEAU	14

PART I VARIETIES OF CONSCIOUS EXPERIENCE

2. Visual Experience PÄR SUNDSTRÖM	39
3. Non-Visual Perception CASEY O'CALLAGHAN	66
4. Bodily Feelings: Presence, Agency, and Ownership FRÉDÉRIQUE DE VIGNEMONT	82
5. Emotional Experience: Affective Consciousness and its Role in Emotion Theory JULIEN DEONNA AND FABRICE TERONI	102
6. Imaginative Experience AMY KIND	124
7. Conscious Thought TIM BAYNE	142
8. The Experience of Agency MYRTO MYLOPOULOS AND JOSHUA SHEPHERD	164
9. Temporal Consciousness PHILIPPE CHUARD	188

10. The Phenomenal Unity of Consciousness 208
    Farid Masrour

PART II THEORIES OF CONSCIOUSNESS

11. The Neural Correlates of Consciousness 233
    Jorge Morales and Hakwan Lau

12. Beyond the Neural Correlates of Consciousness 261
    Uriah Kriegel

13. Dualism: How Epistemic Issues Drive Debates about the Ontology of Consciousness 277
    Brie Gertler

14. Russellian Monism 301
    Philip Goff and Sam Coleman

15. Idealism: Putting Qualia To Work 328
    Michael Pelczar

16. Eliminativism about Consciousness 348
    Elizabeth Irvine and Mark Sprevak

17. A Priori Physicalism 371
    Frank Jackson

18. A Posteriori Physicalism: Type-B Materialism and the Explanatory Gap 387
    Joseph Levine

19. Representationalism about Consciousness 405
    Adam Pautz

20. Higher-Order Theories of Consciousness 438
    Josh Weisberg

21. Self-Representationalist Theories of Consciousness 458
    Tom McClelland

22. The Epistemic Approach to the Problem of Consciousness 482
    Daniel Stoljar

PART III CONSCIOUSNESS AND NEIGHBORING PHENOMENA

23. Consciousness and Attention — 499
    CHRISTOPHER MOLE

24. Consciousness and Memory — 520
    CHRISTOPHER S. HILL

25. Consciousness and Action: Contemporary Empirical Arguments for Epiphenomenalism — 538
    BENJAMIN KOZUCH

26. Consciousness and Intentionality — 560
    ANGELA MENDELOVICI AND DAVID BOURGET

27. Consciousness and Knowledge — 586
    BERIT BROGAARD AND ELIJAH CHUDNOFF

28. Consciousness, Introspection, and Subjective Measures — 610
    MAJA SPENER

29. Consciousness and Selfhood: Getting Clearer on For-Me-Ness and Mineness — 635
    DAN ZAHAVI

30. Consciousness and Morality — 654
    JOSHUA SHEPHERD AND NEIL LEVY

31. Embodied Consciousness — 673
    MARK ROWLANDS

Index — 689

List of Contributors

Tim Bayne completed an undergraduate degree in Philosophy and Religious Studies at the University of Otago (New Zealand), and a PhD in Philosophy at the University of Arizona. He has taught at Macquarie University, the University of Western Ontario, the University of Manchester, and the University of Oxford. He is currently Professor of Philosophy at Monash University, Melbourne Australia. He is an editor of *The Oxford Companion to Consciousness* and the author of *The Unity of Consciousness* (Oxford 2010), *Thought: A Very Short Introduction* (Oxford 2013), and *Philosophy of Religion: A Very Short Introduction* (Oxford 2018).

David Bourget is associate professor of philosophy and director of the Centre for Digital Philosophy at the University of Western Ontario. He has written numerous articles on the nature of consciousness and its place in the mind. He also manages major services and projects that advance philosophical research through technology, such as PhilPapers.org.

Berit 'Brit' Brogaard is Professor of Philosophy at University of Miami. Her areas of research include philosophy of mind, philosophy of language, and cognitive science. She is the author of the books *Transient Truths* (Oxford 2012), *On Romantic Love* (Oxford 2015), *The Superhuman Mind* (Penguin 2015), and *Seeing and Saying* (Oxford 2018).

Philippe Chuard is associate professor of philosophy at SMU in Dallas (Texas). He has published articles in the philosophy of perception (nonconceptual content, phenomenal sorites) and in epistemology. His current research is on the nature of temporal experience, working on a book entitled *The Temporal Mind: A Philosophical Introduction*, as well as another book defending the snapshot conception of temporal experiences.

Elijah Chudnoff is associate professor of philosophy at the University of Miami. He has written papers and books exploring the role of conscious experience in both a priori and empirical inquiry. He is currently working on a book about expertise.

Sam Coleman is reader in philosophy at the University of Hertfordshire.

Julien Deonna is associate professor in philosophy at the University of Geneva and project leader at the Swiss Centre in Affective Sciences.

Brie Gertler is Commonwealth Professor of Philosophy at the University of Virginia. Her work focuses on epistemic and metaphysical questions about the mind. She is the author of *Self-Knowledge* (Routledge 2011), as well as numerous articles on self-knowledge, dualism, mental content, and the self.

Philip Goff is Assistant Professor of Philosophy at Durham University. His work is focused on how to integrate consciousness into our scientific worldview, and he defends panpsychism on the grounds that it avoids the difficulties faced by the more traditional options of physicalism and dualism. He has published an academic book on this topic – *Consciousness and Fundamental Reality* (Oxford 2017) – as well as a book aimed at a general audience – *Galileo's Error: Foundations for a New Science of Consciousness* (Rider in UK, Pantheon in US). Goff has also published in newspapers and magazines, such the *Guardian*, *Scientific American*, the *Times Literary Supplement* and *Philosophy Now*.

Christopher S. Hill is William Herbert Perry Faunce Professor of Philosophy at Brown University. Hill has written numerous articles and four books: *Sensations* (Cambridge), *Thought and World* (Cambridge), *Consciousness* (Cambridge), and *Meaning, Mind, and Knowledge* (Oxford). He has also edited several collections, most recently joining with Brian McLaughlin to edit *New Essays in the Philosophy of Perception* (*Philosophical Topics*, Volume 44, Issue 2).

Elizabeth Irvine is lecturer in philosophy at Cardiff University. Her research interests are primarily in philosophy of cognitive science and psychology, and philosophy of science. She has published in journals such as *Mind and Language*, *Synthese*, and won the 2016 Sir Karl Popper Essay Prize for an article published in the *British Journal for Philosophy of Science*.

Frank Jackson is an emeritus professor at The Australian National University. His books include *Conditionals*, *From Metaphysics to Ethics*, and *Language, Names, and Information*.

Amy Kind is Russell K. Pitzer Professor of Philosophy at Claremont McKenna College. Her research interests lie broadly in the philosophy of mind, but most of her work centers on issues relating to imagination and to phenomenal consciousness. In addition to authoring the introductory textbook *Persons and Personal Identity* (Polity 2015), she has edited *The Routledge Handbook of Philosophy of Imagination* (Routledge 2016) and *Philosophy of Mind in the Twentieth and Twenty-first Centuries* (Routledge 2018), and she has co-edited *Knowledge through Imagination* (Oxford 2016).

Benjamin Kozuch received his doctorate in philosophy from the University of Arizona in 2013, and is now assistant professor at the University of Alabama. Much of his research involves using neuroscientific data to evaluate philosophical theories of consciousness. He also conducts research regarding visual illusions, and the nature of pain experiences. Before coming to philosophy, Benjamin was a freelance bassist in New Orleans, and he currently competitively mountain bikes.

Uriah Kriegel is the author of many articles on consciousness, as well as four books: *Subjective Consciousness: A Self-Representational Theory* (Oxford 2009), *The Sources of Intentionality* (Oxford 2011), *The Varieties of Consciousness* (Oxford 2015), and *Brentano's Philosophical System: Mind, Being, Value* (Oxford 2018).

Hakwan Lau is associate professor at Hong Kong University, and a member of the State Key Laboratory for Brain & Cognitive Science (HKU). He also holds a tenured position at UCLA, where he directs a laboratory funded partly by the US National Institute of Health.

Joseph Levine is professor of philosophy at the University of Massachusetts Amherst. He received his PhD from Harvard in 1981 and has taught at N.C. State University and the Ohio State University. He works in philosophy of mind, with a focus on the problem of consciousness. He published *Purple Haze: The Puzzle of Consciousness* in 2001, and in 2018 a collection of his papers entitled *Quality and Content: Essays on Representation, Consciousness, and Modality*.

Neil Levy is professor of philosophy at Macquarie University, Sydney, and a senior researcher at the Uehiro Centre for Practical Ethics, University of Oxford. He is the author of seven books, including, most recently, *Consciousness and Moral Responsibility* (Oxford 2014).

Tom McClelland is a lecturer at the University of Cambridge. He works in various topics in philosophy of mind, including mental action, cognitive phenomenology, perceptual content, and the explanatory gap. He also dabbles in philosophy of film.

Farid Masrour is Vilas Associate Professor of Philosophy at University of Madison-Wisconsin. His primary area of research is philosophy of mind, epistemology, and Kant's theoretical philosophy. He is currently working on a Kant-inspired book on perception.

Angela Mendelovici is associate professor of philosophy at the University of Western Ontario. She works in philosophy of mind, focusing on consciousness, intentionality, and the relationship between consciousness and intentionality. Her recent book, *The Phenomenal Basis of Intentionality*, argues for a version of the phenomenal intentionality theory, on which all intentionality ultimately derives from phenomenal consciousness.

Christopher Mole teaches in the Department of Philosophy at the University of British Columbia, where he is also the chair of the Programme in Cognitive Systems.

Jorge Morales is a postdoctoral research fellow at the Psychological and Brain Sciences Department at Johns Hopkins University. His research lies on the intersection of philosophy of mind and cognitive science. In philosophy, he works on consciousness and introspection. In his research in cognitive neuroscience, he studies the psychological and neural mechanisms of metacognition, consciousness, perception, and attention.

Myrto Mylopoulos is assistant professor in the Department of Philosophy and the Institute of Cognitive Science at Carleton University in Ottawa, Canada. Her research interests include the phenomenology of agency, action control, skill, consciousness, and self-control.

Casey O'Callaghan is professor of philosophy at Washington University in St Louis. He is author of *Sounds* (Oxford 2007), *Beyond Vision* (Oxford 2017), and A *Multisensory Philosophy of Perception* (Oxford 2019).

David Papineau is professor of philosophy of science at King's College London and distinguished professor of philosophy at the City University of New York. He has served as president of the Aristotelian Society, the Mind Association, and the British Society for the Philosophy of Science. His most recent books are *Thinking About Consciousness* (Oxford 2003), *Philosophical Devices* (Oxford 2012) and *Knowing the Score* (Little Brown 2017).

Adam Pautz is a Professor of Philosophy at Brown University specializing in philosophy of mind and metaphysics. He has recently been pursuing a 'consciousness-first' program in the philosophy of mind. His book *Perception* is forthcoming with Routledge.

Michael Pelczar is associate professor of philosophy at the National University of Singapore. His main interests are in metaphysics, philosophy of mind, and philosophy of language. He is the author of *Sensorama: A Phenomenalist Analysis of Spacetime and Its Contents* (Oxford 2015).

Mark Rowlands (D.Phil., Oxford University) is Professor of Philosophy at the University of Miami. He is the author of nineteen books, translated into more than twenty languages, and over a hundred journal articles, book chapters, and reviews, which incorporate interests in the philosophy of mind, ethics, moral psychology, and phenomenology.

Joshua Shepherd is assistant professor in the Philosophy Department at Carleton University. He is also a research professor at the University of Barcelona, where he is the principal investigator on the project Rethinking Conscious Agency. In the past he has been a Wellcome Trust Research Fellow at the Oxford Uehiro Centre for Practical Ethics, and a junior research fellow at Jesus College, Oxford.

Maja Spener is lecturer in the Department of Philosophy at the University of Birmingham (UK). She is writing a book on introspection and introspective method in philosophy and scientific psychology.

Mark Sprevak is senior lecturer in philosophy at the University of Edinburgh. His primary research interests are in philosophy of mind, philosophy of science, and metaphysics, with particular focus on the cognitive sciences. He has published articles in, among other places, *The Journal of Philosophy*, *The British Journal for the Philosophy of Science*, *Synthese*, *Philosophy, Psychiatry & Psychology*, and *Studies in History and Philosophy of Science*. He is also the author of *The Computational Mind*, published by Routledge.

Daniel Stoljar is professor of philosophy at the Australian National University. He is the author, among other things, of *Ignorance and Imagination: The Epistemic Origin of the Problem of Consciousness* (Oxford University Press), *Physicalism* (Routledge) and *Philosophical Progress: In Defence of a Reasonable Optimism* (Oxford University Press).

Pär Sundström is professor of philosophy at Umeå University. He has published articles on consciousness, perception, colour, and the connections (and lack of connections) between thought and experience.

Fabrice Teroni is associate professor at the universities of Geneva and Fribourg. He works in the philosophy of mind and epistemology, with a special interest in affective states. He is the coauthor of *The Emotions: A Philosophical Introduction* (2012) with Julien Deonna and *In Defense of Shame* (2012) with Julien Deonna and Raffaele Rodogno. Recently, he coedited *The Ontology of Emotions* (2018) with Hichem Naar and *Shadows of the Soul: Philosophical Perspectives on Negative Emotions* (2018) with Christine Tappolet and Anita Konzelmann Ziv.

Frédérique de Vignemont is a CNRS research director at the Jean Nicod Institute in Paris. Her major current works focus on bodily awareness, self-consciousness, and social cognition. She has published widely in philosophy and psychology journals on the first-person, body schema, agency, empathy, and more recently on pain. She is the recipient of the 2015 Young Mind & Brain prize. She is also one of the executive editors of the *Review of Philosophy and Psychology*.

Josh Weisberg is associate professor in philosophy at the University of Houston. He is the author of *Consciousness* (Polity 2014).

Dan Zahavi is professor of philosophy at the University of Copenhagen and the University of Oxford and director of the *Center for Subjectivity Research* in Copenhagen. He is author and editor of more than twenty-five volumes including *Husserl's Phenomenology* (2003), *Subjectivity and Selfhood* (2005), *The Phenomenological Mind* (with S. Gallagher) (2008/12), *Self and Other* (2014), *Husserl's Legacy* (2017), and *Phenomenology—The Basics* (2019). He is co-editor-in-chief of the journal *Phenomenology and the Cognitive Sciences*.

INTRODUCTION

What is the Philosophy of Consciousness?

URIAH KRIEGEL

CONSCIOUSNESS is one of the most elusive phenomena of the natural world. But it is, after all, *part* of the natural world. It has presumably evolved at some point, as a result of certain natural processes taking place within the causally integrated spatiotemporal system we call Nature. What need is there, then, for a *philosophy* of consciousness? As a *natural* phenomenon, should it not submit to theoretical explanation by the *natural* sciences? There is no philosophy of owls; owls are natural phenomena, so the theory of owls is part of a natural science—zoology. We now also have a lively science *of consciousness*, conducted by cognitive psychologists and neuroscientists among others. What do philosophers have to contribute here?

One might answer: our empirical knowledge about consciousness is so fragmentary and incomplete, at this early stage of scientific inquiry, that philosophers may be called upon to offer more or less disciplined speculations about the part of the story where we simply do not as yet have sufficient scientific knowledge. It would follow that, as scientific knowledge of consciousness grows, the need for a philosophy of consciousness will recede—until it will disappear and be entirely replaced by the science of consciousness.

The assumption behind the present volume is that philosophy may have a more significant role to play in shaping our understanding of consciousness; that even a complete science of consciousness may involve certain lacunae calling for philosophical supplementation. The plausibility of this notion depends in part on what one calls 'a science.' To bracket verbal issues, we will concern ourselves here with three areas in which the science of consciousness *as pursued today* leaves certain questions unaddressed. The next three sections introduce and discuss these three areas; each serves as a motivating introduction to one of the volume's three parts.

1.1 Phenomenal Grounding: The Varieties of Conscious Experience

Science tries to explain. But to get busy explaining, we first need to be clear on what the phenomena are which need explaining. That is, we need to be clear on our *explananda* before launching our explanatory enterprise. A science of consciousness, in particular, needs a clear list of the kinds or types of conscious experience that may occur in the natural world, the scientific explanation of which would be welcome.

Early psychologists in the 1870s, alive to this dual task, distinguished between *descriptive psychology* and *explanatory psychology*. Descriptive psychology had the task of *describing* psychological phenomena—manifest mental occurrences—as well as providing an initial taxonomy of them; in this task *introspection* had a central role. Explanatory psychology, in contrast, had the task of providing causal explanations for the occurrence of the relevant phenomena, to record regularities in their occurrence, and to articulate the natural laws governing their occurrence; here introspection was comparatively subsidiary, with 'physiology' (in essence: neuroscience) playing the more central role. Many psychological phenomena (e.g., visual experiences) are introspectible, but they occur as the result of subpersonal neurophysiological processes that are not themselves introspectible.

In this division of labor, descriptive psychology had the job of delineating the domain of phenomena to which explanatory psychology is answerable. However, the introspective method on which it relied soon fell into disrepute. The two main issues were (i) the persistent irresolvability of introspective disagreements and (ii) the apparent theory-ladenness of introspective judgments. Behaviorists were incensed about 'psychology exceptionalism': the sense that psychology just did not look like a regular, bonafide natural science, in which objective standards of testing and replication could be discerned and certain methods were available for resolving disagreements (Watson 1913: 163). This story is familiar. What is less understood is the way the behaviorist critique effectively and decisively banished the research area of *descriptive* psychology from the science of the mind. Explanatory psychology, with its neurophysiological methods and goals, was relatively unaffected by the behaviorist turn. What needed radical reframing, for the behaviorist, was not our conception of *how to explain* in psychology, but our conception of *what needs explaining* in psychology. The new explananda were not subjectively experienced internal occurrences, but pieces of publicly observable behavior.

Crucially, when cognitivists mounted their critique of behaviorism, starting in the late 1950s, their critique was in truth very partial: they insisted that psychological *explanation* could advert to internal, genuinely psychological posits ('internal' as opposed to behavioral, 'genuinely psychological' as opposed to merely neurological). But they left intact the behaviorist's conception of the *explananda* of psychology. Still today, what psychologists (or 'cognitive scientists') try to explain are just bits of *behavior* (including verbal reports). Internal mental processes *are* invoked in post-behaviorist psychology, but they are treated as *explanatory posits*—theoretical entities posited in the context of trying to make sense of behavioral phenomena, not phenomena with which we have pre-scientific acquaintance and for which we would like to provide scientific explanation.

In this respect, consciousness science differs markedly from other scientific disciplines. Chemistry tries to explain chemical phenomena, zoology tries to explain zoological phenomena, and so on. But psychology does not try to explain psychological phenomena; it tries to explain *behavioral* phenomena. Furthermore, while the zoologist works with certain theoretical posits, such as DNA, with which we have no pre-scientific familiarity, she also recognizes manifest zoological phenomena, such as owls and wings, with which we do have pre-scientific familiarity; these she treats as observable explananda rather than as unobservable, purely theoretical explanatory posits. In contrast, the psychologist treats subjective experiences as theoretical posits, as though we have no pre-scientific familiarity with them. But in truth, it is evident that we very much *do* have pre-scientific and indeed pre-theoretic familiarity with experiential phenomena, such as feeling embarrassed at a party, smelling a camembert, suddenly understanding what the speaker meant in response to our question, and so on. If DNA did not help explain anything, we would never suspect its existence. But if the experience of sadness did not help explain anything, we would all still believe that there is such a thing as feeling sad.

In taking behavioral rather than psychological phenomena as its explananda, and in treating *all* psychological occurrences as mere theoretical posits, mainstream academic psychology involves a form of exceptionalism after all. No other scientific discipline banishes its own proprietary phenomena from its domain of explananda, substituting to them alternative explananda; and none proceeds as though its proprietary phenomena are purely theoretical posits even when we clearly have pre-scientific familiarity with them. Perhaps this exceptionalism is ultimately justified, say on methodological grounds. Still, none of this makes the experiential phenomena with which we have pre-scientific familiarity *go away*. Descriptive psychology may have been banished from scientific psychology, but the experiential phenomena themselves—the *subject matter* of descriptive psychology—cannot be banished by fiat.

This opens up a first area where philosophers have had a crucial contribution to make to our understanding of consciousness. Wearing the moth-eaten cap of the descriptive psychologist, the philosopher may hope to produce a respectable inventory of experiential phenomena, as well as to impose initial order in it (through taxonomy and topology).

Two central questions define the core of this endeavor. First: of all the possible forms of conscious experience, which ones have psychological reality in our conscious life? (Depending on one's ambition, the 'our' could be interpreted in a variety of ways, from ranging only over normal human adults to ranging over every sentient being.) Second: of all the psychologically real phenomena of conscious life, which ones can be analyzed into combinations of other, more fundamental experiential phenomena, and which ones must be treated as fundamental, unanalyzable, primitive types of conscious experience? The types of experience which are not only psychologically real but also fundamental and unanalyzable—the 'experiential primitives' in our stream of consciousness, if you will—are the holy grail of descriptive psychology. Collectively, they constitute the complete fund of experiential ingredients the combinations and recombinations of which yield every subject's total conscious experience at a time.

It is the fashion of the day to frame philosophical issues in terms of *grounding*, the metaphysical relation canonically picked out by the locution 'in virtue of' in its philosophical use. Not to be deficient in this particular, let us frame the second issue just presented in terms of a distinction between (a) types of experience which are grounded in (combinations of) other types of experience, and (b) types of experience which are grounded in no others. The latter are the *ungrounded grounds* of the experiential realm, the 'building blocks' of our stream of consciousness. Early introspectionist psychologists referred to these as the *elements of consciousness*, and had indulged in bold speculations about their number. (Edward Titchener, probably the most prominent of all introspectionist psychologists, proffered that there were around 42,415 'elements of consciousness'!) But although such questions are incredibly hard to settle, or even address in an epistemically responsible way, they answer to certain *facts of the matter* that empirical cognitive science does not, perhaps judiciously, venture to contend with.

Part I of this volume is dedicated to philosophical discussions of some of the most central candidate ungrounded grounds of the sphere of experiential phenomena. It opens with two chapters on perceptual experience: a chapter by Pär Sundström on visual experience and another by Casey O'Callaghan on the varieties of nonvisual perceptual experience. There follow three chapters on three other types of phenomenologically lively kinds of experience: a chapter by Frédérique de Vignemont on bodily experience, a chapter by Julien Deonna and Fabrice Teroni on emotional experience, and a chapter by Amy Kind on imaginative experience. Few philosophers would deny the very *existence* of these types of experience, but plenty of philosophers have maintained that these types of experience can be accounted for entirely in terms of the coming-together of other, more basic types of experience. We close Part I with four chapters on more controversial types of experience, ones the very existence of which has often been called into question: a chapter by Tim Bayne on the experience of thinking, a chapter by Myrto Mylopoulos and Josh Shepherd on the experience of agency, a chapter by Philippe Chuard on the experience of time, and a chapter by Farid Masrour on the experiential unity of consciousness. For each of these putative experiential phenomena, we can ask whether it is (a) an ungrounded primitive of conscious life (call this an 'experiential primitive'), (b) a psychologically real phenomenon but one grounded in combinations of other, more fundamental phenomena (an 'experiential derivative'), or (c) not a psychologically real phenomenon at all (a mere 'experiential putative,' if you will).

Consider the experience of conscious thinking. One possible view is that there is simply no such thing—thought processes are never *experienced*, though they may be systematically *accompanied* by certain experiences, say of auditory imagery. Another view is that we do experience some of our thoughts, but the relevant experience consists in some cocktail of perceptual, imagistic, and emotional feelings coming together just so. A third view is that the experience of conscious thought sometimes brings into the picture a new, sui generis kind of irreducibly cognitive feeling—a type of proprietary cognitive phenomenology. According to this third view, there is at least one aspect to the experience of conscious thought that constitutes an experiential primitive, an experiential ingredient that goes beyond any combination of ingredients found in other kinds of experience.

A similar dispute between three such positions—one broadly eliminativist, one broadly reductivist, and one broadly primitivist—can be framed for any of the putative types of conscious experience discussed in Part I of this volume. The collection of all phenomena for which the primitivist view is the correct one would give us the fundamental furniture of the experiential realm—the 'elements of consciousness.' Clearly, settling on the right collection or inventory of such elements is a foundational task of first importance in our understanding of consciousness. And it is the philosophy of consciousness that attends to this task. (To repeat, one could use the term 'science' in such a way that descriptive psychology is part of the science of consciousness. My point is just that very few academics in science departments engage in descriptive psychology; it is typically academics in philosophy departments who do.)

I.2 Physical Grounding: Theories of Consciousness

When we speak of scientific research into consciousness, we speak in truth of research which targets in the first instance salient *correlates* of consciousness. Neuroscientific research is transparently framed in those terms, since its official aim is to identify the 'neural correlates of consciousness.' But as we will see in the next section, research into consciousness *in cognitive psychology* can similarly be framed as targeting, in the first instance, the *cognitive correlates* of consciousness. It is possible, of course, to hold that consciousness is in fact *nothing over and above* its neural correlates and/or *nothing over and above* its cognitive correlates. A certain kind of physicalist would hold the former and a certain kind of functionalist would hold the latter. But these additional claims—these nothing-over-and-above claims—are not themselves scientific claims, and the arguments bearing on their plausibility are not on their face empirical arguments based on laboratory results. On the contrary, nothing-over-and-above claims are paradigmatically philosophical claims and the considerations typically brought in their support tend to be adduced rather from the armchair.

In other areas, what scientists provide us with makes it *straightforward* whether a nothing-over-and-above claim is appropriate. Once told that H_2O molecules are present wherever water is present, and that sufficiently large coalitions of them exhibit all the features and behaviors water does, it is straightforward that H_2O constitutes not only the 'molecular *correlate* of water' but water itself. Nonetheless, it is still a non-empirical, *philosophical* claim that water is nothing but H_2O—albeit one that courts no controversy. In the case of consciousness, in contrast, the corresponding claim that consciousness is nothing but its neural (and/or cognitive) correlate does engender a kind of intellectual discomfort.

How best to frame this discomfort is itself a topic of lively debate among philosophers; the opening chapter of this volume, by David Papineau, offers one potential diagnosis. According to Papineau, there is simply a specially resistant pre-doxastic 'intuition of distinctness' that makes it hard for us to take seriously the proposition that consciousness might be nothing but its neural correlate. This diagnosis is offered as an alternative to the most popular philosophical diagnosis of the challenge presented by consciousness, namely, the notion that even absolutely complete knowledge of a person's brain, or for that matter of the totality of physical reality, would be insufficient to derive any knowledge of what specific kind of conscious experience a person is undergoing, and even of whether she is undergoing any experience at all (more on this in §I.3).

(My own view may be put in terms of an 'intuition of *categorical* distinctness': the reason we cannot see how the subjective quality of conscious experience could be generated, let alone *constituted*, by the silent transactions of so many brain cells inside the darkness of the skull, is that the two appear to belong to two different ontological categories. All these brain cells ever do, after all, is increase and decrease the rates at which they transmit an electrical impulse to each other; the notion that the subjective quality of feeling sad, or smelling coffee, or being visited with an insight, *just is* such a change in cells' firing rates strikes our intuition as a *category mistake*. Anaxagoras claimed that consciousness is a 'self-moving number,' which is almost certainly false, it is natural to think, given that consciousness and numbers belong to different ontological categories, as indeed do numbers and movement. But as far as our intuition is concerned, the transmission of an electrical pulse among cells is just as categorically foreign to the conscious experience of sadness or insight as numbers, self-moving or otherwise.)

However we ultimately choose to frame the relevant intellectual discomfort, its result is that there *is* a controversy over the non-empirical, philosophical nothing-over-and-above claim(s) associated with consciousness. Addressing and resolving this controversy is a second area where philosophical research is indispensable for a complete understanding of the nature of consciousness. Accordingly, Part II of this volume is dedicated to discussions of some of the most prominent philosophical positions on the ultimate relationship between consciousness and its physical (notably neural) correlates.

Part II opens with two chapters about the neural correlates of consciousness: one chapter by Jorge Morales and Hakwan Lau on the state of the art in this area of scientific inquiry, and another chapter by me about the different possible 'philosophical explanations' of the very existence of a correlation between neural activity and consciousness. There follow six chapters about the most prominent such explanations, three physicalist and three anti-physicalist: a chapter by Brie Gertler on dualism, the view (roughly) that the experiential and the physical are mutually (metaphysically) independent, such that any links between consciousness and its neural correlate are at most causal and contingent, not constitutive and necessary; a chapter by Philip Goff and Sam Coleman on so-called Russellian monism, the view (roughly) that all we know of physical properties is their dispositional or relational character, not their underlying intrinsic nature, which nature may in fact be experiential or at least proto-experiential; a chapter by Michael Pelczar on idealism, according to which (roughly) consciousness is ontologically prior to matter (or else matter does not exist at all); a chapter by Liz Irvine and Mark Sprevak about eliminative physicalism, which denies the very existence of consciousness; a chapter by Frank Jackson on a priori physicalism, the idea that consciousness is not only grounded in its physical correlate, but is so in an epistemically transparent way, such that complete knowledge of the physical facts regarding some person *would* make it possible to derive knowledge of the conscious experience she is undergoing; and finally a chapter by Joe Levine on a posteriori physicalism, which holds that although experiential facts are grounded in physical facts, this link is epistemically opaque to us, in that complete knowledge of physical facts does not suffice to derive facts about conscious experience. (Note well: not all of these authors *endorse* the position on which they write!) The next three chapters of Part II explore three specific strategies often adopted by physicalists in trying to account for consciousness (but sometimes embraced without a physicalist agenda): a chapter by Adam Pautz about representationalist theories, according to which conscious mental activity is characterized essentially by its distinctive way of representing the world; a chapter by Josh Weisberg on higher-order theories, according to which conscious mental activity is characterized rather by the way it is targeted by representations *of it*; and a chapter by Tom McClelland on self-representational theories, according to which the crucial characteristic of conscious states is that, whatever else they represent, they always also represent *themselves*. The final chapter of Part II, by Daniel Stoljar, is dedicated to the so-called epistemic approach to the problem of consciousness, the view (roughly) that we simply lack knowledge of certain key empirical facts that would shed light on whether and how consciousness might 'arise' from physical processes; in some versions, our ignorance of the relevant facts is principled and insurmountable, in others it is potentially merely temporary.

This selection of philosophical theories on the connection between consciousness and its physical correlate is perforce partial. There are many more options and sub-options for understanding the relationship between consciousness and matter. A more systematic and more nearly complete map of the available options is presented in Figure I.1. It divides philosophical takes on the consciousness–matter relationship into monist and dualist. The dualist approaches it divides into substance dualism and property dualism, and property dualism it divides into naturalistic and nonnaturalistic versions: the former insists on a causal or nomic dependence of consciousness on physical facts, while the latter rejects *any* dependence of consciousness on matter. Naturalistic dualism is then divided into interactionist and epiphenomenal: the former grants, while the latter denies, causal efficacy to conscious experiences. In this organization of logical space, the four main dualist theories are substance dualism, nonnaturalistic property dualism, interactionist naturalistic property dualism, and epiphenomenalist naturalistic property dualism.

Monist theories are divided in Figure I.1 into three groups: physicalist monism, neutral monism, and idealist monism. All three hold that reality is 'at bottom' unified (i.e., unified at the fundamental level, the level of 'ontological bedrock'). But, roughly speaking, one view is that reality is at bottom physical, another is that it is at bottom mental, and a third that it is at bottom something else, something which is neither physical nor mental but is both proto-physical and proto-mental. Ignoring important subdivisions of idealist and neutral-monist views, Figure I.1 goes on to divide physicalist views into three further groups: eliminative physicalism, reductive physicalism, and nonreductive physicalism. The first claims that there are no experiential properties or types; the second that experiential properties or types are identical to physical ones; the third that experiential properties/types are not identical to physical properties/types, but the former are nonetheless *constitutively dependent* (and not merely causally or nomically dependent) upon the latter. This constitutive dependence was traditionally framed in terms of supervenience, a relationship whereby one family of properties (the supervenient ones) cannot vary without corresponding variation in another family of properties (the subvenient ones, the 'supervenience base'). Traditionally, a further important distinction between a priori and a posteriori physicalism is then framed as a distinction between two different potential modal forces with which the experiential may supervene on the physical: a priori physicalism holds that the experiential supervenes on the physical with *conceptual* necessity, a posteriori physicalism that it supervenes with merely *metaphysical* necessity. (Incidentally, naturalistic dualism has sometimes been characterized as holding that the experiential supervenes with merely *nomic* necessity on the physical, and nonnaturalistic dualism can be seen as rejecting *any* supervenience of the experiential on physical.)

It is worth noting that in recent philosophy supervenience relations have come to be seen as mere symptoms of the aforementioned more robust underlying metaphysical relation of *grounding*. Accordingly there emerged in recent philosophy of mind an interest in 'grounding physicalism' as a potential position, either on the mind–body problem or on the associated 'consciousness–matter problem' on which we have focused here. It is not always clear in the relevant literature how grounding physicalism is related to the more traditional versions of physicalism, but my own sense is that it is best viewed as a potentially better and more accurate reformulation of nonreductive physicalism. For grounding relations are not typically eliminative about the grounded, so grounding physicalism is not a version of eliminative physicalism. Meanwhile, reductive physicalism is naturally seen as requiring the identification of consciousness with something physical, whereas an important feature of grounding is that it differs from identity in being asymmetric. (This difference is moreover crucial to grounding physicalism's ability to capture the ontological priority of the physical over the mental without subsuming or absorbing the mental in the physical.) So I think grounding is best seen as that which metaphysical or conceptual supervenience is the symptom of, and accordingly grounding physicalism is best seen as what nonreductive physicalism was always supposed to be. Now, if we do frame nonreductive physicalism in terms of grounding rather than supervenience, then the distinction between a priori and a posteriori physicalism becomes a distinction between two kinds of grounding, or two different ways in which the experiential can be grounded in the physical. The idea is that there are distinctions between grounding relations that mirror the distinction between conceptual and metaphysical supervenience. Consider: the fact that Jimmy is a bachelor is grounded in one way in the fact that Jimmy

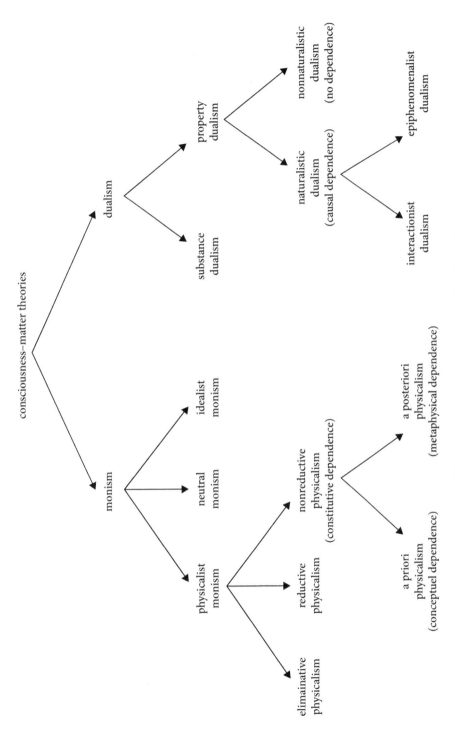

FIGURE 1.1 Taxonomy of consciousness–matter theories—fragment

is an unmarried man, but grounded in another way in the fact that the person who originated in the relevant sperm and the relevant egg is a bachelor. (I am indulging here, merely for the sake of illustration, the essentiality-of-origin thesis.) The first kind of grounding has conceptual (hence a priori) supervenience for a symptom, the second has metaphysical (hence a posteriori) supervenience for a symptom.

Figure I.1 thus distinguishes, alongside the aforementioned four types of dualism, four central forms of physicalism: eliminative physicalism, reductive physicalism, a priori nonreductive physicalism, and a posteriori nonreductive physicalism. In addition it recognizes a fifth and sixth type of monism: idealism and neutral monism. Then there is the epistemic approach, which allows that we may simply not know, and may even be constitutionally incapable of knowing, which of these positions is correct. With this plethora of options, certain decisions had to be made to keep Part II of this volume manageable—decisions which were guided not only by intellectual but also by practical and sociological considerations.

I.3 Psychological Grounding: Consciousness and Neighboring Phenomena

At least historically, the problem of whether there is more to consciousness than its physical correlate has been the most central in the philosophy of consciousness. Indeed, this problem is often referred to in the philosophical literature simply as 'the problem of consciousness.' As noted, there are different ways of understanding the source of the problem. But a recurring theme in many presentations is that although the problem concerns in the first instance the relationship between consciousness and its *physical realizer*, it ultimately passes through worries concerning the relationship between consciousness and its *functional or psychological role* (see Levine 1983: 357, Chalmers 1995: 64).

It is sometimes said that there is nothing more to physical matter than *structure and dynamics*, whereas there *is* something more to consciousness than structure and dynamics, namely, *intrinsic feel*. The point can be put more informally and impressionistically as follows: there is no gap between what a physical phenomenon *does* and what it *is*, whereas there is more to what consciousness *is* than what it *does* (there is also how it *feels*). A physical phenomenon, system, mechanism, process, or property *is* what it does—its essence or nature is to do just that which it does. But although a conscious experience does various things—it performs many psychological functions, that is, plays a certain psychological role—its nature is not exhaustively captured by a complete enumeration of all it does. There appears to be a 'para-functional residue' in consciousness; the term 'phenomenal consciousness' can be seen as designating precisely the aspect of consciousness that appears to go beyond the totality of its psychological functions (Block 1995).

To bring the point out, let us compare consciousness and memory. Both of them *do* something: they play a causal or functional role in the subject's overall psychological economy. Crushing many subtleties, let us say that what memory does is store information. What is important to note is that storing information is so essential to memory that it is natural to say that memory just is an *information-storer*. Now, the complete psychological profile of memory is surely more nuanced than this; but whatever it is, once we know exactly what memory does, we can identify memory with that-which-does-*that*. Any system or mechanism that did the same thing—that played the relevant psychological role—would ipso facto count as a memory system. This is why we have no problem attributing memory to such inanimate objects as desktop computers from the 1970s. (To say this is not take a stand on whether computers could ever be conscious; it is only to take a stand on whether desktop computers from the 1970s were conscious—the stand that they were not!)

Consciousness has its own functional or psychological profile, which seems considerably more multifaceted than memory's. Some attempt to unify that profile around the notion of *cognitive access*: consciousness makes information more available to a wide variety of downstream mechanisms, modules, and subsystems. Again, a full specification of the functional or psychological role of consciousness would surely be more nuanced than this, but whatever it turns out to be, it is what I referred to in §I.2 as the 'cognitive correlate of consciousness': it is the specific, singular contribution consciousness makes to cognition. What is important for our purposes is that it seems perfectly possible, indeed rather *easy*, to imagine a system or mechanism that does exactly *that* (whatever consciousness does within our cognitive system) and yet does not amount to consciousness at all. If one day we isolate the complete psychological role of consciousness, construct a system made of silicon chips that perform the exact same cognitive functions, and embed that system in a computer, we will not immediately take this to *settle the question* of whether that computer is conscious. There seems to be an *open question* left over: Does the computer's performance of these functions involve a subjective quality, a phenomenal character, an experiential feel? The very fact that this question makes sense, even where the psychological role of consciousness has been fully replicated, shows that there is more to our concept of consciousness than the idea of *that-which-does-such-and-such*. In other words, our concept of consciousness allows for potential daylight between what consciousness is and what consciousness does—a daylight that our concept of memory, for instance, does not tolerate.

A philosopher could of course maintain that although this is true of our naïve, prescientific concept of consciousness, a more sophisticated scientific understanding of consciousness will reduce consciousness to its cognitive correlate, that is, will construe consciousness as exhausted by the sum total of its psychological functions. To this, another philosopher will respond that such a reconceptualization of consciousness is so radical, leaving out the very essence of consciousness (namely, its subjective feel), that it amounts to effectively denying the existence of consciousness as we ordinarily think of it. The first philosopher may then come back with the complaint that unless we accept her radical reconceptualization of consciousness, we will end up with a mysterian, nonnaturalist picture of the world overly welcoming of scientifically intractable, vaguely supernatural phenomena. Here we approach the great looming terror of the philosophy of consciousness: that all said and done, the only *stable* positions on the nature of consciousness are eliminative physicalism and nonnaturalistic dualism—and that the tremendous industry of fashioning clever intermediate positions is but an expression of a futile hope to have the cake and eat it too.

The point I want to make is that this is a paradigmatically philosophical debate, not a scientific one. At the end of inquiry, if you please, the cognitive psychology of consciousness will identify the complete cognitive correlate of consciousness. But the question of the ultimate relationship between consciousness and its cognitive correlate cannot be settled by cognitive psychology itself—just as the question of the ultimate relationship between consciousness and its neural correlate cannot be settled by neuroscience (and indeed, just as the question of the ultimate relationship between voting patterns and the behavior of sub-atomic particles cannot be settled by particle physics). The claim that consciousness is *nothing but* its cognitive correlate, and the claim that it is *not* nothing but its cognitive correlate, are *philosophical* claims. Here too, then, we find a distinctive role for philosophy to play in our overall understanding of the nature of consciousness.

Part III of this volume is dedicated in large part to studies of the relationship between consciousness and some of the psychological phenomena or mechanisms with which it is functionally bound. It includes chapters on consciousness' relationship with attention (Chris Mole), memory (Chris Hill), action guidance (Benjamin Kozuch), intentionality (Angela Mendelovici and David Bourget), perceptual knowledge (Berit Brogaard and Eli Chudnoff), the self (Dan Zahavi), introspection and self-knowledge (Maja Spener), and even moral knowledge (Josh Shepherd and Neil Levy); the volume closes with a chapter (by Mark Rowlands) on consciousness' embodiment.

There are surely other psychological functions of relevance to consciousness' functional role. But this partial list captures some of the most salient ones: conscious awareness tends to display a foreground/background attentional structure; consciously perceived stimuli tend to stay in short-term memory longer and more vividly than stimuli perceived subliminally or in blindsight; conscious experiences seem to guide certain of our on-the-fly actions; they tend to be intentionally directed at objects and features in the external world; they tend to induce and justify perceptual beliefs about the external world, as well as introspective beliefs about oneself and one's 'inner world.' So much is beyond serious doubt. The question is whether these intimate relations consciousness bears to attention, memory, action, intentionality, perceptual judgment, introspection, and the self are *causal and contingent* or on the contrary *constitutive and necessary*. Causal and contingent relations are to be studied by cognitive science; the philosopher's distinctive contribution is to examine the prospects for constitutive, essential connections between consciousness and these neighboring psychological phenomena.

Again, we may also put the question in terms of grounding: Is consciousness grounded in some of its neighboring psychological phenomena, such that once a cognitive system performs the relevant psychological functions, it is *guaranteed* to also exhibit (phenomenal) consciousness? Or does consciousness ultimately outstrip any collection of psychological functions and is thus a sui generis mental phenomenon? Grounding being a metaphysical relation, such questions of grounding pertain to the metaphysics of consciousness, not to the empirical science of consciousness. There is no laboratory instrument that can detect grounding relations in nature. The question is not *empirically tractable*.

I.4 CONCLUSION

Given a certain conscious experience—say, feeling grief-stricken about a relative's death, or nervous about an upcoming appointment—there are at least three kinds of question about relations of grounding or constitutive dependence that the experience bears to (increasingly removed) other phenomena: (1) Is the experience grounded in/constitutively dependent upon other types of conscious experience? (2) Is it grounded in/constitutively dependent upon psychological phenomena other than conscious experience? (3) Is it grounded in/constitutively dependent upon certain physical (or otherwise non-mental) processes or states? These questions define a sphere of inquiry where philosophical reflection on consciousness seems indispensable. This volume attempts to cover some of the most prominent issues that arise concerning each of these distinctively philosophical questions.

REFERENCES

Block, N. J. (1995), 'On a Confusion About the Function of Consciousness', *Behavioral and Brain Sciences* 18: 227–47.
Chalmers, D. J. (1995), 'The Puzzle of Conscious Experience, *Scientific American* (December): 62–8.
Levine, J. (1983), 'Materialism and Qualia: The Explanatory Gap', *Pacific Philosophical Quarterly* 64: 354–61.
Watson, J. B. (1913), 'Psychology as the Behaviorist Views It', *Psychological Review* 20: 158–77.

CHAPTER 1

THE PROBLEM OF CONSCIOUSNESS

DAVID PAPINEAU

1.1 INTRODUCTION

CONSCIOUSNESS raises a range of philosophical questions. We can distinguish between the *How?*, *Where?*, and *What?* questions. First, *how* does consciousness relate to other features of reality? Second, *where* are conscious phenomena located in reality? And, third, *what* is the nature of consciousness?

In line with much philosophical writing over the past fifty years, this chapter will focus mostly on the *How?* question. Towards the end I shall also say some things about the *Where?* question. As for the *What?* question, a few brief introductory remarks will have to suffice.

This is not to deny that the *What?* question raises a range of philosophically interesting issues. There is much to ask about the nature of consciousness. Must conscious states always involve some reflective awareness of themselves? Do all conscious states have an intentional content? Must consciousness always be consciousness for some subject, and if so for what kind of subject? In what sense, if any, are the conscious experiences of a subject at a given time always unified into some whole?

However, in order to keep my task manageable, I shall leave issues like these for the essays that follow in this volume. For my purposes, it will be enough if we simply characterize consciousness in the normal way, as states that are 'like something' for the subjects that have them. If examples are wanted, simply reflect on the difference between having your eyes open, and enjoying a range of conscious visual experiences, and closing your eyes and eliminating those conscious experiences. Or, more generally, contrast the conscious life you enjoy when you are awake, in all its rich variety, with its complete disappearance when you are given a general anaesthetic.

1.2 The Case for Physicalism

Let us make a start on the *How?* question. How does consciousness relate to other features of reality? At first pass, it might be unclear why there is any special issue here. Why is there a puzzle about conscious states, as opposed to other kinds of states? Reality contains many different kind of things, biological, meteorological, chemical, electrical, and so on, all existing alongside each other, and all interacting causally in various ways. There seems no immediate reason why consciousness should be singled out as posing some special puzzle about its relation to the rest of reality.

If conscious properties did interact causally with non-conscious states, then there would indeed be no special problem about its relation to other features of reality. We could all be happy interactionists, in the style of Descartes. We could hold that conscious mind influences non-conscious matter, by controlling bodily behaviour, and similarly that matter influences mind, giving rise to sensory experiences, pains, and other conscious mental states.

There is a compelling argument, however, against this kind of interactionist stance. This derives from the so-called 'causal closure of the physical'. The problem is that the physical realm seems causally sufficient unto itself. Physical effects always issue from physical causes. This applies to bodily movements, and the neural processes which prompt them, as much as to any other physical effects. Scientists studying neural processes take it as given that the events they observe are effects of electromagnetic and chemical causes, not of independent mental influences exerting an influence from outside the physical realm.[1]

The 'causal closure of the physical' thus implies that, if there is a separate realm of mental states, it cannot exert any influence on bodily behaviour or other physical processes. One possible move at this point is to continue to uphold the existence of a distinct mental realm, and accept that it indeed has no influence on the physical world. However, this 'epiphenomenalist' option is not only intrinsically implausible, but faces various internal difficulties.[2]

Given this, most contemporary philosophers have opted instead for some form of physicalist monism. There are not two separate realms, mind and matter. Rather mental states are themselves a species of physical states. You might initially think of your pains or your desires as something separate from the cerebral and other physical states that

---

[1] Perhaps the thesis of 'causal' closure is better formulated as the claim that (the chances of) all physical events are *determined* by prior physical events according to physical law. On some views of causation, these prior determiners do not necessarily count as causes (Woodward 2005; Menzies 2008). Still, determinational closure itself sustains an argument against metaphysically independent mental influences. I shall ignore this complication in what follows.

[2] In particular, epiphenomenalism is arguably *self-stultifying*, in that it implies that the conscious realm has no casual impact on the views of those who believe in it (Robinson 2015: sect 2.4).

accompany them. But in truth, so the physicalist thought goes, your mental states are one and the same as those physical states. On this view, of course, there is then no difficulty about pains, desires, and other mental states causally influencing bodily behaviour or other physical processes. If your conscious mental states are no different from your cerebral physical states, then they will have just the same physical effects that those physical states do.

If there is such a compelling argument for a physicalist view of the mind, why hasn't physicalism always been the dominant philosophical position, rather than only becoming so in the middle of the last century? The answer is that the causal closure of the physical was not generally accepted until relatively recently. Note that the closure-based argument against dualism is not just the traditional objection put to Descartes by his contemporaries, that if mind and matter are so different, it is difficult to understand how they can causally interact. Even if this was a problem in Descartes' time, it is not clear that it greatly perturbed subsequent thinkers. Rather the problem is that modern science has definite views about the kinds of things that do affect the movement of matter, and independent mental influences are not among them.

To repeat, this exclusion of independent mental causes is a relatively recent phenomenon. Through most of the modern period, science had no problem with fundamental conscious causes. Orthodox physical science, from the time of Newton through to the twentieth century, was generally open-minded about the kinds of things that could influence the movements of matter. In addition to mechanical forces of impact, and gravitational forces, it allowed distinctive chemical forces, magnetic forces, forces of cohesion, vital forces—and conscious mental forces. It was only in the middle of the twentieth century that a detailed understanding of the electro-chemical workings of neurons convinced the scientific mainstream that there is no place for sui generis mental forces.[3] It is noteworthy that all the familiar modern arguments for physicalism were developed in the middle of the twentieth century, and all appealed to some version of the causal closure of the physical.[4]

1.3 THE EXPLANATORY GAP

There is a huge contemporary literature on physicalist views of the mind, covering a range of questions. How exactly should we define 'physical'? Can mental properties be identified with basic physical properties, or should we instead embrace some version of 'non-reductive physicalism', according to which mental properties supervene on, or are grounded in, or are otherwise constituted by basic physical properties, without being

---

[3] For a more detailed account of the history of causal arguments for physicalism since the seventeenth century, see the Appendix to my *Thinking about Consciousness* (2002).

[4] See Feigl 1958; Oppenheim and Putnam 1958; Smart 1959; Lewis 1966; Armstrong 1968; Davidson 1970.

strictly identical to them? Do these non-reductionist options succeed in avoiding the epiphenomenalist threat that prompted physicalism in the first place? And so on.

However, we can by-pass all these issues here. This is because *any* version of physicalism about conscious states seems to generate pressing philosophical problems. Despite the strength of the argument for physicalism, the equation of the lived experience of perceptions, emotions, and pains with neuronal oscillations in the brain strikes many philosophers as effectively incomprehensible. As Thomas Nagel puts it in *The View from Nowhere* 'We have at present no conception of how a single event or thing could have both physical or phenomenological aspects, or how if it did they could be related' (1986: 47). Or, in the more direct words of Colin McGinn, 'How can technicolour phenomenology arise from soggy grey matter?' (1991: 1). To Nagel, McGinn, and many other philosophers, the idea that conscious states are at bottom physical seems obviously problematic.

This is the central problem of consciousness for contemporary philosophy. Arguments from causal closure provide compelling reasons to view conscious states as physical. But any such physicalist view of consciousness strikes many as little short of unintelligible. (Since this problem arises for all versions of physicalism, non-reductive as well as reductive, I shall often simplify the exposition from now on by talking of conscious states as physical, or as identical to physical states; everything that follows will apply equally to physicalist positions that view conscious states as supervenient on, or grounded in, or constituted by, physical states.)

If we are to make any progress with this central problem of consciousness, we need to articulate the nature of the resistance to physicalism illustrated by the quotations from Nagel and McGinn. One useful way to do this is to compare putative mind-brain identities with similar scientific identity claims in other areas. When we are told that common salt is NaCl, or lightning is atmospheric electrical discharge, we happily accept these claims as telling us about the underlying physical nature of these everyday phenomena. But when we are told that pains are the firing of prefrontal nociceptive-specific neurons, or that visual experiences of red are neuronal oscillations in the V4 area of the visual cortex, we react quite differently. Even after we are given this information, we still want to know *why* those brain states are accompanied by those feelings. Why do the nociceptive-specific neurons, or the oscillations in V4, feel like that, rather than some other way, or no way at all? As Joseph Levine has put it, mind-brain identities seem to leave us with an *explanatory gap*, in a way that other scientific identities do not (Levine 1983). We remain puzzled about why the brain states give rise to the feelings, in a way that we do not feel puzzled about why NaCl gives rise to salt, or electrical discharges to lightning.

Now, as a social or psychological phenomenon, the existence of an explanatory gap is quite uncontentious. There is no doubt that most people react to mind-brain identity claims with demands for further explanation, in a way they don't react to other scientific identity claims. However, the philosophical significance of this social fact is far less straightforward. Philosophers disagree widely about the source of the reaction and about what, if anything, it implies about the relation between conscious and physical states.

There are two distinct questions here. The first is a psycho-social question. What is the *source* of the explanatory asymmetry? Why do people feel that mind-brain identities, unlike scientific identities, leave something unexplained? The second is a philosophical question. What *follows* from this explanatory asymmetry? Does the puzzlement occasioned by mind-brain identities imply that there is some deficiency in the physicalist view of consciousness?

I shall address these issues in turn. The next three sections will be devoted to the source of the explanatory asymmetry. After that I shall turn to the philosophical implications.

1.4 The Derivability Gap

The psycho-social question first. My own view on this is a straightforward one. I think that the feeling of an explanatory gap is simply an upshot of the fact that we all—including professed physicalists like myself—find mind-brain identities almost impossible to believe. Even after we are shown plenty of evidence that pains and nociceptive-specific neuronal firing always accompany each other, and have the same causes and effects, we still intuitively resist the conclusion that they are identical. How could that urgent feeling possibly be one and the same as neuronal activity, we ask? We find it hard to escape the spontaneous dualist thought that the feeling and the physical state are not one thing, but two different states that somehow invariably accompany each other.

And, to the extent that we do think this, then of course we feel a need for more explanation. Why is the neuronal activity accompanied by the nasty feeling of pain, rather than a pleasant sense of floating, say? Indeed, why is it accompanied by any feeling at all? Once we slip into the dualist way of seeing things, we cannot avoid a range of demands for further explanation. (See Papineau 2010.)

Most philosophers currently working on consciousness, however, take a quite different and less straightforward view of the feeling of an explanatory gap. In their view, this feeling is not a consequence of an intuitive resistance to physicalism. Rather, it stems from an internal feature of the way we think of conscious states, and would persist even if we were able fully to embrace physicalism.

This mainstream view attributes the feeling of an explanatory gap to the impossibility of *deriving* mind-brain identities a priori from the physical facts. This is supposed to mark a contrast with the scientific cases. While we can often derive scientific identities a priori from the physical facts, so the thought goes, we cannot so derive mind-brain identities, and this creates a feeling of puzzlement about them.

The reason for the difference, on this mainstream account, lies in the different ways in which we ordinarily *conceive* of scientific properties and conscious properties. Consider our everyday concept of *common salt*. According to the mainstream view, we think of salt as the stuff that is white, crystalline, granular, with a distinctive taste, that dissolves in water, and is found in the oceans. Now imagine someone who has a fully detailed account of the physical make-up of the world, in terms of the distribution of matter, arrangement of elementary particles, the deployment of fields, and so on. In principle, such a person could arguably put this knowledge together with their prior conceptual grasp of *salt* to figure out that salt must be NaCl, on the grounds that NaCl is the stuff that fits the conceptual requirements for salt—white, crystalline,...However, we can't do this with pain, say, or with visual experiences of red. The problem is that our everyday concepts of *pain* or *visual experience* do not pick out their objects via some descriptive role, like white, crystalline,...but in terms, so to speak, of what the states feel like. We typically think of conscious states directly, by focusing on the feelings involved, and not as the states, whatever they may be, that play some descriptively specified role. And this blocks any a priori derivation of mind-brain identities from the physical facts, of the kind that is arguably available for identities like salt = NaCl. Scrutinize the physical facts as much as you like, and they won't tell you that pains are the firing of prefrontal nociceptive-specific neurons. Since we don't think of pains in terms of some specified role, but in terms of the feelings involved, there is no way to connect the physical facts with the phenomenon of pain.

Given this, our knowledge of mind-brain identities can only be based on some kind of a posteriori abductive inference, rather than a principled a priori demonstration that a certain physical state fills some specified role. For example, we might observe that pains occur whenever prefrontal nociceptive-specific neurons fire, and vice versa; we might also note that, if pains were the firing of nociceptive-specific neurons, then this would account for a number of other observed facts about pain, such as that it can be caused by trapped nerves, and can be blocked by aspirin; and we might conclude on this basis that pains are indeed identical to the firing of nociceptive-specific neurons.

Still, to repeat, there is no question of deriving this identity a priori from the physical facts, by showing that the nociceptive-specific neuronal firing fills the pain role—for we do not think of conscious pains in terms of roles to start with. And this, says the view under examination, is why we feel an explanatory gap in the mind-brain case. The peculiarly direct nature of our concepts of conscious states stops us deriving mind-brain identities a priori from the physical facts.

1.5 Doubts about Derivability

This lack-of-derivability account of the source of explanatory-gap feelings is widely taken for granted in contemporary philosophy of mind. Despite this, I think it is clearly mistaken, and shall explain why in a moment. One part of the story, however, is relatively uncontentious. This is the idea that we have direct, non-descriptive concepts of conscious states that preclude any a priori derivation of mind-brain identities from physics.

Some initial mid-twentieth-century versions of physicalism did not accept this, and so held that mind-brain identities could indeed be read off from the physical facts.

But this stance was dealt a critical blow by Frank Jackson's 'Knowledge Argument' (1986). Jackson pointed out that someone who has never experienced colours could be in possession of all the physical facts about colour vision, and yet not 'know what it is like' to see something red. The overall philosophical significance of Jackson's argument is a complex matter, to which we shall return in due course. But it is pretty much agreed on all sides that, at a mimimum, Jackson's argument does demonstrate the existence of a special range of 'phenomenal concepts', ways of thinking about conscious states directly, in terms of the feelings involved, which are normally only available to subjects who have experienced those states themselves, and which block any physics-based derivation of mind-brain identities.[5]

So far so good. We cannot derive mind-brain identities a priori from the physical facts. Still, is this really the source of the feeling that the identities leave something unexplained, as claimed by the suggestion currently under examination? This suggestion faces an obvious objection. Plenty of other identities similarly cannot be derived from physics, but generate no corresponding impression of an explanatory gap.

After all, as the above remarks make clear, a priori derivations from physics will be blocked whenever we have concepts that refer directly, rather than by association with some described role. On the face of things, phenomenal concepts are by no means the only such cases. Proper names ('Cary Grant'), demonstrative constructions ('that dog'), and simple terms for observable properties of objects ('round') are all arguably terms that refer directly, rather than by description. Given this, when we accept identity claims involving these terms (such as 'Cary Grant = Archie Leach', or 'that dog = her pet', or 'round = locus of constant distance from some point'), it can only be on the basis of an abductive inference from direct empirical evidence, such as that the two things in question are found in the same places and the same times, and are observed to bear the same relations to other things, not because we can deduce the identities a priori from the physical facts.

Yet we feel no explanatory disquiet when presented with these identities. Even though they must perforce be based on some form of abductive inference, for lack of any descriptive roles associated with the relevant terms, they certainly do not leave us with a feeling that something has been left unexplained.

Come to think of it, it is doubtful that many scientific identities are based on anything more than abductive inferences either. When nineteenth-century scientists first figured out that salt is NaCl, they certainly did not do so by inferring a priori from basic physical theory that NaCl molecules will appear white, form crystals, dissolve in water, and so on, and hence concluding that NaCl must be the substance that fits the specifications for salt. The sub-atomic understanding required for such derivations was more than a

---

[5] Among the exceptions who resist phenomenal concepts are David Lewis (1988) and Daniel Dennett (1992). Curiously, they have now been joined by Jackson himself, who has come to view dualism as untenable while continuing to maintain that it would follow from the existence of phenomenal concepts (2007). Other recent writers reject phenomenal concepts on the grounds that no concepts can constitutively depend on prior conscious experiences (Ball 2009; Tye 2009); in my view, this argument sets the standards for phenomenal concepts too high.

century in the future. Rather the original scientists simply noted that NaCl molecules were present whenever salt was, and vice versa, and had some of the same causes and effects, and identified them on that basis.[6]

The same goes for the identification of lightning with electrical discharge, or consumption with tuberculosis infection, or nearly all other scientific identities. Scientists did not derive these identities a priori from physical theory, but based them largely on simple observations of co-occurrence and matching casual relations to other things.

Yet this did not make the scientists feel something was left unexplained. Even though the identities were based on abductive inference, rather than derived a priori from the physical facts, the scientists were not left unhappily puzzled about why NaCl gives rise to salt, rather than to something else, or to nothing at all, or why lightning arises from electrical discharge, or consumption from tuberculosis infection. Once more, the absence of a priori derivations did not seem to engender any feelings of things left unexplained.

Perhaps these counterexamples are less than conclusive. Still, there are further grounds, apart from possible counterexamples, for doubting the mainstream thesis that the feeling of an explanatory gap arises from our inability to derive the relevant identities a priori from the physical facts.

Note how this mainstream account implies that *something is left unexplained* when we embrace mind-identities on the basis of abductive inferences, something that *does get explained* when we supposedly derive scientific identities from the physical facts. But what exactly is that? What exactly does get explained, according to the mainstream account, when we derive scientific identities a priori from the physical facts, but not when we embrace mind-brain identities on the basis of abductive inferences?

One first thought might be that it is the identities themselves that are explained. We can explain *why* salt is NaCl, or *why* lightning is electrical discharge, once we can derive the identities a priori from the basic physical facts, in a way these identities would be left unexplained if we simply based them on abductive inferences.

But this seems odd. We do not normally regard identities as in need of explanation. Since they are necessary, they could not have been otherwise, and did not need anything to make them so. (To repeat a familiar example, when we discover that Mark Twain = Samuel Clemens, we might reasonably ask *why* he had two names, or *why* nobody told us before. But it would make no sense to ask—*why* was Mark Twain the same man as Samuel Clemens? (Block 1978.))

A second thought would be that it is not the identities per se that get explained, but the behaviour displayed by everyday kinds. So, for example, once we can derive the identity of salt with NaCl a priori from the physical facts, then we will in principle be able to explain why salt displays such defining characteristics as whiteness, crystallinity, solubility in water, and so on, in a way we can not do if the identity is based on brute correlations.

But this second thought does not hold water either. Sure, we can explain the behaviour of salt if we derive its identity with NaCl a priori from the physical facts, by appealing to

---

[6] In any case, a derivation from the strictly *physical* facts alone was never really on the cards, given the presence of such observational terms as *white* in the conceptual role of *salt*. See Levine 2010.

our physical understanding of how NaCl molecules work. But, by just the same coin, we can explain the behaviour of pain if we accept its identity with nociceptive neuronal firings on the basis of an a posteriori abductive inference. As I observed above, an identification of pain with the firing of prefrontal nociceptive-specific neurons, even if based on an abductive inference, will happily allow us to explain such things as why pain is caused by trapped nerves, or why it is relieved by aspirin.

So, once more, it does not look like the impression of an explanatory gap can really be due to a lack of a priori derivation. Such derivations do not allow us to explain anything that cannot be explained without them.

Much of the contemporary literature on the 'explanatory gap' simply reads this phrase as referring to the impossibility of deriving mind-brain identities a priori from the physical facts. But we have now seen that, in truth, this understanding quite fails to answer the psycho-social question of why mind-brain identities leave most people with the feeling of an *explanatory* gap. For a start, people do not seem to have any feeling of non-explanation with other identities that cannot be derived a priori from the physical facts. Moreover, nothing extra would seem to be explained when we can derive identities a priori from the physical facts.

In the end, though, there is an even more powerful reason for rejecting the idea that the feeling of an explanatory gap is something to do with a priori underivability. This is the availability of the alternative account mentioned earlier, an account that avoids all the difficulties raised in this section.

1.6 The Intuition of Distinctness

On the alternative account I favour, the issue is not that we feel that something still remains to be explained *after* we have accepted mind-brain identities. It is rather that we all find mind-brain identities very difficult to accept in the first place.

As I observed above, even after we are given all the abductive evidence, we still find mind-brain identity claims almost impossible to believe. We cannot resist the dualist conviction that conscious feelings and the physical brain states are two different things. And this, in my view, is the real reason why we feel a need for further explanation. We want to know why the neuronal activity is accompanied by *that* conscious feeling, rather than by some other, or by no feeling at all. Our dualist intuitions automatically generate a hankering for further explanation.

On my diagnosis, then, the demand for explanation arises, not because something is lacking in physicalism, but because something is lacking in us. Even after we are shown the arguments for physicalism, and are perhaps moved to embrace physicalism at a theoretical level, we continue to experience the pull of the dualistic perspective, and so intuitively feel that something remains to be explained.

If only we could fully embrace physicalism, this diagnosis suggests, the feeling of an explanatory gap would disappear. If we could fully accept that pains are nociceptive-specific neuronal firings, then we would stop asking why 'they' go together—after all, nothing can possibly come apart from itself. The feeling of a gap is simply a corollary of the intuitive grip of dualism.

From this perspective, then, a properly thorough-going physicalism promises to dissolve 'the problem of consciousness'. The committed physicalist will simply deny that any puzzle is raised by the fact that it feels painful to be a human with active nociceptive-neurons. Why shouldn't it feel like that? That's how it turns out. Why regard this as puzzling?

Note how my diagnosis in terms of intuitive dualism offers a far better account of the feeling of an *explanatory* gap than the appeal to lack of a priori derivability. For a start, it is now clear why we feel something has been left *unexplained*—we want to know specifically why brain states give rise to extra conscious states. Moreover, the feeling of a gap is now specifically about mind-brain relations, and so there is no puzzle about why we do not feel it in other cases where a priori derivability is blocked.

By way of further support for the idea that the feeling of an explanatory gap stems from intuitive dualism, we need only attend to the phraseology normally used to discuss the relation between mind and brain. Brain processes are said to 'generate', or 'yield', or 'cause', or 'give rise to' conscious states. ('How can technicolour phenomenology *arise from* soggy grey matter?') These expressions are common currency in writings on consciousness, including by thinkers who say they are not dualists. But the phraseology itself is not consistent with physicalism. Fire 'generates', 'causes', 'yields', or 'gives rise to' smoke. But NaCl does not 'generate', 'cause', 'yield', or 'give rise to' salt. It *is* salt. The point is clear. To speak of brain processes as 'generating' conscious states, and so on, only makes sense if you are implicitly thinking of the conscious states as separate from the brain states.

If yet further evidence is needed, consider our intuitive reaction to whether zombies are possible. Could a being share all your physical properties but have no conscious life? Everybody's first thought is, 'Sure. Just duplicate the physical stuff and leave out the feelings.'

Reflective physicalists will of course realize, on second thoughts, that they must deny that this is really possible. (If conscious states *are* physical states, the 'two' cannot come apart.) But it is the initial reaction that I want to focus on here. Compare our response to the idea of Marilyn Monroe existing without Norma Jean Baker, say. I take it that our initial reaction to this suggested possibility would be puzzlement. What are we being asked to posit? That she exist without herself? That makes no sense.

This contrast is a reflection of our intuitive dualism. Zombies strike us as initially possible simply because all of us, physicalists included, intuitively think of conscious feelings and physical states as distinct existents. If we fully embraced the idea that they are one and the same, then we would find the idea of zombies simply puzzling. How could there be nociceptive-specific neuronal firing without pains? What are we being asked to posit? That the state exist without itself? That would not make any more sense than Marilyn Monroe without Norma Jean Baker. (Cf Papineau 2007.)

If the feeling of an explanatory gap stems from our intuitive dualism, as I have been arguing, then the obvious next question is about the cause of these persistent dualist thoughts. Why do dualist ideas maintain such a firm grip, even on thinkers who are fully persuaded of the strength of the arguments for physicalism?

Plenty of possible answers to this question offer themselves, but before considering them I would like first to return to the issue left hanging earlier, namely whether the feeling of an explanatory gap is associated with any good *arguments* against a physicalist view of consciousness. After all, one possible explanation for why many people feel intuitively convinced that physicalism is false might be that they can all see that there is a strong argument against it.

Of course, even if there were a good philosophical argument against physicalism, it might not be the reason most people instinctively reject physicalism; the argument might not be apparent to them. But, even so, it will be useful to get clear about the nature of the arguments against physicalism, before discussing the possible causes of persistent dualist intuitions.

1.7 Arguments Against Physicalism

The best place to begin assessing the argumentative case against physicalism is with Jackson's 'Knowledge Argument'.

As I explained earlier, Jackson's argument hinges on the observation that someone could know all the physical facts about colour vision, and yet not 'know what it is like' to see something red. And, as I said, this observation is generally agreed to demonstrate the existence of a special range of 'phenomenal concepts' that refer directly to conscious states and are normally only available to subjects who have experienced those states themselves.

Jackson original intention, however, was not just to argue for an extra set of phenomenal *concepts*, but in addition for an extra set of phenomenal *properties*. That is, he was arguing for the dualist conclusion that conscious states are metaphysically distinct from and additional to any physical states.

Even so, once phenomenal concepts are on the table, physicalists would seem to have a ready initial response to his argument. They can say that 'not knowing what some conscious states are like', even when you are completely knowledgeable about the physical facts, is simply a matter of not being able to represent certain physical states (the relevant conscious states) *using phenomenal concepts*. Once you know all the physical facts, then you know about all of reality. If, despite this, you still 'don't know what some states are like', that is just a matter of your not being able to represent those states in the special direct way that only becomes available once you are in possession of the relevant phenomenal concepts.

From the point of view of physicalists who take this line—'a posteriori' physicalists—there are thus two distinct kinds of concepts that refer to conscious states. On the one hand are phenomenal concepts—like *pain* or *seeing something red*—that pick out their referents directly, in terms of what they feel like, so to speak. And on the other are physical concepts—like *nociceptive-specific neuronal firing* or *oscillations in V4*—that refer to just the same states in terms of their physical nature. Scientific investigation can then show us that the former concepts pick out the same things as the latter ones, just as it establishes such other a posteriori identities as *salt = NaCl*, or *lightning = atmospheric electrical discharge*.

However, a second line of anti-physicalist argument now comes into play. This focuses on the particular nature of phenomenal concepts, and contends that certain features of these concepts are incompatible with their referring to physical states.

The basic thought is that, if physicalism were true, the *directness* of phenomenal concepts ought to render its falsity inconceivable—yet it does not. Consider once more a 'zombie', a being who shares all my physical properties yet has no conscious life. Physicalists must deny that zombies are *possible*, given that the mind is ontologically inseparable from the brain. But a posteriori physicalists have no choice but to allow that they are at least *conceivable*. (If phenomenal concepts refer directly, and my feelings are therefore not a priori derivable from my physical properties, then there is no conceptual contradiction in ascribing a being all my physical properties, but denying it my conscious ones.)

The argument against physicalism now hinges on the thesis that impossibilities are only conceivable when presented using concepts that refer *indirectly*. For example, take *salt = NaCl*. Even though this could not be otherwise—salt *is* NaCl—someone can certainly conceive of (indeed believe in) NaCl not being salt. However, according to the argument at issue, they can only do this because they are thinking of salt at second hand, as *the* substance, whatever it is, that is white, crystalline, ... This way of thinking leaves it open whether or not salt is in fact NaCl, and thus whether it is necessarily identical to that substance.

But a phenomenal concept like *pain* is not indirect in this way. Phenomenal concepts do not pick out their referents indirectly, by some association with a role, as with *salt*, but directly, in terms of what they are like. So there is no room, the argument goes, for claims made using phenomenal concepts, such as *nociceptive-specific firing is pain*, to be necessarily true, yet appear conceivably false. If this claim were true, it would have to be a priori. Yet it is not.

The crucial premise in this argument is that necessary facts can only appear conceivably false when they are presented using indirect concepts. Or, putting it the other way around, once everything is formulated directly, no necessary truths will appear conceivably false. In short, the crucial premise is that direct concepts are *revelatory*, in the sense of displaying all the necessary properties of their referents a priori. (And then the anti-physicalist reasoning goes: the concept *pain* is direct, so it must be revelatory; so, if my physical nature necessitated my pains, this ought to be knowable a priori; but it is not; therefore pains cannot be physical.)

A posteriori physicalists deny the crucial premise of this argument. They do not accept that direct concepts are always revelatory. Directness is a semantic matter—the concept picks out its reference directly, rather than as the item that satisfies some descriptive role. Revelatoriness is epistemological—the concept renders all necessary features of its referent a priori knowable. A posteriori physicalists insist that the former does not imply the latter.

In particular, they hold that phenomenal concepts are direct but not revelatory. They accept that phenomenal concepts are direct. And as physicalists they of course hold that pains have a physical nature. But they deny that this essential feature of pains must be revealed to us by the phenomenal concept *pain*. You can grasp this direct concept fully, yet not appreciate that pains are necessitated by the relevant brain processes.

An extensive literature is devoted to the question of whether all direct concepts are revelatory, and all directly formulated necessary claims are therefore knowable a priori. (See e.g., Block and Stalnaker 1999; Chalmers and Jackson 2001; Chalmers 2002; Levine 2001, 2010.) A posteriori physicalists and other opponents of this thesis contend that there are plenty of counterexamples. What about identity claims involving proper names, indexical constructions, or observational concepts—'Cary Grant = Archie Leach', 'that dog = her pet', 'round = locus of constant distance from some point'? Earlier I cited the apparent a priori underivability of such claims from the physical facts as an argument against attributing the explanatory gap to this kind of underivability. In the present context, the same cases offer putative examples of directly formulated necessities that are not a priori knowable.

At this point the arguments get messy. Anti-physicalists respond that, despite the prima facie absence of descriptive content, the terms in question should properly be understood as functioning indirectly, and that this is why they do not reveal the identity claims involving them a priori. Some physicalists counter by questioning the way their opponents are drawing the distinction between direct and indirect terms. An alternative physicalist strategy is to grant that in general direct concepts are revelatory and directly formulated necessities a priori, and that a posteriori phenomenal mind-brain claims are therefore an exception to this rule, but maintain that there is nothing wrong with that. And so on. (See Levine 2001: ch 2.4.)

Fortunately, it is possible to cut through much of this dialectic. What really matters for the anti-physicalist argument is whether *phenomenal concepts* are revelatory, not any more general thesis about some wider category of 'direct' concepts. The anti-physicalists say that phenomenal concepts are revelatory, and in particular that they reveal conscious states not to be physical. Physicalists respond that there is no reason to suppose that phenomenal concepts have the power to reveal such things.

Given this, it makes sense for us to address the revelatoriness of phenomenal concepts head on, and by-pass the further issue of whether this can be seen as a special case of some more general principle involving direct concepts. As far as the anti-physicalist argument goes, all that matters is the workings of phenomenal concepts themselves. (Cf Nida-Rümelin 2007; Goff 2011.)

At an intuitive level, it is certainly not implausible that phenomenal concepts are revelatory. Consider what it is like to think at first hand about a stabbing pain, or a visual experience of seeing something red. Does not such thinking acquaint you with the very nature of these conscious states? It certainly seems as if such phenomenal thinking lays bare all essential aspects of the relevant experiences.

A posteriori physicalists will respond that appearances are deceptive. We should not be distracted, they will say, by the close association between phenomenal thinking and the experiences being thought about. Often the experience itself (the pain, the awareness of red) is present when we think about it phenomenally. In other cases, an imagined version of the experience (a 'faint' copy, as Hume put it) accompanies our phenomenal thinking. And, because of this, it can seem that everything is revealed. A version of the experience is right there, before our minds. How can anything essential remain hidden?

But it is one thing, physicalists will object, to *have* an experience. It is another to *know* everything about its nature. Phenomenal thinking might characteristically *give* us the experience, in the sense that we undergo some version of it while thinking about it. But this does not mean it tells us everything about its nature. In particular, it does not mean it will reveal that the experiences are at bottom physical, if they are.

Moreover, the physicalist can continue, there is something deeply mysterious about the idea that merely thinking about something can reveal all its necessary properties. Of course, in the case of complex concepts with internal structure, mere thinking can deliver analytic knowledge; for example, someone who possesses complex concept *square* can work out, just by analysing this concept, that *squares have four sides*. But this model does not seem relevant to the putative power of phenomenal thinking. Phenomenal concepts like *pain* or *seeing something red* do not seem complex; nor, correspondingly, do anti-physicalists maintain that the non-physicality of their referents is an analytic consequence of their internal structure.

Perhaps anti-physicalists can appeal to a different model. Instead of invoking analytic knowledge, they can construe phenomenal thinking as a kind of direct acquaintance, appealing to the point that such thinking is characteristically accompanied by versions of the experiences thought of. The idea would be that we find out about phenomenal states by thinking about them introspectively. We scrutinize our experiences internally, and thereby uncover their nature.

But the mystery remains. Introspection is certainly able to tell us what experiences we are having, and various other things about them. But why should it be guaranteed to tell us about *all* their necessary properties? How is that supposed to work? Any normal information-delivering process is inevitably fallible and only partially informative about the nature of its objects. To hold that introspection is guaranteed to reveal all necessary properties of experience would seem to take us beyond the realm of naturally explicable faculties.

1.8 Neutral Monism

Suppose for the moment that the argument from revelation did hold water. This would scarcely leave the anti-physicalist in a comfortable position. As I observed earlier, modern scientific findings seem to leave epiphenomenalism as the only viable alternative to physicalism. Yet the epiphenomenalist relegation of conscious states to inefficacious causal 'danglers' is not an attractive option. If this is where the argument from revelation ends up, that would itself be a reason for thinking it must have gone wrong somewhere.

But perhaps there is another way out. An increasing number of contemporary philosophers favour an alternative view, known as 'Russellian monism', which offers a way of embracing the argument from revelation while avoiding the entanglements of epiphenomenalism. In effect, this position aims to maintain the causal significance of phenomenal states by viewing both the phenomenal and the physical as grounded in some more fundamental reality.

Let us go back to the argument from revelation. This said that a truth of the form *pains = nociceptive-specific firing* can only be conceivably false if it is formulated in indirect terms. The route from this to Russellian monism hinges on the thought that perhaps it is *nociceptive-specific firing* that is the indirect term, rather than *pain*.

So far I have not queried the idea that physical terms like *nociceptive-specific firing/ NaCl/electric discharge* are direct and revelatory. But there is no reason to take this for granted. A standard account of scientific terms has them referring via theoretical descriptions—to that property, or quantity, that plays such-and-such a theoretically specified role. (So for example, *mass* might be equated with *that quantity that is inversely proportional to acceleration and obeys the law of gravitation*.)

This now offers a different way of squaring the conceivable falsity of *pains = nociceptive-specific firing* with the principle that necessary truths can only be conceivably false if formulated in indirect terms. Suppose that the term *nociceptive-specific firing* refers indirectly to that underlying property, whatever it is, that plays the role specified by neurophysiological theory. Russellian monism now views the conscious feeling of pain as itself grounded in this underlying property (Russell 1927).

This allows us to account for the conceivability of zombies, beings who have nociceptive-specific firing but no pains, as possible beings in whom the relevant theoretical role is filled, not by the underlying property that constitutes pain in the actual world, but by some different and non-conscious property. Since we are thinking of the nociceptive-specific firing only indirectly, as the filler of a theoretically specified role, this leaves it open that this role could possibly be played by something other than its actual filler, indeed by something that fails to constitute any conscious feeling at all.

At the same time, this Russellian move promises to eliminate any worries about the epiphenomenality of pain. After all, pain is now constituted by a basic property, the property that fills the *nociceptive-specific firing* role in the actual world. At first pass, such basic properties look like just the kind of items to enter into fundamental causal relations.

This Russellian position is often associated with some version of the *panpsychist* doctrine that consciousness permeates all parts of the natural world. For some thinkers, this further commitment is motivated by the thought that our introspective awareness of our conscious experience is the only point at which we are directly acquainted with the underlying nature of reality. Since introspection shows reality to be conscious in all cases where its underlying nature is revealed, the thought continues, we should therefore conclude that it is conscious throughout (Goff 2017).

A further motivation for panpsychism derives from a perceived need to *explain* the consciousness that is present in beings with brains like ours. Russellian monists accept the orthodox view that the underlying physical processes that constitute our conscious life are complex, and in particular that they are built up from the same simple components (fundamental field and particles) that compose the rest of nature. Given this, many feel that it would be mysterious for consciousness to emerge in complex brain processes if it were not already present in the simple parts. (Cf Strawson 2003.)

Despite Russellian monism's current popularity, it is questionable whether it marks any real advance on ordinary a posteriori physicalism. On further analysis, it turns out to leave us with many of the same issues, and moreover to generate a number of problems of its own.

An initial difficulty relates to the explanation of macroscopic conscious states in terms of their microscopic parts. Even if the microscopic components are credited with some conscious nature, this will presumably be different in kind from the conscious nature of the wholes they compose. So why is the relation between the conscious parts and the differently conscious wholes any less mysterious than the supposedly puzzling emergence of conscious wholes from non-conscious parts? (Stoljar 2006.)

A converse puzzle involves our phenomenal knowledge of macroscopic conscious states with microscopic parts. If phenomenal concepts reveal all the necessary properties of their referents, then why do they not show pains and other conscious states to be composite? If some state is built from parts, then this is presumably part of its nature. Yet introspection presents conscious states like pains as simple and unified, not composite (Lockwood 1993).

A further worry is that Russellian monism seems to end up flirting with the very epiphenomenalism it is designed to avoid. It is essential to the Russellian position that the *nociceptive-specific firing* role, say, might possibly be filled by a number of different underlying states, including ones that have no conscious nature (as in the zombie version of me). But now it looks as if the conscious differences between these alternative fillers make no difference to their causal powers. After all, by hypothesis these different fillers all display just the same behaviour and conform to just the same scientific laws. If, in addition, the fillers involve variations in consciousness, these variations would thus seem condemned to causal inertness.[7]

Finally, and relatedly, the general metaphysical position on which Russellian monism rests is itself highly contentious. As the Russellians see it, scientific terms are non-revelatory because the specification of a theoretical role leaves it open which underlying entity fills that role. But it is not obvious, to say the least, that we should accept this thesis. Consider the case of mass. As I said, science arguably picks this out as *that quantity that is inversely proportional to acceleration and obeys the law of gravitation*. From the

---

[7] For this line of objection see Howell (2015), and for a Russellian response see Alter and Coleman (2018).

Russellian perspective, then, there is another possible world, just like the actual world, save that some different quantity, *schmass*, plays the mass role there. But this seems a perverse commitment. Surely that would simply be another world that contains *mass*, the same quantity as is present in our world.

This is not the place to resolve the debate about the metaphysical relation between properties and laws (cf Bird 2007). Still, on the face of things, the more natural view would seem to be that basic scientific properties are necessarily attached to their nomological roles. Fix the profile of laws that governs the entity, and you have fixed the entity itself.[8] Why multiply complexity unnecessarily by positing differences that have no further consequences?

All in all, then, Russellian monism seems to generate more problems than it solves. In my view, we would do better to stick with simple a posteriori physicalism, and forget about the supposed argument from relevation. Abductive evidence establishes certain phenomenal-physical identities. Even if both the phenomenal and physical concepts involved pick out their referents directly, the conceivable falsity of these identities does not discredit them. Why ever should we suppose that directly referring terms will reveal all the necessary features of their referents a priori?

1.9 Explaining the Intuition of Distinctness

Let us return to the feeling of an 'explanatory gap'. My earlier diagnosis was that this is simply a manifestation of a widespread intuitive conviction that dualism is true. Even those who take themselves to be persuaded of physicalism cannot shake off the intuition that consciousness is non-physical, and so find themselves hankering for some explanation of how the brain 'gives rise' to conscious feelings.

This diagnosis then left us with a different explanatory need. Why does the intuition of dualism exert such a grip on our minds? One possibility was that we are all persuaded by our awareness of a sound argument for dualism. If there is no such argument,[9] however, then the explanation for the intuition of dualism must lie elsewhere.

---

[8] This is not to deny that some coarse-grained theoretical roles—that of an electrical insulator, say—can be variably realized by different states of affairs with different fine-grained specifications. But that isn't enough for the Russellian monist, who needs even the most fine-grained theoretical roles to be variably realized.

[9] Doesn't a persistent intuition of dualism itself amount to an argument against physicalism? No. E is only evidence against T if E is less probable given T than not-T. However, if the alternatives to physicalism are epiphenomenalism or Russellian monism, then they make dualist intuitions no more likely than physicalism does, at least insofar as we think of these intuitions as publicly expressed. After all, it is agreed on all sides that the conscious realm makes no causal difference to views about it: epiphenomenalists and Russellian monists agree with physicalists about the way the brain works, and so in particular about the processes that give rise to expressions of intuitive dualism. (Cf footnote 2 above.)

As it happens, there is no shortage of existing hypotheses about dualist intuitions. In a moment I shall describe some of these suggestions.

But first it is worth observing that these hypotheses are not in competition. A number of different factors may work together in persuading us against physicalism. Perhaps this itself is a large part of the reason dualist thinking is so persistent. The different psychological pressures favouring dualism gain strength by acting in concert. For each dualist influence that is identified and resisted, others are waiting in the wings, ready to capture our thinking again.

I shall now briefly run through six different theories that have been put forward to account for the prevalence of dualist thinking.[10]

Culture. Perhaps the widespread commitment to dualism is simply a reflection of the influence of religious metaphysics on much everyday thinking. The inherited culture of most societies is shaped by religious beliefs in non-physical realities. It might not be easy to shed the metaphysical ideas we acquire early on from such influences.

Natural-Born Dualists. Many anthropologists and developmental psychologists attribute cultural dualism, including the dualism of religious beliefs, to a more fundamental psychological source. As they see things, the very structure of human thinking inclines us to what they call 'intuitive dualism'. From infancy onwards, the human mind automatically categorizes everything it sees as *either* active self-moving entities directed by minds *or* as passive physical processes triggered by external influences. This categorization thus excludes the possibility of anything that is simultaneously both mental and physical.

Cognitive Architecture. According to many philosophers of mind, when people come to believe an identity of the form $a = b$, they typically 'merge their files' for *a* and *b*. That is, they reorganize their cognitive architecture so that all the items of information previously associated with *a* and *b* respectively are now unified in a single *a/b* file. Perhaps, however, something blocks this merging in the special case of phenomenal-physical identities. Maybe phenomenal concepts are housed in the sensory cortex, while physical concepts are associated with linguistic areas of the brain. This might prevent us from performing the usual 'merge' operation with phenomenal-physical identities, and consequently make us feel that something is amiss with the identities themselves.

The Antipathetic Fallacy. Recall a point made earlier, that phenomenal thinking about a conscious state is typically accompanied by some version of the state itself: when we think phenomenally about pain, we normally either have a pain, or we recreate a 'faint copy' in imagination. Now consider a thought like *pains = nociceptive-specific firing*. When we contemplate this thought, we might naturally enough form the impression that the pain itself, the feeling, is present on the left hand side—given that a version of the pain itself is likely to accompany this phenomenal thinking—whereas by contrast there is no such feeling on the right hand side—exercising the

---

[10] For a more detailed discussion of the literature on explanations for dualist intuitions, see Papineau (2010 sect 7). I would like to thank Dara Ghaznavi for drawing my attention to Place's 'phenomenological fallacy'.

physical concept *nociceptive-specific firing* does not itself generally activate any pain. And we might for this reason conclude that the right hand side 'leaves out' the pain, and so does not succeed in referring to it. Now, of course this is a fallacy (I have dubbed it 'the antipathetic fallacy', Papineau 1993): even if the concept on right hand side does not *use* the pain, as the left hand side does, this is no reason to conclude that it does not *mention* it. But for all that, it is still a highly seductive fallacy.

The Phenomenological Fallacy. Everyday thinking (along with some philosophical theories) takes the view that sensory experiences are constituted in part by ordinary worldly properties: when you see a green circle, the properties of greenness and roundness are in some sense literally present in your experience. However, it is clear that these worldly properties are not instantiated in the brain—nothing in the brain is green or round. So the natural inference is that the sensory experiences must be distinct from brain processes. U. T. Place called this inference 'the phenomenological fallacy' and located the mistake in the initial premise that worldly properties are constituents of experiences (Place 1956). Perhaps Place was too quick to diagnose a fallacy. Maybe there are good senses in which worldly properties are constituents of sensory experience, and indeed senses in which this is consistent with physicalism. Still, however these niceties work out, the point remains that the manifest absence of properties like greenness and roundness from the brain might be the reason why many people are convinced that sensory experiences cannot be physical.

Revelation. Finally, recall the suggestion that phenomenal concepts are revelatory. In an earlier section I argued again this suggestion. But, as I said at the time, it is a highly intuitive idea. When you think at first hand about a stabbing pain, or visual experience of seeing something red, it certainly seems as if you are acquainted with the very nature of these conscious states, and that this reveals them to be non-physical. In my view, of course, introspection lacks the power to show us that experiences are non-physical. But I have no doubt that many people think it does show this, and embrace dualism for that reason.

1.10 Final Thoughts on the 'Where' Question

I have argued that a clear-headed physicalism resolves the 'how' question about consciousness. Conscious states are simply one and the same as physical states. The supposed 'explanatory gap' between brain and mind is nothing but a corollary of dualist intuitions. Certainly some physical states are like something for the beings that have them. But what is so surprising about that? That's how it is.

I would now like to conclude by briefly raising some doubts about the 'where' question. Much contemporary research is concerned with the location of conscious phenomena. Such research aims to discover which neural processes are like something for their subjects, and which are not. For instance, is early visual processing in cortical area V2 conscious for humans? Are neural processes in fish conscious? What about activity in insect brains?

Queries like these are the focus of a great deal of contemporary debate. But I am not sure that they are good questions. It seems to me possible that they too are a misplaced consequence of intuitive dualist commitments.

Ned Block has distinguished *phenomenal* from *access* consciousness (Block 1995). A state is phenomenally conscious if it is like something. It is access conscious if the subject can make use of it for reasoning and control of action. In beings who are capable of introspectively reporting their own mental states, the accessible conscious states will thus be the ones that normal subjects can report.

Access consciousness is certainly an interesting and significant category. Prior to the relevant research, who would have thought that people cannot always report the dorsal stream information that guides their hands' grasping movements (Milner and Goodale 2008), or that patients given morphine remain aware of their pains even after they cease to be distressing? We certainly want to know which cerebral states are accessible to subjects, and which not.

Still, given that we have this distinction, do we need any further division between states that are and are not *phenomenally conscious*? Why suppose that this concept draws a significant line in nature, now that we have taken care to distinguish it from the clearly-defined cognitive role of accessibly in the sense of contributing to reasoning and the control of action?

Of course, if phenomenal consciousness were constituted by some extra mind stuff, something additional to the physical realm, then there would be a real difference between the presence and absence of this mind stuff. However, once we free ourselves from the intuitive myth of such extra mind stuff, should we continue to think of phenomenal consciousness as constituting a distinctive physical kind?

I don't entirely want to rule out this possibility. By way of comparison, the notion of *life* used to be associated with the idea of an *élan vital*, some non-physical substance that animates living beings. But, even though we now reject any such non-physical substance, we still recognize animate beings as a significant sub-category of physical systems.

I doubt, however, whether an analogous point applies to consciousness. In the case of life, we can point to a well-defined range of features that make it worth differentiating living beings: self-sustaining, anti-entropic, reproductive. It is not clear that anything similar gives us a hold on phenomenal consciousness. We can of course distinguish some cerebral states as those to which we have introspective access. But it is not clear that, beyond that, we have any clear ideas about what distinctive features distinguish states that are phenomenally 'like something' from other physical processes.[11]

---

[11] Lee 2014 argues similarly that a committed physicalism undermines any distinctive role for phenomenal consciousness. But see Shea and Bayne (2010) for an attempt to identify such a role.

Isn't the reality of phenomenal consciousness simply manifest? What about the technicolour phenomenology of visual experience, or the vicious unpleasantness of intense pain? Well, of course I don't want to deny these things. But this doesn't necessarily mark out visual experiences or pains as different in kind from other physical processes.

It is tempting to think of our introspective gaze as being attracted by some kind of inner illumination. The reason some states, but not others, are accessible, we suppose, is because they glow with a special light. But this is not the only way to see things. By way of analogy, consider the items that appear on the television news. We don't think that they are distinguished from the ordinary run of events by some distinctive radiance. They are just events that happen to attract the attention of the cameras. Similarly there is no reason to think of our conscious states as being distinguished by some extra lustre. They appear to us as they do in virtue of our having access to them, not because they have some distinctive luminosity.

In some ways, the picture I am here recommending is not unlike panpsychism. In my view, the idea of phenomenally 'being like something', as opposed to being introspectively accessible, fails to draw a line in nature. We should not think of this idea as distinguishing events lit up by phenomenology from those that are mere darkness. But I adopt this even-handedness, not because I think something needs to be added to the physical realm, as do orthodox panpsychists, but because I think that physical states as such are already adequate to account for the nature of conscious experience. Ordinary physical states are perfectly well-qualified to be like something for subjects. To achieve this, they need only play a role in reasoning and action planning, and so feature in the integrated mental lives of the beings that have them.

References

Alter, T. and Coleman, C. (2018), 'Panpsychism and Russellian Monism' in W. Seager (ed.), *Routledge Handbook of Panpsychism*. London: Routledge.
Armstrong, D. (1968), *A Materialist Theory of the Mind*. London: Routledge and Kegan Paul.
Ball, D. (2009), 'There Are No Phenomenal Concepts', *Mind* 118: 935–62.
Bird, A. (2007), *Nature's Metaphysics. Laws and Properties*. Oxford: Clarendon Press.
Block, N. (1978), 'Reductionism: Philosophical Analysis' in *Encyclopedia of Bioethics*. London: Macmillan.
Block, N. (1995), 'On a Confusion about a Function of Consciousness', *Behavioral and Brain Sciences* 18: 227–87.
Block, N. and Stalnaker, R. (1999), 'Conceptual Analysis, Dualism, and the Explanatory Gap', *Philosophical Review* 108: 1–46.
Chalmers, D. (2002), 'Does Conceivability Entail Possibility?' in J. Hawthorne and T. Gendler (eds), *Conceivability and Possibility*. Oxford: Oxford University Press.
Chalmers, D. and Jackson, F. (2001), 'Conceptual Analysis and Reductive Explanation', *Philosophical Review* 110: 315–61.
Davidson, D. (1970), 'Mental Events' in L. Foster and J. Swanson (eds), *Experience and Theory*. London: Duckworth.
Dennett, D. (1992), *Consciousness Explained*. London: Allen Lane.

Feigl, H. (1958), 'The "Mental" and the "Physical"' in H. Feigl, M. Scriven, and G. Maxwell (eds), *Minnesota Studies in the Philosophy of Science vol II*. Minneapolis: University of Minnesota Press.

Goff, P. (2011), 'A Posteriori Physicalists Get Our Phenomenal Concepts Wrong', *Australasian Journal of Philosophy* 89: 191–209.

Goff, P. (2017), *Consciousness and Fundamental Reality*. Oxford: Oxford University Press.

Howell, R. (2015). 'The Russellian Monist's Problems with Mental Causation', *Philosophical Quarterly* 65: 22–39.

Jackson, F. (1986), 'What Mary Didn't Know', *Journal of Philosophy* 83: 291–5.

Jackson, F. (2007), 'The Knowledge Argument, Diaphonousness, Representationalism' in T. Alter and S. Walter (eds), *Phenomenal Concepts and Phenomenal Knowledge*. Oxford: Oxford University Press.

Lee, G. (2014), 'Materialism and the Epistemic Significance of Consciousness' in U. Kriegel (ed.), *Current Controversies in Philosophy of Mind*. London: Routledge.

Levine, J. (1983), 'Materialism and Qualia: The Explanatory Gap', *Pacific Philosophical Quarterly* 64: 354–61.

Levine, J. (2001), *Purple Haze. The Puzzle of Consciousness*. Oxford: Oxford University Press.

Levine, J. (2010), 'The Q Factor: Modal Rationalism vs Modal Autonomism', *Philosophical Review* 119: 365–80.

Lewis, D. (1966), 'An Argument for the Identity Theory', *Journal of Philosophy* 63: 17–25.

Lewis, D. (1988), 'What Experience Teaches', *Proceedings of the Russellian Society of Sydney University* 13: 29–57.

Lockwood, M. (1993), 'The Grain Problem' in H. Robinson (ed.), *Objections to Physicalism*. Oxford: Oxford University Press.

McGinn, C. (1991), *The Problem of Consciousness*. Oxford: Basil Blackwell.

Menzies, P. (2008), 'Causal Exclusion, the Determination Relation, and Contrastive Causation' in J. Kallestrup and J. Hohwy (eds), *Being Reduced: New Essays on Reductive Explanation and Special Science Causation*. Oxford: Oxford University Press.

Milner, A. and Goodale, M. (2008), 'Two Visual Systems Reviewed', *Neuropsychologia* 46: 774–85.

Nagel, T. (1986), *The View from Nowhere*. Oxford: Oxford University Press.

Nida-Rümelin, N. (2007), 'Grasping Phenomenal Properties' in T. Alter and S. Walter (eds), *Phenomenal Concepts and Phenomenal Knowledge*, Oxford: Oxford University Press.

Oppenheim, P. and Putnam, H. (1958), 'Unity of Science as a Working Hypothesis' in H. Feigl, M. Scriven, and G. Maxwell (eds), *Minnesota Studies in the Philosophy of Science vol II*. Minneapolis: University of Minnesota Press.

Papineau, D. (1993), 'Physicalism, Consciousness, and the Antipathetic Fallacy', *Australasian Journal of Philosophy* 71:169–83.

Papineau, D. (2002), *Thinking about Consciousness*. Oxford: Oxford University Press.

Papineau, D. (2007), 'Kripke's Argument is Ad Hominem Not Two-Dimensional' in *Philosophical Perspectives* 21: 475–94.

Papineau, D. (2010), 'What Exactly is the Explanatory Gap?', *Philosophia* 39: 5–19.

Place, U. (1956), 'Is Consciousness a Brain Process?', *British Journal of Psychology* 47: 44–50.

Robinson, W. (2015), 'Epiphenomenalism' *Stanford Encyclopedia of Philosophy*.

Russell, B. (1927), *The Analysis of Matter*. London: Kegan Paul.

Shea, N. and Bayne, T. (2010), 'The Vegetative State and the Science of Consciousness', *British Journal for the Philosophy of Science* 61: 459–84.

Smart, J. (1959), 'Sensations and Brain Processes', *Philosophical Review* 68: 141–56.
Stoljar, D. (2006), *Ignorance and Imagination: The Epistemic Origin of the Problem of Consciousness*. Oxford: Oxford University Press.
Strawson, G. (2003), 'Real Materialism' in G. Strawson (ed.), *Real Materialism and Other Essays*. Oxford: Oxford University Press.
Tye, M. (2009), *Consciousness Revisited*. Cambridge, MA: MIT Press.
Woodward, J. (2005), *Making Things Happen*. Oxford: Oxford University Press.

PART I

VARIETIES OF CONSCIOUS EXPERIENCE

CHAPTER 2

VISUAL EXPERIENCE

PÄR SUNDSTRÖM

2.1 INTRODUCTION

A visual experience, as understood here, is a sensory event that is conscious, or *like something* to undergo. I include among visual experiences veridical perceptions, illusions, and hallucinations, but I leave open whether these form a common kind. (That issue will not be discussed at length, but will be touched on in Section 2.4.)

It is standardly accepted that visual experiences—or at least those that are veridical perceptions—have an 'act-object structure'. For example, in an experience of red, we can distinguish (i) red, which is the 'object' of the experience, and (ii) the *experience of* red (the 'act'). However, the character of the 'acts' is disputed, and the character and the range of the 'objects' of these acts are also disputed. Are the acts *representations* of some kind? Or non-representational relations? What kind of awareness do we, and can we, have of visual experience *acts* as opposed to what they are of? An experience of red is an awareness *of red*, but does it also involve an awareness of *the experience of* red? Regarding the 'objects' of visual experiences, it is widely accepted that they include properties like red. But exactly which properties are among the objects of visual experiences? Was, for example, Hume right that we never experience necessary causal connections between events? And, do the objects of visual experiences include *particulars*, and if so which particulars? Do we sometimes visually experience mind-independent particulars like trees? Do we sometimes visually experience mind-dependent, particular 'sense-data'?

This chapter will make contact with all the just-mentioned issues, but the focus will be selective. Section 2.2 discusses in what sense, if any, visual experiences are 'transparent', and what in turn follows from that. Section 2.3 discusses which properties we are presented with in visual experiences. Section 2.4 briefly discusses whether we are ever presented with spatiotemporal outer particulars—or other kinds of particular—in visual experiences.

2.2 Transparency

Much recent literature has debated whether visual experiences are 'transparent', and what what further conclusions one can, or cannot, draw from settling that issue. Despite the frequent talk about '*the* transparency of experience', there are, as this section will illustrate, many different transparency claims. They raise quite different issues, and figure in quite different arguments.

2.2.1 Varieties of Transparency Claims

Let us first acquaint ourselves with some formulations of 'the' transparency idea. Current discussions often trace back to the following passage from Gilbert Harman:

> When Eloise sees a tree before her, the colors she experiences are all experienced as features of the tree and its surroundings. None of them are experienced as intrinsic features of her experience. Nor does she experience any features of anything as intrinsic features of her experience. And that is true of you too.... Look at a tree and try to turn your attention to intrinsic features of your visual experience. I predict you will find that the only features there to turn your attention to will be features of the presented tree.   (Harman 1990: 39)

A few years later Michael Tye picks up the thread:

> Focus your attention on a square that has been painted blue. Intuitively, you are directly aware of blueness and squareness as out there in the world away from you, as features of an external surface. Now shift your attention inward and try to become aware of your experience itself, inside you, apart from its objects. Try to focus your attention on some intrinsic feature of the experience that distinguishes it from other experiences, something other than what it is an experience *of*. The task seems impossible: one's awareness seems always to slip through the experience to blueness and squareness, as instantiated together in an external object. In turning one's mind inward to attend to the experience, one seems to end up concentrating on what is outside again, on external features or properties   (Tye 1995: 30).[1]

These passages, and others like them, make transparency claims that vary in several dimensions. Let me note five dimensions of variation.

(1) Transparency claims vary with regard to what we may call their *modality*. For example, one type of claim concerns what we *are*—or are typically—aware or not aware of. Another type of claim concerns what we *can* or *cannot* be aware of.

---

[1] See also Moore (1903: 450) for a much-cited, earlier transparency formulation, and Pasnau (2016) for a review of such ideas in pre-contemporary philosophy.

(2) Transparency claims vary with regard to the *mental acts* they focus on. For example, some are claims about what we *experience*, others about what we can *attend* to, and yet others about what we can be *aware* of.
(3) Transparency claims vary with regard to the *objects* of the mental acts they focus on. For example, some say that we are not aware of our *experiences*, others that we are not aware of *properties of* our experiences or of *intrinsic* properties of them.
(4) Some transparency claims are ('positive') assertions about what we *are or can* be aware of (e.g., colours of external objects). Others are ('negative') assertions about what we are *not or cannot* be aware of (e.g., intrinsic properties of experiences).
(5) Some transparency claims stay within a 'phenomenological bracket': they are claims about how, say, experiences or introspections *present*—or do not present—things to us. Other transparency claims go beyond such a bracket, asserting, for example, that when we try to attend to an experience, we end up focussing on what (not just *seems* to us to be but) *actually are* properties of external objects.

The remainder of this section will revolve around two transparency claims. These claims or close kin of them have been central in recent discussions. I will consider if the claims are correct, and what follows if they are.

2.2.2 Transparency and the Whereabouts of Colours

Let me start with this claim, which some have tried to establish on the *basis* of 'transparency':

Non-Colour-Mentalism: No experienced colour is a property of a mental or mind-dependent object.

Non-Colour-Mentalism stands opposed both to the view that experienced colours are properties of mind-dependent *sense-data* that are the immediate objects of our visual experiences (see, e.g., Russell 1912; Jackson 1977; Robinson 1994), and to the view that experienced colours are properties ('qualia') of visual experiences themselves (see, e.g., Robinson 2004).[2]

One 'transparency strategy' for defending *Non-Colour-Mentalism* appeals to the following claim, which echoes the first two sentences from Harman above:

Transparency-1: We experience colours as properties of external objects like trees, and not as properties of experiences or other mind-dependent things.

---

[2] That is one but not the only theory that goes by the name 'qualia theory'. See Crane (2000) and Sundström (2014) on different 'qualia theories'.

Transparency-1 is a conjunction of a 'positive' claim about how we experience colours, and a 'negative' claim about how we do not experience them. Both conjuncts remain within a 'phenomenological bracket'. As formulated, *Transparency-1* can be read with stronger or weaker 'modalities'. I will tinker with some variations along this dimension, but for the time being, I will operate with a strong-modality version according to which we *inevitably* experience colours as properties of external objects and *cannot* experience them in other ways.

How might one argue for *Non-Colour-Mentalism* on the basis of *Transparency-1*? It is clear that even a strong-modality version of *Transparency-1* does not *by itself* provide much support for *Non-Colour-Mentalism*. *Transparency-1* is a claim about how we *experience* and do not experience colours. Meanwhile, *Non-Colour-Mentalism* is a claim about what experienced colours *are*—or are not—properties of. And things are not always as we experience them. One can therefore consistently (a) accept *Transparency-1* and (b) with, a sense-datum or 'qualia' theorist, deny *Non-Colour-Mentalism*.[3] An argument for *Non-Colour-Mentalism* on the basis of *Transparency-1* requires an explanation of why the combination of (a) and (b) should be a bad idea.

One reason that has been offered in this context is that perceptual experiences are *trustworthy* when it comes to the whereabouts of colours. For example, Tye has argued for something like *Non-Colour-Mentalism* on the basis of something like *Transparency-1* and such a 'trustworthiness'-claim:

> Intuitively, the surfaces you see directly are publicly observable physical surfaces.... In seeing these surfaces, you are immediately and directly aware of a whole host of qualities.... you experience them as being qualities of the surfaces. None of the qualities of which you are directly aware in seeing the various surfaces look to you to be qualities of your experience.... To suppose that the qualities of which perceivers are directly aware in undergoing ordinary, everyday experiences are really qualities of the experiences would be to convict such experiences of massive error. This is just not credible.   (Tye 2000: 46)

One can develop at least two different arguments from this suggestion. The first argument appeals to the 'positive' claim that we experience colours as properties of external objects, and adds this trustworthiness claim, which rules out 'universal false positives':

Sometimes-Correct: If we experience colours as properties of external objects, then some experienced colour is a property of an external object.

To get to *Non-Colour-Mentalism* from this, one must also add:

---

[3] This often-made observation goes back at least to Hume (1758: sect 12).

Not-Both: It is not the case that some experienced colour is a property of an external object *and* that some experienced colour is a property of a mental or mind-dependent object.

The second argument appeals to the negative claim that we do *not* experience colours as properties of mental objects and adds the following, quite different trustworthiness claim, which rules out false negatives:

No-Misses: If we do not experience colours as properties of mental or mind-dependent objects, then no experienced colour is a property of a mental or mind-dependent object.

I shall here make only some brief remarks about the strengths of these arguments.

It is clear that, even if one takes *Transparency-1* as given, each argument requires at least one substantial additional assumption. It is arguable that the burden of defending such assumptions is often underplayed in the literature. For example, Tye does not defend any such assumptions in the context of the above-quoted passage.

Moreover, *Transparency-1* is itself controversial, at least on the strong-modality reading that we have so far assumed. For example, Paul Boghossian and David Velleman argue that *colours of after-images* are experienced as belonging to 'figments of one's eyes' (1989: 87), which I take to imply the negation of strong-modality *Transparency-1*. Similarly, Hilary Putnam (2014) argues, on the basis of empirical and clinical observations (reported in Held and Hein 1963, Held et al. 2011, and Ostrovsky et al. 2009), that 'transparent experience' is something learned and that we do not experience colours as being 'out there' in early developmental stages.[4]

Transparency-1 is less controversial on a weak-modality reading according to which we (mature human adults) *typically* experience colours as properties of external objects and typically not in other ways. But that version of *Transparency-1* can also carry lesser burdens in arguments for *Non-Colour-Mentalism*. Consider, for example, the first of the two arguments spelled out above. If we can establish a strong-modality version of *Transparency-1*, we need in the next step appeal to nothing more than a *strong-modality-antecedent* version of *SometimesCorrect*. That commits us to the claim that, if no experienced colour is a property of an external object, then it is *possible* for us to not experience colours as properties of external objects. If by contrast we can establish only a weak-modality version of *Transparency-1* we must in the next step defend a *weak-modality-antecedent* version of *SometimesCorrect*. That commits us to the less plausible claim that, if no experienced colour is a property of an external object, then it is *atypical* for us to experience colours as properties of external objects.

---

[4] See also Kind (2003) for doubts specifically about *strong-modality* transparency claims.

2.2.3 Transparency and Introspection of Properties of Experiences

Here is another transparency claim, which is suggested by the quotes from Harman and Tye in Section 2.2.1:

Transparency-2: There is no property P such that P is a property of a visual experience E and one can become aware of the P-ness of E by introspecting E.[5]

By 'introspection' I here understand our peculiar way of accessing our own mental states, *however* that peculiar way is understood. To be 'aware of the P-ness' of something is understood in a distinct sense. In the intended sense, you can be aware of *a fact* of the form x is P without being aware of the *P-ness* of x—or the P-ness of anything. For example, waiting at a traffic light, you may be aware *that* the light facing away is green. But there is a sense in which you are not aware of the *greenness* of that light. You are aware of the *fact* that the light facing away is green by being aware of *motions* of certain cars (compare Dretske 1999).

To appreciate what *Transparency-2* claims and does not claim, it is crucial to bear in mind the distinction, from Section 2.1 above, between experiences and their objects. Take an experience of red. Even though the experience is *of* red, it may not itself *have* the redness that it is *of*—or be red at all (compare Harman 1990: 35 and Dretske 1995: 36). And if the experience does not have the redness that it is of, *Transparency-2* allows that by introspecting the experience one can become aware of that redness. Consider on the other hand the property *being a visual experience*. This is a property that any visual experience has. *Transparency-2* therefore rules out that one can, by introspecting an experience, become aware of its *visual experienceness*. Consider also the fact that one can have blurry experiences of red. The property *being blurry* is plausibly a property of experiences. If it is, *Transparency-2* rules out that one can, by introspecting an experience, become aware of its blurriness.

Transparency-2 is thus a quite substantive claim. It is arguable that *Transparency-2* makes a more substantive and interesting claim on its own than *Transparency-1* does on its own. *Transparency-2* can also be used to support significant conclusions about visual consciousness. I will shortly discuss whether *Transparency-2* might be defensible, and what one might be able to infer about visual consciousness on the basis of it. But let me first make two sets of observations about the 'lay of the land' around *Transparency-2*.

First: Claims in the vicinity of *Transparency-2* often feature in conjunction with *intentionalist* views according to which experiences are representations. However, *Transparency-2* can be naturally combined with other views as well. Consider, for example, a naïve realist theory according to which having a visual experience of red amounts to standing in a non-representational relation to a mind-independent red

---

[5] Speaks (2009, 2015) defends transparency claims closely related to this.

object or its redness. This view can be combined with *Transparency-2*; they jointly entail that one cannot by introspecting a visual experience become aware of any property-instance of the relevant experiencing relation. *Transparency-2* can similarly be combined with a sense-datum theory according to which having a visual experience of red amounts to standing in a relation to a mind-independent sense-datum.[6]

Second and relatedly: There is a two-way independence between *Transparency-1* and *Transparency-2*. For example, an intentionalist or naïve realist can accept the *Transparency-1* claim that colours are inevitably experienced by us as properties of mind-independent external objects and never in other ways, and maintain, contra *Transparency-2*, that we sometimes become introspectively aware of property-instances of our experiences, like blurriness. For the converse independence, one may think that we *sometimes*—for example, in having after-images—experience colours as belonging to mind-dependent objects, and still accept the *Transparency-2* claim that we can never—even in having after-images—become introspectively aware of property-instances of our experiences; that we inevitably 'see through' our experiences to what they are *of*, which are sometimes mind-dependent objects.[7]

Let us now consider whether *Transparency-2* might be plausible. I will first discuss two candidate counter-examples.

Consider to begin with the property *being a visual experience*.[8] It is indisputable that we can, on the basis of introspection, become aware *that we are having a visual experience*. But as we have noted, one can grant this and still maintain that we are never, in the intended sense, introspectively aware of the *visual experienceness* of an experience that one has. To repeat, one can in general be aware that some x is P by being, in the intended sense, aware not of the P-ness of x or the P-ness of anything, but of some other property of some other thing. Now, Dretske (1994, 1995), Tye (2000: sect 3.2, 2014a: sect 2), and Byrne (2005, 2012) all argue that when we are introspectively aware of the fact that we have a visual experience, we gain this awareness, not by being introspectively aware of *visual experienceness*, but by being visually aware of the colours, shapes, and motions of

---

[6] See Martin (1998: sect 1), and Tye (2000: 47) for related observations.

[7] There is, however, one important connection between *Transparency-2* and issues from the preceding section. The preceding mentioned a type of 'qualia' theory according to which experienced colours are properties of experiences. It is difficult to combine that qualia theory with *Transparency-2*. For it seems very plausible that, *if* experienced colours are properties of experiences, then one can by introspecting a visual experience become aware of its experienced colour. And, it is doubtful that *Transparency-2* can ground a strong case against this kind of qualia theory (compare Sundström 2014: sect 7). If that is right, then *Transparency-2* is plausible only if there are *independent* grounds for rejecting that kind of qualia theory. Now Section 2.2.2 outlined two *Transparency-1* based arguments against—*inter alia*—this kind of qualia theory. If either of these arguments is the *best* argument against that kind of qualia theory, then the acceptability of *Transparency-2* relies on the acceptability of *Transparency-1*. One might understand Tye (2000: 45 ff., partly cited above) as arguing in such stages, although he does not explicitly break down his discussion that way. For *non-transparency based* arguments against the relevant qualia theory, see Mehta (2013) and Sundström (2014: sect 7).

[8] Lycan (2004: sect 6.2) cites this property as a counter-example to a transparency claim that he finds in Tye (2002).

external objects like trees and cars. If that is correct, the property *being a visual experience* is not a counter-example to *Transparency-2*.

Let us next consider *blurriness*. And let us again start with some indisputable facts.

The boundaries of objects are more or less distinct. Furry things have less distinct boundaries than knives for example. And visual experiences can be more or less sharp. There are often similarities between (a) a sharp visual experience of an indistinctly bounded object and (b) a blurry experience of a distinctly bounded object. For example, both experiences may—as we may put it—'fail to present a distinct boundary'. But there is an important difference between these cases. A sharp visual experience of an indistinctly bounded object fails to present a distinct boundary *because* of how the object is while a blurry experience of a distinctly bounded object fails to present a distinct boundary because of how the experience is. A further fact is that when we are in a situation of one of these types, we can often easily tell which type of situation we are in.

Blurry vision is a counter-example to *Transparency-2* if we sometimes tell that we see a distinctly bounded object blurrily by being, in the relevant sense, introspectively aware of the blurriness of our experience. Tim Crane seems to promote such a view. He asks whether blurry seeing of a distinctly bounded object is not

> a straightforward case of where one can be 'directly' aware of an aspect of one's experience which is not an aspect of the objects of experience? It is natural to say that I am aware of blurriness; but I am not aware of blurriness by being aware of any other properties; and blurriness does not seem to be a property of objects of experience. (Crane 2006: 130)[9]

However, there are alternative explanations of the indisputable fact that we can often easily tell whether we see a distinctly bounded object blurrily or see an indistinctly bounded object sharply. One alternative explanation is that we tell such cases apart on the basis of a variety of (typically easily accessible) cues. One kind of cue derives from the boundaries characteristic of various types of objects. If an object looks knife-like but is not seen to have a distinct boundary when one focuses on it, that raises the chance that it is seen blurrily. Another cue is whether there are *some or no* distinct boundaries in the visual field. Blurry vision typically affects the whole visual field. Thus, if *some* object in the visual field is seen to have a distinct boundary, that raises the chance that the visual experience is sharp. If the availability of cues like these always suffice to explain our ability to tell apart blurry seeing of distinct boundaries and sharp seeing of indistinct boundaries, then (putative) introspective awareness of the blurriness of one's experience is not required to explain this.[10]

---

[9] See Bach (1997: 467) and Smith (2008) for similar views.

[10] This proposal develops a suggestion by Schroer (2002). The proposal can be combined with various suggestions about the content of blurry vision. I would be most inclined to combine it with something like the proposal from Dretske (2003: 77) that blurry vision incorrectly represents objects as having less distinct boundaries than they have. For a recent discussion of this and some competing proposals, see Allen (2013).

The above provides, I hope, a flavour of how *Transparency-2* can be defended against purported counter-examples. Let me add one remark relevant to the assessment of the claim.

I have so far explained 'awareness of the P-ness' of something only by *example*. I have not tried to analyse this phenomenon. Nor will I. But it *might* be plausible that 'awareness of P-ness', in the sense exemplified, is best understood as a kind of *perceptual* awareness.[11] And, it *might* be plausible that perception is in some ways a bad model for introspection; in particular, that introspection is always and only an awareness *that* so-and-so is the case, and never awareness of P-ness, in the present sense.[12] If all this is right, that provides reason to accept *Transparency-2*.

I will conclude this section by briefly discussing a line of argument concerning visual *consciousness* based on *Transparency-2*.

Let us take it as given that what a visual experience is *like* is at least *partly* constituted by its being *of* such-and-such. For example, what my current visual experience is like is at least partly constituted by its being of red. We can then go on to ask whether or not the following is correct:

Nothing-Other-Than-Of: What a visual experience is like is not constituted by any factor other than its being of such-and-such.

There is a natural line of thought leading from *Transparency-2* to *Nothing-Other-Than-Of*. It is natural to think that there is a close connection between consciousness and introspection (compare for example Kriegel 2002: 175–6). Consider now the following specification of that thought (*C* and *I* for *consciousness* and *introspection* respectively):

CI-Link: If what a visual experience E is like is constituted by some factor other than its being of such-and-such, then that factor is a property P such that P is a property of E and one can become aware of the P-ness of E by introspecting E.

CI-Link rings somewhat plausible, to my ears, and together with *Transparency-2* it entails *Nothing-Other-Than-Of*.

Now, a problem with this line of thought is that there are serious worries about *Nothing-Other-Than-Of*. I will focus on one. It is standardly accepted that there are cases of unconscious perception. And, any unconscious perception differs from any conscious

---

[11] Stoljar (2004: 371) claims that this is 'the usual way' of understanding such awareness, and Dretske (1999), after highlighting that one can be *aware that x is F* without being *aware of F*, moves without comments between locutions like '*sees F*', '*perceives F*', '*senses F*' on the one hand, and 'is *aware of F*' on the other.

[12] Compare Shoemaker (1994, especially lecture 1) and Dretske (1999). Perceptual models of introspection go back at least to Locke (1689). For some relevant recent discussion of differences and similarities between introspection and perception, see (besides the just-mentioned Shoemaker and Dretske) also Armstrong (1968: ch 15), Lycan (1996: ch 2; 2004), Rosenthal (2002: sect 2), Goldman (2006: ch 9), and Picciuto and Carruthers (2014).

perception in what it *is like*: any conscious perception is like *something*, but no unconscious perception is. Yet, it may be possible that some unconscious perception is *of* exactly the same that some conscious perception is of. For example, each may be of a red square. If so, then contrary to *Nothing-Other-Than-Of*, what a conscious perception is *like* must be partly constituted by some factor other than what it is of. And if *Nothing-Other-Than-Of* is incorrect, then either *CI-Link* or *Transparency-2* must be incorrect.

I will briefly outline one strategy (i) for retaining *Nothing-Other-Than-Of*, *Transparency-2*, and *CI-Link* in view of this objection, and two strategies (ii–iii) for retaining as much as possible, as it were, of this package.

The first strategy, (i), is to argue that an unconscious perception cannot, after all, be *of* what a conscious perception is of. For example, Ian Phillips (2016 and in Phillips and Block 2017) questions that there are any cases of unconscious perception. To the extent that that is doubtful, it may also be doubtful that some unconscious perception could possibly be of exactly what some conscious perception is of.[13] If there is promise in this thought, then one might after all be able to retain the whole package of *Nothing-Other-Than-Of*, *Transparency-2*, and *CI-Link*.

Barring that option, one must give up either *Transparency-2* or *CI-Link*. But each alternative has room for a kind of minimal retreat.

Beginning with *Transparency-2*, one might—this is strategy (ii)—urge that the property *being conscious*—or *like something at all*—is the *sole* exception to *Transparency-2*. One will then urge that we should accept, instead of *Transparency-2*:

Transparency-2*: Except for the property *being conscious*, there is no property P such that P is a property of a visual experience E and one can become aware of the P-ness of E by introspecting E.

One can then retain *CI-Link* without getting committed to *Nothing-Other-Than-Of*. *CI-Link* and *Transparency-2** commits one to only the following, more cautious claim, which has a significant following in the literature:

Nothing-Other-Than-Of-and-Conscious: What an experience is like is not constituted by any factor other than its being of such-and-such and its being conscious.[14]

The retreat to *Transparency-2**, *CI-Link*, and *Nothing-Other-Than-Of-and-Conscious* suggests that a visual experience has exactly two properties that constitute what it is like: the property *being conscious* and the property *being of such-and-such*. The former property is one that we can become aware of by introspection. The second is not, but we can

---

[13] Thau (2002: ch 5) may be sympathetic to this view.
[14] *Nothing-Other-Than-Of-And-Conscious* is accepted by Tye (1995, 2000), Byrne (2001), Chalmers (2004), and Kriegel (2009), but it is not clear that they all accept it together with *Transparency-2** and *CI-Link*. An alternative way of accepting it follows momentarily.

become aware *that* an experience has it by being aware of other properties, for example, by being *visually* aware of the redness and squareness of an outer object.

An alternative, minimal-retreat strategy, (iii), is to urge that the property *being conscious* is the sole exception to *CI-Link*. One will then urge that we should accept:

CI-Link*: If what a visual experience E is like is constituted by some factor other than its being of such-and-such and its being conscious, then that factor is a property P such that P is a property of E and one can become aware of the P-ness of E by introspecting E.

Then one can retain *Transparency-2* without getting committed to *Nothing-Other-Than-Of*. *CI-Link** and *Transparency-2* commit one, again, to nothing more than *Nothing-Other-Than-Of-and-Conscious*. This package suggests that a visual experience has exactly two properties that constitute what it is like: the property *being conscious* and the property *being of such-and-such*. But we cannot become aware of either of these by introspecting an experience. This position requires that we become aware *that* an experiences has both these properties by being aware of other properties.

2.3 Which Properties Are we Presented with in Visual Experience?

We operated above with the idea that what an experience is *like* is partly constituted by its *being of* such-and-such. But what are visual experiences of? As we have seen, it is natural to think that visual experiences are in a sense of less than what we can come to know on the basis of them. To re-employ the earlier example, I can come to know on the basis of visual experience that the traffic light facing away is green although I do not experience any greenness. Now greenness is a property that I plausibly *sometimes* experience. But there may be cases where I come to know something of the form x is P on the basis of visual experience and where P is a property I *never* experience. For example, I sometimes come to know on the basis of visual experience that my neighbour forgot to cancel the newspapers before she left town. But it might be natural to think that I never visually experience the property *having forgotten to cancel the newspapers before leaving town* (compare Dummett 1976: 95). If that is right we can ask: which properties do we sometimes visually experience, and which properties do we never visually experience?

I shall say that a *sparse* theory is a theory according to which we never visually experience any property other than colours, shapes, locations, orientations, sizes, illuminations, motions, and textures; I will sometimes call these the *sparse* properties. An *abundant* theory says that we sometimes visually experience some property other than the sparse ones. I will restrict myself to the 'anthropological' question of which properties *we* (humans) sometimes visually experience; I set aside questions about which properties other actual or possible creatures or systems *could* visually experience.

The issue has a long history. One historical landmark is Berkeley's (1709) argument that distance in the depth dimension is not seen. Another is Hume's (1739) argument that we never observe necessary causal connections. It is natural to associate these arguments with *sparse* theories even if they do not explicitly aim for that conclusion. For it is natural to think that, if we do not visually experience *distance in the depth dimension* then we never visually experience any property beyond the sparse ones; similarly for necessary causal connections.

In recent debates, there has been a tendency for abundant theorists to try to establish their view and for sparse theorists to try to rebut these arguments rather than offer positive arguments for their view. The discussion here will largely reflect this tendency.

In particular, much recent debate has revolved around a family of arguments by Susanna Siegel (2006, 2011) for an abundant theory. Whether or not Siegel's arguments succeed—I shall suggest that they do not—they have done much to highlight and sort out data and hypotheses that both abundant and sparse theorists must take into account. I will therefore discuss a representative argument by Siegel in some detail.

Siegel discusses the issue within the frame of an *intentionalist* theory according to which visual experiences are representations with 'contents' that are 'accuracy conditions' (2011: ch 2). But as she notes (2006: 483), her discussion could be reconstructed within other theories of perception, like disjunctivist or sense-datum theories.

'Contents of visual experiences', as Siegel understands them, supervene on what visual experiences *are like*: If two visual experiences have different contents, then they must differ in what they are like; equivalently, sameness in what two visual experiences are like guarantee sameness in their contents (2011: 88).

Many philosophers agree that visual experiences have *a* kind of content, *phenomenal content*, that thus supervenes on what they are like, but claim that visual experiences also have non-phenomenal contents that do not.[15] Given such a distinction, one can accept different types of theory of the different types of content; for example, one can combine a *sparse* theory about the phenomenal contents of visual experiences with an *abundant* theory about their non-phenomenal contents.[16] It is not clear that Siegel has any stake in denying that visual experiences have a kind of content in addition to the phenomenal one that she focuses on. In any case, the present focus will be on contents of experiences that supervene on what experiences are like.

The argument from Siegel that I will focus on revolves around the following case of 'perceptual learning':

> Suppose you have never seen a pine tree before and are hired to cut down all the pine trees in a grove containing trees of many different sorts. Someone points out to you which trees are pine trees. Some weeks pass, and your disposition to distinguish

---

[15] See for example Kriegel (2002), Chalmers (2006), Prinz (2006), Bayne (2009), and Briscoe (2015).

[16] Prinz (2006) develops such a view. Chalmers (2006) develops a view on which phenomenal and non-phenomenal contents differ, though do not clearly differ in that one is sparse and the other abundant.

the pine trees from the others improves. Eventually, you can spot the pine trees immediately: they become visually salient to you.[17]

Siegel takes it as given that *what it is like* for you when you experience pine trees at the end of this process is different from what it was like for you when you experienced pine trees at its beginning. She takes this assumption to be 'minimal' (2011: 101). The claim is not that your *visual experiences* differ in what they are like. It is only that there is a difference in the *totality* of what it is like when you view pine trees at the beginning and end of this process; as Siegel puts it, there is a difference in the 'overall' experiences of which the visual experiences are 'parts'. Siegel then *argues* that the difference between what the overall experiences are like is best *explained* on the assumption that the visual experience at the expertise stage represents some non-sparse property.

What non-sparse property might be such that it is visually represented at the expertise stage and this explains—or contributes to explaining—the relevant 'phenomenal contrast'? A salient candidate is: the property *being a pine tree*. I will assume that there is no more plausible candidate than this.[18]

Siegel's argument can be construed as concerning experience *types* or experience *tokens*. I will touch on both readings, but I will concentrate on the token reading, and take that argument to aim for the conclusion that *some actual token* visual experience of some expert pine spotter represents some non-sparse property. Admittedly, there are parts of Siegel's discussion that are more naturally understood as concerned with experience types. But not all parts are.[19] Moreover, the token conclusion by itself amounts to an abundant theory, as I have specified things; the conclusion of the type argument, which is more committal, is not needed.[20]

---

[17] Siegel (2011: 100). The phenomenon of perceptual learning is often traced to Gibson (1963), who characterizes it as a 'relatively permanent and consistent change in the perception of a stimulus array, following practice or experience with this array' (1963: 29).

[18] This assumption will play a rather marginal role in the discussion. I will highlight it wherever it comes into play. It is not always essential where it is in play. Note that Siegel does not assume that her conclusion is made true by the representation of the property *being a pine tree* (2011: 114-15).

[19] Perhaps most importantly, the starting assumption of the argument is not—or not clearly—as 'minimal' as Siegel suggests on the type reading. The *overall* experiences of which expert visual experiences of pine trees are parts belong to all kinds of types. For the expert who is in pain, the overall experience will be of the pain type. For another expert, it will be of the itchy type. Presumably these typings are not relevant for purposes of Siegel's argument (construed as concerning types). But what then is the relevant typing? Presumably, the *visual phenomenology* characteristic of expert pine tree spotting is relevant. But on that typing, it is hard to see any important difference between the starting assumption concerning overall experiences and the claim that the *visual phenomenology* characteristic of experts' pine-tree experiences differs from the visual phenomenology characteristic of non-experts' pine-tree experience. And, as mentioned above, Siegel intends the starting assumption to be importantly more minimal than a claim about visual phenomenology. Perhaps there is another relevant typing that does secure a minimal starting point for the argument, but it is not clear to me that there is.

[20] On the type reading of the argument, the aimed-for conclusion would be, I take it, that (a) there is a type of visual experience characteristic of an expert pine spotter, and experiences of that type represent some non-sparse property. It would be crazy to accept this conclusion and deny that (b) there is some actual token visual experience of some expert pine spotter that represents some non-sparse property. To maintain (b) and deny (a) may not be appealing, but is clearly not as crazy.

On the token reading, we may formulate Siegel's central claim thus:

Siegel's Central Claim: There is a pair of token overall experiences, OE1 and OE2; and pair of token visual experiences, VE1 and VE2, such that:

(i) VE1 is a visual experience of a pine tree by an expert pine spotter,
(ii) VE2 is a visual experience of a pine tree by a non-expert,
(iii) VE1 and VE2 are parts of OE1 and OE2 respectively,
(iv) there is a difference in what OE1 and OE2 are like, and
(v) the 'abundant hypothesis' that VE1 represents some non-sparse property is part of the best explanation of the difference in what OE1 and OE2 are like.

There are clearly *many* actual cases that satisfy (i)–(iv). The question is whether at least one such case also satisfies (v). To assess this claim, we need to consider what alternative explanations there might be of the phenomenal contrast of (iv) in the cases that satisfy (i)–(iv).

Following Siegel, we can divide the factors that could figure in such alternative explanations into the following three types:

(A) Differences in *non-visual phenomenology* between OE1 and OE2.
(B) Differences in visual phenomenology between VE1 and VE2 that do not derive from differences in the *contents* of the experiences.
(C) Differences in visual phenomenology between VE1 and VE2 that derive from differences in the contents of the experiences but do not include that VE1 represents some non-sparse property.

I will largely set aside differences of type (B). It is controversial that there are differences of this type.[21] And, as I think will emerge, taking into account any differences of type (B) that there may be makes only a marginal difference to the assessment of Siegel's argument.

Here are some examples of differences of type (A):

(A1) The expert might have phenomenology deriving from bodily sensations—e.g. tensions in muscles around the eyes—that the non-expert lacks (cf. Siegel 2011: 102).
(A2) The expert might have phenomenology deriving from imagery—e.g., visual imagery of similar-looking (pine) trees—that the non-expert lacks (cf. Siegel 2011: 102; Price 2006: ch 1, 2009: sect 3; Prinz 2013: 830; Strawson 1971; Hume 1739: sect 1.1.7).
(A3) The expert might have phenomenology deriving from judgements—e.g., the

---

[21] The existence of such differences is denied by the 'intentionalist' view that two experiences with same content must be the same in what they are like. That view is an instance of *Nothing-Other-Than-Of* and of *Nothing-Other-Than-Of-and-Conscious* above. See also this volume, Chapter 19.

judgement *that is a pine tree*—that the non-expert lacks (Siegel 2011: 103ff.; Price 2006: ch 1, 2009: sect 3).

(A4) The expert might have phenomenology deriving from emotions—e.g., the emotion naturally expressed in terms like, 'how nice to see one of these familiar pines again'—that the non-expert lacks (Siegel 2011: 112; Price 2006: ch 1; 2009: sect 3; Prinz 2013: 830).

And here is one example of a difference of type (C):

(C1) The expert might allocate her attention to some constellation of 'sparse' properties that are distinctive of pine trees, like the shapes and orientations of the branches, the colours and texture of the bark, and the shapes, sizes, and colours of the cones and needles, and as a consequence of this visually represent sparse properties other than those that the non-expert represents (Price 2006: ch 1; 2009: sect 3; Nanay 2011: sect 3; Prinz 2013: 830; Connolly 2014, 2019: ch 3).[22]

It is clear enough that, for *any* relevant pair of *actual* pine tree experiences, the *overall* experiences of which they are parts *will* differ in some of the respects (A1)–(C1). (In fact, this understates things. Any actual overall experiences of this kind will differ in their auditory phenomenology, and/or olfactory phenomenology, and/or tactile phenomenology as well.) Therefore, it is clear that at least a *part* of the 'phenomenal contrast' between any relevant pair of overall experiences *will* be explained by factors other than that one visual experience represents a non-sparse property.[23] The relevant question is then whether these factors make up the *whole* contrast in *every* case, or whether there is in *some* case a *residual* contrast that cannot be thus explained. *Siegel's Central Claim*—and in particular the crucial component (v)—requires that the latter is correct.

It is not evident to me that this is correct. It is also doubtful that Siegel provides any reason to think that it is. Siegel concentrates on three alternatives to her abundant hypothesis: that the relevant phenomenal contrast is explained *exhaustively* by differences of type (A); that it is explained *exhaustively* by differences of type (B); and that it is explained *exhaustively* by differences of type (C). She does not—or not clearly—address the hypothesis that the relevant contrast is explained by the *sum total* of differences

---

[22] Siegel does not consider (C1). The only difference of type (C) that she considers is that the expert might visually represent a 'pine tree shape gestalt', which is something different from a complex of *specific* colours and shapes. A pine tree gestalt is something that is: 'general enough that it can be shared by different-looking pine trees. But it is specific enough to capture the look shared by exemplary pine trees. The pine-tree-shape gestalt is invariant across differences in the shape of particular pine trees' (2011: 111). It is not clear to me that visual experiences represent pine tree shape gestalts thus understood. (Though it may be plausible that such gestalts play a role in the identification of pine trees on the basis of visual experience. It may also be plausible that they play a role in generating visual imagery accompanying pine tree experiences.) In any case, I do not think it matters much for the assessment of Siegel's argument whether or not this is so. It is clear, I take it, that visual experiences represent complexes of *specific* colours and shapes.

[23] Koksvik (2015: 325) makes a closely related observation.

of these three types. But it is clear, I think, that this is the most important alternative to her view.[24]

It is arguable, I think, that there is ultimately better reason to accept a sparse explanation than an abundant explanation of the phenomenal contrasts of the pine tree case. Let me first review one consideration that I believe both theories can handle equally well, and then two considerations that seem to me to speak in favour of the sparse theory.

It might be plausible—and here we touch on the type reading of Siegel's argument—that there is a type of visual experience that expert pine spotters sometimes have and that non-experts *cannot* have; an experience that is not in the 'repertoire' of non-experts. This can be explained on an abundant theory. For example, it can be explained by the hypothesis that expert pine spotters sometimes visually represent the property *being a pine tree*, and that non-experts cannot do so. But a sparse theory can provide the relevant explanation as well.[25] It is natural to think that an expert's visual identification of a pine tree involves a trained skill to allocate visual attention to shapes, colours, sizes, orientations, and textures that are distinctive of pine trees (compare (C1) above). Now, trained skills differ with respect to how easy or hard it is to 'mimic' them on a single occasion. A mediocre dart player can largely mimic the skill of an expert on a single occasion. By contrast, a mediocre juggler cannot largely mimic the skill of an expert

---

[24] Siegel's focus on three alternatives that (I claim) do not include the most important one can perhaps be traced to her break-down of her argument into the following steps (rendered with innocent liberty from 2011: 101):

(0) There is a difference in the phenomenology of OE1 and OE2.
(1) If there is a difference in the phenomenology of OE1 and OE1, then there is a difference in the phenomenology of VE1 and VE2.
(2) If there is a difference in the phenomenology of VE1 and VE2, then there is a difference in content of VE1 and VE2.
(3) If there is a difference in the content of VE1 and VE2, then VE1 represents some non-sparse property.

(0) is the minimal starting point. And each of (1)–(3) in a sense 'addresses' each of the three types of factor, (A)–(C), that might contribute to explaining that starting point. And, (1) is true as long as the contrast of (0) is not explained exhaustively by (A)-type differences in non-visual phenomenology. One might then think that (2) is similarly guaranteed if we can in addition rule out that the contrast of (0) is exhaustively explained by differences of type (B), and that (3) is guaranteed if we can further rule out that the contrast of (0) is exhaustively explained by differences of type (C). But this is not so. Suppose we rule out both that the contrast of (0) is exhaustively explained by differences of type (A), and that it is exhaustively explained by differences of type (B). We still need not accept (2). Our suppositions allow that, contra (2), the phenomenological differences between VE1 and VE2 consists entirely in differences of type (B), and that the phenomenological difference between OE1 and OE2 consists in *that* difference *together with* differences of type (A). One might perhaps suspect that, in offering (0)–(3), Siegel has in mind an argument different from the one I discuss in the text. But I think it is clear that, when Siegel defends the consequents of (1), (2), and (3), the focus is consistently on what best explains the contrast of (0), which is in effect the argument I discuss.

[25] The following is inspired by Connolly (2014, 2019: ch 3), who in turn draws on work by Goldstone (1998) and Goldstone et al. (2011). See also Briscoe (2015: 178–9) and Siewert (1998: 256) for related thoughts.

even on a single occasion. Now, it is not implausible that an expert spotter's skill at allocating attention to sparse properties that are distinctive of pine trees is more like the latter skill than the former, and that a non-expert in practice cannot imitate it even on a single occasion. It is also not implausible that, if non-experts cannot imitate this capacity for attention allocation, then expert spotters sometimes visually experience constellations of sparse properties that a non-expert *cannot* experience.

I now turn to the two considerations that, I think, provide some support for sparse explanations of the phenomenal contrasts of pine tree cases.

First, it seems plausible that pine tree spotting expertise comes in all kinds of degrees: there are mediocre pine tree spotters, good ones, and experts, and there are pairs of perceivers such that one is ever so slightly better than the other. Relatedly, it seems plausible that there is a range of token visual experiences that reflect the expertise of their subject (just as there is a range of juggling performances that reflect the skills of jugglers). Now, even supposing that there is a well-marked phenomenal contrast between the typical expert experience and the typical experience of a very poor pine spotter, it is plausible, I think, that the development of pine tree spotting expertise, and of the phenomenology that goes with it, is a gradual, continuous process without significant 'jumps' (compare again the development of juggling expertise, and see Siegel 2011: 100, for an observation in this vicinity). All of this is compatible with a sparse theory. Connecting again to (C1), it is plausible that the best version of a sparse theory says that the relevant development centrally involves improving the ability to allocate attention to, and thus visually represent, complexes of sparse properties that are distinctive of pine trees, and that this development is continuous. By contrast, it is unclear that what we have supposed is compatible with an abundant theory. The best version of an abundant theory says—I have assumed—that expert pine spotters represent the property *being a pine tree*. It is hard to see that one could *halfway* visually experience that property. If this is not possible, then this theory predicts—questionably—an important 'jump' in the development in pine spotting expertise.

Second, suppose there had been no pine trees but instead twin-pine trees that replicated all the sparse properties of pine trees, or at least all the sparse properties that we encounter in normal viewing circumstances, from which I exclude, for example, viewings of the cellular structure of trees. Suppose further that things were in other relevant respects the way they actually are. In particular, in the counter-factual scenario, there are people who gradually develop expertise at identifying twin-pine trees, and at the end of this learning process have overall experiences that include visual experiences of twin-pine trees and that differ in their phenomenology from overall experiences that include visual experiences of twin-pine trees by non-experts.

Now consider the following two claims:

(1) If no phenomenal contrast in this counter-factual scenario is best explained on the assumption that some expert visually represents the property *being a pine tree*, then no actual phenomenal contrast is best explained on this assumption.

(2) No phenomenal contrast in this counter-factual scenario is best explained on the assumption that some expert visually represents the property *being a pine tree*.

(1) and (2) entail:

(3) No actual phenomenal contrast is best explained on the assumption that some expert visually represents the property *being a pine tree*.

If, as I have assumed, the most plausible abundant explanation of phenomenal contrasts in pine tree cases includes the proposal that some expert visually represents the property *being a pine tree*, (3) in turns vindicates a sparse explanation of these phenomenal contrasts.

And, (1) seems plausible. It is, I think, more plausible than it might sound. The kind of 'explanation' we have discussed throughout is (evidently) an explanation of what the relevant phenomenal contrasts *are*, or *consist* in. And it seems plausible that the phenomenal contrasts in the counter-factual scenario are the same as the actual phenomenal contrasts; if instead of pine trees there had been sparse-property-replicating twin-pine-trees, there would plausibly have been no difference in *what it is like* for anyone of us (in normal viewing circumstances). And if the contrasts are the same, it is plausible that the explanations of what the contrasts consist in are the same.

Finally, (2) is beyond dispute. (2) is correct if all phenomenal contrasts in the twin scenario are fully explained by factors like (A1)–(C1). But (2) does not require this; (2) allows that some phenomenal contrast in the twin scenario is partly explained by the fact that some visual experience represents the property *being a twin-pine tree*. (2) just rules out that some contrast in the twin scenario is best explained on the assumption that some visual experience represents the property *being a* pine *tree*. This we can rule out with as much confidence as we can rule out that any *actual* case is best explained by some expert visually representing the uninstantiated property *being a twin-pine tree*.[26]

The preceding has focused on perceptual learning and the case of pine trees. One might think there are other perceptual learning cases that are better suited to support an abundant theory. Some hearsay about chicken sexing suggests as much. It is sometimes said that chicken sexers have no clue how they distinguish male and female baby chicks on the basis of sensory encounters with them.[27] This might be taken to suggest that there is no difference in which sparse properties they visually represent in the two cases, and that there is therefore a phenomenal contrast here that is best explained on the assumption that chicken sexers visually represent the non-sparse properties *being male* and *being female*.[28]

---

[26] For similar defences of a sparse theory, see Price (2006: ch 1, sect 3, 2009: sect 5), Pautz (2009: 505–7), Prinz (2013: 832–3), Silins (2013: 21–2), and Byrne in Siegel and Byrne (2017: part 2).
[27] See for example Turri (2014: 176–7).
[28] Bayne (2009: 398–9) outlines such an argument but does not whole-heartedly endorse it.

However, as far as I can tell, such an argument would be based on a myth. Chicken sexers distinguish male and female baby chicks (primarily) by getting a good angle on the copulatory organ and viewing its size and shape—and they are able to tell that this is what they do.[29] There is therefore, I believe, no reason to think that the chicken sexing case differs from the pine tree case in any way that matters for present purposes. The same goes, I conjecture, for other cases of perceptual learning.

Perceptual learning cases need not be the only source of evidence on the present issue. Recent work has explored other ways of moving the issue forward. Here I can do no more than briefly review two such attempts.[30]

First, William Fish (2013: sect 3) and Ned Block (2014) both try to advance the discussion by considering 'adaptational effects'. An example of such an effect is the waterfall illusion. If you watch downward motion for a period of time your visual system will adapt to that stimulus, and if you shift your gaze to a still stimulus, like a wall, you will as a consequence of the adaptation typically experience upward motion. The general idea of Fish and Block is that adaptation to a property might be a sign that the property is presented in your experience, and that therefore, if we were to find an adaptational effect stemming from some property beyond the sparse ones, that would support an abundant theory. For example, if we were to find an adaptational effect stemming from the property *being a pine tree* (a property not had by *twin*-pine trees) rather than from the property *having such-and-such constellation of sparse properties* (which happens to be distinctive of pine trees but does not distinguish them from twin-pines), that would provide support for an abundant hypothesis. It is not clear to me that any such thing has been found, and it might be a sign of the strength of the sparse theory that it is hard to imagine it being shown. In any case, the prospects of this approach might well be further illuminated over the next few years.

Second, Bence Nanay (drawing on work by Humphrey and Riddoch 2001 and Riddoch et al. 1998) claims that patients with symptoms of unilateral neglect sometimes 'are unaware of the shape, size and color properties of the objects presented to them in the contralateral side of their visual field' (2012: 238). Although Nanay focuses on 'shape, size and color properties', the suggestion is that some of the relevant patients are more broadly not aware of *any* sparse properties of objects in the relevant part of their visual field (2012: 237, 242). Yet, Nanay claims, the same subjects sometimes 'consciously see' objects in these parts of their visual field, and are aware of some of their 'action properties', like the property *being edible* or *being climbable* (2012: 237, 238). Nanay argues that the best explanation of these data is that action properties are parts of these patients' 'visual phenomenology' (2012: 242; see also Nanay 2011).

---

[29] Specifically, they do so in 'vent sexing', which (I presume) is the sexing method that people who have suggested the above have had in mind. See Masui and Hashimoto (1933), Canfield (1940, 1941), Lunn (1948), and Biederman and Shiffrar (1987). See also various videos explaining vent sexing on the internet.

[30] For further recent attempts to defend an abundant theory, see Bayne (2009), Masrour (2011), Fish (2013: sect 1–2), Speaks (2015: ch 20), McClelland (2016), Bayne and McClelland (2019), and Toribio (2018). For arguments in favour of a sparse theory, see Byrne (2009, sect 7) and Prinz (2012: 166–8).

As I understand it, Nanay's argument appeals to something like the following principle: If some subject S has a visual experience of some object x, then there is some property P such that: x is P and S has a visual experience of P. If such a principle is correct, and Nanay's account of the unilateral neglect data accurate, that would make up a strong case for an abundant theory, because the account suggests that there are cases of this type: an object is visually experienced and there is no property other than some action property that the subject plausibly experiences.

The relevant principle may be plausible.[31] I am less convinced by Nanay's account of the data. In particular, I do not find clear support in his sources for the suggestion that some of the relevant patients lack awareness of *all* sparse properties (including, say, the *locations*) of objects they 'consciously see'.[32] But here again, the issues may well get further clarified over the next few years.

2.4 WHICH PARTICULARS ARE WE PRESENTED WITH IN VISUAL EXPERIENCES?

Recall the idea that visual experiences have at least *a* type of content, phenomenal content, that is determined by what the experience is like. Substituting the technical 'content'-terminology for the more ordinary 'of'-terminology, we can formulate the idea thus: Necessarily: If what two experiences *are like* is the same, then what they are in the phenomenal sense *of* must be the same; or, as I will say, they must be *phenomenally of* the same. Specifically, I will take the idea to be that if two experiences *in any two possible worlds* are the same in what they are like, they must be the same in what they are phenomenally of.

There is a powerful argument that no visual experience is in this sense *phenomenally of* any spatiotemporal outer object like a fork or a tree. Suppose I turn my eyes and attention towards a particular fork, F_1, and have a visual experience that in some sense 'concerns' it. Call this the *F_1 situation*. Now, it is possible that a numerically distinct fork, F_2, with the exact same colour, size, and shape as F_1 had been in the same location and that the viewing circumstances had been otherwise exactly the same. Call such a situation an *F_2 situation*. It seems plausible that:

(1) For some possible F_2 situation, what my visual experience would have been like in that situation = what it is like for me in the F_1 situation.

From the specification of phenomenal-of-ness it follows that:

---

[31] For defence of something like it, see Burge (2010: 33–4, and 539 ff.).
[32] See Raftopoulos (2015) for some related discussion.

(2) Therefore: What my visual experience would have been phenomenally of in that F2 situation = what my visual experience is phenomenally of in the F1 situation.

Moreover, it is clear that:

(3) My visual experience in the F2 situation would not have been phenomenally of the fork F1.

This is clear because my experience in this situation would not have been of F1 *at all*. Therefore it would not have been *phenomenally* of F1.
2 and 3 entail that:

(4) Therefore: My visual experience in the F1 situation is not phenomenally of F1.

The argument generalizes. There is nothing special about the fork F1. If my visual experience in the F1 situation is not phenomenally of F1, then it is safe to suppose that no visual experience is ever phenomenally of any spatiotemporal outer particular.

In fact, the arguments generalizes further. Let me note two further generalizations.

First: My visual experience in the F2 situation may have been phenomenally of the property *being silver coloured*. But it would not have been phenomenally of the particular *silver colouredness of F1*. From this and (2) one can infer that my visual experience in the F1 situation is not phenomenally of the particular silver colouredness of F1. And similarly for any *property instance* of any spatiotemporal outer object.

A second dimension of generalization involves sense-datum theory. Suppose a sense-datum theory allows the following.

(5) There could be two distinct sense-data, S1 and S2, such that: what it is like for a subject of one visual experience to encounter S1 = what it is like for a subject of another visual experience to encounter S2.

Then, by reasoning no more controversial than (1)–(4), one can infer that no visual experience is phenomenally of any particular sense-datum. An equally strong, parallel argument can be made concerning property instances of sense-data.

These generalizations suggest that, if one accepts (1)–(4), one will be committed to accepting that our experiences are phenomenally of nothing more than abstract, non-spatiotemporally located properties (or 'universals'), like the property *being silver coloured*.

So far we have nothing more than a set of conclusions couched in terms of the technical notion of 'phenomenal-of-ness'. However, it is somewhat natural to suppose that phenomenal-of-ness, as specified, captures what is 'present', or 'directly present', or at least in *one important sense* 'directly present' to us in our conscious experiences. Insofar as it does, we can conclude from the arguments above that particular objects and their particular property instances are, in one important sense, not directly present to us in our conscious experiences. A number of philosophers have accepted conclusions along these lines (see for example McGinn 1982: ch 4; Davies 1992; Tye 1995, 2000; Pautz 2009; and Mehta 2014).

There is remarkably limited room to resist these arguments. Specifically, it seems they can be challenged on two, and no more than two, points.

First, one can question premise (1). One might urge that the seeming plausibility of (1) stems from the correct observation that (a) one may be unable to *distinguish* an experience of the fork F1 from an experience of the fork F2, but that it does not follow from this that (b) these experiences are the same in what they *are like*. Michael Martin (2004) defends this kind of divorce between what experiences *are like*—or what he calls their 'phenomenal properties'—and what we can *tell apart*, arguing that such a divorce is demanded by a 'suitable modesty' about what we can know about our conscious life. John Campbell (2002: ch 6), Bill Brewer (2011) and Jeff Speaks (2015: part 7) defend similar views.

Second, one can question that there is a link between phenomenal-of-ness and *any* important notion of what is present or directly present to us in experience. Why, after all, should I accept that the fork F1 is, in any important sense, not 'directly present' to me on the grounds that that there is a possible experience of another fork that is exactly like my experience of F1? Inspired by Mark Johnston, one might urge that this thought reflects nothing more than 'an influential but unhappy stipulation about how to use the terms "direct" and "indirect". To which the response should be to simply avoid these terms, at least when they are intended in the stipulated sense' (2004: 154).[33]

Barring these two responses, there seems to be no alternative to accepting that there is one important sense in which particular objects and property instances are not directly present in our experiences. For the argument for (4) is valid: (4) follows from (2) and (3), and the step from (1) to (2) is guaranteed by the specification of 'phenomenal-of-ness'. The premise (3) is indisputable. And the generalizations from the argument seem to not involve anything more controversial than the argument itself.

Much recent work in the vicinity of these issues has tried to reconcile 'common-factor theories', which accept claims like (1), with the view that experiences can in some sense put us in direct contact with particular objects. For example, David Chalmers (2006: sect 12) proposes to reconcile these ideas in terms of experiences involving a 'demonstrative modes of presentation'. Tye (2009: ch 4) proposes that the content of an experience is a kind of 'schema' that gets 'filled' by whatever object one experiences, if one experiences an object at all, and otherwise—if one hallucinates—contains a gap in the

---

[33] Johnston's target here is a principle that connects (i) *qualitative indistinguishability* between experiences and (ii) what one is *directly presented* with in experiences, and it is not entirely clear whether, in challenging this principle, Johnston would wish to sever the connection between *qualitative indistinguishability* and sameness in what it is like, or the connection between sameness in what it is like and sameness in what one is 'directly presented' with.

object 'slot'. Susanna Schellenberg (2010, 2011a, 2011b, 2016) develops a similar view. Alan Millar (2007) and Neil Mehta (2014) also develop views in this neighbourhood.[34]

Such a project can be understood in two ways. It can be understood as conceding everything in our family of arguments and as trying to merely *supplement* that concession with an explanation of how experiences can still in some sense put us in direct contact with particulars objects, although such objects are, in one important sense, never 'directly present' in our conscious experience (I think Chalmers 2006 and Mehta 2014 should be understood in this way).

Alternatively, one can understand such a project as denying that there is any important sense in which particulars fail to be 'directly present' in our conscious experiences. As we have seen, that requires denying that phenomenal-of-ness connects with *any* important notion of what is directly present in experience. It is possible that Tye or Schellenberg should be understood in this way; however, neither of them clearly takes issue with the common idea that there is such a connection.

It is worth noting that while much literature has been concerned to avoid a 'threat of indirectness' arising from *mental* or *inner* intermediaries,[35] no argument under consideration here has arrived at an intermediary of that kind. And, given the generalization involving sense-datum theory above, it is arguable that this kind of intermediary does not pose the only—or even the most serious—threat to the idea that we are in direct experiential contact with outer, spatiotemporal objects. Another threat comes from the possibility that what our experiences are most directly of are abstract, non-spatiotemporally located properties (or universals).[36,37]

References

Allen, K. (2013), 'Blur', *Philosophical Studies* 162/2: 257–73.
Armstrong, D. (1993 [1968]), *A Materialist Theory of the Mind*, 2nd revised edn. Abingdon: Routledge.
Bach, K. (1997), 'Engineering the Mind', *Philosophy and Phenomenological Research* 57/2: 459–68.
Bayne, T. (2009), 'Perception and the Reach of Phenomenal Content', *Philosophical Quarterly* 59/236: 385–404.

---

[34] Tye (2014b) criticizes his own view from 2009, and sketches two alternatives to it.
[35] See for example Tye (2009: 77), Millar (2007: 183–4), and Genone (2016: sect 2).
[36] Kriegel (2011) develops and discusses this kind of 'veil of abstracta' threat to 'intentionalist' views of perception.
[37] For very helpful comments on earlier drafts, many thanks to Torfinn Huvenes, Uriah Kriegel, Neil Mehta, Bence Nanay, Jessica Pepp, Susanna Schellenberg, Daniel Stoljar, Inge-Bert Täljedal, Bram Vaassen, and two anonymous reviewers for this publisher.

Helton (2016) provides an overview of recent issues in 'high-level perception'. There is significant overlap in selection of issues between that article and Section 2.3 above. To the best of my knowledge, the selections were made entirely independently. I submitted the 'first final' version of the present chapter, and did not thereafter revise the selection of issues, shortly before the publication of Helton's article, of which I had not seen any earlier draft.

Bayne, T. and McClelland, T. (2019), 'Ensemble Representation and the Contents of Visual Experience', *Philosophical Studies* 176/3: 733-53.
Berkeley, G. (1948-1957 [1709]), *An Essay Towards a New Theory of Vision*, in A. A. Luce and T. E. Jessop (eds), *The Works of George Berkeley, Bishop of Cloyne*, vol. 1. London: Thomas Nelson and Sons.
Biederman, I. and Shiffrar, M. (1987), 'Sexing Day-Old Chicks: A Case Study and Expert Systems Analysis of a Difficult Perceptual-Learning Task', *Journal of Experimental Psychology: Learning, Memory, and Cognition* 13/4: 640-45.
Block, N. (2014), 'Seeing-As in the Light of Vision Science', *Philosophy and Phenomenological Research* 89/1: 560-72.
Boghossian, P. and Velleman, D. (1989), 'Color as a Secondary Quality', *Mind* 98/389: 81-103.
Brewer, B. (2011), *Perception and Its Objects*. Oxford: Oxford University Press.
Briscoe, R. (2015), 'Cognitive Penetration and the Reach of Phenomenal Content' in A. Raftopoulos and J. Zeimbekis (eds), *The Cognitive Penetrability of Perception: New Philosophical Perspectives*. Oxford: Oxford University Press, 174-99.
Burge, T. (2010), *Origins of Objectivity*. Oxford: Oxford University Press.
Byrne, A. (2001), 'Intentionalism Defended', *Philosophical Review* 110/2: 199-240.
Byrne, A. (2005), 'Introspection', *Philosophical Topics* 33/1: 79-104.
Byrne, A. (2009), 'Experience and Content', *Philosophical Quarterly* 59/236: 429-51.
Byrne, A. (2012), 'Knowing What I See' in D. Smithies and D. Stoljar (eds), *Introspection and Consciousness*. Oxford: Oxford University Press, 183-210.
Campbell, J. (2002), *Reference and Consciousness*. Oxford: Oxford University Press.
Canfield, T. H. (1940), 'Sex Determination of Day-Old Chicks', *Poultry Science* 19/4: 235-38.
Canfield, T. H. (1941), 'Sex Determination of Day-Old Chicks: II. Type Variations', *Poultry Science* 20/4: 327-28.
Chalmers, D. (2004), 'The Representational Character of Experience' in B. Leiter (ed.), *The Future for Philosophy*. Oxford: Oxford University Press, 153-81.
Chalmers, D. (2006), 'Perception and the Fall from Eden' in T. Gendler and J. Hawthorne (eds), *Perceptual Experience*. Oxford: Oxford University Press, 49-125.
Connolly, K. (2014), 'Perceptual Learning and the Contents of Perception', *Erkenntnis* 79/6: 1407-18.
Connolly, K. (2019), *Perceptual Learning: The Flexibility of the Senses*. Oxford: Oxford University Press.
Crane, T. (2000), 'The Origins of Qualia' in T. Crane and S. Patterson (eds), *The History of the Mind-Body Problem*. Abingdon: Routledge, 169-94.
Crane, T. (2006), 'Is There a Perceptual Relation?' in T. Gendler and J. Hawthorne (eds), *Perceptual Experience*. Oxford: Oxford University Press, 126-46.
Davies, M. (1992), 'Perceptual Content and Local Supervenience', *Proceedings of the Aristotelian Society* 92: 21-45.
Dretske, F. (1994), 'Introspection', *Proceedings of the Aristotelian Society* 94: 263-78.
Dretske, F. (1995), *Naturalizing the Mind*. Cambridge, MA: MIT Press.
Dretske, F. (1999), 'The Mind's Awareness of Itself', *Philosophical Studies* 95/1-2: 103-24.
Dretske, F. (2003), 'Experience as Representation', *Philosophical Issues* 13/1: 67-82.
Dummett, M. (1976), 'What is a Theory of Meaning (II)' in G. Evans and J. McDowell (eds), *Truth and Meaning*. Oxford: Oxford University Press, 67-137.
Fish, W. (2013), 'High-Level Properties and Visual Experience', *Philosophical Studies* 162/1: 43-55.
Genone, J. (2016), 'Recent Work on Naïve Realism', *American Philosophical Quarterly* 53/1: 1-25.

Gibson, E. (1963), 'Perceptual Learning', *Annual Review of Psychology* 14: 29–56.
Goldman, A. (2006), *Simulating Minds*. Oxford: Oxford University Press.
Goldstone, R. (1998), 'Perceptual Learning', *Annual Review of Psychology* 49: 585–612.
Goldstone, R., Landy, D., and Brunel, L. (2011), 'Improving Perception to Make Distant Connections Closer', *Frontiers in Psychology* 2: 1–10.
Harman, G. (1990), 'The Intrinsic Quality of Experience', *Philosophical Perspectives* 4: 31–52.
Held, R. and Hein, A. (1963), 'Movement-Produced Stimulation in the Development of Visually Guided Behavior', *Journal of Comparative and Physiological Psychology* 56/5: 872–76.
Held, R. et al. (2011), 'The Newly Sighted Fail to Match Seen with Felt', *Nature Neuroscience* 14/5: 551–3.
Helton, G. (2016), 'Recent Issues in High-Level Perception', *Philosophy Compass*, 11/12: 851–62.
Hume, D. (1975 [1758]), *Enquiry Concerning Human Understanding*, L. A. Selby-Bigge and P. Nidditch (eds). Oxford: Oxford University Press.
Hume, D. (1978 [1739]), *A Treatise of Human Nature*, P. Nidditch (ed.). Oxford: Oxford University Press.
Humphreys, G., and Riddoch, J. (2001), 'Detection by Action: Neuropsychological Evidence for Action-Defined Templates in Search', *Nature Neuroscience* 4/1: 84–88.
Jackson, F. (1977), *Perception: A Representative Theory*. Cambridge: Cambridge University Press.
Johnston, M. (2004), 'The Obscure Object of Hallucination', *Philosophical Studies* 120/1–3: 113–83.
Kind, A. (2003), 'What's so Transparent about Transparency?', *Philosophical Studies* 115/3: 225–44.
Koksvik, O. (2015), 'Phenomenal Contrast: A Critique', *American Philosophical Quarterly* 52/4: 321–34.
Kriegel, U. (2002), 'Phenomenal Content', *Erkenntnis* 57/2: 175–98.
Kriegel, U. (2009), *Subjective Consciousness: A Self-Representational Theory*. Oxford: Oxford University Press.
Kriegel, U. (2011), 'The Veil of Abstracta', *Philosophical Issues* 21: 245–67.
Locke, J. (1975 [1689]), *An Essay Concerning Human Understanding*, P. Nidditch (ed.). Oxford: Oxford University Press.
Lunn, J. (1948), 'Chick Sexing', *American Scientist* 36/2: 280–287.
Lycan, W. (1996), *Consciousness and Experience*. Cambridge, MA: MIT Press.
Lycan, W. (2004), 'The Superiority of HOP to HOT' in R. Gennaro (ed.), *Higher-Order Theories of Consciousness: An Anthology*. Amsterdam: John Benjamins, 93–113.
Martin, M. (1998), 'Setting Things before the Mind' in A. O'Hear (ed.), *Current Issues in Philosophy of Mind*. Oxford: Oxford University Press, 157–79.
Martin, M. (2004), 'The Limits of Self-Awareness', *Philosophical Studies* 120/1–3: 37–89.
Masrour, F. (2011), 'Is Perceptual Phenomenology Thin?', *Philosophy and Phenomenological Research* 83/2: 366–97.
Masui, K. and Hashimoto, J. (1933), *Sexing Baby Chicks*. Vancouver: Journal Printing Company, Limited.
McClelland, T. (2016), 'Gappiness and the Case for Liberalism about Phenomenal Properties', *Philosophical Quarterly* 66/264: 536–58.
McGinn, C. (1996 [1982]), *The Character of Mind: An Introduction to the Philosophy of Mind*, 2nd edn. Oxford: Oxford University Press.

Mehta, N. (2013), 'Beyond Transparency: The Spatial Argument for Experiential Externalism', *Philosophers' Imprint* 13/8: 1–19.
Mehta, N. (2014), 'The Limited Role of Particulars in Phenomenal Experience', *Journal of Philosophy* 111/6: 311–31.
Millar, A. (2007), 'What the Disjunctivist Is Right about', *Philosophy and Phenomenological Research* 74/1: 176–99.
Moore, G. E. (1903), 'The Refutation of Idealism', *Mind* 12/48: 433–53.
Nanay, Bence. (2011), 'Do We See Apples as Edible?' *Pacific Philosophical Quarterly* 92/3: 305–22.
Nanay, Bence. (2012), 'Perceptual Phenomenology', *Philosophical Perspectives* 26/1: 235–46.
Ostrovsky, Y. et al. (2009), 'Visual Parsing After Recovery From Blindness', *Psychological Science* 20/12: 1484–91.
Pasnau, R. (2016), 'Therapeutic Reflections on Our Bipolar History of Perception', *Analytic Philosophy* 57/4: 253–84.
Pautz, A. (2009), 'What Are the Contents of Experiences? *Philosophical Quarterly* 59/236: 483–507.
Phillips, I. (2016), 'Consciousness and Criterion: On Block's Case for Unconscious Seeing', *Philosophy and Phenomenological Research* 92/3: 419–51.
Phillips, Ian and Ned Block. (2017), 'Debate on Unconscious Perception' in B. Nanay (ed.), *Current Controversies in Philosophy of Perception*. Abingdon: Routledge, 165–92.
Picciuto, V. and Carruthers, P. (2014), 'Inner Sense', in D. Stokes, M. Matthen, and S. Biggs (eds), *Perception and Its Modalities*, Oxford: Oxford University Press, 277–94.
Price, R. (2006), *The Ways Things Look*. D.Phil Thesis, Oxford University.
Price, R. (2009), 'Aspect-Switching and Visual Phenomenal Character', *Philosophical Quarterly* 59/236: 508–18.
Prinz, J. (2006), 'Beyond Appearances : The Content of Sensation and Perception' in T. Gendler and J. Hawthorne (eds), *Perceptual Experience*. Oxford: Oxford University Press, 434–60.
Prinz, J. (2012), *The Conscious Brain*. Oxford: Oxford University Press.
Prinz, J. (2013), 'Siegel's Get Rich Quick Scheme', *Philosophical Studies* 163/3: 827–35.
Putnam, H. (2014), 'Visual Experiences aren't Always Transparent', in *Sardonic Comment*, online at http://putnamphil.blogspot.se/2014/08/visual-experiences-arent-always.html. Accessed 30 January 2020.
Raftopoulos, A. (2015), 'What Unilateral Visual Neglect Teaches Us About Perceptual Phenomenology', *Erkenntnis* 80/2: 339–58.
Riddoch, J. et al. (1998), 'Visual Affordances Direct Action: Neuropsychological Evidence from Manual Interference', *Cognitive Neuropsychology* 15/6–8: 645–683.
Robinson, H. (1994), *Perception*. Abingdon: Routledge.
Robinson, W. (2004), *Understanding Phenomenal Consciousness*. Cambridge: Cambridge University Press.
Rosenthal, D. (2002), 'Explaining Consciousness' in D. Chalmers (ed.), *Philosophy of Mind: Classical and Contemporary Readings*. Oxford: Oxford University Press, 406–21.
Russell, B. (1912), *The Problems of Philosophy*. London: Williams and Norgate.
Schellenberg, S. (2010), 'The Particularity and Phenomenology of Perceptual Experience', *Philosophical Studies* 149/1: 19–48.
Schellenberg, S. (2011a), 'Ontological Minimalism about Phenomenology', *Philosophy and Phenomenological Research* 83/1: 1–40.
Schellenberg, S. (2011b), 'Perceptual Content Defended', *Noûs* 45/4: 714–50.

Schellenberg, S. (2016), 'Perceptual Particularity', *Philosophy and Phenomenological Research* 93/1: 25–54.

Schroer, R. (2002), 'Seeing It All Clearly: The Real Story on Blurry Vision', *American Philosophical Quarterly* 39/3: 297–301.

Shoemaker, S. (1994), 'Self-Knowledge and 'Inner Sense', *Philosophy and Phenomenological Research* 54/2: 249–314. Reprinted in *The First-Person Perspective and Other Essays* (Cambridge: Cambridge University Press, 1996).

Siegel, S. (2006), 'Which Properties Are Represented in Perception?' in T. Gendler and J. Hawthorne (eds), *Perceptual Experience*. Oxford: Oxford University Press, 481–503.

Siegel, S. (2011), *The Contents of Visual Experience*. Oxford: Oxford University Press.

Siegel, S., and Byrne, A. (2017), 'Rich or Thin?' in B. Nanay (ed.), *Current Controversies in Philosophy of Perception*. Abingdon: Routledge, 59–80.

Siewert, C. (1998), *The Significance of Consciousness*. Princeton, NJ: Princeton University Press.

Silins, N. (2013), 'The Significance of High-Level Content', *Philosophical Studies* 162/1: 13–33.

Smith, A. D. (2008), 'Translucent Experiences', *Philosophical Studies* 140/2: 197–212.

Speaks, J. (2009), 'Transparency, Intentionalism, and the Nature of Perceptual Content', *Philosophy and Phenomenological Research* 79/3: 539–73.

Speaks, J. (2015), *The Phenomenal and the Representational*. Oxford: Oxford University Press.

Stoljar, D. (2004), 'The Argument from Diaphanousness' in M. Escurdia, R. Stainton, and C. Viger (eds), *Language, Mind and World. Canadian Journal of Philosophy Supplement* 30. Calgary: University of Calgary Press, 341–90.

Strawson, P. (1971), 'Imagination and Perception' in L. Foster and J.W. Swanson (eds), *Experience and Theory*. Amherst, MA: University of Massachusetts Press and Duckworth, 31–54. Reprinted in *Freedom and Resentment and Other Essays* (London: Methuen, 1974).

Sundström, P. (2014), 'Two Types of Qualia Theory', *Harvard Review of Philosophy* 20: 107–31.

Thau, M. (2002), *Consciousness and Cognition*. Oxford: Oxford University Press.

Toribio, J. (2018), 'Visual Experience: Rich but Impenetrable', *Synthese* 195/8: 3389–406.

Turri, J. (2014), *Epistemology: A Guide*. Oxford: John Wiley & Sons.

Tye, M. (1995), *Ten Problems of Consciousness: A Representational Theory of the Phenomenal Mind*. Cambridge, MA: MIT Press.

Tye, M. (2000), *Consciousness, Color, and Content*. Cambridge, MA: MIT Press.

Tye, M. (2002), 'Representationalism and the Transparency of Experience', *Noûs* 36/1: 137–51.

Tye, M. (2009), *Consciousness Revisited: Materialism Without Phenomenal Concepts*. Cambridge, MA: MIT Press.

Tye, M. (2014a), 'Transparency, Qualia Realism and Representationalism', *Philosophical Studies* 170/39: 39–57.

Tye, M. (2014b), 'What Is the Content of a Hallucinatory Experience?' in B. Brogaard (ed.), *Does Perception Have Content?* Oxford: Oxford University Press, 291–308.

CHAPTER 3

NON-VISUAL PERCEPTION

CASEY O'CALLAGHAN

3.1 Introduction: Perception beyond Vision

This chapter addresses perceptual consciousness beyond vision. An impressive reach of human perceptual consciousness is non-visual. From this perspective, it is odd that philosophers have so persistently focused on visual forms at the expense of others. This oversight has potential costs. Nothing guarantees that claims about perceptual consciousness or its phenomenology founded on vision alone generalize to non-visual ways of perceiving. Moreover, critical features may be missed by dwelling on vision. If we are after a general and comprehensive account of perceptual consciousness and its phenomenology, it is poor methodology to focus exclusively on vision.

This chapter aims to provide the background that is relevant to understanding and appreciating the significance of varieties of consciousness associated with other sensory modalities, such as hearing, touch, smell, and taste. Section 3.2 clarifies the target phenomena. Section 3.3 discusses the diverse characteristics of non-visual experiences in various sense modalities, describing distinctive features of experiences in several senses and how each compares with vision. It asks whether the prospects are good for a shared account of perceptual consciousness across the senses. Then, the chapter turns to multisensory forms of perceptual experience. Section 3.4 asks what unifies perceptual awareness among the senses, and it describes the consequences of several varieties of multisensory experience for theorizing about the structure of perceptual consciousness.

3.2 Extra-Visual Perceptual Consciousness

This chapter treats a relatively focused domain of consciousness: non-visual varieties of exteroceptive sense perception. Sense perception is a paradigm of human consciousness, and it plays a critical role in philosophical debates about the mind. It is the most vivid form of lived human consciousness, and it is illuminated by advanced scientific accounts of sensory processing. Sense perception impacts justification for empirical beliefs, and it guides world-directed action. Much of it extends beyond vision.

It is worth clarifying my target. First, the focus throughout this chapter is on conscious perception. Allow that some perception occurs subconsciously in otherwise conscious subjects. Perhaps information about an object or feature is registered psychologically in a way that impacts thought, emotion, or action. In such cases, the psychological impact of a process of registering information may warrant attributing perception. However, this does not occurrently impact the subject's present waking consciousness in a manner that could be noticed as such by the subject.

Some perception occurs consciously. A subject who is awake can consciously hear a sound, smell an odor, feel a textured surface, or taste bitterness. There is something it is like for the subject to undergo these perceptual episodes, and they typically are recognizable as such. Moreover, consciously perceiving typically provides reasons for belief and action that subjects can appreciate. This chapter's focus is on conscious perception.

The primary target is exteroceptive forms of perception, which involve perceiving things other than oneself. By this I mean to include candidates such as consciously seeing, hearing, touching, tasting, and smelling. First, there is disagreement about whether interoception counts as perception. Some philosophers hold that perceiving requires awareness of something in a manner that makes evident that it is distinct from the perceiving subject. Thus, pains and the sensation of hunger do not count as forms of perception. Awareness of the position of one's own body presents a difficult intermediate case, turning on whether the self is understood as purely psychological, in which case the body is distinct from oneself, or as including one's body. I propose to avoid these difficulties by focusing on exteroceptive perception.

Moreover, my discussion treats only sensory forms of perceptual consciousness. If there are other, non-sensory forms of conscious perception, such as perceptual consciousness of arithmetical, logical, modal, semantic, or moral objects or facts, this chapter at best informs their discussion. This chapter also does not consider the sorts of consciousness associated with emotions by accounts that treat them as forms of perception, whether interoceptive or exteroceptive (e.g., Prinz 2004).

This discussion aims to be neutral among philosophical theories of the nature of conscious perception, including those that may be classified as relationalist, adverbialist, or intentionalist, such as naïve realism, sense data theories, representationalism, or disjunctivism.

Furthermore, this chapter is neutral about whether or not there is a distinctive phenomenology of thought or cognition. If there is, that is a form of consciousness that is extra-perceptual. If there is not, it still may be that the phenomenology associated with thinking shares a format or character with consciously perceiving or sensing—perhaps it is sensory-affective, to use Galen Strawson's (1994) term. This chapter sets aside such forms of consciousness, along with conscious imagination and sensory memory, in favor of focusing on the varieties of consciousness to which such forms are compared. It treats only the sort of consciousness associated with occurrently perceiving or merely seeming occurrently to perceive, as in perfect philosophical hallucinations (see Kriegel 2015 for discussion of further varieties).

Finally, just because a conscious perceptual episode is auditory, tactual, gustatory, or olfactory does not preclude its being visual, or visual in some respects. It would be misleading to describe most multisensory episodes as non-visual, since, except in blindness, they typically involve seeing. A better description is extra-visual or other-than-visual perceptual consciousness. This chapter concerns forms of perception other than vision, rather than non-visual perceptual consciousness, strictly understood.

3.3 DIVERSITY ACROSS THE SENSES

Attention to the varieties of exteroceptive perceptual consciousness may raise doubts about the prospects for a unified account of their phenomenology, their contents, or their objects. What do catching a glimpse of a falling maple leaf, hearing the din of the refrigerator, or detecting a rancid smell all share?

3.3.1 Features

The senses differ in which specific features they reveal. This is a difference in detail. Each sensory modality has its proper sensibles, features revealed in the first instance only by perceptual experiences belonging to that modality: colors for vision, pitches and timbres for audition, pressure and warmth for touch, scents for olfaction, and tastes for gustation. Each of these properties has a qualitative dimension that contributes a distinctive character to experiences of its corresponding sense modality. Some senses also reveal common sensibles, features that may be perceived through other modalities and for which there is not just one distinctive sense-specific qualitative character.

There is an open question about which sorts of features may figure in perceptual consciousness in each of the senses. For instance, many philosophers hold that humans visually experience causality, in part due to empirical research suggesting we visually detect causality and in part because this sensitivity is reflected in visual phenomenology (e.g., Siegel 2010). What about other senses? It is plausible that causality may be heard. Think of hearing screeching tires followed by a crash, a cracking branch followed by a booming collapse, the trajectory of vocalizations during speech, sounds in a musical melody, or a sound and its echo. However, it is not clear that this extends to other senses. What is a compelling example of consciously perceptible causality in taste, smell, or even touch?

Two related issues concern the perception of semantic properties and kind properties. Some have argued that humans visually experience meanings or natural kind properties (e.g., Bayne 2009; Siegel 2010; Speaks 2015). It is intelligible that people could hear meanings when listening to speech, but typically we do not taste or smell semantic properties. Kind properties, however, are better examples of features that may be perceptible in other senses if they are perceptible in vision. Once you learn to recognize the sound of a viola in contrast with a violin, the scent of patchouli in contrast with citronella, the flavor of spearmint in contrast with peppermint, the feeling of velour in contrast with velvet, or the taste of brussels sprouts in contrast with broccoli, each may contribute to your perceptual consciousness in a way best explained by awareness of 'higher-level' kind properties, such as being a brussels sprout or being a viola.

Indiscernible confounds appear just like recognizable kind members but lack the relevant kind property. For instance, a wax figure could look just like a human. Beyond vision, too, indiscernible confounds present potential counterexamples to perceptual consciousness of kind properties as such. Unless you are prepared to say that hearing the sound of a perfectly synthesized viola or tasting a convincing synthetic brussels sprout compound involves a kind illusion, it may be that the best account of the character of auditory or gustatory consciousness does not appeal to the experience of kind properties. This instead suggests that perceptual experience associated with other senses reveals complex analogs to the typical visual looks or appearances of things that belong to specific kinds. These appearance analogs are aptly called sounds, smells, feels, and tastes.

3.3.2 Space

Structural differences across the senses have greater potential for revisionary consequences concerning perceptual consciousness. Space provides one example. Kant said space is the form of outer intuition, or sensory presentation. Accordingly, each modality of perceptual consciousness ought to be spatial. So, we can ask whether each sense involves spatial awareness. Furthermore, we can ask whether each of the spatial modalities is spatial in the same respects. For instance, we can ask whether each shares the same spatial structure.

Does each sense involve spatial awareness? Intuitively vision and touch are both spatial. You can see shapes, directions, distances, and movement. You can feel shapes, locations in the space you can reach with your body or a contact tool, and motion on your skin. On the other hand, taste itself, abstracted from touch, lacks spatial structure. At best, with the aid of touch, tastes seem located in food in the mouth. Orthonasal olfaction conveys more spatial information than taste. Active sniffing over time reveals spatial features such as directions, locations, and boundaries of odors. But static olfaction in humans is a deficient or parasitic form of spatial consciousness. Olfaction in other creatures, such as dogs or hammerhead sharks, may be spatially richer.

Audition is more contentious. P. F. Strawson (1959) famously denied that hearing is inherently spatial. According to Strawson, a purely auditory experience would be non-spatial. Nudds (2001) and O'Shaughnessy (2009) share Strawson's skepticism about spatial audition. Nevertheless, some philosophers argue that hearing does have a spatial phenomenology and that humans hear sounds or their sources as located in some direction and at some distance (Pasnau 1999; O'Callaghan 2007; Casati and Dokic 2009). This claim is supported by contemporary research on locational hearing and auditory space, which details sophisticated spatial hearing capacities (e.g., Blauert 1997). An intermediate position is that hearing presents directions but not distances.

Human audition, however, differs from vision and touch in two noteworthy respects. First, its spatial resolution is poorer than vision's by an order of magnitude, and it provides neither the detail nor the accuracy of vision or touch. Directionally, audition is prone to errors in the cone of confusion, where interaural cues are ambiguous, and distance hearing suffers in reverberant environments because it relies heavily on secondary reflections. Second, auditory consciousness does not present its objects as having a richly detailed internal spatial structure. Sounds may seem located in three-dimensional space and to move or stand in spatial relations to each other; however, we do not typically hear things to have spatial parts that stand in spatial relations to each other, and humans generally do not resolve clear spatial edges or boundaries auditorily (O'Callaghan 2008). Nonetheless, we may hear volumes of space, such as the interior of a cathedral, a gymnasium, or a shower (Young 2017). Echolocators have uncommonly developed auditory spatial capacities (Thaler and Goodale 2016).

These differences in detail raise questions about the spatial structure of perceptual consciousness. Martin (1992) argues that vision and touch differ in spatial structure in the following respect. Vision is capable of presenting unoccupied locations as empty, but touch is not. Because touch requires contact (cf. Fulkerson 2014), you cannot feel the empty space in the middle of a donut itself as empty, but you can see the space inside the hole to be unoccupied. Thus, touch does not involve a spatial field in the same way vision does, as an array of distal objects appearing to occupy otherwise unoccupied space. Touch does not present things as filling space that extends beyond the body.

Nudds makes a similar claim about hearing. He maintains that audition, unlike vision, does not situate sounds in relation to the space they occupy. Nudds concludes that audition lacks spatial structure: 'I am attempting to draw attention not merely to the fact that the auditory experience has a different spatial structure, but that it has a structure that is non-spatial' (Nudds 2001: 213).

One important question concerns whether or not spatial experience in one sense ever depends on spatial experience in another. For instance, a Berkeleyan might contend that three-dimensional visual spatial awareness depends on touch. Strawson maintained that the spatial characteristics of typical, mature auditory experience depend on the inherently spatial modalities, vision and touch.

3.3.3 Objectivity

Spatial characteristics of consciousness across the senses bear on whether or not a sense counts as a perceptual modality. Some philosophers hold that spatial awareness is required for apparent objectivity and that such objectivity is necessary for consciousness to count as exteroceptive and thus as perceptual. The idea is that perception presents its objects as independent from oneself and one's experiences or states of consciousness.

Space is a Kantian requirement on objectivity. Objectivity requires being aware of a thing or feature in a manner that encodes or appreciates that its existence does not depend on being perceived. Strawson (1959) interpreted this to require that subjects must be able to experience places where a thing could be or exist even while it is not being perceived, thus enabling reidentification. Suppose, with Strawson, that vision and touch are inherently spatial. Taste and smell, however, may not meet the spatial requirement on objectivity, and thus may not count as fully perceptual. Perhaps they do not make room on their own for the distinction between self and non-self (see also Burge 2010).

According to the Strawsonian account, in which audition is not inherently spatial, a purely auditory experience does not furnish the materials for spatial concepts, and thus audition all on its own does not count as a fully perceptual form of consciousness. Nonetheless, Strawson holds that mature hearing in the context of other senses does involve awareness of locations, so audition embedded among inherently spatial senses may amount to perceptual consciousness and full-fledged hearing. Something similar might hold of other senses, such as olfaction and taste, in multisensory contexts.

Beyond disputing the spatial status of a sense, or recognizing the spatial dependence of one sense on another, one might challenge the Kantian requirement on objective experience. We should clearly distinguish the spatial and mind-independent notions of 'out there.' Apparent distal location and apparent objectivity could come apart. Afterimages may seem distally located but experience-dependent, and perhaps olfaction is objective but non-spatial (see Smith 2002: ch 5). For instance, apparent objectivity may require only the capacity to discern experiential changes that result wholly from changes to oneself—mere experiential changes—from experiential changes resulting from changes to that of which one is aware. This criterion has a significant benefit: it can be investigated by studying perceptual constancies (cf. Burge 2010).

3.3.4 Objects

The structure of perceptual consciousness may vary in other respects across perceptual modalities. One such respect concerns apparent objects and their features. For instance, seeing involves visually experiencing objects, their parts, and their properties.

Some maintain that visual consciousness has a predicative structure, in which features are attributed perceptually to objects (e.g., Clark 2000; Matthen 2005). Predication involves something akin to judgment or entertainment, and it entails having truth conditions. My view is that it is wrong to think of the visually apparent relation between visible attributes and visible objects as that of predication. Instead, objects appear to bear or to instantiate features. In either case, one perceptually experiences objects and the features that appear to qualify them. This is an aspect of the structure of visual consciousness. Furthermore, it is an aspect of vision's structure that it can involve consciousness of multiple objects at a time that appear distinct from each other.

Accordingly, one question about each non-visual sense is whether or not the features it reveals appear to be attributed or to belong to perceptible objects. For instance, taste on its own might be thought to reveal the sensible qualities of saltiness, bitterness, sourness, sweetness, and umami, without itself ascribing them to individual objects. Batty (2011) argues that olfaction differs in this respect from vision. First, Batty contends that olfaction's content is existentially quantified in structure. Olfaction reveals properties, and it reveals them as instantiated, but olfactory experience does not represent individual objects that appear olfactorily to bear the features you smell. Second, according to Batty, olfaction is incapable of distinguishing distinct items to which features belong. So, you only smell that something is smoky, sweet, and citrusy. You cannot smell that something is smoky and sweet while something else is citrusy. Olfactory content employs only one quantifier at a time, according to Batty.

I have argued elsewhere that auditory consciousness does involve experiencing objects and features and that we can hear multiple objects at a time (O'Callaghan 2008). Audible features, such as pitch, timbre, location, and duration, appear to belong to sounds or sound sources. And it is possible to hear something loud, high-pitched, and distant while hearing something soft, low-pitched, and nearby. Audition thus solves what Jackson (1977) calls 'the many properties problem,' requiring items to which such attributes audibly appear to belong. Audition, like vision, requires perceptible individuals, or feature-bearers (see also Clark 2000).

Nonetheless, perceptual objects need not be of the same sort across the various sensory modalities. It is plausible to think that visual consciousness reveals three-dimensional, extended individuals that appear to persist by enduring or being fully present at each moment at which they exist, rather than by comprising distinct temporal parts over time. Visual experience thus reveals bodies, including material bodies. And the same is plausible for touch. (I set aside whether objects such as rainbows, holes, and clouds mistakenly appear solid, in the sense that they visually appear to exclude other wholly distinct things from the space they occupy, or merely seem visually extended, in the sense that they appear to occupy space.)

Auditory consciousness in humans, however, does not typically reveal material bodies as such. Most people do not in the first instance hear three-dimensional, spatially extended individuals that appear to occupy space as such. I cannot auditorily make out sharp boundaries or rich internal spatial structure. Echolocating humans, marine mammals, and bats have an advantage in this respect.

Moreover, auditory objects do not usually appear to persist in the same manner as visible or tactual objects. Audition's objects generally do not strike one as persisting by being wholly present at each moment at which they exist. Instead, subjects hear things as having temporal parts, and the identities of sounds are determined by the features they display over time. The pattern of sounds in time is relevant to being the sound of a spoken utterance, a police siren, an aspen quaking in the breeze, or a melody. What matters in audition is the pattern of features over time. This suggests that auditory objects are event-like individuals. They are happenings or occurrences, rather than typical material objects. This helps to capture the space:time::vision:audition analogy (O'Callaghan 2008).

Olfaction is a curious case. Again, it does not seem that human olfactory consciousness involves experiencing scents to belong to ordinary or material objects, such as roses or candles. The qualities do not seem 'bound up' with such individuals; you do not discern the rose's edges or smell the rose to occupy space; and the scent can outlast the object itself without producing any time lag illusion. Olfactory consciousness does not enable you to differentiate material objects from their surroundings, and the material body itself does not strike you as olfactorily present to consciousness, as it is in vision (in the sense of Valberg 1992).

If anything, olfactory objects are odors, which exist as something like clouds in the air. You can actively explore them and discern their spatial parts and boundaries diachronically. However, at a moment, olfaction on its own does not seem to reveal objects in any familiar sense. One lesson we might extrapolate from Batty's work is that static olfactory individuals lack the defining spatial or temporal structure of visual, tactual, or auditory objects. Momentary olfactory consciousness in isolation lacks the kind of spatio-temporal structure found in vision, touch, and hearing. Static human olfaction is thus a degenerate form of object perception.

Finally, consider taste. Taste on its own is worse off than olfaction. Nonetheless, in multisensory contexts, and over time, tastes appear to qualify food in the mouth. The object or substance you nosh is salty and sweet. Active tasting, with the aid of other senses, such as touch, in fact may involve perceptual consciousness of individuals' bearing gustatory features. Thus, ordinary episodes of gustatory consciousness may have an object-involving structure.

This section has considered four sorts of differences in perceptual consciousness across the senses. One concerns differences in the qualities and attributes revealed by different senses. The other three concern aspects of the structure of experience in the several senses. The first of these is whether and how perceptual consciousness is spatial in different sensory modalities. The second is whether a sense involves objective awareness and thus is fully perceptual. The third is whether a modality reveals objects and features and which perceptual objects each sense reveals.

3.4 UNITY AMONG THE SENSES

Perceptual consciousness involves the joint use of several senses. Humans can see, hear, touch, taste, and smell at the same time. The previous section articulated differences in the qualities and in the structure of perceptual consciousness across sense modalities. This section addresses what unifies perceptual consciousness between senses. In particular, it focuses on the ways in which perceptual consciousness may be multisensory.

3.4.1 Unisensory Views

If humans could only use one sense at a time, then perceptual consciousness would be unisensory. Spence and Bayne (2015) defend the view that human perceptual experience at each moment is unisensory, or associated with at most one sense, but that it rapidly switches back and forth from sense to sense with shifts in attention. Against this type of view, it is natural to think not just that multiple sensory systems operate at once, but that perceptual consciousness at a moment can be associated with more than one sense. If the temporal grain of momentary consciousness (the specious present) is coarser than that of some rapid shift in attention from one sense to another, then there is some conscious moment during which one's experience is associated with more than one sense (O'Callaghan 2017).

3.4.2 Co-consciousness

Typical subjects enjoy experiences of different senses that are co-consciously unified (Tye 2003; Bayne 2010). That is, they do not constitute wholly separate fields or realms of consciousness. Instead, they belong to a single consciousness, perhaps that of a single subject. Thus, typically, when you have a visual experience while having an auditory experience, those experiences are co-consciously unified into an experience that is both visual and auditory.

Any two conscious experiences at a time may be co-consciously unified. For instance, a sensation, an emotional experience, and even a conscious thought may be subsumed by a single consciousness when each belongs to a single conscious subject. Mere co-consciousness among the senses is nothing special. Accordingly, it could be that one's overall perceptual consciousness at a time is exhausted by that which is associated with each of the respective senses. What I mean is that perceptual consciousness may involve no more than a co-consciously unified collection or fusion of sense-specific parts or attributes.

It is controversial whether experiences involve parts that also are experiences. If experiences are events, it is not clear that a multisensory experience decomposes into sense-specific experiences that also are events. Thus, one might prefer to speak neutrally of features of experiences, which includes parts or attributes. Thus, a co-consciously unified multisensory experience is compatible with the claim that perceptual consciousness at each moment is exhausted by features that are associated with each of the respective sense modalities along with whatever accrues thanks to simple co-consciousness. The latter may include complex features that supervene on those that are sense-specific.

3.4.3 Crossmodal Coordination

Crossmodal illusions demonstrate that stimulation to one sense can impact experience that is associated with another sense. Here are three examples. Ventriloquism is an auditory spatial illusion produced by a visible apparent sound source. Video of a speaker articulating /ga/ can make audio of /ba/ sound instead like /da/, due to the McGurk effect. In the sound-induced flash illusion, a disk that flashes once, presented with two quick beeps, looks like it flashes twice.

Crossmodal illusions show that perception conforms to principles that reduce or eliminate conflicts between the senses. For instance, ventriloquism, the McGurk effect, and the sound-induced flash effect involve the resolution of conflicting information about spatial location, phonemes, and number, respectively. In general, resolving intersensory discrepancies helps to deal with noisy and asynchronous sensory signals. It helps to minimize error and improve overall reliability. Sometimes, as with the intersensory discrepancy paradigm in experimental psychology, and at the movies, it leads to illusions.

Performing conflict resolution suggests something more. Conflict requires a common subject matter. This suggests that perceptual systems have a grip on the common sources of sensory stimulation, despite differences in how information about those sources is transmitted and sensorily encoded. But appreciating the identity of an object or feature across senses could not be sense specific. Thus, if appreciating intersensory identity is reflected as such in perceptual consciousness, then not every aspect of exteroceptive sensory perceptual consciousness is associated with one of the senses or accrues thanks to mere co-consciousness. So, not all perceptual experience is modality specific.

Nevertheless, a system could perform conflict resolution without appreciating that it is doing so and without grasping its common sources or subject matter as such. So, it is possible that crossmodal illusions show only that perceptual systems serve to coordinate experiences across distinct senses without reflecting the identity of their shared objects and features as such in perceptual consciousness. If so, then the features of each conscious perceptual episode could be exhausted by those that are associated with each of the respective sense modalities and those that accrue thanks to mere co-consciousness. Therefore, the existence of crossmodal illusions is compatible with the claim that overall perceptual consciousness is a sum of sense-specific experiences.

3.4.4 Binding

Awareness of intermodal feature binding is a form of multisensory perceptual consciousness that is not merely a co-conscious fusion of experiences belonging to several senses.

Through awareness of *intra*modal feature binding, it is possible consciously to see an object's being both red and rough, or to have a vertical part and a horizontal part, as in the letter 'T' (Jackson 1977; Clark 2000; Treisman 2003). In addition, some philosophers maintain that there is *inter*modal feature binding awareness (Bayne 2014; O'Callaghan 2014). Thus, it is possible multisensorily to perceive an object's being both round and rough, or to perceive an explosion's being both loud and bright. Just as seeing something's being red and round may differ from seeing something's being red and something's being round, multisensorily perceiving something's being both loud and bright may differ phenomenologically from hearing something's being loud while seeing something's being bright. Defenders of intermodal binding contend that it is possible multisensorily to perceptually experience a single individual's bearing features perceived using different senses. This difference, however, is not simply a matter of differing apparent spatio-temporal features or extra-perceptual judgments. Skeptics maintain that apparent binding is a matter of inference, judgment, or mere association (Fulkerson 2011; Connolly 2014; Spence and Bayne 2015).

If intermodal binding is reflected in perceptual consciousness, a significant result follows. There is an aspect of perceptual consciousness that unifies multisensory experiences but which does not stem from mere co-consciousness. This is an intermodal variety of what Bayne and Chalmers (2003) call 'objectual unity' that involves multisensory perceptual objects.

If perceptual experiences have contents, intermodal binding awareness involves contents that are not simple conjunctions of contents belonging to separate senses. Perceiving something's being jointly red and rough is not simply seeing something's being red and feeling something's being rough. Instead, it involves attributing features from several senses to a single perceptible item. Such multisensory contents involve items that are shared or identified across the senses, rather than just collections or conjunctions of sense-specific contents.

Nevertheless, someone might contend that, phenomenologically, binding awareness is just an aspect of the structure of perceptual experience and that it does not involve some novel feature or component of perceptual consciousness. After all, binding awareness reveals nothing new in the world. It only reveals the identity of an object that is perceived through multiple senses.

3.4.5 Novel Features

Suppose there were features only perceptible multisensorily. For instance, there could be novel feature instances that one could perceive only through the joint use of multiple senses.

Suppose that you could multisensorily perceptually experience intermodal spatial relations; intermodal apparent motion; intermodal temporal features such as simultaneity, order, rhythm, or musical meter; or intermodal causality. In any such case, you could have conscious multisensory awareness as of a new feature instance that you could not otherwise have experienced unisensorily. The coordinated use of several senses would reveal new features in the world.

As illustration, here are two plausible examples. Philosophers have argued that visual consciousness reveals causality (e.g., Siegel 2010; Peacocke 2011). In addition, Nudds (2001) argues that we sometimes perceptually experience something visible to generate or to produce a sound. This is an audiovisual experience of a causal relation that could not otherwise be perceived through separate senses working independently, and it is not a matter of having visual and auditory experiences that are simply co-conscious.

As a second example, consider hearing one musical meter, then feeling another meter tapped on your skin. Now, imagine hearing and feeling the two at the same time. It has been reported that subjects in psychophysics experiments are able to detect and discern a novel audio-tactual meter that is distinct from both the audible and the tactual metrical pattern (Huang et al. 2012). Consciously experiencing such a novel intermodal meter audio-tactually could not be just a matter of having co-conscious auditory and tactual experiences. Instead, it is a novel, emergent variety of audio-tactual consciousness.

Nevertheless, causality and meter each can be experienced unisensorily. In that respect, then, perceiving intermodal instances of causality and meter is not a wholly new sort of perceptual consciousness. However, there could be wholly novel types of features revealed only thanks to the joint operation of several senses. Flavors, for instance, can only be perceived fully thanks to taste and smell working together. That is why being stuffed up with a cold dulls your flavor experiences. No instance of a flavor property is perceptible in the first instance unisensorily because flavors are complex multisensory properties. Experiencing flavors thus involves a novel variety of multisensory phenomenology. Balance, which integrates visual and vestibular information, is another plausible example of a novel multisensory variety of perceptual consciousness.

Any such episode involving multisensory awareness of a novel feature instance or novel feature type is one in which the phenomenal character of an episode of multisensory consciousness is not exhausted by that which is associated with each of the respective sense modalities on that occasion plus whatever accrues thanks to mere co-consciousness. Phenomenal character overflows the several senses.

3.4.6 Multisensory Qualities

None of the above establishes that conscious multisensory perception involves novel phenomenal qualities, understood as qualitative properties in virtue of which conscious perceptual episodes may resemble each other in respect of what it is like for a subject to undergo them. Qualia and sensible qualities are examples. For instance, flavor might be a complex, structured multisensory property with only sense-specific qualitative ingredients. So, experiencing flavor might involve no new qualitative phenomenal ingredient. If each qualitative component or ingredient involved in perceptual consciousness is associated with some sense or another on each occasion, then that is an important respect in which perceptual consciousness is sense specific.

It is worth noting that the phenomenal character of a conscious perceptual episode may outstrip such simple qualitative features and those that supervene on them. It could, for example, involve structural properties. So, even if each phenomenal quality were sense specific, that would not entail that phenomenal character is exhausted by that which is associated with each of the respective senses.

Even so, it could be that multisensory consciousness does involve novel qualitative components beyond those associated with the several senses. Consider again a flavor experience. Take the distinctive spiciness of capsaicin. It is not obvious that the distinctive qualitative character associated with the experience of a spicy smoked pepper is exhausted by qualities associated with taste, smell, and somatosensation. Instead, it could involve something further—some new qualitative ingredient that results from taste, smell, and trigeminal somatosensation working in concert. This coordinated activity could reveal a novel qualitative feature that none could reveal independently.

If so, then we have a counterexample even to the claim that each qualitative characteristic revealed in a conscious multisensory perceptual episode is associated with some sense or another, or else is a matter of mere co-consciousness. Not even sensible qualities and not even qualia must be sense specific.

3.4.7 Crossmodal Dependence

The previous cases show that overall perceptual consciousness is not exhausted by what is associated with each of the respective senses. Crossmodal illusions show that the character of an experience of one sense can depend causally on concurrent stimulation to another sense. But even experiences associated with one sense that occur in unisensory contexts can depend on other senses. Unisensory consciousness is reshaped over time thanks to multisensory perception.

Perceptual consciousness associated with one sense can depend historically on another sense. Strawson said that auditory awareness of space depends on vision or touch. While Strawson held a purely auditory experience would be non-spatial, he granted that typical audition involves the experience of space. If so, spatial audition is parasitic on vision or touch. Empirical researchers have recently argued that congenital blindness leads to auditory spatial deficits, partially vindicating Strawson. Some aspects of spatial hearing depend on vision. However, lacking vision also can improve spatial hearing in other respects (see Thaler and Goodale 2016).

Moreover, there could be crossmodal forms of amodal completion that shape one's auditory experience of a sound or one's visual experience of an event, even in unisensory contexts. For instance, auditory cortex is active while silently lip-reading, and it affects visual processing in turn. And, plausibly, the auditory experience of someone who has been blind since birth, especially an echolocator, can differ in character from that of someone who has always been able to see. Research on perceptual learning suggests that some such sort of crossmodal dependence is possible. Furthermore, if beliefs and judgments penetrate perceptual experiences, having an experience of one sense might depend indirectly on forms of experience associated with another.

There could be other forms of crossmodal dependence. An experience of one sense might depend constitutively for its character on experiences of another sense. For instance, visually experiencing material objects as such—as solid bodies that exclude wholly distinct items from the space they occupy—could depend constitutively on touch. De Vignemont (2014) has argued that some forms of bodily awareness depend constitutively on vision. We might say something similar about olfactory awareness of odors as voluminous objects in space. Synesthetic experiences in which audible sounds are attributed colors may provide another sort of example in which the character of an experience belonging to one sense in a unisensory context is parasitic on another.

Any such crossmodal dependence means that there exist experience types that are associated with a given sense on an occasion that would not have been possible under typical conditions if not for another sense. If so, then the features of an experience that are associated with a given sense modality are not limited to those that could be instantiated by experiences belonging to creatures who could only ever consciously perceive using that sense alone.

3.4.8 Experiential Modalities

The lesson of this section is that perceptual consciousness is not necessarily a simple co-conscious sum or fusion of experiences associated with the several sense modalities. Consciously perceiving could be more than co-consciously seeing, hearing, touching, tasting, and smelling at the same time.

In what respects, then, does perceptual consciousness correspond to separate sensory modalities? Some may reject that there exist differing modes of experience. Speaks (2015), for instance, opts for a single mode of consciously experiencing rather than several distinct modes of experience corresponding to the several senses (see also Tye 2003).

My own view is that experiences can be typed according to sense modalities, and that they can be typed as such according to their phenomenology (O'Callaghan 2015). But this is subject to two significant qualifications. First, modalities of perceptual experience, understood as types of perceptual episodes, are not mutually exclusive. Being auditory, for instance, does not preclude being visual. An experience may belong to more than one sense. Second, you may not be able to tell of each feature of your perceptual consciousness the sense to which it belongs. While introspection may reveal that you are having a visual experience or a tactual experience (thanks to your awareness of color or of warmth), introspection need not reveal the boundaries between experiences associated with different senses—it may not tell you where vision ends and touch begins. Modality, in my view, is thus not phenomenally basic.

Unisensory approaches, which investigate perceptual experiences of one sense in abstraction or in isolation from the others, therefore face noteworthy methodological challenges. In multisensory contexts, one sense may causally or constitutively impact experience associated with another. Thus, nothing rules out that some feature of perceptual consciousness that seems to be associated with one sense has as part of its explanation phenomena stemming from another sense. Moreover, no complete account of the character of perceptual experience can be assembled one sense at a time, and it is not possible to draw sharp boundaries between experiences belonging to distinct senses based on phenomenology.

Fruitful topics for future work include whether, how, and in which respects the coordinated use of multiple senses makes possible novel forms of multisensory perceptual consciousness.

References

Batty, C. (2011), 'Smelling Lessons', *Philosophical Studies* 153: 161–74.
Bayne, T. (2009), 'Perception and the Reach of Phenomenal Content', *The Philosophical Quarterly* 59/236: 385–404.
Bayne, T. (2010), *The Unity of Consciousness*. Oxford: Oxford University Press.
Bayne, T. (2014), 'The Multisensory Nature of Perceptual Consciousness', in D. Bennett and C. Hill (eds), *Sensory Integration and the Unity of Consciousness*. Cambridge, MA: MIT Press, 15–36.
Bayne, T. J. and Chalmers, D. J. (2003), 'What Is the Unity of Consciousness?' in A. Cleeremans (ed.), *The Unity of Consciousness: Binding, Integration, and Dissociation*. Oxford: Oxford University Press.
Blauert, J. (1997), *Spatial Hearing: The Psychophysics of Human Sound Localization*. Cambridge, MA: MIT Press.
Burge, T. (2010), *Origins of Objectivity*. Oxford: Oxford University Press.
Casati, R., and Dokic, J. (2009), 'Some Varieties of Spatial Hearing' in M. Nudds and C. O'Callaghan (eds), *Sounds and Perception: New Philosophical Essays*. Oxford: Oxford University Press, 97–110.
Clark, A. (2000), *A Theory of Sentience*. Oxford: Oxford University Press.
Connolly, K. (2014), 'Making Sense of Multiple Senses' in R. Brown (ed.), *Consciousness Inside and Out: Phenomenology, Neuroscience, and the Nature of Experience*. Berlin: Springer, 351–64.
de Vignemont, F. (2014), 'A Multimodal Conception of Bodily Awareness', *Mind* 123/492: 989–1020.
Fulkerson, M. (2011), 'The Unity of Haptic Touch', *Philosophical Psychology* 24/4: 493–516.
Fulkerson, M. (2014), *The First Sense: A Philosophical Study of Human Touch*. Cambridge, MA: MIT Press.
Huang, J., Gamble, D., Sarnlertsophon, K., Wang, X., and Hsiao, S. (2012), 'Feeling Music: Integration of Auditory and Tactile Inputs in Musical Meter', *PLoS ONE* 7/10: e48496.
Jackson, F. (1977), *Perception: A Representative Theory*. Cambridge: Cambridge University Press.
Kriegel, U. (2015), *The Varieties of Consciousness*. Oxford: Oxford University Press.
Martin, M. (1992), 'Sight and Touch.', in T. Crane (ed.), *The Contents of Experience. .*(Cambridge: Cambridge University Press.), 196–215.

Matthen, M. (2005), *Seeing, Doing, and Knowing: A Philosophical Theory of Sense Perception*. Oxford: Oxford University Press.
Nudds, M. (2001), 'Experiencing the Production of Sounds', *European Journal of Philosophy* 9: 210–29.
O'Callaghan, C. (2007), *Sounds: A Philosophical Theory*. Oxford: Oxford University Press.
O'Callaghan, C. (2008), 'Object Perception: Vision and Audition', *Philosophy Compass* 3/4: 803–29.
O'Callaghan, C. (2014), 'Intermodal Binding Awareness', in D. Bennett and C. Hill (eds), *Sensory Integration and the Unity of Consciousness*. Cambridge, MA: MIT Press, 73–103.
O'Callaghan, C. (2015), 'The Multisensory Character of Perception', *The Journal of Philosophy* 112/10: 551–69.
O'Callaghan, C. (2017), 'Grades of Multisensory Awareness', *Mind & Language* 32/2: 155–81.
O'Shaughnessy, B. (2009), 'The Location of a Perceived Sound' in M. Nudds and C. O'Callaghan (eds), *Sounds and Perception: New Philosophical Essays*. Oxford: Oxford University Press, 111–25.
Pasnau, R. (1999), 'What Is Sound?', *Philosophical Quarterly* 49: 309–24.
Peacocke, C. (2011), 'Representing Causality' in T. McCormack, C. Hoerl, and S. Butterfill (eds), *Tool Use and Causal Cognition*. Oxford: Oxford University Press, 148–68.
Prinz, J. J. (2004), *Gut Reactions: A Perceptual Theory of Emotion*. Oxford: Oxford University Press.
Siegel, S. (2010), *The Contents of Visual Experience*. Oxford: Oxford University Press.
Smith, A. D. (2002), *The Problem of Perception*. Cambridge, MA: University Press.
Speaks, J. (2015), *The Phenomenal and the Representational*. Oxford: Oxford University Press.
Spence, C. and Bayne, T. (2015), 'Is Consciousness Multisensory?' in D. Stokes, M. Matthen, M. and S. Biggs (eds), *Perception and Its Modalities*. Oxford: Oxford University Press, 95–132.
Strawson, G. (1994), *Mental Reality*. Cambridge, MA: MIT Press.
Strawson, P. F. (1959), *Individuals*. London: Routledge.
Thaler, L. and Goodale, M. A. (2016), 'Echolocation in Humans: An Overview', *WIREs Cognitive Science* 7/6: 382–93.
Treisman, A. (2003), 'Consciousness and Perceptual Binding' in A. Cleeremans (ed.), *The Unity of Consciousness: Binding, Integration, and Dissociation*. Oxford: Oxford University Press, 95–113.
Tye, M. (2003), *Consciousness and Persons: Unity and Identity*. Cambridge, MA: MIT Press.
Valberg, J. J. (1992), *The Puzzle of Experience*. Oxford: Clarendon Press.
Young, N. (2017), 'Hearing Spaces', *Australasian Journal of Philosophy* 95/2: 242–55.

CHAPTER 4

BODILY FEELINGS
Presence, Agency, and Ownership

FRÉDÉRIQUE DE VIGNEMONT

4.1 INTRODUCTION

AT the sensory level we continuously receive a flow of information about our own body through external and internal perceptions. Not only can we see our body and touch it, but we also have several inner receptors that convey information about the position of our limbs, the balance of our body, and its physiological condition. Unlike external perception, the inner sensory flow never stops and cannot be voluntarily controlled: we can close our eyes, but we cannot shut our interoceptive system. Thus, an important amount of information is constantly available whether we want it or not, whether we pay attention to it or not. In that respect, our body qualifies as the object that we know best. Yet, despite numerous sources of information, the phenomenology of bodily awareness is limited. In painful and learning situations, our body appears at the core of our interest, but when we walk in the street, we are rarely aware of the precise position of our legs and while typing on our laptop, we do not vividly experience our fingers on the keyboard. Our conscious field is primarily occupied by the content of what we are typing, and more generally by the external world, instead of the bodily medium that allows us to perceive it and to move through it. We use the body, but we rarely reflect upon it.

This is not to say that we are completely unaware of it. Except in very rare illusory or pathological cases, we never feel fully disembodied. Instead, we are constantly conscious of the presence of our body, although at the margin of the stream of our consciousness.

> We are immediately and directly aware of our body, at least in marginal form, at every moment of our lives, under all circumstances, and at whatever place we might happen to find ourselves. (Gurwitsch 1985: 60)

But what is the content of this continuous marginal body consciousness? At first sight, it appears to be less luxuriant and detailed than visual phenomenology, for instance, which can be analysed as full of fine-grained colour shades and well-individuated 3D shapes that move around. It seems to be reducible to the 'feeling of the same old body always there' or to a mere 'feeling of warmth and intimacy' (James 1890: 242). But can we go beyond this rough and metaphorical description?

Here I shall focus on what I call bodily feelings, which express the various facets of the enduring relation that the subject has with her body in relation to the world. In this chapter, I will focus on three such feelings:

(i) The body in the world: the feeling of bodily presence;
(ii) The body in action: the feeling of bodily capacities;
(iii) The body and the self: the feeling of bodily ownership.

After describing these bodily feelings in more detail, I will ask to what extent they are feelings at all, and if they are, how to best interpret their phenomenology: in sensory, affective, cognitive, or even metacognitive terms.

4.2 Beyond Bodily Sensations

Let us imagine that I wake up in the middle of the night. I feel my heart beating too fast. The position of my left arm feels uncomfortable and painful. It feels nice to stretch on the bed and to feel the contact of the cold sheet on my skin. I feel too warm. I am thirsty. I get up but I lose my balance.

All those bodily sensations describe the 'anecdotal' state of the body, so to speak, that is, the state of the body that keeps changing (e.g. its posture, its temperature, its movement, and so forth). They qualify as sensory insofar as they depend on sensory channels that are specifically dedicated to one's body. Touch, which is sensitive to the pressure between the world and the body, provides information about both terms of the relation (Katz 1925). Proprioception, which is sensitive to muscle stretch, tendon tension, and joint position, provides information about the position and movement of the body. Nociception responds to dangerously intense stimuli (Melzack and Wall 1983). Interoception, which is based on cardiovascular, respiratory, gastrointestinal, and urogenital systems, provides information about the physiological condition of the body in order to maintain optimal homeostasis (Sherrington 1906). The vestibular system in the inner ear, which is sensitive to the pull of gravity and to motion acceleration as our head moves in space, provides information about the balance of the body (Ferrè and Haggard 2016). There has been a recent booming of interest in these bodily senses, and in the experiences they give rise to. However, one should not believe that these bodily sensations exhaust the phenomenology of bodily awareness and it is important also to consider other types of experiences that are less directly connected to sensory receptors, what I call bodily feelings (also known as existential feelings, Ratcliffe 2008).

Let us now imagine that before waking up in the middle of the night I was having a terrible nightmare in which I was floating in the sky but then suddenly started falling down. When I wake up leaving my bad dream for the reality of my bed, I become aware that I am alive and that all my limbs are intact. I am aware of my body being here in my bedroom, no longer floating up in the sky. I also become aware that this body has two legs and two arms that can cycle and swim, but that cannot fly. I am finally aware that this body is of a highly peculiar significance for me: it is mine, or maybe even it is me.

In what sense do these experiences differ from the experience of being seated for instance? One can first note that the sensation of being seated depends on the proprioceptive system, but there does not seem to be the equivalent of such a sensory system for the feeling of being alive. Arguably, bodily feelings cannot be directly derived from sensory inputs but involve more complex computations.[1] Furthermore, bodily sensations fluctuate all the time. You feel in pain and then you do not and then you do again; you are thirsty, you drink, you no longer feel thirsty until next time, and so forth. But there is a core of bodily awareness that is relatively permanent. This core is rarely at the forefront of consciousness, precisely because it normally does not change, and thus does not attract attention. It includes all these bodily feelings that describe what may be conceived of as the 'fundamental' state of the body, that is, the enduring relation of the body with the world and with the self. Here my objective is not to provide an exhaustive list of these feelings, and I shall simply focus on three main aspects: bodily presence, bodily capacities, and bodily ownership.

4.3 VARIETIES OF BODILY FEELINGS

The notion of *feeling of presence* has originally been proposed to characterize the distinctive visual phenomenology associated with actual scenes, which is lacking in visual experiences of depicted scenes (Matthen 2005; Noë 2005; Dokic 2010). When I see a picture of my son, my experience of him feels different from the experience that I have when I see him in front of me: he does not feel as though he is here. Seeing an object as present involves being aware of it as a whole object located in three-dimensional space, as an object that one can explore from different perspectives and that one can grasp, while seeing a picture of the same object only involves being aware of its material surface with certain configurational properties. In the same way that there is a feeling of presence associated with visual experiences of actual objects, I suggest that there is a feeling of *bodily presence* normally associated with bodily sensations. Most of the time we are only dimly aware of the various parts of our body, but as soon as we feel sensations in them, we become aware of their presence. For instance, when something brushes our knee, not only do we feel a tactile sensation, we also become suddenly aware of the presence of our knee, a body part that is rarely at the forefront of consciousness.

---

[1] Pain may be more complex insofar as it does not seem to be directly sensory-driven. But even then there remains a difference between suffering from a toothache and feeling alive. Unless for chronic pain, one varies while the other does not.

The feeling of bodily presence is well illustrated by the experience of phantom limbs. Many amputees experience from the inside the continuous presence of their lost limbs, as described by the neurologist Mitchell, who first coined the term 'phantom limb':

> There is something almost tragical, something ghastly, in these thousands of spirit limbs haunting as many good soldiers, and every now and then tormenting them with the disappointments which arise when the memory being off guard for a moment, the keen sense of the limb's presence betrays the man into some effort, the failure of which of a sudden reminds him of his loss. (Mitchell 1871: 565–6)

The reverse may also happen, a kind of mental amputation, as in depersonalization disorder. Patients who suffer depersonalization feel as if their body is no longer present: 'The top part of my head often seems to disappear' (Sierra 2009: 29) and to reassure themselves of the presence of their body they often feel the urge to touch their body or to pour hot water on it: 'As I sense it I have the need to make sure and I rub, touch, and hurt myself to feel something' (Sierra 2009: 29).

Let us now turn to the awareness of one's own bodily capacities. Amputees with phantom limb syndrome not only experience the missing body part as being here but they often also experience it either as something that escapes their control or on the contrary, as something that they can move at will. Interestingly, their experience of control of their phantom limb differs from their experience of control of their prosthesis: the limb—although it is not real—feels as if it is *immediately* present to them to carry their actions. As famously noted by Descartes (*Meditation IV*), 'I am not only lodged in my body as a pilot in a vessel'. Surprisingly, however, although agentive feelings have been extensively explored (Bayne 2008), their embodied dimension has been largely ignored.[2] Most computational models and philosophical theories of action do not even mention the body, although action planning and control requires information about the posture of the limbs, their size, their strength, their flexibility, and so forth. It is often more optimal for bodily information to be left unconscious because the motor system needs to adjust very quickly and cannot afford the time that it takes to become aware of it. Nonetheless, we have some awareness of our body in action: we feel our arm raising, our legs kicking, our head turning. These kinaesthetic sensations normally accompany some—although not all—of our bodily movements. But is that all there is to the phenomenology of the acting body?

The notion of the sense of agency usually refers to the awareness of oneself as the cause of a particular action. I suggest here that there is also a more enduring notion of agency, which does not concern the punctual occurrence of a movement at time t, but the long-term capacity to move.

---

[2] With the notable exception of O'Shaughnessy (1980) and Wong (2015).

> The self-awareness of a self-consciously competent bodily agent includes a familiarity with the possibilities for bodily acting that come with having the kind of body she has: for instance, a familiarity with the different movements that are feasible at different joints. (McDowell 2011: 142)

Here I shall leave aside skill-based capacities (how to ride a horse or dance tango) and the associated feeling of competence, and focus exclusively on what may be called built-in capacities, which are determined by bodily configuration, size and strength, and by the flexibility of the joints. It is thanks to the awareness of bodily possibilities that one does not attempt to move in biologically impossible or painful ways. It is also thanks to it that one does not over- or under-reach when trying to get an object. One may not be aware of the exact strength of one's limbs or the precise degree of freedom of the joints. Nonetheless, one has some rough awareness of one's capacities, which can be used to explain one's course of actions (e.g. I chose this complex series of movements to reach my goal because I was not strong enough to do it otherwise).

Sometimes this awareness can be mistaken. Patients suffering from hysterical conversion have perfectly preserved motor abilities but they are convinced that they are partly paralysed and thus, they do not even intend to move. Conversely, patients suffering from anosognosia for hemiplegia are paralysed on the left side of their body but remain unaware of their paralysis. When asked to raise their left arm, they claim that they can do it, and even that they are performing the movement (although the arm remains still). An anosognosic patient, who is in a wheelchair, even claimed that he could go surfing: 'Why not, if the wind is strong enough' (Cocchini et al. 2002: 2031). Finally, some schizophrenic patients experience what is known as the omnipotence delusion: they take themselves to have divine powers, such as the ability to fly or to run faster than light. In all these cases, patients fail to be aware of what they can and cannot do.

The agentive dimension of bodily awareness brings to light the intimate relation between the body and the self, but one can go a step further: one does not normally experience *a* body that immediately responds to one's intentions; one normally experiences *one's own* body. Any account of the phenomenology of bodily awareness must thus also include an account of its first-personal character. I do not mean here the subjectivity of my bodily experiences (*I* feel), but the sense of bodily ownership (*my own* body). The notion of bodily ownership carries with it no specific metaphysical assumption one way or the other.[3] It only states that this particular body has a special significance for the subject. The challenge is to spell out in what sense this body is special.

One should avoid an interpretation in terms of *familiarity*, which would be too weak. Bodily awareness includes a feeling of familiarity with one's own body, but the sense of bodily ownership cannot be reduced to it. There are indeed many bodies that we are

---

[3] It does not express that the self is embodied or, on the contrary, that it is not (it might seem that an object that is owned must be distinct from its owner).

familiar with and that have a personal significance. The function of the feeling of familiarity is to track any body with which one has had sufficiently many previous encounters. Therefore, it cannot ground self-ascriptive bodily judgements (e.g. this is my own body). One should also avoid an interpretation that would be too strong: the special relationship that is expressed by the sense of bodily ownership is not of *identity*. The sense of identity and the sense of bodily ownership normally go together. However, they play different epistemic roles: the former can ground judgements of the type '*I* am raising my hand' whereas the latter can ground judgements of the type 'This is *my* hand raising'. In the case of face transplant, the issue is not only of recognizing the new face as one's own, but also of recognizing *oneself* when looking at the mirror.[4] This is why face transplant has been allowed only recently (Dubernard et al. 2007).

The sense of bodily ownership should thus be reduced neither to the feeling of familiarity nor to the sense of identity. But then what is it? The most neutral definition is to say that it consists in the feeling that one experiences when one is aware of a body as being one's own. One may go a step further and propose that the feeling of ownership is a feeling *in virtue of* which one is aware of a body as being one's own. Most of the time it targets only the body that belongs to the subject. In some rare contexts, however, it can concern an extraneous object, as in the Rubber Hand Illusion (hereafter RHI). In the classic experimental set up, one sits with one's arm hidden behind a screen, while fixating on a rubber hand presented in one's bodily alignment; the rubber hand can then be touched either in synchrony or in asynchrony with one's hand. After a few of minutes, one can report that it seems as if the rubber hand was one's own hand (Botvinick and Cohen 1998). Conversely, one can lack a sense of ownership for one's own body. Patients with depersonalization not only feel that their limb has disappeared but also that it no longer belongs to them. It can also occur in patients with somatoparaphrenia, who after a lesion in the right parietal lobe deny that their limbs belong to them. When shown her own limb and asked whose hand it was, a patient replied: 'How am I supposed to know whose hand is this? It's not mine' (Gandola et al. 2012: 1176).

4.3.1 Lack of Presence or Absence?

We have just seen that bodily awareness normally includes the awareness of one's body as being present in the world, as being able to carry actions, and as being one's own body. We have also seen that in some pathological conditions these various aspects of bodily awareness can be replaced by the opposite experience: the sense of presence by the sense of absence and disappearance in depersonalization, the sense of bodily capacities by the sense of bodily incapacities in hysterical conversion, and the sense of bodily ownership by the sense of bodily disownership in somatoparaphrenia. One may then wonder

---

[4] By face transplant, one means the transplantation of new composite tissue on the underlying bones and muscles that have remained intact. The new face never resembles the old face, but it neither resembles the donor's face.

whether these pathological forms of bodily awareness merely express the lack of the corresponding bodily feeling or whether there is more to these pathological senses. In other words, can we reduce the sense of absence to the absence of the sense of presence and the sense of disownership to the absence of the sense of ownership?

Consider the case of internal organs. They are parts of our body and we can feel painful sensations there. Yet the awareness we have of them is very limited. More specifically, we do not experience them as being present, nor do we experience them as being parts of our body in the same way we experience our arms or our legs. For all that we do not experience them as disappearing, nor do we experience them as alien. What this example shows is that the lack of the sense of bodily presence and ownership does not necessarily entail the sense of bodily disappearance and alienation. Why, then, do some patients experience their limbs as absent and foreign to them? Arguably, they have no sense of presence and ownership for these limbs. In that respect, there is no difference with their awareness of their internal organs. Yet there is a major difference: it is normal to lack these feelings in the case of their internal organs but it is not in the case of their limbs. The sense of disappearance and of disownership therefore expresses not only the lack of bodily feelings, but also some degree of awareness of the abnormality of the situation. Then the question is: what conclusions about normal bodily awareness can we draw on the basis of these pathological feelings? More specifically, can one appeal to these disorders in order to show that there is a distinctive phenomenology associated with the sense of presence, capacities, and ownership?

4.3.2 Feeling or Merely Knowing?

The notion of awareness is ambiguous insofar as it can refer both to what the subject feels and to what she judges. One may then question whether the various components of bodily awareness that I have described so far have an experiential counterpart or whether they are manifested to the subject only in the form of beliefs or judgements (Bermúdez 2010, 2011, 2015; Martin 1992, 1995; Alsmith 2015; Mylopoulos 2015; Wu forthcoming). For instance, Bermúdez claims that there is no 'distinctive experience of agency' (Bermúdez 2010: 588) and that 'the feeling of ownership is just a philosophical fiction' (Bermúdez 2017). On such an apparent eliminativist account, we have beliefs about what we do and about whose body is ours, but these beliefs are not grounded in some specific feelings of agency or ownership. Instead they are grounded in some fundamental facts about kinaesthetic and bodily experiences. This hypothesis is parsimonious insofar as it does not posit extra phenomenal properties. But it might be too parsimonious and, thus, fail to account for the reports that subjects give in borderline situations.

Consider again the case of phantom limbs. Why should we take patients at their word when they claim that they *feel* the presence of their phantom hands, that they *feel* them as being parts of their bodies and that they *feel* they could (or could not) control them? One reason is that they make such reports although they are fully aware that their limb is missing. One patient described his experience as follows: 'To anyone looking at me, I have no arm. But I can feel the entirety of my phantom hand and arm' (Mezue and Makin 2017). Hence, it can seem to one that the limb is present while correctly judging that it is not. Such a decoupling between appearance and knowledge calls to mind classic visual illusions, such as the Müller-Lyer illusion: one has a visual experience of the two lines as being different, while having the belief that they are actually of the same size. One may then provide a similar explanation to the phantom presence: one *experiences* the limb as being present in the same way as one *experiences* the lines as being different. The argument schema has been called the argument from cognitive impenetrability (Mylopoulos 2015). It assumes that there is a feeling of x if it seems to one that x while one correctly judges that there is no x (Harcourt 2008).

However, the argument from cognitive impenetrability has been criticized on the ground that attitudes other than feelings and sensations can be encapsulated and immune to the influence of beliefs and judgements (McDowell 2011; Bermúdez 2015; Mylopoulos 2015). But what attitudes precisely? The eliminativists often remain relatively vague when it comes to describing their positive view. It is true that one can *suppose* that x while one knows that x is not true, and that supposition is not a feeling. However, I doubt that they would claim that the amputee *supposes* his hand to be here. Imagination may be a better candidate. However, imagination is generally under voluntary control, whereas the patients cannot stop feeling the presence of their limb. Furthermore, imagination involves mentally recreating selected experiences (Goldman 2006). If one does imagine the missing hand as being here, it means that one imagines *experiencing* it as being here (for further discussion, see de Vignemont 2020).

To recapitulate, the argument from cognitive impenetrability is not conclusive: it does not state that there must be a feeling of x if it seems to one that x while one correctly judges that there is no x. There may be alternative interpretations of the dissociations in cognitive terms but the crucial question is whether these cognitive interpretations fare better than the interpretations in experiential terms. Whether there are bodily feelings or not will thus eventually depend on an inference to the best explanation. Furthermore, it is worth mentioning that those who question the validity of the argument from cognitive impenetrability primarily target *sensory* phenomenology: a person does not need to have a *sensory* experience of x just because it seems to her that x although she knows that x is false. However, some of them at least seem to be willing to accept a non-sensory phenomenology of x, and more particularly of a cognitive type (Alsmith 2015; Mylopoulos 2015). Consider the case of the feeling of déjà vu. Suppose I have a déjà vu experience although I perfectly know that I have never been here before. In this case, it seems legitimate to assume that it feels like something specific when I have this experience. Arguably, this feeling is not sensory and its grounds are relatively complex, involving metacognitive monitoring of visual processing. Still, there is a distinct phenomenology associated with the feeling of déjà vu. One can also mention the feeling of familiarity. It cannot be reduced to the recognition of the visual features of the face, but involves autonomic responses, which result in increased arousal in front of familiar faces (Ellis and Lewis 2001). But again it is characterized by a specific phenomenology, which can be conceived of in affective terms (Dokic and Martin 2015). Here I will suggest that some bodily feeling should be analysed in the same way as these non-sensory types of feelings.

There are, then, two ways such feelings might be understood in representational terms. First, they can be conceived of as affective colouring, or specific modes of presentation, of the sensory content of perceptual experiences (Matthen 2005). This solution, however, raises more questions that it answers. Alternatively, feelings can be conceived of as proper experiences distinct from the sensory experiences that they are bound to (Dokic and Martin 2015). In favour of the latter view, Dokic and Martin (2015) appeal to the feeling of *déjà vu*. They suggest that it should be interpreted as a free-floating feeling of familiarity without any associated sensory experience. If this is the correct interpretation, then affective feelings can be fully independent from sensory experiences. However, Dokic and Martin's claim seems too strong: the feeling of *déjà vu* is not completely disconnected from any sensory experience; it is bound to the global sensory content of a scene, although one does not know which particular object or event in this scene triggers the feeling. If we now turn to bodily experiences, it seems even more difficult to conceive of free-floating feelings of ownership, for instance. There is thus no clear answer to this debate so far and I shall thus leave it open here. I shall now leave these general issues to analyse in detail each bodily feeling.

4.4 THE SENSE OF BODILY PRESENCE

Let us first consider the feeling of bodily presence. As argued in the previous section, one can feel the limb as still being here while one knows that it is not true, as in the case of phantom limbs. The feeling of phantom presence cannot be reduced to the experience of phantom sensations. According to the neurologist Melzack (1992), the feeling of the presence of phantom limbs is only 'reinforced' by the kinaesthetic, tactile, thermal, and painful sensations that the amputees experience as being located in their phantom limbs, but it goes beyond them. Let us now consider the mirror phenomenon, namely, depersonalization disorder. As for amputees, it seems difficult to account for the patients' reports in purely cognitive terms. They are indeed greatly disturbed by what they experience and yet they know that their body is still here, it only seems to them as if it were not. How could mere 'as if' judgements account for such an emotional impact? It rather seems that they do *feel* their limbs as missing. Furthermore, depersonalized patients can still feel sensations in their body that they feel as disappearing: 'Even if I touch my face I feel or sense something but my face is not there' (Sierra 2009: 29). Hence, the feeling of presence (or the lack of it) cannot be simply explained away by bodily sensations (or the lack of them). One can still experience sensations to be located in a body part and still not feel this body part as being present. How, then, should one account for the feeling of bodily presence? As mentioned earlier, the notion of presence has been discussed primarily in the context of visual experiences. Several theories have then been proposed and I shall not review them here. Instead I shall focus only on the sensorimotor conception and highlight both its insights and its limits.

Noë (2005) notes that when facing a tree, one sees only one side of it and yet one is aware of the whole tree. On his view, to be aware of the presence of the tree is then to know that if one walks around the tree, one can see the other side. By contrast, when facing the painting of a tree, there is no hidden side of the tree that one could access. Thus, one does not experience the depicted tree as being present. Likewise, Matthen (2005) claims that one feels an object as visually present thanks to the fact that one knows one can act on it, whereas one cannot act on the object depicted in a picture. He thus suggests that the source of the feeling of visual presence can be found in the involvement of visuo-motor processing in visual experiences. One may then propose a sensorimotor account of the feeling of *bodily* presence. When I have an itching sensation on a small spot at the back of my knee, I am aware not only of the limited area of the body in which I localize the sensation but of the whole three-dimensional knee, both sides included. On a sensorimotor account, the feeling of the presence of the whole knee consists in knowing how to act on this body part. My itching sensation is just about a small area on the two-dimensional sheet of my skin, but my scratching it involves being aware of the volume of the whole joint.

The sensorimotor account of bodily awareness faces many problems and I shall not list them all here (for discussion, see de Vignemont 2011). Let us simply note that knowing how to access the unfelt part of one's body does not suffice for the feeling of bodily presence. Consider first the case of visual experience (Kind 2018). There is a bottle in front of you. You may feel the whole bottle as being present, including the side hidden from sight, but you do not feel the liquid in it as being present in the same way. Yet you do know that if you look inside the bottle, you will see the liquid. You thus have the right sensorimotor expectations, but no feeling of presence. Similar examples can be offered for the feeling of bodily presence. For instance, a surgeon knows how to access a tumour inside him but for all that he may not feel his tumour as being present. Hence, there is more to the feeling of presence than some kind of know-how.

A further issue concerns Noë's starting point: how are we aware of the hidden side of perceived objects? But this question only highlights the fact that we are aware of objects in their entirety as three-dimensional volumes and it is not clear that it fully captures the phenomenology of presence (Dokic 2018). Indeed what appears as crucial for the feeling of presence is the awareness of externality rather than of volume, what one may call a feeling of 'here-ness': one is aware of the object as being here, that is, as occupying a portion of the external world.[5] It may then seem that the feeling of presence is an *enabling condition* for actions. If you do not feel the object to be here, you do not plan to act on it. No matter how minimal the involvement of consciousness can be for action, it seems that some awareness of the presence of the object is

---

[5] Here I use a relatively minimal notion of presence, which does not entail reality. On this view, the feeling of presence can be part of the phenomenology of imagination and dream (Nanay 2016).

required. Hence, the feeling of presence is tightly linked to action but its relationship should not be conceived of in constitutive terms.

What therefore seems to provide both externality and this link to action is the egocentric perspective. On the one hand, it localizes the perceived objects in their spatial relation to the perceiver's body or parts of his body. On the other hand, it is required to plan movements in the direction of the objects. However, one may question whether the notion of egocentric frame of reference can be applied to bodily awareness insofar as one cannot provide a centre of this frame, nor suggest axes on which one could compute distances and directions for bodily sensations (Bermúdez 1998). Still, when experiencing bodily sensations one should not believe that we are locked in the space of our body. The body that we experience is not only an inside; it has also an outside in which it navigates. For instance, when we feel touch on our hand, not only do we experience the pressure in a specific location within our long-term body image (e.g. our right hand), we also experience this part of our body in a specific location in the external world (e.g. on the left). Another way to put it is to say that bodily sensations have two types of felt location, which I respectively call *bodily location* and *egocentric location* (de Vignemont 2018). Bodily location is the location in a specific part of the body, no matter where the body part is located: when I move my hand, the bodily location does not change. By contrast, egocentric location depends on bodily posture, and is thus given within an egocentric frame of reference: it is the location relative to the other parts of the body at the time of the sensation. The spatial duality of tactile sensations is well illustrated by the Japanese illusion. Cross your wrists, your hands clasped with thumbs down. Then turn your hands in toward you until your fingers point upward. If now I touch one of your fingers, you will have difficulty not only in moving the finger that is touched, but also in reporting which finger it is. If tactile sensations had only bodily locations, then this complex posture should make no difference (a touch on the right index finger remains on the right index finger no matter where the finger is located). The difficulty that you have in the Japanese illusion thus shows that the relative location of body parts matters. Thanks to their egocentric locations, bodily sensations can be said to be anchored in external space: one is aware of the body part in which one feels sensations in a space larger than one's body. Thanks to their egocentric locations, one can act on the body part that hurts or itches.

In summary, the feeling of bodily presence expresses the awareness of the relationship between one's body and the external world. This relationship should be understood in spatial terms: one experiences one's body as being 'here' in three-dimensional space. But it has sensorimotor consequences: in this external world, this is a body that one can act upon. On this view, the feeling of presence is relatively primitive. It results from *sensory* processes of spatial remapping from a bodily frame to an egocentric frame. This account is thus at odds with other more sophisticated conceptions that describe the feeling of presence in terms of cognitive or affective phenomenology (Dokic and Martin 2015; Dokic 2018). The difficulty that the affective conception faces, is that there is no clear valence or motivational role that is intrinsic to the feeling of presence. As said earlier, presence is only the background condition for motivation. On its own the feeling of bodily presence is simply neutral: you can act on it or not; it does not invite you to choose a course of action. Nonetheless, Dokic (2018) suggests that feelings of presence do play a motivational role: 'They have a non-sensory, affective-like phenomenology, in the sense that we feel motivated to form specific judgments about what we perceive'. This definition of affective phenomenology, however, may be too liberal and many states that bear no relation with emotions may end up being 'affective-like'. Instead I want to propose that the nature of the phenomenology of bodily presence is simply sensory. It has a clear mind-to-world direction of fit: it expresses that something is here and it is accurate only if this thing is here.

4.5 THE SENSE OF BODILY CAPACITIES

Let us now turn to a more directly sensorimotor dimension of bodily awareness, namely, the awareness of one's own bodily capacities. To some degree we are aware of what our body can and cannot do. What is the origin of such awareness? One may be tempted to reply that I know that I can move on the basis of the simple fact that I am moving and I know that I am moving on the basis of proprioceptive, tactile, visual, and vestibular information, as well as on the basis of efferent information.[6] This is different, however, in the case of the awareness of one's bodily incapacities: I am not entitled to conclude that I cannot move from the fact that I am not moving. In that case indeed, I also need to be aware that I intended to move and that no external constraints prevented me from moving. It is only the discrepancy between my intention and the absence of movement in this specific context that entitles me to conclude that I cannot move. The comparison between efferent and afferent information then enables me to decide how much my body obeys or betrays me. However, the awareness of bodily capacities should not be reduced only to the awareness of *bodily obedience*. As said earlier, I am interested in a more enduring notion of agency, one that is not tied to the occurrence of a movement, nor of a motor intention.

There are two complementary sources of information for this enduring sense. On the one hand, one has information about the various bodily parameters that are necessary to plan action, which are represented in what is known in the literature as the body schema (de Vignemont 2010). For instance, my son can know whether he can reach the chocolate bar in the cupboard by comparing the estimated sizes of his body and of the cupboard. Several studies have shown how reachability judgements can be modulated by altering the body schema (Bourgeois et al. 2014). This solution works well for specific movements that have never been achieved before. But imagine now that every day after

---

[6] When one moves, one anticipates the sensory consequences of one's movements, which allows anticipatory control (Desmurget and Grafton 2000). Such sensory prediction can then give rise to kinaesthetic experiences. This explains how one can feel that one is moving before the movement has even started (Libet et al. 1983).

school my son grabs a chocolate bar in the cupboard. It seems that his reachability judgement is then grounded in the memory of the series of his previous successes: he knows that he can do it because he did it before. By monitoring one's performance, one can indeed become aware of what one can do. More specifically, one can exploit two cues: the ratio of success to failure and the ease or difficulty associated with performing the movement. Compare linguistic ability: you know that you can speak a foreign language if you were able to communicate without too much effort before.

The sense of one's capacities then results from monitoring one's own performance, and thus qualifies as being metacognitive.[7] Metacognitive awareness, however, can be either theory-based or experience-based (Koriat 2000). Consider the following example. If you are asked about the date of the end of the Roman Empire, you may be able to give a reply although you are not certain that you are right. Your lack of confidence can result from the fact that you know that you have a poor memory for dates and that you have always disliked history. Alternatively, you have a kind of intuitive feeling, something akin to a 'gut feeling', which tells you that you do not really know. This feeling of confidence (or its absence) is what some call a noetic feeling, along with feelings of knowing, feelings of 'déjà vu', and tip-of-the-tongue experiences (Dokic 2012). It involves implicit monitoring of one's cognitive capacities, for instance how rapidly and easily our memory system retrieves the answer. The question is: is there another type of metacognitive feeling, something like a 'Yes, I can', which gives rise to the awareness of one's bodily capacities? Unfortunately, we cannot use the argument from cognitive impenetrability here. In hysterical conversion, in anosognosia for hemiplegia and in schizophrenia, patients are delusional: they believe, and not only feel, that their body can or cannot do this or that. Furthermore, as far as I know, no Superman illusion has been tested (one would be made to feel as if one could do more than one knows to be physically possible).[8] Consequently, one may argue that metacognitive judgements about one's bodily capacities are exclusively theory-based: one *infers* what one can or cannot do on the basis of past actions; this is not something that one experiences.

Still, one might be tempted by an experiential account of the sense of bodily capacities. More specifically, I propose to interpret it in terms of the metacognitive experience of *global fluency*. Fluency can be defined as 'the subjective experience of ease or difficulty associated with completing a mental task' (Oppenheimer 2008: 237). One may then distinguish between local and global fluency. Whereas local fluency concerns a specific process at the time it occurs, global fluency concerns a series of similar processes over time. More specifically, in the case of action it has been shown that the sense of agency can partly result from fluency in action selection: the easier the process is to select which movement to perform, the more in control one feels (Chambon and Haggard 2012). This experience of fluency is local: it exclusively concerns the action in progress. However,

---

[7] For a metacognitive account of the sense of agency, see Carruthers (2015).

[8] A couple of studies used virtual avatars with superpowers (such as the ability to fly, Rosenberg et al. (2013)) or with anatomically incongruent limbs (such as having very long arms, Kilteni et al. (2012)) but they did not investigate the sense of capacities.

one needs first to learn through expertise that selection fluency is a reliable cue for successful outcome. Hence, one needs to keep track for each action that fluency is associated with good control (Chambon et al. 2014). In the case of the feeling 'Yes, I can', the hypothesis is that the accumulation of local fluency experiences generates fluency expectancies and that these expectancies give rise to a diffuse experience of global fluency. Roughly speaking, you feel that things will go smoothly in the future because you feel that they have been going smoothly so far. This is not only something that you know; this is something that you feel. Insofar as agentive phenomenology remains largely 'thin' and 'evasive' (Metzinger 2006), one can conceive that one can easily miss this specific metacognitive feeling. Yet it is part of our mental life in the same way as the feeling of confidence.

In summary, one can experience a sense of agency while controlling the movements of a cursor on a screen, but when one controls the movements of one's own body, its phenomenology becomes richer, including kinaesthetic experiences of the body in movement based on the integration of efferent and afferent information (from proprioception, vision, and touch), a sense of bodily obedience based on the comparison between what one intends to do and what one does, and finally a metacognitive sense of the possibilities open to one's body based on the monitoring of one's past performance.

4.6 The Sense of Bodily Ownership

Among bodily feelings, the feeling of bodily ownership has been the most investigated as well as the most controversial. The main question is whether there is a primitive non-conceptual awareness of ownership. The RHI has been taken as evidence that there is such a thing as a feeling of bodily ownership because participants are fully aware that the hand that they report as their own is a mere piece of rubber (de Vignemont 2013; Peacocke 2014). Further dissociation between feelings and judgements of ownership can also be found in depersonalization as well as in xenomelia (also known as Body Identity Integrity Disorder). Little is still known about xenomelia, but patients describe an overwhelming desire to be amputated of one of their perfectly healthy limbs because it does not feel part of their body. Yet they know the limb that they want to cut is their own: 'Inside I feel that my legs don't belong to me, they shouldn't be there (…) I would almost say as if they're not part of me although I feel them, I see them, I know they are' (Corrine in 'Complete Obsession', BBC, 17 February 2000).

It is true, however, that these illusory and pathological dissociations are open to interpretation and some claim that they can be accounted for in purely cognitive terms (Alsmith 2015; Bermúdez 2015; Wu forthcoming). They may further argue that there cannot be feelings of bodily ownership (Bermúdez 2011, 2015). In order to defend his view, Bermúdez appeals to Anscombe's (1962) epistemological argument. She claims that sensations must be able to ground knowledge, and in order to do so, their internal content must be 'independently describable': there is a sensation of x if its description has a different content than x and this content is taken as a sign that indicates x. For example, there is a sensation of going down in a lift since one can provide an independent description of its internal content in terms of lightness and of one's stomach lurching upward. By contrast, it is not legitimate to talk of sensation of sitting cross-legged, Anscombe claims, because there is no such independent description that can be given. Likewise, Bermúdez (2015) assumes that one cannot describe the sense of ownership without referring to the fact that this is one's own body (i.e. myness), and thus there are no feelings of ownership:

> It is highly *implausible* that there is a determinate quale of ownership that can be identified, described and considered independently of the myness that it is supposed to be communicating. (Bermúdez 2015: 39, my emphasis)

The problem, however, is that each step of Anscombe's argument can actually be questioned. In particular, it is unclear why sensations require independent content and how we should interpret this notion of independent content. It is even less clear why there cannot be independent descriptions for bodily awareness. Neither Anscombe nor Bermúdez give arguments for this claim on which their whole argument rests. They merely state it. Bermúdez (2015: 44) further adds that ownership is 'a phenomenological given' and that it is impossible to ground it in further non-conceptual content. But this seems to be simply begging the question. By offering no principled reasons for their assumption, they undermine their own objection.

A different type of objection against the feeling of ownership arises from the assumption that there is no additional feeling beyond the felt location of bodily sensations (Martin 1992, 1995). Martin proposes that the distinction between what is one's own body and what is not one's own body should be phrased exclusively in spatial terms, between inside and outside bodily boundaries in which one can experience bodily sensations. He makes the following metaphysical assumption, which he calls the Sole Object view: there is an identity between one's own body and the body in which one locates bodily experiences. This identity, he claims, enables the spatial content of bodily experiences to ground bodily self-ascriptions. Consequently, it is sufficient to feel sensations as being located in a body part to experience this body part as one's own: 'this sense of ownership, in being possessed by all located sensations, cannot be independent of the spatial content of the sensation, the location of the event' (Martin 1995: 277).

However, one may wonder whether Martin does not eliminate the first-personal character of the sense of bodily ownership by trying to reduce it in such a way. One may indeed question the validity of the Sole Object view, and without this background metaphysical assumption, there is nothing in the spatial content of the sensation itself that justifies bodily self-ascription. Contrary to what he claims, it does not suffice for one to feel sensation in a body part to experience this body part as one's own. Some patients actually experience a sense of bodily disownership despite the fact that they still feel sensations in their so-called 'alien' limb. This is the case of patients with somatoparaphrenia who can feel touch and cry out in pain if the examiner pinches their 'alien' hand

(Melzack 1990; Bottini et al. 2002; Moro et al. 2004; Maravita 2008; Cogliano et al. 2012). Despite feeling these sensations to be located in their 'alien' hand, they maintain that it does not belong to them.

To recapitulate, the debate is still open whether they are—or not—feelings of bodily ownership. It is true that the argument from cognitive impenetrability is not a sufficient proof, but it is still *a* proof in favour of ownership feelings and it is not clear that there is any plausible alternative account of illusory and pathological ownership. Furthermore, there have not yet been any fatal objections against ownership feelings. It rather seems that the phenomenology of ownership is over and above the spatial phenomenology of bodily sensations. The question now is how best to characterize it.

I propose here to describe it on the model of the feeling of familiarity. As discussed earlier, the feeling of familiarity that is elicited by the perception of a face that has personal significance can be conceived of as a specific type of affective phenomenology that goes beyond the sensory recognition of the face. The phenomenology of visual experiences can thus be dual, both sensory and affective, and because of this duality, it is possible to have dissociations, as in the Capgras syndrome (Dokic and Martin 2015). Patients with Capgras syndrome can see that a person is visually identical to their spouse, for example, but they do not feel that she is their spouse and they believe that this person must be an impostor. Their sensory phenomenology is thus intact, but they lack the affective responses normally associated with it. Their delusion of an impostor is only an attempt to explain their 'incomplete' perceptual experiences of their spouse. By contrast, patients with Frégoli delusion have an anomalously heightened affective responsiveness for unknown individuals, and thus believe that they are surrounded by familiar persons in disguise (Langdon et al. 2014).

I claim that the feeling of bodily ownership can be conceived of as another type of affective phenomenology, which goes beyond the sensory phenomenology of bodily sensations and which involves autonomic responses. We can now reinterpret cases of somatoparaphrenia and xenomelia in which patients can still feel bodily sensations located in the body part that feels alien. As in Capgras syndrome, these patients have their sensory phenomenology preserved, while their affective one is missing. It was indeed found that when patients with somatoparaphrenia and with xenomelia saw their 'alien' hand threatened, they did not react to protect it (Romano et al. 2014, 2015). By contrast, participants who experience the RHI have their sensory phenomenology preserved, while their affective one is misguided (directed towards the wrong hand), and the illusion should thus be compared to Fregoli delusion. Indeed, subjects in the RHI react vividly when they see the rubber hand threatened and the strength of their reaction is correlated with their ownership rating in questionnaires (Ehrsson et al. 2007).

One should not believe, however, that the hypothesis that I defend, which I call the Bodyguard hypothesis, is that the body that one protects is the body that one experiences as one's own. Since one protects many things besides one's body and since one does not always protect one's body, this latter thesis is indeed clearly untenable. Instead I propose that the sense of bodily ownership is grounded in a specific type of body representation, which I call the *protective body map*. Because of the significance of the body for survival, there is a specific representation to fix what is to be protected. One does not protect one's biological body; one protects the body that one takes oneself to have and the protective body map, like any representation, can misrepresent one's biological body and include a phantom and a rubber hand, or fail to include one's own hand. This protective body map commands us to protect the body that it represents, but we can always disobey its command and our disobedience does not show a deficit of protective body schema; it merely shows that we have ceased to act on it. The Bodyguard hypothesis thus only claims that one experiences as one's own any body parts that are incorporated in the protective body map (for more details, see de Vignemont 2018).[9]

4.7 Conclusion

To conclude, although elusive, bodily awareness is rich, especially when things go wrong. It includes not only sensations of touch and tickles, of heat and cold, of pain and fatigue, of hunger and thirst, of postures and movements, but also a range of bodily feelings that express the presence of one's body in the world, ready to act on it and to protect itself from it. The phenomenology of bodily awareness should thus not be conceived of simply in sensory terms, but also in affective and metacognitive terms.

References

Alsmith, A. J. T. (2015), 'Mental Activity & the Sense of Ownership', *Review of Philosophy and Psychology* 6/4: 881–96.

Anscombe, G. E. M. (1962), 'On Sensations of Position', *Analysis* 22/3: 55–8.

Bayne, T. (2008), 'The phenomenology of agency', *Philosophy Compass* 3/1: 182–202.

Bermúdez, J. L. (1998), *The Paradox of Self-Consciousness*. Cambridge, MA: MIT Press.

Bermúdez, J. L. (2010), 'Action and awareness of agency: comments on Chris Frith', *Pragmatics and Cognition*, 18: 576–88.

Bermúdez, J. L. (2011), 'Bodily awareness and self-consciousness', in S. Gallagher (ed.), *Oxford Handbook of the Self*. Oxford: Oxford University Press.

Bermúdez, J. L. (2015), 'Bodily ownership, bodily awareness, and knowledge without observation', *Analysis* 75/1: 37–45.

Bermúdez, J. L. (2017), 'Ownership and the space of the body', in F. de Vignemont and A. Alsmith (eds), *The Subject's Matter: Self-consciousness and the Body*. Cambridge MA: MIT Press.

Bottini, G., Bisiach, E., Sterzi, R., and Vallar, G. (2002), 'Feeling touches in someone else's hand', *Neuroreport* 13: 249–52.

Botvinick, M. and Cohen, J. (1998), 'Rubber hands "feel" touch that eyes see', in *Nature* 391: 756.

---

[9] Here I limit the scope of the Bodyguard hypothesis to humans and assume that the protective body schema can ground the sense of bodily ownership only given the suite of cognitive capacities that human beings normally have. I leave aside the delicate issue of the sense of bodily ownership in other animals.

Bourgeois, J., Farnè, A., and Coello, Y. (2014), 'Costs and benefits of tool-use on the perception of reachable space', *Acta Psychologica (Amst)*, 148: 91–5.

Carruthers, G. (2015), 'A metacognitive model of the feeling of agency over bodily actions', *Psychology of Consciousness: Theory, Research, and Practice*, 2/3: 210–21.

Chambon, V. and Haggard, P. (2012), 'Sense of control depends on fluency of action selection, not motor performance', *Cognition* 125/3: 441–51.

Chambon, V., Sidarus, N., and Haggard, P. (2014), 'From action intentions to action effects: how does the sense of agency come about?' *Frontiers in Human Neuroscience* 8: 320.

Cocchini, G., Beschin, N., and Sala, S. D. (2002), 'Chronic anosognosia: a case report and theoretical account', *Neuropsychologia*, 40/12: 2030–8.

Cogliano, R., Crisci, C., Conson, M., Grossi, D., and Trojano, L. (2012), 'Chronic somatoparaphrenia: a follow-up study on two clinical cases', in *Cortex* 48/6: 758–67.

de Vignemont, F. (2010), 'Body schema and body image: pros and cons', *Neuropsychologia*, 48/3, 669–80.

de Vignemont, F. (2011), 'A mosquito bite against the enactive view to bodily experiences', *Journal of Philosophy*, CVIII, 4, 188–204.

de Vignemont, F. (2013), 'The mark of bodily ownership', *Analysis*, 73/4: 643–51.

de Vignemont, F. (2018), *Mind the Body*. Oxford: Oxford University Press.

de Vignemont, F. (2020), 'What phenomenal contrast for bodily ownership?' Journal of the APA.

Descartes, R. (1724), *Les méditations métaphysiques*. Paris: Garnier Flammarion, 1979.

Desmurget, M. and Grafton, S. (2000), 'Forward modeling allows feedback control for fast reaching movements', Trends in Cognitive Sciences, 4/11: 423–31.

Dokic, J. (2010), 'Perceptual Recognition and the Feeling of Presence', in Bence Nanay (ed.), *Perceiving the World*. Oxford University Press.

Dokic, J. (2012), 'Seeds of self-knowledge: noetic feelings and metacognition', in M. J. Beran, J. L. Brandl, J. Perner, and J. Proust (eds), *Foundations of Metacognition*. Oxford: Oxford University Press, 302–21.

Dokic, J. (2018), 'Visual awareness and visual appearances: a dual view', in Fiona Macpherson and Fabian Dorsch (eds), *Phenomenal Presence*, Oxford: Oxford University Press.

Dokic, J. and Martin, J.-R. (2015), "Looks the same but feels different": a metacognitive approach to cognitive penetrability', in A. Raftopoulos, and J. Zeimbekis (eds), *Cognitive Effects on Perception: New Philosophical Perspectives*. Oxford: Oxford University Press.

Dubernard, J. M., Lengelé, B., Morelon, E., Testelin, S., Badet, L., Moure, C., Beziat, J.L., Dakpé, S., Kanitakis, J., D'Hauthuille, C., El Jaafari, A., Petruzzo, P., Lefrancois, N., Taha, F., Sirigu, A., Di Marco, G., Carmi, E., Bachmann, D., Cremades, S., Giraux, P., Burloux, G., Hequet, O., Parquet, N., Francès, C., Michallet, M., Martin, X., Devauchelle, B. (2007), 'Outcomes 18 months after the first human partial face transplantation', *New England Journal of Medicine* 357/24: 2451–60.

Ehrsson, H. H., Wiech, K., Weiskopf, N., Dolan, R. J., and Passingham, R. E. (2007), 'Threatening a rubber hand that you feel is yours elicits a cortical anxiety response', *Proceedings of the National Academy of Sciences of the United States of America*, 104/23, 9828–33.

Ellis, H. D. and Lewis, M. B. (2001), 'Capgras delusion: a window on face recognition', *Trends in Cognitive Sciences*, 5/4, 149–56.

Ferrè, E. R., Haggard P. (2016), 'The vestibular body: Vestibular contributions to bodily representations', *Cognitive Neuropsychology* 33/1–2: 67–81.

Gandola, M., Invernizzi, P., Sedda, A., Ferrè, E. R., Sterzi, R., Sberna, M., Paulesu, E., and Bottini, G. (2012), 'An anatomical account of somatoparaphrenia', *Cortex*, 48/9: 1165–78.

Goldman, A. I. (2006), *Simulating Minds*. Oxford: Oxford University Press.

Gurwitsch, A. (1985), *Marginal Consciousness*. Athens: Ohio University Press.

Harcourt, E. (2008), 'Wittgenstein and Bodily Self-Knowledge', in *Philosophy and Phenomenological Research*, 77/2.

James, W. (1890), *The Principles of Psychology*, Vol 1. New York: Holt.

Katz, D. (1925), *The World of Touch*. Hove: Psychology Press.

Kilteni, K. L., Normand, J. M., Sanchez-Vives, M. V., Slater, M. (2012), 'Extending body space in immersive virtual reality: a very long arm illusion', *PLoS One*, 7/7: e40867.

Kind, A. (2018), 'Imaginative presence', in Fiona Macpherson and Fabian Dorsch (eds), *Phenomenal Presence*, Oxford: Oxford University Press.

Koriat, A. (2000), 'The feeling of knowing: Some metatheoretical implications for consciousness and control', in *Consciousness and Cognition*, 9/2: 149–71.

Langdon, R., Connaughton, E., and Coltheart, M. (2014), 'The Fregoli delusion: a disorder of person identification and tracking', in *Topics in Cognitive Science*, 6/4: 615–31.

Libet, B., Gleason, C. A., Wright, E. W., and Pearl, D. (1983), 'Time of unconscious intention to act in relation to onset of cerebral activity (Readiness-Potential)', in *Brain*, 106: 623–42.

McDowell, J. (2011), 'Anscombe on bodily self-knowledge', in A. Ford, J. Hornsby, and F. Stoutland (eds), *Essays on Anscombe's Intention*, Cambridge, MA: MIT Press.

Maravita, A. (2008), 'Spatial disorders', in S. F. Cappa, J. Abutalebi, J. F. Demonet, P. C. Fletcher, and P. Garrard (eds), *Cognitive Neurology: A Clinical Textbook*. New York: Oxford University Press, 89–118.

Martin, M. G. F. (1992), 'Sight and touch', in T. Crane (ed.), *The Content of Experience*. Cambridge: Cambridge University Press, 199–201.

Martin, M. G. F. (1995), 'Bodily awareness: a sense of ownership', in J. L. Bermúdez, T. Marcel, and N. Eilan (eds), *The Body and the self*. Cambridge, MA: MIT Press.

Matthen, M. P. (2005), *Seeing, Doing, and Knowing: A Philosophical Theory of Sense Perception*. Oxford: Oxford University Press.

Melzack, R. (1990), 'Phantom limbs and the concept of a neuromatrix', *Trends in Neuroscience*, 13/3: 88–92.

Melzack, R. (1992), 'Phantom limbs', *Scientific American*, 266/4: 120–6.

Melzack, R. and Wall, P. D. (1983), *The Challenge of Pain*. New York: Basic Books.

Metzinger, T. (2006), 'Conscious volition and mental representation: Toward a more fine-grained analysis', in N. Sebanz and W. Prinz (eds), *Disorders of Volition*. Cambridge, MA: Bradford Books, 19–48.

Mezue, M. and Makin, T. (2017), 'Immutable body representations: lessons from phantoms in amputees', in F. de Vignemont and A. Alsmith (eds), *The Subject's Matter: Self-consciousness and the Body*. Cambridge, MA: MIT Press.

Mitchell, S. W. (1871), 'Phantom limbs', *Lippincott's Magazine of Popular Literature and Science*, 8: 563–9.

Moro, V., Zampini, M., and Aglioti, S. M. (2004), 'Changes in Spatial Position of Hands Modify Tactile Extinction but not Disownership of Contralesional Hand in Two Right Brain-Damaged Patients', *Neurocase*, 10/6: 437–43.

Mylopoulos, M. (2015), 'Agentive awareness is not sensory awareness', *Philosophical studies*, 172/3: 761–80.

Nanay, B. (2016), 'Imagination and perception', in Amy Kind (ed.), *Routledge Handbook of the Philosophy of Imagination*. Abingdon: Routledge.

Noë, A. (2005), 'Real Presence', *Philosophical Topics*, 33: 235–64.

Oppenheimer, D. M. (2008), 'The secret life of fluency', *Trends in Cognitive Science*, 12/6: 237–41.

O'Shaughnessy, B. (1980), *The Will*. Volume 1. Cambridge: Cambridge University Press.

Peacocke, C. (2014), *The Mirror of the World: Subjects, Consciousness, and Self-Consciousness*. Oxford: Oxford University Press.

Ratcliffe, M. (2008), *Feelings of Being : Phenomenology, Psychiatry and the Sense of Reality*. Oxford; Oxford University Press.

Romano, D., Gandola, M., Bottini, G., and Maravita, A. (2014), 'Arousal responses to noxious stimuli in somatoparaphrenia and anosognosia: clues to body awareness', *Brain*, 137/4: 1213–23.

Romano, D., Sedda, A., Brugger, P., and Bottini, G. (2015), 'Body ownership: When feeling and knowing diverge', *Consciousness and Cognition*, 34: 140–8.

Rosenberg, R. S., Baughman, S. L., and Bailenson, J. N. (2013), 'Virtual superheroes: using superpowers in virtual reality to encourage prosocial behavior', *PLoS One*. 8/1: e55003.

Sherrington, C. S. (1906), *The Integrative Action of the Nervous System*. New Haven, CT: Yale University Press.

Sierra, M. (2009), *Depersonalization: A New Look at a Neglected Syndrome*. Cambridge: Cambridge University Press.

Wong, H. Y. (2015), 'On the Significance of Bodily Awareness for Action', *Philosophical Quarterly*, 65/261: 790–812.

Wu, W. (forthcoming), 'Mineness and Ownership in Action', in Marie Guillot and Manuel Garcia-Carpintero (eds), *The Sense of Mineness*. Oxford: Oxford University Press.

CHAPTER 5

EMOTIONAL EXPERIENCE

*Affective Consciousness
and its Role in Emotion Theory*

JULIEN DEONNA AND FABRICE TERONI

It is uncontroversial that subpersonal, neurophysiological processes subtend the emotions. This is what leads some prominent neuroscientists to claim that emotions are identical with such processes (Damasio 2000; LeDoux 1998). In these models, we may or may not feel the emotions we undergo. Others, first and foremost the philosophers, tend to speak of emotions as experiences (James 1884; Descartes 1989; Stocker 1996). Emotions, they say, are necessarily felt. One may think that these alternative ways of demarcating the territory are innocuous terminological choices and as such equally acceptable. After all, both camps agree that there are happenings at the subpersonal level that may be felt. To a large extent, this is true: researchers in the area tend to apply the term 'emotion' to the focus of their investigation and these terminological choices are reflective of the distinctive interests of neuroscience and philosophy.

This conciliatory standpoint is easily put under pressure, however, since an important family of approaches to consciousness seems to imply that the understanding of emotions as felt experiences is fundamentally misguided. According to these approaches, something is conscious if and only if it is the object of a psychological state. We become conscious of a tree when we see or touch it. Similarly, we become conscious of a psychological state when it is the object of another, higher-order psychological state.[1] In the light of these approaches, there is indeed pressure to demarcate the territory in the way neuroscientists do. For one may reason as follows: while botanists should be concerned with trees and not with our consciousness of them, emotion scholars should be concerned with emotions and not with our consciousness of them.

---

[1] These so-called higher-order theories of consciousness come in two fundamental varieties: those according to which the relevant higher-order states are thoughts (e.g. Rosenthal 2005) and those according to which they are perception-like experiences (e.g. Lycan 1996). For an introduction to the issues, see Carruthers (2011).

Observe that these approaches, when applied to the emotions, rest on a specific understanding of the expression 'the experience of an emotion', according to which the 'of' is that of *intentionality* (Alston 1969). The idea is that there is a higher-order state that is about the emotion, viz. that takes it as its object. In and of themselves, emotions are not experiences. We see here at work a traditional conception of consciousness as capturing the subject's *reflective perspective* on her own psychological states. The role of emotional consciousness so conceived primarily consists in providing the subject with a perspective from which she can attend to her affective life, hopefully making sense of it and perhaps channelling it in new directions.[2] This perspective can be claimed to rest on more or less cognitively demanding activities. At one end of the spectrum, it might depend on the deployment of socially acquired emotional labels. This is the case of Robert Roberts' idea that experiencing an emotion consists in construing oneself as having a given emotion (2003: 319–28). At the other end of the spectrum, the reflective perspective might be a less demanding affair, as in Michelle Montague's approach (2014) on which emotional consciousness consists in experiencing one's own emotional experiences. In psychology, the same understanding of consciousness as reflectivity transpires from the way consciousness is operationalized as self-report in a variety of questionnaire-based studies.

Not surprisingly, the intentional reading of 'the experience of an emotion' is not the only one available—actually, it has not been prevalent in the study of emotional consciousness. It is customary to distinguish between two fundamental varieties of consciousness (Block 1995; Lambie and Marcel 2002). There is not only *reflective* consciousness, there is also *phenomenal* consciousness, i.e. what it is like to be in given psychological states (Nagel 1974). As important as reflective consciousness is, there may not be something distinctively emotional about it. Reflective consciousness sometimes happens to be directed at emotions. Yet, when it is so, we may face no more than the deployment of a multi-purpose capacity to a specific domain. This is why—in philosophy at least—the bulk of the effort has been targeted on phenomenal consciousness.

Within a phenomenology-based approach to consciousness, the 'of' in for example 'the experience of anger' is not that of intentionality. Rather, it is the 'of' of *specification* (as in 'a church of Gothic style')—the expression refers to the specific kind of experience that anger involves, without this implying that it is the object of a higher-order psychological state. Emotional consciousness is here understood as an aspect of emotions as first-order experiences. That being the case, the study of consciousness does not look any more like a domain of research disconnected from the study of emotions themselves. In the same way as botanists should be concerned, amongst other things, with the different species of trees, emotion scholars should be concerned with the different species of emotional experiences.

With this distinction in hand, it looks like the issue of phenomenal consciousness does not boil down to that of whether emotions are reflectively conscious: one may have

---

[2] This is the kind of consciousness that is necessary for the ability to reappraise one's own emotional reactions, see e.g. Gross and Thompson (2007).

emotional experiences without thinking about them or attending to them. In the same spirit, observe that the majority of emotional responses that are indirectly measured (e.g. by brain or behavioural measures as opposed to self-reports) are not reflectively conscious. The next question is whether emotions, in addition to sometimes being *reflectively* unconscious, can also be *phenomenally* unconscious, that is, whether they need not be (or include) experiences.[3] The answer to this question cannot be inferred from indirect measurement of emotions, and it is not easy to appreciate what is at stake (Dretske 2006). In a sense, we are back to square one in trying to decide whether we can type emotions at the subpersonal level. We have already said that we can, since this is in large part a terminological issue. Note, however, that for those who emphasize phenomenal consciousness, the relevant subpersonal processes are fixed by the occurrence of that sort of consciousness. So, as opposed to what happens with reflective consciousness, the fact that these processes sometimes do not reverberate in phenomenal consciousness cannot be due to the subject's failing to label or to attend to what happens in his inner life. It must rather be due to a disruption of the natural covariation between neural processes and their phenomenological correlates. For that reason, maintaining that emotions occur when subpersonal goings-on do not reverberate in consciousness is similar to maintaining that a blindsighter is visually aware of his environment.[4] How should we understand the motivation for endorsing such a view?

First, it may manifest general scepticism with regard to the existence (Dennett 1988), the explanatory role (e.g. Jackson 1982), or the autonomy (Lycan 1996; Rosenthal 2005) of phenomenal consciousness. Whether or not (part of) this scepticism is warranted—we obviously cannot go into that here—observe how surprising it would be to take it as a point of departure when dealing with the emotions. Of course, human beings respond to well-being relevant stimuli by quickly allocating their cognitive resources so as to deal with them. This can be claimed without any reference to emotional experience. Still, given the saliency of emotional phenomenology, identifying at the outset such responses with emotions is to run the risk of missing one of their fundamental aspects.

Second, scepticism vis-à-vis phenomenal consciousness may rest on more local reasons. Exclusive focus on the subpersonal level may thus be supported by the existence of subjects deprived of emotional phenomenology (Berridge and Winkielman's (2003) 'blindfeelers'), or, less dramatically, by the observation that such phenomenology is inherently flimsy and poor (Russell 2003).

To assess scepticism regarding the import of emotional phenomenology and whether we can rest content with the subpersonal level, we have to move away from the abstract considerations that make up this introduction. We have to explore substantive accounts

---

[3] Although it will become obvious that we do not think that the possibility of phenomenally unconscious emotions is genuine, some important suggestions in this direction are offered in Lacewing (2007).

[4] Subjects in a blindsight condition have had a portion of their primary visual cortex destroyed, and claim to have become, as a result, blind in a region of their visual field. Since subjects forced to guess at the properties of their 'blind' field (e.g. whether it contains an 'X' or an 'O') prove remarkably accurate, one may insist that they are visually aware of their environment despite not having (or not reporting) visual phenomenal consciousness. For more on blindsight, see Weiskrantz (1986).

of emotional phenomenology in order to see whether it sheds light on key features of emotions. To this end, we shall focus on four features that can be introduced by way of an example. Say Sam is angry at Maria's nasty remark. The first feature relates to the fact that anger is a negative emotion, by contrast with positive emotions such as joy and admiration (*valence*). The second feature is how anger differs from other emotions such as sadness, fear, and joy (*individuation*). The third concerns the objects of anger and the sense in which anger discloses the significance of Maria's remark to Sam (*intentionality*). Fourth and finally, there is anger's relation to behaviour (*motivation*). Does focusing on emotional phenomenology encourage specific accounts of these features? We shall see that there are reasons to think it does. Are these reasons of sufficient import to dispel the scepticism of those who think that nothing of consequence plays out at the personal level of emotional experience? Given the role of emotional experience in our evaluative practices, we shall conclude that they are. Our discussion is structured as follows: Section 5.1 focuses on feeling approaches to phenomenology, Section 5.2 on componential approaches, Section 5.3 on perceptual approaches, and Section 5.4 on attitudinal approaches. Section 5.5 concludes with some observations regarding the significance of emotional phenomenology.

5.1 Feeling Accounts

Two things spring to mind when we think about how it feels to experience emotions. First, emotions are more or less pleasant or unpleasant. Second, they involve various degrees of felt excitation. For example, the contentment that one may feel after one hour of meditation can be very pleasant but low in excitation; the joy of scoring a goal will be as pleasant and very high in excitation; terror at meeting a ghost will be extremely unpleasant and high in excitation; while regret at having forgotten a lunch box is slightly unpleasant and low in excitation. These two dimensions are probably what we have in mind when we metaphorically speak of the emotions' 'warmth'. Not surprisingly, a very influential approach to emotional phenomenology revolves around these two dimensions (Russell 2003). Each type of emotion occupies, it is claimed, its own niche within a two-dimensional valence/arousal space, which the advocates of this view call 'core affect'.

Let us start by observing that this approach is apt to illuminate the *valence* of emotions through their phenomenology: emotions are (more or less) positive or negative depending on how more or less (un-)pleasant it is to experience them. Things are less straightforward as soon as we consider the other features, however. Consider *individuation*. The core affect approach has two striking consequences regarding the capacity of phenomenology to illuminate distinctions we draw within the affective domain generally, and amongst emotions in particular. First, if the only thing to be said about emotional experience is that it occupies a point (or a series of points) within a two-dimensional space, phenomenology would shed no light on the distinctions we ordinarily draw between affective categories. Indeed, the way it feels to be in an algedonic state (pain, pleasure), in a mood (irritation, anxiety), or in a general bodily condition (nauseous, energized) can be plotted against the same two dimensions.[5] Second, this is also true of a substantial number of the distinctions we make between types of emotions. Two episodes of anger and fear, or of admiration and amusement, may be equally (un-)pleasant and involve the same degree of excitation.

These consequences will strike some as a *reductio* of the core affect approach. Others will maintain that distinctions within the affective domain are not primarily based on phenomenology. According to an influential line of thought that we shall have the opportunity to discuss in Section 5.2 (Schachter and Singer 1962; Russell 2003; Reisenzein 2012; Barrett and Russell 2014), they are based on purely cognitive components of the emotions.

A lot may be said about why it is often claimed that emotional phenomenology is insufficiently rich to help draw these distinctions. Our suspicion is that these reasons have nothing to do with what can be gathered from experience itself.[6] What is in any case striking is that this deflationary take on emotional phenomenology clashes with another influential approach emphasizing its riches:

> But not even a Darwin has exhaustively enumerated all the bodily affections characteristic of any one of the standard emotions. More and more, as physiology advances, we begin to discern how almost infinitely numerous and subtle they must be.... Not only the heart, but the entire circulatory system, forms a sort of sounding-board, which every change of our consciousness, however slight, may make reverberate.... The various permutations and combinations of which... these organic activities are susceptible, make it abstractly possible that no shade of emotion, however slight, should be without a bodily reverberation as unique. (James 1884: 191–2)

Reading this passage, we should be struck by the difficulty of reducing bodily phenomenology to a single dimension of variation, that of arousal. According to James, bodily phenomenology originates on the contrary from the activation of several systems, which all contribute to making emotional experience a textured and complex affair. Emotional experience, it is widely acknowledged nowadays, results from the reverberation of distinct patterns of changes in facial and skeletal muscles, as well as in the autonomic and endocrine systems (e.g. Izard 1992; Ekman 1999; Scarantino 2014a).

A Jamesian approach holds the promise of getting from phenomenology much more than is possible from the core affect picture. But it will deliver on this promise only if it correctly assumes that a substantial number of emotion types, as we recognize them in ordinary language, correspond to differentiated profiles of bodily responses. How plausible is this assumption? As a matter of fact, it has in recent years been the target of numerous criticisms (e.g. Russell 2003; Barrett 2006; Lindquist et al. 2012). The critics insist that specific types of emotions are not associated with specific patterns of bodily

---

[5] Teroni (2019) explores the relations between algedonic states and emotions in the context of the core affect approach.

[6] For detailed discussions of this issue, see Deonna and Teroni (2017) and Teroni (2017).

changes, and that emotions anyway often occur in the absence of bodily feedback (see Reisenzein and Stephan 2014 for a review). The evidence for the existence of emotion-specific patterns of physiological reactions, facial expressions, and feelings (e.g. Levenson 1992; Kreibig 2010; Stephens et al. 2010; Laird and Lacasse 2014) is claimed by the critics to be fragmented and controversial. To this, the Jamesian replies that the fragmentation of the evidence is due to methodological problems (see Reisenzein 2000 and Mauss et al. 2005 for discussions). This is not the place to adjudicate between these positions—suffice it to say that whether emotional phenomenology is rich or poor remains an open question.

Individuation *of emotions* is only one feature for which phenomenology may be pressed into service. As we have seen, we may want phenomenology not only to individuate emotions from one another, but also to demarcate emotions from other affective states. It is less clear that the body is apt to this task: moods, algedonic states, and more general conditions of the body all involve bodily feelings. More generally, whether we appeal to rich patterns of felt bodily changes or to a poorer two-dimensional understanding of phenomenology, the resulting accounts are markedly silent regarding the other features we singled out: *intentionality* and *motivation*. These accounts foster a conception of emotions according to which their relation to the environment outside the body is at best indirect and contingent (e.g. Kenny 1963; Thalberg 1964). Whether emotions are conceived on the model of moods—feeling good or bad, alert or aloof, open or closed, etc.—or of feelings of the body, they may be *caused* by environmental events and are in turn likely to channel the interpretation of these events in specific directions, but they are not *ways of being engaged with* these events.[7] Without denying that affective phenomenology sometimes fits that description, emotions as a rule feel to the subject like responses to significant environmental events that prepare her to efficiently deal with them. This is why so many insist on the intentional and motivating aspects of emotions, aspects upon which the approaches to emotional experience under discussion are ill equipped to shed light.

5.2 Componential Accounts

Starting where we left off, the obvious move to bring in the systematic relation that emotions entertain with the environment is to supplement core affect or the felt body (we shall henceforth refer to these as 'feelings') with additional components. The move consists in conceiving of emotions as composites of emotional feelings and cognitive elements. An episode of anger would bring together a negatively valenced feeling with a high level of arousal and an anger-related thought. This componential strategy, which

---

[7] Ratcliffe (2008) has done a lot to draw attention to how deep and rich moods can be. He is careful not to identify them with emotions, however. For a less sharp distinction between emotions and moods, see Price (2006) and Tappolet (2018).

has enjoyed considerable success in both philosophy and psychology, comes in two different flavours.

The first has it that the relevant thoughts are about the feelings one is experiencing. An emotion would consist in the categorization of a feeling as belonging to a given emotion type—the categorization being driven by considerations pertaining to how the feeling came about. Sam is angry when he labels his negative feeling as one of anger, given his conviction that it issues from Maria's nasty remark. This is in essence the influential conceptual act theory advocated by Lisa Feldman Barrett (2006, 2014) and inspired by one possible reading of the literature on arousal misattribution initiated by Schachter and Singer's (1962) experiments.[8] In light of the distinction between reflective and phenomenal consciousness, note that here we are not exclusively dealing with the latter: the approach in fact proposes to distribute emotional consciousness over first-order phenomenology (which is not about the environment) and higher-order thoughts (which diagnose feelings as resulting from given environmental events). Now, while we have acknowledged the role of reflective consciousness in regulating inner life, we have contended that this is not the right entry point to emotional experience. It is true that we sometimes introspect our affective life in order to make sense of it, but emotional experience of the environment does not come down to taxonomy-oriented introspection (Deonna and Scherer 2010). All in all, the distinctive worry raised by the conceptual act theory is that it excludes the possibility of emotional relations to the environment that do not boil down to complex aetiological thoughts.

The second variant of the componential strategy rests on a much simpler view of the aetiological story. It conceives of emotions as being composed of a causal sequence originating in a thought about an external event and culminating in a feeling (Lyons 1980; Russell 2003; Whiting 2011). No need here for higher-order thoughts about feelings and their place within the sequence. This alternative to the conceptual act theory turns out to be an unsatisfactory way of accommodating the claim that emotional experience connects us with significant events in the environment, however. As we have already acknowledged, feelings typically result from the perception of such events and this surely is essential to understanding how they end up connecting us with the environment. Still, is it right to conceive of emotional experience as being made of a thought about an event causing a feeling that in itself has no relation to the environment (Aquila 1975; Maddell 1997)? Does using the term 'emotion' to cover both the feeling and the thought that precipitated it achieve more than rearranging the deck chairs on the Titanic?

To answer this question, let us revisit the two variants of the componential strategy with this phenomenological concern in mind. Do the cognitive elements they add on to feelings contribute to emotional phenomenology and, if so, do they have the right phenomenological profile? Up to this point, we have intentionally left the issue vague in speaking of the addition of thoughts. All now depends on what sort of phenomenology these added thoughts themselves have. One of two things must be true.

---

[8] For discussion, see Deonna and Teroni (2017).

On the one hand, the added thoughts may have a rich phenomenological profile, involving detailed sensory imagination or deep immersion. If so, the issue is whether all emotions involve exercises in imaginative immersion. Consider what happens upstream of emotions. Immersion sometimes helps elicit emotions, for example. when you feel compassion because you picture a situation in its gruesome sensory details. But the claim hardly generalizes, as many run of the mill emotions are not prefaced by such imaginings. Consider next what happens downstream of emotions. Emotions often induce imaginings from which new emotions arise. Still, emotions need not always have such consequences. An episode of anger may generate immediate action without room for imagination to set in. And, in any case, these imaginings are best seen as consequences of the emotions than as components of them.

On the other hand, the added thoughts may have no phenomenology or the sort of thin cognitive phenomenology that is, according to some philosophers, characteristic of all thoughts (Bayne and Montague 2011, Pitt 2004). Plausible candidates are evaluative thoughts, that is, thoughts that identify the object of the emotion and its significance—in fear it would be the thought that a given situation is dangerous, in amusement the thought that it is funny, etc. Observe in passing that these evaluative thoughts will help *individuate* emotions from one another and from other affective phenomena, which will prove important within componential approaches resting on core affect. That being said, appeal to such thoughts has one key consequence for the issue of intentionality under discussion: the phenomenology of being engaged with the environment in emotions would not be specific to them, since it would take the shape of thoughts that could occur in non-emotional contexts.[9] Of course, when emotions take place, such thoughts are followed by feelings. Still, this may be insufficient to accommodate the idea we emphasized in criticizing feeling accounts, viz. that emotional experiences feel like ways of being engaged with significant environmental events. Many will indeed dig in their heels at this stage, insisting that emotions feel like specific intentional relations to these events: it is a non-negotiable fact about emotional phenomenology that, from the perspective of someone who is afraid, fear seems to be a specific, affective, intentional relation to danger (Maddell 1997; Pugmire 1998; Goldie 2000). This, it is claimed, cannot be maintained if intentionality and phenomenology are distributed in the way characteristic of componential approaches: the phenomenology of fear is not that of merely thinking that one is facing a dangerous event and having feelings as a consequence.

Advocates of the componential strategy are not without resources to respond to these observations, which assume that the experience of emotional engagement with the environment is so unified that it cannot be distributed over an unemotional thought and a non-intentional emotional feeling (Herzberg 2012). This assumption may be challenged, since we often undergo emotions that feel like they are composed of various ingredients failing to coalesce into coherent wholes. If we think that such episodes of emotional turmoil are pervasive, we embrace the idea that emotional phenomenology always

---

[9] We leave aside here the possibility canvassed by Mendelovici (2013), according to whom the relevant thoughts cannot occur in non-emotional contexts.

consists in the separate contribution of various components of emotions to phenomenal consciousness. Although this response is not without merit, it is an overreaction to the cases at hand: emotional phenomenology is not characterized by such disorganization. This is simply not how ordinary episodes of fear, shame, amusement, or gratitude manifest themselves in consciousness. Everyday experiences of these emotions do not seem to be distributed over two (or more) components, one relating us to the environment, the other providing emotions with their warmth. For this reason, componential approaches do not rest on an adequate picture of the phenomenology.[10]

5.3 Perceptual Accounts

If this diagnosis is along the right track, this means that we are still looking for ways to understand emotional phenomenology apt to do justice to the idea that emotions are experiences that relate us to meaningful aspects of the environment. The three perceptual accounts that we shall now introduce all proceed from the conviction that the componential strategy is misguided since emotional phenomenology is a *unitary* phenomenon in which feelings themselves play the role of connecting subject and environment. What is shared by these accounts comes down to two basic insights. First, that the meaningful aspects of the environment are evaluative (or well-being relevant) properties such as the dangerous, the funny, the offensive, the admirable, etc. Second, that emotions are experiences that are about or represent these properties: fear would be an experience that represents the dangerous, amusement an experience that represents the funny, etc. Since all then rest on the specific way one elaborates on these insights, the issue of *intentionality* has understandably been prominent in the development and criticism of perceptual accounts. We shall follow suit, but want first to say a few words regarding how these accounts can deal with *individuation* and *valence* (we shall have the opportunity to discuss *motivation* later on).

As regards *individuation*, perceptual accounts will typically claim that emotions differ from one another, as well as from other affective states, in virtue of the properties they represent. The claim could be that general conditions of the body, moods, and algedonic states do not represent evaluative properties, and that types of emotions are differentiated in virtue of representing distinct evaluative properties. Anger and no other emotion but anger would be the experience of the offensive, etc. As regards *valence*, perceptual accounts can either maintain that it is a phenomenologically salient aspect of emotional experience or deny that this is the case. If the former, they will appeal to the fact that evaluative properties themselves are positive (the funny, the admirable) or negative

[10] Some componentialists have tried to account for the unitary nature of emotional experience in terms of phenomenal properties emerging from the 'fusion' of the various components such as beliefs, desires and feelings (Aquila 1975; Castelfranchi and Miceli 2009). In the absence of further detail on how to understand the nature of these emerging properties, it remains unclear whether this account falls prey to the objections just pressed or if it rather qualifies as a perceptual account (see Section 5.3).

(the dangerous, the offensive) and claim that the distinction between positive and negative emotions is derivative on the nature of what they represent.[11] If the latter, they may adopt a variety of strategies to understand valence in non-phenomenological terms.[12]

This being said, let us now turn to the crux of the matter, the issue of *intentionality*—if emotions are unitary phenomena that qualify as experiences that represent evaluative properties, what sort of experiences are they exactly?

Let us start with Jesse Prinz (2004), whose account is famous for putting forward an understanding of emotions as unitary phenomena. According to Prinz, emotions are nothing more than what James thought they were, namely felt bodily changes. To appreciate how emotions connect us with the environment, this account, he claims, needs only be supplemented by a story about how these felt bodily changes come about. The story begins with the observation that different types of bodily changes correspond to different types of situations that impinge on well-being. The perception of types of evaluative situations systematically produces types of felt bodily changes (those associated with fear, anger, admiration, etc.). Since co-variation has been set up by evolutionary pressure, Prinz insists that the *function* of these patterns of bodily feelings is to *indicate* the types of situations that cause them. Now, according to the teleosemantic programme (Dretske 1981; Millikan 1984), if x has the function of indicating y, then x *represents* y. The feelings associated with fear, anger or admiration then *represent* the dangerous, offensive or admirable character of the events that trigger them. On this account, phenomenology is conceived exclusively in terms of bodily feelings, which happen to represent evaluative properties. So, as promised, feelings are recruited to connect the subject and the environment.

This ingenious account fails to the extent that it gets things the wrong way round. For while we should not overstate the clarity with which emotional feelings manifest themselves in consciousness, it seems that they relate us to meaningful aspects of the environment and not to changes within our own bodies. They are, to quote Peter Goldie's (2000) apt phrase, first and foremost 'feelings towards' the world. Ironically, Prinz reveals what is wrong with his account when he tries to illustrate the insight behind it. According to the analogy he puts forward, perception of bodily changes in emotion is to the representation of evaluative properties what visual awareness of water is to the representation of H_2O: we represent the latter through experiencing the former (Prinz 2004: 67–9). This is odd. H_2O is not phenomenologically present as such within visual awareness of water, but the same cannot be said of the significance of the events with which emotions co-vary. There is something in the experience of fear or amusement that makes the dangerous or the funny phenomenologically salient. Prinz avoids the pitfalls of componential accounts, but fails to capture the way emotional engagement with the environment is manifest in consciousness.[13]

---

[11] For discussion, see Teroni (2018) and (2019).
[12] To take just two examples, one may understand valence in terms of approach or avoidance behaviour (MacLean 1993) or in terms of imperative subpersonal states (Prinz 2004).
[13] As we shall see in Section 5.4, something like the reverse of his account may be more convincing.

The second perceptual account that will interest us is that of Robert Roberts. Emotions, he says, qualify as evaluative experiences because they represent the environment in the light of specific concerns—they are 'concern-based construals'. A subject's attachments, desires, wishes, and personality traits explain why events take this or that emotional meaning. More specifically, Roberts claims that emotions *represent* the impact of specific aspects of the environment on the subject's concerns. In being afraid of a lion, say, the lion is construed in terms of its aversive consequences regarding the desire to be safe from harm. A crucial feature of the account, we are told, is that the construal at stake should be understood on the model of *aspectual* perception: in emotion, we perceive the environment *in the light of* concerns for safety, honour, justice, beauty, etc. This is what evaluative perception comes down to, and the account attempts in this way to circumvent the worries raised by the componential strategy. Indeed, the affective (the represented concerns) and the cognitive (what is construed) dimensions of emotions are claimed to constitute a unitary experience of the environment as being imbued with significance.[14]

Is this a faithful picture of emotional phenomenology? Let us start by considering whether, in emotional experience, the subject is struck by how events impact on her concerns. We are not asking whether emotions *result* from such impact—this is in all probability true—but whether this is something we *experience*. Here are two interrelated reasons to doubt it.[15] First, something akin to the aforementioned scepticism regarding the idea that emotional phenomenology features an identification of the emotion we are undergoing applies here to the idea that it features an identification of the relevant concerns. The claim that, in emotion, events always appear to the subject as satisfying or thwarting one of her attachments or desires just is unfaithful to the phenomenology. Second, the relevant concerns not only seem to be absent from the content of emotions, they may in addition not be accessible at all to the subject. This happens when emotions come as a surprise and several explanations in terms of concerns are open. The concerns that actually drive emotions sometimes come to light only after more or less sustained reflection, which would be impossible if they were available from emotional content.

On a different note, which is especially significant given our interest in phenomenology, the account raises a worry regarding the *format* of concerned-based construals. Moulding emotional experience into aspectual perception leaves little doubt about the answer. While Roberts insists that, as opposed to *judging*, *construing* the world as being so and so is not to commit oneself to how the world is, he is clear that the terms in which the world is construed are conceptual in nature. In the standard cases, the subject perceives something, which she then construes in a specific way by applying the concept of the relevant concern. This is unattractive, however, for the familiar reasons that have contributed to judgement theories of the emotions coming to be out of favour. It not only intellectualizes emotions in ways that end up depriving animals and infants from having

---

[14] Roberts himself does not put forward his conception as an account of emotional phenomenology. This is because he approaches, as we have observed at the outset of our discussion, the issue of emotional experience exclusively in terms of higher-order states. But the conception of emotions as concern-based construals can be severed from this further commitment so as to apply to first-order phenomenology.

[15] For more details, see Teroni (2016).

them, it is also unfaithful to the phenomenology for reasons that should by now be familiar. Indeed, the account looks like a slightly modified version of the componential strategy discussed in Section 5.2. The conceptual act theory conceives of emotional experience in terms of the conscious impact of higher-order thoughts about the origin of non-intentional feelings. We are now asked to think of it in terms of the conscious impact of construals, that is, higher-order thoughts regarding how events perceived or thought about affect the subject's concerns (Vance 2018).

Two observations are in order. First, this account may fare worse than the conceptual act theory given that what we have called the warmth of emotions is now altogether out of the picture. According to Roberts, emotions are no more than construals of the environment in conceptual terms. Second, observe that any approach to emotional phenomenology that takes aspectual perception as its model will face the same difficulty. More specifically, focusing on the environmental side (i.e. the lion is construed *as dangerous*) rather than on the subject side (i.e. it is construed *in terms of one's concern for safety*) will not help. It will not, because the construals—which explain why emotions are experience of the environment as being imbued with significance—do no more than apply concepts to objects or events that are, in the most favourable cases, perceived.[16] Even in these cases, emotions turn out to be composed of perceptual *experiences* representing objects and emotional *thoughts* about these objects. So, we have not yet extricated ourselves from the componential strategy.[17]

This conclusion regarding aspectual perception may suggest that the conception of emotions as experiences of meaningful aspects of the environment should be more radical than we have so far envisaged. Some philosophers hold that the prospects for such a conception are good once we insist on evaluative properties (rather than concerns) and on simple or non-conceptual (rather than aspectual) perception (Tappolet 2000, 2016; Tye 2008; Mendelovici 2013; Mitchell 2018). According to this third perceptual account, emotions are quite literally thought to be perception-like experiences that make evaluative properties manifest to us. Being afraid is not thinking of a perceived objet or event as threatening a desire to be safe or even as dangerous, it is perceiving that object's or event's dangerousness.

Let us take a step back to fully appreciate the idea. If, to take a simple example, sight allows us to apprehend the shape and colour of a given lion, and hearing allows us to apprehend the sounds it emits, the emotions, so the idea goes, allow us to apprehend the values it exemplifies. The claim that emotions are perceptual experiences of values amounts therefore to the claim that distinct emotions (fear, anger, admiration, etc.) track distinct values (danger, offense, excellence, etc.). To the question of whether and how emotional phenomenology reflects the fact that emotions relate us to meaningful aspects of the environment, the account gives a straightforward answer: emotional experience

---

[16] The claim is not that all construals are instances of concept application (this may not be the case of the duck–rabbit Gestalt switches), but that it is the case when evaluative construals are concerned.

[17] It seems to us that Peter Poellner's (2016: 16–17) claim according to which emotions are experiences that present themselves as merited or justified in the circumstances also qualifies as a view of emotions as aspectual perceptions. As such it may fall prey to the kind of criticisms developed here.

makes values manifest to the subject undergoing the emotion. One is then in a position to circumvent the worry raised by the distribution of the intentional and phenomenal aspects of emotions over distinct components characteristic of the componential strategy we have discussed in Section 5.2. These are claimed to be two aspects of the intentional experiences that make up the emotions—these experiences are about something significant and make themselves manifest as such. The analogy with familiar ways of thinking about perception is complete. In the same way as the phenomenology of perceptual experience essentially consists in making perceived properties manifest to the subject, the phenomenology of emotional experience essentially consists in making evaluative properties manifest to her (e.g. Tye 2008).

This picture is attractive. First, the idea that no other emotional experience than that of fear is a suitable candidate for *presenting* the world in terms of danger is intuitive. Although we have no difficulty imagining a scenario in which we end up reacting to a dangerous situation with, say, amusement, it hardly makes sense to think that amusement might present danger or make it manifest to us. The case is strictly analogous to perception. It makes sense to suppose, as in inverted spectrum scenarios, that red surfaces elicit in Joanna experiences of the kind red surfaces typically elicit in us and in Michael experiences of the kind blue surfaces typically elicit in us. But it hardly makes sense to say that Michael's visual experiences make redness experientially manifest to him (Price 2009). The intuition is the same, perhaps even stronger, regarding the emotions.

Second, the picture is also attractive for theoretical reasons, since it fits nicely within an influential approach according to which phenomenology essentially consists in various ways (perceptual, mnesic, emotional, etc.) the world makes itself manifest to us. In the words of Max Scheler, perhaps the first explicit exponent of this approach in the realm of emotions, 'the value quality is not a feeling state or a relation to some such state…, just as the quality "blue" is not a visual sensation or a relation to some such sensation state' (Scheler 1980: 249, as translated in Poellner 2016). In this passage, Scheler points to the shortcomings of core affect approaches to emotional experiences and claims that perceptual and emotional phenomenology are both *transparent* (e.g. Harman 1990; Martin 2002): attempts to describe the phenomenology of experience (be it perceptual or emotional) always end up in the description of worldly properties (colours, forms, or values).

Although we agree that emotional phenomenology is a unitary phenomenon in which feelings connect subject and environment, it is unclear whether appealing to the *presentational* character of simple perception is adequate to capture emotional phenomenology. Proponents of simple perception typically insist that attention to perceptual phenomenology should lead us to distinguish a level of non-conceptual representation upon which the subject may then deploy her conceptual resources (e.g. in construing what she perceives in terms of a given concept). This is plausible insofar as we think that, in perception, one can be struck by properties like colours and shapes without mastering and deploying the relevant colour or shape concepts. To extend this diagnosis to emotions would thus require a firm grasp on emotional experience as a non-conceptual presentation of values. The worry here is twofold. First, advocates of the simple perception model are not very forthcoming in that respect. Second, the claim that emotional experience is transparent comes under pressure once we examine it head-on. Let us expand on this last point.

Pace Mendelovici (2013) and Tye (2008), attention to emotional experience does not support the view that it is transparent. In emotion, the litmus test for transparency, namely the exercise of attending to the experience as opposed to what it is about, does not end up in the contemplation of the same evaluative properties in both instances. On the contrary, attending to experience seems to disrupt the intentional structure of the emotion: we are no more related to the object and its significance, but to various disturbances within our body. This suggests in our opinion that emotional experience is not transparent and, hence, that it cannot be modelled on simple perception. It also seems to indicate that we cannot give up on bodily feelings as easily as we might have thought, an idea we substantiate in section 5.4.

Finally, observe that perceptual accounts in general, and this third account in terms of simple perception in particular, are vulnerable to the charge that they are not faithful to the *motivational* aspect of the emotions. The perceptualist can maintain that emotions, being perceptual experiences of evaluative properties, represent reasons for action—something appearing dangerous is a reason to avoid it (justificatory reason) and may prompt an avoidance strategy (motivating reason). What she cannot maintain is that they are in and of themselves motivational states. Being presented with a reason to act is not yet being motivated to act (Brady 2013). This may well constitute another reason why the simple perception view is not faithful to the nature of emotional experience. Some will insist with some plausibility that experiencing an emotion is not experiencing a reason to act, but rather experiencing *a specific way of being engaged with something in the world*.[18] As we shall see in Section 5.4, this conclusion and the claim that emotional experience is not transparent but somehow incorporates bodily feelings are actually two sides of the same coin.

Before we turn to that, let us bring this review of the perceptual approach to emotional experience to an end. We have explored three ways of channelling the core insights motivating this approach into specific accounts and have seen reasons to conclude that these either fail to deliver on the promise that emotional experiences are unitary, or do not rest on adequate models of these experiences.

5.4 Attitudinal Accounts

It looks as if our journey into emotional phenomenology takes us back to what we dismissed almost at the outset of our discussion, namely the felt body. This may look like bad news, until we realize that the worries attached to the claim that the phenomenology of emotions is that of the felt body all stem from the idea that this phenomenology is

---

[18] On the pitfalls associated with the Jamesian idea that emotions are in themselves motivational states, see Deonna and Teroni (2017). See also Vanello (2019).

revealed to us when attention is directed towards changes occurring in the body. The project of illuminating emotional phenomenology through reflective consciousness may well be a mistake, however. We shall first explain why it is a mistake and next offer a suggestion as to how the felt body actually features in emotional experience. We shall see that this is best understood as characteristic of emotional *attitudes*, a claim that sharply contrasts with the perceptual accounts we have just reviewed.

As we have observed in our criticism of the simple perception view, inward-looking attention actually disrupts the nature of emotional experience and what comes into view is a fragmented landscape of modifications in various bodily parts. Here is how Claparède, an early supporter of James, expresses dissatisfaction with the way the latter conceived of bodily phenomenology:

> Permit yourself to become absorbed in [the object of] your anger;...then you no longer experience distinctly the trembling of your lips, your pallor, or the isolated sensations arising from the different parts of your contracted muscular machinery.
> (Claparède 1928: 129)

According to Claparède, then, in emotional experience the subject's attention is typically directed outward. When this is the case, he argues, the body feels altogether differently, viz. it is experienced in a holistic rather than atomistic fashion: 'The emotion is nothing other than the consciousness of a form, of a "Gestalt" of these multiple organic impressions.... This confused and general perception of the whole...is the primitive form of...emotional perception' (1928: 128).[19]

Reference to a 'Gestalt' is evocative, but we surely need something more specific. The most promising option is to appeal to states of action readiness.[20] There is a preparedness to act in a particular direction which harnesses the subject's resources at the expense of her other goals and/or activities (Scarantino 2014b). This preparedness to act is sustained by changes in a variety of organismic systems including facial and skeletal muscles, the autonomic nervous system (e.g., heart rate, perspiration, respiration digestion), and the endocrine system (e.g., adrenaline). These changes not only happen, but are typically felt and so contribute to shaping distinctive emotional experiences, which are as many *stances or attitudes* that one can take towards the world. In fear, we feel the way our body is poised to act so as to contribute to the neutralization of what provokes the fear. In anger, we feel the way our body is prepared for active hostility to whatever causes the anger. In an episode of loving affection, we feel the way our body is prepared to move towards cuddling the beloved object. In sadness, the body is felt as though it were prevented from entering into interaction with a certain object. Since these descriptions of bodily reactions—if they capture the way emotions manifest themselves in

---

[19] On the same topic, see Lambie and Marcel (2002) and Frijda's (2005: 482) discussions of the impact of different modes of attention on phenomenology.

[20] States of action readiness feature already in McDougall's (1923), Bull's (1951) and Arnold's (1960) emotion theories. They have been systematically explored by Frijda (1986) and have more recently been put to use by philosophers (Deonna and Teroni 2012; Scarantino 2014b).

consciousness—appear to be quite rich, advocates of this attitudinal account will insist that emotional phenomenology is apt to *individuate* emotions from one another as well as from other affective states. But what does appeal to attitudes exactly amount to?

Addressing the features of *intentionality* and *motivation* will help us to make progress. As regards *intentionality*, it is important to appreciate how distinct the account is from the representational understanding of emotional phenomenology characteristic of the perceptual approach. The present suggestion is that the way it feels to have an emotion is not to be described in terms of how the world is presented, but rather, as we have just illustrated, in terms of a felt way of being engaged with what is represented (see also Mueller 2018). This may be successful in avoiding the two worries raised by the perceptual approach. First, according to the attitudinal account, emotional phenomenology is not in the business of representing values, and so the question of transparency does not even arise. Second, and this regards *motivation*, the specific way the body features in emotional experience, that is, as a felt engagement with the environment, reflects the fact that emotions are, in themselves, motivational states. The claim is that experiencing an emotion is experiencing a specific way of being engaged with something, which contrasts with the perceptual approach according to which it consists in experiencing a reason to act.

We now have all the ingredients to see why understanding emotional phenomenology in terms of 'feelings of the body' need not end up in the claim that this phenomenology is that of feeling changes occurring in various bodily parts. When appeal is made to feelings of the body here, the 'of' is not that of intentionality. It is rather that of specification and does not refer to the representation of changes in bodily parts, but to the sort of felt bodily engagement we have been discussing. If this is correct, then states of action readiness do not point to the body: they are attitudes that we adopt in relation to external objects or situations, and this is precisely how they feel.

Are we finally out of the woods? Perhaps not, as you may recall that the main difficulty attending theories appealing to bodily phenomenology is that they fail to conform to the idea that emotions are experiences that relate us to meaningful aspects of the environment. The strength of perceptual theories is that they conceive of emotions directly as representations of these meaningful aspects. Does the outward-looking intentionality of states of action readiness also qualify as evaluative? Here is how Frijda introduces the phenomenology of action readiness as that of a felt evaluative attitude:

> Action readiness transforms a neutral world into one with places of danger and openings towards safety, in fear, with targets for kissing and their being accessible for it, in enamoration, with roads stretching out endlessly before one, in fatigue, misery, and despair, with insistent calls for entry or participation or consumption, in enjoyment.   (Frijda 2007: 205)

The idea that emotions are felt bodily stances we take towards aspects of the environment is amenable to the idea that they are evaluative attitudes. To illustrate, fear is a danger-related evaluative experience because, as we have seen above, it consists in feeling one's body's readiness to act so as to diminish an object's likely impact on one (flight, preemptive attack, etc.). This is why this attitude is both fitting and reasonable if the dog is dangerous. Similarly, anger is an offence-related evaluative experience because it consists in feeling one's body's readiness to act so as to retaliate one way or another. This is why this attitude is both fitting and reasonable if there has been an offence.[21]

5.5 Emotional Experience and Understanding

At the outset of our discussion, we took notice of some reasons for scepticism about the import of phenomenology. To assess whether the study of emotions would benefit from attention to what happens at the personal level, we said, requires that we explore emotional phenomenology and see if it encourages adopting specific views on key features of emotions. We hope that the foregoing discussion has confirmed that it does. Emotional phenomenology is key to assessing the merits of various theoretical frameworks. We have argued that many of these frameworks turn out to be unsatisfactory because they are unfaithful to how we live emotions. In the process, we have illustrated how phenomenology can come to play a constitutive role in accounting for central features of the emotions (valence, individuation, intentionality, motivation).

Now, this might only reflect our focus in this chapter: exploring emotion theory through the prism of phenomenology inevitably revolves around views about the felt aspect of emotions. Perhaps an attitudinal approach is in this respect best suited to shed light on some of their central features, but have we done anything to show that such an approach—and phenomenology more generally—is of real import for our understanding of the emotions? If emotions are fundamentally responses to well-being relevant stimuli, what would be lost if they were to remain hidden at the subpersonal level?

According to us, attention to the personal level of emotional experience is essential to accounting for our *understanding* of evaluative concepts and, ultimately, to accounting for the specific way human agents respond to well-being relevant stimuli by passing evaluative judgements. Let us explain why. Being a competent user of evaluative concepts may require more than the mere ability to apply them in the correct circumstances. Classifying something as comical or shameful is essentially linked to the understanding that we tend to favour or reject it. Now, it seems to us that if we were deprived of the relevant emotional experiences, our understanding of these sorts of 'favouring' or 'rejecting' would become quite elusive. The approach to emotional experiences we favour, that is, as experiential attitudes consisting in one's readiness to act in various and distinctive ways vis-à-vis given objects or situations, makes this especially salient. It is because our emotional experiences are such felt attitudes that our evaluative concepts are anchored

---

[21] One important issue this raises is whether the fact that the phenomenology involved is not representational means that it does not contribute to the intentionality of emotions. On this, see Deonna and Teroni (2012, 2015). For criticisms, see Dokic and Lemaire (2015) and Tappolet and Rossi (2019).

in them: it is by experiencing the former that we come to be aware of the canonical conditions of application pertaining to the latter (Peacocke 1996; Zagzebski 2003).

Imagining an emotional zombie, a creature deprived of emotional experience, will drive this point home. She handles our evaluative practices because dedicated subpersonal mechanisms track the relevant values and she links her application of evaluative concepts to the verdicts of these mechanisms. But does she understand the evaluative judgements she makes? For her, judging that something is amusing, degrading, or offensive consists in realizing that these subpersonal mechanisms align with the emotional responses of others. While her evaluative verdicts are in line with ours, the canonical conditions of application of her evaluative concepts are radically different from ours. Perhaps we can describe the verdicts of her subpersonal mechanisms as some form of understanding, but we can hardly maintain that she understands the point of our evaluative practices. Her lack of felt engagement with the world means that she does not experience objects as moving her to act in various and distinctive ways. Being deprived of the capacity to experience situations as offensive, shameful, or amusing for herself, the sense in which we may think of her as animated by concerns, such as staying decent, or cultivating her sense of humour, is elusive to say the least. What does it mean for a creature who has never felt shame or amusement that she has a concern for staying decent or for cultivating her sense of humour? If there is any point for her in making evaluative judgements, it is simply not the same as ours. This suggests that our understanding of value is indeed anchored in the personal perspective offered by emotional experience.[22]

References

Alston, W. (1969), 'Feelings', *Philosophical Review*, 78/1: 3–34.
Aquila, R. (1975), 'Causes and Constituents of Occurrent Emotion', *Philosophical Quarterly*, 25: 346–9.
Arnold, M. (1960), *Emotion and Personality*. New York: Columbia University Press.
Barrett, L. F. (2006), 'Emotions as Natural Kinds?', *Perspectives on Psychological Science*, 1: 28–58.
Barrett, L. F. (2014), 'The Conceptual Act Theory: A Précis', *Emotion Review*, 6: 292–7.
Barrett, L. F. and Russell, J. (eds) (2014), *The Psychological Construction of Emotions*. New York: The Guilford Press.
Bayne, T. and Montague, M. (eds) (2011), *Cognitive Phenomenology*. New York: Oxford University Press.
Berridge, K. C. and Winkielman, P. (2003), 'What is an Unconscious Emotion: The Case for Unconscious "Liking"', *Cognition and Emotion*, 17: 181–211.
Block, N. (1995), 'A Confusion about a Function of Consciousness', *Behavioral and Brain Sciences*, 18: 227–47.

---

[22] We would like to thank Margherita Arcangeli, Richard Dub, Uriah Kriegel, Moritz Mueller, Tristram Oliver-Skuse, Joel Smith, Jona Vance, and colleagues at the Swiss Center for Affective Sciences for their helpful comments on a previous version of this article.

Brady, M. (2013), *Emotional Insight: The Epistemic Role of Emotional Experience*. New York: Oxford University Press.
Bull, N. (1951), *The Attitude Theory of Emotion*. New York and London: Johnson Reprint Corporation.
Carruthers, P. (2011), 'Higher-Order Theories of Consciousness', *The Stanford Encyclopedia of Philosophy* (Fall 2011 Edition), E. N. Zalta (ed.), URL = <http://plato.stanford.edu/archives/fall2011/entries/consciousness-higher/>.
Castelfranchi, C. and Miceli, M. (2009), 'The Cognitive-Motivational Compound of Emotional Experience', *Emotion Review*, 1/3, 223–31.
Claparède, E. (1928), 'Feelings and Emotions', in M. L. Reymert (ed.), *Feelings and Emotions: The Wittenberg Symposium* Clark University Press, 124–39.
Damasio, A. (2000), *The Feeling of What Happens: Body and Emotion in the Making of Consciousness*. New York: Harcourt Brace.
Dennett, D. (1988), 'Quining Qualia', in Anthony J. Marcel and E. Bisiach (eds), *Consciousness in Modern Science*. New York: Oxford University Press, 42–77.
Deonna, J. and Scherer, K. (2010), 'The Case of the Disappearing Intentional Object: Constraints on a Definition of Emotion', *Emotion Review*, 2/1: 44–52.
Deonna, J. and Teroni, F. (2012), *The Emotions: A Philosophical Introduction*. New York: Routledge.
Deonna, J. and Teroni, F. (2013), 'What Role for Emotions in Well-being?', *Philosophical Topics*, 41/1: 123–42.
Deonna, J. and Teroni, F. (2015), 'Emotions as Attitudes', *Dialectica*, 69/3: 293–311.
Deonna, J. and Teroni, F. (2017), 'Putting Bodily Feelings into Emotional Experience in the Right Way', *Emotion Review*. doi.org/10.1177/1754073916639666
Descartes, R. (1649/1989), *The Passions of the Soul* (transl. by S. H. Voss). Indianapolis: Hackett.
Dokic, J. and Lemaire, S. (2015), 'Are Emotions Evaluative Modes?', *Dialectica*, 69/3: 271–92.
Dretske, F. (1981), *Knowledge and the Flow of Information*. (Cambridge, MA: MIT Press.
Dretske F. (2006), 'Perception Without Awareness', in Tamar S. Gendler and John Hawthorne (eds), *Perceptual Experience*. New York: Oxford University Press, 147–80.
Ekman, P. (1999), 'Basic Emotions', in T. Dalgleish and M. Power (eds), *Handbook of Cognition and Emotion*. New York: John Wiley and Sons, 38–60.
Frijda, N. (1986), *The Emotions*. Cambridge: Cambridge University Press.
Frijda, N. (2005), 'Emotion Experience', *Cognition and Emotion*, 19/4: 473–97.
Frijda, N. (2007), *The Laws of Emotion*. Mahwah, NJ: Lawrence Erlbaum.
Goldie, P. (2000), *The Emotions: A Philosophical Exploration*. Oxford: Oxford University Press.
Gross, J. and Thompson, R. (2007), 'Emotion Regulation: Conceptual Foundations', in J. Gross (ed.), *Handbook of Emotion Regulation*. New York: Guilford Press, 3–24.
Harman, G. (1990), 'The Intrinsic Quality of Experience', in J. Tomberlin (ed.), *Philosophical Perspectives* 4. Atascadero, CA: Ridgeview, 31–52.
Herzberg, L. (2012), 'To Blend or to Compose: a Debate About Emotion Structure', in P. Wilson (ed.), *Dynamicity in Emotion Concepts*. Bern: Peter Lang, 73–94.
Izard, C. E. (1992). 'Basic Emotions, Relations Amongst Emotions and Emotion–cognition Relations', *Psychological Review*, 99: 561–65.
Jackson, F. (1982), 'Epiphenomenal Qualia', *The Philosophical Quarterly* 32: 127–36.
James, W. (1884), 'What is an Emotion?', *Mind*, 9: 188–205.
Kenny, A. (1963), *Action, Emotion and Will*. London: Routledge.
Kreibig, S. (2010), 'Autonomic Nervous System Activity in Emotion: A Review', *Biological Psychology*, 84/2: 394–421.

Lacewing, M. (2007), 'Do Unconscious Emotions Involve Unconscious Feelings?', *Philosophical Psychology*, 20/1: 81–104.
Laird, J. and Lacasse, K. (2014), 'Bodily Influences on Emotional Feelings: Accumulating Evidence and Extensions of William James's Theory of Emotion', *Emotion Review*, 6: 27–34.
Lambie, J. A. and Marcel, A. J. (2002), 'Consciousness and the Variety of Emotion Experience: A Theoretical Framework', *Psychological Review*, 109/2: 219–59.
LeDoux, J. (1998), *The Emotional Brain: The Mysterious Underpinnings of Emotional Life*. New York: Simon and Schuster.
Levenson, R. (1992), 'Autonomic Nervous System Differences Among Emotions', *Psychological Science*, 3: 23–7.
Lindquist, K., Wager, T. D., Kober, H., Bliss-Moreau, E., and Barrett, L. F. (2012), 'The Brain Basis of Emotion: A Meta-analytic Review', *Behavioral and Brain Sciences*, 35/2: 121–43.
Lycan, W. (1996), *Consciousness and Experience*. Cambridge, MA: MIT Press.
Lyons, W. (1980), *Emotion*. Cambridge: Cambridge University Press.
McDougall, W. (1923), *An Outline of Psychology*. London: Methuen.
MacLean, P. (1993), 'Cerebral Evolution of Emotion', in M. Lewis and J. Haviland (eds), *Handbook of Emotions*. New York: The Guilford Press, 67–83.
Madell, G. (1997), 'Emotion and Feeling', *Proceedings of the Aristotelian Society*, Suppl. 71: 147–62.
Martin, M. (2002), 'The Transparency of Experience', *Mind and Language*, 17: 376–425.
Mauss, I., Levenson, R., McCarter, L., Wilhelm, F., and Gross, J. (2005), 'The Tie that Binds? Coherence Among Emotional Experience, Behavior, and Autonomic Physiology', *Emotion*, 5: 175–90.
Mendelovici, A. (2013), 'Pure Intentionalism about Moods and Emotions', in U. Kriegel (ed.), *Current Controversies in Philosophy of Mind*. New York: Routledge, 135–57.
Millikan, R. G. (1984), *Language, Thought and Other Biological Categories*. Cambridge, MA: MIT Press.
Mitchell, J. (2018), 'On the Non-conceptual Content of Affective-Evaluative Experience', *Synthese*. DOI 10.1007/s11229-018-1872-y
Montague, M. (2014), 'Evaluative Phenomenology', in S. Roeser and C. Todd (eds), *Emotion and Value*. New York: Oxford University Press, 32–51.
Mueller, M. (2018), 'Emotion as Position-Taking', *Philosophia*, 46/3: 525–40.
Nagel, T. (1974), 'What is It Like to Be a Bat?', *Philosophical Review* 83: 435–50.
Peacocke, C. (1996), 'Précis of a Study of Concepts'. *Philosophy and Phenomenological Research*, 56/2: 407–11.
Pitt, D. (2004), 'The Phenomenology of Cognition or What is It Like to Think That P?', *Philosophy and Phenomenological Research*, 69/1: 1–36.
Poellner, P. (2016), 'Phenomenology and the Perceptual Model of Emotion', *Proceedings of the Aristotelian Society*, 116/3: 261–288.
Price, C. (2006), 'Affect Without Object: Moods and Objectless Emotions', *European Journal of Analytic Philosophy*, 2/1: 49–68.
Price, R. (2009), 'Aspect-switching and Visual Phenomenal Character', *The Philosophical Quarterly* 59/236: 508–18.
Prinz, J. J. (2004), *Gut Reactions: A Perceptual Theory of Emotion*. Oxford: Oxford University Press.
Pugmire, D. (1998), *Rediscovering Emotions*. Edinburgh: Edinburgh University Press.
Ratcliffe, M. (2008), *Feelings of Being: Phenomenology, Psychiatry and the Sense of Reality*. New York: Oxford University Press.

Reisenzein, R. (2000), 'Exploring the Strength of Association Between the Components of Emotion Syndromes: The Case of Surprise', *Cognition and Emotion*, 14/1: 1–38.

Reisenzein, R. (2012), 'What is an Emotion in the Belief-Desire Theory of Emotion?', in F. Paglieri, L. Tummolini, R. Falcone, and M. Miceli (eds), *The Goals of Cognition: Essays in Honor of Cristiano Castelfranchi*. London: College Publications, 181–211.

Reisenzein, R. and Stephan, A. (2014), 'More on James and the Physical Basis of Emotion', *Emotion Review*, 6: 35–46.

Roberts, R. (2003), *Emotions: An Essay in Aid of Moral Psychology*. Cambridge: Cambridge University Press.

Rosenthal, D. (2005), *Consciousness and Mind*. Oxford: Oxford University Press.

Russell, J. (2003), 'Core Affect and the Construction of Emotions', *Psychological Review*, 110: 145–72.

Scarantino, A. (2014a), 'Basic Emotions, Psychological Construction and the Problem of Variability', in L. Barrett and J. Russell (eds), *The Psychological Construction of Emotion*. New York: Guilford Press, 334–76.

Scarantino, A. (2014b), 'The Motivational Theory of Emotions', in D. Jacobson and J. D'Arms (eds), *Moral Psychology and Human Agency*. New York: Cambridge University Press, 156–85.

Schachter, S. and Singer, J. (1962), 'Cognitive, Social, and Physiological Determinants of Emotional States', *Psychological Review*, 69: 379–99.

Scheler, M. (1980), *Der Formalismus in der Ethik und die materiale Wertethik*. Berne and Munich: Francke.

Stephens, C. L., Christie, I. C., and Friedman, B. H. (2010), 'Autonomic Specificity of Basic Emotions: Evidence from Pattern Classification and Cluster Analysis', *Biological Psychiatry*, 84: 463–73.

Stocker, M. (1996), *Valuing Emotions*. New York: Cambridge University Press.

Tappolet, C. (2000), *Emotions et valeurs*. Paris: Presses Universitaires de France.

Tappolet, C. (2016), *Emotions, Value and Agency*. Oxford: Oxford University Press.

Tappolet, C. (2018), 'The Metaphysics of Moods', in H. Naar and F. Teroni (eds), *The Ontology of Emotions*. New York: Cambridge University Press, 169–86.

Tappolet, C. and Rossi, M. (2019), 'What Kind of Evaluative State Are Emotions? The Attitudinal Theory vs. the Perceptual Theory of Emotions', *Canadian Journal of Philosophy*, 49/4: 544–63.

Teroni, F. (2016), 'Emotions, Me, Myself and I', *International Review of Philosophical Studies* 4: 1–19.

Teroni, F. (2017), 'In Pursuit of Emotional Modes: The Philosophy of Emotion after James', in A. Cohen and R. Stern (eds), *Thinking About the Emotions: A Philosophical History*. Oxford: Oxford University Press, 291–313.

Teroni, F. (2018), 'Emotionally Charged: The Puzzle of Affective Valence', in C. Tappolet, F. Teroni, and A. Konzelmann Ziv (eds), *Shadows of the Soul: Philosophical Perspectives on Negative Emotions*. New York: Routledge, 10–19.

Teroni, F. (2019), 'Valence, Bodily Displeasure and Emotion', in D. Bain, M. Brady, and J. Corns (eds), *Philosophy of Suffering: Metaphysics, Value and Normativity*. New York: Routledge, 103–22.

Thalberg, I. (1964), 'Emotion and Thought', *American Philosophical Quarterly*, 1: 45–55.

Tye, M. (2008), 'The Experience of Emotion: An Intentionalist Theory', *Revue Internationale de Philosophie*, 1/243: 25–50.

Vance, J. (2018), 'Phenomenal Commitments : A Puzzle for Experiential Theories of Emotion', in H. Naar and F. Teroni (eds), *The Ontology of Emotions*. New York: Cambridge University Press, 90–109.

Vanello, D. (2019), 'Affect, Motivational States, and Evaluative Concepts', *Synthese*. DOI: 10.1007/s11229-019-02120-0.

Weiskrantz, L., (1986), *Blindsight*. Oxford: Oxford University Press.

Whiting, D. (2011), 'The Feeling Theory of Emotion and the Object-Directed Emotions', *European Journal of Philosophy*, 19/2: 281–302.

Zagzebski, L. (2003), 'Emotion and Moral Judgment'. *Philosophy and Phenomenological Research*, 66/1: 104–24.

CHAPTER 6

IMAGINATIVE EXPERIENCE

AMY KIND

A few years ago when I was on a work-related trip to Ohio, one of my hosts convinced me to take a brief detour so that I could see what she described as a cultural landmark. She wouldn't tell me anything more about it until we arrived. And indeed, it was quite a sight to behold: An office building designed to look like a giant woven wooden picnic basket—complete with two basket handles attached at the top. The seven story building was built in 1997 to serve as the corporate headquarters of the Longaberger Basket Company. Consisting of stucco-over-steel construction, it weighs in at about 9000 tons, with the handles alone weighing in at 150 tons.

Perhaps you too might have been lucky enough to have visited this architectural marvel, and you might now be remembering it and your experience of having seen it. But assuming you've not had the pleasure—and I suspect that many readers of this chapter have probably never driven on that section of State Route 16 in Newark, Ohio—you might well have imagined the building as you read my description of it. If you didn't, then pause for a moment and try to do so now. Next, let's reflect on your mental activity. How is what you are doing when you're imagining the building different from what you would be doing if you were just thinking about the building? Do you picture it before your mind's eye, so to speak? What is your experience like as you do so? Is it vivid and clear—almost like you are right there seeing the building—or is it instead hazy and dim?

These questions—about the phenomenal character of our imaginative experience, about how it is and is not like the phenomenal character of perceptual experience, about how it is and is not like the phenomenal character of other mental activities—have a long history in philosophical discussions of imagination. Philosophers have also long asked parallel questions about the nature of imagination. But in this chapter, our focus will not be on *what imagination is* but rather on *what it is like*. Rather than exploring the various accounts of imagination on offer in the philosophical literature, we will instead be exploring the various accounts of imaginative experience on offer in that literature. In particular, our focus in what follows will be on three different sorts of accounts that have played an especially prominent role in philosophical thinking about these issues.

When developing accounts of imaginative experience, philosophers generally (though not universally) accept two pieces of phenomenological data and take them as a starting point: (1) the experiential character of imagining is importantly similar to that of perceiving; (2) despite this similarity, the experiential character of imagining is nonetheless importantly different from perceiving.[1] Corresponding to these two pieces of data, someone who aims to explain imaginative experience must discharge two principal tasks: first to explain the similarity between the experiential character of imagination and the experiential character of perception, and second, to explain the difference. Though to some extent we will address both of these tasks in what follows, our focus will be on the second. All three of the views that we will consider aim principally to explain how the character of imaginative experience differs from the experiential character of related mental states like perception.

Along these lines, the first of these three views draws attention to various ways in which the phenomenology of imagination is thought to be impoverished in relation to that of perception and other mental states. Imagination is claimed to be less vivid, less clear, less forceful. While this account—what I will call the *impoverishment view*—has been explored by various philosophers across the centuries, it is probably most closely associated with David Hume.

The second view that will be considered relies on the operation of the will to distinguish the experiential character of imagining from the experiential character of perceiving. It is perhaps a bit of an overstatement to call this an account, since it has not been fully developed in the philosophical literature. But, that said, we see an exploration along these lines—what I will call the *will-dependence view*—in the work of Ludwig Wittgenstein.

The third view to be considered relies on the fact that imagination is in some way distanced from reality; as noted above, our imaginings take us away from the here and now. On what I will call the *non-existence view*, this fact about imagination is claimed to imprint itself on the character of imaginative experience, and moreover, to do so in such a way that differentiates it from the character of perceptual experience. A version of this account was suggested by Jean-Paul Sartre.

While there are important insights to be drawn from all of these views, each seems to me to be importantly flawed in various ways. As I will suggest, close examination reveals that none of them gives us an adequate account of the character of imaginative experience. Ultimately, in the final section of the chapter, I briefly explore what their failure teaches us about the project of giving an account of imaginative experience.

Before I begin, however, I need to say something about what imagination is. For indeed, given some ways of understanding imagination, it might seem to be a mistake to talk of the experience of imagining. Thus, before I turn to the three different views of imaginative experience, I will first take up the issue of why we should believe there is such a thing as imaginative experience at all.

---

[1] Russell (1921) is an important exception with respect to (2). I return to Russell's view in Section 6.4.

6.1 Imagination

Here it will be helpful to begin with René Descartes' discussion of imagination in the Sixth Meditation:

> if I want to think of a chiliagon, although I understand that it is a figure consisting of a thousand sides just as well as I understand the triangle to be a three-sided figure, I do not in the same way imagine the thousand sides or see them as if they were present before me.... But suppose I am dealing with a pentagon: I can of course understand the figure of a pentagon, just as I can the figure of a chiliagon, without the help of the imagination; but I can also imagine a pentagon, by applying the mind's eye to its five sides and the area contained within them. And in doing this I notice quite clearly that imagination requires a peculiar effort of mind which is not required for understanding. (Descartes 1641/1986: 50–1)

For the purpose of this chapter, we can leave aside the question of whether Descartes is right that we cannot imagine a chiliagon. Rather, what is important is the 'peculiar effort of mind' to which he adverts at the end of the passage. Here Descartes seems to be suggesting that imagination requires mental imagery, and indeed, an imagery-based understanding of imagination has played an important role in the philosophical literature.[2]

At this point, however, an obvious worry immediately arises, since an understanding of imagination in terms of imagery might seem to limit imagination to the visual domain. Can we not engage in non-visual imaginings, as when someone imagines the thunderous applause she hopes to receive at the end of her presentation or the smooth surface of the lectern she will be standing before? To account for these kinds of cases, we might reinterpret 'imagery' in broad terms, such that there can be auditory imagery, olfactory imagery, and so on. But insofar as even this broadening of the notion still seems too restrictive—we can also engage in imaginings of emotions, pain, and other bodily sensations, and it might seem to stretch the notion of imagery too far to allow for emotional imagery and pain imagery—it is perhaps best to understand the 'peculiar effort of mind' in terms of sensory (or quasi-sensory) presentation.[3]

This Cartesian-inspired understanding of imagination fits well with the idea that imagination has a phenomenological character, that is, that we are right to talk of imaginative experience. But we find in the philosophical literature several worries about this Cartesian picture. One concerns how we should best taxonomize a group of what might broadly be called 'speculative' mental activities, that is, how we should best understand the connections between imagining, supposing, and conceiving. Another, related

---

[2] See Kind (2001) for one development of an imagery-based account of imagination.
[3] White, for example, is willing to extend the notion of imagery to include auditory imagery but refuses to do so for our imaginings of aches and pains (1990: 89–90).

to the first, concerns the alleged existence of imaginings that seem to proceed without the involvement of any sensory presentation whatsoever.

As we go about our everyday activities, our thoughts often extend far beyond what is presently going on around us. Did my students understand the material I covered this morning in class, or will I have to review it again next time? How is my spouse handling what was predicted to be a particularly tough day at work? When I get home tonight, will I be able to scrounge together a decent dinner from what's in the house or do I need to stop by the store? In asking these questions, I take myself out of the here and now in which I find myself and speculate about what is happening elsewhere, about what has already happened, or about what will happen. Sometimes this speculation might proceed via the production of the sorts of sensory presentations that we were considering above. I might try to visualize the contents of my fridge and pantry, for example. But sometimes this speculation seems to occur in other ways, via a chain of reasoning. I might simply start with the supposition that I have only an assortment of vegetables of questionable freshness, some leftover rice, a couple of eggs, and so on, and then try to work out whether I can throw together an adequate meal from the things on that list. In making this supposition, I need not visualize the food items themselves. Rather, I might proceed much as one does in a logic class when one puts forth a certain proposition for the sake of a reductio proof.

And now the question arises: Should we treat these different ways of speculating as fundamentally different mental activities, or are they essentially the same, perhaps with one a sub-class of the other? While many philosophers, and especially those in the Cartesian tradition discussed above, tend to draw a sharp distinction between imagining and supposing, other philosophers argue that supposition should be treated as a special type of imagination.[4] If this latter view is right, then we have a problem in accounting for imaginative experience, since supposition seems to lack the kind of sensory character associated with other types of imagining. In fact, many philosophers have treated supposition as lacking experiential character at all.[5] But even if it has some kind of experiential character along the lines of conscious thought—what is typically referred to as *cognitive phenomenology*—we would still face a problem in providing a *unitary* account of imaginative experience.[6]

As for the second worry about the Cartesian picture, philosophers have often suggested that there are many instances of imagination that do not involve the production of sensory presentations. As Alan White argues, although we can just as easily imagine a difficulty or an objection as we can imagine an elephant or a bus, only for the latter examples 'would the presence of imagery be at all plausible' (White 1990: 89). Or consider a case offered by Neil Van Leeuwen: 'When I imagine, on reading *Lord of the Rings*, that elves can live forever, I'm fictionally imagining a proposition that I couldn't imagine

---

[4] Philosophers distinguishing imagination and supposition include Gendler (2000) and Balcerak Jackson (2016); philosophers treating supposition as a special kind of imagination include Currie and Ravenscroft (2002), Ichikawa and Jarvis (2012), and Arcangeli (2014).

[5] For discussion of the differences between imagination and supposition see Gendler (2011).

[6] See Chapter 7, this volume, for a discussion of cognitive phenomenology.

using mental imagery. It would take too long! So presumably I represent this in a more abstract symbolic code' (Van Leeuwen 2013: 222). Like supposings, these instances of imagining would also lack the kind of experiential character associated with other types of imagining, so they too pose a problem for the attempt to provide a unitary account of imaginative experience.

To my mind, the defender of the Cartesian picture has several resources available for answering these two kinds of worries.[7] For our purposes here, however, this doesn't really matter. Rather, we can simply sidestep the debate. Even if supposing forms a sub-class of imagining, and even if there are examples of imagining that proceed without the use of any sensory presentation, there is reason to set these cases aside. Importantly, the kind of experiential character associated with supposing or with the kinds of examples posed above by White and Van Leeuwen seems to borrow from other types of experience; it is not proprietary to imagining. Yet there is still a large class of imaginings that proceed by way of sensory presentation and thereby seem to share an experiential character, and it is this experiential character that is similar to, but in some ways also different from, the experiential character of related mental states like perception and memory. It is this experiential character that is proprietary to imagining, and it is this experiential character that will be our focus in what follows.

Thus, these two worries do not suggest that our investigation into imaginative experience is unwarranted. Rather, they simply suggest that our investigation should be understood as an investigation into what we might call *proprietary imaginative experience*.[8] To investigate it we will focus on those imaginings that proceed by way of sensory presentation. Whether these imaginings capture the entirety of the class of imaginings—as assumed by those in the Cartesian-inspired tradition considered above—is a question that we do not need to settle for our purposes here. However that question is settled, it remains appropriate to investigate the nature of imaginative experience.

6.2 THE IMPOVERISHMENT VIEW

As I noted above, philosophers attempting to provide an account of imaginative experience want to explain the difference between imaginative experience and other types of conscious experience like perceptual experience and memory experience. One particularly well-known attempt at such an explanation comes from Hume's *Treatise*. In the

---

[7] See Balcerak Jackson (2016) for a persuasive case that supposition should be treated differently from imagination; see Kind (2001) for an attempt to accommodate the alleged examples of non-imagistic imaginings.

[8] There is some cost to proceeding this way. In particular, one might worry about the existence of imaginings that lack the kind of experiential character that is proprietary to imagining. But insofar as an account of the nature of imaginative experience is different from an account of the nature of imagination, perhaps this cost is not too high.

opening section, Hume claimed that ideas could be distinguished from impressions on the basis of 'force and vivacity' (1739/1985: 1.1.1). He then uses similar descriptors to distinguish ideas of memory from ideas of imagination:

> We find by experience, that when any impression has been present with the mind, it again makes its appearance there as an idea; and this it may do after two different ways: either when in its new appearance it retains a considerable degree of its first vivacity, and is somewhat intermediate betwixt an impression and an idea: or when it entirely loses that vivacity, and is a perfect idea. The faculty, by which we repeat our impressions in the first manner, is called the MEMORY, and the other the IMAGINATION. 'Tis evident at first sight, that the ideas of the memory are much more lively and strong than those of the imagination, and that the former faculty paints its objects in more distinct colours, than any which are employ'd by the latter. When we remember any past event, the idea of it flows in upon the mind in a forcible manner; whereas in the imagination the perception is faint and languid, and cannot without difficulty be preserv'd by the mind steddy and uniform for any considerable time.   (Hume 1739/1985: Treatise 1.1.3)

Hume here draws the contrast specifically between imagination and memory, but most discussions of imaginative phenomenology tend to focus on the contrast between imagination and perception, where the same point can be made. Doing so gives us a version of what I am calling *the impoverishment view* of imaginative experience:

THE IMPOVERISHMENT VIEW: Imaginative experience is an impoverished form of perceptual experience.

Hume was neither the first nor the last to characterize imaginative experience in this way. A century before, for example, Hobbes had referred to imagination as 'decaying sense' (Hobbes 1651/1968: 88). More recently, Alex Byrne has argued that we can best capture the phenomenological similarity between perception and imagination in their sharing the same kind of content; what explains the phenomenological difference is that the content of imagining is 'degraded' in comparison to the content of perception (Byrne 2010: 19). Likewise, Colin McGinn has argued that images can be distinguished from percepts at least partly on grounds of saturation; in contrast to a percept, an image is 'gappy, coarse, discrete' (McGinn 2004: 25). But this way of accounting for imaginative experience—in terms of its impoverishment—is most commonly associated with Hume.

The kind of impoverishment that Hume focuses on concerns an impoverishment of force and vivacity—imaginative experience is less forceful, and has less vivacity, than perceptual or memory experience. Unfortunately Hume does not tell us much about what the central notions employed—that of force and vivacity—are supposed to mean.[9]

---

[9] Nor has the matter received much attention by Hume scholars; as Traiger (2008: 61) notes, 'There are surprisingly few detailed interpretations of Hume's notion of vivacity.' Govier (1972), which I will briefly discuss in this section, is one notable exception. For a discussion of the coherence of the notion of vividness, see Kind (2017).

And to make matters even worse, while his initial use of these terms suggests they are meant to pick out two different (if complementary) phenomenological aspects of mental states, he later explicitly equates them:

> An idea assented to *feels* different from a fictitious idea, that the fancy alone presents to us. And this different feeling I endeavour to explain by calling it a superior *force*, or *vivacity*, or *solidity*, or *firmness*, or *steadiness*. This variety of terms, which may seem so unphilosophical, is intended only to express that act of the mind, which renders realities more present to us than fictions, causes them to weigh more in the thought, and gives them a superior influence on the passions and imagination. Provided we agree about the thing, 'tis needless to dispute about the terms.   (Hume 1739/1985: Appendix)

To contemporary ears, however, the term 'force' seems to pick out something phenomenologically rather different from 'vivacity'—even if we do not have a good handle on what is being picked out.[10] In a helpful discussion of Hume's use of phenomenological descriptors for ideas and impressions, Trudy Govier argues that he could have overcome various objections and counterexamples to some of the associated epistemological claims he wants to make about ideas and impressions had he divided the phenomenological descriptors into two categories. In the first category, we have terms that refer to a mental state's 'staying power'—here we find Hume using words like *strong, forceful, vigorous, steady, solid,* and *firm*. In the second category, we have terms that refer to a mental state's 'clarity or amount of detail'—here we find Hume using terms like *vivacious, vivid, lively,* and *intense* (Govier 1972: 45).

For our purposes here, we fortunately do not have to worry too much about what exactly Hume meant—or even what he should have meant—by 'force' and 'vivacity.' On any likely way of unpacking these terms, the impoverishment view seems implausible. Perhaps the easiest way to diagnose its failure is simply to point to the numerous people who claim that their imaginative experiences are in no way less vivid or forceful than their perceptual experiences. Consider Francis Galton's famous 'Breakfast Table Questionnaire.' In the late nineteenth century, Galton asked 100 adult men (and, later, an additional 172 schoolboys) to 'think of some definite object—suppose it is your breakfast-table as you sat down to it this morning—and consider carefully the picture that rises before your mind's eye.' (Galton 1880: 301) He then asked a series of specific questions, including ones focused on illumination, definition, and coloring:

> 1. Illumination.—Is the image dim or fairly clear? Is its brightness comparable to that of the actual scene? 2. Definition.—Are all the objects pretty well defined at the same time, or is the place of sharpest definition at any one moment more contracted than it is in a real scene? 3. Colouring.—Are the colours of the china, of the toast, breadcrust, mustard, meat, parsley, or whatever may have been on the table, quite distinct and natural?   (Galton 1880: 302)

---

[10] For a related point, see Brann (1991: 196-7).

In response, though many of the subjects did indeed report that their imaginative experience was dim and indistinct in relation to the comparable perceptual experience, many others claimed to find no difference with respect to these factors between the two. As one subject remarked, 'I can see my breakfast table or any equally familiar thing with my mind's eye, quite as well in all particulars as I can do if the reality is before me.' (1880: 305) Quite apart from Galton's study, there are plenty of other people—people often described as highly imaginative—who also deny that their imaginative experiences are impoverished in comparison to their perceptual experiences. Consider Temple Grandin, an author and professor of animal science who has become particularly well-known for her writing and thinking about her experience with autism. Grandin describes herself as 'thinking in pictures'—when she imagines the front of a shop she often goes to, for example, she *sees* it in her mind. Moreover, she sees it in a way that could be described as 'perfectly clear and as vivid as normal vision' (Grandin and Panek 2013).[11]

But however vivid or forceful Grandin's imaginings—or those of any gifted imaginer—there remains a phenomenological difference between these imaginings and the corresponding percepts. Thus, the impoverishment view cannot give us the right account of what is distinctive about imaginative experience. And the problem doesn't seem to be limited to the specific phenomenological descriptors that Hume was working with. For whether we try to spell out the difference in terms of vividness or intensity or resolution or accuracy, it is hard to believe that the 'best' imagining could not be at the same level as the 'worst' perception. As Uriah Kriegel has aptly noted, 'when we consider the lowest resolution a perceptual experience can have consistently with the laws of nature, it is hard to believe that no imaginative experience can match *that* level of accuracy' (Kriegel 2015: 189).

6.3 The Will-Dependence View

Underlying the impoverishment view is a commitment to what has often been called the *continuum hypothesis* (see Savage 1975: 260). On this hypothesis, perceptual experience and imaginative experience differ in degree and not in kind. Perception and imagination are simply at different points on the same experiential spectrum, a spectrum that contains not only memory but also hallucinations and dreams. As we have seen, different versions of the impoverishment view cash out this phenomenological continuum in different ways, but however it is explicated, the fact remains that imagination and perception are thought to be experientially continuous with one another. In this section and the next, we will consider two views that deny this claim. On these views, perceptual experience and imaginative experience differ not in degree but in kind.

---

[11] This description comes from the Vividness of Visual Imagery Questionnaire, an influential measure of imagery vividness developed by David Marks (1973).

To flesh out the first of these two views, it will be helpful to begin with Wittgenstein's discussion of imagination. Exploring the similarities and differences between visual impressions (percepts) and visual images in the second volume of his *Remarks on the Philosophy of Psychology*, Wittgenstein relies heavily on a point that, as we saw above, poses trouble for the impoverishment view: However similar our imaginings and our percepts, they cannot be mistaken for one another. As he notes, 'One can't take an image for reality nor things seen for things imaged' (1948/1980: §85; see also §97).[12] But why are we unable to make this mistake? His answer draws upon the operation of the will: Imagination is subject to the will in a way that perception is not. As Wittgenstein puts it, imagining is a *doing* and not a *receiving* (1948/1980: §111): 'When we form an image of something we are not observing. The coming and going of the pictures is not something that *happens* to us' (1967: §632). And this sets imagining in sharp contrast to perception. Though I can will myself to imagine a picnic basket, I cannot through sheer force of will bring myself to see a picnic basket. Of course, I can take certain actions that will put me in a position to see one—I can travel to a local picnicking site or to a store carrying household goods. And more generally, there are actions that I take to enable myself to have visual impressions, like opening my eyes. But I cannot bring myself to have a perception simply by willing it to be the case.[13] This gives us what I'm calling the *will-dependence view*:

> THE WILL-DEPENDENCE VIEW: Imaginative experience is a type of sensory experience marked by its dependence on the will.

What seems to be the same basic point is given various formulations in the literature on imagination. It is sometimes put by classifying imagination as an action: To imagine something is to perform an action; to perceive is not. It is also sometimes put in terms of voluntariness: Imagination is voluntary while perception is not.[14] And it is also sometimes put in terms of control: Imagination is under our control while perception is not. That these different formulations are meant to be capturing the same basic point is

---

[12] See also Sartre, who suggests that we '*never* take our images for perceptions' (1936/1962: 87). For a contrary view, see Russell's claim that the difference between the two 'is by no means always obvious to inspection' (1921: 145). In support of this claim, Russell notes: 'When we are listening for a faint sound—the striking of a distant clock, or a horse's hoofs on the road—we think we hear it many times before we really do, because expectation brings us the image, and we mistake it for sensation' (1921: 145). Also relevant here is C. W. Perky's experiment in which subjects took themselves to be imagining an object in cases in which they were presented with a faint image of that object (Perky 1910). Whether this experiment shows that we can mistake imagining for perceiving has of late been a matter of considerable dispute (see Hopkins 2012).

[13] See McGinn (2004: 13) for further discussion of this point. More generally, Budd (1989: ch 5) provides a helpful exploration of Wittgenstein's will-dependence view.

[14] Wittgenstein does not like this way of formulating the point because it suggests that we are picking out a property extrinsic to the act; see §83. The *very same* arm movement may sometimes be voluntary and sometimes not, but in the case of imagining and perceiving, we do not have the very same act. On Wittgenstein's view, the fact that imagining is subject to the will and perception is not makes them different kinds of acts.

supported by the fact that they are often intermixed. For example, Jonathan Ichikawa notes that 'To imagine is to act—our imagery is in some important sense under our control; this is not so with percepts' (Ichikawa 2009: 107).

The will-dependence view is sometimes associated with Jean-Paul Sartre, who takes spontaneity to be a key characteristic of imagining (what he calls the *imaging consciousness*):

> A perceptual consciousness appears to itself as passive. On the other hand, an imaging consciousness gives itself to itself as an imaging consciousness, which is to say as a spontaneity that produces and conserves the object as imaged.... [T]he image consciousness is not given as a piece of wood that floats on the sea, but as a wave among the waves. (Sartre 1940/2010: 14)

We also see hints of the will-dependence view in the work of Brian O'Shaughnessy, who makes much of the will-susceptibility of imaginings and who seems to take this will-susceptibility to play a role in making an imagining be experienced as an imagining (O'Shaughnessy 2000). Likewise, having noted that 'images and percepts are asymmetrically related to the will, and that this is an important difference between them,' Colin McGinn suggests that this difference impacts their experiential natures: 'there does seem to be some sense in which the phenomenology of images is affected by their voluntariness: what it is like to have them seems affected by the fact they are products of will; their causation is somehow imprinted on their phenomenology' (McGinn 2004: 16).

Note that this latter claim—that the operation of the will imprints itself upon imaginative phenomenology—is essential to the will-dependence view. To distinguish imaginative experience from perceptual experience, it is not enough merely to find a difference between imagination and perception. Rather, we must find a difference that impacts the phenomenology. So we can really see the will-dependence view as consisting of two parts: (1) imagining and perception differ in their relation to the will; and (2) this difference in relation to the will makes a phenomenological difference. Correspondingly, there are two different kinds of objections that might be raised by an opponent of the view. First someone might argue that imagining and perceiving do not fundamentally differ along the dimension of will-dependence. Second, someone might grant that imagining and perceiving differ along this dimension but deny that this difference impacts the phenomenology.

Perhaps the most plausible way to pursue an objection of the first sort is to point to the phenomenon of unbidden imaginings, as when an image just pops into your head or you find a catchy tune running through your mind. Often these unbidden imaginings are unwelcome ones—horrific or disgusting or embarrassing—but they might equally be innocuous. It is also often difficult to banish them.[15] Once you find yourself picturing some unpleasant situation, it can be very hard—even seemingly impossible—to get

---

[15] McGinn notes that there are three different stages at which imaginings are subject to the will. The will may be involved in their inception, in their maintenance, and in their termination (2004: 14).

yourself to stop; likewise, that catchy tune might not only be running through your mind but stuck there. In what sense, then, are these imaginings subject to the will? Not only were they unwilled to begin with, but they also seem unable to be willed away.

In addition to these kinds of examples that suggest that will-dependence is not a necessary feature of imagining, an opponent of the will-dependence view might also try to suggest that will-independence is not a necessary feature of perceiving. Along these lines, Nigel J. T. Thomas has argued that we have more voluntary control of perception than proponents of the will-dependence view would have us believe. As he notes, 'Something may be there in front of you, but, if you don't want to see it, it is easy enough to shut your eyes, or turn them away; or if you *do* want to see what is not *quite* in front of you, it usually takes no great effort to turn your eyes or move your body toward it' (Thomas 2014: 139). More generally, Thomas suggests that the claim that perception is not subject to the will derives much of its plausibility from a mistaken and outdated view of perception, one that sees perception as something that passively happens to us rather than something we do. Though Thomas ultimately grants that there is some difference between imagination and perception with respect to their relation to the will, he sees it as a difference in degree rather than a difference in kind.

Several different but related responses are available to proponents of the will-dependence view. First, they may note that the kind of control we have over our percepts seems importantly different from the kind of control that we have over our imaginings. As Ichikawa notes, the control that we have over our percepts is only *indirect*: 'we can take action that we know will result in a changed perceptual experience, but we cannot change our perceptual experience directly' (Ichikawa 2009: 107). This kind of difference is likely also what Wittgenstein has in mind when he notes that 'Seeing is subject to the will *in a different way* from forming an image' (Wittgenstein 1948/1980: §141). Second, they may also note that even when we cannot successfully subject imagination to our will, it nonetheless makes sense for us to try to do so, and this marks a significant difference with perception. As Wittgenstein notes, to say that imagining is subject to the will is to say that 'it makes *sense* to order someone to "Imagine that", or again: "Don't imagine that"' (1948/1980: §83)—it makes sense, that is, even if someone is unable to comply with the order. In contrast, it is not just that the orders 'See that!' or 'Don't see that' can't be complied with but that they don't even make any sense. To put this point another way: Perception does not just fail to be subject to the will in practice; rather, it fails to be subject to the will even in principle. In contrast, while there may be cases where imagination fails to be subject to the will in practice, even in these cases it remains subject to the will in principle.[16]

These kind of responses do seem to bolster the first claim of the will-dependence account, that is, they bolster the claim that imagining and perceiving differ with respect to their relation to the will. In doing so, however, they open up the second claim to attack. The problem? Once we see more clearly exactly how imagining and perceiving differ from one another with respect to their relation to the will, it becomes considerably

---

[16] See also Budd (1989: 109).

harder to see this difference as being phenomenologically relevant. Even those imaginings that come to us unbidden, those that were not actually produced by the will, have the phenomenology of imagining. We might grant that such imaginings are nonetheless in principle subject to the will, but it is hard to see how this in itself could give rise to a phenomenology that is different in kind from the phenomenology of perceiving. While we might find it plausible to think that the will can leave its mark on imaginative experience when it has actually been in operation, it is considerably less plausible that the will can leave its mark on imaginative experience when, though it hasn't actually been in operation, in principle it might have been.

In fact, there are some who would argue that to grant even this would be to concede too much to the will-dependence view. For no matter how this view is spelled out, however exactly it turns out that imagining and perceiving differ from one another with respect to their relation to the will, it will fundamentally come down to a difference in causal origin. But why should we think a difference in causal origin amounts to a phenomenological difference? To use an example employed by David Sosa in a similar context, whether the burn on your skin results from too much time in the sun or too much time in the tanning booth need not make a difference to the pain you feel; the causal origin of your skin condition is different, but the resulting phenomenology is the same (Sosa 2006: 320). On this line of objection, then, even if proponents of the will-dependence view are able to make good on their first claim, doing so is not enough to establish their second claim, that is, we have no reason to think imagining's will-dependence accounts for its distinctive experiential character.

6.4 THE NON-EXISTENCE VIEW

As we saw in Section 6.3, Sartre takes spontaneity to be an essential feature of imaginative phenomenology, and we thus might treat him as a proponent of the will-dependence account. But there is also the development of a different kind of account in Sartre's work. While this account shares with the will-dependence view the sense that imaginative phenomenology differs in kind from perceptual phenomenology, it traces this difference not to the operation of the will but to the way in which imagination presents its object's existential status. On this view, perception 'posits its object as existing' while imagining does not: 'However lively, appealing, strong the image, it gives its object as not being' (Sartre 1940/2010: 12, 14). Compare, for example, seeing the Longaberger basket building with imagining it. For Sartre, when the building is perceived, the perceptual phenomenology presents it as existing. In contrast, when the building is imagined, the imaginative phenomenology presents it as not existing—as 'a nothingness' (1940/2010: 11). This gives us what I am calling the *non-existence view*:

> THE NON-EXISTENCE VIEW: Imaginative experience is marked by the fact that it presents its object as non-existent.

It may help our understanding of this view to contrast it with a different view in the same general vicinity. In *The Analysis of Mind*, Bertrand Russell argues that percepts and imaginings share all their intrinsic qualities; there is no difference between them that's intrinsic to the phenomenology (Russell 1921: see especially Lecture VIII). Insofar as there seems to be a phenomenological difference between them, this can be explained in terms of their attendant beliefs. While percepts are accompanied by beliefs about the existence of their objects, there is an absence of such beliefs in the case of imaginings.[17] Call this the *attendant belief view*. The non-existence view shares with the attendant-belief view the intuition that the existential status of the objects is an important factor in understanding the difference between perception and imagination. The two views differ, however, on whether this factor makes its way into the phenomenology itself.

So why should we adopt the non-existence view rather than the attendant-belief view? Here Sartre puts considerable weight on the fact that we can immediately and effortlessly apprehend whether we are perceiving or imagining. For a theory of imagination to be plausible, 'it must account for the spontaneous discrimination made by the mind between its images and perceptions' (Sartre 1936/1962: 117). To convince us that we should accept this requirement, Sartre suggests that we each consult our own inner experience. As he reports of his own inner experience, 'I am seated, writing, and see the things around me. Suddenly I form an image of my friend Peter. All the theories in the world are helpless against the fact that I *knew*, the very instant of the appearance of the image, that it was an image' (1936/1962: 96). As he also notes, 'a host of strange little occurrences take place about us at every moment, objects which apparently move of their own accord, cracking or groaning, appearing or disappearing, and the like' (1936/1962: 98). Yet even when confronted with these 'fantastic occurrences' we are not the least bit tempted to treat these as imaginings:

> I was sure that I put my hat in the closet, and there it is on the chair. Do I fall into doubt, 'disbelieving my eyes'? Not for a second. I might wear myself out looking for explanations, but I would take for granted in all my reflections from start to finish, without even bothering to go over and touch the felt, that the hat I see is *my real hat*. I think my friend Peter is in America. There he is at the corner of the street. Do I say, 'It's an image'? Not at all. My first reaction is to wonder how he could possibly be back already. (Sartre 1936/1962: 98)

In fact, in addition to supporting the immediacy requirement, these reflections seem to support a further requirement. Not only is there an immediacy to our imagistic apprehension, but there is also a degree of certainty to it (see also Sartre 1936/1962: 96).[18] But it

---

[17] Russell also denies that there is any phenomenological difference between imaginings and memories: 'Memory-images and imagination-images do no differ in their intrinsic qualities, so far as we can discover' (Russell 1921: 176). Rather, the difference consists in the fact that memory-images, unlike imagination-images, are accompanied by a belief of the sort, 'this happened.'

[18] Kriegel (2015: 187-8) takes Sartre to have offered four related epistemological arguments: one about immediacy, one about effortlessness, one about certainty, and one about incongruity.

should be clear that the attendant-belief view is unable to meet either of these requirements. The consultation of attendant beliefs requires an additional step—a step that, at least in many cases, can be neither instantaneous nor effortless since it requires the balancing of various considerations and probabilities. Moreover, in typical instances this kind of consultation and balancing would not carry with it the degree of certainty inherent in our imagistic apprehension. Thus, the attendant-belief view must be rejected.

Of course, even if we reject the attendant-belief view, that is not enough to establish the non-existence view. The will-dependence view, for example, might also be thought to account for the immediacy and certainty requirements laid out by Sartre. Moreover, the claim that a presentation of non-existence is built into the phenomenology of imagining faces an obvious objection, because we frequently imagine objects that we know to exist. Uriah Kriegel, who has recently defended a version of the non-existence view, suggests that this objection can be easily answered: When I imagine something that I know to exist, as when I imagine the Longaberger basket building, my imaginative experience itself still plausibly presents the building as nonexistent, but 'it is just accompanied by an overriding belief that the imagined object in fact exists' (Kriegel 2015: 192). To flesh out this response, Kriegel draws a comparison to a case of optical illusion: 'looking at a Müller-Lyer display, I have a visual experience that presents-as-existent a pair of uneven lines; but the experience is accompanied by a belief that "disendorses" that content' (2015: 192). Likewise, if I close my eyes and imagine the Longaberger basket building having been relocated to my college's football field, and I abstract away from my belief that the building exists, the building of my imagining is arguably something I am aware of as unreal (and as such stands in contrast to the real building that's located in Ohio).

To see the problem with this line of response, however, compare imagining something that we know exists with imagining something that we know does not exist. Having heard about the Longaberger basket building, we might want to imaginatively explore other companies having headquarters that resemble their products, so we might imagine a Maybelline lipstick building. But when we compare the imagining of the Maybelline lipstick building to the imagining of the Longaberger basket building, it seems plausible that there is a difference in the imaginative phenomenology with respect to the presentation of their existential status. While the imagined Maybelline lipstick building may be presented-as-non-existent—while this could plausibly be said to be built into the imaginative phenomenology—this does not seem true of the imagined Longaberger basket building. It is not just that I believe the one building to exist and the other not to exist but rather that the imaginings present the buildings differently. (Indeed, if they did not, if my imagining of the Longaberger basket building presents its object as non-existent in exactly the way that my imagining of the Maybelline lipstick building presents its object as non-existent, then my imagining of the Longaberger basket building would be importantly misleading in a way it does not seem to be.) The fact that the non-existence view must deny any such difference counts against it.[19]

---

[19] I pursue this kind of objection against Kriegel's view in Kind (2016).

Presumably, the proponent of the non-existence view will deny that there is any such difference. Consider, for example, Sartre's discussion of a case in which he imagines his (actual) friend Pierre who is presently far away in Berlin. For Sartre, an imagining of Pierre as he is at this moment is more like an imagining of a centaur, an object known not to exist, than like a memory of Pierre: 'What is common between Pierre as imaged and the centaur as imaged is that they are two aspects of Nothingness' (Sartre 1940/2010: 182). But this suggests a related problem for the non-existence view, namely, that of explaining how an imagining of Pierre is really an imagining *of Pierre* at all. Compare, for example, Kriegel's claims about his own imagining of Barack Obama: 'As I close my eyes and picture him, the Obama hovering just there on the other side of my desk is something I am aware of as unreal; the real Obama is in the White House talking to more important people' (2015: 192).

Despite these criticisms, there does seem to be something importantly right underlying the non-existence view, or at least in the vicinity of the non-existence view. For imagining does take us away from the here and now, and there does seem to be a sense in which imagined objects, unlike perceived objects, are not presented as being before the senses. While they may not be presented as non-existent, they do seem to be presented as not present, that is, not before the senses. Since Sartre himself sometimes speaks of the imagined object being presented as *absent*, this view would seem to be very much in line with the motivations behind the non-existence view.

In exploring this sort of suggestion, McGinn explicates it in terms of embodiment and spatial-relatedness. While a percept always specifies a spatial relation to the perceiver's body, an imagining 'is neutral about spatial relatedness' (McGinn 2004: 30). As such, the intentional content of imagining departs from that of perceiving: 'The "absence" of which Sartre speaks could as well be described as the absence of the body from imaginative intentionality, in contrast to the presence of the body in all perception' (2004: 30). But this way of construing the point opens it up to an analogous sort of criticism to one we raised against the impoverishment view above. When gifted imaginers produce images that are just as vivid as percepts, there is still an experiential difference between imagining and perceiving. Likewise, when gifted imaginers produce imaginings about spatial locations—when someone imagines her friend Pierre to be sitting across from her at the table, exactly four feet away from her, there is still an experiential difference between this imagining and the corresponding perception, even though this imagining is not at all neutral about spatial relatedness.

What should we make of this criticism? While it seems a compelling one, we might take it to show only that McGinn has not adequately captured the kind of absence that Sartre had in mind. Perhaps there is still something to the insight about absence that can lead us to a better view of imaginative phenomenology. In the final section of this chapter I will briefly explore this thought, but my conclusion will ultimately be a pessimistic one. Indeed, as I will go on to suggest, we seem to have reason for a more far-reaching pessimism as well.

6.5 A Pessimistic Conclusion

Our discussion of the non-existence view ended with a speculative thought: Even if the view as stated is problematic, might there nonetheless be a related view in the vicinity that is more promising? In particular, can we build on the insight that imagined objects do not seem to present themselves to the senses in the way that perceived objects do? Though McGinn's notion of spatial relatedness does not seem to work, might there be a nearby alternative that does better?

As compelling as the basic insight seems to be, however, I think it is unlikely to bear fruit. In particular, I worry that there can be no way to spell out this insight in a contentful way. For what is it to say that the imagined objects are not presented as being before the senses other than to say that the imagined objects are not presented as being perceptually available? Rather than *explaining* the difference between imaginative phenomenology and perceptual phenomenology, we have simply restated it: Perceptual phenomenology presents objects as being perceptually available while imaginative phenomenology does not.

Attempts to spell out the phenomenal difference between different kinds of perception—between vision and audition, for example—often seem to face a similar problem. How do we explain the difference in phenomenology between seeing a plane flying overhead and hearing a plane flying overhead? Though there is no question that these two experiences are phenomenologically different, it is hard to say anything contentful about the difference. Rather, all we end up being able to say is that the one experience presents the plane in a visual sort of way while the other does not. Finding the words to explain what makes something have a visual feel rather than an auditory feel proves to be an enormously difficult task. Qualia—the phenomenal properties of experience—have generally been thought to be ineffable. Ned Block makes this point, for example, when he invokes Louis Armstrong's famous comment about defining jazz—'If you got to ask, you ain't never gonna get to know'—as an analogy for the enterprise of defining qualia. (Block 1978: 281) We can experience qualia but there are no adequate words to describe them.

Though it is hard to anticipate what other accounts of imaginative phenomenology could be devised, I suspect that they will suffer from analogous problems to those that have faced the three accounts considered in this chapter. While we are very good at recognizing the difference between different kinds of phenomenal experience, we are much less good at capturing this difference in a meaningful way. This difficulty is not one that is unique to imaginative phenomenology, and it thus should not be terribly surprising that the accounts of imaginative phenomenology that we have considered have seemed in various ways inadequate. Thus, though I am pointing us towards a pessimistic conclusion about the project of providing an account of imaginative phenomenology, this should not be seen as an indictment of imagination, or our understanding of it. Rather, it can be seen as part and parcel of a more general pessimism about descriptive phenomenology.

Thomas Nagel has famously argued that we cannot know what it is like to be a bat. In contrast, we can—and we do—know what it is like to imagine. But knowing what it is like and being able to explain what it is like are two different matters. And just as Nagel thinks that we lack the kinds of concepts that we would need to be able to explain the subjectivity of consciousness in terms of the objective vocabulary of science, resulting in our present inability to explain what conscious experience *really is*, so too it may seem that we lack the kinds of concepts that we would need to be able to capture the nature of our phenomenology, resulting in our present inability to explain what our conscious experience *really is like*. Perhaps there is work that can be done to sharpen and deepen our phenomenological vocabulary, but in advance of that work, our attempts to capture imaginative phenomenology—like our attempts to capture phenomenology in general—seem doomed to fall short.[20]

REFERENCES

Arcangeli, M. (2014), 'Against Cognitivism About Supposition', *Philosophia*, 42: 607–24.
Balcerak Jackson, M. (2016), 'On the Epistemic Value of Imagining, Supposing, and Conceiving', in A. Kind and P. Kung, *Knowledge Through Imagination*. Oxford: Oxford University Press, 41–60.
Block, N. (1978), 'Troubles with Functionalism', *Minnesota Studies in the Philosophy of Science*, 9: 261–325.
Brann, E. (1991), *The World of the Imagination*. Lanham, MD: Rowman & Littlefield.
Budd, M. (1989), *Wittgenstein's Philosophy of Psychology*. London: Routledge.
Byrne, A. (2010), 'Recollection, Perception, Imagination', *Philosophical Studies*, 148: 15–26.
Currie, G. and Ravenscroft, I. (2002), *Recreative Minds: Imagination in Philosophy and Psychology*. Oxford: Oxford University Press.
Descartes, R. (1641/1986), *Meditations on First Philosophy With Selections from the Objections and Replies*, trans John Cottingham. Cambridge: Cambridge University Press.
Galton, F. (1880), 'Statistics of Mental Imagery', *Mind*, 5: 301–18.
Gendler, T. (2000), 'The Puzzle of Imaginative Resistance', *Journal of Philosophy*, 97/2: 55–81.
Gendler, T. (2011), 'Imagination', in *Stanford Encyclopedia of Philosophy* (Fall 2013 ed.), edited by Edward N. Zalta, available at <http://plato.stanford.edu/archives/fall2013/entries/imagination/>.
Grandin, T. and Panek, R. (2013), *The Autistic Brain: Helping Different Kinds of Minds Succeed*. New York: Houghton Mifflin Harcourt Publishing.
Govier, T. (1972), 'Variations on Force and Vivacity in Hume', *The Philosophical Quarterly*, 22: 44–52.
Hobbes, T. (1651/1968), *Leviathan*, edited by C. D. Macpherson. Harmondsworth: Penguin Books.
Hopkins, R. (2012), 'What Perky Did Not Show', *Analysis*, 72/3: 431–9.

---

[20] For helpful comments on a previous draft of this essay, I am grateful to Uriah Kriegel, Peter Kung, and Frank Menetrez.

Hume, D. (1739/1985), *A Treatise of Human Nature*, edited by P. H. Nidditch. Oxford: Oxford University Press.

Ichikawa, J. (2009), 'Dreaming and Imagination', *Mind and Language*, 24 (1): 103–21.

Ichikawa, J. and Jarvis, B. (2012), 'Rational Imagination and Modal Knowledge', *Noûs*, 46: 127–58.

Kind, A. (2001), 'Putting the Image Back in Imagination', *Philosophy and Phenomenological Research*, 62 (1): 85–110.

Kind, A. (2016), 'Imaginative Phenomenology and Existential Status', *Rivista Internazionale di Filosofia e Psicologia*, 7: 273–8.

Kind, A. (2017), 'Imaginative Vividness', *Journal of the American Philosophical Association*, 3: 32–50.

Kriegel, U. (2015), *The Varieties of Consciousness*. Oxford: Oxford University Press.

McGinn, C. (2004), *Mindsight: Image, Dream, Meaning*. Cambridge, MA: Harvard University Press.

Marks, D. (1973), 'Visual Imagery Difference in the Recall of Pictures', *British Journal of Psychology*, 64/1: 17–24.

O'Shaughnessy, B. (2000), *Consciousness and the World*. Oxford: Clarendon Press.

Perky, C. W. (1910), 'An Experimental Study of Imagination', *The American Journal of Psychology*, 21/3: 432–52.

Russell, B. (1921), *The Analysis of Mind*. London: George Allen & Unwin Ltd.

Sartre, J.-P. (1936/1962), *Imagination*, translated by Forrest Williams. Ann Arbor, MI: The University of Michigan Press.

Sartre, J.-P. (1940/2010), *The Imaginary*, translated by Jonathan Webber. London: Routledge.

Savage, C. W. (1975), 'The Continuity of Perceptual and Cognitive Experiences', in R. K. Siegel and L. J. West, *Hallucinations: Behavior, Experience, and Theory*. New York: John Wiley, 257–86.

Sosa, D. (2006), 'Scenes Seen', *Philosophical Books*, 47/4: 314–25.

Thomas, N. J. T. (2014), 'The Multidimensional Spectrum of Imagination: Images, Dreams, Hallucinations, and Active, Imaginative Perception', *Humanities*, 3: 132–84.

Traiger, S. (2008), 'Hume on Memory and Imagination' in E. Radcliffe (ed.), *A Companion to Hume*. Oxford: Wiley-Blackwell, 58–71.

Van Leeuwen, N. (2013), 'The Meanings of "Imagine" Part I: Constructive Imagination', *Philosophy Compass*, 8/3: 220–30.

White, A. (1990), *The Language of Imagination*. Oxford: Basil Blackwell.

Wittgenstein, L. (1948/1980), *Remarks on the Philosophy of Psychology, Vol. II.*, edited by G. H. von Wright and Heikki Nyman. Chicago: The University of Chicago Press.

Wittgenstein, L. (1967), *Zettel*, edited by G. E. M. Anscombe and G.H. von Wright. Berkeley: The University of California Press.

CHAPTER 7

CONSCIOUS THOUGHT

TIM BAYNE

> A gentleman friend and I were dining at the Ritz last evening and he said that if I took a pencil and a paper and put down all of my thoughts it would make a book. This almost made me smile as what it would really make would be a whole row of encyclopediacs. I mean I seem to be thinking practically all of the time. I mean it is my favorite recreation and sometimes I sit for hours and do not seem to do anything else but think. So this gentleman said a girl with brains ought to do something else with them besides think.
>
> <div align="right">(<i>Gentlemen Prefer Blondes</i>, p.1)</div>

7.1 INTRODUCTION

Pick up any introduction to the philosophy of mind, and you might well be forgiven for doubting the very existence of conscious thought. The said textbook will no doubt contain chapters on both consciousness and thought, but the chapters on consciousness will almost certainly focus on sensation and perception, while those on thought are likely to mention consciousness only in passing if at all.

The neglect of conscious thought is puzzling, for a catalogue of any ordinary 5-minute interval of waking awareness will surely include thoughts of many kinds. One realizes that one has just slept in; one infers that one will now miss one's flight to Tucson; one wonders whether there is some other way of getting to Uncle Max's wedding, and so on. Conscious thought is no theoretical posit; rather, it is something with which we are each intimately acquainted. As Kriegel (2015) and Strawson (2011) have observed, our capacity to appreciate stream-of-consciousness literature surely presupposes some degree of first-person familiarity with conscious thought.

The neglect of conscious thought is also unfortunate, for an account of conscious thought is surely integral to any comprehensive understanding of the mind. (Some theorists—e.g. Jackendoff (1997); Carruthers (2017)—argue that thought per se is never conscious, but they are in the minority.) An account of consciousness that had nothing to say about the nature of thought would be as deficient as an account of thought that was silent about the nature of consciousness.

Conscious thought has been neglected, but it has not been entirely overlooked. Discussion of the topic has focused on three sets of questions. The first set of questions focuses on the kinds of states (events, episodes) that qualify as forms of conscious thought. What might a taxonomy of conscious thought look like? A second set of questions concerns the kind(s) of consciousness that characterizes thought. Are thoughts conscious in the same fundamental way that other mental phenomena are, or is 'cognitive consciousness'—that is, the kind of consciousness associated with thought—*sui generis*? A third set of questions concerns the relationship between consciousness and thought. Is consciousness essential to thought, or is it an accidental and contingent feature of thought—a feature that some thoughts possess but others lack? This chapter provides an opinionated point of entry into these and other questions.

7.2 THE VARIETIES OF CONSCIOUS THOUGHT

Talk of conscious thought is likely to evoke the image of Auguste Rodin's *'Le Penseur'*—'The Thinker'. (Ryle subtitled one of his essays on thought, 'What is "*Le Penseur*" doing?'.) Whatever it is that *Le Penseur* is doing, he does not appear to be *en rapport* with his immediate environment. One might say that *Le Penseur's* thoughts are 'perceptually disengaged'. In this respect, his thoughts can be contrasted with (say) thoughts about the cause of a sound that one has heard, the identity of an animal that one sees, or the origin of a pungent odour that one smells. These thoughts are 'perceptually engaged': they are prompted by and focused on perceptually salient objects. In many cases, the content of perceptually engaged thought contains demonstratives that refer to perceptual objects, as in 'What is *that*?'

A second distinction to be made here concerns the role that a thought plays in the context of one's cognitive aims. Some thoughts arise in response to problems. One might search for the solution to a crossword puzzle, look for the missing link in a proof, or deliberate about which of two paths on a hiking trail to take. In such cases thinking is a mental activity, something that one does. The reply 'I'm thinking' is sometimes a perfectly legitimate response to the question, 'What are you doing?' But thought is not always goal-directed and thinking is not always a mental activity (or at least, not in the way that looking and listening are.) Consider thoughts that arise in the context of what is variously called 'day-dreaming' or 'mind-wandering' (Christoff et al. 2016; Smallwood and Schooler 2015), a phenomenon that is surely not unfamiliar to any student of philosophy. The thoughts that populate the stream of consciousness during such episodes are unsupervised. They are not related to one's projects, nor are they attempts to secure one's cognitive aims. Studies have suggested that mind-wandering occupies up to 50 per cent of waking life (Klinger and Cox 1987; Kane et al. 2007; Killingsworth and Gilbert 2010). (What were you thinking about *just now*? A vacation in the south of France? Picking the kids up from school? An upcoming meeting with the Dean?) Interestingly, mind-wandering often goes undetected, even when one has a standing intention to guard against it (Schooler 2002). If we assume that undirected thoughts are themselves events in the stream of consciousness, these data indicate that it is one thing for a thought to be conscious and another for one to be conscious of it. In short, a conscious thought is not to be identified with a thought of which one is conscious.

The two distinctions that we have considered thus far are relatively straightforward, for the distinctions themselves are clearly relevant to the analysis of conscious thought and the categories in question clearly have members. We turn now to distinctions that are more controversial when considered in this context.

One distinction that is often made in discussions of thought is between linguistic / sentential accounts of thought (e.g. Fodor 1975, 2008; Carruthers 1996; Davies 1998) and non-sentential accounts of thought—accounts that regard thoughts as maps or models of reality (e.g. Johnson-Laird 1983; Lewis 1994; Braddon-Mitchell and Jackson 2007). Although these two conceptions of thought are typically contrasted with each other, it might turn out that some types of thought are sententially structured whereas others are non-sententially structured. It might also turn out that certain types of thoughts have a hybrid structure, in the sense that they resemble sentences in certain respects and (say) maps in other respects (Camp 2007).

With respect to our current concerns, the central question is not which of these two approaches to thought is most promising, but what implications—if any—the debate between them might have for the *conscious* dimensions of thought. One question here is whether conscious thoughts in particular (as opposed to thoughts in general) have one kind of structure rather than another. A second question concerns the implications of the debate between sentential and non-sentential accounts for the consciously experienced aspects of thought. Fodorian versions of the language of thought hypothesis are pitched at the sub-personal level, and as such they do not seem to have any particular implications for thought as a conscious phenomenon. However, versions of the sentential view that identify thinking with the deployment of natural language sentences (e.g. Carruthers 1996) are pitched at the personal-level, and as such do appear to have implications for our understanding of what it is like to think.

Reference to thinking as a matter of inner-speech brings us to another distinction that is often invoked in discussions of conscious thought: the distinction between 'imagistic thought' and 'non-imagistic thought'. Some theorists use the term 'imagistic thought' to refer only to thoughts that involve visual imagery, such as those that might be involved in (say) working out whether a sofa will fit in one's living room. However, it is more common for the term to be used for any thought that has sensory form, where this includes inner-speech. Thus understood, the controversial issue here is whether all conscious thought is imagistic, or whether there are conscious thoughts that involve no sensory content whatsoever. Some authors claim not to be aware of any non-imagistic thoughts within their stream of consciousness (e.g., Heil 2009; Prinz 2012), whereas others take the existence of such thoughts to be introspectively evident (e.g. Kobes 1995; Siewert 1998; Pitt 2004).[1]

Thus far we have focused on distinctions between thoughts considered as particular mental states or events—'thinkings', as it were. A final distinction concerns the ways in which thoughts are related to each other in chains of thought. Some thoughts are connected to each other via relations of association. For example, thoughts about Japan might lead to thoughts about Kurosawa films, which might in turn lead to thoughts about lonely samurai. Episodes of mind-wondering are characterized by associative chains of this kind. Other thoughts are linked by chains of inference, and constitute episodes of reasoning. For example, one might realize that since North road is parallel to Grant street, and since Grant street is parallel to Johnston street, it follows that Johnston street must in turn be parallel to North road.

How is the contrast between associative transitions and inferential transitions reflected in consciousness? Arguably, a conscious inference of the form 'If P then Q', 'P', 'Therefore Q' involves awareness of the fact that the two premises conjointly entail the conclusion. In other words, a (conscious) inference cannot be equated with a temporally-ordered sequence of conscious thoughts, but requires some form of conscious sensitivity to the logical relationship between the members of the sequence. It is one thing to entertain a series of conscious thoughts that happen to be inferentially connected, and another to engage in a conscious inference (Boghossian 2014; Nes 2016). What exactly rational inference involves is a contested matter, but it is plausible to suppose that the notion of consciousness will lie at its heart. And that in turn suggests that an account of reasoning and rationality requires an account of conscious thought.

7.3 WHAT WE TALK ABOUT WHEN WE TALK ABOUT CONSCIOUS THOUGHT

Let us turn now from distinctions between conscious thoughts to the more fundamental question of what notion(s) of consciousness are at issue when considering thought. As Carruthers (2005) has noted, theories of consciousness are not theories of the concept consciousness. Nonetheless, an account of conscious thought ought to begin with the concept(s) of consciousness, if only because it is far from clear just what concept(s) of

---

[1] The debate about the existence of non-imagistic thought was at the heart of the crisis that marked the demise of introspectionism (Ogden 1911; Boring 1953; Lyons 1986;). On one side were Titchener and his followers at Cornell, who claimed that introspection provides no evidence of non-imagistic thought; on the other side were the members of the Würzburg school—notably Külpe, Ach, and Bühler—who claimed to have discovered introspective evidence of non-imagistic thought. It is chastening to realize how little progress we have made in understanding the nature of conscious thought.

consciousness are being employed when we talk about thought. To fix ideas, I will refer to the kind of consciousness that is relevant to thought as 'cognitive consciousness' without assuming that cognitive consciousness is a *sui generis* type of consciousness.

7.3.1 Consciousness as Phenomenality

Some theorists identify cognitive consciousness with phenomenal consciousness. On this view, conscious thoughts are properly grouped together with sensory and perceptual states as a species of a single mental kind. Just as there is 'something that it's like' (Farrell 1950; Nagel 1974) to consciously sense and perceive, so too—these theorists hold—there is something that it is like to consciously think.

We can distinguish two very different positions within the ranks of those who think of cognitive consciousness as phenomenal consciousness. Some take the phenomenal properties that characterize thought to be purely sensory. This is the kind of view that might be held by someone who thinks of conscious thought as a matter of inner-speech, for example. Other theorists take thoughts to be characterized by a distinctive range of non-sensory phenomenal properties—properties that have come to be associated with the phrase 'cognitive phenomenology' (or 'cognitive phenomenality'). Section 7.4 ('Cognitive Phenomenology') examines the debate between the proponents of cognitive phenomenology and their detractors in some detail.

Treating cognitive consciousness as a species of phenomenal consciousness is undeniably attractive. For one thing, it allows us to see debates about conscious thought as essentially continuous with debates about conscious perception and sensation. However many theorists hold that, although some thoughts have a sensory phenomenology of some kind, it is a mistake to identify cognitive consciousness with phenomenal consciousness. As Nelkin once put it:

> There are propositional attitudes, and we are sometimes noninferentially conscious about our attitudinal states. But such consciousness does not *feel* like anything. A propositional attitude and consciousness about that attitude have no phenomenological properties. The mistake is to think they must. There are different sorts of states we call "conscious states," and the most important sorts are not like having sensations.   (Nelkin 1989: 430; see also Nelkin 1997)[2]

Cognitive consciousness, on this view, is a species of non-phenomenal consciousness (Lormand 1996). But if cognitive consciousness is not a form of phenomenal consciousness how then should we understand it?

---

[2] Consider also: 'Bodily sensations and perceptual experiences are prime examples of states for which there is something it is like to be in them. They have a phenomenal feel, a phenomenology, or, in a term sometimes used in psychology, raw feels. Cognitive states are prime examples of states for which there is not something it is like to be in them, of states that lack a phenomenology' (Braddon-Mitchell and Jackson 2007: 129).

7.3.2 Consciousness as Cognitive Accessibility

Some theorists identify the kind of consciousness that is exemplified by thought with 'access consciousness' (Block 1995). According to Block's original explication of 'access consciousness', a state is access conscious 'if, in virtue of one's having the state, a representation of its content is inferentially promiscuous, that is, poised for use as a premise in reasoning, poised for rational control of action, and poised for rational control of speech' (Block 1995: 231).[3] Thoughts are clearly access conscious in this sense of the term.[4] Indeed, it is arguable that occurrent thoughts *must* be access conscious, for if the content of a representation was not poised for use as a premise in the rational control of thought and action, then what grounds could we have for treating it as a genuine, fully-fledged thought, as opposed to a sub-personal representation of some kind?[5]

The controversial issue is not whether thoughts are access conscious, but rather whether they are *merely* access conscious. Those who regard thoughts as phenomenally conscious can certainly grant that they are often (perhaps even necessarily) access conscious. Indeed, they might even suggest that thoughts are access consciousness in virtue of being phenomenally consciousness, and that it is their phenomenal character that in some way 'greases the wheels' of cognition, and thus accounts for the fact that the content of the state is available for the rational control of thought and behaviour. What they deny is that the notion of access consciousness (or 'cognitive access') captures the central notion of conscious thought. A purely functional characterization of conscious thought omits its subjective aspects. It has seemed evident to many that the conscious grasp of a proposition is not just a matter of what one is in a position to do with it, but involves an experiential dimension that cannot be reduced to any set of functional relations, no matter how complex they might be.

7.3.3 Consciousness as Awareness

A third conception of cognitive consciousness equates it with awareness. Carruthers (2005: 138) writes, 'In the case of conscious thinking *the* phenomenon to be explained is

---

[3] Block's later characterizations of access consciousness depart from this one in various ways, but these departures do not affect the point being made here.

[4] Carruthers (2017) appeals to global neuronal workspace accounts of consciousness to argue that only sensory states are (first-order) access conscious. However, it is hard to see how thoughts could in general fail to be access conscious given Block's original characterization. Carruthers must thus be using 'access conscious' in some sense other than the one that Block associated with the term.

[5] In describing thoughts as access conscious, Block did not deny that they are also phenomenally conscious, although he was agnostic about the nature of thought's phenomenal character. 'One possibility is that it is just a series of mental images or subvocalizations that make thoughts P-conscious. Another possibility is that the contents themselves have a P-conscious aspect independent of their vehicles' (1995: 232).

the way that we (seem to) have immediate and non-inferential awareness of (some of) our own thought processes.' This view comes in two very different forms, paralleling a debate between two views of perceptual consciousness. Some theorists embrace higher-order accounts of conscious thought, equating conscious acts of thinking with events whose occurrence and content the subject has immediate and non-inferential awareness of (Rosenthal 1993; Carruthers 1996; see also Kirk 1994). Other theorists—'first-order theorists'—conceive of conscious thoughts as thoughts that provide one with a certain kind of awareness of features of one's environment.

Leaving to one side for the moment the contrast between the first-order and higher-order versions of this view, let us consider how we might understand the notion of awareness. Although theorists often treat this notion as an unexplained primitive, that approach is unsatisfactory in this context given that we are here considering how this conception of conscious thought differs from its rivals.

Is awareness simply to be understood in terms of representation, so that a conscious thought is simply a thought that one represents oneself as being in? That is one account of awareness, but it fails to capture the sense in which awareness is a 'personal-level' phenomenon. Sub-personal representations of various kinds guide the formation and evolution of one's thoughts without thereby making one aware of them.

What if we move to personal-level representation, so that a conscious thought is a thought that is represented in thought? This moves us close to Rosenthal's view of conscious thought, although Rosenthal requires not only that the target thought and the monitoring thought belong to one and the same subject of experience but also that the relationship between the two thoughts is direct and immediate. These qualifications are motivated by the need to deal with potential counter-examples (the fact that you might happen to be monitoring my thoughts obviously does not make them conscious), but it is unclear what their internal motivation is. If a thought's being conscious is, most fundamentally, a matter of one being conscious of it, why should the manner of one's access to the thought matter? Why precisely should a thought not qualify as conscious merely because one's access to it is indirect?

A further objection to monitoring approaches is that they open up the possibility of a certain kind of gap between thoughts themselves and our awareness of them. If a thought is conscious in virtue of how we represent it, then it would be conceptually possible for us to misrepresent our conscious thoughts. However, it is far from clear that misrepresenting one's conscious thoughts *is* conceptually possible. One can of course misrepresent one's dispositional states and sub-personal occurrent states, but it is far less obvious that one can misrepresent one's current thoughts. There is a strong temptation to think that someone who takes themselves to be wondering whether there are an infinite number of primes must indeed be wondering whether there are an infinite number of primes.

7.4 THE COGNITIVE PHENOMENOLOGY DEBATE

Let us return now to the phenomenal dimensions of conscious thought. Everyone grants that thoughts are often associated with phenomenal states of various kinds. Wondering whether to go on holiday might give rise to images of crystalline beaches; realizing the solution to a long-standing puzzle might be accompanied by a buzz of jubilation; deciding to sign a contract might involve feelings of anxiety and foreboding. None of this is particularly controversial. What is controversial is how these sensory states are related to thoughts, and whether their phenomenal character exhausts that of thought.

As we noted earlier, some theorists ('conservatives') hold that the only phenomenal states that are associated with thought are sensory, and that there are no distinctively cognitive forms of phenomenal consciousness. Other theorists ('liberals') hold that thoughts are characterized by various kinds of non-sensory phenomenology—what has come to be known as *cognitive phenomenology* (Bayne & Montague 2011a; Smithies 2013; Chudnoff 2015a; Montague 2016)—in addition to whatever sensory phenomenology might accompany them.[6]

Running parallel to the debate between conservatives and liberals is a debate about the relationship between the phenomenal dimensions of thought and the essential nature of thoughts themselves. Starting first with conservative views, some conservatives hold that the sensory phenomenology of a thought is not merely associated with it, but in some way constitutes it. For example, Prinz holds that the deployment of concepts involves sensory phenomenology, because 'in occurrent acts of conceptualization, we use the high-level representations that are stored in long-term memory to construct temporary mental images of what our concepts represent' (Prinz 2011: 181; see also Heil 2009). Other conservatives insist on a strict distinction between thoughts themselves and their sensory accompaniments (e.g. Carruthers and Veillet 2011). A similar contrast can be drawn within the ranks of the liberals. Most liberals seem to regard cognitive phenomenology as in some way constituting thought. However, such a commitment is not inherent in the very idea of cognitive phenomenology, and one could hold that thoughts themselves are fundamentally distinct from the cognitive phenomenology that accompanies them.

---

[6] Note that this usage of 'cognitive phenomenology' differs in important ways from other usages that are current. Some theorists, such as Prinz (2011), Smithies (2013), Kriegel (2015), use 'cognitive phenomenology' to refer to the kind of phenomenology that characterizes thought, irrespective of whether that phenomenology is irreducible to sensory phenomenology or whether it is distinctively non-sensory. Other theorists employ 'cognitive phenomenology' for non-sensory phenomenology that is constitutively related to thought (Carruthers and Veillet 2011).

Let us return to the question that is at the heart of the cognitive phenomenology debate: are there any non-sensory phenomenal properties? The first point to note is that liberals differ in the kinds of non-sensory phenomenal properties that they posit. Some liberals hold that there are phenomenal properties associated with particular cognitive attitudes (for example, judging, desiring, entertaining), but they are either agnostic or overtly sceptical about the existence of phenomenal properties associated with the contents of thought (e.g., Goldman 1993; Klausen 2008; Koksvik 2015). Other theorists are silent on the question of attitude-specific phenomenology, but posit phenomenal properties that are specific to thought contents in various ways (e.g., Pitt 2004; Nes 2016;). But perhaps the most widely-discussed versions of liberalism take the phenomenology of thought to have both attitude-specific and content-specific dimensions:

> There are phenomenologically discernible aspects of...cognitive phenomenology, notably (i) the phenomenology of *attitude type* and (ii) the phenomenology of *content*. The former is illustrated by the phenomenological difference between, for instance, *occurrently hoping* that Hillary Clinton will be elected U. S. President and *occurrently wondering* whether she will be—where the attitude-content remains the same while the attitude-type varies. The phenomenology of content is illustrated by the phenomenological difference between occurrently thinking that Hillary *will* be elected and occurrently thinking that she will *not* be elected—where the attitude-type remains the same while the content-type varies.
> (Horgan and Graham 2012: 334; see also Horgan and Tienson 2002: 522)

The following discussion focuses on this relatively demanding form of liberalism, but the existence of less demanding forms of liberalism should be kept in mind in what follows.

7.5 Arguments For and Against Cognitive Phenomenology

This section surveys a number of arguments for and against the existence of cognitive phenomenology. Some of these arguments have been discussed extensively in the literature; others have received relatively little attention.

7.5.1 Phenomenal Contrast Arguments

Perhaps the most widely discussed arguments for cognitive phenomenology are phenomenal contrast arguments (Kriegel 2007; Siegel 2007; Chudnoff 2015b). Liberals who employ this method present two mental states that allegedly differ in phenomenal character (this is the 'contrast'), and then go on to argue that the difference between the two states is best explained by appealing to the existence of a certain type of non-sensory phenomenal character.

Familiar contrast cases appeal to the phenomenal perspectives of two subjects who hear the same utterance, one of whom understands it and one of whom does not (either because they are unfamiliar with the relevant language or because they fail to parse it properly) (see e.g. Moore 1910/1953: 58–9; Strawson 1994: 6–7; Siewert 1998: 275–6). In this vein, Pitt (2004) invokes garden-path sentences, such as 'The boat sailed [by someone] down the river sank' to argue for the existence of what he calls the phenomenology of understanding. Subjects often find this sentence incomprehensible until they realize that it is equivalent to 'The boat that was sailed down the river, sank.' Another kind of case involves the phenomenal contrast between failing to 'get' a joke or an inference and then 'getting it', where the experiential state that one is in before getting a joke or an inference is very different from that which one is in after the penny has dropped.

Conservatives can respond to contrast arguments in one of two ways. One option is to simply deny that the scenario in question involves any phenomenal contrast. The conservative who adopts this response might grant that the contrasted scenarios differ in 'what it's likeness', but deny that the relevant what-it's-likeness is *phenomenal* 'what-it's-like-ness'. In practice, however, conservatives tend to grant that the scenarios invoked in contrast arguments do differ in phenomenal character, but that such differences are exhausted by changes in the 'sensory manifold', to use Levine's (2011) useful expression. Prinz (2011) provides one of the most thorough-going responses of this form, appealing to the phenomenal effects of prototypicality, verbal labelling, the generation of images, and the allocation of attention to category-relevant sensory features in order to explain the kinds of phenomenal contrasts that liberals appeal to (see also Carruthers and Veillet 2011; Tye and Wright 2011).[7]

Are these conservative responses compelling? Consider the following contrast case, presented by Chudnoff (2015b: 98):

> *Case 1*: You entertain the proposition that if $a < 1$, then $2 - 2a > 0$ and do not "see" that it is true. In particular you do not "see" how a's being less than 1 makes $2a$ smaller than 2 and so $2 - 2a$ greater than 0.
>
> *Case 2*: You entertain the proposition that if $a < 1$, then $2 - 2a > 0$ and do "see" that it is true. In particular you do "see" how a's being less than 1 makes $2a$ smaller than 2 and so $2 - 2a$ greater than 0.

Conservatives such as Prinz will argue that the phenomenal contrast between *Case 1* and *Case 2* involves nothing over and above the phenomenology associated with (say) inner speech or the bodily sensations associated with emotional relief. I myself doubt whether that is true, and am strongly inclined to think that Case 2 involves an intellectual

---

[7] Prinz (2011: 189) describes inner speech and sensory imagery as 'mutually supporting resources' when it comes to accounting for the experiential character of thought, which can, as he puts it, 'pick up for the other's limitations'.

experience that is absent from Case 1. But as an *argument* for cognitive phenomenology this contrast case seems to fail. In order to establish the existence of cognitive phenomenology, liberals need cases in which it is implausible to suppose that there are any differences in sensory phenomenology. It is difficult to rule out the possibility of such differences, even when considering abstract domains such as this one. In other words, even if the scenarios that liberals present do involve differences in cognitive phenomenology, contrast arguments suffer from dialectical shortcomings insofar as it is difficult to rule out the possibility that the contrast between the relevant cases can be accounted for in purely sensory terms (Koksvik 2015).

7.5.2 The Grounding Argument

A second line of argument for the existence of cognitive phenomenology appeals to the idea that such properties are needed to account for the determinacy of intentional content. An early version of this argument can be found in Loar (2003), with more recent discussions in Horgan and Tienson (2002); Strawson (2011); Goff (2012); Horgan and Graham (2012); and Kriegel (2013). This argument is closely associated with what has been called the phenomenal intentionality research programme (Kriegel 2013).

The grounding argument has three premises. The first premise involves the claim that our thoughts have determinate contents. We can entertain the thought <rabbits have tails>, a thought that is distinct from other thoughts in the neighbourhood, such as <undetatched rabbit-parts have tails>. The second premise is the assumption that we cannot account for the determinacy of content without appealing to consciousness. Some authors defend this premise by invoking Quine's (1960) arguments for the indeterminacy of translation or Kripke's (1982) worries about rule-following; others point to the history of attempts to ground intentional content in causal, functional, and teleological properties, arguing that the failures of Dretske, Fodor, and Millikan to provide an adequate semantics for thought is strong inductive evidence that attempts to ground content without appealing to consciousness are doomed to fail. The third step of the argument involves the claim that an appeal to phenomenal properties *can* account for the determinacy of content. As Graham et al. (2007) put it, 'content determinacy is fixed phenomenally'.

As an argument for cognitive phenomenology this seems to me to be less than compelling. For one thing, it is not entirely clear that our thoughts do have a determinacy over and above what they acquire through their anchors to perception, behaviour, and public language. Consider Stich's case of an elderly woman, Mrs T, who gradually loses beliefs as the result of a degenerative disease.

> Before the onset of the disease, [Mrs. T] believes that McKinley was assassinated, and she has a whole slew of related beliefs of just the sort one would expect. But as the disease progresses, she loses the belief that McKinley was a U.S. President; then she loses the belief that assassinated people are dead; then she loses most of her

beliefs about the differences between the living and the dead—she no longer has any idea what death is. Even at this advanced stage of her disease, she is still capable of answering the question: 'What happened to McKinley?' by saying 'McKinley was assassinated.' (Stich 1996: 24)

Do Mrs T's beliefs have determinate content? That is far from obvious. Of course, one might deny that Mrs T continues to have beliefs of any kind about McKinley (indeed, Stich argues for precisely that conclusion), but it is not implausible to suppose that she has beliefs of some form, at least in the early stages of her disease. Similar questions about content determinacy can be raised by considering non-human animals. My dog has thoughts about my postman, but what exactly are their contents? How precisely does my dog represent him? Does she represent him as a postman? That does not seem plausible? As a human being? Perhaps not. As a physical object? Again, that does not seem quite right either. These terms seem to impose a determinacy on the thoughts of my dog that ill fits them. One wonders if what is true of my dog is not true of any creature that lacks natural language capacities.

A further problem with the grounding argument is that it is far from clear that attempts to provide a non-conscious ground for intentional content are doomed. There are certainly serious problems with all extant attempts to 'naturalize' intentionality, but it does not follow from this fact that the project itself is doomed. After all, there are surely avenues for naturalizing semantic content that have yet to be explored in detail.

In my view, however, the main problem with the grounding argument concerns the suggestion that the intentional content of a thought could be grounded in its phenomenal properties. The problem is that there are only two viable accounts of phenomenal properties, and on neither of these accounts is there a plausible story as to *how* phenomenal properties could ground intentional content (see Pautz 2013 for related discussion).

Some theorists conceive of phenomenal properties in non-intentional terms—as 'mere sensations', 'raw feels', or 'pure qualia'. If phenomenal properties are understood in this way, then it is completely unclear how they might necessitate intentional properties. Why should one kind of raw feel ground the thought that rabbits have tails while another grounds the thought that undetached rabbit parts have tails? Attempts to derive intentionality from phenomenality are no more plausible than are attempts to derive phenomenality from functional relations—there is no intelligible or a priori scrutable bridge from the one set of properties to the other. Another tradition thinks of phenomenal properties as inherently intentional—as having conditions of satisfaction 'baked into them'. The problem with this approach is that it presupposes what we are trying to explain. If phenomenal properties are inherently intentional then we cannot think of them as grounding the determinacy of content, for grounding is surely an irreflexive relation (X cannot ground itself). On this conception of phenomenal properties, the problem of accounting for the determinacy of content simply re-emerges as the problem of accounting for the determinacy of phenomenal properties.

7.5.3 The Self-Knowledge Argument

A third argument for cognitive phenomenology appeals to the role that such states might be thought to play in accounting for self-knowledge. The basic idea here is that the only (or at least the best) explanation for the kind of knowledge we have of our own thoughts must posit non-sensory forms of phenomenology associated with thought (Peacocke 1998; Siewert 1998; Pitt 2004).

It is quite plausible to suppose that knowledge of one's own bodily sensations and perceptual experiences involves direct acquaintance with their phenomenal properties. Advocates of the self-knowledge argument hold that we can extend this account of self-knowledge from knowledge of sensations and perceptual experiences to knowledge of our cognitive states. Alvin Goldman (1993) was an early proponent of this position, arguing that we know what propositional-attitude states we are in on the basis of their phenomenal character.[8] Central to his argument was the claim that awareness of one's own mental states must involve properties that are both intrinsic (non-relational) and categorical (non-dispositional), and that the only properties that meet these conditions are phenomenal properties. A more recent defence of the self-knowledge argument for cognitive phenomenology can be found in the work of David Pitt (2004, 2011), who focuses on first-person access to the contents of thought.

The self-knowledge argument has not met with much enthusiasm in the literature. Some theorists deny that we have introspective access to our propositional-attitude states, and hence that there is no problem that phenomenal properties need be invoked in order to solve. For example, Carruthers (2010) argues that we have no direct or privileged access to our conscious judgments or conscious intentions (see also Gopnik 2013). Other theorists allow that we have introspective access to our thoughts, but deny that such access as we have involves the detection of phenomenal properties. Phenomenal properties may explain how we know our sensations and perceptual states, but—such theorists claim—they play no such role in accounting for knowledge of our own *thoughts* (see e.g. Nichols and Stich 2003; Prinz 2004; Schwitzgebel 2012).

The key claim in Pitt's argument—or indeed in any self-knowledge argument—is that only phenomenal states are introspectable. Advocates of the argument from self-knowledge seem to find this premise obvious, but none of their critics do. Furthermore, a number of theorists have developed accounts of introspection that do not appeal to phenomenal properties in order to account for our first-person access to thoughts. Drawing on a broadly Fodorian account of thought according to which propositional attitudes involve distinctive functional relations to 'mentalese' sentences, Levine (2011) argues that what it is to have knowledge of one's thoughts involves tokening a higher-order mentalese sentence that expresses what one is thinking. This counts as 'immediate self-knowledge' because the higher-order state is reliably caused by the first-order state and some functionally defined internal monitoring process.

---

[8] See Goldman (2006) for his second thoughts about this view.

7.5.4 The Argument from Chauvinism

The three arguments examined thus far have been the subject of extensive discussion. By contrast, what we might call the 'argument from chauvinism' has received only cursory treatment to date (see Bayne and Montague 2011a).

At the heart of this argument is the idea that leading accounts of perceptual phenomenology suggest that thoughts should also be phenomenally conscious. Consider two very influential theses associated with the analysis of phenomenal consciousness. The first thesis—we might call it 'functionalism'—is that perceptual states that have a certain functional status are phenomenally conscious. (The perceptual states associated with blindsight are not phenomenal because they lack this status.) How best to characterize this functional status is something of an open question, but as a first pass we might think of it in terms of availability for the global control of thought and action—roughly equivalent to Block's notion of access consciousness.

The second thesis—we might call it 'intentionalism'—is that the phenomenal character of a perceptual state supervenes on its intentional content, such that distinctions between various kinds of perceptual phenomenology correspond to distinctions in perceptual content. As the intentionalist thinks of things, phenomenal character is nothing over and above some amalgam of intentional content and functional role.

Let us call the conjunction of these two theses 'the basic package'. Note that although the labels that I have used in connection with the basic package have reductive connotations, the view itself is not inherently reductive.

Given the basic package, the existence of cognitive phenomenology would seem to be extremely plausible. After all, thoughts are often access conscious (as we have already observed); thus, if being access conscious is sufficient for being phenomenally conscious then thoughts are phenomenally conscious. Furthermore, thoughts clearly have intentional content; thus, it would be very natural for theorists who regard the phenomenal character of perceptual states as supervening on their intentional content to suspect that the phenomenal character of thoughts might also supervene on their intentional content. From the perspective of the basic package, recognizing the existence of perceptual phenomenology while also denying the existence of cognitive phenomenology might seem to be unmotivated.

The argument is, of course, far from being conclusive. A critic might argue that although access consciousness suffices for phenomenal consciousness when it comes to perceptual states, other kinds of mental states can be globally available for the control of thought and action without being phenomenally conscious. This position is certainly not incoherent, but it does seem to be at odds with the spirit of functionalism. A second response would be to accept that thoughts are phenomenally consciousness, but to hold that the phenomenology of a thought has nothing to do with its nature as a thought, but derives entirely from its sensory accompaniments. Again, although this response is not incoherent, it does seem to be at odds with the spirit of intentionalism: if the phenomenal character of a perceptual state supervenes on its intentional content, should we not also expect the phenomenal character of a thought to supervene on its intentional content?

7.5.5 The Processive Argument

For the most part conservatives have focused on trying to undermine liberal arguments for cognitive phenomenology, and positive arguments against cognitive phenomenology are scarce on the ground. However, a couple of such arguments have been offered. One of the most interesting is Tye and Wright's (2011) processive argument. The argument draws on ideas that have been developed by Soteriou (2007; 2009), who was himself indebted to the work of Geach (1969).

The processive argument involves two claims. The first claim is that experiences 'unfold over time'— they are events or processes rather than states. The second claim is that thoughts do not unfold over time. To use their example, in thinking the thought 'The claret is delightful' one does not first grasp the noun 'claret', followed by 'is', and then finally the adjective 'delightful'. Instead, they claim, the entire thought arrives 'all at once'. It is, Tye and Wright hold, only the various phenomenal goings-on that accompany thoughts—for example, linguistic sub-vocalizations and images—that unfold over time. Thoughts themselves do not, and as a result they cannot feature in the stream of consciousness.

There are two points at which the processive argument is vulnerable to criticism (see Forrest 2017 for further discussion). First, one might allow that the stream of consciousness is limited to events and processes, but deny that thoughts are always 'static'. We certainly describe ourselves as thinking through a problem or deliberating about what to do. Do such episodes involve only sequences of states, so that one transitions from one 'fully formed' thought to another? That's hardly obvious. Even if thoughts themselves are 'static', perhaps there is a *sui generis* form of cognitive phenomenology which concerns the transitions between thoughts—a kind of phenomenology associated with episodes of conscious thinking.

A second response to the processive argument denies that the stream of consciousness is limited to events and processes. One way to put pressure on the assumption that consciousness is limited to events and processes is to argue that perceptual experience includes elements that are non-processive and do not 'unfold over time'. Consider perceptual recognition. Although perceptual recognition might be embedded in processes that unfold over time, acts of recognition do not themselves seem to unfold over time. The experience of seeing an assortment of dots as (say) a Dalmatian or recognizing a sequence of notes as the theme to *Star Wars* seems to occur 'all at once'. Whatever the merits of these responses, it is clear that there are important points of contact between the cognitive phenomenology debate and questions concerning the temporal structure and the ontology of consciousness.

7.5.6 Coda

Before leaving the topic of cognitive phenomenology, let us pause to consider the fact that arguments for and against its very existence appear to be necessary. This fact, it seems to me, is worthy of reflection, for it is by no means obvious why there should be a (long-standing, perhaps intractable) debate about the status of cognitive phenomenology. After all, phenomenal states are not usually regarded as elusive or difficult-to-identify. Introspective access to one's character traits and dispositional states might be a vexed matter, but we tend to assume that questions about the phenomenal character of one's current conscious states can be answered merely by attending to the relevant experiences. Why can't the debate about the existence of cognitive phenomenology be settled by direct appeal to introspection?[9]

One possibility is that cognitive phenomenology is elusive. It exists, but it is not easily identified as such, and that is why conservatives fail to recognize it (Horgan 2011). Another possibility is that there is no such thing as cognitive phenomenology, and that what liberals mistakenly describe as cognitive phenomenology is nothing more than certain concatenations of sensory phenomenology (Prinz 2011). A third possibility—and one that I am sympathetic to—is that conservatives and liberals are in some important sense arguing past each other: liberals and conservatives disagree about what introspection reveals because they have different conceptions of what cognitive phenomenology would be, perhaps because they have different conceptions of phenomenal consciousness itself. Consider the fact that certain conservatives allow that there is 'something that it's like' to have a conscious thought, but they insist that this kind of 'what it's likeness' is not the kind of 'what it's likeness' that is constitutive of phenomenality (see e.g. Tye 1997: 312, n. 3). Perhaps, however, this kind of 'what it's likeness' is precisely the kind of 'what it's likeness' that liberals take to be constitutive of phenomenality.

Given the short-comings with ostensive definitions of phenomenal consciousness, a number of theorists have explored ways in which appeal to the various epistemic puzzles associated with consciousness—the explanatory gap (Levine 1983), the knowledge argument (Jackson 1982), and the hard problem (Chalmers 1996)—might be used to address the question of whether cognitive consciousness is a species of phenomenal consciousness (Bayne and Montague 2011b). The basic idea here involves arguing that

---

[9] Some theorists think that it can. The trouble, of course, is that the answers that they give do not converge. For example, Horgan and Tienson claim that 'the phenomenology of intentional content and the phenomenology of attitude type are phenomenal aspects of experience *that you cannot miss if you simply pay attention*' (Horgan and Tienson 2002: 523; my emphasis), but pretty much every article published by conservatives contains claims to the effect that there is no introspective evidence for cognitive phenomenology. For example, Tye and Wright (2011: 328) justify the claim that phenomenal consciousness is exclusively sensory by reference to 'introspective unfamiliarity' with any kind of cognitive phenomenology (see also Nichols and Stich 2003: 196; Wilson 2003; Carruthers and Veillet 2011; Prinz 2011).

thoughts do (or do not) possess a distinctive form of cognitive phenomenology on the grounds that they do (or, as the case may be, do not) generate versions of these puzzles.

Although this approach to the cognitive phenomenology debate represents an important step forward, it has yet to deliver any consensus. One problem is that there is debate about whether thoughts generate versions of the epistemic puzzles associated with consciousness: some theorists argue that they do (e.g. Goff 2012; Kriegel 2015; McClelland 2016), others that they do not (e.g. Carruthers and Veillet 2011). A second issue concerns the relationship between these epistemic puzzles and phenomenal consciousness. Although there is clearly a connection of some kind here, the fact that certain forms of perceptual phenomenology clearly generate straightforward versions of these puzzles whereas other forms of perceptual phenomenology do not indicates that the nature of this connection is not a simple one (Bayne 2009).

7.6 CONSCIOUSNESS AND THE NATURE OF THOUGHT

What connection is there between consciousness and the fundamental nature of thought? Is understanding consciousness central to understanding thought, or should the analysis of thought proceed in relative—or indeed, complete—independence from the analysis of consciousness?

As Horgan and Tienson (2002) note, philosophy of mind has by-and-large accepted a 'separatist' agenda since the middle decades of the twentieth century, in which the analysis of thought and that of consciousness have proceeded along relatively independent lines. Theorists rarely invoke consciousness when trying to account for either the content of thoughts or their identity as states of a particular kind (e.g., judgements, desires, intentions). Standard computational and functional accounts of thought give every indication that consciousness has no bearing on the fundamental nature of thought, and that there is no reason to assume that a thinking creature must also be a conscious creature. From a computational perspective, conscious thought emerges as something of a mystery, and the notion of consciousness struggles to gain a foothold in a theory of thought.

There are, however, voices of dissent—theorists who have argued that an understanding of consciousness is fundamental to understanding thought. Perhaps the most influential of such voices belongs to John Searle, whose 'connection principle' claims that thoughts must be potentially conscious. We have, Searle says, 'no notion of the unconscious except as that which is potentially conscious' (1992: 152). The details of Searle's view are somewhat obscure, but its broad contours are clear enough. At the heart of his position is the claim that genuine thought requires what he calls 'aspectual shape'. Thought does not represent an object as such, but instead represents it in a certain manner or way. But—Searle argues—no appeal to a thought's behavioural, functional, or neural dimensions can account for its aspectual shape (Searle 1992: 158). Therefore, Searle concludes, thoughts must be potentially conscious, for it is only in virtue of being conscious that a thought can possess aspectual shape.

There are a number of puzzling things about this argument. For one thing, Searle provides no account of *how* consciousness might ground the aspectual nature of thought. Searle seems to assume that it is obvious how appealing to consciousness might succeed in explaining the aspectual nature of thought when appeals to behaviour, functional, or neural properties of thought have failed, but the connection is anything but obvious. As Fodor and Lepore (1994) note, Searle does not explain why intentionality might depend on consciousness rather than (say) relative humidity or time of day. Second, even if an explanatory link can be drawn between consciousness and aspectual shape, Searle requires only that thoughts are potentially conscious, and thus allows for unconscious occurrent thought. How might consciousness account for the aspectual shape of unconscious thought? Searle does not say, and it is not easy to concoct a plausible story here. Finally, it is difficult to square the connection principle with Searle's own commitment to a biological account of consciousness. If neural properties account for consciousness, and if consciousness in turn accounts for aspectual shape, what grounds could there be to assume that neural properties cannot account for aspectual shape directly?

Although Searle's case for the connection principle is unconvincing, it is hard to shake the conviction that there is an internal (necessary, deep) connection between consciousness and genuine, personal-level, thought. An unconscious creature might be able to process information in complex ways, but thought itself—one might be tempted to hold—is the exclusive domain of conscious creatures. How might such a position be defended?

I can think of only two possible lines of defence. The first appeals to the idea that genuine thought involves a grasp of a proposition, and that grasping a proposition requires an act of consciousness. Although this line of thought is certainly appealing, it hardly qualifies as a defence of the idea that consciousness is essentially implicated in thought, for the claim that the grasp of a proposition involves an act of consciousness is unlikely to be accepted by anyone who does not already embrace the conclusion of the argument.

A second line of defence appeals to Gareth Evans' (1982) 'Generality Constraint', according to which any subject that has the capacity to think <F is a> and <G is b> must also have the capacity to think <F is b> and <G is a>. Although the Generality Constraint is not uncontroversial, it is widely taken to capture a necessary condition on genuine thought. How might we get from the Generality Constraint to the idea that only a conscious creature is capable of thought? The idea is that only a conscious creature can freely integrate the concepts that it has at its disposal in the manner required by the Generality Constraint. An unconscious creature might be able to integrate representations concerning a single domain, but—so this line of thought runs—it will not be able to integrate representations that concern very different domains.

I suspect that if there is an argument linking consciousness to thought it will need to appeal to the Generality Constraint, or at least something very much like it. There is, however, one glaring problem with this argument as sketched: we lack an account of why or how consciousness might play the integrative role that the argument assigns to it. Those who think of consciousness in functional terms may not find this worry particularly pressing, but those who think of consciousness in phenomenal terms are likely to see here yet another manifestations of the explanatory gap between consciousness and the brain.

What, finally, of unconscious thought? Are there any such states? Could there be any such states?

We can certainly grant that much of our behaviour is under the control of representations of which we are not conscious, and I see no reason to complain if someone wishes to call such states 'unconscious thoughts'. However, I myself would wish to reserve the term 'thought' for events that occur within the stream of consciousness—for events that characterize one's life 'from the inside'. It is surely states of this kind that the protagonist of *Gentlemen Prefer Blondes* had in mind when she described herself as thinking 'practically all of the time'. There may indeed be many commonalities between the thoughts that occur as events in the stream of consciousness and those thought-like events that, although unconscious, influence our behaviour, but there are also profound differences between them. Perhaps describing states of both kinds as 'thoughts' risks overplaying the commonalities and underplaying the contrasts.

References

Bayne, T. (2009), 'Perception and the reach of phenomenal content', *Philosophical Quarterly*, 59: 385–404.
Bayne, T. and Montague, M. (2011a), *Cognitive Phenomenology*. Oxford: Oxford University Press.
Bayne, T. and Montague, M. (2011b), 'Introduction' in T. Bayne and M. Montague, *Cognitive Phenomenology*. Oxford: Oxford University Press, 1–34.
Block, N. (1995), 'On a confusion about a function of consciousness', *Behavioural and Brain Sciences*, 18: 227–87.
Boghossian, P. (2014), 'What is inference?' *Philosophical Studies*, 169: 1–18.
Boring, E. G. (1953), 'A history of introspection', *Psychological Bulletin*, 50/3: 169–89.
Braddon-Mitchell, D. and Jackson, F. (2007), *Philosophy of Mind and Cognition* (2nd edn). Oxford: Blackwell.
Camp, E. (2007), 'Thinking with maps', *Philosophical Perspectives, 21: Philosophy of Mind*, 145–82.
Carruthers, P. (1996), *Language, Thought and Consciousness*. Cambridge: Cambridge University Press.
Carruthers, P. (2005), 'Conscious experience versus conscious thought', in P. Carruthers, *Consciousness: Essays from a Higher-Order Perspective*. Oxford: Oxford University Press, 134–56.
Carruthers, P. (2010), 'Introspection: Divided and partly eliminated', *Philosophy and Phenomenological Research*, 80/1: 76–111.
Carruthers, P. (2017), 'The illusion of conscious thought', *Journal of Consciousness Studies*, 24/9–10: 228–52.

Carruthers, P. and Veillet, B. (2011), 'The case against cognitive phenomenology', in T. Bayne and M. Montague (eds), *Cognitive Phenomenology*. Oxford: Oxford University Press, 35–56.
Chalmers, D. (1996), *The Conscious Mind*. Oxford: Oxford University Press.
Christoff, K., Irving, Z. C., Fox, K., Spreng, R. N., and Andrews-Hanna, J. (2016), 'Mind-wandering as spontaneous thought: a dynamic framework', *Nature Reviews Neuroscience*, 17: 718–31.
Chudnoff, E. (2015a), *Cognitive Phenomenology*. London: Routledge.
Chudnoff, E. (2015b), 'Phenomenal contrast arguments for cognitive phenomenology', *Philosophical and Phenomenological Research*, XCI/1: 82–104.
Davies, M. (1998), 'Language, thought, and the language of thought (Aunty's own argument revisited)' in P. Carruthers and J. Boucher (eds), *Language and Thought*. Cambridge: Cambridge University Press, 226–47.
Evans, G. (1982), *The Varieties of Reference*. Oxford: Clarendon Press.
Farrell, B. (1950), 'Experience', *Mind*, 49: 170–98.
Fodor, J. (1975), *The Language of Thought*. Cambridge, MA: Harvard University Press.
Fodor, J. (2008), *LOT 2: The Language of Thought Revisited*. Oxford: Oxford University Press.
Fodor, J. and Lepore, E. (1994), 'What is the connection principle?', *Philosophy and Phenomenological Research*, 54/4: 837–45.
Forrest, P. V. (2017), 'Are thoughts ever experiences?', *American Philosophical Quarterly*, 54/1: 46–58.
Geach, P. (1969), *God and the Soul*. London: Routledge and Kegan Paul.
Goff, P. (2012), 'Does Mary know I experience plus rather than quus? A new hard problem', *Philosophical Studies*, 160: 223–35.
Goldman, A. (1993), 'The psychology of folk psychology', *Behavioral and Brain Sciences*, 16/1: 15–28.
Goldman, A. (2006), *Simulating Minds: The Philosophy, Psychology, and Neuroscience of Mindreading*. Oxford: Oxford University Press.
Gopnik, A. (1993), 'How we know our minds: The illusion of first-person knowledge of intentionality', *Behavioral and Brain Sciences*, 16/1: 1–14.
Graham, G., Hogran, T., and Tienson, J. (2007), 'Consciousness and intentionality', in M. Velmans and S. Schneider (eds), *The Blackwell Companion to Consciousness*. Oxford: Basil Blackwell, 468–84.
Heil, J. (2009), 'Language and thought' in A. Beckermann, B. P. McLaughlin, and S. Walter (eds), *The Oxford Handbook of Philosophy of Mind*. Oxford: Oxford University Press, 631–47.
Horgan, T. (2011), 'From agentive phenomenology to cognitive phenomenology: A guide for the perplexed' in T. Bayne and M. Montague (eds), *Cognitive Phenomenology*. Oxford: Oxford University Press, 57–78.
Horgan, T. and Graham, G. (2012), 'Phenomenal intentionality and content determinacy' in R. Schantz (ed.), *Prospects for Meaning*. De Gruyter, 321–44.
Horgan, T. and Tienson, J. (2002), 'The intentionality of phenomenology and the phenomenology of intentionality' in D. J. Chalmers (ed.), *Philosophy of Mind: Classical and Contemporary Readings*. Oxford: Oxford University Press, 520–33.
Jackendoff, R. (1997), *The Architecture of the Language Faculty*. Cambridge, MA: MIT Press.
Jackson, F. (1982), 'Epiphenomenal qualia', *Philosophical Quarterly*, 32: 127–36.
Johnson-Laird, P. N. (1983), *Mental Models: Towards a Cognitive Science of Language, Inference and Consciousness*. Cambridge: Cambridge University Press.

Kane, M. J., Brown, L. H., McVay, J. C., Silvia, P. J., Myin-Germeys, I., and Kwapil, T. R. (2007), 'For whom the mind wanders, and when: an experience-sampling study of working memory and executive control in daily life', *Psychological Science*, 18: 614–21.

Killingsworth, M. A. and Gilbert, D. T. (2010), 'A wandering mind is an unhappy mind', *Science*, 330: 932.

Kirk, R. (1994), *Raw Feeling*. Oxford: Oxford University Press.

Klausen, S. (2008), 'The phenomenology of propositional attitudes', *Phenomenology and the Cognitive Sciences*, 7: 445–62.

Klinger, E. and Cox, W. M. (1987), 'Dimensions of thought flow in everyday life', *Imagination, Cognition and Personality*, 7/2: 105–28.

Kobes, B. (1995), 'Access and what it is like', *Behavioral and Brain Sciences*, 18: 260.

Koksvik, O. (2015), 'Phenomenal contrast: A critique', *American Philosophical Quarterly*, 52/4: 321–34.

Kriegel, U. (2007), 'The phenomenologically manifest', *Phenomenology and the Cognitive Sciences*, 6: 115–36.

Kriegel, U. (2011), *The Sources of Intentionality*. Oxford: Oxford University Press.

Kriegel, U. (ed.) (2013), *Phenomenal Intentionality*. Oxford: Oxford University Press.

Kriegel, U. (2015), *The Varieties of Consciousness*. Oxford: Oxford University Press.

Kripke, S. (1982), *Wittegenstein on Rules and Private Language*. Oxford: Blackwell.

Levine, J. (1983), 'Materialism and qualia: The explanatory gap', *Pacific Philosophical Quarterly*, 64: 354–61.

Levine, J. (2011), 'On the phenomenology of thought' in T. Bayne and M. Montague (eds), *Cognitive Phenomenology*. Oxford: Oxford University Press, 103–20.

Lewis, D. (1994), 'Reduction of mind' in S. Guttenplan (ed.), *A Companion to Philosophy of Mind*, Oxford: Blackwell, 412–31.

Loar, B. (2003), 'Phenomenal intentionality as the basis of mental content' in M. Hahn and B. Ramberg (eds), *Reflections and Replies: Essays on the Philosophy of Tyler Burge*. Cambridge, MA: MIT Press, 229–58.

Lormand, E. (1996), 'Nonphenomenal consciousness', *Noûs*, 30: 242–61.

Lyons, W. E. (1986), *The Disappearance of Introspection*. Cambridge, MA: MIT Press.

McClelland, T. (2016), 'Gappiness and the case for liberalism about phenomenal properties', *The Philosophical Quarterly*, 264: 536–58.

Montague, M. (2016), 'Cognitive phenomenology and conscious thought', *Phenomenology and the Cognitive Sciences*, 15/2: 167–81.

Moore, G. E. (1953), 'Propositions', in his *Some Main Problems of Philosophy*. London: Routledge.

Nagel, T. (1974), 'What is it like to be a bat?', *Philosophical Review*, 83/4: 435–50.

Nelkin, N. (1989), 'Propositional attitudes and consciousness', *Philosophy and Phenomenological Research*, 49/3: 413–30.

Nelkin, N. (1997), *Consciousness and the Origins of Thought*. Cambridge: Cambridge University Press.

Nes, A. (2016), 'The sense of natural meaning in conscious inference' in T. Breyer and C. Gutland (eds), *The Phenomenology of Thinking. Philosophical Investigations into the Character of Cognitive Experiences*. London: Routledge, 97–115.

Nichols, S. and Stich, S. (2003), 'How to read your own mind: A cognitive theory of self-consciousness' in Q. Smith and A. Jokic (eds), *Consciousness: New Philosophical Essays*. Oxford: Oxford University Press, 157–200.

Ogden, R. M. (1911), 'Imageless thought: Résumé and critique', *The Psychological Bulletin*, 8/6: 183–97.

Pautz, A. (2013), 'Does phenomenology ground mental content?' in U. Kreigel (ed.), *Phenomenal Intentionality*. Oxford: Oxford University Press, 194–234.
Peacocke, C. (1998), 'Conscious attitudes, attention, and self-knowledge' in C. Wright, B. C. Smith, and C. Macdonald (eds), *Knowing Our Own Minds*. Oxford: Oxford University Press, 63–98.
Pitt, D. (2004), 'The phenomenology of cognition Or What is it like to think that P?' *Philosophy and Phenomenological Research*, 69: 1–36.
Pitt, D. (2011), 'Introspection, phenomenality, and the availability of intentional content' in T. Bayne and M. Montague (eds), *Cognitive Phenomenology*. Oxford: Oxford University Press, 141–73.
Prinz, J. (2004), 'The fractionation of introspection', *Journal of Consciousness Studies* 11/7–8: 40–57.
Prinz, J. (2011), 'The sensory basis of cognitive phenomenology' in T. Bayne and M. Montague (eds), *Cognitive Phenomenology*. Oxford: Oxford University Press, 174–196.
Prinz, J. (2012), *The Conscious Brain*. New York: Oxford University Press.
Quine, W. V. O. (1960), *Word and Object*. Cambridge, MA: MIT Press.
Rosenthal, D. (1993), 'Thinking that one thinks', in M. Davies and G. Humphreys (eds), *Consciousness*. Oxford: Blackwell.
Schooler, J. W. (2002), 'Re-representing consciousness: dissociations between experience and meta-consciousness', *Trends in Cognitive Sciences*, 6: 339–44.
Schwitzgebel, E. (2012), 'Introspection, what?' in D. Smithies and D. Stoljar (eds), *Introspection and Consciousness*. Oxford: Oxford University Press.
Searle, J. (1992), *The Rediscovery of the Mind*. Cambridge, MA: MIT Press.
Siegel, S. (2007), 'How can we discover the contents of experience?' *The Southern Journal of Philosophy*, XLV, 127–42.
Siewert, C. (1998), *The Significance of Consciousness*. Princeton, NJ: Princeton University Press.
Smallwood, J. and Schooler, J. (2015), 'The science of mind wandering: empirically navigating the stream of consciousness', *Annual Review of Psychology*, 66: 487–518.
Smithies, D. (2013), 'The nature of cognitive phenomenology', *Philosophy Compass*, 8/8: 744–54.
Soteriou, M. (2007), 'Content and the stream of consciousness', *Philosophical Perspectives*, 21/1: 543–68.
Soteriou, M. (2009), 'Mental agency, conscious thinking, and phenomenal character' in L. O'Brien and M. Soteriou (eds), *Mental Actions*. Oxford: Oxford University Press, 231–52.
Stich, S. (1996), *Deconstructing the Mind*. Cambridge, MA: MIT Press.
Strawson, G. (1994), *Mental Reality*. Cambridge, MA: MIT Press.
Strawson, G. (2011), 'Cognitive phenomenology: Real life' in T. Bayne and M. Montague (eds) *Cognitive Phenomenology*. Oxford: Oxford University Press, 285–325.
Tye, M. (1997), 'The problem of simple minds: Is there anything it is like to be a honey bee?' *Philosophical Studies*, 88: 289–317.
Tye, M. and Wright, B. (2011), 'Is there a phenomenology of thought?' in T. Bayne and M. Montague (eds) *Cognitive Phenomenology*. Oxford: Oxford University Press, 326–44.
Wilson, R. (2003), 'Intentionality and phenomenology', *Pacific Philosophical Quarterly*, 84/4: 413–31.

CHAPTER 8

THE EXPERIENCE OF AGENCY

MYRTO MYLOPOULOS AND JOSHUA SHEPHERD

IN this chapter we reflect on questions about the nature and sources of agentive phenomenology—that is, the set of those experience-types associated with exercises of agency, and paradigmatically with intentional actions. Our discussion begins with pioneering work in psychology and neuroscience that dates to the early 1980s (Section 8.1). As we will see, much of the current work on agentive phenomenology in both psychology and philosophy draws motivation from this work, and the questions it raises.[1] After discussing empirical work relevant to agentive phenomenology, we turn to consideration of its nature. We cover questions about the scope of agentive phenomenology, about its relationship to other types of experiences (Section 8.2.1), about the best way to characterize aspects of agentive phenomenology, and about the function of various types of agentive experience (Section 8.2.2).

8.1 THE SCIENCE OF AGENTIVE PHENOMENOLOGY

8.1.1 Consciously Deciding

In a now-classic study, Libet et al. (1983) asked six participants each to perform a 'quick, abrupt flexion of the fingers/and or wrist' (1983: 625) with their right hand, at a time of

---

[1] Certainly one also finds motivation stemming from work on agentive phenomenology in the history of psychology and philosophy. Regarding psychology, see de Biran (1812) and James (1880). Regarding philosophy, see, e.g., Brentano (1874), Sartre (1969), Merleau-Ponty (1996), and Ricoeur (1966). For an interesting recent discussion of Hume's phenomenology of agency, see Wood (2014).

their own choosing. They were instructed not to decide in advance on a time at which to perform the act, but rather 'to let the urge to act appear on its own at any time without any preplanning or concentration on when to act' (1983: 625). Participants were seated facing a specialized clock, around which a dot would revolve every 2.56 seconds. They were instructed to report the time at which they first became aware of deciding or having the 'urge' to move based on the position of the dot on the clock (the 'W judgment'). They were also asked to report the time at which they were aware that they had 'actually moved' (1983: 627) (the 'M judgment'). During the task, they were hooked up to an electroencephalogram (EEG) that measured their brain activity, as well as an electromyogram (EMG) that measured their muscle activity.

The most striking result that Libet and colleagues uncovered was this.[2] A slow build-up of neural activity preceding the onset of spontaneous movements (known as the 'Readiness Potential or 'RP'), and which has been widely associated with the neural signature of action initiation (though see Mele 2010; Schurger et al. 2012; and Schurger et al. 2016 for competing interpretations), precedes the time at which participants report being aware of an urge or decision to act by an average of approximately 350 ms. (The reported time of the urge or decision itself precedes the onset of the action by about 200 ms.) As Libet and colleagues put it, 'the brain evidently "decides" to initiate or, at least, prepare to initiate the act at a time before there is any reportable subjective awareness that such a decision has taken place' (Libet et al. 1983: 640). This result, and especially the interpretation that Libet and colleagues offer, has garnered an astounding amount of scholarly and popular attention. This is largely due to assumed implications regarding free will. But it is important to note that these implications depend on assumptions regarding the phenomenology of deciding. For the natural thought is that if 'the brain decides' such that the phenomenology of deciding is illusory, the person must not be in control, and must not therefore be free.

Libet's work, coupled with the many studies that followed from Libet's original one, has prompted a surge of interest in the phenomenology of deciding (see, e.g., Carruthers 2007; Mele 2009; Shepherd 2013). While some have broadly taken Libet's side, arguing that the phenomenology of deciding is in some sense illusory (e.g., Carruthers 2007), most have argued that Libet's results at best demonstrate the existence of early bias in decision-making processes (e.g., Mele 2009). How best to understand the processes underlying decision-making, and the relationship of the phenomenology of deciding to those processes, remains undetermined (though see Bear and Bloom 2016 for an interesting recent study).

---

[2] Another notable result from the Libet study is this. Participants reported awareness of acting on average 86 ms prior to the onset of bodily movement as measured by EMG. This might be viewed as *prima facie* support for accounts that take agentive phenomenology to arise prior to any sensory feedback from bodily movement, thus providing motivation for cognitive accounts of agentive phenomenology based on intentions, tryings, or doxastic states. Others are skeptical that the results can be interpreted in this way, arguing that the subjective reports provided by participants are not conclusive (e.g., Carruthers 2012).

8.1.2 The Feeling of Doing

A second relevant research program was led primarily by the psychologist Daniel Wegner. Wegner focused on the psychological mechanisms giving rise to what he called the 'feeling of doing'. Wegner (2002) argues on the basis of folk theoretical observations, as well as work demonstrating that priming for certain action outcomes influences the degree to which agents report feeling in control of their behavior (Wegner and Wheatley 1999), that our experience of consciously willing our actions is illusory. For Wegner, the underlying causes of our behaviour are unconscious processes in the brain, and not our conscious intentions themselves. He develops a view on which we infer that our intentions cause our actions when we are aware of them occurring prior to the action, they are consistent with the action, and there are no salient alternative causes. In this way, 'The experience of will may be a result of the same mental processes that people use in the perception of causality more generally' (Wegner 2004: 654).

Regarding the influence of Wegner's work, three similarities with Libet deserve mention. First, as with Libet, much of the scholarly and popular attention devoted to Wegner's results has centered on assumed implications for free will. Second, these implications depend on assumptions regarding agentive phenomenology—in this case, the feeling of doing. As with Libet, the evident importance of agentive phenomenology to questions of broad societal interest motivated renewed interest in agentive phenomenology. Wegner himself characterized the 'feeling of doing' in multiple ways (see Nahmias 2005 for discussion). In response to Wegner's work, thinkers interested in agentive phenomenology have thus been forced to consider just what we might mean by speaking of a feeling of doing, and how best to characterize the kinds of experiences that constitute it. Third, as with Libet, the majority of philosophers have argued that these results, while interesting, pose little threat to free will (see especially Mele 2009, Bayne 2011b, Shepherd 2015a).

8.1.3 The Comparator Model and Agentive Phenomenology

A third line of work attempts to understand agentive phenomenology by anchoring it to the states and processes underlying sensorimotor control. This approach leans heavily on a popular neurocomputational model, known as the Comparator Model (CM), of how such control functions. According to this model, several computational mechanisms work together to anticipate upcoming segments of action execution, to check for possible mistakes, and to correct for mistakes in real time. One mechanism, called the inverse model, computes motor commands—representations that specify the fine-grained aspects of bodily movement, such as grip aperture and grip force—on the basis of the current state of the body in order to satisfy a given goal state. Another mechanism, called the forward model, is thought to take as input a copy of the motor command, known as the efference copy, as well as a representation of the current state of the body, and output a prediction of the sensory consequences that executing that command would yield. In addition, a series of comparisons involving the goal state, the forward model prediction, and the sensory feedback from the bodily movement are posited in order to explain various control operations.

First, there is a comparison between the forward model prediction and the sensory feedback. Second, just prior to movement, there is a comparison between the forward model prediction and the goal state. If a mismatch results, then an error signal is sent to the inverse model, and a new motor command is computed. Lastly, a third comparison between the goal state, that is, a proximal intention, and sensory feedback is posited. This comparison plays a role in motor learning, since it allows the training up of the inverse model, but also ongoing correction and adjustment of the action as it unfolds, if needed (Blakemore et al. 1999; Blakemore and Frith 2003; Blakemore et al. 2003).

Agentive phenomenology is typically thought to arise as a result of a match between the forward model prediction and sensory feedback from bodily movement (Bayne and Pacherie 2007; Pacherie 2008; Bayne 2011a).[3] As Bayne (2011a) describes it, 'when there is a match between predicted and actual state, the comparator sends a signal to the effect that the sensory changes are self-generated; when there is no match (or an insufficiently robust match), sensory changes are coded as externally caused' (2011a: 495).

Motivation for this model arises in part from the observation that disruptions in agentive phenomenology seem to correlate with deficits in generating accurate forward model predictions. Perhaps one of the most celebrated findings in support of this view is that, while healthy individuals experience sensory attenuation in relation to a self-generated tactile stimulus, but not an externally generated tactile stimulus (Blakemore et al. 2003), schizophrenic individuals with delusions of control do not experience such attenuation to the same degree (Blakemore et al. 2003). The thought is that the mechanism behind sensory attenuation is forward model prediction—when a sensory consequence is predicted by the forward model it is 'canceled out'—and schizophrenic individuals are impaired in their ability to form just such states, leading to a failure of attenuation, and thereby a lack of agentive phenomenology.

Another set of widely-cited studies in support of the CM account of agentive phenomenology uses action-monitoring paradigms. In these paradigms, participants are tasked with performing a simple act (e.g., moving a joystick, reaching towards a target), and presented with visual feedback that is distorted to varying degrees relative to their movement (e.g., Daprati et al. 1997; Fourneret and Jeannerod 1998; Farrer et al. 2003). Participants are then asked whether it is their movement that they see, or one caused by

---

[3] Some theorists propose a division of phenomenal labor, according to which the comparison between the goal state and the forward model prediction underlies one's sense of *initiating* an action and the comparison between the forward model prediction and sensory feedback underlies one's sense of *control* over an action (e.g., Synofzik et al. 2008). But the main evidence appealed to in support of positing the former comparison is not compelling. It is that a number of studies have found that people tend to report anticipatory awareness of acting—that is, they report having started acting before any sensory feedback from the action is available (Lau et al. 2004; Libet et al. 1983). Such reports, however, could just as well be based on intentions or decisions to start acting, rather than the output of any comparison involving a forward model prediction.

an external source. The thought here is that participants base their judgments on the comparison between the forward model prediction and the visual feedback they receive. Again, schizophrenic individuals with delusions of control tend to perform poorly on this task compared to healthy controls and schizophrenic individuals without such delusions (Daprati et al. 1997). Moreover, the accuracy of their performance even correlates with the severity of their symptoms (Synofzik et al. 2010).

Here we suggest, in agreement with others (e.g., Synofzik et al. 2008), that though the CM may be a suitable model for explaining sensorimotor control, it faces some difficulties when it comes to explaining agentive phenomenology. Concerning the sensory attenuation results, it has been found that sensory attenuation of an auditory tone following a voluntary action is modulated by the presence or absence of a belief that one's action is the cause of the tone. But if so, then it would seem that forward model prediction, which is present across conditions, cannot be the source of the attenuation. So insofar as sensory attenuation is linked to agentive phenomenology (more on this in Section 8.2), it does not seem that the CM can explain it. Other results that are linked to both forward model predictions and agentive phenomenology, such as the 'intentional binding effect' (Haggard et al. 2002)—that is, the finding that the effects of one's actions are subjectively perceived as occurring earlier in time than the effects of one's involuntary movements—can also arguably be divorced from the CM in this way (see Mylopoulos 2012).

Second, it has been pointed out that without case-by-case adjustments to how different states (e.g., visual vs. proprioceptive feedback) are weighed in the comparison, the CM has difficulty consistently accounting for a range of experimental results (Carruthers 2012). For example, deafferented individuals who lack proprioceptive feedback arguably experience agentive phenomenology in virtue of a match between visual feedback from their bodily movements and forward model predictions. But in other studies, proprioception seems to play a key role in agentive experience (Balslev et al. 2007).

Such difficulties have led some theorists to assert that 'there are many cases where the comparator output is neither a sufficient nor a necessary condition for the [feeling of agency]' (Synofzik et al. 2008: 226). An alternative model that has been offered is the so-called multifactorial weighting model, on which a range of action-related cues such as efference copy, forward model prediction, and multimodal sensory feedback, are used as inputs in a multifactorial weighting process that determines agency according to a Bayesian learning framework (Synofzik et al. 2008).

While this model may hold promise, at this point it is not yet known how to determine in a principled way what the appropriate weights are for given cases. As such, this model does not currently enable predictions for or explanations of when or why agentive phenomenology arises, and may even be unfalsifiable (see Carruthers 2012 for discussion on this point).

Third, it is remarkable that the CM approach is such that the subpersonal states and processes that purportedly give rise to agentive phenomenology operate to some degree independently of the agent's intentions, as well as action-related beliefs and perceptions. This relegates such states to the backseat in driving agentive phenomenology. But it seems unlikely that, central as they are to intentional control, these states would not make a more direct contribution to our experiences of acting. Accounts of agentive experience pitched in terms of these personal-level states (e.g., Wegner 2002) or a mix of personal-level states and the subpersonal states of the CM (e.g., Pacherie 2008) may therefore be preferable to those that focus exclusively on the CM.

Finally, we emphasize that it is not at all clear *which* aspects of agentive phenomenology the studies and paradigms that are frequently appealed to in support of the CM are actually measuring. For instance, in the case of the intentional binding effect, only the participants' subjective timing judgments relating to the consequences of their bodily movements are explicitly probed, leaving it open as to whether the effect also indicates a sense of mineness, a sense of control, or some other aspect of agentive phenomenology. Similarly, when it comes to the action-monitoring paradigm, though it is often claimed to examine the 'sense of agency' (more on various usages of this term later in the discussion) it seems primarily to measure action perception, that is, whether one's proprioceptive feedback matches with the visual feedback one receives. Insofar as 'the sense of agency' is thought to refer to a sense of executing one's intention, or a sense of purposiveness, it is not being directly measured by this study. (Consider that the task could be performed with entirely passive movements as well.) We attempt to clear up some of these issues in Section 8.2.2.

8.1.4 Metacognition and Agentive Phenomenology

We turn now to consider a fourth line of work gaining traction lately, suggesting that aspects of agentive phenomenology can be explained by appeal to metacognitive states and processes (e.g., Wenke et al. 2010; Metcalfe et al. 2013; Chambon et al. 2014; Carruthers 2015). In particular, some have recently suggested that agentive phenomenology reflects the metacognitive monitoring of aspects of our action-producing mechanisms as they are being engaged (see also Section 82.2.5 for discussion of a metacognitive account of mental agency).

One attractive feature of this view is that it can plausibly account for the subjective character of agentive phenomenology. After all, many metacognitive states are construed as subjective feelings, such as the 'feeling of knowing' (Koriat 2000). Moreover, these are hardly robust experiences like the feeling of pain or a typical visual experience. It is not unreasonable, then, that agentive phenomenology, which is often itself characterized as 'thin'—perhaps an indication that its subjective character is difficult to capture in virtue of being typically located at the margins rather than the center of one's total experience at a time—might be assimilated to this class of feelings as well.

Though this view holds considerable appeal, a central question concerns the aspects of the action-producing mechanisms to which agentive phenomenology is sensitive. Here we examine the recent proposal that agentive phenomenology is the result of the metacognitive monitoring of 'fluency' signals generated during the process of action selection (Wenke et al. 2010; Chambon et al. 2014).

Wenke et al. (2010) explore this possibility with an elegant study asking participants to perform a left or right keypress in response to a left- or right-facing target arrow. Prior to the target arrows, participants are presented with a masked prime arrow that is either compatible or incompatible with the target. Once they press the key, a color patch appears after a certain delay interval. The color of the patch corresponds to whether the target arrow is compatible or incompatible with the masked prime. At the end of each block, participants are asked to rate how much control they felt they had over the specific colors that appeared. Participants reported feeling more control over prime-compatible colors, that is, those occurring after actions that were primed and therefore more easily selected, versus prime-incompatible colors, despite the predictability of the colors being the same—namely zero.[4]

Some argue on the basis of such results that (i) agentive phenomenology relies on the evaluation and monitoring of action selection processes prior to action execution, and (ii) agentive phenomenology should thus be construed as a form of metacognition.

In particular, it has been suggested (Chambon et al. 2014) that fluent action selection is a reliable predictor of control over action *effects*, and in this way the monitoring of fluency signals can be construed as a metacognitive process insofar as it serves as a capacity 'through which an operating cognitive subsystem [in this case the action-producing system] is evaluated or represented in a context-sensitive way' (Proust 2013: 13). Here we would have an analog of the 'feeling of knowing', which evaluates the potential success of mnemonic retrieval operations, in the 'feeling of doing', which evaluates the potential success of action-production processes.

While a proposal along these lines may ultimately prove fruitful, important questions remain to be settled. For one, though the most widely-discussed empirical studies in this area only explicitly ask about participants' feelings of control over the effects of their actions, it is reasonable to suppose that the monitoring of fluency signals contributes to a sense of control over the executed actions themselves, and not just the effects that these paradigms happen to focus upon. But to our knowledge this possibility has yet to be directly examined. Second, fluency is not the only candidate for what is being monitored here. Another option is that it is the extent to which the executed action—again, rather than its effect—is predicted by one's action producing mechanism, with the subliminal prime serving as a predictive representation. Third, there is a question regarding whether the metacognitive monitoring being posited involves an explicit self-attribution of agency via a metarepresentation or, rather, is simply sensitive to fluency cues in some way that falls short of explicit self-attribution.

On this last point, indeed, it may be that these different forms of metacognition that are potentially at play here would respectively track different aspects of agentive phenomenology, some requiring explicit self-attribution and some not. We further stress

---

[4] In a subsequent study, Chambon et al. (2012) found that participants reported feeling more in control of prime-compatible colors than prime-incompatible colors even when reaction times were slower for the former, thus dissociating the monitoring of fluency signals from performance monitoring that uses reaction times as a cue to performance.

that the terms 'sense of agency' and 'sense of control' are often used interchangeably in describing what is being examined in this work, and it is sometimes unclear what exactly theorists have in mind when they use these terms and whether or not they are being consistent in their usage. Without more precision here, it is difficult to evaluate what specific contributions are being made to the enterprise of understanding agentive phenomenology. In Section 8.2, we reflect on ways that philosophy has attempted to contribute to such precision, and suggest some further refinements of our own.

8.1.5 Summary

Work in psychology and neuroscience has been responsible for increased interest in the sources of agentive phenomenology. But as we have seen, it is debatable just what aspects of agentive phenomenology this work seeks to, and in fact does, elucidate. We have noted issues surrounding Libet's characterization of the phenomenology of deciding, Wegner's characterization of the feeling of doing, and attempts to explain the agentive phenomenology via the comparator model and metacognitive processes. These issues are not insurmountable, but they do suggest that greater clarity is needed regarding the explananda. Just what is the structure of this thing, agentive phenomenology, the sources of which science is attempting to reveal?

8.2 THE PHILOSOPHY OF AGENTIVE PHENOMENOLOGY

Two broad issues have occupied philosophical attention to agentive phenomenology. The first issue has to do with the structure of consciousness in general, and in particular with the relationship between agentive phenomenology and the rest of conscious mental life. Is agentive phenomenology proprietarily agentive, that is, not reducible to perceptual, emotional, or cognitive phenomenology? The second issue has to do with the structure of agentive phenomenology more specifically. What kinds of experience-types qualify as agentive, how ought we to taxonomize them, and how do they relate to each other? We discuss both issues in turn.

8.2.1 Is any Phenomenology Proprietarily Agentive?

Consider this sequence of activity, as described by an amateur skier:

> To my alarm, I recognized that the control that I had over the direction of my skis, never anything near total, was now nothing more than feeble. Each turn required immense concentration and exhausting effort.... I became aware that I was shaking

not simply through physical exhaustion but also because I was beginning to get quite frightened.... In the half-light, the surface of the mountain appeared to be tablecloth smooth but I knew this to be nothing more than a mirage. In the daylight, every contour would be clearly visible, but now I had to try and relax enough to ride any invisible bump, hillock or mogul. Leaning forward against all my natural instincts, I bent my knees a little further trying to absorb any nasty shocks with my aching legs. Momentarily, I thought that I had skied off the edge of a cliff as my internal organs, operating on some different system of gravity to the rest of my leaden body, rose in my stomach. Several minutes later, or so it seemed, my skies came back to earth.... Feeling delighted that I was still upright, I thumped my ski sticks back into the freezing surface. As I did so, I suddenly sensed, to my alarm, that I was sliding rapidly backwards. (Randall 2009: 5–6)

Is this an episode of *agentive* phenomenology? That depends on what it means to call a bit of phenomenology agentive. We might gloss agentive phenomenology as the conscious experiences surrounding (both bodily and mental) action. But this is a fairly weak gloss. Perceptual, emotional, and cognitive experiences (among others) surround action, and figure in the above description. Is there anything special or unique in virtue of which a bit of phenomenology might be considered agentive?

Drawing on Uriah Kriegel's recent discussion (Kriegel 2015: 73), here is one way to approach this question. Let us say that a bit of phenomenology can be considered obviously agentive if it instantiates a phenomenal property that is proprietarily agentive. And let us say that a phenomenal property is proprietarily agentive if it is instantiated by a state or process central to some actional episodes, and not instantiated by states and processes that occur outside of actional episodes.

Why believe that any phenomenal property is proprietarily agentive in this sense? One reason would have to be based on introspecting one's conscious experiences. Accordingly, philosophers who endorse proprietarily agentive phenomenology advance largely phenomenological arguments. Horgan et al. (2003) and Horgan (2007) develop contrast cases based on observations about what the phenomenology of agency is not like.

> [I]t is certainly not like this: first experiencing an occurrent wish for your right hand to rise and your fingers to move into clenched position, and then passively experiencing your hand and fingers moving in just that way. Such phenomenal character might be called the phenomenology of fortuitously appropriate bodily motion. It would be very strange indeed, and very alien. Nor is the actional phenomenological character of the experience like this: first experiencing an occurrent wish for your right hand to rise and your fingers to move into clenched position, and then passively experiencing a causal process consisting of this wish's causing your hand to rise and your fingers to move into clenched position. Such phenomenal character might be called the passive phenomenology of psychological state-causation of bodily motion. (Horgan 2007: 8)

Horgan and colleagues take it, then, that what the phenomenology of agency is like cannot be characterized without reference to a proprietarily agentive property. They call this property self-as-source—'the what-it's like of self as source of the motion' (Horgan 2007: 8).

Uriah Kriegel (2015) offers a different characterization of proprietarily agentive phenomenal properties. Rather than self-as-source, Kriegel emphasizes the phenomenology of deciding, which involves a 'felt pull' to action, and of trying, which satisfies the tension inherent in decision's felt pull and involves the experience of 'mobilizing force in the face of resistance' (2015: 90). Kriegel considers a number of proposals that would reduce such phenomenal properties to perceptual or emotional properties, and argues they are all inadequate. Perhaps the most plausible such proposal is due to William James and emphasizes anticipatory imagery (for a similar proposal, see Prinz 2007). As Kriegel notes, 'on this view, the key element for capturing the conative dimension of the experience of clenching one's fist is the feel of imaginatively anticipating one's fist muscles contracting' (2015: 80). Against this proposal, Kriegel argues, first, that it gets the timing of the phenomenology wrong, placing it before the doing takes place. Second, it 'seems false to our experience'. Kriegel elaborates:

> We experience a representation of the act to follow, but also of the act following, and following because we *make* it follow. That is, we experience not only an anticipation of the act, but also the causing of the act in real time.   (Kriegel 2015: 80)

Although introspection has to play some role in an argument for proprietarily agentive phenomenology, it is important to note that empirical considerations can be brought to bear as well. In a recent paper Shepherd (2016) offers an empirically based argument against reductive proposals like James's. Shepherd observes that the best empirical reason to adopt a proposal like James's requires a close connection between phenomenology and the kinds of computational models posited to explain action control. Our best such models give an important functional role to states of anticipatory imagery. As we discussed earlier in the context of forward model predictions, such states are used to compare anticipated with actual perceptual feedback, in order to identify and correct errors in real time. But is there good reason to tie phenomenology to such states (and not others)?

Against such a move, Shepherd (2016) appeals to studies involving temporary paralysis. In these studies, participants try to perform various actions with various body parts. They report strong experiences of trying to move, but very little in the way of anticipatory imagery. Shepherd comments:

> The experiences of trying reported in these [experiments] cannot be explained by matches between predicted and actual feedback, since there was no actual feedback. Nor can they be explained by internally simulated feedback, or anticipations of feedback. For such feedback, if centrally involved in the experiences of trying, should produce experiences of the feedback simulated or anticipated. That is, such experiences should be (presumably, sensory) experiences of things happening at the relevant bodily sites. But...very little sensory experience was reported. The experiences reported were largely directive in nature, concerning the direction of effort to the body parts. And...experiences of trying were clearly distinct from

(though seemingly causally linked with) the sensory experience of body parts moving. (Shepherd 2016: 425–26)

Mylopoulos (2015) advances a different set of empirical considerations against views that would attempt to explain agentive phenomenology in terms of purely sensory phenomenology. Mylopoulos notes that such views come in reductive and non-reductive varieties. Reductive views attempt to identify agentive phenomenology with the phenomenology of familiar sensory modalities—most plausibly, proprioception, vision, or some combination. But such proposals have problems accommodating the full range of empirical data on action and experience. For example, stimulation of the motor cortex produces movement (as well as proprioceptive and visual experience of the body movement) but not—according to those whose motor cortex has been stimulated—any agentive phenomenology. Indeed, as Mylopoulos notes, it is difficult to see how a reductive proposal could account for the distinction we readily make between action and passive movement, for there seems to be no set of sensory qualities that mark the difference between 'actions as against non-actions' (2015: 774; see also Bermúdez 2010 for further discussion of this argument).

Non-reductive attempts at redescription must identify agentive phenomenology with a novel sensory modality. Bayne (2011a) makes a case for such a modality, connecting it to the Comparator Model of action control discussed above. In response, Mylopoulos (2015) observes that it is not clear why we should consider phenomenology attached to this model *sensory*. Further, Bayne's proposal makes failed predictions. Patients with anarchic hand syndrome display sophisticated sensorimotor control while denying that the movements of their hands are their own actions. But if agentive phenomenology is closely tied to the computational mechanisms responsible for sensorimotor control, anarchic hand patients should have agentive phenomenology. Mylopoulos notes that those sympathetic to Bayne's proposal might wish to invoke some additional element at some point—perhaps the presence of an intention in addition to low-level sensorimotor control. Doing so, however, further undermines the thought that the relevant phenomenology is sensory.

At the very least, then, it appears that the skeptic about proprietary agentive phenomenology faces serious problems. The skeptical view appears to lack empirical motivation. Further, the skeptical view is phenomenologically inadequate. The case for proprietarily agentive phenomenology appears strong.

8.2.2 Describing Agentive Phenomenology

Agentive phenomenology is complex. In addition to involving proprietarily agentive aspects, agentive phenomenology often involves a wide range of perceptual, emotional, and cognitive (as well as, arguably, metacognitive: see Section 8.1.4) experiences. Further, agentive phenomenology involves these experience-types in dynamic relationships that differ depending upon the agent's action-type, skill-level, and circumstances. Taxonomizing the relevant experience-types, and explaining their dynamic relationships with one another, is thus a difficult task. Unsurprisingly, those writers who have attempted the task have often used idiosyncratic terminology, and have frequently placed the emphasis in different places.

Agentive phenomenology is often referred to simply as 'the sense of agency'. A glance at the literature reveals the many different aspects of agentive phenomenology that this term has been used to capture. Some authors use it to emphasize the subjective feeling of control, as when Haggard and Chambon (2012) describe it as 'the experience of controlling one's own actions, and, through them, events in the outside world' (2012: R390). At other times, the focus is on self-attributing an action, as when Jeannerod (2007: 64) writes that it is 'the ability to identify oneself as the agent of a behavior or a thought' and Gallagher (2000: 15) glosses it as '[t]he sense that I am the one who is causing or generating an action'. Some prefer to focus on authorship or ownership, as when Marcel (2003: 54) depicts it as '[a] sense of oneself as an actor or a sense that actions are one's own', and Pacherie (2007: 2) defines it as 'the sense the agent has that he or she is the author of that action'. Finally one also finds the term being used to single out the sense of initiating or causing an action, as when Synofzik et al. (2008: 219) state that it is 'the registration that we are the initiators of our own actions' and Sato (2009: 74) characterizes it as the 'sense that one is causing an action'. At times there is also some focus not just on causing bodily actions, but the consequences of such actions, as when Blakemore and Frith (2003: 220) portray it as 'the feeling that we cause movements and their consequences'. In light of all the various ways that 'the sense of agency' has been used, we suggest retiring it in favor of more precise terminology.

To that end, in this section we propose an opinionated taxonomy that does as much justice as possible to what others have said. Our aim is to identify areas of implicit agreement and disagreement, and to make progress towards a more refined understanding of the descriptive shape of agentive phenomenology.[5]

In our view, reflection on agentive phenomenology—and reflection on what others have said about it—suggests six somewhat dissociable clusters. We will call these clusters the phenomenology of purposiveness (Section 8.2.2.1), the phenomenology of mineness (Section 8.2.2.2), the phenomenology of execution (Section 8.2.2.3), the phenomenology of action perception (Section 8.2.2.4), the phenomenology of action assessment (Section 8.2.2.5), and the phenomenology of free will (Section 8.2.2.6). Understanding the nature of these clusters, and how they conjoin and overlap in full-blown agentive phenomenology, is the central descriptive task facing the phenomenologist.

---

[5] Further questions include the ways these aspects of agentive phenomenology appear in various domains of action. For example, what is the best characterization of the phenomenology of expert (or skilled) action (see Shepherd 2015b; Christensen et al. 2016, Dow 2017)? What is the phenomenology of joint action like, and how does it differ from that of individual action (Pacherie 2012)? These questions deserve separate treatment, and as such will not occupy our attention here.

8.2.2.1 *Purposiveness*

A number of authors emphasize the purposiveness of agentive phenomenology. For example, David Hume (2000: 257) speaks of 'the internal impression we feel and are conscious of, when we knowingly give rise to any new motion of our body or new perception of our mind'. His language suggests that he regards the 'giving rise to' as fundamentally purposive.

Paul Ricoeur seems to echo the same idea. Contrasting the experience of willing with the experience of the body in action, Ricoeur writes 'the personal body presents itself as body-moved-by-a-willing, that is, as the terminus of a movement which *comes down from the "I" to its mass*' (1966: 220).

Both Carl Ginet and Brian O'Shaughnessy invoke cases without perceptual feedback to assert a similar view.

> It could seem to me that I voluntarily exert a force forward with my arm without at the same time its seeming to me that I feel the exertion happening: the arm feels kinesthetically anesthetized. (Ginet 1990: 28)

> Consider now the event of trying to move an arm whose psychologicality was revealed nakedly to view because of the complete absence of kinaesthetic experience...where was that psychological event, of which one was immediately aware, experienced as taking place? One is perhaps inclined to say one experienced it as being at the felt location of the arm. However, it seems to me that to do so would be to confuse the site of the target-object for the will, with the event of willing that is directed to that place. (O'Shaughnessy 2003: 351)

More recently, Uriah Kriegel characterizes the experience of trying—which as mentioned is a part of what Kriegel regards as the core of agentive phenomenology—in purposive terms, as 'a nonsensory analog of innervation (a feeling of a kind of nonsensible current traveling from will to muscle)' (2015: 95).

Regarding purposive phenomenology, a number of questions remain open. It is natural to consider purposiveness as that aspect of agentive phenomenology that is most clearly proprietary in the sense described above. But is this right? What is the relationship between purposiveness and intention? What is the relationship between purposiveness and the mechanisms that enable action control? We cannot discuss these questions here—we mention them as bookmarks for future research.

A further interesting question concerns the relationship between purposiveness and other aspects of agentive phenomenology—in particular, what we describe below as mineness phenomenology. Many of the passages above invoke the 'I' or the agent or some central place from which the experience emanates in describing the structure of purposive phenomenology. How are we to understand such language?

8.2.2.2 *Mineness*

It is often asserted that in consciously acting, agents experience their activity as in some sense their own. Horgan et al. (2003) call this feature self-as-source phenomenology.

According to them, 'You experience your arm, hand, and fingers as being moved by you yourself, rather than experiencing their motion either as fortuitously moving just as you want them to move or else as being transeuntly caused by your own mental states' (2003: 329). Similarly, Bayne and Levy (2006) emphasize what they call the experience of authorship, maintaining that 'it is not unlikely that the experience of authorship is essential to the experience of agency—that to experience a movement as one's own action necessarily involves an experience of oneself as the author of the movement' (2006: 56).

Beyond such initial assertions, how ought we to understand the phenomenology of mineness? One attractive option is to understand the phenomenology of mineness as implicit in the phenomenology of purposiveness. Consider the following characterization of the experience of trying.

> The directive character of experiences of trying...does not emanate from any bodily location. It is not incorrect to call it an experiential mandate. But in this case the mandate seems to emanate from the agent. When I have an experience of trying to raise my arm, I have an experience as of mandating that my arm rise. It is this fundamentally directive character that marks the experience out as an experience of trying. (Shepherd 2016: 421)

On the option under consideration, the experience as of mandating or directing bodily activity is at once purposive and implicitly agent-involving. That is to say, there need be no experience of a substantive self involved—the directive aspect of the phenomenology suffices to mark out the experience as both purposive, and as the agent's own.

A second option maintains that mineness and purposiveness are distinct, and that mineness is a primitive feature of agentive phenomenology. The italics in the following passage suggest that this is how Terry Horgan views mineness phenomenology.

> How...should one characterize the actional phenomenal dimension of the act of raising one's hand and clenching one's fingers, given that it is not the phenomenology of fortuitously appropriate bodily motion and it also is not the passive phenomenology of psychological event-causation of bodily motion? Well, it is the what-it's-like of *self as source* of the motion. You experience your arm, hand, and fingers as being moved *by you yourself*—rather than experiencing their motion either as fortuitously moving just as you want them to move, or passively experiencing them as being caused by your own mental states. You experience the bodily motion as caused by *yourself*. (Horgan 2007: 8)

A third option is to understand mineness phenomenology as a kind of cognitive or thought-like phenomenology, attached to a belief, knowledge-state, or thought to the effect that one is producing the action in question. In a recent paper Mylopoulos (2017) defends this option at length, arguing that agentive thoughts that one is A-ing can be viewed as anchoring mineness phenomenology in virtue of deploying the essential indexical.

It is worth noting that in addition to the intrinsic interest one might take in describing mineness phenomenology, one's descriptive account might have philosophical ramifications elsewhere. For example, agent causalists—those who hold that actions are caused by agents, as opposed to events or facts—might appeal to the phenomenology of mineness as support for their view. Whether such a move is sound will depend in part upon the nature of the phenomenology (see Bayne 2008 for discussion).

8.2.2.3 *Execution*

A third aspect of agentive phenomenology, closely related to purposiveness, is that of *execution*. Purposiveness involves aiming or directing one's efforts towards a certain outcome. But the phenomenology of agency often involves the sense that one is *doing* what one intends to do—not merely the sense of striving towards some goal, but of successfully achieving it.

Empirical work, too, suggests a dissociation between the subjective awareness of purposiveness and of action execution. In Libet's (Libet et al. 1983, Libet 1985) classic subjective timing studies, participants reported a feeling of 'deciding' or having an 'urge' to act that clearly preceded any awareness of performing the action in question (see footnote 2).

Having the sense that one is executing one's intended action is often intimately tied to an awareness of what one's body is doing and an evaluation of how *well* one is performing the action in question. We will discuss each of these further facets of agentive phenomenology in what follows, but first we address the question of how execution is tied to mineness.

Do mineness and execution dissociate? Here it is good to keep clear on the distinction between executing just *any* behavior and executing an intention in particular. It would seem that one can be aware of executing some behavior without an accompanying sense of mineness. For instance, in anarchic hand syndrome (AHS), a condition caused by a lesion to the supplementary motor area that results in loss of control over the movements of the contralesional limb, the agent is aware of executing various behaviors with that limb, for example, picking up objects, grasping at things, while lacking the subjective sense that the behaviour is theirs. Such patients say things like, 'I know it's me, it just doesn't *feel* like me' (as reported in Marcel 2003: 79). But importantly, this is not a case of executing *willed* behavior. Typically the anarchic limb does things that are at cross-purposes with the agent's conscious intentions. The agent may be trying to turn the page of a book, for example, while the anarchic hand closes it (Banks et al. 1989: 457). We emphasize that it is the sense of executing *willed* behaviour that we take to capture the executive component of agentive phenomenology.

A natural way of understanding the relationship between mineness and action execution is that awareness of executing one's intention is intimately—perhaps necessarily—connected with mineness phenomenology. This might be because an awareness of intention execution grounds mineness phenomenology in some way (yet to be understood). Or it could be because mineness phenomenology is in part constitutive of the awareness of intention execution.[6] These questions remain to be settled in future work.[7]

8.2.2.4 *Action Perception*

A fourth important aspect of agentive phenomenology involves the primarily perceptual experience of what is happening in the world, with the body, and with certain aspects of the mind, as one acts. Regarding perceptual experience in action, two broad areas are relevant. The first concerns the relative importance of perceptual experience to action control. Following the pioneering work of Milner and Goodale (1995) on conscious vision in action, some philosophers—most prominently Andy Clark (2001)—have suggested that contrary to appearances, conscious perception is of little importance for action control. Clark has maintained that 'although it may sometimes seem as if conscious seeing is what continuously and delicately guides our fine-tuned motor activity, such online control may be largely and typically devolved to distinct, nonconscious, visual-input-using systems' (2001: 511). Other philosophers have pushed back against this interpretation of Milner and Goodale, arguing instead that while conscious perception is not the only source of information for action control, for many action-types it remains functionally important (see Wallhagen 2007; Mole 2009; Shepherd 2016; Briscoe and Schwenkler 2015).

A second area of interest concerns the relationship between the phenomenology of perception and that of action.[8] In this connection, one interesting question raised recently in Shepherd (2016) is this. What is the relationship between one's proprietarily agentive phenomenology and the perceptual experiences one has while acting? Shepherd argues that in experiences of acting, experiences of trying and perceptual experiences fit together in a certain way.

---

[6] A further question surrounds cases of deviant causation. Could an agent experience both mineness and execution in spite of deviant causal chains linking intention and behavior? In our view, the answer to this question must proceed via examination of the kinds of mechanisms that generate both mineness and execution phenomenology. It is at least possible that these mechanisms do not depend directly on the causal chains linking intention and behavior. If so, one could have the illusion of execution and mineness in spite of deviant causal chains.

[7] Mylopoulos' (2017) aforementioned treatment of agentive phenomenology can be viewed as an attempt to explain how this might work via agentive thoughts that represent oneself as performing the intended action via the essential indexical, thus inextricably linking the experience of mineness to the experience of execution.

[8] Here we note two interesting issues that are beyond the present scope. The first concerns attempts to characterize actional aspects of perceptual experience. For example, Siegel (2014) argues that some perceptual experiences contain action mandates—something like commands that the agent do such-and-such. And Nanay (2013) has argued that perceptual experiences attribute action-properties (e.g., attribute climb-ability to a tree) that enable perceptual experiences to play the role of the immediate psychological precursors to action. The second concerns the proper role of attention in agentive phenomenology. One plausible view is that attention plays signature roles in structuring an agent's perception in action (Wu 2011). But it is possible that attention has a broader role than this. We leave this possibility for future research.

> The experience of acting typically consists of temporally extended experiences from more than one [perceptual] modality. These experiences are easily associated with the action being performed in virtue of the fact that their contents fit coherently into the agent's broader plan for action. And their contents fit coherently in virtue of the fact that they are functionally integrated and structured by what the agent is trying to do. (Shepherd (2016: 436))

On this view, the perceptual experiences that are typically co-conscious with agentive experiences are distinct from, but structured by what the agent is trying to do.

We flag a more radical option, while admitting that it remains unclear how best to explicate it. Consider the much-discussed claim that perceptual experiences are transparent in a certain way. On a standard construal of transparency, it is said that 'We normally "see right through" perceptual states to external objects and do not even notice that we are in perceptual states; the properties we are aware of in perception are attributed to the objects perceived' (Lycan 2015). Might the same thing be true of experiences of acting? On this view, one does not simply experience agentive aspects and perceptual aspects co-consciously. One 'sees through' these elements and experiences to the action itself—the agentive and perceptual aspects are attributed to the same unfolding event, namely, the action. The idea needs further development, but it is worth noting that on such a view, it could be that perceptual phenomenology plays a role in at least some experiences of execution and mineness. Execution, recall, is the experience of actually doing what it is one intends to do. And certainly what one intends to do often constitutively involves events in the body and the world beyond it. On such a view, then, phenomenology associated with mineness, execution, and perception in action would turn out to be very closely related. Such a prospect is tantalizing, but developing it is well beyond the present scope.

8.2.2.5 *Action Assessment*

A fifth cluster concerns experiences that seem to assess the action or some of its subcomponents. Here we have in mind experiences of error in action, experiences of success in action, of control over the action, of the ease (or difficulty) of the action, experiences of fatigue, frustration, or anxiety associated with the action, and experiences of engagement in the action, of exhilaration in acting, and more.

The experience-types mentioned above may not form a unified cluster. Consider the experience of error in action. Above our amateur skier recalled sensing, 'with alarm', that he was sliding backwards. This was not supposed to happen—it signaled a mistake. This experience seems clearly to have a function of assessment, although it is not clear how exactly to parse it—is the experience emotional, cognitive, or something else? Other experience-types in this cluster seem to involve sensory and bodily perception, in combination perhaps with the emotions. Notice the combination of bodily perception with a positive emotion of exhilaration in Hemingway's description of skiing: 'The rush and the sudden swoop as he dropped down a steep undulation in the mountainside plucked Nick's mind out and left him only the wonderful flying, dropping sensation in his body' (Hemingway 1995: 121).

We cannot offer a full account of this cluster here. We do, however, wish to highlight an interesting account of a subset of action assessment experiences, due to Joelle Proust (2013). According to Proust, a certain class of nonconceptual metacognitive experiences plays an important role for mental acts, and by extension for agency (insofar as mental acts are crucial for exercises of agency more generally; see Section 8.1.4 for discussion of metacognition and the sense of bodily agency). Proust calls these 'noetic feelings'— feelings associated with the feasibility of performing a mental act like remembering some content. For Proust these feelings are nonconceptual in the sense that one need not deploy or possess concepts to have them. And these feelings are metacognitive in the sense that the psychological mechanisms that produce them 'have the function of assessing one's cognitive dispositions as such' with respect to their ability to fulfill various epistemic functions (2013: 165). That is, these feelings track '"cognitive adequacy," that is, the correct evaluation of the resources available/needed for a given mental task, of such and such import' (2013: 224). These feelings are critical for initiating, sustaining, and guiding the operation of various mental actions.

> In a mental action...the subject needs to appreciate the normative status of the output of the mental act: is the name retrieved correct? Has the list been exhaustively reproduced? Here...a subject is sensitive to the norms involved in self-evaluation through a global impression, including feelings of fluency, coherence, and so on... (Proust 2013: 155)

There is much more to Proust's account than this. Here, it suffices to note that she has identified an interesting class of experiences that are, if she is right, crucial for the kinds of mental actions that make up a large part of agentive phenomenology. Reflection on Proust's account, and on these kinds of 'noetic feelings' generally, seems like a worthwhile endeavor for the agentive phenomenologist.

8.2.2.6 *Freedom*

A sixth cluster revolves around the phenomenology of free will. Philosophers are divided on a number of questions surrounding this phenomenology. Is there a phenomenology of free will for all actions, or only for certain ones (e.g., decisions) (see Mylopoulos and Lau 2014 for some doubts on both counts)? Is the phenomenology better understood as a component of another cluster (e.g., of mineness: see Horgan et al. 2003), or is it a separate, primitive element of agentive phenomenology? Is there a phenomenology of free will at all? On these questions, there is no consensus.[9]

Certainly the primary question regarding the phenomenology of free will concerns how it maps onto philosophical positions on the nature of free will. Many philosophers appear to believe that the phenomenology is libertarian in the sense that if the

---

[9] For a more expansive treatment of the phenomenology of freedom, see the appendix in Kriegel (2015).

experience were veridical, libertarianism—the view that free will is incompatible with determinism, and that we possess free will—would be true. Here is C. A. Campbell in a representative passage.

> Everyone must make the introspective experiment for himself: but I may perhaps venture to report...that I cannot help believing that it lies with me here and now, quite absolutely, which of two genuinely open possibilities I adopt.   (Campbell 1951: 463)

Other philosophers find nothing in their phenomenology suggesting libertarianism, although different reasons are offered for this position. Horgan (2012) argues that introspection is not powerful enough to tell us whether agentive phenomenology includes libertarian contents. Grünbaum (1952: 672) argues that the phenomenology is straightforwardly compatibilist: 'this feeling simply discloses that we were able to act in accord with our strongest desire at that time, and that we could indeed have acted otherwise if a different motive had prevailed at the time'.[10]

Finally, there are those who adopt an intermediate position, according to which our phenomenology involves *both* compatibilist and libertarian elements. Strawson (2010), for instance, maintains that our unreflective stance towards our desires involves the full awareness that we cannot choose them—that they are 'just there' (2010: 92). And yet, he urges that we have a compatibilist reaction to this, on which 'it remains true that their just-thereness is not seen as posing any sort of threat to our freedom' (2010: 93). Still, there remains another aspect to our experience that according to Strawson is 'profoundly libertarian' (2010: 90) in character, centrally involving a sense of oneself as a 'self-determining "agent-self"' (2010: 93) that is 'separate from, and somehow irreducibly over and above, all its particular desires, pro-attitudes, and so on' (2010: 93).

How might we resolve this dispute? Suppose that there is at least some phenomenology suggestive of free will attached to experiences of deciding and acting. Even if so, it remains unclear how to further characterize this phenomenology: and it is notable in this connection that libertarians typically rest content with the assertion that the phenomenology is libertarian, rather than providing further description. But a range of descriptive options are available. Is the relevant phenomenology cognitive or thought-like in nature, attached to anticipatory imagery of action-possibilities, perceptual, proprietarily agentive, or something else? Offering a further characterization of this experience may help us to see whether or how the experience could have a content that rules out deterministic causation.

Here is one example of what we have in mind. In a recent paper Chandra Sripada (2016) argues that elements of the phenomenology of freedom are connected with the

---

[10] In a similar vein, Oisin Deery (2015), drawing on a view of David Chalmers's regarding the content of color experience, has developed an intermediate view on behalf of the philosophical (but not the phenomenological) compatibilist. On Deery's view, the phenomenology of free will may contain both libertarian and compatibilist contents. The view is offered to the compatibilist as a way of maintaining that the phenomenology of freedom could be veridical even if determinism is true, thus blocking one libertarian route to the existence of libertarian free will. We refer interested readers to Deery's paper.

activity of deliberation. As Sripada has it, in deliberation we go about constructing sets of options relevant to the decision problem(s) we face. In three different senses, Sripada uses the language of space to characterize features of these sets of options. First, some option sets are narrow or spacious in the sense that the relevant options are few or many. Second, some option sets are narrow or spacious in the sense that the distance between the relevant options—roughly, it seems, the different kinds of futures associated with taking one or another option—is great or small. Third, some option sets are narrow or spacious in the sense that the options one could include within them are many or few.

Building slightly on what Sripada says, it appears that different experience-types are associated with these features of option set construction. We sometimes experience our options as narrow or constricting. We sometimes experience what Sripada calls the spaciousness of our options. We sometimes experience what Sripada calls movement between options. When the distance between options is great, Sripada observes that 'the gap that separates [options] is massive; it is dizzying to traverse it' (2016: 16). And when we recognize that the options we could include in our set are many, we experience what Sripada calls unboundedness.

Sripada stresses that all of this is consistent with compatibilism. Moving beyond Sripada, one might suggest that these elements of the phenomenology of freedom could be deployed in a deflationary explanation of claims regarding libertarian phenomenology. Could it be that the experience of relative unboundedness in deliberation, or relative spaciousness and movement at the time of a decision, are wrongly interpreted as a libertarian ability to do otherwise? The suggestion has at least some plausibility, especially for those who find it difficult to see how phenomenology could be suggestive of indeterministic causation.

8.3 Conclusion

At the beginning of this chapter we glossed agentive phenomenology as the set of those experience-types associated with exercises of agency, and paradigmatically with intentional action. Given the many ways agents act intentionally, one might expect the relevant experience-types to form a broad and diverse class. Our discussion here bears that out. Empirical work on the sources of agentive phenomenology has made some progress in elucidating the kind of psychological mechanisms that undergird it. But as we noted, this work has often suffered from a lack of clarity regarding the target of explanation. One and the same study might measure and probe multiple aspects of phenomenology simultaneously, some proprietarily agentive and others not. In order to both make salient this concern, and make some progress in addressing it, we divided the experience-types that we take to constitute (exhaustively or at least nearly so) agentive phenomenology into six clusters, which we called the phenomenology of purposiveness, mineness, execution, action perception, action assessment, and freedom. Each cluster raises its own interesting questions, and questions remain about the relationships between the clusters. We are hopeful that progress on these questions may serve to help guide future empirical work.

References

Balslev, D., Cole, J., and Miall, R. C. (2007), 'Proprioception contributes to the sense of agency during visual observation of hand movements: evidence from temporal judgments of action', *Journal of Cognitive Neuroscience*, 19/9: 1535–41.

Banks, G., Short, P., Martínez, A. J., Latchaw, R., Ratcliff, G., and Boller, F. (1989), 'The Alien Hand Syndrome: Clinical and Postmortem Findings', *Archives of Neurology*, 46/4: 456–9.

Bayne, T. (2008), 'The Phenomenology of Agency', *Philosophy Compass*, 3/1: 182–202.

Bayne, T. (2011a), 'The Sense of Agency', in F. Macpherson (ed.), *The Senses*. Oxford: Oxford University Press, 490–524.

Bayne, T. (2011b), 'Libet and The Case for Free Will Scepticism', in R. Swinburne (ed.), *Free Will and Modern Science*. Oxford: Oxford University Press.

Bayne, T. and Levy, N. (2006), 'The Feeling of doing: Deconstructing The Phenomenology of Agency', in W. P. N. Sebanz (ed.), *Disorders of Volition*. Cambridge, MA: MIT Press, 49–68.

Bayne, T. and Pacherie, E. (2007), 'Narrators and Comparators: The Architecture of Agentive Self-awareness', *Synthese*, 159: 475–491.

Bear, A., and Bloom, P. (2016), 'A Simple Task Uncovers a Postdictive Illusion of Choice', *Psychological Science*, 1: 9.

Bermúdez, J. L. (2010), 'Action and Awareness of Agency: Comments on Christopher Frith', *Pragmatics and Cognition*, 18/3: 584–96.

Blakemore, S. J. and Frith, C. (2003), 'Self-awareness and Action', *Current Opinion in Neurobiology*, 13/2: 219–24.

Blakemore, S. J., Frith, C. D., and Wolpert, D. M. (1999), 'Spatio-temporal Prediction Modulates the Perception of Self-produced Stimuli', *Journal of Cognitive Neuroscience*, 11/5: 551–9.

Blakemore, S. J., Oakley, D. A., and Frith, C.D. (2003), 'Delusions of Alien Control in The Normal Brain', *Neuropsychologia*, 41/8: 1058–67.

Brentano, F. (1874), *Psychologie vom empirischen Standpunkte* (Vol. 1). Duncker & Humblot.

Briscoe, R. and Schwenkler, J. (2015), 'Conscious Vision in Action', *Cognitive Science*, 39/7: 1435–67.

Campbell, C. A. (1951), 'Is Free Will a Pseudo-Problem?' *Mind*, 60/240: 441–65.

Carruthers, G. (2012), 'The Case for The Comparator Model as An Explanation of The Sense of Agency and its Breakdowns', *Consciousness and Cognition*, 21: 30–45.

Carruthers, G. (2015), 'A metacognitive model of the feeling of agency over bodily actions', *Psychology of Consciousness: Theory, Research, and Practice*, 2/3: 210–21.

Carruthers, P. (2007), 'The Illusion of Conscious Will', *Synthese*, 159/2: 197–213.

Chambon, V., Wenke, D., Fleming, S. M., Prinz, W., and Haggard, P. (2012). 'An online neural substrate for sense of agency', *Cerebral Cortex*, 23/5: 1031–7.

Chambon, V., Filevich, E., and Haggard, P. (2014), 'What is the Human Sense of Agency, and is it Metacognitive?' in S. M. Fleming and C. D. Firth (eds), *The Cognitive Neuroscience of Metacognition* Springer Berlin Heidelberg, 321–42.

Christensen, W., Sutton, J., and McIlwain, D. J. (2016), 'Cognition in Skilled Action: Meshed Control and The Varieties of Skill Experience', *Mind & Languag,e* 31/1: 37–66.

Clark, A. (2001), 'Visual Experience and Motor Action: Are the Bonds Too Tight?' *Philosophical Review*, 110: 495–519.

Daprati, E., Franck, N., Georgieff, N., Proust, J., Pacherie, E., Dalery, J., and Jeannerod, M. (1997), 'Looking for the Agent: An Investigation into Consciousness of Action and Self-Consciousness in Schizophrenic Patients', *Cognition*, 65: 71–86.

de Biran, F. M. M. (1932), 'Essai sur les fondements de la psychologie (1812)', *Edition Tisserand des Œuvres de Maine de Biran, tomes VIII et IX*, Alcan.

Deery, O. (2015), 'The Fall from Eden: Why Libertarianism Isn't Justified by Experience', *Australasian Journal of Philosophy*, 93/2: 319–34.

Dow, J. M. (2017), 'Just Doing What I Do: On the Awareness of Fluent Agency', *Phenomenology and the Cognitive Sciences*, 16/1: 155–77.

Farrer, C., Franck, N., Georgieff, N., Frith, C. D., Decety, J. and Jeannerod, M. (2003), 'Modulating the Experience of Agency: A Positron Emission Tomography Study', *Neuroimage* 18/2: 324–33.

Fourneret, P. and Jeannerod, M. (1998), 'Limited Conscious Monitoring of Motor Performance in Normal Subjects', *Neuropsychologia* 36/11: 1133–40.

Gallagher, S. (2000), 'Philosophical conceptions of the self: implications for cognitive science', *Trends in Cognitive Sciences*, 4/1, 14–21.

Ginet, C. (1990), *On Action*. Cambridge: Cambridge University Press.

Grünbaum, A. (1952), 'Causality and the Science of Human Behavior', *American Scientist*, 40/4: 665–76.

Haggard, P. and Chambon, V. (2012), 'Sense of Agency' *Current Biology*, 22/10: R390–R392.

Haggard, P., Clark, S., and Kalogeras, J. (2002), 'Voluntary Action and Conscious Awareness', *Nature Neuroscience*, 5/4: 382–5.

Hemingway, E. (1995), 'Cross Country Snow', in J. Fenton (ed.), *Ernest Hemingway: The Collected Stories*. London: Everyman's Library.

Horgan, T. (2007), 'Agentive Phenomenal Intentionality and the Limits of Introspection', *Psyche*, 13/1: 1–29.

Horgan, T. (2012), 'From Agentive Phenomenology to Cognitive Phenomenology: A Guide for the Perplexed', in T. Bayne and M. Montague (eds), *Cognitive Phenomenology*. New York: Oxford University Press, 57–78.

Horgan, T., Tienson, J., and George, G. (2003), 'The Phenomenology of First-person Agency', in S. Walter and H. Heinz-Dieter (eds.), *Physicalism and Mental Causation*. Exeter: Imprint Academic, 323–40.

Hume, D. (2000), *A Treatise of Human Nature*, D. F. Norton and M. J. Norton (eds), Oxford: Oxford University Press.

James, W. (1880), *The Feeling of Effort* (Vol. 14), The Society.

Jeannerod, M. (2007), 'Being Oneself', *Journal of Physiology—Paris*, 101/4: 161–8.

Kriegel, U. (2015), *The Varieties of Consciousness*. New York: Oxford University Press.

Koriat, A. (2000), 'The feeling of knowing: Some Metatheoretical implications for consciousness and control', *Consciousness and Cognition*, 9/2: 149–71.

Lau, H. C., Rogers, R. D., Haggard, P., and Passingham, R. E. (2004), 'Attention to Intention', *Sciencei*, 303/5661: 1208–10.

Libet, B. (1985), 'Unconscious cerebral initiative and the role of conscious will in voluntary action', *Behavioral and Brain Sciences*, 8/4: 529–39.

Libet, B., Gleason, C. A., Wright, E. W., and Pearl, D. K. (1983), 'Time of Conscious Intention to Act in Relation to Onset of Cerebral Activity (Readiness-potential). The Unconscious Initiation of a Freely Voluntary Act', *Brain*, 106: 623–42.

Lycan, W. (2015), 'Representational Theories of Consciousness', in E. N. Zalta (ed.), *The Stanford Encyclopedia of Philosophy* (Summer 2015 Edition), <http://plato.stanford.edu/archives/sum2015/entries/consciousness-representational/>.

Marcel, A. (2003), 'The Sense of Agency: Awareness and Ownership of Action', in J. Roessler and N. Eilan (eds), *Agency and Self-awareness: Issues in Philosophy and Psychology*. Oxford: Oxford University Press, 48–93.

Mele, A. (2009), *Effective Intentions: The Power of Conscious Will*. Oxford: Oxford University Press.

Mele, A. (2010), 'Conscious Deciding and the Science of Free Will', in R. Baumeister, A. Mele, and K. Vohs (eds), *Free Will and Consciousness: How Might They Work?* Oxford: Oxford University Press.

Merleau-Ponty, M. (1996), *Phenomenology of Perception*, C. Smith (trans.). (New Delhi: Motilal Banarsidass Publishers).

Metcalfe, J., Eich, T. S., and Miele, D. B. (2013), 'Metacognition of Agency: Proximal Action and Distal Outcome', *Experimental Brain Research*, 229/3: 485–96.

Milner, R. D. and Goodale, M. A. (1995), *The Visual Brain in Action*. Oxford: Oxford University Press.

Mole, C. (2009), 'Illusions, Demonstratives and the Zombie Action Hypothesis', *Mind*, 118/472: 995–1011.

Mylopoulos, M. (2012), 'Evaluating the Case for the Low-level Approach to Agentive Awareness', *Philosophical Topics*, 40/2: 103–27.

Mylopoulos, M. I. (2015), 'Agentive Awareness is Not Sensory Awareness', *Philosophical Studies*, 172/3: 761–80.

Mylopoulos, M. (2017), 'A Cognitive Account of Agentive Awareness', *Mind & Language*, 32/5: 545–63.

Mylopoulos, M. I. and Lau, H. (2014), 'Naturalizing Free Will', in A. Mele (ed.), *Surrounding Free Will: Philosophy, Psychology, Neuroscience*. Oxford: Oxford University Press.

Nahmias, E. (2005), 'Agency, Authorship, and Illusion', *Consciousness and Cognition*, 14: 771–85.

Nanay, B. (2013), *Between Perception and Action*. Oxford: Oxford University Press.

O'Shaughnessy, B. (2003), *Consciousness and the World*. Oxford: Clarendon Press.

Pacherie, E. (2007), 'The sense of control and the sense of agency', *Psyche*, 13/1: 1–30.

Pacherie, E. (2008), 'The Phenomenology of Action: A Conceptual Framework', *Cognition*, 107: 179–217.

Pacherie, E. (2012), 'The Phenomenology of Joint Action: Self-Agency vs. Joint-Agency', in Axel Seemann (ed.), *Joint Attention: New Developments*. Cambridge, MA: MIT Press.

Prinz, J. J. (2007), 'All Consciousness is Perceptual', in B. P. McLaughlin and J. Cohen (eds), *Contemporary Debates in Philosophy of Mind*. Malden, MA: Blackwell Publishing Ltd.

Proust, J. (2013), *The Philosophy of Metacognition: Mental Agency and Self-awareness*. Oxford: Oxford University Press.

Randall, W. (2009), *Another Long Day on the Piste: A Season in the French Alps* (London: Little, Brown Book Group).

Ricoeur, P. (1966), *Freedom and Nature: The Voluntary and the Involuntary* (Vol. 1). Evanston, IL: Northwestern University Press.

Sartre, J. P. (1969), *Being and Nothingness: An Essay on Phenomenological Ontology*, H.E. Barnes (trans.). New York: Washington Square Press.

Sato, A. (2009), 'Both motor prediction and conceptual congruency between preview and action-effect contribute to explicit judgment of agency', *Cognition*, 110/1: 74–83.

Schurger, A., Sitt, J. D., and Dehaene, S. (2012), 'An Accumulator Model for Spontaneous Neural Activity Prior to Self-initiated Movement', *Proceedings of the National Academy of Science*, 109/42: E2904–13.

Schurger, A., Mylopoulos, M., and Rosenthal, D. (2016), 'Neural Antecedents of Spontaneous Voluntary Movement: A New Perspective', *Trends in Cognitive Sciences*, 20/2: 77–9.

Shepherd, J. (2013), 'The Apparent Illusion of Conscious Deciding', *Philosophical Explorations*, 16/1: 18–30.

Shepherd, J. (2015a), 'Scientific Challenges to Free Will and Moral Responsibility', *Philosophy Compass*, 10/3: 197–207.

Shepherd, J. (2015b), 'Conscious Control over Action', *Mind & Language*, 30/3: 320–44.

Shepherd, J. (2016), 'Conscious Action/Zombie Action', *Noûs*, 50/2: 419–44.

Siegel, S. (2014), 'Affordances and the Content of Perception', in B. Brogaard (ed.), *Does Perception Have Content?* Oxford: Oxford University Press, 51–75.

Sripada, C. (2016), 'Free Will and the Construction of Options', *Philosophical Studies*, 173/11: 2913–33.

Strawson, G. (2010), *Freedom and Belief (Revised Edition)*. Oxford: Oxford University Press.

Synofzik, M., Vosgerau, G., and Newen, A. (2008), 'Beyond the Comparator Model: A Multifactorial Two-step Account of Agency', *Consciousness and Cognition*, 17/1: 219–39.

Synofzik, M., Thier, P., Leube, D. T., Schlotterbeck, P., and Lindner, A. (2010), 'Misattributions of Agency in Schizophrenia are Based on Imprecise Predictions about the Sensory Consequences of One's Actions', *Brain*, 133/1: 262–71.

Wallhagen, M. (2007), 'Consciousness and Action: Does Cognitive Science Support (Mild) Epiphenomenalism?' *British Journal for the Philosophy of Science*, 58/3: 539–61.

Wegner, D. M. (2002), *The Illusion of Conscious Will*. Cambridge, MA: Bradford Books.

Wegner, D. M. (2004), 'Précis of the Illusion of Conscious Will', *Behavioral and Brain Sciences*, 27/5: 649–59.

Wegner, D. M. and Wheatley, T. P. (1999), 'Apparent Mental Causation: Sources of the Experience of Will', *American Psychologist*, 54: 480–92.

Wenke, D., Fleming, S. M., and Haggard, P. (2010), 'Subliminal Priming of Actions Influences Sense of Control over Effects of Action', *Cognition*, 115/1: 26–38.

Wood, J. M. (2014), 'Hume and the Phenomenology of Agency', *Canadian Journal of Philosophy*, 44/3–4: 496–517.

Wu, W. (2011), 'What is Conscious Attention?' *Philosophy and Phenomenological Research*, 82/1: 93–120.

CHAPTER 9

TEMPORAL CONSCIOUSNESS

PHILIPPE CHUARD

You saw the crash, all of it: the cyclist swerving left to avoid a duckling on the trail, then losing control and heading straight for the tree. You heard it too: the duck quacking in fright, the cyclist swearing, the collision against the tree trunk. Perceptual experiences like these seem to relate to time in at least two ways.

First, conscious experiences *occur in time*, occupying temporal locations and intervals. If experiences are psychological *events*, they persist by *perduring*, the assumption goes: spreading out though time in virtue of their distinct temporal parts. Experiences, like their temporal parts, instantiate temporal properties and relations: duration, succession, etc.

Second, sensory experiences relate to time by way of their *intentional* or *representational content*.[1] Seeing the crash involves seeing the cyclist's *trajectory*, *speed*, how the collision *succeeds* their zooming out of the trail, how long it took to reach the tree. The temporal features of perceived events—change, succession, order, duration—appear to be presented in conscious sensory experience.

These 'temporal' aspects of experience—and their possible interactions—raise three related questions, central to our understanding of temporal consciousness:

Q1: how do sensory experiences carry information about, or make us aware of, some of the temporal features of perceived events (if at all)—in what format, by what mechanisms?
Q2: do the temporal properties of conscious experiences—including the arrangement of their temporal parts—play any role in how these experiences present or represent the temporal properties of perceived events?
Q3: how does such temporal representation manifest itself in the phenomenology of the relevant experiences?

---

[1] I aim to remain neutral on whether perceptual experiences have representational contents or consist instead of a direct intentional relation of the sort naïve realists posit.

Most theories of temporal consciousness, we shall see, can be divided in terms of how they treat these questions. This chapter begins with a brief sketch of the main theories currently on the market (Section 9.1) and some of their background assumptions (Section 9.2); it then moves to a—also brief—critical review of some of the arguments at the center of the dispute (Section 9.3).

9.1 THE THEORETICAL LANDSCAPE (OR PARTS THEREOF)

Accounts of temporal experiences tend to converge on the following, at least. Most grant that (i) conscious experiences are events, some extended in time with proper temporal parts. All agree that (ii) worldly events can be perceived and that (iii) some perceptual experiences cause, or serve as bases for, perceptual judgments about the temporal properties of those events. Finally, there is little disagreement over whether (iv) phenomenologically, many such experiences strike us in the following manner: perceived events and their successive temporal parts appear to 'flow in a seamless fashion' with 'constant' 'renewal of content', where each experience or temporal part thereof 'flows into' the next in a 'subjectively continuous' manner 'without any apparent gap' (Dainton 2000: 114, 119, 2014a: 125; 2017: sect 3). Beyond that, there are relatively subtle disagreements over how (i)–(iv) ought to be accounted for, involving different conceptions of the temporal ontology of experiences and of their temporal content.

9.1.1 Snapshots

One account goes back to several remarks of Locke (1690), Hume (1739), and Reid (1855). As I understand it (read: according to a version I find more promising), perceptual experiences amount to no more than very short-lived—perhaps even instantaneous—conscious events occurring in succession.[2] Should it seem counterintuitive that we have such short *experiences*, no harm is done replacing the term 'experience' by 'sensory event' or 'experiential snapshot'.[3] What matters is that these short psychological events instantiate some typically *experiential*—especially phenomenal and intentional—

---

[2] In principle, the shortest temporal parts of experience could be strictly unextended, 'chunky' (with a tiny extension, either fixed or variable, and a minimum to be determined empirically), or gunky (extended but infinitely divisible): see Dainton (2000: sect 7.3; 2014a: 113–19; 2017: Appendix 1, sect 2; Appendix 2, sect 5) and Le Poidevin (2007: ch. 7).

[3] *Genuine* experiences, Grube (2014) insists, meet 'downstream' requirements, like the ability to refer to experienced objects (2014: 26) and to form beliefs about them (2014: 25). If temporal parts of experiences (taken individually) are too short to meet such desiderata, they are not really *experiences*, he concludes. Note: Grube does not argue that those shortest temporal parts lack phenomenal or intentional properties, only that their having them has no impact on cognitive functions: they cannot be introspected,

properties. One could of course label the *successions* of such short experiential events 'experiences'. Those successions, however, are just *that*: temporally ordered mereological fusions of their briefest temporal parts—a 'continued train of distinguishable ideas' in Locke's terms (1690: ch. XIV, sect 6).

A propos their intentional features, no snapshot presents or represents temporal relations between non-simultaneous events, the view insists: each such snapshot presents only the briefest temporal part of a perceived event and some of its features, whichever causally prompted it (its distal stimulus). When things go well, an experiential snapshot is generated by a neurological process resulting from the stimulation of a sensory organ by some temporal part of a perceived event.[4]

The bare-bones of this 'snapshot' view thus include:

The snapshot conception:[5]
(i) *metaphysical thesis*: there are very brief experiential events occurring in succession.
(ii) *intentional thesis*: no short-lived experiential event presents/represents any temporal relation between non-simultaneous perceived events.[6]

In a sense, then, we do not sensorily perceive temporal relations between non-simultaneous worldly events or their temporal parts (no succession, order, duration, or change), the snapshot theorist has it: none of the snapshots making up successions thereof presents or conveys any explicit information about such temporal features of perceived events. As Hume put it: 'The idea of time is not deriv'd from a particular impression mix'd up with others, and plainly distinguishable from them; but arises altogether from the manner, in which impressions appear to the mind, without making one of the number' (Hume 1739: Book I, part II, sect 3)[7]

That is not to say we do not perceive extended events: we do, by successively perceiving their successive temporal parts, for one. Likewise with motion and change, if '[m]otion isn't something that takes place *at* a single point, it is essentially *interval-bound*' (Dainton 2014a: 113): we successively perceive *successive stages constitutive* of motion or change.

Nor does the view imply that we cannot form perceptual judgments and beliefs about such events or *their temporal features*. Successions of experiential snapshots, along with various types of memories thereof (episodic as well as iconic or echoic memories,

---

do not ground thoughts about what they represent—though he seems to grant that successive experiential snapshots could jointly meet such 'downstream' requirements (2014: 28).

[4] The proposal rests only on causal constraints on perception, and should be kept separate from Reid's contention that snapshots are 'confined to the present moment of time' (1855, essay 3, ch 5).

[5] Also: the 'cinematic view', the 'Lockean view', 'atomism', the 'zoetrope conception' (James 1890: 200; Phillips 2011), or the 'flipbook account' (Justin Fisher, p.c.).

[6] See Koch (2004), Kelly (2005a, 2005b), Chuard (2011, 2017), and Le Poidevin (2007: chs 6–7). And for a useful review, Dainton (2017: sect 4).

[7] Compare Le Poidevin (2007: 98–9).

for instance), together with background beliefs and expectations, can lead one to recognize—automatically or immediately, as it were—a succession of perceived temporal parts of an event as those of a cyclist swerving around a duck, say. In the same manner, the perceived temporal parts of an event can be recognized as succeeding other temporal parts experienced earlier. And noticeable differences between successively experienced temporal parts can be recognized as changes in the motion, speed, and trajectory of a swerving cyclist (*ditto* with other perceptible qualities).

As for the phenomenology of temporal experiences, the snapshot theorist views it as *supervening* upon (a) the successive arrangement of the phenomenal properties of successive experiential snapshots, together with the fact (*when* it is one) that (b) there is no *apparent gap* between adjacent snapshots (even *if* there *are* gaps, they might be too short or too fast to be detected), and (c) the succession of contents of successive snapshots appears smooth and gradual, with a relatively high degree of similarity and overlap from one content to the next (no apparent jump in content).[8] Hence, the seeming continuity of the flow of experience, on this view, owes largely to the seemingly smooth pace of transition between successive snapshots: it does not call for substantive connections between adjacent snapshots other than the *mere absence of noticeable disunity or discontinuity*.[9]

Yet, at least since William James (1890: 628–9) observed that 'a succession of feelings, in and of itself, is not a feeling of succession', the snapshot conception hasn't enjoyed much of a positive reception, at least in philosophical circles. Its critics, mostly on phenomenological grounds (see Section 9.3), have rejected the view as 'bold, even heroic' but not 'very promising' (Dainton 2014b: 177), so as to 'proceed on the assumption that the Snapshot View is wrong' (Lee 2014a: 2) and alternatives much preferable.

9.1.2 Extended Experiences

The extensionalist alternative treats temporal experiences as *essentially extended in time*: the relevant experiences have a duration of a few seconds or so, perhaps less, corresponding to the longest limit within which non-simultaneous events can be jointly 'present in consciousness' (Dainton 2000: 122), 'experienced together', or 'apprehended as unified' (Dainton 2017: sect 1.2)—this is the 'specious present' (Dainton 2000: 113).[10] Extended experiences have temporal parts, yet it is the whole experience composed of those parts which has *explanatory priority*: since perceived events often are temporally extended, experiences of such events must be extended too, the extensionalist rationale goes (Dainton 2000: 114, 2014b: 178; Phillips 2014a: 149–50, 2018: 293–4). But it isn't *just*

---

[8] Note how this version ascribes no role to memory in characterizing the phenomenology of successions of snapshots: memory only serves a cognitive function in the transition from successions of snapshots to the formation of perceptual beliefs—presumably, memory is also crucial for the introspection of such successions.

[9] Compare Dennett (1991: 356).

[10] On this notion, see Dainton (2017: appendix 1) and Strawson (2009: 250–5).

that such experiences have duration, as we shall see—after all, successions of snapshots do too: whole extended experiences are the prime unit of extensionalist explanation since, the thought seems to go, they are not *fully reducible* to their successive temporal parts.[11]

The *content* of extended experiences is said to be 'dynamic' at least in the sense that, being extended in time, such experiences can represent the dynamic features of objects and events—such as a 'ball moving and falling' (Dainton 2008: 372). In short, extensionalists reject the snapshot theory in both the following respects:

Extensionalism:
(i) *metaphysical thesis*: perceptual experiences are temporally extended and irreducible to mere successions of their temporal parts.
(ii) *intentional thesis*: such experiences, by virtue of their extension, can present or represent temporal relations between non-simultaneous perceived events.[12]

Beyond this skeletal portrayal, the details of the extensional view can be developed in different ways—here I focus on two recent contenders.[13]

On Dainton's 'overlap' model, what needs to be added to a succession of temporal parts of experience is a primitive relation of 'co-consciousness' between adjacent temporal parts (2000: 113): these relations, the absence of which would result in a 'disruption in experienced phenomenal flow' (2000: 131), are meant to explain how parts linked by co-consciousness combine into 'unified' whole experiences (2000: 166; 2008: 370–1; 2014b: 178). Any pair of adjacent co-conscious parts will form a unified whole, which overlaps previous and subsequent similar wholes, by sharing some of the very same temporal parts. This overlapping structure, Dainton claims, is 'responsible for the moment-to-moment phenomenal continuity' characteristic of temporal experiences (2008: 372; 2014a: 125; 2014b: 179, 184).

Yet co-consciousness and overlap are not enough, Dainton sometimes insists (2000: 173–6; 2014a: 107): the 'phenomenal flow' of experience has a direction, though the mereological structure of the overlap model is 'symmetrical with respect to time' (2000: 173). An additional ingredient comes from the *contents* of temporal experiences: 'most contents of immediate experience are not momentary, they possess some short duration, and consequently these contents possess an intrinsic temporal organization', which is 'dynamic'—in the sense, this time, that 'the flow of passage in experience is included in the phenomenal content of experience' (2000: 175–7). It is this 'inherent directional dynamism' of temporal contents that is supposed to explain how an experienced temporal part of a perceived event seems to be 'flowing into' the next (2014a: 107).

---

[11] Note that extended successions of snapshots also are 'the unit of explanation' for the snapshot theorist.

[12] Dainton (2000, 2008, 2014a, 2014b, 2017), Hoerl (2012, 2013), Phillips (2010, 2011, 2014a), as well as Soteriou (2010, 2013) and Strawson (2009: Part 5).

[13] For a broader survey: Dainton (2000: chs 6–7; 2017: sect 5).

While Dainton exploits the mereological structure built upon co-consciousness relations between parts of experience, he has appeared reluctant to embrace any substantive holistic proposal according to which whole experiences determine the phenomenal and intentional features of their temporal parts (2000: ch. 8; 2010). This contrasts with Phillips' avowedly *holistic* version of extensionalism: he advocates that, insofar as temporal representation is concerned, 'the content of our experience at very short timescales is metaphysically dependent on the content of experience over longer timescales' (2011: 810).[14] For instance,

> Thus, imagine that, over a half-second period, a batsman experiences a ball's motion from one end of the wicket to the other. It will not be true that, at an *instant* during this period, the batsman has *an experience* of any of the ball's motion. Nonetheless, it may be true that he is *experiencing* the ball's motion at that instant in virtue of that instant being a temporal subpart of a longer experience that has the ball's motion as object. (Phillips 2014a: 150)

Are the overlap and holistic models incompatible? What do their differences amount to? Phillips need not deny that successive temporal parts of experience can be co-conscious and form unified, overlapping, wholes as a result. Nor does Dainton need to balk at the suggestion that the dynamic contents of *parts* of temporal experiences are a function of the wholes they compose and their overlapping structure.[15]

Perhaps, then, the difference is merely one of emphasis: of what is strictly needed to best explain the phenomenology and content of temporal experiences—where one version of extensionalism renders the other superfluous, and *vice versa*. Or perhaps the difference is mereological after all: while the overlap approach only adds extra structure grounded in co-consciousness relations to mere successions of temporal parts of experience, it preserves the sort of 'bottom-up' approach favored by the snapshot theorist—whereas the holist, by focusing on the 'metaphysical priority' of whole experiences, completely reverses the order of metaphysical determination. Accordingly, even if Dainton and Phillips agree that whole experiences are explanatorily central, they might disagree about the nature of such wholes and how they relate to their parts.[16]

9.1.3 Extended Contents

Another alternative is concerned almost exclusively with the *contents* of temporal experiences: their intentional or representational properties. If such contents are extended in time, presenting what occurs during certain intervals, the conscious psychological states bearing such intentional properties need not be extended at all, retentionalists insist. It should be possible, that is, to perceive a temporally extended event *via* an instantaneous perceptual experience (Tye 2003: 88; Pelczar 2010a, 2010b;

---

[14] Compare Soteriou (2007, 2013: 102–6, 144–6).
[15] Indeed, see Dainton (2000: 175–7; 2014a: 107, 113).
[16] See also Dainton (2017: sect 5.4, 69–70).

Lee 2014a: 6). Possible, but not necessary: as Lee (2014a: 4–5) allows, temporal experiences may be extended in time, at least as long as it takes for neurophysiological processes to produce or realize such experiences, *provided* their extension does not imply that such experiences can be factored into distinct temporal parts differentiated by their phenomenology or content.

So construed, this form of retentionalism denies the snapshot theory's intentional thesis, as well as the metaphysical thesis at the heart of extensionalism:

Retentionalism:
(i) *metaphysical thesis*: perceptual experiences need not be extended temporally.
(ii) *intentional thesis*: such experiences can have contents which present or represent temporally extended portions of reality, including temporal relations between non-simultaneous perceived events.[17]

In short, the temporal features of experiences themselves play hardly any role in the retentionalist account. For longer events, however, the duration of which stretches beyond the intervals which can plausibly figure in the content of a single experience (Kelly 2005b), some retentionalists (Lee 2014b) acknowledge that several successive experiences, each with their own extended content, might contribute to representing the successive segments of such longer events. And the extended contents of single experiences might well overlap (Lee 2014b: 155): a temporal part y of a perceived event may figure, first, in the extended content of an experience e as *occurring now* and as immediately succeeding an earlier temporal part x of that same event. The very same part (y) of that perceived event might then figure in the extended content of the next experience e*, as having *occurred earlier* and preceding the next temporal part z of the same event, which is experienced as *occurring now* in e*. No matter how the temporal 'profile' or relative location of these distinct temporal parts of a perceived event is represented in experience (Lee 2014a: 6), a succession of extended contents is thus likely to involve some *constant updating* of that profile.

Finally, the phenomenology of temporal experience, on this view, is determined solely by the temporally extended representational contents of experience: most retentionalists appear to endorse some form of *representationalism*, whereby the phenomenal properties of experiences are grounded in their contents (see, e.g., Tye 2003).

9.2 Some Clarifications (or an Attempt Thereat)

This brief survey raises a range of questions. I concentrate on two of the most pressing ones.

---

[17] See Tye (2003); Grush (2007, 2008), Pelczar (2010a, 2010b), Lee (2014a, 2014b). For historical precedents, see Dainton (2000: ch. 6; 2017: sect 6).

9.2.1 Perception?

One bone of contention between the three theories reviewed is whether we *perceive* temporal relations between non-simultaneous worldly events, and in what sense exactly. Is there a univocal enough and shared conception of *perception* to underpin the dispute, or could it collapse as a mere verbal disagreement?[18]

What is at stake appears to presuppose a broad contrast between (i) a kind of perceptual awareness essentially influenced by other non-perceptual states, and (ii) another kind, entirely devoid of such non-perceptual influence. Where the latter is *purely sensory* in this relative sense, the former results not just from sensory processing, but may be imbued by contributions from different types of memories, background beliefs and expectations, inferences, and even introspection.

Thus, no one denies, not even the snapshot theorist, that temporal relations between separate events can be perceived in the sense of (i). One axis of disagreement—between the snapshot view and its two rivals—is whether such relations are perceived in some purely sensory manner *à la* (ii).[19] It is only in this (narrow) sense that there is a dispute about temporal *perception*.

9.2.2 Resemblance and Temporal Isomorphy?

All three theories of temporal experience surveyed make a claim, not just about the *content* of such experiences, but about their *temporal ontology*. So how does the former relate to the latter? Retentionalists provide the simplest answer on this count: temporal content, on their view, has little to do with an experience's temporal features (and everything to do with underlying neural mechanisms processing perceptual information).[20] For extensionalists, on the other hand, the duration of a whole experience matters greatly to its content, as we saw: but what is the nature of that connection, exactly?

At the very least, the temporal extension of a whole experience is clearly meant as a *necessary* condition upon temporal representation, yet it is not *sufficient*, presumably:

---

[18] It is doubtful, on the other hand, that the dispute owes ultimately to different commitments between a 'naïve' or 'relational' picture of perception (concerned exclusively with a relation of direct perceptual awareness) and a representationalist one (with representational contents as the main explanatory tools), as Hoerl (2013: 380–4; 2017: 177–80) suggests. Even if it were historically accurate, the suggestion is misleading in presenting extensionalism as wedded to a naïve or relational view, while retentionalists are mainly guided by their representationalism: just as extensionalism can naturally be phrased in terms of representational contents, retentionalism is easily construed *via* a direct relation of perception, *albeit* one where the perceptual relation ranges over an extended interval comprising distinct events (where the events perceived may appear *in different temporal guises* because of their relative temporal locations).

[19] Retentionalists like Lee (2014a: 3, 6) explicitly insist that retentions are elements of the content of conscious *perceptual* experiences, not memories.

[20] With longer events, successive experiences (each with their own extended content) of partial segments of such longer events may, of course, match the order of these segments, as we saw. But this plays hardly any explanatory role on the extensionalist picture.

something else is required for extensionalists, such as the overlapping structure grounded in co-consciousness relations highlighted in Dainton's version, or the holistic dependence of the parts upon the whole experience at play in Phillips' version.

Does this mean extensionalists are committed to some 'explanation-by-resemblance' thesis, according to which 'time as presented in experience is in some way represented by time itself' (Lee 2014a: 1–2; Dainton 2017: sect 7.1)?[21] Though Dainton and Phillips explicitly deny that *every* temporal feature of conscious experiences affect their temporal content (Phillips 2014b: 695–7; Dainton 2017: sect 7.1, 116), this is nevertheless consistent with a qualified endorsement of the 'explanation-by-resemblance' thesis for a smaller subset of such temporal features (Lee, 2014a: 8–9). Likewise, adherence to James' slogan—that the mere successive arrangement of the temporal parts of an experience is not quite enough to represent succession—remains perfectly compatible with the suggestion that, *when combined* either with a structure of overlapping wholes unified by co-consciousness, or some holistic determination relation, succession and duration as instantiated by experiences themselves somehow serve to represent succession and duration.[22]

Caution is required when it comes to relations of *temporal isomorphy* between conscious experiences and the events they represent, however, since there is a range of distinct such relations in the vicinity. First, claims of temporal isomorphy might involve different *relata*: on the side of experience, they might connect (i) the *objective* temporal structure of a conscious experience, or (ii) its 'subjective' temporal features—as they strike one in introspection. On the other side, the *relatum* might consist in (iii) the *objective* temporal features of those worldly events that are perceived (distal stimuli), or (iv) the *represented* temporal features ascribed—accurately or not—to perceived events in the temporal content of experience. Second, temporal resemblance might bear upon different temporal properties: order, duration, or both (Lee 2014a: 8), perhaps change too (Phillips 2014c: 133–4), and may involve differences in degree, from perfect similarity to something much looser.

More importantly, a mere *temporal match* between conscious experiences and their temporal content ought to be distinguished from explanatorily more ambitious claims to the effect that the temporal structure of one *asymmetrically depends* on that of the other, with the different directions of explanation such claims might take. For instance, it may be that, since worldly events and experiences thereof are both events occurring

---

[21] One version of such a resemblance approach might be developed along *projectivist* lines—where the temporal ontology of an experience is somehow projected onto the perceived events it represents (Dennett and Kinsbourne 1992: Hurley 1998: 29; Phillips 2014a: 146).

[22] It is unclear to what extent extensionalists are prepared to claim this much. Phillips (2013: 697, n. 12) seems to suggest that what explains *how* experiences represent the temporal features of worldly events may remain 'an empirical matter'. Dainton, we saw, claims that the overlapping structure of whole extended experiences grants them an 'intrinsic dynamic patterning' (2000: 177), apparently meant to explain our awareness of dynamic features like movement (2000: 175–6). But he has little to say about how exactly the *order* and *direction* of successive co-conscious temporal parts of experience somehow make their way into their contents so as to *represent* the order and flow of the temporal parts of perceived events.

in the same temporal dimension with the same metrical structure, they naturally instantiate the same temporal structure, decomposing into parallel successions of their temporal parts—temporal match without one determining the other. Contrast this with the stronger thesis that conscious experiences *owe* their temporal properties and structure to those of their distal stimuli, as they causally depend (with temporal regularity) on the latter. Conversely, the 'explanation-by-resemblance' thesis aims to account for the *represented* temporal structure of perceived events as a function of the temporal features—whether objective or subjective—of conscious experiences (Watzl 2013: 1010–1; Lee 2014a: 1–2, 8–9; Phillips 2014b: 695, 2014c: 133; Dainton 2017: sect 7.1). And there may well be other such relations, like Phillips' 'inheritance principle', whereby the direction of dependence appears to go the opposite way from that in 'explanation-by-resemblance': namely, 'the temporal structure of experience matches the *apparent* temporal structure of the world presented' (2014a: 142) in the sense that an 'experience itself inherits the [temporal] properties apparently presented in experience' (2014c: 131, 2014b: 695).[23]

Even if Dainton and Phillips seem rather coy on this matter, one should take care not to conflate one relation of dependence for another in assessing whether extensionalism carries with it a commitment to 'explanation-by-resemblance'. If some versions of extensionalism clearly manifest some sympathy towards this type of explanation of temporal content, it remains unclear that all extensionalists need to.

The snapshot view, too, exploits several relations of temporal isomorphy—some occupy a crucial explanatory function. To begin with, the temporal structure of successions of experiential snapshots *causally depends* upon that of the events prompting our experiences: the order and relative duration of individual snapshots, as well as the duration of the whole successions they compose, are largely a function (both in veridical and non-veridical cases) of (a) the respective order and duration of the distinct temporal parts making up the events we perceive, together with (b) causal and temporal constraints upon the neural mechanisms underpinning sensory perception. This highlights what limitations there are on the sensory perception of events: we are bound, given (a) and (b), to perceive one temporal part of a worldly event at a time, one experiential snapshot at a time.

More significantly, successions of experiential snapshots also gain certain 'dynamic' features—their order, direction, how many snapshots occur in a given interval, how their contents vary and overlap from one snapshot to the next, etc.—out of such causal interactions. And these features fulfill distinct explanatory roles, for the snapshot theorist: here are two, by way of illustration. First, regarding the *phenomenology* of successions of experiential snapshots: their 'dynamic' features contribute to the sense of 'experiential flow' such successions seem to generate—*a* appears to flow into *b* primarily

---

[23] Phillips insists his inheritance principle only presents a 'necessary condition' (2014b: 695–7, 697, 2014c: 133) on temporal experience and the phenomenal adequacy of its content, and is independent from the extensionalist requirement that temporal experiences be extended in time (2014c: 133). The rationale behind the principle has to do with considerations of 'phenomenal transparency', he argues (2010: 183–4, 2014b: 695, 2014c: 132)—though compare Tye (2003: 96), as well as Lee (2014a: 8–9).

because the snapshot representing b smoothly (i.e., without a noticeable gap or jump in content) follows that representing a, to simplify somewhat (see Section 9.3.1). Second, in relation to the *perception* of events: *when things go well*, the order and duration of successions of experiential snapshots can be said to 'track', at least to some degree, the order and duration of the successive temporal parts of perceived events.[24]

Temporal isomorphy, then, plays rather different roles for the snapshot and extensionalist views. Extensionalists are mostly concerned with the match between the temporal *content* and the temporal features of experiences—whereas there is no such content for the snapshot view (hence, no need for any 'explanation-by-resemblance' of such content). On the other hand, the snapshot theory I have sketched *does* rest upon a general representational mechanism of a sort, grounded in temporal isomorphy: *albeit* one essentially constrained by causal dependence of the temporal features of successions of experiential snapshots upon worldly events and their successive temporal parts (together with temporal constraints on underlying neural processes).

9.3 Succession, Constant Change, and Phenomenal Continuity (Some Arguments)

We can now ask what evidence might help decide between these rival conceptions of temporal experience. The following—a very selective sample—speak directly to the issue of how the temporal structure of experience might affect perception of the temporal features of perceived events.

9.3.1 Successions of Experiences and Experience of Succession

First, a word about James and his famous slogan: of the three theories reviewed, everyone can embrace the observation that mere successions of experiences are *not* experiences *of* succession. If it was meant as an objection, it is not entirely clear who the target is.[25] The snapshot view sketched here, in particular, is not it: to repeat, insofar as

---

[24] This is not to say that the 'dynamic' features of successions of snapshots determine the temporal content of snapshots, since the latter lack such content. The claim is only that, in veridical cases at least (and perhaps in many non-veridical cases too), a rough correspondence holds between the temporal structure of perceived events and that of successions of experiential snapshots—without entailing that *every* temporal feature will match, or that it will match perfectly—compare Dainton (2017: sect 7.1, 114), Hoerl (2017: 176).

[25] See, e.g., Dainton (2008: 371; 2017: sect 4.1, 39–41). But compare Dainton's (2017: sects 4.1–2) distinction between 'cinematic realism' and 'anti-realism'.

the *temporal content of purely sensory experiences* goes, succession (or duration, or change) does not figure in it, snapshot theorists insist. It is perfectly true for the snapshot theory, in other words, that successions of experiential snapshots *do not constitute* sensory contents representing succession, more precisely. (In a more trivial sense, on the other hand, successions of experiential snapshots do represent, one after another, some of the successive temporal parts of extended events and successions. In *that* weaker sense, they can be characterized as 'experiences of succession': just like successively seeing small segments of a long, dark, and narrow tunnel from the inside can be described, somewhat imprecisely, as an 'experience of a tunnel', even though one is never really in a position to see the whole tunnel as such.)

Perhaps, what informs appeals to James' slogan is the assumption that ascription of a rich enough *temporal content*—representing succession, change, duration—is the end all of any account of temporal experiences and their phenomenology. The snapshot view rejects that there is any real explanatory need for such temporal content (at the purely sensory level, that is), let alone that it is made mandatory by the phenomenology of temporal experiences, or that the accurate description of such phenomenology demands anything more substantive than mere absence of noticeable discontinuities and gaps between successive snapshots.

In this respect, note also that attempts to press James' point—not uncommonly—come hand-in-hand with distinctively impoverished characterizations of the descriptive resources the snapshot view deploys. For instance, should successions of experiential snapshots really be described as akin to those of a 'timeless subject...whose experience is not stream-like at all' (Dainton 2014b: 177–8), when successions of experiential snapshots are, indeed, *successions*, ordered through time in a given direction, one snapshot after the other at a certain pace, in a perfectly 'stream-like' and 'dynamic' manner?[26] Are these successions really 'utterly static and devoid of change' (Dainton 2014b: 176)? If the *contents* of individual snapshots admittedly are, the 'constant renewal' of successive contents characteristic of successions of experiential snapshots—one snapshot immediately following another, and so on—is not. Are 'episodes of awareness' really 'durationless' (Dainton 2017: sect 4.1, 39–40), when they consist of *temporally extended successions* of either short-lived or instantaneous snapshots?

It goes on: should we expect individual experiential snapshots to appear as 'stills' which 'register...as static images' (Dainton 2017: sect 4.1, 41–2) when introspected? Why should we, if snapshots are quite short-lived, immediately replaced by the next snapshot in tightly packed successions thereof? There is no reason to assume, in other words, that we could *introspectively* identify *single* snapshots—as opposed to slightly longer stretches thereof—let alone detect their boundaries with adjacent snapshots, owing to their very short duration, close contiguity, high degree of similarity in content, and the fast pace of their succession.[27] Are experiential snapshots really 'discrete' and 'experientially isolated from one another' as a result (Dainton 2017: sect 4.1, 40–1)?

---

[26] At least in one sense, seemingly akin to Dainton's (2000: 175–7).
[27] Compare Rashbrook's interesting suggestion regarding phenomenal continua (2013: sect 4).

If they are likely discrete in some sense, that does not mean they should *appear* as such, again, for the same reasons. Nor is it clear why, and in what sense exactly, a visual experience of, say, some object o with visible properties F, G, H, at some location L should seem 'experientially isolated' from the next experience, only a tiny fraction of a second later (without any detectable gap in-between), recognizably of the very same object o with the same properties F, G, H, but at location L^*, where L^* massively but not perfectly overlaps L? What would such *experiential isolation* amount to, exactly—and how does it manifest itself phenomenologically?

As for phenomenological considerations thought to underpin the Jamesian point, even if no *single* snapshot represents, as such, 'the explosive roar of a crowd, or the sound of an approaching car, or the barking of a dog' (Dainton 2017: sect 4.2, 44) *in their entirety*, we nevertheless experience *in succession* most (if not all) of the successive temporal parts making up these events. Successions of experiential snapshots like these ground the very phenomenology—seemingly continuous, constantly flowing—described earlier (Section 9.1). Yet there is *no sensory content* representing succession *as such*: only the continuous, successive, experiencing of those successive temporal parts, one after the other. That is all there is to experience sensorily anyway, and this is exactly how we typically experience such events, the snapshot view has it.[28]

9.3.2 Constant Change

Another standard objection also misconstrues its target somewhat. Locke noted how experiences of change and motion seem affected by the rate at which change or motion occur: too slow and nothing appears to change, too fast and things seem to whiz in a blur (Locke 1690: book II, ch XIV, sects 9–11; see Kelly 2005b: 223). Between these limits, change and motion become *apparent* throughout: as when looking at the second-hand of a clock, in contrast to the slow motion of the hour-hand (Broad 1923: 351).

Experiences of constant apparent change are regularly invoked against the snapshot theory: they seem essentially dynamic, the objection goes, so how could they possibly reduce to the essentially static or 'frozen-snapshot like instants' (Dainton 2014b: 177) posited by snapshot theorists? Not only that, but how could the snapshot theory even account for the significant phenomenological differences between experiences of slow change and those of constant change (Dainton 2008: 364; Hoerl 2017: 174; Prosser 2017: 147)? Again, this ignores the dynamic features of successions of experiential snapshots (Section 9.2.2, Section 9.3.1).

More importantly, it ignores the gradual differences in content between successive experiential snapshots, and their phenomenological significance. In cases of slow change, one salient characteristic of the phenomenology of a succession of experiential

---

[28] The snapshot theorist, note, does not aim to reduce the phenomenology of such successions to our beliefs at all (Dainton 2017: sect 4.5: 54), only to suggest that some introspective descriptions of the relevant phenomenology may be informed by questionable theoretical assumptions. Compare Hoerl (2017: 176–7).

snapshots is that the contents of successive snapshots seem to be largely the same: successive representations of the location of the hour-hand do not noticeably vary in this respect, from one snapshot to the next, over relatively long intervals. With constant apparent change, on the other hand, there is far more variation in content over much shorter periods. If experiential snapshots are temporally tiny and quickly replaced by subsequent ones, there may not be any representational difference regarding the location of the second-hand between *adjacent* snapshots. But there will be between close enough—even partly overlapping—extended 'packets' of experiential snapshots. And such small representational differences can increase across successive snapshots to become salient and noticeable: at very short time frames, how quickly small representational differences become noticeable will affect the apparent smoothness of the transitions. This difference in the representational variability of successive contents across successions of experiential snapshots highlights a central phenomenological difference between the two cases—one that is perfectly amenable to the snapshot view.

Interestingly, experiences of constant apparent change raise a general difficulty, according to Phillips (2011): one he takes to threaten *all* accounts of temporal experience. Start with slow motion: the hour-hand of a clock, which *is* in fact moving, does so too slowly to *appear* to be moving. The standard explanation operates in terms of perceptual limitations upon our discriminatory abilities. The hour-hand is moving constantly, yet its motion is too slow to be detected by our visual system: small changes in location, falling below some discriminatory threshold D, cannot figure in the content of experience. Consequently, the hour-hand does not look to be moving.

This standard explanation leads to what Phillips (2011: 810) calls 'Fara's Puzzle', after Fara (2001: 926). In cases of *constant perceptible* change, as with the second-hand of a clock, the second-hand *also* goes through changes in location so small as to fall below the very same threshold D for perceptual discrimination—*albeit* for shorter intervals. If the standard explanation works in cases of slow motion, it should apply to cases of constant motion just as well, the thought goes. At least for those slightly shorter intervals during which its changes in location fall below the same discriminatory threshold D, the second-hand should move in a perceptually *undetectable* manner, and hence not appear to move. Phenomenologically speaking, however, it seems we experience the second-hand as moving *constantly*, even during the shortest intervals. But how could this be, if the standard explanation of slow motion holds?

The problematic assumption behind the standard explanation, Phillips alleges, lies with the idea of 'decomposing change experience into "instantaneous exposures" or "stages", and analyzing it in terms of the presentation of successive static clock hand positions' (2011: 814). In short, the problem according to Phillips owes essentially to a remaining commitment to what is in fact a central ingredient in the snapshot view— dubbing it the 'zoetrope picture' (2011: 809). The solution, the argument continues, draws on Phillips' own holistic account: it is because a whole extended experience has a dynamic content that its temporal parts do too (2011: 819, 821–2). There may still be 'instantaneous exposures' but their contents are not 'static', being entirely determined by the whole dynamic contents in which they figure.[29] Phillips advertises his solution as being available to retentionalists too, provided their version is 'focused on the *contents* of experience, as opposed to experience itself' (Phillips 2011: 818).

It is unclear, however, why cases of constant change should force us to renounce the idea, central to the snapshot theory, that very brief temporal parts of extended experiences have static contents[30]—that is, no change, motion, or succession, figure in those contents.[31] Experiential snapshots, to repeat, are temporal parts of experience, and there is no limit, in principle, to how short they could be: even if not instantaneous, the briefest temporal parts may last no longer than a few milliseconds or even less. This means, again, that those briefest temporal parts of experience likely occur in tightly packed successions thereof, surrounded by similarly very brief other temporal parts, where one such temporal part is immediately replaced by the next. Indeed, this much holds not just for the snapshot view, but any other view of temporal experience, whether the briefest temporal parts of experience are instantaneous, chunky, or gunky.

In this light, *perceptual* discriminatory limitations are not the only limitations we face:[32] again, it should seem unreasonable to expect that one can ever reliably tell by introspection precisely what figures in the contents of individual snapshots, whether the contents of adjacent snapshots are exactly the same or not, whether they present a static scene or not, let alone when such snapshots begin and cease, etc. Thus, a single

---

[29] Dainton (2014a: 108) considers a similar challenge from Pelczar (2010b: 279), specifically against extensionalism. For extensionalists, experiences can have *dynamic contents*, only if such experiences are *extended in time*. But if extended experiences occupy *every* instant in the interval through which they occur, they should have instantaneous temporal parts, the argument goes. Being *unextended*, these temporal parts should lack a dynamic content, by the extensionalist's own lights. Thus, extensionalism threatens to collapse into the snapshot theory, if extended experiences ultimately reduce to successions of unextended temporal parts with purely static contents. In response, Dainton ventures that 'experienced change (or motion, or succession) is not determined solely by the phenomenal features our streams of consciousness possess at an instant t: what matters is the content and character the stream possesses over the brief interval in which t occurs' (2014a: 113). To which he adds a gunky view of experience: 'no matter how small the parts are, they always have a finite, non-zero, size' (Dainton 2014a: 113), which is 'infinitely divisible' (Dainton 2014a: 117).

[30] Nor is it clear why a *holistic explanation* is preferable, if the puzzle owes essentially to the *sensitivity* of our perceptual faculties and how it affects perceptual contents. One significant difference between cases of slow and constant change is the *size of the intervals* during which small differences in location fall below discriminatory threshold D. Hence, perceptual representation of such small differences may not just depend on the *spatial size* of the differences in location, but on the *temporal size* of the intervals during which they present themselves—as Phillips (2011: 817) rightly points out. It could simply be that a small difference in spatial location below threshold D is not represented perceptually when it happens through an interval longer than *temporal threshold T*, but does make it into the content of experience when it lasts less than T. Perceptual representation of such differences, in other words, may be constrained by *both* spatial and temporal thresholds, and inversely so. No holistic determination of the content of a part by its whole is needed—let alone any consideration of the *overall intervals* spanning the motion such small changes contribute to.

[31] Though other considerations might: for an alternative account of motion perception, see Prosser (2016: ch 5; 2017).

[32] Compare Fara (2001: 927–8) and Chuard (2010) for some discussion, as well as Rashbrook (2013: sects 3.3 & 3.5) and Dainton (2014a: 117, 119).

snapshot may well represent only the static location of the second-hand at an instant—an instantaneous temporal part of its motion. Only it is quite unlikely to *appear* as such in any way, given its very brief duration, and the fact that it is immediately replaced by many subsequent snapshots. The same goes for differences in content between adjacent snapshots: small jumps in content, when small enough, may simply not *appear* as such, in these conditions.

This is, after all, the very idea behind the *cinematic metaphor* often associated with the snapshot view: small differences in the static contents of successive snapshots—let alone the fact that these contents are static—may not be detectable, owing to the snapshots' brief duration and the pace of their succession. Moreover, longer successions of snapshots can generate an impression of smooth 'dynamic' flow: across several successive experiential snapshots or 'packets' thereof, this constant replacement of different contents can add up to noticeable enough differences which, at the right pace, appear gradual and smooth.[33]

9.3.3 Phenomenal Continuity

The phenomenal continuity distinctive of experiences of succession and constant change has also been used as the basis for a phenomenological objection to the snapshot conception: if Dainton grants that snapshot theorists can explain the seemingly 'gapless' continuity of such experiences, they cannot account, he insists, for the 'experiential connectedness' of successive experiences of succession—how one experienced phase 'flows into' the next.[34] Yet, we saw (Section 9.3.1), what 'experiential connectedness' amounts to exactly—other than the instantiation of *co-consciousness* relations—and how it (or its absence) is phenomenologically manifested, remains rather unspecified and a little mysterious.[35]

Dainton has leveled a similar complaint regarding phenomenal continuity against retentionalism. Start with Dainton's own overlap model, for contrast: the shortest experiences are linked *via* co-consciousness to adjacent experiences, thus forming small overlapping wholes (Section 9.1.2). It matters to Dainton's (2014a: 127–8, 2014b) extensionalism that such wholes overlap, thus sharing some of *the very same temporal*

---

[33] The fact that snapshots are experiential states, rather than the objects of such states (as in movies), is not an intended part of the analogy, note—compare Dainton (2017: sects 4.1, 4.9). The thought, rather, is that the dynamic aspects of a *succession* of snapshots can be responsible for the *impression* of a dynamic succession of perceived events: the perceptual mechanism behind the apparent motion of cinematic images is an instance of a more general mechanism underlying consciousness too, in other words.

[34] He labels the first 'moderate continuity', the second 'strong continuity' (2014a: 125, 2017: sect 3, 36–7). So construed, either form of phenomenal continuity is not quite equivalent with the mathematical notion—a continuous series is dense and gapless—which Rashbrook seems to presuppose (2013: 110): see also Dainton (2017: Appendix 2, sect 5, 2014a: sects 6.5–6.6).

[35] Especially if, for Dainton, the direction with which one event is experienced as 'flowing into' the next depends ultimately on the 'dynamic' temporal structure of experience (Section 9.1.2): something similar can be exploited by the snapshot theory.

parts. For instance, experience e_2 might be a constituent part in two successive overlapping wholes, the whole composed of e_1 and e_2, followed by that composed of e_2 and e_3. This is meant to guarantee that it is *the very same experience* which e_1 'flows into', and which then 'flows into' e_3. This, Dainton argues, allows the extensionalist to explain how:

> If one hears a rapid "do-re-mi", it is perfectly clear that the "re" which is experienced as following directly on from "do" is the *same token experience* (or same instance of auditory content) that one experiences as flowing into "mi". As far as I can see, few features of our experience are more obvious than this   (Dainton 2014a: 127–8).

The trouble for retentionalists, Dainton continues, is that, across successive experiences with distinct extended contents, some such contents may well partially overlap in representing some of the same notes (Section 9.1.3). Thus, the very same event (the token note 're') might be represented by distinct successive token experiences, with somewhat different extended contents. What is problematic about this for retentionalists, Dainton insists, is that it cannot be *the very same experience* of the same note, on their view, which 'is experienced as flowing into' the experience of the next note (2014a: 128). This means, Dainton concludes, that 'it is impossible for contents in distinct but neighboring specious presents to be directly phenomenally unified' and so, the retentionalist explanation 'inevitably fragments our streams of consciousness' (Dainton 2014a: 126).[36]

There are at least two reasons for skepticism, I think. For one thing, note that, in running the objection, Dainton visibly shifts from (a) the innocuous phenomenological datum that it is *the same note* ('re') which is experienced as flowing from 'do' and seems to flow into 'mi', to (b) the more demanding and contentious requirement that it should be the *same token experience* of the same note—as opposed to (c) successive experiences presenting the same note twice but in such a way that it *appears* to be very same token—which is 'experienced' as flowing into its predecessor and successor. Of course, (b) has its natural home in Dainton's overlap model. That is no reason, however, to assume that retentionalists cannot make sense of (a) without (b), but in terms of (c) instead.

Another reason is that objections of this sort merely reveal, to my mind, divergent preferences for different styles of phenomenological explanation. On Dainton's approach, the way in which successive experiences phenomenally flow into one another demands at the very least some metaphysical relation (co-consciousness) which bears most of the weight of phenomenological explanation, connecting successive experiences into unified overlapping wholes. It is as if the phenomenological features of extended experiences ought to be 'read off' from their mereology.

An alternative is to have phenomenological relations supervene upon the contents of experiences: for retentionalists, the distinct contents of successive experiences might simply present the same event (a note) in a manner that it should appear numerically and qualitatively identical across adjacent experiences. This might well suffice for phenomenal continuity: without any detectable difference between the first presentation of

---

[36] For an earlier version, see Dainton (2014b: 180–3), and Lee (2014b: 155) for a response.

an event to the subsequent (and overlapping) presentation of the same event, there is no reason to expect any manifest phenomenal discontinuity across such successive experiences. *Ditto* with the snapshot view, if successive snapshots are so arranged that no gap—and no noticeable jump in content—is salient.

What we have here, it seems, is yet another significant difference between these three theories of temporal consciousness. The more substantive question, of course, is why prefer one type of phenomenological explanation to another. But that is a question for another day.

9.4 CONCLUSION

It is still wide open, I think, which of the three theories surveyed here best explains various features of our temporal experiences. None of the considerations reviewed appear decisive in that regard. What I hope this survey illustrates, however, is how deciding between these theories depends for a large part upon an entanglement of additional assumptions and side issues: including conceptual questions about the nature of perception, as well as a host of empirical considerations, ranging from the stringency of temporal constraints on perceptual processing (and how brief the shortest experiences can be, how many occur in some interval), to whether some of the experiential features of these experiences outstrip what we introspectively access, etc. To what extent genuine progress can be achieved without properly addressing some of these side issues remains to be seen.[37]

REFERENCES

Broad, C. D. (1923), *Scientific Thought*. London: Kegan Paul).
Chuard, P. (2010), 'Non-transitive Looks & fallibilism', *Philosophical Studies*, 149: 161–200.
Chuard, P. (2011), 'Temporal Experiences and their Parts', *Philosophers' Imprint*, 11(11).
Chuard, P. (2017), 'The Snapshot Conception of Temporal Experience', in I. Phillips (ed.), *The Routledge Handbook of Philosophy of Temporal Experience*. Abingdon: Routledge.
Dainton, B. (2000), *The Stream of Consciousness*. Abingdon: Routledge.
Dainton, B. (2008), 'Sensing Change', *Philosophical Issues*, 18: 362–84.
Dainton, B. (2010), 'Phenomenal Holism', *Philosophy*, 67: 113–39.
Dainton, B. (2014a), 'The Phenomenal Continuum', in D. Lloyd and V. Arstila (eds), *Subjective Time: the Philosophy, Psychology, and Neuroscience of Temporality*. Cambridge, MA: MIT Press.
Dainton, B. (2014b), 'Flow, Repetitions, and Symmetries: Replies to Lee and Pelczar', in N. Oaklander (ed.), *Debates in the Metaphysics of Time*. London: Bloomsbury Continuum.
Dainton, B. (2017), 'Temporal Consciousness', *The Stanford Encyclopedia of Philosophy*.

---

[37] All my gratitude to Eric Barnes, Justin Fisher, Robert Howell, as well as Uriah Kriegel and two anonymous referees, for helpful comments and suggestions.

Dennett, D. (1991), *Consciousness Explained*. Harmondsworth: Penguin.

Dennett, D. and Kinsbourne, M. (1992), 'Time and the Observer: the Where and When of Consciousness in the Brain', *Behavioral and Brain Sciences*, 15: 183–247.

Fara, D. G. (2001), 'Phenomenal Continua and the Sorites', *Mind*, 110: 905–35.

Grube, E. (2014), 'Atomism and the Contents of Experience', *Journal of Consciousness Studies*, 21/7-8: 13–33.

Grush, R. (2007), 'Time and Experience', in T. Müller (ed.), *Philosophie Der Zeit*. Frankfurt: Klosterman.

Grush, R. (2008), 'Temporal Representation and Dynamics', *New Ideas in Psychology*, 26: 146–57.

Hoerl, C. (2012), 'Husserl, the Absolute Flow, and Temporal Experience', *Philosophy and Phenomenological Research*, 86/2: 376–411.

Hoerl, C. (2013), 'A Succession of Feelings, in and of Itself, is Not a Feeling of Succession', *Mind*, 122/486: 373–417.

Hoerl, C. (2017), 'Temporal Experience and the Philosophy of Perception', in I. Phillips (ed.), *The Routledge Handbook of Philosophy of Temporal Experience*. Abingdon: Routledge.

Hume, D. (1739), *A Treatise of Human Nature*, ed. P. Nidditch. Oxford: Oxford University Press.

Hurley, S. (1998), *Consciousness in Action*. Cambridge, MA: Harvard University Press.

Jackson, F. (1977), *Perception*. Cambridge: Cambridge University Press.

James, W. (1890/1952), *The Principles of Psychology*. New York: Dover.

Kelly, S. (2005a), 'The Puzzle of Temporal Experience', in A. Brook and K. Akins (eds), *Cognition and Neuroscience*. Cambridge: Cambridge University Press.

Kelly, S. (2005b), 'Temporal Awareness', in A. Thomason and D. W. Smith (eds), *Phenomenology and Philosophy of Mind*. Oxford: Oxford University Press).

Koch, C. (2004), *The Quest for Consciousness*. New York: W.H. Freeman.

Lee, G. (2014a), 'Temporal Experience and the Temporal Structure of Experience', *Philosophers' Imprint*, 14/3: 1–21.

Lee, G. (2014b), 'Extensionalism, Atomism, and Continuity', in N. Oaklander (ed.), *Debates in the Metaphysics of Time*. London: Bloomsbury Continuum.

Le Poidevin, R. (2007), *The Images of Time: An Essay on Temporal Representation*. Oxford: Oxford University Press.

Locke, J. (1690), *An Essay Concerning Human Understanding*, ed. P. Nidditch. Oxford: Oxford University Press, 1975.

Pelczar, M. (2010a), 'Must an Appearance of Succession involve a Succession of Appearances?', *Philosophy and Phenomenological Research*, 131/1: 49–63.

Pelczar, M. (2010b), 'Presentism, Eternalism, and Phenomenal Change', *Synthese*, 176: 275–90.

Phillips, I. (2010), 'Perceiving Temporal Properties', *The European Journal of Philosophy*, 18/2: 176–202.

Phillips, I. (2011), 'Indiscriminability and Experience of Change', *The Philosophical Quarterly*, 61/245: 808–27.

Phillips, I. (2013), 'Perceiving the Passing of Time', *Proceedings of the Aristotelian Society*, 113/3: 225–52.

Phillips, I. (2014a), 'The Temporal Structure of Experience', in D. Lloyd and V. Arstila (eds), *Subjective Time: the Philosophy, Psychology, and Neuroscience of Temporality*. Cambridge, MA: MIT Press.

Phillips, I. (2014b), 'Breaking the Silence: motion silencing and experience of change', *Philosophical Studies*, 168: 693–707.
Phillips, I. (2014c), 'Experience of and in Time', *Philosophy Compass*, 9/2: 131–44.
Phillips, I. (2018), 'Consciousness, Time, and Memory', in R. Gennaro (ed.), *The Routledge Handbook of Consciousness*. Abingdon: Routledge.
Prosser, S. (2016), *Experiencing Time*. Oxford: Oxford University Press.
Prosser, S. (2017), 'Rethinking the Specious Present', in I. Phillips (ed.), *The Routledge Handbook of Philosophy of Temporal Experience*. Abingdon: Routledge.
Rashbrook, O. (2013), 'The Continuity of Consciousness', *The European Journal of Philosophy*, 21/4: 611–40.
Reid, T. (1855), *Essays on the Intellectual Powers of Man*. Derby.
Soteriou, M. (2007), 'Content and the Stream of Consciousness', *Philosophical Perspectives*, 21: 543–68.
Soteriou, M. (2010), 'Perceiving Events', *Philosophical Explorations*, 13/3: 223–41.
Soteriou, M. (2013), *The Mind's Construction*. Oxford: Oxford University Press.
Strawson, G. (2009), *Selves*. Oxford: Oxford University Press.
Tye, M. (2003), *Consciousness and Persons*. Cambridge, MA: MIT Press.
Watzl, S. (2013), 'Silencing the Experience of Change', *Philosophical Studies*, 165: 1009–32.

CHAPTER 10

THE PHENOMENAL UNITY OF CONSCIOUSNESS

FARID MASROUR

It is early in the morning of a cold winter day. I am hearing the regular ticking of the wall clock. My back is a little sore from shoveling the snow yesterday and my fingers are cold. But it is a pleasant moment. Writing is going well and I'm happy. I can smell the rooibos that is brewing in the glass cup sitting next to the laptop and occasionally check if it is ready by shifting my attention to how its color is intensifying. I stop writing for a moment and check the shape of the glass. It has an ordinary cylindrical shape. But the proportions are perfect. It looks nice!

This is a partial description of what I am experiencing now. To complete the description, I should add more experiences. But there is an important item that is needed to give a complete description of my phenomenology that we would not normally regard as an experience. There is a sense in which my experiences are *phenomenally unified* with each other. In other words, my experiences seem to form some sort of unified field. I will refer to this as the *phenomenal unity of consciousness*, or for short, *phenomenal unity*.

Philosophical interest in unity of consciousness goes back, at least, to Kant's work in the *Critique of Pure Reason*. But there has been a recent revival of interest among analytic philosophers of mind that focuses on unity of consciousness, construed as phenomenal unity. My first goal in this chapter is to survey some of the issues and questions that have been central to this recent work. I do so in Section 10.1, after clarifying what I mean by phenomenal unity.

My second goal is to sketch an alternative to what I see as a dominant, though implicit, tendency in the recent literature on unity. This is the tendency to formulate the idea that phenomenal unity is a natural feature[1] of consciousness in terms of what I will call the

---

[1] By a natural feature of consciousness I simply mean something that belongs to its nature. I will be treating 'X belongs to the nature of Y' and 'X is a natural feature of Y' as equivalent.

Unity Thesis, according to which all synchronous experiences of a conscious subject at a moment are phenomenally unified with each other.[2] This thesis has received substantial attention. But there has not been much explicit discussion of its philosophical significance, and in particular whether it provides the best formulation of the idea that unity belongs to the nature of conscious. In Section 10.2, after arguing that the *Unity Thesis* does not offer the best way of formulating this idea, I offer an alternative construal.

My third goal is to rebut another common trend in recent literature, namely, the tendency to understand phenomenal unity as obtaining in virtue of a type of oneness or singularity. I have argued against this tendency in previous work and advanced an alternative that sees phenomenal unity as obtaining in virtue of connectivity conditions over relations among phenomenal experiences. In Section 10.3, I discuss how the connectivity view can handle potential problems presented by cases of fusion and fission. The two last sections contribute to the broader project of offering a comprehensive account of the fundamental connection between phenomenal unity and consciousness. I end the chapter with a brief discussion of the theoretical burdens associated with this project and how the present discussion may contribute to their resolution.

10.1 Phenomenal Unity

10.1.1 What is Phenomenal Unity?

I started this chapter with a sketch of my experiences and used it to point to our target phenomenon, namely, phenomenal unity. Let me now make three points about what phenomenal unity is not—or at least what it cannot, at the outset of inquiry, be assumed to be.

First, when I say that my conscious experiences are phenomenally unified, I do not mean that they are *subjectively unified*, where conscious experiences are *subjectively unified* when they belong to, or are attributable to, the same conscious subject. Arguably, two experiences can belong to the same subject without being phenomenally unified. So, we should distinguish the concept of phenomenal unity from the concept of subjective unity.

Second, phenomenal unity should be distinguished from *objectual unity*, where experiences are objectually unified when they together present something *as a* single object. For example, my experiences of the shape and color of the tea cup are objectually unified, but this seems distinct from, and over and above, their phenomenal unity.

---

[2] Bayne and Chalmers (2003), Bayne (2010).

Third, phenomenal unity should be distinguished from *access unity*, where conscious experiences are *access unified* when they are accessible to the same subject or cognitive process. When I say that my conscious experiences are phenomenally unified, I do not mean that they are accessible to the same subject (me) or cognitive process (whatever it might be).[3]

These remarks leave it open that there might be substantive a posteriori connections between phenomenal unity and subjective, objectual, or access unity. They also leave it open that at the end of theoretical enquiry one might decide that the concept of phenomenal unity has to be revised and thus analyzed in terms of these concepts.

Discussions of phenomenal unity usually confine themselves to a two-step manner of identifying the target phenomenon: they ostensively identify phenomenal unity with the aid of examples and then sharpen the target by distinguishing it from other forms of unity. This is what I have done so far. However, I believe we can also do more. Specifically, we can provide a positive characterization of phenomenal unity, in the form of a set of data points (or if you like, platitudes). Although they function as data in the sense that they are (non-trivial) ideas that any adequate account of phenomenal unity must somehow handle or take into account, as we will see, they are not all universally accepted.

First, phenomenal unity is a *monadic property* of some but not all sets of experiences, where at least some such sets have more than one member. For example, the set of experiences that I have at the moment contains more than one experience and is phenomenally unified, but the set of experiences that contains both my experiences and your experiences is not.

Second, phenomenal unity is *phenomenally manifest* in the sense that there is a phenomenal contrast between its presence and its absence. In other words, what it is like to have a set of experiences when this set is phenomenally unified is different from what it is like to have the same set of experiences when the set is not phenomenally unified.[4]

Third, phenomenal unity is a *phenomenally singularizing* property. What I mean by this is that a set of experiences is unified only if its members together form a single phenomenal item. Note that this is a claim about a necessary condition for phenomenal unity. It should not be read as the claim that the single unified experience emerges from, or is less fundamental than, the experiences that are unified with each other. Whether the claim that phenomenal unity is phenomenally singularizing is a highly substantive claim depends on one's view about the phenomenal item and its individuation. A common assumption is that this item is an experience. Other phenomenal items that can serve the same purpose are streams of consciousness or phenomenal fields, where a

---

[3] This is a partial list. Other forms of unity that are often distinguished from phenomenal unity include introspective unity, spatial unity, Gestalt unity, and representational integration. For a more in-depth discussion of these distinctions see Bayne and Chalmers (2003), Tye (2003), and Dainton (2006).

[4] For an interesting analysis of the different ways in which this condition can be satisfied see Koksvik (2014).

phenomenal field is a momentary slice of a temporally extended stream of consciousness.[5] We will revisit this issue below.

Fourth, phenomenal unity is a *uniformly grounded* property. By the claim that phenomenal unity is grounded I mean that when a set of experiences is phenomenally unified it is so in virtue of the instantiation of more fundamental person-level properties or relations. In saying that phenomenal unity is uniformly grounded I mean that phenomenal unity is not grounded in a disjunction of several distinct properties or relations. We can call the question about the uniform ground of unity the *grounding question*: when experiences are unified, what are the more fundamental uniform personal-level facts, if any, in virtue of which they are unified? One's answer to the grounding question should be distinguished from a proposal concerning the necessary and sufficient conditions for unity. As we shall soon see, theorists disagree about the correct answer to the grounding question.

Fifth, as indicated at the outset, phenomenal unity belongs to the nature of consciousness. There is a sense in which we cannot conceive of an occurrence of consciousness that lacks phenomenal unity and this strongly indicates that phenomenal unity belongs to the nature of consciousness. This datum inspires the question of how best to formulate the idea that phenomenal unity is a natural feature of consciousness. Call this the *articulation question*. As we saw earlier, a common, though implicit, answer to this question is in terms of the *Unity Thesis*. I will argue in Section 10.2 that this is not a good answer.

I have introduced five data concerning phenomenal unity. They tell us that phenomenal unity is a property of a set of experiences that is phenomenally manifest, uniformly grounded, singularizing, and natural to phenomenal consciousness. I think each datum is prima facie justified by extended introspection, by which I mean introspection supplemented with reflection and a bit of philosophical ideology (for example, views about the individuation of experience, and the conceptual framework of grounding and natures). The data can serve as constraints that help to identify the target phenomenon. But this is not to say that they are sacrosanct; we can regard them as theoretically negotiable constraints in the sense that at the end of theoretical enquiry one might reject some or even all of them. In fact, some current debates and implicit disagreements about unity can be understood as debates over these data, or as centering on questions that emerge once they are accepted. What follows is a quick survey of some of these debates and questions.

10.1.2 Debates about Phenomenal Unity

Some theorists deny our first datum. Such denial is common among theorists who endorse what I will call the *one-experience view*, according to which the cases that we

---

[5] This characterization of the notion of a phenomenal field was suggested to me in a conversation by Christopher Hill. For an interesting alternative analysis of the notion of a phenomenal field see Roelofs (2014).

normally describe as cases in which experiences are unified are, strictly speaking, cases in which there is only one single experience with a complex content. So phenomenal unity is not a monadic property of a set of experiences that can contain more than one member.[6] Accordingly, the proponent of the one-experience view would reject our first datum, though they can replace it with the thesis that phenomenal unity is the monadic property of a set of items other than experiences, items such as phenomenal contents, or experience parts.

There are also some theorists who deny that unity is phenomenally manifest.[7] On these views, there are cases in which phenomenally conscious experiences are unified and cases in which they are not. But the difference between these cases should be understood in non-phenomenal terms, for example, in terms of the failure of other forms of unity such as access unity or subjective unity.

Many theorists accept that unity is singularizing in that when experiences are unified we have a single phenomenal entity that encompasses those experiences. But there is disagreement about the kind of entity in question. Many regard this entity as a single experience, but there are some dissenters.[8] I shall revisit this issue in Section 10.2, where I side with the dissenters.

The idea that unity is uniformly grounded is also denied by some theorists. Hill (2014), for example, defends a multiple property account of unity on which phenomenal unity is a disjunctive property that can be grounded in several distinct properties. Most other theorists disagree with Hill and offer uniform accounts of the grounds for unity.

We can find a variety of explicit or implicit answers to the grounding question among these theorists. These answers fall into two broad categories namely, those that ground unity in a primitive form of oneness and those that ground it in certain relations among experience. I call the generic thesis that phenomenal unity is grounded in a fundamental form of oneness *Newtonianism* because it structurally resembles Newton's account of relations of co-spatiality.[9] Newtonian answers to the grounding question can be contrasted with *Leibnizian* answers that ground phenomenal unity in unity relations.

---

[6] See Tye (2003). See also Guistina (2017) who defends the view and also interprets Brentano as endorsing it. Bayne (2010: 29–32) responds to Tye's argument for the one experience view. See also this chapter, Section 10.2.3.

[7] See Hurley (1998). See Masrour (2014a) for a response.

[8] Hill (2014), for example, denies that unified experiences always form a single experience. See Bayne (2014) for a response.

[9] Bayne (2014), for example, defends the view that when experiences are unified they are so in virtue of being parts or components of one encompassing experience. Many other accounts of unity have the same structural profile, though they differ in their conceptions of the oneness that grounds unity. Tye (2003) proposes that the oneness of experience obtains in virtue of the oneness of content, and Peacocke (2014) maintains that experiences are unified in virtue of belonging to the same single subject. Newtonian tendencies also figure in interpretations of historical figures. The idea that phenomenal unity is grounded in the oneness of an act of synthesis is commonly attributed to Kant. Giustina (2017) interprets Brentano as adopting the view.

Here again, the label marks a structural similarity between these views and Leibniz's view about what grounds the fact that a set of points belong to one space.[10]

Tracking the debate about whether unity is a natural feature of conscious experiences is not straightforward. This is partly because this idea has been in the background of the debates; it has not been explicitly discussed, at least not as such. As remarked earlier, a common construal of the idea is the Unity Thesis. As we shall soon see, the status of this thesis depends on the exact sense of 'subject' that is involved in its formulation. There are several options here, but it is common to regard the subject either in a biological sense or as one who is capable of having cognitive attitudes such as beliefs and desires. Understood in either of these ways, many theorists deny the Unity Thesis, though they do not conclude from this that unity is not a natural feature of consciousness.[11]

If we assume that phenomenal unity has to satisfy all five of the above data, then we might be tempted to think any theorist who denies one of the data should be regarded as a skeptic about unity. But philosophical inquiry rarely proceeds in ways that would justify this way of using the labels 'data' and 'skeptic'. In many cases, we start with a set of prima facie warranted assumptions about a target domain, some of which will be subsequently revised as theoretical enquiry proceeds.

This said, I think two of the above data are so central that denying them would qualify one as a skeptic about phenomenal unity. The first is the idea that unity is phenomenally manifest (the second datum) and the second that it is phenomenally singularizing (the third datum). It should be clear why denying the former would amount to skepticism: if unity is not phenomenally manifest, then it would not be *phenomenal* unity. The reason for regarding the idea that unity is singularizing as central is that this feature distinguishes unity from other features of consciousness that belong to its nature. If we do not accept this datum, then we would not be able to distinguish unity from other phenomenally manifest natural features of consciousness—such as temporal extension, intensity, and subject–object dichotomy—that are uniformly grounded. Accordingly, I will call any position that denies either that unity is phenomenally manifest or that it is singularizing *skepticism* about phenomenal unity.

Understood in this restrictive way, skepticism about phenomenal unity does not seem to have many advocates among those who are not generally skeptical about phenomenal consciousness.[12] In what follows, I will assume that skepticism conflicts with

---

[10] Dainton (2006) defends a primitivist version of Leibnizinanism that grounds unity on relations of co-consciousness. I, on the other hand, have defended a non-primitivist version that grounds unity on connectivity conditions defined over a relation of attachment; see Masrour (2014a, 2014b). Watzl (2014) also defends a Leibnizian view that grounds unity in foreground–background relations in attentional structure, though he puts things in terms of the nature of unity as opposed to its uniform grounds. Roelofs (2014) defends a somewhat similar view.

[11] Among philosophers, Moor (1982), Davis (1997), Tye (2003), and Schechter (2010) deny the Unity Thesis. A notable exception here is Bayne (2010: 189–221) who mounts an impressive defense of the idea that unity is maintained in split brain cases, and offers an excellent review of the philosophical and scientific literature on split brains.

[12] As noted earlier, Hurley (1998) denies that unity is phenomenally manifest and would therefore qualify as a skeptic about phenomenal unity, even though she is not a skeptic about phenomenal character/consciousness more generally.

extended introspection and should therefore be rejected. This is not to say that the move from extended introspection to positing unity as a phenomenally manifest and singularizing property is straightforward and uncontroversial. But arguably, the controversies that are involved here are the general controversies about the reliability of introspection and reflection; they are not specific to phenomenal unity. So, I will set skepticism aside here.

The rest of this chapter focuses on the articulation and the grounding questions. Section 10.2 argues that the Unity Thesis and other similar answers to the articulation question that appeal to the notion of a subject (or some other entity) fail to properly capture the fundamental connection between consciousness and unity. We should, I will argue, aim to articulate a *direct* link between consciousness and unity, one that is not mediated by a third element.[13] I call this approach Purism. After motivating Purism, I propose and defend a specific purist thesis. Section 10.3 focuses on the grounding question. Building on previous work, I propose and defend a Leibnizian view.

Two last remarks before we turn to the articulation and grounding questions. First, it has become customary in the recent literature on phenomenal unity to distinguish between *synchronic* and *diachronic* phenomenal unity, where the former applies to the unity of experiences at one moment of time and the latter concerns unity among experiences at different times. I will not make much of this distinction here. So, in what follows, unless explicitly stated, all claims about phenomenal unity should be understood as applying equally to synchronic and diachronic unity.

Second, many issues about phenomenal unity are intimately related to issues about the individuation of experiences. This paper assumes a specific individuation scheme and I want to end this section by making this individuation scheme explicit. This will help to clarify the proceeding discussion. I started this chapter by describing some of the things that I was experiencing. The list included the sound of the ticking of the clock, my back pain, the smell of the tea and the color and contour of the tea inside the glass, etc. How many experiences did I undergo? Let me outline three different approaches to this question in broad strokes.

One possible answer is that for any quality that is experientially presented to me, I have at least one experience that presents only that quality. For example, I have an experience that presents the color of the tea, another experience that presents the shape that it takes in the glass, an experience of the quality of my back pain, and yet another experience that presents its location, so on and so forth. Let us call this the *quality-based individuation scheme*. This individuation scheme gives us a very fine-grained experiential structure.

At the opposite end, we have the view that I have as many experiences as I have unified streams of consciousness. Assuming that my consciousness is unified, I have only

---

[13] A purist does not have to deny that there are deep links between the notion of unity and the notions of a conscious subject. She could even accept that unity relations among experiences are necessary conditions for the existence of conscious subjects to whom the experiences belong. But a purist would hold that the fundamental connection between consciousness and unity holds even if we deny the connection between unity and subjects.

one experience with a very rich content; it presents to me the color of the tea, its smell, the quality and location of my back pain, the sound of the clock, so on and so forth. We can call this the *unity-based individuation scheme*. This individuation scheme would give us what we earlier called the one-experience view.

In between these poles, there are many possible individuation schemes on which we get more than one experience during a unified stream of consciousness but fewer than the qualities that are experientially presented. I think the most plausible among these is that during a period of time, there are as many experiences as there are experientially presented intentional objects, where abstracta or property instantiations do not count as intentional objects. We can call this the *intentional object individuation scheme*. It is plausible to assume that a set of phenomenal items together present an intentional object if and only if they present the qualities that they present as belonging to the same object. Our scheme thus entails that a set of phenomenal items together form one experience if and only if they present the qualities that they present as belonging to the same object.[14] In other words, to determine the number of experiences in a stream of consciousness, we need to look at what we earlier called objectual unity. In our example, my pain is presented by my experience as having a location and a quality. My experience also presents the tea as having a color, a location, and a shape (a shape that it acquires from the shape of the cup). Thus, on the intentional object individuation scheme, I have at least two experiences, namely, the pain experience and the tea experience. In what follows, I will assume the intentional object individuation scheme without arguing for it.

10.2 PURE EXTRINSIC UNITY AND THE ARTICULATION QUESTION

How should we articulate the idea that phenomenal unity is a natural feature of consciousness? This is a multi-faceted question with at least two dimensions. One dimension concerns the general issue of how to articulate theses about natures. Here, a common trend has been to put things in terms of necessities. A second, more recent, trend is to put things in terms of essences. Thus, the idea that phenomenal unity belongs to the nature of consciousness can be put either in terms of the thesis that consciousness is necessarily unified or in terms of the thesis that consciousness is essentially unified. These two formulations are not equivalent. But in what follows I will be ignoring their difference and, though I believe that we should go with the essentialist formulation, will put things in terms of necessities.

---

[14] Note that since the relevant notion of object here is the intentional notion, the scheme allows for the presentation of objects that do not in fact exist. This notion also allows for the possibility that the number of intentional objects that are presented by experience might diverge from the number of objects that are perceived.

My focus will be on a second dimension pertaining to the different ways in which the idea that consciousness is necessarily unified can be made more precise. There are a variety of options here. To mention two examples, one answer is that necessarily all conscious experiences of a subject at a time, or during a continuous stream of consciousness, are unified with each other. Another possible answer is that necessarily every occurrence of consciousness is unified.

The Unity Thesis, that is the thesis that necessarily all conscious experiences of a subject at a time are unified, expresses a connection between consciousness and unity but it contains a third element, namely, a subject. We can say that this is an *impure* articulation of the idea that unity is a natural feature of consciousness. In contrast, the thesis that necessarily all occurrences of consciousness are unified, as incomplete and ambiguous as it might be, is a *pure* thesis because it expresses an unmediated connection between consciousness and unity. An important question is whether our answer to the articulation question should be a pure or an impure answer. My contention is that our answer has to be pure. The goal in this section is to motivate this claim and defend a specific pure answer. I start by arguing that the Unity Thesis is either very likely false or trivial. I then argue that the considerations against the Unity Thesis generalize to other impure theses. This motivates purism. I then turn to proposing and defending a pure thesis.

10.2.1 Why Purism?

To see why the Unity Thesis is not a good response to the articulation question, let us distinguish between two senses of a subject. Under one construal, a subject is a being capable of having cognitive attitudes such as beliefs and desires. We can call this the cognitive sense of a subject, henceforth called $subject_{cog}$.[15] Most discussions of the Unity Thesis assume either the cognitive sense of the subject or a watered-down version of it that allows us to attribute subjectivity to some creatures who do not possess cognitive attitudes. For our purposes here, I will ignore the difference between $subject_{cog}$ and its watered-down version. A different notion of a subject builds on the idea that every conscious experience is essentially given or presented to a phenomenally conscious perspective. This gives us the perspectival sense of a subject according to which subjects are identical with the phenomenal perspectives to which conscious experience are presented. On this construal the number of perspectival subjects contained in a body at a moment corresponds to the number of phenomenally conscious perspectives contained in that body at the moment. The cognitive and perspectival notions of subjects are conceptually distinct and might also fail to be co-extensive.

---

[15] As noted earlier, another option is to construe the subject in the biological sense. Everything that I say here about subjects in the cognitive sense would generalize to subjects in the biological sense. Therefore, I will be ignoring this sense of subjects here.

The two senses of subject give us two different versions of the Unity thesis that I shall refer to as Unity$_{cog}$ and Unity$_{pers}$. Unity$_{cog}$ is the thesis that necessarily all of the synchronic experiences of a subject$_{cog}$ are unified. On Unity$_{pers}$, necessarily all the synchronic experiences that are given to the same conscious perspective are unified.[16]

Many theorists reject Unity$_{cog}$ because they hold that in some experimental settings split brain patients have two disunified streams of consciousness yet constitute one subject$_{cog}$.[17] This should disqualify Unity$_{cog}$ as a good articulation of the idea that phenomenal unity belongs to the nature of consciousness. For there is no clear reason to assume that one who accepts that cases like split brain are cases of disunified consciousness within a subject$_{cog}$ should reject this connection between consciousness and unity. It is no wonder that many who reject Unity$_{cog}$ still accept that there is a fundamental connection between unity and consciousness.[18] So, there must be a way to articulate the connection that does not commit us to Unity$_{cog}$.

What about Unity$_{pers}$? According to this thesis, necessarily, all synchronic experiences that are given to the same conscious perspective are unified with each other. This thesis is intuitively plausible. The problem, however, is that under the natural way of understanding the notion of a phenomenal perspective, phenomenal perspectives have to be individuated in terms of unity relations. Under this natural understanding, Unity$_{pers}$, though true, does not say much. For example, the thesis would be true even in a condition where the set of all conscious experiences that I have at this moment is fully disunified in that none of its members are unified with each other because they are given to different perspectives.[19] Suppose that this set consists of experiences $E_1, E_2, \ldots, E_n$. Since a subject$_{pers}$ is identified with the conscious perspective to which an experience is given, the set of experiences that I have is associated with at most the same number of subjects in the perspectival sense as the number of experiences that I have, where E1 is given to Subject$_{1pers}$, E2 to Subject$_{2pers}$, and so on. Now, even if none of these experiences are unified with each other, it is still true that all conscious experiences that are given to any of the perspectival subjects in me are unified because there is one experience given to every subject.

Neither Unity$_{cog}$ nor Unity$_{pers}$, therefore, seem to fit the bill. In a sense, Unity$_{cog}$ demands too much. We want a thesis that tells us that unity is a fundamental feature of consciousness. But in order to get this, we do not need to demand that all the conscious experiences of a subject$_{cog}$ have to be unified with each other. Unity$_{pers}$, on the other hand, seems to ask for too little. It secures the connection between subjects and

---

[16] Obviously, this dichotomy does not exhaust the space of possible versions of the Unity Thesis. But, as we shall soon see, focusing on these two notions will do for our purposes here.

[17] This view is popular among both philosophers and cognitive scientists. Among philosophers, Moor (1982), Davis (1997), Tye (2003), and Schechter (2010), hold this view. A notable exception here is Tim Bayne who puts up an impressive defense of unity in split brain cases. See Bayne (2010: 189–221) for his defense and an excellent review of the philosophical and scientific literature.

[18] Tye (2003) is a good example.

[19] One might argue that even in such a case, there is a sense in which we find unity because each of my experiences are in an intrinsic sense unified. I explain why this move is unsatisfactory in Section 10.2.2.

unity by deflating the notion of a subject, but in doing so it becomes too non-committal. It is true even in a situation where we have a totally fractured state of consciousness. A good articulation of the fundamental connection between unity and consciousness should avoid both pitfalls.

One possible reaction to the above observations is to look for different construals of the Unity Thesis based on alternative notions of the subject. Another option is to appeal to alternative impure theses that appeal to items other than subjects, items that might have intuitive connections to unity and consciousness.[20] However, I suspect that the resulting theses would be subject to similar problems. To avoid the problem that afflicts Unity$_{cog}$, that is, in order to avoid expressing a thesis that is not necessarily true, the relevant notion has to be derived from the notion of unity of consciousness. But if we rely on such a notion it is unclear how we can avoid the problem that afflicts Unity$_{pers}$; the thesis would express something rather uninteresting and trivial. So, it is unclear how any third item, whether it be another construal of a subject or a distinct third element, could serve our purpose. Obviously, this claim requires careful defense. But my purpose here is only to provide an intuitive motivation for abandoning appeals to third elements, not to conclusively establish that all ways to do so would fail. I therefore propose that we look for a purist articulation of this connection.

10.2.2 Pure Extrinsic Unity

Assuming that unity belongs to the nature of consciousness, we should find unity wherever we find consciousness. Put modally, a pure articulation of this idea would be that necessarily all conscious experiences are unified. But this thesis is rather ambiguous. So, let us start by distinguishing between two senses of unity.

> **Extrinsic Unity**
> An experience, E, is extrinsically unified iff there is some experience, F, such that F is numerically distinct from E, is unified with E, and is neither a part of E nor contains E as a part.
>
> **Intrinsic Unity**
> An experience, E, is intrinsically unified iff either E is simple (has no parts) or all of its simple parts are extrinsically unified with each other.

Drawing on the above distinction, we get two different pure theses.

> **Pure Intrinsic Unity**
> Necessarily, all experiences are intrinsically unified.
>
> **Pure Extrinsic Unity**
> Necessarily, all experiences are extrinsically unified.

---

[20] A list of potential candidates would include items such as an 'I think' that accompanies all experiences, for-me-ness (Kriegel 2005; Zahavi and Kriegel 2015), and higher order or same order self-representations (Rosenthal 1997; Kriegel 2009).

Pure Intrinsic Unity avoids the first pitfall that we discussed earlier; it does not ask for too much and is therefore compatible with the idea that experiences of split brains are at times disunified. Moreover, it seems hard to see how parts of the same experience may not be unified with each other. Since every occurrence of consciousness is either simple or complex in that it has parts, it follows that every occurrence of consciousness exhibits intrinsic unity.

However, Pure Intrinsic Unity does not seem to be a substantive thesis that reveals a deep connection between unity and consciousness that is grounded in the specific natures of consciousness and unity. To see this, note that Pure Intrinsic Unity can be regarded as an implication of a general thesis that applies to nearly all forms of existence. By this, I mean the thesis that necessarily every K is either simple or its parts are united in a K-wise relation, where two things stand in a K-wise relation when they are part of the same particular that is of kind K. For example, my nose and my eyes stand in a face-wise relation. Pure Intrinsic Unity does not logically follow from this general thesis, but it is too close to it. This is because it is a near triviality that experiences that are parts of the same experience are phenomenally unified. In other words, being experience-wise related is a trivially sufficient condition for phenomenal unity. But this triviality in conjunction with the thesis that necessarily every K is either simple or its parts are united in a K-wise relation entails Pure Intrinsic Unity. So, Pure Intrinsic Unity would be a consequence of a thesis that is universally true and a near triviality. The upshot is that although Pure Intrinsic Unity implies that we should find unity whenever we find consciousness, it does so at the expense of making the thesis non-specific. The thesis therefore demands something that is satisfied by nearly every form of existence. In a sense, the thesis does not avoid our second pitfall; it still demands too little.

The above observations motivate a closer look at Pure Extrinsic Unity. According to Pure Extrinsic Unity, necessarily for any experience, E, there is some numerically distinct experience, F, that is unified with E and does not stand in part–whole relations with E. The thesis obviously avoids the above two pitfalls and is clearly substantive. For one thing, it entails that lonely experiences are impossible, where a lonely experience is an experience that is not extrinsically unified with any other experience. Therefore, if true, the thesis would indicate a deep and substantive feature of consciousness that does not apply to many other forms of existence.

The thesis also seems to resonate with what we find under introspection. I have never had lonely experiences and I do not have any reason to think that this does not generalize to other subjects.[21] In fact, my intuition that there is a fundamental connection between unity and consciousness is grounded in the introspective observation that whenever I find an experience through introspection, I find other experiences that are unified with it. In other words, my conscious experiences are always marked by *unity within a complexity*. This conforms to the demand for complexity that is inherent

---

[21] Some meditators claim that deep meditation can result in states of consciousness that are devoid of any complex content. Perhaps these could be regarded as examples of lonely experiences. If this is the case then Pure Extrinsic Unity is false. But, of course, there are several other ways to interpret the phenomenology of deep meditative states that is compatible with the impossibility of lonely experiences.

in Pure Extrinsic Unity. Pure Extrinsic Unity therefore seems be an attractive formulation of the connection between unity and consciousness.

Despite its attractiveness, however, Pure Extrinsic Unity faces some rather obvious challenges. This is perhaps why the thesis has not received the attention that it deserves. In what follows, I discuss some of these difficulties and argue that they are surmountable.

10.2.3 The Subsumption Challenge for Pure Extrinsic Unity

It might be argued that Pure Extrinsic Unity runs into what is sometimes called the bloat problem. Let us assume that E_1 and E_2 are extrinsically unified. Since they are unified, there must be a third experience E_3 that contains E_1 and E_2 as parts. But if Pure Extrinsic Unity is true, there must be another experience, E_4, that is extrinsically unified with E_3. This will in turn give rise to another experience E_5 that contains E_4 and E_3 as parts. But again, we need another experience that is extrinsically unified with E_5 and the chain continues ad infinitum. Thus, Pure Extrinsic Unity leads to an unbearable ever-growing bloat.[22]

A related problem is that Pure Extrinsic Unity seems to have many counterexamples. Take the totality of experiences that you have at this moment. Assuming that these experiences are all unified with each other, let T be the single experience that contains all of them as parts. T is not extrinsically unified with any other experience. But then T would be a lonely experience, which is a counterexample to Pure Extrinsic Unity.[23]

These two problems are related, because they both rely on the following assumption:

Subsumption
A set of experiences is extrinsically unified only if there is an experience that contains all of its members as parts.[24]

According to Subsumption, whenever you have extrinsic unity you have a total experience that contains the unified experiences as parts. This is just a logical relation between the existence of total experiences and extrinsic unity. It is therefore weaker than the thesis that experiences are extrinsically unified in virtue of being parts of a total experience.

---

[22] An argument of this nature is one of the main reasons that Tye (2003) denies that there can be phenomenal unity relations among experiences and embraces the one-experience account of unity.

[23] We cannot solve this problem by assuming that T is diachronically unified with some of your experiences in the immediate past and the future because we can use those experiences to generate another counterexample. Let T* be the experience that contains all your experiences during the uninterrupted continuous stream of consciousness that includes T. T* is a lonely experience because it is not extrinsically unified with any other experience. So T* is a counterexample to Pure Extrinsic Unity.

[24] I borrow the term 'subsumption' from Bayne and Chalmers (2003), although they do not characterize it in terms of extrinsic unity.

Subsumption is a more specific version of the general thesis that phenomenal unity is singularizing, that is, the thesis that experiences are unified only if they together form a single phenomenal item. According to Subsumption this item is an experience. But why should we accept Subsumption? We do not accept the general principle that entities of some kind are connected in some intimate sense only if another entity of the same kind contains them as parts. For example, mountains can form a mountain range together, but a mountain range is not a mountain. Analogously, although all of one's experiences at a moment might be unified with each other, this may not entail that the resulting unity is itself an experience. So, the motivation behind Subsumption cannot be a general metaphysical principle and, in the absence of reasons to the contrary, the proponent of Pure Extrinsic Unity can reject Subsumption. Further support for this comes from the principle of individuation discussed in the previous section. On this principle there are as many experiences as there are experientially presented objects. So my experience of the tea in the glass and my mood experience, although phenomenally unified, do not together form an experience because they do not together form a single object. Another line of support for rejecting Subsumption comes from the Connectivity view developed in the next section. Although this view is compatible with Subsumption, it sheds light on how Subsumption might be false. As we shall see, the Connectivity view gives us a detailed account of how experiences can be unified just in virtue of their relations and without forming a single total experience. Connectivity gives us unity without a single total experience.

This said, I think it is important to note the connection between Subsumption and a somewhat deeper issue. To see this, it helps to consider the following phenomenological argument for Subsumption. Let S be a subject in the cognitive sense, and let S have only two disunified experiences E_1 and E_2 at t_1 and undergo a change in t_2 that consists only in E_1 and E_2 becoming extrinsically unified and whatever other change might come about in virtue of this unity. Let T_1 and T_2 be the total phenomenology of S at t_1 and t_2 respectively. The argument would go as follows:

1. Since extrinsic unity is a phenomenal relation it must make a difference to the overall phenomenology of S at t_2.
2. The phenomenal character of E_1 and E_2 does not change from t_1 to t_2.
3. Therefore, there must be a third experience, E_3, that exists in t_2 and is absent in t_1.
4. Either E_3 is an encompassing experience that has E_1 and E_2 as parts or it is extrinsically unified with E_1 and E_2.
5. On pain of infinite regress, we should assume that there is some encompassing experience that has E_1 and E_2 as parts.

A realist about phenomenal unity would accept the first premise. If unity is a phenomenal relation, it must be phenomenally manifest. So there must be a phenomenal contrast between T_1 and T_2. One who rejects certain forms of holism would also accept 2.[25] The move to 3 can be defended by relying on the idea that whenever there is a phenomenal difference between two situations there must be an experience that explains the difference. This might strike many as plausible, but it is incompatible with several theoretical views about experience. Before getting into this issue, however, let us see the rationale behind the rest of the argument. If E3 is neither extrinsically unified with E1 and E2 nor has them as parts, then it is very paradoxical why it is relevant to explaining the phenomenal difference between T1 and T2. But if E3 is extrinsically unified with E1 and E2 then, by the same pattern of reasoning applied in 1–4, there must be another experience E4 that is either extrinsically unified with E1, E2, and E3 or contains them as parts. To stop an infinite regress, we have to assume that at some point there is an experience that contains the previous experiences as components.

How could the proponent of Pure Extrinsic Unity reject this argument? As I noted, the suspect is the idea that motivates the move from 1 and 2 to 3: whenever there is a phenomenal difference between two situations there must be an experience in virtue of which the difference obtains. There are several theoretical perspectives that can help us see how one might reject this idea. For example, one who holds that experiences essentially involve phenomenal perspectives might also hold that when experiences are unified their phenomenal perspectives overlap and this overlap explains the phenomenal difference between unity and disunity. Thus, the difference between T1 and T2 can be explained by citing the fact that in t1 the phenomenal perspectives inherent in E1 and E2 are separate but in t2 they are overlapping. Similar moves can be made by appealing to the emergence of phenomenal subjects, for-me-ness, and the manner in which an experience is given. On closer look, all of these views are committed to the same generic principle: some phenomenal differences between two situations can be simply explained in terms of relations among experiences. This suggests that the simplest version of this strategy can appeal to the relation of phenomenal unity. The phenomenal difference between T1 and T2 simply consists in the fact that E1 and E2 are phenomenally unified at t2 but are not unified at t1. So, there is no reason to posit a new experience to explain the difference between T1 and T2.

My goal in this section has been to motivate and defend a substantive purist thesis about the fundamental connection between consciousness and unity. I motivated purism by arguing that it is hard to see how impure theses could be both substantive and true. I then advanced Pure Extrinsic Unity according to which, necessarily, every experience is extrinsically unified with another experience. This thesis captures the idea that unity is present in every occurrence of conscious experience. I also explained the Subsumption challenge for this thesis and discussed how it can be blocked. Rejecting Subsumption, as noted earlier, does not have to amount to a rejection of the platitude that phenomenal unity is singularizing. For one does not have to identify the single

---

[25] Some hold that the phenomenal character of E1 and E2 would slightly change when they are unified. For discussion see Koksvik (2014).

phenomenal item in this platitude with an experience. There are a variety of options here. My own view is that the single item is a stream of consciousness.

10.3 Connectivity

This section focuses on the grounding question: when consciousness is unified, what are the uniform fundamental person-level facts,[26] if any, in virtue of which it is unified? Earlier, I distinguished between Newtonian and Leibnizian answers to this question. To get an intuitive idea of the difference between these answers, let us consider the following example. Jack and Jill are family members. What are the more fundamental facts in virtue of which they are family members? One possible answer is that there is an entity called the Anderson family and Jack and Jill are both members of this family. Let us call this answer Family. According to Family, the fact that Jack and Jill are family members obtains in virtue of the fact that there is a single entity and they stand in a membership relation to this single entity. This answer is intuitively unappealing. It is natural to hold that families emerge from family relations, but Family reverses the order. A more plausible answer is that Jack and Jill are family members, in virtue of being connected through a continuous chain of parent–child relations. For example, Jack's mom is Jill's cousin, where the relationship of being a cousin is also grounded in a chain of parent–child relations. Let's call this answer Kinship.

The distinction between Family and Kinship exemplifies a structural difference that can be seen in several everlasting philosophical debates. For example, on Newtonian views of space, objects stand in spatial relations in virtue of being located in a single space. On this view, facts about spatial relations are grounded in facts about locatedness in a single space. Leibniz reverses the order. On his view, spatial relations are more fundamental than locatedness in a single space. In fact, on Leibniz's view, space is grounded in and derivative from the fact that spatial relations among objects satisfy certain conditions. The same structural differences distinguish Family from Kinship. The former is Newtonian, the latter Leibnizian.

I have defended a Leibnizian answer to the grounding question about phenomena unity in previous work.[27] This section explains the intuitive case for adopting this approach and the original connectivity view that is defended in earlier work. I then argue that in

---

[26] By person-level facts I mean facts that are somehow manifest at the conscious level. The view that unity obtains when this or that condition fashioned in terms of brain processes are satisfied, for example, would not be an answer to the grounding question because facts about brain processes are not manifest at the conscious level as such.

[27] In Masrour (2014b), I argue that Newtonian answers to the grounding question are dialectically undesirable in that (a) the explanans of these views are not sufficiently removed from their explananda, (b) they are more susceptible to skepticism about phenomenal unity, and (c) they are not easily generalizable to diachronic unity relations.

order to offer a uniform treatment of synchronic and diachronic unities, the original version of the view has to be revised. I propose a revised version at the end.

10.3.1 The Original Connectivity View

The intuition behind the connectivity approach to unity is that relations of phenomenal unity can be accounted for in a way that is structurally analogous to Kinship. So, let me highlight the structural features of Kinship that Connectivity shares. We have already discussed one crucial feature: Kinship has a Leibnizian structure. The second feature is that Kinship is a non-primitivist view. The fundamental parent–child relations that Kinship appeals to do not necessarily connect all members of the Anderson family. The relation that is at the bottom of this account is therefore different from the relation that the account aims to explain. On a primitivist Leibnizian account, however, being family members would be a primitive relation that is not grounded in a more fundamental relation. The third feature of Kinship is that it gives us a uniform treatment of diachronic and synchronic family relations. Suppose that Charles is an Anderson who lived in the eighteenth century. Jack and Jill stand in a synchronic family relation to each other and a diachronic family relation to Charles. An interesting feature of Kinship is that it accounts for these synchronic and diachronic relations in exactly the same way. In both cases, facts about family relations are grounded in the existence of a continuous chain of parent–child relations. Kinship is therefore a uniform account of synchronic and diachronic family relations. To summarize, Kinship is Leibnizian; it is non-primitivist; and it provides a uniform account of synchronic and diachronic family relations.

Connectivity, similarly, is Leibnizian, non-primitivist, and offers a uniform account with respect to synchronic and diachronic unity. The key is to find an element in experience that plays a role that is similar to parent–child relations. In the connectivity approach, this role is played by experiences of specific relations. What are these experiences? An example might help. I just heard the song that the ice cream truck that frequents our neighborhood plays and, looking through the window, I cut a glimpse of the truck slowly passing by. I did not just experience the sound and the visual profile of the truck; I experienced the sound as originating from the same spatial location as the truck and I experienced the truck as the cause of the sound. So, I experienced spatial and causal relations between the sound and the truck. Let us call the experiences exemplified in these cases experiences of specific relations.[28] The connectivity approach grounds unity in continuity conditions defined over experiences of specific relations.

We can use experiences of specific relations to define a relation among experiences called binding:

---

[28] There can be disagreement about whether we experience specific relations and if we do which specific relations we can experience. But for the purposes of this chapter I take it for granted here that there is a non-empty set of specific relations that we can experience.

Binding
Two experiences are bound together iff they are attached by an experience of a specific relation.

In the previous example, my auditory experience of the truck's sound and my visual experience of its visual profile are bound together by the experience of the specific causal and spatial relations that I experience between the truck and its sound. Three points about binding deserve highlighting. First, we can sometimes experience relations among our experiences, or between our experiences and objects and events in the world. But in normal perceptual cases experiences of specific relations are not experiences of relations among our experiences. Rather, they are experiences of relations among the items that we experience. Second, for our current purposes we can treat attachment as a primitive relation that connects experiences of specific relations with other experiences. In pointing out that this relation is a primitive relation, I want to emphasize that it is a relation that cannot be reduced to content relations. The mere existence of an experience of a specific relation is not sufficient for binding two experiences with each other. The experience of a specific relation has to be *attached* to the experiences that it binds together. Third, although this does not follow from the characterization of binding, it is not the case that all of our unified experiences are bound together. This is clear in the case of diachronic experiences within a unified stream that do not succeed each other. But I think it applies to synchronic experiences too. The melody that the ice cream truck plays usually invokes a sense of nostalgia in me and I experience this emotion as caused by the melody. My emotional experience is bound with my auditory experience of the melody. But my emotional experience is not directly bound with the visual experience of the truck through an experience of a specific relation.[29] I do not experience my emotional reaction as caused by what I see; I experience it as caused by what I hear.

It follows from the third point that a simple Leibnizian view that identifies unity with binding cannot account for diachronic unity and arguably not even synchronic unity relations. Therefore, we should not identify unity with binding. Nevertheless, there can be an intimate connection between the two notions. We can use the binding relation to define the notion of a unity path in the following manner:

Unity Paths
There is a unity path between two experiences E_m and E_n iff E_m is bound with E_n or there is an E_r such that E_m is bound with E_r and there is a unity path from E_r to E_n.[30]

---

[29] In general, one can consistently maintain that although we can experience relations of temporal succession, not all of our experiences that succeed each other are bound by experiences of temporal succession.

[30] This is obviously a recursive definition. The occurrence of 'unity path' in the second disjunct is discharged by repeated applications of the first.

A path consists in a chain of experiences of specific relations and the experiences that are bound by the path. An experience can be a member of a unity path in either of two ways. It can either be a binder or one of the experiences that are bound by the binders in the path.

The notions of a unity path and path membership can be used to offer an analysis of unity:

Connectivity
Two experiences are unified in virtue of the fact that they belong to the same unity path as members.

Connectivity is attractive in many respects. However, the view suffers from a problem. What follows explains this problem and proposes a revision that would address it.

10.3.2 The Revised Connectivity View

The main problem for Connectivity is that it cannot accommodate phenomenal fission and fusion. By phenomenal fusion I mean a case in which two disunified streams of consciousness become unified. If fusion is possible, then two experiences, E_1 and E_2, that are not unified before fusion can be members of a diachronic unity path that results from fusion. The original version of Connectivity, would imply that these experiences are unified and this clashes with the intuitive sense that E_1 and E_2 are not unified. A similar problem emerges in the case of fission where one unified stream breaks into two disunified streams. It is intuitive to say that the experiences in the two streams after the fission are disunified, but there is a unity path that connects them through the unified stream in the past.

It is possible to solve this problem by providing different accounts of synchronic and diachronic unity relations. For example, we can distinguish between synchronic and diachronic binding and use this distinction to define different relations of synchronic and diachronic connectivity. Doing so would enable us to say that in the fusion and fission cases E_1 and E_2 are synchronically disunified but diachronically unified. But if we go with this option, we have in effect given up on the ambition to provide a uniform treatment of diachronic and synchronic unity relations.

Another option would be to index claims about unity relations to times or temporal periods. For example, we might say that E_1 and E_2 are disunified during the period before fusion and unified after fusion. But this seems implausible. For E_1 and E_2 may not even exist at the time of fusion and afterwards. So it would make no sense to say that they are unified after fusion.

The best strategy, in my view, is to revise Connectivity in order to block the implication that disunified experiences before fusion or after fission satisfy the conditions for unity. The key here is that the unity paths that result from fusion and fission change their temporal direction; they contain a *diachronic turn*.

Diachronic Turn
There is a diachronic turn in a unity path when there are experiences En, Em, and Ep in the path such that (a) En is between Em and Ep, and (b) En is either temporally prior or temporally posterior to both Em and Ep.

An experience, En, is between experiences Em and Ep in a unity path, U, iff there is a sub-path of U that starts with Em and ends with Ep and En is a member of this sub-path. A path that has a diachronic turn travels in time in one direction and then turns back.

We can solve the fission/fusion problem by restricting Connectivity to unidirectional paths, where a unidirectional path is one that does not contain a diachronic turn.

Revised Connectivity
Two experiences are unified in virtue of the fact that there is a unidirectional unity path that they both belong to as members.

As a thesis about the fundamental facts in virtue of which unity obtains, Revised Connectivity has many advantages.[31] The thesis also has implications for our understanding of the neural correlates of consciousness in that it suggests a distributed model of these correlates as opposed to models on which the correlates of consciousness have to relate to a core or center.[32]

10.4 CONCLUSION

My goal in this chapter has been three-fold. In the first section, I surveyed some of the issues and questions that have been central to recent work on phenomenal unity. In the second section, I argued that the Unity Thesis and other impure answers to the articulation question fail to properly capture the intuitive sense in which phenomenal unity belongs to the nature of consciousness. I proposed and defended a purist alternative. Finally, I proposed and defended a Leibnizian answer to the grounding question.

The articulation and the grounding questions have independent philosophical significance, but they also play an important role in a project whose main goal is to offer an account of how phenomenal unity belongs to the nature of consciousness. To get the project off the ground, we need first to properly formulate the thesis that corresponds to the intuitive idea that unity belongs to the nature of consciousness. Thus, we need to answer the articulation question. I have argued here that the Pure Extrinsic Unity thesis is the best answer to the articulation question and defended the thesis from various

---

[31] For discussion see Masrour (2014a).
[32] Bayne (2010) refers to this distinction as the distinction between the Federalist and the Imperialist models of consciousness. For discussion see Masrour (2014a).

objections. But this does not amount to showing *why* the thesis is true. In order to do so, one needs to explain how Pure Extrinsic Unity flows from the nature of consciousness. Approached systematically, this is a two-fold task. First, we need an account of the facts in virtue of which unity obtains; in other words, we need an answer to the grounding question. Second, we need to show how the presence of the facts that ground unity relations is a consequence of facts about the nature of consciousness. Doing so would help us see why unity is present wherever consciousness is present. I have not attempted this second task. But let me end this chapter with the promissory note that this can be done in full satisfaction if one could demonstrate that consciousness has a necessary (or if you like essential) structure that is grounded in experiences of relations. Establishing this claim is the task of future work.

References

Bayne, T. (2010), *The Unity of Consciousness*. Oxford: Oxford University Press.
Bayne, T. (2014), 'Response to Commentators', *Analysis*, 74/3: 521–9.
Bayne, T. and Chalmers, D. (2003), 'What is the Unity of Consciousness?', in A. Cleeremans (ed.), *The Unity of Consciousness: Binding, Integration, and Dissociation*. Oxford: Oxford University Press, 23–58.
Dainton, B. (2006), *Stream of Consciousness: Unity and Continuity in Conscious Experience*. Abingdon: Taylor & Francis.
Davis, L. (1997), 'Cerebral Hemispheres', *Philosophical Studies*, 87: 207–22.
Giustina, A. (2017), 'Conscious Unity from the Top Down: A Brentanian Approach', *The Monist*, 100:15–36.
Hill, C. (2014), 'Tim Bayne on the Unity of Consciousness', *Analysis*, 74/3: 499–509.
Hurley, S. L. (1998), *Consciousness in Action*. Cambridge, MA: Harvard University Press.
Koksvik, O. (2014), 'Three Models of Phenomenal Unity', *Journal of Consciousness Studies*, 21/7–8: 105–31.
Kriegel, U. (2005), 'Naturalizing subjective character', *Philosophy and Phenomenological Research*, 71/1: 23–57.
Kriegel, U. (2009), *Subjective Consciousness: A Self-Representational Theory*. Oxford: Oxford University Press.
Masrour, F. (2014a), 'Unity of Consciousness: In Defense of a Leibnizian View', in C. Hill and D. Bennett (eds), *Sensory Integration and the Unity of Consciousness*. (Cambridge, MA: MIT Press, 323–47.
Masrour, F. (2014b), 'Unity, Mereology and Connectivity', *Analysis*, 74/3: 509–20.
Moor, J. (1982), 'Split Brains and Atomic Persons', *Philosophy of Science*, 49: 91–106.
Peacocke, C. (2014), *The Mirror of the World: Subjects, Consciousness, and Self-Consciousness*. Oxford: Oxford University Press.
Roelofs, L. (2014), 'What are the Dimensions of the Conscious Field?', *Journal of Consciousness Studies*, 21/7–8: 88–104.
Rosenthal, D. M. (1997), 'A theory of consciousness', in N. Block, O. Flanagan, and G. Guzeldere (eds), *The Nature of Consciousness*. Cambridge, MA: MIT Press.
Schechter, E. (2010), 'Individuating mental tokens: The split-brain case', *Philosophia*, 38/1:195–216.

Tye, M. (2003), *Consciousness and Persons: Unity and Identity*. Cambridge, MA: MIT Press.
Watzl, S. (2014), 'Attentional organization and the unity of consciousness', *Journal of Consciousness Studies*, 21/7–8: 56–87.
Zahavi, D. and Kriegel, U. (2015), 'For-me-ness: What it is and what it is not', in D. Dahlstrom, A. Elpidorou, and W. Hopp (eds), *Philosophy of Mind and Phenomenology*. Abingdon: Routledge, 36–53.

PART II
THEORIES OF CONSCIOUSNESS

CHAPTER 11

THE NEURAL CORRELATES OF CONSCIOUSNESS

JORGE MORALES AND HAKWAN LAU

Our understanding of the neural basis of consciousness has substantially improved in the last few decades. New imaging and statistical techniques have been introduced, experiments have become more sophisticated, and several unsuccessful hypotheses have been quite conclusively ruled out. However, neuroscientists still do not entirely agree on the critical neural features required for sustaining perceptual conscious experiences in humans and other primates. In this chapter, we discuss a selection of influential views of the neural correlates of consciousness (NCC) and the predictions they make. For example, neural activity synchronized at 40Hz used to be considered a serious candidate for the NCC. Among current views, some expect activity in the ventral stream of the visual processing pathway to be crucial for consciousness, others expect recurrent activity in visual areas, distributed activity across frontoparietal areas, or specific activity in prefrontal cortex (PFC). In particular, we focus on the predictions these views make with respect to the role of PFC during visual experiences, which is an area of critical interest and some source of contention. Our discussion of these views will focus mainly on the level of functional anatomy, that is, the level at which we consider different brain regions, rather than at the neuronal circuitry level. We take this approach because we currently understand relatively more about experimental evidence at this coarse level, and because these results are appropriate for arbitrating between current theoretical frameworks. For instance, while the Neural Synchrony Theory (Crick and Koch 1990), the Two-Visual-Systems Hypothesis (Milner and Goodale 1995, 2006), and the Local Recurrency Theory (Lamme 2010, 2006) predict that PFC activity is not critical for perceptual consciousness, the Higher Order (Lau 2008; Lau and Rosenthal 2011) and Global Workspace (Baars 1997, 2005; Dehaene and Naccache 2001; Dehaene 2014) Theories confer activity in PFC a crucial role in enabling conscious perception. Moreover, while Global

Workspace Theory requires global and elevated activity distributed in a frontoparietal network, Higher Order Theory expects specific computations in PFC to be responsible for visual conscious experiences.

While it is sometimes described as a 'brain mapping' issue (for example, in the form of questions like '*Where* is the neural basis of consciousness?'), finding the NCC is hardly a simple 'localization' job. This is not to say that identifying certain areas differentially involved during conscious experiences is not part of what is required for finding the NCC. But the theoretically interesting quest for the NCC goes beyond straightforward 'brain mapping'. Success in finding the NCC is likely to involve describing how multiple brain areas work in conjunction to sustain conscious experiences, as well as the neural computations and the computational architecture behind them. Importantly, there are also important conceptual and experimental design issues that are relevant, where philosophy can play a key role. By highlighting some neurobiological and computational modeling results, we will argue that the currently available evidence favors a hierarchical processing architecture that confers a crucial, if subtle and specific, role to PFC. After presenting the relevant results, we discuss some methodological and functional implications of this neural architecture supporting conscious experiences. To anticipate, we note that despite the apparent stark differences between conscious and unconscious perceptual processing, available evidence suggests that their neural substrates must be largely shared. This indicates that the difference in neural activity between conscious and unconscious perceptual processing is likely to be subtle and highly specialized. In consequence, imaging techniques that focus only on marked differences between conscious and unconscious levels of activity are likely to be insensitive to the relevant neural activity patterns that underlie conscious experiences. Finally, it follows from the evidence we discuss that the functional advantages of conscious over unconscious perceptual processing may be more limited than commonly thought.

11.1 Finding the Neural Correlates of Consciousness

Scientists study the neural difference between being conscious versus unconscious in at least two different ways. First, they may focus on the neural differences of being conscious versus unconscious overall (e.g. wakefulness, anesthesia, coma, sleep, etc.), also referred to as 'state-consciousness'. Alternatively, they may focus on the neural activity that determines whether someone is conscious of something or not (e.g. seeing or not seeing a face, seeing a face versus seeing a house, hearing or not hearing a sound, feeling or not feeling pain, etc.). This is often referred to in the literature as 'content-consciousness' and it will be the main focus in this chapter.[1]

---

[1] See (Hohwy 2009) for discussion of problems with the study of content- and state-NCC. See (Noe and Thompson 2004) for discussion of problems with the content-NCC approach. For a recent review of state-NCC research, see (Gosseries et al. 2014). Note that neuroscientists' terms 'content-' and

When studying the NCC, scientists seek necessary and sufficient neural events that cause conscious experiences.[2] However, it has been acutely pointed out that finding necessary conditions for consciousness can be challenging (Chalmers 2000). First, after damage to a specific part of the brain (e.g. stroke, surgery, etc.), mental functions—including consciousness—may be lost. But they may also be recovered thanks to neuroplasticity: the brain's capacity to 'rewire' itself. In some rare cases, cognitive functions and consciousness are never lost at all, even after massive, albeit slow, destruction of neural tissue (Feuillet et al. 2007).

Second, redundancy makes finding necessary conditions for consciousness unlikely. It is not uncommon that the brain has redundant or backup mechanisms for performing the same function. This means that consciousness could be sustained by more than one neural mechanism. If mechanism x causally sustains consciousness, x is undoubtedly an NCC. But consciousness may be overdetermined if mechanisms x and y can cause the same type of conscious event independently. In this case, if x is damaged but y is spared, consciousness would still take place. This would demonstrate that x is not a necessary condition for that type of conscious event, even though it is *ex hypothesi* its neural correlate (or one of them). Thus, preservation of consciousness when a brain region is destroyed, impaired, or when it does not display any measurable activity does not in and of itself show that normal activity in that region is not an NCC.

Third, convergent evolution could have produced independent mechanisms for consciousness in two species whose common ancestor lacked either mechanism. It may be the case that something as complex as consciousness emerged during evolution just once, but it is not necessary. If different species (say, humans and octopuses) sustain conscious experiences via different types of neural mechanisms, neither would be necessary for consciousness in a strong metaphysical sense. For all these reasons, establishing strict necessary conditions for consciousness is unlikely to be successful. If anything, we can aspire to restricted necessity claims that include clauses like 'in humans' or 'in normal conditions'.[3]

Finding sufficient neural conditions for consciousness is not without challenges either. For instance, everything else being the same, the whole brain is likely to be sufficient for sustaining conscious experiences. Yet, postulating the whole brain as the NCC would not be informative. Instead, neuroscientists are interested in the '*minimal* set of neural events jointly *sufficient* for a specific conscious experience (given the appropriate enabling conditions)' (Koch 2004: 97); or 'core realizers' of consciousness for short (see Shoemaker 1981). Delimiting what counts as a core realizer is far from straightforward (Chalmers 2000; Aru et al. 2012). For instance, when comparing a condition in which subjects report being conscious of a stimulus against a condition in which subjects report no consciousness of it, the difference between these two conditions should be

---

'state-consciousness' are often described by philosophers as 'state-' and 'creature-consciousness', respectively (Rosenthal 1993).

[2] The term 'correlate' falls short of capturing necessary and sufficient conditions. We just follow the terminology used in the field at least since Crick and Koch (1990).

[3] Establishing what counts as a normal condition is complicated too, but we sidestep this issue here.

conscious awareness only. Yet, distilling stimulation and cognition from consciousness is not easy. Controlling for stimulation, attention, and performance capacity (e.g. accuracy, reaction time, etc.), such that these are matched across conscious and unconscious conditions is hard to achieve experimentally (Lau 2008; Morales et al. 2015; Morales et al. 2019). During imaging experiments, prerequisites (e.g. stimulus processing, attention) and consequences (e.g. performance, attention, working memory, motor preparation, verbal report, etc.) of consciousness can be easily confounded with the actual NCC (Lumer and Rees 1999; Tse et al. 2005; Aru et al. 2012; Bachmann 2015). Using lesion patients for whom performance is constant across subjective judgments of awareness and unawareness without experimental manipulation does not eliminate all the problems. Not only are these patients rare and their deficits often constrained in specific ways, their lesions are hardly ever limited to clear-cut anatomical or functional regions. Moreover, these patients' brains often rewire and recover functions in peculiar ways, which hinders making general inferences.

A practical limitation when studying the NCC is the methods currently available for detecting neural activity in the relevant functional networks. In the last few decades, sophisticated non-invasive imaging techniques such as functional magnetic resonance imaging (fMRI) have been added to decades-old technology like electroencephalography (EEG), magnetoencephalography (MEG), and positron emission tomography (PET). These technologies, however, have strong limitations with respect to either their spatial or temporal resolutions, or both. They are also indirect measurements of neural activity: oxygenated blood, electrical and magnetic signals measured outside the skull, or glucose consumption detected via positron-emitting radioactive tracers. Electrocorticography (ECoG) allows making measurements with better signal-to-noise ratio and good temporal resolution by placing electrodes directly over the cortex, but it requires risky surgical intervention. For obvious medical and ethical reasons, the use of this technology in humans is very limited. In contrast, direct single- and multi-unit recording of neural activity offers unsurpassable spatiotemporal resolution. Unfortunately, it requires inserting electrodes directly into or right next to neurons, making it an extremely invasive method. In consequence, it is available almost exclusively in other animals such as monkeys or rats. Working with animal models offers multiple advantages (Passingham 2009), but the study of consciousness may be challenging even when ingenious solutions have been devised (Leopold and Logothetis 1996). We will come back to some of the limitations of these methods when assessing the available empirical evidence for the NCC.

Finally, restricted necessary and sufficient conditions should ideally be established via causal interventions. By directly manipulating neural activity, we may reveal the causal mechanisms underlying conscious states (Craver 2007; Neisser 2012). Manipulating the brain safely and effectively, however, is a major challenge—especially in humans. Genetic, chemical, and surgical interventions are risky, almost exclusively available in other animals and likely to affect more than just conscious awareness. More promising may be the use of non-invasive technology such as transcranial magnetic stimulation (TMS). TMS pulses project a small magnetic field onto the surface of the brain through a coil placed outside the skull. Depending on the number and frequency of pulses, the magnetic field can enhance or inhibit neural activity in the target region. This allows researchers to create reversible 'virtual lesions' for short intervals and test whether the target region was subserving the function of interest, including conscious awareness. While promising, the precise mechanisms of action of TMS are still poorly understood and its effects can only be coarsely controlled (Sandrini et al. 2011).

11.2 Theoretical Predictions Regarding the NCC

Different theories about the nature and localization of the NCC place their explanatory power at different levels (Hardcastle 2000). The emphasis has sometimes been laid on neurochemistry ([e.g. activation of the NDMA neuroreceptor that forms large neural assemblies (Flohr 1995)), neuronal types (e.g. spindle neurons (Allman et al. 2005; Butti et al. 2013)), systemic properties (e.g. integrated information (Tononi 2008)) and functional neuroanatomy (e.g. specific neurophysiological markers and neural activity in specific regions or networks; for recent reviews see (Dehaene and Changeux 2011; Lau and Rosenthal 2011; Koch et al. 2016)). In this section, we briefly discuss some of the main recent functional neuroanatomical theories. In no way is this an attempt at a thorough review. Not only we do not discuss other viable empirical theories of the NCC, we only make succinct presentations of the ones discussed. Rather, our goal is to show that the theories we discuss predict different neural implementations of consciousness, especially regarding the role of PFC, providing an opportunity to arbitrate empirically between several theoretical frameworks.

11.2.1 Neural Synchrony Theory

Much of the recent interest in finding the NCC was set off by the introduction of Neural Synchrony Theory (Crick and Koch 1990). According to this theory, at the psychological level consciousness depends on short-term memory and attention. At the neural level, attention makes groups of relevant neurons fire in a coherent way giving rise to conscious percepts. Neurons in different areas often fire independently of each other. However, attention can make their firing rates become synchronized in fast waves (between 40 and 70 times per second). This temporal coherence achieves a global unity imposed on different areas of the brain that activates short-term (working) memory. Crick and Koch hypothesize that this basic oscillatory mechanism underlies all kinds of consciousness (e.g. visual, auditory, tactile, or painful experiences). Thus, the NCC is identified in their theory with a special type of activity (i.e. neural firings oscillating at 40–70Hz). The specific contents of conscious experiences depend on the specialized cortex where the activity takes place. In the case of vision, different features of visual stimuli are processed by different areas of visual cortex (e.g. V1/orientation, V4/color, MT-V5/motion). The brain binds together all these features in a single, coherent, and conscious percept by synchronizing the neural activity in these areas. Moreover, this activity is coordinated by zones in sensory cortices that are rich in feedback neurons (i.e. neurons that project from a higher area to a lower area). These feedback projecting zones also exist in other regions, such as the thalamus or the claustrum, which may play a major coordination role (Crick and Koch 2005). Thus, synchronized firing at about 40–70Hz is proposed as a necessary and sufficient condition for consciousness (provided enabling conditions such as attention and activation of working memory are met). Importantly, even though the NCC in Crick and Koch's proposal are highly distributed across brain areas, PFC is not predicted to play any significant role in sustaining conscious activity. At most, PFC may be relevant for attention, sustaining contents in working memory, and reporting conscious contents.

11.2.2 Two-Visual-Systems Hypothesis

According to an influential theory advanced by Milner and Goodale (1995, 2006), the neural correlates of visual awareness are restricted to activity in the ventral stream of the visual processing pathway. There are corticocortical projections from early visual cortex (V1) that later split into two processing streams (Ungerleider and Mishkin 1982). One stream is located dorsally and ends in parietal cortex, the other stream runs on a ventral pathway that ends in inferior temporal cortex. The Two-Visual-Systems Hypothesis relies on neurophysiological and anatomical evidence in monkeys, as well as neuropsychological evidence in humans, to suggest activity in the dorsal stream is associated with visually-based action (for example, saccades or visually guided hand movements) and egocentric representations (i.e. representations of objects from the subject's point of view). Despite involving complex computations, activity in this stream is not normally available to awareness according to this view. In contrast, activity in the ventral stream is typically associated with allocentric representations (i.e. objective representations independent of the subject's perspective) and visual object recognition. Objective visual representations have shape, size, color, lightness, and location constancies that allow subjects to re-identify objects independently of viewpoint (Burge 2010). Milner and Goodale argue that 'visual phenomenology...can arise only from processing in the ventral stream' (2006: 202). In other words, activity in the ventral stream is necessary for awareness. Additionally, attentional modulation that selects a represented object is required. Object representations in the ventral stream and attention are jointly sufficient for conscious awareness. Importantly, they think prefrontal cortex exerts 'some sort of top-down executive control...that can initiate the operation of attentional search' (2006: 232), guide eye movements and motor control. However, activity in prefrontal cortex would be considered in and of itself irrelevant for conscious awareness.

11.2.3 Local Recurrency Theory

Local Recurrency Theory (LRT) proposes three stages involved in visual information processing. First, after stimulus presentation there is a rapid, unconscious feedforward sweep (~100–200ms) of activity from visual cortex (V1) to motor and prefrontal cortex. Immediately after, in a second processing stage, an exchange of information within and across high- and low-level visual areas starts taking place. This fast and widespread information exchange is achieved by means of so-called recurrent processing, namely, neural activity in horizontal connections within a visual area, and activity in feedback connections from higher level areas back to lower levels (all the way back to V1). Local recurrent processing enables the exchange of information of different visual properties (e.g. orientation, shape, color, motion, etc.) that are processed independently in different visual areas. This facilitates the required 'perceptual grouping' (Lamme 2006: 497) for forming coherent conscious representations of objects. According to LRT, this second stage of recurrent processing is the NCC as it is both necessary and sufficient for phenomenal consciousness (Lamme and Roelfsema 2000; Lamme et al. 2002): 'That recurrent processing is necessary for visual awareness is now fairly well established, and supported by numerous experiments' (Lamme 2010: 216); 'According to such empirical and theoretical arguments, [local recurrent processing] is the key neural ingredient of consciousness. We could even define consciousness as recurrent processing' (Lamme 2006: 499). Finally, in a late third stage, this reverberating activity becomes a widespread co-activated network involving visual and fronto-parietal areas through attentional amplification. Motor and prefrontal cortex activity enables response preparation, keeping information in working memory and other types of cognitive control like attending, changing response strategies, or inhibiting response. For LRT, this later frontoparietal activity is required exclusively for report and cognitive control (what Block (2007) calls 'access consciousness'), not for supporting conscious experiences themselves (what Block (2007) calls 'phenomenal consciousness'). One surprising consequence of the view is that conscious experiences take place even if they are not reportable or accessible to the subject (Landman et al. 2003; Block 2007; Sligte et al. 2008; Vandenbroucke et al. 2015). In other words, it would be possible to be conscious without knowing it and without any possible behavioral and cognitive manifestation of such phenomenal experiences (Block 2019).[4] In many cases, according to LRT, when subjects report unawareness, they may just be reporting their lack of access to otherwise conscious experiences.

11.2.4 Global Workspace Theory

According to Global Workspace Theory (GWT), after stimulus presentation, activity in visual areas starts accumulating in two independent processing streams, one that can

---

[4] See (Cohen and Dennett 2011; Kouider et al. 2012; Phillips and Morales 2020) for criticisms of the scientific viability of this position.

lead to consciousness and another that supports unconscious processing (Del Cul et al. 2009; Charles et al. 2013; Charles et al. 2014).[5] Evidence accumulation through visual information processing in each stream races to a threshold in a 'winner-takes-all' fashion (Wald 1947; Pleskac and Busemeyer 2010; Shadlen and Kiani 2013). If activity in the conscious stream reaches its threshold first, a sudden ignition 'mobilizes' perceptual representations to a widespread global workspace implemented in frontoparietal interconnected neurons. This global broadcasting makes visual representations available for report and cognitive control, which results in a visual conscious experience (Dehaene and Naccache 2001; Dehaene and Changeux 2011). It is this globally broadcasted activity that GWT identifies as the NCC (Dehaene et al. 2006). Simultaneously, an unconscious stream processes the same visual stimulus. In case global ignition fails, the perceptual representation in the unconscious stream can be used if the subject is forced to provide a response, accounting for the commonly-observed capacity of subjects to perform above chance even when they are unaware of stimuli. Global workspace theorists appeal to a wealth of studies showing that all sorts of cognitive processing can be performed unconsciously to a certain extent: visual judgments, word meaning extraction, performing simple arithmetic operations, cognitive control, etc. (Dehaene et al. 2014). Note that this dual-stream approach makes the surprising assumption that every stimulus is processed twice simultaneously, which imposes stringent and possibly unnecessary computational requirements on the brain.

Global workspace theorists note that unconscious performance and neural activity associated to it are rarely at the same level as during conscious conditions. Thus, global ignition provides a necessary and minimally sufficient signature of consciousness, which according to the view, increases and maintains performance and cognitive flexibility. This signature is identified by GWT with frontoparietal activity in fMRI studies and with sudden, widespread activity in a late (~270–650ms) positive voltage in frontoparietal areas in EEG studies (also known as the P300 component) (Sergent et al. 2005; Del Cul et al. 2007; Lamy et al. 2009).

11.2.5 Higher Order Theory

The Higher Order Theory (HOT) of consciousness holds that a mental state is conscious by virtue of its relation to some higher-order state. A perceptual representation alone is never in and of itself conscious. Rather, it becomes conscious when it is somehow 'tagged' or meta-represented by another, higher-order state. According to some versions of HOT, this relation is achieved by means of the higher-order state's representing the first-order state in ways similar to thought or perception (Lycan 2004; Rosenthal 2004; Brown 2015). What different versions of higher-order theories have in common is that

---

[5] Not to be confused with the dorsal and ventral streams discussed by the Two-Visual-Systems Hypothesis. According to GWT, the conscious and unconscious streams may be implemented in largely overlapping anatomical regions.

'a mere change in the higher order representation or process is sufficient to lead to a change in subjective awareness, even if all first-order representations remain the same' (Lau and Rosenthal 2011: 365).

HOT holds that first-order representations depend on neural activity in early visual areas, whereas higher-order processes (whether these re-represent first-order content or not) are implemented mainly in prefrontal (and parietal) cortex in both human and other primates (Lau and Rosenthal 2011; Brown et al. 2019). More specifically, consciousness emerges from a hierarchical processing architecture in which unconscious visual information processed in early areas gets selected by downstream mechanisms in PFC. One of HOT's main predictions, then, is that disrupting the activity responsible for sustaining higher-order processes in prefrontal cortex should affect or eliminate visual experiences without affecting performance (because performance is driven mainly by unconscious first-order representations in early sensory cortex). Importantly, disruptions to PFC should affect conscious experiences themselves, not just report or access to visual experiences, as expected by LRT. In contrast to GWT, HOT does not expect global activity to be predictive of conscious awareness. PFC activity related to consciousness may be very subtle as it may just need to select relevant visual processes in early areas (Lau 2019; see also Gershman 2019). Thus, HOT predicts that massive alterations to PFC may not be sufficient to disrupt consciousness as long as specific PFC activity is preserved. Perhaps more surprisingly, some versions of HOT predict that specific activity in PFC is necessary and minimally sufficient for consciousness. In other words, if the 'tagging' activity normally responsible for consciousness takes place in the absence of a 'tagged' state, conscious experiences may still occur (e.g., this might be a mechanism for explaining hallucinations).

In summary, these theories make very different general predictions about the nature and location of the NCC. They also make very different specific predictions regarding the role of PFC in consciousness, behavior, and the computational architecture underlying conscious processing. Neural Synchrony Theory, Two Visual Systems Hypothesis, and Local Recurrency Theory focus on activity in sensory areas in fact denying any role in consciousness for PFC.[6] GWT accepts PFC plays an important role, emphasizing the heightened level of activity and its distribution through frontoparietal areas. In contrast, HOT confers PFC a dominant role in consciousness because of the specific and subtle function it plays within a hierarchical processing architecture.

A clear sign of progress in the scientific quest for the neural correlates of consciousness is that despite their initial popularity, some theories are completely abandoned in light of subsequent evidence. The Neural Synchrony Theory, for example, has lost credibility thanks to multiple studies finding oscillations at 40Hz in the absence of awareness and failing to detect these same oscillations during reports of conscious experiences (for a brief review, see Koch et al. 2016). The Two-Visual-Systems Hypothesis (at least with respect to its commitment to the ventral stream being the NCC) has also been the

---

[6] Neural Synchrony Theory and Local Recurrency Theory further specify that consciousness is associated with a specific type of feedback activity.

subject of strong skepticism after considering the mounting evidence against the independence of the dorsal and ventral streams and their proposed clear-cut roles (Wu 2014; Briscoe and Schwenkler 2015).

In Sections 11.3 and 11.4, we discuss neuroscientific and computational evidence relevant for arbitrating between the theoretical frameworks of the other three theories discussed in this section—LRT, GWT, and HOT—and their predictions regarding the NCC and PFC's involvement.

11.3 THE NCC: EVIDENCE FOR PFC'S INVOLVEMENT

Activity in PFC is crucial for supporting conscious perceptual experiences.[7] Multiple neuroimaging studies have systematically found increased activity in prefrontal and parietal cortex when comparing conscious versus unconscious conditions, often even when performance capacity is controlled for (Dehaene et al. 2001; Gross et al. 2004; Sergent et al. 2005; Lau and Passingham 2006; for recent reviews see Dehaene and Changeux 2011; Lau and Rosenthal 2011; Boly et al. 2017; Odegaard et al. 2017;). Some researchers minimize PFC's importance in the NCC arguing that it plays an important function in attention, report, and cognitive control, but that it has a negligible role in consciousness (Tsuchiya et al. 2015; Koch et al. 2016). While these ideas are not new (Lumer and Rees 1999; Tse et al. 2005), they have sparked a renewed interest in the topic.

Admittedly, interpreting imaging results can be challenging. During an imaging experiment, reasons other than a causal role in supporting conscious experiences might lead to statistically significant results (e.g. noise or different functions performed by the same areas). As discussed in Section 11.1, a more robust way of determining if an area of the brain is necessary for supporting a function is to permanently or temporarily impair it. If the function is lost, a constrained necessity claim may be warranted. Relatedly, if the function is not lost, not only are constrained necessity claims harder to maintain, the non-affected areas become candidates for being sufficient for supporting that function.[8] With this logic in mind, recent studies with carefully controlled psychophysical methods have investigated how PFC lesions (Del Cul et al. 2009; Fleming et al. 2014) and temporarily induced impairments by transcranial magnetic stimulation (Rounis

---

[7] For simplicity we refer collectively to PFC, but activity relevant for consciousness is likely to be found in more specific areas, such as dorsolateral PFC, insula, and other orbitofrontal and rostrolateral regions.

[8] Necessity claims or denials in this context have to be constrained for the reasons discussed in Section 11.1. Other species may implement consciousness differently, preventing any unconstrained necessity claim. But, perhaps more importantly for the neuroscientific study of consciousness, failures to eliminate a function—consciousness in this case—need not imply that the area was not necessary (in a constrained way) for supporting the function. The impairment might not have been specific enough or the brain might have repurposed other circuits to implement that function which, otherwise, would have been implemented in the impaired area under normal conditions.

et al. 2010) impact visual experiences. The results of these studies have been univocal: permanent and temporary impairments to PFC do not abolish objective visual task performance capacity, while they affect subjective judgments. Either the percentage of visible stimuli decreased despite constant performance (Del Cul et al. 2009; Rounis et al. 2010) or these subjective judgments became less diagnostic of task performance (Fleming et al. 2014). In the case of lesion patients, the capacity to use subjective ratings to diagnose task performance (i.e. metacognitive capacity) was impaired by 50 per cent (Fleming et al. 2014).

Nevertheless, several objections are often raised against this evidence. First, it is argued that these impairments only affect subjective judgments mildly, while damage to early visual areas like V1 abolish visual consciousness completely; second, that PFC does not represent conscious content specifically, which confers it a limited role (if any); and, third, that the activity detected in PFC during imaging studies pertain to attention and report, not consciousness per se. We address these objections in order.

11.3.1 PFC Activity Related to Consciousness is Highly Specific

Lesions to V1, in fact, can often completely abolish visual experiences (Weiskrantz 1997; Melnick et al. 2016). When V1 is affected, as in blindsight, the sensory signal is degraded to the point of preventing subjective judgments of consciousness. In blindsight patients, the lateral geniculate nucleus (LGN) is spared. This relay center of visual information from the retina to early visual areas in the occipital lobe is located in the thalamus, and is likely responsible for driving objective performance of blindsight patients (Schmid et al. 2010). This does not rule out that in normal cases the proper functioning of early visual areas is required even if not sufficient, for consciousness.

A second point to highlight is that PFC functions very differently from sensory cortices. For instance, neuronal coding in PFC is relatively distributed, is rarely linear and shows a high degree of mixed selectivity (Mante et al. 2013; Rigotti et al. 2013). This means that, unlike visual cortex whose function is highly specialized for processing visual information, PFC's role in consciousness is performed by highly specific patterns of activity as it is responsible for carrying out many other functions as well. Therefore, to exclusively produce a large disruption of perceptual experience, neural patterns of activity in PFC would need to be affected in highly specific ways.

Relatedly, frontal and parietal cortices are densely connected and frontal regions display high neuroplasticity (Barbas and Mesulam 1981; Petrides and Pandya 1984; Andersen et al. 1985; Cavada and Goldman-Rakic 1989; Miller and Cohen 2001; Croxson et al. 2005). This implies that the brains of patients with frontal impairments can rewire rapidly by the time they can be tested, often several months after the lesion. Lesions produced by trauma, stroke, or ablation are often too unspecific, but sometimes they are extended enough to likely include all regions responsible for consciousness. However, because these same regions support many central cognitive functions (Duncan and

Owen 2000; Miller 2000; Badre and D'Esposito 2009; Passingham and Wise 2012), patients may be so generally impaired that testing them immediately following the brain damage may not be straightforward (Mettler 1949; Knight and Grabowecky 1995). As further support for this point, chemical inactivation in rodent and monkey PFC and regions strongly connected to PFC (e.g. pulvinar) lead to strong effects in subjective confidence judgments without affecting performance in perceptual and even memory tasks. In these cases, the animals are tested immediately after PFC or pulvinar are inactivated, preventing compensatory rewiring (Romanski et al. 1997; Shipp 2003; Pessoa and Adolphs 2010; Komura et al. 2013; Lak et al. 2014; Miyamoto et al. 2017). This background makes the specific effects of lesions or temporary impairments of PFC on subjective judgments indeed quite robust.

11.3.2 PFC Encodes Specific Content

Another recent objection is that PFC activity does not encode specific content (Koch et al. 2016), making its role as the NCC likely to be limited. First, specific content representation of visual experiences in PFC is not explicitly predicted by all theories (Lau 2019). For instance, PFC may enable conscious perception through connections to early visual areas where the specific content is supported (Lau and Rosenthal 2011). Second, and perhaps more importantly in terms of interpreting the available neuroscientific evidence correctly, denying that PFC represents explicit contents of conscious experiences is empirically unsupported.

Researchers often perform simple contrastive univariate analysis with fMRI data. In this kind of analysis, the overall levels of activity belonging to one experimental condition are simply compared to (subtracted from) the overall levels of activity in another condition (e.g. conscious versus unconscious trials). But univariate fMRI analysis provides limited sensitivity. As mentioned above, activity in PFC is hardly linear and neurons exhibit mixed selectivity, which varies widely upon contextual changes. Measuring the overall levels of activity is at best a coarse approximation to the relevant neural activity. Hence, visual content supported by specific patterns of activity may only be decoded effectively with careful analysis and sophisticated modeling strategies (Ester et al. 2015; Stokes 2015). This includes multivariate analyses that go beyond a simple subtraction of overall activity. One example of this is multi-voxel pattern analysis (MVPA), where a decoder is trained to classify the *patterns* of activity in two conditions of interest. For example, if subjects are presented with two types of stimuli in different trials, say, houses and faces, the decoder can be trained to distinguish between patterns of activity pertaining to houses and patterns pertaining to faces. A successful decoder classifies above chance a novel set of data (usually data from the same subject that was left out during training) as belonging to house- or face-trials. MVPA reveals that perceptual content can be decoded from PFC in a simple perceptual decision task (Cortese et al. 2016), and that the pattern of activity in PFC reflects specific perceptual content even under several straining conditions (Wang et al. 2013). In another recent study, patterns of activity specific to subjective confidence judgments in perceptual and memory trials were successfully decoded from PFC (Morales et al. 2018).

Finally, it could be objected that the spatiotemporal resolution of fMRI offers only a limited insight into neural activity, even when these sophisticated multivariate analyses are used. After all, it only gives us access to ~2 second snapshots of indirect blood-oxygen level dependent (BOLD) activity driven by the hundreds of thousands of neurons found in each voxel (i.e. the minimum resolution in fMRI, equivalent to a 3D pixel of approximately 3 × 3 × 3mm). However, direct single- and multi-unit neural activity recording in monkeys offer a significantly higher spatiotemporal resolution (i.e. in the order of milliseconds and down to a single neuron) and multiple studies have unambiguously confirmed that specific perceptual decisions can be decoded from PFC (Kim and Shadlen 1999; Mante et al. 2013; Rigotti et al. 2013).

11.3.3 PFC is Crucial for Consciousness, not just Attention or Report

Together, the aforementioned evidence indicates that activity in PFC is necessary for visual consciousness. However, most of the fMRI studies mentioned above involved subjects explicitly reporting their conscious experience. A legitimate worry is that this activity does not reflect conscious perception per se and that, rather, it is confounded by the task demand to report or attend the stimulus (Tsuchiya et al. 2015; Koch et al. 2016). Some of these concerns have recently been rekindled by neuroimaging studies where subjects were not required to make explicit subjective judgments about visual stimuli and activity in prefrontal cortex previously related to consciousness was significantly diminished or undetected (Frässle et al. 2014; Brascamp et al. 2015; Tsuchiya et al. 2015).

The issues concerning limited sensitivity of methods commonly used in fMRI studies, specifically univariate analysis concerning PFC, are relevant here. Using more sensitive methods in humans, such as direct intracranial electrophysiological recording (electrocorticography, or ECoG), reveals activity related to visual consciousness in PFC even when subjects were not required to respond to the stimulus (Noy et al. 2015). Perhaps more importantly, in direct neuronal recordings in nonhuman primates who viewed stimuli passively, activity specifically related to the stimulus was detected in PFC (Panagiotaropoulos et al. 2012). It could be argued, however, that even under passive viewing an over-trained animal may still attend the stimuli or implicitly prepare a report (which could increase prefrontal activity for reasons unrelated to consciousness (Block 2019)). But even unreported features of a visual stimuli can be decoded from PFC activity. That is, even when the animal had to report on a different, orthogonal stimulus feature, the unattended and unreported feature was encoded in PFC (Mante et al. 2013). It is very unlikely that the monkeys prepared to attend or report on both features, especially considering that the task was challenging and involved near-threshold stimuli.

It is important to note that this does not mean that in studies of conscious perception making explicit reports does not further drive activity in PFC. PFC activity is involved in all sorts of higher cognition, not just conscious awareness. But this is consistent with the hypothesis that most univariate imaging techniques will only reveal the most heightened activity. It is also consistent with the observation by Noy and colleagues (2015) that their positive ECoG findings in PFC were subtle when no report was required. Still, in more direct recordings unreported stimulus features were robustly decoded, almost at the same level as attended and reported features (Mante et al. 2013). Thus, we conclude that objections from the so-called 'no-report' paradigms may have been exaggerated (Michel and Morales 2019).

In summary, the important role of PFC in visual conscious experiences resists common objections. As anticipated in the first section, when looking for the NCC, methodological hurdles have to be considered with utmost care. When studying consciousness, non-invasive tools like fMRI may seem ideal for making inferences about neural function in humans. However, its spatiotemporal limitations as well as the prevalence of simple statistical approaches should give us pause, especially when confronted with null findings. When ECoG and single- and multi-unit cell recordings along with multi-voxel pattern decoding analysis are incorporated, the picture that emerges is that activity in PFC is a serious candidate for being the NCC. We note that this is incompatible with the main predictions made by LRT. Also, despite predicting an involvement of PFC during global ignition, GWT's requirement of global, heightened activity does not fit well with the evidence presented in this section. This evidence points towards a subtler and more specific role of frontal activity during conscious awareness. HOT also predicts an important role of PFC as the NCC but, in contrast to GWT, it does not require the relevant activity to be particularly heightened or distributed.

11.4. The Architecture of the NCC: Computational Considerations

Neuroimaging as well as direct cortical recordings offer evidence for determining where activity supporting conscious experiences is located in the brain. Multivariate analyses can even distinguish specific patterns of conscious and unconscious activity, rather than merely detecting a difference in levels of activity. Nevertheless, finding the NCC is not only a 'localization' problem. At the level of analysis we are focusing on, it also involves finding the computational architecture most likely to account for the available neurophysiological and behavioral evidence. Computational modeling offers a non-invasive, formal way of comparing different models' capacities to account for behavioral data obtained in normal experimental conditions. Unlike neuroimaging and neurophysiology, where different conditions prevail across different experiments, in computational modeling the same data from a single experiment can be fed to a range of models. This is especially important for comparing the likelihood of rival possible computational architectures of the NCC, giving them an equal chance to fit the data.

Some possible models of how perceptual processing and conscious processes interact in the brain are directly ruled out by the neurophysiological evidence. For example, a model that does not predict unconscious and conscious perceptual processing to take place in two distinct regions, like the one implied by LRT, is not particularly promising when evidence of the importance of frontal regions for visual consciousness is considered. Nevertheless, multiple computational architectures may be compatible with the extant neurophysiological evidence that privileges PFC. Unconscious and conscious processes could be instantiated in different fashions. For example, on one model these distinct processes could operate in parallel. On another model, perceptual conscious processing could operate hierarchically such that later activity associated with consciousness operates as if evaluating the quality of unconscious visual processes.

We explore this issue with the illustrative case of experiments in which performance is matched while subjective judgments differ. Humans and some nonhuman animals make perceptual decisions about the external world all the time, and they are also capable of making subjective judgments regarding the quantity, quality, or reliability of their evidence regarding such perceptual decisions (e.g. by making one decision over another, by extending or suspending a search for resources, by providing visibility or confidence ratings, by placing bets regarding their likelihood of being correct, etc.) (Smith 2009; Beran et al. 2012; Fleming and Frith 2014).

Notoriously, objective perceptual decisions and subjective judgments about the stimuli can come apart in the laboratory and in clinical contexts. For instance, blindsight patients can objectively discriminate visual stimuli while denying having any subjective experience of them (Weiskrantz 1997). In experimental conditions, humans (Lau and Passingham 2006; Rounis et al. 2010; Rahnev et al. 2011; Vlassova et al. 2014; Koizumi et al. 2015; Maniscalco and Lau 2016; Samaha et al. 2016) and some other animals (Komura et al. 2013; Fetsch et al. 2014; Lak et al. 2014) can exhibit similar dissociations: subjects achieve comparable performance levels in a perceptual task while providing different subjective reports in different conditions. For example, in masking experiments (Lau and Passingham 2006; Del Cul et al. 2009; Maniscalco and Lau 2016), long and short gaps between stimulus presentation and the presentation of a mask allow subjects to identify the stimulus correctly at similar rates, while their subjective ratings of how visible the stimulus was differ significantly. These dissociations offer a unique opportunity to assess the specific processes involved in consciousness while distinguishing them from mere perceptual processing.

Here we consider three models recently used to fit data from a masking experiment (Maniscalco and Lau 2016): a single-channel, a dual-channel, and a hierarchical model (Figure 11.1). The single-channel model holds that subjective and objective judgments are different ways of evaluating the same underlying evidence generated by a single perceptual process. This sensory evidence consists on the sensory signal that arises in the brain after stimulus presentation plus the internal noise always present in neural processing. This sensory evidence is processed by the perceptual system and both objective and subjective systems tap into the same processing stream.

According to the dual-channel model, objective perceptual judgments are based on the same sensory evidence as subjective judgments when the subject is conscious of the

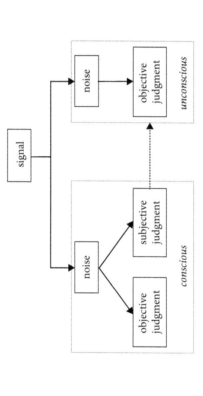

FIGURE 11.1 Diagrams of three computational models of objective and subjective judgments. *Single-channel model.* The same evidence (sensory signal + internal noise) gives rise to objective and subjective judgments. *Dual-channel model.* Two parallel streams of conscious and unconscious perceptual processing run simultaneously, each influenced by independent sources of noise. If the subjective judgment is given the lowest rating (e.g. 'not seen', 'not confident', 'guess') the unconscious stream is used for objective classification, otherwise the conscious stream is used. *Hierarchical model.* Objective and subjective judgments are driven by different processes organized in a serial hierarchy. An early stage produces objective judgments and a later stage of processing produces subjective judgments, as if evaluating the quality of the former. The second stage inherits the noise of the first, influenced by the early stage, but not vice versa.

Source: Adapted from Maniscalco and Lau (2016).

stimulus, while unconscious perceptual judgments are based on an independent, parallel source of evidence. 'Conscious' and 'unconscious' streams receive the same sensory signal but this gets affected independently by different sources of noise. If the conscious processing stream reaches a threshold first, the stimulus is classified by the brain as 'seen' and the sensory evidence is amplified and made available in working memory for further cognitive control (e.g. making a perceptual judgment about the stimulus and report that it was consciously seen). If the consciousness threshold is not crossed, the stimulus is classified by the brain as 'not seen' and the evidence accumulated in the conscious channel is discarded. If the subject still has to provide an answer—for instance, if prompted by the experimenter—the sensory evidence accumulated in the unconscious channel is used to provide a forced response.

Finally, according to the hierarchical model, the sensory evidence available for objective and subjective judgments differ, but it is not independent. The sensory signal (plus noise) is used to make objective perceptual judgments. Then, subsequent processing of this same evidence, in addition to a new source of noise, is used to make subjective judgments (Cleeremans et al. 2007; Fleming and Daw 2017). Thus, the accumulated evidence at the late stage might become degraded by the time it is tapped by subjective mechanisms due to signal decay or accrual of noise, or it may be enhanced due to further processing.

We note that these models have been proposed based on conceptually reasonable grounds. In other words, a model that fits the empirical data better provides us with substantial insight regarding the computational architecture behind conscious perception. After performing formal model comparison, Maniscalco and Lau (2016) found that the hierarchical model provided the best and more parsimonious fit to the data of the masking experiment, and it was also superior in reproducing the empirical data pattern in a series of simulations. The hierarchical model was able to account for the dissociation between performance and subjective visibility ratings by supposing that early-stage perceptual processing is better transmitted to late-stage processing when the gap between stimulus and mask is longer. Since the early stage influences task performance and the late stage governs subjective judgments, longer gaps allow more evidence accumulation. This results in higher subjective visibility judgments in trials with longer gaps between the stimulus and the mask than in trials with short gaps, in spite of having similar task performance.

The last point is of importance for arbitrating between the theories of consciousness discussed in the previous sections. LRT does not make the prediction that the manipulation of the second processing stage changes subjective judgments without affecting task performance, bearing more functional resemblance to a single-channel model. Although GWT allows for unconscious above-chance performance, it does not predict unconscious performance will be at the same level if global workspace activity, likely implemented in fronto-parietal regions, is disrupted. Some global workspace theorists explicitly endorse this dual-channel model which, at least for the masking dataset reported above, does not account well for the dissociation of objective and subjective judgments (Del Cul et al. 2009; Charles et al. 2013; Charles et al. 2014). The dual-channel model espoused by GWT, then, does not aptly account for the data presented in the previous section, where altering PFC normal functioning affects subjective judgments but preserves performance at normal levels (Fleming et al. 2014; Rounis et al. 2010). In any case, the idea of perfectly parallel processing routes for conscious and unconscious visual stimuli is unlikely to reflect the real neural circuitry involved in visual processing. As discussed above, for a long time the dorsal and ventral streams of visual processing were taken to be exclusively involved in unconscious and conscious visual representation, respectively (Milner and Goodale 2006). However, information within both streams is likely to be integrated (Wu 2014), and unlikely to be sufficient for consciousness. In sharp contrast to LRT and GWT, HOT predicts that late stage activity can be disrupted without affecting task performance. HOT explicitly proposes that downstream brain areas like PFC render sensory activity conscious by evaluating it. This puts HOT in close functional proximity to the hierarchical model, whose performance was far superior to the other two.

It is important to note that these results are limited to the analyzed dataset in Maniscalco and Lau (2016) and only further testing may confirm whether they generalize to other datasets, other experimental paradigms, or whether the hierarchical model outperforms other models. Nevertheless, it is also important to highlight that these results fit well with the data presented in the previous section according to which activity in PFC is crucial for conscious experiences. The second stage in the hierarchical model may be played by specific patterns of activity in PFC, while the earlier processing stage takes place in early visual areas.

11.5. Further Implications for the NCC

The neuroscientific and computational evidence presented in the previous sections suggests that the NCC may be found in a hierarchical processing architecture of perceptual signals in the brain. In this section, we explore some relevant implications of this architecture of the NCC.

11.5.1 Conscious and Unconscious Neural Circuitry Is Largely Shared

The Hierarchical model favored by the formal model comparison results holds that unconscious and conscious objective performance is based on the same perceptual evidence. Combined with the available neuroscientific evidence, this suggests early visual and association areas support objective judgments while PFC taps onto this evidence later in the processing hierarchy, as if evaluating it, to give rise to consciousness. One consequence of this architecture is that, as far as visual information processing is concerned, unconscious and conscious mechanisms are mostly shared. PFC conscious-related engagement with visual representations constitutes only a late portion of the conscious processing stream, otherwise shared with unconscious representations. This important realization should impact how we study consciousness as well as how we think about the function of consciousness.

11.5.2 Distinguishing Conscious and Unconscious Activity Requires Subtle Methods

The fact that these mechanisms are largely shared points towards a subtle difference between conscious and unconscious processing. When controlling for stimulus strength and performance in an experimental setting, which is crucial for discovering the NCC, neural activity levels are not likely to differ greatly between conscious and unconscious trials. Unlike activity in visual cortex, activity in PFC is often not linearly correlated with behavior or stimulus properties and frontal neurons often have mixed selectivity properties that code distinct properties in a highly contextual manner (Mante et al. 2013; Rigotti et al. 2013). This suggests that we need to be very careful when interpreting results of purported elevated and distributed activity in conscious conditions (Lamy et al. 2009; Railo et al. 2011; Dehaene 2014; Pitts et al. 2014; Koivisto et al. 2016; Koivisto and Grassini 2016). In some of these experiments, it is often the case that stimulus strength and performance is inadequately controlled for and, sometimes, dated conceptions of the nature of perception hinder the interpretation of these results (Morales et al. 2015). For instance, it is easy to mistakenly include activity related to objective stimulus processing as part of activity responsible for consciousness.

The interpretation of null findings also demands caution. Detecting subtle neural activity specifically involved in consciousness requires highly sensitive methods. Current, non-invasive imaging technologies like univariate fMRI, MEG, or EEG are not ideal for such a task as they are only able to detect the strongest signals from the brain. Because of their particular limitations and their indirect nature, subtle yet critical activity in prefrontal cortex is easily missed when comparing activity from conscious and unconscious conditions. In other words, while there may be nothing wrong with positive results when these methods detect strong activity in prefrontal cortex, we should be conservative about the meaning of null findings. The computational and empirical evidence gathered from more powerful methods suggest that, for the most part, only subtle and highly specific patterns of activity are relevant for consciousness. It should not be surprising then, that crude methods—advanced as they are— often turn out to be unsuited for detecting critical activity for consciousness in PFC.

11.5.3 The Function of Consciousness May Be Limited

If the mechanisms for unconscious and conscious processing are mostly shared and their difference is expected to be subtle and specific, it is possible that consciousness per se does not contribute significantly to visual information processing, task performance or behavior in general (Rosenthal 2005, 2008; Robinson et al. 2015). It is hardly contested that the brain can perform lots of perceptual and cognitive tasks unconsciously (but see Peters and Lau 2015; Phillips 2016): anything from stimulus detection (Tsuchiya and Koch 2005) and word identification (Dehaene et al. 2001), to processing word meanings (Luck et al. 1996; Gaillard et al. 2006) or performing basic arithmetic (Van Opstal et al. 2011). Even high-level cognitive functions, such as cognitive control (Koizumi et al. 2015) or working memory (Samaha et al. 2016) show no apparent benefit from conscious awareness in controlled experimental conditions.

Denying the role of consciousness in behavior might strike as rather counterintuitive. Conscious experiences, it would seem, allow us to make fine-grained discriminations and to increase performance, and even to form beliefs, reason, and act (Tye 1996). In fact, in experiments showing above-chance performance in unconscious trials, the effects tend to be small and elicited only in forced-choice contexts. However, unconscious stimuli often differ from conscious ones in other ways besides consciousness. For instance, stimuli are often rendered unconscious by weakening perceptual stimulation (e.g. lower contrast, shorter presentation, higher noise, inattention, etc.), which has the effect of reducing the signal-to-noise ratio of the perceptual evidence. A lower signal-to-noise ratio alters first-order representations, expectedly decreasing performance capacity and the effect of attentional magnification. In these cases, it is the decreased signal-to-noise ratio elicited by the stimulation conditions rather than the stimulus being unconscious that accounts for the difference in performance capacity. This is why it is crucial to insist that performance capacity is a confound that needs to be controlled for when searching for the NCC (Morales et al. 2015; Morales et al. 2019). This, of course, is not to deny consciousness has *some* function; although it does invite a rethink of what the functions of consciousness might be (e.g. the initiation of action or availability for rational thought). Here we just point out that it is not a necessary trait of conscious experiences to enable better performance than during unconscious processing.

11.6 Conclusions

The current science of consciousness is gradually achieving maturity. Fair assessments of empirical evidence related to the NCC, however, require subtle and thorough theoretical work. Determining necessary and sufficient neural conditions for consciousness goes beyond merely 'mapping' conscious-related activity (or lack thereof) onto certain brain areas. First, detecting or failing to detect activity in a brain area is not immediately uncontroversial evidence in favor or against that area being the NCC. For instance, activity in certain areas during conscious conditions may be confounded with activity of some other cognitive capacities related to performance, attention, or cognitive control. Also, activity supporting consciousness in normal situations may be subtle and, hence, hard to detect with traditional methods. In consequence, scientists and philosophers need to be cautious as a few null results may not be sufficient for ruling out certain area as an important NCC. Second, a simple mapping of relevant brain areas is insufficient for explaining the overall computational architecture supporting consciousness. Even if a certain brain area is found to be related to consciousness, activity in that area could be consistent with different processing architectures. So, the NCC is probably better understood as brain-wide interconnected processing rather than isolated activity in a single brain area.

Importantly, the empirical efforts behind the search for the NCC go beyond functional localization as they can also shed light on theoretical issues. As different theories make distinct predictions regarding the neurofunctional and computational architecture involved in consciousness, we can use empirical findings to arbitrate between these theories. Here we found that the main predictions made by the Local Recurrency Theory regarding the NCC are not supported by currently available evidence. A vast body of evidence using different methodologies privileges PFC as a crucial area for consciousness, which is incompatible with its central predictions. In contrast, both the Global Workspace and Higher Order Theories predict PFC must have a major function in conscious awareness. We argued from a study involving a formal model comparison that a hierarchical computational model akin to HOT's prediction of a serial processing stream is better supported than a dual-channel model akin to some versions of GWT's prediction that objective and subjective processes are implemented in parallel. While this result is limited to the analyzed dataset, when considered along with the systematic findings of PFC's relevant role for consciousness, confidence in a hierarchical implementation of the NCC may be bolstered.

Finally, the data we presented point towards some important, although perhaps unexpected, features of the study of the NCC and consciousness itself. First, we argued that the neural activity involved in conscious and unconscious perception may be largely shared. This suggests that the NCC involve subtle activity differences from unconscious processing which are detectable only by highly sensitive methods. Second, the function of consciousness may be limited. While a subtle difference in neural activity does not necessarily imply a subtle difference at the psychological, behavioral, or phenomenal level, it does make it a possibility. Only future research will be able to confirm or reject this hypothesis.

References

Allman, J. M. et al. (2005), 'Intuition and Autism: A Possible Role for Von Economo Neurons', *Trends in Cognitive Sciences*, 9/8: 367–73.
Andersen, R. A., Asanuma, C., and Cowan, W. M. (1985), 'Callosal and Prefrontal Associational Projecting Cell Populations in Area 7A of the Macaque Monkey: A Study Using Retrogradely Transported Fluorescent Dyes', *The Journal of Comparative Neurology*, 232/4: 443–55.

Aru, J. et al. (2012), 'Distilling the Neural Correlates of Consciousness', *Neuroscience and Biobehavioral Reviews*, 36/2: 737–46.

Baars, B. J. (1997), 'In the Theatre of Consciousness. Global Workspace Theory, A Rigorous Scientific Theory of Consciousness', *Journal of Consciousness Studies*, 4/4: 292–309.

Baars, B. J. (2005), 'Global Workspace Theory of Consciousness: Toward a Cognitive Neuroscience of Human Experience', in S. Laureys (ed.), *Progress in Brain Research* Amsterdam: Elsevier, 45–53.

Bachmann, T. (2015), 'On the Brain-Imaging Markers of Neural Correlates of Consciousness', *Frontiers in Psychology*, 6: 868.

Badre, D. and D'Esposito, M. (2009), 'Is the Rostro-Caudal Axis of the Frontal Lobe Hierarchical?' *Nature Reviews. Neuroscience*, 10/9: 659–69.

Barbas, H. and Mesulam, M. M. (1981), 'Organization of Afferent Input to Subdivisions of Area 8 in the Rhesus Monkey', *The Journal of Comparative Neurology*, 200/3: 407–31.

Beran, M. J. et al. (2012), *Foundations of Metacognition*. Oxford: Oxford University Press.

Block, N. (2007), 'Consciousness, Accessibility, and the Mesh Between Psychology and Neuroscience', *Behavioral and Brain Sciences*, 30/5-6: 481–99.

Block, N. (2019), 'What Is Wrong with the No-Report Paradigm and How to Fix It', *Trends in Cognitive Sciences*, 23/12: 1003–13.

Boly, M. et al. (2017), 'Are the Neural Correlates of Consciousness in the Front or in the Back of the Cerebral Cortex? Clinical and Neuroimaging Evidence', *The Journal of Neuroscience*, 37/40: 9603–13.

Brascamp, J., Blake, R., and Knapen, T. (2015), 'Negligible Fronto-Parietal BOLD Activity Accompanying Unreportable Switches in Bistable Perception', *Nature Neuroscience*, 18/11, 1672–78. doi:10.1038/nn.4130.

Briscoe, R. and Schwenkler, J. (2015), 'Conscious Vision in Action', *Cognitive Science*, 39/7: 1435–67.

Brown, R. (2015), 'The HOROR Theory of Phenomenal Consciousness', *Philosophical Studies*, 172: 1783–794.

Brown, R., Lau, H., and LeDoux, J. E. (2019), 'Understanding the Higher-Order Approach to Consciousness', *Trends in Cognitive Sciences*, 23/9: 754–68. doi:10.1016/j.tics.2019.06.009.

Burge, T. (2010), *Origins of Objectivity*. Oxford: Oxford University Press.

Butti, C. et al. (2013), 'Von Economo Neurons: Clinical and Evolutionary Perspectives', *Cortex*, 49/1: 312–26.

Cavada, C. and Goldman-Rakic, P. S. (1989), 'Posterior Parietal Cortex in Rhesus Monkey: II. Evidence for Segregated Corticocortical Networks Linking Sensory and Limbic Areas with the Frontal Lobe', *The Journal of Comparative Neurology*, 287/4: 422–45.

Chalmers, D. J. (2000), 'What Is a Neural Correlate of Consciousness' in T. Metzinger (ed.) *Neural Correlates of Consciousness* Cambridge, MA: MIT Press, 17–40.

Charles, L. et al. (2013), 'Distinct Brain Mechanisms for Conscious Versus Subliminal Error Detection', *Neuroimage*, 73: 80–94.

Charles, L., King, J.-R. and Dehaene, S. (2014), 'Decoding the Dynamics of Action, Intention, and Error Detection for Conscious and Subliminal Stimuli', *The Journal of Neuroscience*, 34/4: 1158–70.

Cleeremans, A., Timmermans, B., and Pasquali, A. (2007), 'Consciousness and Metarepresentation: A Computational Sketch', *Neural Networks*, 20/9: 1032–9.

Cohen, M. A. and Dennett, D. C. (2011), 'Consciousness Cannot Be Separated From Function', *Trends in Cognitive Sciences*, 15/8: 358–64.

Cortese, A. et al. (2016), 'Multivoxel Neurofeedback Selectively Modulates Confidence Without Changing Perceptual Performance', *Nature Communications*, 7: 13669.

Craver, C. (2007), *Explaining the Brain*. Oxford: Oxford University Press.

Crick, F. and Koch, C. (1990), 'Towards a Neurobiological Theory of Consciousness', *Seminars in the Neurosciences*, 2: 263–75.

Crick, F. C. and Koch, C. (2005), 'What Is the Function of the Claustrum?' *Philosophical Transactions of the Royal Society of London. Series B, Biological Sciences*, 360/1458: 1271–9.

Croxson, P. L. et al. (2005), 'Quantitative Investigation of Connections of the Prefrontal Cortex in the Human and Macaque Using Probabilistic Diffusion Tractography', *The Journal of Neuroscience*, 25/39: 8854–66.

Dehaene, S. et al. (2001), 'Cerebral Mechanisms of Word Masking and Unconscious Repetition Priming', *Nature Neuroscience*, 4/7: 752–8.

Dehaene, S. (2014), *Consciousness and the Brain: Deciphering How the Brain Codes Our Thoughts*. Harmondsworth: Penguin.

Dehaene, S. and Changeux, J.-P. (2011), 'Experimental and Theoretical Approaches to Conscious Processing', *Neuron*, 70/2: 200–27.

Dehaene, S. and Naccache, L. (2001), 'Towards a Cognitive Neuroscience of Consciousness: Basic Evidence and a Workspace Framework', *Cognition*, 79/1–2: 1–37.

Dehaene, S. et al. (2006), 'Conscious, Preconscious, and Subliminal Processing: A Testable Taxonomy', *Trends in Cognitive Sciences*, 10/5: 204–11.

Dehaene, S. et al. (2014), 'Toward a Computational Theory of Conscious Processing', *Current Opinion in Neurobiology*, 25: 76–84.

Del Cul, A., Baillet, S., and Dehaene, S. (2007), 'Brain Dynamics Underlying the Nonlinear Threshold for Access to Consciousness', *Plos Biology*, 5/10): E260.

Del Cul, A. et al. (2009), 'Causal Role of Prefrontal Cortex in the Threshold for Access to Consciousness', *Brain*, 132: 2531–40.

Duncan, J. and Owen, A. M. (2000), 'Common Regions of the Human Frontal Lobe Recruited By Diverse Cognitive Demands', *Trends in Neurosciences*, 23/10: 475–83.

Ester, E. F., Sprague, T. C., and Serences, J. T. (2015), 'Parietal and Frontal Cortex Encode Stimulus-Specific Mnemonic Representations During Visual Working Memory', *Neuron*, 87/4: 893–905.

Fetsch, C. R. et al. (2014), 'Effects of Cortical Microstimulation on Confidence in a Perceptual Decision', *Neuron*, 83/4: 797–804.

Feuillet, L., Dufour, H., and Pelletier, J. (2007), 'Brain of a White-Collar Worker', *The Lancet*, 370/9583: 262.

Fleming, S. M. and Daw, N. D. (2017), 'Self-Evaluation of Decision-Making: A General Bayesian Framework for Metacognitive Computation', *Psychological Review*, 124/1: 91–114.

Fleming, S. M. and Frith, C. D. (2014), *The Cognitive Neuroscience of Metacognition*. Berlin: Springer.

Fleming, S. M. et al. (2014), 'Domain-Specific Impairment in Metacognitive Accuracy Following Anterior Prefrontal Lesions', *Brain*, 137: 2811–22.

Flohr, H. (1995), 'Sensations and Brain Processes', *Behavioural Brain Research*, 71/1–2: 157–61.

Frässle, S. et al. (2014), 'Binocular Rivalry: Frontal Activity Relates to Introspection and Action But Not to Perception', *The Journal of Neuroscience*, 34/5: 1738–47.

Gaillard, R. et al. (2006), 'Nonconscious Semantic Processing of Emotional Words Modulates Conscious Access', *Proceedings of the National Academy of Sciences of the United States of America*, 103/19: 7524–9.

Gershman, S. J. (2019), 'The Generative Adversarial Brain', *Frontiers in Artificial Intelligence*, 2 September, 3059–8. doi:10.3389/frai.2019.00018.

Gosseries, O. et al. (2014), 'Measuring Consciousness in Severely Damaged Brains', *Annual Review of Neuroscience*, 37: 457–78.

Gross, J. et al. (2004), 'Modulation of Long-Range Neural Synchrony Reflects Temporal Limitations of Visual Attention in Humans', *Proceedings of the National Academy of Sciences of the United States of America*, 101/35: 13050–5.

Hardcastle, V. G. (2000), 'How to Understand the N in NCC' in T. Metzinger (ed.), *The Neural Correlates of Consciousness*. Cambridge, MA: MIT Press, 259–64.

Hohwy, J. (2009), 'The Neural Correlates of Consciousness: New Experimental Approaches Needed?' *Consciousness & Cognition*, 18/2: 428–38.

Kim, J. N. and Shadlen, M. N. (1999), 'Neural Correlates of a Decision in the Dorsolateral Prefrontal Cortex of the Macaque', *Nature Neuroscience*, 2/2: 176–85.

Knight, R. and Grabowecky, M. (1995), 'Escape From Linear Time: Prefrontal Cortex and Conscious Experience' in M. Gazzaniga (ed.), *The Cognitive Neurosciences*. Cambridge, MA: MIT Press, 1357–71.

Koch, C. (2004), *The Quest for Consciousness: A Neurobiological Approach*. New York: WH Freeman.

Koch, C. et al. (2016), 'Neural Correlates of Consciousness: Progress and Problems', *Nature Reviews. Neuroscience*, 17/5: 307–21.

Koivisto, M. and Grassini, S. (2016), 'Neural Processing Around 200 Ms After Stimulus-Onset Correlates with Subjective Visual Awareness', *Neuropsychologia*, 84: 235–43.

Koivisto, M. et al. (2016), 'Subjective Visual Awareness Emerges Prior to P3', *The European Journal of Neuroscience*, 43/12: 1601–11.

Koizumi, A., Maniscalco, B., and Lau, H. (2015), 'Does Perceptual Confidence Facilitate Cognitive Control?' *Attention, Perception & Psychophysics*, 77/4: 1295–306.

Komura, Y. et al. (2013), 'Responses of Pulvinar Neurons Reflect a Subject's Confidence in Visual Categorization', *Nature Neuroscience*, 16/6: 749–55.

Kouider, S., Sackur, J., and Gardelle, V. De (2012), 'Do We Still Need Phenomenal Consciousness? Comment on Block', *Trends in Cognitive Science*, 16/3: 140-1.

Lak, A. et al. (2014), 'Orbitofrontal Cortex Is Required for Optimal Waiting Based on Decision Confidence', *Neuron*, 84/1: 190–201.

Lamme, V. A. F. (2010), 'How Neuroscience Will Change Our View on Consciousness', *Cognitive Neuroscience*, 1/3: 204–20.

Lamme, V. A. F. (2006), 'Towards a True Neural Stance on Consciousness', *Trends in Cognitive Sciences*, 10/11: 494–501.

Lamme, V. A. F. and Roelfsema, P. R. (2000), 'The Distinct Modes of Vision Offered By Feedforward and Recurrent Processing', *Trends in Neurosciences*, 23/11: 571–9.

Lamme, V. A. F., Zipser, K., and Spekreijse, H. (2002), 'Masking Interrupts Figure-Ground Signals in V1', *Journal of Cognitive Neuroscience*, 14/7: 1044–53.

Lamy, D., Salti, M., and Bar-Haim, Y. (2009), 'Neural Correlates of Subjective Awareness and Unconscious Processing: An ERP Study', *Journal of Cognitive Neuroscience*, 21/7: 1435–46.

Landman, R., Spekreijse, H., and Lamme, V. A. F. (2003), 'Large Capacity Storage of Integrated Objects Before Change Blindness', *Vision Research*, 43/2: 149–64.

Lau, H. (2008), 'A Higher Order Bayesian Decision Theory of Consciousness', *Progress in Brain Research*, 168: 35–48.

Lau, H. (2019), 'Consciousness, Metacognition, & Perceptual Reality Monitoring', *PsyArXiv*, 10 June, doi:10.31234/osf.io/ckbyf.

Lau, H. and Passingham, R. E. (2006), 'Relative Blindsight in Normal Observers and the Neural Correlate of Visual Consciousness', *Proceedings of the National Academy of Sciences of the United States of America*, 103/49: 18763–8.

Lau, H. and Rosenthal, D. (2011), 'Empirical Support for Higher-Order Theories of Conscious Awareness', *Trends in Cognitive Sciences*, 15/8: 365–73.

Leopold, D. A. and Logothetis, N. K. (1996), 'Activity Changes in Early Visual Cortex Reflect Monkeys' Percepts During Binocular Rivalry', *Nature*, 379/6565: 549–53.

Luck, S. J., Vogel, E. K., and Shapiro, K. L. (1996), 'Word Meanings Can Be Accessed But Not Reported During the Attentional Blink', *Nature*, 383/6601: 616–18.

Lumer, E. D. and Rees, G. (1999), 'Covariation of Activity in Visual and Prefrontal Cortex Associated with Subjective Visual Perception', *Proceedings of the National Academy of Sciences of the United States of America*, 96/4: 1669–73.

Lycan, W. G. (2004), 'The Superiority of HOP to HOT', in R. J. Gennaro (ed.), *Higher-Order Theories of Consciousness: An Anthology*. Amsterdam: John Benjamins, 93–114.

Maniscalco, B. and Lau, H. (2016), 'The Signal Processing Architecture Underlying Subjective Reports of Sensory Awareness', *Neuroscience of Consciousness*, 2016/1.

Mante, V. et al. (2013), 'Context-Dependent Computation by Recurrent Dynamics in Prefrontal Cortex', *Nature*, 503/7474: 78–84.

Melnick, M. D., Tadin, D., and Huxlin, K. R. (2016), 'Relearning to See in Cortical Blindness', *The Neuroscientist*, 22/2: 199–212.

Mettler, F. A. (1949), *Selective Partial Ablation of the Frontal Cortex: A Correlative Study of Its Effects on Human Psychotic Subjects*. Ismaning: Hoeber.

Michel, M. and Morales, J. (2019), 'Minority Reports: Consciousness and the Prefrontal Cortex', *Mind & Language*, Online First, https://doi.org/10.1111/mila.12264.

Miller, E. K. (2000), 'The Prefrontal Cortex and Cognitive Control', *Nature Reviews. Neuroscience*, 1/1: 59–65.

Miller, E. K. and Cohen, J. D. (2001), 'An Integrative Theory of Prefrontal Cortex Function', *Annual Review of Neuroscience*, 24: 167–202.

Milner, D. and Goodale, M. (1995), *The Visual Brain in Action*. Oxford: Oxford University Press.

Milner, D. and Goodale, M. (2006), *The Visual Brain in Action*, 2nd edn. Oxford: Oxford University Press.

Miyamoto, K. et al. (2017), 'Causal Neural Network of Metamemory for Retrospection in Primates', *Science*, 355/6321: 188–93.

Morales, J., Chiang, J., and Lau, H. (2015), 'Controlling for Performance Capacity Confounds in Neuroimaging Studies of Conscious Awareness', *Neuroscience of Consciousness*, 2015/1.

Morales, J., Lau, H., and Fleming, S. M. (2018), 'Domain-General and Domain-Specific Patterns of Activity Support Metacognition in Human Prefrontal Cortex', *The Journal of Neuroscience*, 38/14: 3534–46.

Morales, J., Odegaard, B., and Maniscalco, B. (2019), 'The Neural Substrates of Conscious Perception Without Performance Confounds', *PsyArXiv*, 26 November, doi:10.31234/osf.io/8zhy3.

Neisser, J. (2012), 'Neural Correlates of Consciousness Reconsidered', *Consciousness and Cognition*, 21/2: 681–90.

Noe, A. and Thompson, E. (2004), 'Are There Neural Correlates of Consciousness?' *Journal of Consciousness Studies*, 11/1: 3–28.

Noy, N. et al. (2015), 'Ignition's Glow: Ultra-Fast Spread of Global Cortical Activity Accompanying Local "Ignitions" in Visual Cortex During Conscious Visual Perception', *Consciousness and Cognition*, 35: 206–24.

Odegaard, B., Knight, R. T., and Lau, H. (2017), 'Should a Few Null Findings Falsify Prefrontal Theories of Conscious Perception?' *The Journal of Neuroscience*, 37/40: 9593–602.

Panagiotaropoulos, T. I. et al. (2012), 'Neuronal Discharges and Gamma Oscillations Explicitly Reflect Visual Consciousness in The Lateral Prefrontal Cortex', *Neuron*, 74/5: 924–35.

Passingham, R. (2009), 'How Good Is the Macaque Monkey Model of the Human Brain?' *Current Opinion in Neurobiology*, 19/1: 6–11.

Passingham, R. E. and Wise, S. P. (2012), *The Neurobiology of the Prefrontal Cortex: Anatomy, Evolution, and the Origin of Insight*. Oxford: Oxford University Press.

Pessoa, L. and Adolphs, R. (2010), 'Emotion Processing and the Amygdala: From a "Low Road" to "Many Roads" of Evaluating Biological Significance', *Nature Reviews. Neuroscience*, 11/11: 773–83.

Peters, M. A. K. and Lau, H. (2015), 'Human Observers Have Optimal Introspective Access to Perceptual Processes Even for Visually Masked Stimuli', *Elife*, 4: E09651.

Petrides, M. and Pandya, D. N. (1984), 'Projections to the Frontal Cortex from the Posterior Parietal Region in the Rhesus Monkey', *The Journal of Comparative Neurology*, 228/1: 105–16.

Phillips, I. (2016), 'Consciousness and Criterion: On Block's Case for Unconscious Seeing', *Philosophy and Phenomenological Research*, 93/2: 419–51.

Phillips, I. and Morales, J. (2020), 'The Fundamental Problem with No-Cognition Paradigms', *Trends in Cognitive Sciences*, January 24, doi:10.1016/j.tics.2019.11.010.

Pitts, M. A. et al. (2014), 'Gamma Band Activity and the P3 Reflect Post-Perceptual Processes, Not Visual Awareness', *Neuroimage*, 101: 337–50.

Pleskac, T. J. and Busemeyer, J. R. (2010), 'Two-Stage Dynamic Signal Detection: A Theory of Choice, Decision Time, and Confidence', *Psychological Review*, 117/3: 864–901.

Rahnev, D. et al. (2011), 'Attention Induces Conservative Subjective Biases in Visual Perception', *Nature Neuroscience*, 14/12: 1513–15.

Railo, H., Koivisto, M., and Revonsuo, A. (2011), 'Tracking the Processes Behind Conscious Perception: A Review of Event-Related Potential Correlates of Visual Consciousness', *Consciousness and Cognition*, 20/3: 972–83.

Rigotti, M. et al. (2013), 'The Importance of Mixed Selectivity in Complex Cognitive Tasks', *Nature*, 497/7451: 585–90.

Robinson, Z., Maley, C. J., and Piccinini, G. (2015), 'Is Consciousness a Spandrel?' *Journal of the American Philosophical Association*, 1/02: 365–83.

Romanski, L. M. et al. (1997), 'Topographic Organization of Medial Pulvinar Connections with the Prefrontal Cortex in the Rhesus Monkey', *The Journal of Comparative Neurology*, 379/3: 313–32.

Rosenthal, D. M. (1993), 'State Consciousness and Transitive Consciousness', *Consciousness and Cognition*, 2/4: 355–63.

Rosenthal, D. M. (2004), 'Varieties of Higher-Order Theory' in R. J. Gennaro (ed.), *Higher-Order Theories of Consciousness: An Anthology*. Amsterdam: John Benjamins, 17–44.

Rosenthal, D. M. (2005), *Consciousness and Mind*. Oxford: Oxford University Press.

Rosenthal, D. M. (2008), 'Consciousness and Its Function', *Neuropsychologia*, 46/3: 829–40.
Rounis, E. et al. (2010), 'Theta-Burst Transcranial Magnetic Stimulation to the Prefrontal Cortex Impairs Metacognitive Visual Awareness', *Cognitive Neuroscience*, 1/3: 165–75.
Samaha, J. et al. (2016), 'Dissociating Perceptual Confidence From Discrimination Accuracy Reveals No Influence of Metacognitive Awareness on Working Memory', *Frontiers in Psychology*, 7, P.851.
Sandrini, M., Umiltà, C., and Rusconi, E. (2011), 'The Use of Transcranial Magnetic Stimulation in Cognitive Neuroscience: A New Synthesis of Methodological Issues', *Neuroscience and Biobehavioral Reviews*, 35/3: 516–36.
Schmid, M. C. et al. (2010), 'Blindsight Depends on the Lateral Geniculate Nucleus', *Nature*, 466/7304: 373–7.
Sergent, C., Baillet, S., and Dehaene, S. (2005), 'Timing of the Brain Events Underlying Access to Consciousness During the Attentional Blink', *Nature Neuroscience*, 8/10: 1391–400.
Shadlen, M. N. and Kiani, R. (2013), 'Decision Making as a Window on Cognition', *Neuron*, 80/3: 791–806.
Shipp, S. (2003), 'The Functional Logic of Cortico-Pulvinar Connections', *Philosophical Transactions of the Royal Society of London. Series B, Biological Sciences*, 358/1438: 1605–24.
Shoemaker, S. (1981), 'Some Varieties of Functionalism', *Philosophical Topics*, 12/1: 93–119.
Sligte, I. G., Scholte, H. S., and Lamme, V. A. F. (2008), Are There Multiple Visual Short-Term Memory Stores?' *Plos One*, 3/2: 1699.
Smith, J. D. (2009), 'The Study of Animal Metacognition', *Trends in Cognitive Sciences*, 13/9: 389–96.
Stokes, M. G. (2015), '"Activity-Silent" Working Memory in Prefrontal Cortex: A Dynamic Coding Framework', *Trends in Cognitive Sciences*, 19/7: 394–405.
Tononi, G. (2008), 'Consciousness as Integrated Information: A Provisional Manifesto', *The Biological Bulletin*, 215/3: 216–42.
Tse, P. U. et al. (2005), 'Visibility, Visual Awareness, and Visual Masking of Simple Unattended Targets Are Confined to Areas in the Occipital Cortex Beyond Human V1/V2', *Proceedings of the National Academy of Sciences of the United States of America*, 102/47: 17178–83.
Tsuchiya, N. and Koch, C. (2005), 'Continuous Flash Suppression Reduces Negative Afterimages', *Nature Neuroscience*, 8/8: 1096–101.
Tsuchiya, N. et al. (2015), 'No-Report Paradigms: Extracting the True Neural Correlates of Consciousness', *Trends in Cognitive Sciences*, 19/12: 757–70.
Tye, M. (1996), 'The Function of Consciousness', *Noûs*, 30/3: 287–305.
Ungerleider, L. G. and Mishkin, M. (1982), 'Two Cortical Visual Systems' in D. J. Ingle, M. A. Goodale and R. J. W. Mansfield (eds), *Analysis of Visual Behavior*. Cambridge, MA: MIT Press, 548–86.
Van Opstal, F., De Lange, F. P., and Dehaene, S. (2011), 'Rapid Parallel Semantic Processing of Numbers Without Awareness', *Cognition*, 120/1: 136–47.
Vandenbroucke, A. R. E. et al. (2015), 'Neural Correlates of Visual Short-Term Memory Dissociate Between Fragile and Working Memory Representations', *Journal of Cognitive Neuroscience*, 27/12: 2477–90.
Vlassova, A., Donkin, C., and Pearson, J. (2014), 'Unconscious Information Changes Decision Accuracy But Not Confidence', *Proceedings of the National Academy of Sciences of the United States of America*, 111/45: 16214–18.
Wald, A. (1947), *Sequential Analysis*. London: John Wiley & Sons.

Wang, M., Arteaga, D., and He, B. J. (2013), 'Brain Mechanisms for Simple Perception and Bistable Perception', *Proceedings of the National Academy of Sciences of the United States of America*, 110/35: E3350–9.

Weiskrantz, L. (1997), *Consciousness Lost and Found: A Neuropsychological Exploration*. Oxford: Oxford University Press.

Wu, W. (2014), 'Against Division: Consciousness, Information and the Visual Streams', *Mind & Language*, 29/4: 383–406.

CHAPTER 12

BEYOND THE NEURAL CORRELATES OF CONSCIOUSNESS

URIAH KRIEGEL

12.1 INTRODUCTION

THE centerpiece of the scientific study of consciousness is the search for the neural correlates of consciousness (NCC; see Morales and Lau, Chapter 11 this volume). Yet science is typically interested not only in correlation relations among natural phenomena, but also in causal and constitutive relations. Often, these causal and constitutive relations are posited as *explanations* of why certain phenomena correlate. To treat correlations as brute and inexplicable is to acquiesce in mysterious aspects of nature, somewhat as the spiritualist revels in 'weird coincidences'. It is surely the mandate of intellectual inquiry in general and science in particular to address such coincidences and shed light on why they hold.

Consider Leibniz's 'pre-established harmony theory' of the connection between mind and body (i.e., the hypothesis that at the beginning of time God established a correlation between the two, so that whenever certain changes occur in some creature's brain activity, certain events will take place simultaneously in the creature's stream of consciousness, and vice versa). In an obvious sense, this is an extremely anti-scientific approach to the correlation between consciousness and brain activity. Yet even this approach ventures *some* kind of explanation. It does not posit the correlation as brute and inexplicable. Instead, it offers a *reason* for the correlation. In so doing, it tries to make it *intelligible*. Insofar as the 'brute correlation' approach we find in current scientific research on consciousness does not even attempt to do that, it might be claimed to be even more mysterian.

With this in mind, it is natural for us to hope that the current science of consciousness could offer more than just an *identification* of the neural correlates of consciousness—that it might offer an *explanation* of why the correlation holds. The purpose of the chapter is twofold. In the first half (Sections 12.2–12.3), I want to lay out the various *possible* explanations of the correlation between consciousness and its neural correlate. The idea is to provide a sort of 'menu' of options from which we would probably have to choose—and to link it to traditional metaphysical positions on the problem of consciousness. In the chapter's second half (Sections 12.4–12.5), however, I will raise considerations suggesting that, under certain reasonable assumptions, the choice among these various options may be in principle underdetermined by the relevant scientific evidence, so that the traditional metaphysical positions may be *empirically equivalent*. I should stress that I am not entirely persuaded that the claim is true; still, the considerations supporting it strike me as quite powerful and worth contending with. If it is true, however, then the choice between different explanations of phenomenal–cerebral correlations cannot in principle be a scientific one. It must be a matter of *philosophical*-theory choice.

12.2 Neural Correlates and Explanatory Hypotheses

It is widely thought that materialism and dualism about consciousness are both compatible with the eventual discovery of the neural correlates of consciousness (NCC). One way to think of this is in terms of what we can *infer from* a correlation. Suppose, purely for the sake of exposition, that the NCC is neural synchronization with above-baseline activity in the dorsolateral prefrontal cortex (dlPFC) (Lau and Passingham 2006; Kriegel 2009: ch.7; Rounis et al. 2010). Often—though, of course, not always—correlation is an indicator of *causation*. When we notice a correlation between the striking of matches and their lighting up, we infer that striking a match *causes* it to light. This is a fairly standard form of so-called inference to the best explanation, arguably the central mode of scientific inference (Harman 1965; Lipton 1991). The reasoning proceeds as follows:

(1) Match-striking correlates with match-lighting;
(2) The best explanation of this is that match-striking *causes* match-lighting; therefore, plausibly,
(3) Match-striking causes match-lighting.

In a similar vein, we might infer from the correlation between neural synchronization with dlPFC activity and consciousness that synchronization with dlPFC activity *causes* consciousness—that this particular neural activity brings about, is responsible for the production of, consciousness. More generally, the reasoning is this:

(1) The NCC correlates with consciousness;
(2) The best explanation of this is that the NCC *causes* consciousness; therefore, plausibly,
(3) The NCC causes consciousness.

This is often the most natural explanatory hypothesis for the correlation between two phenomena: that one is simply the cause of the other.

As is well known, however, the direction of causation is often in question when explanatory inferences are performed. The largest concentration of asthmatics in the US lives in Tucson, Arizona, despite the fact that the Sonora desert's extraordinarily dry air is supposed to *help* with asthma. Obviously, the explanation of this tight correlation between dry air and incidence of asthma is not that Tucson's dry air causes people to develop asthma. On the contrary, it is that sufficiently severe asthma causes people to relocate to Tucson. By the same token, a perfectly coherent possibility is that synchronization with dlPFC activity is not so much the *cause* of consciousness as its *effect*. In this picture, there is a sort of 'downward causation' by which consciousness alters the state of the brain, a downward causation characteristic of what Chalmers (2002) calls 'type-D dualism'.[1] It is thus epistemically possible to pursue the following piece of reasoning:

(1) The NCC correlates with consciousness;
(2) The best explanation of this is that consciousness *causes* the NCC; therefore, plausibly,
(3) Consciousness causes the NCC.

The difference between this 'reverse causal hypothesis' and the 'more straightforward' causal explanation concerns what causal direction is taken to *better* explain the correlation between consciousness and the NCC. In this section I do not comment on the question of the possible hypotheses' relative merits; my goal is merely to set out the menu of options.

A further option, when faced with a correlation between two phenomena, is to maintain that there is a *third cause* responsible for the occurrence of each phenomenon independently—and thus responsible for their correlation. The correlation between lightning and thunder, for example, is best explained neither by the hypothesis that lightning causes thunder nor by the hypothesis that thunder causes lightning. Rather, there is a third element that causes both: the collision of ice and water particles inside a cloud causes lightning, on the one hand, and thunder, on the other. Since it causes both, it also causes their correlation. Likewise, one might hold that some third factor might

---

[1] At this point, I do not wish to comment on the plausibility of this view. The present discussion is intended merely to lay out the *possible* explanations.

cause the occurrence of the NCC, on the one hand, and of consciousness, on the other. Here the general explanatory inference looks like this:

(1) The NCC correlates with consciousness;
(2) The best explanation of this is that there is some third element that causes both the NCC and consciousness; therefore, plausibly,
(3) There is some third element that causes both the NCC and consciousness.

In itself, this explanatory inference is neutral on what the third cause is—what the 'X factor' is. This means that there are as many versions of this inference as there are potential X factors. One way to understand 'quantum-mechanical approaches' to consciousness (e.g., Hameroff and Penrose 1996) might be as a version of the above causal inference. The thesis is that certain quantum-mechanical events cause both changes in the brain and changes in consciousness, thus accounting for the correlation between the two. Another version is of course Leibniz's pre-established harmony theory, where God's will acts as the third cause.

Sometimes causal hypotheses are not the best explanations of correlation at all. There is a tight correlation between lifting something out of a shop and breaking the law. But this is not because shoplifting *causes* lawbreaking, but because shoplifting *is* lawbreaking. We may say that the relation between shoplifting and lawbreaking is not causal but *constitutive*: shoplifting *constitutes* breaking the law. In this case, the shoplifting breaks the law *by definition* rather than by *causation*. But arguably, there are cases where a constitutive hypothesis explains correlation better than a causal hypothesis even where no definitions are involved. When scientists first observed the remarkable correlation between water and the molecular structure known as H_2O, they did not infer that H_2O must *cause* water; instead, they inferred that H_2O must *be* water—that there is nothing more to water over and above H_2O. That is, large enough collections of H_2O molecules *constitute* bodies of water. Here the inference is from correlation to constitution. The same reasoning can be applied to the correlation between consciousness and the NCC (see Hohwy 2011):

(1) The NCC correlates with consciousness;
(2) The best explanation of this is that the NCC *constitutes* consciousness; therefore, plausibly,
(3) The NCC constitutes consciousness.

There is thus a competition between two interpretations of the correlation between consciousness and its neural correlate: a *causal* interpretation and a *constitutive* interpretation. It is the latter that characterizes physicalist theories of consciousness (see Jackson, Chapter 17 this volume).

Moreover, just as the causal interpretation admits of two opposing 'directions'—the NCC causes consciousness and consciousness causes the NCC—so the constitutive interpretation does. In addition to the above constitutive hypothesis, the opposite hypothesis according to which neural structures are themselves ultimately constituted by consciousness is coherent as well. This is, in effect, the view of idealists—such as Michael Pelczar (2015, and Chapter 15 this volume)—who maintain that ultimate reality is in fact phenomenal. Here the reasoning proceeds as follows:

(1) The NCC correlates with consciousness;
(2) The best explanation of this is that consciousness *constitutes* the NCC; therefore, plausibly,
(3) Consciousness constitutes the NCC.

This reasoning may also be taken to characterize the view of certain panpsychists—such as Greg Rosenberg (2005)—who hold that some phenomenal properties underlie all physical properties.

Likewise, corresponding to the 'third cause' explanatory hypothesis, there is certainly the option of a *third constitutor* hypothesis. That is, there might be an 'X factor' that in one manifestation (perhaps in combination with some micro-properties) constitutes the NCC and in another (with other properties) constitutes consciousness. Here the reasoning is:

(1) The NCC correlates with consciousness;
(2) The best explanation of this is that there is some third element that constitutes both the NCC and consciousness; therefore, plausibly,
(3) There is some third element that constitutes both the NCC and consciousness.

As we will see later in the chapter, certain versions of 'neutral monism', a view that goes back at least to Spinoza, are in effect committed to such a third-constitutor view (see Coleman and Goff, Chapter 14 this volume).

In summary, I have presented six possible explanations, or interpretations, of the correlation between consciousness and whatever turns out to be its neural correlate (e.g., synchronization with dlPFC). These are:

(1) CAUSATION: consciousness is caused by the NCC.
(2) REVERSE CAUSATION: the NCC is caused by consciousness.
(3) THIRD CAUSE: consciousness and the NCC are both caused by some third element.
(4) CONSTITUTION: consciousness is constituted by the NCC.
(5) REVERSE CONSTITUTION: the NCC is constituted by consciousness.
(6) THIRD CONSTITUTOR: consciousness and the NCC are both constituted by some third element.

In Section 12.3, I link this menu to contemporary philosophical theories about the mind–body problem.

12.3 Explanatory Hypotheses and Metaphysical Positions

Of the six explanatory hypotheses just laid out, the most important may well be CAUSATION and CONSTITUTION. For something like it appears to mark the crucial disagreement between moderate forms of materialism and moderate forms of dualism. There are radical forms of materialism according to which consciousness does not exist (see Irvine and Sprevak, Chapter 16 this volume), and therefore has no correlates, as well as radical forms of dualism according to which conscious activity unfolds in complete freedom from brain activity. We may call these *eliminative materialism* and *non-naturalistic dualism*. In modern philosophy of mind, *non-eliminative* forms of materialism and *naturalistic* forms of dualism are the more dominant views. Both agree that conscious activity depends in some way on brain activity. The disagreement concerns the type of dependence involved. For the materialist, consciousness depends ontologically, metaphysically, or constitutively, on brain activity. For the dualist, the dependence is merely 'natural', nomological, or causal.

There are many different ways to try to capture this difference more precisely. In late twentieth-century philosophy of mind, the notion of supervenience played a crucial role in this area. In particular, the distinction between (non-eliminative) materialism and (naturalist) dualism was taken to come down to the choice between *metaphysical* and merely *nomological* supervenience (Chalmers 1996). Roughly, the idea is that for the materialist, in no metaphysically possible world could there be variation in conscious activity without corresponding variation in brain activity, whereas for the dualist, this could happen in some metaphysically possible world, though not in any nomologically possible world (i.e., in any world that has the same laws of nature as the actual world).

In more recent philosophy of mind, the notion of supervenience is often taken to point at a mere *formal symptom* of underlying substantive connections between the supervenient and the subvenient. We might distinguish between 'metaphysical grounding' and 'natural grounding' as the two substantive connections underlying metaphysical and nomological supervenience; in which case (non-eliminative) materialism would claim that consciousness is metaphysically grounded in the NCC whereas (naturalistic) dualism would claim that consciousness is naturally grounded in the NCC. Alternatively, we might call 'grounding' the connection whose diagnostic symptom is metaphysical supervenience and 'emergence' the connection whose diagnostic symptom is nomological supervenience; in which case materialism would claim that consciousness is grounded in the NCC whereas dualism would claim that consciousness merely emerges from the NCC.

However we mark this difference, the distinction between causal and constitutive connections seems to go to the core of the distinction. The notion that a conscious state is *constituted* by its neural correlate is of a piece with the ideas that the former is grounded in, or metaphysically supervenes upon, the latter. The notion that a conscious state is *caused* by its neural correlate is of a piece with the ideas that the former emerges from, or nomologically supervenes upon, the latter. Indeed, a constitutive connection would presumably have metaphysical supervenience for a symptom and a causal connection would presumably have nomological supervenience for a symptom (since causation certainly obeys the principle 'same causes, same effects'). Thus we may take CONSTITUTION and CAUSATION to capture the key difference between non-eliminative materialism and naturalistic dualism.

As for non-naturalistic dualism, it can play out in two very different ways. The first is that there is no correlation whatsoever between consciousness and the NCC. This view can be seen as making the prediction that the scientific search for the NCC will end with failure. The second option, however, is that although conscious activity unfolds in complete freedom from brain activity, the opposite does not hold, perhaps because REVERSE CAUSATION is true: conscious activity casually determines what neural process our brain undergoes. Both views, to repeat, are non-naturalistic forms of dualism. They do not represent a significant background position on the mind–body problem in contemporary philosophy and cognitive science. I am airing them here just for the sake of completeness.

In the same vein, we may note that REVERSE CONSTITUTION is a very natural development of traditional *idealism*. Some care is needed here, however. Some idealists, such as Berkeley, hold that the physical does not exist—nothing is physical (Berkeley 1710). A fortiori, then, there are no brains and no neural processes. Accordingly, there is no neural correlate of consciousness. All there is is consciousness. This is to be distinguished from the view, perhaps Plato's and/or Leibniz's, that the physical does exist but is ultimately constituted by the phenomenal. We may distinguish the two views by calling the former view *eliminative idealism* and the latter *non-eliminative idealism*. Now, while eliminative idealism denies the existence of phenomenal–neural correlations (just as eliminative materialism does), non-eliminative materialism appears to be committed to REVERSE CONSTITUTION.

What about THIRD CAUSE and THIRD CONSTITUTOR? The latter fits rather naturally with certain forms of Russellian monism, namely, those that posit fundamental properties of the universe that are neither phenomenal nor physical but at the same time are both *proto*-phenomenal and *proto*-physical: some combinations or aggregates of them somehow constitute phenomenal properties, others somehow constitute physical properties (including neural properties). If this is one's view of the ultimate connection between consciousness and brain activity, then one takes there to be a third type of ingredient in the universe that constitutively underlies both consciousness and its correlated neural processes. That is, one is committed to THIRD CONSTITUTOR. Now, there are also versions of Russellian monism in which the proto-physical properties are taken to be phenomenal rather than *proto*-phenomenal properties. Those versions are rather committed to REVERSE CONSTITUTION, and essentially collapse into non-eliminative idealism.

Insofar as THIRD CONSTITUTOR is a kind of Russellian monism, we could think of THIRD CAUSE as corresponding to a kind of 'Russellian dualism'. The idea is that there is some third type of property, neither phenomenal nor physical, different combinations of which somehow *causally* bring about instantiations of phenomenal properties and instantiations of physical properties. As noted, quantum theories of consciousness may be seen to be committed to something like this.

Thus we can map the six explanatory hypotheses laid out at the end of Section 12.2 onto six metaphysical positions on the ultimate connection between phenomenal and neural properties: CAUSATION corresponds to naturalistic dualism; REVERSE CAUSATION corresponds to (some versions of) non-naturalistic dualism; THIRD CAUSE corresponds to certain quantum theories; CONSTITUTION corresponds to non-eliminative materialism; REVERSE CONSTITUTION corresponds to non-eliminative idealism; THIRD CONSTITUTOR corresponds to (certain versions of) Russellian monism. What this suggests is that many of the competing metaphysical positions on the mind–body problem can be paired with specific interpretations of the correlation between consciousness and the NCC.[2]

In this way, our sixfold scheme allows us to see how the choice among various metaphysical positions on the problem of consciousness reduces to a choice among different explanatory hypotheses regarding the correlation between consciousness and its NCC. It allows us to reframe the philosophical problem of consciousness as the following question: Which is the best explanatory inference to make from the correlation between consciousness and the NCC? Which offers the most plausible explanatory hypothesis about why this correlation exists?

12.4 EXPLANATORY HYPOTHESES AND EMPIRICAL EQUIVALENCE

How should we go about choosing among the options before us? In general, choosing among alternative explanatory hypotheses is based on two kinds of consideration. First, there is the question of *empirical adequacy*: which of the competing hypotheses accommodates the empirical data best. Second, there is the question of *theoretical adequacy*: which of the competing hypotheses scores highest with respect to the theoretical (or 'superempirical') virtues, such as simplicity, parsimony, conservatism, modesty, cohesion/coherence, unity, elegance, fecundity, testability, and so on (see Quine and Ullian 1970). In this section, I want to raise the epistemic possibility that at least CONSTITUTION and CAUSATION—arguably, the two leading explanatory hypotheses in our scheme—may be empirically equivalent, in the sense of being exactly equal in

---

[2] Note, though, that our sixfold distinction is not exhaustive of the logical landscape on the mind–body problem. It notably leaves out eliminative materialism and eliminative idealism. It also fails to make certain distinctions, e.g. between reductive and non-reductive materialism and between epiphenomenalist and downward-causation versions of dualism.

empirical adequacy. In Section 12.5 I will briefly consider the consequences such empirical equivalence would have for the choice between them.

In trying to pull CAUSATION and CONSTITUTION apart experimentally, the first order of business should be to seek empirical symptoms of the difference between causal and constitutive relations in general—in the hope that we might be able to exploit these in the present context as well. There are two main empirical symptoms of the causal/constitutive difference: one has to do with time lag, the other with mediating mechanism. The hope is that at least one of these could help us produce *discordant predictions* out of CAUSATION and CONSTITUTION.

Let us start with the issue of time lag. It is plausible to suppose that, while there is always a time lag between cause and effect (the former *precedes* the latter), constitutor and constitutee (if you will) are always *simultaneous*. Thus, the presence of H_2O in some location does not precede the presence of water, but the striking of a match does precede its lighting up. Of course, like everything else in philosophy, the temporal lag between cause and effect *has* been contested (Huemer and Kovitz 2003). If there is no temporal lap between cause and effect, then temporal considerations will offer no empirical symptom of the difference between causal and constitutive connection. Let us grant for the sake of argument, however, that causes do precede their effects, whereas constitutors do not precede their constitutees. Applied to the choice between CAUSATION and CONSTITUTION, we might suppose that if the NCC is *causally* connected to consciousness, then its occurrence will precede the onset of consciousness ever so slightly, whereas if it is *constitutively* connected to consciousness, it will be strictly simultaneous therewith. This is one empirical symptom of the difference between causal and constitutive connections.

As for mechanism, causal connections are typically mediated by a mechanism, whereas constitutive connections are not. Thus, when investigating the connection between match-striking and match-lighting, it is possible to 'go deeper' and discover the mechanism that mediates the causing of the latter by the former. Typically, this means exposing a series of intermediary causal transactions at a more fundamental level of reality—in this case, chemical interactions involving sulfur, phosphorus, oxygen, and so on. In general, when A causes B, it is often the case that this is mediated through a series of finer-grained causal transactions—A constitutes E_1, E_1 constitutes E_2, E_2 causes E_3,..., E_{n-1} causes En, and En causes B. The only exception to the existence of a mediating mechanism concerns causal transactions at the 'bottom level' of reality, which must be brute and unmediated, since we cannot 'go deeper' and seek even more fundamental transactions mediating them. (More on that presently.) In contrast with all this, when A *constitutes* B, such that B is *nothing but* A, there is no expectation that there be 'intermediate stages' of 'nothing-but-ness.' For A to constitute B, it is not necessary that there be some series $X_1 \ldots X_n$ such that A constitutes X_1, X_1 constitutes X_2,..., X_{n-1} constitutes Xn, and Xn constitutes B. Accordingly, to choose between CAUSATION and CONSTITUTION, we might seek a series of intermediary correlates between consciousness and the NCC. If such a series can be found, however short, this could indicate a causal connection between the two. If none can be found (despite sustained attempts to reveal one), that could indicate a constitutive connection.

Unfortunately, I think both of these empirical symptoms of the causal/constitutive distinction—temporal lag and mediating mechanism—face outstanding challenges when applied to the case of consciousness and the NCC. These challenges make it unlikely that they can help us discriminate between CAUSATION and CONSTITUTION.

When it comes to temporal lag, there is of course the problem that no technology we can envisage at present has the sort of temporal resolution necessary to tell apart the difference between exact simultaneity and slight precedence at the time scales with which we are concerned here. (Certainly fMRI and EEG do not, but nor does optical imaging.[3]) More importantly, there are at least two *more principled* problems with appeal to temporal lag in the present context.

An initial problem is this. Imagine a time lag characteristic of the relevant kind of causal transaction—a lag between times t_1 and t_2. Imagine also that at t_1 the neural state N_1 occurs and the phenomenal state P_1 does, and that at t_2 neural state N_2 occurs and phenomenal state P_2 does. Here there are both materialist/constitutive and dualist/causal hypotheses regarding the neural correlate of P_2. The materialist hypothesis is that the neural correlate of P_2 is N_2, which is simultaneous with P_2 and indeed constitutes it. The dualist hypothesis is that the neural correlate of P_2 is N_1, which precedes it, because it is its cause. At the time scales we are talking about, P_2 is likely to be systematically correlated across different contexts with both N_1 and N_2.[4]

The same point applies to the very onset of consciousness. Suppose two mental states M_1 and M_2 occur at t_1 and t_2, such that M_2 is phenomenally conscious but M_1 is not. Suppose also that N_1 is a neural state exactly contemporaneous with M_1 and N_2 a neural state exactly contemporaneous with M_2. Again, we can hypothesize that N_1 is the neural correlate of M_2, hence a cause of consciousness, or that N_2 is the neural correlate of M_2, hence a constitutor of consciousness. Both hypotheses accommodate the timed observations of N_1, N_2, M_1, and M_2.

There is a further problem, which may be tougher yet. When trying to pinpoint the exact time of two kinds of event, with an eye to comparing these times, it is crucial that we know how much time the measuring instruments take to produce their timing verdicts. Otherwise, there will be an irresolvable confound. If a time lag is detected between A and B, all we know immediately is that the detecting of A preceded the detecting of B. This is consistent with both (a) A really preceding B and (b) A and B being simultaneous but the detecting of B taking longer than the detecting of A. The only way to remove this confound is by having an independent measure of the time it takes each instrument to time its target. Ideally, this problem would be bypassed by using the very same measuring tool for both, or at least overcome by using measuring tools that demonstrably take the same amount of time to do the measuring. Clearly, however, in the present case this ideal set-up is unavailable: the timing of conscious states must ultimately rely on

---

[3] On optical imaging and its resolution, see Gratton et al. 2003.
[4] The problem would be solved if we could somehow 'observe' not only both correlates, but also the actual connection between them. But it is widely held that the connection between cause and effect is unobservable (and presumably so is the connection between constitutor and constitute).

introspection, since introspection is our only direct access to conscious states, whereas the timing of neural states cannot use introspection, since introspection affords us no access to neural states.[5] Sub-ideally, then, we might use two different measuring instruments and find an independent way to measure the time it takes each measuring instrument to detect its target, subtracting this time to identify the likely time of occurrence of the target event. This approach may apply well to the timing of neural states: measuring the time it takes a measuring instrument to time the occurrence of a neural event may be fairly straightforward in principle (if technically challenging in practice). The real problem with the approach, however, is that when it comes to the timing of conscious states by introspection, the approach becomes circular, since introspective states are themselves conscious. We can imagine a future in which we have fully specified the neural mechanisms subserving introspection, and where we have measured precisely the time it takes for information to 'travel up' to the 'introspection center' and trigger the neural state underlying the introspective state. But unless we know whether there is a further bit of travel to be done, because that neural state merely *causes* the introspective state, or the traveling is finished, because the neural state *constitutes* the introspective state, we cannot be certain of the exact time it takes to introspectively detect that which is introspected.

If all this is correct, we are bound to remain stuck with our confound, and therefore with two empirically indistinguishable interpretations of any time lag between the detecting of the NCC and the detecting of consciousness.[6] Bearing in mind Wittgenstein's alleged remark that it is nonsense to suppose that humans will some day walk on the moon, and adopting in consequence a more diffident cast of mind toward the deliverances of armchair reasoning, I hesitate to rule out a priori the idea of a future time in which the timing of corresponding neural and conscious states has been established, in a way as yet elusive to our imagination, and is used to empirically distinguish CAUSATION and CONSTITUTION. Nonetheless, the above challenge to the very possibility of such a future looms large.

So much for using temporal lags to empirically distinguish causal and constitutive hypotheses. What about mediating mechanism? The idea was that causal transactions are mediated by mechanisms involving finer-grained causal transactions, whereas

---

[5] This too has been contested by some philosophers. For example, Churchland (1979) claims that with better (more scientifically based) primary and secondary education, future generations of humans will learn to introspect their conscious life in neural terms. I am going to assume here that this is false.

[6] The confound, to repeat, is this. Suppose we detect consciousness and the NCC, and the detecting of the latter suitably precedes the detecting of the former. One interpretation of this time lag between the two detections is that there was a real time lag between the NCC and consciousness. The other is that there was no time lag between consciousness and the NCC and the lag between their detections is due entirely to the different speeds of operation of our timing devices. The specter I am raising here is that there is no way to experimentally pull apart these two interpretations. (Conversely, suppose we find no time lag between the detecting of the NCC and the detecting of consciousness. This too is consistent with at least two interpretations. One is that the two are simultaneous. The other is that the NCC precedes consciousness but its precedence is masked by a compensatory difference in the speed of timing consciousness and timing the NCC.)

constitutive connections are not normally mediated by a series of finer-grained constitutions. Recall, however, that there was an exception to the rule that causal transactions are mediated by finer-grained transactions. The exception was causal transactions at the fundamental level of reality. At the bottom level of reality, there *are* no finer-grained causal transactions for us to seek. We must treat such transactions as metaphysically brute and ungrounded—somewhat as we treat the gravitational constant, the Avogadro constant, and other fundamental physical constants. Nothing *underlies* the fact that the gravitational constant is approximately 6.673×10^{-11} N·(m/kg)^2, and likewise nothing *underlies* the causal process by which a lepton absorbs a boson and converts into a neutrino. There are causal laws governing such causal transactions, but there are no finer-grained transactions mediating them. The problem this presents in the present context is that according to mainstream versions of naturalistic dualism, consciousness occurs precisely at the fundamental level of reality, where no mediating mechanism is to be found. If so, the fact that CONSTITUTION does not make room for a mediating mechanism linking the NCC and consciousness does not distinguish it from CAUSATION.

Consider Chalmers' (1996) version of naturalistic dualism. Chalmers reasons that since dualists, unlike materialists, hold that phenomenal properties are irreducible to any microphysical properties (or any other fundamental properties there might be), they must posit phenomenal properties as fundamental. If charm and spin are fundamental, then phenomenal consciousness must be construed as belonging at the same level of reality as charm and spin—the 'bottom level'. This means that any causal transactions between microphysical events and phenomenal events are effectively transactions at the 'bottom level' of reality. That, in turn, means that there will be no *more* fundamental transactions mediating them—no mechanism connecting cause and effect. In consequence, the materialist's CONSTITUTION and the naturalistic dualist's CAUSATION make the exact same prediction here: that there will be no 'intermediate correlates' between consciousness and the NCC, or more accurately between consciousness and the microphysical processes that constitute the NCC. Since they make the same prediction, they are empirically equivalent on this score.

There may be some other empirical symptoms of the difference between causation and constitution, other than temporal lag and mediating mechanism. But for my part, I cannot think of any. It would certainly be of great value to identify such potential empirical symptoms. Unless we can do so, we may have to acquiesce in the empirical indistinguishability of CONSTITUTION and CAUSATION, hence of non-eliminative materialism and naturalistic dualism.

12.5 EMPIRICAL EQUIVALENCE AND THE SCIENCE OF CONSCIOUSNESS

As noted, in addition to *empirical* adequacy, scientific theories are also assessed for their *theoretical* adequacy. One could therefore suggest that CAUSATION and

CONSTITUTION may yet be evaluated and compared with respect to the superempirical virtues. Certainly parsimony seems to tell in favor of CONSTITUTION, or materialism more generally, since, obviously, 1 < 2 (see Smart 1959). This approach raises a number of difficulties, however.

First, when two theories are perfectly empirically equivalent, there is an important sense in which choosing among them on the basis of superempirical virtues is a non-scientific endeavor. Doctoral students and postdocs in cognitive neuroscience laboratories are trained by their advisors in the designing and carrying out of experiments, not in the judicious comparison of experimentally indistinguishable hypotheses along superempirical dimensions.

More deeply, there is an ongoing debate in philosophy of science about the proper doxastic attitude toward the superempirical or theoretical virtues (see van Fraassen 1980; Churchland 1982). Consider simplicity. It is intuitive that *mutatis mutandis* we should always prefer simpler theories to more complicated ones. It is thus natural to count the simplicity of a theory as a reason for believing it. However, it is not obvious *why* the simplicity of a theory counts in its favor. In particular, it is very unclear why, indeed whether, a theory's simplicity means that it is more likely to be true. As van Fraassen (1980: 90) puts it, 'it is surely absurd to think that the world is more likely to be simple than complicated.'

Several philosophical ideas underlie this challenge to understanding the status of simplicity in theory evaluation. One idea is that ultimately, the only reason to *believe* a theory is that the theory is likely to be true. We may decide to *adopt* a theory, for pragmatic, aesthetic, or other reasons. But that is not quite the same as *believing* a theory. To believe a theory is to adopt it for *epistemic* reasons, more specifically for the reason that we think it *likely to be true*. Second, what makes a theory true is that it represents correctly the way the world is. Accordingly, for a theory to be more likely to come out true, it must be more likely that it represents the world the way it really is. Third, we do not actually have an independent handle on the objective degree of nature's complexity, in a way that would allow us to compare the complexity of nature and the complexity of theories that purport to describe it. If we take on board all three ideas, it would seem that simplicity is not a reason to *believe* a scientific theory—though it may well be a reason to adopt it on some non-epistemic grounds (i.e., for the sake of other purposes than knowing how the world is).

The worry is that this kind of reasoning may generalize to the other central theoretical virtues, especially parsimony and unity. We do not have some independent grip on the cosmos' degree of unity, one that suggests the cosmos is so inherently unified that the more unified our theory of it, the more likely the theory is to represent the world correctly. Likewise, we do not have an independent handle on the number of entities in the world that recommends keeping the number of posits in our theory thereof to a minimum. Thus whatever the force of unity and parsimony—and it is an open question both what that force exactly is and what it is based on—it cannot be due to their augmenting a theory's likely truth (i.e., the likelihood that it represents the world the way it really is). One way to put the challenge is that the theoretical virtues may not be *truth-conducive*: that a theory T exhibits the theoretical virtues does not make it more likely that T correctly represents the way things are (Beebe 2009; Kriegel 2013).

It might be objected that parsimony reasoning is often used in scientific theory building in what appears to be a truth-conducive way (Sober 2009). Consider this piece of reasoning from evolutionary biology: both humans and monkeys have tailbones; if humans and monkeys have no common ancestry, the tailbone would have had to originate twice; if they have common ancestry, it only had to originate once; the latter hypothesis is thus more parsimonious than the former, and more likely to be true. The idea here is that the occurrence of two independent events is less probable than the occurrence of one (other things being equal). Suppose the probability of E_1 occurring is 70 per cent and that of E_2 is 50 per cent. Then the probability of *both* occurring is 35 per cent—lower than either. Accordingly, the single-event hypothesis is more probable than the dual-event one. So parsimony tracks likely truth.

Observe, however, that the kind of parsimony invoked here is not the kind invoked by materialism and CONSTITUTION. Both evolutionary hypotheses under consideration posit the same types of entity—humans, monkeys, tailbones, originations. They only differ on the *distribution* of those entity types: one posits one token event where the other posits two tokens. Thus the two hypotheses differ in what we might call *token*-parsimony, but are equal in *type*-parsimony: they differ in the number of token tailbone-origination events they posit, but both are ontologically committed to tailbones, originations, and indeed tailbone-originations. In contrast, materialism and dualism differ in *type*-parsimony: they disagree on the *kinds* of things there are in the world.[7] The point is: while it is clear how token-parsimony can be truth-conducive, it is much more mysterious how type-parsimony might be. Yet it is the latter that separates CAUSATION and CONSTITUTION.

If all this is right, then there may be no epistemic grounds for preferring CAUSATION or CONSTITUTION, qua scientific hypotheses about the relationship between consciousness and its neural correlate. On the one hand, there appears to be no way to experimentally disentangle them. On the other, the theoretical virtues do not seem to apply to them in a way that renders one more likely to be true than the other. As already noted, it may well be that our present difficulties in envisaging an experimental test that could separate predictions by CAUSATION and CONSTITUTION are but failures of imagination. It is also possible, of course, that a demonstration of the truth-conduciveness of (some) superempirical virtues will emerge at some point. Still, the considerations above do cast a worrisome shadow over the hope for a scientific resolution of the dualism/materialism debate. If so, the right attitude may be to withhold scientific judgment on whether CAUSATION or CONSTITUTION (or one of the other four hypotheses formulated in Section 12.1) is most likely to be true.

---

[7] Furthermore, the dualist does not posit her two types of property—physical and phenomenal—to explain a single explanandum (as is the case with the tailbones). Rather, she posits the physical brain property to explain neurological data or third-person overt behavior, but phenomenal properties to explain our introspective impressions or first-person grasp on our mental life.

This line of reasoning is in some ways disappointing. But in other ways, it may be thought liberating. The problem of consciousness has led many scientists to ignore consciousness as an improper subject of scientific investigation. Some have even been led to deny the existence of consciousness, more or less to protect the Enlightenment notion that science can account for every aspect of reality. Others have admitted the existence of consciousness and refused to ignore it, but there is a stubborn sense that they nonetheless have deflated somewhat the phenomenon, turning it into a purely functional phenomenon, thin on intrinsic subjective character. The above reflections recommend a humbler approach that relinquishes the mentioned Enlightenment ideal and concedes that we may be unable in principle to reach a scientific resolution of the problem of consciousness. There may be principled methodological and epistemological reasons why we cannot choose among the various possible explanations of the correlation between consciousness and the NCC. Indeed, the above reflections may be seen to offer a *diagnosis* of the elusiveness of scientific progress on the ultimate question of consciousness' place in nature.[8]

References

Beebe, J. R. (2009), 'The Abductivist Reply to Skepticism', *Philosophy and Phenomenological Research*, 79: 605–36.
Berkeley, G. (1710), *A Treatise Concerning the Principles of Human Knowledge*.
Chalmers, D. J. (1996), *The Conscious Mind*. Oxford: Oxford University Press.
Chalmers, D. J. (2002), 'Consciousness and Its Place in Nature', in D. J. Chalmers (ed.), *Philosophy of Mind: Classical and Contemporary Readings*. Oxford: Oxford University Press).
Churchland, P. M. (1979), *Scientific Realism and the Plasticity of Mind*. Cambridge: Cambridge University Press.
Churchland, P. M. (1982), 'The Ontological Status of Observables: In Praise of the Superempirical Virtues', *Pacific Philosophical Quarterly*, 63: 226–36.
van Fraassen, B. C. (1980), *The Scientific Image*. Oxford: Oxford University Press.
Gratton, G., Fabiani M., Elbert, T., and Rockstroh, B. (2003), 'Seeing Right through You: Applications of Optical Imaging to the Study of the Human Brain', *Psychophysiology*, 40: 487–91.
Hameroff, S. R., and Penrose, R. (1996), 'Conscious Events as Orchestrated Spacetime Selections', *Journal of Consciousness Studies*, 3: 36–53.
Harman, G. (1965), 'The Inference to the Best Explanation', *Philosophical Review*, 74: 88–95.

---

[8] I would like to thank David Chalmers, Jakob Hohwy, Benji Kozuch, and Farid Masrour for comments on a previous draft, and Benji Kozuch and Rachel Schneebaum for useful conversations. I have also benefited from presenting one incarnation or another of the chapter at the Berlin School of Mind and Brain, Boston University, CREA, the University of Arizona, the University of Copenhagen, and the University of Strasbourg. I am grateful to the audiences there, in particular Michel Bitbol, Rosa Cao, Carolyn Dicey-Jennings, Ellen Fridland, Rik Hine, Shaun Nichols, Michael Pauen, and Sebastian Watzl. This work was supported by the French National Research Agency's grant ANR-17-EURE-0017, as well as by grant 675,415 of the European Union's Horizon 2020 Research and Innovation program.

Hohwy, J. (2011), 'Mind–Brain Identity and Evidential Insulation', *Philosophical Studies*, 153: 377–95.
Huemer, M. and Kovitz, B. (2003), 'Causation as Simultaneous and Continuous', *Philosophical Quarterly*, 53: 556–65.
Kriegel, U. (2009), *Subjective Consciousness: A Self-Representational Theory*. Oxford: Oxford University Press.
Kriegel, U. (2013), 'The Epistemological Challenge of Revisionary Metaphysics', *Philosophers' Imprint*, 12 (June): 1–30.
Lau, H. C. and Passingham, R. E. (2006), 'Relative Blindsight in Normal Observers and the Neural Correlate of Visual Consciousness' *Proceedings of the National Academy of Science USA*, 103: 18763–8.
Lipton, P. (1991), *Inference to the Best Explanation*. London: Routledge.
Lockwood, M. (1989), *Mind, Brain and the Quantum*. Oxford: Blackwell.
Pelczar, M. W. (2015), *Sensorama: A Phenomenalist Analysis of Spacetime and Its Contents*. Oxford: Oxford University Press.
Quine, W. V. O., and Ullian, J. S. (1970), *The Web of Belief*. New York: Random House.
Rosenberg, G. (2005), *A Place for Consciousness: Probing the Deep Structure of the Natural World*. Oxford: Oxford University Press.
Rounis E., Maniscalco, B., Rothwell, J., Passingham, R. E., and Lau, H. C. (2010), 'Theta-Burst Transcranial Magnetic Stimulation to the Prefrontal Cortex Impairs Metacognitive Visual Awareness', *Cognitive Neuroscience*, 1: 165–75.
Russell, B. (1927), *The Analysis of Matter*. London: Kegan Paul.
Smart, J. J. C. (1959), 'Sensations and Brain Processes', *Philosophical Review*, 68: 141–56.
Sober, E. (2009), 'Parsimony Arguments in Science and Philosophy—a Test Case for Naturalismp', *Proceedings and Addresses of the American Philosophical Association*, 82: 117–55.

CHAPTER 13

DUALISM

How Epistemic Issues Drive Debates about the Ontology of Consciousness

BRIE GERTLER

You feel a tickle in your toe, you taste a tangy lemon drop, you smell coffee brewing. These experiences have a distinctive feel, a qualitative character that constitutes *what it's like* to feel a tickle or taste lemon or smell coffee. Dualism about consciousness says that this qualitative character is something over and above the physical processes associated with such experiences.

Historically, dualism was motivated by theological concerns, such as the need to explain how the soul could persist into an afterlife. But most contemporary philosophical arguments for dualism are entirely naturalistic. And they do not aim to establish the existence of immaterial *substances* such as souls; rather, they aim to show that the qualitative *properties* of conscious experience are non-physical. This chapter will deal exclusively with naturalistic property dualism.

Dualism is a metaphysical view about the nature of consciousness. But it is driven largely by epistemic concerns. Dualism's chief rival, physicalism about consciousness, is also a metaphysical view that is driven largely by epistemic concerns.

A primary goal of this chapter is to correct a widespread misunderstanding about how epistemic issues shape the debate between dualists and physicalists. According to a familiar picture, dualism is motivated by armchair reflection, and dualists accord special significance to our ways of conceptualizing consciousness and the physical. In contrast, physicalists favor empirical data over armchair reflection, and physicalism is a relatively straightforward extension of scientific theorizing. This familiar picture is inaccurate. Both dualist and physicalist arguments employ a combination of empirical data and armchair reflection; both rely on considerations stemming from how we conceptualize certain phenomena; and both aim to establish views that are compatible with scientific results but go well beyond the deliverances of empirical science. My discussion highlights these neglected epistemic parallels between dualism and physicalism.

I begin this chapter by fleshing out the distinctive commitments of dualism, in a way that illuminates the interplay of epistemic and metaphysical elements within the dualist position. Section 13.2 then outlines two influential arguments for dualism and explains how dualists defend those arguments from key criticisms. The next two sections examine the most powerful objections to dualism. Section 13.3 discusses the charge that dualism is inferior to physicalism as regards the theoretical virtue of *simplicity*, and hence dualist arguments bear a special burden of proof. Section 13.4 discusses the worry that, given reasonable assumptions, dualists must deny that our conscious thoughts and feelings genuinely *cause* our decisions and actions. I show that each of these objections to dualism depends on substantial assumptions that cannot be empirically justified. And the objection from mental causation rests on an ambitious assumption about how we conceptualize physical phenomena. Section 13.5 briefly reviews how epistemic considerations inform arguments on both sides of this debate.

13.1 What is Dualism?

13.1.1 Dualism vs. Physicalism

Dualism is the thesis that consciousness is not physical: although it may arise from physical processes, it is something over and above the physical. As mentioned earlier, contemporary naturalistic dualists favor *property* dualism. Property dualism concerns the qualitative character or feel of conscious experiences. It says that these qualitative properties of experience do not consist in, and are not necessitated by, physical properties and phenomena.

Dualism contrasts with physicalism, the thesis that everything, including consciousness, is physical (or necessitated by the physical). It is sometimes assumed that physicalism must be part of any scientific worldview. Naturalistic dualism challenges that assumption.

The dualism at issue is naturalistic in both an ontological and a methodological sense. Ontologically, naturalistic dualism regards consciousness as an aspect of the natural world. It presumably resulted from evolutionary processes, and its relation to the physical is amenable to explanation by laws of nature. Methodologically, naturalistic dualism embraces the idea that the proper way to investigate consciousness is by the use of broadly scientific methods: the acquisition, analysis, and systematization of empirical data.

Given naturalistic dualism's commitment to a scientific outlook, it can be difficult to see how, precisely, this view differs from physicalism. There is now a substantial literature on the question how best to formulate dualism and physicalism, and on 'the' (defining) point at issue between these positions. The formulation of dualism I will propose seems to me promising, in that it captures the spirit of the debate and is faithful to at least the dominant positions on this topic. But contributing to the debate about the proper formulation of dualism is not my purpose here. So I do not claim that my construal is preferable to all others. And I admit that there may be some views legitimately regarded as physicalist that are compatible with the dualist thesis as I construe it; there may even be some versions of dualism that reject that thesis.

I think a useful way to approach the debate between dualism and physicalism is to consider how these competing positions view the prospects for physical science. Dualists can be just as optimistic as physicalists about the prospects for empirical science generally. In particular, dualists can allow that all of concrete reality, including consciousness, is amenable to explanation by empirical science. (I include the qualification 'concrete' because the status of abstract objects is orthogonal to this debate.) But dualists will deny that an account of consciousness will be part of a specifically *physical* scientific theory.

Here is an initial, relatively abstract formulation of dualism that reflects this approach.

Dualism (initial formulation). A true and exhaustive account of consciousness is beyond the reach of physical science.

This initial formulation of dualism draws on the idea that the notion of the *physical* operative in these debates is tied to physical science. This idea is, I think, very plausible; it reflects the inclination of philosophers to defer to scientists as to the particular characteristics of ordinary physical objects and phenomena.

And a link with physical science is present in both of the basic conceptions of the physical that Stoljar (2001) identifies. On the *theory-based conception*, a property is physical if and only if it is, or is necessitated by, 'the sort of property that physical theory tells us about' (2001: 256). On the *object-based conception*, a property is physical if and only if it is, or is necessitated by, 'the sort of property required by a complete account of the intrinsic nature of paradigmatic physical objects and their constituents' (2001: 257).[1] Neither of these conceptions identifies a specific property (such as having spatial extension) as a marker of the physical; they both defer to physical science as to the detailed nature of the properties in its domain. In this way, both of these conceptions tie the notion of the physical to the domain of physical science: what physical science investigates, or what it (ideally) discovers.

Dualism is a metaphysical thesis. So my initial formulation is apt only if the standard defining 'the reach of physical science' is metaphysical: that is, only if the domain of physical science is delineated by the metaphysical features of the items it explains or posits. I will propose a metaphysical standard in Section 13.1.3 below.

However, epistemic standards for physical science also figure prominently in this debate. Epistemic standards construe physical science in terms of certain methods of investigation. Because dualism is a metaphysical position, it is not committed to the epistemic thesis that the methods of physical science are inadequate for understanding consciousness. However, that thesis plays a leading role in some arguments for dualism. So I will discuss it before turning to a fuller explication of dualism.

---

[1] The fact that 'physical' occurs in both conceptions does not challenge their legitimacy, since they are not intended as reductive analyses.

13.1.2 An Epistemic Standard for Physical Science: Objectivity

Physical science is often described as *objective*, by virtue of its methods of data collection and analysis. Following Goldman (1997), we can characterize objective methods as those that could (in principle) be used by different researchers investigating a single phenomenon—and, if so used, would generate the same results.[2] Prohibiting the use of non-objective methods may seem prudent, as it bars scientists from relying on epistemically dubious sources such as mystical visions.

But a restriction to objective methods also excludes introspection. Since introspection can be used only by a single subject—the person undergoing the introspected experience—it is an exclusively first-personal, non-objective method.[3]

At present, some areas of physical science, including psychology and neuroscience, make essential use of introspective reports from experimental subjects. And medical trials standardly rely on subjects' reports, for example about the kind and degree of pain they are feeling. Dualists contend that this reliance on introspection is unavoidable, since one must reflect on one's own experience to appreciate the qualitative features of conscious experiences—for example, what it's like to feel a tickle or smell coffee. Any means of recognizing what someone else is feeling ultimately depends on introspection, to correlate the third-personal data with the experience in question. For example, knowing that certain kinds of neuronal activity are correlated with tickles might enable a scientist to determine, through fMRI, that a particular subject is feeling a tickle. But introspective reports are required to establish the initial correlation between the neuronal activity and those experiences. And tracking neuronal activity would not enable the scientist to comprehend what the subject was feeling, according to the dualist, unless the scientist knew from her own experience *what it's like* to feel a tickle. Since no purely third-personal knowledge will suffice for understanding what it's like to feel a tickle, no purely objective methodology will suffice for recognizing a tickle *as such*.

Dualists maintain that this situation is inescapable. Although developments in neuroscience may enable us to identify conscious experiences in others through fMRI or more advanced techniques, first-personal observations are required both for establishing the initial correlations to such third-personal data and for comprehending the qualitative features that make conscious experiences what they are. Jaynes expresses

---

[2] This is a rough characterization, adapted from Goldman's very useful discussion of the alleged 'publicity requirement' in science (Goldman 1997). Goldman considers various ways of refining this characterization.

[3] The possibility that a single experience might be introspected by multiple persons is raised by some cases of craniopagus twins—twins who are fused at the cranium. A pair of craniopagus twins born in 2006, Krista and Tatiana Hogan, are said to share some sensations. When one twin is tickled both feel the tickle (Dominus 2011). Whether this challenges the claim that an experience can be introspected only by a single subject depends on further details: specifically, whether both twins have introspective access to a single conscious experience, or whether instead the tickling causes each to have her own tickle experience.

this point forcefully, using knowledge of the brain to represent what is available through third-personal methods:

> Though we knew the connections of every tickling thread of every single axon and dendrite in every species that ever existed, together with all its neurotransmitters and how they varied in its billions of synapses of every brain that ever existed, we could still never—*not ever*—from a knowledge of the brain alone know if that brain contained a consciousness like our own. (Jaynes 1976/2000: 18)

By contrast, most physicalists maintain that we could eventually overcome this reliance on introspection. They claim that every genuine property associated with conscious experience could, in principle, be detected without reliance on introspection. Physicalists generally allow that some ways of characterizing or thinking about a given property are available only to the experiencing subject. But they generally deny that any genuine properties of conscious experiences are accessible in principle only through introspection, or that undergoing an experience provides for substantial knowledge about the experience that is not available through other means.[4]

Now if a comprehensive understanding of tickles or other conscious experiences required having had those experiences—or even required having had conscious experiences at all—then conscious experience would differ sharply from other phenomena. After all, one need not undergo photosynthesis or engage in asexual reproduction or experience planetary motion in order to fully comprehend those phenomena. To deny that conscious experience is in principle accessible via third-personal methods is, in effect, to posit a disparity between conscious experience and other phenomena. On this view, conscious experience differs from other phenomena in that one must have had conscious experiences in order to fully understand them.

This methodological issue exposes a fault line in the debate, concerning whether a true and exhaustive account of consciousness requires the use of first-personal methods. Most physicalists reject this idea. Dualists accept it. The corresponding claim is as follows.

The subjectivity of consciousness. A true and exhaustive account of consciousness is beyond the reach of a purely objective science.

This claim interprets the initial dualist thesis in epistemic terms: physical science cannot fully account for consciousness because its domain is limited to what is accessible via objective methods.

---

[4] Physicalists who use the so-called 'phenomenal concept strategy' to block arguments for dualism generally claim that there are ways of conceptualizing the qualitative character of experiences that are available only to those who have had such experiences. But in most versions of this strategy, these conceptualizations—so-called 'phenomenal concepts'—are not required for a comprehensive understanding of the qualitative property itself (e.g. Levin 2006). Some physicalists, such as Balog (2012) and Howell (2013), allow that introspection is required for fully comprehending the qualitative character of conscious experience, but argue that this epistemic fact is compatible with a physicalist view about the nature of consciousness. Chalmers (2006) challenges this general physicalist strategy. I raise doubts about Balog's and Howell's versions of it in a recent paper (Gertler 2019).

As an epistemic thesis, the subjectivity of consciousness does not entail, and is not entailed by, the metaphysical thesis of dualism. Still, this epistemic thesis contributes to some arguments for dualism, and it is difficult to reconcile with physicalism. Physicalists can deny the subjectivity of consciousness. Or they can argue that the presence of an epistemic divide between the physical (which is accessible through objective methods) and consciousness (which is not), does not imply that there is a metaphysical divide between them. Each of these strategies faces difficulties.[5]

13.1.3 A Metaphysical Standard for Physical Science: Structure and Dynamics

On my formulation, the dualist thesis is that an exhaustive account of consciousness is beyond the reach of physical science. The subjectivity of consciousness is an epistemic gloss of this thesis: it construes it in methodological terms. But to express dualism we need a metaphysical standard, one that construes physical science in terms of the kinds of things (objects, properties, and phenomena) it recognizes.

The metaphysical standard I have in mind derives from what is arguably the prevailing conception of physical science. On this conception, phenomena at higher 'levels', such as biological or astronomical phenomena, are explained by identifying phenomena at lower 'levels', such as the phenomena studied in chemistry or physics, that constitute or necessitate them. This conception is driven by the idea that all physical phenomena are ultimately constituted (or necessitated) by fundamental phenomena, falling within the domain of physics. This means that phenomena at higher levels cannot vary independently of fundamental phenomena. To put it metaphorically: once God set in place everything that falls within the domain of physics—all of the most basic entities, with their particular properties and at their particular locations, and all of the laws governing their behavior—nothing more was needed to bring it about that photosynthesis and asexual reproduction occurred, or to set the patterns of planetary motion.

There is no consensus as to what types of entities and phenomena ultimately constitute, and explain, all physical phenomena. The fundamental level may include fermions, bosons, and other 'elementary' particles, with properties of mass, charge, and spin. Or, if string theory is correct, such particles may be ultimately constituted by strings whose vibrations play the roles we assign to mass, charge, and spin. Alternatively, the fundamental level may be composed of things as yet unimagined. What is important is the *form* that physical science explanations take. Physical theory explains higher-level phenomena, such as biological and astronomical phenomena, by reference to lower-level phenomena, such as those studied in chemistry and physics, that constitute or necessitate the higher-level phenomena.

---

[5] The difficulty of the former strategy is reflected in the intuitive appeal of the Jaynes passage above, and in the force of the Knowledge Argument for dualism (section 13.2.1). Difficulties facing the latter strategy include those faced by the second phenomenal concept strategy (see note 4).

Crucially, higher-level phenomena are explained by reference to the *structure and dynamics* of underlying entities. (Throughout this chapter, my discussion of structure and dynamics is deeply indebted to Chalmers 2002.) To get a sense of structural-dynamical explanations, consider a familiar fact: lukewarm water poured into a glass will conform to the shape of the glass, whereas an ice cube placed into a glass will retain its shape. Chemists explain these differing reactions by citing the structural and dynamical properties of H_2O molecules. The relevant structural features include the composition of those molecules (two hydrogen atoms and one oxygen atom) and their polarity (the uneven distribution of negative and positive charges within them). The relevant dynamical factors include the way intermolecular forces bind molecules with that polarity, and how temperature affects these bonds. Together, these structural and dynamical characteristics (combined with the structural-dynamic features of the molecular constituents of glass, etc.) explain why the bonds between H_2O molecules are tighter at lower temperatures and, hence, why ice cubes retain their shape whereas lukewarm water conforms to its container.

Alter provides this helpful summary:

> [S]tructural-dynamic descriptions are those that are analyzable in formal, spatiotemporal, and nomic terms, where the formal is the logical and the mathematical, and the nomic is the domain of laws and causation. (Alter 2016: 795)

Note that in the explanation just given, facts about structure and dynamics are taken to *necessitate* the target phenomena. To return to our earlier metaphor: once God fixed the structural and dynamic facts, nothing more needed to be done to fix the facts about how H_2O at various temperatures reacts to being placed in a container. Those latter facts are necessitated by the structural-dynamic facts.

On the prevailing conception of physical science, physical science explains (higher-level) phenomena by giving structural-dynamic descriptions of (lower-level) phenomena that constitute or necessitate them. Moreover, physical science is restricted to explanations of this sort: the lower-level factors that explain the target phenomena are characterized purely in terms of structure and dynamics. This conception of physical science, applied to my initial, abstract formulation of dualism, yields a more specific thesis:

> A true and exhaustive account of consciousness is beyond the reach of a science that explains its targets purely in terms of structure and dynamics.

Let us use the term 'structural-dynamic phenomena' to refer to phenomena for which structural-dynamic descriptions are *exhaustive*: that is, they capture every aspect of these phenomena. On the conception of physical science just described, explanations identify structural-dynamic phenomena that constitute or necessitate the target phenomena. Combining these points with the thesis just given yields the following dualist thesis.

Dualism. Conscious experience is neither constituted nor necessitated by structural-dynamic phenomena.

This will be our working formulation of dualism. It takes conscious experience to be non-physical by virtue of its defining qualitative properties—those responsible for *what it's like* to feel a tickle or taste lemon (etc.). (Arguably, conscious experience just is the instantiation of those properties in a subject at a time.) As I mentioned earlier, I am not claiming that this is the only reasonable way to formulate dualism. But I believe that it captures the spirit of prominent dualist views and of the larger debate more generally.

The dualist thesis says that conscious experience cannot be analyzed purely in terms of structure and dynamics, and is not constituted or necessitated by anything amenable to structural-dynamic analysis. Of course, the dualist can allow that consciousness *has* structural and dynamic features. Gazing at a blue mug full of steaming coffee, the internal structure of your visual experience may include shifting wispy trails of white above a static blue patch. Similarly, consciousness may be dynamically related to other phenomena: pains may arise from certain types of neuronal activity, and may cause us to say 'ouch!'. But these structural and dynamic features do not constitute or necessitate *what it's like* to have that visual experience or to feel pain, according to dualism. The dualist contends that conscious experience's intrinsic qualitative character is not amenable to structural-dynamic analysis.

More generally, dualists maintain that any attempt to describe conscious experience in purely structural-dynamic terms will leave out a crucial—really, *the* crucial—feature of conscious experience, namely, its qualitative character. Suppose that we had an exhaustive structural-dynamic description of a certain kind of neuronal activity. Suppose further (and less plausibly) that this kind of neuronal activity was perfectly correlated with pain. According to the dualist, the structural and dynamic features of this neuronal activity would not explain the occurrence of a conscious experience with the qualitative character of *pain*. In Levine's terms, there remains an 'explanatory gap' between these structural-dynamic phenomena and consciousness: we can still wonder about *why* pain arises when, and only when, that neuronal activity occurs (Levine 1983). This contrasts with the water example. When we understand the structural and dynamic features of H_2O molecules (and the structural-dynamic features of the molecular constituents of glass, etc.), we no longer wonder why lukewarm water conforms to the shape of the glass.

Dualists draw support for their view from this contrast. The behavior of H_2O is fully explained by underlying structure and dynamics, precisely because we can see how fixing the structural-dynamic facts fixes the facts about how H_2O behaves. In other words, the structural-dynamic facts *necessitate* the facts about how H_2O behaves. But we cannot see how fixing the structural and dynamic characteristics of lower-level phenomena—whether these are neurophysiological or involve fundamental entities treated by physics—fixes the facts about conscious experience. According to the dualist, this suggests that structural-dynamic facts do not necessitate the facts about conscious experience, and hence that consciousness is not physical.

Dualists deny that physical facts *necessitate* the facts about consciousness: that is, they maintain that consciousness *could* vary independently of structure and dynamics. But naturalistic dualists generally allow that, because of contingent laws of nature linking consciousness to structure and dynamics, consciousness will not *actually* vary independently of structural-dynamic phenomena. Dualism is compatible with the idea that conscious experience arises from structural-dynamic phenomena in a lawlike way.

An analogy will illustrate why, compatibly with dualism, conscious experience may arise from structural-dynamic phenomena in a lawlike way. Suppose that there exist non-physical ghostly spirits, whose presence and behavior is not constituted or necessitated by structural-dynamic phenomena. Suppose further that these spirits can be conjured by conducting a séance: lighting candles while reciting certain incantations, say. We can stipulate that these physical activities give rise, in a lawlike way, to the spirits' presence. This latter stipulation is compatible with the spirits being non-physical. If the spirits are non-physical—if they have features not amenable to structural-dynamic explanation—then the laws relating physical phenomena to the spirit world are not those (the 'dynamics') governing interactions among physical entities. In this sense, they are not physical (structural-dynamic) laws.

Astronomical, biological, and chemical phenomena are necessitated by structural-dynamic phenomena at lower levels. But conscious experience is not so necessitated, according to the dualist. This brings out the sense in which dualism is *dualist*. Physical phenomena—phenomena within the domain of physical science—are structural-dynamic phenomena or, at least, necessitated by structural-dynamic phenomena). But according to dualism, consciousness is neither a structural-dynamic phenomenon nor necessitated by structural-dynamic phenomena.

13.1.4 The Epistemic, the Metaphysical, and Brute Necessities

The subjectivity of consciousness thesis (section 13.1.2) is epistemic: it concerns what is required for recognizing conscious experience and grasping its qualitative features. Dualism is a metaphysical thesis: it concerns the nature of consciousness. Still, it might seem that the subjectivity of consciousness implies the truth of dualism. For suppose that dualism were false, and tickle experiences could be exhaustively characterized in terms of structure and dynamics (presumably the structural-dynamic features of neuronal activity or phenomena underlying such activity). In that case, we might expect objective methods to be adequate for understanding and identifying structural-dynamic phenomena. A well-informed investigator could completely understand tickles by grasping those structural-dynamic facts, and could recognize a tickle by recognizing the corresponding structural-dynamic phenomena. So if tickles were simply a matter of structure and dynamics, we would not need to rely on introspection to recognize tickles or to understand how they feel.

This is why dualism seems to follow from the subjectivity of consciousness. If dualism were false, and the qualitative features of conscious experiences were a matter of structure and dynamics, then we should expect that those features would be accessible through objective methods. So if the feel of a tickle is not objectively accessible, this suggests that dualism is true.

However, the subjectivity of consciousness—an epistemic thesis—does not imply the metaphysical thesis of dualism. To say that structural-dynamic phenomena necessitate consciousness is not to say that we can *make sense of* how or why they do so. The necessitation may instead be *brute*, in that there remains an epistemic divide (or 'explanatory gap') between structural-dynamic phenomena and consciousness. So long as conscious experiences are necessitated by structural-dynamic phenomena, dualism is false. Yet consciousness might nonetheless be subjective. It might be that first-personal methods are required for detecting and comprehending conscious experience, even if conscious experience is somehow necessitated, in a way that we cannot comprehend—that is, *brutely*—by structural-dynamic phenomena within the reach of objective methods.

If the necessary link between structural-dynamic phenomena and tickles were unintelligible to us, then even a well-informed investigator could not detect a tickle by relying solely on structural-dynamical evidence. For the investigator could not 'read off' the qualitative features from the structural-dynamical information. On the reasonable presumption that objective methods provide only information about structure and dynamics, the investigator would need to use first-person methods to detect tickles and correlate them with structural-dynamic phenomena such as neuronal activity.

It bears repeating that this situation, in which the structure and dynamics of lower-level phenomena somehow necessitate conscious experiences but this necessitation is opaque to us, differs starkly from paradigm cases of structural-dynamic explanation. Once we know the relevant structural and dynamical facts about H_2O molecules (and about the molecular constituents of glass, etc.), we fully understand why ice cubes retain their shape when placed in glass containers. The dualist will contend that this disparity is systematic, in that brute necessities are not required for structural-dynamic explanations of phenomena other than consciousness. For the dualist, this is reason for skepticism about brute necessities.

This juxtaposition of the epistemic and the metaphysical informs the dialectical structure of the debate over dualism. Dualists generally believe that consciousness is subjective, and take the epistemic disparity between consciousness (as subjective) and the physical (as objective) to point to a metaphysical disparity, and thereby to dualism. The step from the epistemic to the metaphysical is supported by the assumption that there are no brute necessities. For their part, some physicalists deny that there is an unbridgeable epistemic gap between consciousness and the physical. This position is known as *a priori physicalism* (see Jackson, Chapter 17 this volume). Other physicalists allow that there is such a gap, but deny that this epistemic gap provides reason to think that consciousness differs in kind from the physical. This latter position embraces brute necessities, and is known as *a posteriori physicalism* (see Levine, Chapter 18 this volume).

13.2 ARGUMENTS FOR DUALISM

There are three leading arguments for dualism: the Knowledge Argument (Jackson 1982), the Zombie Argument (Chalmers 1996), and the Modal Argument (Kripke 1980). In each of these, epistemic premises play a crucial role in securing the metaphysical thesis of dualism. In fact, these three arguments are all variations on the theme just mentioned: there is an epistemic gap between consciousness and physical phenomena, and hence these are ontologically distinct. I will focus on the Knowledge and Zombie Arguments, which are especially accessible and illuminating.

13.2.1 The Knowledge Argument

Although others had presented similar arguments, the most famous formulation of the Knowledge Argument is Jackson's (1982). Jackson describes Mary, a brilliant neuroscientist of the future, who has spent her entire life in a room that is exclusively black, white, and shades of gray. While in the room, Mary comes to know all of the physical facts about color vision. She knows how the surface properties of objects affect light reflectance, and she knows how the human visual system processes light at various wavelengths. For example, she knows that 'red' is the term for the qualitative property that normal humans experience when their retinas are struck by light with a wavelength of 620–780 nanometers. We can even suppose that she has identified perfect correlations between types of color experiences and types of neuronal activity. But she has never seen any colors.

Jackson invites us to consider what will happen when Mary leaves the room and, for the first time, sees something red (and which she knows to be red), such as a stop sign. He thinks that Mary will learn something new about color experience. She might express this new knowledge by saying, 'Oh, *this* is what it's like to see red!' Jackson argues that, since Mary already knew all of the physical facts about color experience, this fact about the qualitative character of 'seeing red' experiences is not a physical fact. He concludes that physicalism is false, and so dualism is true.

The subjectivity of consciousness is pivotal to this argument. Mary had access to all of the objective facts about color experience before her release: the only thing she lacked was first-person access to color experience, since she had not experienced color herself. So if she learns what it's like to see red only when she first sees something red, this means that objective methods will not reveal the qualitative character of color experience. This implies that objective methods will not yield a full understanding of consciousness; that is, consciousness is subjective. Jackson thus derives metaphysical dualism from the epistemic divide between what can be known via objective methods and what requires first-person experience.

Jackson does not define 'physical', but cashing out the notion of the physical in terms of structure and dynamics preserves the spirit and force of his argument. While in the room, Mary learns all of the structural-dynamic facts about color experience; we may further suppose that she has a comprehensive structural-dynamic description of the human visual system, the behavior of light, etc. But it seems she cannot know what it's like to see red—following standard usage, let us call such facts *phenomenal facts*—except by seeing something red. This means that that phenomenal fact is not deducible from the facts about structure and dynamics. Now if phenomenal facts were necessitated by structural-dynamic facts, then Mary's full knowledge of the structural-dynamic facts should enable her to deduce the phenomenal facts. After all, if Mary knew the structural and dynamic facts about H_2O molecules, she could deduce that ice cubes retain their shapes in containers, even if she had never encountered an ice cube. To maintain that the phenomenal facts are necessitated by the structural-dynamic facts, but are not deducible from them, is to embrace the brute necessities mentioned earlier. So unless there are brute necessities, the claim that Mary learns what it's like to see red only when leaving the room implies dualism. In this way, the 'no brute necessities' assumption licenses the shift from this argument's epistemic premises to its metaphysical conclusion.

13.2.2 The Zombie Argument

The Zombie Argument, developed in its most sophisticated form by Chalmers (1996), also aims to show that phenomenal facts are not deducible from physical facts. But instead of describing the situation of an isolated neuroscientist, Chalmers uses a more direct thought experiment. He asks you to try to conceive of a creature that is identical to you in all physical respects, but that lacks consciousness—a 'zombie'. Chalmers expects that you will be able to conceive of a zombie. That is, he thinks you will detect no incoherence in the idea of a molecule-for-molecule duplicate of yourself, with identical neurophysiology, but which lacks conscious experience. For example, he thinks you can conceive of your zombie twin undergoing c-fiber stimulation without experiencing the pain that you experience when your c-fibers are stimulated.[6] That you can conceive of a zombie—that you find nothing incoherent in the idea of a creature sharing your physical features, but lacking consciousness—means that you cannot deduce, from facts about a creature's physical constitution, that conscious experience is or is not present. As in the Knowledge Argument, this non-deducibility is taken to show that phenomenal facts are not necessitated by physical facts.

Our formulation of dualism is well-suited to this argument. (This is unsurprising, since that formulation is taken from Chalmers' work.) In conceiving of a zombie, one conceives of a creature that is identical to oneself in all structural-dynamic respects but lacks conscious experiences. This means that facts about conscious experience are not deducible from facts about structure and dynamics. After all, you can equally conceive that a creature exactly similar to a zombie, in all structural-dynamic respects, *does* have conscious experiences. For *you* are such a creature. Since you cannot distinguish yourself from your zombie twin *purely* on the basis of structural-dynamic features, you cannot deduce that consciousness is (or is not) present from knowledge of those features. As with the Knowledge Argument, the step from this epistemic premise to the dualist conclusion relies on the 'no brute necessities' assumption. That is, it relies on the assumption that, if the

---

[6] Crucially, we are not to assume that the duplicate is subject to the same laws of nature. For as the séance example illustrated (section 13.1.3), dualism is compatible with the idea that consciousness arises from physical phenomena as a matter of contingent laws.

phenomenal facts were necessitated by structural-dynamic facts, then we could deduce the former from the latter.

It is worth noting that, in contrast to the Knowledge Argument, the Zombie Argument need not rely on the subjectivity of consciousness. Each of these arguments attempts to establish dualism by pointing to an epistemic divide between consciousness and the physical. But in the Zombie Argument, this divide need not be specifically a divide between the subjective and the objective. Consider the point made in the previous paragraph: you cannot distinguish yourself from your zombie twin *purely* on the basis of structural-dynamic features. So facts about consciousness are not deducible from those features. Now it may well be that the best diagnosis of this non-deducibility is that consciousness is subjective whereas the physical is objective. But the Zombie Argument does not strictly require that the epistemic divide is a divide between the subjective and the objective.

We believe that other human beings have conscious experiences. And arguably, we infer that they are conscious from their physical features and behavior: after all, we do not have anything else to go on. (Particularly salient here is the capacity for articulate speech, which zombies also exhibit.) However, the inference from others' physical similarity to the conclusion that they are conscious is not deductive. You can imagine, in a twist on a classic horror film trope, that the human-like creatures around you are zombies, with no conscious inner life. (This scenario is at odds with most versions of naturalistic dualism, which take consciousness to arise from the physical contingently but in a way governed by laws of nature; see note 6.) That others are physically similar to you is strong but not absolutely conclusive evidence that they have conscious experiences roughly similar to your own.

13.2.3 Can We really Perform these Thought Experiments?

Some physicalists charge that these thought experiments are unreliable, as we are not equipped to competently evaluate the scenarios at issue. As applied to the Knowledge Argument, the worry is that even a well-informed scientist does not have the information needed to meaningfully imagine knowing all of the physical (structural-dynamic) facts about color experience. So we are not in a position to determine whether such knowledge would enable us to deduce the phenomenal facts. As applied to the Zombie Argument, the worry is that even a well-informed scientist does not have the information needed to truly conceive of a perfect physical (structural-dynamic) duplicate, and hence we cannot evaluate whether the possibility of a zombie is coherent.

It is true that neuroscience is still in its early days, and theories in fundamental physics remain speculative. In engaging in these thought experiments we must therefore rely on a general conception of what it is to be *physical*. Following Chalmers (2002), I have suggested that we conceive of the physical as what can be exhaustively characterized in terms of structure and dynamics. But this suggestion does not silence the current worry. For we do not know what kinds of structural-dynamic phenomena are yet to be discovered, or how our models of physical phenomena might evolve (while remaining structural-dynamic). So we cannot conceive of all of Mary's knowledge, or all of the properties that would be shared by our structural-dynamic duplicate, in detail.[7]

The dualist will maintain that the details are not needed to perform the thought experiment, as careful reflection on what it's like to feel a tickle or smell coffee enables us to recognize that such qualitative features of experience are not amenable to any structural-dynamic explanation, regardless of the specific structural-dynamic details. This response highlights the significance of conceptual matters in this debate. The dualist arguments rely on the accuracy of our phenomenal concepts, developed through introspective reflection on experience, and also draw on our physical concepts. As we will see in Sections 13.3 and 13.4, conceptual matters are also central to physicalist objections to dualism. These objections are grounded in confidence about our ways of conceptualizing the physical, as expressed in our physical theories. They presume that our conceptualizations are not only useful but represent physical reality accurately and comprehensively.

Perhaps most importantly, our ignorance about the neuroscience of consciousness and the nature of fundamental physics cuts both ways. For the greater our ignorance about these matters, the less confident we should be about what form a comprehensive theory of concrete phenomena will take. In particular, recognizing that advances in fundamental physics may alter our current models of physical phenomena should limit our confidence that all of concrete reality is amenable to explanation in structural-dynamic terms—or perhaps even in any terms that qualify the successful theory as a *physical* theory, in a non-trivial sense.

13.2.4 The Use of Armchair Reasoning

The Knowledge and Zombie arguments rest on the use of introspection and *a priori* reflection. This exposes them to doubts about whether such 'armchair reasoning' is legitimate as a means of discerning metaphysical truths about concrete reality.

The worry is that armchair reasoning seems to reveal only *epistemic* facts. We may discover, through introspective reflection on the feel of a tickle, that phenomenal properties appear not to be a matter of structure and dynamics. Armchair reasoning may also reveal that we cannot deduce phenomenal facts from physical facts, and that we can conceive of zombies. But these are merely epistemic matters, insufficient to establish dualism.

The relation between the epistemic and the metaphysical is a philosophically foundational one. Positions on this issue are grounded in complex accounts of thought, reference, and modality. Fortunately, we need not go into the details of those accounts to determine whether, in the context of this debate, it is legitimate for the dualist to use armchair

---

[7] Another concern is that we may err even in applying those concepts we do possess: that is, in attempting to conceive of a zombie. Chalmers addresses this issue by appealing to an idealized notion of conceivability. As he notes, this notion idealizes away from our cognitive limitations in much the same way as the notion of a priori truths idealizes away from those limitations: a mathematical equation may be a priori even if, because of its complexity, it cannot be properly evaluated by unaided human cognition.

reasoning. This is because the case for physicalism equally rests on armchair reasoning. Let me explain.

According to physicalism, facts about structure and dynamics *necessitate* all facts (about concrete reality—I will omit this in what follows). That is, it is impossible for any facts, including facts about conscious experience, to vary independently of facts about structure and dynamics. Now in order to establish that something is necessary or impossible, armchair reasoning is indispensable. Ordinary observation can establish that something is *possible*: if you see a cat on the mat, you can safely conclude that it is possible for cats to be on mats. But claims about what is necessary or what is impossible cannot be established through observation.

For example, the discovery that every creature undergoing a certain kind of neuronal activity is also experiencing pain would not show that these were linked with metaphysical necessity. This might be simply a coincidence. More plausibly, they may be linked nomologically: laws of nature may ensure that pain arises from neuronal activity of that kind. And if the link between consciousness and the physical is only a matter of contingent laws of nature, then dualism is true (as our séance example illustrated). So nothing that could be established simply through empirical observation—not even perfect correlations between types of neuronal activity and types of conscious states—could resolve this debate in favor of physicalism.[8] The case for physicalism requires going beyond empirical observations (which concern what's actual) and generalizations from those observations. The dualist can allow that, because of contingent but lawlike regularities, conscious experience *will not* vary independently of the underlying physical phenomena. But the physicalist thesis requires more than this. It requires that conscious experience *could not* vary independently of the physical.

As the next two sections will illustrate, the case for thinking that consciousness is *necessitated* by the physical relies on armchair reasoning. Specifically, it relies on significant assumptions about the nature of the physical, assumptions that cannot be verified by empirical science or reasonably inferred from its findings.

13.3 DUALISM AND THEORETICAL SIMPLICITY

We now turn to the first influential challenge to dualism. This challenge stems from the idea that, given the success of physical science generally, a physicalist theory of consciousness will provide for a theory of concrete phenomena that is simpler than dualism, and hence possesses greater explanatory power.

---

[8] Since dualism is a thesis about what is possible, rather than a thesis about what is necessary or impossible, this debate could ostensibly be resolved by empirical observation: e.g., the discovery of two creatures that were exactly similar, physically, but that differed in their conscious experiences. But verifying this would be difficult (to say the least). And it would undermine the standard naturalist form of dualism, which says that there is a lawlike relation between consciousness and the physical.

The physical sciences are rightly regarded as exemplars of knowledge production, given their remarkable success in explaining and predicting a wide range of phenomena. So it is natural to hope that they will someday provide a comprehensive account of all concrete phenomena, including consciousness.

If that hope were realized, the resulting theory would have the virtue of *simplicity*. Suppose that all phenomena, including consciousness, were amenable to explanation in terms of structure and dynamics. In that case, a single explanatory framework could be adequate for explaining all phenomena. The resulting physical theory might well be simpler than dualism in two ways. First, it might include fewer basic kinds of things in its ontology, since all of the basic entities it recognizes will be amenable to structural-dynamic analysis. (This dimension of simplicity is known as *parsimony*.) Second, it might include fewer fundamental laws, since it need not include special fundamental laws linking structural-dynamic phenomena to consciousness. (This is known as *elegance*.)[9]

Simplicity concerns exert a powerful, often covert influence on the dualism-physicalism debate. I suspect that it is the appeal of greater simplicity that is responsible for the sense that dualism faces a greater initial burden of proof.

Whether simplicity considerations provide good reason to favor physicalism depends on how the arguments for dualism fare. In general, simplicity concerns guide theory choice only when the theories being compared accommodate the data equally well. And the arguments for dualism attempt to show that physicalist theories do not accommodate all of the data about conscious experience. The thought experiments in the Knowledge Argument and the Zombie Argument are designed to lead us to conclude that our own introspective data—data we glean from introspecting our own experiences—are not accommodated by a physicalist theory. In our formulation, these data are not accommodated by a theory that explains phenomena purely in terms of structure and dynamics.

In response, the physicalist can argue that we should be wary of the claim that these data cannot be explained by a physicalist theory, precisely because respecting that claim requires sacrificing simplicity. After all, the physicalist might say, the importance of simplicity raises the bar for arguments aiming to establish dualism. And this high bar cannot be cleared simply by observing that some data about experiences appear to resist structural-dynamic explanation.

To assess this issue, we need to understand the importance of simplicity. How much does simplicity matter, in evaluating a theory? And *why* does it matter? These questions are surprisingly difficult to answer. While simpler theories are generally preferred in the

---

[9] That a theory is compatible with physicalism does not *entail* that it is simpler than a dualist theory. Suppose that qualitative features of experience are intrinsic to structural-dynamic entities, but are not themselves fixed by structural-dynamic factors. This entails dualism (on my formulation of dualism). Yet it is compatible with a high degree of both parsimony and elegance: e.g., a kind of monism that allows for a sparse set of basic laws and principles. Views of this kind, often inspired by Russell (1927), have recently grown in prominence. (See Goff and Coleman, Chapter 14 and Stoljar, Chapter 22 of this volume, and the papers in Alter and Nagasawa 2015.) There is some controversy as to whether this monistic view strictly qualifies as dualism or as physicalism; such controversies mean that any formulation of these positions, including mine, will be open to question. But the fact that this view seems, to many, to be closer in spirit to dualism than to physicalism illustrates the inadequacy of the term 'dualism', as that term suggests that dualism is incompatible with monism.

sciences, the preference for simplicity does not translate easily to philosophy. The scientific preference may be driven by instrumental or even aesthetic considerations, whereas the philosopher's exclusive concern is with *truth*. And there is no clear reason to think that a simpler theory is more likely to be true.

A natural thought is that 'simpler theories are more likely to be true' might be established inductively. An inductive argument could cite the fact that simplicity considerations guide theory choice in the sciences, and so take the predictive success of the sciences as a basis for inferring that greater simplicity indicates a greater likelihood of truth. But as Huemer (2009) demonstrates, this strategy is problematically circular. We regard scientific theories as true because the truth of their claims is the *simplest* explanation of their predictive success. The inference from predictive success to truth depends on the assumption that simplicity is linked with truth, and so it cannot (non-circularly) establish that link.

The prospects for an empirical justification for favoring simpler theories, in the search for truth, seem dim. Sober argues that, while favoring simpler theories may be justified as a means of maximizing predictive success, there may be no way of justifying the assumption that a simpler theory is more likely to be true (Sober 2009).[10]

The first challenge to dualism is physical science's record of success, and the corresponding promise of a unified physicalist theory encompassing consciousness and other phenomena. But whether a unified physicalist theory is possible depends on how the dualist arguments fare. Some contributors to this debate take physicalism's greater simplicity to warrant skepticism about data that threaten this unification project—for example, introspective data that support the Knowledge and Zombie arguments. This strategy invests simplicity with an importance and relevance to truth that may be impossible to justify—and seems not to be open to empirical justification. So we should be wary of taking the perceived threat to simplicity as grounds for skepticism about the data used to support dualism.

13.4 Dualism and Mental Causation

The most influential objection to dualism—and, correspondingly, the most influential argument for physicalism—concerns mental causation. The problem of mental causation

---

[10] Sober expresses skepticism about the association of parsimony with truth, as regards 'the mind/body identity theory', a version of physicalism. (The term 'model selection theory' refers to a particular operational interpretation of parsimony.)

> Placing the mind/body identity theory and dualism within the context of model selection theory requires one to think of the contending theories in terms of their predictive accuracy, not their truth. Metaphysicians may balk at this, proclaiming that they don't care about predictive accuracy and want only to figure out what is true. I am not arguing against that preference. Rather, my point is that the parsimony argument for the identity theory finds a natural home in the model selection framework. If there is another treatment of the argument that establishes its connection with truth, I do not know what that treatment is (Sober 2009, 137).

is standardly regarded as the most serious challenge to dualism. This challenge takes many forms. My focus will be on the form that has dominated discussion for the past thirty years or so, namely, the exclusion argument.

13.4.1 The Exclusion Argument

We ordinarily assume that conscious experiences have physical effects. Tickles cause us to laugh; pain causes us to seek analgesics. But a powerful argument suggests that, if conscious experiences are something over and above the physical, then they do not cause physical events. According to this argument, dualism implies that conscious experience is *epiphenomenal*: it may be caused by physical events or processes, but it does not have physical effects. Some dualists embrace epiphenomenalism about consciousness, while others argue that conscious experience, although non-physical, can causally affect the physical realm. The problem of mental causation is widely regarded, by physicalists and dualists alike, as the most serious challenge facing dualism.

Why think that dualism implies that conscious experience has no physical effects? In a nutshell, the worry is this. In order to explain a physical event, we never *need* to invoke anything non-physical—or so it seems. For example, we may one day be able to fully explain how tickles cause laughter and how pain causes us to say 'ouch!' and to seek analgesics. Such explanations would presumably invoke only *physical* causes: in our terms, only phenomena that are amenable to structural-dynamic explanation. (For brevity, I will continue to use 'physical'.) Given the availability of purely physical explanations of human behavior, no explanatory work remains for non-physical factors to perform. So if the qualitative character of tickles and pains—how these sensations *feel*—is non-physical, then reference to this qualitative character is not needed to explain laughter or analgesic-seeking behavior. More generally: if, for every physical event that can be causally explained, a causal explanation in purely physical terms is available (in principle), then the non-physical seems inconsequential as regards causal explanations of physical phenomena.

This problem, which is known as the *exclusion problem*, was developed in its contemporary form by Jaegwon Kim (1989a). The availability of purely physical explanations seems to leave no work to be done by explanations citing non-physical factors, and hence to *exclude* the latter.

Now even if non-physical features of conscious experiences are not *needed* to causally explain physical events, this does not mean that those features are causally inert. Imagine that you are awoken by two simultaneous alarms. Each of these alarms is redundant, in that the presence of the other alarm means that neither one is *needed* for the task of awakening you. But adding the second alarm did not *silence* the first one; neither alarm is robbed of its causal power by the presence of the other. Similarly, a causal explanation of laughter may invoke the (non-physical) *feel* of a tickle even if, given the availability of a physical explanation, the explanation that invokes that non-physical feel is redundant.

Suppose that, for every physical event for which a causal explanation is available, there is an explanation in purely physical terms. Non-physical properties of experience might nonetheless be invoked in (admittedly redundant) causal explanations of physical events. In that case, every physical effect (such as saying 'ouch!') of a non-physical conscious experience (such as feeling a pain) is *overdetermined*: there is a physical cause (perhaps neuronal activity) capable of bringing about the effect all on its own, and an additional non-physical cause (the pain sensation) also capable of bringing about the effect all on its own. The specter of rampant overdetermination—a pervasive redundancy in nature—is unappealing.

The dualist has three unattractive options. The first is to deny that conscious experiences have causal efficacy—that is, to embrace epiphenomenalism. The second is to maintain that conscious experiences are causally efficacious by allowing the type of rampant overdetermination just described. The third option is to deny that every physical effect could be explained purely by reference to physical phenomena.

The physicalist can avoid this problem by saying that conscious experiences *just are* physical events (so qualitative character is a physical feature).[11] In that case, conscious experiences and physical events do not compete for the title 'cause', since they are one and the same. So physical explanations do not *exclude* explanations that cite conscious experiences.

Papineau (2002) provides a tidy formulation of this argument.[12]

(1) Some conscious experiences have physical effects. (This is the rejection of epiphenomenalism.)
(2) All physical effects are fully caused by purely physical prior histories. (That is: for every physical event that can be causally explained, a purely physical explanation is in principle available.)
(3) The physical effects of conscious experiences are not always overdetermined by distinct causes.

Conclusion: The conscious experiences mentioned in (1) must be identical with some part of the physical causes mentioned in (2).

Suppose we want to identify what caused your laughter. To secure a non-superfluous explanatory role for the feel of the tickle, reference to that feeling should be essential to the causal explanation. This requirement is easily met by simply *identifying* that feeling with a type of physical state. On this physicalist proposal, 'tickle sensation' and 'neuronal activity N' refer to the same thing—they are two terms for a single type of state. To say that that state caused your laughter is to provide a physical explanation (consonant

---

[11] On the plausible view that a conscious experience is the instantiation of qualitative properties in a subject at a time, the claim that conscious experiences are physical events implies that qualitative properties are physical.

[12] This formulation is paraphrased from Papineau 2002: ch 1.

with premise 2) that invokes conscious experience (confirming premise 1) but avoids overdetermination (confirming premise 3).

The physicalist thesis that avoids the exclusion problem, and that serves as the conclusion of this argument, is especially strong. The idea that tickle sensations are strictly identical to a certain kind of physical event implies that tickle sensations cannot be realized in other physical types—other types of brains, with different structural-dynamic characteristics. For this reason, most physicalists deny that conscious experiences are strictly identical to physical events. Most favor the more moderate physicalist thesis that conscious experiences are necessitated by, but not identical to, physical events.

Moderate physicalism also faces the exclusion problem (Kim 1989b). If physical effects can be causally explained purely by reference to physical causes, and physical causes are not identical to conscious experiences, then physical explanations exclude explanations invoking conscious states. (See Bennett 2007 for an illuminating discussion of this problem and of the responses available to the moderate physicalist.)

13.4.2 The Completeness Premise

I believe that epiphenomenalism, the denial of premise 1 of the argument, is less damaging to our commonsense views than it initially appears (Gertler 2019). But my discussion here will center on premise 2, which is known as the *completeness* premise. It says that the realm of the physical is explanatorily complete, in that we never need to invoke anything outside that realm to explain any (explainable) physical event.

Applying our conception of the physical yields the following interpretation of the completeness premise.

Structural-Dynamic Completeness:

For every effect that can be exhaustively characterized in structural-dynamic terms, an explanation invoking only structural-dynamic phenomena is (in principle) available.[13]

This statement seems plainly true. By conceptualizing an effect in structural-dynamic terms, we more or less ensure that it is amenable to structural-dynamic explanation. After all, structural-dynamic characterizations of a phenomenon include its causal and nomic properties: the kinds of interactions it enters into, and the laws governing its behavior. So to characterize an event in structural-dynamic terms is already to locate it within the explanatory framework of structure and dynamics. What this shows is that much of the weight of the argument from mental causation is borne by the way that the effects to be explained—the 'physical' effects—are conceptualized.

---

[13] Strictly speaking, on our formulation physical events are constituted *or necessitated* by structural-dynamic phenomena. I elided this qualification for brevity. It does not change the basic point since, trivially, an effect necessitated by structural-dynamic phenomena is explainable in terms of structure and dynamics.

In order for the exclusion argument to succeed, our way of conceptualizing the events to be explained—the 'physical effects'—must be not only accurate but also exhaustive. The argument would fail if there were features of these target effects that were not simply a matter of structure and dynamics. For suppose that the physical effect to be explained had some such features. (These could be characteristics at the fundamental level of physics, which underlie or complement the phenomenon's structure and dynamics.) In that case, the availability of a structural-dynamic explanation would not render other explanations superfluous. These other explanations might do needed explanatory work as regards the aspect of the phenomenon that resists structural-dynamic analysis. This would neutralize the overdetermination worry, and thereby undermine the exclusion argument.[14]

These reflections reveal an assumption of the exclusion argument: that our way of conceptualizing the physical, in terms of structure and dynamics, is not only accurate but also *exhaustive*, in that it captures all explanatorily salient features of physical reality. This assumption seems reasonable enough, so long as we have no reason to think that there is a dimension of physical phenomena that resists structural-dynamic analysis or explanation. But it is worth noting that this is a very substantial assumption. It requires an especially ambitious view about the relation between how we conceptualize reality and reality itself. The previous section discussed a moderate (but still questionable) claim about this relation, namely that if two theories—two ways of conceptualizing and explaining a set of phenomena—accommodate the data equally well, then the simpler theory is more likely to be true. If we had reason to accept that claim, it could be used to establish that the way our physical theories conceptualize (physical) reality, in terms of structure and dynamics, is accurate: that is, physical reality truly has the structural-dynamic features we attribute to it. But even this argument, which relies on a questionable claim about the link between simplicity and truth, is silent on the question whether structure and dynamics *exhaust* the physical. For it says nothing about whether there is anything *beyond* structure and dynamics.

The assumption that there is no aspect of physical phenomena that evades structural-dynamic explanation could be challenged on a variety of grounds. In fact, the worry about causal exclusion could fuel just such a challenge. Positing an aspect of physical effects that is not amenable to structural-dynamic explanations provides a way to avoid both epiphenomenalism and overdetermination.

Let me sum up. The leading form of the problem of mental causation, the exclusion argument, depends on an ambitious assumption: that our conceptualization of physical phenomena, in terms of structure and dynamics, is not only accurate but also exhaustive. This assumption goes well beyond the kind of background assumption required to avoid skepticism, viz. that our concepts correspond (at least roughly) to features of reality itself. It also goes well beyond the idea that simpler theories are more likely to be true.

---

[14] Following Russell (1927), some have suggested that structural-dynamic characterizations neglect the intrinsic or categorical features of physical things. This opens up the possibility of a variety of alternatives to classic dualism and physicalism. See note 9.

And it is a conceptual, philosophical claim, not a scientific one: nothing empirical could establish that physical theory *comprehensively* captures the underlying reality it (perhaps accurately) describes. So this objection to dualism, like the objection from simplicity, relies on confidence that our way of conceptualizing the physical, in physical theories, is linked to the physical itself. But the required link here is particularly robust. It is that there is no aspect of physical phenomena beyond what is captured by our theories; in other words, physical phenomena consist entirely in structure and dynamics (and what is necessitated by structure and dynamics).

13.5 The Epistemic Sources of Dualism and Physicalism

Arguments on both sides of this debate rely on epistemic premises: claims about how we represent, conceptualize, and learn about conscious experience and/or physical phenomena. These arguments also rely on strategies for justifying the inference from their respective epistemic premises to their respective metaphysical conclusions.

For the dualist, the epistemic premises include the subjectivity of consciousness and the (apparent) conceivability of zombies. The metaphysical conclusion is that conscious experience is not identical to or necessitated by structural-dynamic phenomena. The bridge from the epistemic to the metaphysical is the 'no brute necessities' assumption: if there were *necessary* connections between conscious experience and structural-dynamic phenomena, these connections would be intelligible to us.

For the physicalist, the epistemic premises include the claim that conceptualizing physical phenomena in terms of structure and dynamics—the conceptualization embodied in physical theory—is not only accurate but exhaustive. The metaphysical conclusion is that conscious experience is amenable to explanation in these terms: it consists in, or is necessitated by, structural-dynamic phenomena. In the arguments we considered here, the bridge from the epistemic to the metaphysical depends on simplicity considerations. Suppose that all concrete phenomena other than consciousness consist in, or are necessitated by, purely structural-dynamic phenomena (this is the epistemic premise). In that case, a structural-dynamic explanation of consciousness will yield a theory of concrete reality that has a relatively high degree of theoretical simplicity. In particular, given the epistemic premise, a structural-dynamic explanation of consciousness will yield a theory that is simpler than a theory that disavows structural-dynamic explanations of consciousness—that is, a dualist theory. The bridge from the epistemic premise to the metaphysical conclusion is the assumption that if two theories accommodate the data equally well, the simpler theory is more likely to be true.

The exclusion argument fits this pattern. The epistemic premise is that structural-dynamic explanations of non-mental phenomena are accurate and comprehensive—they leave no dimension of the target phenomenon unexplained. In light of that premise, positing alternative explanations—explanations citing phenomena that are not structural-dynamical—compromises theoretical simplicity, by requiring overdetermination. Embracing epiphenomenalism also threatens simplicity. For the causal inefficacy of conscious experience makes it a 'nomological dangler': something that (we presume) arises from physical processes but does not give rise to anything. This picture is plainly inelegant. The threat to simplicity seems to be what Smart has in mind when he complains that 'the laws whereby these nomological danglers would dangle... would be like nothing so far known in science. They have a queer "smell" to them' (Smart 1959: 142–3).

One's position on dualism will not be determined simply by how one regards conceptual arguments, or by the extent of one's deference to physical science and theorizing. Arguments on both sides of this debate presume that the way we conceptualize a phenomenon can justify claims about that phenomenon's metaphysical nature. And arguments on both sides employ distinctively philosophical claims—claims outside the purview of science—about the status and proper domain of physical science. Where one stands on the question of dualism chiefly depends on where one stands on more specific epistemic questions: the epistemic premises of the arguments for and against dualism, and the way these arguments justify the inference from those premises to their respective metaphysical conclusions.[15]

REFERENCES

Alter, T. (2016), 'The Structure and Dynamics Argument against Materialism', *Noûs*, 50: 794–815.
Alter, T. and Nagasawa, Y. (eds) (2015), *Consciousness in the Physical World: Perspectives on Russellian Monism*. Oxford: Oxford University Press.
Balog, K. (2012), 'In Defense of the Phenomenal Concept Strategy', *Philosophy and Phenomenological Research*, 84: 1–23.
Bennett, K. (2007), 'Mental Causation', *Philosophy Compass*, 2: 316–37.
Chalmers, D. J. (1996), *The Conscious Mind: In Search of a Fundamental Theory*. Oxford: Oxford University Press.
Chalmers, D. J. (2002), 'Consciousness and its Place in Nature', in D. J. Chalmers (ed.), *Philosophy of Mind: Classic and Contemporary Readings*. Oxford: Oxford University Press, 247–72.
Chalmers, D. J. (2006), 'Phenomenal concepts and the explanatory gap', in T. Alter and S. Walter (eds), *Phenomenal Concepts and Phenomenal Knowledge: New Essays on Consciousness and Physicalism*. Oxford: Oxford University Press, 167–94.
Dominus, S. (2011), 'Could Conjoined Twins Share a Mind?' *New York Times Magazine*, May 29, 2011. (http://www.nytimes.com/2011/05/29/magazine/could-conjoined-twins-share-a-mind.html)

---

[15] I'm grateful to Uriah Kriegel and Torin Alter, who offered extremely useful comments on a previous draft of this chapter.

Gertler, B. (2019), 'Acquaintance, Parsimony, and Epiphenomenalism', in S. Coleman (ed.), *The Knowledge Argument*. Cambridge: Cambridge University Press, 62–86.

Goldman, A. (1997), 'Science, Publicity, and Consciousness', *Philosophy of Science*, 64: 525–45.

Howell, R. J. (2013), *Consciousness and the Limits of Objectivity: The Case for Subjective Physicalism*. Oxford: Oxford University Press.

Huemer, M. (2009), 'When is Parsimony a Virtue?', *Philosophical Quarterly*, 59: 216–36.

Jackson, F. (1982), 'Epiphenomenal Qualia', in *Philosophical Quarterly*, 32: 127–36.

Jaynes, J. (1976/2000), *The Origins of Consciousness in the Breakdown of the Bicameral Mind*. Boston, MA: Houghton Mifflin.

Kim, J. (1989a), 'Mechanism, Purpose, and Explanatory Exclusion', *Philosophical Perspectives*, 3: 77–108.

Kim, J. (1989b), 'The Myth of Nonreductive Physicalism', *Proceedings and Addresses of the American Philosophical Association*, 63: 31–47.

Kripke, S. (1980), *Naming and Necessity*. Cambridge, MA: Harvard University Press.

Levin, J. (2006), 'What is a phenomenal concept?', in T. Alter and S. Walter (eds), *Phenomenal Concepts and Phenomenal Knowledge: New Essays on Consciousness and Physicalism*. Oxford: Oxford University Press, 87–110.

Levine, J. (1983), 'Materialism and Qualia: the explanatory gap', *Pacific Philosophical Quarterly*, 64: 354–61.

Papineau, D. (2002), *Thinking About Consciousness*. Oxford: Oxford University Press.

Russell, B. (1927), *The Analysis of Matter*. London: Kegan Paul.

Smart, J. J. C. (1959), 'Sensations and Brain Processes', *The Philosophical Review*, 68: 141–56.

Sober, E. (2009), 'Parsimony Arguments in Science and Philosophy—A Test Case for Naturalism', *Proceedings and Addresses of the American Philosophical Association*, 83: 117–55.

Stoljar, D. (2001), 'Two Conceptions of the Physical', *Philosophy and Phenomenological Research*, 62: 253–81.

CHAPTER 14

RUSSELLIAN MONISM

PHILIP GOFF AND SAM COLEMAN

14.1 INTRODUCTION

RUSSELLIAN monism is a new, or rather a rediscovered, approach to the problem of consciousness, which offers a middle way between the more conventional options of physicalism and dualism. It is inspired by some claims made by Bertrand Russell in *The Analysis of Matter* in 1927, on the basis of which he defended a novel approach to the mind–body problem. This approach was mostly forgotten about in the latter half of the twentieth century but has recently been rediscovered in mainstream philosophy of mind, causing considerable interest and excitement.[1]

The view has a negative and a positive aspect. The negative aspect starts from the idea that physical science tells us a lot less than we tend to assume about the nature of the physical world. In the public mind, physical science is on its way to giving us a complete account of the nature of space, time, and matter. However, it turns out upon reflection—at least according to Russellian monism—that physical science is confined to telling us about the *behavioural dispositions* of physical entities. Think, for example, about what physics tells us about an electron. Physics tells us that an electron has mass and negative charge, among other properties. How does physics characterize these properties? Mass is characterized in terms of gravitational attraction and resistance to acceleration. Charge is characterized in terms of attraction and repulsion. All of these characterzations concern how the electron is disposed to behave, and the same is true with respect to the ways in which physics characterizes other physical properties. Physics is silent on

---

[1] See Alter and Nagasawa 2015 for a collection of essays on Russellian monism. Goff 2017 brings together and critically evaluates much of the recent literature on this topic. Half of Pereboom 2011 is a defence of Russellian monism. Although the view has recently sprung into the mainstream, there were sporadic defences of something like Russellian monism throughout the latter half of the twentieth century, for example, Feigl 1971, Maxwell 1978, Lockwood 1989, Strawson 1994, and Griffin 1998.

the features of matter that underlie its behavioural dispositions, generally referred to as the 'categorical properties' of matter.[2]

The positive claim of Russellian monism is that it is these 'hidden' categorical properties of matter that explain consciousness. We can see the advantage of this thesis by reflecting on the problems that beset physicalism on the one hand and dualism on the other:

The Problem with Physicalism—Nothing we have learnt from neuroscience seems to explain why brains are conscious; indeed, everything we know from neuroscience about the brain seems entirely consistent with the complete absence of consciousness. Moreover, there are powerful philosophical arguments—the knowledge argument and the conceivability argument—which seem to demonstrate that the properties of physical science alone could never explain consciousness (Jackson 1982, 1986; Chalmers 2009; Goff 2015b, 2017). If these arguments are sound, then physicalism—understood as the thesis that physical science can in principle give a complete account of reality—is inconsistent with consciousness realism.[3]

The Problem with Dualism—Many philosophers believe that there is strong empirical support for the thesis that the physical world is causally closed, in the sense that every physical event has a sufficient and immediate physical cause. If this is true, it is hard to see how non-physical consciousness could play any role in the production of behaviour. If everything Sarah does has a sufficient physical cause, then there does not seem to be anything left for Sarah's non-physical consciousness to do. A commitment to the non-physicality of consciousness seems to render it causally impotent, a thesis which some are happy to accept but most take to be beyond the pale.[4]

The Russellian monist elegantly avoids both of these difficulties, or so she claims. She agrees with the dualist that the dispositional properties of physical science cannot on

---

[2] Dispositional essentialists (Ellis 2001, 2002; Molnar 2003; Mumford 2004; Bird 2007) hold that all fundamental properties are dispositions, and so deny that there are any categorical properties. Opponents of dispositional essentialism (Russell 1927; Campbell 1976; Robinson 1982; Heil 2003; Lowe 2006; Goff 2017: ch 6) have tried to argue that the view essentially involves either a vicious regress or a vicious circularity. Even if there are possible worlds in which dispositional essentialism is true, the knowledge and conceivability arguments (discussed below in this section), if sound, demonstrate that dispositional properties cannot ground consciousness properties, and hence that dispositional essentialism is false at any possible world containing consciousness. Some have argued that dispositional and categorical properties are identical (Heil 2003; Martin and Heil 1998; Martin 2007; Strawson 2008). Taking this view into account, we can characterize the Russellian monist as holding that physical science tells us nothing about the nature of categorical properties *qua categorical*.

[3] We are here understanding the word 'physicalism' in a narrow sense such that it contrasts with Russellian monism; however, 'physicalism' (or 'materialism') is sometimes defined in a very broad sense such that it is consistent with Russellian monism. Galen Strawson (2003, 2006), for example, defends a form of panpsychist Russellian monism that he refers to as 'real materialism'. In this chapter, we are roughly thinking of 'physicalism' as the view that physical science can in principle give a complete account of the fundamental nature of reality. For a more nuanced definition of physicalism and how it differs from Russellian monism, see Goff (2015a, 2017: ch 2).

[4] See Lowe 2009, Gibb 2015 for attempts to defend dualism against this problem.

their own explain consciousness, and thus she is not threatened by the knowledge and conceivability arguments. But she also agrees with the physicalist that consciousness is part of the causally closed physical world, in virtue of being constituted by the categorical properties of matter.[5] Even critics of Russellian monism have remarked on the beauty of its solution to the problem of consciousness: physicalist Alyssa Ney declares that it is 'at least as bold and exciting as Newton's proposed identification of terrestrial and cosmic reality' (Ney 2015: 349).[6]

Russellian monism is a quite general approach, which comes in a variety of forms depending on what is said about the categorical properties of basic physical entities.[7] We can usefully distinguish between *panpsychist* and *panprotopsychist* forms. Panpsychist Russellian monists hold that the categorical properties of basic physical entities are experiential properties. Panprotosychist Russellian monists hold that the categorical properties of basic physical entities are *proto-experiential*, where proto-experiential properties are not themselves experiential properties but are crucial ingredients in facts that explain the production of consciousness.[8] In the first half of this chapter Philip Goff will discuss panpsychist forms of Russellian monism, and in the second half Sam Coleman will discuss panprotosychist forms.[9]

14.2 Panpsychist Russellian Monism (by Philip Goff)

14.2.1 The Basic Idea

Panpsychism is the view that consciousness is a fundamental and ubiquitous feature of reality. For much of the twentieth century, analytic philosophers treated this view with

---

[5] More specifically, the proposal is that by grounding physical dispositional properties, special categorical properties directly relevant to the grounding of consciousness, and thus macro-level consciousness itself, get intimately involved in physical causation. Howell (2015) argues that these supposed advantages of Russellian monism with respect to mental causation are illusory. See Alter and Coleman 2019, 2020 for a response.

[6] It ought to be said that Ney precedes this declaration with '...suspending disbelief about the...theses that lead up to it...'

[7] We will shortly be considering forms of emergentism, according to which there are fundamental properties at the macro-level, and in this context we need to distinguish the subset of fundamental properties that are *basic*. We can say that a property P is *basic* iff (A) P is fundamental, and (B) P is instantiated by a fundamental individual that is not causally dependent for its existence on an individual(s) at some other mereological level.

[8] See Section 14.3 for further detail on the definition of proto-experiential properties. The distinction between 'panpsychism' and 'panprotopsychism' comes from Chalmers 2015.

[9] Although neither panpsychism nor panprotopsychism entail Russellian monism, we focus on Russellian monist versions of these positions in what follows, and will use the terms 'panpsychism' and 'panprotopsychism' accordingly.

contempt, insofar as they thought about it at all. However, panpsychism has recently become a respected minority position, largely because Russellian monism can be interpreted in panpsychist terms. On the standard form of Russellian panpsychism defended in contemporary philosophy, the fundamental constituents of the physical world—perhaps electrons and quarks—have unimaginably simple experience, whilst the complex experience of the human or animal brain is constituted of, or otherwise dependent on, the simple experience of its parts.[10]

When one first hears about the view that quarks are conscious, it is natural to interpret what is being claimed dualistically. That is to say, one imagines that the quark has its physical properties and its experiential properties sitting side by side, as it were. However, this would not be a Russellian form of panpsychism. For the Russellian panpsychist, the physical properties of the quark—such as mass and charge—*are* forms of consciousness. Those very properties that physics characterizes behaviouristically are, in their categorical nature, forms of consciousness.[11] In this way, the Russellian panpsychist avoids the dualist's difficulties reconciling the efficaciousness of consciousness with the causal closure of the physical world.

What grounds are there for accepting the panpsychist's proposal? First, it is not obvious that we have an alternative; many philosophers hold that the only categorical properties we have a positive conception of are those we find in our conscious experience. It may be that the theoretical choice for the Russellian monist is between the panpsychist's proposal as to the nature of mass and the thesis that mass is 'we know not what'. If we are looking for a picture of reality that is both complete and intelligible, panpsychism may be the only option.[12]

Furthermore, it is arguable that panpsychism is the most theoretically virtuous theory of matter consistent with both the data of physics and our first-person awareness of the reality of consciousness. This is what I have called 'the simplicity argument' for panpsychism (Goff 2016, 2017). Assuming the falsity of dualism, we know that some material entities, that is, living brains, have a categorical nature that involves consciousness. Neither physics nor introspection give us any clue as to the categorical nature of material entities outside of brains, or indeed of the categorical nature of the

---

[10] For recent work on panpsychism see the following Freeman 2006, Skrbina 2009, Blamauer 2011, Alter and Nagasawa 2015, Brüntrup and Jaskolla 2016, Goff 2017, Roelofs 2019, Seager 2020).

[11] Alternately, the Russellian panpsychist may hold that physical property terms refer to dispositional properties, and hence that physical properties are realized by, rather than identical with, forms of consciousness. The disagreement between this view and the view described in the main text is not one of substance but rather regards how terms in physics are defined. I suspect it is indeterminate whether the linguistic use of physical scientists is such that 'mass' refers to a dispositional property or to a categorical property in terms of the dispositions it realizes. There is, however, a substantive dispute between *pure panpsychists*, who hold that the concrete categorical nature of matter is entirely constituted by consciousness, and *impure panpsychists*, who hold that the categorical nature of matter is partly constituted by experiential properties and partly constituted by non-experiential properties. The advantage of the pure view is that it has the potential to give us a complete account of what matter essentially is.

[12] As Coleman discusses in Section 14.3, panqualityism offers an alternative proposal as to the categorical nature of physical properties.

components of brains. And therefore, the most simple, elegant, parsimonious hypothesis is that the categorical nature of the stuff outside of brains is continuous with that of brains in also being consciousness-involving. Or to put it another way: we would need a reason for thinking that matter has two kinds of categorical property rather than one. Special relativity is not entailed by the empirical datum that light is measured to be the same in all frames for reference, but it is arguably the simplest hypothesis consistent with that datum. Similarly, panpsychism is not entailed by the datum of consciousness but it is arguably the simplest hypothesis consistent with that datum.

There is, then, a good case for panpsychism even before we get to thinking about the need to explain human and animal consciousness in more fundamental terms. But, of course, the Russellian panpsychist also aspires to do this. Physicalists believe that consciousness can be explained in terms of processes that do not involve consciousness. There is a general consensus that no one has yet worked out how to do this. The Russellian panpsychist proposes an alternative research programme: Instead of attempting to explain consciousness in terms of non-conscious elements, try to account for the consciousness of humans and other animals in terms of more basic forms of consciousness, basic forms of consciousness that are postulated to exist as essential properties of basic material entities. It is still early days in the panpsychist research project, but the history of failure of physicalist solutions to problem of consciousness makes it rational to explore other options.

Physicalists may object as follows:

The fact that we haven't *yet* managed to give a physical account of consciousness doesn't entail that we will *never* be able to give such an account. Perhaps we are in the situation of scientists puzzling about the existence of complex life before Darwin and Wallace came up with the idea of natural selection. Better to wait for the 'Darwin of consciousness' to point the way to a naturalistic account of consciousness than to turn to supernaturalist pseudo-explanations. (See for example Churchland 2013)

However, to adopt panpsychism is not to *abandon* naturalistic explanation; panpsychism is a naturalistic research programme in its own right. The project is to try to *explain* human consciousness, in terms of more basic forms of consciousness, not just to accept it as a mysterious gift from God. The Russellian panpsychist does not think that consciousness itself can be explained in terms of something more basic. But it is not contrary to the scientific method to add irreducible entities to our ontology; Maxwell for example postulated new fundamental electromagnetic forces (Chalmers 1995 makes this analogy).

Moreover, as we noted in the introduction, there are strong philosophical arguments which purport to show that physical science alone cannot fully explain consciousness. For naturalistically minded philosophers who are persuaded by these arguments, panpsychism may be an attractive middle way between physicalism and dualism. And in any case, those adopting the panpsychist research programme need not insist on the physicalist research programme being abandoned. It is early days in the scientific study of consciousness, and it would be foolish at this stage to rule out paths which may one day lead to progress.[13]

What kind of consciousness is mass, as opposed to charge or spin? What is it like to be a quark? Panpsychism is a broad theoretical framework, and it will take time to fill in the details. Compare: it took decades of hard work to bridge the gap between the basic principles of Darwinian evolution by natural selection and modern genetics.

14.2.2 Problems with Panpsychism I—The Incredulous Stare

In spite of the arguments above, for many the idea that quarks have experience, no matter how basic, is just too crazy to be taken seriously. The incredulous stare panpsychists sometimes receive may not be an argument but it is a powerful force nonetheless. The deep-rooted intuitive resistance to the view is probably to be explained in terms of cultural associations; in popular culture views which sound superficially similar have been defended with less than rigorous reasoning. But it goes without saying that just because a view has been defended with bad arguments, it does not follow that there are no good arguments for that same view. And when the matter is looked at plainly, panpsychism is no more profligate than many other revisionary proposals that are taken seriously in contemporary metaphysics.

Another likely source of intuitive opposition to panpsychism is the often unquestioned assumption that physics is on its way to giving us a complete account of fundamental reality. When in the mindset of thinking that physics is on its way to giving a complete story of matter, a consciousness-filled universe is extremely improbable, as physics does not attribute consciousness to quarks. But if we accept that physics tell us nothing about the categorical nature of matter, and indeed the only thing we really know about the categorical nature of matter is that some of it is experience-involving, panpsychism starts to look much more probable.

At the end of the day, good arguments and the theoretical advantages of a theory ought to be taken more seriously than common-sense intuition. The fact that we have a common ancestor with apes; the fact that time flows slower when travelling at high speeds; the fact that a particle can exist in a superposition between distinct locations; all of these views are highly counter-intuitive, but this gives us little or no reason to think them false. One might object that, in opposition to panpsychism, these other theories are supported by empirical evidence. But the reality of consciousness is a datum in its own right. We know that consciousness exists, and hence any theory of reality with aspirations to be complete must be able to account for it. If panpsychism is able to account for consciousness in a way that avoids the difficulties that plague its more conventional rivals, then this will constitute strong support for its truth.

---

[13] Strawson 2006 argues that panpsychism is the only way of avoiding an unpalatable form of radical emergentism. A similar argument is explored in Nagel 1979, although a close reading reveals that Nagel is using the word 'panpsychism' to denote the disjunction of panpsychism and panprotopsychism. A revised form of Nagel's argument is responded to in McLaughlin 2016.

14.2.3 Problems with Panpsychism II—The Combination Problem

By common consent, the deepest difficulty facing the panpsychist is *the combination problem*. There are in fact multiple forms of the combination problem, but most notorious is the problem of how *little conscious things* combine to make *big conscious things*.[14] Most Russellian panpsychists take the relationship between biological consciousness and consciousness at more basic levels to be one of constitution or grounding: the subject of experience that is me is somehow composed of a large number of micro-level subjects of experience.[15] We seem to be able to make sense of parts of a car engine making up a functioning engine, or bricks and cement constituting a house, but we struggle with the idea of smaller minds combining to constitute a big mind.[16]

There are two ways to take the combination problem. One way is to see it as a *challenge* which the panpsychist must address. Alternatively, one can see it as an *argument* that panpsychism cannot possibly be true. Almost all panpsychists embrace the former understanding of the problem, and indeed one of the major focuses of the panpsychist research programme is to try to meet this challenge.

Before my conversion to panpsychism, I tried to press the combination problem as an argument against panpsychism by construing it as a conceivability argument aimed at demonstrating the impossibility of mental combination (Goff 2009, 2017). The starting point for this argument is the following: For any group of conscious subjects, it seems that we can conceive of *just those subjects* existing in the absence of some *further* subject.

---

[14] Chalmers 2016 catalogues multiple forms of the combination problem.

[15] Some panpsychists defend *constitutive cosmopsychism*, the view that all facts are grounded in facts about the conscious universe (Mathews 2011, Jaskolla and Buck 2012, Shani 2015, Nagasawa and Wager 2016, Albahari 2020 and Goff 2017, 2020). Strictly speaking, this view avoids the combination problem, as, on this view, a macro-level conscious subject derives its existence and nature not from the parts that make it up but from the whole of which it is a proper part. However, it faces an equally pernicious 'de-combination problem' of explaining how facts about 'little' conscious things are grounded in facts about 'big' conscious things. The conceivability combination problem discussed in this section seems to have a perfect analogue that applies against constitutive cosmopsychism: we can conceive of a conscious universe which is such that none of its parts is conscious. See Goff 2017: ch 9 and Miller 2018 for attempts to solve the de-combination problem. Shani 2015 adopts a form of semi-emergentism in response to the de-combination problem.

[16] The term 'combination problem' comes from Seager 1995, but it is generally traced back to James 1890/1981: 160. See Coleman 2014, Chalmers 2016, and Goff 2006, 2009, 2017 for recent versions of the combination problem. As Chalmers (2016) suggests, how serious the combination problem is may depend on how willing one is to be deflationary about conscious subjects. It is perhaps easier to make sense of conscious *states* combining than it is to make sense of conscious *subjects* combining. If, as bundle theorists believe, a conscious subject is nothing more than a bundle of conscious states, then the combining of certain conscious states may be sufficient for the combining of conscious subjects. Perhaps, then, the combination problem is easier for the bundle theorist. On the other hand, one could take the fact that conscious subject combination is more problematic than conscious state combination to be evidence that subjects are something over and above their states.

We can make the case more vivid by imagining a *microexperiential zombie*, which we can define as having the following characteristics:

- Empirically indistinguishable from an actual human being, i.e. it behaves the same, if you cut it open no physical difference from an actual human can be empirically discerned.
- Each of its micro-level parts has conscious experience.
- No macro-level part of the organism has conscious experience.

Such creatures seem to be coherent; from which it would seem to follow that the postulation of conscious subjects at the micro-level sheds no explanatory light on the existence of conscious subjects at the macro-level, undermining the panpsychist's attempt to account for human consciousness.[17] This is an especially worrying problem for the panpsychist, because (i) a key motivation for panpsychism involves rejecting physicalism on the grounds that it cannot account for consciousness, and (ii) the main way of arguing that physicalism cannot account for consciousness is via a conceivability argument of the form we have just used against panpsychism. We seem to have got nowhere.

It is clear that this is a profound challenge to the hopes of Russellian panpsychism. In the rest of my half of this entry, I will briefly consider three responses.

14.2.3.1 *Solution 1: Give us time!*

Most panpsychists agree that there is as yet no perfectly satisfying solution to the combination problem, whilst rejecting the charge that this undermines the motivation for working towards a panpsychist theory of consciousness. The problem of consciousness is perhaps the deepest in contemporary science and philosophy, and none of the proposed solutions is without its problems and challenges.

Moreover, there is good reason to think that the combination problem is more tractable than the explanatory gap faced by the physicalist. The concepts involved in articulating the physical facts are very different from the concepts involved in articulating the consciousness facts: the former concepts are third-personal and quantitative, the latter concepts are first-personal and qualitative. This radical difference provides grounds for thinking there could never be a priori derivations from the physical facts to the consciousness facts, and hence that zombies would remain conceivable even for an ideal reasoner. There is no such support for the conceivability of micro-experiential zombies,

---

[17] The notion of coherence I am working with here is equivalent to Chalmers' (2009) notion of 'negative conceivability': P is negatively conceivable just in case we cannot rule out the truth of P a priori. It follows from the negative conceivability of micro-experiential zombies that there is no a priori entailment from the micro-level consciousness (and micro-physical) facts to the macro-level consciousness facts, and in this sense the micro-level consciousness (and micro-physical) facts shed no explanatory light on the existence of conscious subjects at the macro-level. One might suppose that there is simply a brute necessary connection between the micro-level consciousness (and micro-physical) facts and the macro-level consciousness facts. But, if this is an option, then the postulation of micro-level consciousness starts to look redundant, as we might as well just postulate a brute necessary connection between the micro-physical facts and the macro-level consciousness facts.

given that in this case first-person qualitative concepts are employed in the articulation of both the fundamental and the higher-level facts.

This difference can also be brought out by reflecting on the knowledge argument against physicalism. The knowledge argument imagines a genius neuroscientist, Mary, who has been raised in a black and white room and so never seen any colours apart from black and white and shades of grey. Plausibly, no matter how much she learns about the neuroscience of colour experience, Mary will never be able to work out what it is like to see red. To consider the analogous challenge to the Russellian panpsychist, we must imagine Mary knows not only the physical facts but also the facts about the micro-experience that (according to Russellian panpsychism) underlies human experience of red. It is much less clear that Mary would not be able to work out what it is like to see red from this basis. Hume's 'missing shade of blue' provides us with a plausible example of how one could derive a certain experiential property P—in this case the missing link in a spectrum ranging from dark to light blue—from knowledge of other experiential properties—the other shades of blue in the spectrum—without actually being acquainted with P. And hence there seems to be no principled ground for denying that Mary would be able to deduce facts about human colour experience from facts about its micro-experiential basis.

No one has yet worked out how to close the gap between micro-level experience and macro-level experience, but there are not the same principled reasons as exist in the case of physicalism for thinking that the gap can never be closed. Moreover, there are already numerous very interesting proposals for making progress: those discussed in the next couple of sections, as well as Roelofs 2014, 2016, 2019, 2020, Goff 2017: ch 9, and Miller 2018.

14.2.3.2 *Solution 2: Phenomenal Bonding*

In general, composition involves relationships. Organs cannot form a functioning body, or cogs form a working clock, unless they are related in quite specific ways. It is natural, therefore, to suppose that micro-level subjects must be related in certain quite specific ways in order to constitute a macro-level subject. Perhaps our inability to understand mental combination arises from our ignorance regarding some special relationship essentially involved in mental combination. We can call this special relationship 'phenomenal bonding' (Goff 2016, 2017).

A fully worked out version of this solution must surely involve saying something more about the positive nature of the phenomenal bonding relation. Spatial or physical relations seem to be ruled out, on account of the fact that the parts of a micro-experiential zombie instantiate all of the same spatial and physical relationships as in a normal human being without resulting in mental combination. A number of philosophers sympathetic to panpsychism have proposed *co-consciousness* as the phenomenal bonding relation (Dainton 2011; Miller 2018). Co-consciousness is the relation experiences bear to each other when they are *experienced together*. On this form of the phenomenal bonding view, it is when micro-level experiences come to bear the co-consciousness relation to each other that they are bonded together into a unified macro-level experience.

Insofar as I have defended the phenomenal bonding response (Goff 2016, 2017), I have argued that we have no positive understanding of the nature of the phenomenal bonding relation and perhaps never will. There is admittedly a worry that adopting such a 'mysterian' account of phenomenal bonding could undermine the motivation for panpsychism. If we are relying on some mysterious bonding relation to explain the grounding of human subjects, what reason is there to suppose that that relation can only work its magic on micro-subjects? It seems equally likely that there is some mysterious relation that bonds together *utterly non-conscious* particles to make a conscious human subject (Coleman 2016). We have no idea how a relation could do such a thing, but, on the panpsychist proposal under consideration, nor do we have any idea how a relation could bond conscious particles to make a human subject. The postulation of micro-subjects, in addition to a mysterious bonding relation, starts to look redundant.[18]

14.2.3.3 *Solution 3: Emergentist Panpsychism*

I have so far been assuming a reductionist interpretation of Russellian panpsychism, according to which facts about human and animal consciousness are grounded in or wholly constituted of facts about micro-level consciousness. However, I am increasingly attracted to an emergentist form of Russellian panpsychism, according to which facts about animal consciousness are fundamental facts in their own right, although causally dependent on facts about micro-level consciousness.[19] The emergentist panpsychist avoids the conceivability-based combination problem altogether. She can accept that micro-experiential zombies are conceivable and even possible: such creatures exist in possible worlds which lack the basic principles of nature in virtue of which macro-level animal consciousness emerges from micro-level consciousness.

Is this view consistent with causal closure? In fact, talk of 'causal closure' often lumps together two quite different principles:

- *Broad Causal Closure*—Every (micro-physical, chemical, neurophysiological) physical event has a sufficient, immediate physical cause.
- *Micro Causal Closure*—Every physical event either (A) has a sufficient, immediate micro-physical cause, or (B) is grounded in an event which has a sufficient, immediate *micro-level* physical cause.

---

[18] How strong this criticism is may depend on whether we have independent reason to think that physical relations must have a concrete nature underlying the mathematical characterization we get from physics. If we do have reason to think this (as I argue in Goff 2017: 7.3.2.5), then we have to commit to a 'hidden' real nature of physical relations in any case, and so the panpsychist does not incur an extra cost by investing in the phenomenal bonding relation. In this case, the simplicity argument discussed above may still lead us to favour a panpsychist interpretation of Russellian monism over a panprotopsychist interpretation (this is essentially the case I make in Goff 2017: ch 7).

[19] Rosenberg (2004, 2014) and Brüntrup (2016) defend emergentist panpsychism. Mørch (2014) and Seager (2016) defend a form of emergentism slightly different from the one I have described here, in which micro-subjects 'fuse' into a macro-subject, ceasing to exist in the process.

The former principle is quite consistent with emergentist Russellian panpsychism, as the emergentist Russellian panpsychist can claim that animal conscious states are the categorical nature of certain neurophysiological states. The crucial question is: Which of the above principles do we have reason to accept?

The principle of causal closure is frequently appealed to but rarely defended. In my view, the most plausible defence of it is the 'no-gap' argument, roughly an inductive argument starting from the premise that we do not find gaps in the causal processes studies by neuroscience, contrary to what we would expect if causal closure were false (Papineau 1993: 31–2; McLaughlin 1998: 278–82; Melnyk 2003: 288–90). The reasoning goes like this: if dualism were true, and a non-physical mind were interacting with the brain on a regular basis, then this would show up in neuroscience. There would be all kinds of happenings in the brain that lacked a physical cause; it would appear as though a poltergeist was playing with the brain.

The no-gap argument is support only for broad causal closure. Suppose certain neurophysiological events are fundamental events in their own right, not grounded in micro-level events. Assuming those fundamental neurophysiological events are causally efficacious, it will follow that micro causal closure is false, as any effect of a fundamental neurophysiological event will have neither a (sufficient and immediate) micro-level cause nor a (sufficient and immediate) cause that is grounded in micro-level facts. But if every physical event in the brain has a physical cause *at some level*, then broad causal closure will be true.

Do we have any evidence that micro causal closure is true? An inductive argument for this would have to start from the premise that we have causally explained many macro-level events in the living brain in terms of micro-level facts, and that in the course of doing this have never found a macro-level brain event that cannot be explained in this way. But have we really done this? As far as I know, no empirical defence of micro causal closure in these terms has ever been given.

I am inclined to think, therefore, that emergentist Russellian panpsychism avoids the combination problem whilst remaining perfectly consistent with the data of observation. It is fair to point out, however, that these benefits would also be enjoyed by emergentist forms of *panprotopsychism*, according to which (A) the experiential properties of animals are fundamental properties that are the categorical nature of neurophysiological states, and (B) these experiential properties are causally dependent on micro-level proto-experiential properties of the brain.[20] What then is the motivation for 'going panpsychist'?

---

[20] Although as Coleman notes below, there don't seem to be any defenders of such a view. In the context of emergentist Russellian monism, what is it for a micro-level property to be 'proto-experiential'? Following the definition given by Coleman below, we can say that there is an a priori entailment from truths about the proto-experiential properties at the micro-level to the truths about consciousness properties at the macro-level; in other words, there is an intelligible connection between cause and effect.

I believe the simplicity argument for panpsychism is at its strongest when it comes to comparing panpsychist and panprotopsychist forms of emergentist Russellian monism. The emergentist Russellian monist has to suppose that there is some positive nature to micro-level categorical properties. In my view, the only fundamental categorical properties we have direct access to are the essentially experiential ones instantiated by human brains.[21] If we suppose that micro-level categorical properties are also experiential, then we can confine ourselves to believing in one kind of fundamental categorical property rather than two. There is a clear saving here in terms of quantitative parsimony; and thus, in the absence of any reason to the contrary, emergentist Russellian monists should be panpsychists.

14.3 PANPROTOPSYCHISM (BY SAM COLEMAN)

14.3.1 Introduction to Panprotopsychism

Panpsychists are impressed by the metaphysical heft of consciousness. This shows in their belief that human consciousness is best explained by consciousness of a more fundamental sort (whether microscopic or macroscopic) and that theories positing a non-conscious ground, like physicalism, struggle to explain consciousness. Panprotopsychists are less impressed by consciousness's metaphysical heft, since they posit a grounding base for the world, including human-level consciousness, which lacks consciousness. In that respect panprotopsychists are closer to physicalists than to panpsychists, agreeing that, insofar as consciousness is a real phenomenon, its grounding base need not also instantiate consciousness. But panprotopsychists are closer to panpsychists than to physicalists in their belief that the underlying categorical aspect of the physical world—that element physics does not tell us about, leaving a gap the panpsychist fills with conscious experience—is key to explaining the existence of human-level consciousness. Instead of positing forms of consciousness as providing the categorical nature of fundamental physical entities, the panprotopsychist posits protoconscious (aka protopsychic, protoexperiential, or 'protophenomenal') properties to play this role. There is much to say on the topic of the character of such properties, but for now we can define them as properties that are (i) not identical to or grounded in the dispositional (or otherwise relational) properties revealed by physical science, (ii) not themselves forms of consciousness, but such that (iii) in appropriate combinations they

---

[21] The panqualityist position (discussed by Coleman below) denies this, holding that what we have direct access to are properties that are essentially qualitative but contingently experiential. And, indeed, the argument I am about to give in the main text could be equally put forth by an emergentist panqualityist. I think the challenges the panqualityist faces in bridging the gap between qualities and consciousness, discussed by Coleman in Section 14.3, are insurmountable. But I concede that the simplicity argument in itself gives no support to panpsychism over panqualityism.

constitute consciousness properties. Moreover, (iv) truths about the protoconscious properties a priori entail the truths about human consciousness.[22]

Next, we can define reductive panprotopsychism as follows:

Reductive panprotopsychism: Facts about human and animal consciousness are not fundamental, but are grounded in/realized by/constituted of facts about more fundamental kinds of protoconscious properties, e.g. facts about the protoconsciousness of micro-level entities.[23]

The way we have defined protoconscious properties more or less commits anyone who posits them to reductive panprotopsychism. Nonetheless an emergentist variety of panprotopsychism appears possible, holding that human-level consciousness is a distinct existent produced and sustained by the right arrangement of fundamental protoconscious properties. Clearly, on emergentist panprotopsychism clause (iii) of the definition of protoconscious properties would need to be revised, as human-level consciousness would be something over and above the right arrangement of protoconscious properties.[24] However, I know of no adherents to emergentist panprotopsychism, current or historical. I will therefore equate panprotopsychism with the reductionist variety, and retain the above definition of protoconscious properties.[25]

As well as reductionists about consciousness, panprotopsychists have almost always been 'smallists'—holding that the facts about the world are determined by the facts about its lowest micro-level. Although there are questions about his status as a Russellian monist,[26] Russell (as the name suggests) inspired the current upsurge in Russellian monism, and panprotopsychist views in particular. In many ways Russell is the arch-panprotopsychist,

---

[22] Cf. Chalmers (2015: 259). By contrast, the physicalist either does not believe the world's categorical properties figure in an account of consciousness, or that if they do figure the transition from their nature to the nature of human-level consciousness is strictly a posteriori. See Goff (2015a, 2017: 144) for more on how to distinguish physicalism from panprotopsychism. A physicalist is also unlikely to embrace some of the panprotopsychist's positive suggestions for the categorical natures; e.g. unexperienced qualities, as on panqualityism (see Section 14.3.3).

[23] The human-level facts about consciousness may also be partly grounded in the more conventional facts about physical microstructure, the sorts of facts physics discovers, so that someone deriving the presence of human-level consciousness would need to know both sorts of fundamental fact. However, the panprotopsychist will likely hold that the microstructural facts are ultimately grounded in the protoconscious facts—among other reasons because dispositions are grounded in their categorical bases. In that case no qualification to this statement of reductive panprotopsychism is needed regarding the microstructural properties, and the deriver would only need to know the protoconscious natures to derive human-level consciousness.

[24] Perhaps also clause (iv), depending on one's view regarding the compatibility of emergentism and a priori entailment.

[25] Stubenberg (2016) argues that emergentism is incompatible with a major form of panprotopsychism known as 'neutral monism'. Neutral monism asserts that the mental and the physical are not ultimate ontological categories (being reducible to relations among the fundamental neutral elements), whereas emergentism asserts at least the fundamentality of the mental.

[26] See e.g. Wishon (2015) and Stubenberg (2016) for some discussion of Russell's relation to Russellian monism.

and he certainly viewed the universe as a bucket of shot rather than a bucket of jelly. A priority monist version of panprotopsychism also appears possible,[27] but I will concentrate on the overwhelmingly typical variety: reductive smallist panprotopsychism. In what follows I will refer to this conjunctive position simply as 'panprotopsychism'.

There is no commitment in panprotopsychism that consciousness first arises at the human, or animal, level. Someone who holds that while quarks and leptons have non-conscious categorical properties, these constitute, in their characteristic arrangements, consciousness properties pertaining to atoms is a panprotopsychist not a panpsychist—since no fundamental entities would be conscious on this view. But because human-level consciousness is our explanandum, I will talk as if this is the level where panprotopsychists first expect consciousness, and that happens to accord with all the panprotopsychist positions I know of.

Panprotopsychists agree with panpsychists that an austerely physical universe could not support consciousness—something extra needs adding to the physical raw ingredients.[28] But panprotopsychists agree with physicalists that an explanation of human consciousness does not require consciousness to be fundamental; what needs to be added is therefore something less than consciousness. In thus seeing the universe, especially in its fundamental or categorical nature, as somewhat richer than the physicalist believes it to be, while somewhat less rich than the panpsychist believes it to be, the panprotopsychist's position is rightly seen as intermediate between the two. Proponents are liable to think that, as with many middle roads, it enjoys the benefits of the roads to either side without some of their perils. But of course like any distinctive path in philosophy it faces perils of its own, as we will see in Section 14.3.6.

14.3.2 Awareness vs. Qualities

One further general distinction is useful before getting into the details of specific panprotopsychist positions: the analysis of consciousness into two aspects, awareness and qualities (or content). These aspects can be isolated by saying that the first is what all experiences have in common, while the second is that aspect which allows for comparisons of resemblance and difference between experiences. All experiences, had by experiencers of however exotic a type, involve the *awareness by a subject* of a *content* or a set of *qualities*. In other words, the qualities or content of an experience have the property of being 'for' the subject of the experience. But clearly, the content of experience, the set of qualities experienced on a given occasion—what gives each experience its distinctive character—varies between subjects and also changes for the same subject over time.

---

[27] See Goff (2017) for priority monism in relation to a panpsychist form of Russellian monism. Coleman (2015a) can be read as a priority monist panprotopsychist. Chalmers dubs this view 'cosmoprotopsychism' (personal communication).

[28] See the Introduction to this chapter.

The term 'what-it-is-like-ness' (and relatives) has conventionally been used by philosophers to capture the *whole* of consciousness, awareness as well as content, but it seems more appropriate to restrict its use to the quality/content aspect. After all, the quality of an experience is precisely that which the subject adverts to when asked what her experience is like (e.g. 'bitter', 'painful'). With this terminological restriction in place, applying 'what-it-is-like-ness' to the qualitative or content aspect of experience, the first aspect, awareness, can usefully be labelled 'that-it-is-for-ness': Ascribing awareness denotes the fact that a content or quality is (in the relevant sense) *for* a subject at all, that there is a specific subjective awareness of this particular content or quality. In the philosophy of consciousness it is controversial whether these two aspects of consciousness can come apart in reality, as they plausibly can in thought.[29] If they can really come apart then there could be unconscious what-it-is-like-ness. This is an issue panprotopsychists disagree over.[30] Still, the distinction will be useful below in explaining the panprotopsychist variants.

14.3.3 The Character of the Categorical Properties

Since it eschews what might be thought of as the more obvious answers to the question of what the world's fundamental nature is like, in the form of a conventionally physical nature (for physicalists) or a conscious nature (for panpsychists), there is an onus on panprotopsychists to offer some characterization of the protoconscious properties they posit as the key to the production of consciousness in a physical world. It is just not obvious what kind of properties these are. Taking consideration of the literature, there seem to be three options open (though the possibility of further options should not be ruled out given the early state of the field of panprotopsychist research). Panprotopsychists may say that the fundamental protoconscious properties are:

1. Contingently unknown for creatures like us.
2. Necessarily unknown for creatures like us.
3. Of a non-conscious qualitative nature.[31]

---

[29] See e.g. Kriegel (2009, ch.1), Rosenthal (1991). Many philosophers deny that unconscious qualitative character is even conceivable.

[30] Prominent neutral monists, like Russell (1927, 1959) and Mach (1886), are clear that the contents of experience, sensory, and perceptual appearances, can and do exist entirely apart from subjects, hence outside of awareness. James (1912) seems more cautious on this issue. In general, a panprotopsychist is free to hold that the protopsychic natures must exclusively produce contentful, i.e. qualitative, *states of awareness*, on the ground that the two aspects are inseparable. Such a theorist will not be a panqualityist (see Section 14.3.3). This point links to the distinction below in Section 14.3.4, concerning how panprotopsychists view the generation of the awareness aspect of consciousness.

[31] It should be noted that there is controversy over whether all the positions featuring in camps one and two count as non-physicalist, more specifically over whether the categorical properties they posit are necessarily non-physical properties. Some panprotopsychists, and we will see such examples shortly, posit categorical properties with a physical look about them, and even more panprotopsychists at least

Panprotopsychists in camp one accept that the class of protoconscious properties may be presently unknown to us, but they are somewhat optimistic that we may have, or find, ways to infer, or even somehow to observe, their character. A line of thought that plausibly derives from Kant encourages agnosticism about the nature of fundamental categorical properties: Since our epistemic commerce with the outside world is causation-based—we know of external things, ultimately, as they impact causally on our senses—the precise nature of the categorical properties is bound to be elusive. As noted above, that is because what we know of are the *effects* of these properties, hence also their dispositions; but this does not tell us about the intrinsic character of the natures that ground these dispositions (Langton 2004). But camp one panprotopsychists believe we may nonetheless devise methods, through special use of the imagination, say, to make informed speculations about the categorical characters. And perhaps in the future science or philosophy will develop novel techniques by means of which these speculations could be tested or informatively assessed for theoretical power. Maybe such techniques will eventually enable us to pin down a strong candidate for the protoconscious categorical properties.[32]

Members of camp two see no way to surmount the aforementioned Kantian predicament regarding our knowledge, or else have their own reasons for pessimism based on the human psychological/conceptual endowment, and conclude that we are forever closed off from knowing what the fundamental categorical properties are like.[33] This thesis obviously prevents them from endorsing panpsychism, since panpsychists believe we do know which determinable the categorical properties correspond to as a class—

---

take themselves to be offering a physicalist position (e.g. Montero (2015); certain proponents of camp three positions are also known to claim this, e.g. Coleman (2015a)). Here I follow Goff in defining physicalism as denying that there is an a priori story to be told connecting the world's fundamental categorical properties, if such there be, with human-level consciousness. Since all panprotopsychists claim there is such a story, at least in principle, indeed this is one of their reasons for positing panprotopsychic categorical properties, they are anti-physicalists by Goff's lights. Panprotopsychists are at least physicalists of an unusual sort, likely to be seen as outside the more mainstream herd. And it is useful to collect together the theorists who say non-conscious categorical properties matter deeply and transparently to consciousness under a single term: the policy of labelling all panprotopsychists anti-physicalists prevents (at least a portion of) an interesting cluster of theories from being lost blurrily in the larger and cruder classification of 'physicalism'. For more detail on this distinction and its utility see Goff (2015a, 2017).

[32] Pereboom (2011) makes this suggestion. He considers whether an absolute form of Lockean *solidity* could play the required role, but concludes it could not. Pereboom considers the position he develops 'Russellian physicalism': Russellian because it acknowledges Russell's insight that the intrinsic nature of the physical is up for grabs, and is likely to be relevant to solving the mind–body problem: see Russell (1927). Stoljar (2001) seems to think the relevant natures are conceptualizable, at least for some conceivable being, but I am not clear whether he is optimistic about our abilities; he is plausibly interpreted as agnostic between camps one and two, as is Montero (2015).

[33] McGinn (1989) argues that our various conceptual schemes make it impossible to grasp the deep nature that unifies matter and mind, and his position is plausibly panprotopsychist. McClelland (2013) is also in camp two, although he holds that the awareness aspect of consciousness is reducible (see Section 14.3.4).

kinds of consciousness. Camp two theorists may still allow that some conceivable knower could have access to the natures in question.[34]

Camps one and two characterize protoconscious properties by their relation to our knowledge. There is something frustrating about such descriptions, since they do not really say anything informative about the protoconscious natures themselves. Camp three members, like panpsychists, make a distinctive positive suggestion about the protoconscious categorical natures. These are *panqualityists*:[35] they believe that qualities, of the broad sort we know from conscious experience (e.g., blue, red), provide the fundamental intrinsic character of the material world. But they are not panpsychists: they do not think that *conscious* qualities provide the categorical characters, where a conscious quality is a quality some subject is experiencing. Conscious qualities have the projector-light of awareness shining through them, as it were. The panqualityist, taking the separation of awareness and qualities as aspects of experience with full metaphysical force, posits unexperienced or unconscious qualities as the fundamental categorical properties. Pursuing the cinematic metaphor, these qualities are more akin to colourful celluloid reels not currently being projected (cf. Stubenberg 1998). Though the light of awareness is not upon them, they fully possess the qualitative characters that manifest in awareness.[36] Like the panpsychist, the panqualityist may want to say the determinates of the fundamental qualities are unfamiliar to us.[37] Nonetheless, they share with the qualities we know from experience the broad recognizable determinable of *qualitative character* (what-it-is-like-ness)—which is to say that they are at least potential contents of experience for some conceivable (perhaps very small!) subject, and would help to constitute what experience is like for such a being.[38]

---

[34] God's epistemic access to these natures might be via constitution, not causation. Coleman (2019a) suggests we bear a similar 'acquaintance' relation to the categorical properties of which we are conscious.

[35] Chalmers (2016) has reintroduced this term, which he finds in Feigl (1971), who credits in turn S. C. Pepper.

[36] Thus the panqualityist, uniquely among panprotopsychists, plausibly evades the 'simplicity argument' for panpsychism—see Section 14.2.

[37] See e.g. Rosenberg (2004). Feigl (1971: 308), toying with panqualityism, rules that the fundamental qualities are 'incomparably more "colorless" than the qualities of human experience'. But see Coleman (2016) for reasons why this may be unhelpful to panqualityism when it comes to treating qualitative aspects of the combination problem, as highlighted by Chalmers (2016).

[38] Coleman (2014, 2015a, 2016) is a contemporary proponent of panqualityism. Feigl (1971) entertains the position. Sellars (1981) comes close, but prefers qualities to emerge as primitive properties in the context of a brain. He could be considered an emergentist panqualityist, perhaps. Mach (1886) seems to be a panqualityist: his 'elements' can feature as experiential contents, items like blueness and smells, but can equally exist outside of experience. The same is true of the James of radical empiricism (1912). Russell, at least in his neutral monist phase (e.g. 1927), seems well described as a panqualityist: he suggests that physical events outside the brain may well be intrinsically of the same character as those brain events we experience, i.e. qualitative. And he, like Coleman, is concerned to fill in the microphysical natures using such qualitative properties. Nagel (1979) is usually read as tentatively endorsing (or not ruling out) panpsychism, but some of his remarks suggest panprotopsychism. Retaining his commitment to the irreducibility of experienced qualities, that could make him a panqualityist. Plato of *Timaeus* ascribes qualities to his geometrical atoms in an attempt to explain macroscopic secondary qualities—he thus has something of a panqualityist streak, at least.

14.3.4 Awareness

Panprotopsychists, unlike panpsychists, incur a burden to explain how conscious awareness first enters the world. This is a burden panprotopsychists expressly take on by tying their position to a transparent explanation of human-level consciousness, in both its aspects.[39] Two answers seem available to panprotopsychists on the question of how awareness is generated from a fundamental protoconscious level that lacks it. Either:

(A). Awareness is a purely structural property, a matter only of the right system of relations between complexes of protoconscious categorical properties and/or their bearers.

(B). Awareness is not a purely structural property: the intrinsic character of the protoconscious categorical properties is directly implicated in the production of awareness.

Group B panprotopsychists view the fundamental categorical properties as *latently conscious*; somehow, when they are assembled in the right way as a group, their merely protoconscious inner natures combine and begin to 'glow'—referring to some kind of intrinsic modification—with the light of conscious awareness. These panprotopsychists take human-level consciousness much as panpsychists, non-eliminativist physicalists, and dualists do, that is, in a non-deflationary way, and think of it as resting somehow dormant within the categorical protophenomenal properties themselves.[40] The protoconscious properties are 'consciousness seeds'.

Group A panprotopsychists are more deflationary about awareness, viewing it not as an intrinsic property of experienced qualities at all, nothing like a phenomenal 'glow', but merely as a matter of what relations a qualitative property enters into (see Hume 1739/1975: 207–8, Mach 1886, Russell 1927, James 1912, Lockwood 1989, Stubenberg 1998, Coleman 2012, 2014, 2015a, 2016, McClelland 2013). Specifically, the consciousness-supporting relation involves being in the right position with respect to a

---

[39] In this respect their position resembles that of 'a priori' physicalists, see e.g. Kirk (2005), Jackson (2006). No other theorists in the field promise an explanatory reduction of awareness.

[40] There is an emergentist whiff about this account not present for group A relationalists about awareness. But perhaps there could be such a fundamental disposition for awareness, manifested only in group dynamics, that would still provide a reductive and a priori account of awareness. Meehl (1966) reports a thought experiment from Feyerabend of a universe consisting of two electrons at such a distance that their gravitational attraction is exactly counterbalanced by their electric repulsion. Not moving, their electromagnetic capacity is only latent—there is no electromagnetic field. But if they start to move for some reason (disturbed by fluctuations in the quantum field, or by God's finger), an electromagnetic field will result. It seems that something like this model—it is the altered relations between the electrons that elicit the exercise of a certain power—must be what Group B panprotopsychists have in mind. A close relation is the position Strawson (1994: 76) calls 'asymmetric panpsychism' where any *arrangement*, however small, of basic matter, non-experiential in its intrinsic nature, 'realizes' experiential properties. This position, which sees experience as a latency dependent on group relations, deserves to be considered a form of panprotopsychism.

mind, so as to become a content for it in the requisite way.[41] For example the right relation to a mind might be playing a certain causal or functional role within it.[42] For group A panprotopsychists, unlike group B panprotopsychists, nothing *happens to* qualities when they are arranged in the right manner to be experienced; they are not modified in any way. Rather, their being experienced—becoming objects of awareness— simply consists in their standing in the relevant relation.

As long as the actual-world relational structures that implement awareness obtain in some world, the group A panprotopsychist is bound to say awareness is present in that world. Group B panprotopsychists, by contrast, are free to hold that only special kinds of categorical properties are suited to produce consciousness when appropriately arranged, so that a world that replicates the actual structures of awareness will not necessarily instantiate awareness if its categorical properties are sufficiently different from actuality. For group A panprotopsychists, such radically different categorical properties would merely supply a different kind of content for awareness than features actually.

Group A panprotopsychists can embrace reductionist physicalist attempts to analyse the awareness relation, for instance in terms of higher-order cognition,[43] or could leave it as a brute 'acquaintance' relation.[44] For panprotopsychists who embrace physicalist-style explanations of awareness, it is primarily their anti-reductionist attitude towards the qualities of experience that makes them non-physicalists. We briefly consider what panprotopsychists say about qualities next.

14.3.5 Qualities

All panprotopsychists excepting panqualityists incur a burden to explain how qualities, the properties that provide the what-it-is-like-ness aspect of human experience, arise in the world. These theorists take what-it-is-like-ness to be non-basic, so must explain it in terms of something else. It seems that the options available are to claim that quality is a mere relational affair, or that it directly implicates the intrinsic characters of the protoconscious categorical properties.[45] Panprotopsychists who take the first option are in

---

[41] James (1912), somewhat sceptical about minds and subjects, held that his neutral 'pure experiences' can get into subjective and objective 'taking' relations with each other, and that the subjective relation (as we would say) realizes consciousness. Consciousness is a function, he maintains.

[42] This broad characterization covers for instance McClelland's (2013) HOT-style reduction of awareness. Coleman (2019a) combines a HOT-style theory with a Russellian acquaintance relation to implement awareness of qualities.

[43] For higher-order cognitive theories of awareness see Rosenthal (2005), Coleman (2015b). For attempts to incorporate such a theory into panprotopsychism see Coleman (2015a, 2016), McClelland (2013). A related proposal is Stubenberg's (1998) constitution relation.

[44] Russell seems to vacillate on whether the awareness relation is acquaintance, or analysable into a more mundane relation.

[45] Panqualityism can be seen as the limit case of the second option. An issue I have ignored concerns the location of the qualities: e.g. early Russell held the qualities we experience to belong to external events, and later Russell held them to be instantiated in brains. But this issue is self-contained, and not central to panprotopsychism—even panqualityism—per se.

group B regarding awareness, seeing it as latent in protoconscious properties: they cannot view qualities *and* awareness as reducible to relational properties, for that would make them physicalists.[46] It must be said that this faction is likely to be on the small side, since panprotopsychists typically find physicalist treatments of qualities unsatisfactory; they consider Jackson's Mary—who cannot deduce what red is like from complete scientific information[47]—a serious problem for physicalism, for instance. In fact I know of no current or historical panprotopsychist who endorses option one regarding qualities. Panprotopsychists typically agree with panpsychists that qualitative character is not a mere relational property, but are more sanguine about the possibility of a relational reduction of awareness. Accordingly, the majority of panprotopsychists belong to group A regarding awareness, and take option two when it comes to qualities. Though they must hold that one or the other is irreducible to relations, panprotopsychists may allow that either awareness or what-it-is-like-ness is so reducible.[48] Of course, a panprotopsychist may also hold that awareness and qualities, though not fundamental properties, are alike irreducible to pure relational goings on—this would be a combination of selecting group B as regards awareness and option two as regards qualities.

14.3.6 Objections to Panprotopsychism

For those who crave an explanation of human-level consciousness, and turn away from physicalism due to its apparent failure to provide such an account, embrace of panprotopsychism can be motivated by observing panpsychist struggles with the combination problem (see Section 14.2). Since it does not posit micro-subjects of experience, panprotopsychism faces no problem of explaining how those jointly constitute a macro-subject.[49] But of course it must now *generate* subjects—loci of awareness—and, for non-panqualityists, qualities from scratch. The panpsychist takes these two aspects of consciousness for granted as fundamental and ubiquitous. The non-panqualityist panprotopsychist, like the physicalist, can only seek to explain them in other terms. Even if the panprotopsychist has more resources at her disposal than the physicalist, in the form of the protoconscious categorical properties she posits, the explanatory challenge is great. But it is one the panprotopsychist is committed to overcoming.

Taking these challenges in reverse order: It may be urged against non-panqualityist panprotopsychists that experienceable qualities cannot be grounded in non-qualitative categorical properties, since Jackson's Mary could surely know all about these, as well as

---

[46] Included here are those panprotopsychists who hold that the qualities of experience cannot exist without experience, and so make their entry to the world along with consciousness.

[47] Jackson (1982).

[48] What prevents the availability of a strain of panpsychism that holds that-it-is-for-ness, but not quality, to be fundamental and ubiquitous is the widely held belief that there cannot be a content-less awareness. But see Albahari (2020).

[49] Coleman (2014) argues that panpsychists should instead become panprotopsychists because the subject combination problem is insuperable. But see Roelofs (2016).

about the micro-relations between non-qualitative protophenomenal properties, without being able to know what red is like.[50] The non-panqualityist panprotopsychist has two available responses to this objection. She will want to say either that qualities can be given a purely relational analysis, exactly mirroring 'a priori physicalist' responses to Mary,[51] or that the additional panprotopsychic properties make the difference to Mary's derivation base despite being non-qualitative—that once Mary adds knowledge of the non-qualitative categoricals to her physical database, a derivation of redness becomes open to her.[52] After all, panprotopsychist Mary's derivation-base of information is much richer than the physicalist's, and contains a wealth of detail about the fundamental categorical properties that on panprotopsychism constitute the qualities we experience. Moreover, since we do not currently know what such non-panqualityist protoconscious categorical properties are like, it is hard to say definitively that knowledge of them will not enable Mary to work out what it is like to experience red (Alter and Coleman 2020).

How plausible these responses are remains to be seen. There will be a suspicion that no amount of knowledge concerning non-qualitative properties would permit deduction of what a colour quality is like (Coleman 2015a), hence that non-panqualityist versions of panprotopsychism make little advance over physicalism regarding Jackson's argument. Since panqualityists view qualities of the sort we experience as irreducible to the non-qualitative—this is the moral they glean from Mary's story—in so far as the knowledge argument is a motivation for panprotopsychism, they will feel that panqualityism is the particular variant it supports.

The panqualityist faces her most severe difficulty in accounting for awareness. The panpsychist takes this property as basic, and the physicalist seems to struggle to explain it.[53] It is not obvious that the addition of fundamental qualitative categorical properties gives the panqualityist the resources to do what neither of these other theorists can do, that is, explain awareness in other terms. But it must be said that since this is a problem all other panprotopsychists also face, and as they *additionally* face a problem regarding qualities, a relative lack of problems seems to make panqualityism an especially strong version of panprotopsychism. In addition, it has the only viable positive proposal as to the protoconscious natures. Still, a relative strength will count for little against a decisive objection, so we must consider the force of the objection that panqualityism cannot handle awareness. No way of relating irreducible qualities to each other, however sophisticated, it is said, suffices to constitute awareness of those qualities. One can always conceive of a duplicate panqualityist human being, one whose qualitative protoconscious

---

[50] As Lewis (1988/2004) notes, the knowledge argument seems to show not just that *physical* lessons won't help Mary, but that *lessons* won't help her, whatever the subject matter. He was making the point against dualism, but it seems to apply here. The panqualityist will likely agree with Jackson that the relevant knowledge of qualities requires experience.

[51] See e.g. Jackson (1998, 2006), and Kirk (2005). As noted, she cannot also say this about the awareness aspect of consciousness, on pain of embracing physicalism.

[52] Although he does not spell it out in this way, not least because he does not commit to our being able to grasp the categoricals, this would seem to be Stoljar's (2001) take on Mary's epistemic situation.

[53] Panpsychists may purport to explain *human* awareness in terms of a more basic sort, but the issue here is awareness per se.

categorical properties are related in all the ways allegedly needed for awareness, for whom the light of consciousness remains off: this is the panqualityist 'awareness-zombie'.[54] He instantiates all the micro- and macro-qualities we do, but lacks awareness of them. The conceivability of such a being is taken to show that all panqualityist attempts to reduce awareness fail (see Chalmers 2016).

For the panqualityist who is a relationalist about awareness, a clash of intuitions is generated here that reproduces a pattern familiar from discussions of physicalist attempts to explain consciousness. The analytic functionalist, for one, holds that experiences can be analysed in terms of a certain functional profile: for instance, pain is whichever physical state of a creature meditates appropriately between bodily damage and protective behaviour (Lewis 1966). Such a physicalist may feel, in the grip of her theory, that were the relevant functions implemented in a brain, consciousness would of necessity be instantiated—there could be no zombies then, not even conceivably (see Kirk 2005). The panqualityist who is a relationalist about awareness is likely to have similar misgivings about the conceivability of awareness-zombies, while reclining under the agreeable shade of her theory. It is not easy to see how to make progress from this stalemate: one of the most difficult things is to prod philosophers from positions they comfortably occupy.[55] But the panqualityist need not be a relationalist about awareness: she may be a member of group B above (Section 14.3.4). In this case, imagining the ingredients of the panqualityist zombie world will involve imagining awareness-latent qualities, awaiting only the right relational arrangement to excite their hidden power. Since, by hypothesis, our panqualityist duplicates' brains instantiate that arrangement, they will be aware of their brain-qualities, so not zombies after all.[56]

The objector to panqualityism will doubtless feel such moves do nothing to block the threat of awareness zombies (especially if they are impressed by Goff's panpsychist zombies—see Section 14.2 and Goff 2009), but how this debate progresses remains to be seen.[57] Part of the issue hangs on whether deflationism about awareness, which tends to go with the relational or functional analysis, has any plausibility. Clearly, awareness zombies also threaten non-panqualityist panprotopsychists, although it is harder to assess the resources they can bring to the problem given our ignorance of the non-qualitative

---

[54] This reasoning is analogous to that of the conceivability argument against panpsychism, discussed in Section 14.2.6. Chapter 7 of Goff (2017) compares panpsychism and panprotopsychism as regards their capacity to respond to such conceivability arguments.

[55] Coleman (2016) advocates panqualityist relationalism about awareness. Against Chalmers's awareness zombies, he argues that awareness simply does not show up in conceived scenarios because it has no proprietary or associated quality. This means we strictly cannot (positively) conceive of awareness as missing from a zombie world, leaving zombie thought experiments irrelevant to the relationalist panqualityist analysis. See Mihalik (2016) for criticism.

[56] This move resembles Goff's 'phenomenal bonding' solution to panpsychist zombies (Section 14.2 and Goff 2016). The panpsychist who invokes phenomenal bonding augments the relations between conscious categorical properties, whereas the panqualityist here augments the categorical properties themselves (with a disposition to collective awareness).

[57] One might worry that we have no grasp of 'awareness latency', and that to posit it is simply to package up the mysterious residue of consciousness into an inscrutable property.

protoconscious properties they posit. Perhaps these unknown non-conscious natures have just what it takes to constitute awareness in combination, whereas it might seem we already know that merely re-arranging qualities does not yield awareness (otherwise, the joke might go, a very skillful painter could make a conscious canvas). On the other hand, if a panqualityist can defend deflationism about awareness, she at least has irreducible qualities—the contents of consciousness—already in play, on her view, lessening the perceived shortfall in explaining consciousness as a whole.

Even if she can overcome awareness zombies, the panqualityist faces the further objection that, as is widely believed, the qualities she posits as the fundamental categoricals cannot in fact exist unexperienced. On this view, the qualities we are conscious of are essentially conscious. There is no such thing, for example, as an instance of the kind of redness we experience ('phenomenal red') existing just as redly but without any subject experiencing it. This is a point on which philosophers have wildly differing opinions, and it is hard to say whether a greater number consider it intuitively obvious that a quality of experience could also exist unexperienced than deem that to be an evidently false, or even incoherent, suggestion.[58] It is not clear, anyhow, what consensus would establish: we need some arguments. Arguments that qualities must be conscious are surprisingly hard to come by, given the commonness of the intuition (e.g., Strawson 1994). On the other side, proponents of unconscious qualities will point to phenomena such as blindsight, sleep headaches and itching, and unconscious emotions as plausible instances of unfelt qualities.[59] Moreover, common sense undoubtedly conceives of the qualities we know through consciousness as persisting outside of our experience, albeit thought of as belonging to external objects like facing surfaces. Whatever else may be wrong with common sense, this conception does not seem to be obviously problematic in itself.

14.4 CONCLUSION

Physicalism dominated Anglo-American philosophy in the latter half of the twentieth century, and is perhaps still the most popular view among analytic philosophers. However, there are two deep problems with the theory: (i) it does not provide an account of the concrete categorical nature of matter, (ii) it does not seem to have the resources to provide an adequate explanation of human and animal consciousness. Panpsychism and panprotopsychism offer solutions to these problems that deserve investigation. It may turn out that the combination problem renders panpsychism no advance over physicalism; time will tell. Such a failure, combined with physicalism's perceived lack of

---

[58] In the former camp see Lockwood (1989), Coleman (2015a) and Chalmers (2016). In the latter see Strawson (1994), Stubenberg (1998), Kriegel (2009).

[59] Rosenthal (1991), Jennum and Jensen (2002), Sack and Hanifin (2010); see Coleman (2019b) for an account of unconsciously suffered pain.

explanatory resources, would motivate exploration of panprotopsychist alternatives. However, all variants of panprotopsychism also face objections. What is clear is that, as things stand, both panpsychism and panprotopsychism are views worth taking seriously. Physicalism's problems suggest that our conception of the nature of matter needs enriching, and these two families of theories provide natural ways of doing that.

REFERENCES

Albahari, M. (2020), 'Beyond Cosmopsychism and the Great I Am: How the World might be Grounded in Universal "Advaitic" Consciousness', in W. E. Seager (ed.), *Routledge Handbook of Panpsychism*. Abingdon: Routledge.

Alter, T. and Coleman, S. (2020), 'Panpsychism and Russellian Monism', in W. E. Seager (ed.), *Routledge Handbook of Panpsychism*. Abingdon: Routledge.

Alter, T. and Coleman, S. (2019), 'Russellian Monism and Mental Causation', in *Noûs* Available at: https://doi.org/10.1111/nous.12318.

Alter, T. and Nagasawa, N. eds (2015), *Consciousness and the Physical World*. Oxford: Oxford University Press.

Bird, A. (n.d. 2007), *Nature's Metaphysics: Laws and Properties*. Oxford: Oxford University Press.

Blamauer, M. ed., (2011), *The Mental as Fundamental*. Berlin: Ontos Verlag.

Brüntrup, G. (2016), 'Emergent panpsychism' in G. Brüntrup and L. Jaskolla (eds), *Panpsychism*. Oxford: Oxford University Press, 48–71.

Brüntrup, G. and Jaskolla, L. eds (2016), *Panpsychism*. Oxford: Oxford University Press.

Campbell, K. (1976), *Metaphysics: An Introduction*. Dickenson.

Chalmers, D. J. (1995), 'Facing up to the problem of consciousness', *Journal of Consciousness Studies* 2/3: 200–19.

Chalmers, D. J. (2009), 'The Two-Dimensional Argument Against Materialism', in B. McLaughlin (ed.), *Oxford Handbook of the Philosophy of Mind*. Oxford: Oxford University Press, 313–39.

Chalmers, D. J. (2015), 'Panpsychism and Panprotopsychism', in T. Alter and S. Nagasawa (eds), *Consciousness and the Physical World*. Oxford: Oxford University Press, 246–76.

Chalmers, D. J. (2016), 'The Combination Problem for Panpsychism', in G. Brüntrup and L. Jaskolla (eds), *Panpsychism*. Oxford: Oxford University Press, 19–47.

Churchland, P. S. (2013), *Touching a Nerve*. New York: W. W. Norton and Company.

Coleman, S. (2012), 'Mental Chemistry: Combination for Panpsychists', *Dialectica*, 66/1: 137–66.

Coleman, S. (2014), 'The Real Combination Problem: Panpsychism, Micro-Subjects and Emergence', *Erkenntnis*, 79/1: 19–44.

Coleman, S. (2015a), 'Neuro-Cosmology', in P. Coates and S. Coleman (eds), *Phenomenal Qualities: Sense, Perception, and Consciousness*. Oxford: Oxford University Press, 66–102.

Coleman, S. (2015b), 'Quotational Higher-Order Thought Theory', *Philosophical Studies*, 172/10: 2705–033.

Coleman, S. (2016), 'Panpsychism and Neutral Monism: How to Make Up One's Mind', in G. Brüntrup and L. Jaskolla (eds), *Panpsychism*. Oxford: Oxford University Press, 249–82.

Coleman, S. (2019a), 'Natural Acquaintance', in J. Knowles and T. Raleigh (eds), *New Essays on Acquaintance*. Oxford: Oxford University Press.

Coleman, S. (2019b), 'Painfulness, Suffering, and Consciousness', in D. Bain, J. Corns and M. S. Brady (eds), *The Philosophy of Suffering*. Abingdon: Routledge.

Dainton, B. (2011), 'Review of *Consciousness and its Place in Nature*', *Philosophy and Phenomenological Research*, 83/1: 238–61.
Ellis, B. (2001), *Scientific Essentialism*. Cambridge: Cambridge University Press.
Ellis, B. (2002), *The Philosophy of Nature: A Guide to the New Essentialism*. Montreal: McGill-Queen's University Press.
Feigl, H. (1971), 'Some Crucial Issues of Mind-Body Monism', *Synthese*, 22/3–4: 295–312.
Freeman, A. (ed.), (2006), *Consciousness and its Place in Nature: Does Physicalism Entail Panpsychism?* (Imprint Academic). (This volume is a special issues of the Journal of Consciousness Studies).
Gibb, S. (2015), 'Defending Dualism', *Proceedings of the Aristotelian Society*, 115/2pt2: 131–46.
Goff, P. (2006), 'Experiences Don't Sum', *Journal of Consciousness Studies*, 13/10–11: 53–61.
Goff, P. (2009), 'Why Panpsychism Doesn't Help Explain Consciousness', *Dialectica*, 63/3: 289–311.
Goff, P. (2015a), 'Against Constitutive Panpsychism', in T. Alter and S. Nagasawa (eds), *Consciousness and the Physical World*. Oxford: Oxford University Press, 370–400.
Goff, P. (2015b), 'Real Acquaintance and Physicalism', in P. Coates and S. Coleman (eds), *Phenomenal Qualities: Sense, Perception, and Consciousness*. Oxford: Oxford University Press, 121–43.
Goff, P. (2016), 'The Phenomenal Bonding Solution to the Combination Problem,' in G. Brüntrup and L. Jaskolla (eds), *Panpsychism*. Oxford: Oxford University Press, 283–302.
Goff, P. (2017), *Consciousness and Fundamental Reality*. Oxford: Oxford University Press.
Goff, P. (2020), 'Micropsychism, cosmopsychism, and the grounding relation,' in W. E. Seager (ed.), *Routledge Handbook of Panpsychism*. Abingdon: Routledge.
Griffin, D. R. (1998), *Unsnarling the World-Knot: Consciousness, Freedom, and the Mind-Body Problem*. Berkeley, CA: University of California Press.
Heil, J. (2003), *From an Ontological Point of View*. Oxford: Clarendon Press.
Howell, R. (2015), 'The Russellian Monist's Problems with Mental Causation', *The Philosophical Quarterly*, 65/258: 22–39.
Hume, D. (1739), *A Treatise of Human Nature*, edited by L. A. Selby-Bigge, 1975. Oxford: Clarendon Press.
Jackson, F. (1982), 'Epiphenomenal Qualia', *Philosophical Quarterly*, 32/127: 127–36.
Jackson, F. (1986), 'What Mary Didn't Know', *Journal of Philosophy*, 83/5: 291–5.
Jackson, F. (1998), *From Metaphysics to Ethics*. Oxford: Oxford University Press.
Jackson, F. (2006), 'On Ensuring that Physicalism is not a Dual Attribute Theory in Sheep's Clothing', *Philosophical Studies*, 131/1: 227–49.
James, W. (1890/1981), *Principles of Psychology*, vol. 1. Cambridge, MA: Harvard University Press.
James, W. (1912), *Essays in Radical Empiricism*. London: Longmans, Green and Co.
Jaskolla, L. and Buck, A. J. (2012), 'Does panexperientialism solve the combination problem', *Journal of Consciousness Studies*, 19/9–10: 190–9.
Jennum, P. and Jensen, R. (2002), 'Sleep and Headache', *Sleep Medicine Reviews*, 6/6: 471–9.
Kirk, R. (2005), *Consciousness and Zombies*. Oxford: Clarendon Press.
Kriegel, U. (2009), *Subjective Consciousness: A Self-Representational Theory*. Oxford: Oxford University Press.
Langton, R. (2004), 'Elusive Knowledge of Things in Themselves', *Australasian Journal of Philosophy*. 82/1: 129–36.
Lewis, D. (1966), 'An Argument for the Identity Theory', *Journal of Philosophy*. 63: 17–25.

Lewis, D. (1988/2004), 'What Experience Teaches', in P. Ludlow, Y. Nagasawa, and D. Stoljar (eds), *There's Something about Mary: Essays on Frank Jackson's Knowledge Argument Against Physicalism*. Cambridge, MA: MIT Press, 77–103.

Lockwood, M. (1989), *Mind, Brain and the Quantum*. Oxford: Blackwell.

Lowe, E. J. (2006), *The Four-Category Ontology: A Metaphysical Foundation for Natural Science*. Oxford: Oxford University Press.

Lowe, E. J. (2009), *Personal Agency: The Metaphysics of Mind and Action*. Oxford: Oxford University Press.

McClelland, T. (2013), 'The Neo-Russellian Ignorance Hypothesis: A Hybrid Account of Phenomenal Consciousness', *Journal of Consciousness Studies*, 20/3–4: 125–5.

McGinn, C. (1989), 'Can we Solve the Mind-Body Problem?', *Mind*, 98/391: 349–66.

Mach, E. (1886/1984), *The Analysis of Sensations and the Relation of Physical to the Psychical*, translated by C. M. Williams. Chicago, IL: Open Court.

McLaughlin, B. (1998), 'Epiphenomenalism', in S. Guttenplan (ed.), *A Companion to the Philosophy of Mind*. Oxford: Blackwell.

McLaughlin, B. (2016), 'Mind Dust, Magic, or Conceptual Gap Only?', in G. Brüntrup and L. Jaskolla (eds), *Panpsychism*. Oxford: Oxford University Press.

Martin, C. B. (2007), *The Mind in Nature*. Oxford: Oxford University Press.

Martin, C. B. and Heil, J. (1998), 'Rules and Powers', *Noûs*, 32/12: 283–312.

Matthews, F. (2011), 'Panpsychism as Paradigm?', M. Blamauer, *The Mental as Fundamental*. Berlin: Ontos Verlag, 141–56.

Maxwell, G. (1978), 'Rigid Designators and Mind-Brain Identity', *Minnesota Studies in the Philosophy of Science*, 9: 365–403.

Meehl, P. E. (1966), 'The Compleat Autocerebroscopist: A Thought-Experiment on Professor Feigl's Mind-Body Identity Thesis', in P. K. Feyerabend and G. Maxwell (eds), *Mind, Matter, and Method: Essays in Philosophy and Science in Honor of Herbert Feigl*. Minneapolis: University of Minnesota Press, 103–80.

Melnyk, A. (2003), *A Physicalist Manifesto: Thoroughly Modern Materialism*. Cambridge: Cambridge University Press.

Mihalik, J. (2016), '*Consciousness in Nature: A Russellian Approach*. PhD Thesis, Charles University Prague.

Miller, G. (2018), 'Forming a Positive Concept of the Phenomenal Bonding Relation for Constitutive Panpsychism', *Dialectica*, 71/4, 541–62.

Miller, G. (2018), 'Can Subjects Be Proper Parts of Subjects? The De-Combination Problem', *Ratio*, 31/2, 137–54.

Molnar, G. (2003), *Powers: A Study in Metaphysics*. Oxford: Oxford University Press.

Montero, B. (2015), 'Russellian Physicalism', in T. Alter and S. Nagasawa (eds), *Consciousness and the Physical World*. Oxford: Oxford University Press.

Mørch, H. H. (2014), *Panpsychism and Causation: A New Argument and A Solution to the Combination Problem*. PhD Thesis, University of Oslo.

Mumford, S. (2004), *Laws in Nature*. Abingdon: Routledge.

Nagasawa, Y. and Wager, K. (2016), 'Panpsychism and Priority Cosmopsychism', in G. Brüntrup and L. Jaskolla (eds), *Panpsychism*. Oxford: Oxford University Press.

Nagel, T. (1979), 'Panpsychism', in Nagel's *Mortal Questions*. Cambridge: Cambridge University Press, 181–95.

Ney, A. (2015), 'A physicalist critique of Russellian monism', in T. Alter and S. Nagasawa (eds), *Consciousness and the Physical World*. Oxford: Oxford University Press.

Papineau, D. (1993), *Philosophical Naturalism*. Oxford: Blackwell.
Pereboom, D. (2011), *Consciousness and the Prospects of Physicalism*. Oxford: Oxford University Press.
Robinson, H. (1982), *Matter and Sense*. Cambridge: Cambridge University Press.
Roelofs, L. (2014), 'Phenomenal Blending and the Palette Problem', *Thought*, 3/1: 59–70.
Roelofs, L. (2016), 'The Unity of Consciousness, Within Subjects and Between Subjects', *Philosophical Studies*, 173/12: 3199–221.
Roelofs, L. (2019), *Combining Minds: How to Think About Composite Subjectivity*. Oxford: Oxford University Press.
Roelofs, L. (2020), 'Can We Sum Subjects? Evaluating Panpsychism's Hard Problem', in W. E. Seager (ed.), *Routledge Handbook of Panpsychism*. Abingdon: Routledge.
Rosenberg, G. H. (2004), *A Place for Consciousness*. Oxford: Oxford University Press.
Rosenberg, G. H. (2014), 'Causality and the combination problem', in T. Alter and S. Nagasawa (eds), *Consciousness and the Physical World*. Oxford: Oxford University Press, 224–45.
Rosenthal, D. M. (1991), 'The Independence of Consciousness and Sensory Quality', *Philosophical Issues*, 1: 15–36.
Rosenthal, D. M. (2005), *Consciousness and Mind*. Oxford: Oxford University Press.
Russell, B. (1927), *The Analysis of Matter*. London: Kegan Paul.
Russell, B. (1959), 'My Present View of the World' in Russell, *My Philosophical Development*. New York: Simon and Schuster, 16–27.
Sack, R. and Hanifin, J. (2010), 'Scratching below the surface of sleep and itch', *Sleep Medicine Reviews*, 14: 349–50.
Seager, W. E. (1995), 'Consciousness, information, and panpsychism', *Journal of Consciousness Studies*, 2: 272–88.
Seager, W. E. (2016), 'Panpsychism, aggregation and combinatorial infusion', in G. Brüntrup and L. Jaskolla (eds), *Panpsychism*. Oxford: Oxford University Press, 229–248.
Seager, W. E. (2020), *Routledge Handbook of Panpsychism*. Abingdon: Routledge.
Sellars, W. (1981), 'Foundations for a Metaphysics of Pure Process', *The Monist*, 64: 3–90.
Shani, I. (2015), 'Cosmopsychism: A Holistic Approach to the Metaphysics of Experience', *Philosophical Papers*, 44: 3.
Skrbina, D. (ed.), (2009), *Mind That Abides: Panpsychism in the New Millennium*. Amsterdam; Benjamins.
Stoljar, D. (2001), 'Two Conceptions of the Physical', *Philosophy and Phenomenological Research*, 62/2: 253–81.
Strawson, G. (1994), *Mental Reality*. Cambridge, MA: MIT Press.
Strawson, G. (2003), 'Real Materialism', in L. Antony and N. Hornstein (eds), *Chomsky and his Critics*. Oxford: Blackwell; reprinted in G. Strawson (ed.) (2008) *Real Materialism and Other Essays*. Oxford: Oxford University Press, 19–52.
Strawson, G. (2006), 'Realistic materialism: Why physicalism entails panpsychism', *Journal of Consciousness Studies*. 13/10–11: 3–31.
Strawson, G. (2008), 'The Identity of the Categorical and the Dispositional', *Analysis*, 51/4, 209–13.
Stubenberg, L. (1998), *Consciousness and Qualia*. Amsterdam: Benjamins.
Stubenberg, L. (2016), 'Neutral Monism', in E. N. Zalta (ed.), *Stanford Encyclopaedia of Philosophy* available at https://stanford.library.sydney.edu.au/entries/neutral-monism/
Wishon, D. (2015), 'Russell on Russellian Monism', in T. Alter and S. Nagasawa (eds), *Consciousness and the Physical World*. Oxford: Oxford University Press, 91–118.

CHAPTER 15

IDEALISM

Putting Qualia To Work

MICHAEL PELCZAR

15.1 INTRODUCTION

METAPHYSICAL idealism is the mirror-image of physicalism about the mental: where physicalists contend that the mental facts of our world supervene on the physical facts (but not vice versa), idealists contend that the physical facts of our world supervene on the mental facts (but not vice versa).[1]

Like physicalism, idealism is a kind of monism. According to idealists, the fundamental features of our world (or at least its fundamental contingent features) are all of one kind—the mental kind. Unlike physicalists, however, idealists try to achieve monism without reducing consciousness to something ostensibly more basic, or identifying consciousness with something that we previously didn't realize was consciousness (like brain states).

It has been a long time since idealism was part of the mainstream philosophical conversation. To get a feel for the theory, and to see its attractions, it helps to go back to the days when most philosophers considered idealism a live option.

A good starting point is Kant, whose metaphysics, though not itself strictly idealistic, is a watershed divide between two major idealist world-views: the traditional idealism of Leibniz and Berkeley, and the phenomenalism of J. S. Mill and the sense-datum theorists of the early twentieth century. Section 15.2 of this chapter presents Kantian metaphysics in its bare essentials. Section 15.3 presents traditional idealism as a view that results from modifying Kantian metaphysics in one direction; Section 15.4 presents phenomenalism

---

[1] Here and throughout, 'supervene' is used in its minimal metaphysical sense: the X features of our world supervene on its Y features just in case metaphysically possible worlds exactly like ours in terms of their Y features contain all the X features that our world contains. (Those who prefer grounding to supervenience can substitute the ensuing supervenience-talk with its closest approximation in terms of grounding.)

as a view that results from modifying Kantian metaphysics in the opposite direction. In Section 15.5, we consider some important challenges to the supervenience claim that lies at the heart of all idealist theories. Section 15.6 concludes with some brief speculation about what it would take for idealism to reverse its long-declining fortunes.[2]

15.2 KANTIAN METAPHYSICS

Beliefs about the ultimate causes of our experiences have changed dramatically over the millenia, from combinations of the Four Elements, to geometric configurations of Democritean atoms, to dynamical systems of Newtonian bodies, to excitation states of quantum fields. By contrast, beliefs about what the physical world contains have remained highly stable. The ancient Greeks, the natural philosophers of the Enlightenment, and scientists of the twenty-first century all agree that the world contains trees, despite having profoundly different beliefs about the nature of what gives us our experiences of trees.

A natural explanation for this agreement is that people throughout history have thought, and continue to think, that in order for there to be trees, it is enough for our world to be a place where experiences tend to occur in ways that are suggestive of trees. What has changed over the years are people's opinions about what accounts for that tendency.

This suggests a metaphysics. Our world has the power to cause experiences. For each physical state of affairs that holds in our world, our world has an experience-causing power, or combination of such powers, the existence of which is metaphysically sufficient for that physical state of affairs.

David Chalmers has proposed a metaphysics along these lines. According to Chalmers, ostensibly skeptical hypotheses, such as the hypothesis that all our experiences arise from interactions between some envatted brains and a supercomputer, are really just quirky metaphysical hypotheses consistent with the truth of our everyday beliefs about the world's physical contents. Assuming that the computer has the same experience-causing powers as whatever it is that actually gives us our experiences (of trees and other things), it follows that there really are trees in the envatted brains scenario. In this view, discovering that we were, in fact, envatted brains, would be like discovering that physical objects are fundamentally constituted by protons, neutrons, and electrons, rather than Earth, Water, Air, and Fire.[3]

The best-known proponent of this style of metaphysics is Kant.[4]

---

[2] The correct interpretation of historic idealists' views is controversial. The interpretations I assume here are, I hope, recognizably mainstream, but I've chosen them mainly for the light they shed on idealism as a living theory, and when I choose one interpretation over another, it's without any pretense of settling the associated scholarly debate.

[3] See Chalmers (2010).

[4] On one common interpretation of Kant (the 'one world' or 'two aspects' interpretation).

Here is the Kantian picture: there are entities that broadcast signals. The only thing we can know about these entities is that they broadcast such signals. The signals do not exist in a physical form, and they do not propagate through time or space. The only things capable of receiving the signals (as far as we know) are conscious minds, like ours. But the entities that broadcast the signals do so regardless of whether there are any minds to receive them. For physical things—say, trees—to exist is for it to be the case that if there were minds receptive to all such signaling, then the signals would cause those minds to have experiences that were collectively suggestive of trees.

What does it mean, to say that a collection of experiences is 'suggestive of trees'? Kant does not offer much detail on this, but we can think of it in terms of how the experiences in the collection contribute to a complete picture of a physical world. A collection of experiences is suggestive of trees, we might say, just in case it is a *worldlike* totality of experiences that includes treeish experiences that *cohere* with the other experiences in the totality, where 'worldlikeness' and 'coherence' are understood as follows.

When you walk through a house, the experiences you have are what we might call 'houselike': they fit together, phenomenologically, in a way that is analogous to how the frames in a video walk-through of the house would fit together. This is a quality that is missing from a totality of experiences comprising those you have had in the various kitchens you have occupied. The most you could achieve by attempting to fit those together in a houselike way would be something analogous to a video montage of various houses' kitchens.

Just as we can distinguish houselike collections of experiences from non-houselike collections, we can distinguish worldlike collections from non-worldlike collections. A *worldlike* collection comprises experiences of the sort that would characterize the conscious mental lives of beings who collectively explored the whole of some maximal region of space or spacetime. The details need not detain us here. The important point is that we do judge ourselves to have explored more or less of actual time and space, based on our experiences; the phenomenology that makes for worldlikeness is the kind that informs such judgments.

Worldlikeness is a property that a totality of experiences can have. Phenomenal coherence is a way that one experience in a totality of experiences can relate to the other experiences in the totality.

An experience *coheres* with a given totality of experiences, just in case it relates to the experiences in that totality as the experiences you are having now relate to the rest of the experiences you have had, rather than as the experiences you have when dreaming or hallucinating relate to the rest of your experiences. (For brevity's sake, we can also speak of a totality of experiences containing a 'coherent experience', meaning an experience that coheres with the other experiences in the totality.)[5]

---

[5] Here and throughout, 'experience' is a catch-all for any purely phenomenological event, process, or state of affairs. So, a totality of experiences needn't be just a set of individual sensations; for example, it might include entire streams of consciousness.

Another important concept for idealism is that of a potential for experience or *phenomenal potential*, as I will call it.[6]

It is uncontroversial that there are phenomenal potentials. Their existence is implicit in our talk of 'observable', 'perceptible', 'audible', 'visible', and 'tangible' things. However, the exact nature of phenomenal potentials, like the nature of potentials in general, is controversial. Are potentials (or some of them) ontologically primitive? If not, to what do they reduce? One popular idea is that the existence of a potential reduces to the truth of a suitable subjunctive conditional. Alternatively, we might construe potentials as unconditional probabilities that exceed a certain threshold, or try to analyze them in terms of nomological necessity.[7]

Not all accounts of potential sit equally well with all idealist theories, and this is not the place to investigate the choice-points that an idealist faces in this regard. There are, however, three propositions about phenomenal potential that every idealist must accept: (1) all physical things come with associated phenomenal potential (realized or unrealized), (2) facts about phenomenal potential are metaphysically prior to physical facts, and (3) some phenomenal potentials can exist in the absence of anything non-mental (or at least, in the absence of any contingent non-mental entity).

Define the *sensational facts* as the facts about what phenomenal potentials exist in our world. The first tenet of Kantian metaphysics is that any metaphysically possible world that duplicates our world in terms of which sensational facts hold in it is a world in which there hold all of the physical facts that hold in our world (the actual world). Call this tenet of Kantian metaphysics 'sensational supervenience'.[8]

Sensational Supervenience: the physical facts supervene on the sensational facts.

Define the *phenomenal field* of a possible world, W, as the total phenomenology that would exist in W, if all the phenomenal potential that exists in W were realized. Then we can put the basic idea behind sensational supervenience like this: our world's phenomenal field is a worldlike totality of experiences that contains, for every physical feature of our world, a coherent experience as of that feature, and this circumstance is metaphysically sufficient for the existence of that feature.

The second tenet of Kantian metaphysics is that the phenomenal potentials that exist in our world have some categorical basis, meaning that for every phenomenal potential,

---

[6] We could also speak of 'phenomenal powers', 'phenomenal tendencies', or 'phenomenal dispositions' in this connection, although disposition-talk strongly connotes something that is disposed, which is inconvenient when it comes to characterizing phenomenalist versions of idealism (see later in this section).

[7] Mumford (1998) and Molnar (2003) discuss many of the options in this area.

[8] 'Sensational' is a term of art. The sensational facts aren't necessarily limited to facts about potentials for sensory experience; they might include facts about potentials for other forms of phenomenology, such as cognitive or affective phenomenology. But it is sensory phenomenology that is most relevant to a Kantian construction of the physical world.

there is some irreducibly non-modal entity that explains why that potential exists. (By an irreducibly non-modal entity, I mean an entity whose existence does not reduce to the existence of one or more potentials, dispositions, powers, or possibilities.)

The idea behind the second tenet of Kantian metaphysics is that you cannot just have free-floating experience-causing powers: the powers must be powers that something *has*, and this something cannot just be more powers.

Categorical Hypothesis: phenomenal potentials have some categorical basis.

Kant calls the categorical bases of experience 'noumena'. The third tenet of Kantian metaphysics is that the only thing we can know about the noumena is that they exist, and give us various experiences. As Kant puts it, we can know nothing whatsoever about the 'inner nature' of the noumena. This is what Rae Langton calls 'Kantian humility'.[9]

Kantian Humility: the only thing we can know about the categorical basis of phenomenal potential is that such a basis exists and accounts for whatever experiences actually occur.

The final tenet of Kantian metaphysics concerns the nature of conscious experience. Kant does not have much to say about this, but it is pretty clear that he does not think of consciousness as a physical phenomenon. Anyway, Kantian metaphysics is most interesting when considered as an alternative to physicalism, so it makes sense to include among its tenets one that explicitly excludes physicalism:

Anti-physicalism: the mental does not supervene on the physical.[10]

Kantian metaphysics is the conjunction of these four tenets:

Kantian Metaphysics = Sensational Supervenience + Categorical Hypothesis + Kantian Humility + Anti-physicalism.

Kant calls his theory 'transcendental idealism', but that is misleading. Idealism is best understood as one of four theories we can classify by how they answer two questions about the relationship between the mental and the physical:[11]

---

[9] See Kant (1781/1998: A277/B333) and Langton (1998: 41–3).

[10] By calling this tenet 'anti-physicalism', I don't mean to imply that physicalism is equivalent to the claim that the mental supervenes on the physical. The falsity of psychophysical supervenience is sufficient for the falsity of physicalism, but the truth of psychophysical supervenience isn't sufficient for the truth of physicalism.

[11] Fans of grounding can replace the two questions with, respectively, 'Does the mental ground the physical?' and 'Does the physical ground the mental?'

	Does the physical supervene on the mental?	Does the mental supervene on the physical?
Russellian Monism	Yes	Yes
Idealism	Yes	No
Physicalism	No	Yes
Dualism	No	No

We cannot classify the Kantian position according to this scheme, because it is neutral on the question of whether the physical supervenes on the mental. All that the Kantian can say is that the physical supervenes on the noumenal, and that this *might* imply that the physical supervenes on the mental, but then again it might not: it depends on whether the noumena are mental, which, by Kantian Humility, we can never know.

15.3 TRADITIONAL IDEALISM

From the standpoint of the philosophy of consciousness, the most we can say about Kantian metaphysics is that it is incompatible with physicalism (by definition), and compatible with an idealist form of monism, but also compatible with a non-monistic world-view. Maybe this is the best we can do (Kant thought so), but one might try to do better, by casting something mental in the role of Kant's noumena. The result would be a frankly monist theory in which mental facts formed the subvenient base of physical reality.

Traditional idealism is just such a theory. It is what you get when you start with Kantian metaphysics, drop Kantian Humility, and replace the Categorical Hypothesis with the stronger *Mental Hypothesis*.

Mental Hypothesis: phenomenal potentials have a mental categorical basis.

Traditional idealism is the conjunction of Sensational Supervenience, the Mental Hypothesis, and Anti-physicalism:

Traditional Idealism = Sensational Supervenience + Mental Hypothesis + Anti-physicalism.

The main proponents of traditional idealism are Leibniz and Berkeley.

Where Kant thinks of physical reality as a potential for certain things (the noumena) to *cause* experiences in suitable patterns, Leibniz thinks of physical reality as a potential for certain things (the monads) to *have* experiences in suitable patterns. For Kant, phenomenal potential has its basis in the unknowable categorical nature of the noumena; for Leibniz, it has its basis in the input–output architecture of the monads.

Leibniz describes the monads as 'very exact immaterial automata'. Basically, a monad is a phenomenological Turing machine that takes phenomenal states of the monad as inputs, and returns further phenomenal states of the monad as outputs. The input–output routines that the monads run have neither beginning nor end, so that associated with each monad is an infinitely long stream of consciousness. Furthermore, the monads are isolated, in that no monad affects or is affected by anything else.[12]

Despite their mutual isolation, the mental lives of the monads 'harmonize', in the following sense. You can arrange the monads' streams of consciousness as rows in a table (one row per monad), in such a way that each column of the table contains a worldlike totality of coherent experiences as of physical things, and successive columns are phenomenal representations of successive stages of a world evolving according to the laws of physics.[13]

Leibniz was working on the assumption that spacetime was Newtonian, but we could update his theory to accommodate a relativistic account of spacetime. We could say that instead of there being just one collation of monadic experience that yields a picture of a world evolving according to the laws of physics, there are many such collations (one for each foliation of spacetime), where the columns of each collation (each table) correspond to Cauchy surfaces rather than classical time-slices.

Leibniz's idealism is actualistic, in the sense that it takes our world's phenomenal field to consist entirely of *realized* potentials for experience, so that for each physical state of affairs that holds in our world, there are actual experiences as of that state of affairs that cohere with the remainder of monadic experience. In Leibniz's view, no potential for monadic experience goes unrealized.

Leibniz takes this view because he believes that our world is the best possible world, and thinks that the best possible world has to be the one that is richest in fundamental content (and so, in Leibniz's view, richest in monadic experience). But if we set aside these theologically motivated views, we can consider a potentialist alternative to Leibniz's theory, in which the physical facts of our world supervene on facts about the monads' experience-having potential, there being no assumption now that all (or any) of that potential gets realized.[14]

---

[12] See §§1–25 of Leibniz (1714/1989a) and §§10–12 of Leibniz (1698/1998).

[13] See Leibniz (1712/1989, 1712/2007: 249, 257, and 1714/1989a: 220). This interpretation of Leibniz's doctrine of the harmony of the monads takes seriously Leibniz's view that facts about time, like facts about space and physical objects, reduce to facts about monadic experience (see Leibniz 1714/1989b: 307, 1712/1989: 199, and 1703/1989: 178). Since the temporal facts reduce to facts about monadic harmony, we can't characterize the harmony in terms of a synchrony of monadic experience.

[14] For Leibniz's actualism, see §§57–8 of Leibniz (1714/1989a). Leibniz also offers an explanation for the harmony of the monads, proposing that God created them so as to have experiences that harmonize in the way described above. However, one could dispense with this explanation, and just posit the harmony of the monads as a fundamental regularity of the world, analogous to the tendency for certain quantum events occurring in causal isolation from one another to occur in correlated patterns, as in the famous Bell test experiments.

The best-known version of traditional idealism is Berkeley's, according to which all phenomenal potential has its basis in the mind of God.

Like Leibniz, Berkeley is an actualist, in the sense explained above, but Berkeley's commitment to actualism runs deeper than Leibniz's, since Berkeley identifies physical objects with combinations of experiences. If physical objects are combinations of experiences, you cannot very well have the objects without the experiences. Berkeley takes this to be a compelling argument for the existence of God, as a repository for all the physical things that non-divine minds fail to perceive. Most people take it to be a reductio of Berkeley.[15]

One could modify Berkeley's idealism to escape the commitment to actualism. Berkeley hints at such a modification when he suggests that the existence of an unperceived thing might be a matter of what sorts of experiences *would* occur, if God saw fit to cause certain other experiences. Howard Robinson and John Foster develop potentialist versions of Berkeleyan idealism along these lines.[16]

Unlike Kantian metaphysics, traditional idealism is plainly monistic as regards mind and body. But it achieves monism only by replacing Kant's Categorical Hypothesis with the stronger Mental Hypothesis. The question is: why should we accept the Mental Hypothesis?

Each of us knows from his own case that some experiences, and some potentials for experience, have a mental basis, namely a basis in his own mind. It follows that a world in which some phenomenal potentials have their bases in something other than minds is more complicated, ontologically, than a world in which all phenomenal potentials have their bases in minds. Since we should always prefer the simpler of two competing hypotheses, other things being equal, we should prefer the Mental Hypothesis over any alternative hypothesis about the categorical basis of experience.[17]

The problem with this argument is that it is far from clear that other things *are* equal. The idea that our world consists fundamentally of minds does have a certain simplicity to it, but the simplicity comes at a cost: all those minds.

How high is this cost? Once you have worked your way inside the traditional idealist world-view, it might not look like a cost at all. From the standpoint of the unconverted, however, the benefits of monism are not sufficient to justify the unexpected introduction of so many minds (or, such a special Mind). Traditional idealists have always touted their theory as the metaphysics of common sense. But common sense is that physical things existed long before there were any minds, and would have existed even if there had never been any minds. Maybe Berkeley would say that this is one point on which common sense must yield to metaphysical insight.

---

[15] For Berkeley's view that physical objects comprise experiences ('ideas,' in his vernacular), see §1 of Berkeley (1710/1901). Berkeley denies the existence of matter, but by 'matter' he apparently means physical phenomena that don't reduce to anything experiential. Berkeley is best read as a reductionist about the physical, not an eliminativist: see the first ten sections of Berkeley (1710/1901).
[16] See §3 of Berkeley (1710/1901), Robinson (1994: 213–38), and Foster (2008: 107–22, 199–245).
[17] See §§26–29 of Berkeley (1710/1901). This argument assumes that minds are categorical features of the world. That's debatable—Mill, for example, disagrees Mill (1865/1989, 240–9)—but let's set this aside.

It was precisely because traditional idealism relied so heavily on speculation about the world's mental contents that Kant rejected it in favor of his more cautious position. People sympathetic to traditional idealism might see Kant's caution as a sign of cowardice. Others are more likely to see it as a sober refusal to take a hit from the bong that Berkeley and Leibniz were passing around.

Wherever we come down on this, it is important to recognize that something was lost in the historical shift from theistic idealism to Kantian noumenalism. The shift left Kantians without any satisfying explanation for why there exist the particular potentials for experience that do, in fact, exist. A Kantian can say that these particular potentials exist because the noumena broadcast the particular signals they do, but as long as he adheres to Kantian Humility, this is a purely nominal explanation. It does not rationalize the sensational facts of our world in terms of some deeper unifying principle (like a divine plan, carried out directly or via pre-programmed monads). It is like saying that the tide rises and falls for some reason, adding that there is no possibility of learning anything about that reason, besides that it accounts for the tide's rise and fall.

Physicalists and dualists take various physical entities as the categorical basis of experience, and explain why experiences tend to occur as they do by reference to physical features of those entities. Traditional idealists take various minds as the categorical basis of experience, and explain why experiences tend to occur as they do by reference to mental features of those minds. But a Kantian cannot say anything illuminating about the supposed categorical basis of experience. All he can say about the noumena is that they exist—the ghosts of departed deities.

15.4 Phenomenalism

One reason to posit categorical bases for phenomenal potentials is to explain why there exist the particular potentials that do; however, as we have just seen, this is not a reason that is available to Kantian metaphysicians. If Kantians have a reason to posit a categorical basis for the phenomenal potentials of our world, it can only be that it is in the very nature of potentials to have categorical bases.

The idea that potentials, tendencies, or dispositions—'modality', for a catch-all—must have categorical bases was an important doctrine of late twentieth century metaphysics. David Armstrong was probably the doctrine's staunchest advocate, insisting throughout his long career that if a potential exists, it must be due to the existence of something that is not a potential. Call this the 'Armstrong Doctrine'.[18]

If the Armstrong Doctrine is true, we have no choice but to accept the Categorical Hypothesis. Whether it *is* true is a matter of ongoing debate; however, there are reasons to doubt it.

The possibility of potentials that have no categorical basis—'base-free' potentials, as I'll call them—would appear to be established by the possibility that our own world is

---

[18] See Armstrong (1961: 56–8) and 1993, 187); also Lewis (1992: 218–19, 1998).

fundamentally chancy. As far as we know, it is a physially fundamental fact that there is about a 50 percent chance that the quantum tunneling involved in the decay of a radon atom occurs within four days of the genesis of the atom. Presumably, about 50 percent of the radon atoms that come into existence in our world decay within four days. But we can imagine a world categorically indistinguishable from ours, in which there is only about a 10 per cent chance that a radon atom decays within four days of its genesis. We need only imagine that due to a colossal statistical fluke, about 50 percent of the radon atoms in this other possible world decay within four days, despite there being only about a 10 percent chance that any given radon atom decays within four days. In this other world, there exist potentials for radioactive decay that do not exist in our world, despite the worlds' being categorically indistinguishable.[19]

One philosopher who definitely would have rejected the Armstrong Doctrine is J. S. Mill. Unlike Leibniz, Kant, and Armstrong, Mill sees no reason to think that our world is not potentials all the way down. This leads Mill to reject Kant's Categorical Hypothesis (and with it the stronger Mental Hypothesis of traditional idealism), and to eschew Kantian Humility in favor of what we might as well call Millian Humility.

Millian Humility: for all we know, phenomenal potentials have no categorical basis.

In effect, Mill out-Kants Kant: whereas Kant assumes the existence of a categorical basis for experience and merely suspends judgment as to its more particular categorical nature, Mill suspends judgment on the question of whether a categorical basis for experience exists at all.

Phenomenalism is what you get when you start with Kantian metaphysics, drop the Categorical Hypothesis, and replace Kantian Humility with Millian Humility. It is the conjunction of Sensational Supervenience, Millian Humility, and Anti-physicalism:

Phenomenalism = Sensational Supervenience + Millian Humility + Anti-physicalism.

Just as you can think of Berkeleyan idealism as the result of replacing Kant's noumena with Berkeley's God, and Leibnizian idealism as the result of replacing Kant's noumena with Leibniz's monads, you can think of Millian phenomenalism as the result of replacing Kant's noumena with Mill's 'permanent possibilities of sensation'—potentials for experience that might have categorical bases, but might not, and can serve as the subvenient base of physical reality either way.[20]

---

[19] Stephen Mumford argues for the reality of 'ungrounded' (i.e., base-free) dispositions along these lines; (Mumford 2006). Jennifer McKitrick argues for the metaphysical possibility of bare dispositions in McKitrick (2003); her arguments translate naturally into arguments for the metaphysical possibility of base-free potentials.

[20] For Mill's phenomenalism, see Chapter XI of Mill (1865/1989), and the Appendix to Chapters XI and XII. Other sympathetic discussions of phenomenalism include Price (1932), Lewis (1946: 203–53), Ayer (1946–1947), Fumerton (1985: 131–73), and Pelczar (2015). If we replace Millian Humility in the definition of phenomenalism offered above with the claim that the sensational facts have no categorical basis, we get

Unlike Kantian metaphysics, which is compatible with idealism but also with its denial, phenomenalism is best classified as an idealist theory. This is because phenomenalists, unlike Kantians, do not put anything into their fundamental ontology that they do not classify as mental. A phenomenalist allows that there might be (unbeknownst to us) something non-mental that somehow explains phenomenal potentials, but, if so, its relationship to the potentials is analogous to the relationship of physical brains to conscious experiences in dualist theories—a relationship that is consistent with classifying the experiences as purely mental.

It is true that phenomenalism is a kind of idealism only if the existence of a potential for experience is a mental state of affairs. But since we classify potentials for physical events (like radioactive decay) as physical, it seems reasonable to classify potentials for experience as mental.

It is also true that in the phenomenalist view, facts about potential experience underdetermine facts about actual experience (and vice versa). But in the traditional idealist view, facts about minds underdetermine facts about actual experience (and vice versa), and this does not deter us from counting traditional idealism as a kind of monism.

A commitment to phenomenalism does not carry with it a commitment to suspending judgment on whether phenomenal potentials have any explanation. It just carries a commitment to suspending judgment on whether they have any *categorical* explanation. It is consistent with phenomenalism for one sensational fact (or collection of sensational facts) to explain another sensational fact.

Actually, a phenomenalist has to allow for this kind of explanation, in order to avoid the absurdity of holding that physical facts are universally inexplicable.

The existence of a delta at the mouth of the Mississippi River is not a miracle. It is the result of thousands of years of silt- and sand-deposits occurring where the river slows as it enters the Gulf of Mexico. Like anyone else, a phenomenalist recognizes that the delta is a natural consequence of these hydrological processes. It is just that a phenomenalist sees both the delta and the processes that created it as *metaphysical* consequences of the existence of various potentials for experience.

The motions of water and sediment are a metaphysical consequence of certain sensational facts, the delta is a metaphysical consequence of certain other sensational facts, and the latter sensational facts are a natural, non-metaphysical consequence of the former sensational facts. For a phenomenalist, to say that the delta is a 'natural consequence' of the hydrological circumstances (the water flow, the sediment, etc.) is to say that it is a natural law, or a consequence of natural laws, that if the sensational facts that entail those hydrological circumstances obtain, so do sensational facts that entail the existence of a delta.[21]

---

a theory we might call 'ambitious phenomenalism'. The problem with ambitious phenomenalism is that it's hard to see what justifies the claim that the sensational facts have no categorical basis. If Mill is right, considerations of theoretical simplicity compel us not to posit such a basis, but that's different from positing its non-existence.

[21] As Mill puts it, 'Whether we are asleep or awake the fire goes out, and puts an end to one particular possibility of warmth and light. Whether we are present or absent the corn ripens, and brings a new

A phenomenalist holds that many (perhaps all) sensational facts have non-reductive explanations *in terms of other sensational facts*. This is compatible with Millian Humility, which only requires us to suspend judgment on whether any sensational fact is based in (or explained by) something that is not itself a sensational fact.

Phenomenalism avoids the ontological extravagance of traditional idealism. In Mill's view, the existence of a physical object does not require the existence of a mind capable of having or causing experience, any more than the existence of a Kantian noumenon requires the existence of a mind capable of receiving its signals. Nor, in Mill's view, does the existence of a physical object require any actual experience. According to Mill, the natural world is just a big potential for experience, some of which happens to be realized, but most of which is not (at least, as far as we know).

A theory can be more or less simple along either of two dimensions. One dimension of simplicity is ontological: the less fundamental stuff a theory gets by with (or, the fewer fundamental *kinds* of stuff), the better, all else being equal. The other dimension of simplicity is architectural: a theory that gets by with less-complicated fundamental laws is better, other things being equal, than a theory that requires more complicated fundamental laws.

Ontologically, phenomenalism is very simple. How about architecturally?

For fundamental laws, physicalism gets by with the laws of physics alone. Taking this as our baseline, we see that dualism is architecturally more complex than physicalism, but not dramatically so: it just supplements the laws of physics with some psychophysical bridge laws, to account for observed correlations between experiences and their neural correlates. Traditional idealism is on an architectural par with physicalism; it is just that instead of taking the laws of physics as fundamental, it takes as fundamental the principles that govern the underlying mental reality on which the laws of physics supervene.

Like the traditional idealist, the phenomenalist does not regard the laws of physics as metaphysically fundamental. But unlike the traditional idealist, the phenomenalist cannot base the laws of physics on a deeper level of minds governed by laws that are metaphysically fundamental. What *can* the phenomenalist offer by way of fundamental laws?

We are told that it is a law of physics that for every action, there is an equal and opposite reaction. If that is true, a phenomenalist will say that it is a law of experience that if the phenomenal field contains a coherent experience of an action, it contains a coherent experience of an equal and opposite reaction. Likewise for all other laws. If the Einstein Field Equations express a physical law, then it is a law of experience that the phenomenal field contains coherent experiences of whatever physical phenomena inspire the physicists who contemplate them to accept the Einstein Field Equations.[22]

Where the physicalist has laws of physics, and the traditional idealist laws of minds (or Mind), the phenomenalist has laws of experience.

---

possibility of food. Hence we speedily learn to think of Nature as made up solely of these groups of possibilities, and the active force of Nature as manifested in the modification of some of these by others' (Mill 1865/1989: 230). See also Ayer (1940: 229–31, 1946–1947: 146–50).

[22] The reference to physicists' contemplations here is only to gesture towards the actual content of the relevant law of experience; the law itself would make no reference to physicists or their contemplations.

We can state the laws of physics in terms of a few dozen (at most a few hundred) properties, relations, and natural kinds—physically fundamental fields, forces, particles, etc. Is a similar economy of terms possible in the expression of a phenomenalistic law of experience?

It depends on how rich the phenomenal field must be, in order to serve as the subvenient base of the physical regularities that correspond to physical laws. If it is enough for the field to contain experiences characterized by a smallish range of qualia—perhaps the qualia by virtue of instantiating which our experiences present things as having various geometric and temporal features—then phenomenalism may be on a par with physicalism or traditional idealism, architecturally. If the phenomenal field must be significantly richer than that to support the regularities that physical laws describe, phenomenalism may be at an architectural disadvantage to alternative metaphysical schemes.

15.5 Challenges to Sensational Supervenience

We have saved the biggest challenges to idealism for last. These are objections to sensational supervenience, the central tenet of all idealist metaphysics (and of Kantian metaphysics too). We can state the objections as conceivability arguments against sensational supervenience, of which we will consider three.[23]

Consider first the *Matrix Argument*:

> We can conceive of a world in which there holds every sensational fact that holds in our world, but in which those facts hold only because of the operations of a supercomputer connected to some envatted brains. Furthermore, we can conceive of this world—call it Matrix World—as being physically very different from ours; e.g., as containing no trees. This gives us a compelling reason to believe that the sensational facts about our world (the actual world) do not metaphysically entail the physical facts about our world.

An idealist can respond to this argument by granting the whole thing.

Sensational supervenience says that any metaphysically possible world that is indistinguishable from ours with respect to the sensational facts that hold in it is a world that has all the physical features that our world has. A counterexample to sensational supervenience would be a metaphysically possible world characterized by all *and only* the

---

[23] Conceivability arguments are controversial, but a main motive for taking idealism seriously is dissatisfaction with physicalism, and a main source of dissatisfaction with physicalism is its vulnerability to conceivability arguments against psychophysical supervenience. So, an idealist has to take conceivability arguments against his own theory seriously.

sensational facts that characterize our world (the actual world), but that lacked some of our world's physical features.

Matrix World is not such a world: in Matrix World, there are many sensational facts that do not hold in our world. For example, in Matrix World, the phenomenal field includes coherent experiences as of a powerful computer attached to some brains; this is a sensational fact that presumably does not hold in our world (or if it does, then Matrix World might duplicate ours physically after all, in which case the argument collapses).

What if we suppose that the supercomputer, vats, and related paraphernalia of Matrix World are for some reason imperceptible? Suppose we stipulate that in Matrix World, nothing can perceive the supercomputer and so forth 'from the outside' (i.e., other than in the ways that the envatted brains perceive the computer, if they can be said to perceive it). This version of Matrix World still fails to contain trees, but unlike the earlier version, it contains no more phenomenal potential than our world, and therefore escapes the idealist come-back offered above.

The idealist response to this is that we cannot conceive of such a world.

We can conceive of a world that contains vats, supercomputers, etc. despite containing no conscious experience. (Berkeley thought otherwise, for reasons that are pretty clearly fallacious.) The question here, though, is whether we can conceive of a world that contains vats, supercomputers, etc. despite containing no *potential* for experience.[24]

It is hard to do justice to this question without saying more about the nature of phenomenal potential than there is room to say here. Still, there is reason to be skeptical about the suggestion that we can conceive of a world that contains vats and so forth but no potential for relevant experiences (as of vats and so forth).

If we want to conceive of a world that contains vats without any corresponding potential for experience, how should we go about it? We could imagine some kind of cloaking device that causes anyone who wanders into the vats' vicinity to hallucinate an absence of vats. But then the cloaking device would itself have to be imperceptible, in order for its presence not to entail a difference between Matrix World and our world, at the level of sensational facts.[25]

A better way to try to conceive of an imperceptible vat without simply shifting the focus of discussion (to an imperceptible cloaking device, or whatever) is by trying to conceive of it in purely structural terms. If, as proponents of ontic structural realism contend, the existence of any physical entity reduces to the satisfaction of some purely structural description—a description, like '$\exists \varphi \exists x (\varphi x)$', that employs only logical and mathematical terms—then one could, in theory, conceive of a world containing vats just by conceiving of a world that satisfies certain purely structural descriptions. Assuming, plausibly, that we can conceive of a purely structural description being satisfied in the

---

[24] Even if vats and other middle-sized dry goods can't exist in the absence of a corresponding potential for experience, there might be other physical entities (like subatomic particles) that can; we consider the challenge that such entities (or alleged entities) pose to idealism below.

[25] What about a self-cloaking device that ensures that the only experiences that occur are ones that contribute to a totality suggestive of a device-free world physically indistinguishable from our own? There is room for such a device in an idealist world-view. Kantians call it a noumenon.

absence of any potential for experience, it would follow that we can conceive of a counterexample to sensational supervenience by conceiving of the vats and so forth in Matrix World in purely structural terms, and stipulating that there is no corresponding potential for experience.[26]

This is not the place to debate the merits of structuralist metaphysics. The important point is that there is a real threat to idealism here, and that meeting it requires a close engagement with the structuralist world-view. At the end of the day, idealists might have more to fear from structuralism than from physicalism, dualism, or Russellian monism.[27]

A different modification of the Matrix Argument replaces the envatted brains with disembodied minds, and the supercomputer with interactions among those minds. Thus we have the *Ghost Argument*:

> We can conceive of a world consisting of a multitude of disembodied minds; call it Ghost World. The minds are capable of interactions that result in their having various experiences, and these interactions, or potential interactions, are governed by laws that determine the patterns in which the resulting experiences occur. The laws and minds are such that all and only the phenomenal potentials that exist in our world (the actual world) exist in Ghost World. Since Ghost World contains nothing physical, despite duplicating our world at the level of sensational facts, our ability to conceive of Ghost World gives us a compelling reason to believe that the physical facts don't supervene on the sensational facts.

In response, an idealist can deny that there is any physical difference between Ghost World and the actual world.

From an idealist standpoint, the difference (assuming there is one) between our world and Ghost World is not that our world but not Ghost World contains physical things. The difference is in what ultimately explains why there exist the physical things that do— these being the same physical things (or indistinguishable physical things) in the case of each world. In Ghost World, the existence of physical things has its ultimate explanation in certain lawlike interactions among various minds; in a Leibnizian world, it has its ultimate explanation in a Divine Plan; in a Kantian world, it has its ultimate explanation in the causal powers of the noumena; in our world, it has its ultimate explanation in— well, who knows? Maybe nothing.

This response might not be available to all idealists. Berkeley contends that most physical things in our world consist of divine experiences. If, as many hold, it is essential to a physical object that it consist of whatever sort of stuff it actually consists of, then Ghost World does not contain all the physical things that exist in our world, since Ghost World contains no divine experiences. But if we equate a physical object with a

---

[26] For structuralism about the physical, see Russell (1927), Ladyman *et al.* (2007), and Tegmark (2014). The general idea goes back at least to Boscovich (1763/1922).

[27] That said, proponents of sensational supervenience have reason for optimism *vis à vis* the structuralist threat, since structuralism about the physical faces a serious objection due to Max Newman. In effect, Newman shows that structuralism, at least in its purest form, implies that it is impossible for two worlds that contain the same number of things to differ from one another physically; see Newman (1928).

combination of phenomenal potentials, and individuate such potentials by the experiences for which they are potentials, rather than by the potentials' categorical bases (if any), we can say that Ghost World does contain the same physical things as our world, since it contains the same potentials, even if the potentials have a categorical basis in Ghost World that they do not have in ours.

A final argument against sensational supervenience targets a perennial source of dissatisfaction with idealist metaphysics, which is its treatment of unobservable phenomena. Call it the *Argument from Unobservables*:

We can conceive of a world, WYSIWYG ('what-you-see-is-what-you-get') World, that has all the same observable features as our world, but no unobservable features. Since WYSIWYG World has the same observable features as our world, it includes the same potentials for experience as our world. But since WYSIWYG World lacks the unobservable things that exist in our world (subatomic particles, etc.), it differs from our world physically. So WYSIWYG World is a counterexample to sensational supervenience.

One possible idealist response is to allow that our world has whatever unobservable features science tells us it has, but deny that a world could duplicate ours sensationally without having all those features. The idea here is that the distinction between observable and unobservable phenomena is not a distinction between phenomena for which there are corresponding potentials for experience and phenomena for which there are not, but rather a distinction between two kinds of potential for experience.

We can put this in terms of the phenomenal field. An observable thing, like the Statue of Liberty, is a conspicuous pattern in the phenomenal field. It is a pattern that consists of experiences that all resemble one another in obvious ways—they are all experiences as of a statue with a certain shape, size, color, etc. An unobservable thing, like an electron or gravitational wave, is an inconspicuous pattern in the phenomenal field. It is a pattern consisting of experiences that do not resemble one another in any obvious way, but exhibit some order, symmetry, or regularity that emerges when we subject the experiences to an appropriate mathematical description. In this view, unobservable phenomena are, so to speak, hidden patterns in experience.[28]

An alternative response to the argument from unobservables is to deny that there are any unobservable things (or at least, any that a hidden patterns account cannot handle).

One way to do this would be to hold that although many things are unobservable to us humans, no physical entity is absolutely unobservable, since (one might argue) there is always the possibility of a Laplacean Demon who observes subatomic particles, the interiors of black holes, etc.

But what if our world contains physical entities that are not just unobservable to this or that sentient being, but unobservable in principle? (Perhaps one could argue

---

[28] Theoretical physicists obviously don't work directly from the experiences of observational physicists: they work primarily from the observationalists' records of their observations. But those records are a reflection of the observationalists' experiences, and by discovering a pattern in the records, the theoretician implicitly discovers a pattern in the corresponding experiences.

that subatomic particles and the interiors of black holes are such things.) And what if it is impossible to construe these in-principle unobservable things as hidden patterns in experience?

An idealist has to deny that such things exist. Is this a problem for idealism?

Thinking of the world as containing various unobservable things obeying various rules definitely helps us make sense of what we observe. But it does not follow that the world actually contains unobservable things. It might be that the alleged unobservables are really just accounting devices, like the international dollar, or, if you like, fictional characters in the scientific narrative.

The suggestion is far from new: it is scientific antirealism.

Scientific antirealism is controversial, but an idealist might not have to buy into it lock, stock, and barrel in order to overcome the argument from unobservables. He can adopt a wait-and-see policy of suspending judgment on whether unobservable things exist *until and unless we can make good idealistic sense of them*, either by forming a clear conception of what it would be like to observe the things, or by finding a way to construe the things as hidden patterns in experience.

Before there were microscopes, people could not observe microbes. Still, a visionary Renaissance doctor might have proposed a germ theory of disease, positing germs to explain the transmission and progression of various illnesses.

We can imagine a debate arising over the reality of these so-called 'germs', with some people inclined to think that they are a genuine biological phenomenon, and others inclined to think of them as convenient fictions.

The germ-antirealists will be forced to admit they are wrong, when people start actually observing germs through microscopes. But if they adopt the wait-and-see policy described above, there is no harm done: what they used to regard as convenient fictions, they can now regard as realities supervening on sensational facts involving (among others) the kinds of experiences people have when looking through microscopes.

Similarly, if there comes a time when we can make sense of perceiving a quark (assuming we can't make sense of this already), an idealist can give an account of quarks in terms of the phenomenology of such perceptions. Until then, or until he finds a way to construe quarks as hidden patterns in the phenomenal field, an idealist can treat them as convenient fictions.

Is the wait-and-see policy a reasonable one? That is debatable, but it may have to be, if idealism is to survive the argument from unobservables.

15.6 Conclusion

It is possible that idealism will always be one of those theories that looks compelling from the inside, but implausible from the outside. If so, it is in reputable company: physicalism, arguably, is also such a theory. For those who prefer a metaphysics that looks equally good from all angles, at the cost of not looking particularly stunning from any angle, there is always dualism.

Today, of course, the philosophy of consciousness is almost entirely a conversation between physicalists and dualists. What would it take to get idealism back into the game?

For one thing, it would help to dissociate idealism from some questionable arguments that people have made for it.

One such argument goes like this: we know that there is an external world; idealism is the only metaphysics that is compatible with our having such knowledge; therefore, idealism is true.[29]

The problem here is the second premise. Like any defensible theory, idealism has to recognize a distinction between veridical and non-veridical experience. A skeptical hypothesis for idealism is just one in which all of our experiences fall into the latter category—that is, in which the phenomenal field contains no experiences that cohere with the other experiences in the field. There is nothing in idealism to rule this out (or at least, nothing that wouldn't serve to rule out the corresponding possibility in any other metaphysical setting). If physical objects are woven into a veil of ideas, it is only because the veil has an overall pattern that it could fail to have, consistent with all our actual experience.[30]

Another traditional argument for idealism goes like this: the world (or its non-abstract part) consists ultimately of its categorical contents; the only non-abstract things capable of having categorical natures are conscious minds or experiences; therefore, the world (or its non-abstract part) consists ultimately of conscious minds or experiences.[31]

This argument is better than the epistemic one, but hardly compelling. Not even all idealists agree with its first premise (recall Mill), and convincing arguments for its second premise are elusive.[32]

The best argument for idealism is probably this: some form of idealism is the simplest defensible metaphysics; we should accept the simplest defensible metaphysics; therefore, we should accept some form of idealism.

Making this argument work requires defending idealism from the principal objections to it, and showing that idealism is simpler than any defensible alternative. That is a tall order, but nothing less is likely to put idealism back on the map.[33]

REFERENCES

Adams, Robert M. (2007), 'Idealism vindicated' in P van Inwagen and D. Zimmerman (eds), *Persons: Human and Divine*. Oxford: Oxford University Press, 35–54.

Armstrong, David. (1961), *Perception and the Physical World*. London: Routledge & Kegan Paul.

---

[29] See §§87–91 of Berkeley (1710/1901) and Part IV of Book I of Hume (1739/1978).

[30] There might be a better epistemic argument for idealism, though: see Smithson (2017).

[31] See Leibniz (1686/1998), Eddington (1928, 247–72), Hartshorne (1946, 413), Adams (2007, 40), Foster (2008, 42–82), and Strawson (2008, 19–51).

[32] If there is a good argument for the second premise, it's probably along the lines of Robinson (1982, 108–23).

[33] Thanks to Bob Beddor, Ben Blumson, Brian Cutter, Uriah Kriegel, Abelard Podgorski, Qu Hsueh Ming, Neil Sinhababu, and Rob Smithson for their comments on earlier drafts of this chapter.

Armstrong, David. (1993), 'Reply to Martin' in John Bacon, Keith Campbell, and Lloyd Reinhardt, (eds), *Ontology, Causality, and Mind: Essays in Honour of D.M. Armstrong*. Cambridge: Cambridge University Press, 186–94.
Ayer, A. J. (1940), *The Foundations of Empirical Knowledge*. London: Macmillan.
Ayer, A. J. (1946–1947), 'Phenomenalism', *Proceedings of the Aristotelian Society*, 47: 163–196.
Berkeley, George. (1710/1901), 'A Treatise Concerning the Principles of Human Knowledge' in *The Works of George Berkeley*, ed. A. C. Fraser, Vol. 1. Oxford: Clarendon Press, 233–347.
Boscovich, Roger Joseph. (1763/1922), *A Theory of Natural Philosophy*, J. M. Child, trans. Chicago & London: Open Court Publishing Company.
Chalmers, David. (2010), 'The Matrix as metaphysics' in D. J. Chalmers, *The Character of Consciousness*. Oxford: Oxford University Press, 455–94.
Eddington, A. S. (1928), *The Nature of the Physical World*. New York: Macmillan.
Foster, John. (2008), *A World for Us: The Case for Phenomenalistic Idealism*. Oxford: Oxford University Press.
Fumerton, Richard A. (1985), *Metaphysical and Epistemological Problems of Perception*. Lincoln, NE: University of Nebraska Press.
Hartshorne, Charles. (1946), 'Leibniz's greatest discovery', *Journal of the History of Ideas*, 7/4: 411–21.
Hume, David. (1739/1978), *A Treatise of Human Nature*. Oxford: Clarendon Press.
Kant, Immanuel. (1781/1998), *Critique of Pure Reason*. Cambridge: Cambridge University Press.
Ladyman, James, Ross, Don, and David Spurret, with John Collier. (2007), *Every Thing Must Go: Metaphysics Naturalized*. Oxford: Oxford University Press.
Langton, Rae. (1998), *Kantian Humility: Our Ignorance of Things in Themselves*. Oxford: Clarendon Press.
Leibniz, G. W. (1686/1998), 'Leibniz to Arnauld, 4/14 July 1686' *G.W. Leibniz: Philosophical Texts*, translated by R. Francks and R.S. Woolhouse. Oxford: Oxford University Press, 105–14.
Leibniz, G. W. (1698/1998), 'A Letter from M. Leibniz to the Editor, Containing an Explanation of the Difficulties Which M. Bayle Found with the New System of the Union of the Soul and Body' *G.W. Leibniz: Philosophical Texts*, translated by R. Francks and R. S. Woolhouse. Oxford: Oxford University Press, 201–8.
Leibniz, G. W. (1703/1989), 'Leibniz to de Volder, 20 June 1703 [excerpts]' Roger Ariew and Daniel Garber (eds), *Philosophical Essays*. Indianapolis and Cambridge: Hackett Publishing Company, 174–8.
Leibniz, G. W. (1712/1989), 'Notes for Leibniz to Des Bosses, 5 February 1712' Ariew, Roger, & Garber, Daniel (eds), *Philosophical Essays*. Indianapolis and Cambridge: Hackett Publishing Company, 199–200.
Leibniz, G. W. (1712/2007), 'Leibniz to Des Bosses, 16 June 1712' Look, C. Brandon and Donald Rutherford (eds), *The Leibniz–Des Bosses Correspondence*. New Haven: Yale University Press, 255–7.
Leibniz, G. W. (1714/1989a), 'Monadology' Roger Ariew and Daniel Garber (eds), *Philosophical Essays*. Indianapolis and Cambridge: Hackett Publishing Company, 213–25.
Leibniz, G. W. (1714/1989b), 'Remarks on Berkeley's *Principles*' Roger Ariew and Daniel Garber (eds), *Philosophical Essays*. Indianapolis and Cambridge: Hackett Publishing Company, 307.
Lewis, Clarence Irving. (1946), *An Analysis of Knowledge and Valuation*. La Salle: Open Court.
Lewis, David. (1992), 'Critical notice of *A Combinatorial Theory of Possibility*', *Australasian Journal of Philosophy*, 70/2: 211–24.
Lewis, David. (1998), 'The truthmakers', *Times Literary Supplement*, 4948: 30.

McKitrick, Jennifer. (2003), 'The bare metaphysical possibility of bare dispositions',. *Philosophy and Phenomenological Research*, 66/2: 349–69.
Mill, John Stuart. (1865/1989), *An Examination of Sir William Hamilton's Philosophy, and of the Principal Philosophical Questions Discussed in his Writings*. London: Longman, Green, and Co.
Molnar, George. (2003), *Powers: A Study in Metaphysics*. Oxford: Oxford University Press.
Mumford, Stephen. (1998), *Dispositions*. Oxford: Oxford University Press.
Mumford, Stephen. (2006), 'The ungrounded argument', *Synthese*, 149/3, 471–89.
Newman, M. H. A. (1928), 'Mr Russell's "Causal Theory of Perception"', *Mind*, 37/146, 137–48.
Pelczar, Michael. (2015), *Sensorama: A Phenomenalist Analysis of Spacetime and Its Contents*. Oxford: Oxford University Press.
Price, H. H. (1932), *Perception*. London: Methuen & Co.
Robinson, Howard. (1982), *Matter and Sense: A Critique of Contemporary Materialism*. London: Cambridge University Press.
Robinson, Howard. (1994), *Perception*. London: Routledge.
Russell, Bertrand. (1927), *The Analysis of Matter*. London: Kegan Paul, Trench, Trubner & Co.
Smithson, Robert. (2017), 'A new epistemic argument for idealism' Tyron Goldschmidt and Kenneth L. Pearce (eds), *Idealism: New Essays in Metaphysics*. Oxford: Oxford University Press, 17–33.
Strawson, Galen. (2008), *Real Materialism: and Other Essays*. Oxford: Clarendon Press.
Tegmark, Max. (2014), *Our Mathematical Universe: My Quest for the Ultimate Nature of Reality*. New York: Alfred A. Knopf.

CHAPTER 16

ELIMINATIVISM ABOUT CONSCIOUSNESS

ELIZABETH IRVINE AND MARK SPREVAK

16.1 Introduction

In this chapter, we examine a radical philosophical position about consciousness: eliminativism. Eliminativists claim that consciousness does not exist and/or that talk of consciousness should be eliminated from science. These are strong positions to take, and require serious defence. To evaluate these positions, the chapter is structured as follows. In Section 16.2 we introduce the difference between entity eliminativism and discourse eliminativism and outline the typical strategies used to support each. Section 16.3 provides a brief overview of the kinds of consciousness we refer to throughout the chapter. Section 16.4 focuses on entity eliminativist arguments about consciousness: Dennett's classic eliminativist argument (16.4.1); a rebooted version of Dennett's argument (16.4.2); and recent arguments for 'illusionism' (16.4.3). In Section 16.5, we examine discourse eliminativist arguments about consciousness: methodological arguments from scientific behaviourism (16.5.1); arguments based on the empirical accessibility of phenomenal consciousness (16.5.2); and a stronger version of discourse eliminativism aimed at both phenomenal and access consciousness (16.5.3). In Section 16.6, we offer a brief conclusion.

16.2 Eliminativism

If you meet an eliminativist, the first question to ask is, 'What do you want to eliminate: *entities* or *talk* about entities?' For any given X, an eliminativist might say either or both of:

1. Xs do not exist.
2. We should stop engaging in X-talk, using X-concepts, or other practices ostensibly associated with X in science.

We will call (1) *entity eliminativism* and (2) *discourse eliminativism*. Entity eliminativists claim that we should expel a specific entity from the catalogue of entities assumed to exist. This may be a matter of removing a particular individual from our ontology (e.g. Zeus), but it may also involve removing a property (e.g. being phlogisticated), an event (e.g. spontaneous generation), a kind (e.g. ghosts), or a process (e.g. extrasensory perception). In contrast, a discourse eliminativist seeks to rid science of certain ways of talking, thinking, and acting (e.g. talk about, and practices that attempt to investigate, gods, being phlogisticated, spontaneous generation, ghosts, or extrasensory perception).[1]

Entity and discourse eliminativism are distinct but obviously not unrelated positions. What we think regarding an entity's existence does not, and should not, float free from what we say, think, and do in science. However, the relationship between the two is not so tight that one form of eliminativism can be inferred from the other as a matter of course.[2] Someone might endorse one form of eliminativism but not the other. An entity eliminativist might do away with some entity (e.g. atoms) but decide to preserve talk, thought, and practices associated with that entity in science. For example, Mach claimed that atoms do not exist but he argued that physicists should continue to engage in atomic talk, thought, and action for their predictive and heuristic benefits: the atom 'exists only in our understanding, and has for us only the value of a *memoria technica* or formula' (Mach 1911: 49). Conversely, a discourse eliminativist might root out ways of talking, thinking, and acting from science but say that the entity underlying this rejected discourse nonetheless exists. In Section 16.5, we will see an example of this position with regard to scientific behaviourism's treatment of conscious experience.

Let us examine entity eliminativism and discourse eliminativism more closely.

Entity eliminativism is defined by how it diverges from realism and agnosticism. A realist says, 'Xs exist', an agnostic says, 'We are not in a position to know whether Xs exist or not', and an eliminativist says, 'Xs do not exist'. In order for an entity eliminativist to defend her position, she needs to have a genuine, not merely a verbal, disagreement with the realist and agnostic. To this end, the eliminativist needs to make assumptions

---

[1] In focusing on 'serious' science, the discourse eliminativist makes no claim about whether this or similar talk, thought, and practice should be eliminated from other aspects of human life. What might be unacceptable to serious science may be tolerated, or even welcomed, in popularisations of science, folk tales, religious practice, jokes, or science fiction. The boundary between 'serious' science and other aspects of human enquiry is not sharply defined. For the purposes of this chapter, we do not attempt to define it. We provisionally identify 'serious' science as work currently recognised as such by the scientific community, in contrast to, say, popular exposition of scientific research, adaptation of that scientific research for other ends, or training that is merely propaedeutic to conducting scientific research.

[2] Quine (1980) offered a bridge from discourse eliminativism to entity eliminativism with the quantificational criterion of ontological commitment. However, this bridge fails to link the two forms of eliminativism in a deductively certain way. It relies on numerous assumptions that are contentious in this context: assumptions about the aims of the scientific discourse, about the overriding importance of stating truth in science, and about the correct semantics for the discourse. Quine also only proposed his criterion for fundamental theories. Participants in this debate (realists and eliminativists about consciousness) are unlikely to agree about whether the theories in question are fundamental.

about what Xs are and those assumptions need to be shared with the realist and the agnostic. The realist, agnostic, and eliminativist should agree on what Xs *would be like if they were to exist*. What they disagree about is then whether Xs *do* exist. Consequently, an argument for entity eliminativism generally involves two ingredients. The first is some way to identify the subject matter under dispute that is acceptable to all sides (realist, agnostic, and eliminativist). This is often done by providing a *description* of the essential properties of the entity, but, as we will see in Section 16.4.2, that is not the only way to do it. The second ingredient is an argument to show that no such entity exists. If the entity is identified by description, the second step may involve showing that no entity satisfies this description. According to Mallon et al. (2009), this kind of argument was used to defend eliminativism about beliefs (and other propositional attitudes): first, claim that in order for something to be a belief, it must satisfy a certain description D (given in this case by folk psychology); second, argue that nothing satisfies description D (because folk psychology is false); third, since nothing satisfies D, conclude that beliefs do not exist.

In contrast to entity eliminativism, discourse eliminativism targets talk, thought, and behaviour in science. Let us say that the concept 'ding dong' refers to nanoscale, spherical, tentacled lifeforms. A discourse eliminativist about ding dongs says that scientists should stop talking, thinking, and pursuing research programmes about ding dongs. One motivation for this may be the conviction that there are no ding dongs (i.e. one is an entity eliminativist about them). But being an entity eliminativist is neither necessary nor sufficient for being a discourse eliminativist about them. One might think that ding dongs exist (or be agnostic about them) but argue that scientists should avoid 'ding dong' talk because it is unproductive, misleading, or otherwise unhelpful. Conversely, one might think that ding dongs do not exist but argue that 'ding dong' talk, thought, and practice is useful to science and should be preserved: perhaps the ding dong concept is a useful way to group lifeforms or encourages useful practices (looking for entities at certain spatial scales).

Arguments for discourse eliminativism typically consist in defending a negative and a positive thesis. The negative thesis aims to establish that the talk, concepts, and practices targeted for elimination are somehow unhelpful, damaging, misleading, or otherwise problematic. In the case of conscious experience, a discourse eliminativist might argue that discourse about conscious experience is too subjective, hard to verify, does not generalize well, does not pick out a natural kind, produces intractable disagreements, does not cohere with other scientific talk, or otherwise leads to a degenerative scientific research programme. However, even if these points land, they rarely suffice to motivate discourse eliminativism. Science seldom switches course unless a better alternative is available. The positive part of a discourse eliminativist's argument aims to show that an alternative way of talking, thinking, and acting is available. The discourse eliminativist argues that this proposed alternative discourse is, on balance, better for achieving our scientific goals than the one targeted for elimination. Diverse virtues may weigh in this decision, including purely epistemic virtues (e.g., telling the truth, not positing things that do not exist) but also predictive, pragmatic, theoretical, and cognitive virtues.

16.3 CONSCIOUSNESS

In this chapter, we make use of Block's distinction between access consciousness and phenomenal consciousness (Block 1990, 2007). 'Access consciousness' refers to the aspects of consciousness associated with information processing: storage of information in working memory, planning, reporting, control of action, decision making, and so on. 'Phenomenal consciousness' refers to the subjective feelings and experiences that conscious agents enjoy: the feel of silk, the taste of raspberries, the sounds of birds singing, and so on. The latter is the 'feel-y', subjective, qualitative, what-it-is-like-ness, 'from the inside' aspect of consciousness. We use the term 'qualia' to refer to this subjective feeling.[3] Following Frankish (2016a), we define 'experience' in a purely functional way: mental states that are the direct output of the sensory system. This means that we do not assume that experience necessarily involves phenomenal consciousness.[4]

This chapter focuses on eliminativism about *phenomenal consciousness*. Access consciousness will make an appearance in the final section (16.5.3). For the purposes of this chapter, we do not presuppose anything about the relationship between access and phenomenal consciousness, although some of the eliminativist arguments discussed below do take a stand on this.

One of the striking features of entity eliminativism about consciousness is that it is perceived as a philosophical position that is self-evidently wrong. Critics say that questioning the existence of phenomenal consciousness is impossible. Each of us knows, by introspection, that we have phenomenal consciousness—what is more, we know this in a way that is not open to rational doubt. Not even Descartes doubted the existence of his subjective experience. Yet the eliminativist does. Assessments of eliminativist claims have been correspondingly harsh. Frances writes, 'I assume that eliminativism about feelings really is crazy' (Frances 2008: 241). Searle, 'Surely no sane person could deny the existence of feelings' (Searle 1997). Strawson says that eliminativists 'seem to be out of their minds', their position is 'crazy, in a distinctively philosophical way' (Strawson 1994: 101). Chalmers, 'This is the sort of thing that can only be done by a philosopher, or by someone else tying themselves in intellectual knots!' (Chalmers 1996: 188). How can anyone deny such a self-evident truth about our mental life? (As we will see in Section 16.4, entity eliminativism is typically combined with an attack against the reliability of our introspective access.)

The discourse eliminativist about phenomenal consciousness faces a similar, though perhaps not quite so daunting, challenge. Discourse eliminativists identify problems with a scientific discourse and seek to offer a better alternative. The challenge faced by a discourse eliminativist about phenomenal consciousness is that phenomenal consciousness

---

[3] This is how Dennett uses 'qualia' but departs from the usage of some authors who take 'qualia' to refer to non-representational aspects of conscious experience.

[4] Other authors (including Block) equate phenomenal consciousness with experience. We adopt Frankish's usage here for (slightly better) ease of exposition.

appears to be an overwhelmingly important part of our mental life. Humans care about their phenomenal feelings: about the feelings that accompany eating their favourite dish, scoring a winning goal, being punched in the kidneys, or having their toes tickled. These feelings play a valuable, although hard to specify, role in our cognitive economy. For this reason, it seems that *some* reference to phenomenal consciousness should be made by any scientific psychology. A science that *never* talked about phenomenal consciousness would be incomplete. Even if phenomenal feelings do not exist (as an entity eliminativist says), science should still talk about phenomenal consciousness in order to explain why we (falsely, according to the entity eliminativist) take ourselves to be motivated by such feelings. Eliminating talk of phenomenal consciousness appears to ignore a significant aspect of human mental life and amounts to a failure of ambition for scientific psychology.

16.4. Entity Eliminativism about Consciousness

In this section, we examine three entity eliminativist arguments about phenomenal consciousness. The first is Dennett's (1988) 'Quining qualia' argument. The second is a rebooted version of Dennett's argument that aims to avoid the standard objection to that argument (namely, that Dennett mis-characterizes phenomenal consciousness). The third is the recent research project of 'illusionism', which is related to Dennett's 'Quining qualia' argument but motivated on somewhat different grounds.

16.4.1 Dennett's Eliminativism about Qualia

Dennett's 'Quining qualia' paper looks, at least at first glance, like a classic entity eliminativist argument: it describes the essential properties of the alleged entity; shows that nothing satisfies this description; and concludes on this basis that no such entity exists. The description that Dennett gives of phenomenal consciousness ('qualia') is that it is ineffable (not describable in words), intrinsic (non-relational), private (no inter-personal comparisons are possible), and directly accessible (via direct acquaintance). The final property is related to the idea that we have privileged, incorrigible, or infallible access to qualia. Dennett argues that no entity satisfies this description. As a result, 'Far better, tactically, to declare that there simply are no qualia at all' (Dennett 1988: 44).

Dennett uses a number of 'intuition pumps' to get to this conclusion, which we summarize here.

First, it is plausible that how things subjectively feel is bound up with how you evaluate, or are able to categorize or discriminate between, your experiences. Someone's first taste of a particular wine may be different to how it tastes to them after having become a wine aficionado. At first, my taste of wine was bound up with judgements of yukkiness and an inability to easily tell one wine from another. My current taste of wine is bound up with gustatory enjoyment and an ability to finely discriminate between different wines. This suggests that qualia are not intrinsic properties of experience: that the taste of this specific wine does not have a particular qualitative feeling (quale) for me independently of how I evaluate or categorize it. Instead, the way that wine (and other things) consciously tastes to me is at least partly determined by relational properties, such as whether I like it, and whether I can tell a Pinot Grigio from a Chardonnay.

This also puts pressure on qualia being directly accessible: it looks like I can't tell very much about my qualia from introspection. Say that as you get older, you start liking strong red wine more. One possibility is that your sensory organs have changed, making strong reds taste different and more pleasurable compared to how they used to. On this scenario, you now have different qualitative feelings (more pleasant ones) on tasting strong reds than you had before. Another possibility is that your sensory organs have stayed the same but your likings for specific experiences have changed. You have roughly the same conscious feelings but now you like those feelings more. On the first scenario, your qualia change; on the second scenario, your qualia stay the same. Dennett puts it to us that we would not be able to tell, merely from introspection, which scenario we are in. Yet this should be easy to do if we really had direct (or infallible or incorrigible) access to our qualia.

With respect to the putative ineffability and privacy of qualia, Dennett refers to Wittgensteinian arguments that render entirely private and incommunicable states senseless. Dennett goes on to argue that there is a way in which experiences are practically ineffable and private, just not in the 'special' way intended by qualiaphiles. Imagine two AI systems that learn about their environment in a fairly unsupervised manner and so go on to develop different internal systems of categorizing colour (adapted from Sloman and Chrisley 2003). These two systems will end up with some states that are (at least to some degree) private and ineffable. One system's 'blue' states will be somewhat different to the other system's 'blue' states just in virtue of the internal differences in the systems (e.g. the 'blue' states of each system will be triggered by a slightly different range of hues). In the same way, humans can be in distinct (practically) ineffable and private states because of idiosyncrasies in their perceptual and cognitive processing. Some of these differences one may discover empirically (e.g. that you and I disagree about whether a particular paint chip is blue), and so we can make our experience more 'effable', and less private. Dennett's point is that ineffability and privacy of experience only amounts to this: practical and graded difficulties in assessing which internal state we are in, not essential properties of our experience.

In light of Dennett's considerations, it looks like our supposedly phenomenal experiences do not satisfy the description associated with them: there is nothing ineffable, intrinsic, private, and directly accessible to an experiencer that determines the way that things (phenomenally) seem to them. Whatever produces our judgements and reports about phenomenal experience, it is not an entity of the hypothesized kind. Qualia, as characterized by Dennett's description, do not exist.

A popular response to Dennett is to say that qualia were not successfully characterized by his description. This effectively undermines his argument at the first step. Perhaps partly for this reason, qualiaphiles nowadays tend to favour a minimalistic characterization of qualia. Qualia need only have a *phenomenal character* (a 'what-is-it-like-ness' or subjective feel) (Carruthers 2000; Kind 2001; Levine 2001; Tye 2002). They need not be intrinsic, private, ineffable, or directly accessible properties of experience. Frankish (2012) describes this as the move from 'classic qualia' to 'diet qualia'.[5] Classic qualia are controversial entities; diet qualia are not:

> Philosophers often use the term 'qualia' to refer to the introspectively accessible properties of experiences that characterize what it is like to have them. In this standard, broad sense of the term, it is very difficult to deny that there are qualia. There is another, more restricted use of the term 'qualia', under which qualia are intrinsic, introspectively accessible, nonrepresentational qualities of experiences. In my view, there are no qualia, conceived of in this way. They are a philosophical myth. (Tye 2002: 447)

Dennett's intention is to eliminate *both* classic qualia and diet qualia.[6] His argument, however, does not seem to engage with diet qualia: his description fails to pick out what qualiaphiles have in mind here.[7] In the next section, we rework Dennett's eliminativist argument to explicitly target diet qualia.

16.4.2 'Quining Qualia' Rebooted

Dennett's 'Quining qualia' argument attempted to identify qualia by description. Once we switch to diet qualia, appeal to description appears to be of questionable use as nothing identifies qualia apart from their (contested) phenomenal feel. So, rather than attempt to identify the target for elimination (or realism) by description, we should identify it in some other way.

A common strategy is to identify qualia by a kind of ostension: ask one to consider specific examples of qualia and then generalize to the kind they have in common.[8] One

---

[5] Frankish (2016a) describes a similar distinction between *weak* and *strong* illusionism, and Levine (2001) describes a distinction between *modest* and *bold* qualophilia.

[6] 'Philosophers have adopted various names for the things in the beholder (or properties of the beholder) that have been supposed to provide a safe home for the colors and the rest of the properties that have been banished from the "external" world by the triumphs of physics: "raw feels," "sensa," "phenomenal qualities," "intrinsic properties of conscious experiences," "the qualitative content of mental states," and, of course, "qualia," the term I will use. There are subtle differences in how these terms have been defined, but I'm going to ride roughshod over them. In the previous chapter I seemed to be denying that there are any such properties, and for once what seems so is so. I am denying that there are any such properties' (Dennett 1991: 372).

[7] Although we will not consider his reasoning here, Frankish (2012) argues that the concepts of diet qualia and classic qualia are not, on closer inspection, distinct and so Dennett's 'Quining qualia' argument works against both.

[8] The specific examples cited in Chalmers (1996: ch 1) appear to play this role. Schwitzgebel (2016) outlines a similar strategy, although with the commitment that there should be a 'single obvious

identifies the subject matter at issue by asking one's interlocutor to consider those of her experiences that allegedly have qualia (consider the feel of silk, . . .), drawing her attention to the supposedly felt aspects of these experiences, and saying *more aspects of mental life of this kind*. A set of examples, and how they are relevantly similar, are thus intended to fix the meaning of 'qualia'. The realist and eliminativist may agree on this strategy: they may agree on the set of examples and how we take them to be similar (for example, they may have no difficulty in generalizing to new cases). What the realist and eliminativist disagree about is whether the phenomenal feelings that *appear* to be present in these cases *really are* present. The realist claims that the experiences have, or instantiate, a property, 'what-it-is-like-ness', which should be added to our ontology. The 'what-it-is-like-ness' or phenomenal character is a real property of experience—as real as anything. The realist says that explaining what this phenomenal property is, how it comes about, and how it relates to physical and neural properties is the job of a theory of consciousness. In contrast, the entity eliminativist says that no such property exists (or is instantiated in the relevant cases). According to her, the examples are, in a sense, deceptive: they *appear* to show instantiation of a property, but that appearance is wrong. There is no such property of experience.

An entity eliminativist denies the existence of qualia, but she does not deny the existence of many of our judgements, beliefs, and desires about qualia. This allows her to agree with much of what a realist says about experience. She can agree that we *believe* that our experience has qualia, that it is hard for us to *doubt* that our experience has qualia, and that our beliefs and judgements *motivate* us to act in appropriate ways. Nevertheless, the eliminativist says, these beliefs and judgements are false. They are comparable to the beliefs and judgements that the ancient Greeks held about Zeus: deeply held and capable of motivating action, but fundamentally mistaken. We should no more take on the project of explaining what qualia are, how they arise, and how they relate to physical properties than we should for Zeus.

We divide the rebooted version of Dennett's argument into two steps. The first step aims to defend a sceptical claim: that we do not know which (diet) quale our current experience instantiates. This claim goes beyond a mere failure of infallibility or incorrigibility. The claim is that we lack *any knowledge at all* about which quale our current experience instantiates. The second step leverages this epistemic claim to argue for qualia eliminativism. If the instantiation of one quale rather than another is unknowable, then instantiation of a quale is a difference that would make no difference to the world; on that basis, qualia should be eliminated.

---

folk-psychological concept or category that matches the positive and negative examples'. (We do not think that either the realist or eliminativist need admit this.) Nida-Rümelin (2016: sect 3) outlines a similar strategy to identify 'experiential' properties, although she argues that if this strategy works, there can be no possibility of failure to refer so eliminativism is precluded. The general strategy of reference fixing by ostending examples from a single kind follows roughly the model used by a causal theory of the reference, although in the case of qualia, the subject's relationship to the examples need not be causal (e.g., it could be some sort of non-causal acquaintance relation).

As a starting point, notice that it is sometimes hard to tell which quale your current experience instantiates. Slow, subtle changes in experience may leave one uncertain about which subjective feeling you have—is the quale you have on looking at an Yves Klein blue painting now the same as the one you had a minute ago? Examples like this may present us with epistemically 'bad' cases of qualia knowledge: situations where for some reason we are unsure about which quale we have. Showing that there are some 'bad' cases, however, does not show that we can never know which quale we have.[9]

Focus instead on the apparently 'good' cases of qualia knowledge: cases where we appear to know whether our qualia have changed or are the same. Such cases often involve sudden or dramatic changes in one's experience. If the Yves Klein painting facing you were suddenly exchanged for a bright yellow painting, you would know, not only that the painting had changed, but also that your qualia had changed (perhaps you would regard the latter as evidence for the former). Dramatic changes in experience seem to provide good cases of qualia knowledge. However, even in these 'good' cases, there are reasons to think that one lacks knowledge about which quale one has.

Suppose that while Lara is asleep a neurosurgeon operates on her brain. On waking, she finds that the world looks different: objects that before looked blue now look yellow. No one else notices the change, so Lara concludes that something must have happened to her. *Prima facie*, Lara appears to have justification to think that her qualia have changed. However, the change she notices is compatible with two hypotheses:

(Q) Lara's qualia have changed from those she had yesterday.

(R) Lara's qualia remain the same but her memories of her past experiences have changed.

Lara's post-surgery experiences are consistent with either hypothesis Q or R. On the basis of introspection, Lara knows that things 'look different', but she cannot tell what is responsible: a change in her memory, a change in her qualia, or some combination of both. The problem is more serious than a lack of certainty or failure of infallibility. Q and R appear to be *equally well supported* by Lara's introspective evidence. Introspection alone appears to give her *no knowledge at all* about whether her qualia have changed.

Lara, however, has access to sources of knowledge other than introspection. What if she were to look at changes in her brain? For the sake of argument, put Lara into the strongest possible epistemic position with regard to the physical state of her brain. Suppose she has perfect neuroscientific knowledge and full scans of her brain before and after surgery. Furthermore, suppose (unrealistically, but helpfully for Lara) that there is a clear separation in the neural basis of Lara's sensory systems and the neural

---

[9] It is unfortunate that many of Dennett's intuition pumps involve subtle and slow changes in qualia. This has focused attention on failures of infallibility and incorrigibility in 'bad cases'. The more worrisome lesson from his argument is that there is no knowledge of qualia even in supposedly 'good' cases.

basis of her memory systems, and that this is known to her. She can then reason as follows:

> If the brain scans reveal that the neural change affected only my sensory systems and left my memory systems intact, I have reason to favour Q over R because only the systems that support my current experience, and not those that support my memories of past experiences, have been affected. Conversely, if the scans reveal that the neural change affected only my memory systems and left my sensory systems intact, then I have reason to favour R over Q because only the systems that support my memories, and not those that support my current experience, have been affected.

Thus it seems that empirical evidence can do for Lara what introspection alone cannot: it can give her reason to favour Q over R. (Of course, it is possible that both Lara's sensory and memory systems have been affected by the surgery, but we will ignore this possibility as it would not help her.)

The problem is that the brain scans only provide Lara with information about changes to her *neural events*. This can help her in deciding between Q and R only if she knows *where* in the causal chain of those neural events her qualia experience is instantiated. Lara, however, does not know this, and by hypothesis it is not part of the (thin, minimal) concept of diet qualia. Consider two competing hypotheses about where her qualia experience occurs in the causal order of the neural events:

1. Sensation → *qualia experience* → memory access
2. Sensation → memory access → *qualia experience*

Lara's reasoning assumed something like (1) is true: her qualia are instantiated *after* sensation but *before* memory access. Memory access is causally downstream from the qualia experience. This suggests that any surgery-induced change to the neural basis of her memory system should have a different effect on her qualia experience to any surgery-induced change to the neural basis of her sensory system: one affects something after her qualia experience, the other affects something before. If Lara were to discover that the neural change exclusively targeted her memory system, that suggests her current qualia experience has been unaffected, because the causal antecedents of that experience would be identical to what they were yesterday. However, if she discovers a neural change to her sensory system (e.g., that sensory channels that carry colour information have been swapped), and no change to the neural basis of her memory system, that suggests that a change to her sensation and hence to her current experience.

Unfortunately, this justification vanishes if (2) were true. On (2), Lara's qualia experience is causally downstream from both her sensation and her memory access. A surgery-induced change to the neural basis of *either* system could then potentially affect her current qualia experience. A change to the neural basis of her memory could produce a change in her current qualia or a change in her memory of past experiences, or both. A change to the neural basis of her sensory system could produce a change in her current qualia or a change in the outputs of her memory systems, or both. The two factors about which Lara can detect change (the neural bases of her memory and sensation) both lie causally upstream from her qualia experience, and so are confounded in any causal inference about that experience.

No one knows whether (1), (2), or any number of other proposals about the location of qualia in the causal order is correct. This is not a limitation of the scientific resources we supply Lara—a better scanner or more neuroscientific data would not help. Nor is it something with which the concept of diet qualia can help: that concept is silent about where qualia are instantiated in neural events.

One might attempt to remedy this by correlating Lara's introspective reports of qualia with her neural events to find out where among those events her qualia experience falls. However, we have already seen that there is no reason to trust Lara's introspective reports about her qualia (when they occur or when they change) in this context.[10] Thus, neither introspection, nor empirical knowledge, nor some combination of the two tells Lara which quale her current experience instantiates. Even in an apparently 'good' case, there is no reason to favour Q or R. Given that our own epistemic position is usually worse than Lara's, our own qualia may, for all we know, be changing without us noticing.[11]

This accounts for Step 1 of the argument. Step 2 says that if changes in one's qualia are unknowable (either by introspection or by methods available to science), then we should eliminate qualia from our ontology. The thought behind this is that Step 1 has shown that qualia are an extra 'wheel' that do not turn anything. Qualia have no discernible or characteristic effects on the world—for if they did, Lara could exploit those effects to detect changes in her qualia. A quale's effect on us is always confounded with that of other factors (such as memory). Therefore, affirming the existence of qualia as independent entities/properties in our ontology seems unmotivated. Like Wittgenstein's 'beetle',

> [This] thing in the box has no place in the language-game at all; not even as a something; for the box might even be empty—No, one can 'divide through' by the thing in the box; it cancels out, whatever it is.   (Wittgenstein 1958: sect 293)

It is open to a qualia realist to insist that qualia should still be included in our ontology irrespective of our inability to independently track them (similarly, a beetle realist could insist that there really is a beetle in the box). But the realist's position now begins to look unmotivated. The eliminativist has grounds, in contrast, to deny that qualia exist. Qualia do not earn their ontological keep. As inessential cruft, they should be eliminated.

---

[10] Other problems with such efforts are described in Section 16.5.2.
[11] Dennett (2005: ch 4) presents a similar argument for eliminating qualia using the phenomenon of change blindness, which again relies on cross-time comparisons.

Unlike Dennett's original argument, the rebooted argument does not rely on the assumption that qualia are intrinsic, private, ineffable, or directly accessible. Before closing, we wish to flag two problems with the rebooted argument.

First, one might wonder why, even if the argument is correct, it nevertheless still *seems* to us that qualia exist. This 'seeming' does not go away even if one accepts the eliminativist's conclusion. On this basis, one might press for a residual role for qualia that provides more than an eliminativist would allow: more than merely being associated with a set of dispositions to make judgements, or with having a set of beliefs about qualia (both compatible with those judgements and beliefs being false). Our relationship to qualia appears to be more primitive than this. It *seems* to us that our experiences have qualia and this 'seeming' is the evidence for our beliefs about qualia. How can this impression, this pre-doxastic 'seeming', be produced? One might tell a mechanistic and adaptationist story about how humans arrive at their false beliefs about qualia (Dennett 1991; Humphrey 1992). But what mechanistic story can be told that explains the production of *seemings* that generate and appear to confirm these beliefs? This is the 'illusion problem', discussed in Section 16.4.3, and it remains an unsolved challenge for eliminativists.

Second, one might object to the qualia scepticism of Step 1. Step 1 relies on questioning the reliability of memory-based comparisons. A realist might, however, concede that Lara does not know whether a quale she has today is the same as one she had yesterday (perhaps because of confounds with memory), but deny that she lacks *any knowledge at all* of which quale she currently has. Imagine looking out on a mountain scene with green grass, grey rock, and blue sky. Multiple qualia are instantiated in your current experience: *what-it-is-like to see green, what-it-is-like to see grey, what-it-is-like to see blue*, and so on. You can tell the difference between these qualia (you can make similarity judgements, detect that there are many qualia instantiated versus a few, distinguish between your visual, auditory, and proprioceptive qualia, and so on). None of these judgements appear to rely on memory comparisons. Within the domain of current experience, therefore, you appear to have *some* knowledge about which qualia your experience instantiates. But then, why think that qualia are wheels that turn nothing or are always confounded with memory in their effect on you?

16.4.3 The Illusionist Movement

Recently, interest in eliminativist approaches to phenomenal aspects of consciousness has been rekindled by Frankish, in particular in a special issue of the *Journal of Consciousness Studies*. Frankish outlines 'illusionism' as the view that experiences have no phenomenal properties and that our phenomenal feelings are 'illusory'. We think we have experiences with phenomenal properties, but in fact we do not. Illusionism is a form of entity eliminativism about phenomenal consciousness even if the label 'eliminativism' is avoided for rhetorical reasons. It is motivated somewhat differently to

Dennett's entity eliminativism, and has a slightly different focus, so is worth discussion in its own right.[12]

First, illusionism is partly motivated by taking seriously the idea that phenomenal properties, and phenomenal consciousness, cannot be accounted for scientifically. Illusionism is seen as a way out of this problem. Second (and relatedly), the reasons for favouring illusionism are mainly rather general, theoretical reasons. The theoretical virtue of simplicity, or conservativism, suggests that the fewer entities/properties the better. Since illusionism gets rid of the metaphysically and epistemically problematic phenomenal properties, illusionism is better than alternative realist positions. Third, illusionism is often argued to be a research programme rather than a set of worked-out claims, and that this research programme is worth pursuing more than its alternatives. As we will see, illusionism comes with a range of difficult open questions.

Illusionism follows a slightly different tack to the typical argument for entity eliminativism described in Section 16.2. The first step is supposed to be to identify the contested entity/property in a way that can be generally accepted. This is not straightforward for phenomenal properties (see discussion in both this section and the preceding one). Second, the arguments motivating illusionism are not direct arguments to the effect that phenomenal properties, as described, do not exist; the position is largely motivated on other grounds (e.g. theoretical simplicity). The third step of the classic argument is to conclude that phenomenal properties do not exist. This is also concluded by some proponents of illusionism, but one could arguably also treat illusionism as a promising research programme without committing to this conclusion in advance.

Challenges to illusionism come in roughly three forms (the first two roughly track two of the steps in Section 16.2).

First, one might argue that it is neither obvious nor universally accepted what phenomenal consciousness is, or what phenomenal properties are, such that a proposal to eliminate them is comprehensible. Mandik (2016) states that 'phenomenal' is a technical (not folk) term, but one that is not clearly defined. As such, both eliminativist and realist talk about 'phenomenality' is unwarranted; in neither case is there a clear target to be eliminativist or realist about. Schwitzgebel (2016) tries to provide a minimal 'definition by example' that is not committed to any particular (troublesome) metaphysical or epistemic commitments, but as Frankish (2016b) points out, this is not substantive enough to sway the debate one way or the other.

Second, one might reject some of the main theoretical motivations for thinking that illusionism is the best or most reasonable philosophical position available. For example, Balog (2016) defends the phenomenal concept strategy, which preserves realism about

---

[12] Dennett-style eliminativism treats our ontological commitment to phenomenal consciousness as a theoretical mistake: there is nothing that satisfies the description of qualia, or qualia are ontologically inert and therefore it is safe to eliminate them. Somewhat differently, one can see illusionism as treating our ontological commitment to phenomenal consciousness as an introspective or perceptual mistake: we 'perceive' (via introspection) that our experience has phenomenal properties but it does not (hence the illusionism title). However, see Frankish (2016b) for ways of blurring the boundary between theoretical and introspective/perceptual mistakes.

phenomenal properties but concedes the existence of an explanatory gap. Prinz (2016) also defends a realist account of phenomenal properties, but one that tries to close the explanatory gap by providing neuroscientific explanation of at least some aspects of phenomenal consciousness. More generally, unless one is convinced that the theoretical virtues of illusionism (ontological parsimony, fit with existing non-phenomenal science, avoidance of the hard problem of consciousness) are superior to rival positions on consciousness, one is unlikely to be persuaded of illusionism.

Third, a cluster of worries arise around the 'illusion problem'. This concerns how to account for the alleged illusion of phenomenality. How can one have experiences that appear to have phenomenal properties without any phenomenal properties existing? Frankish (2016a) labels those physical properties (perhaps highly disjunctive and gerrymandered) that typically cause us to misrepresent ourselves as having phenomenal qualities, 'quasi-phenomenal properties'. Quasi-phenomenal redness is, for example, the physical property that typically causes (false) representations of phenomenal redness in introspection. According to Frankish, it is the tokening of these false introspective representations that is responsible for the illusion of phenomenal consciousness. He likens their effect on us to that of other resilient, mistaken perceptual representations such as those of impossible figures like the Penrose triangle (Humphrey 2011) or of colours as 'out there' in the world (Pereboom 2011).

The worry is how exactly this is supposed to work. It is not clear how a false representation caused by non-phenomenal properties could produce an appearance or 'seeming' of phenomenality. And as Prinz puts it, 'what is it about beliefs in experience that causes an illusion of experience?' (2016: 194). How is it that these representations cause illusions of subjective experience when other sorts of false representations do not? Related to this is a worry about how such false introspective representations get their content (Balog 2016). Representations of phenomenal feelings are not like other empty or non-referring representations ('unicorn', 'the largest prime'), which seem to get their content by being semantic composites from representations that do refer ('horse', 'horned', 'largest', 'prime'). Representations of phenomenal experience do not seem to decompose into representations of non-phenomenal properties at all.

Illusionism promises to get us away from the hard problem. It effectively eliminates the 'data' the hard problem asks us to explain—phenomenal feelings. Prinz (2016) argues that the illusion problem and the hard problem in fact face similar difficulties. In both cases, we need to identify what phenomenal properties are. In the hard problem, we need to explain how phenomenal properties come out of 'mere matter': how feelings arise in an apparently non-phenomenal system. In the illusion problem, we need to explain how (vivid!) illusions of phenomenality come about in entirely non-phenomenal systems. The challenge is to explain how an illusion of phenomenality (worthy of that name) arises in a non-phenomenal system. In both cases then, one needs to explain how something suitably like phenomenality arises from 'mere matter'. By the time one has done this, it might be just as easy to be a realist as an illusionist.

Frankish (2016a) briefly discusses the relationship between illusionism and discourse eliminativism: 'Do illusionists then recommend eliminating talk of phenomenal properties and phenomenal consciousness? Not necessarily' (2016a: 21). We agree. However, Frankish goes on to suggest that a commitment to discourse eliminativism can only be avoided by an illusionist if the phenomenal terms in science are redefined to refer to quasi-phenomenal properties. This seems to us neither necessary nor likely.

First, as Frankish says, it would depart from what these terms usually mean in other contexts, and so would invite confusion. Second, although we agree with Frankish that an illusionist scientific psychology is likely to need to talk about quasi-phenomenal properties, this could most naturally be done with a response-dependent characterization of those properties: refer to the physical properties that typically give rise to specific (false) phenomenal representations. Keeping track of quasi-phenomenal properties does not require changing the meaning of phenomenal terms in science. Third, as Frankish (2016b) says, it is no part of illusionism to say that the illusion of conscious experience is not important or useful to the experiencer. Graziano (2016) and Dennett (1991) argue that phenomenal consciousness plays an important and evolutionarily explicable role in our mental lives. It is reasonable to expect that scientific psychology would therefore want to study it. This study could be done while bracketing questions about the existence of phenomenal properties.[13] In a similar way, a scientific psychology that studied childhood dreams might talk about the role of representations of Santa Claus and unicorns in a child's cognitive economy without attempting to redefine those terms to refer to the disjunctive collection of physical properties that typically cause the child to token those false representations. Talk of phenomenal feels can remain in science, albeit with the disclaimer that the entities that allegedly stand behind this talk do not exist.

16.5 Discourse Eliminativism about Consciousness

We now turn to discourse eliminativism. Discourse eliminativism seeks to rid science of talk, concepts, and practices associated with phenomenal consciousness. In this section, we look at three discourse eliminativist arguments. The first is based on concerns raised by psychologists at the start of the twentieth century. The second is based on more contemporary concerns about how to study phenomenal consciousness independently of access consciousness and the mechanisms of reportability. The third is based on the worry that the concept of consciousness fails to pick out a scientifically usable category of phenomena.

16.5.1 Scientific Behaviourism

One of the goals of scientific psychology in the first half of the twentieth century was to redefine psychology, not as the study of the mind, but as the study of observable behaviour.

---

[13] Dennett's (1991) heterophenomenology provides one model for how an illusionist might do this.

Scientific behaviourists argued that scientific psychology should avoid talk of internal mental states, and in particular, talk of conscious states (Hull 1943; Skinner 1953; Watson 1913).

The rise of behaviourism in science was at least partly due to the perceived failure of an earlier attempt to pursue scientific psychology via use of introspection (Titchener 1899). The debate on the nature of imageless thought was held up as an example of how unproductive that research programme was. One side in the debate appealed to introspection to argue that all thoughts were analysable into images; the other used similar evidence to argue for the opposite conclusion. The disagreement was widely seen as impossible to resolve because the evidence from the two sides could not be compared in an unbiased way. By the mid-twentieth century, introspective methods were discredited and study of conscious experience in science largely abandoned (Humphrey 1951).

Scientific behaviourists sought to reform psychology in such a way as to avoid these methodological difficulties. The subject matter of scientific psychology should be publicly observable, publicly verifiable, or independently experimentally controllable events. Scientific psychology should eliminate talk of conscious experience and use of introspective methods. However, this did not mean that behaviourists thought that mental states, including states of phenomenal consciousness, did not exist: 'The objection to inner states is not that they do not exist, but that they are not relevant in a functional analysis' (Skinner 1953: 35).[14] Scientific behaviourists proposed an alternative way of talking, thinking, and acting that they argued was superior (in predictive, explanatory, and methodological terms) to a scientific psychology than one that appealed to, or attempted to study, conscious experience. Phenomenal consciousness, notwithstanding its ontological status, should be excluded from the realm of scientific psychology.

Positivistically-inclined philosophers argued, based on related considerations about verification and public accessibility, for various ontological and/or semantic lessons about conscious experience (Ryle 1949; and less clearly, Wittgenstein 1958). This prompted them to redefine mental state language in terms of behavioural dispositions and/or to eliminate qualitative conscious feelings from ontology. However, connecting these two lines of thought—one about utility to scientific practice and the other about ontology/semantics of ordinary language—requires accepting auxiliary claims about verifiability, the role of science, and the scope of our knowledge. Such links are widely questioned today. Many scientific behaviourists did not perceive such links at the time either and they argued for the elimination of talk of conscious experience from science based on pragmatic rather than ontological/semantic concerns.

16.5.2 Eliminativism via Independent Access

A different methodologically motivated form of discourse eliminativism about phenomenal consciousness is found among some consciousness researchers today. It stems

---

[14] See Hatfield (2003) for discussion of the views of other behaviourists.

from problems involved in trying to operationalize consciousness, or in finding ways to experimentally probe it.

One way of operationalizing consciousness is via some kind of reportability: a subject is conscious of a stimulus if and only if they report it or respond to it in some way. This sounds fairly straightforward, but there are problems with using reportability as a marker for the presence of phenomenal consciousness, rather than as a marker for the cognitive capacities associated with consciousness. These problems can motivate a position of discourse eliminativism about phenomenal consciousness.

First, consider the distinction between phenomenal and access consciousness. Phenomenal consciousness refers to felt conscious experiences, (diet) qualia, raw feels, and so on. Access consciousness refers to the aspects of consciousness that are associated with, or that can be used in, cognitive capacities like reasoning, action, verbal report, and so on. If we somehow knew that access and phenomenal consciousness were always bound together (no cognitive access without phenomenal consciousness and vice versa), then scientific ways of probing access consciousness would also function as scientific ways of probing phenomenal consciousness. That is, if phenomenal consciousness and access consciousness always go together, then probing access consciousness just is to probe phenomenal consciousness. In this case (absent any other problems), it would be perfectly legitimate for the term 'phenomenal consciousness' to figure in scientific discourse, because the phenomenon it picks out is scientifically accessible.

The problem is that it is not obvious whether the aspects of consciousness picked out by access and phenomenal consciousness are always co-present. According to Block (1995), there may be instantiations of phenomenal consciousness (raw feels) without any related cognitive access (ability to respond to or report about these raw feels). Block has outlined a number of examples where this might happen, including situations where subjects may have highly detailed and specific phenomenal experiences, but be unable to report the details of them (Sperling paradigm); cases of phenomenal consciousness of unattended items; and possibly cases of hemi-spatial neglect, where subjects do not appear to have access to phenomenal experiences from some part of their visual field (see Block 2007, 2011, 2014; Irvine 2011; Phillips 2011 for discussion). In most of these cases, there is evidence that subjects are at least processing sensory information that they are unable to report about. Block's claim is that there is a layer of untapped and unaccessed phenomenal consciousness present in these cases, in addition to whatever can be overtly reported or measured.

The lack of a way to probe the phenomenal aspect of consciousness independently of the accessibility aspect makes it difficult (or impossible) to scientifically assess these claims. It looks like any way of probing phenomenal consciousness requires that the experience have some measurable effect on the subject, possibly such that she can report it in some way. That is, accessing phenomenal consciousness relies on it being associated with some kind of cognitive function or capacity, therefore accessing phenomenal consciousness relies on it being associated with access consciousness. So, if an instance of phenomenal consciousness is not associated with access consciousness, then it looks as though we cannot tell if it is present or not. As Dehaene et al. (2006) note, whether participants in an experimental situation 'actually had a conscious phenomenal experience but no possibility of reporting it, does not seem to be, at this stage, a scientifically addressable question' (2006: 209).

Partly in response to this worry, Block, Lamme, and colleagues have argued for the possibility of *indirectly* investigating these purported instances of phenomenal consciousness without accessibility (Block 2011, 2014; Lamme 2006; Sligte et al. 2010). The idea here is to find some reasonable and measurable marker for the presence of consciousness in cases where phenomenal (and access) consciousness is clearly present (call this marker, M). The marker could be a particular neurophysiological signature (e.g., evidence of strong feed-forward processing), or a behavioural marker (e.g., ability to complete a particular type of task based on a set of visual stimuli). One then argues that if the special marker M is present in a subject, then regardless of whether the subject appears to be conscious of the test stimulus according to other standard measures of (access) consciousness, the subject is phenomenally conscious of that stimulus. That is, marker M's presence guarantees that a subject is phenomenally conscious of the test stimulus, even if they do not report seeing it, or cannot perform a range of actions that we usually associate with being conscious of a stimulus. The subject is phenomenally conscious of the stimulus without having cognitive access to that experience.

However, problems of interpretation abound here. Such behavioural and neurophysiological evidence could be taken as indirect evidence of phenomenal consciousness without access consciousness, but it could also be interpreted as evidence of unconscious processing (i.e., that we got the special marker M wrong), or of graded cognitive access and phenomenal consciousness of the stimulus (see replies to Block 2007). There are no direct scientific grounds on which to choose between these interpretations, because there is no direct way to assess whether marker M has anything to do with phenomenal consciousness.

One response to these discussions is to advocate discourse eliminativism about phenomenal consciousness. This is based on accepting that there is no direct way to probe phenomenal consciousness independently of cognitive access, and that there are no straightforward empirical ways of testing the claim that phenomenal consciousness can be present independently of cognitive access. In this case, the only aspect of consciousness that can definitely be probed scientifically is cognitive access, that is, access consciousness. In terms of scientific practice, the safest methodological route is to drop talk of phenomenal consciousness. Something like this position appears to be taken by a number of consciousness researchers (possibly including Dehaene).

This position is compatible with a range of claims about the ontology of phenomenal consciousness. One might say that phenomenal consciousness can (possibly or probably) exist without cognitive access, or be agnostic about this possibility. Alternatively, one might argue, with Cohen and Dennett (2011), that if a phenomenally conscious state is not accessible to scientific enquiry or to the subject having it (e.g., via some kind of report), then it is (evolutionarily, cognitively) implausible to call it a state of consciousness at all. In this case, if phenomenal consciousness exists, it always co-occurs with cognitive access.

16.5.3 Eliminativism via Identity Crisis

The argument for discourse eliminativism about phenomenal consciousness outlined above is based on a problem with *accessing* the phenomenon in question. Another kind of discourse eliminativism is based on the problem of *identifying* the phenomenon in question. For the sake of argument, ignore the problem of access raised in the previous section. Assume that phenomenal consciousness always co-occurs with access consciousness (perhaps for the reasons suggested by Cohen and Dennett), so that we can (for the minute) work just with the term 'consciousness' which will pick out both. Even with the problem of access out of the way, it is still questionable whether the concept of consciousness picks out a clear category of phenomena that is scientifically useful. If it does not, this provides a new motivation for discourse eliminativism about consciousness, and (by assumption) discourse eliminativism about phenomenal consciousness.

It was suggested above that there is a reasonably broad consensus that assessing the presence or absence of consciousness has something to do with reportability. Reportability can be realized in a number of ways, however, some of these are incompatible with each other (see Irvine 2013 for review). One 'objective measure' (taken from psychophysics) of consciousness relies on forced-choice tasks: for example, subjects are shown a masked stimulus for a short period of time and are 'forced' to choose between two response options (stimulus present/absent, stimulus was a square/circle). On the basis of their response, the subjects' underlying 'sensitivity' to the stimuli is calculated. The resulting objective measure of consciousness is highly stable and not subject to biases, but it is liberal, and often attributes consciousness of stimuli to subjects who explicitly deny having any. As a result, it is sometimes criticized as merely being a measure of sensory information processing and not of consciousness (e.g. Lau 2008). Despite being acknowledged as problematic, objective measures tend to be used in studies of consciousness because of their desirable properties as scientific measures (they are stable, bias-free).

In contrast, 'subjective measures' of consciousness use free reports or similar responses generated by experimental participants. The experimental methodology may be based around emphasizing careful use of introspection, assessing subject's confidence in their reports (sometimes using wagering), or just recording simple, untutored responses. Subjective measures get closer to what the subjects themselves acknowledge about their conscious experience. However, the precise ways that subjective measures are generated can have a significant impact on whether consciousness is deemed to be present or absent (or somewhere in between) (Sandberg et al. 2010; Timmermans and Cleeremans 2015). As scientific measures, they are highly unstable and subject to bias. They also regularly conflict with objective measures (except under artificial training conditions), and they are generally thought to be conservative (they normally do not capture all instances of conscious experience).

These difficulties reappear in debates about the neural correlate(s) or mechanism(s) of consciousness. Behavioural measures of consciousness are key in identifying these correlates and mechanisms. Roughly speaking, one chooses a behavioural measure; identifies the neural activity that occurs when the measure says that consciousness is present; and treats this as 'the' correlate or mechanism of consciousness. However, using different behavioural measures (unsurprisingly) leads to the identification of different neural correlates. The latter span all the way from 'early' neural activity for some liberal measures of consciousness (which may capture early sensory processing), to 'late' and attention-based neural activity for conservative measures (which may capture later cognitive uptake of the conscious experience) (see Irvine 2013). Without agreement about what counts as the 'right' behavioural measure of consciousness, there can be no agreement about what the neural correlates and mechanisms of consciousness are.

The plethora of measures and mechanisms of consciousness is not necessarily problematic in itself, but Irvine (2012) argues that there is no methodologically viable way of resolving disagreements between them when they conflict. Each measure has its pros and cons, but none is both scientifically adequate (i.e., fairly stable over repeated measures and bias-free) and fits with pre-theoretic commitments about consciousness. To choose one measure would be to (operationally) define consciousness by fiat, which would undermine the motivations for engaging in 'real' consciousness science in the first place. Furthermore, the mechanisms that correlate with these varied measures do not form a well-demarcated scientific kind, or even a well-demarcated group of kinds. They have no more in common than any arbitrary group of mechanisms within perception and cognition. They range across sensory processing, attention, decision making, report, and meta-cognition.

This suggests a reason for eliminating talk of consciousness from science. There are a wide range of incompatible things that 'consciousness' could pick out, and no methodologically acceptable way of deciding between them. If a scientific concept is surrounded by such problems, then (if they are bad enough) that is motivation for eliminating the concept. These methodological problems are compounded by pragmatic ones. Given that it is unclear what 'consciousness' refers to, talk of consciousness generates unproductive debates and miscommunication; it blocks the generation of useful predictions and generalizations; and it promotes misapplications of research methodologies and heuristics. That is, there are negative practical consequences from continued use of the concept 'consciousness' in science.

There is also a better alternative. This alternative demands that researchers use terms that clearly demarcate the phenomena under study, potentially by referring to how they are experimentally operationalized. This could be done by splitting up phenomena previously grouped under the single heading 'consciousness' by how they are measured (e.g., forced-choice tasks, confidence ratings, or free report). Using these more specific terms avoids the problems above. By precisely specifying what the phenomena are and how they are measured, there is no ambiguity about which phenomenon is picked out. This would also make it possible to identify the neural mechanism that generates the phenomenon, make robust predictions and generalizations about the phenomenon, and avoid miscommunication.

As before, discourse eliminativism is not tied to entity eliminativism (for example, Irvine's (2012) position does not entail entity eliminativism of any sort). Discourse eliminativism is about which representations, concepts, methods, and practices are appropriate and useful to science. Whatever consciousness (access or phenomenal) is may still be out there, even if the concept of 'consciousness' is not a useful one for science.

16.6 Conclusion

In this chapter, we have reviewed a variety of arguments for entity and discourse eliminativism. Entity eliminativists deny the existence of phenomenal consciousness; discourse eliminativists deny the utility of talking about phenomenal (and perhaps access) consciousness in science.

Entity eliminativism can be defended in a number of ways. A standard method is to describe the entity in question, then show that nothing satisfies that definition (Section 16.4.1). This can be expanded to the method of using examples to fix the subject matter (Section 16.4.2). A third approach, taken by illusionists (Section 16.4.3), is to use a loose definition of the relevant entity/property, but argue that whatever this refers to, it is theoretically and metaphysically simpler and more productive to assume that the entity does not exist. A problem that faces entity eliminativists of all types is the 'illusion problem', a mirror image of the hard problem faced by realists, which requires an eliminativist to explain how something non-phenomenal can give rise to something that seems phenomenal.

Discourse eliminativism concerns the net benefit to science of various ways of talking, thinking, and acting. Classic scientific behaviourism focused on what could be measured in a public and 'observable' way, eradicating talk of mental states (Section 16.5.1). More recent scientific work on consciousness has tended to move away from discussion of phenomenal consciousness on the basis that it is not clear whether scientific methodology can probe it independently of the cognitive abilities associated with access consciousness (Section 16.5.2). An argument can also be made that the general concept of consciousness should be eliminated from scientific talk given the problems in clearly demarcating the phenomenon in question (Section 16.5.3). Eliminating discourse about phenomenal consciousness from science might seem to remove a key concept in explaining human behaviour. However, this is not necessarily the case: specific reports and judgements about phenomenal consciousness can still function in explanations, and as explanatory targets in their own right.[15]

---

[15] We would like to thank Uriah Kriegel and Tim Bayne for helpful comments on an earlier draft of this chapter.

References

Balog, K. (2016), 'Illusionism's discontent', *Journal of Consciousness Studies*, 23: 40–51.
Block, N. (1990), 'Consciousness and accessibility', *Behavioral and Brain Sciences*, 13: 596–8.
Block, N. (1995), 'On a confusion about a function of consciousness', *Behavioral and Brain Sciences*, 18: 227–47.
Block, N. (2007), 'Consciousness, accessibility, and the mesh between psychology and neuroscience', *Behavioral and Brain Sciences*, 30: 481–548.
Block, N. (2011), 'Perceptual consciousness overflows cognitive access', *Trends in Cognitive Sciences*, 15: 567–75.
Block, N. (2014), 'Rich conscious perception outside focal attention', *Trends in Cognitive Sciences*, 18: 445–7.
Carruthers, P. (2000), *Phenomenal Consciousness*. Cambridge: Cambridge University Press.
Chalmers, D. J. (1996), *The Conscious Mind*. Oxford: Oxford University Press.
Cohen, M. A., and Dennett, D. C. (2011), 'Consciousness cannot be separated from function', *Trends in Cognitive Sciences*, 15: 358–64.
Dehaene, S., Changeux, J.-P., Naccache, L., Sackur, J., and Sergent, C. (2006), 'Conscious, preconscious, and subliminal processing: A testable taxonomy', *Trends in Cognitive Sciences*, 10: 204–11.
Dennett, D. C. (1988), 'Quining qualia' in A. J. Marcel and E. Bisiach (eds), *Consciousness in Contemporary Science*. Oxford: Oxford University Press, 42–77.
Dennett, D. C. (1991), *Consciousness Explained*. Boston, MA: Little, Brown & Company.
Dennett, D. C. (2005), *Sweet Dreams: Philosophical Obstacles to a Science of Consciousness*. Cambridge, MA: MIT Press.
Frances, B. (2008), 'Live skeptical hypotheses' in J. Greco (ed.), *The Oxford Handbook of Skepticism*. Oxford: Oxford University Press, 225–44.
Frankish, K. (2012), 'Quining diet qualia', *Consciousness and Cognition*, 21: 667–76.
Frankish, K. (2016a), 'Illusionism as a theory of consciousness', *Journal of Consciousness Studies*, 23: 11–39.
Frankish, K. (2016b), 'Not disillusioned: Reply to commentators', *Journal of Consciousness Studies*, 23: 256–89.
Graziano, M. S. A. (2016), 'Consciousness engineered', *Journal of Consciousness Studies*, 23: 98–115.
Hatfield, G. (2003), 'Behaviourism and psychology' in T. Baldwin (ed.), *Cambridge History of Philosophy, 1870–1945*. Cambridge: Cambridge University Press:, 640–8.
Hull, C. L. (1943), *Principles of Behavior*. New York: Appleton-Century.
Humphrey, G. (1951), *Thinking*. London: Methuen.
Humphrey, N. (1992), *A History of the Mind: Evolution and the Birth of Consciousness*. New York: Simon; Schuster.
Humphrey, N. (2011), *Soul Dust: The Magic of Consciousness*. Princeton, NJ: Princeton University Press.
Irvine, E. (2011), 'Rich experience and sensory memory', *Philosophical Psychology*, 24: 159–76.
Irvine, E. (2012), *Consciousness as a Scientific Concept: A Philosophy of Science Perspective*. Dordrecht: Springer.
Irvine, E. (2013), 'Measures of consciousness', *Philosophy Compass*, 8: 285–97.
Kind, A. (2001), 'Qualia realism', *Philosophical Studies*, 104: 143–62.

Lamme, V. A. (2006), 'Towards a true neural stance on consciousness', *Trends in Cognitive Sciences*, 10: 494–501.
Lau, H. (2008), 'Are we studying consciousness yet?' in L. Weiskrantz and M. Davies (eds), *Frontiers Of Consciousness*. Oxford: Oxford University Press, 245–58.
Levine, J. (2001), *Purple Haze: The Puzzle of Consciousness*. Oxford: Oxford University Press.
Mach, E. (1911), *The History and Root of the Principle of Conservation of Energy*. Chicago, IL: Open Court.
Mallon, R., Machery, E., Nichols, S., and Stich, S. P. (2009), 'Against arguments from reference', *Philosophy and Phenomenological Research*, 79: 332–56.
Mandik, P. (2016), 'Meta-illusionism and qualia quietism', *Journal of Consciousness Studies*, 23: 140–8.
Nida-Rümelin, M. (2016), 'The illusion of illusionism', *Journal of Consciousness Studies*, 23: 160–71.
Pereboom, D. (2011), *Consciousness and the Prospects of Physicalism*. Oxford: Oxford University Press.
Phillips, I. (2011), 'Perception and iconic memory', *Mind and Language*, 26: 381–411.
Prinz, J. (2016), 'Against illusionism', *Journal of Consciousness Studies*, 23: 186–96.
Quine, W. V. O. (1980), 'On what there is' in W. V. O. Quine, *From a Logical Point of View*. Cambridge, MA: Harvard University Press, 1–19.
Ryle, G. (1949), *The Concept of Mind*. London: Hutchinson.
Sandberg, K., Timmermans, B., Overgaard, M., and Cleeremans, A. (2010), 'Measuring consciousness: Is one measure better than the other?', *Consciousness and Cognition*, 19: 1069–78.
Schwitzgebel, E. (2016), 'Phenomenal consciousness, defined and defended as innocently as I can manage', *Journal of Consciousness Studies*, 23: 224–35.
Searle, J. R. (1997), *The Mystery of Consciousness*. London: Granta Books.
Skinner, B. F. (1953), *Science and Human Behavior*. New York: Macmillan.
Sligte, I. G., Vandenbroucke, A. R., Scholte, H. S., and Lamme, V. A. (2010), 'Detailed sensory memory, sloppy working memory', *Frontiers in Psychology*, 1: 175.
Sloman, A. and Chrisley, R. (2003), 'Virtual machines and consciousness', *Journal of Consciousness Studies*, 10: 113–72.
Strawson, G. (1994), *Mental Reality*. Cambridge, MA: MIT Press.
Timmermans, B. and Cleeremans, A. (2015), 'How can we measure awareness? An overview of current methods' in M. Overgaard (ed.), *Behavioural Methods in Consciousness Research*. Oxford: Oxford University Press, 21–46.
Titchener, E. B. (1899), *A Primer of Psychology*. New York: Macmillan.
Tye, M. (2002), 'Visual qualia and visual content revisited' in D. J. Chalmers (ed.), *Philosophy of Mind: Classical and Contemporary Readings*. Oxford: Oxford University Press, 447–56.
Watson, J. (1913), 'Psychology as a behaviorist views it', *Psychological Review*, 20: 158–77.
Wittgenstein, L. (1958), *Philosophical Investigations*, 2nd edn. Oxford: Blackwell.

CHAPTER 17

A PRIORI PHYSICALISM

FRANK JACKSON

17.1 INTRODUCTION: THE HISTORICAL BACKGROUND

THERE are very close connections between what goes on in our brains and what goes on in our minds. One way to explain the very close connections is to identify mental states with brain states, as is done in the mind–brain identity theory. Since the late 1950s, this has been a prominent version of materialism, championed by, for instance, Jack Smart, David Armstrong, and David Lewis.[1] These supporters made a point of insisting that the brain states that they held to be identical with mental states were brain states as conceived of in the physical sciences. Their view was not a kind of dual attribute position according to which mental states are brain states with 'extra' properties, where the extra properties are typically invoked to explain phenomenal consciousness.[2] To mark this, the mind–brain identity theorists sometimes called their view physicalism: mental states are brain states with only physical properties, where roughly—we will discuss this in more detail shortly—a physical property is a property that has a place in the account the physical sciences give of what our world is like, where the physical sciences are physics, chemistry, biology, neuroscience, and the like.[3]

However, a 'no extra properties' view of the mind need not be tied to the identity theory. Any theory of mind that insists that a complete account of the mind can be given in terms of physical properties alone can be thought of as a species of physicalism—maybe it also holds that mental states are brain states, or maybe it holds that mental states are functional states realized by brain states (in creatures like us), or maybe it has some

---

[1] Smart (1959), Lewis (1966), Armstrong (1968).
[2] For a view of this kind, see, e. g., Campbell (1971).
[3] Sometimes a physical property is specified in terms of having a place in physics, but we will understand the notion in the more inclusive way.

other account altogether of mental states. This is what we will mean by physicalism in this chapter, and is what is typically meant by physicalism these days.

17.2 FROM METAPHYSICS TO A PRIORI ENTAILMENT

Physicalism as just specified is a thesis in metaphysics: the nature of the mind and its states are such that we need no more than the physical properties to give a complete account of them. However, according to a priori physicalism, this thesis in metaphysics implies a thesis about a priori entailment. If the thesis in metaphysics is true, then a sufficiently rich account of a subject—you, me, or…—given in physical terms a priori entails how that subject is mentally. Here are two illustrative analogies. Density is mass divided by volume. That is a thesis in metaphysics about the nature of density. However, it is also true that facts about mass and volume a priori entail facts about density—or, in other words, facts about density can be deduced from facts about mass and volume. Here is our second illustration. To be the tallest person in one's class is to be taller than anyone else in one's class. That is a thesis in metaphysics about the property of being the tallest in one's class. However, it is also true that facts about the relative heights of people in a class a priori entail who is the tallest person in that class; one can deduce who is the tallest from enough information about relative heights (provided the information includes that it is complete information about the heights of the people in the class). As it is for density and being the tallest, so it is for the mind, is the thought of a priori physicalists. More precisely: a priori physicalists hold the *conjunction* of (i) physicalism, and (ii) physicalism can only be true if the way things are physically a priori entails the way things are mentally. I highlight this because some who are not physicalists also hold (ii), and are not physicalists partly because they are convinced, for one reason or another, that the way things are mentally cannot be deduced from the way things are physically.[4]

This can make things difficult for physicalists. Many find a functionalist analysis of belief and desire plausible. Belief and desire are states defined by their roles in carrying putative information about the world and in influencing our movements with respect to that world, respectively. If this or anything along these lines is right, we can see, broadly speaking, how the physical way things are might a priori entail the belief-desire way things are. It is plausible that enough detail about a subject's physical make up can enable the deduction of how that subject does and would interact with the environment and of the putative information its states carry. The thought is that the situation with belief and desire is akin to that with, for example, thermostats, while being much more complicated. It is plausible that a detailed account of the physical workings of a refrigerator

---

[4] Examples are Chalmers (1996) and a past temporal part of Jackson (1982).

that reveals, first, how a device inside it is causally sensitive to changes in the internal temperature of the refrigerator in ways that turn the refrigerator's motor on and off, and, second, that it does this in a manner that controls the temperature inside the refrigerator, would allow one to deduce that the refrigerator has a thermostat. The situation is, however, very different for mental states especially associated with consciousness, states with a phenomenology—pains, things looking bright red to one, pangs of hunger, and so on. This is because there are appealing although, as is par for the course in philosophy, controversial arguments directed to the conclusion that it is impossible to deduce the nature of conscious experiences like these from the physical account of how we and our world are.[5] This has been a major factor in leading many physicalists to argue that they are not committed to the a priori entailment thesis, as we will call it. These physicalists hold that although the a priori entailment of the mental by the physical may be a sufficient condition for the truth of physicalism, it is not a necessary condition for the truth of physicalism and, moreover, that the thesis is in fact false. These physicalists call their view a posteriori physicalism.

Why do some physicalists want to make things difficult for themselves by embracing a priori physicalism; why do they believe that a posteriori physicalism is not an option? This is the topic of this chapter. As we will see, there are a number of reasons that have or might be given.

We start by saying something about what is, or ought to be, meant by a physical property in these discussions. We need this as background. Moreover, one reason for favouring a priori physicalism arises more or less directly from a consideration of this issue, as we will shortly see.

17.3 WHAT IS A PHYSICAL PROPERTY?

It has long been appreciated that physicalists need to explain what they mean by physical properties; it is, after all, the notion they appeal to in distancing their view from dual attribute views of the mind, as we noted earlier. Unfortunately for our purposes, there is much debate about how the explanation should go. It is in fact a topic for a chapter in its own right. What follows is one way of looking at the question (obviously, it is the way I favour). I think it is, implicitly or explicitly, what many physicalists have had in mind when they talk of physical properties.

In spelling it out, we start from some common ground among physicalists, be they a priori or a posteriori physicalists. The common ground is that creatures with minds are made out of non-minds. Every creature with a psychology is made of bits that lack a psychology. The neurons, cells, veins, organs, bones, blood, etc. out of which we are

---

[5] Two examples are the zombie argument and the knowledge argument. For the first, see, e. g., Kirk (1974) and Chalmers (1996). For the second, see, e. g., Broad (1925) and Jackson (1982). Kirk and Jackson have had second thoughts.

composed lack a mental life. What has a mind is some suitable assembly or arrangement of those bits. What is a suitable arrangement? One answer is that it is the arrangement that is the outcome of the process that leads from conception to you and me, the process described in medical textbooks. We can think of this process as a kind of assembly line for making creatures with a psychology out of items that lack a psychology.

From this perspective, a central question in the philosophy of mind is how assembling items without a psychology can make something with a psychology and, especially, something that has conscious experiences like pain. One motivation for panpsychism—the view that the bits that make us up as well as we ourselves have mental natures—is the conviction that it is not possible to make something with, in particular, consciousness by assembling bits that lack consciousness. We have no choice, some say, but to accept that the bits that make us up, and items in the world more generally, have mental natures.[6] However, matters are not that simple, as panpsychists acknowledge. Panpsychism does not hold the very implausible view that the bits that make up creatures with minds like ours have the same kinds of mental natures that we have. It holds, rather, that the bits that make us up have proto-consciousness and proto-mentality, and that, somehow or other, putting bits with proto-mental natures and proto-consciousness together in the right way delivers creatures with the kind of mental natures and, in particular, the kind of conscious experiences that we have. The upshot is that everyone has to solve the combination problem, as it is often called.[7] However, what is important for us in this section are the implications of the fact that we are composites or aggregations for the question of how to specify the notion of a physical property.[8]

The fact that we are composites means that there are two questions that have to be addressed when we ask what physicalists should mean by a physical property. One concerns what counts as a physical property of the bits that make us up, where we include as properties of the bits the relations between the bits and their relations to the environment. It is, for example, just as much part of the account of how we are composed that some given neuron causally influences another neuron in a certain way, that cells in the eye react to incident light, and how the brain is connected to the spinal cord, as is the fact that our brains contain many neurons and hearts weigh around 300 grams (or whatever). The other concerns what counts as a physical property of the aggregations, the composites, themselves. We start with the first question. Earlier we said that a physical property is any property that has a place in the account the physical sciences give of what our world is like, where the physical sciences are physics, chemistry, biology, neuroscience, and the like. Is this the needed account of what it takes for a property of the bits to be a physical property? It depends on how we read the reference to the physical sciences. If we read it as referring to the physical sciences as they currently

---

[6] See, e. g., Nagel (1979).   [7] James (1890).

[8] In saying that persons are composites, I am not saying that a person is *identical* to some aggregation of bits. What is common ground among physicalists is that a person is composed of, is constituted by, suitably arranged and connected (non-mental) bits. The relation is like that between a table and the parts that make it up.

are, the answer is famously no.[9] We know that those bits have properties that do not have a place in the physical sciences as they currently are, for we know that the physical sciences have unsolved problems and it is certain that, somewhere along the line, they will need to introduce new properties, and no doubt some of these new properties will be properties of the bits that make up creatures with minds. We need to read the reference to the physical sciences as to those sciences in their final, completed forms, thought of as something we are aiming for whether or not we ever in fact get there. This leaves it vague exactly which properties count as physical, but, arguably, physicalists can live with the vagueness. We have here and now a reasonable grasp of the sorts of properties that will appear in the physical sciences in their final form, especially as regards the sorts of properties relevant to our mental natures. What is more, physicalists may reasonably suppose that none of these properties will themselves be mental properties and, in particular, phenomenal consciousness properties. They need to suppose this in order to hold onto their basic thought that, in some good sense, the mental is made out of the non-mental. For, although, as we noted, both physicalists and panpsychists face the combination problem, this does mean that physicalism is a version of panpsychism. The upshot is that physicalists are leaving things a bit vague and are making a supposition that might be challenged. I think that they can, and in any case have to, live with this.

The above, however, says nothing about the second question, the question concerning what makes some property of the composites—you and me, as it might be—count as physical. Composites have properties that outrun the properties of their bits. Indeed, that is a principal rationale for constructing bigger things out of smaller things. In particular, the composites that are persons have properties like being in pain and hoping for world peace, and these are properties of them, not of their bits. This is true independently of whether or not pain, say, is identical with some neural state, as some hold. The neural state is not in pain, although a person with their brain in the neural state may be. Moreover, these additional properties of the composites will include ones that are not the kinds of properties talked about in physics, chemistry, biology, neuroscience, etc.—the sciences we are calling the physical sciences. They will instead include properties of another science, namely, psychology, but of course to count them as physical on that account would empty physicalism of any interest. The thesis that consciousness and belief can be accounted for in physical terms is no news if consciousness and belief count as physical by virtue of appearing in psychology. We have always known that.

The challenge, then, is to explain what it is for a property of the composites to count as physical, given that the composites have properties that are distinct from those appealed to in the physical sciences, and to do so in a way that gives us a doctrine worth serious attention. One way of meeting this challenge leads directly to a priori physicalism, as we will now see.

---

[9] Hempel (1969).

17.4 A priori Physicalism and the Meaning of 'Physical'

Here is where we are. Physicalists have to hand an account of what they mean by physical properties as applied to the bits—where this includes the relations that the bits have to each other and to the surroundings—that make up creatures with mental states; and their view is that such creatures are made up of bits that have only physical properties in this sense. But what about the properties of the composites, the aggregations of those purely physical bits, the things that include you and me according to physicalism, and in particular the psychological properties of those composites? Those properties will not be physical in the specified sense.

This last claim might be queried. Why can the psychological properties, one and all, not be identified with physical properties in the specified sense? We mentioned earlier that some hold that pain is identical with a certain neural state. Could we, then, identify the property of being in pain with, say, one's brain being in neural state P, identify believing in God with one's brain being in neural state G, and so on? One reason for rejecting this suggestion are the various arguments against exactly this kind of proposal, the best known of which is the multiple realizability argument.[10] However, the most compelling reason adverts to something we commented on earlier: the rationale for the existence of composites. Why do we build cars? Why do we build computers? Why did evolution favour creatures with such and such a make-up over those with different make-ups? The answer lies in the fact that composites have properties, sometimes very important properties, in addition to the properties of the bits that make them up. It would be extraordinary if none of our psychological properties were examples of such additional properties. There are bound to be properties distinctive of the discipline of psychology.

The upshot is that physicalists must grant an extended sense in which a property can count as being physical, and there is an obvious way to do this. To see this, take physicalism thought of as a thesis about our world in general, not just about the minded creatures that inhabit it, and imagine someone arguing against global physicalism as follows: 'Having mass is a physical property for it appears in the physical sciences as currently conceived and will no doubt retain its place in some recognizable form in final science. I grant you that. But what about the property of being more massive than at least fifty objects and less massive than at least ten objects. We know enough about our world to be certain that this property is instantiated, but it is not a property that has a place in any physical theory.' The objector is technically correct—that property is too uninteresting to play a role in one of the physical sciences, but it is a priori entailed by properties that do play a role in the physical sciences. That is to say, the obvious response to the objection

---

[10] To be found in many places, e. g., Putnam (1975), but, in my not entirely disinterested view, a stronger argument to the same conclusion draws on the epistemology of psychological properties, see, e. g., Jackson (2012).

is to extend the notion of a physical property so as to count not only properties that play a role in the physical sciences but also any that are a priori entailed by properties that play a role in the physical sciences. Applied to the mind, this gives us a simple argument for holding that a priori physicalism is the only viable form of physicalism. The properties of the composites are physical in the wider sense just if they are a priori entailed by how things are physically in the narrower sense. Those properties of the composites include their psychological properties. We have, accordingly, reached the conclusion that physicalism has to hold that persons' psychological properties are a priori entailed by the physical way they are. For that is a requirement on what it is for their psychological properties to count as physical.

17.5 Determination without a priori Entailment?

Can it really be that easy to show that the only viable version of physicalism is a priori physicalism? It all depends on the availability of a viable alternative account of what a physical property is, in the wider sense. For the purposes of this section, we will dub the wider sense 'physicalw', and the narrower sense, the one in which to be physical is to play a role in the physical sciences (in their final form) 'physicaln'. So the question we are addressing is whether or not there is a viable notion of the physicalw that is not simply being a priori entailed by a rich enough account in physicaln terms of the way things are. In addressing this question, one thing is clear: physicalists have to hold that the physicaln way a person is, along with the physicaln way their environment is,[11] determines without remainder their mental nature. Physicalism is not simply the doctrine that there is a physicaln side to our mental nature. Everyone who isn't an idealist holds that. As we said right at the beginning, physicalism is a completeness claim about the mental—the physicalists' view is that a complete account of our mental nature can be given in physicaln terms, or, as it is sometimes put, our mental nature is nothing over and above our physicaln nature, or, again, the mental is not an addition to the physicaln side of us.

So the issue on the table is: How should physicalists cash out the talk of completeness, of nothing over and above, of determination without remainder and all that, of the mental by the physical? One way is in terms of the a priori entailment of the mental by the physicaln—the thesis distinctive of a priori physicalism, but is there a viable alternative to that answer? There are two possible suggestions we need to discuss. The first is that the physicaln way persons are completely determines in the causal sense the

[11] Different versions of physicalism, be they versions of a priori or a posteriori physicalism, take different stances on the internalism–externalism issue of the relative contributions from a person's physicaln nature and the physicaln nature of their environment in settling their mental nature. We will sometimes talk simply of the physicaln way a person is on the understanding that this includes as much as is needed of the physicaln way their environment is.

mental way persons are—completely determines in the way that, in a Newtonian world, the distribution of mass completely determines the gravitational force acting on any given mass. This answer obviously will not do. It is what those dualists who embrace epiphenomenalism hold: the mental is causally determined by the physicaln while being quite distinct from the physicaln.

The second alternative to a priori physicalism's answer is that the physicaln way persons (and their environments) are strongly necessitates, in the sense often dubbed 'metaphysical', the mental way persons are, but without a priori entailing the mental way persons are, without, that is, conceptually necessitating the mental way persons are. Any discussion of this suggestion is complicated by a controversy over the relationship between metaphysical necessity and conceptual necessity. There is wide agreement that the concept of metaphysical necessity is distinct from the concept of conceptual necessity: to be metaphysically necessary is to be true come what may in the strongest possible sense, whereas to be conceptually necessary is for this to be knowable a priori. The live issue is whether or not there are possibilities, ways things might be, that are metaphysically necessary without being conceptually necessary, and, correspondingly, whether there are possibilities that are conceptually possible without being metaphysically possible.[12] Or, to put the live issue in terms of possible worlds, does the set of conceptually possible worlds have the set of metaphysically possible worlds as a proper sub-set, or is there just one set of possible worlds, each member of which is both conceptually and metaphysically possible.[13]

This live issue also needs to be distinguished from the question of whether there are *sentences* that are necessary a posteriori true. It is widely agreed that there are, a favourite example being 'Water is H_2O'.[14] Although water could not fail to be H_2O, it took empirical research to show that water is H_2O. Of course, granting that this sentence is a necessary a posteriori truth invites the thought that there is an easy answer to the question of whether or not there are conceptual possibilities that are not metaphysically possible. Here is one—water's not being H_2O. However, matters are not that simple. If water's not being H_2O is metaphysically impossible, how can it differ from H_2O's not being H_2O, and that is conceptually impossible? In what follows, we stay neutral on the live issue. What we will see is that whichever way one goes on the live issue, the news is not good for a posteriori physicalism.

Suppose, first, that the answer to the live question is no, and, in particular, that the metaphysically possible ways things might be is co-extensive with the conceptually possible ways things might be. In that case, metaphysical determination coincides with conceptual determination. For determination is the sub-set relation between the ways things might be—if the A way things might be determines the B way things might be,

---

[12] For someone who says that there are, see Lycan (2009: 78); for someone who says that there aren't, see Jackson (2010: lecture four). The importance of Kripke (1980) to the debate goes without saying, but I make no claim concerning where he stands on this particular question.

[13] Conceptually possible worlds are sometimes called epistemically possible worlds.

[14] The chemistry of water is complex and it may be that philosophers should have chosen another example. We will neglect this complication.

the set of A ways things might be is a sub-set of the set of B ways things might be. Now, if the metaphysically possible ways things might be is co-extensive with the conceptually possible ways things might be, any sub-set relation that holds across metaphysically possible ways things might be holds across conceptually possible ways things might be, and conversely. In particular, metaphysical determination of such and such mental ways things might be by so and so physical ways things might be will coincide with conceptual or a priori determination of such and such mental ways things might be by so and so physical ways things might be. Thus, the core idea that underpins the suggestion under discussion will rest on a false presumption, namely that metaphysical determination of the mental by the physical can come apart from conceptual determination of the mental by the physical.

Suppose, secondly, that the answer to the live question is yes, and, in particular, that there are conceptually possible ways things might be which are not metaphysically possible. In that case, the proposal on the table—metaphysical determination of the mental by the physicaln but without conceptual or a priori determination—is a viable one for a posteriori physicalists to embrace. However, there are, all the same, two problems. First, some dualists hold a necessitarian version of the dual attribute theory of mind mentioned earlier (Section 17.1): mental states are brain states with special 'consciousness' properties, with the wrinkle that these special properties are metaphysically necessitated but not a priori entailed by physicaln properties. It is hard for a posteriori physicalists to explain exactly how their view differs from this view.[15] To highlight the difficulty, think of a relatively common view in ethics. A version of Moorean cognitivism in ethics holds that the supervenience of the moral on the non-moral means that the non-moral necessitates the moral, while insisting that the open question argument and the argument from real disagreement tell us that the determination is not a priori and that moral properties are distinct from non-moral properties in some strong sense. This picture of the relationship between non-moral and moral properties is obviously not a model for how physicalists think of the relationship between physicaln and mental properties.

The second problem concerns our knowledge of other minds. Anyone who holds that the conceptually possible ways things might be outruns the metaphysically possible ways things might be allows that empirical research can reveal a conceptual possibility to be a metaphysical impossibility. This indeed is why they hold the position in question. They believe that empirical research has shown a number of conceptual possibilities to be metaphysically impossible and often give water's not being H_2O as an example. Now, on the version of a posteriori physicalism we are considering, it is conceptually possible that everyone apart from, let us say, you yourself, is exactly as they in fact are in physicaln-terms but have no conscious mental life at all, that they are, as it is often put, zombies. What empirical evidence do you have that they are not zombies? This is a hard question for an a posteriori physicalist to answer. For they, the zombies, will pass any and every test for being conscious—for example, their screams will be just as loud as yours, and will be underpinned by the same sorts of neural activity as yours—or at least physicalists

---

[15] For more on this, see Jackson (2006).

must grant this. It follows from the causal closure of the physical_n, which is one of the main reasons they are physicalists in the first place. Would it help to appeal to your own, first person knowledge that you are conscious? Could an a posteriori physicalist argue that this gives you a reason for holding that your own physical_n nature metaphysically necessitates consciousness? But that would hardly help with the *other* minds question. Your physical_n nature differs from that of other people, in some cases by a good margin, not to mention the differences between humans, on the one hand, and dogs and dolphins, for example, on the other hand.

From now on, we will drop the subscript: by 'physical' we will mean physical_n.

17.6 A Message from the History of Astronomy

We have seen that one way for physicalists to spell out their basic thought that the mental is not an addition to the physical is by embracing a priori physicalism, and that, perhaps surprisingly, there is good reason to hold that it is the only way to do so. We now turn to a simpler line of thought—a less philosophical one, if you like—in support of the same conclusion. It draws on a famous example in the history of astronomy.

Uranus has a slight wobble in its orbit. This was successfully explained by postulating the existence of Neptune. Mercury also has a slight wobble in its orbit. Partly inspired by the example of Uranus and Neptune, some astronomers postulated a planet between Mercury and the Sun to explain this wobble. They named it 'Vulcan'. In doing this, these astronomers took it for granted that what was required to explain Mercury's orbit was a deduction of that orbit from data about the masses, positions, and motions of the planets and the sun, plus the relevant laws. Vulcan was postulated precisely in order to allow them to deduce the orbit. Why did they later abandon Vulcan? They found another and better way to deduce the orbit: replace the Newtonian laws by the General Theory of Relativity.

This is not an isolated example. When scientists seek to explain some phenomenon, they seek initial conditions and laws that allow the phenomenon in question to be deduced. They take it for granted that if one cannot deduce the phenomenon, there is something missing somewhere—in the laws or in the data. This remains true even if irreducible probabilities need to be incorporated into scientific theories.[16] The difference will be that the deductions will, in that case, involve probabilities. From this perspective, a priori physicalism is following best scientific practice. The message from the history of science is that to the extent that one cannot deduce the mental from the physical— where, recall, the physical includes both all the physical data and laws—an account of the mental in terms of the physical is incomplete.

---

[16] For discussion of probability in physics, see the papers in Beisbart and Hartmann (2011).

There is, of course, also a message here for non-physicalists. Earlier (Section 17.3) we talked briefly about the combination problem. As we noted, you do not have to be a physicalist to recognize that we are composites made up of bits that lack the kind of mental properties that we composites have. Thus very many philosophers of mind face the question: What is the relationship between the properties of the bits that make us up and how they are connected to each other and to surroundings, on the one hand, and the kinds of mental properties that we composites have but the bits lack, on the other? The message is that any account of this relationship should allow us to see how the mental properties of we composites can be deduced from the properties of the bits that make us up, along with how they are connected to each other and to surroundings.

We also mentioned earlier that although one can see, broadly speaking, how one might deduce the belief and desire way things are from the physical way things are, the situation with consciousness is different. Some argue that it is different in principle, not just in degree. There will always be an explanatory gap in the passage from detailed information in physical terms about a subject to that subject's seeing something as say red, or feeling pain. Some who hold this position conclude that the nature of conscious experience refutes physicalism, others that physicalists can live with the gap. The history of science suggests that if it is indeed the case that there is an unbridgeable explanatory gap, that is a sign of incompleteness, and so that the right conclusion would be to abandon physicalism.[17]

17.7 Is the Relation between H_2O and Water a Good Way to Think of the Relation between the Physical and the Mental?

We spent a little time earlier (Section 17.5) detailing problems for the view that physicalists should hold that the physical way we are metaphysically necessitates without a priori entailing the mental way we are. However, the view has proved perennially attractive and the example of H_2O and water is so often appealed to by a posteriori physicalists in explaining it, that the example deserves a section in its own right. What I say in this section can be read independently of the discussion in Section 17.5, although at one point I refer back to that discussion.

The basic line of thought can be outlined as follows. Science has shown that water is H_2O. In doing this, it revealed water's essential nature. It follows that it is a necessary a

---

[17] The term 'explanatory gap' comes from Levine (1983). His view then was that physicalists can live with it, but its existence means they should be a posteriori physicalists. His view now (Levine 2014) is that the best explanation of the gap is that physicalism is false, but if one is to be a physicalist, the gap means one should be an a posteriori one.

posteriori truth that water is H_2O—necessary because what was discovered was water's essential nature, a posteriori because it was an empirical discovery. This implies that the H_2O way things are metaphysically necessitates without a priori entailing the water way things are. For example, the global distribution of H_2O necessitates, without a priori entailing, the global distribution of water. Likewise, runs the line of thought, science has shown that the mental is the physical. In doing this, it has revealed the mental's essential nature. This implies, by analogy with the H_2O–water case, that the physical way things are metaphysically necessitates without a priori entailing the mental way things are.

There is no denying the immediate appeal of the thought that the example of H_2O and water is good news for a posteriori physicalists. For example, we noted earlier that it can be hard for a posteriori physicalists to distinguish their view from a necessitarian version of a dual attribute theory of mind. This can make it seem a virtue of the H_2O–water example that it is a case of a posteriori necessitation without distinctness: H_2O and water are one and the same. This would, however, be a mistake. As we noted earlier, physicalists have to believe that at least some mental properties are distinct from any physical (physicaln) properties. For the process of aggregation from conception to the way you and I are today led to the instantiation of new properties, and it would be strange indeed to hold that none of these new properties are mental ones. What physicalists have to say is that mental properties, or anyway some mental properties, are distinct from the physical properties of the items being aggregated, but in a way that honours the spirit of what is meant by insisting that mental properties are not additions to the physical account of us of the kind that dualists believe in. One way to do this is to hold that mental properties are a priori determined by physical properties. A key question is whether there is another way to do this, a way that a posteriori physicalists can appeal to. It is not an answer to this question to offer the water–H_2O case as an illustrative model at the same time as insisting that water and H_2O are not distinct.

However, the principal problem for the example is that it is very far from clear that we cannot go a priori from the H_2O way things are to the water way they are; the example lacks exactly the feature that is supposed to recommend it to a posteriori physicalists. Think of what happened when various chemists, in the late 1700s and early 1800s, carried out the experiments that showed that water is H_2O. They took samples of stuff that they knew to be potable, liquid at room temperature, to fill the lakes and oceans, and all that—the stuff that they knew to be watery, as it is often put—passed an electric current through it and got two parts of hydrogen at the cathode and one part of oxygen at the anode. Well of course it was more complicated than that, and there was considerable debate about how to interpret the results. But what is important for us is that the chemists assembled a body of information about the watery stuff that led them to conclude that the watery stuff is H_2O. The exact nature of that body of information is not crucial; what is crucial is that it is a body of information about the watery stuff and its relation to H_2O. For the one thing that the founders of modern chemistry did *not* do were experiments dedicated to showing that the watery stuff is water. The information they had when they did the experiments was enough to assure them that they were experimenting on water. Indeed, one might wonder what experiments to show specifically that some stuff is water could possibly look like, and that is as true today as it was back then. Experiments can reveal how liquid some stuff is, how hot it is, where it is to be found—in lakes, on the moon or wherever, whether it is a natural kind or a mixture like air, how much one needs to drink each day, what it is made of, when it freezes, and so on and so forth. But there is no experiment that tells you, as an extra bit of information, that the stuff is or is not water. Discovering some stuff to be or not to be water is not to discover something in addition to where it is, what its composition is, and all the rest. What this tells us is that discovering H_2O to be water is nothing over and above discovering that H_2O has the right watery properties, where we do not need to adjudicate what, exactly, those watery properties might be. It is sufficient that they do not include being water as such. It follows that we can go a priori from the H_2O way things are—that is, from all the watery information about H_2O—to the water way they are.

17.8 A priori Physicalism and Conceptual Analysis

When Smart (1959) argued for the identity theory of mind, he included a discussion of reports of sensations and offered a rough analysis of them, thought of as an account of what we are saying about how things are when we say, as it might be, 'I am in pain' or 'I am having a yellow after-image'. Armstrong's (1968) major work in defence of materialism advances conceptual analyses for a whole range of mental states. In both cases, it is clear that they took this, or something like this, to be an important part of making the case for materialism. (Armstrong and Smart typically referred to their identity version of physicalism as materialism.) Why did they think this, and how does the enterprise of seeking conceptual analyses of the mental bear on the debate over a priori physicalism?

Smart's interest in offering an analysis of sensation reports was in part sparked by his desire to play due homage to introspection. He was sensitive to the difference between belief, for example, and those mental states with a distinctive phenomenology like having a yellow after-image and being in pain, the ones we have been noting make life difficult for a priori physicalists. On his view, having a yellow after-image is a brain state, and the phenomenology comes from the way this brain state presents itself to us. It presents itself to us as the kind of state that we are in when we see a yellowish patch on the wall. If that is right, that will be what we are reporting when we report having a yellow after-image. Likewise, pain is a certain kind of brain state, but what is available to introspection is the fact that we are in the kind of state that we are in when a pin is stuck in us, and that is what we report when we say that we are in pain.

Anyone—and I am one of them—convinced that the kinds of mental states we are talking about are essentially representational states—for example, to have a pain in one's foot is to be in a state that represents that things are amiss in one's foot, and to have a yellow after-image is to be in a state that represents (non-veridically) that there is a yellow patch on the wall in front of one—will reject this way of thinking of the phenomenology.[18] On the representationalist way of thinking, the phenomenology lies in how things are being represented to be. However, be this as it may, Smart was addressing a question that very much needs to be addressed. Smart (and identity theorists in general) have to allow that there is a sense in which the folk do not know what they are talking about when they talk about bodily sensations and perceptual experiences. In his view, they are talking about our brain states, and that is not something the folk (*qua* folk) know. However, there is also a sense in which the folk do know what they are talking about. When the folk hear a dentist utter the words 'This is going to hurt', they know what to expect; that is why they look worried. When travellers get up early to see a famously spectacular sunrise, they know why it is worth the effort. A question Smart, and philosophers of mind in general, have to answer is, What are we talking about when we use mental language, in the sense of 'about' in which the folk do know what we are talking about. You may not like Smart's answer but he correctly identified a question that needs to be answered.

Armstrong's analyses are much more in the spirit of those offered by analytical functionalists.[19] He thought of mental states as central states of persons, brain states as it happens, which play distinctive causal roles with respect to the environment, one another and bodily movements. Our perceptual experiences, for example, are typically caused by events around us, play distinctive roles in modifying our beliefs, which in turn combine with our desires to cause our bodies to move in ways that tend to satisfy our desires if our beliefs are true. The difference between his view and functionalism can be put as follows: Armstrong held that mental states are brain states, and that what makes those brain states the mental states that they are are the functional roles they play. Analogy: minus 273.15 Celsius is absolute zero; what makes minus 273.15 Celsius absolute zero is that it is the lowest temperature possible. Functionalists hold instead that mental states are functional states realized by brain states. The extent to which this difference is a material one is debatable and debated. Armstrong himself thought of his view as akin to functionalism.[20]

Armstrong's way of thinking of mental states is a promising approach to the question we have lately insisted needs to be answered, namely: What are the folk claiming about how things are when they use mental vocabulary?[21] Consider the sample causal roles I give in the previous paragraph. Plausibly they are applied common-sense and are not a discovery of cognitive science or philosophy. Do the folk need to be told that cats often cause the seeing of cats, that the seeing of cats often causes beliefs about their colour and where they are located relative to the perceiver, and that these beliefs cause behaviour

---

[18] For an exposition and defence of representationalism about experience, see, e. g., Tye (1995).

[19] Accounts of analytical functionalism are to be found in many places; one location is Braddon-Mitchell and Jackson (1996).

[20] See Armstrong (1993: xiv.)

[21] Armstrong (1993: xv) expresses regret at having talked of giving accounts of mental concepts in his 1968, and makes a number of suggestions about different ways of thinking of what he was doing. I think what he was doing was giving an account of what we are claiming about how things are when we use mental vocabulary, and this is in fact offering an analysis of mental concepts in one good sense of analysis.

relative to the cat which is a function of the perceiver's desires—that cat lovers will move their bodies in a way that gets them nearer the cat, cat haters will do the opposite? The same is true of the whole range of causal analyses that Armstrong offers of the various mental states. In this sense, what Armstrong was doing was very much in the spirit of analytical functionalism, as is clear when one remembers that the other name of that view is common-sense functionalism.[22]

However, this is not the place to debate the merits of analytical functionalism. What is to the point here is the bearing of an Armstrong-type analysis of the mental to a priori physicalism.[23] If it is along the right lines, what we noted earlier is plausible for belief and desire will be possible for all mental states. It is one thing to insist that physicalists have to hold that the physical way things are a priori entails the mental way things are— adding that, as a good physicalist, one is thereby committed to holding that the physical way things are does indeed a priori entail the mental way things are—it is quite another to specify how one might deduce subjects' mental states from a suitably detailed body of information about their physical natures. If Armstrong is right, one can see how the deduction might go, broadly speaking at least. One would collect detailed information about the ways in which our surroundings cause various states in our brains and how our brains process these states. One would add to this complex body of information, information about the ways in which these states do or would cause our bodies to change their orientations with respect to their surroundings in various systematic ways. One would then examine which states, if any, play the role distinctive of mental state M, say, and if one found a state that did play that role, one could then infer that the subject is in mental state M. This fits nicely with the working assumption of many neuroscientists investigating memory. They take it for granted that to find memory is to find that which does what memory does. Armstrong's thought, and the thought of analytical functionalists, is an extension of this presumption to mental states across the board.

17.9 WHAT WE HAVE NOT TALKED ABOUT

I have told you why I think that a priori physicalism is the physicalism of choice. If a priori physicalism is the physicalism of choice, there are two ways to go: embrace a priori physicalism, or conclude that physicalism is false on the ground that there are arguments that show that the physical does not a priori entail the mental and, most especially, does not a priori entail the phenomenal conscious side of our mental lives. Nothing I say here gives one a reason to go one way rather than the other, although I in fact (now) go the first way.[24]

---

[22] For more on all this, see Braddon-Mitchell and Jackson (1996).
[23] What follows applies equally to analytical or common-sense functionalism.
[24] I am indebted to far too many people to list, but must mention David Braddon-Mitchell, David Chalmers, David Lewis, Daniel Stoljar, and Galen Strawson. I am also indebted to the editor for very helpful comments. None should be held responsible.

REFERENCES

Armstrong, D. M. (1968), *A Materialist Theory of the Mind*. London: Routledge & Kegan Paul.
Armstrong, D. M. (1993), *A Materialist Theory of the Mind*. London: Routledge & Kegan Paul, pb ed. of Armstrong (1968) with a new preface.
Beisbart, C. and Hartmann, S. (eds) (2011), *Probabilities in Physics*. Oxford: Oxford University Press.
Braddon-Mitchell, D. and Jackson, F. (1996), *The Philosophy of Mind and Cognition*. Cambridge, MA: Blackwell.
Broad, C. D. (1925), *The Mind and its Place in Nature*. London: Routledge & Kegan Paul.
Campbell, K. (1971), *Body and Mind*. London: Macmillan.
Chalmers, D. J. (1996), *The Conscious Mind: In Search of a Fundamental Theory*. New York: Oxford University Press.
Hempel, C. G. (1969), 'Reduction: Ontological and linguistic facets', in S. Morgenbesser, P. Suppes, and M. White (eds), *Philosophy, Science, and Method: Essays in Honor of Ernest Nagel*, New York: St. Martins Press, 179–99.
Jackson, F. (1982), 'Epiphenomenal qualia', *Philosophical Quarterly*, 32: 127–36.
Jackson, F. (2006), 'On ensuring that physicalism is not a dual attribute theory in sheep's clothing', *Philosophical Studies*, 131: 227–49.
Jackson, F. (2010), *Language, Names, and Information*. Oxford: Wiley-Blackwell.
Jackson, F. (2012), 'Leibniz's law and the philosophy of mind', *Proceedings of the Aristotelian Society*, CXII/3: 269–83.
James, W. (1890), *The Principles of Psychology*, vol. 1. New York: Henry Holt and Co.
Kirk, R. (1974), 'Zombies v. materialists', *Proceedings of the Aristotelian Society*, 48, Supp. vol.: 135–52.
Kripke, S. (1980), *Naming and Necessity*. Oxford: Basil Blackwell.
Levine, J. (1983), 'Materialism and qualia: the explanatory gap', *Pacific Philosophical Quarterly*, 64: 354–61.
Levine, J. (2014), 'Modality, semantics, and consciousness', *Philosophical Studies*, symposium on David Chalmers, *The Character of Consciousness*, 167/3: 775–84.
Lewis, D. (1966), 'An argument for the identity theory', *Journal of Philosophy*, 67: 17–25.
Lycan, W. G. (2009), 'Serious metaphysics: Frank Jackson's defence of conceptual analysis', in I. Ravenscroft (ed.), *Ethics and Conditionals: Themes from the philosophy of Frank Jackson*. Oxford: Oxford University Press, 64–84.
Nagel, T. (1979), 'Panpsychism', in T. Nagel, *Mortal Questions*. Cambridge: Cambridge University Press.
Putnam, H. (1975), 'The nature of mental states', in H. Putnam, *Mind, Language and Reality*. Cambridge: Cambridge University Press, 215–71.
Smart, J. J. C. (1959), 'Sensations and brain processes', *Philosophical Review*, 68: 141–56.
Tye, M. (1995), *Ten Problems of Consciousness: A Representational Theory of the Mind*. Cambridge, MA: MIT Press.

CHAPTER 18

A POSTERIORI PHYSICALISM

Type-B Materialism and the Explanatory Gap

JOSEPH LEVINE

18.1 INTRODUCTION

CHALMERS (2002) famously categorizes versions of materialism into various 'types'. For our purposes the only distinction that matters is between 'Type A' and 'Type B'. According to Type A materialism, (ideal) reflection on our mental and physical concepts reveals that the possibility of a being physically identical to a fully conscious human but without conscious experience can be ruled out a priori. Put another way, so-called 'zombies' are not even conceivable. According to Type B materialism, however, zombies are conceivable, but they are not metaphysically possible. The idea is that since the possibility of zombies cannot be ruled out a priori, they count as conceivable, but since in fact the mental supervenes on the physical,[1] zombies are not genuinely possible. I will not be concerned further with Type A materialism in this chapter, only mentioning it to contrast it with Type B, my focus here.

In the past (Levine 1998, 2001) I have argued that though the conceivability of zombies (along with several other thought experiments) manifests the existence of an explanatory gap between the physical and the mental (specifically consciousness—let that be understood in what follows unless otherwise stated), there was still good reason to adopt materialism, though the lack of explanatory import posed a problem. In other words, I claimed that Type B materialism had a serious epistemic defect—the explanatory

---

[1] Here, and in the rest of the chapter, by 'supervenience' I mean *metaphysical* supervenience, a stronger relation than *nomological* supervenience. The latter is consistent with dualism, as it only posits a lawful relation between the physical and the mental, and so allows for basic laws of nature that link the two.

gap—but it was still philosophically coherent and viable. In order to maintain Type B materialism in the face of zombie conceivability it is necessary to open another gap—between conceivability and possibility. Much of the debate over the viability of Type B materialism has concerned the connection between conceivability and possibility. I have mostly taken the side of Type B materialists on this particular question.

More recently (Levine 2014), I have come to doubt the viability of materialism in the face of the explanatory gap. As I see it, the inference to the rejection of materialism takes the form of an inference to the best explanation; the best explanation of the existence and persistence of the explanatory gap is that there is a genuine metaphysical gap. I now favor some version of emergentism. However, though I no longer defend materialism, I still believe that the conceivability argument does not by itself show materialism to be false. I still hold that the original defense against the conceivability argument, the one that relies upon opening a space between conceivability and possibility, works.

In this chapter I want to do three things: In Section 18.2 I will outline what I take to be the principal argument that the rejection of materialism follows rather directly from the conceivability of zombies and explain why I do not accept that argument. In Section 18.3 I will consider a related argument against materialism that might seem to follow from premises that I explicitly endorse, and show that it does not after all. In Section 18.4 I will then turn to an argument that some materialists have presented, and seems to follow from the considerations presented in Section 18.3, that the explanatory gap is not really such a problem for materialists after all. I will try to explain why my inference to the best explanation still goes through in the face of this argument.

18.2 The Conceivability Argument against Materialism

As there is a vast literature on the conceivability argument and its effect on Type B materialism, some of which I have contributed to already, I will keep my discussion here brief.[2] Here is how I see the dialectic. The anti-materialist argues that since zombies are conceivable—which means that any statement to the effect that a zombie exists cannot be ruled out a priori—this shows that they are possible. If zombies are possible, even if not actual, this undermines the commitment of materialists to the claim that phenomenal consciousness (metaphysically) supervenes on the physical facts. If there is a possible world in which the physical facts are as they are in the actual world, and yet a physical twin of a conscious person in the actual world is a zombie in this possible world, then phenomenal consciousness has been demonstrated not to supervene on the physical facts and so a core commitment of materialism is false.

---

[2] For starters, see the works by Chalmers and myself mentioned already, Block and Stalnaker (1999), Chalmers and Jackson (2001), and the collection of papers in Gendler and Hawthorne (2002).

The first move in defense of the supervenience thesis is to assimilate materialist identity claims (whether with neural states or functional states) to other theoretical identity claims discussed by Kripke (1980) and Putnam (1975). Just as it is conceivable that heat not be the motion of molecules, or water not be H_2O, and yet no one doubts the truth of these identity claims, so too the conceivable falsehood of materialist identity claims does not undermine their acceptability. Clearly, then, conceivability of some proposition P does not entail that P is possible.

Anti-materialists, however, have a comeback. There are a lot of different ways to characterize this response, but for my purposes the following works best. While undoubtedly we can coherently conceive of a situation in which water turns out not to be H_2O—for instance, it could have turned out to be XYZ—what does not seem conceivable is that a certain conditional, call it a 'supervenience conditional', should turn out to be false. We can form the relevant supervenience conditional as follows: Take all the basic, fundamental facts about a world—all the physical facts, and whatever else provides the supervenience base for all non-basic facts—and put them in the antecedent of the conditional, and then make the statement that water is H_2O, or that heat is the motion of molecules, the consequent. Let us symbolize this as B → M (where 'B' represents all the basic facts, and 'M' represents non-basic macro-facts). The claim, then, is that B → M is a priori. So if you were given a description of all the basic facts about a world, then from this description and your grasp of the relevant concepts, you could infer what water is, what heat is, etc.

There is nothing in the standard Kripke–Putnam story that explicitly conflicts with this claim about the a priori status of these supervenience conditionals, and so appeal to the conceivability of water not being H_2O does not undermine the claim. But once armed with this claim—let us call it the 'a priori entailment thesis'—it then follows that the conceivability of zombies presents a serious challenge to the claim that phenomenal consciousness supervenes on the physical facts. After all, put in all of the physical and functional facts you think are those on which consciousness must supervene, the resulting supervenience conditional will still not be a priori. Hence there is a principled difference between the zombie case and the cases of water and heat, and so the original conceivability argument for the possibility of a zombie remains intact.

There are two standard lines of reply by Type B materialists in the literature (and another two that are not so standard). I call one of the two standard lines the 'exceptionalist' line and the other the 'non-exceptionalist' one. The non-exceptionalist line is to deny the a priori entailment thesis in general, arguing that conditionals like 'B → M', even where the substituend for 'M' is about some non-mental, middle-sized object like water, are not a priori. The exceptionalist line allows that in most cases conditionals like 'B → M' are a priori, but argues that when it comes to phenomenal states the situation is different. The reason is that when we think about phenomenal states we employ so-called 'phenomenal concepts', and these concepts have special features that block a priori inferences from statements employing non-phenomenal concepts.

Now the 'phenomenal concept strategy', as it has been called, is employed not only to counter the conceivability argument but also to defend materialism against the challenge of the explanatory gap.[3] Elsewhere (Levine 2007) I have criticized the phenomenal concept strategy as a response to the explanatory gap, and from that critique it follows that it does not serve to undermine the conceivability argument either. However, I do think the non-exceptionalist strategy works; that is, the Type B materialist should just reject the entire semantic framework on which the a priori entailment thesis is based.

As I see it, the principal division here is between a Fregean, or neo-Fregean theory that provides a substantive role for a mode of presentation in doing the meta-semantic work of connecting our concepts to their referents (whether objects, properties, or entities of some other ontological category), and a Russellian (or neo-Russellian) theory that does not. On the neo-Fregean theory part of what determines reference for a concept are a priori accessible conditions that must be satisfied by a candidate entity in order to qualify as the referent. Thus, when considering some supervenience conditional of the form 'B → M', one employs one's knowledge of the reference-determining conditions that constitute the modes of presentation of the relevant concepts in order to determine the truth of the conditional. On the neo-Russellian theory, there is no mode of presentation grasped by the subject that determines the referent. Rather, the meta-semantic conditions that connect concepts to their referents work 'behind the scenes', as it were, out of the ken of the subject. The standard conditions appealed to are causal chains and nomic dependencies. If there are no a priori accessible modes of presentation (for most atomic concepts, that is) then there is no semantic knowledge on which to draw to make supervenience conditionals a priori. If the inference from a complete description of the micro-physical facts to the statement that there is water in the glass is not a priori, then the fact that the inference from the micro-physical facts to the phenomenal facts is not a priori should not be a problem. After all, if water supervenes on the micro-physical despite the fact that the relevant supervenience conditional is not a priori, then phenomenal consciousness can supervene on the micro-physical as well.

As I said, I favor the non-exceptionalist response to the conceivability argument. On the neo-Russellian semantic framework the a priori entailment thesis never holds, so therefore there is no reason to expect it to hold in the case of the psycho-physical connection. A description of the entire supervenience base for some phenomenon—indeed, include the entire supervenience base for all non-basic phenomena—need not a priori entail a description of the relevant phenomenon despite necessitating it. Having said that, I will address one line of argument supporting the a priori entailment thesis in the next section. In the remainder of this section I want to briefly characterize the two non-standard replies to the conceivability argument/a priori entailment thesis mentioned above.

The first line of reply starts by accepting the neo-Fregean semantic framework.[4] Let us assume that we have a restricted stock of primitive concepts within which the modes of

---

[3] Again, there is an extensive literature on phenomenal concepts. The locus classicus is Loar (1997). See also the papers in Alter and Walter (2007).

[4] This line of argument is presented in Levine (2014).

presentation of all other concepts can be expressed. When the mode of presentation of a non-primitive concept is applied to the characterization of a possible world in terms of the primitive concepts (what Chalmers calls a 'scenario') the reference of that concept in that world is determined. (This applies only to 'worlds considered as actual', as the 2D theorists put it.) So, if you have a conditional of the form S → M, where 'S' stands for an exhaustive scenario description and 'M' is any statement involving non-primitive concepts, the truth value of the conditional, on this view, is a priori. Hence, it might seem, this view entails the a priori entailment thesis.

However, notice that earlier we used the schema 'B → M' to represent a supervenience conditional, and now we have used the schema 'S → M' to represent what I will call a 'scenario conditional'. What is the difference between 'S' and 'B'? 'S' stands for a complete description of a world in terms of our cognitive system's primitive concepts, while 'B' stands for a complete description of a world in terms of the concepts that represent its basic, or fundamental properties. The a priori entailment thesis concerns the supervenience conditionals, not the scenario conditionals. So if the neo-Fregean semantic framework is to lend support to the a priori entailment thesis, it must be that 'S' and 'B' amount to the same thing. But this would be so only if the concepts that are primitive for us represented the properties that are metaphysically basic for our world. But why think this is the case? In fact, it seems highly unlikely that evolved creatures like ourselves, living in the medium-sized and relatively slow-paced world that we do, would have as primitive concepts ones that represented the most fundamental properties of our world. What a coincidence that would be!

To make this a little less abstract and bring it more directly to bear on Type B materialism, let me put the point another way. What is supposed to be problematic for Type B materialism is the alleged conflict between the following two claims: (1) that a conditional of the form 'P → Q' (where 'P' stands for all the physical facts and 'Q' the phenomenal qualitative facts) is metaphysically necessary, and (2) that this conditional is a posteriori (which is why zombies are conceivable). But suppose, as Chalmers and Jackson (2001) themselves argue, that phenomenal concepts, the ones in which 'Q' is couched, are among our primitive concepts, and therefore among those that, in a sense, define all our non-primitive concepts. Then of course if you put the phenomenal concepts, together with whatever other primitive concepts there are (perhaps spatial concepts, the concept of cause, etc.), into the antecedent of a scenario conditional it will be a priori. But since the concepts within which 'Q' is couched are themselves primitive, if 'Q' is put in the consequent of a conditional—as in 'P → Q'—there is no reason to expect the resulting conditional to be a priori. Therefore, the fact that 'P → Q' is a posteriori does not provide any reason for doubting its necessity, and Type B materialism is off the hook.

There is one final line of reply that is more speculative than the others but still, I think, worth putting out there. Advocates of the conceivability argument, particularly Chalmers and Jackson, emphasize that when presented with a scenario conditional people have the ability to decide, or infer, what the referent of their various non-primitive concepts are, such as 'water' and 'heat'. One might object that even if people can normally do this (which involves a lot of idealization, but let that go for now), what they are doing may be engaging in non-demonstrative, or empirical reasoning. If so, then there would be no basis for considering the relevant conditionals to be a priori. However, they retort that since all the empirical information has already been put into the antecedent of the conditional, any reasoning from the antecedent to the consequent must be a priori, as no empirical considerations remain (outside the characterization of the antecedent) to influence one's reasoning.

Suppose one admits that, for the reason just cited, that the inference from the antecedent to the consequent must be a priori. Still, one may not be forced to locate the source of its a priority in the semantic competence of the subject (or at least not solely). Perhaps our most fundamental rules of reasoning themselves—not derived from semantic analyses but from epistemic norms—are a priori. It might be that whenever one reasons from empirical premises to an empirical conclusion one is employing an a priori epistemic rule system. This rule system differs from demonstrative reasoning in that it is not truth-preserving; nevertheless, it may be a priori. I can imagine independent reasons for thinking this must be the case.[5] While I do not myself have a firm position on this question, it does seem to me a not implausible path for the Type B materialist to take.

18.3 Avoiding Brute Necessity

Above I described the non-exceptionalist reply to the conceivability argument. On this view, we reject the neo-Fregean assumptions underlying the argument, instead opting for a neo-Russellian semantics that more firmly severs the connection between the epistemic status of a proposition and its metaphysical status. However, it is just this severance of the connection between the epistemic and the metaphysical that some argue manifests the weakness in the Type B materialist's position.

The problem revolves around the notion of what Chalmers calls a 'strong necessity', and which others (including myself) have called a 'brute necessity'. Many philosophers find the idea that a metaphysical necessity could be a brute, inexplicable fact to be extremely implausible, if not downright incoherent. Here is how I see the argument for this view. The world is constituted by a set of facts, organized in such a way that some are basic and others are realized in, or constituted by, other facts. We can add laws of nature into the set of basic facts if we are non-Humeans about laws. When we explain various empirical phenomena, we do so by appeal to more basic phenomena, and this process eventually bottoms out in facts and laws that are brute and inexplicable. Why is the gravitational constant what it is and not some other value? Maybe there is an explanation in terms of deeper phenomena, but maybe there is not. It could just be that it is what it is and that is just a brute fact about our world.

---

[5] See Biggs and Wilson (2017) on the a priori nature of inference to the best explanation.

That there should be brute facts about our world is not surprising. After all, if there were not it would mean that the world really had to be the way it is, and then in some sense its structure should be both necessary and accessible a priori. But we know we need experience of the world—we have to get data from it—in order to figure out what it is like. Some aspects of our world, particularly involving its most fundamental structure, just happen to be the way they are, and they are what distinguish it from all of the other possible worlds there could have been. We might say that each possible world is distinguished from every other by the particular constellation of brute facts and laws that constitute it.

So that contingent propositions might be brutely, inexplicably true is not a problem. We expect there to be such propositions. But the point is that a contingent proposition's being brute makes sense precisely because a contingent proposition is specifically about the actual world. But could a necessary proposition be brute? Could some brute fact hold necessarily? Modal facts are not specifically about the actual world, but rather about the entire space of possible worlds. So could some fact about the entire space of possible worlds plausibly be brute? Many philosophers, myself included, think not. If bruteness is constitutively tied to what *just happens to be* the case—the realm of the empirical—then it cannot be a feature of what *must be* the case. Hence necessities require some explanation for their necessity.

What could explain a necessity? Well the traditional conception—that is, pre-Kripke—was that the three distinctions, analytic–synthetic, a priori–a posteriori, and necessary–contingent were all aligned. The notions of being true by virtue of meaning (and logic), being knowable independently of experience, and being true in all possible worlds went perfectly together. That some fact/proposition is necessary is then explicable by appeal to its logical/semantic/epistemic status. The explanation would go something like this. Why is P necessary? Well, because P is a priori. But how does the epistemic status underwrite the metaphysical status? What connects a proposition's being a priori to its being necessary? The answer lies in logic and semantics. It is because of its logical/conceptual structure that the proposition in question is a priori, as mere competence with the concept and with logic renders its truth self-evident. If it is self-evidently true, without need to consult the way the world actually is through experience, then it must be because it has to be that way. Hence we understand why it is necessary.

Now of course this picture has to be complicated in the light of the generally accepted examples of a posteriori necessities made famous by Kripke and Putnam. However, making the accommodation to fit these examples while keeping the constitutive connections just described is not that hard to do. All we need to add is a dimension of modality that allows for a contextual element to determine the referents of concepts with which we have an a priori competence. So, knowing that water is whatever in this world satisfies the 'watery' description is a priori, and when we add the a posteriori information that it is H_2O that in fact satisfies the watery description, we know that water is necessarily H_2O. The point is that it is our a priori accessible competence with the concept of water that bears the burden of explaining the necessity in question. Thus it is not a brute necessity.

Chalmers (2006) has put this relationship in characteristically vivid terms: he calls it the 'golden triangle', with modality, rationality, and semantics occupying the vertices of this triangle. He argues that our very notion of the modal is constitutively tied to our notion of rationality—thus ruling out brute necessity—and that semantics, or our semantic competence, is the link that connects the a priori and the necessary. The Type B materialist, by classifying zombies as impossible despite their conceivability, is guilty, then, of positing a brute necessity, and thus violating this constitutive link between the necessary and the a priori.

We can get to the same conclusion by a slightly different line of reasoning (though ultimately connected to the argument above). The fight over materialism concerning conscious experience has been fought, for the most part, over the question of supervenience. If zombies are possible, then phenomenal consciousness does not supervene on the physical facts and, since materialism entails supervenience, materialism would be false. The reason that supervenience has been the focus of the debate is that the anti-materialist arguments challenge it. However, most materialists admit that supervenience is too weak a relation to adequately capture the thesis of materialism. Instead, most opt for realization (or, nowadays, grounding, which, as far as I can tell, comes to the same thing).

Now one of the principal ways that realization is supposed to go beyond supervenience is that the former, as opposed to the latter, entails that there is an explanatory relation between the realization (and supervenience) base and the facts it realizes (and therefore, which supervene on it). As Jeffrey Poland (1994) puts it, if one set of facts realizes another, then there must exist a 'realization theory' that explains how the instantiation of the realizing facts guarantees the instantiation of the realized facts. What a realization theory provides, then, would be a way of seeing how the base necessitates what is based on it, and this would amount to an a priori derivation of the realized from a description of the realizer. But then this entails that the a priori entailment thesis has to hold, at least if we are committed to there being a realization relation between the physical and the phenomenal, which seems to be a core commitment of materialism.

Of course these two lines of reasoning are connected. One of the main reasons that materialists believe that the psycho-physical relation must be realization (or grounding), and not the weaker supervenience, is that supervenience alone would bring with it a brute necessity. If the phenomenal only supervened on the physical, but were not realized by it, then this would mean the physical would necessitate the phenomenal without there being an explanation of this necessity, and this is to be avoided if possible. So if materialism is committed to a realization relation holding between the physical and the phenomenal, and realizations entail explanatory connections, and these connections entail an a priori inference from the description of the base to a description of what is based on it, then it looks like the conceivability of zombies presents a real problem for Type B materialists after all.

Despite appearances, Type B materialists can maintain both that zombies are conceivable and that phenomenal consciousness is realized by, not just supervenient on, the physical facts. The key to reconciling these two claims lies in the dual nature of identity.

Where Chalmers locates semantics as the third vertex of the golden triangle that connects rationality to modality, I put identity instead.

By identity's 'dual nature' I mean that identity claims are normally a posteriori, established empirically, but, when true, have the stronger modal status of necessity. The necessity of identity, as both Kripke and Hume emphasized, is a priori: it is a matter of logic that everything is what it is and not something else. So if water is identical to H_2O, then it could not be anything other than H_2O. In other words, the schema, $\forall x \forall y (x=y \rightarrow \Box x=y)$, is a priori.

In fact, I would say that the entire phenomenon of a posteriori necessity comes down to this dual nature of identity. Rather than there being a complete break between epistemic and metaphysical modality, as some might interpret the results of the Kripke–Putnam thought experiments, in fact that connection remains secure. It is just that there is this one kind of necessary claim—an identity claim—which, due to its special nature, can be established by a posteriori reasoning. This dual nature of identity is in turn a straightforward consequence of the fact—made so much of by Frege—that it is possible for us to have two (or more) distinct representations for the same entity without realizing it. Once we pin a posteriori necessity on this dual nature of identity, we see how the Type B materialist can maintain both that phenomenal consciousness is realized by physical facts and also that zombies are conceivable.

Let us see how this works. The Type B materialist claims that the physical facts necessitate the conscious facts—that is, the latter supervene on the former. Yet, it is conceivable that all the physical facts are as they are and still there is no consciousness—zombie worlds are conceivable. How do we avoid being committed to brute necessity here? Well first, we identify phenomenal consciousness with some functional, or computational, or neural state (pick your favorite). Once that identification is made, we now have a redescription of phenomenal consciousness in (say) functional terms. When we compare our full description of the physical facts with our new description of phenomenal consciousness in functional terms we see (idealizing, of course) that the functional description follows a priori from the basic physical description. Hence we conclude that phenomenal consciousness is indeed realized by, and not merely supervenient on, the physical facts. Having established this realization relation, we see that the necessity in question here is not brute but quite explicable by an a priori derivation after all.

The idea here is that the necessity of phenomenal consciousness, given the physical facts, is indeed explicable, but just not under the description we usually employ to represent it. There are no brute necessities here, since there is a description for every phenomenon that is necessitated under which it is a priori derivable from some description of what necessitates it. It is the identity claims, themselves established empirically, but, as a matter of logic (and thus a priori), carrying modal import, that allow us to substitute the one description for the other and therefore explain the necessity in question; in this case, the supervenience of the phenomenal on the physical.

As I said above, it seems to me that all a posteriori necessities derive in this way from an empirically established necessary identity. So, take the proposition that water contains hydrogen. This is an a posteriori necessity that is not itself an identity claim. Still, one can explain its necessity by appeal to an identity. First we discover that water is H_2O. Once we know they are the same thing, and therefore are so in every possible world, we are then rationally licensed to substitute the term 'H_2O' for the term 'water' in modal contexts. So from 'Necessarily water contains hydrogen' we get, by substitution, 'Necessarily H_2O contains hydrogen'. The latter statement is clearly a priori, and so not a brute necessity. Given the way we derived it from the former statement, this shows that the former statement is not a brute necessity either. The space of possible worlds is still governed by rational, a priori accessible principles. Brute necessity has been banished.

Of course the obvious response to this method of ridding Type B materialism of the curse of brute necessity is to object that all that has happened is that the bruteness of the necessity of the supervenience relation has been displaced onto the necessity of the identity relation. If identities are indeed the real source of a posteriori necessities, then they too require explanation. While the advocate of the conceivability argument has their favored explanation for these necessities, deriving them from the requisite conceptual analyses of the macro concepts, the (non-exceptionalist, neo-Russellian) Type B materialist leaves these identity claims brute and unexplained.

In reply, the Type B materialist can insist that nothing is really being left unexplained. Consider an identity like water is H_2O. There are two claims that might call out for explanation here. First, what explains its modal status, its necessity? Well, for this we have an a priori explanation, embodied in the a priori nature of the schema presented above. It is a priori that something is what it is and nothing else; it is just logic. Second, what explains its truth? Why is water H_2O? Well, this is something for which we do not expect an explanation. Call it 'brute' if you like, but it is a completely benign sort of bruteness, and not one that in any way undermines the constitutive connection between rationality and modality. After all, things are what they are; how can you explain that? You can explain how something came to exist (for concrete entities anyway), you can explain why it is rational to believe a certain identity claim, and you can explain how it is that this one thing happened to have two distinct representations of it, but it is not at all clear what it would mean to actually explain the identity itself. Things are what they are and nothing else—period.

Here is another way to put the argument between the conceivability challenger and the Type B materialist. If one wants to maintain some version of 'modal rationalism' (Chalmers's term), on which there is a constitutive connection between the a priori and the necessary, and thus brute necessities are banished, you have to come to terms with the (close to) universally acknowledged examples of a posteriori necessities somehow. This means that somewhere in the justification for these necessary truths an empirical element must be introduced. The question then is where to locate that empirical element so as not to undermine the constitutive connection between the a priori and the necessary.

What we have seen is that there are two ways to introduce this empirical element. The first way is the one advocated by the conceivability challengers to Type B materialism.

On this view, we have an a priori grasp of the satisfaction conditions for the relevant concept(s), and the empirical element comes into play in determining which entity in this world meets these conditions. So, for example, we know that water is whatever is the local entity that plays the watery role, and then it takes empirical discovery to determine that it happens to be H_2O. If we take this option, then, for all the reasons rehearsed by the advocates of the conceivability argument, there is no corresponding room for empirical discovery to enter into the justification for psycho-physical necessities, and so one cannot treat Type B materialism in the same way as other a posteriori necessities. Hence Type B materialism seems committed to brute necessities.

On the second way, the one presented above, there is no appeal to an a priori grasp of a concept's satisfaction conditions. What is a priori is just logic, which includes the logic of identity—specifically, that identities are necessary (if true), as in the schema presented earlier. Where the empirical element comes into play is in providing justification for the identity claim in question, for believing it true in the first place. So, for example, we do not identify water with H_2O by bringing to bear our a priori conception of the watery role and seeing which entity in the world satisfies it. Rather, we find that identifying water with H_2O is the best hypothesis to explain the behavior of water, and so is a straightforward application of inference to the best explanation. Once that identity is empirically established, we then get modal consequences from our a priori knowledge of the logic of identity. If viewed this way, then there is no obvious barrier to applying the same reasoning to the identification of phenomenal consciousness with some functional or physical state, and then we get the very same modal consequences as we did in the case of water. Again, the point is that empirical information has to come into play somewhere in the etiology of an a posteriori necessity. By locating the empirical component in the justification of the identity statement that licenses the redescription of the target phenomenon, whether it be redescribing water as 'H_2O' or phenomenal consciousness in physical/functional terms, the Type B materialist can employ the very same reasoning to avoid a commitment to brute necessities.

While I believe this is a perfectly plausible defense of Type B materialism in response to the challenge of the conceivability argument, it presents my overall position with a serious problem. At the outset I presented my commitment to two claims: First, I rejected the conceivability argument as an a priori refutation of Type B materialism. In Sections 18.2 and 18.3 I have defended that claim. But second, I also claimed that there is an explanatory gap between the physical and the phenomenal, and that one was warranted, by inferring to the best explanation, in rejecting materialism despite the defense of it just presented. However, given the argument just presented, that identities do not require explanations, how do I defend the claim that there is an explanatory gap after all? And if there is an explanatory gap, does that not mean I should accept the original conceivability argument? So what I need is an account of psycho-physical identities that leaves room for an explanatory gap but not in a way that provides support for an a priori refutation of materialism. I turn to that task in Section 18.4.

18.4 Explanation and Psycho-Physical Identity

The defense against the conceivability argument I have laid out for the Type B materialist crucially involves an appeal to the claim that identities do not require explanation.[6] This claim is crucial to the defense because psycho-physical identities are both necessary and, by hypothesis, not explicable, so if they did require an explanation they would constitute just the sort of brute necessities we want not to be committed to. But if identities do not require an explanation, where do we locate the explanatory gap?

Prima facie, the claim that identities are not apt for explanation makes good sense. Consider our standard example, water is identical to H_2O. Suppose someone asked, 'but why is water (identical to) H_2O'? I, for one, and not just because of my poor knowledge of chemistry, would not know how to answer such a question; it is unclear what the questioner is after. Why is water H_2O? Why is the Evening Star the Morning Star? Why is Mark Twain Samuel Clemens? In all of these cases it seems the only answer is, 'well, because they are'.

Of course the neo-Fregean can come up with an answer to these why questions. She can say that the answer to the question why water is H_2O is that H_2O satisfies the conditions conceptually constitutive of being water. That is what makes water H_2O. But as I see it, the question is an odd one and the fact that the (neo-Russellian) Type B materialist must consider such questions odd is not at all an embarrassment. In the end, of course, everyone will point to the fact that H_2O manifests the relevant superficial properties of water to justify the claim that they are identical. But for the Type B materialist pointing to these facts comes in by way of justifying acceptance of the identity claim, not explaining what makes it true.

This last point is worth emphasizing. Nobody denies that the reason we think water is in fact H_2O is that its being so explains its superficial behavior: why it is liquid at room temperature, freezes and boils at the temperatures it does, quenches thirst, etc. The disagreement concerns what role these facts play in establishing the identity claim. As I said above, for the neo-Fregean they play the role of determining which entity in the actual world (or the world of the scenario being considered) plays the role that is conceptually constitutive of being water. On this view it is a priori that water is whatever plays the watery role, so once one finds out which entity in the world in question plays that role, it just follows, a priori, that it is water. But for the neo-Russellian, the features that are collectively described as 'playing the watery role' are not conceptually constitutive of being water—nothing is, as on this view it is an atomic concept. However, the watery features are attributed to water as a matter of experience, and what we call 'the watery role' embodies extremely well-confirmed beliefs about the behavior of water. Thus, when we

---

[6] This section has been influenced by reading O'Conaill (unpublished) and subsequent correspondence.

find that H₂O explains these features, we have excellent, but still non-demonstrative reasons for identifying water with it.

So there is, then, a sense one can attach to the question 'why is water H₂O?' for the neo-Russellian, but it is not really a question about why water is H₂O, rather a question about why we should believe that water is H₂O. However this interpretation of the 'why' question will not support there being an explanatory gap when dealing with psycho-physical identities. To the question, why believe that (say) pain is c-fiber firing (or some functional state realized by c-fiber firing), the Type B materialist has an apparently easy answer: we should believe it because there is so much about the behavior of pain that is explained if we identify it with c-fiber firing. So on this picture it does not look as if there is room for the explanatory gap.

There is, however, another sort of question one can ask about an identity. Instead of why the identity holds—which, for the moment, we are granting is not an apt question—we can ask *how* the identity *could* hold. In other words, we can ask a 'how possible?', or 'how could it be?' question about an alleged identity.[7] So, to quote an example of E. J. Lowe (2000), suppose a Pythagorian tells you that standard middle-sized concrete objects, like tables and chairs, are in fact really numbers. One's query in response is not going to concern *why* that is the case, but rather *how it could be* the case. If an identity is claimed to hold and one cannot really see how it could, that certainly seems appropriately described as an explanatory gap. The idea is that explanations make their explananda intelligible, and what seems to be lacking with psycho-physical identities, according to this line of argument, is intelligibility. What we seek is a way to make the identity claim intelligible.

While I think in the end the explanatory problem with psycho-physical identity claims is of the 'how possible?' variety rather than of the 'why is it?' variety, the dialectic around this is complicated. So, consider the example above, the Pythagorian theory. If someone seriously proposed that, say, the chair I am sitting on is in fact identical to a number, I would of course reply that the very idea of the chair being a number is unintelligible. But what makes it unintelligible? Well, I might say the following. The chair has mass and is extended in three spatial dimensions, while numbers are abstract and lack such properties. In other words, when the claim that A is identical with B seems unintelligible, the lack of intelligibility can be attributed to one (or both) of A and B possessing properties that it is difficult to see how the other could instantiate. A number is not extended in space, has no mass, and the like, so how could it be identical to a chair that clearly instantiates these properties?

But now, let us try to apply this to psycho-physical identities. Someone proposes that pain is identical to the firing of c-fibers, or that the phenomenal experience of seeing red is identical to a pattern of firing in V4. One might then ask in response, 'but how could an experience of a color just be a pattern of neural firing?' Well, why could it not be?

---

[7] This is how O'Connail (unpublished) puts it. In early formulations of the explanatory gap I had also described the issue as making the identity 'intelligible', seeing 'how it could be true', which I take to be two ways of saying the same thing.

Presumably, one would appeal to certain properties of an experience that seem not to be attributable to a pattern of neural firing. For instance, experiences of red have a certain qualitative character that seems not appropriately attributed to neural states. If we know one side of the identity claim represents something that has a certain property and the other side represents something that does not have that property, then, by Leibniz's Law, we know the identity claim is false. So the explanatory question here is, how could a pattern of neural firing instantiate this reddish qualitative character? Explain that and then the how-possible question is answered (assuming this can be done for all the relevant properties).

The problem with this way of characterizing the explanatory gap is that the Type B materialist (e.g. Papineau 2002) will reply that we have misunderstood the original identity claim. It is not that there is some state that has a qualitative character and we are identifying that state with a neural state, which then commits one to making intelligible how the neural state could instantiate the qualitative character. Rather, the property in question—the qualitative character itself—is being identified with the relevant neural property. So the kind of how-possible question we want to ask, which relies on specifying a property instantiated by what is represented on one side of the identity that seems unintelligibly attributed to what is represented on the other side of the identity, cannot even be asked.

So here is the dilemma. If you ask a how-possible question about any alleged psycho-physical identity, it is incumbent upon you to find some property clearly instantiated by one term that it seems unintelligible to attribute to the other term. But as soon as you present such a property, the reply will be that it is that very property itself that is being identified with its counterpart across the identity sign. So we seem to be left with only the why question, and that we already admitted, when it comes to identity claims, cannot be asked.

Yet, one wants to say, clearly there is a question here, and it is evident from the contrast we can draw between the psycho-physical case and the standard examples of theoretical identities. I really do not have any idea what someone has in mind if they ask either why water is H_2O or how possibly water could be H_2O.[8] However, when someone finds unintelligible the identity between a visual experience of color and some neural state I perfectly well understand what puzzles them.

In the past I have addressed this question in two ways. In Levine (2001) I distinguished between what I called 'gappy identities' and 'non-gappy identities'. A gappy identity is one for which the question 'why?' or 'how?' is intelligible, whereas a non-gappy one is one for which such questions did not really make sense. Of course this is really to name the problem rather than solve it. I am convinced there is a distinction here, but the distinction itself does not provide much insight into what it is. In Levine (2007) I leaned in

---

[8] Note that I would understand if someone thought, like Aristotle, that water was continuously divisible, and so therefore couldn't be swarms of H_2O molecules, which aren't. But then we would explain that water doesn't actually have that property; instead, it has the property of *appearing* continuously divisible. We can then explain how swarms of H_2O molecules could instantiate that appearance property.

Papineau's direction and acknowledged that what underlies the explanatory gap is really what he called an 'intuition of distinctness', but then, unlike him, argued that there were good reasons to take this intuition seriously and not consider it question-begging, as the standard explanation for the intuition, involving the phenomenal concepts strategy, did not work. Again, I think there is something right about this response too, but it still does not feel adequate to me. So let me try again.

Here is the structure of the problem. Consider property P, which supervenes on property B. If the necessitation of P by B is not to be brute and inexplicable, then there must be some representation of P, R,[9] such that one can derive P's instantiation from B's instantiation under those representations; that is, something like 'Bx → Rx' is a priori. But in order for this to be an explanation of how P, as originally represented (say, as 'P'), is necessitated by B, it must be that P = R is true.

Now, take 'P = R'. Suppose we cannot see how it could be true. Given our model of what it is to find an identity claim unintelligible, what this means is that P and R each have properties that it is hard to see how the other could instantiate. Let us say P has Q and it is difficult to see how R could have Q. But then maybe the problem is that Q is identical to S, R has S (or we can understand how it might have S), and so therefore it has Q. But then one might have a problem with the identity of Q and S, asking, again, how is that possible?

Now, on the model we have come up with for what it is to ask a 'how possible' question, questioning the intelligibility of the identity between Q and S would have to rest on specifying some further property, X, that Q has and for which it is difficult to see how it could be instantiated by S. It does seem that this has to give out at some point. Then the question is, can one just say that the identity does not make sense without appealing to yet further properties? If not, then why can the Type-B materialist not just keep proposing identities of this sort until we have no more properties to play the game with? At that point a brute 'intuition of distinctness' is all the anti-materialist can point to and it can easily seem question-begging.

In Levine (2007) I argued that given the 'core contrast' between standard theoretical identities and psycho-physical identities, it was incumbent on the materialist to explain why we have this intuition of distinctness, and not rest complacent with the claim that relying on a mere intuition is question-begging. I further argued that the phenomenal concept strategy does not explain this contrast, at least not so long as one is restricted to materialist implementations of phenomenal concepts, as of course Type-B materialists are.

A few paragraphs from the end of the paper, I said the following:

> One might say that there now is a second explanatory gap: between implementations of cognitive architecture and whatever it is about phenomenal concepts—in my terms, that they afford genuine cognitive presence to phenomenal properties—that is responsible for the original explanatory gap. If one thought the original

---

[9] We also need an appropriate representation of B, but let's just assume that 'B' (or what goes in for that schematic letter) is the one we want.

> explanatory gap was a problem and needed to be explained away, then one ought to be bothered by this one as well...Suppose I'm right that we can't now imagine how a materialist story of phenomenal concepts would go. No mere physical-causal mechanism can provide the kind of cognitive presence we seem to enjoy with respect to our phenomenal experience. So what is it we need? It seems to me that we need something like the old-fashioned relation of acquaintance. We are acquainted with our experience, and as acquaintance *presents* properties, not merely represents them, we find it difficult to integrate what is presented with what is only represented in a way that allows the latter to explain the former. If acquaintance itself cannot be explained in terms of physical-causal mechanisms, as I claim (at least so far) it can't, then we have to contemplate the possibility that it is a brute relation. If so, then the Materialist Constraint is violated, and materialism is false. (Levine 2007)

I think in the end the proper location for the explanatory gap is precisely at this second level, so it is not that there are two gaps, but rather the real source of the gap is the one identified in this passage. Here is how I want to put it now.

Let us assume we have reached the stage in questioning the intelligibility of an identity claim where there do not seem to be any further properties to appeal to. As in the model above, we hit the point where we have an 'intuition of distinctness' concerning Q and S. It is important to emphasize that the intuition of distinctness is not just an intuition to the effect that the properties in question are distinct, but that one does not see how they could be the same. After all, if it were not for the lack of intelligibility attaching to the identity claim, what would be the basis of the intuition?

To get concrete, what might be the relevant property to put in for 'Q' here? I think something like being a determinate *quality*, where reddishness, painfulness, itchiness are examples of what I mean by qualities. Neural firing patterns or causal roles, or whatever physico-functional properties are the proposed candidates for materialist identity claims, do not seem to have this feature of being qualitative. Now suppose the materialist finds some property of neural firing patterns, or functional roles, and says this is what being qualitative is and the response is, but how can that be? How can being qualitative be just identical to playing a certain functional role?

Given our initial assumption, there is now no other property of being qualitative that we can point to which does not seem intelligibly instantiated by the functional role (or neural firing pattern) property. We just hit bedrock and want to say that we just do not see how being qualitative could be that. The materialist wants to say at that point that if you cannot come up with another property to use in a Lebniz's Law argument against the proposed identity, then your resistance is merely intuitive and has no probative value. But I come back and say that indeed there does not seem to be another property to appeal to for a Leibniz's Law argument, and yet we cannot shake the feeling that there is something unintelligible about the identity. This requires explanation.

In any other case where we have a how-possible problem about an identity there is some further property to appeal to. Once those are exhausted, the intuitive problem disappears as well. So long as our concepts have run out of associations with other concepts and now function—à la the neo-Russellian view—as mere labels, there does not seem to be any basis for intuitive resistance. So it must not be a matter of further properties, but rather the form of access to the property in question. Here is where the appeal to acquaintance comes in. It looks as if the kind of cognitive relation we bear to the contents of our experience is different in kind from that we bear to other sorts of properties, and it makes sense that it is due to this fundamental difference in modes of access that we persist in our intuitive resistance.

Now once we admit that the mode of access itself is a way of revealing difference, or creating an intuition of distinctness, we have to ask ourselves whether acquaintance is plausibly a physical (or physically realized) relation or not, and whether what is presented by that relation—that with which we are acquainted—is plausibly physical, or physically realized. At this point of course the materialist can still insist that they are identical to physical properties and we just cannot see it. I grant this is a consistent position and do not rule it out on a priori grounds. But I find it implausible, and think inference to the best explanation is that we have transcended the physical at this point.

I want to point out again, for emphasis, just where the move to acquaintance is doing the work I need to solve the problem I faced at the beginning of this section. My problem was that I could not provide an account of how one could find the proposed identity of qualitative character with a physico-functional property unintelligible—subject to a how-possible worry—unless there was yet another property of qualitative character that could support a Leibniz's Law objection. By appealing to a fundamentally different mode of cognitive access to qualitative character—acquaintance—I can make sense of the how-possible worry without recourse to another property. If conscious experience involves acquaintance with the contents of experience, and we are acquainted with nothing else, then this explains why the bare intuition of distinctness (that is, one that is not based on a Leibniz's Law objection) arises here and nowhere else. What explains this aspect of acquaintance? Well, this is, again, where I would use inference to the best explanation to support the claim that it is because, with acquaintance, we are not dealing with a purely physical phenomenon.

References

Alter, T. and Walter, S. (2007), *Phenomenal Concepts and Phenomenal Knowledge*. Oxford: Oxford University Press.

Biggs, S. and Wilson, J. (2017), 'The A Priority of Abduction', *Philosophical Studies*, 174/3: 735–58.

Block, N. and Stalnaker, R. (1999), 'Conceptual Analysis, Dualism, and the Explanatory Gap', *Philosophical Review*. 108: 1–46.

Chalmers, D. (2002), 'Consciousness and Its Place in Nature', in D. Chalmers (ed.), *Philosophy of Mind: Classical and Contemporary Readings*. Oxford: Oxford University Press.

Chalmers, D. (2006), 'The foundations of two-dimensional semantics' in M. Garcia-Carpintero and J. Macia (eds), *Two-dimensional Semantics: Foundations and Applications*. Oxford: Oxford University Press.

Chalmers, D. and Jackson, F. (2001), 'Conceptual Analysis and Reductive Explanation', *Philosophical Review*, 110: 315–61.

Gendler, T. and Hawthorne, J. (eds) (2002), *Conceivability and Possibility*. Oxford: Oxford University Press.

Kripke, S. (1980), *Naming and Necessity*. Cambridge, MA: Harvard University Press.

Levine, J. (1998), 'Conceivability and the Metaphysics of Mind', *Noûs*, 32/4: 449–80.

Levine, J. (2001), *Purple Haze: The Puzzle of Consciousness*. Oxford: Oxford University Press.

Levine, J. (2007), 'Phenomenal Concepts and the Materialist Constraint', in T. Alter and S. Walter (eds), *Phenomenal Concepts and Phenomenal Knowledge*. Oxford: Oxford University Press.

Levine, J. (2014), 'Modality, Semantics, and Consciousness', *Philosophical Studies*, symposium on David Chalmers, *The Character of Consciousness*, 167/3: 775–84.

Loar, B. (1997), 'Phenomenal States', in N. Block, O. Flanagan, and G. Güzeldere (eds), *The Nature of Consciousness*. Cambridge, MA: MIT Press.

Lowe, E. J. (2000), *An Introduction to the Philosophy of Mind*. Cambridge: Cambridge University Press.

O'Conaill, D. (unpublished manuscript). 'Identity and the Explanatory Gap'.

Papineau, D. (2002), *Thinking About Consciousness*. Oxford: Oxford University Press.

Poland, J. (1994), *Physicalism: The Philosophical Foundations*. Oxford: Clarendon Press.

Putnam, H. (1975), 'The Meaning of Meaning', in K. Gunderson (ed.), *Language, Mind, and Knowledge*. Minneapolis: University of Minnesota Press, 131–93.

CHAPTER 19

REPRESENTATIONALISM ABOUT CONSCIOUSNESS

ADAM PAUTZ

To a first approximation, representationalism about sensory consciousness holds that sensory consciousness (for instance, being conscious of a red and round thing, or being conscious of the aroma of coffee) is a bit like *belief* or *judgment*. Having a belief is a matter of representing the world to be a certain way. Likewise, according to representationalists, sensory consciousness is a matter of representing the world to be a certain way.

Representationalism is important because it changes the shape of the mind–body problem, the problem of explaining how the brain engenders conscious experience. Once we accept representationalism, the hard problem of consciousness becomes a special case of the hard problem of representation, the problem of how the brain enables us to represent the world. Some (Armstrong, Tye, Dretske) have suggested that representationalism fits well with the idea that consciousness can be reduced to something physical. Others think that representationalism makes the mind–body problem harder because our usual models for reducing representation do not apply in the special case of conscious representation.

In Section 19.1, I formulate the basic theory. In Section 19.2, I explain an argument for it. In Section 19.3, I consider objections. In Sections 19.4 and 19.5, I describe two ways of developing the basic theory: *reductive* and *nonreductive* representationalism.

19.1 WHAT IS REPRESENTATIONALISM ABOUT CONSCIOUSNESS?

Here is one way to get an initial sense of representationalism. Suppose you have a hallucination as of a tiger in the room (as one does). Suppose it is more like a dream or imagery than ordinary sensory consciousness. On a traditional view, you are presented with a tiger-like 'mental image' or 'visual field region' arrayed with 'qualia' on a peculiar sort of internal cinema screen (Russell 1912; Peacocke 2008). But this view is implausible for such a degraded hallucination. If such an 'image' really exists, how many stripes does it have? A better view is that you are just in a 'belief-like' state with an impoverished content according to which a tiger-like thing is present, even though no such (mental or physical) thing is present. And once we accept this 'belief-like' view for such degraded hallucinations, it then becomes natural to generalize the view to all sensory consciousness: even an ordinary veridical experience of tiger is just a belief-like state of the same kind, only with a much richer content. There is nothing more to the reality of your experience. While in a hallucination case, the belief-like state occurs 'off-line', in a veridical case it is controlled by the impact of the environment on the visual system. Your neural patterns somehow enable you to have belief-like states in which it seems to you that the external world is thus-and-so. But you do not have any access to these neural patterns; you only have access to what they are about.

So far, I have tried to give you an initial sense of representationalism. But we need a more precise formulation. I have said that, according to representationalism, sensory consciousness is *analogous to* belief. So, we will start with some remarks about belief; then we can formulate representationalism more exactly.

To believe is to represent things as being a certain *way*. For instance, if you believe that the thing on the table in the next room is a red ball, then you represent it as being a certain way: as *red* and *round*. In other words, in believing, you generally *predicate properties of things*. As Scott Soames says, 'we predicate redness of o, when we form the belief that o is red' (2010, 81). Let us say that in having beliefs we *cognitively* predicate properties of things. Here is an important fact: you can cognitively predicate a property quite independently of whether anything has that property; your belief may be false. Indeed, you can predicate redness even if there does not really exist anything you predicate it of (Soames 2010: 117).[1]

Now we can turn to representationalism. Let us start with hallucination. For instance, suppose you hallucinate a blue ball. It seems to you that there is a thing before you with the properties *being bluish*, *being round*, and *being before me*. Yet these properties do not characterize any physical thing in your environment or brain. How is this possible? Above we noted that you can cognitively predicate a property even if nothing has that property. Representationalists conjecture that sensory consciousness has a similar nature. In particular, they suggest that sensory consciousness involves *phenomenally predicating properties*. (I will also sometimes call it the relation of *phenomenal representation*.) When you hallucinate a blue ball, nothing before you really has the properties *being bluish*, *being round*, and *being before me*. Still, these *properties* exist.

---

[1] In formulating representationalism, I will assume the existence of properties understood as 'abstract objects'. I assume 'realism' about properties as against 'nominalism'. For an argument for this assumption, see Yi 2017. However, I think that representationalism could also be formulated in a higher-order language acceptable to nominalists. I will touch on this issue later in the chapter: see the discussion of 'relation-to-abstract-items representationalism' and 'concrete representationalism' in Section 19.3.

Representationalists propose that your hallucination consists in your phenomenally predicating such properties as a result of aberrant activity in your visual system, in the absence of anything that has the properties. Your brain is 'telling you' that those properties are out there, even though they are not out there. Hallucination is the appearing of properties, in the absence of anything that has the properties. In particular, your hallucination consists in your phenomenally predicating the complex property λx(x is round and x is bluish and x is before me).[2] This is a first approximation: the content of the hallucination is much more rich and detailed than this.

In one respect, then, phenomenal predication is similar to cognitive predication: you can phenomenally predicate properties that nothing has. But, in another respect, phenomenal predication is *radically different* from cognitive predication: unlike cognitively predicating properties, *phenomenally* predicating properties necessarily involves undergoing a state with *presentational phenomenology* (that is why I call it *phenomenal* predication). For instance, when you phenomenally predicate λx(x is round and x is bluish and x is before me), it seems to you that something with those properties is 'present'. This need not be so when one *cognitively* predicates λx(x is round and x is bluish and x is before me). For instance, you could guess that such a thing is before you with your eyes closed.

Representationalists hold that, in normal cases as in the hallucination case we have discussed, having the ball-experience consists in nothing but phenomenally predicating the complex property λx(x is round and x is bluish and x is before me). The only difference is that in the normal case, unlike in the hallucination case, something really *does* have these properties. The way you phenomenally represent things to be is the way that they are.

Representationalists generalize their view beyond vision. For instance, those who lose a limb often continue to feel a pain where the limb used to be. It is part of the phenomenology of their experience that a pain quality seems bound together with a bodily location. A representational view of pain accounts for this nicely. On this view, having phantom pain consists in phenomenally predicating the complex property λx(x is throbbing pain and x is at location l). Or again, representationalism can be applied to the experience of *smell* (Batty 2010). Having a smell experience consists in phenomenally predicating an olfactory quality (*minty, citrus-like*, etc.) together with a certain diffuse location. In a smell hallucination (phantosmia) nothing in the relevant location possesses the relevant quality.

According to representationalists, qualitative similarities and differences in sensory consciousness are similarities and differences in the properties we phenomenally predicate. For instance, if I view a ball, and you view an identical-looking but distinct ball, we might have the same experience because we phenomenally predicate the same properties, even if we see distinct balls. The character of sensory consciousness is indifferent to the identities of the things we experience (if any); what matters is the way we experience the things to be.

---

[2] I use λ-abstraction to refer to complex properties. See Sider 2010.

So far, we have developed an initial formulation of representationalism:

Representationalism (first pass): undergoing an episode of sensory consciousness with a certain character is identical with *phenomenally predicating* a complex array of perceptible properties. All differences in the character of sensory consciousness consist in nothing but differences in what arrays of perceptible properties we phenomenally predicate.[3]

However, there is a problem with this formulation. It contains a made-up technical term, namely 'phenomenally predicating'. We need to say what this term means. Until we do, representationalism is not a clear thesis; we have no idea how we can determine whether it is true or false. As a matter of fact, representationalists have not really adequately explained what they mean by terms like 'phenomenally predicate' or 'phenomenally represent'. So the debate over representationalism has proceeded in the absence of any adequate explanation of what it is saying. This has made the debate over 'representationalism' unclear and difficult to resolve (see note 13 for an example).

Here is a solution. To formulate representationalism without using any unexplained technical terms, we can employ the general *Ramsey–Carnap–Lewis method* for defining theoretical terms. Representationalists think that the postulated relation of phenomenally predicating plays *the character* role: having an experience with a certain character *consists in* phenomenally predicating a certain array of perceptible properties. It also plays *the cognitive-access* role: if a thinker phenomenally predicates a perceptible property at time, then at that time they thereby have the capacity to have beliefs according to which a thing has that property and the capacity to know what that property is like. Another key feature of the phenomenal predication relation is *neutrality*: you can phenomenally predicate a property, so that it *seems* to you that an item has the property, even if nothing in your vicinity does in fact have that property. Given all this, here is all that representationalism amounts to:

Representationalism (final formulation): There is a unique relation R such that: (I) R plays the cognitive-access role, (II) R plays the character role, and (III) R is neutral.

Representationalism is now clear. This formulation does not appeal to the undefined notion that sensory consciousness is representational. In fact, it does not even contain the word 'representation'. But, if we like, we can now introduce the technical term 'phenomenally predicating' (and its synonym 'phenomenally representing'): we can use it to denote the unique relation R (*if there is one*) that satisfies (I)–(III). On this approach,

---

[3] For defenses of representationalism, see Armstrong 1968; Dretske 1995; Tye 1995; Byrne 2001; Chalmers 2010; Pautz 2010; Horgan 2014; Speaks 2015; and Mendelovici 2018. I have formulated representationalism in terms of the predication of *properties*. More often, representationalism is formulated in *propositional* terms. However, there is in fact no big difference between these formulations (Perkins and Bayne 2013: 74).

talk of the representational content of experience stands or falls with the truth of a substantive theory of the nature of experience.[4]

Bare-bones representationalism leaves open some big questions. How does the activity of soggy grey matter in the brain enable us to 'reach out' and phenomenally predicate sensible colors and shapes and other sensible properties that need not be instantiated *in the brain*? And are all these properties really out there? For instance, maybe *colors* have never been out there, but our brains evolved to 'tell us' they are out there, in order to help us isolate objects in scenes, remember these objects, and communicate about them with other observers.

We will address these questions later (Sections 19.4–5). First, we must look at the argument for the bare-bones theory (Sections 19.2–3).

19.2 THE CASE FOR REPRESENTATIONALISM: AN INFERENCE TO THE BEST EXPLANATION

The argument we will consider puts forward representationalism as the best *empirical hypothesis* about the nature of sensory consciousness, akin to the hypothesis that water is H$_2$O or that energy is mass. Representationalism provides the simplest explanation of a host of facts: the fact that many forms of sensory consciousness are essentially spatial and 'externally-directed', the fact that states of visual consciousness can be indeterminate, the fact that they can depict 'impossible' scenarios, and much else. Here I will present the argument informally in a series of steps.

Step 1: The essentially spatial character of visual consciousness. We start with a pretheoretical datum. Consider the *ball-experience* again. This experience-type is essentially spatial. Having the ball-experience *essentially* involves the *seeming* presence of a *round* item. So spatial terms like *round* must be used in any complete definition of what it is to have the experience. Moreover, necessarily, if you have enough experiences like this, this directly enables you to acquire a concept of the shape *round*. It directly enables you to think about the property *being round*, and predicate it of things in thought. In general, so-called 'color qualia' (like *being bluish*) necessarily *appear to* fill spatial regions. And when you experience many color qualia at the same time, they appear to stand in certain *spatial relations* to each other.[5]

---

[4] Travis (2004: esp 85 and 92) and Brewer (2017: sect 2.3) object to representationalism on the grounds that it requires—what they think cannot be supplied—a general algorithm (e.g. in terms of 'looks'-reports or in terms of underlying facts about causal-covariation) for determining the representational content of any given experience. Against this, the availability of the present Ramsey–Carnap–Lewis formulation of representationalism shows that talk of the representational content of experience can be perfectly intelligible even in the absence of such an algorithm.

[5] Here and in what follows, I use 'color qualia' and similar expressions (like 'sensible colors') to refer to properties involved in experience that we can get a grip on from examples, while remaining entirely neutral on their nature. For instance, as we shall see, sense datum theorists hold that they are always

This pretheoretical datum is generally accepted, which testifies to its truth. For instance, even Christopher Peacocke, who opposes representationalism, says, 'visual experience is intrinsically [essentially] spatial...if we do not use spatial properties in characterizing the visual [experience], we omit a subjective feature of the experience' (2008: 10).

The point applies equally to non-veridical visual experiences. Imagine that all your actual experiences are hallucinatory: you are a life-long 'brain in the void' (BIV). Even if your experiences are hallucinatory, they involve the seeming presence of items with shapes. And they are still enough to give you concepts of shapes. They still enable you to think about shape *properties*. For instance, you might still *have a favorite shape*. In fact, even if you are a BIV, your hallucinatory visual experiences still give you plenty of *knowledge* about shapes. They do not give you knowledge about particular physical *things* with shapes—if you are really a hallucinating BIV in empty space, you are not touch with any physical things at all. But they are still enough to enable you to know general things about shape *properties*, for instance, the timeless, necessary truth that being round is more like being oval than being square (Russell 1912: ch X; Yi 2017). And your experiences still help you to know certain other general, necessary geometrical truths.

In fact, there are real-world examples. A person with 'Charles Bonnet Syndrome' might hallucinate an extremely unusual and detailed shape. Before having the hallucination, she could not think of that *very fine-grained, detailed* shape property (unaided by experience, her powers of description and imagination are not so acute). It is her *hallucinatory experience* that explains her now having that fine-grained capacity for as long as the hallucination lasts. She can now wonder: 'Is there something shaped *that way* there?' And this shape property is not a property of any physical thing in her brain or the environment. Nor is it a property of her experience (her experience does not have a shape).

This may seem strange. How could visual experiences 'put you in touch with' spatial properties, even in hallucination cases where they do not 'put you in touch' with physical things having the properties? Maybe it is strange, but it is a fact. And it is a fact that any adequate theory of visual consciousness must somehow accommodate.

Next we will see that the spatial character of experience is not plausibly accommodated by non-representational theories. It is not accommodated at all by the 'internal physical state theory' of visual consciousness (step 2). It *is* accommodated by the 'sense datum view', but this view faces other problems (step 3). Representationalism accommodates the spatial character of experience while avoiding these problems (step 4).

Step 2: Against the internal physical state theory. The *internal physical state theory* holds that experience-types are (necessarily) identical with intrinsic physical-functional types. For instance, to have the ball-experience is just to undergo a distinctive, distributed system of neural patterns (e.g. McLaughlin 2012; Papineau 2016).

---

instantiated by sense data 'in the mind'; by contrast, representationalists hold that they are properties *represented by* experience, and that they are either properties of ordinary physical things (Section 19.4) or nothing at all (Section 19.5). They are talking about the same salient properties, even if they disagree about where to locate them in the world.

The spatial character of visual consciousness rules this view out. The argument is an application of Leibniz's Law:

1. Visual experience-types *essentially* involve the seeming presence of items with shapes (*round, oval*, etc.), and *necessarily* directly enable individuals to have concepts of shapes. (Essential spatial character.)
2. These things are *not* true of mere neural pattern-types.
3. Therefore, visual experience-types are not *identical with* neural-pattern types; for instance, it is not the case that to have the ball-experience is just to undergo a neural state.[6]

The case for Premise 2 is this. Unlike visual experience-types, the essential nature of neural patterns can be fully described without mentioning shapes like *round, oval,* and *square*. They are not *themselves* essentially round, oval, and so on. They only involve neural properties, and visible shapes are evidently distinct from neural properties. (This is so even if visible shapes are 'Edenic'. See note 30.) It also could not be said that neural patterns essentially *represent* such shape properties (*round, oval, square*) so that they *seem* present. This view is inconsistent with the fact that the essential nature of a neural pattern can be fully described in terms of *types of neurons* and the *times, directions,* and *intensities* at which they fire, without mentioning such *shapes* at all. (Analogy: it cannot be said that the *linguistic expressions* 'round', 'oval', and so on *essentially* represent the relevant shapes.) Moreover, neural patterns could not, all by themselves, necessarily endow individuals with concepts of shapes. Imagine the neural patterns occurring at random in an isolated BIV. How could undergoing a series of neural patterns *alone* necessarily be enough to give BIV concepts of *shapes* and put BIV 'in touch with' *shape properties*? The isolated system could not think about shapes and know what they are like directly by virtue of undergoing these neural patterns alone. In this respect, too, visual experience-types differ from neural patterns, since visual experience-types *are* enough to directly endow individuals with concepts of shapes. Therefore, visual experiences must be *something more* than neural patterns.

True, neural states are part of the *enabling-conditions* for visual experiences. It may even be that neural states are *sufficient for* experiences. But the spatial argument shows that visual experiences are *something* more than neural states, something that essentially involves apparent *spatial properties* that need not be instantiated *in* the brain.[7]

---

[6] For discussion of the spatial argument against the internal physical state theory, see Pautz 2010: 266–72; and Block 2019.

[7] Papineau (2014, 2016) accepts the internal physical state view. He rejects Premise 1 (essential spatial character) of the spatial argument against this view (personal discussion). On his view, having visual experiences only essentially involves being in contact with *non-spatial neural properties*, so that having visual experiences alone *only* necessarily endows thinkers with concepts of such neural properties (2016, sects 10 and 15). (Papineau calls these neural properties *square*, round*, oval** and so on. But this is misleading, since they are *nothing like* shapes. For instance, *being round* has the definition *having edges equidistant from a common point*, but this is not true of the neural property *being round**.) Thus, according to Papineau, a life-long, accidentally-created brain in a vat that *has all the same experiences as you* can only

Step 3: Against the sense datum view. According to the *sense datum theory* (Russell 1912; Jackson 1977; Peacocke 2008), to explain the spatial character of visual experience, we must indeed say that visual experiences are 'something more' than neural patterns, contrary to the internal physical state theory.

For instance, suppose that you have the ball-experience during a hallucination. According to the sense datum view, this experience-type is not a mere neural-type, although it is dependent on one. In particular, on this view, it essentially involves being presented with a 'visual field' containing a region (a 'visual sense datum') that has the properties *being bluish* and *being literally round*. And this visual sense datum is not a physical item in your brain (there is no bluish and round item in the brain in such a hallucination case), even if it might be 'created' by your brain. It is something else.[8]

In general, sense datum theorists hold that *all* visual consciousness essentially involves standing in a relation *R* to shapes and colors. Russell (1912) called this relation *sensory acquaintance*. You always stand in this relation to shapes and colors by being presented with sense data *instantiating* those shapes and colors. We might call this the *instantiation principle*. Even in normal visual consciousness, you are presented with a mental visual field that is distinct from the physical layout of objects before you. It is like a peculiar sort of internal cinema screen. This is what determines the character of visual consciousness.

This view is seductive. If you had a vivid hallucination of a blue ball, then it would seem obvious that there is *something* present to your consciousness that is *round*—if not a physical thing, then an 'image' or 'visual field region'. It would seem to be a denial of reality to suggest there is *nothing* round there (Price 1932: 3; Campbell and Cassam 2014: 10).

However, the arguments against the sense datum view are overwhelming.

First, regions of the visual field ('visual sense data') must be peculiar non-physical objects. As mentioned, if you have the ball-experience in a hallucination, there is no literally round and bluish item in your brain or your environment. So if there really exists such an item, it must be a *non-physical* region in a *non-physical* 'visual field'.[9]

---

think about such neural properties, and entirely lacks the ability to think about any *shapes* distinct from neural properties. But Papineau's view seems to go against a phenomenologically manifest fact about ordinary visual experience. As Peacocke (2008: 10) says, 'if we do not use spatial properties in characterizing the visual [experience], we omit a subjective feature of the experience'. So even a life-long BIV could think and know about *shapes*, where shapes are evidently not neural properties.

[8] A terminological note. As I have said, on the sense datum view, the familiar, salient bluish property you are presented with as you view the ball is in fact a property of a round 'sense datum'. Traditional sense datum theorists (Russell 1912; Jackson 1977) called it 'the color blue'. However, for reasons I will not go into, Peacocke (2008: 10) says it should *not* be called a 'color', even though it has hue and saturation. He calls it blue*. (Peacocke, though, is happy to say that the sense datum is literally 'round'.) I take this to be a trivial verbal issue. These different sense datum theorists have the same familiar property in mind, and just refer to it differently. In what follows, I will follow the traditional sense datum theorists, and simply call it 'the color blue'.

[9] Peacocke (2008: 14) tries to avoid this problem. He writes that, for such a hallucinating individual, 'it is *as if* there is something [a "visual field"] parts of which enjoy the relevant sensational properties [e.g. being round, being bluish], even though there is no such thing.' Thus, Peacocke says that, in this case, there does not *really* exist a round and bluish 'visual field region'; it only *seems* that such a thing exists.

Second, if you look a waterfall, and then a stationary rock, you have an experience as of the rock staying in place, but at the same time you have an experience as of movement upwards. How might sense datum theorists like Russell and Peacocke explain this 'impossible' experience? On their view, your visual field contains a blackish and rock-shaped region that is distinct from the rock. Is this region stationary? If so, what accounts for the experience as of movement upwards?

Third, the sense datum view does not apply to 'indeterminate' visual experiences, for instance, experiences of things in the periphery, dream-like hallucinations, and imagery. In such cases, it can seem to you that something is (say) roughly triangular, even if there is no *specific* triangular shape that it seems to you to have. Your experience just does not go into that much detail. Would proponents of this view like Russell and Peacocke say that a 'region of the visual field' can be roughly triangular, without having any particular triangular shape? That seems incoherent. But if we do not apply the theory to such degraded cases, then considerations of uniformity suggest that we should not apply it to more 'vivid' experiences either.

For these reasons, while it may *seem* that there exist 'sense data' or 'visual field regions', we should deny the real existence of such things.

Step 4: Representationalism to the rescue. The conclusion of the spatial argument was that visual experiences are *something* more than neural states, something that essentially involves *shape properties* that need not be instantiated in the brain. We have seen that the 'something more' cannot be the presentation of 'sense data' or 'visual field regions' *possessing* spatial properties. That idea faces big problems. But then what is the alternative?

Enter representationalism about visual consciousness. On this view, the 'something more' is a matter of *phenomenally representing* spatial properties, sensible colors, and so on. Such representational states are *enabled by* our neural states but are *distinct from* those neural states. On representationalism, in hallucination cases, it *seems* that there exist 'sense data' or 'visual field regions' replete with qualia, but there do not *really* exist such things. In such cases, there is misrepresentation. So representationalism avoids the real existence of 'sense data' and 'visual field regions'.[10]

Since he says it does not exist, Peacocke avoids commitment to a 'non-physical object' in this case. But this is just a straight representationalist account of the case. And so the question arises: why does Peacocke not apply this account to *all* cases, and so accept a version of the kind of representationalism we are leading up to? In that way, he could avoid positing 'visual field regions' *in normal as well as abnormal cases.* (For a similar point in a different connection, see the reply to the first objection in Section 19.3, and also note 13.)

[10] Experiences are distinct from neural states even on 'internalist representationalism'. For instance, Ned Block (2019) is an internalist about experience; in particular, he thinks that our experiences are totally fixed by our neural states (so that even a life-long BIV could have all the same experiences as you). To explain the essentially spatial character of visual experience, Block also accepts a form of representationalism: he suggests that visual experiences essentially involve standing in an irreducible phenomenal predication (representation) relation to arrays of spatial properties (for discussion see Section 19.5). (This is why, for a BIV, it *seems* that there exists a visual field whose parts have various spatial properties and qualities, even though in reality there exists no such field.) The result is a kind of internalist representationalism. Even though this view holds that visual experiences are wholly determined by neural states, it implies that they are something more than neural states. This is because it implies that having experience

Taken together, the points we have covered lead straight to this view. The spatial character of visual consciousness means that, in both good cases and hallucination cases, the ball-experience involves the seeming presence of a round thing, and necessarily grounds the ability to think about the property of being round. The simplest explanation is that, in every case, having this experience involves standing in a relation R to the property *being round*; when you bear this relation to a property, then you can easily thereby predicate this property of things in thought. That is, R plays the *cognitive-access role*. As we saw, sense datum theorists also posited such a relation, and they thought that it obeys a kind of *instantiation principle*. Russell (1912) called it *acquaintance*. But we also saw that the instantiation principle leads to disaster—it requires peculiar non-physical objects ('sense data', 'visual field regions'). So now we add to our proto-theory a clause that goes against the sense datum theory: you can stand in R to a property, such as the property of being round, even if you are not related to an item (a physical thing, an image, or visual field region) that instantiates the property. That is, R satisfies *neutrality*. When you have the ball-experience, you stand in the *same* R relation to the property *being bluish* (or *being bluish**, or whatever you want to call it). After all, we might as well explain color experience and spatial experience in the same way. So we have arrived at the view that having the ball-experience *necessarily* involves standing in a relation R to the complex property $\lambda x(x$ is round and x is bluish and x is before me), both in hallucination cases and in normal cases. Now, the simplest explanation of this necessary connection is that having the ball-experience *just is* standing in R to this complex property. There is *nothing more to having the ball-experience*. In particular, standing in R to $\lambda x(x$ is round and x is bluish and x is before me) is not grounded in any additional, more basic mental condition ('intrinsic properties of the experience', 'undergoing a sensation', 'being presented with a visual field region with qualia', etc.). That is, R plays the character-role.

We have given an argument for the theory that the ball-experience involves a relation R that has certain features: it is 'neutral', grounds cognitive access, and constitutes phenomenal character. As we have formulated 'representationalism', this hypothesized relation thereby counts as 'phenomenal representation', and this thesis counts as 'representationalism'. The claim that experience is representational is *not* a pretheoretical claim that lies at the surface (*pace* Speaks 2017: 493). It cannot be established just by pointing out that differences in experience are accompanied by differences in how things seem (*pace* Byrne 2001). (After all, even sense datum theorists could agree with this.) It is a totally non-obvious empirical hypothesis about the hidden nature of experience, akin to the hypothesis that matter is energy.

Representationalism accommodates the spatial character of visual experience. Contrary to the internal physical state view, the definition of what it is to have the ball-experience involves more than *types of neurons* and the *times*, *directions*, and *intensities*

---

essentially involves standing in a non-neural, phenomenal predication relation to spatial properties that are not instantiated in the brain. (Compare how the sense datum view implies that experiences are something more than neural states even if they wholly determined by neural states.) We will discuss internalist representationalism in Section 19.5.

at which they fire. Rather, we must use spatial terms to fully characterize what it is to have the ball-experience. For to have the ball-experience is to phenomenally predicate λx(x is round and x is bluish and x is before me). At the same time, since phenomenal predication is a 'neutral' relation to properties, representationalism avoids 'sense data' or 'visual field regions'. There need not exist anything (a sense datum or a visual field region) that has those spatial and other features. So representationalism avoids the problems confronted by the sense datum view. For instance, representationalism allows a very natural explanation of 'indeterminate' experiences (peripheral vision, dream-like hallucinations, dreams, imagery): they involve information loss. Just like beliefs, experiences can be more or less rich in informational content. No 'indeterminate sense data' or 'indeterminate visual field regions' are required. As for 'impossible' experiences like the waterfall illusion, the explanation of the peculiar phenomenology is now straightforward: you phenomenally represent that the rock is standing still and, at the same time, you phenomenally represent that *something in the same region (not necessarily the rock) is moving upward* (without phenomenally representing anything else about this moving item). The movement is not 'bound' to the rock.[11]

Step 5: Generalizing to all forms of sensory consciousness. Representationalism is a very strong thesis. It says that *every* type of sensory-perceptual experience is identical with standing in a relation R to a distinct complex of perceptible properties. To support this, we note that the previous steps apply equally to all other sensory-perceptual experiences. Different types of experiences provide cognitive access to different arrays of sensible properties (pain qualities, olfactory qualities, audible qualities) bound with various spatial properties. The most economical and most uniform hypothesis is that different types of visual experiences consist in nothing but *bearing R—the same relation involved in the ball-experience—*to different complexes of properties.

Step 6: Against naïve realism. So, a strong argument can be made for representationalism. Nevertheless, many think we should instead accept *naïve realism* (e.g. Brewer 2011: Campbell and Cassam 2014; Allen 2016). Naïve realists agree with representationalists that what it is to have the ball-experience, unlike what it is to have a neural state, can only be defined by using spatial terms like *round* and *three-feet away*. So they agree with representationalists that having the ball-experience is something more than undergoing a neural state. But they disagree with representationalists about what this 'something more' is. On one version of naïve realism, to have the ball-experience is (roughly) to *either* see the blueness and roundness as an external item *or* be in a state that is indiscriminable from seeing the blueness and roundness of an external item. This is a kind of 'disjunctivism'. The first clause provides a naïve realist account of normal perception and the second clause provides a 'negative epistemic' account of illusion and hallucination.

How are we to decide between representationalism and naïve realism of this sort? This is a big issue but let me mention two points.

---

[11] Although I call this an 'impossible' experience, it is not really the case that its content is impossible. For instance, it would be true in a case where the rock is not moving, but an invisible thing in the vicinity is moving upward.

First, naïve realists have problems with illusion and hallucination. Return to the example (mentioned in step 1 above) in which someone with Charles Bonnet Syndrome has a vivid and long-lasting hallucination of a very idiosyncratic and complex shape S and that this explains her new capacity to (for example) wonder whether anything really has *that specific shape*. According to the 'negative epistemic' account of hallucination that many naïve realists favor, all that is going on is that she is in a state that cannot be discriminated from seeing. But how could this negative epistemic condition *explain* her new capacity to think uniquely of this idiosyncratic and complex shape S? (She could not think of it prior to having such an experience: her experience-independent powers of thought are not so discriminating.) If her hallucination explains this new cognitive capacity, does it not have to have a more 'positive' nature, as we said in step 4 of the foregoing argument for representationalism? Do we not have to say that her having the hallucination involves her standing in *some interesting perceptual relation R* to this specific idiosyncratic shape S, a relation that is fit to play the 'cognitive access role' (for example, *perceiving a sense datum with the shape*, or *phenomenally predicating the shape*)? Otherwise, how does the hallucination *explain* her capacity to think of S and not some other shape? (For discussion of these issues, see Brewer 2011: 112ff and Alford-Duguid and Arsenaul 2017.)

In addition, naïve realists face empirical problems. They cannot accommodate in a plausible way the role of internal neural processing in shaping sensory consciousness. (For discussion, see Logue 2017; Beck 2018; and Campbell 2018.) By contrast, representationalists can easily accommodate the role of the brain, by accepting an 'internalist' form of representationalism.

We will be discussing the forms of representationalism, and how they might accommodate the role of the brain, in Sections 19.4–5. But first let us consider some objections to the basic theory of representationalism.

19.3 Objections to Representationalism about Sensory Consciousness

I will put each objection in the mouth of a hypothetical opponent, and then offer a possible representationalist rejoinder.

Objection. How can you be so confident in representationalism's strong thesis that *all* phenomenal differences among experiences are representational differences?

For instance, what about blur? You look at a blue ball with your glasses on. Then you take your glasses off. There is a phenomenal difference in the character of your experience. Yet to a mature perceiver it does not look as if any mind-independent object has really changed. So (the objection continues) there is no difference in the properties you phenomenally predicate (Boghossian and Velleman 1989; Burge 2003; Smith 2008).

Reply. There are two plausible representationalist explanations of blur: the under-representation view (Tye 2000) and the over-representation view (Allen 2003). However, here I will not go into them. Instead, I will make a more general point. For the sake of argument, suppose that the representationalist explanations of blur due to Tye and Allen fail. Then opponents will demand an alternative account of blur from representationalists. But we can turn the tables and ask them *what is their own account? Whatever* account they offer, it might be co-opted by the representationalist and turned into a representationalist account.

For instance, anti-representationalists might suggest a sense datum theory of blur. They might say that, when you take off your glasses, what is going on is that you are presented with a 'visual field region' that has the following trio of properties: *round*, *bluish* (or *bluish**), and *'blurry'*. Here the property of being blurry is a property of regions of the visual field and not physical things. This anti-representationalist account, then, appeals to the property of being blurry without saying much about its nature.[12]

Now if anti-representationalists can appeal to such a special property (without saying much about its nature), there is no obvious bar to representationalists appealing to such a property too. While anti-representationalists can say it is a property of a non-physical 'visual field region', representationalists can say it is a property of *nothing* at all. That is, when one has a blurry experience of a blue ball, all that is going on is that one is phenomenally representing the co-instantiation of the properties *being bluish* (or *being bluish**), *being round*, and the special property *being blurred*. But nothing—no physical thing and no region of the visual field—has this trio of properties.

This representationalist account describes the content of the blurry experience *in exactly the same way* as the anti-representationalist account. It just adds that the content is not real. It merely *seems* that there is a blurry visual field region, according to this view. So how could it be *inferior* to the anti-representationalist account? If anything, it is vastly superior, since it avoids the real existence of a peculiar, non-physical 'visual field region'.

The point here is general. If you have reason to believe that there is a difference in character between two of your experiences, then you must be aware of a *difference*, or an *apparent difference*, of some kind. (If not, you have no reason to think that there was a difference in the character of your experiences in the first place!) But a difference is just a difference in *properties*. So it will always be possible to hold that the relevant difference in character consists in a difference in what properties you bear the representational relation *R* to. That is, it will always be possible to say that the different properties are *represented* properties. For the Ramsey–Carnap–Lewis version of representationalism

---

[12] Boghossian and Velleman (1989: 96) suggest a sense datum view of this kind (but in his 2008 Boghossian takes it back and suggests a representational view). Burge (2003) criticizes representationalism on the grounds that it cannot handle blur but he does not offer his own positive, illuminating account of blur. In fact, he nowhere proposes any theory of the phenomenal character of visual experience and its built-in spatial structure (although at p. 444 he does suggest, without argument, that it supervenes on the internal chemical properties of the brain). However, he does repeatedly speak of a 'visual field' (2003: 408, 440), which suggests something like the sense datum theory.

is a very minimal thesis which does not by itself place any restrictions on what properties can be phenomenally represented.[13] (True, it may sometimes be difficult to *specify* or *characterize* the different properties; but this does not affect my present point.) So it is hard to see how there *could* be a counterexample to the bare-bones representationalist theory. If there is a good objection to representationalism, it must take a different form.[14]

Objection. You representationalists give a lousy *explanation* of the ball-experience. Your explanation is that you stand in this mysterious relation, 'phenomenal predication', to λx(x is round and x bluish and x before me). When asked to define this term, you say it is a theoretical term, and define it as 'the relation such that having an experience consists in standing this relation to some property-complex'. But this makes the explanation look trivial or circular. How is this progress? (John Campbell pressed this objection in discussion. See also Langsam 2018.)

Reply. This objection misunderstands representationalism. Representationalism, as we have formulated it, is not an *explanation* of experience. To explain X is to cite *something else*, Y, that stands in an explanatory relation (causation, grounding) to X. But representationalism does not do that. Representationalism is an existentially-quantified *identity claim*. It only says this: there is a relation R with certain features (it is 'neutral' and grounds 'cognitive access') and having the ball-experience (for instance) is identical with standing in R to λx(x is round and x bluish and x before me). This cannot be criticized for giving a trivial or circular *explanation* of experience—it is not trivial, it is not circular, and it does not even pretend to be an explanation of experience. It is just a remark about the structure of experience.

Objection. Ok, but we can still criticize the *identity claim* proposed by representationalism. For starters, it fails to account for the sense in which the properties that characterize what it is like to have the ball-experience are *present* when one has this experience. This is a way in which having the ball-experience is different from merely *believing* that a bluish and round thing is there. (See Papineau 2016 and Campbell 2018.)

Reply. What do you mean by 'present'? *Instantiated*? In that case, the claim here is not true of all experiences. Suppose you have the ball-experience in hallucination. As we

---

[13] For example, against representationalism, Peacocke (2008: 9–10) suggests that *after-image experiences* do not involve phenomenally representing *anything at all*, on the grounds that in such cases 'it *does not look [to us] as if there are [mind-independent] objects or events in your spatio-temporal environment*'. This relies on the assumption that you phenomenally predicate a property in visual experience just in case it looks to you as if some *mind-independent* object or event has the property. But representationalism is not committed to this assumption. In fact, it does not require that the content of experience is 'looks-indexed' (Travis 2004) in any such simple way (see note 4 of this chapter). So representationalists are free to characterize the content however they like. In fact, they could *agree* with sense datum theorists like Peacocke that the content is such that it looks to mature perceivers as if after-images are *mind-dependent visibilia*, but they will just add that the content is unreal (does not really obtain), thereby avoiding Peacocke's reification of 'visual field regions'. That is, they can also talk of visual field regions, but place all such talk within an intensional context, thereby avoiding ontological commitment (see note 9).

[14] This representationalist move ('just stick the different properties in the representational content') may always be available, but it may not always be plausible. For instance, Speaks (2015: 191) notes the availability of this move in the case of *covert attention shifts*, but suggests that in this case it may be more plausible to revise or supplement representationalism.

saw above ('step 1'), the spatial feature *round* must be mentioned in any complete characterization of what it is like. But here nothing is actually round—at least if we reject sense data ('visual field regions'). So there is a strong case against the 'presence' claim if it requires *actual instantiation*.[15]

At this point, the objector might say, 'well, what I meant is that, necessarily, in every case of having the blue-experience, it vividly ("phenomenally") *seems* that an instance of the relevant properties is "present". That is different from merely believing.'

But, of course, this is something representationalists can and do accept; in fact, truth be told, bare-bones representationalism *does not go far beyond this!* It just adds that this can happen even if nothing with the relevant properties *is* really present. In that minimal sense, the 'seeming' state is a 'representational' state. And (as a 'common factor theory') representationalism holds having the experience, in both veridical and hallucination, is nothing more than being in this representational state.

Objection. I am still not appeased. When you formulated representationalism, you said more: you brought in 'abstract items'. You said that having the ball-experience is nothing more than standing in a relation to a *non-spatial, abstract item*, the complex property λx(x is round and x is bluish and x is before me). How weird is that? I just think that this is obviously false—like the claim that Julius Caesar is identical with the number three. I have got an 'intuition of distinctness'. To be more specific, I object to the idea that experiences are identical with relations to *abstract items*. (See Pautz 2010: 292–3; Papineau 2014.)

Reply. This objection does count against representationalism, but several points soften the blow.

(i) Consider an analogy. The right account of *exact resemblance* mentions abstract items: for two things to *resemble exactly* is for them to instantiate the same *properties*. This is somewhat surprising. Maybe, then, the right account of *experience* mentions abstract items, even if this is surprising.

(ii) Even though I formulated representationalism as the view that experiences are relations to abstract items, there is another way of thinking about the view. On this alternative formulation, to have the ball-experience (for instance) is to *phenomenally represent that a bluish and round item is present*, where this representational state is *not* understood to be a relation to any kind of abstract item.

---

[15] The thesis that the spatial feature *round* must be mentioned in any complete characterization of what it is to have the ball-experience is generally accepted. It is accepted by sense datum theorists, representationalists and naïve realists. This testifies to its truth. True, internal physicalist state theorists, such as David Papineau, will reject this claim; instead, they will say that what it is to have the ball-experience can be specified entirely in terms of *types of neurons* and the *times, directions* and *intensities* at which they fire, without mentioning spatial properties at all. But, as we saw in step two of the argument for representationalism, if we have to choose between the essential spatiality of the ball-experience and the internal physical state view, we should keep essential spatiality and reject the internal state view. So our counterexample to the 'instantiation' claim stands: if someone were to have the ball-experience in a hallucination, *round* would essentially enter into a characterization of what the hallucination is like, yet nothing in the vicinity would actually be round.

(Notice that the specification in italics does not contain a singular term referring to an abstract property. True, it contains a 'that'-clause, but the view I have in mind denies that this is a singular term referring to a proposition understood as an abstract item.) This kind of 'concrete representationalism' avoids the specific objection that 'relations to entities in a Platonic realm outside space and time cannot matter to consciousness', as Papineau (2014: 8) puts it. In fact, concrete representationalists absolutely agree with Papineau's remark here. Indeed, they might be nominalists who altogether reject the existence of abstract entities in Plato's realm.[16]

(iii) At this point, the objector might rephrase the objection. It is not just that it cannot be that to have the ball-experience is to stand in a relation to an abstract item—an objection that is avoided by concrete representationalism. It is more general than that: it is a general 'intuition of distinctness' to the effect that having the ball-experience must be distinct from representing that a blue and round thing is present (where that can happen even if nothing blue and round is present). This intuition, it might be said, counts equally against 'concrete' representationalism and 'relation-to-abstract-items' representationalism. In reply: it would be odd if opponents of representationalism relied on this kind of basic 'intuition of distinctness'. For equally forceful intuitions of distinctness tell against their own views. For instance, such an intuition counts against the internal physical state view: how could this technicolor phenomenology *just be* a pattern of neural activity in soggy grey matter? And such an intuition counts against naïve realists' 'negative epistemic theory' of phenomenal character in hallucination cases (which we briefly discussed in step 6 of the argument for representationalism). How could a mere negative epistemic property constitute technicolor phenomenology?[17]

---

[16] I said in the text that concrete representationalists might be nominalists who altogether reject the existence of abstract items. It is worth remarking that they could also accept the existence of abstract items. Analogy: it is natural to think that the fact that an apple is red is a wholly concrete fact, involving only the apple. It is not identical with the fact that it instantiates an abstract item, the property of being red (Lewis 1986: 190, fn. 13). But you could accept this and then go onto say that the fact the apple is red *grounds* the fact that it stands in the *instantiation relation* to an abstract item in Plato's realm, the property of being red. Likewise, concrete representationalists hold that the fact that you have the blue experience is identical with the wholly concrete fact that you phenomenally represent that a blue thing is present. But they might then go on to say that this *grounds* your standing in a derivative phenomenal representation relation to the property of being blue, an abstract item. They would still evade the specific objection 'it cannot be that the fact that you have the ball-experience is *identical with* the fact that you stand in a relation to an abstract item'.

[17] Only an across-the-board act-object view—such as the sense datum view or 'Austinian disjunctivism' (Moran 2018, 2019)—does not face the 'intuition of distinctness' objection. For, on this view, having the ball-experience is identical with experiencing the blueness and roundness of some presented object. And, if anything, intuition *favors* this view (Price 1932: 4). But this theory faces the problems mentioned in step 3 of the inference-to-the-best-explanation argument for representationalism.

Objection. There are metaphysically necessary restrictions on how things can appear—'laws of appearance'. For instance, it is metaphysically impossible that a surface should seem both *round* and *square*, or *pure red* and *pure yellow* at the same place and the same time. (Of course, something can look *reddish* and *yellowish*—that is, *orange*—but that is not a counterexample.) And it is metaphysically impossible that something should seem red but not extended. It is metaphysically impossible that something should appear either red or green but nothing more specific. How might representationalists explain all this? It is not clear. Why could your (or some possible individual's) visual system not get really screwed up and phenomenally predicate incompatible properties of something? Some philosophers—'Meinongians'—*believe* that there are round squares, and pure red and green things; so if experience is representational like belief, why can you not have *experiences* with these weird contents? By contrast, sense datum theorists have an explanation ready to hand, since they endorse the 'instantiation principle'. Their explanation is that something's perceptually seeming to have incompatible properties would require that there actually be something—a 'sense datum' or 'visual field region'—having incompatible properties. But nothing—not even a sense datum or 'visual field region'—could have incompatible properties. So it looks like we have stumbled upon a new argument for the sense datum view. Maybe we should accept the sense datum view after all, in spite of its problems, because it explains the laws of appearance.[18]

Reply. This is indeed a puzzle for representationalists. One option for them is to reject the metaphysical necessity of the laws of appearance, if they can find no explanation of their metaphysical necessity.[19] Alternatively, they might just accept the laws of appearance as basic, inexplicable metaphysical necessities.

One point worth noting here is that this a problem for other views too—including the sense datum view. The laws of appearance are many and various, and *no* view can explain them all. Even sense datum theorists cannot explain certain 'laws of appearance'.

---

[18] For the problem of explaining the laws of appearance, see Pautz (2017), Speaks (2017), Morgan (ms). It is worth mentioning that the hypothesis that experience is 'non-propositional' and 'feature-placing' (Block ms) is not enough to explain the laws of appearance. For, whatever it may mean, it faces the very same explanatory problem. Why should experience not 'place' incompatible features (*pure red* and *pure green*) in one place, or super-disjunctive properties (*pure red or pure green*), or merely negative properties (*not pure red*)? Block (ms: ch 3) rejects some ostensible laws of appearance, and then suggests that the remaining laws of appearance can be explained by the thesis that phenomenal representation is realized in an *iconic format*. For difficulties with this suggestion see Pautz 2017.

[19] For example, Speaks (2017: 495) and Block (ms: ch 3) favor the option of *rejecting* the metaphysical necessity of some of the laws of appearance: for instance, it is metaphysically *possible* that a surface look pure red and pure yellow all over, or round and square. (As mentioned in the previous note, Block accepts some few *other* laws of appearance but suggests that they are explained by the thesis that phenomenal representation is realized in an *iconic format*.) But in that case why do we *think* it is so obviously metaphysically impossible that a surface look pure red and pure yellow, or round and square? Block (ms) and also E. J. Green and Jacob Beck (in discussion) suggested to me that the explanation might be that, given the way the visual system works, this never happens in humans (though it could happen in other possible creatures), and so we have difficulty imagining the relevant experiences. But this may be insufficient, for there are many experiences that no one has ever had and that we have difficulty imagining (e.g. experiences of unusual shapes or alien colors) but that we take to be metaphysically *possible*.

Why must everything that looks colored also look extended in space? Why could you not be perceptually acquainted with the color of a sense datum 'neat', without being acquainted with its extent in space or its location? That does not seem to be a possible visual experience, but why not? Furthermore, a sense datum has loads of properties: for instance, the relational property *being created by so-and-so brain process*, various logically complex properties (e.g. disjunctive properties), and so on and so forth. Why ca you not be perceptually acquainted simply with *these* properties of the sense datum? Why are some properties (color and shape) 'acquaintables', while these other properties are not? Since all views face a version of the puzzle of the laws of appearance, the puzzle does not provide a strong reason to accept the sense datum view or any other view over representationalism. It remains the case that representationalism achieves an overall better 'balance sheet' than the alternatives.

19.4 Reductive-Externalist Representationalism

We have looked at a defense of representationalism. However, representationalism is incomplete until it is combined with an answer to the question of how the brain enables us to phenomenally predicate sensible colors and shapes and other sensible properties that need not be instantiated *in* the brain.

In our final two sections, we will look at two different answers to this question. We begin in the present section with *reductive-externalist representationalism*, which has been defended by Armstrong (1968), Dretske (1995), Tye (1995), and Byrne and Hilbert (2003).

Consider the world before the evolution of conscious creatures. Reductive-externalist representationalism maintains that even at this time external objects and events were rich with sensible properties ('qualia'). For instance, tomatoes were red, the sky was blue, a falling tree made a sound (even though no one was around to hear it), methane had a bad objective smell, and so on. The sensible beauties (and the sensible nasties) are not creations of the brain; they were out there even before brains came on the scene. The so-called 'qualia' are not features of 'sense data' or 'sensory field regions' in the head; they are just features of physical things in the world. They are just as objective as shape and size. In fact, this view holds that sensible properties are *reducible to* physical properties that things had even before conscious creatures came on the scene:

> **The Reduction of Sensible Properties.** Colors are reflectance properties (ways of reflecting light), odor qualities are molecular properties (see Figure 19.1A), audible qualities are complex physical properties, and so on.

Compare: water is H_2O, which was on the scene long before sentient creatures showed up.

So, before the evolution of consciousness, all these sensible properties were out there, but no one was around to appreciate them. Then we and other creatures evolved the capacity to be *conscious of* them. How did that happen? Reductive-externalist representationalists hold that we came to be conscious of them by *phenomenally representing* them. So the notorious 'hard problem of consciousness' becomes the hard problem of representation: how do we manage to represent these properties so that they seem *present* to us?

Here reductive-externalist representationalists appeal to a standard *externalist model* for reducing representation of the kind that many philosophers developed in the 1990s. Analogy: thermometers came to represent temperatures by undergoing states that have the function to indicate those temperatures. Likewise, we came to phenomenally represent, and thereby be conscious of, the objective sensible properties of things by undergoing states that have the (biological) function of indicating them. Roughly, you stand in the indication relation to property just in case you are in a brain state that *normally* occurs only when that property is present before you (Dretske 1995: 48).

This origin story for sensory consciousness is still incomplete. The phenomenal representation relation cannot be a mere biological indication relation. Take an early single-celled organism. Suppose it had states that indicate *light* and *dark*. We do not think it was *conscious of* these features. It may 'represent' them in some sense but it does not *phenomenally* represent them. So reductive-externalist representationalists need to address the question of what turned mere *indication* into the magic of conscious presentation.

In response, reductive-externalist representationalists hold that phenomenal representation is indication *plus cognitive-rational accessibility*:

The Reduction of Phenomenal Representation Relation. The dyadic mental relation *x phenomenally (consciously) represents property y* is identical with the following complex indication relation: x is in a internal physical state that has the biological function of indicating property y and *that internal state is poised to be fed into a 'cognitive system' for the rational control of thought and action.* (Tye 1995; Dretske 2006)

On this view, consciousness was not present in single-celled organisms; it came into existence only when creatures became capable of *thought* and *reason* (Tye 2000: ch 8). Since this account explains consciousness in terms of thought and reason, it needs to be supplemented by an account of thought and reason that is independent of consciousness, in order to avoid circularity. But we will leave this difficult issue to one side.

In a nutshell, then, that is reductive-externalist representationalism. It implies a radical externalism about the qualities of experience. As Michael Tye puts it:

Peer as long as you like at the detailed functioning of the brain...that is not where phenomenal character is to be found. Neuroscientists are looking in the wrong place (Tye 199:, 162–3)...phenomenal character is in the world (Tye 2009: 119).

For instance, suppose that you look at the ball. On reductive-externalist representationalism, the bluish *quale* that you are conscious of *just is* its *reflectance-type* (its distinctive way of reflecting light), and you are conscious of it by undergoing a neural state that indicates it. Any possible creature that indicates the same reflectance-type must experience the same bluish quale, *no matter what its internal neural processing is like.*[20]

Reductive-externalist representationalists provide a parallel account of other experiences. For instance, suppose you smell a cloud of R-limonene molecules (Figure 19.1A). It will smell *citrus-like* to you. On reductive-externalist representationalism, the citrus-like *quale* that you are conscious of *just is* this *molecular-type*, and you are conscious of it ('phenomenally represent' it) by undergoing a neural state that normally indicates it. This implies that *any possible creature that undergoes a state indicating the same molecular-type must experience the same citrus-like quale, no matter what its internal neural processing is like.*

Likewise, reductive-externalist representationalists hold that, if you have a pain in your leg, your pain-system detects, and thereby phenomenally represents, some disturbance-type down there. The felt quality is identical with the disturbance-type, and its sensory intensity is constituted by the extent and size of the disturbance. Pain is not in the brain.

A consequence is that a life-long *brain in a void* could not be conscious of any olfactory qualia, or color qualia, or even pain qualia, because qualia are in the world or the body, and such a brain would not be connected to them in the right way (its internal states do not have a history of indicating them). The brain needs *help from the world* to generate the consciousness of qualia; it cannot do it all on its own.

It may be wondered how reductive-externalist representationalism explains *perceptual variation*. Reductive-externalist representationalism provides a *selectionist* explanation. The pre-conscious world was rich with sensible properties. Different creatures have different experiences because their visual systems indicate, and thereby enable them to phenomenally represent, different external properties. For example, dogs' olfactory systems indicate different ranges of molecular-types (and hence, different smell qualia) than our own. Or again, pigeon visual systems have the function of indicating reflectances involving UV light, which (on this view) constitute alien color *qualia* that we cannot imagine. We are all conscious of the real world—only we are conscious of different aspects of that world (Cohen 2009: 78ff).

Reductive-externalist representationalism also explains illusion and hallucination. For instance, suppose you have the ball-experience in a hallucination. On this view, the vivid impression that there is *right there* before you a bluish and round thing essentially consists in the fact that you are undergoing an internal neural pattern that *normally* (but not in the present circumstances) indicates an object with a blue-reflectance and a round

---

[20] Because of 'metamerism', reductive-externalist representationalists must identify sensible colors with reflectance-types that are *highly disjunctive* (see Byrne and Hilbert 2003). A similar point applies to *smell qualities* (to be discussed below). However, I will ignore this complication, since it is irrelevant to the points to be discussed.

shape. The ball-experince is a wide physical state that can only be fully characterized by mentioning features of external things like *round* and *bluish*. This explains the essentially spatial character of the hallucination without positing a bluish and round 'visual field region' or 'sense datum'.

Reductive-externalist representationalism is attractive. But there is reason to think that it just does not agree with the facts. Its basic idea—as expressed by Tye in the above quotation—is that the explanation of phenomenal character is to be found in the external world, not the brain. But decades of studies in psychophysics and neuroscience suggest exactly the opposite.

This point is especially clear in the case of *smell*. To illustrate, suppose that you consecutively smell *citral*, *R-limonene*, and *R-carvone*, as shown in Figure 19.1A. You will then experience the smell qualities $citrus_1$, $citrus_2$, and *minty* (where $citrus_1$ and $citrus_2$ are two similar but distinct citrus smell qualities). Howard et al. (2009) used fRMI to look at the neural patterns (distributed spatial-temporal patterns of neural firing) caused by these odorants in a normal human such as yourself. Recall that reductive-internalist representationalism holds that the smell qualities ($citrus_1$, $citrus_2$, and minty) that you experience are *identical with* the corresponding molecular-types in the air. It is the *molecular-types indicated*—and *not* your distributed neural patterns—that constitutes what olfactory qualities you experience. But what Howard et al. (2009) found seems to show that the *opposite* is true. There is a *big mismatch* between the resemblances among the smell qualities you experience and the resemblances among the corresponding molecular-types in the external world, as Figure 19.1A illustrates. In general, olfactory scientists have found that there is *no* measure of molecular similarity that predicts qualitative similarity (Cowart and Rawson 2001: 568).[21] On the other hand, Figure 19.1A also illustrates the finding of Howard et al. (2009) that there is, by contrast, a *perfect agreement* between the resemblances among the smell qualities you experience and the resemblances among the distributed neural patterns in your olfactory system. Many other studies have supported the same basic finding: while *molecular* similarity-space totally fails to match qualitative similarity space, *neural* similarity-space nicely matches qualitative similarity space (e. g. Youngentob et al. 2006). This seems to directly contradict the externalist position of reductive-externalist representationalists.

We can make vivid the conflict between these empirical findings and reductive-externalist representationalism by considering a hypothetical scenario (illustrated in Figure 19.1B). In particular, consider a counterfactual scenario where everything is the same but for one thing: humans naturally evolved so that, in this scenario, your neural

---

[21] Some have proposed that a molecule's *vibrational frequency* in the infrared range predicts its quality. Against this, enantiomers (mirror-image molecules) can smell quite different but have the same vibrational frequency. For other problems, see Pautz 2014b: 276, fn. 11. In general, 'numerous chemical and molecular features (e.g., molecular weight, molecular mass and shape, polarity, resonance structure, types of bonds and sidegroups) can all influence the odorous characteristics of a chemical [but] no systematic description of how these characteristics relate to particular odor qualities has been developed' (Cowart and Rawson 2001: 568). It is only in the brain that we find good predictors of smell quality. (Here I am indebted to Alex Byrne.)

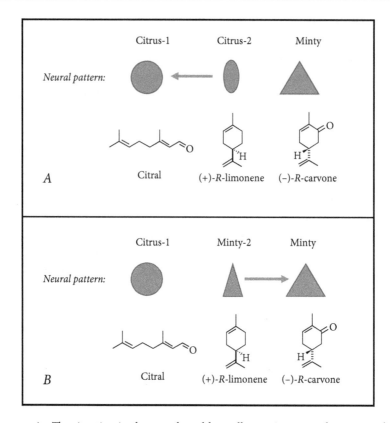

FIGURE 19.1 A: The situation in the actual world: smell experiences are better correlated with internal neural patterns than with external molecular-types. B: A counterfactual situation in which you have a different neural representation of R-limonene, occupying a different position in neural similarity-space for smell.

Source: Adapted from Margot (2009).

representation of R-limonene is neurally more similar to (but distinct from) your neural representation of the *minty-smelling, third molecular-type* than your neural representation of citrus-smelling, first molecular-type—the exact opposite of how things stand in the actual world (Figure 19.1A). As a result, in this scenario, you categorize R-limonene, not with the citrus-smelling first molecular-type, but with the minty-smelling third molecular-type. Let us also stipulate that your (different) neural representation of R-limonene in this scenario has the function of indicating the very *same* molecular-type as humans' actual neural representation of R-limonene. Analogy: different words, in different languages, can indicate the same thing. We can call this a *coincidental variation case*: in the actual situation and the counterfactual situation, there is a complete coincidence in what your olfactory system has the function of indicating, but there is variation in the realizing neural states. Clearly, given the empirical findings, in this scenario, R-limonene would smell similar to (but distinct from) the *minty-smelling*, third molecular-type. That is, it would smell *minty* to you, and not citrus-like as in the actual world.

But this verdict contradicts reductive-externalist representationalism. For, on this view, in both the actual situation and the counterfactual situation, you should *phenomenally represent* the *same smell quale*, despite radical difference in your neural pattern and behavioral dispositions, because those different neural patterns have the *function of indicating* the *same molecular-type*. The case for the possibility of this counterexample is not based on its conceivability; it is supported empirically.

The moral: when it comes to the qualities of olfactory consciousness, our internally neural processing is running the show, not the molecular-types that this internal-neural processing has the function of indicating in the world. If the empirical findings mentioned above do not convince of this, what empirical findings *would*? Call this the *argument from neuroscience* against reductive-externalist representationalism.

The argument from neuroscience is general. For instance, pain researchers generally hold that pain intensity is fixed by neural firing rates in the pain-matrix (this is linearly related to sensory pain intensity), not by 'the size and extent' of the bodily disturbance indicated by the firing rate (this is an extremely poor predictor of pain intensity and is not even well-defined). From an empirical point of view, reductive-externalist representationalism about pain is a non-starter (Price and Barrell 2012: 203). In fact, the empirical findings are much the same in the domain of color experience (Byrne and Hilbert 2003: Figure 5; Brouwer and Heeger 2009; Bohon et al. 2016). If you agree that the empirical findings about smell and pain do support an 'internalist' approach in these cases, then consistency demands you take these similar empirical findings to support a parallel internalist approach in the case of color experience. For instance, contrary to reductive-externalist representationalism, a creature's visual system could indicate the very same reflectance property of the ball, and yet that creature will be conscious of a totally different color quale (say, *green* rather than blue), because of differences in its color-processing. (This would be another *coincidental variation case* with the structure indicated in Figure 19.1B.)[22] True, our *naïve, pretheoretical* view of color experience may be resolutely externalist. But, given the empirical facts, externalism about color experience is no more sustainable than externalism about the experience of pain and smell.[23]

---

[22] For recent discussion of the argument from neuroscience against externalism about the qualities of experience, see Chalmers 2005; Cohen 2009: 81ff; Pautz 2014b; Allen 2016: 71–2; Logue 2017; Beck 2018; Berger 2018; Campbell 2018.

[23] There are a few arguments against reductive-externalist representationalism besides the argument from neuroscience described in the text. (i) *The argument from the internalist intuition* (Horgan and Tienson 2002: n. 23; Hawthorne 2004: 352). One problem with this argument is that 'internalism' about experience is *not* pretheoretically intuitive—it can only be supported empirically (Pautz 2014a). (ii) *The conceivability of spectrum inversion* (Levine 1997: 109; Chalmers 2010: 400 n. 17 and 415–16; Shoemaker 2019). In response, Tye (2000: 110) questions the conceivability-possibility link on which this argument relies. (iii) *The ancient problem of perceptual variation*, for instance due to shifted spectra (Shoemaker 2019) and attention shifts (Block 2010). Byrne and Hilbert (1997: 272–3) first defended a *selectionist* response to this problem and then later (2003: 17) converted to a *misrepresentation* response.

19.5 Nonreductive-internalist Representationalism

Finally, we turn to a radically different way of developing representationalism: *nonreductive-internalist representationalism*.[24]

Reductive-externalist representationalism is radically externalist. But the argument from neuroscience reviewed in Section 19.4 supports *internalism* about the experience of traditional 'secondary qualities', such as pain, smell, and color. In particular, it supports the following picture: external physical properties—types of bodily disturbance, molecular-types, reflectance-types—cause our internal neural states; then those internal neural states totally fix the character of our experiences of secondary qualities.

If we now combine internalism with the representationalist view that experiences are representational states, then we reach *internalist representationalism*: what pain-qualities, smell-qualities, and color-qualities we phenomenally represent 'out there' are somehow entirely fixed by our neural states 'in here'. For instance, what smell qualities you phenomenally represent in the region before your nose is entirely fixed by your neural processing (see Figure 19.1B), and what pain qualities you phenomenally represent in regions of your body is entirely fixed by your neural processing. This is a very natural view. Since this view is internalist, it accords with the empirical results. Since it is representationalist, it explains the possibility of illusion (e.g. phantom-limb illusion). It differs from the *internal physical state view* criticized in Section 19.3: on internalist representationalism, experiences are not *identical with* internal neural states; rather, they are representational states that are *dependent on* but not identical with internal neural states (see Figure 19.2).

The empirical evidence for internalism and against externalism is strongest for the experience of 'secondary qualities'. It is weaker when it comes to the experience of 'primary qualities' (shape, size, distance, number, motion).[25] But, once we accept internalism for the experience of traditional secondary qualities, considerations of uniformity suggest generalizing it to the experience of primary qualities. For instance, since the phenomenal representation of sensible colors is inseparable from the phenomenal representation of extension and location (a 'laws of appearance' of the kind discussed at the end of Section 19.3), internalism about the phenomenal representation of sensible

---

[24] Proponents of nonreductive internalist representationalism include Chalmers 2010; Kriegel 2011; Horgan 2014; Pautz 2014b; and Mendelovici 2018.

[25] For instance, if the apparent length of a line doubles, then the length that your neural state has *the function of indicating* doubles. (This is true even if the experience of the line is a total hallucination.) So here, unlike in the case of smell, there *is* a good correlation between the character of experience and the character of the physical properties in the world that our neural states have the function of indicating.

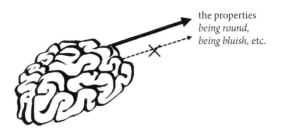

FIGURE 19.2 In having a hallucination of a blue ball, BIV stands in the phenomenal representation relation (the solid arrow) to spatial properties and color properties. But BIV bears no interesting physical relation (such as the indication relation) to these properties (the dashed arrow).

colors leads to internalism about the phenomenal representation of extension and location. Reductive-externalist representationalism fails even here.[26]

Recall that reductive-externalist representationalists hold that the phenomenal representation relation (the 'conscious-of relation') is reducible to the *indication relation*. Internalist representationalists cannot accept this view. According to internalist representationalists, phenomenal representation is unique: it is internally-determined. Therefore, no such standard externalist model for reducing representation applies in the special case of phenomenal representation. In fact, internalist representationalism requires a *non-reductive* picture of sensory consciousness.

One way to see this is to return to the kind of *coincidental variation case* mentioned at the end of Section 19.4 (Figure 19.1). You and your twin in the hypothetical scenario bear the indication relation to the same molecular-type. But, on nonreductive-internalist representationalism, you bear the phenomenal representation relation to different smell qualities. Therefore, the phenomenal representation relation must be distinct from the indication relation.

Or consider the 'brain in the void' (BIV). Recall that on reductive-externalist representationalism BIV cannot have *any* experiences. By contrast, on *internalist* representationalism, BIV has all the same experiences as you. For instance, BIV has experiences of pain. And, just like you, BIV has the ball-experience. In having this experience, BIV has a vivid impression as of a round thing being present. On representationalism, this is because BIV phenomenally represents *being round and in front of me* (and not because, say, BIV is presented with a round 'visual field region'). The brain, then, does not need 'help from the world' in order to enable us to phenomenally represent a range of basic properties; rather, it has an *intrinsic capacity* to represent those properties. See Figure 19.2.

---

[26] On the need for a uniform theory, see Cutter (2016: 7–8) and Pautz (2014b: 286–91). For some independent lines of argument against externalism and for internalism about the experience of 'primary qualities', see Chalmers (2012: 296–7, 333), Masrour (2015), and McLaughlin (2016: 292).

If the BIV-example is possible, then the phenomenal representation relation is an irreducible, non-physical relation. The argument for this is simple:

1. BIV bears the phenomenal representation relation to the property *being round*.[27]
2. BIV does not bear the indication relation, or indeed *any* interesting physical relation, to the property being round.
3. Therefore, the phenomenal representation relation is distinct from any physical relation.

As Ned Block (2019) says in a discussion of this argument, 'we internalists must acknowledge an irreducible representation relation'. (See also Speaks 2015: 271–2.)

Nonreductive-internalist representationalism may seem to require a bizarre dualism. This is not true. It is also compatible with *grounding physicalism*. Even if the phenomenal representation relation is irreducible, it may yet be that, whenever an individual (e.g. you or your BIV twin) bears this relation to some cluster of properties, then this is fully grounded in that individual's internal brain state. In fact, there might be systematic 'grounding laws' of the form: if one undergoes brain state B, then this grounds one's phenomenally representing property $f(B)$, where f is a systematic function from brain states onto perceptible properties. In that sense, there is an explanation of consciousness; it just does not take the form of a reductive definition. Compare: some hold that normative facts about what *ought* to be the case are irreducible to, but still *fully grounded in*, non-normative facts about what *is* the case. Nonreductive-internalist representationalism is like dualism in one respect: just as dualists need 'psychophysical laws', so this view needs special 'grounding laws'. This adds to the complexity of the view. But in another way, it is like physicalism and unlike dualism: by contrast to dualism, it implies that the facts about consciousness cannot 'float free' from the underlying physical facts.

I have said that internalist representationalism requires a *non-reductive* view of phenomenal representation (the 'arrow' in Figure 19.2). It is also naturally combined with an *illusionist* view of the sensible properties, like sensible colors, smell qualities, tickle-qualities, and so on (the properties that the arrow is 'pointed at'). On this view, such sensible properties are *neither* properties of external physical items (objects' surfaces, odorants, bodily regions, and so on) nor are they properties of internal items (e.g. brain states or 'sense data'). They only live in the content of experience.

This is a big issue, but let me briefly explain why internalist representationalism is most naturally combined with illusionism. The basic point is that, if you take an inventory

---

[27] Some internalist representationalists with nominalists sympathies (Kriegel 2011: ch 3; Mendelovici 2018) might reject premise 1; they might agree that BIV has an experience according to which a round thing is present but deny that this means that BIV stands in a representation relation to the abstract property, *being round*. (This is an example of 'concrete representationalism' which we discussed in Section 19.3.) As against this kind of nominalism, by having visual experiences, BIV is in a position to know timeless, necessary truths about the *resemblances* of shapes. And these truths have no nominalistically acceptable paraphrases; they are truths about shape *properties* (Yi 2017). So BIV *is* mentally related to shape properties like *being round*.

of the properties instantiated in the external world or in the brain, you find that they are all poor candidates to constitute the sensible properties. Let us look at a few options.

(I) To begin with, the kind of empirical results mentioned in Section 19.4 clearly suggest that sensible properties cannot be identified with objective, physical properties, contrary to reductive-externalists. For instance, look back at Figure 19.1A. Given the mismatch, the smell qualities cannot be identified with the corresponding molecular-types.[28] Further, *internalist representationalists* certainly cannot identify the sensible properties with such physical properties. They hold that BIV phenomenally represents sensible properties (sensible colors, smell qualities, etc.), but it is impossible to see how BIV could phenomenally represent any such external physical properties (reflectance properties, molecular-types, etc.), as it is has never interacted with them.

(II) Some internalist representationalists hold that sensible properties are identical with *dispositions of external objects to produce neural states in us* (e.g. Kriegel 2009: 90). But this approach faces several problems.[29]

(III) Finally, some have suggested the strange view that sensible properties are *neural properties of our own brain states*. For instance, smell qualities are just identical with neural patterns (see Figure 19.1A). Or again, when one has the blue-ball experience, the bluish (or bluish*) quality one experiences is a *neural property of one's own brain state* (Block 2010: 24, 56, fn. 2). (Of course, this differs from the view of Jackson 1977 and Peacocke 2008, criticized in Section 19.2, that it is a property of a *literally round visual field region or sense datum*.) One problem with this concerns the spatial character of experience. For instance, if the bluish quality is in fact a neural property of one's own (non-round) brain state, then (absent some kind of projective-binding error) it becomes difficult to explain the phenomenologically obvious fact that it *seems* to one to fill a round region. Another point is that internalist representationalists *already* hold that the brain has the innate capacity to phenomenally represent certain properties that are not properties *of* the brain and that may not be properties of anything at all (Block 2019). That is their view in the case of the property *being round* in the BIV case (see Figure 19.2)? So why should it be any different for the property of being bluish (or the quality of being minty, and so on)? Should they not take a *parallel* representationalist view here: that the brain has an innate capacity to phenomenally represent *being bluish* (or being bluish*), even

---

[28] In reply, realists might concede that smell qualia are *distinct from* molecular-types (because of the mismatch), but then try to save realism by holding that they are *grounded in* molecular-types (Allen 2016: 128-9). But this view would require a giant mismatch between the resemblances among the small qualia and the resemblances among the distinct molecular-types they are grounded in. While this view is logically coherent, it is very odd; it would require an endless raft of highly irregular, unsystematizable grounding connections between distinct properties (one for each *smell quale*). Alternative views avoid this.

[29] For a 'psychosemantic' problem with this view, see Byrne and Hilbert 2017: 182-3; McGrath ms; Pautz 2014b: 292-3.

though it is *not* a property *of* the brain? Why insist that *being bluish* needs to be a property of the brain (but somehow 'projected outward'), if one thinks that other properties involved in the phenomenal character of experience (namely, spatial properties like *being round*) need *not* be properties of the brain.

In sum, sensible properties ('qualia') cannot be plausibly located in the external world or in mind-brain. The best view may be that they are not located anywhere, even if they *appear to be* located in regions and surfaces in space.

Nonreductive-internalist representationalism tells a totally different origin story for sensory consciousness than externalist-reductive representationalism. Recall that, on the externalist picture, the sensible properties were in the world before brains evolved; the brain enabled us to be conscious of ('phenomenally represent') sensible properties only because it had a history of indicating their occurrence in the world. The brain, then, did not generate the experience of sensible properties all on its own; it needed help from the world. By contrast, the kind of internalist representationalism I have described holds that the sensible properties were *not* in the world before sentient creatures evolved. (In fact, on an illusionist version, they are not in the world *now*.) The physical world is intrinsically devoid of qualities like *red-as-we-see-it*, *citrus-like*, and so on; it is only filled with quantitative properties like mass, charge, and spin. So, in generating the phenomenal representation of sensible properties, the brain did not have any help from the world. It evolved to enable us to phenomenally represent properties of a wholly novel sort that never have been instantiated in the world. Most would agree that the brain enables us to experience *pain qualities* that were not antecedently out there. Internalist representationalists just extend the same view to the experience of olfactory qualities, audible qualities, color qualities. The brain is inventive. It provides a useful but false model of the physical world. Much of our experience of the world is a case of adaptive illusion. The overriding function of the sensory systems is to enhance adaptive fitness, not to represent the way the world really is. However, internalist representationalists need not say that experience is *wholly* illusory. We also evolved brain states that enable us to phenomenally represent *shapes* and other spatial properties. Here, they might say, there is a happy agreement between appearance and reality. For here enhancing adaptive fitness amounted to enhancing veridicality. The result is an updated version of the traditional Lockean thesis that our ideas of primary qualities resemble external objects while our ideas of sensible qualities do not.[30]

That, then, is nonreductive-internalist representationalism. Why believe it? One of the most puzzling features of sensory consciousness is its Janus-faced nature. On the one hand, we have seen that sensory consciousness is essentially externally-directed

---

[30] For a priori arguments for illusionist forms of internalist representationalism, see Chalmers 2010 and Horgan 2014. For empirical arguments, see Pautz 2014b. Chalmers (2012: 296–7, 333) generalizes illusionism to the *spatial properties* that we phenomenally represent. He calls them 'Edenic'. Russell (1912, 29) advocated the same view (except that Russell was a sense datum theorist while Chalmers is a representationalist).

(Section 19.2): experiences essentially present qualities arrayed in *space*. On the other hand, we have seen that empirical investigation shows that sensory consciousness is also internally-dependent (Section 19.4). Experiences spring from the inside but they also point outwards. Nonreductive internalist representationalism explains this while at the same time avoiding problematic items such as 'sensory field regions' and 'sense data' in a private space.

Nonreductive-internalist representationalism has another advantage over reductive-externalist representationalism. Recall that reductive-externalist representationalists hold that phenomenal representation (and hence phenomenal consciousness) is reducible to *indication plus cognitive-rational accessibility*. So they think that thought and reasons are *explanatorily prior* to consciousness. In particular, Tye (2000: 62) advocates a *cognitive analysis* of consciousness and Dretske (2006: 174) advocates a *reasons-based analysis* of consciousness. On pain of circularity, they must also think that there is an account of thought and reasons that does not advert in any way to consciousness: for instance, an account in terms of reliable indication relations to the external environment. (Compare: *being a man* is explanatorily prior to, and can be explained independently of, *being a bachelor*.) But it is just intuitively implausible that thought and reasons could be explained independently of consciousness. Moreover, such accounts are open to counterexamples and other problems. Nonreductive-internalist representationalists can reverse the direction of explanation. Since they do not reductively explain phenomenal representation (sensory consciousness) in terms of thought and reason (indeed they think it is an irreducible relation), they are free to hold that phenomenal representation explains, and is prior to, thought and reason. They can take a *consciousness-first* approach, on which our conscious experience as of basic properties (itself grounded in our internal brain states) grounds our most cognitive-capacities and reasons. This is by far the more natural view.[31]

True, nonreductive-internalist representationalism may be more complex than reductive-externalist representationalism. Reductive-externalist representationalism *identifies* the phenomenal representation relation with the indication relation. And it *identifies* the sensible properties with external physical properties. Identities are unique in that they do not add to the complexity of our theory; in fact, they conduce to simplicity. By contrast, nonreductive-internalist representationalism says that the phenomenal representation relation is irreducible. It requires basic 'grounding laws' (as yet unknown) linking quite different states: brain states and states of bearing this irreducible relation to certain basic perceptible properties (see Figure 19.2). And these grounding laws add to the complexity of our theory of the world, in much the same way as the 'psychophysical laws' of traditional dualism. But maybe that is just the way the world is.

---

[31] For the idea that consciousness is the source of our most basic reasons and cognitive capacities, see Russell 1912; Pryor 2000; Chalmers 2012: 467; Kriegel 2011. See also Bourget and Mendelovici (Chapter 26, this volume) and the references therein.

19.6 CONCLUSION

Representationalism can provide an excellent account of a host of otherwise puzzling perceptual phenomena (Sections 19.2–3). If true, it changes the mind–body problem. It posits a dyadic mental relation, the relation of *phenomenally representing* ('predicating') a property. Some think that we can reductively explain this relation using one of our standard externalist models for reducing representation (Section 19.4). Others think that it makes a new problem for reductive physicalism (Section 19.5). In particular, phenomenal representation may be unique in that it is internally-determined. If so, our usual models for reductively explaining representation do not apply in the special case of phenomenal representation.[32]

REFERENCES

Alford-Duguid, D. and Arsenault, M. (2007), 'On the Explanatory Power of Hallucination', Synthese, 194: 1765–85.
Allen, K. (2003), 'Blur', *Philosophical Studies*, 162: 257–73.
Allen, K. (2016), *A Naïve Realist Theory of Colour*. Oxford: Oxford University Press.
Armstrong, D. (1968), *A Materialist Theory of Mind*. London: Routledge.
Batty, C. (2010), 'A Representational Account of Olfactory Experience', *Canadian Journal of Philosophy*, 40: 511–38.
Beck, O. (2018), 'Rethinking Naïve Realism', *Philosophical Studies*, https://doi.org/10.1007/s11098-018-1030-x
Berger, J. (2018), 'A Defense of Holistic Representationalism', *Mind and Language*, DOI: 10.1111/mila.12163.
Block, N. (2010), 'Attention and Mental Paint',. *Philosophical Issues*, 20: 23–63.
Block, N. (2019), 'Arguments Pro and Con on Adam Pautz's External Directedness Principle' in A. Pautz and D. Stoljar (eds), *Blockheads! Essays on Ned Block's Philosophy of Mind and Consciousness*. Cambridge, MA: MIT Press.
Block, N. ms. 'The Border Between Seeing and Thinking'.
Boghossian, P. (2008), 'Introduction' in his *Content and Justification*. Oxford: Oxford University Press.
Boghossian, P. and Velleman, D. (1989), 'Colour as a Secondary Quality', *Mind*, 98: 81–103.
Bohon, K, Hermann, K., Hansen, T., and Conway, B. (2016), 'Representation of perceptual color space in macaque posterior inferior temporal cortex (the V4 Complex)', *eNeouro* preprint.
Brewer, B. (2011), *Perception and Its Objects*. Oxford: Oxford University Press.
Brewer, B. (2017), 'The Object View of Perception', *Topoi* 36: 215–27.
Brouwer, G. and Heeger, D. (2009), 'Decoding and reconstructing color from responses in human visual cortex', *Journal of Neuroscience*, 29: 13992–14003.

---

[32] I am very grateful to two referees for their incisive and helpful comments on an earlier version of this essay.

Burge, T. (2003), 'Qualia and Intentional Content: Reply to Block' in M. Hahn and B. Ramberg (eds), *Reflections and Replies: Essays on the Philosophy of Tyler Burge*. Cambridge, MA: MIT Press, 405–15.
Byrne, A. (2001), 'Intentionalism Defended',. *Philosophical Review*. 110: 199–240.
Byrne, A. and Hilbert, D. (1997), 'Colors and Reflectances' in A. Byrne and D. Hilbert, *Readings on Color: Volume 1*. Cambridge, MA: MIT Press.
Byrne, A. and Hilbert, D. (2003), 'Color Realism and Color Science', *Behavioral and Brain Sciences*, 26: 3–21.
Byrne, A. and Hilbert, D. (2017), 'Color Relationalism and Relativism', *Topics in Cognitive Science*, 9: 172–92.
Campbell, K. (2018), 'Does That Which Makes a Sensation of Blue a Mental Fact Escape Us?' in Derek Brown and Fiona MacPherson (eds), *The Routledge Handbook of Philosophy of Colour*. Abingdon: Routledge.
Campbell, J. and Cassam, Q. (2014), *Berkeley's Puzzle*. Oxford: Oxford University Press.
Chalmers, D. (2005), Representationalism Showdown. http://fragments.consc.net/djc/2005/09/representationa.html
Chalmers, D. (2010), *The Character of Consciousness*. Oxford: Oxford University Press.
Chalmers, D. (2012), *Constructing the World*. Oxford: Oxford University Press.
Cohen, J. (2009), *The Red and the Real*. Oxford: Oxford University Press.
Cowart, B. J. and Rawson, N. E. (2001), 'Olfaction' in E. Goldstein (ed.), *The Blackwell Handbook of Perception*. Oxford: Blackwell Publishers.
Cutter, B. (2016), 'Color and Shape: A Plea for Equal Treatment', *Philosophers' Imprint*, 16: 1–11.
Dretske, F. (1995), *Naturalizing the Mind*. Cambridge, MA: MIT Press.
Dretske, F. (2006), 'Perception without Awareness',. in J. Hawthorne and T. Szabo Gendler (eds), *Perceptual Experience*. Oxford: Oxford University Press, 147–80.
Hawthorne, J. (2004), 'Why Humeans Are Out of their Minds', *Noûs*, 38: 351–8.
Horgan, T. (2014), 'Phenomenal Intentionality and Secondary Qualities' in B. Brogaard (ed.), *Does Perception Have Content?* Oxford: Oxford University Press.
Horgan, T. and Tienson, J. (2002), 'The Intentionality of Phenomenology and the Phenomenology of Intentionality'. in D. Chalmers (ed.), *Philosophy of Mind: Classical and Contemporary Readings*. Oxford: Oxford University Press.
Howard, J. D., Plailly, J., Grueschow, M., Haynes, J. D., and Gottfried, J. A. (2009), 'Odor Quality Coding and Categorization in Human Posterior Piriform Cortex', *Nature Neuroscience* 12: 932–9.
Jackson, F. (1977), *Perception: A Representative Theory*. Cambridge: Cambridge University Press.
Kriegel, U. (2009), *Subjective Consciousness: A Self-Representational Theory*. Oxford: Oxford University Press.
Kriegel, U. (2011), *The Sources of Intentionality*. Oxford: Oxford University Press.
Langsam, H. (2018), 'Why Intentionalism Cannot Explain Phenomenal Character', *Erkenntnis*. DOI 10.1007/s10670-018-0031-7
Levine, J. (1997), 'Are Qualia Just Representations?' *Mind and Language*, 12: 101–13.
Lewis, D. (1986), *On the Plurality of Worlds*. Oxford: Blackwell.
Logue, H. (2017), 'Are Experiences Just Representations?' in B. Nanay (ed.), *Current Controversies in the Philosophy of Perception*. New York: Routledge, 43–56.
Margot, C. (2009), 'A Noseful of Objects', *Nature Neurosciencei*, 12: 813–14.

Masrour, F. (2015), 'The Geometry of Visual Space and the Nature of Visual Experience', *Philosophical Studies*, 172: 1813–32.
McGrath, M. ms. The Metaphysics of Looks.
McLaughlin, B. (2012), 'On Justifying Neurobiologicalism for Consciousness' in S. Gozzano and C. Hill (eds) m *New Perspectives on Type Identity*. Cambridge: Cambridge University Press, 206–28.
McLaughlin, B. (2016), 'The Skewed View from Here: Normal Geometrical Misperception'm *Philosophical Topics*, 44: 231–99.
Mendelovici, A. (2018), *The Phenomenal Basis of Intentionality*. Oxford: Oxford University Press.
Moran, A. (2018), *Austinian Disjunctivism Defended: A Presentational Theory of Visual Experience*. Ph.D. Thesis, University of Cambridge.
Moran, A. (2019), 'Naive Realism, Hallucination and Causation: A New Response to the Screening Off Argument', *Australasian Journal of Philosophy*, 97: 368–382.
Morgan, J. ms. The Representational Limits of Perception.
Papineau, D. (2014), 'Sensory Experience and Representational Properties', *Proceedings of the Aristotelian Society*, 114: 1–33.
Papineau, D. (2016), 'Against Representationalism (about Experience)', *International Journal of Philosophical Studies*, 24: 324–47.
Pautz, A. (2010), 'Why Explain Experience in terms of Content?' in B. Nanay (ed.), *Perceiving the World*. Oxford: Oxford University Press, 254–309.
Pautz, A. (2014a), 'The Real Trouble with Armchair Arguments Against Phenomenal Externalism' in M. Sprevak and J. Kallestrup (eds), *New Waves in Philosophy of Mind*. Houndmills: Palgrave Macmillan, 153–84.
Pautz, A. (2014b), 'The Real Trouble for Phenomenal Externalists: New Empirical Evidence for a Brain-Based Theory of Sensory Consciousness' in R. Brown (ed.), *Consciousness Inside and Out*. New York: Springer, 237–98.
Pautz, A. (2017), 'Experiences are Representations: An Empirical Argument' in B. Nanay (ed.), *Current Debates in Philosophy of Perception*. New York: Routledge, 23–42.
Peacocke, C. (2008), 'Sensational Properties: Theses to Accept and Theses to Reject', *Revue Internationale de Philosophie*, 62: 7–24.
Perkins, R. and Bayne, T. (2013), 'Representationalism and the Problem of Vagueness', *Philosophical Studies*, 162: 71–86.
Price, D. and Barrell, J. (2012), *Inner Experience and Neuroscience*. Cambridge, MA: MIT Press.
Price, H. H. (1932), *Perception*. London: Methuen.
Pryor, J. (2000), 'The Skeptic and the Dogmatist', *Noûs*, 34: 517–49.
Russell, B. (1912), *The Problems of Philosophy*. London: Williams and Norgate.
Shoemaker, S. (2019), 'Phenomenal Character and Physicalism' in A. Pautz and D. Stoljar (eds), *Blockheads! Essays on Ned Block's Philosophy of Mind and Consciousness*. Cambridge, MA: MIT Press.
Sider, T. (2010), *Logic for Philosophers*. Oxford: Oxford University Press.
Smith, A. (2008), 'Translucent Experience', *Philosophical Studies*, 140: 197–212.
Soames, S. (2010), *What is Meaning?* Princeton, NJ: Princeton University Press.
Speaks, J. (2015), *The Phenomenal and the Representational*. Oxford: Oxford University Press.
Speaks, J. (2017), 'Reply to Critics', *Philosophy and Phenomenological Research*, 95: 492–506.
Travis, C. (2004), 'The Silence of the Senses', *Mind*, 113: 57–94.

Tye, M. (1995), *Ten Problems of Consciousness*. Cambridge, MA: MIT Press.
Tye, M. (2000), *Consciousness, Color and Content*. Cambridge, MA: MIT Press.
Tye, M. (2009), *Consciousness Revisited*. Cambridge, MA: MIT Press.
Yi, B. (2017), Nominalism and Comparative Similarity. *Erkenntnis* , https://doi.org/10.1007/s10670-017-9914-2.
Youngentob, S. L., Johnson, B. A., Leon, M., Sheehe, P. R., and Kent, P. F. (2006), 'Predicting Odorant Quality Perceptions from Multidimensional Scaling of Olfactory Bulb Glomerular Activity Patterns', *Behavioral Neuroscience*, 120: 1337–45.

CHAPTER 20

HIGHER-ORDER THEORIES OF CONSCIOUSNESS

JOSH WEISBERG

HIGHER-ORDER (HO) theories of consciousness hold that a mental state is conscious when it is appropriately represented by a 'higher-order' state, a state about another mental state. The higher-order perception (HOP) theory holds that HO representation is best modeled on perceptual processes, while the higher-order thought (HOT) theory holds that it is best modeled on thought. In addition, some HO theories hold that to be conscious, a state must be actively represented by an HO state, while others maintain that the mere disposition to be represented by an HO state is enough. The HO theory, if successful, offers a reductive explanation of mental state consciousness in terms of nonconscious HO representation.[1] In this chapter, I will first spell out the general motivation for the HO view and the differences between HOP and HOT. Then I will consider key objections to the approach, as well as possible empirical support. I will close by looking at how the view addresses the explanatory gap and the hard problem of consciousness.

20.1 THE TRANSITIVITY PRINCIPLE

20.1.1 The Transitivity Principle Explained

HO theories are motivated by what David Rosenthal (2000) terms the 'transitivity principle', the idea that *conscious states are states we're conscious of*. On the face of it, the

---

[1] Though there are nonreductive versions of the HO theory (see for example Chalmers 2013), in this chapter I will focus only on those arguing for a reduction of consciousness to HO representation.

principle looks circular. However, the term 'consciousness' has both a transitive and intransitive use. In the transitive sense, we are conscious *of* something; in the intransitive sense, a mental state is either conscious or nonconscious. The transitivity principle characterizes the intransitive consciousness of a mental state in terms of a subject's transitive consciousness *of* that mental state.[2] There are plausible explanations of transitive consciousness in terms of representation, explanations independent of intransitive mental state consciousness.[3] So it is open to the HO theorist to explain intransitive mental state consciousness in terms of representational transitive consciousness.

But what reason is there to accept the transitivity principle? First, the principle is folk-psychologically plausible, especially in its contrapositive form: we would intuitively deny that a state is conscious if we are in no way aware of it.[4] This seems to point to a folk-theoretic way of distinguishing conscious and nonconscious states: implicit in our folk psychology is the idea that conscious states are states we are aware of. If the initial data for theorizing about the mind is given by a 'rough and ready' analysis of our everyday folk-psychological concepts,[5] then the transitivity principle plausibly captures at least one everyday sense of 'consciousness'. Second, we can appeal to phenomenology. First-person reflection may reveal that consciousness possesses the sort of inner- or self-awareness characterized by the transitivity principle. When I am aware of my backyard, for example, there also seems to be a kind of awareness of myself as seeing the back yard, or an awareness that I am seeing it. This awareness may be more or less focused and it may even fade into the background when I am fully absorbed in a task. Still, it is claimed, this 'for-me-ness' is always present in experience to some degree. Different conscious states may involve the rich colors of my backyard, or the pain in my upper back, or even my troubled reflections on the hard problem, but they will share the kind of reflexive awareness characterized by the transitivity principle.[6] Third, one might appeal to the theoretical utility of embracing the transitivity principle. It may provide a useful way of empirically individuating conscious states—in experimental psychology, for example, taking conscious states to be states we are aware of being in may facilitate experimental design or avoid conceptual confusion. Or it may provide the best overall theoretical 'fit' for conscious states, given our commonsense, empirical, and metaphysical commitments. That is, the task of finding a global equilibrium between these various concerns may best be served by embracing the transitivity principle. Fourth, the transitivity principle may best connect a theory of consciousness to certain historical antecedents, like the views of Aristotle, Locke, or Sartre.[7] And finally, it may be that the transitivity principle provides the best opening wedge to reductively explaining

---

[2] Another use of 'consciousness' picks out the consciousness of creatures: a creature can be conscious or unconscious. The HO theory focuses on 'state consciousness' and leaves 'creature consciousness' to one side. Cf. Rosenthal 1986.

[3] For example, Fodor 1990; Dretske 1981; Millikan 1984.

[4] In what follows, I will use the terms 'aware of' and 'conscious of' interchangeably, and I intend them to pick out transitive consciousness characterized independently of intransitive state consciousness.

[5] Lewis 1972; Cf. Braddon-Mitchell and Jackson 2007.   [6] See Zahavi and Kriegel 2015.

[7] See, e.g., Caston 2002; Güzeldere 1995; Gennaro 2002.

consciousness. Remaining explanatory worries might then be tackled within the framework developed to capture the transitivity principle. Taken together, these reasons provide support for the claim that the transitivity principle appropriately fixes the data a theory of consciousness must explain.

Two refinements of the transitivity principle are needed. In its basic form, the principle states that we are conscious of our conscious states. But we can be conscious of our mental states in ways that fail to make those states conscious. If I am in a state of anger and I am informed of this fact by someone I trust, I may come to be conscious of my anger. But that may not make the anger itself conscious. I may still be in denial or otherwise unable to directly access the state. My awareness of the state must, therefore, occur in a seemingly direct way. I cannot be aware of any mediating inference or observation leading to the awareness—it must seem from the first-person perspective to be spontaneous and unmediated. This is captured in the transitivity principle by adding 'appropriately': a mental state is conscious when one is *appropriately* aware of it. The right way to cash out this sort of awareness is a matter for the theory to determine, but it is clear that not just any awareness of one's state will do.

A second refinement concerns whose state one is aware of. It seems that even if I become aware of one of your states in a seemingly direct way, that will not make your state conscious. I must be appropriately aware of *myself* as being in the state. So some sort of self-reference needs to be captured in the transitivity principle. This delivers the full transitivity principle:

> TP: A mental state is conscious when one is appropriately conscious of oneself as being in that state.

This characterization of consciousness is meant to be pretheoretic, offered prior to the theoretical positing of any mechanism that might explain how this process is instantiated in us. HO theorists take the transitivity principle as fixing the data a theory of mental state consciousness must explain and develop their theories accordingly.

20.1.2 Challenges to the Transitivity Principle

The use of the transitivity principle in fixing the data can be challenged in a number of ways. Charles Siewert (1998: sect 6.3) argues that while there is a sense in which we use 'conscious of' language to refer to an awareness of our conscious states, more often we use the phrase to report awareness of objects in the world.[8] This suggests that we should not rush to take 'conscious of' talk as implying anything about state- or self-awareness. Instead, it normally marks off the worldly content we are aware of. But the HO theorist can accept this claim without giving up the idea that the transitivity principle properly

---

[8] See also Byrne 2004.

fixes the data. The principle is not justified on the basis of frequency of use; rather, it is justified as a (likely implicit) folk-psychological distinction between conscious and unconscious states. The intuitive difference between a conscious and nonconscious visual representation of a ball is that we are suitably aware of ourselves as seeing the ball in the conscious case. And this justifies the transitivity principle, even if there are many contexts where we use 'conscious of' to pick out things other than our own states.

Fred Dretske (1993) directly challenges the transitivity principle by presenting a case allegedly showing that we can be in a conscious state we are not conscious of. He calls this the 'spot' case. Consider an array containing thirteen similar spots in a random pattern. We might look at the array and have a conscious experience of it. Later, we might be presented with an array with only twelve of the previously seen spots and consciously experience that as well. However, we often will not be aware of any difference between two arrays, even though one spot is missing. Dretske contends that the experience of the thirteenth spot must have been conscious, because we were looking at in good light, attending to the array, etc. But we are not conscious of the difference between our two experiences. It follows that we are conscious of the thirteenth spot even though we are not conscious of our experience of it. Thus, the transitivity principle is wrong. However, the defender of the transitivity principle can hold that we can be conscious of our states without being conscious of them in every respect. Importantly, we might be conscious of our states but not conscious of the property that makes the difference between two experiences. We might even be conscious of the relevant spot, but not under the description of 'difference maker'. So the spot case does not contradict the transitivity principle.[9]

More pressing is the charge that the transitivity principle, while reasonably picking out one kind of consciousness, is not about the one most relevant to the study of consciousness: consciousness characterized in terms of 'what it's like for the subject'.[10] In response, proponents of the transitivity principle point to Thomas Nagel's initial 'what it's like' characterization of consciousness (Nagel 1974). Nagel writes that 'an organism has conscious mental states if and only if there is something that it is like to *be* that organism—something it is like *for* the organism' (Nagel 1974: 436, emphasis in original). Nagel himself stresses that there must be something it is like *for* the organism. Defenders of the transitivity principle argue that the best explanation of there being something it is like *for* the organism is that the organism is aware of its states. If we are in no way aware of being in a state, there is nothing it is like *for us* to be in that state. So, the transitivity principle does not leave out what it is like; indeed, it makes clear just why there is something it is like for us when we are in conscious states.

But recently, Daniel Stoljar has challenged this 'reflexive' reading of Nagel's 'what it's like' characterization (Stoljar 2016). He argues for what he terms the 'affective approach'

---

[9] See Seager 1999: ch 3, for a detailed discussion of this case.
[10] This kind of consciousness is known as 'phenomenal consciousness'. See Block 1995; Chalmers 1996: ch 1.

to interpreting 'what it's like' talk in general and Nagel's phrase in particular. Stoljar's analysis of Nagel's phrase is as follows:

> For any subject S and any psychological state X of S, X is a phenomenally conscious state if and only if X is constitutively such that there is some way that S feels in virtue of S's being in X   (Stoljar 2016: 1190).

Stoljar's analysis reveals no connection between what it is like and state- or self-awareness. Further, the 'for' emphasized by Nagel drops away as irrelevant. What matters, rather, is that a subject is in a conscious state when that state, because of its nature, makes her feel a certain way. As Stoljar puts it, there is no 'easy implication' to a reflexive theory—a theory embracing the transitivity principle. But this does not block the transitivity reading of Nagel's what it is like phrase. First, it was not the claimed that there was an *entailment* from Nagel's phrase to the transitivity principle. Rather, the transitivity principle provides a good interpretation of the phrase, one revealing its deeper structure. Further, Stoljar's 'affective approach' is flawed. There are plausible cases of states that make us feel ways based on their constitution that nonetheless are not conscious states. If I have an unconscious pain, it may alter my overall mood, it may influence my behavior, etc. precisely because it is a pain and not some other state. But that does not entail that there will be something it is like for me to be in that state. Stoljar's analysis falls short just where we need it to mark the distinction between conscious and nonconscious states. This suggests a revised analysis: one adding to Stoljar's characterization *that we are aware of the state*. But this just is a version of the transitivity principle. We can conclude that the principle does not leave out what it is like and so stands as the right way to fix the data a theory of consciousness must explain.

20.2 Varieties of HO Theory

20.2.1 HOP versus HOT

Given the transitivity principle, we can sketch an argument to the best explanation for the HO theory:

1. A mental state is conscious when one is appropriately conscious of oneself as being in that state. (Transitivity Principle)
2. The best explanation of this process is HO representation.
3. Therefore, the best explanation of conscious states is in terms of HO representation.

A key question for HO theory concerns the format of the HO representation. Two main options have been defended in the literature, the higher-order perception (HOP) view (Armstrong, Lycan) and the higher-order thought (HOT) view (Rosenthal, Carruthers;

see also Gennaro).[11] Armstrong, defending the HOP theory, notes that inner awareness can provide a directed scanning of our experience, in much the way perception provides a directed scanning of our environment. Lycan, too, sees the functional profile of higher-order awareness as analogous to perceptual monitoring of our environment. Further, he contends that the range of features we can be aware of in experience outstrips conceptual resources, suggesting that the monitor employs perception-like nonconceptual representations.

A key part of Rosenthal's case for HOT theory involves undermining HOP. He argues that perceptual processes are marked by distinctive sensory qualities: mental colors, tastes, smells, etc. However, when we consider conscious experience, we only find the qualities of first-order states. We never experience any higher-order sensory qualities. This suggests that HO representation lacks sensory quality and thus is better viewed as thought-like. In response to Lycan's worry that experience outstrips conceptual resources, Rosenthal argues that this underestimates the range of conceptual resources. If we include comparative concepts like 'lighter than' or 'darker than' we can conceptually represent a vast range of colors, for example, even if we lack distinct concepts like 'red' or 'green' for each quality experience. Further, thought, too, can serve to monitor a domain, as when we monitor our thought for error or bias. Note, however, that since all three theorists are functionalists and representationalists, broadly construed, in the final analysis the difference between HOP and HOT may not be so great.[12]

Another dimension along which HO theorists differ is the question of whether the HO state must be occurrent or whether it can be merely dispositional. Peter Carruthers (2000), in defending a dispositional version of the HO theory, contends that it is implausible that a HO state re-represent all of the detail present in a conscious first-order perceptual state. For one, the information is already present in the first-order state. Why would it need to be re-represented? What evolutionary purpose would that fulfill? And such complete recapitulation at the HO level may well threaten cognitive overload. How could a higher-order cognitive system take up all that data? Instead, Carruthers argues, we should view the presence of the HO state as dispositional. First-order states are conscious when they can be accessed by a higher-order 'mind reading' system. But they need not be occurrently taken up by the system, nor need it re-represent them in all detail.

However, an 'occurrent' HO theorist can respond with several points. First, it is not clear that at any given moment of experience we are actually aware of all that much detail. We can take in a range of properties 'at a glance' by representing them in grouped 'ensembles'.[13] For example, we can be aware of a pile of colored books in the periphery of our vision without being able to make out the details of the colors and shapes. The actual burden on HO representation at a given time is not so great. Further, there is evidence

---

[11] Armstrong 1968, 1981; Lycan 1987, 1996; Rosenthal 1986, 2005; Carruthers 2000, 2005; Gennaro 2012.
[12] See Rosenthal 2004; Lycan 2004, for further discussion of the differences between HOP and HOT theories.
[13] Cohen et al 2016; Ward et al 2016.

that we systematically overestimate just how much we can see at a given time. People are surprised to find just how little detail is actively present in parafoveal vision when we are not attending to periphery.[14] This suggests that we may not actively represent many details until we need to, lessening the cognitive burden on HO states. What is more, there are problems with the dispositional approach. One worry is that we are disposed to become aware of many states that do not in fact enter awareness at a given time. I may be disposed to become aware of some sensation of mine if I am prompted to attend to it. For example, can you feel your big toe right now? If the feeling of your big toe was not conscious prior to the prompt, one is nonetheless disposed to become aware of it in the right circumstances. We are left wanting to know which dispositions matter and why. But even if that challenge can be met, it remains unclear that a disposition to represent is enough to make us aware of being in a state. If there is no active, occurrent change in the state or in our awareness of it beyond the potential to represent it, how can that account for the change from a nonconscious state to a conscious one? Thus, it seems an occurrent account is to be preferred.

20.2.2 HOT Theory Detailed

I will now provide a brief sketch of David Rosenthal's HOT theory, to show in more detail how the HO view might be developed.[15] Rosenthal argues that a mental state is conscious when we form an appropriate HOT about the state. The HOT must possess an assertoric attitude, as other attitudes like wondering or doubting need not make us aware of anything. Further, the state must be formed without any inference or observation the subject is aware of—it must seem spontaneous and immediate from the subject's point of view. Rosenthal contends that the HOT employs descriptive, conceptual content to represent the target state. Recall that conceptual thought may include comparative concepts to extend the range of conceptual description. Finally, the HOT must make reference to the self. This delivers the following characterization:

> HOT: A mental state of seeing a red ball, for example, is conscious when we token the following roughly co-occurrent assertoric HOT: 'I, myself, am seeing a red ball.'

In addition to picking out intentional contents like 'ball', HOTs must be able to pick out the distinctive qualities of sensations. To do so, Rosenthal appeals to 'quality space' theory, one characterizing qualities in relational terms, by way of their role in similarity and difference judgments.[16] Further, note that the HOT must be able to pick out mental states as such: I am in a state of seeing or hearing, etc. It may at this point seem that the HOT view cannot be right, as we are never aware of such complex cognitive states when we have ordinary conscious experience. However, according to Rosenthal's view, HOTs

---

[14] See Land and Tatler 2009: ch 3. [15] See Rosenthal 2005.
[16] Rosenthal 2005: chs 5–7; Cf. Clark 1993.

are generally *nonconscious*, so we will not ordinarily be aware of their presence.[17] This also serves to block a potential regress of conscious states making us aware of our conscious states. HOTs, on Rosenthal's view, are posited to explain the awareness we have of our conscious states. They are not justified on phenomenological grounds, at least not directly. The end result is a nonconscious HOT, formed in a seemingly spontaneous manner, to the effect that 'I, myself, am seeing a red ball.' When this HO state is tokened, I become appropriately aware of myself as seeing a red ball—my visual state of seeing a red ball becomes conscious. Armstrong and Lycan offer variations on this sort of theoretical structure, but the broad strokes are the same: a nonconscious first-order state is represented by a separate HO representation, rendering the first-order state conscious.

20.3 Objections to the HO theory

20.3.1 Rock States and Liver States

The first objection we will consider challenges the idea that mere representation is enough to explain the transition from unconscious to conscious mental state. Why is it that when one is conscious of a mental state it becomes conscious, but when one is conscious of a rock, say, it does not? Indeed, we can represent a seemingly unlimited number of things without those things themselves becoming conscious rocks, conscious trees, conscious eggplants, and what have you. If representation does not produce this sort of transformation in the usual case, why think it occurs in the case of mental states? And if more is needed to explain the transition, this suggests that the real work of consciousness is being done by the additional factors, rendering the representational explanation irrelevant. This objection is known as 'the problem of the rock.'[18]

In response, Rosenthal and Lycan argue that the key difference is that mental states are being represented—it is in their nature that when we are conscious of them, they become conscious. But this answer, even if true, needs more support. What is it about the nature of mental states that explains this difference? Here, the HO theorist can point to the self-ascribing character of the HO state. It is an awareness that *I, myself,* am in such-and-such a state. I can be aware of myself as being in a visual state or a state of desire, but it is not clear how I could be aware of myself as being in a rock state (or as being a rock, etc.). Self-ascription thus limits the range of HO awareness. Further, the way we are built may limit what can trigger the HO representational system. Mental states are causally poised to trigger this system; rocks, trees, and eggplants are not. Even though the HO system employs representation, and thus in principle could represent these other things, the way the system is actually instantiated in us limits its application.

---

[17] HOTs themselves can become conscious when targeted by further '3rd-order' states. Rosenthal labels this phenomenon 'introspection'.
[18] Goldman 1993.

And this helps deal with a variation of the rock objection, the 'liver state objection'.[19] It does seem that we might self-ascribe states of our own livers: 'I, myself, am metabolizing bilirubin slowly', if I have jaundice, say. But such states do not ever become conscious states. Again, it might be that such states are not in a position to trigger the HO system. We are just not built that way. Or perhaps we can form thoughts that we are in such states, but not in a seemingly immediate way. To generate a thought in the spontaneous manner required by the transitivity principle, the right triggering conditions may need to be present. Liver states plausibly fail to meet those conditions. Thus, although liver states may be self-ascribable, they are not properly placed to spontaneously trigger the HO awareness required by the transitivity principle.

20.3.2 Over-sophisticated HOTs

A different set of objections argues that the HOT theory in particular requires a high degree of conceptual sophistication and this in turn rules out many creatures, including perhaps babies or young children, from having conscious mental states.[20] The HOT theory demands that we employ concepts picking out mental states as such, as states of seeing, hearing, feeling, and so on. What is more, the requirement that HOTs involve self-representation further limits the creatures that might have conscious states. It may be that most nonhuman animals and children up to three years old lack such conceptual sophistication. But it seems highly implausible that children and animals lack conscious pains or perceptions. Perhaps the HO theorist can bight the bullet here (see Carruthers 1989), but a better tack challenges the claim that the concepts required for HOT are really so sophisticated. Rosenthal contends that nonlinguistic creatures might refer in a minimal way to their sensory states by way of their position in the relevant sensory field. Further, there is evidence of the presence of 'theory of mind' capacities in a range of nonhuman animals, including ravens.[21] Such capacities implicate the employment of an implicit appearance/reality distinction. And this in turn may provide the resources needed by HOT to pick out mental states. So it is not clear that the HOT theory denies consciousness to nonhuman animals and babies.

Further, there is similar evidence of at least a minimal self-concept present in nonhuman animals.[22] Social animals in particular need to have ways to track themselves and their conspecifics in terms of their social relations. And an even more basic ability to distinguish one's own body from the external world is clearly present far down the phylogenetic scale. Are such minimal self-concepts sufficient to explain the sort of self-reference present in consciousness as characterized by the transitivity principle? It appears so, especially when we distinguish between the sort of implicit self-reference present in consciousness and a more full-blown conscious *introspective* awareness of self, present more rarely in us. This sort of introspective self-awareness perhaps does require cognitive

---

[19] Block 1995.   [20] Block 1995: 280.
[21] Bugnyar et al 2016; see also Allen and Bekoff 1997.   [22] Bekoff 2003.

resources beyond that of young children. But that is not the kind of self-awareness at issue. Rather, all that is required is the background self-awareness marking our mental states as ours, as integrated into our background awareness of ourselves. This kind of awareness distinguishes my states from the states of others and it provides a background sense of 'for me-ness', the phenomenal impression that I subjectively own my conscious states.[23] This more restricted kind of self-awareness is plausibly present in babies and some nonhuman animals, suggesting that the HO theory is not overly restrictive in the way indicated by the objection. The issue is largely empirical, but it is not clear that the HO theory entails an objectionable result.

20.3.3 Misrepresentation and Empty HOTs

A third objection focuses on the representational connection between conscious mental states and our awareness of them. This objection has received the most attention in recent literature, so I will consider it in some detail. The HO theory holds that we represent our conscious states. But by its nature, representation can go astray—successful representation plausibly requires the possibility of misrepresentation.[24] So what happens if an HO state misrepresents its target? In particular, what happens to phenomenal character, to 'what it's like' for the subject? Consider the following three scenarios:

1. A subject accurately represents herself as being in a red visual state, by way of an HO representation to the effect that 'I, myself, am seeing red', when she is seeing red. (Accurate)
2. A subject inaccurately represents herself as being in a red visual state, by way of an HO representation to the effect that 'I, myself, am seeing red', when she is in fact seeing green. (Inaccurate)
3. A subject inaccurately represents herself as being in a red visual state, by way of an HO representation to the effect that 'I, myself, am seeing red', when she is in fact in no visual state whatsoever. (Empty)

We can call these scenarios 'accurate', 'inaccurate', and 'empty' scenarios, respectively. What, according to the HO theory, is it like for the subject in each of these cases? In the accurate scenario, it is like seeing red—this is the standard case the theory is designed to explain. But in the inaccurate case, what it is like for the subject is arguably just the same as in the accurate scenario: what it is like for a subject is plausibly a matter of how that subject represents her state. And, by parity of reasoning, what it is like for the subject in the empty case is again the same: it is like seeing red. These results are seen as having devastating consequences for the theory.

First, it seems that the first-order state has been rendered unnecessary for the presence of a conscious state. Conscious experience indistinguishable from the accurate

---

[23] See Zahavi and Kriegel 2015.   [24] Dretske 1981.

case can occur without a first-order state.[25] The relational structure posited to explain state consciousness has collapsed. We are left with a single state accounting for experience, a view with no obvious structural advantage over rival 'first-order representational' theories.[26] And how could a mere HO state, particularly a nonsensory state like a HOT, explain the richness of conscious experience, in the total absence of the relevant sensation?[27]

But more seriously, there seems to be an incoherence exposed at the heart of HO theory if the empty scenario can occur. The transitivity principle defines a conscious state as one we are conscious of. In the empty scenario, the state we are conscious of is a red visual state. But that state does not exist. But surely to be a conscious state, the state must exist. So there is no conscious state in the empty scenario. Yet the HO theory holds that what it is like in the empty scenario is subjectively indistinguishable from the accurate case. And if something is subjectively indistinguishable from a conscious experience, it too must be a conscious experience. So in the empty scenario we are in a conscious state! Thus, the empty scenario seems to force the HO theory into an out-and-out contradiction, not a happy result.[28] Perhaps the HO theory can hold that it is the HO state itself that is conscious in all cases, but that does not seem to provide an effective explanation of the transitivity principle, of how we are conscious of our conscious states.[29] We are not generally aware of our HO states and this is indeed important in blocking a potential regress of conscious states in the theory (see Section 20.2.2 above). And if HO states are conscious for some other reason, we have lost the explanatory power of the theory. We can no longer explain the intransitive consciousness of mental states in terms of HO representation. We are left without an explanation at all. Taken altogether, HO misrepresentation appears to badly undermine the HO theory.

What, then, can the HO theory offer in response? One move is to argue that, at least for the more serious empty case, the lack of a first-order target would block the stable formation of an HO representation. The brain is filled with backward-projecting connections, connections from the higher back to the lower levels. These plausibly create feedback loops which sustain the co-activation and coordination of brain states. It may be that the HO state is connected in this manner to the lower-order areas it monitors. In the empty scenario, the lack of appropriate feedback from the lower-level might block the activity of the targetless HO state. Thus, for architectural reasons we can conclude the empty scenario could not occur. And it might even be that a severe enough mismatch between the HO state and its first-order target would block sustained formation of the HO state, limiting the damage of the inaccurate case.[30] While it may seem counterintuitive that our experience of green could be as of red, it is not so implausible that our experience of green might be misrepresented as turquoise or aquamarine. If normal

[25] See Wilberg 2010 for a challenge to this claim. See also Gennaro 2012, 59–66.
[26] Dretske 1995 and Tye 1995 defend first-order representational theories. See Byrne 1997 for details of this objection.
[27] See Byrne 1997; Neander 1998 for extended treatments of the objection. See also Van Gulick 2004.
[28] Kriegel 2003. Cf. Kriegel 2009.   [29] Though see Brown 2015.
[30] See Gennaro 2012: ch 9, for elaboration and defense of these claims.

brain functioning serves to limit the possibility of the troubling phenomena, perhaps the HO theory can avoid the objection.

But this sort of response may seem to miss the point. We want to know what accounts for what it is like for the subject according to the HO theory. If it is a matter of how the HO state represents things, we can reasonably ask about cases of misrepresentation even if they are limited in practice (or even nomologically impossible). This is a question of how the theory explains things even in the accurate case. If the HO theory hopes to reductively explain state consciousness in terms of HO representation, we need to know how HO representation accounts for what it is like. And the answer seems to be that it is the content of the HO state alone that explains what it is like. The misrepresentation objection calls out this claim for scrutiny.

There is a fork in the road for HO theorists here. Either they can try to strengthen the relational link between HO and first-order states or they can embrace the idea that HO content is fully sufficient for an explanation of what it is like. The first move leads to either a noncausal (and so, plausibly, nonreductive) view of representation, or it leads to a 'self-representational' theory, where a conscious states represents both itself and the world. Either move will block the empty scenario, but they incur the costs of explaining the strengthened notion of representation or the new self-representational relation. And there is the further problem of restricting the inaccurate scenario, if that worry retains its force in the absence of the empty case. I will not pursue these alternatives further here, though see Chapter 21 on the self-representational approach.[31]

Instead, I will pursue the second option, the claim that HO content is sufficient to fully explain what it is like. There are two related ways of defending this move. First, note that the content of the HO state makes reference to the self: 'I, myself, am in such-and-such a state.' Whenever a subject tokens such a state, the state will successfully refer to that very subject. So there is a sense in which an 'empty' HO state is never really empty. It is always about the very subject thinking that thought. And it then ascribes (in this case erroneously) properties to that subject: that she has the property of being in this or that state. What is more, there will always be various states present in a self-representing subject to serve as an inaccurately-described target. It is not that there is nothing else going on in the mind of the subject when she misattributes a state to herself. And at a minimum, the HOT itself will be present, though misdescribed. So, by the structure of the theory, the empty scenario is impossible: the subject and some state of hers will always be present whenever she tokens a HO state, even if she is inaccurate about which state she is in. And this is not for contingent reasons of neural architecture but because of the nature of the HO states posited.

But we might take a more radical tack. Some HO theorists have defended the idea that in all cases, accurate and inaccurate, the target of the HO state is merely an intentional object.[32] The idea here is that all that is required by the transitivity principle for a state to be conscious is that we are aware of ourselves as being in it. And that can occur even if

---

[31] See, for example, Kriegel 2009. See Weisberg 2008, 2011a, 2014a for criticisms of this approach.
[32] Rosenthal 2004, 2011; Weisberg 2011b, 2011c.

the state does not exist. We can in some sense be aware of something that is not there. As Gil Harman (1990) notes, there is a decent sense in which Macbeth is aware of a dagger before him, even though there is no such dagger. This explains how things *seem* to Macbeth. In the empty scenario, we represent ourselves as being in a state we are not actually in. But it will seem to us, because we represent things to ourselves that way, that we are in that very state. And so, we will be aware of the state in the sense that counts. It follows that one can be in a conscious state that does not exist, because all that matters for being in a conscious state is how things seem to one, and this is a matter of how we represent our mental lives to ourselves by way of HO representation.

Two further points need to be stressed to make this claim palatable. First, the counter-intuitive nature of this claim can be explained without denying HO representation. We are generally unaware of the HO state making us aware of our conscious states. So that awareness will seem immediate and direct. And because of this, there will not seem to be any 'space' between us and our conscious experience to allow for error. But that is because we remain unaware of the HO mechanism and its workings. The appearance of immediacy misleads us into an overly strong view about the accuracy of inner awareness. What is more, there is no similarly direct means of noticing error because the only seemingly-direct access we have is by way of HO states. We have no cross-modal check on inner awareness in the way we do with perceptual awareness. There is no direct evidence that could undermine our confidence in the deliverances of consciousness, so we conclude that misrepresentation cannot occur. But that does not mean there cannot be theoretical reasons to allow for error.

And this leads to the second point supporting the intentional object view: as general matter, theory sometimes prompts us to give up intuition. We start with the transitivity principle. This pins down the data to be explained by a theory of consciousness. We then posit HO representation as the best explanation of the transitivity principle: this is a theoretical claim, not an a priori analysis or a claim based on intuition. It turns out that HO representation allows for counterintuitive misrepresentation in the ways specified. But so long as the HO theory is well-supported in general, this gives us reason to doubt the intuitions against misrepresentation. In the same sense that it is counterintuitive, though not false, that the earth is in rapid motion, it may be counterintuitive, though not false, that HO representation explains state consciousness, even though it can misrepresent. Sometimes, theory overrides intuition, so long as we have a plausible story saving the appearances. Misrepresentation, though counterintuitive, is not fatal to the HO theory.

20.4 Empirical Support for the Higher-Order Theory

The objections considered thus far have largely been a matter of conceptual coherence. They are not matters to be decided by direct empirical test. This may raise doubts about the empirical status of the HO theory: is it merely a species of a priori analysis, to be accepted or rejected based on imagined counterexamples? Though much of the literature on HO theory focuses on conceptual matters, this is not the case. While the transitivity principle is a matter of pretheoretical analysis, the HO theory is offered as the best explanation of the transitivity principle, one ultimately open to empirical confirmation or refutation. Scientific theories may be challenged both on conceptual and empirical grounds, so it is not a mark against the empirical credentials of the HO view that debate at this stage focuses largely on possible conceptual coherence. Considerable further clarification and refinement will be needed, no doubt, to connect so-called philosophical theories of consciousness with experimental data powerful enough to separate rival views. Still, even at this stage, we can consider how data from psychology and neuroscience meshes with the HO approach.

The HO theory is committed to the claim that the state accounting for what it is like for us is separate and 'upstream' from our sensory systems. For example, the view appears committed to the idea that activity in primary visual areas alone is insufficient for conscious experience. Rather, there must be activity either in temporal or frontal regions, regions which might realize the sort of metacognitive state required for HO representation. Areas in prefrontal cortex associated with 'theory of mind' representations are a reasonable candidate for HO states,[33] as are regions in the dorsolateral prefrontal cortex associated with monitoring conflicting activity at lower levels. Work by Lau and Passingham involving a disparity between accuracy in a perceptual task and judgments of confidence concerning perception implicate activity in dlPFC as corresponding to HO monitoring.[34] Lau and Rosenthal argue that these results (and related results) provide evidence for HO theory.[35] In addition, Lau and Brown exploit the possibility of HO 'empty' misrepresentation to argue that phenomenal illusions like those in Charles Bonnet syndrome offer evidence of consciousness accounted for solely by the presence of the HO state.[36] This in effect turns the 'bug' of empty representation into an evidential feature. Such claims are controversial and theorists opposed to HO theory have alternative ways of interpreting this data. Still, it seems clear that empirical evidence is relevant to the defense of HO theory. It is not just old-fashioned armchair analysis.[37]

What is more, there are existing empirical views which may map relatively well to the HO view, broadly considered. The work of Antonio Damasio, for example, involves higher-order self-monitoring mapping activity in bodily and sensory systems.[38] And the 'higher-order syntactic' view of Edmond Rolls makes explicit connection to HO theory.[39] Finally, the work of Hans Flohr offers a way that HO representation might be realized when the right sorts of activation patterns are present in neurons possessing NMDA receptors.[40] This research has its basis in considerations of the effects of various anesthetics, including the breakdowns in experience that occur under the influence of

---

[33] Medial PFC, for example; see Saxe 2009.   [34] Lau and Passingham 2006.
[35] Lau and Rosenthal 2011.   [36] Lau and Brown 2019.
[37] See Sebastián 2014 for an interesting empirical challenge to HO theory. See Weisberg 2014b for an HO response.
[38] Damasio 1999.   [39] Rolls 2004.   [40] Flohr 1995, 1999.

ketamine. While it is clear that these views can be developed independently of HO theory, the authors have generally recognized the connection and some see it as providing a psychological explanation of the neurological phenomena they have been considering. This further strengthens HO theory's connection to empirical data, and it recommends the theory as an alternative to the lower-order re-entrant views and global workspace theories popular in neuroscience.[41]

20.5 THE HARD PROBLEM OF CONSCIOUSNESS

There remains, however, an outstanding worry, even if the earlier objections can be defused. Philosophers who hold that no reductive physicalist theory can close the 'explanatory gap' between the physical and the phenomenal, or those who think no physicalist theory can handle the 'hard problem' of consciousness—the problem of saying why any physical state is conscious at all—will conclude that HO theory falls short in explaining consciousness. It provides no narrowing of the explanatory gap and it fails to convincingly rule out the possibility of zombies, beings physically identical to us that nonetheless lack conscious states. It seems that zombies can have HO states of the relevant kind without being conscious. The view thus fails to explain consciousness in the deep sense required by the gap and the hard problem.

Since this is a challenge that hits all reductive physicalist views, the HO theorist might argue that more general considerations about modality and explanation are the proper place to look for answers to the gap and the hard problem. The conceivability of zombies and the lack of an a priori deduction of the phenomenal facts from the physical facts may in the end prove irrelevant to the prospects of a successful theory of consciousness.[42] Still, the HO theory has certain advantages in blocking these objections. First, the HO theory is committed to the claim that the transitivity principle fixes the data a theory of consciousness must explain. This in itself may counter the gap and hard problem. If being in a conscious state is simply being appropriately aware of yourself as being in a state, then the gap falls away. How do we explain consciousness in physical terms? We explain how physically-instantiated higher-order representation makes us aware of our mental states. That is what consciousness amounts to—there is no further question about how that could be, assuming higher-order representation provides an explanation of the appropriate awareness. Further, if some creature represents its first-order states in this way, then it, too, is in conscious states. That is, zombies are inconceivable on the HO theory, because all there is to consciousness is the right sort of awareness of our states and purported zombies can possess this sort of awareness. There is nothing more to a consciousness, so characterized. We have already seen that one can challenge the

---

[41] See Dehaene et al 2006; Lamme 2006.   [42] See, e.g., Block and Stalnaker 1999.

transitivity principle's claim to adequately fix the data (see Section 20.1.2 above), so I will not revisit the issue here. Suffice to say that *if* one accepts the transitivity characterization, then the gap and the hard problem dissolve.

But it might be argued that the strong intuition of a gap or of the conceivability of zombies remains, even if one accepts the transitivity principle and the positing of HO representation. Indeed, it could be claimed that the transitivity principle is but a necessary condition for consciousness, but it is not sufficient, as the persistence of gap intuitions shows. It may be countered that we should therefore discount the intuitions in the face of a successful theory. But a stronger move is available to the HO theory. The theory itself plausibly predicts the intuitions of an explanatory gap and zombies. And this helps weaken the relevance of those intuitions—if they are to be expected even if the HO theory is true, they lose their undermining force.

So what, according to the HO theory, accounts for the robust presence of these intuitions? First, the mechanism of awareness posited by the theory is generally hidden from first-person access. We are not usually conscious of ourselves as being in higher-order states during conscious experience. They operate unconsciously, behind the scenes. Further, we are unaware of any triggering conditions for the relevant HO states. The awareness they engender appears immediate and noninferential. This means that subjects will not find it intuitive that all conscious states are states represented by HO representation. Thus, we will be surprised to learn of its presence. Further, as noted in discussing intuitions about misrepresentation, the hidden nature of the HO state, as well as the lack of any accessible mediating factor, will support the intuition that we cannot be wrong about what conscious state we are in. There will not seem to be any of the distance or intervening process that explains error in the ordinary perceptual or cognitive case. It will seem to us that we have got direct and incorrigible access to our conscious experience and any claim that there is further background machinery accounting for such awareness will seem counterintuitive. There will thus seem to be a gap between the physically-realized processes posited by the HO theory and phenomenal consciousness. And it will be easy to imagine conscious beings who lack HO representation, because it is counterintuitive that we have such machinery, even if we in fact do.

But what of the distinctive qualities of experience, the 'qualia' supposedly lacking in zombies, unknown by color-deprived super-scientist Mary, etc.? Even if we can explain our seemingly direct access to these things, the things so accessed seem problematic in and of themselves. Qualia have seemingly simple natures: they do not seem to allow decomposition into something more basic, nor do they seem amenable to reductive explanation. They form the basic building blocks of experience and lack any apparent structure to provide the needed 'hooks' for explanation. Further, there is something indescribable or 'ineffable' about qualia. If you have never had an experience with certain basic qualities, there is little informative about the qualities that can be conveyed to you. If you have never tasted sweetness or seen red, for example, no amount of explanation will provide you with what you are missing. And taken in conjunction with the seeming directness of our first-person access to qualia, they seem only contingently connected to structural, functional, or dynamical properties, properties amenable to physicalist reduction. Directly-accessed qualia are what make consciousness really intractable, it seems.

Again, however, the HO theory can explain why qualia appear intractable when they are not. A guiding principle of cognitive science, one gaining further support in experimental and social psychology, is that the bulk of mental processing occurs outside of conscious awareness.[43] We monitor and process a range of stimuli at a given time, but only a select set of features makes it into experience. What is more, there is evidence that unconscious processing is more information-rich, and that consciousness effects a kind of bottleneck in the cognitive stream.[44] Consciousness seems to be a limited-bandwidth system, one that only takes up features as needed.[45] Taking these facts into account, it follows that HO representation would have a compressing, limiting effect on the flow of information. There would be pressures to reduce to a minimum the information needed to make the subject aware of relevant features of her conscious states. It is plausible, then, that the HO state would abstract away from the range of causal and functional connections constitutive of physically-reducible sensory qualities. All that HO states would register would be a compressed version of the information, that the state possesses this or that quality, without making explicit the connections to other features of the mind. Or a complex battery of associations, exemplars, and contextual cues might be reduced down to a representation of a single, constant quality, the one must likely to track salient and useful features. Doubtless, this compressing and limiting process occurs throughout the perceptual processing stream, but awareness of our states filtered through HO representation would add to this effect.

The result of this ongoing compressing and limiting would be the appearance of seemingly simple qualities, qualities without the sorts of relational connections needed to provide an informative description. And, for that reason, we would be unaware of connections between the qualities and any structural, functional, or dynamical properties of mental states—they would seem only contingently connected to such things. We would have the appearance of simple, indescribable qualities, only contingently connected to the mind. Further, because these qualities are known in a seemingly direct manner, our knowledge of them would seem special and privileged. We would find it counterintuitive that we could be in error about them. There would therefore seem to be an unbridgeable explanatory gap and zombies would be easy to conceive. But because this is predicted by the constraints of architecture and resources imposed by HO theory, we can reasonably discount the importance of these intuitions. They are just what we would expect if the HO theory is true. And this further vindicates the claim made in Section 20.1.1 above that the transitivity is a full and adequate characterization of the data a theory must explain. It predicts that we would find a phenomenal 'what it's like' characterization appealing, even though the transitivity principle captures the data without remainder. Thus, the HO theory disarms the gap and the hard problem, clearing the way for a satisfying explanation of consciousness in physical terms.

---

[43] See, for example, Wilson 2002.   [44] Norretranders 1991.
[45] See O'Regan 2011; Cf. Cohen et al 2016.

REFERENCES

Allen, C. and Bekoff, M. (1997), *Species of Mind: The Philosophy and Biology of Cognitive Ethology.* Cambridge, MA: MIT Press.
Armstrong, D. M. (1968), *A Materialist Theory of Mind.* London: Routledge and Kegan Paul.
Armstrong, D. M. (1981), 'What is Consciousness?' in *The Nature of Mind.* Ithaca, NY: Cornell University Press.
Bekoff, M. (2003), *Minding Animals: Awareness, Emotions, and Heart.* Oxford: Oxford University Press.
Block, N. (1995), 'On a Confusion about the Function of Consciousness', *Behavioral and Brain Sciences*, 18: 227–87.
Block, N. and Stalnaker, R. (1999), 'Conceptual Analysis, Dualism, and the Explanatory Gap', *Philosophical Review*, 108: 1–46.
Braddon-Mitchell, D. and Jackson, F. (2007), *Philosophy of Mind and Cognition*, 2nd edn. Oxford: Blackwell Publishing.
Brown, R. (2015), 'The HOROR Theory of Phenomenal Consciousness', *Philosophical Studies*, 172/7: 1783–94.
Bugnyar, T., Reber, S., and Buckner, C. (2016), 'Ravens attribute visual access to unseen competitors', *Nature Communications.* 7.
Byrne, A. (1997), 'Some like it HOT: Consciousness and higher-order thoughts', *Philosophical Studies*, 2/2:103–29.
Byrne, Alex (2004), 'What phenomenal consciousness is like' in R. J. Gennaro (ed.), *Higher-order Theories of Consciousness.* Amsterdam: John Benjamins Publishers, 203–25.
Carruthers, P. (1989), 'Brute experience', *Journal of Philosophy*, 86: 258–69.
Carruthers, P. (2000), *Phenomenal Consciousness.* Cambridge: Cambridge University Press.
Carruthers, P. (2005), *Consciousness: Essays from a Higher-Order Perspective.* New York: Oxford University Press.
Caston, V. (2002), 'Aristotle on consciousness', *Mind*, 111/444: 751–815.
Chalmers, D. J. (1996), *The Conscious Mind: In Search of a Fundamental Theory.* New York: Oxford University Press.
Chalmers, D. J. (2013), 'How can we construct a science of consciousness?', *Annals of the New York Academy of Sciences*, 1303: 25–35.
Clark, A. (1993), *Sensory Qualities.* Oxford: Clarendon Press.
Cohen, M. A., Dennett D. C., and Kanwisher, N. (2016), 'What is the Bandwidth of Perceptual Experience?' *Trends in Cognitive Science*, 20/5: 324–35.
Damasio, A. (1999), *The Feeling of What Happens.* New York: Houghton Mifflin Harcourt.
Dehaene, S., Changeux, J.-P., Naccache, L., Sackur, J., and Sergent, C. (2006), 'Conscious, preconscious, and subliminal processing: a testable taxonomy', *Trends in Cognitive Science*, 15/8: 365–73.
Dretske, F. (1981), *Knowledge and the Flow of Information.* Cambridge, MA: Bradford Books/MIT Press.
Dretske, F. (1993), 'Conscious experience', *Mind*, 102/406: 263–83.
Dretske, F. (1995), *Naturalizing the Mind.* Cambridge, MA: Bradford Books/MIT Press.
Flohr, H. (1995), 'Sensations and brain processes', *Behavioral Brain Research*, 71: 157–61.
Flohr, H. (1999), 'NMDA-receptor-mediated computational processes and phenomenal consciousness' in T. Metzinger (ed.), *Neural Correlates of Consciousness.* Cambridge, MA: MIT Press, 245–58.

Fodor, J. A. (1990), *A Theory of Content and Other Essays*. Cambridge, MA: Bradford Books/MIT Press.

Gennaro, R. J. (2002), 'Jean-Paul Sartre and the HOT theory of consciousness', *Canadian Journal of Philosophy*, 32/3: 293–330.

Gennaro, R. J. (2012), *The Consciousness Paradox: Consciousness, Concepts, and Higher-Order Thoughts*. Cambridge, MA: Bradford Books/MIT Press.

Goldman, A. I. (1993), 'Consciousness, Folk Psychology, and Cognitive Science', *Consciousness and Cognition*, 2: 264–82.

Güzeldere, G. (1995), 'Is consciousness the perception of what passes in one's own mind?' in T. Metzinger (ed.), *Conscious Experience*. Paderborn: Ferdinand Schoningh, 335–57.

Harman, G. (1990), 'The intrinsic quality of experience', *Philosophical Perspectives*, 4: 31–52.

Kriegel, U. (2003), 'Consciousness as intransitive self-consciousness: Two views and an argument', *Canadian Journal of Philosophy*, 33: 103–32.

Kriegel, U. (2009), *Subjective Consciousness: A Self-Representational Theory*. Oxford: Oxford University Press.

Lamme, V. A. (2006), 'Towards a true neural stance on consciousness', *Trends in Cognitive Science*, 10: 494–501.

Land, M. F. and Tatler, B. W. (2009), *Looking and Acting: Vision and Eye Movements in Natural Behavior*. New York: Oxford University Press.

Lau, H. and Brown, R. (2019), 'The Emperor's New Phenomenology? The Empirical Case for Conscious Experience without First-Order Representations', in A. Pautz and D. Stoljar (eds.), *Blockheads! Essays on Ned Block's Philosophy of Mind and Consciousness*. Cambridge, MA: MIT Press, 171–98.

Lau, H, and Passingham, R. (2006), 'Relative blindsight and the neural correlates of visual consciousness', *Proceedings of the National Academy of Science*, 103: 18763–9.

Lau, H. and Rosenthal, D. (2011), 'Empirical support for higher-order theories of conscious awareness', *Trends in Cognitive Sciences*, 15/8: 365–73.

Lewis, D. K. (1972), 'Psychophysical and Theoretical Identifications', *Australasian Journal of Philosophy*, L/3: 249–58.

Lycan, W. G. (1987), *Consciousness*. Cambridge, MA: MIT Press.

Lycan, W. G. (1996), *Consciousness and Experience*. Cambridge, MA: MIT Press.

Lycan, W. G. (2004), 'The Superiority of HOP to HOT' in R. J. Gennaro (ed.), *Higher-Order Theories of Consciousness*. Amsterdam: John Benjamins Publishers.

Millikan, R. (1984), *Language, Thought, and Other Biological Categories*. Cambridge, MA: Bradford Books/MIT Press.

Nagel, T. (1974), 'What is it like to be a Bat?' *Philosophical Review*, 83: 435–56.

Neander, K. (1998), 'The Division of Phenomenal Labor: A Problem for Representational Theories of Consciousness', *Noûs*, 32/S12: 411–34.

Norretranders, T. (1991), *The User Illusion: Cutting Consciousness Down to Size*. Viking Penguin.

O'Regan, J. K. (2011), *Why Red Doesn't Sound Like a Bell: Understanding the Feel of Consciousness*. Oxford: Oxford University Press.

Rolls, E. T. (2004), 'A higher order syntactic thought theory of consciousness' in R. J. Gennaro (ed.), *Higher-Order Theories of Consciousness*. Amsterdam: John Benjamins Publishers.

Rosenthal, D. M. (1986), 'Two concepts of consciousness', *Philosophical Studies*, 49/3: 329–59.

Rosenthal, D. M. (2000), 'Consciousness and Metacognition' in D. Sperber (ed.), *Metarepresentation: Proceedings of the Tenth Vancouver Cognitive Science Conference*. New York: Oxford University Press.

Rosenthal, D. M. (2004), 'Varieties of Higher-Order Theory' in R. J. Gennaro (ed.), *Higher-Order Theories of Consciousness*. Amsterdam: John Benjamins Publishers, 19–44.
Rosenthal, D. M. (2005), *Consciousness and Mind*. Oxford: Clarendon Press.
Rosenthal, D. M. (2011), 'Exaggerated reports: reply to Block', *Analysis*, 71/3: 431–7.
Saxe, R. (2009), 'Theory of mind: Neural basis' in W. Banks (ed.), *Encyclopedia of Consciousness*. Oxford: Academic.
Seager, W. (1999), *Theories of Consciousness: An Introduction and Assessment*. New York: Routledge.
Sebastián, M. Á. (2014), 'Not a HOT Dream' in R. Brown (ed.), *Phenomenology and the Neurophilosophy of Consciousness*, Studies in Brain and Mind, Vol. 6. New York: Springer.
Siewert, C. (1998), *The Significance of Consciousness*. Princeton, NJ: Princeton University Press.
Stoljar, D. (2016), 'The Semantics of "What it's like" and the Nature of Consciousness', *Mind*, 125/500: 1161–98.
Tye, M. (1995), *Ten Problems of Consciousness: A Representational Theory of the Phenomenal Mind*. Cambridge, MA: MIT Press.
Van Gulick, R. (2004), 'Higher-order global states (HOGS): An alternative higher-order model' in R. J. Gennaro (ed.), *Higher-Order Theories of Consciousness*. Amsterdam: John Benjamins Publishers.
Ward, E. J., Bear, A., and Scholl, B. J. (2016), 'Can you perceive ensembles without perceiving individuals?: The role of statistical perception in determining whether awareness overflows access', *Cognition*, 152: 78–86.
Weisberg, J. (2008), 'Same old, same old: The same-order representation theory of consciousness and the division of phenomenal labor', *Synthese*, 160/2: 61–81.
Weisberg, J. (2011a), 'Review of *Subjective Consciousness: A Self-Representational Theory*, by Uriah Kriegel', *Mind*, 120/478: 538–42.
Weisberg, J. (2011b), 'Misrepresenting Consciousness', *Philosophical Studies*, 154: 409–33.
Weisberg, J. (2011c), 'Abusing the notion of "what-it's-like-ness": A reply to Block', *Analysis*, 71/3: 438–43.
Weisberg, J. (2014a), 'Review of The Consciousness Paradox: Consciousness Concepts, and Higher-Order Thoughts, by Rocco J. Gennaro', *Australasian Journal of Philosophy*, 92/2: 401–4.
Weisberg, J (2014b), 'Sweet Dreams are Made of This? A HOT Response to Sebastián' in R. Brown (ed.), *Consciousness Inside and Out: Phenomenology, Neuroscience, and the Nature of Experience*, Studies in Brain and Mind, Vol. 6. (New York: Springer), 433–43.
Wilberg, J. (2010), 'Consciousness and false HOTs', *Philosophical Psychology*, 23/5: 617–38.
Wilson, T. D. (2002), *Strangers to Ourselves: Discovering the Adaptive Unconscious*. Cambridge, MA: Harvard University Press.
Zahavi, D. and Kriegel, U. (2015), 'For-me-ness: What it is and what it is not' in D. Dahlstrom, A. Elpidorou, and W. Hopp (eds), *Philosophy of Mind and Phenomenology*. Abingdon: Routledge, 36–53.

CHAPTER 21

SELF-REPRESENTATIONALIST THEORIES OF CONSCIOUSNESS

TOM McCLELLAND

21.1 INTRODUCTION: THE META-REPRESENTATIONALIST FAMILY

To understand Self-Representationalism (SR) you need to understand its family. Self-Representationalism is a branch of the Meta-Representationalist family, and according to theories in this family what distinguishes conscious mental representations from unconscious mental representations is that conscious ones are themselves the target of a mental *meta*-representational state. A mental state M_1 is thus phenomenally conscious in virtue of being suitably represented by some mental state M_2. What distinguishes the Self-Representationalist branch of the family is the claim that M_1 and M_2 must be the same token mental state, so a mental state is phenomenally conscious in virtue of suitably representing itself.[1] This Self-Representationalist branch of the family divides into further branches, giving us specific implementations of the Self-Representationalist approach. But before asking whether we should adopt Self-Representationalism, and in

---

[1] Some Meta-Representationalist theories of consciousness are not specifically presented as theories of *phenomenal* consciousness (see Block 2011 for discussion of some of the complications surrounding this fact). Interestingly though, Self-Representationalist theories seem to be universally presented as theories of phenomenal consciousness, so I will continue on the assumption that the target of all the theories under discussion is indeed phenomenal consciousness. To that end, I will generally drop the 'phenomenal' qualifier from here on.

what form, we should reflect on why Meta-Representationalism is an attractive family in the first place. After all, Self-Representationalist theories trade on their family name, claiming to deliver on the promises that drive the Meta-Representationalist approach. The two most important promises of Meta-Representationalism are: (a) the promise of capturing the *transitivity* of consciousness; and (b) the promise of rendering consciousness *naturalizable*. I discuss each in turn.

What is the difference between conscious mental states and non-conscious mental states? A plausible initial answer is that conscious mental states are those of which you are aware. In other words, a mental state of yours is conscious in virtue of you being conscious *of* it. There are two different senses of 'conscious' in play here that need to be distinguished (see Rosenthal 1986; Kriegel 2009). 'Consciousness' can be used in a *transitive* sense to designate the relation of being conscious *of* something. But the same term can also be used in an *intransitive* sense to designate the non-relational property of being a conscious state. Equipped with this distinction, we can frame the foregoing a little more precisely: the question is what the difference is between mental states that are intransitively conscious and mental states that are not; the plausible initial answer is that intransitively conscious mental states are those mental states of which we are transitively conscious. According to this 'transitivity principle', transitive and intransitive consciousness are two sides of the same coin. Every theory in the Meta-Representationalist family makes the following promise:

> **The Transitivity Promise:** We promise to offer a theory of consciousness that conforms to the principle that intransitively conscious mental states are those mental states of which the subject is aware.[2]

How do Meta-Representationalist theories hope to deliver on that promise? They do so by making the simple claim that when we talk of being aware *of* a mental state, the 'of' is the 'of' of intentionality (Lycan 2001). Just as being a picture *of a house* is a matter of representing a house, so too being aware *of a mental state* is a matter of representing that state. Meta-Representationalists thus vindicate the principle that conscious mental states are those mental states of which we are aware by cashing out 'awareness-of' in

---

[2] For a useful examination of arguments for and against the transitivity principle, see the entry on Higher-Order Theories of Consciousness in Chapter 20, this volume. A number of arguments for the principle are helpfully catalogued in the Appendix to Kriegel's (2009). Thomasson (2006) offers a particularly insightful critique of the main arguments. Many critics of Self-Representationalism object to the transitivity principle (e.g. Seager 2006; Lyyra 2008; Gertler 2012; Siewert 2013). Though these objections deserve to be taken seriously, I will not discuss them here. Whether the transitivity principle is well-motivated is a problem for the whole Meta-Representationalist family. In order to determine the relative merits of Self-Representationalism, it will be best to focus on the issues that distinguish it from its relatives, and that distinguish different versions of Self-Representationalism from each other. As such, I will continue on the assumption that the Transitivity Promise is a promise worth delivering on.

representational terms, and claiming that conscious states are those mental states that we suitably represent.[3]

Can phenomenal consciousness be naturalized? A common response is that the answer *ought* to be yes, but that we are not sure how it *could* be. The answer ought to be yes because naturalism is an incredibly successful world view that we should be reluctant to compromise, and because anti-naturalist views face a swathe of problems regarding how consciousness fits into an otherwise naturalistic world. Yet we are not sure how the answer *could* be yes because phenomenal consciousness is peculiarly and recalcitrantly resistant to naturalization. Consequently, if a theory can improve the prospects for naturalizing consciousness it would be a major point in its favour. This leads us to the second promise of Meta-Representationalism.

> **The Naturalizability Promise:** We promise to offer a theory of consciousness amenable to naturalization.[4]

How does Meta-Representationalism hope to deliver on this promise? The key is the naturalizability of mental representation. We have already seen how Meta-Representationalists aim to account for consciousness in representational terms, so if representation can in turn be explained naturalistically we will have a naturalistic account of consciousness. It must be conceded that an adequate naturalistic theory of mental representation has not yet been developed. However, many feel that the prospects for naturalizing mental representation are strong, so if Meta-Representationalist theories can explain consciousness in representational terms they will have made good on their promise. They might not have actually explained consciousness in naturalistic terms, but they will have offered an account of consciousness amenable to naturalization in the long run.[5]

Having familiarized ourselves with what characterizes and motivates the Meta-Representationalist family as a whole, we are now ready to start distinguishing the different households that make up that family. Figure 21.1 shows the Meta-Representationalist family tree.

---

[3] The 'suitably' clause is designed to accommodate the fact that not just any representation of one's mental state suffices to make that state conscious. Chapter 20 on Higher-Order Theories of Consciousness discusses some of the details of this clause.

[4] Unlike the Transitivity Promise, not every Meta-Representationalist promises to offer a naturalistic theory. Although we will be looking at some non-naturalist theories later on, the point remains that the Naturalizability Promise is a key motivation for the majority of Meta-Representationalists, and Self-Representationalist theories ought to be evaluated with respect to their capacity to deliver on that promise.

[5] This move needs to be taken with a hefty pinch of salt (Kidd 2011). Debates around the naturalization of intentionality have been raging for some time and have no immediate end in sight. It is an open possibility that intentionality will transpire to be unnaturalizable, meaning that representational theories of consciousness will ultimately fail to deliver on their promise of naturalization. Nevertheless, the prospects of naturalizing intentionality are better than the immediate prospects of naturalizing consciousness, so explaining consciousness in representational terms at least *improves* the prospects of naturalizing consciousness.

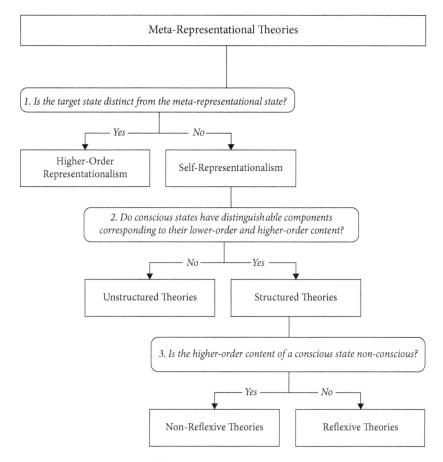

FIGURE 21.1 The Meta-Representationalist Family Tree

As you can see, the Meta-Representationalist family tree is structured around three choice-points. The first choice-point is where Self-Representationalism differentiates itself from its well-established relatives: the Higher-Order Representationalist (HOR) theories of consciousness. The second and third choice-points allow us to differentiate the various households in the Self-Representationalist branch of the family. As we work our way down the family tree, we will introduce the key members of each household and identify the problems that plague each of them. Although different theories face different problems, the overarching theme of the chapter is that no existing version of Meta-Representationalism can satisfy all three of the following desiderata:

(i) To deliver on the Transitivitiy Promise
(ii) To deliver on the Naturalizability Promise
(iii) To respect the 'intimacy' of consciousness

After exploring the main existing forms of SR, I make some suggestions about how Self-Representationalists might develop a version of the theory that satisfies all three desiderata.

21.2 THE FIRST CHOICE-POINT: IS THE TARGET STATE DISTINCT FROM THE META-REPRESENTATIONAL STATE?

Take a subject S who is enjoying a visual experience of the sunset. Meta-Representationalists explain the subject's experience in terms of her having a mental state M_1 that perceptually represents the sunset, and a mental state M_2 that represents her as being in M_1. The first choice-point for Meta-Representationalism concerns whether M_1 and M_2 are distinct, or whether they are one and the same token mental state. Higher-Order Representationalism chooses the former: it explains S's experience in terms of two mental states, one with the lower-order content and the other with the higher-order content. Self-Representationalism chooses the latter: it explains S's experience in terms of her having a single mental state that represents both the sunset *and* itself.

21.2.1 Option 1: Higher-Order Representationalism (HOR)

HOR comes in many different flavours, and different versions tell different stories about the format of the higher-order representation required for consciousness. Some claim that the higher-order state is a *thought* about the lower-order state (e.g. Rosenthal 1986; Carruthers 2004). Others claim it is more akin to an inner *perception* of the lower-order state (e.g. Armstrong 1981; Lycan 2004). A case can also be made for regarding the higher-order state as having a status somewhere between that of ordinary thoughts and ordinary perceptual states. HOR theorists also tell different stories about the exact relationship between M_1 and M_2 required for consciousness. What each of these views has in common is the claim that M_1 and M_2 are distinct.[6]

Why do Higher-Order Representationalists claim that M_1 and M_2 are distinct states? Some explicit arguments can be found in the literature, but the main reason seems to be that this is the *default* way of formulating Meta-Representationalism. If M_1 is conscious in virtue of being targeted by a mental state M_2, it is natural to assume that M_2 will be a distinct mental state. Meta-Representationalists should only make the bolder claim that a mental state is only conscious when it is represented *by itself* if there are specific reasons to do so. Of course, Self-Representationalists claim to have just such reasons for taking the other branch of this choice-point. Although a number of problems have been raised against the view that M_1 and M_2 are distinct, the most serious is that HOR theorists have trouble with intimacy.[7] When we are in a conscious state we have a distinctively intimate

---

[6] For a more detailed survey of the varieties of position available, see Chapter 20 on Higher-Order Theories of Consciousness.

[7] I borrow this phrase from Weisberg (2008). The intimacy problem for Higher-Order Representationalism has been put forward (in varying forms) by: Neander (1998); Levine (2003; 2010); Gennaro (2006); Kriegel (2009); Block (2011); Kidd (2011); Picciuto (2011); Van Gulick (2012); Coleman (2015); and others.

relationship with that state: our conscious state seems to be immediately disclosed to us. One way of putting this is that there can be no gap between how a conscious state *seems* to us and how it *really is*.[8] The apparent intimacy of consciousness has two aspects.

First, consciousness is *qualitatively* intimate insofar as the qualities that we experience our conscious state as having are necessarily qualities it really has. For instance, if we experience our conscious state as having a painful quality, then it must actually have that quality. Consciousness does not allow for a mismatch between the qualities that we experience our conscious state as having and the qualities it really has. Second, consciousness is *existentially* intimate insofar as experiencing ourselves as being in a conscious state guarantees that we really are in a conscious state. Experiencing a conscious state guarantees the existence of that state. Consciousness does not allow for cases where we experience ourselves as being in a conscious state when no such state exists.

The problem for HOR theorists is that the relation they posit between the distinct states M_1 and M_2 falls short of the intimacy of consciousness. Where a representation is distinct from what it represents, there is the possibility of error. It might be that the object represented lacks the properties attributed to it, like when a perceptual state represents a pencil in water as bent. Or it might be that the object represented does not exist at all, like when Macbeth's perceptual state represents a dagger before him. Since M_1 and M_2 are distinct, there is nothing to preclude M_2 from misrepresenting M_1 in either of these ways.

First, M_2 might misrepresent the qualities of M_1. Perhaps M_1 is a tactile representation of itchiness, but M_2 misrepresents it as a tactile representation of pain. In such a case, the pain quality that we represent our conscious state as having diverges from the itchy quality that it actually has. Second, M_2 might misrepresent the very existence of M_1. Perhaps M_2 is a targetless state that represents the subject as being in pain, but fails to represent any actual lower-order state of the subject. The intimacy of consciousness seems to preclude these kinds of error, yet HOR is committed to the possibility of such errors occurring. Note, it will not help to insist that the processes responsible for higher-order representation are so reliable that such misrepresentations will never actually occur. The point is that the apparent intimacy of consciousness seems to make such errors *impossible*, but if M_2 and M_1 are distinct states then it is at least possible for M_2 to misrepresent M_1. The representation relation described by HOR is consistent with such error, but the transitive consciousness relation is not, so HOR has not successfully captured the transitive consciousness relation.

HOR theorists have responded to the problem of intimacy by proposing a constitutive connection between how a subject's higher-order state represents their mental life as being and the phenomenology they actually undergo (e.g. Rosenthal 2011; Weisberg 2011b). On this view, if you *represent* yourself as having a pain experience then you thereby *really have* a pain experience. If the lower-order state you represent is actually a

---

[8] Note, the claim here is that there is no gap between how a conscious state *phenomenally* seems to us and how it really is. This is quite consistent with the possibility of our *judgements* about our conscious states being in error: a state might phenomenally seem to be an itch and yet cognitively seem to be a pain. The intimacy of consciousness should not be confused with claims about the infallibility of phenomenal judgements.

representation of an itch, your experience will still be painful because what matters is how the lower-order state *seems* to you. It does not even matter if your higher-order state fails to target any actual lower-order state, you will still have a pain experience because it appears to you that you are in pain. There is a sense in which this constitutive view collapses the distinction between how a conscious state seems and how a conscious state is: how your higher-order state represents things as being cannot diverge from the experience you actually have.[9]

This response goes at least some way to accommodating the apparent intimacy of consciousness, but at what cost? By proposing a constitutive link between the content of a subject's higher-order state and her phenomenology, the HOR theorist risks reneging on the Transitivity Promise. Remember, HOR theory promises to capture the principle that conscious states are those mental states of which we are aware. But on the current picture, the state of which we are aware drops out as irrelevant. A subject's pain experience cannot plausibly be identified with her represented lower-order state in either scenario: in the first scenario the represented state is an itch not a pain, and in the second scenario the represented state does not even exist. If the pain experience cannot be identified with a lower-order state, perhaps it should be identified with the higher-order state? After all, the HOR theorist is claiming that the subject's higher-order state is wholly responsible for her pain experience. The problem with this move is that this higher-order state is not represented. This leaves the HOR theorist with a choice of reneging on the claim that being in a conscious state requires one to be aware of that conscious state, or reneging on the claim that being aware of our conscious state requires us to suitably represent it. Either way, HOR will have gone back on the Transitivity Promise.

Can the HOR theorist take a different tack and simply deny that we have the proposed intimate relation to our conscious states? Some say that the intimacy of consciousness is guaranteed *conceptually*: that it is part of our concept of phenomenal consciousness, and of phenomenal qualities, that the way a conscious state appears to us is the way it is (e.g. Kidd 2011). I recommend allowing that how best to conceptualize consciousness is still up for grabs (after all, we do not want to accidentally define features into consciousness that it might not really have). A better response to the HOR theorist who denies the intimacy of consciousness is that such a denial is *phenomenologically* implausible. Reflection on our experience strongly suggests that we have an intimate relationship with our conscious states that precludes the kinds of error countenanced by HOR. There is an open possibility that our phenomenology is misleading, but the burden is on the HOR theorist to explain why consciousness has this misleading appearance. So as things stand, there is a pervasive phenomenological feature of experience—its apparent intimacy—for which HOR theory has difficulty accounting.

---

[9] This move is discussed in more detail in Chapter 20 on Higher-Order Theories of Consciousness.

Overall, the claim that M_1 and M_2 are distinct is plausibly undermined by the intimacy problem.[10] Consequently, we should go down the other branch of this choice-point to see whether matters are any better if M_1 and M_2 are held to be token identical.

21.2.2 Option 2: Self-Representationalism (SR)

As we will see, there are a number of different households on the SR branch of the family tree. What unites these households is the claim that a mental state is conscious in virtue of suitably representing itself.[11] What motivates the claim that the state of which we are aware is token identical with the state in virtue of which we are aware of it: that $M_1 = M_2$? The key motivation is the promise of capturing the intimacy of consciousness. HOR theory had trouble with intimacy because M_2 was independent of M_1 so could misrepresent it. By proposing that a conscious state is just a single state M^*, SR theorists hope to give the higher-order content of that state the requisite dependence on its lower-order content. Regarding qualitative intimacy, the hope is that since M^* is a single state there is no room for a mismatch between the lower-order content that M^* represents itself as having and the lower-order content it actually has. Regarding existential intimacy, the hope is that since the target of M^* is itself there is no possibility of M^* being targetless. SR thus adds a third promise to its list of motivations:

The Intimacy Promise: We promise to accommodate the apparent intimacy of the relationship between a conscious state and the subject's awareness of that conscious state.

---

[10] Although other objections to the distinctness route have been offered, they have less bite than the intimacy objection. For instance, some have suggested (Dretske 1995; Van Gulick 2004; Kriegel 2009) that if M_1 is made conscious by being represented by a distinct state, then by parity of reasoning non-mental entities should also become conscious when represented, yet consciousness is clearly restricted to mental entities. Rosenthal (unpublished) rightly responds that this objection rests on a misconstrual of what Higher-Order Representationalism says about consciousness: consciousness is how your mental life appears to you, so if non-mental entities appear some way to you then that does not make them conscious (this response is explored in Chapter 20 on Higher-Order Theories of Consciousness). Another objection (Kriegel 2009: 139) is that if M_1 is made conscious by a distinct mental state then M_1's causal powers would remain the same, yet becoming conscious clearly changes a mental state's causal powers. However, this problem is plausibly dealt with by noting other cases in which relations confer new causal powers on an object (say, Boris Johnson entering into a new relation to the British state).

[11] This should not be confused with the claim that a conscious mental state is conscious in virtue of suitably representing *the* self, i.e. the subject of the mental state. Some SR theories propose that the self is at least implicitly represented in consciousness (e.g. Ford 2009; Sebastian 2012), but this is by no means characteristic of the theory. One can be in a state that represents itself without being in a state that represents you as its bearer. For the purposes of this chapter, I bracket questions about what role (if any) the self plays in experience, though see McClelland (forthcoming).

With these considerations in place, we can present the *Master Argument* for Self-Representationalism:

MA1 A mental state is intransitively conscious in virtue of being suitably represented.
MA2 It is not the case that a mental state is intransitively conscious in virtue of being represented by a numerically distinct state.
MA3 Therefore, a mental state is intransitively conscious in virtue of being suitably represented by itself.[12]

The motivations for the first premise are the motivations for Meta-Representationalism discussed earlier, viz. the promise of accommodating the transitivity principle and giving a naturalizable account of consciousness. The key motivation for the second premise is that if consciousness involves two distinct states then you run into the troubles with intimacy considered above. From these two premises, the conclusion follows that conscious states are self-representing. As things stand, this is only an argument built on promises. Whether SR can actually deliver on those promises depends on how exactly it is cashed out, and, in order to understand the different ways it might be cashed out, we need to work our way down the family tree to the second and third choice-points.

21.3 Second Choice-Point: Do Conscious States have Distinguishable Components Corresponding to their Lower- and Higher-order Content?

The self-representing states posited by SR are multifaceted—they have both higher-order and lower-order content. Self-Representationalists explain a subject's perceptual experience of the sunset in terms of a single state that represents both the sunset and itself. Structured theories propose that conscious states have an internal structure, and that within this structure one can isolate the components responsible for the lower-order and higher-order content of the state. So within the conscious state that constitutes the sunset-experience, one can isolate a component that represents the sunset and a component that represents that very state. Unstructured theories deny that conscious states have this internal structure. Although they hold that the subject's conscious state does indeed represent both the sunset and itself, they deny that this state is divisible into one component that represents the sunset and another component that represents the state. On this view, the conscious state is analogous to the sentence "this very sentence is about the sunset". The sentence represents a sunset and represents itself but it cannot be

---

[12] Adapted from Kriegel (2009: 15–16).

divided into a sentential representation of the sunset and a sentential representation of itself. Rather, it is an indivisible representation with complex contents. Unstructured theories claim that conscious states are analogously indivisible.

21.3.1 Option 1: Unstructured Self-Representationalism

Some accounts of consciousness clearly qualify as Unstructured Self-Representationalist accounts. Brook and Raymont (2006: 9), for example, claim that conscious states are self-representing but explicitly deny that they have a composite structure. Williford (2006) and Block (2011) can also be put under this umbrella. A strong case can be made for reading Brentano this way too, although complex issues of interpretation abound (Zahavi 2004, 2005, 2006; Textor 2006, 2015; Kriegel 2016). However, there are a large set of views according to which: (a) conscious states do not have a composite structure; (b) those states confer awareness of themselves, but (c) the awareness conferred is non-representational. Claims (a) and (b) certainly put such views in the neighbourhood of Unstructured SR, but claim (c) looks like a deal-breaker: if you deny that conscious states represent themselves you cannot qualify as a Self-Representationalist. One way of putting this position is that conscious states are self-*presenting* but not self-*representing*. This position is influentially articulated by Zahavi (2004, 2005, 2006) who denies that our awareness of our own conscious states is 'intentional'. In this he claims to have the support of just about every major phenomenologist besides Brentano, including Husserl, Scheler, Heidegger, Sartre, Merleau-Ponty, Henry, and Ricoeur (Zahavi 2004: 82).[13] Going further back in history, Caston (2002) attributes this kind of view to Aristotle. Or more recently, Levine (2006, 2015) and Janzen (2006) have offered accounts in line with this outlook.

One could take these self-presentational theorists at their word that they do not think conscious states represent themselves. However, I suggest that the disagreement might be dismissed as merely verbal. Terms like 'representation' and 'intentionality' are notoriously unclear, so it is an open possibility that when the proper sense of 'representation' is specified these theorists *do* think conscious states are self-representing. For instance, when Zahavi claims that conscious states are not self-representing, his driving claim seems to be that our conscious state is not an *object* for us in the way that perceived objects are.[14] This seems quite consistent with claiming that conscious states represent themselves, just not in the same way that they represent worldly objects. Although these interpretative issues are beyond the scope of the chapter, it is worth noting that the Unstructured SR household plausibly extends beyond its card-carrying members.

---

[13] Lyyra (2008) offers an interesting alternative interpretation of these phenomenologists according to which what is special about conscious states is not that we are aware of them, but that we 'live through' them: a notion that certainly cannot be understood in self-representational terms.

[14] Zahavi himself (2004: 74) seems to acknowledge there is a terminological issue here. Williford (2006: 3) notes the same issue and concludes that Zahavi is Self-Representationalist in every way that matters.

What difficulties does Unstructured SR face? Rosenthal introduces a number of general objections to SR that seem to have particular bite against the unstructured form of the view. First, he suggests SR is unable to explain how an unconscious mental state becomes conscious. On HOR, a state becomes conscious when it enters into an extrinsic relation to a distinct mental state. But on SR, consciousness is intrinsic to a state, so entering into different relations cannot explain how that state becomes conscious. Second, he suggests that SR is at odds with empirical evidence indicating a time-lag between the occurrence of a mental event and a subject's consciousness of that event. Libet's experiments (e.g. Libet 1985; Haggard and Libet 2001), found that subjects only became conscious of a volition a short time after the on-set of that volition. If the state of which we are conscious, and the state through which we are conscious of it, are one and the same then such a time-lag would be impossible. Third, he suggests that SR's claim that a conscious state is a single state with both lower- and higher-order content cannot be reconciled with the fact that the lower- and higher-order content might involve different propositional attitudes. Consider a case in which we are conscious of our doubt. HOR explains this in terms of our having a lower-order state with an attitude of doubt toward some content, and a higher-order state with an assertoric attitude to the content that one is undergoing such a doubt. SR is forced into the potentially paradoxical position that we have a single state that has both a propositional attitude of doubt *and* a propositional attitude of assertion.

Although these objections deserve to be taken seriously, the most important objection to Unstructured SR is that it fails to deliver on the Naturalizability Promise. Indeed, the majority of the theorists identified above as advocates of Unstructured SR have no commitment to naturalism. The problem for Unstructured SR is that naturalistic accounts of representation revolve around causation. Even if the details of natural representation are yet to be worked out, a plausible core principle is that a state represents an object in virtue of being suitably causally responsive to that object. However, causation is an irreflexive relation: nothing is a cause of itself. This seems to preclude mental states from representing themselves.[15] Structured SR attempts to overcome this problem by claiming that conscious states have composite parts that stand in the requisite causal relations. However, by denying that conscious states have such a compositional structure, Unstructured SR is unable to avail itself of this response.

Unstructured SR delivers on the Transitivity Promise by claiming that conscious states confer an awareness of that very state. And it delivers on the Intimacy Promise by claiming that a pain state represents both the bodily pain and itself. This seems to preclude any mismatch between the qualities you are aware of a conscious state as having

---

[15] Interestingly, Buras (2009) draws the opposite conclusion from this situation. He claims that some mental states represent themselves despite not being causes of themselves, and infers that causal theories of mental content must therefore be mistaken. However, for this move to overcome worries about naturalizability, we would need reason to believe that a non-causal naturalistic theory of representation is available. But the prospects of finding such a theory are poor.

and the qualities it really has. It also seems to preclude the possibility of being aware of oneself as being in a state that does not exist. However, by denying that conscious states have internal structure Unstructured SR makes it naturalistically inexplicable how conscious states could represent themselves. As such, it fails to deliver on the Naturalizability Promise.[16]

21.3.2 Option 2: Structured Self-Representationalism

According to Structured SR, a conscious state is a complex state with both lower-order and higher-order components that stand in some integration relation in virtue of which they constitute a single mental state. When a lower-order state M_1 such as a perceptual representation of a sunset is suitably related to a higher-order state M_2 that represents M_1, the two components form a single state M^* that represents both the sunset and itself. Although M^* cannot be a cause of itself as such, parts of M^* can be causes of other parts of M^*. As such, there is no obstacle to M_1 standing in the causal relation to M_2 required for natural representation. Structured SR thus has far better prospects of delivering on the Naturalizability Promise than its unstructured counterpart.

Structured SR also promises to avoid some of the objections to SR broached by Rosenthal. Advocates of Structured SR can agree with Rosenthal that a state's becoming conscious must be explained in terms of it entering into new relations to other mental states. They only diverge from Rosenthal by proposing that these relations integrate the original state into a new complex state that is intrinsically conscious. Similarly, they can agree with Rosenthal that there might be a time-lag between a volition occurring and a subject becoming conscious of it, but diverge from Rosenthal by explaining this transition in terms of the volition coming to enter a complex self-representing state. Finally, they can accommodate Rosenthal's case of the incompatible propositional attitudes by holding that the doubting attitude belongs to M_1 while the assertoric attitude depends on M_2. M_1 and M_2 constitute a single representation, but the constituent components of that representation can still exemplify different propositional attitudes. So it seems that SR can dodge Rosenthal's worries by attributing conscious states a compositional structure.

The foregoing provides some preliminary reasons to prefer Structured SR over Unstructured SR. However, to properly evaluate Structured SR we need to distinguish the different versions of the view. To that end, we should move down the family tree to our third and final choice-point.

---

[16] A further objection I have not considered is the threat of regress. Unstructured SR seems to be committed to all of the content of a conscious state being represented by that state. The problem is that representing all of that content is also part of the content of the state, so must itself be represented. But then that content too must be represented and so on. This issue goes back at least to Brentano and is insightfully discussed by e.g. Williford (2006); Siewert (2013); Schear (2009); and Textor (2006).

21.4 THE THIRD CHOICE-POINT: IS THE HIGHER-ORDER CONTENT OF A CONSCIOUS STATE NON-CONSCIOUS?

According to SR, by being in a suitably self-representing state M* we are conscious of that very state. According to Structured SR, this is to be explained in terms of a higher-order component of M* that represents the lower-order component of M* thereby making us conscious of that state's lower-order content. All forms of Structured SR thus agree that when we are in a conscious state we are aware of the lower-order content of that state. What they disagree on is whether we are ever also aware of the higher-order content of that state. Non-Reflexive Theories (as I will call them) claim that we are never aware of the higher-order content of our conscious states. Reflexive Theories claim that we are, at least sometimes, aware of the higher-order content of our conscious states.

21.4.1 Option 1: Non-Reflexive Self-Representationalism

According to HOR, in ordinary cases of consciousness we are aware of a first-order mental state but are not aware of the second-order state that bestows this awareness. In order to be aware of our second-order state, we would need to have a third-order state that represents it. Such third-order representation is quite possible—HOR theorists claim that this is exactly what happens when we introspect—but even then the higher-order state in virtue of which we are conscious would not figure in our introspective awareness. Perhaps we could climb up to a fourth-order state to represent this, but it will always be the case that the *highest*-order state is outside of our awareness. Through our highest-order state, we can be aware of lower-order states but the highest-order state itself remains off the phenomenological stage.

Non-Reflexive Theories inherit the principle that the higher-order representation in virtue of which we are conscious inevitably falls outside of our awareness. One might think that the core tenets of SR preclude such an inheritance from HOR. According to SR, the state of which we are conscious and the state in virtue of which we are conscious are one and the same, so we cannot fail to be conscious of the state in virtue of which we are conscious. However, when we zoom in on the internal components of M* posited by Structured SR we find a situation akin to that of HOR. M_1 is the component of M* of which we are aware, and M_2 is the component in virtue of which we are aware. So even though M_2 is a constituent of M* it remains off-stage: by being in M* we are aware of the lower-order content of M* but not its higher-order content. We might become aware of the higher-order content of a state when we introspect, but even then the *highest*-order component of our conscious state will inevitably be unconscious.

The foregoing captures what unifies the theories in the Non-Reflexive household. Now what differentiates them? Non-Reflexive theories differ mainly with respect to the account they give of what unifies a lower- and higher-order representation into a self-representing state. Let us start with Gennaro's (2004, 2006) Wide Intrinsicality View (WIV), which he describes as follows:

> On the WIV, we have two parts of a single conscious state with one part directed at ('aware of') the other. In short, there is a complex conscious mental state with an inner, intrinsic relation between parts.   (Gennaro 2004: 60–1)

What makes the lower-order and higher-order components part of a single complex? Gennaro suggests that we have higher-order concepts that *synthesize* the content of the lower-order component, and thereby constitute a single self-representing complex. Moreover, he speculates that these complex representations are realized by neural feedback loops in the brain that display the kind of cross-level integration one might expect from such a complex.

Van Gulick's (2004, 2006) Higher-Order Global State (HOGS) theory holds that the relevant self-representing states are constituted by the integration of a lower-order state into a subject's wider mental economy. A subject is aware of a lower-order mental state insofar as the contents of that state are appropriately linked to that subject's other mental states. Van Gulick's theory displays something of the spirit of the global workspace theory, which equates a state's consciousness with its availability to higher mental processes. His proposal is that this mental network—which has the lower-order state as an integrated part—constitutes a single state that implicitly represents its own lower-order component. He explains:

> The transformation from unconscious to conscious state is not a matter of merely directing a separate and distinct meta-state onto the lower-order state but of 'recruiting' it into the globally integrated state that is the momentary realization of the agent's shifting transient conscious awareness.   (Van Gulick 2004: 74–5)

Like Gennaro, Van Gulick has a story to tell about how such states are realized in the brain. He suggests that non-conscious states are realized in relatively localized areas of the brain, but when they become conscious they are integrated into a complex neural network that is globally distributed.

Both WIV and HOGS face serious difficulties that may well be endemic to the Non-Reflexive household. First, there is a worry that neither theory offers an account in which the lower- and higher-order components are genuinely unified into a single mental state.[17] When a lower-order state is 'synthesized' by higher-order concepts in the

---

[17] This objection is pushed by Weisberg (2008, 2011a); Kriegel (2009); Kidd (2011); and Picciuto (2011).

manner proposed by WIV, it is not clear why we should not regard the resulting scenario as an interaction between two distinct states. Similarly, when a lower-order state is integrated with a wider mental network, it is not clear why we should not regard it as an individual state that has entered into new relations to other distinct mental states. Appealing to the neurological processes that underwrite these states will not help: it is one thing for the neural processes that underwrite a pair of representations to be integrated, but quite another for the representations themselves to form a single representational state. Van Gulick and Gennaro might be tempted to resort to the claim that the integration relation is a kind of primitive property that joins mental representations. However, both are committed to the Naturalizability Promise, so cannot appeal to an unexplained integration relation (Kidd 2011).

There is also a worry that WIV and HOGS lose sight of the Transitivity Promise. A driving principle of Meta-Representationalism is that conscious states are represented, but doubts can be raised over whether either theory respects this principle. Is Gennaro's conceptual synthesis a species of representation? If not, then we no longer have a meta-representational theory and the transitivity of consciousness is left unaccounted for. If it is a kind of representation, it is unclear how such conceptual synthesis differs from the conceptual higher-order representations posited by higher-order thought theory. Does being integrated into a network of mental states constitute higher-order representation of the integrated state? Van Gulick has a teleosemantic story to tell in which the integrated state alters the dispositions of a subject's wider mental network, and the network thereby implicitly represents that state (2004, 2006). However, objectors have pointed out that such a dispositional account of implicit higher-order representation is at odds with awareness being an *occurent* and *explicit* phenomenon (e.g., Weisberg 2008).

More could be said about whether WIV and HOGS manage to successfully implement the Non-Reflexive approach. At the very least, the foregoing shows that implementing this approach is far from straightforward. However, the most dialectically salient objection to Non-Reflexive SR pertains not to how it is implemented but to its essential commitments. Remember, the characteristic feature of Non-Reflexive SR is the claim that the higher-order content of a conscious state is always unconscious. Kriegel suggests that any theory with this commitment will be unable to explain a crucial feature of our phenomenology that he describes as *inner awareness*. Inner awareness is the awareness we have *of our own awareness*:

> I cannot envisage what it would be like to have a phenomenology lacking the kind of inner awareness that constitutes for-me-ness. Even the simplest visual experience—say, a homogenously bluish experience—folds within it an outer awareness of blue and an inner awareness of that very outer awareness. (Kriegel 2009: 175)

Here Kriegel is making the strong claim that consciousness is *always* characterized by inner awareness. However, even the weaker claim that consciousness is *sometimes* characterized by inner awareness is enough to cause trouble for Non-Reflexive SR.

According to Non-Reflexive SR, a conscious state never represents its own higher-order component. Because awareness is to be understood representationally, we are therefore never aware of that higher-order component. But since that higher-order component is what constitutes our awareness at that time, we are therefore never aware of our concurrent awareness. So by making the higher-order content of a conscious state non-conscious, Non-Reflexive theories are committed to the impossibility of inner awareness. If Kriegel is right that there are at least some cases in which our awareness figures in our phenomenology, then Non-Reflexive SR is false.

Can Non-Reflexive theorists simply reject Kriegel's phenomenological claim? Many have stated that reflection on their own phenomenology fails to reveal anything akin to Kriegel's inner awareness. Others, however, have agreed whole-heartedly with Kriegel's phenomenological report.[18] Attempts have been made by each side of this dispute to explain away the phenomenological reports of their opponents, but none of these attempts stand up to scrutiny (McClelland 2015). A more promising route is to cite theoretical considerations in favour of the thesis that we are at least sometimes aware of awareness. However, the theoretical assumptions that drive these arguments are no less contentious than the putative phenomenological datum itself, so this strategy too has proved inconclusive (McClelland 2015).

One argument for inner awareness that deserves special consideration is Kriegel's 'epistemic argument' (2009: 115–29). In line with the transitivity principle, everyone in the Meta-Representational family agrees that all conscious states are represented. But *how* do we know this about conscious states? Kriegel suggests that we know this precisely because it is manifest to us in our experience: when we are in a conscious state, we are aware of that very state being represented. He goes on to claim that this direct phenomenal justification is the *only* justification we could have for the transitivity principle. There are four other potential sources of evidence for the principle—indirect phenomenological evidence (including evidence from introspection), a posteriori experimental evidence, a priori conceptual analysis, and general philosophical principles—but Kriegel argues that none of them can provide what is needed. If Kriegel is right about this, then it would be extremely difficult for Meta-Representationalists to deny that consciousness is characterized by inner awareness. Meta-Representationalists are motivated by the transitivity principle, so by denying that consciousness is characterized by an inner awareness that directly justifies the principle, they inadvertently undermine their own position. Critics have responded to Kriegel by saying that he underestimates introspection as a source of evidence (Levine 2010; Van Gulick 2012). This gets us into difficult issues about the warrant of generalizations based on introspective judgement, and it again seems that the theoretical assumptions of the disputants are no less contentious than the phenomenological datum they are contesting. Kriegel's epistemic argument

---

[18] Detractors include Gennaro (2008); Schear (2009); Gertler (2012); Mehta (2013); Coleman (2015). Supporters include Zahavi (2004, 2005, 2006) and Strawson (2011).

thus captures one reason we might have for concluding that consciousness is characterized by inner awareness, but it does not settle the matter entirely.

Given the recalcitrance of this phenomenological disagreement, it would be premature to say that Non-Reflexive SR faces a fatal objection here. Insofar as you find it plausible that your concurrent awareness sometimes figures in your phenomenology, you should reject Non-Reflexive SR. If, on the other hand, you find this phenomenological claim implausible then Non-Reflexive SR will survive Kriegel's objection. However, we will see shortly that a problem with intimacy faced by all Structured SR theories might undermine the Non-Reflexive household. In the meantime, we should explore whether the other branch of this choice-point better enables SR to accommodate inner awareness.

21.4.2 Option 2: Reflexive Self-Representationalism

Reflexive SR claims that the higher-order content of a conscious state can itself be conscious. Reflexive SR is driven by the following promise:

> **The Inner Awareness Promise:** We promise to accommodate the fact that inner awareness characterizes at least some phenomenological episodes.

Reflexive SR thus accumulates a fourth promise on top of the three already accrued: the Transitivity Promise; the Naturalizability Promise, and the Intimacy Promise. An influential Reflexive Self-Representational theory has been developed in detail by Kriegel. According to Kriegel's Cross-Order Integration (COI) theory, a conscious self-representing state is formed by the integration of a lower- and higher-order state. Kriegel proposes that this integration is achieved in the same way that different perceptual contents are integrated in perceptual binding. The early visual system has discrete representations of, say, an object's red colour and its circular shape. These signals must then be bound in order to form a representation of a red circle. Our best understanding of how these neural signals are bound is that they synchronizse the frequency of their oscillations. Kriegel suggests that neural synchrony is also what binds a lower- and higher-order representation into a single self-representing state.

How does Kriegel hope to accommodate inner awareness on this model? The challenge for Kriegel is to offer an account that is naturalizable. We have already seen that on a naturalistic understanding of representation it is likely to be an irreflexive relation. Although this was a problem for Unstructured SR, Structured SR gets around this problem by proposing that a conscious state has components M_1 and M_2 that are causally related. Although this might explain how M_2 represents M_1, it cannot straightwardly explain how M_2 could represent M_2 as this component of the conscious state cannot be a cause of itself. Kriegel's strategy is to appeal to indirect representation. He notes that a painting may represent a whole house in virtue of representing part of that house, and that a perceptual state may represent a whole apple in virtue of representing the facing surface of that apple. In other words, by directly representing an integrated part of a thing, one can thereby indirectly represent the whole of which it is a part.[19] According to COI, M_1 is an integrated part of M^*. Since M_2 *directly* represents M_1, it thereby *indirectly* represents M^*. Since M_2 is part of M^*, there is thus a sense in which M^* represents its own higher-order component. By representing its own higher-order component, M^* thus makes one aware of one's awareness. COI thus entails that we can be aware of our awareness. In fact, it yields the stronger conclusion that *whenever* we are aware we are aware of our awareness.

Kriegel's proposal faces a number of objections. The first objection is that the binding relation cited by COI does not bind distinct representations into a single representational state. In vision, the neural synchrony of a red-signal and a circle-signal binds them to a single object, viz. the red circle. But binding of contents to a single object is not equivalent to the joining of representations into a single representation.[20] Like WIV and HOGS, worries can thus be raised about whether COI really yields the result that consciousness is underwritten by a single self-representing state rather than a pair of distinct states as in HOR.

COI's appeal to neural synchrony raises further problems (see e.g. Sebastian 2012 and Coleman 2015). However, a deeper problem for Kriegel is that even if we grant his account of what binds the components of a conscious state, COI is still unable to deliver on the Inner Awareness Promise. Kriegel relies on a number of claims about indirect representation that can be called into doubt.

First, some doubt that there is even such a phenomenon as indirect representation. When we represent the surface of an apple we also represent the whole apple, but why can this not be understood in terms of a direct representation of the surface bringing about a *distinct* direct representation of the whole apple? The notion of indirect representation may not be needed at all (Levine 2010; Phillips 2013).

Second, even if we grant that there is such a thing as indirect representation, it is doubtful that direct representation of a part suffices for indirect representation of the whole. Phillips (2013) offers an example of seeing a lemon that, unbeknownst to you, is an integral part of a lemon battery. It is implausible that by seeing the lemon you thereby see the lemon battery. But this raises doubts about why representing M_1 should suffice for representing M^*.[21] Perhaps Kriegel can respond by claiming that if there are further

---

[19] Here parthood has to be understood as a substantive relation. One cannot simply stipulate that there is a complex entity Z consisting of X and Y. X and Y are only parts of a single whole if there is a contingent relation between X and Y that is necessary for the existence of Z but not for the existence of X or Y (Kriegel 2009).

[20] See Weisberg (2008; 2011a); Levine (2010); Kidd (2011); Van Gulick (2012); and Rosenthal (unpublished).

[21] It is also worth noting that being part of a complex is not plausibly a *necessary* condition of indirect representation either. Coleman (2015) and Weisberg (2011a) each provide cases in which we represent an object via something other than an integrated part of that object.

conditions that must be met for indirect representation, they are met in the case of M*. But even if that is granted, a third problem remains.

To accommodate inner awareness our representation of M* must be *phenomenal* representation: Kriegel's promise is, after all, to explain our *awareness* of our own awareness. However, indirect representation is most plausibly *non*-phenomenal. When you phenomenally represent the surface of an apple, you might thereby represent the whole apple but you do not thereby represent the whole apple phenomenally (Levine 2010; Sebastian 2012). Your visual experience seems to be exhausted by the appearance of the apple's surface, so even if there is a sense in which the whole apple is indirectly represented, it is not a sense that has any bearing on your phenomenology. So if M* does indirectly represent itself, the phenomenology of M* ought to be exhausted by what it directly represents, that is, by its represented lower-order content. Overall then, COI is unable to convincingly deliver on the Inner Awareness Promise.

I noted earlier that the existence of inner awareness is a contentious phenomenological datum. Might Structured SR fare better if it denied that datum and scrapped the Inner Awareness Promise? I suggest not. A promise with which no version of SR can dispense is the Intimacy Promise, but there are reasons to think that Structured SR is unable even to deliver on that promise. Structured SR sidesteps the naturalizability worries faced by Unstructured SR by proposing that the higher- and lower-order content of a conscious state are underwritten by distinct components. However, as soon as this move is made the possibility emerges of the higher-order component misrepresenting the lower-order component. And if such misrepresentation is possible, Structured SR can ensure neither qualitative intimacy nor existential intimacy.

Let us consider qualitative intimacy first. If the lower-order component of the self-representing state is an itch, there is nothing to prevent the higher-order component from representing it as a pain. This is evident in each of the Structured SR theories we have examined. On WIV nothing precludes the higher-order component from conceptualizing a representation of an itch as a representation of a pain. On HOGS, the global network of mental states that are responsive to the lower-order state might *misconsume* that state as if it were a pain. On COI, by Kriegel's own admission a lower-order representation of an itch might be neurally synchronized with a higher-order state that represents it as a pain. The Structured SR theorist might respond by insisting that on a proper understanding of the state-integrating relation, one would see that misrepresentation is impossible. However, the relations actually sketched by the three theories discussed do nothing to guarantee accuracy, and it is difficult to see how any naturalizable relation *could* yield such infallibility.

Perhaps Structured SR can respond to this problem by claiming that there is a constitutive link between the qualities that a conscious state *represents* itself to have and the qualities that it actually has. Indeed, Kriegel makes this move explicitly and claims this COI thereby accommodates qualitative intimacy (2009: 110). Gennaro could make a parallel move by saying that our phenomenology is fixed by how the higher-order component of a state represents itself as being. Van Gulick would have to say that what fixes our phenomenology is how your wider mental economy takes your lower-order state to be. The problem with such an account of qualitative intimacy is that it is indistinguishable from the account offered by HOR theorists: an account on which the qualities of the lower-order state drop out as irrelevant. We saw reasons to regard that account as unsatisfactory, but even if it was to be deemed satisfactory this would justify the adoption of HOR theory, and render the digression into SR entirely pointless.

A further problem with this constitutive response is that it compromises Structured SR's ability to accommodate existential intimacy. It seems that the higher-order component of a self-representing state can exist in the absence of any lower-order component.[22] Advocates of Structured SR say that a state is conscious only if it is a composite that has an actual lower-order component, but are they entitled to this claim? Remember, on the constitutive view our phenomenology is fixed entirely by how the higher-order component of the complex represents things as being: if it represents us as being in a lower-order state of pain, then we thereby have a pain experience. But if our pain experience is constituted by the higher-order component of our conscious state, why would that component need to be integrated with a lower-order state before constituting a pain experience? Remember, the lower-order state is explanatorily idle on the constitutive approach. The Structured SR theorist would have to say that an unintegrated state that represents us as being in a pain state would not yield a pain experience, but that if this state was then integrated with a lower-order representation of an itch, we would thereby have a pain experience. This seems at best *ad hoc* and at worst absurd. Advocates of Structured SR might respond by just *stipulating* that consciousness requires the higher-order component to be integrated with some lower-order component. But if such a stipulation is permissible, the HOR theorist can simply stipulate that higher-order states only yield consciousness when they target an actual lower-order state.[23] Again, Structured SR fails to yield any advantage over the HOR branch of the family.

---

[22] On WIV, the lone higher-order state would be a conceptual representation to the effect that one is in some lower-order state. For HOGS, the lone higher-order state would be some global state of one's mental network such that the network is disposed to take it to be the case that one is in some lower-order state. For COI, self-representation involves a higher-order state being bound through neural synchrony to a lower-order state, so a lone higher-order state would be whatever that state is prior to binding.

[23] Kriegel hopes to have an advantage over his competitors here because being bound to a lower-order state is a necessary condition of the indirect self-representation constitutive of consciousness, so the higher-order component of a conscious state cannot fail to have a target. However, Weisberg (2008) points out that nothing in Kriegel's account precludes a higher-order state from being bound with some lower-order state other than the one it represents. So even if the theory entails that it has to be bound to some real state, it does not entail that this real state must be its target. Kriegel might respond that if the higher-order component referred to a non-existent state, it would fail to directly refer to any part of the conscious state of which it is a component, and so fail to achieve the indirect self-representation necessary to consciousness. However, Weisberg (2008) proposes that the requisite indirect self-representation can be achieved through reference to a non-existent target state, meaning that COI is vulnerable to the possibility of targetless conscious states after all.

21.5 Moving Forward

Having worked our way down the Meta-Representationalist family tree, we can now see that no existing version of SR is adequate. Along the way we have accrued three promises on which any adequate version of SR must deliver:

(1) The Transitivity Promise
(2) The Naturalizability Promise
(3) The Intimacy Promise

HOR theory delivered on 1 and 2 but not 3. Unstructured SR delivers on 1 and 3 but not 2. Structured SR appeals to a natural representation relation between the components of a conscious state, so promises to deliver on 1 and 2. However, we have just seen that it is ill-equipped to deliver on 3. Perhaps the specific character of the relation that unifies the two components into a single state can put some distance between Structured SR and HOR and allow it to deliver on the Intimacy Promise. However, by moving too far away from an ordinary representation relation Structured SR risks violating 1 by positing a relation that does not amount to representation, or violating 2 by positing a representation relation that cannot be accounted for naturalistically.

We also discussed a fourth promise: the Inner Awareness Promise. The putative phenomenological datum that drives this promise is contentious, so a case could be made for not factoring it into our assessment. It is worth noting, however, that neither HOR nor Structured SR show any real potential to accommodate inner awareness. Unstructured SR fares better: there is no reason why an unstructured conscious state's *sui generis* representation of itself could not yield inner awareness. However, it remains the case that this kind of self-representation is unnaturalizable.

How should we deal with the fact that no existing theory can deliver on the three main promises? The pessimistic strategy would be to concede that Meta-Representationalism is unable to yield all three results, and then to a pick a theory that delivers on the promises that we value most. We might dispute the apparent intimacy of consciousness and endorse HOR, or we might scrap any aspiration to naturalizability and endorse Unstructured SR. Different versions of SR would deliver on different combinations of promise, but none will deliver on all. This pessimistic strategy should not be dismissed out of hand. It is, after all, an open possibility that the assumptions that drive the three main promises are in error. That said, I would recommend a more optimistic approach.

There is nothing formally inconsistent about the three main promises, so we should not shy away from the ambition of delivering on every one of them. Structured SR fell down on the relations it posited between the higher- and lower-order components of a conscious state. To the extent that they posit an ordinary representation relation, they fail to gain any advantage over HOR. But to the extent that they posit a more distinctive close connection between the two components, they move away from giving an account of awareness that is both meta-representational and naturalizable. This suggests that what we need to do is to find a relation that, like ordinary representation, is representational and naturalizable but, unlike ordinary representation, is able to accommodate the intimacy of consciousness.

To do this, I suggest that we need to reconceive the higher-order component of a conscious state as *disclosing* the lower-order component of the state as it is in itself rather than as attributing the lower-order component properties in a way that might misfire. To account for such a relation in natural representational terms, one might follow Kidd (2011) in appealing to *indexicals*. Indexical reference is normally taken to have a kind of context-relative infallibility, and this might help account for the intimacy of consciousness. Furthermore, there is little threat of indexical reference being unnaturalizable. Alternatively, one might follow Coleman (2015) or Picciuto (2011) in appealing to *quotation*. When we quote something that very thing stands for itself in a way that precludes at least some kinds of misrepresentation. And again, quotation seems open to naturalization.[24]

Such a self-representational account would face many challenges. It would have to explain why indexical or quotational reference to a state would yield consciousness of that state. It would also have to reassure sceptics that such a relation can indeed be naturalized. And since such an account shows little hope of delivering on the Inner Awareness Promise, it would have to undermine the claim that our phenomenology is ever characterized by inner awareness. I can see no immediate reason to doubt that such challenges can be met. Meta-Representationalism is an attractive family, and the Self-Representationalist branch of that family holds the most appeal. The members of the family to which we have been introduced might not be what we wanted, but there remains reason to hope that we can find another member of the family that provides exactly what we need.

REFERENCES

Armstrong, D. M. (1981), 'What is Consciousness', in D. M. Armstrong, *The Nature of Mind* Brisbane: University of Queensland Press.

Block, N. (2011), 'The Higher Order Approach to Consciousness is Defunct', *Analysis*, 71/3: 419–31.

Brook, A. and Raymont, P. (2006), 'The Representational Base of Consciousness', *Psyche*, 12/2.

Buras, T. (2009), 'An Argument Against Causal Theories of Mental Content', *American Philosophical Quarterly*, 46/2: 117–29.

Carruthers, P. (2004), 'HOP over FOR, HOT Theory', in R. J. Gennaro (ed.), *Higher-Order Theories of Consciousness*. Amsterdam: John Benjamins, 115–35.

---

[24] Appeals to acquaintance (Williford 2006; Hellie 2007), or to a direct awareness relation akin to that posited by naïve realists (Kidd 2015), might also fit the bill. However, in these cases one might worry: (a) that the relation is no longer representational and; (b) that the relation has poor prospects of naturalization. Again though, it would be premature to rule these options out.

Caston, V. (2002), 'Aristotle on Consciousness', *Mind*, 111/444: 751–815.
Coleman, S. (2015), 'Quotational Higher Order Thought Theory', *Philosophical Studies*, 172/10: 2705–33.
Dretske, F. (1995), *Naturalizing the Mind*. Cambridge, MA: MIT Press.
Ford, J. (2009), 'Review of Self-Representational Approaches to Consciousness', *Minds & Machines*, 19: 283–7.
Gennaro, R. J. (2004), 'Higher-order thoughts, animal consciousness, and misrepresentation: A reply to Carruthers and Levine', in R. J. Gennaro (ed.), *Higher-Order Theories of Consciousness*. Amsterdam: John Benjamins, 45–56.
Gennaro, R. J. (2006), 'Between Pure Self-Referentialism and the (extrinsic) HOT theory of consciousness', in U. Kriegel and K. Williford (eds), *Consciousness and Self-Reference*. Cambridge, MA: MIT Press, 221–48.
Gennaro, R. J. (2008), 'Representationalism, peripheral awareness, and the transparency of experience', *Philosophical Studies*, 139: 39–56.
Gertler, B. (2012), 'Conscious states as objects of awareness: on Uriah Kriegel, Subjective Consciousness: a Self-representational Theory', *Philosophical Studies*, 159: 447–55.
Haggard, P. and Libet, B. (2001), 'Conscious intention and brain activity', *Journal of Consciousness Studies*, 8/11: 47–64.
Hellie, B. (2007), 'Higher-Order Intentionality and Higher-Order Acquaintance', *Philosophical Studies*, 134: 289–324.
Janzen, G. (2006), 'Phenomenal Character as Implicit Self-Awareness', *Journal of Consciousness Studies*, 13/12: 44–73.
Kidd, C. (2011), 'Phenomenal Consciousness with Infallible Self-Representation', *Philosophical Studies*, 152: 361–83.
Kidd, C. (2015), 'The Idols of Inner Sense', *Philosophical Studies*, 172: 1759–82.
Kriegel, U. (2009), *Subjective Consciousness: A Self-Representational Theory*. Oxford: Oxford University Press.
Kriegel, U. (2016), 'Brentano's Dual-Framing Theory of Consciousness', *Philosophy and Phenomenological Research*, doi:10.1111/phpr.12327.
Levine, J. (2003), 'Experience and Representation', in Q. Smith and A. Jokic (eds), *Consciousness: New Philosophical Perspectives*. Oxford: Oxford University Press, 58–76.
Levine, J. (2006), 'Conscious Awareness and (Self-)Representation', in U. Kriegel and K. Williford (eds), *Self-Representational Approaches to Consciousness*. Cambridge, MA: MIT Press, 173–98.
Levine, J. (2010), 'Review of *Subjective Consciousness: A Self-Representational Theory*', *Notre Dame Philosophical Review*.
Levine, J. (2015), 'A "Quasi-Sartrean" Theory of Subjective Awareness', in S. Miguens, G Preyer, and C. B. Morando (eds), *Pre-Reflective Consciousness: Sartre and Contemporary Philosophy of Mind*. Abingdon: Taylor & Francis, 242–62.
Libet, B. (1985), 'Unconscious Cerebral Initiative and the Role of Conscious Will in Voluntary Action', *The Behavioral and Brain Sciences*, 8: 529–66.
Lycan, W. G. (2001), 'A simple argument for a higher-order representation theory of consciousness', *Analysis*, 61/269: 3–4.
Lycan, W. G. (2004), 'The Superiority of HOP to HOT', in R. J. Gennaro (ed.), *Higher-Order Theories of Consciousness*. Amsterdam: John Benjamins, 93–113.
Lyyra, P. (2008), 'Two Senses for "givenness of consciousness"', *Phenomenology and Cognitive Science*, 8: 67–87.
McClelland, T. (2015), 'Affording Introspection: An Alternative Model of Inner Awareness', *Philosophical Studies*, 172/9: 2469–92.

McClelland, T. (forthcoming), 'Do We Experience Our Conscious States as Belonging to Us?' in M. Guillot and M. García-Carpintero (eds), *Consciousness and the Sense of Mineness*. Oxford: Oxford University Press.

Mehta, N. (2013), 'Is there a phenomenological argument for higher-order representationalism?' *Philosophical Studies*, 164: 357–70.

Neander, K. (1998), 'The Division of Phenomenal Labour: A Problem for Representational Theories of Consciousness', *Philosophical Perspectives*, 12: 411–34.

Phillips, B. (2013), 'Indirect representation and the self-representational theory of consciousness', in *Philosophical Studies*, 167/2; doi:10.1007/s11098-012-0087-1

Picciuto, V. (2011), 'Addressing Higher-Order Misrepresentation with Quotational Thought', *Journal of Consciousness Studies*, 18/3–4: 109–36.

Rosenthal, D. (1986), 'Two concepts of consciousness', *Philosophical Studies*, 49: 329–59.

Rosenthal, D. (2011), 'Exaggerated reports: reply to Block', *Analysis*, 71/3: 431–7.

Rosenthal, D. (unpublished), 'Intrinsicalism and its Discontents' https://sites.google.com/site/davidrosenthal12/ last accessed 7 October 2016.

Schear, J. K. (2009), 'Experience and self-consciousness', *Philosophical Studies*, 144: 95–105.

Seager, W. (2006), 'Is Self-Representation Necessary for Consciousness?', *Psyche*, 12/2.

Sebastian, M. A. (2012), 'Review of Uriah Kriegel, *Subjective Consciousness*', *Disputatio*, 32: 413–7.

Siewert, C. (2013), 'Phenomenality and Self-Consciousness', in U. Kriegel (ed.), *Phenomenal Intentionality*. Oxford: Oxford University Press, 235–60.

Strawson, G. (2011), 'Radical Self-Awareness', in M. Sidertis, E. Thompson, and D. Zahavi (eds), *Self, No Self?: Perspectives from Analytical, Phenomenological and Indian Traditions*. Oxford: Oxford University Press, 274–307.

Textor, M. (2006), 'Brentano (and Some Neo-Brentanians) on Inner Consciousness', *Dialectica*, 60/4: 411–32.

Textor, M. (2015). '"Inner Perception Can Never Become Inner Observation": Brentano on Awareness and Observation', *Philosophers' Imprint*, 15/10.

Thomasson, A. L. (2006), 'Self-Awareness and Self-Knowledge', *Psyche*, 12/2.

Van Gulick, R. (2004), 'Higher Order Global States (HOGS): An Alternative Higher-Order Model of Consciousness', in R. J. Gennaro (ed.), *Higher-Order Theories of Consciousness*. Amsterdam: John Benjamins, 67–92.

Van Gulick, R. (2006), 'Mirror, mirror—is that all?', in U. Kriegel and K. Williford (eds), *Self-Representational Approaches to Consciousness*. Cambridge, MA: MIT Press, 11–40.

Van Gulick, R. (2012), 'Subjective consciousness and self-representation', *Philosophical Studies*, 159: 457.

Weisberg, J. (2008), 'Same old, same old: the same-order representation theory of consciousness and the division of phenomenal labour', *Synthese*, 160: 161–81.

Weisberg, J. (2011a), 'Review of Subjective Consciousness: A Self-Representational Theory', *Mind*, 120/478: 538–42.

Weisberg, J. (2011b), 'Abusing the notion of what-it's-likeness: A response to Block', *Analysis*, 71/3: 438–43.

Williford, K. (2006), 'Zahavi versus Brentano: A Rejoinder', *Psyche*, 12/2.

Zahavi, D. (2004), 'Back to Brentano', *Journal of Consciousness Studies*, 11/10–11: 66–87.

Zahavi, D. (2005), 'Intentionality and Experience', *Synthesis Philosophica*, 40: 299–318.

Zahavi, D. (2006), 'Two Takes on a One-Level Account of Consciousness', *Psyche*, 12/2.

CHAPTER 22

THE EPISTEMIC APPROACH TO THE PROBLEM OF CONSCIOUSNESS

DANIEL STOLJAR

22.1 INTRODUCTION

AT the end of a *Time* magazine summary of the present state of thinking on the hard problem of consciousness, Steven Pinker writes:

> And then there is the theory put forward by philosopher Colin McGinn that our vertigo when pondering the Hard Problem is itself a quirk of our brains. The brain is a product of evolution, and just as animal brains have their limitations, we have ours...[and so we]...can't intuitively grasp why neural information processing observed from the outside should give rise to subjective experience on the inside.
>
> (Pinker 2007: 6)

Concerning this theory, Pinker remarks (2007, 6): 'This is where I place my bet, though I admit that the theory could be demolished when an unborn genius—a Darwin or Einstein of consciousness—comes up with a flabbergasting new idea that suddenly makes it all clear to us.'

It is not so easy to interpret what Pinker is saying here. McGinn's view is that it is biologically impossible for humans to solve the hard problem (McGinn 1989; see also McGinn 1991, 2004).[1] A consequence of this is that there could be no Darwins or

---

[1] McGinn uses the phrase 'mind–body problem' rather than 'hard problem' but we can assume that his view applies to both (if indeed there is a difference). I will describe in more detail what the hard problem is immediately below.

Einsteins of consciousness, not at any rate if that means a *human* Darwin or Einstein. And while McGinn does not rule out that a *non-human* (e.g., a Martian) Darwin or Einstein might solve the problem—indeed, it is consistent with his view that even the dullest Martian might do so—a further consequence of his view is that no Martian could make the solution clear to us humans, for that too is biologically impossible.

What then does Pinker think? When he says he would place a bet on McGinn's view, it sounds like he thinks it is probably true. But when he says that he admits McGinn's view *could*[2] be demolished, it sounds like he thinks it is probably false.

Despite this, there is no doubt that Pinker is highly sympathetic to the general direction of McGinn's position. Both suppose that we are ignorant at least for the time being of something important and relevant when it comes to the hard problem, and that this fact has a significant implication for its solution. They both hold, as I will put it, an *epistemic view* of the hard problem of consciousness.

Moreover, they are not alone in doing so. The epistemic view is a common one in the history of philosophical and scientific thought about the hard problem. One can detect it or something similar in Arnauld's (1641) criticism of Descartes, in Locke's (1975[1689]) suggestion that God may 'super-add' the capacity of thinking to matter, in Priestley's (1777) discussion of organized matter, in Du Bois-Reymond's (1872) distinction between ignoramus and ignorabimus, and in Russell's (1927) views on 'the causal skeleton of the world'. Versions of the view are also present in Chomsky's (1975) distinction between mysteries and problems, in Nagel's (1974) discussion of whether the pre-Socratics could understand the identity of matter and energy, and in Jackson's (1982) example of the super-slugs, all three of which are the immediate precursors of McGinn's paper.

I too am a proponent of the epistemic approach, though the kind of position I favour is different again from those advanced by these writers. In the first part of this chapter, I will outline in elementary terms the version of the view I think most plausible. In the second part, I will respond to two objections to the view. The first is that, while we may be ignorant of various features of the world, we are not ignorant of any feature that is *relevant* to the hard problem. The second is that, even if the epistemic approach is true, properly understood it is not an *answer* to the hard problem; indeed, it is no contribution to that problem at all. In the concluding part, I will offer some brief reflections on why the epistemic approach, despite its attractiveness, remains a minority view in contemporary philosophy of mind.

22.2 Which Question is at Issue?

Suppose we are asking for the explanation of some natural phenomenon. It does not matter for present purposes what it is—let it be the origin of some disease, or the operation of a particular enzyme, or the fluctuation of wool prices in medieval England.

---

[2] I take it 'could' is important here; if Pinker had said 'would' no interpretative difficulty would arise.

Now suppose somebody—Bill, let us call him—announces that he has finally arrived at a theory. 'Bravo and congratulations', we say, gathering round, waiting for further details. Imagine then our disappointment when Bill steps up to the podium and says, 'My theory is...wait for it...I have none. I have no theory at all. In fact, I haven't a clue about what explains the phenomenon in question.' Perhaps some of us with commend Bill for his honesty. But most of us will feel cheated. 'It's fair enough to be ignorant', we might say, 'but it's outrageous to call it a theory. Even more outrageous is that people get paid by universities to say such things.'

Is the epistemic view any better than this? At first glance you may think not. Surely the hard problem of consciousness is just the problem of explaining what consciousness is. And surely the epistemic view is just the 'theory' that we do not know what that explanation is. If so, a proponent of that view is no better than Bill, and should be subject to the same kind of opprobrium.

But this impression is misleading. The hard problem is not a single problem but a cluster of related questions and issues. It is true that one question in the cluster—call it Question A—is, 'What is the explanation of consciousness?' But a different question—call it Question B—asks not *what* the explanation of consciousness is, but rather *whether* there is, or could be, a certain sort of explanation, a sort sometimes called a reductive explanation. The notion of a reductive explanation may be spelled out in different ways, but here we may assume that there is a reductive explanation of consciousness if and only if there is a set of physical facts—perhaps facts about the brains and bodies of sentient creatures—that necessitate the facts of consciousness.[3] So from this point of view, Question B is, 'Is there a physical fact, or set of such facts, that necessitate the facts about consciousness?'

From a logical point of view, Question A and Question B are distinct. Question B is a yes/no question, Question A is not. Question B explicitly concerns the notion of a reductive explanation, Question A does not. Nevertheless they are also related. For example, often but not always, when people raise Question A, they presuppose a positive answer to Question B; that is, they assume that there is some relevant set of physical facts, and are simply asking what these are. Moreover, if the answer to Question B is negative, this constrains the sort of answers we might give to Question A, since we could not in that case answer it by providing a reductive explanation.

While the questions are distinct, one might think there is no need to discuss them separately. 'Just work on Question A', you might say, 'and the answer to Question B will come out automatically.' This advice is plausible on the surface but it forgets that there are persuasive reasons for supposing that there *must* be a negative answer to Question B, reasons which are apparently quite independent of Question A. The reasons I have in mind are the famous arguments in philosophy of mind about zombies, Mary, inverted

---

[3] By 'fact' here I mean a true proposition; by 'necessitate' here I mean what is sometimes called metaphysical or logical necessitation; on this view one fact necessitates another just in case in all possible worlds in which the first obtains, the second does too. This notion of reductive explanation is similar to but is not quite the same as that discussed in Chalmers and Jackson 2001.

spectra, and the rest. If successful, these arguments all suggest the same conclusion, namely, that there is no reductive explanation and hence that Question B must have a negative answer.

The epistemic view, in the form I think is most plausible, is concerned with Question B, and in particular, with these arguments that it must be answered in the negative. In brief, its suggestion is that these arguments presuppose that we have a complete knowledge of the facts relevant to answering them—that 'all the facts that concern us lie open before us' as Wittgenstein memorably put it in a related context (see Wittgenstein 1960: 6). Since, according to the epistemic view, that presupposition is false, the arguments fail, and we are free to suppose that there is a reductive explanation of consciousness.

I have said that the epistemic view is concerned with Question B. I have not said that it is *not* concerned with A—a view may be concerned with two questions at once after all. Is it or is it not? Well, suppose it is not; then the proponent of the epistemic view is clearly not in the position of Bill above, and that problem at least is answered. But you might reasonably insist that no genuine contribution to the hard problem can avoid dealing with Question A somewhere along the line. If so, it looks as if the proponent of the epistemic view is in the same position as Bill after all. This brings us close to the second of the two objections I mentioned at the outset, namely, the problem of whether the epistemic view is a genuine contribution to the hard problem at all. However, let me postpone this issue until we have looked in more detail at the view.

22.3 THE CONCEIVABILITY ARGUMENT

I spoke just now of the 'famous arguments in philosophy of mind about zombies, Mary, the inverted spectra'. Let us examine one of these arguments—namely, the conceivability argument—and how the epistemic view seeks to answer it. (Here my discussion will be very brief since there is a huge literature dealing with the ins and outs of these arguments.)[4]

The first premise of the argument is that it is conceivable or imaginable that there is a possible world identical to the actual world as regards all physical facts but is different from it as regards some fact about consciousness. The second premise is that if this is conceivable, it is possible. The conclusion is that this is indeed possible, and in consequence there can be no reductive explanation of consciousness.

The epistemic view has a two-part response to this argument. The first part supposes that there is a type of physical fact that is relevant to consciousness but of which we are ignorant; I refer to this part of the response as *the ignorance hypothesis* (see Stoljar 2006).[5]

---

[4] For a recent selection of this literature, see Alter and Howell 2012.
[5] It bears emphasis that the ignorance hypothesis concerns types of facts, rather than individual facts; for discussion of this point see Stoljar 2006: 70–2.

This part of the epistemic view is a contingent claim, since it makes a claim about our epistemic capacities and achievements, and the relation between these capacities and achievements and the world. But it is a contingent claim that is rather plausible—at least prima facie. Surely we can assume that there are facts about consciousness of which we are ignorant!

The second part argues that, *if* the ignorance hypothesis is true, the conceivability argument is unpersuasive. To illustrate this second part, let us focus on the quantifier phrase 'all physical facts' that occurs explicitly or implicitly in both premises of the conceivability argument. If the ignorance hypothesis is true, this quantifier may be understood in two ways: it might be interpreted so that the physical facts that are relevant but unknown to us are included in its domain; or it might be interpreted so that those facts are not included. Either way, the argument is unpersuasive. For suppose the relevant but unknown physical facts *are* included in its domain; in that case it is not true that we can conceive of the possibility in question, and the first premise of the argument is false. Suppose instead they are *not* included in the domain; in that case the conclusion of the argument shows only that the facts about consciousness come apart from *some* physical facts, not that they come apart from *all*. But by itself that conclusion is unsurprising; certainly it does not entail that consciousness is a fundamental element in nature, which is the conclusion that proponents of the conceivability argument are usually interpreted as wanting to establish.[6]

22.4 THE EPISTEMIC APPROACH AND OTHER RESPONSES

How does this answer to the conceivability argument relate to other, more traditional, answers?

The dualist responds to the argument by accepting it, and then supposing that consciousness *is* a fundamental element of nature, rather like space, time, and gravity (or at any rate like space, time, and gravity are often taken to be). The proponent of the epistemic view is clearly not a dualist, since he or she does not accept the argument. Moreover, the dualist is naturally understood as inferring that consciousness is fundamental from the claim that it is not derivative on known features of matter. The proponent of the epistemic view denies this, pointing out that, from the premise that something is not derivative on known features of matter, it does not follow that it is not derivative on anything; hence it does not follow that it is fundamental.

The eliminativist responds to the argument by agreeing with the dualist, conditional on the existence of consciousness—and then denies the condition. According to the eliminativist, in other words, consciousness does not exist. The proponent of the

---

[6] For extensive discussion of this view, see Stoljar 2006 and references therein; see also Stoljar 2015.

epistemic view is clearly not an eliminativist, since nothing in that view denies that consciousness exists.

The materialist[7] responds to the argument by rejecting it, and asserting that materialism is true. Of course a proponent of the epistemic view rejects the argument as well—how then is this view to be distinguished from materialism?

Well, the *standard* materialist, the sort you usually find in the literature on these matters, denies the claim I mentioned above, the ignorance hypothesis. The standard materialist thinks that all the relevant facts are in, or at any rate that one can assume that they are in when discussing the conceivability argument. Rather than appealing to the ignorance hypothesis, the standard materialist tries to disarm the conceivability argument in a different way.

How does the standard materialist try to disarm the argument? There are a large number of ideas about this in the literature: the ability hypothesis, the phenomenal concept strategy, various acquaintance views, appeals to the necessary a posteriori, to the distinction between concepts and properties, to representationalism, and so on and so forth. I will not go into these ideas here. Suffice it to say that I am persuaded that none of them is successful; that is, none of them explains where the conceivability argument goes wrong (see, e.g., Stoljar 2006: 175–217). So at this point, I am in agreement with dualists and eliminativists who likewise think that none of these ideas can be made to work. Conclusion: standard materialism should be rejected. Further conclusion: if dualism and eliminativism are likewise rejected, the remaining option is materialism of a non-standard kind, a kind that combines materialism with the ignorance hypothesis.

Should a non-standard materialist be called a 'materialist' in the first place? That depends on an interpretative question that turns out to be surprisingly difficult, namely, what *exactly* you have to believe in order to count as a materialist. By very weak standards, it is sufficient to count as a materialist if you hold only that consciousness is not fundamental. By that standard a proponent of the epistemic view can certainly be called a materialist. By much stronger, but more historically accurate, standards, a materialist is someone who thinks that everything is determined by the physical, where the notion of the physical is understood in the light of a well-known historical theory—for example, the sort of atomism articulated by the Greeks and revived in the early (pre-Newtonian) renaissance period by philosophers such as Gassendi. By that standard, non-standard materialism is certainly not a kind of materialism—but then again nor are the versions of 'materialism' held by philosophers such as David Lewis or J. J. C. Smart, who are usually thought of as the paradigm contemporary examples of materialist philosophers.

My own view is that observations like this cause a major problem for the attempt to provide a clear statement of materialism; that is why the interpretative question I mentioned is so difficult.[8] However, for present purposes, we can afford to be relaxed: if you adopt weak standards, non-standard materialism is indeed a version of materialism; if you

---

[7] By 'materialist' I will mean 'non-eliminativist materialist'.
[8] For discussion of these issues see Stoljar 2010.

adopt strong standards, non-standard materialism does not look much like materialism—but then again neither do the contemporary theses that usually go by that name.

22.5 Varieties of the View

We have set out the epistemic view, and explained its relation to other responses to the conceivability argument. Let me bring this brief sketch of it to a close by noting that there are various different versions of the view.

One version is that advanced by McGinn in the work Pinker comments on in Section 22.1. As we have seen, McGinn's view is that it is biologically impossible for us to solve the hard problem. As McGinn develops this idea, it contains some elements that distinguish it from the view we have been looking at. For one thing, he does not bring the issue of ignorance to bear on the conceivability argument and similar arguments quite in the way that I do; moreover, he thinks of these arguments as having a conceptual, rather than an epistemic, origin.[9] Still, if we transpose what he says into our framework, the result is something like this: (a) we are ignorant of some of the physical facts that necessitate the facts about consciousness; and (b) this ignorance is not something that can be overcome in a way that is consistent with our biological nature. Following Owen Flanagan (1992), we may call this the 'mysterian' version of the epistemic view.

There is no doubt that mysterianism is interesting and well worth exploring. But there is no need for a proponent of the epistemic view to be a mysterian: one can assert (a) without asserting (b). After all, to say that there are unknown relevant properties of matter is not to say that these properties will remain forever unknown to humans or to rational agents in general—it is not to say that we are *cognitively closed* with respect to these properties, in McGinn's well-known phrase.

Indeed, when you focus on it, this last suggestion is extremely speculative. You can say that we are cognitively closed with respect to something only if you also know two further things: what the limits of human knowledge are, and whether the thing in question falls outside those limits. But we know neither of those things, and that is why the epistemic view I favour leaves the issue of cognitive closure open.[10]

Another version of the epistemic view, which has been getting a lot of attention in recent years, is a view inspired by Bertrand Russell's (1927) *The Analysis of Matter*. In that book, Russell outlines an epistemological position according to which in empirical inquiry we are limited to knowing only the logical or causal structure of the world—structural facts, as we might put it in more contemporary language. But he also thought that it was possible that there are non-structural facts in addition to structural facts, and went on to suggest, in effect, that facts that necessitate consciousness might include these non-structural facts. Transposing this into our framework, the result is something

---

[9] For some discussion of these points, see Stoljar 2005.
[10] For an interesting exchange on whether we should even leave it open, see Kriegel 2003 and Demircioglu 2017.

like this: (a) we are ignorant of some of the physical facts that necessitate the facts about consciousness; and (b) the physical facts in question are non-structural facts that our epistemological framework does not permit us to know.

Like mysterianism, the Russellian version of the epistemic view is interesting and well worth exploring. But again no proponent of the epistemic view needs to be a Russellian: one can assert (a) without asserting (b). For one thing, to endorse the ignorance hypothesis is not to presuppose any special epistemology like the one sketched by Russell—*any* epistemological theory at all must acknowledge possibilities of the kind the ignorance hypothesis makes salient. Moreover, Russell's epistemological position taken absolutely literally is quite implausible. Take fish, for example. On the face of it, we know plenty of facts about fish—for example that they have fins—that seem to be neither logical nor causal facts about them. Hence we know facts about fish that are not structural in the relevant sense. Of course, the phrase 'structural' is, like fish, extremely slippery. Someone might interpret it in such a way that facts about fish of the kind I just mentioned count. But there is trouble ahead for the Russellian version of the epistemic view if this line is adopted. For the broader you make the notion of 'structural', the narrower the notion of 'non-structural' becomes, that is, because these are a package deal. Consequently, the less likely it is that these non-structural facts can play a role in necessitating the facts about consciousness.[11]

22.6 THE RELEVANCE OBJECTION

So much for saying what the epistemic view *is*—turning now to objections, like any other position in philosophy, there are several different potential concerns to pursue. Here I will concentrate on two: the relevance objection and the no answer objection.

According to the relevance objection, while we are ignorant of certain types of fact, we are not ignorant of any type of fact that is *relevant* to consciousness. There are a number of different ways to develop this idea. Jerry Fodor, for example, in a review of Chomsky's (2000) *New Horizons*, argues that consciousness 'seems to depend, not on the "ultimate" nature of matter, but on its macrostructure' (Fodor 2000: 3).[12] The point underlying this remark can, I believe, be stated as follows.

> Premise 1: all facts relevant to consciousness are macrostructural facts.
> Premise 2: there are no macrostructural facts of which we are ignorant.
> Conclusion: there are no facts relevant to consciousness of which we are ignorant.

This argument is certainly valid and we may agree with Premise 1. But someone who advances the ignorance hypothesis and the epistemic view will immediately deny

---

[11] For some discussion of these points, see Stoljar 2015 and Alter 2016, and the references therein.
[12] It is not clear that Fodor has consciousness specifically in mind here, but we may adapt what he says to this case.

Premise 2. After all, their whole point is that there are relevant facts of which we are ignorant. If so, this argument is no good against the epistemic view, since its second premise is no better than an assertion that the view is mistaken.[13]

Someone may try to motivate Premise 2 by pointing out (a) that there are *microstructural* facts of which we are ignorant—for example, facts associated with quantum mechanics—but (b) that this seems not to have an impact on macrostructural facts—for example, that quantum indeterminacy seems to be a feature of the micro-world rather than the macro-world. But even if these claims are true, they lend no plausibility to Premise 2, a point that comes out best if we consider the matter abstractly. Suppose we are ignorant of a particular type of fact, say A-facts. And suppose A-facts are irrelevant to a distinct type of fact, say B-facts. It scarcely follows that we are *not* ignorant of B-facts. In general, you do not get to know a type of fact simply by *not* knowing some quite distinct type of fact!

A different way to develop the relevance objection is suggested by David Lewis when he remarks, 'the physical nature of ordinary matter under mild conditions is very well understood' (1999: 292). Lewis is here talking about the brain, and his point is that *its* physics is well understood, since it is an example of ordinary matter. This suggests the following version of the relevance objection.

> Premise 1: all facts relevant to consciousness are facts about the brain.
> Premise 2: there are no facts about the brain of which we are ignorant.
> Conclusion: there are no facts relevant to consciousness of which we are ignorant.

Once again the argument is valid, and we may agree with Premise 1. But why believe Premise 2? Of course *some* physical features of the brain are well understood—we know how its mass or shape, for example, is a function of the mass or shape of its parts. (It is these features of the brain that Lewis is talking about when he mentions 'ordinary matter under mild conditions'.) But other features of the brain—to take an obvious example, how exactly consciousness depends on it—are clearly not understood; indeed it is a scientific truism that this is so.[14]

One might try to bolster Lewis's version of the relevance objection by pointing out that we have a good understanding of what the individual parts or constituents of the brain are. At least since the work of Ramon y Cajal at the end of the nineteenth century, it has been known that the brain is made up of cells, which are themselves made up of molecules and so on and so forth (cf. Shepherd 1991). However, for the epistemic view

---

[13] It is worth emphasizing here that the ignorance hypothesis does not require that we are ignorant of facts concerning macrostructural *objects* or *first-order* macrostructural properties (i.e., properties of objects). It is enough for the thesis that we are ignorant of facts concerning *second*-order macrostructural properties, i.e., properties of first-order properties. For some discussion of this using a slightly different terminology, see Stoljar 2006: 72–4.

[14] One might object that the point in the text would be stronger if there were examples of a principled incompleteness in our theory of the brain or of the physical that's independent of consciousness. For a number of historical cases along these lines, see Stoljar 2006: 123–41.

the crucial issue is not what the individual parts of the brain are. It is rather what the properties of those parts are, and indeed what the properties of the properties of those parts are. In fact, it is precisely for this reason that Lewis makes his point by speaking of the 'physical nature' of the brain rather than its constituents.

A final way to develop the relevance objection appeals to the idea in philosophy of mind known as *functionalism*, which says, roughly, that mental states are identical to functional states.[15] The key thing about functional states, according to this line of thought, is that they make no (or at least very few) demands on the matter that makes them up; hence even if we are ignorant about underlying features of matter, we may know exactly what the functional states are. This suggests a third version of the relevance objection, as follows.

> Premise 1: all facts relevant to consciousness are functional facts, i.e., facts about functional states.
> Premise 2: there are no functional facts of which we are ignorant.
> Conclusion: there are no facts relevant to consciousness of which we are ignorant.

But the problem here is that the notion of a functional fact can be interpreted in many different ways. Formally speaking, functionalism is not so much a theory as a technique of definition; it says, for example, that a mental state M is the nth state in a sequence of states that satisfies the relevant description. Everything depends, therefore, on what the relevant description is. If there are no constraints on the description, Premise 1 of the above argument is certainly plausible, but Premise 2 is implausible, since even unknown and unknowable facts may be functional facts in this general sense. If there *are* constraints on the relevant description, however, we get the reverse problem. For example, in philosophy of mind, people who describe themselves as 'functionalists' typically assume that the descriptions at issue are limited to those concerning causal processes, which results in the idea that mental states are exhausted by their causal roles. This view renders Premise 1 plausible, but equally it renders Premise 2 *im*plausible, since it is implausible that all facts relevant to consciousness are functional facts in this restricted sense. Indeed, the idea that all facts relevant to consciousness are functional facts in this restricted sense is itself refuted by the conceivability argument. Either way, therefore, this version of the relevance objection is unpersuasive.

22.7 THE NO ANSWER OBJECTION

For these reasons, the epistemic view is in a good position as regards the relevance objection. What then of the other objection I mentioned, that properly understood the view is no answer to the hard problem at all?

---

[15] For a very good presentation of functionalism, see Braddon Mitchell and Jackson 2007.

We may formulate this objection by looking back at the two questions I distinguished earlier. Question A was: what is the explanation of consciousness? Question B was: does consciousness have a reductive explanation? I suggested before that, while the epistemic view is focused on Question B, one may well insist that a genuine contribution to the hard problem should focus on Question A. And it is this observation that sets up the no answer objection, which we may state as follows.

> Premise 1: something is a genuine contribution to the hard problem of consciousness only if it answers Question A.
> Premise 2: the epistemic view does not answer Question A.
> Conclusion: the epistemic view is not a genuine contribution to the problem.

How to react? I think the weakness here comes to light when we focus on what exactly Question A is asking; that is, what question is at issue when people ask for 'the explanation of consciousness', and, connected to this, what an answer to that question might be. For while we sometimes take ourselves to know intuitively what an explanation of consciousness would be, this becomes much less clear when you focus on it.

One attractive way to approach this issue starts from the observation that consciousness is something that has both a history and a constitution.[16] As regards history, each and every conscious event stands at the end of a huge causal history leading all the way back to the beginning of the universe. As regards constitution, each and every conscious event stands at the apex of a huge constitutive hierarchy leading all the way down to the basic elements of the universe. One thing you could be asking for when you ask for 'the explanation of consciousness' is total information about both the history and constitution of consciousness. Hence an answer to Question A would be a proposition expressing this total information.

Now, if that is how Question A is to be understood, there is no doubt that the epistemic view does not answer it; that is, Premise 2 of the no answer objection is correct. Indeed, more than not answering it, the epistemic view entails that it cannot now be answered, since it entails that at least some of the relevant facts here are unknown to us.

By the same token, however, Premise 1 on this interpretation is very implausible, since it is very implausible that something is a genuine contribution to the hard problem only if it provides total information in this sense. For one thing, *no* contribution to the hard problem has *ever* provided total information; hence nothing *ever* said about the hard problem constitutes a contribution by that standard.

Moreover, many of the most interesting questions about consciousness can be pursued in the absence of total information. We have already noted that the hard problem is a cluster of related questions, and singled out Questions A and B as members of that cluster. Several further questions in the cluster are as follows:

---

[16] This way of looking at things owes a lot to Lewis's discussion of causal explanation; see Lewis 1986. For further discussion see Stoljar 2017.

Question C: What is it that makes a mental state conscious?
Question D: Are you always aware of your conscious states?
Question E: How do those states interact with other psychological features?
Question F: How do they evolve over time?
Question G: What is their epistemological and rational role?
Question H: In what ways, if any, are they valuable?
Question I: What neural and computational structures are associated with them?

We may profitably formulate and assess answers to these (and other) questions without having total information about the history and constitution of consciousness. Hence no answer to these questions would count as contributions to the hard problem either given the standard we have just set out.

If we interpret Question A as asking for total information about the constitution and history of consciousness, therefore, Premise 1 above should be rejected. Of course, one might say now that Question A should *not* be interpreted as asking for total information but rather for partial information, or better partial information of a contextually relevant sort. If so, Premise 1 certainly becomes plausible. But, unfortunately for the proponent of the no answer objection, now Premise 2 is *im*plausible! For the epistemic view *does* provide partial information of this sort. If they are sound, the famous arguments in philosophy of mind about zombies, Mary, inverted spectra, and the rest will tell us something extremely dramatic, namely, that consciousness marks a major constitutional and historical break in the system of nature. The suggestion of the epistemic view is that we can reject those arguments so long as we agree that we are ignorant of certain features of the situation—something that is highly plausible in any case.

22.8 Conclusion

My main aim has been to set out the elements of the epistemic approach to the problem of consciousness, and to respond to two objections. Obviously there are further objections to consider; I will not take them up here. Let me instead end by asking why the epistemic approach is not more common than it is.

In saying this, I am not denying the view has had defenders; on the contrary, we noted a number of extremely distinguished ones at the outset. What I mean rather is that the bulk of contemporary philosophers and scientists of mind these days give it short shrift, or at least so it seems to me. Why so?

Partly the answer is that people are not clear enough on what the view is, on what questions it is trying to answer and, more importantly, what questions it is not trying to answer. For example, one common mistake is that the proponent of the epistemic view is no better than Bill whom we met before. But I think there are also deeper issues at work here, issues having to do with some of the dominant ways we have had in the last hundred years of framing and pursuing philosophical problems.

It is not too much of an exaggeration to say that philosophy of mind, and philosophy in general, in the last hundred years has had two main phases: a positivist phase and a post-positivist phase. The positivist phase is typified by Carnap and has been recently revived and reimagined in interesting ways by David Chalmers (see Carnap 1967; Chalmers 2012). The main idea of this approach is to assume, first, that there is a base language whose constituent expressions we understand and, second, that every truth about the world bears the right kind of relation to a truth that can be formulated in this base language—base truths, as we may call them for short. Obviously, views of this kind may differ on what exactly the base language is, and what relation must obtain between all truths and base truths.

The post-positivist phase is typified by Quine and is widely represented in contemporary philosophy (see, e.g., Quine 1953, 1960). The main idea of this approach is to assume, first, that we have a set of base facts given to us by contemporary science and, second, that something is a fact only if it bears the right sort of relation to one of these base facts. Obviously again, views of this kind may differ on what exactly the base facts are, and what relation other facts must bear to these base facts.

On the surface there is a lot that differentiates the Carnapian and the Quinean. The Carnapian view lends itself to the formal mode, the Quinean view to the material mode. Quineans tend to interpret themselves as privileging science over philosophy and criticize Carnapians for doing the opposite. Carnapians tend to be more sympathetic to conceptual analysis and the a priori than Quineans.

But these differences should not blind us to the fact that there is also something deeply similar here. Both views tend to assume that philosophical problems take the form of explaining various problematic sentences or facts by relating them in acceptable ways to sentences or facts of an approved sort. This sets up a very strong expectation about what a contribution to the hard problem of consciousness will look like: in the Carnapian case, it will be an account of how sentences about consciousness relate to sentences in the base language which we understand; in the Quinean case, it will be an account of how facts about consciousness relate to facts presented to us in contemporary science which again we understand.

I think there is no doubt that the epistemic view of the hard problem violates expectations of this sort. It does not 'explain' consciousness in this sense. However, this is more a problem for these expectations than for the epistemic view. Of course we would like an explanation of consciousness in the sense mentioned in the previous section: the provision of contextually relevant information about the history and constitution of consciousness. But nothing here requires that the information in question be provided in ways recommended either by Carnap or Quine. A more plausible view is that this information will be provided over the long term by a combined effort of various different disciplines and enterprises. Philosophy of mind is one of these disciplines, and an important one, but not the only one.

It is at points like these that we arrive at one of the most interesting aspects of the epistemic approach to the hard problem of consciousness. Not only is the view historically important, and extremely plausible from a scientific and philosophical point of view. It also represents a way of doing philosophy that is quite different from the ways we have settled into in the last hundred years.

References

Alter, T. (2016), 'The Structure and Dynamics Argument Against Materialism', Noûs [OR 2016, 50/4: 794–815]

Alter, T. and Howell, R. (eds.) (2012), *Consciousness and the Mind-Body Problem: A Reader*. Oxford: Oxford University Press.

Arnauld, A. (1641), 'Fourth Set of Objections to Descartes' *Meditations*' in J. Cottingham et al (eds) (1985b), *The Philosophical Writings of Rene Descartes*, Volume II. Cambridge: Cambridge University Press.

Braddon Mitchell, D. and Jackson, F. (2007), *Philosophy of Mind and Cognition*, 2nd edn. Oxford: Wiley-Blackwell.

Du Bois Reymond, E. (1872), 'The Nature of Scientific Knowledge' in E. Du Bois-Reymond (1886), *Reden von Emil Du-Bois-Reymond* [Addresses of Emil du Bois-Reymond]. Leipzig: Erste Folge, Verlag von Veit & Comp.

Carnap, R. (1967), *The Logical Structure of the World*. Berkeley, CA: University of California Press (Original publication in German: 1928).

Chalmers, D. (2012), *Constructing the World*. Oxford: Oxford University Press.

Chalmers, D. and Jackson, F. (2001), 'Conceptual Analysis and Reductive Explanation', *Philosophical Review*, 110/3: 315–61.

Chomsky, N. (1975), *Reflections on Language*. London: Pantheon Books.

Chomsky, N. (2000), *New Horizons in the Study of Mind and Language*. Cambridge: Cambridge University Press.

Demircioglu, E. (2017), 'Human Cognitive Closure and Mysterianism: Reply to Kriegel', *Acta Analytica*, 32/1: 125–32.

Flanagan, O. (1992), *Consciousness Reconsidered*. Cambridge, MA: MIT Press.

Fodor, J. (2000), Review of Chomsky's *New Horizons in the Study of Language and Mind*, Times Literary Supplement.

Jackson, F. (1982), 'Epiphenomenal Qualia', *Philosophical Quarterly*, 32: 127–36. Reprinted in P. Ludlow, Y. Nagasawa, and D. Stoljar (eds), *There's Something About Mary: Essays on Phenomenal Consciousness and Frank Jackson's Knowledge Argument*. Cambridge, MA: MIT Press, 2004; references to the reprinted version.

Kriegel, U. (2003), 'The new mysterianism and the thesis of cognitive closure', *Acta Analytica*, 18/30–31: 177–91.

Lewis, D. (1986), 'Causal Explanation' in D. Lewis, *Philosophical Papers, Vol. II*. New York and Oxford: Oxford University Press, 214–40.

Lewis, D. (1999), 'Reduction of Mind' in *Papers in Metaphysics and Epistemology* (Cambridge: Cambridge University Press, 1999), 291–324. First published in S. Guttenplan, (ed.), *A Companion to Philosophy of Mind*. London: Blackwell, 1994.

Locke, J. (1975), *An Essay Concerning Human Understanding* ed. P. H. Nidditch. Oxford: Oxford University Press. Original Publication: 1689.

McGinn, C. (1989), 'Can We Solve the Mind-Body Problem?' *Mind*, 98: 349–66.

McGinn, C. (1991), *The Problem of Consciousness*. Cambridge: Blackwell.
McGinn, C. (2004), *Consciousness and Its Objects*. Oxford: Clarendon Press.
Nagel, T. (1974), 'What Is It Like to Be a Bat?' *Philosophical Review*, 83: 435–50.
Pinker, S. (2007), The Brain: The Mystery of Consciousness Time, available at: http://content.time.com/time/magazine/article/091711580394-600.html
Priestley, J. (1777), 'Of the Properties of Matter', in J. Passmore, (ed.), *Priestley's Writings on Philosophy, Science and Politics*. New York: Collier Books, 1965, 103–7.
Quine, W. V. O. (1953), *From a Logical Point of View*. Cambridge, MA: MIT Press.
Quine, W. V. O. (1960), *Word and Object*. Cambridge, MA: MIT Press.
Russell, B. (1927), *The Analysis of Matter*. London: Kegan Paul.
Shepherd, G. M. (1991), *Foundations of the Neuron Doctrine*. Oxford: Oxford University Press.
Stoljar, D, (2005), 'Review of McGinn's *Consciousness and Its Objects*', *Notre Dame Philosophical Reviews*.
Stoljar, D. (2006), *Ignorance and Imagination*. New York: Oxford University Press.
Stoljar, D. (2010), *Physicalism*. London and New York: Routledge.
Stoljar, D. (2015), 'Russellian Monism or Nagelian Monism?' in T. Alter and Y. Nagasawa (eds), *Consciousness in the Physical World: Perspectives on Russellian Monism*. New York: Oxford University Press, 324–45.
Stoljar, D. (2017), *Philosophical Progress: In Defence of Reasonable Optimism* Oxford: Oxford University Press.
Wittgenstein, L. (1960), *The Blue and Brown Books*. Oxford: Basil Blackwell.

PART III

CONSCIOUSNESS AND NEIGHBORING PHENOMENA

CHAPTER 23

CONSCIOUSNESS AND ATTENTION

CHRISTOPHER MOLE

According to one tradition of philosophical theorizing, it is attention that transforms the stream of consciousness into a place where epistemically significant business can be transacted. It is only in the *attentive* mind that decisions are consciously reached, and personal-level inferences drawn; only there that complex properties are consciously experienced as belonging to temporally extended objects (of a sort that can be tracked and reencountered over time); and only there that stored information gets consciously recollected. According to this tradition—which has its roots in Saint Augustine's *De trinitatae* (Book 11, Chapter 2)—an inattentive mind is not yet the mind of a person who consciously perceives, or makes judgements about, any *thing* in particular. The inattentively experienced world is not yet perceived as a coherently structured set of things, and the inattentively remembered world is not yet recollected as a coherently structured set of facts. Information in the inattentive mind may exert a rationally appropriate influence, and it may enter into consciousness whilst doing so, but the inattentive subject does not act in conscious recognition of her reasons. The inattentive mind is one in which 'the sounds of the world melt into confused unity,... and the foreground of consciousness is filled, if by anything, by a sort of solemn sense of surrender to the empty passing of time' (James 1890/1981: 382).

The ideas motivating this line of thought can be developed in several ways, and they have been developed quite differently at different moments in the history of our theorizing (Ward 1918; Deutsch and Deutsch 1963; Evans 1970; Smithies 2011). Some ways of developing them are made clearer by construing 'attention' broadly, so that people who are distracted by a thing thereby count as giving it some part of their attention. Others are made clearer by construing attention more narrowly, so that a thing only counts as receiving our attention if it has been the cynosure of (some relevant subset of) our psychological activities (Mole 2011). The English language allows both strict and narrow uses of the word 'attention': it allows us to speak of a distracted person as exhibiting one sort of attention (by paying fleeting attention to the things by which he is distracted); but it allows us to speak just as properly as if this person were a paradigm of *in*attention (since it is only in a willy-nilly fashion that his psychological resources are allocated). This can create the appearance of contradictions where the only real disagreement is between two precisifications of a vague term (de Brigard 2010). There is therefore a risk that merely verbal disagreements will be mistaken for substantive ones. To minimize this risk it is helpful to keep empirical results at the centre of our philosophical enquiry.

Many such results have been established, the majority of which pertain to *perceptual* attention, the presence of which is indicated by a speeding up of our reaction times to visually (or sometimes auditorily) presented stimuli. In the discussion that follows I focus almost exclusively on the form of attention that is indicated by such behavioural measures, saying nothing about the considerable body of empirical literature employing electroencephalography and magnetic resonance imaging.

Perceptual attention (of the sort that has speeded reaction times as its behavioural signature) has always been a central topic for experimental psychologists. Their research into it has often been conducted in the hope of illuminating the relationship between attention and consciousness. During certain phases of psychology's history that hope tended not to be avowed, since 'consciousness' was a trouble-making word, but even in those periods the relationship of attention to consciousness remained a matter of concern, with the researchers who studied attention sometimes being accused of using 'attention' as 'a code word for consciousness' (Allport 1980).

The wealth of data that has been generated by this psychological research does not prevent verbal disagreements from arising. On some occasions it serves only to reclothe disputes about definition, so that these appear in the guise of disputes about operationalization. The benefit that comes from focusing on the data is that doing so enables disputes about the meanings of 'attention' and 'consciousness' to become disputes over which conceptualization gives the best account of the empirically attested phenomena. Our disputes are thereby prevented from descending into *mere* clashes of semantic taste, even if the points that are at issue must remain, in part, semantic ones.

In the last decades of the twentieth century the main stream of psychological research into attention was strongly influenced by Anne Treisman's Feature Integration Theory (a theory that can be thought of as a refinement of Donald Broadbent's 'Early Selection Theory', by which the topic of attention was established as a central explanandum for post-behaviourist psychology, following the cognitive-revolution that Broadbent himself helped to precipitate (Broadbent 1958; Treisman and Gelade 1980). Treisman tentatively suggested that some theory descended from this line 'should give us all the information there is about the conditions that create consciousness' (Treisman 2003: 111). Some philosophers have been inclined to agree, and have given psychological theories of attention a central role in their accounts of the way in which consciousness is achieved (Baars 1988; Prinz 2011, 2012). Among psychologists the supposition that attention should play some role in the explanation of consciousness is widespread, although there is little consensus as to the form that this role should take.

23.1 INATTENTIVE CONSCIOUSNESS

Treisman's 'Feature Integration Theory' is a theory of the way in which information from partly independent processing streams gets bound together into the representation of a single object, so that the perceiver is not only aware of which colours and shapes are present, but also of the ways in which those colours and shapes belong together, as the colours and shapes of distinct objects. The evidence supporting this theory is of the first importance for understanding the way in which consciousness might be structured in the absence of focal attention. It is therefore important for understanding the way in which the focusing of attention influences the structure of consciousness.

One early source of evidence, on which Treisman builds, is our ability quickly to detect boundaries between visual stimuli of various types. If the visual field is divided into two halves because only vertical lines appear on one side and only horizontal lines appear on the other then this will be perceived as a divided scene, even before attention has been focused on any of the individual lines. The boundary between horizontal and vertical lines—and therefore the difference between verticality and horizontality—seems to be registered without attention needing to be paid. (The registration of these orientations might still be modulated by attention, even though attention is not always necessary for it (Yeshurun and Carrasco 1998).) If the division between the two halves of the visual field is instead marked by Ts appearing on one side and Ls appearing on the other—so that it is the way in which vertical and horizontal lines are *combined* that is crucial—then this division will become perceptually apparent only once attention has been given to some of these letters (Beck 1967; Treisman and Gelade 1980). The same is true if vertical and horizontal lines appear on both sides of the screen, but with black verticals and white horizontals on one side, and white verticals and black horizontals on the other (Wolfe 1992). This suggests that attention has a role in facilitating the recognition of properties *in combination*.

Treisman finds further support for that suggestion by considering the response times of people who are searching for some specified item among a field of distractors. These response times indicate that items are easy to find if they differ from the accompanying distractors in some one feature. Items of that sort are easy to find, whether they occur in a field of many distractors or few. In this respect such items contrast with those that share each one of their individual features with the surrounding distractors, but which differ from those distractors in the way in which these features are combined. The response time data indicate that items of the latter sort take very much longer to find, and that the task of finding them gets progressively harder as the number of distractors increases. For an example that illustrates this, consider the task of finding a red circle, somewhere on a computer screen. This will be easy if the other items on the screen are all blue circles, and will be just as easy if they are all red triangles. In those cases the target circle's unique redness or unique circularity will 'pop out' from the surrounding field of distractors, so that the red circle can be located straightaway, even if this surrounding field is large. A red circle will, however, be hard to find if redness and circularity are both present among the distractors surrounding it. In that case the addition of more distractors will tend to make the search take longer, and the experience of searching will be one of checking each potential target in turn, rather than of surveying the field and allowing the target to pop out (Treisman and Gormican 1988).

Many variations on these results have been investigated, and the basic effect that they illustrate has been found to generalize well, needing only slight qualifications (Quinlan 2003). Even once these qualifications are in place, the results suggest that most *combinations* of perceptible properties can be identified only once attention has been paid to the things by which those properties are instantiated, whereas the *simple* properties of a scene can be identified immediately that the scene is perceived. This can be taken as empirical support for one version of the traditional idea with which we began: it can be taken as showing that consciousness in the absence of attention does not yet have many-propertied objects among its contents (except, perhaps, in the case where there is only one perceptible object present, and so no possibility that this object's properties will be misascribed to some other object). It can also be taken as showing that some part of the structure that makes consciousness epistemically useful is dependent on attention being paid.

Experiments that have been inspired by Treisman's work often require their participants to search for items in a crowded scene. The completion of such a search requires these participants to form a judgement about where the searched-for item occurs. It indicates that this searched-for item has figured in the participant's consciousness, but also that the participant has made a judgement about its having done so. The results of such experiments are therefore compatible with a range of positions concerning the consequences for consciousness of attention's not having yet been paid. Some of these positions emphasize the consequences of inattention for *consciousness*. Others emphasize the consequences of inattention for the possibility of *making judgements*. One position says that conscious awareness in the absence of attention is still the awareness of many-propertied objects, although those properties are not reliably assigned to the *correct* objects (Cohen and Ivry 1989). A different position says that consciousness in the absence of attention is not consciousness of objects at all, but only consciousness of unstructured gist (Rensink 2005). A third says that consciousness in the absence of attention is absolutely empty (and this last position is perhaps equivalent to saying that there is no such consciousness (Mack and Rock 1998; Noë and O'Regan 2000)). Various other positions also become tenable once certain distinctions have been drawn, such as a distinction between the consequences of attention being withdrawn from a stimulus, and the consequences of the stimulus having never yet been attended (Wheeler and Treisman 2002); or between the consequences of a stimulus falling outside the locus of attention, and the consequences of that stimulus being presented on an occasion when no attention is being paid to the perceived world.

One of these more various positions follows Treisman in saying that properties falling outside the locus of attention are merely strung together, and are not yet differentially assigned to different objects, but it adds that the same is true for properties falling within the locus of attention, if attention is spread across several objects: On this view the consequence of attending is to structure the field of consciousness into a two-part 'Boolean Map', so that one subset of currently experienced properties is consciously experienced as being instantiated in one portion of the perceived space, with the complement set of these properties being assigned, without any further differentiation, to the remainder of that space (Huang and Pashler 2007; Campbell 2011).

These several conceptions of inattentive consciousness are quite different from each other, but they can nonetheless be difficult to distinguish empirically. A much-publicized series of experiments, showing that people often fail to notice unexpected events if these occur whilst attention is directed elsewhere, were once thought to favour the view that inattentive consciousness is empty (Simons and Levin 1997; Simons et al. 2002). The extent of such failures has, however, been prone to overstatement. It is true that many people fail to notice the appearance of a pantomime gorilla if they are engaged in a task that involves ignoring the other black-clad figures who surround him, but it is also true that plenty of participants do notice this gorilla, especially if they have relevant expertise (Memmert 2006). It might be that those who notice the gorilla happen to give him some attention. It might also be that these people have an inattentive consciousness of gist, the contents of which include some indication of the gorilla's presence, even before their attention has been shifted to it. The effects that have been observed in these experiments therefore fail to adjudicate between those who think that unattended consciousness is empty and those who think that it has some gist as its content (Schwitzgebel 2007; Mole 2008). To settle that dispute a more subtle experimental design is needed. The dual task paradigm adopted by Li, VanRullen, Koch, and Perona employs one (Li et al. 2002). The tasks that are performed in it are unusually demanding, involving hours of training and thousands of stimuli, but the logic of the paradigm is nonetheless straightforward. The results of a single experiment can never be conclusive, but the results of this one are far less equivocal than the experiments demonstrating inattentional blindness or change blindness. Its details are worth considering.

23.1.1 The Li, VanRullen, Koch, and Perona Experiment

The participants in Li et al.'s experiment were first given the task of discerning whether a set of five letters are all the same, or have an odd-one-out amongst them. All the letters were either Ls or Ts. They were presented at random orientations, in a somewhat randomly arranged cluster, in the centre of the visual field. Very shortly after they had been presented, each of these letters was masked by an F.[1] Detecting an odd-one-out amongst them was therefore difficult.

---

[1] The use of one stimulus to mask a previously presented one—as here, where Fs are used to mask Ts and Ls, and patterns of textured noise are used to mask photographs—is a standard technique in experimental psychology. The rationale for using this masking procedure is that the appearance of the mask not only removes the previous stimulus, but also removes any residual information about that stimulus that might persist on the retina, or at other stages of very early visual processing (Kahneman 1968).

To ensure that this task had a similar level of difficulty for each participant the time for which these letters were displayed, prior to being masked, was adjusted for each of the experimental participants individually: each started out with a 500ms exposure to the letters; this was reduced progressively if they were able to perform the odd-one-out detection with better than 85 per cent accuracy. All of the participants were eventually making reliable judgements about whether the cluster of five letters contained an odd-one-out, in conditions where these letters had been masked after less than 250ms. (Only one participant was excluded from this experiment because its tasks proved too demanding.)

Since the letters in this first task are presented in the centre of the visual field, there is plenty of space in the periphery of the screen on which they appear. In the second part of the experiment—which is the interesting part—this space is also used. In this second part of the experiment clusters of five letters continue to be presented in the centre of the screen, and—exactly as before—the participants have to indicate whether these are the same or include one letter that is different. Fifty-three milliseconds after each cluster has appeared a photograph is flashed for 27ms, at some random location on the screen's periphery. After a few more tens of milliseconds (with the precise duration again being adjusted to fit the ability of each participant) a pattern mask is presented in the place where this photograph has been shown. In addition to judging whether the central letters contain an odd-one-out, the participants are now asked to indicate, using a mouse button, whether an animal was present in this peripherally-flashed photograph.

It bears emphasis that the durations involved in this experiment are extraordinarily brief. There is scarcely more than one twentieth of a second between the letters having first appeared and the photograph appearing on the screen beside them. That photograph remains on screen for an even briefer period. It gets masked whilst the letters remain present, and this mask remains where the picture was shown until the end of the trial. Shortly after the photograph is masked the letters are too. All of these things happen within one quarter of a second. The participants then have two responses to make. With a keypress of the left hand they indicate whether the letters were the same or included one that is different (pressing 'S' for same and 'D' for different). By releasing a mouse button with the right hand they indicate whether an animal was present in the photographed scene.

The results show that subjects can reliably indicate the presence of animals in these briefly flashed photographs, whether or not they are performing the odd-letter-out task concurrently. Their performance in these two concurrent tasks is not correlated, positively or negatively, and does not get noticeably worse or better if less information-rich black and white photographs are used, nor if two photographs are shown, with an animal in at most one of them (Li et al. 2005). That is all the more remarkable because the same subjects *cannot* perform the odd-letter-out task concurrently with perceptual tasks that are considerably simpler than photographed-animal detection. Crucially, their performance on the odd-letter task drops back to chance if these concurrent tasks are attention-demanding: If, instead of photographs from natural scenes, the participants are asked to judge the vertical or horizontal orientation of a half red and half green circle, their performance goes from being good, when this circle is presented on its own, to being at chance when it is presented concurrently with the letter task. If, instead of photographs from natural scenes, the participants are peripherally presented with one additional letter, and are asked to judge whether this is a T or an L, their performance is, again, a matter of chance, or else it detracts from their performance on the central task. In sum: the participants in this experiment show an ability to detect the presence of animals in peripherally-flashed photographs, without thereby reducing their concurrent performance on a central task the difficulty of which has been adjusted so that it apparently demands their full attention. They have no such ability to detect the orientation of a two-coloured circle, or the identity of an additional letter. The authors of this study claim that its results indicate a conscious experience of gist in the '*near*-absence' of attention. There is room to dispute whether that is the correct interpretation, but the results do at least show that the depiction of an animal in a photograph registers somehow with subjects, even when such resources of attention as would be required for the detection of a circle's orientation are not available to be directed onto that photograph.

23.1.2 Interpreting the Li et al. Results

The presence of an animal might seem to be a special sort of content, of sufficient importance in our evolutionary history that it might feasibly be processed by an independent processing channel. One might therefore think that Li et al.'s result can be explained away—as showing only that some special processing resources are held in reserve for the detection of animals (but not for the detection of oriented circles). A variation of the basic result rules out this interpretation: Li et al. were able to replicate their finding in a version of their experiment where it was the presence of *vehicles* that needed to be detected, and where their animal-including photographs were among the distractors in their set of photographic stimuli. Since the presence of vehicles can be detected in the same conditions as the presence of animals, and since vehicles played no special role in our evolutionary history, specially evolved channels seem not to have any role here. Nor could it be that this finding depends on the fact that there are special processing resources dedicated to the processing of faces (resources that might sometimes be activated by the face-like features of certain vehicles (Gauthier et al. 2000)). The animal pictures used in the study showed animals in various naturalistic scenes. They included such things as birds on the wing, and a caterpillar on a leaf. They were not photographs of animal faces. Since a role for special face- or animal- specific processing channels is ruled out, the results of these experiments do seem to indicate that, even when attention cannot be directed to a part of the visual field, there is some experience of the gist of things that are, very briefly, presented there. The content of this gist is sufficiently rich that it can provide information about the presence of animals or of vehicles. This suggests that consciousness in the absence of attention is neither impossible nor empty. If one wants to reject this suggestion one must maintain either that the presence of animals is *not* consciously registered by these experimental participants, or else one must claim that attention *is* paid to the pictures in which the animals appear. Both claims have been mooted in the literature; the first by Kentridge (2011: 235) the second by Cohen et al. (2012).

Maintaining that participants have no conscious awareness of the animals whose presence they report leaves us needing to give an explanation for the accuracy of those reports. Following a suggestion of Kentridge, one might attempt to explain it with the conjecture that the responses voluntarily made by these experimental participants should be thought of on the model of a blindsighter's guesses. This conjecture is hard to assess, partly because it is hard to know whether there was anything guess-like about the mouse-button responses by which the presence of animals was accurately indicated. Participants in this experiment were not kept in ignorance of the hypothesis being tested. (Two of them were the experimenters themselves.) Their introspective judgements as to whether they were guessing or reporting on the basis of a conscious experience would therefore have been susceptible to bias. It is perhaps for this reason that the authors report no introspective data that might indicate whether the participants' animal-indicating responses were experienced as guess-like. Even if this experiment were replicated with unbiased subjects, the question of whether one's response to a fleeting stimulus is guess-like would seem to be at the limits of what introspective judgement could resolve. The introspective judgements of unbiased participants—if there could be such things—would not settle the question of whether the accuracy of their voluntary performance is explained by information that figures in the conscious experience by which that performance is triggered.

We might look for evidence of the photographs being consciously experienced by looking for evidence of their presentation being consciously *recollected*. There is evidence suggesting that very fleetingly presented stimuli *can* be consciously recollected (VanRullen and Koch 2003), but this evidence is somewhat controversial (Liu and Jiang 2005), and the experiments from which it comes made no particular efforts to ensure that attention was kept away from the fleetingly-presented stimuli that were used. That being so, we can say only that the capacity of participants to respond accurately to the presence of animals in Li et al.'s photographs provides defeasible evidence that the gist of those photographs was consciously perceived. It must be admitted that— until the possibility of blindsight-like guessing is ruled out—this evidence is less than conclusive.

The alternative route by which one might hope to block the inference from Li et al.'s result to the conclusion that there is inattentive consciousness of gist would be by claiming that the photographs in which animals are detected do receive some of the participant's attention. This would require attention to be *divided* between the photographs and the letter task. Postulating a division of attention might seem to be avoidable were one able to maintain that attention is switched very rapidly from one set of stimuli to the other, but a switching account cannot be maintained in the current case: there is insufficient time for a switch of attention to be executed—(such shifts take about 175ms to complete (Egeth and Yantis 1997))—and the participants need all of the time that is available in order to maintain their level of performance in the letter task. It is here that the individual adjustment of stimulus timings is crucial: When the participants were asked to increase the speed at which they performed the letter task (in some additional trials, immediately after the main experiment) they were unable to perform successfully at higher speeds. In order to maintain that attention has been paid to the photographs one must therefore maintain that attention is paid to them whilst the letter task is *also* receiving attention. One must maintain that this division of attention results in no deterioration in the performance of either task, despite the fact that performance on the letter task *does* become disrupted when attention is divided between that task and the task of detecting the orientation of a two-coloured circle, or the task of recognizing a further letter. To defend the claim that attention is necessary for consciousness one must therefore say that the participants in this experiment are paying attention to the photographs of whose gist they are conscious, but one must also maintain that the processes by which this attention is constituted are not general-purpose attention-processes (since the inability of those same participants to detect the orientation of the two-coloured circle shows that these experimental conditions are ones in which no *general* attention resources are available).

As ever when a single experiment is at issue, there is room for manoeuvre in determining exactly which positive lessons should here be drawn. The experiment of Li et al. does, nonetheless, provide good evidence for something important. If one is committed to the view that consciousness without attention is impossible then the results of the Li et al. experiments require that you endorse at least one of the following two positions. The first says that voluntary responses to rapidly presented stimuli can show a blindsight-like tendency to carry accurate information that has never been registered in consciousness, including information about the presence of vehicles or animals. The second rejects the idea that there is some single channel of attention-constituting processes by which stimuli are brought into conscious awareness (since any attention-constituting process that brings the photographs to consciousness must be distinct from any attention-constituting process that might bring the orientation of the circle into consciousness).

Even if they do not refute the claim that consciousness is empty in the absence of attention, these experiments do undermine one conception of attention that has led some theorists to make that claim. They are incompatible with the conception of attention as a general-purpose process for the promotion of stimuli into consciousness, where consciousness is taken to be the place in which concepts like 'animal' and 'vehicle' are applied.

Our attempt to extract a moral from this experiment reveals one of the complications in the semantic dispute that was mentioned at the beginning of this chapter, and from which a focus on empirical results cannot entirely liberate us. That dispute was between an understanding of 'attention' on which one counts as paying attention to distracting things, to which one's mental resources are allocated only fleetingly, and an understanding on which one does not count as paying attention to such things, but only to things on which one has focused. The photographs that are peripherally flashed in Li et al.'s experiment have the character of penumbral cases in this dispute, falling on the borderline over which the different understandings disagree. A theorist who was hoping to avoid semantics might have hoped that the dispute could be settled by empirically discoverable facts about whether some particular process gets instantiated when these photographs are perceived. They might have thought that there must be some natural kind of process to which the English word 'attention' refers. They would then have thought that there must be a fact about whether this process is or is not involved when the penumbral cases occur, with such cases being included in the extension of the word 'attention' if and only if this process is involved. The results of Li et al.'s experiments do not settle our semantic question, but they do provide evidence that this conception of 'attention' as a natural kind term would be incompatible with the idea that attention is necessary for consciousness: if it were necessary then consciousness of the gist of the photographs would entail that attention had been paid to those photographs, and so would entail that processing resources of the relevant natural kind are available to be deployed in the contexts where those photographs are presented, but this would leave us without an explanation for the evidence indicating that attention cannot be paid to a two-coloured circle, when it is present in a similar context.

23.1.3 Inattentive Consciousness: Open Questions

The most plausible accounts of inattentive consciousness take it to be consciousness of *gist*. This concept of gist remains undefined. Even if we take the Li et al. results to indicate that consciousness in the absence of attention cannot be entirely empty, those results tell us rather little about the sorts of gist-like contents that such consciousness might have. To be told that it includes animal-relevant gist, and vehicle-relevant gist, is not yet to be told very much. Experiments by Evans and Treisman have indicated that, when stimuli are presented for such brief periods, the inattentive perception of gist does not include content that is rich enough to enable subjects to make reliable judgements about *which* animals are present, or about where (Evans and Treisman 2005). This suggests that the gist perceived in these experiments is only very schematic, but it does not enable us to conclude that unattended consciousness has content that is always impoverished in this way: its impoverishment in the present case might be attributed to the extraordinarily brief presentation of the stimuli, rather than to their unattendedness. Since any stimulus that is presented for a longer time would be around for long enough that attention might be directed to it, we do not yet have a paradigm that enables this confound to be resolved.

The experiments that we have been considering are consistent with (and suggestive of) the traditional thought with which we began: They suggest that in the absence of attention the stream of consciousness is not yet in a position to do certain sorts of epistemic work, and so they provide some corroboration for the idea that attention does something for consciousness: something that endows it with a new structure, or with new representational capacities. They do not tell us much about what this structure might be. Conjectures concerning it can be found in Koralus (2014); Jennings (2015); and Watzl (2017).

Other explanatory relations between consciousness and the paying of attention remain possible, and these relations might be intimate ones, even if we exclude the idea that attention to a thing is necessary for consciousness of it. One suggestion that has recently been made is that—rather than explaining how items in the perceived world come to be *objects* of consciousness—the paying of attention might explain how the persons who perceive those items come to be aware of themselves as conscious *subjects*. Proponents of this suggestion claim that consciousness involves forming an internal model of one's own perceiving, where this model can be used in exerting control over the direction of that perceiving (Graziano 2013). Controlled perception and the representation of oneself as a subject of perception are therefore taken as coming together, in the sense that the representations required for perceptual control play a central role in the explanation of both; with 'controlled perception' being understood as an essential part of attention, and 'the representation of oneself as a subject' being understood as an essential part of consciousness. Some of philosophy's established claims about the relationship between consciousness and higher order thought would be applicable to this proposal, but philosophers have not yet engaged directly with it. Empirical investigations of it are in their infancy (Webb et al. 2016).

23.2 Unconscious Attention

Section 23.1 made the case against thinking of attention as a single limited-capacity process by the operation of which information enters consciousness. (It also acknowledged that this case is not a conclusive one.) In retreating from the view that attention explains consciousness, one might be tempted by a theory that inverts that explanatory order: rather than thinking of attention as coming first, and of consciousness as being explained or partly explained by it, one might be tempted by a view according to which consciousness comes first, and 'attention' is taken to be a name for the thing that happens when consciousness takes a certain form. One version of this approach would identify attention with conscious foregrounding (Wundt 1912). Such a view would take attending to a thing to be one special way of being conscious of it. Since a thing cannot be in the foreground if that thing is nowhere in the picture, such views must take attention to operate entirely within the field of consciousness.

The second half of this chapter shows that this alternative view of the relationship between attention and consciousness also needs to be rejected. Just as it would leave something out from our theory of consciousness if that theory applied only to attentive consciousness (for there may be inattentive consciousness of gist), so it would leave something out from our theory of attention if that theory applied only to conscious attention (for there may be processes of attention that operate entirely beyond the reach of consciousness). We should therefore reject the claim that consciousness is necessary for attention, together with the claim that attention is necessary for consciousness. This requires us to reject the idea that attention is identical to conscious foregrounding.

The rejection of these views is compatible with maintaining that it will very often be the case that attention plays a role in explaining why it is that a person is conscious of something, rather than being oblivious to it; why it is that a person is conscious of one thing, rather than another; and why a person's consciousness is structured in the particular way that it is. These latter claims should be relatively uncontroversial, since a great many well-entrenched explanatory practices depend upon them. Those are not practices that we need to give up. We do not need to give up the idea that distracted drivers are dangerous, that preoccupied students get lost in lectures, and that misdirected audiences fail to notice the magician's sleight of hand, *because*, in each case, their lack of attention makes them unaware of certain things (Forster and Lavie 2016). These explanations require attention to play some role in the orchestration of our conscious resources, but it can play that role without being necessary or sufficient for those resources to operate.

The argument against taking attention to be an entirely conscious phenomenon proceeds by showing that there are at least two ways in which such a view would go wrong. It would go wrong by implying that the things to which attention is paid must themselves be things that are consciously experienced; and it would go wrong by implying that the effects of attention must be effects that manifest themselves within the conscious field. It might also go wrong by implying that an attentive subject must be conscious of the way in which her attention is directed. The evidence showing that these implications are mistaken comes from three different empirical sources. The following sections consider them.

23.2.1 The Allocation of Attention Need not be Consciously Experienced

More than one line of evidence indicates that subjects may be unaware of the way in which their attention is directed, and unaware of the stimulus-properties (and perhaps also of the stimuli) that cause it to be so directed. One property that can cause attention to be directed onto a stimulus is the suddenness of its appearance. An experiment by Mulckhuyse, Talsma, and Theeuwes required participants to respond as soon as possible to a target that was flashed up on a screen where three grey circles had previously appeared (Mulckhuyse et al. 2007). In some trials one or other of those circles had appeared 16ms earlier than the others. That is too small a difference to be consciously noticed, and each of the participants in this experiment performed at chance when asked to indicate whether any early onset had occurred. Targets that subsequently appeared at the location of the circle that had had an earlier onset were nonetheless responded to more rapidly than targets that appeared elsewhere. The early onset of a circle therefore seems to draw the attention, without the attentive subject being conscious of it.

Early onset is a very simple attention-drawing property; so simple that one might think that the reaction-time benefits observed in this experiment could be understood as being the result of some early-perceptual priming, of a sort that is more basic than the allocation of attention. That interpretation becomes untenable in the light of evidence indicating that more complex properties can also influence the allocation of attention without needing to make an appearance in the conscious awareness of the attentive subject. Zhao, Al-Aidroos, and Turk-Browne presented their subjects with four different meaningless symbols, one at the top of the screen, one at the bottom, one at the left, and one at the right (Zhao et al., 2013). These were presented for three quarters of a second. A brief pause followed, after which four more symbols appeared in the same locations. This continued for several minutes. Occasionally these four streams of symbols would be interrupted, and the four locations would instead show three L shapes and one T, with participants being asked to locate this T as quickly as possible. Each of the four locations had its own repertoire of nine meaningless hieroglyphs, with each location's hieroglyphs having a particular typographical style. At three of the locations these hieroglyphs were drawn from that location's repertoire at random, so that all nine of the symbols belonging to that location were shown in some order, before being shown again in some other order (with the only constraint being that no symbol ever followed itself). At the one remaining location the ordering of the hieroglyphs was rather less random: hieroglyphs one, two, and three were always given in that order, as were four, five, six, and seven, eight, nine. The order in which these complete triples followed one another was random, with the only constraint being that no ordered-triple ever followed itself. When the T that needed to be located among the Ls was shown in the less random location, the time taken to find it was relatively brief. This suggests that the subjects' attention had been drawn towards the one location in which the ordering of symbols was somewhat structured.

Here again the experimental participants seemed not to be conscious of the way in which their attention had been allocated: Even when the existence of a regularity in the ordering of symbols was mentioned during the experimental debriefing, only seven of the twenty-five participants claimed to have noticed any regularities in the stimuli, and only one of these correctly identified the location in which the regularity had been present. The difference in reaction time to targets that occur in the less-random location remains significant if the data from these seven participants are omitted. The effect of temporal structure on the allocation of attention therefore seems not to require that that structure be consciously registered. This suggests that even complex properties can unconsciously influence the direction of attention, and that they can do so even when they involve diachronic patterns, and therefore require for their detection that some sort of memory is put to work.

One further demonstration of attention being unconsciously modulated is given in a memorable experiment by Jiang, Costello, Fang, Huang, and He (Jiang et al. 2006). In this experiment a more complex technique was used to keep the attention-modulating stimuli from coming to consciousness, and a more complex method was also used to gauge the direction in which attention is paid. Jiang et al. presented their stimuli on a screen that was divided into two halves. They probed which side of this screen received more attention by measuring their participants' performance of a task that required them to judge the direction in which a briefly presented Gabor patch was tilted. Some of these patches appeared on the right-hand side of the screen, others on the left. Since the patches were tilted at an angle of just one degree, and since they were presented for only 100ms, their direction of orientation was hard to see, and it was judged more accurately if attention was directed to the side of space in which the relevant patch appeared. The modulation of this accuracy could therefore be used to indicate where attention was allocated.

Immediately before these Gabor patches appeared, the participants were presented for 800ms with a pair of brightly patterned grids, having been asked to judge if these were the same or different. These grids were shown to only one eye. Another pair of images was presented to the other eye, but because those images were shown at a lower contrast they never dominated in the resulting binocular rivalry, and so never came to be consciously experienced. Jiang et al. were therefore able to present erotic photographs, alongside scrambled versions of such photographs, concurrently with their brightly coloured grids, without the participants having any awareness of a photograph being shown. The presence of those photographs modulated the participants' attention, and the content of the photographs seems to play a role in explaining the way in which it did so, since the direction and magnitude of the attention-effects that were created by them depended on the participant's gender, and on their sexual orientation.

Such results have many implications. The most relevant for our purposes is that the processing which results in attention being directed to one part of the visual field need not be conscious: subjects can be unaware of the attention-modulating contents that are being processed, and they can be unaware that any such processing is taking place. The participants in Mulckhuyse et al.'s (2007) experiment are not aware that one of the circles has onset prior to the others, and yet it is information about this onset that modulates the direction of their attention. The participants in Zhao et al.'s (2013) experiment are not aware that they are encoding the temporal structure of the streams of symbols with which they are presented, and yet it is this information that modulates the direction of their attention. The participants in Jiang et al.'s (2006) experiment are not aware that they are processing any erotic information, and yet it is this information that modulates the direction of their attention. In none of these experiments do participants seem to be aware that their attention is allocated in anything other than a uniform fashion. It therefore seems that the allocation of attention, and the stimuli or stimulus properties that are the causes of it, can be unconscious.

23.2.2 Attention can be Allocated to Objects that are not Consciously Experienced

The experiments discussed above indicate that there are unconscious influences on attention, but the participants in each of those experiments were having normal conscious experience of the circles, or hieroglyphs, or Gabor patches, to which their attention was being directed, even if they were not aware of the rapid onset, the temporal structure, or the nude photographs that caused it to be so directed. These experiments therefore leave room in which one might attempt to maintain that attention is indeed a modification of consciousness, conceding only that it is a modification that is subject to unconscious influences. To refute that view one needs to show that attention can be allocated *to* items that are not consciously experienced, and not merely allocated *by* such items. For this, a different line of evidence is needed.

In order to show that attention has been paid to some particular object, it is not enough to have shown that there has been some change in the allocation of attention from which the perceptual processing of that object benefits. The processing of information pertaining to an object might benefit from attention's being allocated to some larger complex, of which that object is a part, without attention ever being paid to the object per se. The processing of information pertaining to an object might also benefit from attention's being allocated to some part of space within which that object falls, without attention ever being paid to the object per se (Mole 2014). In order to show that attention is being directed *to* some particular object (per se) we need to observe more than just a boosting of that object's processing. One effect that reveals attention's allocation to a particular object is the 'Same Object Advantage'. Before seeing the evidence that attention can be paid to objects that are not consciously perceived, we need to understand what this effect is. The clearest demonstrations of it are found in experiments where participants are presented with a screen similar to that shown in Figure 23.1.

If an attention-grabbing cue appears at location A, at the top of the left-hand rectangle, then the resulting shift of attention will influence the time taken to react to stimuli that are presented shortly afterwards at locations B and C (at the bottom of that rectangle, and at the top of the adjacent one). The reaction time to stimuli at C will be relatively slow. The reaction time to stimuli at B will be relatively fast. This difference is found despite the fact that locations B and C are at the same distance from location A. It depends on

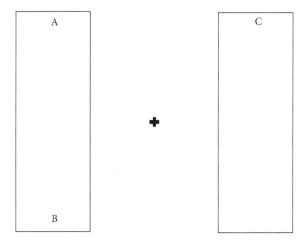

FIGURE 23.1 Stimulus and target locations in demonstrations of the Same Object Advantage (after Egly *et al.* 1994)

the fact that A and B fall within the same visual object, whereas A and C do not. This can be shown by reorienting the rectangles, so that it is now A and C that fall within the same object. Under those conditions the effect is reversed. This suggests that the cue which appears at A causes attention to be allocated *to the rectangle* on which that cue appears, and not just to the space in which that rectangle happens to be (Egly et al. 1994).

The evidence showing that attention can be allocated to objects that are not consciously experienced is evidence showing that this Same Object Advantage can be found, even when the rectangle that defines the attended object is presented unconsciously: such evidence comes from experiments in which cues appearing at A cause attention to be allocated to the rectangle of which A is a part, even when that rectangle does not figure in the conscious experience of the attentive subject.

Special measures need to be taken in order to prevent a pair of rectangles from being consciously seen, even whilst they are being shown in the location where an attention grabbing cue is presented, and where a stimulus to be responded to then appears. In a 2013 experiment by Norman, Heywood, and Kentridge, such rectangles were defined by a contrast of visual texture: the screen on which they were presented was filled by a 22×22 grid of Gabor patches, all of which had the same orientation except for those that fell within the two rectangles, which were perpendicular to the others (Norman et al. 2013). Since it was only this change of visual texture that defined these rectangles, they could be made invisible by alternating vertical and horizontal Gabor patches at a sufficiently high speed for each one of them to become a blur. When asked whether texture-defined rectangles are present on a screen that is filled with these rapidly-alternating Gabor patches, the guesses of participants carry no information at all. That gives good evidence that these rectangles are not being consciously experienced. Reaction-times to targets at locations B and C nonetheless indicate that attention-directing cues that are presented within these rectangles create the Same Object Advantage: when targets are subsequently presented at a location that is separated from the attention-directing cue those targets are detected relatively quickly if their location falls within the same invisible object as the cue, but they are detected relatively slowly if their location falls within a different invisible object. The effect reverses if these invisible rectangles are reoriented. The Same Object Advantage is therefore present, and so attention here seems to be allocated to an object that is not consciously experienced.

The significance of this result is best seen when it is paired with the results that we considered previously. We should distinguish between those stimuli that influence the direction of one's attention, and those to which attention is paid. In the experiments of Mulckhuyse et al. (2007), Zhao et al. (2013), and Jiang et al. (2006) the attention-modulating properties are not registered in consciousness, although the things to which attention is paid are so registered. In the experiments of Norman et al. (2013) it is the second of these that is not registered in consciousness, although the first is. Taken together, these results suggest that consciousness has no essential role to play in the explanation of attention's allocation: attention can be allocated to and by things of which the subject is not conscious, and the subject may be quite unaware of there being any process of allocation taking place.

23.2.3 Attention can Modulate Unconscious Processing

Even whilst rejecting the idea that attention to a thing *suffices* to bring that thing into consciousness, one might think that attention is essentially *conducive* to consciousness. The above results do not refute that position. Advocates of it might claim that consciousness occurs only once some threshold has been passed. Although the effects of attending may not be enough to bring a stimulus over that threshold, they might nonetheless be effects that essentially contribute to a stimulus's aptitude for coming into consciousness. Experiments by Sumner, Tsai, Yu, and Nachev suggest that this would be a mistake. In these experiments the stimuli that influence the direction of a person's attention are consciously experienced, as are the target stimuli about which a judgement must be made, but the processes that attention modulates are nonetheless unconscious ones. The meaning of this should become clearer once we have seen the effect that these experiments demonstrate.

The screen with which Sumner et al. (2006) presented their subjects showed a black background, against which there were two grey-framed rectangles, one above and one below a central fixation cross. Attention was directed to one of these rectangles, by having its grey outline turn white for 50ms. The participants' task was to indicate the direction of a pair of arrowheads, which appeared inside one of these rectangles for 100ms. Before the appearance of these arrowheads, but after the attention-directing cue, a masked prime was presented. This prime was another pair of arrowheads, presented in one or other of the rectangles (sometimes in the rectangle to which attention had been directed, sometimes not). In one experimental condition this prime was presented for 20ms. In another it was presented for 70ms. In both cases it was followed by a pattern mask. When these prime arrows were presented for 20ms, the participants were hardly able to see them, and performed at chance when asked to judge the direction in which they were pointing. When the arrows were presented for 70ms they became much easier to see, and the subjects were able to indicate their direction reliably (being somewhat more reliable when the prime appeared in the cued location than when it appeared in the uncued one).

In these conditions the effects of visible and invisible primes are very different: If subjects have been presented with a left-pointing prime, and are then required to indicate the direction of a subsequent target that is also left pointing, they are faster if this prime has been visible to them, but their reaction times to a subsequent arrow that is pointing in the same direction will be *slower* if this prime has been presented briefly enough to be invisible. Invisible arrows therefore create a kind of negative priming, whereas visible ones prime positively. The crucial finding from this experiment is that both the facilitative effects of consciously experienced arrows and the deleterious effects of unconsciously experienced arrows increase in magnitude when the prime which induces them appears in an attended location: whereas attended visible primes produce a stronger positive priming effect, attended invisible primes produce a stronger negative priming effect. If the effect of attention were to bring stimuli more fully into consciousness, one would expect that directing attention towards invisible primes would make them behave more like visible primes. Since the opposite is true, we should reject any theory according to which attention is essentially a consciousness-enhancing boost (even one in which that consciousness-enhancing boost sometimes fails to bring stimuli over the threshold required for consciousness). The effects of attention are often effects on consciousness, but they can also be effects on unconscious processing. The evidence suggests that these unconscious effects of attention are not sub-threshold versions of their conscious counterparts.

23.3 Conclusion

The introductory section of this chapter noted that the English word 'attention' can be used rather loosely. As a tactic for preventing our enquiry into attention's relationship to consciousness from lapsing into ill-definition, we resolved to treat 'attention' as a term to be defined by the role that is assigned to it in our explanations of empirically established psychological phenomena (especially those involving the modulation of reaction times). The evidence that we have reviewed in this chapter shows that such modulations are associated with processing that stands in various relations to consciousness. The psychological phenomena that explain such modulations should not be identified with the causes of consciousness, nor do they operate exclusively within the field of conscious awareness. If the explanation of those phenomena is to cast explanatory light on how and when consciousness occurs, it will need to do so in the context of some more complex explanatory theory. The development and testing of such theories is a topic for ongoing research.[2]

References

Allport, A. (1980), 'Attention and Performance' in G. Claxton (ed.), *Cognitive Psychology: New Directions*. London: Routledge and Kegan Paul, 112–53.

Augustine, (2012), *The Doctrinal Treatises of Saint Augustine*. Altenmünster, Germany: Jazzybee Verlag.

Baars, B.J. (1988), *A Cognitive Theory of Consciousness*. Cambridge: Cambridge University Press.

Beck, J. (1967), 'Perceptual grouping produced by line figures', *Perception & Psychophysics*, 2/11: 491–5.

Broadbent, D. E. (1958), *Perception and Communication*. New York: Pergamon Press.

Campbell, J. (2011), 'Visual attention and the epistemic role of consciousness' in C. Mole, D. Smithies, and W. Wu (eds), *Attention: Philosophical and Psychological Essays*. New York: Oxford University Press, 323–41.

---

[2] Many thanks to the editor, for providing very helpful comments on a first draft of this chapter.

Cohen, A. and Ivry, R. (1989), 'Illusory conjunctions inside and outside the focus of attention', *Journal of Experimental Psychology: Human Perception and Performance*, 14/4: 650–63.

Cohen, M. A., Cavanagh, P., Chun, M. M., and Nakayama, K. (2012), 'The attentional requirements of consciousness', *Trends in Cognitive Sciences*, 16/8: 411–17.

de Brigard, F. (2010), 'Consciousness, Attention, and Commonsense', *Journal of Consciousness Studies*, 17/9–10: 189–201.

Deutsch, J. A. and Deutsch, D. (1963), 'Attention: Some theoretical considerations', *Psychological Review*, 70/1: 80–90.

Egeth, H. E. and Yantis, S. (1997), 'Visual attention: Control, representation, and time course', *Annual Review of Psychology*, 48/1: 269–97.

Egly, R., Driver, J., and Rafal, R. D. (1994), 'Shifting visual attention between objects and locations: evidence from normal and parietal lesion subjects', *Journal of Experimental Psychology: General*, 123/2: 161–77.

Evans, C. O. (1970), *The Subject of Consciousness*. New York: Humanities Press.

Evans, K. K. and Treisman, A. M. (2005), 'Perception of objects in natural scenes: is it really attention free?' *Journal of Experimental Psychology: Human Perception and Performance*, 31/6: 1476–92.

Forster, S. and Lavie, N. (2016), 'Establishing the attention-distractibility trait', *Psychological Science*, 27/2: 203–12.

Gauthier, I., Skudlarski, P., Gore, J. C., and Anderson, A. W. (2000), 'Expertise for cars and birds recruits brain areas involved in face recognition', *Nature Neuroscience*, 3/2: 191–7.

Graziano, M. S. A. (2013), *Consciousness and the Social Brain*. Oxford: Oxford University Press.

Huang, L. and Pashler, H. (2007), 'A Boolean Map Theory of Visual Attention', *Psychological Review*, 114/3: 599–631.

James, W. (1890/1981), *The Principles of Psychology*. Cambridge, MA: Harvard University Press.

Jennings, C. D. (2015), 'Attention and perceptual organization', *Philosophical Studies*, 172/5: 1265–78.

Jiang, Y., Costello, P., Fang, F., Huang, M., and He, S. (2006), 'A gender-and sexual orientation-dependent spatial attentional effect of invisible images', *Proceedings of the National Academy of Sciences*, 103/45: 17048–52.

Kahneman, D. (1968), 'Method, findings, and theory in studies of visual masking', *Psychological Bulletin*, 70/6, Pt 1: 404–25.

Kentridge, R. W. (2011), 'Attention Without Awareness: A Brief Review' in C. Mole, D. Smithies, and W. Wu (eds), *Attention: Philosophical and Psychological Essays*. New York: Oxford University Press, 228–46.

Koralus, P. (2014), 'The Erotetic Theory of Attention: Questions, Focus and Distraction', *Mind and Language*, 29/1: 26–50.

Li, F. F., VanRullen, R., Koch, C., and Perona, P. (2002), 'Rapid natural scene categorization in the near absence of attention', *Proceedings of the National Academy of Sciences*, 99/14: 9596–601.

Li, F.-F., VanRullin, R., Kohn, C., and Perona, P. (2005), 'Why does natural scene categorization require little attention? Exploring attentional requirements for natural and synthetic stimuli', *Visual Cognition*, 12/6: 893–924.

Liu, K. and Jiang, Y. (2005), 'Visual working memory for briefly presented scenes', *Journal of Vision*, 5/7: p.5.

Mack, A. and Rock, I. (1998), *Inattentional Blindness*. Cambridge MA: MIT Press.

Memmert, D. (2006), 'The effects of eye movements, age, and expertise on inattentional blindness', *Consciousness and Cognition*, 15/3: 620–7.

Mole, C. (2008), 'Attention and Consciousness', *Journal of Consciousness Studies*, 15/4: 86–104.

Mole, C. (2011), *Attention is Cognitive Unison: An Essay in Philosophical Psychology*. New York: Oxford University Press.

Mole, C. (2014), 'Attention to Unseen Objects', *Journal of Consciousness Studies*, 21/11–12: 41–56.

Mulckhuyse, M., Talsma, D., and Theeuwes, J. (2007), 'Grabbing attention without knowing: Automatic capture of attention by subliminal spatial cues', *Visual Cognition*, 15/7: 779–88.

Noë, A. and O'Regan, J. K. (2000), 'Perception, Attention and the Grand Illusion', *Psyche*, 6/15.

Norman, L. J., Heywood, C. A., and Kentridge, R. W. (2013), 'Object-Based Attention Without Awareness', *Psychological Science*, 24/5: 836–43.

Prinz, J. J. (2011), 'Is Attention Necessary and Sufficient for Consciousness' in C. Mole, D. Smithies, and W. Wu (eds), *Attention: Philosophical and Psychological Essays*. New York: Oxford University Press, 174–203.

Prinz, J. J. (2012), *The Conscious Brain*. New York: Oxford University Press.

Quinlan, P. T. (2003), 'Visual feature integration theory: past, present, and future', *Psychological Bulletin*, 129/5: 643–73.

Rensink, R. A. (2005), 'Change Blindness' in L. Itti, G. Rees, and J. K. Tsotsos (eds), *Neurobiology of Attention*. San Diego, CA: Elsevier, 76–81.

Schwitzgebel, E. (2007), 'Do you have constant tactile experience of your feet in your shoes? Or is experience limited to what's in attention?' *Journal of Consciousness Studies*, 14/3: 5–35.

Simons, D. J. and Levin, D. T. (1997), 'Change blindness', *Trends in Cognitive Sciences*, 1/7: 261–7.

Simons, D. J., Chabris, C. F., Schnur, T., and Levin, D. T. (2002), 'Evidence for Preserved Representations in Change Blindness', *Consciousness and Cognition*, 11/1: 78–97.

Smithies, D. (2011), 'Attention is Rational Access Consciousness' in C. Mole, D. Smithies, and W. Wu (eds), *Attention: Philosophical and Psychological Essays*. New York: Oxford University Press, 247–73.

Sumner, P., Tsai, P.-C., Yu, K., and Nachev, P. (2006), 'Attentional modulation of sensorimotor processes in the absence of perceptual awareness', *Proceedings of the National Academy of Sciences*, 103/17: 10520–5.

Treisman, A. (2003), 'Consciousness and perceptual binding' in A. Cleeremans (ed.), *The Unity of Consciousness*. Oxford: Oxford University Press, 95–113.

Treisman, A. M. and Gelade, G. (1980), 'A feature-integration theory of attention', *Cognitive Psychology*, 12/1: 97–136.

Treisman, A. and Gormican, S. (1988), 'Feature analysis in early vision: evidence from search asymmetries', *Psychological Review*, 95/1: 15–48.

VanRullen, R. and Koch, C. (2003), 'Competition and selection during visual processing of natural scenes and objects', *Journal of Vision*, 3/1: 75–85.

Ward, J. (1918), *Psychological Principles*. Cambridge: Cambridge University Press.

Watzl, S. (2017), *Structuring Mind: The Nature of Attention and How it Shapes Consciousness*. Oxford: Oxford University Press.

Webb, T. A., Kean, H. H., and Graziano, M. S. A. (2016), 'Effects of Awareness of the Control of Attention', *Journal of Cognitive Neuroscience*, 28/5: 1–10.

Wheeler, M. E. and Treisman, A. M. (2002), 'Binding in short-term visual memory', *Journal of Experimental Psychology: General*, 131/1: 48–64.

Wolfe, J. M. (1992), '"Effortless" texture segmentation and "parallel" visual search are not the same thing', *Vision Research*, 32/4: 757–63.

Wu, W. (2011), 'Attention as Selection for Action' in C. Mole, D. Smithies, and W. Wu (eds), *Attention: Philosophical and Psychological Essays*. New York: Oxford University Press, 97–116.

Wundt, W. (1912), *An Introduction to Psychology*. Translated by R. Pintner. London: George Allen and Unwin.

Yeshurun, Y. and Carrasco, M. (1998), 'Attention improves or impairs visual performance by enhancing spatial resolution', *Nature*, 396/6706: 72–5.

Zhao, J., Al-Aidroos, N., and Turk-Browne, N. B. (2013), 'Attention Is Spontaneously Biased Toward Regularities', *Psychological Science*, 24/5: 667–77.

CHAPTER 24

CONSCIOUSNESS AND MEMORY

CHRISTOPHER S. HILL

24.1 INTRODUCTION

THIS chapter is concerned with relationships between three forms of consciousness and three types of memory.

The forms of consciousness I have in mind are *introspective consciousness, access consciousness,* and *phenomenal consciousness*. (1) Introspective consciousness occurs when a subject is introspectively aware of one of her own mental states. Just as an object acquires the property of being illuminated when a spotlight is focused on it, so also a mental state acquires the property of being conscious when a subject takes introspective note of it. This form of consciousness has of course been of great interest to people in the psychoanalytic tradition; but long before Freud, novelists, dramatists, and biographers appreciated that there are differences in the degrees to which people are aware of their own motives, expectations, and emotions. (2) According to Ned Block's widely quoted definition of access consciousness, a mental state becomes access conscious when it 'is made available to the brain's "consumer" systems: systems of memory, perceptual categorization, reasoning, planning, evaluation of alternatives, decision-making, voluntary direction of attention, and more generally, rational control of action' (Block 2005: 5–6). This definition is somewhat opaque, due to the expression 'made available', but Block goes on to explain as follows: 'The "made available" terminology is supposed to capture both the occurrent nature of the experience (when something is *made* available, something happens) and the dispositional aspect (availability). There are many somewhat different ways of precisifying access consciousness on this picture. One might think of the crucial feature as representations being *sent*, or else, *received*, or else *translated* from the system of representation of the producing systems to the system of representation of the consuming systems' (Block 2005: 6). (3) Phenomenal consciousness occurs whenever a subject is in a conscious state with a proprietary phenomenology, where phenomenology is constituted by phenomenal properties or qualia. Qualia are properties like pain, the way it feels to be angry, the way oranges taste, and the way red things look when seen in bright sunlight.

There are several forms of consciousness in addition to the ones I have mentioned. Thus, for example, while all of the forms of consciousness noted above are properties of individual mental states, there is also a form of consciousness that is a property of agents. We have this form in mind when we say such things as 'Jon's surgery was successful and he is now conscious and in the recovery room.' I will be setting all such additional forms of consciousness aside because I believe that questions concerning them are to a large extent reducible to questions concerning introspective consciousness, access consciousness, and phenomenal consciousness.

There are three types of memory that are arguably connected, either directly or indirectly, with one or more of the forementioned forms of consciousness—*long-term memory*, *working memory*, and *iconic memory*. (1) Long-term memory is the easiest to describe: it is a form of storage with virtually unlimited capacity and the ability to retain items indefinitely. *Semantic memory* is a form of long-term memory that will be of particular interest to us. It is the repository of concepts and conceptually based general knowledge. (2) Logie and Cowan define working memory

> as the holding mechanism in the mind for a small amount of information that is kept in a temporarily heightened state of availability... [It] is called working memory because it is essential for doing the work of cognition. The work comprises such things as holding on to phonemes and words in speech until they can be recalled in the correct order or be integrated into meaningful ideas; temporary storage of visual properties of objects such as shape, color, or location, and of sequences of arm or body movements to aid actions; holding on to the key information needed to figure out the solution to a problem; supporting mental imagery; and holding on to our immediate plans until we can carry them out. (Logie and Cowan 2015: 315–16)

There are many open questions about working memory, and many claims about it that are highly controversial, but it seems that most contributors to the literature would accept this broad portrayal. There is also wide agreement that working memory has a highly restricted capacity, with room for only a handful of items, and that it preserves items for comparatively short periods of time, extending only briefly beyond the periods during which representations are relevant to ongoing tasks. (3) Iconic memory is quite different. For one thing, its storage capacity is much more extensive: it can retain information about virtually all of the parts of visual stimuli, including information about their sizes, shapes, colors, and locations. Another difference is that the duration of its contents is much more restricted, typically extending to just a few hundred milliseconds. A third difference is that the contents of iconic memory are not immediately available for use by high level consuming systems. They are, however, *indirectly* available to such systems. This was shown by an innovative experiment devised by George Sperling in the 1950s (Sperling 1960). In this experiment, Sperling exposed his subjects to a visual stimulus consisting of a matrix of twelve letters for a very short period (less than 100 milliseconds).

Then, after the stimulus had disappeared, he used a tone to call attention to the letters in one of the rows of the matrix; a low tone meant that the subject was to attend to the letters in the bottom row, and so on. He found that after attention had been drawn to the letters in a particular row, they were promoted to working memory and thus made available to high level agencies. The restriction was that at most four of the constituents of a matrix could be accessed in this way.

Iconic memory is concerned exclusively with the storage of visual stimuli. As that fact may suggest, I will be concerned principally with visual consciousness and consciousness of visual states. But much of the discussion can easily be generalized so as to apply to conscious experiences that are associated with other sensory modalities, for there are counterparts of visual iconic memory for hearing and touch. Researchers often refer collectively to this trio of counterparts as *sensory memory*.

Although distinctions among types of memory are controversial, there is good reason for recognizing a fourth type. *Fragile short-term visual memory* is a relatively new discovery. It has been studied in recent years by I. G. Sligte, Victor Lamme, and their colleagues (Sligte et al. 2008), and their work has provided evidence of several kinds that it can be dissociated both from iconic memory and working memory (Sligte et al. 2009; Vandenbroucke et al. 2015). A short description of it is that it stands somewhere between these two other types of memory in point of capacity and the duration of its contents. Thus, it is capable of holding onto at least fifteen items for 4 seconds (Sligte et al. 2009). Fragile memory could conceivably stand in interesting relations to one or more forms of consciousness. I will not have much to say about it here, however, because its role in information processing is still unclear. In contrast, there are large literatures discussing the distinctive functions of the three types of memory I have distinguished above.

So much for preliminaries! I will now turn to the business of considering how our three forms of consciousness might be related to our three major types of memory.

24.2 Introspective Consciousness

On the view I prefer, introspective consciousness occurs when an agent forms a judgment about one of his or her own mental states. The judgment may be either simple or complex, but in either case it involves classifying the state in terms of concepts. The view denies that there is an essential bond between mental states and the judgments that are directed on them. Indeed, in most versions, it denies that mental states are usually accompanied by introspective judgments. Introspective judgments occur only when the apparatus that constructs such judgments has been primed, and priming occurs only when the agent has special concerns. When it does occur, the resulting judgments are preceded by the states to which they refer, though often only by miniscule amounts of time. I will call this the *judgment theory* of introspective awareness. Related views have been developed by Rosenthal (2006), Carruthers (2013), and Byrne (2018) . In arguing for their respective positions, these authors say a great deal that can be adapted to support the judgment theory.

The judgment theory is not inevitable. At the other end of the spectrum, we find the idea that we have an introspective command of *every* conscious state *as that state occurs*, because being conscious of an item X necessarily involves being conscious of one's consciousness of X. In other words, introspective awareness is built into consciousness itself, because consciousness is necessarily reflexive. I will call this the *reflexivity theory* of introspection.

The claim that consciousness is reflexive has been defended by a number of philosophers, though not all of them have thought of reflexive awareness as a form of introspection. According to Brentano (1973: 127–8), '[i]n the same mental phenomenon in which the sound is present to our minds we simultaneously apprehend the mental phenomenon itself. What is more, we apprehend it in accordance with its dual nature insofar as it has the sound as content within it, and insofar as it has itself as content at the same time. We can say that the sound is the *primary object* of the *act* of hearing, and that the act of hearing itself is the *secondary object*.' This picture has been elaborated with subtlety and insight by Kriegel (2011). (I hasten to add that while Brentano and Kriegel are staunch advocates of the reflexivity of consciousness, they both deny that reflexive awareness counts as introspection.)

There is a strong reason for preferring the judgment theory to the reflexivity theory: the claim that consciousness is reflexive has a certain intuitive appeal, but it is very hard to find evidence that directly supports it. I am now having a fairly typical visual experience. As far as I can tell, when I consider the experience carefully, there is nothing about it which suggests that it is reflexive. On the contrary, it seems that I can exhaustively characterize it by enumerating the external objects that it presents and specifying their apparent sizes, shapes, colors, and so on. This is all there is to the visual phenomenology of the experience. It follows that anything that counts as introspective awareness of the experience must be external to the visual phenomenology, just as the judgment theory maintains. To be sure, the visual phenomenology might be *accompanied by* an introspective judgment. But to say this is to grant that introspective awareness involves judgments, another concession to the judgment theory. Moreover, it is pretty clear that the phenomenology could have occurred without being accompanied by the judgment, since psychology tells us that they have different and independent causes. That is to say, the introspective judgment that accompanies the visual experience is in no sense constitutive of it. This verifies another of the claims made by the judgment theory.

At this point, a defender of the reflexivity theory might chose to maintain that the larger experience consisting of the original visual experience and the judgment involves reflexivity. This would be true if the judgment referred to itself as well as to the original visual experience. But this still concedes that introspection involves judgments. Moreover, it seems very implausible that self-referential judgments routinely occur. It requires considerable conceptual sophistication and very special motivation to construct self-referential judgments. Self-reference occurs when we are playing or experimenting with words or concepts, not when we are conducting serious everyday business.

As noted, additional arguments favoring the judgment theory can be found in the cited works by Byrne, Carruthers, and Rosenthal. I will assume here that it is correct.

Now with this assumption in the background, we can easily see that working memory is required for introspective consciousness. According to the assumption, introspective awareness consists of judgments. When, for example, I am aware that I am seeing a cylindrical object with red and white stripes, it is because I am judging that I am seeing an object with those properties. But judgments involve concepts. In particular, the judgment that I am seeing a cylindrical object with red and white stripes involves the concepts of seeing, the concept of a cylinder, the concept of a stripe, the concept of red, and the concept of white. But working memory plays a crucial role in the process of conceptualization. This is because conceptualization requires time. Thus, to determine which concepts apply to a current stimulus, a range of potentially relevant concepts has to be located in long-term memory, and information deriving from perception has to be compared to the criteria of applicability for these concepts to determine the best fit. While this process is continuing the information has to be preserved. Working memory is the register that has this responsibility. It is the place where the conceptual rubber meets the perceptual road. (There are various theories of how conceptualization works, but they all involve the activation of structures in semantic memory, and the use of working memory to maintain perceptual information while it is determined whether these structures are applicable. (See, e.g., Machery 2009). For example, on the exemplar theory, perceptual concepts consist of memories of past stimuli together with procedures for computing similarities between the members of such sets and current stimuli. Information about stimuli must be held in working memory while the similarities are being computed.)

It appears, then, that we have found a significant connection between a form of consciousness and a type of memory: working memory is a necessary condition for introspective consciousness. We have also noted a connection between introspective consciousness and long-term memory—or more specifically, between introspective consciousness and semantic memory, the register where concepts and conceptually grounded knowledge are stored. On the view I am assuming, introspective awareness consists of judgments, and introspective processing must obtain the constituents of those judgments from semantic memory. This means that semantic memory is also necessary for introspective consciousness, though its involvement is less direct.

So far so good, but before going on we should take note of a phenomenon that might be thought to pose a threat to the view of introspection I am assuming. This is a phenomenon that was first appreciated by Descartes. Descartes in effect maintained that we are *omniscient* with respect to our current experience: nothing happens in the realm of consciousness that is not known to us. This is no doubt a huge exaggeration, but we all feel that the claim harbors a substantial core of truth. Can the judgment theory accommodate this Cartesian intuition? (The intuition is probably the main source of motivation for the reflexivity theory.)

On the face of it, it might seem that the judgment theory is too restrictive to explain the Cartesian insight, even if the latter is pared down quite a bit. After all, the theory implies that actual introspective judgments are comparatively rare. Introspective faculties are expensive to operate, and are therefore activated only when there is a special need for them. (In most cases introspective awareness is not needed because what we need to know about in order to act is the state of the world, not the state of our take on the world.) But reflection shows that the theory has the requisite explanatory capacity provided it is recognized that Cartesian 'omniscience' is grounded in dispositions to make introspective judgments rather than judgments that actually occur. Experiences tend to leave traces in working memory that *can* give rise to introspective judgments *if* our introspective faculties should be activated. That is, it is generally true that we *would* be able to introspectively grasp an immediately preceding experience *if* the context made it desirable to do so. Arguably, it is dispositional facts of this sort that provide the basis of our sense of 'omniscience'. We think that we generally know what we are experiencing because we can generally answer questions about experience when it occurs to us to ask them. (Another way of putting this is to say that our impression of Cartesian 'omniscience' is due to a kind of refrigerator light illusion. It can seem that a refrigerator light is always on because it is always on when we open the door. So also, we can generally answer questions about what we are currently experiencing or have currently experienced.)

Note that this explanation of Cartesian 'omniscience' presupposes another deep connection between introspective consciousness and working memory. We have already seen that working memory is a necessary condition of *actual* introspective consciousness. It supports the conceptualization of perceptual experience. But it also figures prominently in the present explanation of the Cartesian insight. 'Omniscience' is possible only because there is a strong tendency for fragments of experiences to be preserved in working memory independently of whether they are actually objects of introspective awareness.

24.3 Access Consciousness

As may have been evident from the descriptions of access consciousness and working memory that I quoted above, these two things are intimately related. A representation is access conscious if it has been made available for use by high level cognitive agencies, such as the agencies that are responsible for categorizing presented objects, fixing beliefs, making decisions, forming plans, and solving problems. Working memory plays a role in supporting all of these activities. Hence, it is plausible that making a representation available to higher cognitive activities just consists, in some cases, at least, in encoding the representation in working memory.

What do such encodings involve? There appears to be wide acceptance of the view that encoding occurs when a high level goal or task causes attention to be directed onto a representation (Prinz 2012; Ma et al. 2014; D'Esposito and Postle 2015). On this picture, working memory is not a site or a bin into which a representation is moved. Nor is it a separate storehouse that contains copies of representations. Rather, a representation is encoded in working memory when attention operates directly on the site in which the representation occurs, prolonging the neural activity that sustains it. Those processes may be less robust, in terms of level of activity, than they were when the representation first burst into consciousness, and they may also contain less information about the original stimulus. But they support a version of the representation that is adequate to the task at hand. I will presuppose this picture in what follows. For our purposes, its crucial component is the claim that working memory sustains representations by bestowing attention on them.

The idea to be considered, then, is that access consciousness involves working memory, where working memory is a form of storage that has the indicated properties. But how should we explain 'involves'? Here are three proposals:

(1) Being present in working memory is necessary for a representation to be access conscious.
(2) Being present in working memory is minimally sufficient for a representation to be access conscious.
(3) Being present in working memory is necessary and sufficient for a representation to be access conscious.

These proposals have the virtues of being simple and straightforward, but reflection shows that (2) and (3) are *too* simple. The problem is that a representation could conceivably be retained in working memory in a situation in which all of an agent's high level cognitive agencies had been damaged by pathologies, or temporarily neutralized by an abnormal influence like Transcranial Magnetic Stimulation (TMS). In a case of this kind, the representation would not have the dispositional property (availability) that Block cites as constitutive of access conscious. To cope with this difficulty we need to replace (2) and (3) with (2*) and (3*):

(2*) Being present in working memory is minimally sufficient for a representation to be access conscious, provided that the cognitive faculties of the relevant agent are intact and operational.
(3*) Being present in working memory is necessary and sufficient for a representation to be access conscious, provided that the cognitive faculties of the relevant agent are intact and operational.

(1), (2*), and (3*) are worthy of consideration because they promise to clarify the nature of access consciousness. As we saw, Block distinguishes between the occurrent and dispositional dimensions of access consciousness, and he characterizes the occurrent dimension (the *making* available of a representation) as a matter of a representation's being *sent* to high level cognitive agencies, or being *received* by such agencies, or being *translated* into a format that is used by such agencies. This account of the occurrent dimension is helpful, but it suffers from vagueness. We gain clarity if we say that the occurrent dimension of access consciousness consists in being present in working memory. (1), (2*), and (3*) are different ways of developing this thought.

Now (2*) is quite plausible. Consider the description of working memory by Logie and Cowan that I quoted earlier. On that account, working memory plays a crucial role in supporting a broad range of high level cognitive tasks. Since access consciousness is *defined* in terms of such tasks, it follows that being present in working memory is sufficient for access consciousness.

On the other hand, at first sight, at least, there are grounds for concern about (1) and (3*). We can apply high level cognitive operations to representations of past stimuli, but we can also apply them to representations of stimuli that we are currently experiencing. It is a triviality that some form of memory is required in the first case. Why, though, should we think that memory is needed in the second case? If, say, we wish to describe an object that we are currently perceiving, is it not enough for information about the object to flow directly to the linguistic faculties that are responsible for constructing descriptions, without being encoded in working memory? To be sure, *verbal* working memory is required for the process of constructing a description of what we see, but is it necessary to retain a *visual* memory of what we are seeing in order for the constructive process to go forward? On the face of it, the answer should be 'no'. Surely it is important to distinguish between processing a representation of a current stimulus and processing a representation of a stimulus that has disappeared! And surely it is only the latter that warrants the label 'memory'!

This line of thought is initially tempting, but there is good reason to think that the distinction it draws is more notional and linguistic than substantive. What is really at issue here is whether the mind uses the same mechanisms or processes in exploiting representations of current stimuli as in exploiting representations of past stimuli. And there is excellent reason to think that the answer should be affirmative. Consider what happens when an agent is describing a present stimulus. To construct a description, the agent must attend to the stimulus. But as we noticed, it is widely held that attention is the mechanism by which working memory preserves representations for processing by higher faculties. Accordingly, if this view is correct, there is a strong affinity between the two processes. One involves a representation of a current stimulus that is strengthened by attention, and the other involves a representation of a past stimulus that is prevented by attention from fading into an unusable wisp. Attention is the core ingredient in both cases, and in both cases it has the same function—that of making a representation available to higher faculties. Moreover, when one strengthens a representation by attending to it, one also extends its duration, in effect expanding working memory to include it. As is often said, attention is the gatekeeper to working memory.

In view of these facts, it should come as no surprise that cognitive scientists generally use the expression 'working memory' in describing both the processing of current stimuli and the processing of past stimuli.

We can conclude, then, that there is a strong reason to accept (2*), and that despite initial appearances to the contrary, there is also a substantial case for accepting (1) and (3*). Still, there is a matter we should look into before giving any of these propositions our imprimatur.

More specifically, while it clearly is appropriate to speak of items held in working memory as *accessible* to higher faculties, it might be doubted whether it is altogether appropriate to speak of such items as access *conscious*. After all, in everyday life, we tend to distinguish between memories and states of consciousness. Memories are states that *used to be* conscious. Moreover, states of consciousness tend to be highly evanescent; but representations can remain in working memory for upwards of ten seconds. I emphasize that this is not to question the reality or significance of the phenomenon picked out by the predicate 'accessible'. Clearly, accessibility is of immense importance for the enterprise of explaining mental states and behavior. The point is just that it is not immediately clear that we use 'conscious' in a way that tracks the feature. Is it perhaps a kind of linguistic error to combine 'access' with 'conscious' in describing representations stored in working memory?

It is true that there are tendencies in our thought and talk about consciousness that speak against (1)–(3*), but it is also true that there are tendencies to which they are more congenial. I am thinking here of our willingness to apply 'conscious' to activities that extend over time. To illustrate, it can be appropriate at time T to say that someone is consciously pondering how to solve a problem, even though only a few fragments of the problem are actually before his or her mind at T, the rest being currently kept active in working memory by attention, or by being rehearsed in a different memory apparatus that Baddeley calls the 'phonological loop' (Baddeley 2003). Equally, it can be appropriate to say at T that someone is consciously considering what to do next, even though at T she is actively entertaining only one of the several options that she is weighing. It is easy to multiply examples. Accordingly, it would be a mistake to think that ordinary usage poses a substantial challenge to (1)–(3*). As a general rule, it is a mistake to view the ordinary meaning of 'conscious' as a narrow filter that places stringent constraints on theories of consciousness. Our use of the word is much too elastic, multi-faceted, and downright messy for that.

I close this section with a couple of observations about the relationship between access consciousness and semantic memory—which, as we saw, is one of the systems that compose long-term memory. Semantic memory is the principal repository of concepts, and concepts interact with working memory in two ways. First, conceptual structures like plans and expectations play a significant role in determining which aspects of an incoming stimulus, if any, are encoded in working memory. And second, working memory is the locus in which the selected aspects of stimuli are subsumed under concepts, and thereby made ready for exploitation by high level faculties. Interactions of the first type play a role in determining which aspects of stimuli become access conscious, and interactions of the second type play a role in determining what kind of influence those aspects have on high level cognition. Thus, in very different ways, these two forms of interaction provide support for access consciousness.

24.4 Phenomenal Consciousness

Are there any significant relationships between phenomenal consciousness and memory? As a preliminary to discussing this question, I should note that when I speak of representations in the present section, I will be concerned exclusively with perceptual representations and other representations that have a phenomenal character—a proprietary phenomenology. (I will not attempt here to explain what having phenomenal character consists in. My views about that topic are presented in Hill 2009.)

Further, before proceeding to more positive claims, we should take note of a negative fact: there is no chance at all that being present in a memory register is sufficient for phenomenal consciousness. This is because the duration of an episode of phenomenal consciousness is quite different than the duration of a memory. We can appreciate this by noting, first, that episodes of phenomenal consciousness are individuated by their phenomenology, and second, that phenomenology is in constant flux. Even if one is just staring at a wall under conditions of constant lighting, there will at least be minor fluctuations in focus or point of fixation. To put the point in quantitative terms, it is pretty clear that episodes of phenomenal consciousness are measured in milliseconds. But representations can be preserved in fragile memory for 4 seconds and in working memory for much longer. Moreover, they can be preserved in iconic memory for a full second. Try this experiment. Turn your head so that your field of vision sweeps across the room you are in while you mark the passing of a second, perhaps by saying 'one thousand and one'. Note the changes in phenomenology that occur. I predict that they will seem numerous. A second is much too long to correspond to the moving edge of phenomenal consciousness. In view of all this, it is clear that representations can be present in a memory register without being phenomenally conscious.

Fortunately, this negative point leaves plenty of room for positive theses. Thus, even though presence in a memory system is not sufficient for phenomenal consciousness, it could still be true that phenomenal consciousness is causally sufficient for producing traces in one or more memory systems, or at least that phenomenal consciousness *normally* produces memory traces. Suppose that some such possibility obtains, and suppose also that the relevant system or systems of memory can be shown to play crucial roles in downstream processing. Under these assumptions, we could go a long way toward explaining the *value* or *importance* of phenomenal consciousness by describing its causal contributions to memory. Accordingly, there is a substantial philosophical reason for considering exactly how strong the causal relationship between phenomenal consciousness and memory might be. We all want to know why Mother Nature bothered to endow us with phenomenal consciousness.

It will be helpful to begin by returning to Sperling's experiment, because it is pretty clear how phenomenal consciousness influenced our three memory systems in Sperling's subjects. Let us agree that his subjects were phenomenally conscious of a matrix of twelve letters for a very brief interval, lasting less than 100 milliseconds. Let us also agree that this phenomenally conscious state involved a representation that captured the individuality of each of the presented letters. That is, the representation had a part that stood for the letter 'A', a part that stood for the letter 'Z', and so on. (For supporting argumentation, see Block 2011.) Now let us ask: what exactly were the effects of this phenomenally conscious state on memory? The answer is that there were three such effects. In the first place, the subjects generally remembered three or four of the letters long enough to name them. This means that representations of three or four letters made it into working memory without any conscious effort by the subjects. Second, each of the subjects remembered the *gist* of the original display and were able to name it. Thus, in each case, a gist like *letters!* or *matrix of letters!* was transferred to working memory. And third, as we know from the results of Sperling using post-stimulus tones to give retro-cues as to which rows of letters were to be reported, the subjects retained traces of all twelve of the letters in iconic memory. Depending on the cue, the subjects attended to the letters in a specific row, thereby transferring those letters to working memory, where they were appropriately classified by the subjects.

Now if the processing done by Sperling's subjects was typical, we could claim that phenomenal consciousness generally has effects of these three kinds on memory systems. Reflection shows, however, that Sperling's subjects were in very special circumstances. For one thing, the matrix of letters was not embedded in a series of other stimuli that made strong claims on attention. In everyday life, we are generally preoccupied with the stimulus at hand. There is little need, and little opportunity, to respond to retro-cues telling us to reactivate some portion of an immediately preceding experience. In view of this, it is arguable that the contents of iconic memory are irrelevant to visual processing in most contexts. (Reflections of this sort led Haber (1983: 1) to conclude that iconic memory 'cannot possibly be useful in any typical visual information-processing task except reading in a lightning storm'!) This would suggest that iconic memory should not be given much weight in explaining the importance of phenomenal consciousness. Second, when the matrix of letters originally appeared on Sperling's tachistoscope, the subjects were undoubtedly already devoting considerable spatial attention to the whole screen. After all, they had been told to take note of what would appear there! But broadly distributed spatial attention is not characteristic of phenomenal consciousness. Usually, attention is focused on a few items at the center of one's field of vision. Now it might be thought that this heightened level of attention was responsible for the fact that all of the parts of the original matrix were represented in iconic memory (Persuh et al. 2012), and also for the fact that the gist of the whole presentation was represented in working memory. If so, then it would be a mistake to extrapolate from Sperling's subjects to general conclusions about the relationship between phenomenal consciousness and memory.

These concerns need to be considered, but they are hardly the last word on the matter. The first concern is that Sperling's set-up was special in that the subjects were given explicit retro-cues and also the leisure to act on them. Haber and others have maintained that no lessons can be drawn from the results of this procedure concerning the role of iconic memory in everyday life. As Cowan (1993) has emphasized, however, there are reasons for thinking that iconic memory is useful in ways that are entirely independent of retro-cues. For example, it is arguable that iconic memory is generally needed to perceive motion and various other types of transformation. Here is what Cowan (1993) says about this topic:

> [I]t may well be that the visual sensory afterimage is...used to integrate perception across time. Without sensory memory integration, it is thus difficult to understand

how fluid motion can be perceived at all. We know this to be true in the perception of motion pictures, but from the point of view of the visual system, the situation may be essentially the same for ordinary, fluid motions and transformations of objects. Perhaps a fair model of how the world might appear without visual sensory memory is a case study in which a woman with damage to an area at the border of the occipital and cortical regions experienced a 'frozen world' in which changes appeared suddenly, with no fluid motion between them. (Cowan 1993: 67)

The idea that awareness of change depends on iconic memory receives support from experiments on change blindness that use the flicker paradigm. (A subject in a flicker experiment is briefly shown an image followed by a very short mask, and is then briefly shown a second image. The second image is just like the first except for lacking one comparatively large component. The sequence involving these three stimuli is repeated until subjects notice the change. Subjects usually fail to detect it for surprisingly long periods of time.) These experiments are relevant because vision scientists often appeal to iconic memory—implicitly, if not by name—in explaining the results. Their hypothesis is that change blindness occurs because short-lived memory traces of the original image are overwritten by the ensuing mask, and that this precludes comparisons between the two images that would otherwise have occurred automatically. Rensink et al. (1997) were perhaps the first to give an explanation of this sort. Becker et al. (2000) and Landman et al. (2003) give additional grounds for the hypothesis, as do more recent writers. Their claims are at least partially conjectural, but if they were sustained by future research, they would point to a substantial connection between phenomenal consciousness and downstream processing, and thereby help to account for the importance of phenomenal consciousness.

In addition to being unusual because the subjects were prompted with explicit retrocues, Sperling's set-up was special in that it encouraged the subjects to spread their spatial attention across an entire display. As we saw, this feature of the experiment might lead to skepticism about drawing general conclusions from Sperling's results. Perhaps the distribution of attention played an essential role in producing a representation of the whole matrix in iconic memory. Equally, if it had not been for attention, the gist of the original experience might not have been passed on to working memory. Both of these doubts are legitimate, but I think they can be resisted. In the first place, while some level of attention may be required to create iconic memories (Persuh et al. 2012), it seems unlikely that a high level of attention is necessary. As we all know, it is possible to detect significant changes in the periphery of one's field of vision even when one's attention is captured by an item at the center. If we accept Cowan's view that iconic memory plays an essential role in perceiving change, we will have to suppose that representations can produce traces of themselves in iconic memory even when the boost they receive from attention is small. Also, with respect to the concern about gist, we know from a number of studies that gists are perceived even when attention is largely occupied with other matters. In these studies, subjects are given attention-demanding tasks that involve an image at the center of the field of vision. While they are performing these tasks, images of scenes are flashed in peripheral locations. Subjects are generally able to extract gists from these scenes. For example, they can determine whether an image contained an animal, whether it contained a vehicle, and whether it contained a human face of a certain gender (Li et al. 2002; Reddy et al. 2004; and Reddy et al. 2006). These experiments do not establish that gists can be perceived in the complete absence of attention, but they do show that, for certain types of gist, at least, only minimal levels of attention are required.

There is another consideration that should be mentioned. It may well be the case that some minimal level of attention is required for phenomenal consciousness in the first place. That is, it could be that a minimal level of attention is one of the features in virtue of which representations are endowed with phenomenal consciousness. If so, then the attention that Sperling's subjects bestow on the matrix would not distinguish their experience sharply from ordinary cases of phenomenal consciousness. There would be a difference, but it would only be one of degree.

We have been reviewing reasons for thinking that phenomenal consciousness has substantial impacts on iconic memory and working memory. I turn now to consider the idea that phenomenal consciousness can be *analyzed* or *explained* in terms of its relationship to memory systems. As we noticed earlier, it would be a mistake to say that representations are phenomenally conscious in virtue of *being present* in memory systems, due to the fact that representations in memory systems have longer duration than episodes of phenomenal consciousness, but it might still be maintained that phenomenal consciousness consists in standing in some other relation to memory. Thus, it might be claimed that a representation counts as phenomenally conscious in virtue of *causing* copies or traces of itself to be established in memory, or in virtue of *being disposed to cause* such copies or traces. Another view of this sort is that representations are phenomenally conscious in virtue of having whatever *intrinsic* properties normally *support* a disposition to cause copies or traces in a memory system. I will refer to views of these three types as versions of the *memory theory of phenomenal consciousness*.

I have space only to examine one version of the memory theory. According to the version I have in mind, phenomenal consciousness can be explained in terms of the set Σ of intrinsic properties in virtue of which representations normally cause traces or surrogates of themselves in *working* memory. More specifically, according to the theory, a representation is phenomenally conscious just in case it possesses the members of Σ. This *working memory theory of phenomenal consciousness* has been of considerable interest to philosophers. For example, Prinz's 2012 can be understood as a defense of it. (The theory could also be expressed by saying that phenomenal consciousness is the *categorical basis* of dispositions to produce surrogates of representations in working memory.)

Block has criticized the working memory theory on the grounds that the contents of phenomenal consciousness can *overflow* the boundaries of working memory. (See, e.g., Block 2011.) Block supports this thesis by appealing to Sperling's experiment and more recent variations on the same theme. Sperling's subjects told him that they had seen all twelve components of a briefly presented matrix of letters, but he found that the subjects could explicitly remember only four of the letters. Block takes the subjects' memory of having seen twelve letters to show that they originally enjoyed phenomenal consciousness of the entire matrix, and he takes their subsequent inability to recall more than four as evidence that most of the letters were not registered in working memory. His conclusion is that the volume of phenomenal consciousness transcends the volume of working memory, and that as a result, phenomenal consciousness cannot depend on creating traces in working memory. (Block's discussion is not directly concerned with the working memory theory. Rather, it targets the view that a representation counts as phenomenally conscious just in case it is access conscious. As we saw earlier, however, the relationship between access consciousness and working memory is extremely close. Block's key points are easily adapted so as to apply to the working memory theory.)

This overflow objection clearly deserves careful consideration, but it depends on an assumption that can be questioned. Let us grant that Sperling's subjects were phenomenally conscious of the letters in the matrix. Let us also agree that this phenomenally conscious state involved a representation that captured the individuality of each of the presented letters. That is, the representation had a part that stood for the letter 'A', a part that stood for the letter 'Z', and so on. Now according to objection, the fact that this representation was phenomenally conscious cannot be analyzed in terms of a relationship to working memory unless the representation either produced or was capable of producing a surrogate in working memory that explicitly represented each letter in the array. That is, in order to explain the fact that the original representation was conscious in terms of working memory, it would have to be true that the representation either caused or was capable of causing a surrogate that simultaneously represented 'A', 'Z', and all the rest of the letters. And of course, Sperling's subjects did not have surrogates in working memory with that degree of specificity. But why should we insist on a criterion of success for the working memory theory that requires highly specific surrogates? Why is it not sufficient to require that a phenomenally conscious representation produce a memory of a *gist* of the original experience, a gist that can be expressed by saying exactly what Sperling's subjects said—'I was aware of a matrix of letters, and I was aware of the specific natures of the letters that occupied the matrix. I can recall this; I just can't recall the identities of those specific letters.' Such a gist would encode *generic* information about each letter, though not information about its specific identity. Why is this not good enough? Where is it written that specific information about perceptual states is more relevant to phenomenal consciousness than generic information?

There are additional grounds for concern about the overflow objection to the working memory theory, for there are indications in the contemporary experimental literature that the capacity of working memory may not be as limited as has heretofore been supposed. Until recently, it was held that the capacity of working memory is limited to representations of four items. It was thought that attention did the work of sustaining the representations, and that attention was divided equally among them. The result was a kind of 'all-or-none' law for working memory. Here is a summary of this familiar picture:

> The classic view has been that working memory is limited in capacity, holding a fixed, small number (K) of items, such as Miller's 'magical number' seven or Cowan's

> four.... For vision, a highly influential proposal has been that items retained in working memory are held in three or four independent object 'slots', one for each item stored. This slot conceptualization of working memory is all or none: an object either gets into a memory slot and is then remembered accurately, or it does not, in which case it is not remembered at all. (Ma et al. 2014: 347)

In more recent work, this picture has been challenged by one in which the attention available to working memory is a variable quantity—a quantity that can be distributed over large sets of items to different degrees. Here are Ma et al. again (2014), this time describing the alternative picture:

> Recent work has led to substantial advances in our understanding of the structure and organization of working memory. In particular, compelling reasons to reconsider the classic view have arisen from psychophysical studies showing that the precision of recall declines continuously as the number of items to be remembered increases, and increasing the salience or goal relevance of a stimulus causes it to be stored with enhanced precision, at the cost of poorer memory for other stimuli. Although interpretation of these results remains an active area of debate, neither of these findings would have been predicted on the basis of the original slot model, in which every item is either stored with high precision or not at all.
>
> *In contrast, the results are naturally accommodated by models that consider working memory to be a limited resource, distributed flexibly between all items in a scene.* Crucially, although resource models consider working memory to be extremely limited, they do not invoke a fixed item limit on the number of objects that can be stored. Thus, for these models, K is not the fundamental metric with which to measure working memory. According to these views, it is not the number of items remembered, but rather the quality or precision of memory that is the key measure of working memory limits. (Ma et al. 2014: 347)

Van den Berg et al. (2012) express a similar view: '[The Variable Precision] model might reconcile an apparent capacity of about four items with the subjective sense that we possess some memory of an entire scene: Items are never discarded completely, but their encoding quality could by chance be very low' (Van den Berg et al. 2012: 8784).

Evidence is accumulating for this new view. (See, e.g., Huang 2010 and Bays 2015. For opposing arguments see Zhang and Luck 2011.) Suppose that it is true. Then traces are sustained in working memory to different degrees, and correspondingly different degrees of causal oomph are required to establish such traces. These consequences might be comfortably accommodated by a version of the working memory theory of phenomenal consciousness which maintained that phenomenal consciousness comes in degrees.

I have been defending the working memory theory of phenomenal consciousness against the overflow objection. This is not to say the working memory theory is correct. The point is just that if the objection is to be acceptable, there are additional questions that it must address.

Even if the working memory theory fails, our reflections indicate that it is possible to account for much of the *importance* of phenomenal consciousness by appealing to its relationships to memory systems, and this suggests that a memory theory might at least capture part of the truth about phenomenal consciousness. Thus, it is tempting to think that if we knew why phenomenal consciousness is valuable, we could parlay that knowledge into a reductive theory of the *nature* of phenomenal consciousness, *for it is plausible that the essential nature of phenomenal consciousness can be explained in terms of the properties that account for its value—that is, in terms of the properties that explain why Mother Nature bothered to endow us with phenomenal consciousness in the first place*. Suppose that this view is true, and suppose also that Φ is the set of properties of representations that account for the value of phenomenal consciousness. Now it is plausible that Φ will include properties that are causally responsible for creating surrogates of phenomenally conscious representations in various memory systems. Thus, it is clear both from commonsense reflection and from the experimental work we have been reviewing that phenomenally conscious states *do* create such surrogates, and it is also clear that such surrogates play important roles in the cognitive endeavors of agents. It follows that a memory theory of phenomenal consciousness is at least partially true. That is to say, it follows that phenomenal consciousness is partially constituted by the properties that casually explain the ability of phenomenally conscious states to produce surrogates in memory systems. For a memory theory to be entirely true, it would have to be the case that *all* of the members of Φ support causal relations to memory. Depending on one's views about cognitive processing, that might seem unlikely. For example, it might seem that Φ must contain properties that can shape action directly, without any mediating support from memory systems. But even so, given our assumption about the relationship between the value of phenomenal consciousness and its essential nature, the claim of partial truth seems well motivated. It is clear that many of the downstream effects of phenomenal consciousness are mediated by memory. (For a related discussion, see Hill 2016.)

I conclude with three brief remarks about the relationships between phenomenal consciousness and long-term memory. First, obviously, many of the contents of phenomenally conscious states are eventually transferred to long-term memory. We remember what we feel and perceive. Second, long-term memories often play a role in directing the various forms of sensory and perceptual attention, thereby shaping the contents of phenomenal consciousness. And third, it is sometimes maintained that structures in long-term memory like beliefs and long term plans can 'penetrate' phenomenal consciousness, actively shaping the phenomenology of perceptual experiences in ways that go beyond the effects of attention. This is, however, a very controversial claim, and there is no room to evaluate it here. (For discussion see Firestone and Scholl 2016, Siegel 2017, and Block forthcoming.)[1]

---

[1] I thank Steven Sloman and William Warren for illuminating exchanges, and Uriah Kriegel for very helpful comments on an earlier version. My largest debt is to David Badre, who was outstandingly generous with his time and knowledge throughout my work on this project. He steered me to key items in the literature, helped me to understand them, and gently pointed out problems in several earlier drafts.

References

Baddeley, A. (2003), 'Working Memory: Looking Back and Looking Forward', *Nature Reviews Neuroscience*, 4: 829–39.
Bays, P. M. (2015), 'Spikes Not Slots: Noise in Neural Populations Limits Working Memory', *Trends in Cognitive Science*, 19/8: 431–8.
Becker, M. W., Pashler, H., and Yantis, S. M. (2000), 'The Role of Iconic Memory in Change-detection Tasks', *Perception*, 29/3: 273–86.
Block, N. (2005), 'Two Neural Correlates of Consciousness', http://www.nyu.edu/gsas/dept/philo/faculty/block/.
Block, N. (2011), 'Perceptual Consciousness Overflows Cognitive Access', *Trends in Cognitive Sciences*, 15/12: 567–75.
Block, N. (forthcoming). *The Border between Seeing and Thinking*.
Brentano, F. (1973), *Psychology from an Empirical Standpoint*, translated by L. L. McAlister. London: Routledge.
Byrne, A. (2018), *Transparency and Self-Knowledge* (Oxford: Oxford University Press).
Carruthers, P. (2013), *The Opacity of Mind* (Oxford: Oxford University Press).
Cowan, N. (1997), *Attention and Memory*. Oxford: Oxford University Press.
D'Esposito, M. and Postle, B. R. (2015), 'The Cognitive Neuroscience of Working Memory', *Annual Review of Psychology*, 66: 115–42.
Firestone, C. and Scholl, B. J. (2016), 'Cognition Does Not Affect Perception: Evaluating the Evidence for 'Top-down' Effects', *Behavioral and Brain Sciences*, 39, 10.1017/S0140525X15000965.
Haber, R. N. (1983), 'The Impending Demise of the Icon: The Role of Iconic Processes in Information Processing Theories of Perception', *Behavioral and Brain Sciences*, 6: 1–11.
Hill, C. S. (2009), *Consciousness*. Cambridge: Cambridge University Press.
Hill, C. S. (2016), 'Replies to Byrne, McGrath, and McLaughlin', *Philosophical Studies*, 173: 861–72.
Huang, L. (2010), 'Visual Working Memory is Better Characterized as a Distributed Resource rather than Discrete Slots', *Journal of Vision*, 10/14: 1–8.
Jiang, Y., Costello, P., Fang, F., Huang, M., and He, S. (2006), 'A Gender- and Sexual Orientation-dependent Spatial Attentional Effect of Invisible Images,' *PNAS*, 103/45: 1748–52.
Kriegel, U. (2011), *Subjectivity and Consciousness*. Oxford: Oxford University Press.
Landman R., Spekreijse H., and Lamme V. A. F. (2003), 'Large Capacity Storage of Integrated Objects before Change Blindness', *Vision Research*, 43: 149–64.
Li, F. F., Van Rullen, R., Koch, C., and Perona, P. (2002), 'Rapid Natural Scene Categorization in the Near Absence of Attention', *Proceedings of the National Academy of Sciences*, 99/14: 9596–601.
Logie, R. H. and Cowan, N. (2015), 'Perspectives on Working Memory', *Memory and Cognition*, 43/3: 315–24.
Ma, W. J., Husain, M., and Bays, P. J. (2014), 'Changing Concepts of Working Memory', *Nature Reviews Neuroscience*, 17/3: 347–56.
Machery, E. (2009), *Doing without Concepts*. Oxford: Oxford University Press.
Persuh, M., Genzer, B., and Melara, R. D. (2012), 'Iconic Memory Requires Attention', *Frontiers in Human Neuroscience*, 6/126: 1–8.
Prinz, J. J. (2012), *The Conscious Brain*. Oxford: Oxford University Press.
Reddy L., Wilken P., Koch C. (2004), 'Face-gender Discrimination is Possible in the Near-absence of Attention', *Journal of Vision*, 4: 106–17.

Reddy L., Reddy L., and Koch C. (2006), 'Face Identification in the Near-absence of Focal Attention', *Vision Research*, 46: 2336–43.

Rensink, R. A., O'Regan, J. K., and Clark, J. J. (1997), 'To See or Not to See: The Need for Attention to Perceive Changes in Scenes', *Psychological Science*, 8: 368–73.

Rosenthal, D. (2006), *Consciousness and Mind*. Oxford: Oxford University Press.

Siegel, S. (2017), *The Rationality of Perception*. Oxford: Oxford University Press.

Sligte, I. G., Scholte, H. S., and, V. A. F. (2008), 'Are There Multiple Visual Short-Term Memory Stores?', *PLoS One*, 3/2: 1–9.

Sligte, I. G., Scholte, H. S., and Lamme, V. A. F. (2009), 'V4 Activity Predicts the Strength of Visual Short-Term Memory Representations', *Journal of Neuroscience*, 29/23: 7432–8.

Sperling, G. (1960), 'The Information Available in Brief Visual Presentations', *Psychological Monographs*, 74: 1–29.

Vandenbroucke, A. R. E., Sligte, I. G., de Vries, J. G., Cohen, M. X., and Lamme, V. A. F. (2015), 'Neural Correlates of Visual Short-term Memory Dissociate between Fragile and Working Memory Representations', *Journal of Cognitive Neuroscience*, 27/12: 2477–90.

van den Berg, R., Shin, H., Chou, W.-C., George, R., and Ma, W. J. (2012), 'Variability in encoding precision accounts for visual short-term memory limitations', *Proceeding of the National Academy of Sciences*, 109/22: 8780–5.

Zhang, W. and Luck, S. J. (2011), 'The Number and Quality of Representations in Working Memory', *Psychological Science*, 22: 1434–41.

CHAPTER 25

CONSCIOUSNESS AND ACTION

Contemporary Empirical Arguments for Epiphenomenalism

BENJAMIN KOZUCH

25.1 INTRODUCTION: VARIETIES OF EPIPHENOMENALISM

IN its classical form, epiphenomenalism is the view that conscious mental events have no physical effects: while physical events cause mental events, the opposite is never true (Huxley 1874). Stepping on a thorn causes an experience of pain, but the pain is not what causes the person's shriek; a picture of a loved one causes a feeling of longing, but the longing is not what causes the person's sigh. It might be fair to say that epiphenomenalism is a view adopted under duress, its adherents having been philosophers who wanted to hold that phenomenal properties (i.e., the 'what-it's-like' that accompanies conscious mental states; see Nagel 1974) are non-physical[1] while not abandoning the naturalistic view that physical events never have non-physical causes (Jackson 1982; Chalmers 1996).[2] But to many philosophers it is plainly absurd that a thought to raise one's hand is not what caused one's hand to rise, or that a feeling of sadness is not what caused one's tears, and so classical epiphenomenalism has never enjoyed much popularity.

---

[1] The motivation for adopting this kind of property dualism was the failure of phenomenal facts to logically supervene on physical facts; see Chalmers 1995 for a brief treatment of this idea, Chalmers 1996 for one in-depth and technical.

[2] Even this advocacy has been short-lived or tentative: Jackson later recanted epiphenomenalism in favor of materialism (see, e.g., his 2003), and Chalmers just considers the view a live possibility, given the truth of property dualism.

The same is not true of contemporary forms of epiphenomenalism, which are based not on a priori reasoning, but rather results in neuroscience and psychology, and so have not been so casually dismissed. Unlike classical epiphenomenalism, these contemporary forms do not hold that conscious mental states always lack causal efficacy, only that they are epiphenomenal relative to certain kinds of action, ones we pre-theoretically would have thought consciousness to make a causal contribution to. It is two of these contemporary, empirically based challenges to the efficacy of the mental that are the focus of this chapter.

The first originates in research conducted by the psychologist Benjamin Libet and his colleagues. This work has been interpreted by many as showing that the neural events initiating voluntary actions precede our conscious willing of them, meaning the conscious will cannot be what causes them. The second challenge originates in research carried out by vision scientists David Milner and Mel Goodale. These studies, which consist of instances in which the content of visual consciousness and motor action dissociate, have been thought to cast doubt on the intuitive view that visual consciousness guides visually based motor action. In Sections 25.2 and 25.3, we look at each challenge in turn.

25.2 Epiphenomenalism about Conscious Will

It is seemingly hard to question the causal efficacy of conscious will, given the numerous and easily available examples in which the conscious will appears to produce action: I decide to drink my water, and my hand reaches for it; I intend to order a burger instead of salad, and hear myself say 'the burger' to the waiter. However, the last few decades have seen this apparently safe assumption come under increasing empirical pressure, with several lines of evidence suggesting that feelings of conscious willing are but by-products of unconsciously initiated decisions to act (see, e.g., Wegner 2003a, b; Haynes 2011). Most prominent among these lines of evidence would be experiments conducted by Libet and colleagues, ones in which a subject's awareness of an incipient action seems to come only after her brain has initiated it. This section examines these experiments, along with challenges that have been made to the methodology and significance of them.

25.2.1 The Libet Experiments and Free Will

For two millennia, the debate over free will was the exclusive province of philosophers, the issue remaining largely insulated from empirical data. This changed in a dramatic way in the early 1980s when Libet and colleagues (1983) conducted an ingenious series of experiments. The idea was to compare the time at which the brain initiates a voluntary action with the time at which subjects felt that they had consciously willed it. Libet and his collaborators did not explicitly discuss the philosophical implications of their research (but see Haggard and Libet 2001), but the implications were clear enough: if a subject's brain initiated the voluntary action before the subject knew it, then it would look like her conscious intention was not the source of her action; and this in turn might call into question the very idea of free will.

In the experiments, subjects were asked to perform a simple voluntary task, this being to spontaneously ('freely and capriciously') flex their wrist at a time of their choosing.[3] The timing of three events were measured: First, the time at which the wrist flex occurred was measured using an electromagnetogram (EMG), a device that detects the electrical charge created when a muscle contracts. Second, the time at which the subject consciously willed the wrist flex was determined by having the subject watch a computer image in which a dot orbited a central disk, having the subject note the dot's precise position when she decided to flex. The final event whose time needed to be measured was that of the brain initiating the wrist flex. To determine this, the experimenters employed an electroencephalogram (EEG), a device that consists of numerous electrodes taped to a subject's head that are used to measure the electrical activity created when populations of neurons fire. Prior experiments had discovered that voluntary motor actions like those that Libet's subjects were asked to carry out are reliably preceded by something known as a *readiness potential* (Kornhuber and Deecke 1965), a distinctive negative shift in electrical activity in frontal parts of the brain. Libet used this readiness potential as an index of when the brain initiated the wrist flex.

The results were astonishing. While the readiness potential appeared an average of 535ms before wrist flex, subjects reported deciding to flex an average of just 192ms beforehand: The brain initiated the motor action before subjects thought that they had consciously willed it. If the results were as they seemed—that is, if the readiness potential was the initiation of the wrist flex, and if subjects were correct about the time of conscious willing—then the conscious willing could not have caused the wrist flex. And if there was reason to think that the results of the Libet experiments generalized to all or most instances of intentional action, then it looked like there was also reason to question the existence of free will.

It is important to note that the conclusions to be drawn from the Libet experiments are potentially wide-ranging, posing a threat to even less demanding interpretations of free will. Few modern philosophers subscribe to *libertarian* theories of free will, according to which people enjoy a freedom of choice unconstrained by the (more or less)[4] deterministic laws prevailing elsewhere in the universe (e.g., Campbell 1957; Kane 2009). Libertarianism is clearly hard to reconcile with the Libet results, given that they imply

---

[3] More exactly, the subject was asked to 'perform [a] quick, abrupt flexion of the fingers and/or the wrist of his right hand' (Libet et al. 1983: 625).

[4] Of course, according to contemporary quantum theories of physics, microphysical events do not happen deterministically, but only with a certain probability. But few philosophers or scientists think that these microphysical events 'percolate' up to the macrophysical level in such a way as to support libertarian theories of free will.

that these allegedly unconstrained actions are not authored by the agent. But the Libet results even threaten the less stringent *compatibilist* theories of free will, those that do not require an agent's actions to be undetermined. Such theories vary in what they take to be required for an agent's action to be free, with some saying that the agent must be responsive to reasons for acting or not acting (e.g., Dennett 1984; McKenna 2013), others saying that it requires that one's second-order desires mesh with her first-order desires in the proper way (Frankfurt 1988). But a plausible common denominator of the various compatibilist theories would be that an action is free only if it is caused—in some fashion or another—by one's conscious will (cf. Sinnott-Armstrong and Nadel 2010). And if it is true that the Libet experiments show the initiation of the wrist flex to temporally precede the conscious willing, the conscious will cannot be causing the flexion. So the Libet results appear to threaten free will even if we are considering less stringent notions of it.

However, Libet's lab did employ another paradigm the results of which Libet took to save a measured role for conscious will (Libet 1985). Subjects were asked to initiate a wrist flex at a pre-arranged time, but then decide to not follow through with it, instead 'vetoing' the wrist flex just before (100–200ms) it would have occurred. That subjects were capable of doing this was taken by Libet to mean that, while we cannot consciously choose to initiate an action, we can consciously choose to abstain from performing an act that was unconsciously initiated. While we lack free will, we do have 'free won't' (as it is sometimes jocularly put). However, one would expect that this vetoing action itself has a readiness potential, one that precedes the conscious willing of the veto (Dennett and Kinsbourne 1992). In fact, this veto-readiness potential appears to have been recently discovered (Filevich et al. 2013).

Of course, methodological challenges have been raised to the Libet experiments; these are surveyed shortly. But some commentators argue that even if the Libet results are valid, they have little bearing on the free will debate. It has been argued, for instance, that the actions subjects were asked to perform ('Libet-actions') are not paradigmatic acts of free will, since flexing one's wrist at some arbitrary time has little in common with the kind of reason-based and morally significant choices usually associated with free will (Pockett and Purdy 2010; Roskies 2010; see also Breitmeyer 1985; Bridgeman 1985). Put another way, Libet-actions are more like choosing which pant leg to put on first, and less like deciding whether to steal money from a register that one is running. There is the further worry that a Libet-action is not properly considered an instance of conscious willing, it instead being the automatic component of an action that was willed earlier, that of forming the intention to follow the experimenter's instructions to flex her wrist some time in the next few seconds (Breitmeyer 1985; Flanagan 1996, ch 4; van de Grind 2002; Bayne 2011). Going forward, however, we will put aside questions concerning what the Libet results might mean for the free will debate, instead focusing only on what they show (or do not show) about the efficacy of conscious will.

The significance of the Libet experiments comes from their appearing to show the initiation of the wrist flex to occur before subjects think that they consciously willed it. Accordingly, there are two general strategies for undermining the validity of the Libet results, the first being to contest the timing of the initiation of the wrist flex, the second being to contest the timing of the conscious willing. Each of subsections 25.2.2 and 25.2.3 are dedicated to looking at one of these two strategies.

25.2.2 Questioning the Time of Action Initiation

In the Libet paradigm, it is assumed that the moment that the brain initiates the wrist flex can be determined by looking for the readiness potential (hereafter RP), the distinctive type of electrical activity that is thought to precede the wrist flex. Before looking at doubts that have been raised about this assumption, some background is needed on how RP is determined.

Because of the messy nature of neural activity and poor spatial resolution of EEG, it might be difficult to detect the neural signature of some cognitive event on any individual trial. A distinctive pattern of neural activity such as RP is usually found only after analyzing and averaging data from numerous trials, a technique known as 'back-averaging'. In back-averaging, some observable event (like a report or wrist flex) is used as a reference point, and electrical activity preceding the event is analyzed so as to identify the neural signature of the cognitive event that the experimenters want to track. A consequence of using back-averaging to find RP is that trials in which high neural noise would mask an individual RP are treated the same as trials where there is low neural noise but still no detectable RP. This means that it is possible that many individual wrist flexes are not preceded by an RP.

To investigate this possibility, Pockett and Purdy (2010) adopted the unconventional technique of 'eye-scoring' individual trials, searching for low-noise trials that seemed to also lack an RP; 12 per cent of the 390 trials analyzed turned out like this. Upon averaging these trials, there was still no discernable RP preceding the wrist flexes. These are interesting data, but also contentious, since scoring individual trials is frowned upon because of the highly variable nature of neural activity. But if Pockett and Purdy's method were valid, it would mean that a significant portion of wrist flexes are not preceded by an RP, suggesting that RP does not mark the moment of action initiation.

Back-averaging creates another potential problem (Mele 2009; Roskies 2010). Since back-averaging requires some reference point from which to analyze the electrical activity, data are gathered only from those trials in which the wrist flex is carried out. This means that the brain could frequently generate RPs even when no voluntary motor action is performed, leaving open the possibility that RPs are the neural signature of some cognitive process other than the initiation of flexion.

It is because of this that Mele (2010) wonders whether RPs are present on trials where subjects are asked to form the intention to flex but then veto it at the last moment (i.e., trials supposedly exemplifying 'free won't'; see Subsection 25.2.1), since such trials will be among those not recorded for purposes of back-averaging. An explanation as to what RP alternatively might be the neural signature of is offered by Pockett and Purdy (2010), who have pointed out how slow-going negative waveforms similar to RP precede the perception of a stimulus. Pocket and Purdy have argued on the basis of this that RP might be the neural signature not of action-initiation, but rather of the *anticipation* of some event, be this a decision to move, the appearance of the stimulus, or something else. But if RP is not the neural signature of the decision to flex, what neural event is? The beginning of an answer might be found in a study conducted by Haggard and Eimer (1999). Here, experimenters asked subjects to choose to flex either their left or right wrist. Analysis of the EEG data revealed a *lateralized readiness potential* (LRP), one appearing in the hemisphere contralateral to the hand, and which was preceded by the time of conscious willing in about 20 per cent of trials. Such results are suggestive, but at this time it remains unclear what neural event the LRP represents, and whether similar neural activity can be found in the standard Libet paradigm (but see Haggard 2011).

In sum, there is an at least tentative case to be made against RP being necessary and/or sufficient for the wrist flexes that subjects are asked to perform in a Libet paradigm, in which case we cannot be sure that RP reliably signifies the initiation of the wrist flex. This leaves open the possibility that the initiation of the wrist flex does not actually precede the subject's conscious willing of it, potentially undermining the main result of the Libet experiment.

25.2.3 Questioning the Measured Time of Conscious Willing

The time at which subjects report having consciously willed the wrist flex is known as 'W'. One might wonder whether it is worth questioning the validity of W, given that if there is anything one knows, it would be the events in one's own mind, particularly conscious willings. There is, however, a half-century tradition of experiments in cognitive science showing not as much is available to introspection as one might expect (for reviews, see Nisbett and Wilson 1977; Carruthers 2010), research to be revisited later in this subsection. For now, it is enough to note that the results of these experiments provide ample reason to question the validity of W.

One worry about W comes from the well-documented way in which subjects' judgments about a stimulus can be affected by the conditions under which it is perceived (van de Grind 2002). While it is not immediately clear whether we should think that introspection is subject to distortions in the same way that the perception of external events is, some commentators think the processes analogous enough to merit concern (Haggard 2006). One potential problem comes from the 'prior entry effect' (Sternberg and Knoll 1973). This can occur when a subject is asked to compare the relative timing of events in two modalities (e.g., vision and audition), and causes the attended event to appear to occur earlier than it actually did. Given that attention was not controlled for in the Libet experiments, this appears worrying. However, Libet discounts the prior entry effect on grounds that it has been shown to move the perceived temporal location of a stimulus no more than 70ms, far short of closing the roughly 300ms gap between W and RP (Haggard and Libet 2001).

Nonetheless, there are still grounds for wondering whether the Libet paradigm suffers *some* confound or another, given that W displays high variability both between and within subjects (Mele 2010). Haggard and Eimer (1999) calculated each of their subjects' premedian and postmedian average Ws, finding them to be anywhere between 984 and 4ms before flexion. Unless we have reason to think that the temporal relation between the conscious decision and RP is highly variable, this is worrying. However, Trevena and Miller (2002) found mean RP to be not only earlier than mean W, but also earlier than the earliest W that occurred on any individual trial; in which case the essential point of the Libet studies is probably retained. Hopefully future research reveals the reasons for high variability, and whether it is cause for concern.

The possibility must be entertained, however, that W is not a meaningful measure of anything at all. Consider this study by (Banks and Isham 2009). Instead of flexing their wrist, subjects were asked to press a button that responded with a 'beep'. In some trials the tone sounded immediately after the button was pressed, but in others it was delayed by varying amounts. It was found that the longer the interval there was between the button press and the tone, the later W would become.[5] On some trials, W even came after the button press! Banks and Isham take this to mean that subjects were using the tone as a reference for the time of the conscious willing. Going further, Banks and Isham hypothesize that when subjects in Libet paradigms judge the time of conscious willing, it is not an act of introspection at all, but rather a process of 'retrospective inference', one in which the subjects construct the time of conscious willing from whatever cues are available (Banks and Isham 2009, 2010; see also Hallett 2007).[6]

That this would be the case would comport with the tradition of cognitive science research mentioned earlier, the one consisting of an extensive collection of experiments in which subjects appear to not know the workings of their own minds. Subjects, for instance, have been shown to confabulate reasons for why they prefer one of two identical pairs of pantyhose (Nisbett and Wilson 1977), or to be unaware that the presence of others was a factor in their deciding not to seek aid for someone in distress (Latané and Darley 1970). Such experiments are often taken to show that one comes to know what mental states and/or processes one is in in roughly the same way that we come to know those of another person, which is to infer them by applying a folk psychological theory to the person's overt behavior and surrounding circumstances. In fact, another experiment by Banks and Isham (2010) indicates that this might be precisely what is going on in Libet-style experiments: The experimenters had subjects observe another person perform the button-pressing version of the Libet paradigm, asking the subjects to report the time at which they thought that the person had decided to press the button. Subjects' judgments of the timing of the observed person's decisions closely tracked what W had

---

[5] The delayed W-judgments were not quite time-locked to the auditory cue, in that 1ms of delay in the tone produced only an average of .77ms of delay in the perceived time of the decision.

[6] Since in the normal Libet paradigm, there is no tone available as a reference point, Banks and Isham hypothesize that it might be kinesthetic feedback that is determining W.

been in the experiments where the subjects themselves were pressing the button; again, their temporal judgments moved with the tone as it was delayed.

Perhaps the parsimonious explanation of these data—the high variability in the timing of W, the susceptibility of W to the timing of related cues, the symmetry between judgments of W for oneself and for others—is that there is nothing for W to track (Banks and Isham 2010). That is, perhaps the idea that there are such things as conscious willings is just another mistaken tenant of folk psychology, making the Libet experiments a misbegotten attempt to measure something that does not exist.

In this section, we have examined the Libet experiments, which seem to show the time at which one consciously flexes her wrist to come after the brain has already initiated it. These experiments have sometimes been taken to show that free will does not exist, but as seen above, there are probably a number of methodological and philosophical barriers to overcome before this sweeping conclusion could be arrived at. Next we look at another current debate in cognitive science, one concerning the extent to which visual experience guides motor action.

25.3 Epiphenomenalism about Visually Guided Motor Action

Within visual experience, one seems to find very precise information about the location of objects. A glass of water sitting before you, for instance, appears represented in your experience as not merely in some general location or another (e.g., on the table), but rather *right there*, some exact distance and direction from you. Similar observations could be made about the precision with which an object's shape and orientation are represented within visual experience. Notice now that this metrically precise information found within visual experience seems well-suited for use in fine-grained, online motor operations, such as efficiently picking up the water without spilling any. Similar reflections could be made about other precision movements, like catching a Frisbee or hiking a rock-strewn trail.

These observations have been thought by many philosophers to lead rather naturally to the idea that visual experience must play some important, perhaps ineliminable role in visually guided motor action (O'Shaughnessy 1992; Peacocke 1992; Grush 1998; Briscoe and Schwenkler 2015). Such a view is plausibly also part of the commonsense conception of how visual experience and motor action are related (Clark 2001; Wallhagen 2007; Mole 2009; Kozuch 2015). Intuitive as it seems, however, this view has lately come under increasing empirical pressure, in favor of the idea that it is only rarely (if ever) that visual experience guides motor action (Milner & Goodale 1995/2006; Clark 2001, 2007, 2009; Kozuch 2015; cf. Wu 2013). This section surveys the more important arguments and data that have been brought to bear in the currently active debate concerning how visual experience and motor action are related.

25.3.1 The Dissociation Argument

The primary argument for visual experience not being involved in motor action is based on a collection of experiments in which visual experience appears to come apart from motor action. Before looking at this argument, some neuroscientific background is necessary. In the human brain, more advanced kinds of cognition such as perception, memory, or planning take place in the *neocortex*, the brain's outermost layer. Visual information first enters the neocortex in an area known as the *primary visual cortex*, then proceeds via two distinct pathways, a superiorly located *dorsal stream*, and an inferiorly located *ventral stream* (Morel and Bullier 1990; Young 1992; but see Prinz 2012: ch 6). Building on this neuroanatomical division, vision scientists Milner and Goodale (1995/2006; cf. Jacob and Jeannerod 2003) have proposed a *dual visual systems theory*, according to which the two pathways are functionally distinct, with the dorsal stream preparing visual information for use in motor action, and the ventral stream providing the identity of objects for use in goal-oriented cognition. More controversially, the theory also includes the idea that visual consciousness is confined to the ventral stream.

The most well-developed argument for visual experience not guiding motor action is due to Clark (2001, 2007, 2009; see also Milner and Goodale 1995/2006), who builds a case for this by appealing to experiments in which the content driving motor action appears missing from visual experience. We can refer to this as the 'Dissociation Argument'. The Dissociation Argument mainly consists of two lines of evidence, the first consisting of studies of lesions to the ventral or dorsal stream, the second consisting of psychophysical experiments involving visual illusions. We examine each in turn.

Damage to the ventral stream can result in *visual form agnosia*, an inability to consciously perceive things like the shape, size, orientation, or position of an object (Heider 2000). The most extensively studied case of visual form agnosia is patient DF,[7] a Scottish woman who suffered ventral damage when a water heater leaked carbon monoxide as she showered. The case of DF is remarkable because her deficits of visual consciousness apparently do not impede her ability to perform visually guided motor actions: In the 'posting task', the subject is asked to place an envelope-shaped object into a slot whose orientation varies from trial to trial. While DF is at chance when asked to report the orientation of the slot, she effortlessly fits the envelope into the slot each time (Goodale et al. 1991; Milner et al. 1991). DF's ventral damage also resulted in numerous other dissociations between visual experience and motor action, such as picking up objects that differ in shape without being able to tell them apart (Goodale et al. 1994), or stepping over obstacles the height of which she cannot report (Patla and Goodale 1996).[8] On the other hand, *dorsal* lesions sometimes result in converse deficits: Damage here can produce *optic ataxia*, a disorder of motor action unaccompanied by deficits of visual

---

[7] To preserve anonymity, lesion patients are usually called by just their initials in psychological studies.

[8] For further examples of the dissociations that DF displays, see Milner and Goodale 1995/2006: 128–33.

consciousness (Perenin and Vighetto 1983, 1988). Those suffering from optic ataxia are, for instance, unable to succeed at the posting task, but have no difficulty identifying things like the orientation, position, or shape of an object.[9]

The other line of evidence to which the Dissociation Argument appeals comes from experiments in which a consciously experienced visual illusion appears to leave motor action unaffected. The most widely discussed experiment in the context of this debate is due to Aglioti, Desouza, and Goodale (1995), and involves the Ebbinghaus–Titchener illusion, an illusion in which two disks of identical size are made to appear different by the addition of a ring of small circles to the first disk, and a ring of large circles to the second (Haffenden and Goodale 1998). In an interactive version of this illusion created with plastic disks placed on a table, Aglioti and colleagues demonstrated that the visual illusion had significantly less of an effect on subjects' motor actions than it did on their conscious perception, since their grip width would conform much more closely to the interior disks' actual size than did their conscious perception of them. Other visual illusions, such as the Ponzo (Brenner and Smeets 1996; Ellis et al. 1999) or hollow face illusion (Króliczak et al. 2006) have been used to demonstrate similar dissociations. I note that some of these experiments are still considered controversial (see, e.g., Franz and Gegenfurtner 2008); this, however, is a technical issue that we lack space to go into in this short piece.

As we will see in what follows, both lines of evidence are contested. Putting this aside, however, the brain lesion and visual illusion data just surveyed are naturally interpreted as showing visual experience not to have the kind of relationship with motor action that we might have pre-theoretically thought: as observed earlier, the information found in visual consciousness seems to contain the kind of richness and detail required for the fine-grained, online guidance of motor action. In the experiments just described above, however, the content driving motor action seems to be either missing from (DF) or mismatched with (the visual illusions) the content of visual experience, in which case visual experience cannot be what is driving motor action. From this one might infer, as Clark does, that 'a great deal of our daily, fine-tuned motor activity proceeds quite independently of the current contents of conscious visual experience' (2001: 499).

Shortly (Subsection 25.3.3), we look at how some commentators attempt to resist this conclusion. First though, we explore the issue of upon what precise claim the Dissociation Argument should be taken to cast doubt.

25.3.2 The Hypothesis of Experience-Based Control

The Dissociation Argument seeks to overturn a certain conception of how visual experience relates to motor action, but what precisely is this conception? In Clark's original

---

[9] I am presenting a somewhat simplified picture here, since optic ataxics found it difficult to identify some of these properties in (Pisella et al. 2006, 2009); however, these difficulties are probably the result, not of deficits in consciousness, but rather of attention (see Kozuch 2015).

salvo, he called into question what he referred to as the 'Hypothesis of Experience-Based Control'; for short, 'EBC.' EBC, along with other, similar theses at play in the present debate, has been understood in various ways. The key issues at stake can be encapsulated in the following formulation (Kozuch 2015):

> EBC: The content of visual consciousness is what is typically used to directly guide visually based motor action.

A first thing to notice about this formulation is that it contains both a *typicality clause*, and a *directness clause*; that is, for EBC to be considered true in its entirety, visually guided motor actions would need to be both typically and directly guided by information within visual experience. My formulating EBC in this way is motivated by how commentators involved in the debate have described the view that they mean to attack or defend. However, EBC can be understood either as a philosophical thesis, or as an attempt to express the commonsense view of the relationship between visual experience and motor action. In the case of EBC as a philosophical hypothesis, formulating it as it appears above is of course not contentious, since the formulation merely adheres to the stipulated view that commentators in the debate intend to engage with. More controversial is whether the above formulation precisely captures the commonsense view of the relationship between visual experience and motor action, and whether the impression that visual experience guides motor action is something that can be derived from the phenomenology of performing motor actions (Shepherd 2015, 2016). However, these latter two issues are set aside in this short review so that we might focus on whether EBC as a philosophical thesis passes muster.[10]

Let us further precisify what is at issue. Something to note is that opponents of EBC do not hold that visual experience is *wholly* epiphenomenal toward motor action, it instead being the case that visual experience mostly only has high-level, broadly specified influences on motor action. More specifically, it is thought that the function of visual experience (and of the ventral stream) is to merely identify and select the objects that are to be acted upon (e.g., a mug of coffee) and perhaps provide general parameters for the action based upon context or background knowledge (to pick the mug up by its handle since it is hot); once these general goals and parameters are set, the task is handed off to non-conscious dorsal processes for implementation. Detractors of EBC usually also grant that there are times where information from visual experience might be called upon to more directly guide motor action. For example, it is commonly thought that, because visual information in the dorsal stream decays quickly (it has a 'short memory'), certain delayed motor actions are guided by conscious information in the ventral stream (e.g., ones performed after the lights have been shut off for a few seconds; Rossetti et al. 2005). However, according to opponents of EBC, this kind of fine-grained guidance by visual experience is very much the exception rather than rule.

---

[10] But see Kozuch 2015 for some justification for what is probably the more contentious of the two, the directness clause.

Above, we looked at how the original challenge to EBC was raised in the form of the Dissociation Argument. Now we move on to examine how commentators have subsequently attempted to argue for or against EBC. The discussion is organized according to the directness and typicality clauses of EBC, starting with directness.

25.3.3 Does Visual Experience *Directly* Guide Motor Action?

According to Milner and Goodale's dual visual systems theory, just the dorsal stream produces those representations guiding visuomotor action, and just the ventral stream produces conscious representations. Were this true, it would mean that, even if it could be shown that visual experience has a significant causal influence on motor action (an issue taken up in Section 25.3.4), any such contributions would first be routed through the dorsal stream, making them indirect; that is, the *directness* clause of EBC would be false. The question arises then as to whether the relevant empirical data support this tenant of Milner and Goodale's theory. The most systematic argument for this is due to Kozuch (2015), who argues that a close examination of available evidence shows it to be neither the case that the ventral stream ever directly guides motor action, nor that the dorsal stream ever produces conscious representations.

To support the first idea, Kozuch appeals to a variety of neuroimaging and lesion data. A first line of evidence comes from a set of neuroimaging studies in which increased visuomotor task demand produced increased dorsal activity without a corresponding increase in ventral activity (Binkofski et al. 1999; Culham et al. 2003; Prado et al. 2005); these studies include one experiment in which DF's neural activity was measured while carrying out the posting task discussed in Subsection 25.3.1 (James et al. 2003). The results of damage to ventral and dorsal areas are thought to lend further support to the idea that the ventral stream never directly guides motor action, since while it is the case that dorsal damage produces profound, pervasive visuomotor problems, those brought about by ventral lesions manifest only under unusual circumstances, such as when the motor target is viewed monocularly (Dijkerman et al. 1996, 1999), or is removed shortly before the action is performed (Milner et al. 1999);[11] and even in those cases where these ventrally caused motor deficits manifest, the available neuroimaging evidence implies that it is not the ventral stream directly guiding the motor actions, since it is still dorsal areas showing increased activation (see, e.g., Himmelbach et al. 2009).

In arguing for the idea that the dorsal stream does not produce conscious representations, Kozuch mostly appeals to the results of dorsal lesions: While dorsally damaged patients will suffer from those deficits in visuomotor action that constitute optic ataxia,

---

[11] Himmelbach et al. (2012) argue that DF does not actually perform at the level of controls in even some tasks carried out under normal conditions, for example, actions performed toward objects in the periphery (see also Briscoe and Schwenkler 2015), but these deficits could be attributed to dorsal damage more recently discovered in DF (James et al. 2003; Bridge et al. 2013).

their conscious perception appears unaffected, since dorsal patients can successfully report upon things such as the shape, direction, orientation, position, and identity of objects (Perenin and Vighetto 1983, 1988). But if the dorsal stream produced conscious representations, one would think that dorsal damage would bring about deficits in at least some kinds of conscious visual perception. Additionally, Brogaard (2011b) argues that we should think that dorsal representations are not conscious since processes such as changing one's grip aperture happen too quickly to be cognitively accessed, and such access is necessary for consciousness (see also Brogaard 2011a).

However, Wu (2014) recently appealed to neuroimaging (Committeri et al. 2004) and lesion (Berryhill et al. 2009) evidence in order to argue that dorsal areas V3A and V7 might produce conscious representations of object distance (see also Prinz 2012: ch 6), although it is unclear whether these representations feed into visuomotor action. Additionally, brain area MT (mediotemporal) is often classified as being part of the dorsal stream, but is also thought by some to produce conscious motion representations (Zeki 2003; Block 2007; Schenk and McIntosh 2010; Prinz 2012: ch 6); however, Milner and Goodale (1995/2006: 219) argue that MT is instead more aptly considered an early processing area (i.e., not part of the dorsal stream), one akin to the primary visual cortex, and that the representations of MT are probably not conscious until they arrive in the ventral stream (1995/2006: ch 8). Additionally, Brogaard (2012) argues that dorsal representations must sometimes be conscious, since according to one gloss of dual visual systems theory it is only the dorsal stream that produces the kind of viewer-centered representations that we find in visual experience, but Foley, Whitwell, and Goodale (2015) argue that it is only because of a misreading of the dual visual systems hypothesis that some commentators suppose that the ventral stream does not contain these kinds of 'egocentric' representation.

According to the directness clause of EBC, the representations found in visual experience are—at least sometimes—the same as those driving fine-grained, online motor actions. If this were the case, then the ventral stream should directly guide motor action, or the dorsal stream should produce conscious representations. As just seen, the first condition seems rather unlikely to obtain, but whether the second obtains is more controversial. Now we move on to the issue of how frequently the information in visual experience is what—directly or indirectly—guides motor action.

25.3.4 Does Visual Experience *Typically* Guide Motor Action?

The Dissociation Argument proceeds by citing experiments in which the content driving motor action appears mismatched with or missing from the content of visual experience, the idea being that these present instances in which visual experience cannot be driving motor action. One strategy that commentators have used to respond to the Dissociation Argument is to argue that the experiments appealed to in it do not actually present instances of content mismatches, since there is reason to think that subjects' reports about what content appears in their visual experience cannot be taken at face value. If such a strategy succeeds, it would help support the idea that visual experience guides motor action more typically than is often supposed by the critic of EBC.

For an example of this approach, we again consider visual form agnosia.[12] The case of DF is troubling for EBC because DF can perform motor actions that require information about a target object's form, though she is apparently unable to consciously perceive form. Wallhagen (2007), however, argues that we should think that DF actually consciously experiences form, since DF is still able to experience colors, and it would be incoherent to suppose that her experience could contain colors without them being bounded in some fashion (e.g., in areas where two different colors adjoin), in which case she *de facto* has conscious experiences of form (but see Mole 2009). Wallhagen claims that we should instead think that DF merely has a deficit in bringing conscious form representations under concepts, as would be necessary for their report. This is the more natural explanation, argues Wallhagen, since the facility with which she motorically interacts with objects is hard to explain if she cannot experience object form.

Clark's main response to this is to argue that whatever form content DF allegedly enjoys cannot be considered conscious, as it lacks the kind of connection to personal agency required for this (Clark 2007; see also 2009). Clark points out some distinctive limitations on how DF uses form content, such as her inability to sketch an object, or to determine the proper end to pick it up from (in the case of, e.g., a screwdriver). But one would think that content lacking these kinds of connection to an agent and her practical goals does not deserve to be called 'conscious' (see also Evans 1982). Criticizing Clark's response, Kozuch (2015) points out how Clark's argument appears to appeal only to *conceptual* considerations, that is, ones concerning how the term 'conscious' is or should be used, but that it is unclear how conceptual considerations are supposed to bear on the issue of whether DF, as a matter of fact, does or does not have (phenomenally)[13] conscious experiences of form.

In a vein similar to Wallhagen, Mole (2009, 2013) argues that DF's experience contains *embodied demonstrative* content, content representing the slot's orientation in the posting task as something like '*this* way round'. This form content, claims Mole, is difficult to experimentally discover since it arises only in the course of performing motor actions. To support this hypothesis, Mole points out how DF sometimes correctly identifies an object's shape if she attempts to do so while or just before reaching for it (Schenk and Milner 2006). Mole also claims that it would be hard to explain the confidence with which DF performs visually guided motor actions if she lacked conscious form content. In response to this, Wu (2013) argues that DF's ability to identify object form in these

---

[12] Critics of the Dissociation Argument also contest the visual illusion evidence, doing so in a similar manner, but we lack space to consider these objections here.

[13] The word 'phenomenally' is inserted parenthetically to highlight that we are talking about a notion of conscious experience according to which there is no entailment from some mental content being conscious to its being accessible for report; this is in contrast to the idea of so-called access consciousness (see Block 1995, 2002).

situations might come from proprioception and not vision, the result of an 'efference copy' (Wolpert and Ghahramani 2000), that is, a simulation of an incipient motor action generated by the motor system to predict and correct errors. However, Schenk and Milner (2006) take this scenario to be unlikely since the accuracy of DF's grip fails to correlate with the accuracy of her verbal report, something that would be expected if her report was based on a simulation of the motor action about to be preformed.

Another strategy adopted in response to the Dissociation Argument is to appeal to studies or data in which visual experience appears to be guiding or influencing motor action. Briscoe and Schwenkler (2015), for instance, call attention to how in some visual illusion studies that are cited against EBC (e.g., Aglioti et al. 1995) it is not that the visual illusion has *no* effect on motor action, but rather that the effect on motor action is significantly less than the effect on visual experience, something suggesting that even in these cases 'consciously encoded spatial information will make measurable contributions to motor programming' (Briscoe and Schwenkler 2015: 21). Briscoe and Schwenkler argue, furthermore, that this difference between motor action and visual experience presents under only very specific circumstances, viz., when the motor action is well-practiced (Gonzalez et al. 2008), performed rapidly (e.g., Kroliczak et al. 2006), right-handedly (Gonzalez, Ganel & Goodale 2006), *and* with binocular vision (Marotta et al. 1998); Briscoe and Schwenkler claim that outside of these conditions, the motor systems are 'fully susceptible to the effects of visual illusions' (2015: 21). Overall, Briscoe and Schwenkler take the data to which they appeal to make a good case for visual experience playing a far larger role in motor action than detractors of EBC usually allow.[14]

Using a similar strategy, Shepherd cites experiments that he believes show visual experience to make a 'critical causal contribution' to motor action (2015). One is a study in which the experimenters altered the visual illusion while subjects were midway through performing a motor action toward it, the result being that the visual illusion had a greater effect on motor action than it would have otherwise (Caljouw et al. 2011). Another study showed that the amount of time that a golfer visually fixates the hole while putting was positively correlated with success (Vine et al. 2013); since this longer 'quiet eye duration' (Mann et al. 2007) is plausibly construed as successful allocation of attention (something probably closely associated with consciousness), this might present an instance where visual experience is guiding motor action. Both of the studies Shepherd cites are of particular interest, since they are both instances in which visual experience might be involved in the *online* guidance of motor action (i.e., guidance of motor action in the course of its being performed), something detractors of EBC have expressed particular skepticism about ever happening (cf. Milner and Goodale 2010).

The studies cited by Briscoe and Schwenkler and Shepherd indeed seem important to introduce into the debate over EBC. However, the idea that these experiments might lend support to visual experience typically driving motor action is open to several criticisms.

---

[14] Briscoe and Schwenkler also make several notable points about the case of DF, but we lack the space to consider them here.

A first criticism applies to Briscoe and Schwenkler's idea that a visual illusion having any effect on motor action could act as evidence for visual experience playing a role in guiding motor action, even if this effect is less than the one had on visual experience. However, it seems that all one would need to show that visual experience is not guiding a motor action is that there is a *mismatch* between the content of visual experience and the motor systems: plausibly, visual experience could be guiding some given motor action only if the representations appearing in visual experience are the *same* as those guiding the motor action (more carefully, only if the two have type-identical content), something precluded by their being mismatched.

However, even in studies where there is a purported match in content, this falls short of showing that it is visual experience guiding motor action, since it fails to exclude the possibility that the observed motor effects arise because the visual illusions affect representations in early visual areas (e.g., the primary visual cortex), areas tributary to both the dorsal and ventral streams. In such a case, the effects on motor action would arise because it is the (unconscious) representations of early visual areas that are providing the visual information used by the dorsal stream, the conscious ventral stream having been completely bypassed. This might occur because the nature of the visual illusion is such that it is prone to arise within early visual areas (Dyde and Milner 2002; Milner and Dyde 2003), or because of top-down effects from higher areas (Murray et al. 2006; Fang et al. 2008), ones possibly the result of modulation by attention (Tootell et al. 1998; Ito and Gilbert 1999; Somers et al. 1999; Fischer and Whitney 2009). And so many of the studies to which Briscoe and Schwenkler and Shepherd appeal cannot yet be considered instances in which visual experience is driving motor action.

One last criticism applies to the Briscoe and Schwenkler contention that motor actions are less affected by visual illusions only under narrow circumstances. A first difficulty here is that the number of studies used to support this claim is rather small. Putting this aside, there is the further problem that they often interpret these studies in an idiosyncratic fashion.

For instance, what Briscoe and Schwenkler regard as a slowly performed motor action in Kroliczak et al. (2006) is not taken by the study's authors to be a measure of the content of the motor systems, but rather a 'perceptual' measure, that is, a measure of the content of visual experience; similarly, the motor actions in Rossetti et al. (2005) are not taken by the study's authors to be *slow* motor actions, but rather *delayed* motor actions: in the experiment in question, subjects are not asked to perform the action slowly, but rather are not allowed to perform the action until several seconds after the target is presented, the lights having been shut off in the interim. Similar critiques can be made about the manner in which Briscoe and Schwenkler appeal to other experiments to support the claim under consideration.

As discussed earlier, the character of visual experience strongly suggests that it is closely associated with motor action, given that the kind of fine-grained and detailed information found in visual experience seems well-suited for use in precision movement. This view, however, has been thought to be belied by results in vision science, including the way that DF is able to perform motor actions in the absence of normal visual experience, and the way that motor actions appear resistant to the influence of visual illusions. But, as just seen, whether such results make the view that visual experience rarely guides motor action mandatory is an active area of debate, one perhaps not resolved soon.

25.4 CONCLUSION

These days, most philosophers are materialists, and therefore worry not about the type of epiphenomenalism that might arise from dualism about phenomenal properties. The same is not true of contemporary empirically driven cases for epiphenomenalism: Whether the conscious will lacks causal efficacy became a worry when the Libet experiments were first performed, and remains so; whether visual experience only rarely (if ever) drives our motor actions became a worry when DF's residual motor abilities were first discovered, and remains so. Likely these will continue to be open questions until we have not just more data, but also further philosophical argumentation, where the latter plays an integral role in the proper interpretation of the former.

REFERENCES

Aglioti, S., Desouza, J., and Goodale, M. (1995), 'Size-contrast illusions deceive the eye but not the hand', *Current Biology* 5/6: 679.

Banks, W. P. and Isham, E. A. (2009), 'We infer rather than perceive the moment we decided to act', *Psychological Science*, 20/1: 17–21.

Banks, W. P. and Isham, E. A. (2010), 'Do we really know what we are doing? Implications of reported time of decision for theories of volition', in W. Sinnott-Armstrong and L. Nadel (eds), *Conscious Will and Responsibility*. Oxford: Oxford University Press), 47–60.

Bayne, T. (2011), 'Libet and the case for free will scepticism', in R. Swinburne, (ed.), *Free Will and Modern Science*. (Oxford: Oxford University Press/British Academy), 25–46.

Berryhill, M. E., Fendrich, R., and Olson, I. R. (2009), 'Impaired distance perception and size constancy following bilateral occipitoparietal damage', *Experimental Brain Research*, 194/3: 381–93.

Binkofski, F., Buccino, G., Stephan, K. M., Rizzolatti, G., Seitz, R. J., and Freund, H.-J. (1999), 'A parieto-premotor network for object manipulation: evidence from neuroimaging', *Experimental Brain Research*, 128/1–2: 210–13.

Block, N. (1995), 'On a Confusion about the Function of Consciousness', *Behavioral and Brain Sciences*, 18: 227–87.

Block, N. (2002), 'Concepts of Consciousness', in D. Chalmers (ed.), *Philosophy of Mind: Classic and Contemporary Readings*. New York: Oxford University Press.

Block, N. (2007), 'Consciousness, accessibility, and the mesh between psychology and neuroscience', *Behavioral and Brain Sciences* 30/5: 481.

Breitmeyer, B. G. (1985), 'Problems with the psychophysics of intention', *Behavioral and Brain Sciences*, 8/04: 539–40.

Brenner, E. and Smeets, J. B. (1996), 'Size illusion influences how we lift but not how we grasp an object', *Experimental Brain Research*, 111/3: 473–6.

Bridge, H., Thomas, O. M., Minini, L., Cavina-Pratesi, C., Milner, A. D., and Parker, A. J. (2013), 'Structural and functional changes across the visual cortex of a patient with visual form agnosia', *Journal of Neuroscience*, 33/31: 12779–91.

Bridgeman, B. (1985), 'Free will and the functions of consciousness', *Behavioral and Brain Sciences*, 8/04: 540–0.

Briscoe, R. and Schwenkler, J. (2015), 'Conscious vision in action', *Cognitive science*, 39/7: 1435–67.

Brogaard, B. (2011a), 'Are there unconscious perceptual processes?', *Consciousness and Cognition*, 20/2: 449–63.

Brogaard, B. (2011b), 'Conscious vision for action versus unconscious vision for action?', *Cognitive Science*, 35/6: 1076–104.

Brogaard, B. (2012), 'Vision for action and the contents of perception', *The Journal of Philosophy*, 109/10: 569–87.

Caljouw, S. R., Van Der Kamp, J., Lijster, M., and Savelsbergh, G. J. (2011), 'Differential effects of a visual illusion on online visual guidance in a stable environment and online adjustments to perturbations', *Consciousness and Cognition*, 20/4: 1135–43.

Campbell, C. (1957), *On Selfhood and Godhood*. London: The Macmillan Company.

Carruthers, P. (2010), 'Introspection: Divided and partly eliminated', *Philosophy and Phenomenological Research*, 80/1: 76–111.

Chalmers, D. J. (1995), 'Facing up to the problem of consciousness', *Journal of Consciousness Studies*, 2/3: 200–19.

Chalmers, D. J. (1996), *The Conscious Mind: In Search of a Fundamental Theory*. Oxford: Oxford University Press.

Clark, A. (2001), 'Visual experience and motor action: Are the bonds too tight?', *Philosophical Review*, 110/4: 495–519.

Clark, A. (2007), 'What reaching teaches: Consciousness, control, and the inner zombie', *The British Journal for the Philosophy of Science*, 58/3: 563–94.

Clark, A. (2009), 'Perception, action, and experience: Unraveling the golden braid', *Neuropsychologia*, 47/6: 1460–8.

Committeri, G., Galati, G., Paradis, A.-L., Pizzamiglio, L., Berthoz, A., and Lebihan, D. (2004), 'Reference frames for spatial cognition: different brain areas are involved in viewer-, object-, and landmark-centered judgments about object location', *Journal of Cognitive Neuroscience*, 16/9: 1517–35.

Culham, J. C., Danckert, S. L., De Souza, J. F., Gati, J. S., Menon, R. S., and Goodale, M. A. (2003), 'Visually guided grasping produces fMRI activation in dorsal but not ventral stream brain areas', *Experimental Brain Research*, 153/2: 180–9.

Dennett, D. (1984), *Elbow Room: The Varieties of Free Will Worth Wanting*. Cambridge, MA: MIT Press.

Dennett, D. C. and Kinsbourne, M. (1992), 'Time and the observer: The where and when of consciousness in the brain', *Behavioral and Brain Sciences*, 15/2: 183–201.

Dijkerman, H., Milner, A., and Carey, D. (1996), 'The perception and prehension of objects oriented in the depth plane', *Experimental Brain Research*, 112/3: 442–51.

Dijkerman, H., Milner, A., and Carey, D. (1999), 'Motion parallax enables depth processing for action in a visual form agnosic when binocular vision is unavailable', *Neuropsychologia*, 37/13: 1505–10.

Dyde, R. T. and Milner, A. D. (2002), 'Two illusions of perceived orientation: one fools all of the people some of the time; the other fools all of the people all of the time', *Experimental Brain Research*, 144/4: 518–27.
Ellis, R. R., Flanagan, J. R., and Lederman, S. J. (1999), 'The influence of visual illusions on grasp position', *Experimental Brain Research*, 125/2: 109–14.
Evans, G. (1982), *The Varieties of Reference*. Oxford: Oxford University Press.
Fang, F., Boyaci, H., Kersten, D., and Murray, S. O. (2008), 'Attention-dependent representation of a size illusion in human V1', *Current Biology*, 18/21: 1707–12.
Filevich, E., Kühn, S., and Haggard, P. (2013), 'There is no free won't: antecedent brain activity predicts decisions to inhibit', *PloS one*, 8/2: e53053.
Fischer, J. and Whitney, D. (2009), 'Attention narrows position tuning of population responses in V1', *Current Biology*, 19/16: 1356–61.
Flanagan, O. (1996), *Self-Expressions*. Oxford: Oxford University Press.
Foley, R. T., Whitwell, R. L., and Goodale, M. A. (2015), 'The two-visual-systems hypothesis and the perspectival features of visual experience', *Consciousness and Cognition*, 35: 225–33.
Frankfurt, H. G. (1988), 'Freedom of the Will and the Concept of a Person', *What Is a Person?* Springer, 127–44.
Franz, V. H. and Gegenfurtner, K. R. (2008), 'Grasping visual illusions: consistent data and no dissociation', *Cognitive Neuropsychology*, 25/7–8: 920–50.
Gonzalez, C. L., Ganel, T., and Goodale, M. A. (2006), 'Hemispheric specialization for the visual control of action is independent of handedness', *Journal of Neurophysiology*, 95/6: 3496–501.
Gonzalez, C., Ganel, T., Whitwell, R., Morrissey, B., and Goodale, M. A. (2008), 'Practice makes perfect, but only with the right hand: Sensitivity to perceptual illusions with awkward grasps decreases with practice in the right but not the left hand', *Neuropsychologia*, 46/2: 624–31.
Goodale, M. A., Milner, A. D., Jakobson, L., and Carey, D. (1991), 'A neurological dissociation between perceiving objects and grasping them', *Nature*, 349/6305: 154–6.
Goodale, M. A., Meenan, J. P., Bülthoff, H. H., Nicolle, D. A., Murphy, K. J., and Racicot, C. I. (1994), 'Separate neural pathways for the visual analysis of object shape in perception and prehension', *Current Biology*, 4/7: 604–10.
Grush, R. (1998), 'Skill and spatial content', *Electronic Journal of Analytic Philosophy*, 6/6.
Haffenden, A. M. and Goodale, M. A. (1998), 'The effect of pictorial illusion on prehension and perception', *Journal of Cognitive Neuroscience*, 10/1: 122–36.
Haggard, P. (2006), 'Conscious intention and the sense of agency', in N. Sebanz and W. Prinz (eds), *Disorders of Volition*. Cambridge, MA: MIT Press.
Haggard, P. (2011), 'Does brain science change our view of free will?', in R. Swinburne, (ed.), *Free Will and Modern Science*. Oxford: Oxford University Press/British Academy), 15–24.
Haggard, P. and Eimer, M. (1999), 'On the relation between brain potentials and the awareness of voluntary movements', *Experimental Brain Research*, 126/1: 128–33.
Haggard, P. and Libet, B. (2001), 'Conscious intention and brain activity', *Journal of Consciousness Studies*, 8/11: 47–64.
Hallett, M. (2007), 'Volitional control of movement: the physiology of free will', *Clinical Neurophysiology*, 118/6: 1179–92.
Haynes, J. D. (2011), 'Decoding and predicting intentions', *Annals of the New York Academy of Sciences*, 1224/1: 9–21.

Heider, B. (2000), 'Visual form agnosia: neural mechanisms and anatomical foundations', *Neurocase*, 6/1: 1–12.

Himmelbach, M., Nau, M., Zündorf, I., Erb, M., Perenin, M.-T., and Karnath, H.-O. (2009), 'Brain activation during immediate and delayed reaching in optic ataxia', *Neuropsychologia*, 47/6: 1508–17.

Himmelbach, M., Boehme, R., and Karnath, H.-O. (2012), '20 years later: A second look on DF's motor behaviour', *Neuropsychologia*, 50/1: 139–44.

Huxley, T. H. (1874), 'On the hypothesis that animals are automata, and its history', in *Science and Culture, and Other Essays*. New York, 1882, 239.

Ito, M. and Gilbert, C. D. (1999), 'Attention modulates contextual influences in the primary visual cortex of alert monkeys', *Neuron*, 22/3: 593–604.

Jackson, F. (1982), 'Epiphenomenal qualia', *The Philosophical Quarterly*, 32/127: 127–36.

Jacob, P. and Jeannerod, M. (2003), *Ways of Seeing: The Scope and Limits of Visual Cognition*. Oxford: Oxford University Press.

James, T. W., Culham, J., Humphrey, G.K ., Milner, A. D., and Goodale, M. A. (2003), 'Ventral occipital lesions impair object recognition but not object-directed grasping: an fMRI study', *Brain*, 126/11: 2463–75.

Kane, R. (2009), 'Libertarianism', *Philosophical Studies*, 144/1: 35–44.

Kornhuber, H. H. and Deecke, L. (1965), 'Hirnpotentialänderungen bei Willkürbewegungen und passiven Bewegungen des Menschen: Bereitschaftspotential und reafferente Potentiale', *Pflüger's Archiv für die gesamte Physiologie des Menschen und der Tiere*, 284/1: 1–17.

Kozuch, B. (2015), 'Dislocation, not dissociation: The neuroanatomical argument against visual experience driving motor action', *Mind & Language*, 30/5: 572–602.

Króliczak, G., Heard, P., Goodale, M. A., and Gregory, R. L. (2006), 'Dissociation of perception and action unmasked by the hollow-face illusion', *Brain Research*, 1080/1: 9–16.

Jackson, F. (2003), 'Mind and illusion', *Royal Institute of Philosophy Supplements*, 53: 251–71.

Latané, B. and Darley, J. M. (1970), *The Unresponsive Bystander: Why doesn't he help?* Prentice Hall.

Libet, B. (1985), 'Theory and evidence relating cerebral processes to conscious will', *Behavioral and Brain Sciences*, 8/4: 558–66.

Libet, B., Gleason, C. A., Wright, E. W., and Pearl, D. K. (1983), 'Time of conscious intention to act in relation to onset of cerebral activity (readiness-potential)', *Brain*, 106/3: 623–42.

McKenna, M. (2013), 'Reasons-responsiveness, agents, and mechanisms', in D. Shoemaker (ed.), *Oxford Studies in Agency and Responsibility*, Vol. 1. Oxford: Oxford University Press, 1151–83.

Mann, D. T., Williams, A. M., Ward, P., and Janelle, C. M. (2007), 'Perceptual-cognitive expertise in sport: A meta-analysis', *Journal of Sport and Exercise Psychology*, 29/4: 457.

Marotta, J., Desouza, J., Haffenden, A., and Goodale, M. (1998), 'Does a monocularly presented size-contrast illusion influence grip aperture?', *Neuropsychologia*, 36/6: 491–7.

Mele, A. R. (2009), *Effective Intentions: The Power of Conscious Will*. Oxford: Oxford University Press on Demand.

Mele, A. R. (2010), 'Libet on Free Will: Readiness Potentials, Decisions, and Awareness', in W. Sinnott-Armstrong and L. Nadel (eds), *Conscious Will and Responsibility: A Tribute to Benjamin Libet*. Oxford: Oxford University Press.

Milner, D. and Dyde, R. (2003), 'Why do some perceptual illusions affect visually guided action, when others don't?', *Trends in Cognitive Sciences*, 7/1: 10–11.

Milner, D. and Goodale, M. (1995/2006), *The Visual Brain in Action*. Oxford: Oxford University Press.

Milner, A. D. and Goodale, M. A. (2010), 'Cortical visual systems for perception and action', in N. Gangopadhyay, M. Madary, and F. Spicer (eds), *Perception, Action, and Consciousness: Sensorimotor Dynamics and Two Visual Systems*. Oxford: Oxford University Press 71–95.

Milner, A., Dijkerman, H., and Carey, D. (1999), 'Visuospatial processing in a pure case of visual-form agnosia', N. Burgess, K. J. Jeffery, and J. O'Keefe (eds), *The hippocampal and parietal foundations of spatial cognition*. Oxford: Oxford Univesity Press, 443–66.

Milner, A., Perrett, D., Johnston, R., Benson, P., Jordan, T., Heeley, D., Bettucci, D., Mortara, F., Mutani, R., and Terazzi, E. (1991), 'Perception and action in "visual form agnosia"', *Brain*, 114/1: 405–28.

Mole, C. (2009), 'Illusions, demonstratives, and the zombie action hypothesis', *Mind*, 118/472: 995–1011.

Mole, C. (2013), 'Embodied demonstratives: a reply to Wu', *Mind*, 122/485: 231–9.

Morel, A. and Bullier, J. (1990), 'Anatomical segregation of two cortical visual pathways in the macaque monkey', *Vis Neurosci*, 4/6: 555–78.

Murray, S.O., Boyaci, H., and Kersten, D. (2006), 'The representation of perceived angular size in human primary visual cortex', *Nature Neuroscience*, 9/3: 429–34.

Nagel, T. (1974), 'What is it like to be a bat?', *The Philosophical Review*, 83/4: 435–50.

Nisbett, R. E. and Wilson, T. D. (1977), 'Telling more than we can know: Verbal reports on mental processes', *Psychological Review*, 84/3: 231.

O'Shaughnessy, B. (1992), 'The diversity and unity of action and perception', in T. Crane (ed.), *The Contents of Perception*. Cambridge: Cambridge University Press.

Patla, A. E. and Goodale, M. A. (1996), 'Obstacle avoidance during locomotion is unaffected in a patient with visual form agnosia', *NeuroReport*, 8/1: 165–8.

Peacocke, C. (1992), 'Scenarios, concepts, and perception', in T. Crane (ed.), *The Contents of Experience*. Cambridge: Cambridge University Press, 105–35.

Perenin, M. and Vighetto, A. (1983), 'Optic ataxia: A specific disorder in visuomotor coordination', in A. Hein and M. Jeannerod (eds), *Spatially Oriented Behavior*. New York; Berlin; Heidelberg: Springer, 305–26.

Perenin, M. and Vighetto, A. (1988), 'Optic ataxia: a specific disruption in visuomotor mechanisms', *Brain*, 111/3: 643–74.

Pisella, L. et al. (2006), 'No double-dissociation between optic ataxia and visual agnosia: multiple sub-streams for multiple visuo-manual integrations', *Neuropsychologia*, 44/13: 2734–48.

Pisella, L. et al. (2009), 'Optic ataxia and the function of the dorsal stream: contributions to perception and action', *Neuropsychologia*, 47: 3033–44.

Pockett, S. and Purdy, S. (2010), 'Are voluntary movements initiated preconsciously? The relationships between readiness potentials, urges and decisions', in W. Sinnott-Armstrong and L. Nadel (eds), *Conscious Will and Responsibility: A Tribute to Benjamin Libet*. Oxford: Oxford University Press, 34–46.

Prado, J., Clavagnier, S., Otzenberger, H., Scheiber, C., Kennedy, H., and Perenin, M.-T. (2005), 'Two cortical systems for reaching in central and peripheral vision', *Neuron*, 48/5: 849–58.

Prinz, J. (2012), *The Conscious Brain*. Oxford: Oxford University Press.

Roskies, A. (2010), 'Why Libet's studies don't pose a threat to free will', in W. Sinnott-Armstrong and L. Nadel (eds.) *Conscious Will and Responsibility: A Tribute to Benjamin Libet*. Oxford: Oxford University Press, 11–22.

Rossetti, Y. et al. (2005), 'Visually guided reaching: bilateral posterior parietal lesions cause a switch from fast visuomotor to slow cognitive control', *Neuropsychologia*, 43/2: 162–77.

Schenk, T. and McIntosh, R. D. (2010), 'Do we have independent visual streams for perception and action?', *Cognitive Neuroscience*, 1/1: 52–62.

Schenk, T. and Milner, A. D. (2006), 'Concurrent visuomotor behaviour improves form discrimination in a patient with visual form agnosia', *European Journal of Neuroscience*, 24/5: 1495–503.

Shepherd, J. (2015), 'Conscious control over action', *Mind & Language*, 30/3: 320–44.

Shepherd, J. (2016), 'Conscious action/zombie action', *Noûs*, 50/2: 419–44.

Sinnott-Armstrong, W. and Nadel, L. (2010), 'Introduction', in W. Sinnott-Armstrong, and L. Nadel (eds), *Conscious Will and Responsibility: A Tribute to Benjamin Libet*. Oxford: Oxford University Press), xi–xvi.

Somers, D. C., Dale, A. M., Seiffert, A. E., and Tootell, R. B. (1999), 'Functional MRI reveals spatially specific attentional modulation in human primary visual cortex', *Proceedings of the National Academy of Sciences*, 96/4: 1663–8.

Sternberg, S. and Knoll, R. L. (1973), 'The perception of temporal order: Fundamental issues and a general model', i *Attention and Performance IV*, 629–85.

Tootell, R. B., Hadjikhani, N., Hall, E. K., Marrett, S., Vanduffel, W., Vaughan, J. T., and Dale, A. M. (1998), 'The retinotopy of visual spatial attention', *Neuron*, 21/6: 1409–22.

Trevena, J. A. and Miller, J. (2002), 'Cortical movement preparation before and after a conscious decision to move', *Consciousness and Cognition*, 11/2: 162–90.

Van De Grind, W. (2002), 'Physical, neural, and mental timing', *Consciousness and Cognition*, 11/2: 241–64.

Vine, S. J., Lee, D., Moore, L. J., and Wilson, M. R. (2013), 'Quiet eye and choking: Online control breaks down at the point of performance failure', *Medicine & Science in Sports & Exercise*, 45/10: 1988–94.

Wallhagen, M. (2007), 'Consciousness and action: Does cognitive science support (mild) epiphenomenalism?', *The British Journal for the Philosophy of Science*, 58/3: 539–61.

Wegner, D. M. (2003a), *The Illusion of Conscious Will*. Cambridge, MA: MIT Press.

Wegner, D. M. (2003b), 'The mind's best trick: how we experience conscious will', *Trends in Cognitive Sciences*, 7/2: 65–9.

Wolpert, D. M. and Ghahramani, Z. (2000), 'Computational principles of movement neuroscience', *Nature Neuroscience*, 31: 212–17.

Wu, W. (2013), 'The case for zombie agency', *Mind*, 122/485: 217–30.

Wu, W. (2014), 'Against division: Consciousness, information and the visual streams', *Mind & Language*, 29/4: 383–406.

Young, M. P. (1992), 'Objective analysis of the topological organization of the primate cortical visual system', *Nature*, 358/6382: 152–5.

Zeki, S. (2003), 'The disunity of consciousness', *Trends in Cognitive Sciences*, 7/5: 214–18.

Chapter 26

Consciousness and Intentionality

Angela Mendelovici and David Bourget

Philosophers traditionally recognize two main features of mental states: intentionality and phenomenal consciousness. To a first approximation, intentionality is the 'aboutness' of mental states, and phenomenal consciousness is the felt, experiential, qualitative, or 'what it's like' (Nagel 1974) aspect of mental states. In the past few decades, these features have been widely assumed to be distinct and independent. But several philosophers have recently challenged this assumption, arguing that intentionality and consciousness are importantly related. This chapter overviews the key views on the relationship between consciousness and intentionality and describes our favored view, which is a version of the phenomenal intentionality theory, the view that the most fundamental kind of intentionality arises from phenomenal consciousness.[1]

26.1 Introduction: Consciousness and Intentionality

Phenomenal consciousness is the felt, experiential, qualitative, or 'what it's like' (Nagel 1974) aspect of mental states. Some paradigm examples of mental states that exhibit phenomenal consciousness are sensations (e.g., pains, visual experiences) and emotional feelings (e.g., feelings of sadness or elation). For present purposes, we can define *(phenomenal) consciousness* ostensively as the salient feature of such states that is naturally described using terms like 'what it's like' and 'experience'. Mental states, such as the emotion of joy or the perception of a rose, may have multiple properties, some of which are phenomenal and others of which are not. It is useful to have a term

---

[1] This chapter overviews many ideas that are developed in greater depth in Mendelovici 2018.

designating the purely phenomenal features of mental states. We will refer to these features as *phenomenal properties* and to instantiations of phenomenal properties as *phenomenal states*.

Above, we offered a gloss of intentionality as 'aboutness'. This characterization, which is common in the literature, is merely a first approximation rather than a strict definition. It is a fairly loose way of describing a phenomenon that we are able to at least sometimes notice introspectively in ourselves. The phenomenon is exemplified by thoughts, the kinds of mental states that we enjoy when we think, as well as by visual perceptual experiences. Both in thought and in visual experience, our mental states seem to 'say' something, or be 'about', 'of', or 'directed' at something, and it seems that this requires no corresponding external entity or state of affairs. For example, a perceptual experience might be described as being 'about' a cup, and a thought might be described as 'saying' that grass is green. We take *intentionality* to be this phenomenon that we notice introspectively in at least some cases and that we are tempted to describe using representational terms like 'says', 'about', 'of', and 'directedness'.[2] A state's *(intentional) content* is that which we are tempted to describe as what an intentional state 'says' or is 'directed at'. We will say that intentional states *(intentionally) represent* their intentional contents. While we are primarily concerned with intentional contents and intentional representation, we allow that there are other (arguably looser and more permissive) everyday uses of the term 'represent' and that we can speak of the 'contents' that are thus represented. As in the case of phenomenal consciousness, complex mental states might exhibit intentionality along with other features. We will call the purely intentional features of mental states *intentional properties* and the instantiations of intentional properties *intentional states*.[3]

Like our definition of 'consciousness', our definition of 'intentionality' is ostensive. In the case of intentionality, our paradigm cases are thoughts and visual experiences. Standing propositional attitudes, such as beliefs that one counts as having even when not actively entertaining, are also sometimes taken to be central cases of intentionality.

---

[2] See Mendelovici 2010, 2018 and Kriegel 2011b for further development of ostensive ways of defining 'intentionality'. One of us (DB) has tended to prefer a different definition of 'intentionality' as a non-factive relation to propositions, which may or may not pick out the same thing as our present definition. DB's more theoretically-loaded definition is suitable for his project in Bourget 2010a, 2010b, 2015, 2017a, 2017b, 2017c, 2017d, 2019, forthcoming, where his aim is to shed light on consciousness in terms of non-factive relations to propositions. Part of our aim here, however, is to discover the nature of a phenomenon that we can introspectively observe in ourselves, so employing DB's definition, or any other definition making substantive commitments with respect to the nature of intentionality, to capture the introspectively observed phenomenon would beg the question in favor of certain views of the introspectively observed phenomenon. This is why we employ an ostensive definition for our purposes. See Mendelovici 2018 for an explicit defense of such an approach.

[3] The term 'intentional state' is sometimes used to mean a state that has intentional properties. Since we are primarily interested in the relationship between consciousness and intentionality, and not the relationship between consciousness and other features of states exhibiting intentionality, such as their 'modes' or 'attitudes', we use the term 'intentional state' to pick out instantiations of intentional properties. On our usage, an instance of representing that grass is green is an intentional state, while a *belief* that grass is green is a mental state that involves the intentional state of representing that grass is green.

However, we choose not to include standing propositional attitudes in our paradigm cases because they are not immediately observable through introspection in the way that many thoughts and visual experiences are and we believe that, when possible, it is preferable for ostensive notions to be grounded in the most immediately observable cases available.[4] Of course, how we define 'intentionality' is merely a terminological choice. We will discuss this choice again when it becomes relevant in Section 26.4.

26.2 THREE VIEWS OF THE RELATIONSHIP BETWEEN CONSCIOUSNESS AND INTENTIONALITY

Many mental states have both intentional properties and phenomenal properties. For example, when you see a rose, there is something it is like for you to see the rose, and your mind is seemingly directed at something, such as a rose or a possible state of affairs involving a rose. It is natural to ask what is the relationship between these two mental features. Roughly following Horgan and Tienson (2002a), we can distinguish three main views on this question. According to *representationalism*, all actual phenomenal states are nothing over and above, or, as we will say, *arise from*, intentional states (perhaps together with other ingredients).[5] According to the *phenomenal intentionality theory* (PIT), all actual intentional states, or at least all actual originally intentional states (more on this later in this section), arise from phenomenal states.[6] According to *separatism*, neither kind of state arises from the other.

The notion of a set of states A arising from another set of states B is supposed to capture the intuitive idea that the states in A are nothing over and above the states in B. There are different ways in which a set of states A can arise from another set of states B: for instance, every state in A might be identical to, grounded in, constituted by, or realized by some state in B (or some combination of B states).

Representationalism is often thought of as offering a theory of consciousness in that it tells us what consciousness arises from. According to representationalism, some intentional states, by their very nature, and perhaps together with the help of certain further ingredients, are phenomenally conscious or automatically result in phenomenal states. For example, a perceptual state representing a red square might, simply in virtue of representing a red square, automatically have a 'reddish' phenomenal character.

---

[4] See also Mendelovici 2018: sect 1.4.2.
[5] Introductions to representationalism include Lycan 2000; Seager and Bourget 2007; and Bourget and Mendelovici 2014.
[6] Introductions to PIT include Kriegel 2013 and Bourget and Mendelovici 2016.

Similarly, PIT is often thought of as offering a theory of intentionality in that it tells us what intentionality arises from. According to PIT, certain phenomenal states, all by themselves, automatically give rise to intentional states. For example, a perceptual state with a 'reddish squarish' phenomenal character might, all by itself, automatically result in the representation of a red square or of there being a red square.[7]

Separatism denies both representationalism and PIT, maintaining that we cannot have a theory of consciousness in terms of intentionality or a theory of intentionality in terms of consciousness. The separatist might say that although many states are both intentional and phenomenal, the intentional and the phenomenal are largely independent of one another. For example, a separatist might say that it is possible for a perceptual state to have a 'reddish' phenomenal character but to represent the property of being green.[8]

A strong and simple form of representationalism claims that all actual phenomenal states arise from intentional states alone. A strong and simple form of PIT claims that all actual intentional states arise from phenomenal states alone. Most representationalists and phenomenal intentionality theorists do not hold these simple views. The main reason is that these views face challenges with intentional states that are not accompanied by any phenomenal states, such as the standing propositional attitudes that one has on a continuous basis (even when sleeping dreamlessly) and intentional states involved in early visual or linguistic processing that we are not aware of having. Given the reasonable assumption that such states can have the same contents as states that are accompanied by phenomenal consciousness, the simple version of representationalism faces a challenge, since these cases seem to show that phenomenal consciousness is not just a matter of having particular intentional states. Intentional states without accompanying phenomenal states also challenge the simple version of PIT because they seem to show that not all actual intentional states arise from phenomenal states.

These challenges have helped motivate weakened versions of representationalism and PIT. The simple version of representationalism described above is sometimes called *pure representationalism*, since it claims that all phenomenal states arise from intentional states *alone*. According to pure representationalism, all that matters for phenomenal consciousness is intentionality. The weakening of this view that is thought to avoid the above-mentioned problems is *impure representationalism*, which claims that all actual phenomenal states arise from intentional states *combined with other ingredients*, which might include functional roles, ways of representing, or intentional modes similar to the attitude components of propositional attitudes.[9] Impure representationalism can deal with the problem cases mentioned above by denying that standing propositional

---

[7] While PIT is primarily a view of how we represent various contents, many advocates of PIT and nearby views have also argued that the attitude components of propositional attitude states, like the belief component of the belief that grass is green, arise from phenomenal consciousness (Horgan and Tienson 2002a; Pitt 2004; Jorba 2016; Mendelovici 2018: Appendix E, forthcoming).

[8] See especially Block 1990 and 1996 for arguments for such a separatist view.

[9] See Chalmers 2004 for the distinction between pure and impure representationalism.

attitudes and other non-phenomenally conscious states have the extra ingredients required for being phenomenally conscious.[10]

In the case of PIT, a different distinction is typically made. Let us call intentionality that arises from phenomenal consciousness alone *phenomenal intentionality*. A *phenomenal intentional state* is an intentional state that arises from phenomenal states alone, and a phenomenal intentional state's content is its *phenomenal content*. The simple version of PIT mentioned above takes all intentionality to be phenomenal intentionality. We will refer to it as *strong PIT*. *Moderate PIT* is a weakening of this view according to which *some* intentional states are phenomenal intentional states and all other intentional states derive in some way from phenomenal intentional states.[11] While moderate PIT recognizes non-phenomenal intentionality, it nevertheless maintains that phenomenal consciousness is the *source* of all intentionality (Kriegel 2011b, 2013).

Moderate PIT can be stated using a distinction that is sometimes drawn between original and derived intentionality. *Derived intentionality* is intentionality that derives from other actual or merely possible instances of intentionality, while *original intentionality* is intentionality that is not derived. For example, it is sometimes thought that linguistic intentionality is a kind of derived intentionality in that the intentionality of linguistic expressions derives from the original intentionality of mental states. Moderate PIT, then, is the view that all original intentionality is phenomenal intentionality and any other intentionality is (ultimately) derived from phenomenal intentionality.[12]

Impure representationalism and moderate PIT weaken the simple versions of representationalism and PIT, respectively, but in different ways.[13] Impure representationalism denies that all actual phenomenal states arise from intentional states *alone*, allowing that ingredients apart from intentionality matter for phenomenal consciousness.

---

[10] Some versions of impure representationalism take the relevant extra ingredients to merely determine *whether* a phenomenal state arises given the presence of a particular intentional state, maintaining that *which* phenomenal state it is that arises is determined by the content of the corresponding intentional state. Employing Byrne's (2001) distinction between inter- and intramodal representationalism, we might call this kind of impure representationalism *intermodal impure representationalism*. *Intramodal impure representationalism*, then, is a version of impure representationalism that takes the extra ingredients to help determine not only whether a phenomenal state arises given the presence of a particular intentional state but also *which* phenomenal state it is that arises (see Lycan 1987). Bourget (2010a, 2010b, 2015, 2017b, 2017d, and 2019) argues for intermodal representationalism and against intramodal representationalism.

[11] See Bourget and Mendelovici 2016 and Mendelovici 2018 for the distinction between strong PIT and moderate PIT. In Mendelovici and Bourget 2014, we use the terms 'extreme PIT' and 'strong PIT' to mark this distinction.

[12] Proponents of moderate PIT, or something close to it, include Bourget (2010a, 2017c, 2018), Farkas (2008a,b), Horgan and Tienson (2002b), Horgan et al. (2004), Kriegel (2003, 2011a,b), Loar (2003a), Searle (1992), Mendelovici (2010, 2018), Mendelovici and Bourget (2014), Montague (2016), Pitt (2004, 2009, 2011), Pautz (2013), Siewert (1998), and Smithies (2011, 2013a,b, 2014). See Section 26.4 of this chapter and Mendelovici 2018 for a defense of strong PIT.

[13] There are also versions of PIT that weaken PIT by taking intentionality to arise from phenomenal consciousness together with other ingredients. Farkas (2013) and Masrour (2013) defend such views.

Moderate PIT, in contrast, rejects the requirement that *all* actual intentional states arise from phenomenal states alone, allowing that some intentional states do not arise from phenomenal states, so long as they are instances of derived intentionality.

Why does the representationalist deny the 'alone' part of the simple version of her view while the advocate of PIT denies the 'all' part of the simple version of her view? Recall that the representationalist aims to account for all phenomenal states, which involves specifying the conditions under which we have particular phenomenal states. Since intentional states do not uniquely determine phenomenal states, she cannot do so by invoking intentional states *alone*; she must invoke extra ingredients apart from intentionality. So, the simple version of representationalism is most naturally weakened to impure representationalism.

In contrast, the advocate of PIT aims to account for intentional states, which involves specifying the conditions under which we have any given intentional state. But, since phenomenal states are thought not to be necessary for all intentional states, she at best can only use phenomenal states alone to specify the conditions under which we have a subset of intentional states (these are the states with phenomenal intentionality). The intentional states that do not correspond to phenomenal states must be accounted for in some other way. This motivates weakening the simple version of PIT to moderate PIT, which takes some intentional states to be a matter of phenomenal consciousness alone and others to have merely derived intentionality.

The above points show that although the interesting weakenings of the simple versions of representationalism and PIT are superficially quite different with respect to their methods of weakening, there is a deep agreement between the two strategies in that they both aim to accommodate intentional states that do not correspond to phenomenal states.

Before moving on, it is worth noting that, as we have defined the views, some, but not all, forms of representationalism and PIT are compatible with each other. For example, since identity is not asymmetric, some versions of representationalism and PIT taking the relevant arising relations to be identity relations are compatible with each other.[14] In contrast, versions taking the relevant arising relations to be grounding relations are not compatible with each other, since grounding is an asymmetric relation, so intentionality cannot ground consciousness while consciousness grounds intentionality.[15]

Since Chapter 19 in this volume is focused on representationalism, the rest of this chapter will focus on PIT.

---

[14] We believe that identity versions of both views are true and have defended representationalism elsewhere. See Mendelovici 2018: ch 6 for discussion of why the compatibility of representationalism and PIT does not necessarily threaten the claim that the views can be understood as providing theories of consciousness and intentionality, respectively.

[15] We explore other aspects of the relationship between representationalism and PIT in Bourget and Mendelovici 2016.

26.3 Motivating PIT

This section describes what we take to be a central motivation for accepting PIT as a theory of intentionality. Section 26.4 explores challenges to PIT and develops our favored version of PIT in response, which, we will see, is a version of strong PIT.[16]

As mentioned above, PIT can be understood as a theory of intentionality, a theory that tells us what intentionally really *is*, metaphysically speaking. It is not a *naturalistic* theory in the traditional sense of a theory couched in physical-functional language, but it is nonetheless an attempt to explain intentionality, that is, to describe its nature. Arguably, much of the interest in PIT stems from dissatisfaction with alternative theories of intentionality. In our view, one of the most important motivations for PIT is that its main competitors face unforgivable problems of empirical adequacy, while PIT does not.[17]

PIT's two main competitors are tracking theories and functional role theories. *Tracking theories* of intentionality maintain that original intentionality arises from tracking, which is detecting, carrying (or having the function of carrying) information about, or otherwise appropriately corresponding to items in the environment, such as particular objects, properties, or states of affairs. The tracking relations that have been thought to explain intentionality are supposed to be entirely reducible to physical features in the manner championed by such authors as Dretske (1988, 1993), Fodor (1990a,b), and Millikan (1984).

Functional role theories maintain that original intentionality arises from functional roles, where the functional role of an internal state is the sum-total of the causal relations that it is disposed to enter into with other internal states input stimuli (e.g., retinal stimulation), and outputs (e.g., bodily movements). On most versions of the view, it is only a subset of these causal relations that is required and relevant for intentionality, usually those causal relations corresponding to 'correct' inferences. A theory taking original intentionality to arise from a combination of functional roles and relations to the environment is also possible and is sometimes called a *long-arm functional role theory* (see Harman 1987).

Tracking and functional role theories of intentionality have received considerable attention over the past few decades. For some time, it appeared that 'naturalizing' intentionality by accounting for it in terms of tracking or functional roles was one of the most important goals in philosophy of mind. But this research program has lost momentum. Over time, it has become clear that offering an empirically adequate theory of intentionality in terms of tracking or functional role (let alone one that is genuinely explanatory) is very challenging.

---

[16] See Bourget and Mendelovici 2016 and Kriegel 2013 for extensive discussions of a broad range of motivations and Mendelovici 2018 for a more detailed treatment of the arguments presented here.

[17] See also Kriegel 2013 and Mendelovici and Bourget 2014 for a critical assessment of PIT in comparison to alternative theories of intentionality, particularly tracking theories. In Mendelovici and Bourget 2014, we also argue that PIT is naturalistic in the sense of 'naturalism' that matters most.

Many challenges to the empirical adequacy of tracking theories have been lodged, most of which work against some tracking theories but not others. Rather than provide a general overview of these challenges here, we will focus on one kind of challenge to empirical adequacy that tracking theorists themselves have hardly discussed. The problem is that there are large classes of cases in which what a representation represents does not match anything it can plausibly be said to track. Such cases are *mismatch cases*, and the problem that they pose for tracking theories is the *mismatch problem*. Below we will describe one mismatch case, that of perceptual color representations.[18]

We visually represent the color red, we represent the vivid, striking, and warm quality that many of us are familiar with. Let us stipulate that this is what we mean by 'redness'. If our visual states representing redness have their contents in virtue of what they track, they have to represent properties available to be tracked, which, on most tracking theories, are properties that are or have been instantiated in the actual world.[19] According to our best scientific understanding of apparently colored objects, the best candidate properties that are available for perceptual experiences of redness to track are properties such as the property *being disposed to primarily reflect electromagnetic radiation of wavelengths of around 650nm*. Call this property *EM650*. It is not very important here what is the best candidate physical basis of color, so we will assume it is EM650. The problem for tracking theories is that redness, the property that we visually represent, and EM650, the property that our visual states track, seem to be entirely different properties. One is categorical, vivid, striking, and warm. The other is dispositional and has to do with electromagnetic radiation and wavelengths. The two properties differ in *their* properties—that is, there is a difference in higher-order properties—so, by Leibniz's law of the indiscernability of identicals, they are distinct properties. So, perceptual experiences of redness do not track what they represent. The tracking theory cannot accommodate them. The same problem arises in other cases, such as experiences of hotness and coldness, sweetness, moral or other kinds of value, and thoughts about many of these same contents.

There are many objections one might make to this argument.[20] We will only discuss one, which we think might seem particularly compelling: the objection is that apparent differences between EM650 and redness are merely illusory. One might draw an analogy with the case of the apparent distinctness of physical and mental properties. The mental and the physical, one might say, seem different, but, it might be argued, this is compatible with mental properties being identical to physical properties. It is just that we represent mental properties in a special way, perhaps using a special 'mode of presentation', which makes them seem distinct from physical properties. Perhaps, similarly,

---

[18] The mismatch problem for tracking theories is developed in detail in Mendelovici 2018: ch 3.
[19] There are tracking theories that allow us to track properties that have never been instantiated, such as an early version of Fodor's asymmetric dependence view (Fodor 1987). However, this view requires lawful connections between tracked properties and inner representations to obtain and be relatively strong, which is a condition that is not plausibly met in the kinds of cases we will discuss, so it does not help the tracking theorist avoid the mismatch problem. See Mendelovici 2013b, 2016, 2018: Appendix A for more details.
[20] See Mendelovici 2018: ch 3 for some objections and replies.

EM650 and redness are one and the same property, but we do not realize this because we represent it in two different ways. But note that there is an important difference between the argument from the mismatch problem against tracking theories and the well-known arguments against physicalism. The arguments against physicalism rest on the observation that we cannot a priori infer mental facts from physical facts.[21] In contrast, the argument from the mismatch problem rests on the observation that redness and EM650 have distinct higher-order properties. While a lack of inferability might perhaps be explained in terms of ways of representing (as opposed to a real difference in properties), differences in higher-order properties between two properties *entail* non-identity (by Leibniz's law). On the face of it, the typical physicalist reply is not applicable.[22]

One might try to apply the reply at the level of higher-order properties. One might say that properties such as those of being vivid, striking, and warm are, despite appearances, physical features of electromagnetic properties, and having to do with wavelengths and electromagnetic radiation are features of redness. One might also say that redness in fact lacks some of the properties that it seems to have, such as being categorical. By identifying certain higher-order properties that we attribute to EM650 and redness and rejecting others, one might attempt to undermine the argument from Leibniz's law. Of course, one *can* simply make the relevant claims, but, we maintain, there is little motivation independent of saving the tracking theory to think that they are true. It is *always* possible to save a theory by positing errors of judgment and illusions of non-identity like this *without independent evidence*. Absent independent reasons to think we are making such errors in this case, the reply is unconvincing.

Let us now turn to the functional role theory. The idea behind this theory is that the overall pattern of functional relations between mental representations (and perhaps their components) determines their intentional contents. The problem with this is easiest to see if we adopt the framework of the language of thought (Fodor 1975). Let us say that our mental representations are formulas in some inner language L. Causal connections that our inner formulas and their constituent symbols stand in to other formulas and symbols are supposed to determine their intentional contents. Let us model the contents of formulas and their constituent symbols as intensions, which are functions from possible worlds to entities or set-theoretic constructions out of entities (truth values, objects, sets of objects, etc.). Let us assume that the intension of a formula is determined by the intensions of its constituent symbols and their logical arrangement. Causal role is supposed to determine contents through such constraints as this:

---

[21] See, e.g., Chalmers 1996.

[22] There are arguments for dualism that take the same form as the above argument, such as Descartes' argument that the mind and the body must be distinct because the former is unextended while the latter is extended. However, the best physicalist response to such arguments is not to postulate some kind of illusion of non-identity but instead to deny that the mind (or the body) has (or lacks) the relevant property. This kind of reply seems more plausible in the case of the mind than in the case of properties such as colors.

Representations A and B represent contents CA and CB, respectively, in virtue of their functional role only if it is the case that A causes B iff CA entails CB.

A complete theory, of course, would have to provide more such constraints in order to have a hope of providing sufficient conditions for representing any given content.

Whatever the exact content-determining rules that one might want to specify, the causal role account proceeds by mapping causal relations between inner representations (broadly understood) to logical relations between their contents: the causal relations between a certain set of representations determine what logical relations (e.g., entailment) obtain between the contents of representations of this set. The logical relations are then supposed to determine the specific contents.

One problem is that logical relations are not sufficient for determining contents.[23] This can be shown using a method similar to that used in Putnam's model-theoretic arguments (Putnam 1981: Appendix). Let us suppose that there is at least one interpretation I_1 of the symbols in L that is consistent with their causal roles. We can think of I_1 as assigning intensions to all the non-logical symbols in L. Statements in L get their intensions compositionally. Assume that some predicate F_1 in L is non-trivial at some world w_1, in that F_1 is true of some objects at w_1 (e.g., object a) and false of other objects at w_1 (e.g., object b). Now picture the set of all objects in w_1 laid on a surface such as the left rectangle in Figure 26.1.

Imagine the extensions of all names and predicates in L at w_1 specified by I_1 being marked as points (for names) and shapes (for predicates) on this surface, as illustrated in the left-hand rectangle in Figure 26.1 for names 'a' and 'b' and predicates F_1 and F_2 (each symbol is shown next to its extension).[24] Now take two objects such that one is in the extension of F_1 at w_1 and the other is not, for example, the extensions of 'a' and 'b', a and b. If we swap the places of a and b while leaving all labels in place, we obtain new extensions for 'a', 'b', F_1, and any other symbol that has a or b in its extension. The result of swapping a and b is illustrated in the right-hand rectangle of Figure 26.1. The new extension of 'a' is b, the new extension of 'b' is a, and the new extension of predicates are the same as on I_1 except that a and b are swapped. This swapping procedure does not change

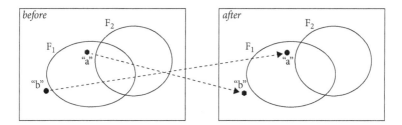

FIGURE 26.1 Constructing alternative interpretations for mental symbols

---

[23] See Bourget MS for the argument that follows.

[24] The extensions of monadic predicates could be non-contiguous shapes without this affecting the argument. A different drawing convention would have to be used for non-monadic properties, whose extensions are sets of n-tuples; we are setting those aside for simplicity.

the truth value of any statement at w_1. We can thus use this procedure to construct an alternative to I_1 that makes all the same statements true at any world and preserves all logical relationships between statements: Let I_2 be the interpretation that assigns to each expression e in L the intension whose values are defined as follows: at w_1, it is the value at w_1 of the intension assigned to e by I_1, except that a and b are swapped as described above; at any other world, it is the value at that world of the intension assigned to e by I_1. By construction, the intensions assigned by I_2 yield the same truth-values as the intensions assigned by I_1 for all sentences of L and all worlds (including w_1). So, all broadly logical relations such as entailment between the sentences of L are exactly the same on I_1 and I_2. However, I_1 and I_2 are clearly different interpretations, since they assign different intensions and extensions to 'a', 'b', and F_1 (and potentially many other mental symbols). This shows that determining logical relations between contents is not sufficient for determining contents. Our Putnam-style procedure constructs minimally differing extensions and intensions, but it is easy to see that we can also construct massively different extensions and intensions, since many worlds contain large numbers of objects, which can be swapped. This is a problem for the functional role theory: even if some of our contents are a little bit indeterminate, it is implausible that they are massively indeterminate in this way.[25]

It might be thought that the long-arm functional role theory avoids the underdetermination worry for functionalism, since it takes functional roles *and* relations to the environment to be relevant to content determination. For example, it can say that certain color representations get determinate color contents from tracking relations, while other color representations get their contents from their relations to these color representations. Tracking relations provide a representational system with determinate contents, which are then transformed and passed around to other representations. However, insofar as external relations are taken to play a role in determining content, long-arm functional

---

[25] One might suggest that functional role theory could determine probabilistic relations rather than logical relations and that it would be harder to generate deviant interpretations consistent with probabilistic relations. Fine (1977) discusses a view in the ballpark, but he does not offer it as a theory of content. It may be that our swapping procedure would not preserve probabilistic relations, but such a theory of mental content would rely on the existence of objective, mind-independent conditional probabilities between arbitrary propositions and we are skeptical that there are such probabilities (for what it's worth, Fine talks only about subjective probabilities).

Another possible response is that interpretations should be limited to functions that assign 'natural' intensions, which would presumably be intensions that assign 'natural' extensions. This is Lewis' 'reference magnetism' reply to Putnam. The resulting view would not be a version of the functional role theory, but a view aiming to account for intentionality in terms of both functional roles and reference magnetism. We are not convinced that facts about natural kinds can play the required roles, since it is unclear why natural kinds should constrain interpretation in the required way—in other words, it is unclear why natural kinds should be 'magnetic'. See Chalmers 2012 (extended edition, 20th excursus) for more objections to reference magnetism.

Other determinacy worries for conceptual role theories arise from 'Kripkenstein'-style considerations (see Kripke 1982). BonJour (1998: 176–7), Graham et al. (2007), Searle (1990), Strawson (2008), and Kriegel (2011b) also raise worries concerning content determinacy for tracking and functional role theories of intentionality. See also Pautz 2013 for critical discussion.

role theories inherit the tracking theory's mismatch problem, since the content allegedly provided by these relations is sometimes the wrong content.[26]

The underdetermination problem and the mismatch problem show that the functional role theory and the tracking theory cannot attribute content correctly, that they are empirically inadequate. The mismatch problem shows that the tracking theory makes the wrong predictions in mismatch cases, while the underdetermination problem shows that the functional role theory cannot give the right answer in all cases of non-trivial predicates for in-principle reasons. These are strong reasons to reject the views.[27]

We believe that PIT can attribute content correctly in all cases. Since it does not take content to be determined by logical relations between representations, it does not face the functional role theory's in-principle worries with correct content attribution. It can also yield the right answer in the tracking theory's mismatch cases. Some versions of PIT simply identify intentional states with phenomenal states, while others take phenomenal states to realize, constitute, or ground intentional states. Either way, PIT has the resources to ascribe the right content in the case of experiences of redness, since they involve a phenomenal character that matches the content we want to ascribe. This phenomenal character might simply be identical to the content, or it might realize, constitute, or in some other way ground it. Similar claims can be made about other mismatch cases for the tracking theory.

The preceding does not conclusively show that PIT ascribes correct, or even determinate, content in all cases. Many objections to PIT concern cases where it appears not to attribute content correctly. We turn to such cases in Section 26.4. If what we say there is correct, then PIT is arguably empirically adequate, which provides significant support for the view, particularly when its main competitors are not.[28]

26.4 CHALLENGING CASES FOR PIT

In Section 26.3, we outlined what we take to be some important motivations for PIT. We now turn to various challenging cases for the view. As we will see, different ways of handling these cases result in different versions of PIT. We will argue for an approach that results in a version of strong PIT, which claims that all intentionality is phenomenal intentionality.

There are four main kinds of challenging cases we will consider: conscious thoughts with complex or abstract contents that do not seem to correspond to phenomenal states,

---

[26] See Mendelovici 2018: ch 4 for this argument against the long-arm functional role theory.
[27] In Mendelovici and Bourget 2014 and Mendelovici 2018: ch 6, we argue that failure of empirical adequacy cannot be made up for by having other virtues, such as that of being naturalistic.
[28] Empirical adequacy, of course, is not enough to show that a view is viable. In order for PIT to succeed, phenomenal consciousness has to be metaphysically sufficient to give rise to intentionality. Another line of argument for PIT aims to establish that while tracking and functional relations do not have the power to give rise to intentionality, phenomenal consciousness does (see Mendelovici 2018: chs 4 and 5).

intentional states with wide contents, standing propositional attitudes, and nonconscious representations of the kind described by cognitive science. We will overview each kind of case in turn before providing a sketch of how proponents of PIT might deal with them.

Thoughts. It seems that we have all sorts of complex or abstract thoughts, some of which represent entities such as political systems, norms of behavior, unobservable particles, and highly abstract mathematical entities. When we have such thoughts, it might not seem that we have correspondingly complex or abstract phenomenal states. Unlike in the case of experiences of redness, where the feel of an experience seems to match what is represented, in the case of complex or abstract thoughts, there seem to be no phenomenal states matching what is represented. This casts doubt on strong PIT, which requires that all intentionality is phenomenal intentionality. Moderate PIT, which takes all intentionality to be phenomenal intentionality or derived from phenomenal intentionality, is not committed to every intentional state corresponding to a matching phenomenal state. But the case of complex and abstract thoughts also casts doubt on moderate PIT, since it is unclear that such thoughts are related to phenomenal consciousness at all.

Wide intentional states. A problem also arises with wide intentional states, which are states whose contents at least partly depend on factors external to the individual whose states they are. If Twin Earth intuitions are right (see Putnam 1975), then Oscar's thought that water is wet represents the content <H_2O is wet>. But, on the plausible assumption that phenomenal states are internally determined, Oscar has no phenomenal state matching <H_2O>. Similarly, wide intentional states involving singular contents, such as the thought you might have with the content <Justin Trudeau is currently in Europe>, do not come with a phenomenology uniquely matching their singular contents. Here, too, the problematic cases directly challenge strong PIT, since wide contents clearly do not seem to be phenomenal contents, but the cases also challenge moderate PIT, since it is not clear how such contents might be related to phenomenal intentional states.

Standing propositional attitudes. Standing propositional attitudes are beliefs, desires, and other propositional attitudes that we count as having even when we are not occurrently undergoing them. The problem with standing propositional attitudes is that there is nothing that it is like to have them. For example, there is nothing it is like to believe that monkeys like bananas, at least when not occurrently entertaining this belief. So, it does not seem that standing propositional attitudes arise from phenomenal states, which makes them problematic for strong PIT. It is also unclear how they might be related to consciousness at all, which makes them problematic for moderate PIT.

Nonconscious representational states. Cognitive science describes all sorts of representational states that seem to be intentional but independent of any phenomenal states we might have. For example, representations occurring in early visual processing and our tacit knowledge of grammar seem to have no echo in phenomenal consciousness, yet one might hold that they are intentional. If these states are intentional, this would directly contradict strong PIT and cast doubt on moderate PIT.

In addition to the above challenges, it might be claimed that phenomenal states that might be thought to lack intentional content, such as feelings of elation and headaches, are a challenge for PIT. Such cases pose a challenge to representationalism, but they are not a problem for most versions of PIT, which only claim that all intentional states arise from phenomenal states, not that every phenomenal state gives rise to an intentional state. For this reason, such cases do not concern us here.[29]

Note that standing states and the nonconscious representational states posited by cognitive science are precisely the kinds of states that motivate impure representationalism over pure representationalism and moderate PIT over strong PIT, as we saw in Section 26.2. In what follows, we will reconsider these motivations for moderate PIT, eventually arguing that strong PIT is in fact correct.[30]

For any problematic state, there are three main strategies that a proponent of moderate PIT might adopt. *Inflationism* claims that the problematic state, despite appearances, has rich phenomenal character from which its content arises. *Eliminativism* denies that the problematic state exists or that it has any intentionality at all. *Derivativism* claims that, while the problematic intentional state does not arise solely from phenomenal consciousness, it derives from intentional states that do. The first two strategies, but not the third, are open both to the proponent of strong PIT and to the proponent of moderate PIT.

We will now consider how each kind of strategy can be applied to the problematic cases, focusing on our favored strategies.

26.4.1 Standing Propositional Attitudes

In the case of standing propositional attitudes, inflationism seems to be a nonstarter: there is clearly no phenomenology associated with most of our standing beliefs and other standing propositional attitudes. A more promising strategy is an eliminativist strategy that flat-out denies the existence of anything answering to the notion of a standing propositional attitude. While we are sympathetic to this strategy, we think a more nuanced eliminativist strategy is preferable. We will turn to it after considering a related derivativist strategy.

One promising derivativist strategy takes propositional attitudes to be dispositions to have certain related occurrent states—such as occurrent beliefs, occurrent desires, or other thoughts—whose contents are either phenomenal contents or derived from phenomenal contents. On this view, which we might call *derivativist dispositionalism*, propositional attitudes and their contents derive from dispositions to have occurrent states whose contents are either phenomenal contents or derived from phenomenal contents.

---

[29] See Block 1996 and Kind 2003, 2013 for worries with representationalism based on moods, pain, and other such cases. See also Harman 1990, Tye 1995, 2008, Dretske 1995, Byrne 2001, Crane 2003, Bain 2003, Seager and Bourget 2007, Mendelovici 2013a, 2014, Bourget and Mendelovici 2014, Bourget 2015, 2017b, and Smithies 2019 for defenses of representationalist treatments of such cases. See Mendelovici 2018: Appendix B for discussion of the relevance of such cases to PIT.

[30] Similar arguments can also show that pure representationalism is defensible. See Mendelovici 2010, 2013a, and 2014 and Bourget 2010a,b.

For example, your belief that monkeys like bananas might amount to a set of complex dispositions to have occurrent beliefs to the effect that monkeys like bananas (or perhaps occurrent beliefs that are entailed by such occurrent beliefs) whenever relevant.[31]

There is also an eliminativist version of the dispositionalist strategy, which we find preferable (though there is another view we are also partial to, which we will describe in Section 26.4.3). This *eliminativist dispositionalism* accepts that we have dispositions to have various occurrent thoughts and that these play many of the roles we associate with standing propositional attitudes. Unlike the derivativist dispositionalist, however, the eliminativist dispositionalist denies that the relevant dispositional states qualify as intentional states. Recall that we defined intentionality ostensively by pointing to paradigm cases in thought and visual experience. Since a disposition to do X is different in nature from doing X, the relevant dispositions are different in nature from our paradigm cases, so our definition plausibly excludes them.[32] Of course, whether or not the relevant dispositional states qualify as intentional states depends on how we define 'intentionality'. If we were to count propositional attitudes as paradigm cases of intentionality, then eliminativist dispositionalism would likely end up being classified as a derivativist dispositionalism.

Unlike the eliminativist strategy that flat-out denies the existence of anything answering to the notion of a standing propositional attitude, both derivativist and eliminativist dispositionalism attempt to be somewhat accommodating to our prior views of standing propositional attitudes, accepting that we have states playing the roles of standing beliefs, standing desires, and other standing states, even though their nature is merely dispositional, and perhaps not even genuinely intentional. In order for these strategies to succeed at accommodating standing propositional attitudes, however, PIT needs to be able to accommodate occurrent thoughts with the relevant contents, which might include contents that are complex or wide. We turn to these challenging cases below, starting with the case of wide thoughts.

26.4.2 Wide Thoughts

In the case of occurrent thoughts with wide contents, inflationism, again, seems to be a nonstarter. Take for example the occurrent thought that monkeys like bananas. The wide content of this thought relates creatures with a certain kind of DNA or evolutionary

---

[31] Searle's (1989, 1990) potentialism is arguably best understood as a form of derivativism about standing propositional attitudes. On his view, standing states that are potentially conscious derive their intentionality from the phenomenal states they are disposed to cause. Kriegel's *interpretivism* (2011a,b) also provides a derivativist view of standing propositional attitudes, taking non-phenomenally conscious intentional states to be derived from the phenomenal intentional states of an ideal observer applying intentional systems theory to subjects based on their phenomenal intentional states and behavior.

[32] See also Strawson 1994: 167 and Mendelovici 2018: ch 8 for applications of the eliminativist strategy in the case of standing propositional attitudes.

history to bananas. It seems implausible that there is a phenomenal character of thought that captures this specific kind of DNA or evolutionary history.

One kind of eliminativist strategy might simply deny that there are any wide contents, perhaps suggesting that we are mistaking referents for wide contents (see Farkas 2008a) or that our intuitions supporting wide contents are mistaken (Pitt 1999, 2011). The view we will ultimately defend is also eliminativist, but it is eliminativist in a slightly more accommodating way.[33]

Here the derivativist strategy is quite plausible and widely endorsed among advocates of PIT. One natural version of this strategy takes thoughts to have both wide and narrow contents, with the wide contents deriving from the narrow contents. These narrow contents are phenomenal contents (or at least derived contents that are derived from phenomenal contents).[34] For example, the thought that water is wet might have a descriptive narrow content like <the clear watery stuff around here is wet>, which, in certain contexts, determines derived wide contents like <H_2O is wet>. We call this strategy the *derivativist descriptivist strategy* for wide thoughts, since it takes wide contents to be derived from broadly-speaking descriptive narrow contents.[35]

As in the case of derivativist dispositionalism, there is also an eliminativist version of the descriptivist strategy. According to *eliminativist descriptivism*, thoughts have narrow descriptive contents which determine wide contents, but these wide contents are not *intentionally* represented by thoughts. While we might represent them on some loose sense of 'represent', our representing them does not qualify as an instance of intentionality. If our paradigm cases of intentionality are all cases of phenomenal intentionality, it is quite likely that the representation of wide contents is of a different nature than our paradigm cases, and so does not qualify as a kind of intentionality. Again, of course, whether a content qualifies as intentional turns largely on how we define 'intentionality'.

Both derivativist and eliminativist descriptivism require that our thoughts represent narrow descriptive contents that determine the desired wide contents, but it is unclear that PIT can accommodate the required descriptive contents. The problem is that many descriptive contents would have to be quite nuanced and complex in order to fix on the desired wide contents, and it is not clear that such contents are phenomenal contents or somehow derived from phenomenal contents. For example, in order to fix on the natural kind *monkey*, we might need causal or metalinguistic descriptive contents like <the species around here that causes such-and-such superficial effects on observers> or <the species called 'monkey' around here>. But, since it does not seem that we have

---

[33] See Siewert 1998, Kriegel 2007, Farkas 2008a, Pitt 1999, 2011, and Mendelovici 2010, 2018 for applications of the eliminativist strategy to wide states.

[34] Such views are defended by Horgan and Tienson (2002a), Horgan et al. (2004), Loar (2003a), Bourget (2010a), and Chalmers (2010), among others. Mendelovici (2010, 2018) defends an eliminativist version of this kind of view.

[35] This strategy requires a broadly descriptivist view such as that defended by Jackson (1998). A view in a similar spirit is developed by Chalmers (2002a). Of course, descriptivism faces well-known objections (e.g., from Kripke 1980). We think these objections have been adequately addressed by descriptivists (see, e.g., Jackson 1998, 2003a,b; Chalmers 2002b, 2012) and focus here on objections to descriptivism that are special to PIT's application of the view.

phenomenal states matching such narrow contents every time we think about monkeys, it is not clear how PIT can accommodate such descriptive contents. This issue for the descriptivist strategy is of a piece with the general problem of thoughts with abstract or complex contents, to which we now turn.

26.4.3 Complex and Abstract Thoughts

Many phenomenal intentionality theorists have applied an inflationist strategy in the case of thoughts with complex or abstract contents, arguing that they have a sufficiently rich phenomenology to account for their rich contents.[36] Proponents of rich cognitive phenomenology have attempted to bring out this phenomenology in various ways. One way is through the use of phenomenal contrast cases. For example, you might be asked to compare your phenomenology when hearing the words 'birds fly' with that of someone who does not know what the word 'bird' means. This person might have some auditory phenomenology corresponding to the word 'bird', but she seems to be missing something that you have. This something is the rich phenomenology of thought corresponding to the (perhaps narrow) idea of a bird.[37]

For our part, we are not entirely convinced of the inflationist strategy. We agree that phenomenal contrast cases show that there is *something* in consciousness when one is thinking about monkeys, birds, or flying, but this something is not the full idea, even the full *narrow* idea, of a monkey, bird, or of flying. It seems to us that the contents that are determined by the phenomenology of conscious thoughts are gisty, partial, or schematic compared to the full narrow contents that we might want to attribute to these thoughts, which might include descriptive contents of the sort described above or even just rough characterizations like <a winged feathery animal that lays eggs and flies>.[38]

An alternative approach to complex thoughts is derivativist: Although the occurrent thoughts we typically have do not have phenomenal properties that capture the full narrow contents that we want to attribute to them, they are inferentially or otherwise connected with complex or abstract thoughts whose phenomenal properties determine these fuller contents. One might say that typical occurrent thoughts have the complex narrow contents they have in virtue of bearing such connections to more complex thoughts. There are different views on what the relevant connections are. We will focus on a view that takes the relevant connections to be determined by our dispositions to take ourselves to mean one content by another. According to this view, which we will call

---

[36] See, e.g., Strawson (1994, 2008, 2011), Siewert (1998, 2011), Horgan and Tienson (2002a), Horgan et al. (2004), Chudnoff (2015), and Pitt (2009, 2011).

[37] For such arguments, see especially Strawson 1994, Siewert 1998, Horgan and Tienson 2002a, Chudnoff 2015, and Pitt 2009. Koksvik (2015) questions the methodology of phenomenal contrast arguments.

[38] We have argued for this claim elsewhere. See especially Mendelovici 2018: ch 8 and 2019a. See also Bourget 2017c and 2018, which argues for the more specific claim that the phenomenal contents associated with abstract or complex thoughts are often largely symbolic, representing words without precise meanings.

derivativist self-ascriptivism, we derivatively represent a content by having a disposition to ascribe it to ourselves or our own mental states in certain circumstances. In order for such an approach to succeed, we must further say that the relevant contents of these self-ascriptions are phenomenally represented.[39]

To see how this view works, suppose, for example, that you are talking about physicalism with a colleague. In the course of this discussion, you say, 'At least we can agree that phenomenal properties supervene on physical properties.' Suppose that your colleague asks what you mean by 'supervene'. You might pause for a brief moment before producing an elucidation of supervenience such as this:

(Supervenience) Properties of class A supervene on properties of class B if and only if any possible worlds that are alike in their B properties are like in their A properties.

It seems clear that, prior to pausing and reflecting on the matter, you did not have an occurrent grasp of supervenience as that relation that Supervenience spells out. For instance, when you had the first thought about supervenience, you didn't have in your consciousness anything like the idea of a possible world. Still, we are inclined to say that Supervenience was involved in the content of your thought because, on reflection, you ascribe this content to your thought. According to derivativist self-ascriptivism, such self-ascriptions have phenomenal intentionality and your thought about supervenience derivatively represents the full definition of supervenience in virtue of your disposition to have such phenomenally conscious self-ascriptive thoughts.

A few points of clarification are in order. First, in order to derivatively represent a particular content, you merely need to be *disposed* to form the relevant self-ascriptions; it does not matter whether you ever actually do so. Second, the view can be refined by specifying the relevant dispositions' conditions of manifestation. The more idealized these conditions are, the less likely we are to ever have the relevant self-ascriptive thoughts but the more likely these thoughts are to capture our all-things-considered best understanding relating to our thoughts and concepts.[40] Third, any given self-ascriptive thought need only *partially* specify the full unpacking of any given thought. On the

---

[39] This kind of self-ascriptivist strategy is developed in detail in Mendelovici 2018, 2019a, and forthcoming, though it is given an eliminativist spin (see below). Bourget 2018 also defends a view along these lines. Pautz (2013) offers an alternative derivativist strategy for complex thoughts, the *consciousness-based best systems theory*, which allows states to derive intentionality from their functional relations with other states with phenomenal intentionality. Kriegel's (2011a,b) interpretivism might also be applied to the case of thought (see n. 31). See also Loar 2003a,b and Bourget 2010a for other derivativist views of thought content.

[40] Thanks to an anonymous reviewer, who worried that self-ascriptivism does not allow us to make mistaken judgments as to what we represent, for prompting this clarification. The worry is avoided because mistakes are possible outside of the relevant dispositions' conditions of manifestation. For example, we might say that the relevant circumstances are 'good' ones in which subjects are awake, alert, and given ample opportunity to reflect. When subjects fail to meet these conditions, their self-ascriptive thoughts do not determine their derived contents and so they can be mistaken about those contents. See also Mendelovici 2010: sect 10.3.1 and 2018: sect 7.3 for further discussion. Woodward (2019) raises a similar objection; see Mendelovici (2019b) for a response.

resulting view, thoughts with relatively impoverished phenomenal contents can manage to derivatively represent rich and complex contents, contents that we might never be able to entertain in a single conscious thought.

As in the case of dispositionalist and descriptivist strategies, there is an eliminativist version of the self-ascriptivist strategy, which is the view that we endorse. *Eliminativist self-ascriptivism* accepts the derivativist self-ascriptivist's story about dispositions to self-ascribe complex contents but denies that we *intentionally* represent these contents. To illustrate and motivate the eliminativist version of self-ascriptivism, note first that there are really two kinds of content at play in situations such as that of your discussion with your colleague above. When you first used the word 'supervenience', you did not grasp the full meaning of this term for you as spelled out in Supervenience, but your mind was not completely empty. There was something before your mind, something that you grasped mentally as you were speaking. Plausibly, you had a gisty sense of what supervenience is. So it seems that your first, fleeting thought about Supervenience has two contents: a gisty content, which you initially grasped, and the full content spelled out by Supervenience, which you only grasped on reflection. We can call the first the *immediate content* of the thought and the second its *reflective content*. Immediate and reflective contents can coincide, but they can also diverge, as seems to be the case in the present example. According to self-ascriptivism, the first kind of content is phenomenal content, while the second kind of content is derived content.

We defined 'intentionality' by pointing to introspectively accessible paradigm cases. Now, it seems that introspection does not reveal anything about reflective contents (though reflection often does). So, our paradigm cases of intentionality are cases of the representation of immediate contents. In order to count as intentional, the having of reflective contents would have to be the same kind of thing as the having of immediate contents. Elsewhere, we have argued that there are important differences between the two kinds of states.[41] If this is right, then the representation of reflective contents are not instances of intentionality. Our disposition to self-ascribe complex and abstract contents might create a vast illusion of our intentionally representing such contents, whereas in fact the *intentional* contents of thoughts are limited to their somewhat impoverished immediate contents. We do, however, have dispositions to self-ascribe more complex or abstract contents, but, so long as we are not occurrently entertaining them, we do not *intentionally* represent them.

Recall that the dispositionalist and descriptivist strategies mentioned above pass the buck to a theory of complex thought content. We are now in a position to see how the self-ascriptivist view of complex thought content can plug into and complete the dispositionalist and descriptivist views. The narrow descriptions required by the descriptivist strategy are a matter of our dispositions to self-ascribe descriptive contents to our

---

[41] Mendelovici (2018: sect 7.5) argues that reflective contents are had only relative to a self-ascriber and are often indeterminate, while immediate contents are not. Bourget (2018) argues that phenomenal intentionality and non-phenomenal intentionality play different causal and rational roles, the former allowing for genuinely content-responsive thinking and the latter allowing only for an emulation of content-responsive thinking.

occurrent thoughts. These descriptions, together with how the world is, fix the wide content of those thoughts. Standing propositional attitudes are a matter of dispositions to have occurrent thoughts with descriptive and/or wide contents. On this picture, one problematic kind of content or state is built up out of another, based on a foundation of dispositions to have self-ascriptions whose relevant contents are purely phenomenal. We call this picture the *scaffolding view*. One can have a derivativist, eliminativist, or mixed version of the scaffolding view, depending on whether one takes any of the relevant non-phenomenal contents to be genuinely intentionally represented or not. As we have already noted, we take each kind of non-phenomenal representation to be different in kind from genuine intentionality, so we prefer the eliminativist version of the scaffolding view to the alternative derivativist and mixed versions.[42]

While we find the scaffolding view attractive, we believe that self-ascriptivism alone can accommodate all the same sorts of states. Self-ascriptivism can directly account for wide intentional states and standing propositional attitudes, since, in both cases, we have dispositions to self-ascribe the relevant states or contents: In the case of the wide thought that water is wet, you are disposed to self-ascribe the content <H_2O is wet> in that you are disposed to take yourself to be thinking that whatever happens to be the clear watery stuff around here (i.e., whatever is the referent of your water description) is wet. H_2O is what happens to be the clear watery stuff around here, so you are disposed to self-ascribe this content to yourself. In effect, we represent wide contents by being disposed to have self-ascriptions that *use* rather than mention narrow descriptive contents. Similarly, self-ascriptivism can accommodate standing propositional attitudes: we self-ascribe standing propositional attitudes in that we are disposed to take ourselves to have them.[43,44]

26.4.4 Nonconscious Representational States

Let us now turn to the case of nonconscious representational states posited by cognitive science. An inflationist strategy might claim that at least some such states are in fact phenomenally conscious and have phenomenal intentionality, even though we are not aware of this. Just as you are not aware of your neighbor's phenomenal states, your brain might house phenomenal states that you are not aware of. Whether these states are *your* states or the states of some other subject depends in part on how we understand subjects of experience, but it is irrelevant for the inflationist's main point, which is that the relevant states might very well have phenomenal intentionality that we are unaware of.

---

[42] For versions of the scaffolding view, see Horgan and Tienson 2002a, Bourget 2010a, and Mendelovici 2010.

[43] See Mendelovici 2018: chs 8–9, 2019a, and forthcoming for an application of self-ascriptivism across the board and for arguments for the claim that derived mental representation requires self-ascription, which provides reason to prefer this overall view over the scaffolding view.

[44] The scaffolding view is compatible with self-ascriptivism across the board; there might be more than one way in which we come to have standing propositional attitudes or wide thoughts.

While this might be plausible for some of the relevant nonconscious representational states (e.g., the states involved in masked priming), it is doubtful that all the relevant states involve hidden phenomenal characters. In general, there are too many kinds of nonconscious representational states representing too many introspectively inaccessible contents for it to be plausible that they are all phenomenal.[45]

The derivativist strategy, which claims that the relevant states are derived from phenomenal intentional states (or from states that are eventually derive from phenomenal intentional states) might stand a better chance of accommodating all of the nonconscious representational states posited by cognitive science. For instance, Kriegel's interpretivism (2011a,b) takes nonconscious intentionality to be derived from the phenomenal intentionality of an ideal interpreter who uses intentional systems theory to ascribe intentionality to nonconscious mental states (see also n. 31). Since this ideal interpreter is motivated by some of the same considerations as cognitive scientists, her content attributions are likely to match up with those of cognitive science.[46]

The main motivation for a derivativist strategy is a desire to be conciliatory with what we might take to be the standard view of the relevant nonconscious states. However, we prefer an eliminativist strategy, which we believe is at least as conciliatory with the standard view. The notions of representation operative in cognitive science are arguably either based on tracking or computational or other functional roles or taken to pick out something that is nothing over tracking relations and functional roles. Although we do not think tracking or functional roles can account for intentionality as we have defined it, we accept that internal states track things and have various functional roles and that these are important features of these states that can serve many explanatory purposes. We also accept that there might be useful notions of representation that are based on such features. So we can agree with most of the claims characterizing the standard view. The only potential disagreement concerns whether the nonconscious representation posited by cognitive science is the same kind of thing as intentionality in our sense, which would require that it be the same kind of thing as the conscious intentionality we can introspect. In Section 26.3, we briefly overviewed reasons for thinking that the conscious intentionality we can introspect is not a matter of tracking or functional roles. If these arguments are sound, then intentionality (in our sense) is not the same kind of thing as the representation exhibited by the nonconscious representational states posited by cognitive science. The key point here is that our disagreement with the standard view concerns the nature of conscious intentionality, not the nature of the nonconscious representational states posited by cognitive science, making the eliminativist strategy quite conciliatory when it comes to the nature of the nonconscious representational states posited by cognitive science.[47]

---

[45] Pitt (2009), Bourget (2010a, 2017c), and Mendelovici (2018: ch 8) argue for an inflationist strategy along these lines for at least some cases.

[46] Bourget (2010a) suggests a derivativist strategy for certain nonconscious occurrent representational states. See also Horgan et al. (2004).

[47] See also Horgan et al. 2004, Mendelovici and Bourget 2014, Bourget and Mendelovici 2016, Bourget 2010a, 2017c, 2018, and Mendelovici 2018: ch 8, 2019a for arguments for the claim that the

26.5 CONCLUSION

In this chapter, we have outlined some possible views on the relationship between phenomenal consciousness and intentionality. Our focus has been on our preferred view, PIT. We suggested that one of the strongest arguments for PIT is based on the empirical inadequacy of its main competitors. We have argued that PIT can avoid the problems facing its competitors, but it too faces some challenges. We have considered four central kinds of challenging cases for PIT and three kinds of strategies that can be applied to each case. For each kind of challenging case, there are several attractive options, yielding a plethora of plausible versions of PIT. We have argued for a largely eliminativist position in all cases, which results in a version of strong PIT. *All* instances of intentionality arise from phenomenal consciousness *alone*.[48]

REFERENCES

Bain, D. (2003), 'Intentionalism and pain', *Philosophical Quarterly*, 53/213: 502–23.
Block, N. (1990), 'Inverted earth', *Philosophical Perspectives*, 4/n/a: 53–79.
Block, N. (1996), 'Mental paint and mental latex', *Philosophical Issues*, 7: 19–49.
BonJour, L. (1998), *In Defense of Pure Reason*. Cambridge: Cambridge University Press.
Bourget, D. (2010a), 'Consciousness is underived intentionality', *Noûs*, 44/1: 32–58.
Bourget, D. (2010b), *The Representational Theory of Consciousness*. PhD thesis, Australian National University.
Bourget, D. (2015), 'Representationalism, perceptual distortion and the limits of phenomenal concepts', *Canadian Journal of Philosophy*, 45/1: 16–36.
Bourget, D. (2017a), 'Intensional perceptual ascriptions', *Erkenntnis*, 82/3: 513–30.
Bourget, D. (2017b), 'Representationalism and sensory modalities: an argument for intermodal representationalism', *American Philosophical Quarterly*, 53: 251–67.
Bourget, D. (2017c), 'The role of consciousness in grasping and understanding', *Philosophy and Phenomenological Research*, 95/2: 285–318.
Bourget, D. (2017d), 'Why are some phenomenal experiences "vivid" and others "faint"? representationalism, imagery, and cognitive phenomenology', *Australasian Journal of Philosophy*, 95/4: 673–87.
Bourget, D. (2018), 'The rational role of experience', *Inquiry*, 61/5–6: 475–93.
Bourget, D. (2019), 'Implications of intensional perceptual ascriptions for relationalism, disjunctivism, and representationalism about perceptual experience', *Erkenntnis*. 84/2: 381–408.

---

eliminativist strategy with respect to nonconscious occurrent representational states is in line with the standard view of such states. Mendelovici (2018: ch 8) also argues that derivativism is less in line with the standard view than eliminativism and that this may be a reason to prefer it.

[48] Thanks to Uriah Kriegel and two anonymous reviewers for this volume for very helpful comments on earlier drafts of this paper.

Bourget, D. (2019). 'Relational vs adverbial conceptions of phenomenal intentionality', in A. Sullivan (ed.), *Sensations, Thoughts, Language: Essays in honor of Brian Loar*. Abingdon: Routledge, 137–66.

Bourget, D. (MS), 'Phenomenal intentionality, underdetermination, and functional role'.

Bourget, D. and Mendelovici, A. (2014), 'Tracking representationalism', in A. Bailey (ed.), *Philosophy of Mind: The Key Thinkers*. London: Continuum, 209–35.

Bourget, D. and Mendelovici, A. (2016), 'Phenomenal intentionality'. in *Stanford Encyclopedia of Philosophy*.

Byrne, A. (2001), 'Intentionalism defended', *Philosophical Review*, 110/2: 199–240.

Chalmers, D. J. (1996), *The Conscious Mind: In Search of a Fundamental Theory*. Oxford: Oxford University Press.

Chalmers, D. J. (2002a), 'The components of content', in D. J. Chalmers (ed.), *Philosophy of Mind: Classical and Contemporary Readings*. Oxford: Oxford University Press.

Chalmers, D. J. (2002b), 'On sense and intension', *Philosophical Perspectives*, 16/s16: 135–82.

Chalmers, D. J. (2004), 'The representational character of experience', in B. Leiter (ed.), *The Future for Philosophy*. Oxford: Oxford University Press, 153–81.

Chalmers, D. J. (2010), *The Character of Consciousness*. Oxford: Oxford University Press.

Chalmers, D. (2012), *Constructing the World*. Oxford: Oxford University Press.

Chudnoff, E. (2015), *Cognitive Phenomenology*. Abingdon: Routledge.

Crane, T. (2003), 'The intentional structure of consciousness', in Q. Smith, and A. Jokic (eds), *Consciousness: New Philosophical Perspectives*. Oxford: Oxford University Press, 33–56.

Dretske, F. (1988), *Explaining Behavior: Reasons in a World of Causes*. Cambridge, MA: MIT Press.

Dretske, F. (1993), 'The nature of thought', *Philosophical Studies*, 70/2: 185–99.

Dretske, F. (1995), *Naturalizing the Mind*. Cambridge, MA: MIT Press.

Farkas, K. (2008a), 'Phenomenal intentionality without compromise', *The Monist*, 91/2: 273–93.

Farkas, K. (2008b), *The Subject's Point of View*. Oxford: Oxford University Press.

Farkas, K. (2013), 'Constructing a world for the senses', in U. Kriegel (ed.), *Phenomenal Intentionality*. Oxford: Oxford University Press, 99.

Fine, K. (1977), 'Logic, meaning, and conceptual role', *Journal of Philosophy*, 74/7: 378–409.

Fodor, J. A. (1975), *The Language of Thought*. Cambridge, MA: Harvard University Press.

Fodor, J. A. (1987), *Psychosemantics: The Problem of Meaning in the Philosophy of Mind*. Cambridge, MA: MIT Press.

Fodor, J. A. (1990a), 'A theory of content I', in J. A. Fodor (ed.), *A Theory of Content and Other Essays*. Cambridge, MA: MIT Press.

Fodor, J. A. (1990b), 'A theory of content II', in J. A. Fodor (ed.), *A Theory of Content and Other Essays*. Cambridge, MA: MIT Press.

Graham, G., Horgan, T. E., and Tienson, J. L. (2007), 'Consciousness and intentionality', in M. Velmans and S. Schneider (eds), *The Blackwell Companion to Consciousness*. Oxford: Blackwell, 468–84.

Harman, G. (1987), '(Nonsolipsistic) conceptual role semantics', in E. LePore (ed.), *Notre Dame Journal of Formal Logic*. London: Academic Press, 242–56.

Harman, G. (1990), 'The intrinsic quality of experience', *Philosophical Perspectives*, 4/n/a: 31–52.

Horgan, T. and Tienson, J. (2002a), 'The intentionality of phenomenology and the phenomenology of intentionality', in D. J. Chalmers *Philosophy of Mind: Classical and Contemporary Readings* New York: Oxford University Press, 520–33.

Horgan, T. and Tienson, J. (2002b), 'The phenomenology of intentionality and the intentionality of phenomenology', in D. J. Chalmers (ed.), *Philosophy of Mind: Classical and Contemporary Readings*. New York: Oxford University Press, 520–33.

Horgan, T. Tienson, J., and Graham, G. (2004), 'Phenomenal intentionality and the brain in a vat', in R. Schantz (ed.), *The Externalist Challenge*. Berlin: Walter De Gruyter.

Jackson, F. (1998), *From Metaphysics to Ethics: A Defence of Conceptual Analysis*. Oxford: Oxford University Press.

Jackson, F. (2003a), 'Narrow content and representation—or twin earth revisited', *Proceedings and Addresses of the American Philosophical Association*, 77/2: 55–70.

Jackson, F. (2003b), 'Representation and narrow belief', *Philosophical Issues*, 13/1: 99–112.

Jorba, M. (2016), 'Attitudinal cognitive phenomenology and the horizon of possibilities', in T. B. C. Gutland (ed.), *The Phenomenology of Thinking. Philosophical Investigations into the Character of Cognitive Experiences*. Abingdon: Routledge, 77–96.

Kind, A. (2003), 'What's so transparent about transparency?' *Philosophical Studies*, 115/3: 225–44.

Kind, A. (2013), 'The case against representationalism about moods', in U. Kriegel (ed.), *Current Controversies in Philosophy of Mind*. Abingdon: Routledge.

Koksvik, O. (2015), 'Phenomenal contrast: A critique', *American Philosophical Quarterly*, 52: 321–34.

Kriegel, U. (2003), 'Is intentionality dependent upon consciousness?' *Philosophical Studies*, 116/3: 271–307.

Kriegel, U. (2007), 'Intentional inexistence and phenomenal intentionality', *Philosophical Perspectives*, 21/1: 307–40.

Kriegel, U. (2011a), 'Cognitive phenomenology as the basis of unconscious content', in T. Bayne and M. Montague (eds), *Cognitive Phenomenology*. Oxford: Oxford University Press, 79–102.

Kriegel, U. (2011b), *The Sources of Intentionality*. Oxford: Oxford University Press.

Kriegel, U. (2013), 'The phenomenal intentionality research program', in U. Kriegel (ed.), *Phenomenal Intentionality*. Oxford: Oxford University Press.

Kripke, S. A. (1980), *Naming and Necessity*. Cambridge, MA: Harvard University Press.

Kripke, S. A. (1982), *Wittgenstein on Rules and Private Language*. Cambridge, MA: Harvard University Press.

Loar, B. (2003a), 'Phenomenal intentionality as the basis of mental content', in M. Hahn and B. Ramberg (eds), *Reflections and Replies: Essays on the Philosophy of Tyler Burge*. Cambridge, MA: MIT Press, 229–58.

Loar, B. (2003b), 'Transparent experience and the availability of qualia', in Q. Smith and A. Jokic (eds), *Consciousness: New Philosophical Perspectives*. Oxford: Oxford University Press.

Lycan, W. G. (1987), *Consciousness*. Cambridge, MA: MIT Press.

Lycan, W. G. (2000), 'Representational theories of consciousness', in E. N. Zalta (ed.), *Stanford Encyclopedia of Philosophy*. Stanford: Metaphysics Research Lab, 66–9.

Masrour, F. (2013), 'Phenomenal objectivity and phenomenal intentionality: In defense of a Kantian account', in U. Kriegel (ed.), *Phenomenal Intentionality*. Oxford: Oxford University Press, 116–36.

Mendelovici, A. (2010), *Mental Representation and Closely Conflated Topics*. PhD thesis, Princeton University.

Mendelovici, A. (2013a), 'Intentionalism about moods', *Thought: A Journal of Philosophy*, 2/1: 126–36.

Mendelovici, A. (2013b), 'Reliable misrepresentation and tracking theories of mental representation', *Philosophical Studies*, 165/2: 421–43.

Mendelovici, A. (2014), 'Pure intentionalism about moods and emotions', in U. Kriegel (ed.), *Current Controversies in Philosophy of Mind*. Abingdon: Routledge, 135–57.

Mendelovici, A. (2016), 'Why tracking theories should allow for clean cases of reliable misrepresentation', *Disputatio*, 8/42: 57–92.

Mendelovici, A. (2018), *The Phenomenal Basis of Intentionality*. Oxford: Oxford University Press.

Mendelovici, A. (2019a), 'Immediate and reflective senses', in S. Gouveia, M. Curado, and D. Shottenkirk (eds), *Perception, Cognition, and Aesthetics*. New York: Routledge, 187–209.

Mendelovici, A. (2019b), 'Reply to Philip Woodward's review of *The Phenomenal Basis of Intentionality*', *Philosophical Psychology*, 32/8: 1261–67.

Mendelovici, A. (forthcoming), 'Propositional attitudes as self-ascriptions', in L. L. G. Oliveira and K. Corcoran (eds), *Commonsense Metaphysics: Essays in Honor of Lynne Rudder Baker*. Oxford: Oxford University Press.

Mendelovici, A. and Bourget, D. (2014), 'Naturalizing intentionality: Tracking theories versus phenomenal intentionality theories', *Philosophy Compass*, 9/5: 325–37.

Millikan, R. G. (1984), *Language, Thought and Other Biological Categories*. Cambridge, MA: MIT Press.

Montague, M. (2016), *The Given: Experience and its Content*. Oxford: Oxford University Press.

Nagel, T. (1974), 'What is it like to be a bat?' *Philosophical Review*, 83/October: 435–50.

Pautz, A. (2013), 'Does phenomenology ground mental content?' in U. Kriegel (ed.), *Phenomenal Intentionality*. Oxford: Oxford University Press, 194–234.

Pitt, D. (1999), 'In defense of definitions', *Philosophical Psychology*, 12/2: 139–56.

Pitt, D. (2004), 'The phenomenology of cognition, or, what is it like to think that P?' *Philosophy and Phenomenological Research*, 69/1: 1–36.

Pitt, D. (2009), 'Intentional psychologism', *Philosophical Studies*, 146/1: 117–38.

Pitt, D. (2011), 'Introspection, phenomenality, and the availability of intentional content', in T. Bayne and M. Montague (eds), *Cognitive Phenomenology*. Oxford: Oxford University Press, 141–73.

Putnam, H. (1975), 'The meaning of "meaning"', *Minnesota Studies in the Philosophy of Science*, 7: 131–93.

Putnam, H. (1981), *Reason, Truth, and History*. Cambridge: Cambridge University Press.

Seager, W. E. and Bourget, D. (2007), 'Representationalism about consciousness', in M. Velmans and S. Schneider (eds), *The Blackwell Companion to Consciousness*. Oxford: Blackwell, 261–76.

Searle, J. R. (1989), 'Consciousness, unconsciousness, and intentionality', *Philosophical Topics*, 17/1: 193–209.

Searle, J. R. (1990), 'Consciousness, explanatory inversion and cognitive science', *Behavioral and Brain Sciences*, 13/1: 585–642.

Searle, J. R. (1992), *The Rediscovery of the Mind*. Cambridge, MA: MIT Press.

Siewert, C. (1998), *The Significance of Consciousness*. Princeton, NJ: Princeton University Press.

Siewert, C. (2011), 'Phenomenal thought', in T. Bayne and M. Montague (eds), *Cognitive Phenomenology*. Oxford: Oxford University Press, 236.

Smithies, D. (2011), 'What is the role of consciousness in demonstrative thought?' *Journal of Philosophy*, 108/1: 5–34.

Smithies, D. (2013a), 'The nature of cognitive phenomenology', *Philosophy Compass*, 8/8: 744–54.
Smithies, D. (2013b), 'The significance of cognitive phenomenology', *Philosophy Compass*, 8/8: 731–43.
Smithies, D. (2014), 'The phenomenal basis of epistemic justification', in J. Kallestrup and M. Sprevak (eds), *New Waves in Philosophy of Mind*. Basingstoke: Palgrave Macmillan, 98–124.
Smithies, D. (2019), *The Epistemic Role of Consciousness*. Oxford: Oxford University Press.
Strawson, G. (1994), *Mental Reality*. Cambridge, MA: MIT Press.
Strawson, G. (2008), 'Real intentionality 3: Why intentionality entails consciousness', in G. Strawson (ed.), *Synthesis Philosophica*. Oxford: Oxford University Press, 279–97.
Strawson, G. (2011), 'Cognitive phenomenology: Real life', in T. Bayne and M. Montague (eds), *Cognitive Phenomenology*. Oxford: Oxford University Press, 285–325.
Tye, M. (1995), 'A representational theory of pains and their phenomenal character', *Philosophical Perspectives*, 9: 223–39.
Tye, M. (2008), 'The experience of emotion: An intentionalist theory', *Revue Internationale*.
Woodward, P. (2019), 'Primer, proposal, and paradigm: A review essay of Mendelovici's *The Phenomenal Basis of Intentionality*', *Philosophical Psychology*, 32/8: 1246–60.

CHAPTER 27

CONSCIOUSNESS AND KNOWLEDGE

BERIT BROGAARD AND ELIJAH CHUDNOFF

27.1 INTRODUCTION

You wonder whether it is raining. So you look out the window, see it raining, and thereby come to know that it is indeed raining. When you see it is raining, you have a perceptual experience. This is a conscious mental state with a distinctive phenomenology. When you come to know that it is indeed raining, you form a new belief about your immediate environment. This is a cognitive mental state for which you have adequate justification. If one is interested in the relationship between consciousness and knowledge, then a good starting point for inquiry is to consider the relationship between perceptual experiences and justified beliefs. That is what we will do here. We will organize this chapter around five questions:

1. Does having a perceptual experience make one have justification for any beliefs?
2. Does having a perceptual experience make one have justification for any beliefs about the external world?
3. Does having a perceptual experience make one have justification for any beliefs about the external world in virtue of its phenomenology?
4. Are perceptual experiences composed of sensations and seemings?
5. What does perceptual experience reveal?

The strongest relationship between consciousness and knowledge that we might reasonably expect to hold is that being conscious in a certain way itself constitutes the basis we have for some of our knowledge about the world. The first three questions and the sections dedicated to them lead up to the view that this relationship does indeed hold in the case of perceptual consciousness and our knowledge about our immediate environment. The last two questions and the sections dedicated to them explore the details of this relationship further, taking up issues about the structure and content of perceptual experience and their bearing on perceptual justification. In the concluding section we indicate how some of the topics pursued in this chapter might generalize beyond perception.

27.2 Does having a Perceptual Experience Make one have Justification for a Belief?

It is worth commenting on the relevant epistemic property. It is one thing to know that it is raining, another thing to have a justified belief that it is raining, and yet a third thing to have justification for believing that it is raining. To have justification for believing that it is raining is to be such that it is reasonable, or epistemically appropriate, for you to believe that it is raining. It does not imply that you do actually believe that it is raining.

If you have a justified belief that it is raining, then you do believe that it is raining and this belief is based on whatever it is that constitutes your justification for believing that it is raining. Suppose your perceptual experience as of rain makes you have justification for believing that it is raining and your belief that it is raining is formed by taking your perceptual experience at face value. Then your belief that it is raining is a justified belief that it is raining.

To know that it is raining requires more than having a justified belief that it is raining. The project of saying what more remains steeped in controversy, but by most accounts the belief at least needs to be true. Suppose your perceptual experience as of rain is a result of a hoax: someone is on your roof spraying water down so as to make it look as if it is raining to anyone looking out the window. Provided that you have no reason to be suspicious, arguably you still have a justified belief that it is raining, but in this case you do not know that it is raining.

Perceptual experiences can be the result of hoaxes and need not be taken at face value. So if they make one have an epistemic property, the relevant epistemic property is having justification for a belief. This should become clearer when we say more about the relevant making relation. What we have in mind is a constitutive, not a causal relation. Here is an illustrative example: I might say, 'the fact that 7 is only divisible by 1 and itself makes it prime'. The fact that 7 is only divisible by 1 and itself does not cause 7 to be prime. Rather, it constitutes 7's primality. Similarly, when we ask whether having a perceptual experience makes one have justification for a belief we are asking whether having a perceptual experience constitutes one's having justification for a belief. Is the perceptual experience itself a justifier?

If the answer to our question is positive, then there is immediate justification. If you have justification for believing *p* and you do so in part because you have justification for believing other propositions *q*, *r*, *s*, etc., then your justification for believing *p* is mediate—it is mediated by your justification for believing *q*, *r*, *s*, etc. If you have justification for believing *p* and you do so independently of justification you have for believing other propositions *q*, *r*, *s*, etc., then your justification for believing *p* is immediate. Now suppose having a perceptual experience makes you have justification for believing *p*. Your perceptual experience itself constitutes your justification for believing *p*, so this is justification you have independently of justification you have for believing other propositions *q*, *r*, *s*, etc. Hence it is immediate justification.

An important qualification is here in order. Imagine you are in the circumstances described above, looking out your window and having a perceptual experience as of rain because of a hoax, but this time you have received information that some such hoax is in the works. In this case you should not believe that it is raining. Having the perceptual experience no longer makes you have justification for believing that it will rain. This observation might raise a worry: given that your perceptual experience justifies you in believing that it is raining only if you do not have information that is likely the result of a hoax, is the justification it makes you have absent this information really immediate? The answer is positive, and the correct response to the observation is to draw a distinction between prima facie and all things considered justification.

Prima facie justification can be defeated or undermined. Consider three cases. You have a perceptual experience as of rain; you have a perceptual experience as of rain after acquiring information that it is likely the result of a hoax; you have a perceptual experience as of rain after listening to a weather report that says it will not rain. In all three cases you have prima facie justification for believing it is raining. In the second case this prima facie justification is undermined. It no longer weighs in favor of believing that it is raining. In the third case this prima facie justification is, or at least might be, defeated. It weighs in favor of believing that it is raining, but it has to be balanced against the weather report. What you have all things considered justification for believing depends on the result of this balancing.

Taking the distinction between prima facie and all things considered justification into account, then, the thesis under consideration is this: having a perceptual experience makes one have prima facie justification for a belief. The main opposition to this thesis comes from philosophers who deny that there is any immediate justification, and in particular any immediate justification deriving from experience (Sellars 1956; Bonjour 1978; Davidson 1986). One of the most influential lines of reasoning against immediate justification deriving from experience is known as 'The Sellarsian Dilemma', after Wilfrid Sellars (Sellars 1956; Bonjour 1978). The basic line of reasoning goes like this:

(1) Either perceptual experiences are belief-like in that they represent the world as being a certain way, or they are not.
(2) If perceptual experiences are belief-like, then they do not immediately justify beliefs, since belief-like states only justify beliefs by inferential transmission of justification one has for them to other beliefs.

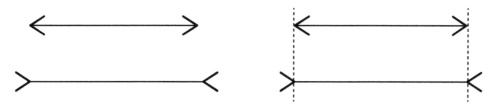

FIGURE 27.1 The Müller-Lyer Illusion. Even when you learn that the line segments on the left have the same length, they continue to appear as if they have different length.

(3) If experiences are not belief-like, then they do not immediately justify beliefs, since the only relations non-belief-like states can stand in to beliefs are causal relations, not inferential relations.

(4) So perceptual experiences do not immediately justify beliefs.

The argument is no longer seen as compelling. Its two key premises, (2) and (3), have been subject to sustained criticism. With respect to (2), many philosophers now believe that perceptual experiences are belief-like in representing, or some sense presenting, the world as being a certain way, but are not belief-like in that they are not the sorts of mental states for which one can have justification.[1]

One reason experiences are thought not to be the sorts of mental states for which one can have justification is that unlike beliefs, experiences are evidence-insensitive: they endure even when we are faced with strong evidence that they are inaccurate. Consider the Müller-Lyer illusion (Figure 27.1).

In the Müller-Lyer illusion the line segments have exactly the same length but because of the fish hooks, they appear as if they have different lengths. This illusion persists even when you measure the line segments and come to the conclusion that they have the same length. Because the experience of the line segments persists despite strong evidence against its accuracy, it is evidence-insensitive. Beliefs are not evidence-insensitive in this way. If you believe it is raining but walk outside only to find that there is not a single cloud in the sky, you do not hold onto your belief but reject it and form the belief that it is not raining.

With respect to (3), some philosophers—including Laurence Bonjour, a former major proponent of the Sellarsian Dilemma—now believe that there are justifying relations other than inferential relations (Bonjour 1999). Having a headache, for example, might

---

[1] See (McDowell 1994) for a sustained confrontation between this view of perceptual experience and the Sellarsian dilemma. The full picture of the current state of play is a bit more complicated than is suggested in the text. First, a vocal group of philosophers, some proponents of the relationalist thesis discussed in Section 27.3, deny that perceptual experiences represent the world as being a certain way, hence the need for the qualification 'or in some sense presenting'. See (Brogaard 2014) for a sampling of the recent literature on this issue. Second, the doxastic view of perceptual experiences according to which they just are beliefs has, after lying dormant for a few decades, become a live option again. See, for example, the defenses of this view in (Byrne 2009) and (Glüer 2009). Third, Susanna Siegel has recently published a book (Siegel 2017) arguing that perceptual experiences themselves are in fact open to rational criticism. This chapter was written before we had a chance to engage with Siegel's most recent work.

justify you in believing that you have a headache, though, on the face of it, it does not do so in virtue of providing you with a basis from which you can infer that you have a headache.

27.3 Does having a Perceptual Experience Make one have Justification for a Belief about the External World?

Suppose having a perceptual experience makes one have justification for a belief. This leaves open what the belief is about. In Section 27.2 we defaulted to the assumption that in the cases under consideration the belief is about a bit of the external world, namely the local weather. But there is disagreement among those philosophers who think that having a perceptual experience makes one have justification for a belief.

Some philosophers—call them Cartesians—think that if a perceptual experience itself justifies a belief, then that belief must be about the character of that perceptual experience (Bonjour 1999). It would be a belief about the internal world. This view is often combined with the view that beliefs about the external world are justified by inferences from such beliefs about the internal world. The combined view is known as classical foundationalism.

Other philosophers think that if a perceptual experience itself justifies a belief, then that belief might be about the ostensible bit of reality presented in the experience. It would be a belief about the external world—the apparently seen, heard, felt, etc. portion of one's immediate environment. This view is associated with two labels, made prominent by two turn of the century formulations (Pryor 2000, 2005; Huemer 2001):

Dogmatism: whenever you have a perceptual experience as of p, you thereby have immediate prima facie justification for believing p.

Phenomenal Conservatism: if it seems to you as if p, then you thereby have at least prima facie justification for believing that p

Three quick observations about phenomenal conservatism in relation to dogmatism. First, as originally formulated, it is about all seemings, not just perceptual seemings. Other seemings might include intellectual seemings, such as seemings about morality, or introspective seemings about one's own mind. Second, some philosophers think that even perceptual seemings are distinct mental states from perceptual experiences (Tucker 2010; Bengson et al 2011; Cullison 2013; Lyons 2015; Conee 2013; Bergmann 2013; Reiland 2015a; Reiland 2015b). We explore this issue in Section 27.5. Third, the 'phenomenal' in the label suggests a commitment about what feature of seemings makes them justifiers—it is their phenomenology. We explore this issue in section 3.

Typically, when one forms a belief on the basis of a perceptual experience, it is a belief about the external world, not the internal world, and such beliefs are, at least by ordinary standards, paradigm cases of justified beliefs. On the face of it, the Cartesian view is a departure from common sense. One motivation for this departure derives from the argument from illusion (Ayer 1963: 3–11). The argument is primarily about the constitution of perceptual experience, but it has traditionally be taken to have implications for the epistemology of perceptual judgment as well (cf. Russell 1912).

Compare veridically perceiving a moving texture with having an illusory perception as of a moving texture due to the waterfall illusion, also known as the motion aftereffect. This is an illusion that a stationary object is moving induced by perceptual adaptation to a previously viewed moving stimulus. The argument from illusion rests on three key ideas:

Indiscernibility: A veridical perception of a quality and an illusory perception as of that quality are introspectively indiscernible.

Common Kind: If two experiences are introspectively indiscernible, then they are constituted in the same way.

Relationalism: Experiences are constituted by awareness relations to objects instantiating the qualities that appear in them.

Taking the example of moving texture as representative, the argument from illusion can be rendered as follows:

(1) By Relationalism, the illusory perception of a moving texture is constituted by awareness relations to objects instantiating motion.
(2) In the illusory perception case, there are no external world objects instantiating motion.
(3) So the illusory perception as of a moving texture is constituted by awareness relations to internal world objects, not external world objects.
(4) By Indiscernibility, veridically perceiving a moving texture and having an illusory perception as of a moving texture are introspectively indiscernible.
(5) By Common Kind, they are constituted in the same way.
(6) So the veridical perception of a moving texture is also constituted by awareness relations to internal world objects, not external world objects.

Suppose one accepts the conclusion, (6). Then one might reason further: since both veridical and illusory perceptions are constituted by awareness relations to internal world objects, perceptual experiences in general are constituted by awareness relations to internal world objects. This is a claim about the constitution of perceptual experience. But if perceptual experiences in general are constituted by awareness relations to internal world objects, not external world objects, having such experiences can, it is tempting to think, at most justify beliefs about the internal world, not the external world. Here we have a claim about the epistemology of perceptual judgment.

Justification for beliefs about the external world existence of a moving texture, say, would depend on the perceptual experience plus some additional reason to think that there is an external world object corresponding to the internal world object it presents. Hence Cartesianism.

There are various ways one can resist this argument. In the contemporary literature, the most popular way of rejecting the argument has been to reject relationalism, viz. the claim that perception is *constituted* by awareness relations to objects instantiating the qualities that appear in them (Dretske 1995; Tye 1995; Chalmers 2004; Pautz 2010; Siegel 2010; Schellenberg 2014). One can reject relationalism, for instance, by arguing that perception is a relation to a proposition, or content, that represents the world in certain ways. Alternatively, one can reject the Common Kind assumption and argue that only veridical cases are cases of genuine perception, whereas illusory cases are cases of some other kind of mental state, such as a believing or being inclined to believe. This view is also known as disjunctivism (Hinton 1967; Snowdon 1980–1; Martin 2002; Fish 2009; Brewer 2011).

One argument for thinking that experience is representational rather than relational turns on the assumption that statements about how things perceptually seem to a person are statements about that person's perceptual experiences (Chudnoff and Didomenico 2015). We will return to this assumption in Section 27.4. Given this assumption, the argument runs as follows (Brogaard, ms. For an argument that does not rely on this assumption see Brogaard 2015):

(1) 'Perceptually seem' is a hyperintensional mental state operator.
(2) Hyperintensional mental state operators operate on representational content.
(3) So, 'perceptually seem' operates on representational content.
(4) If 'perceptually seem' operates on representational content, then the states that usages of it refer to are representational states.
(5) So, perceptual experiences are representational states.

Here 'perceptually seem' is an instance of the kinds of 'seems' locutions that occur in sentences such as 'It seems to John that the rock is moving' and 'it seems to Mary that the table is red'. When 'seems' occurs in sentences like these, it is hyperintensional. Substituting one expression for a necessarily coextensive expression within its scope can yield a change in truth-value. For example, even though 'Hesperus is the brightest object in the evening sky' and 'Phosphorus is the brightest object in the evening sky' are necessarily equivalent, 'it seems to Mary that Hesperus is the brightest object in the evening sky' may be true, while 'it seems to Mary that Phosphorus is the brightest object in the evening sky' may be false. Since Mary cannot stand in a direct relation to Hesperus (i.e., Venus) without standing in the same relation to Phosphorus (i.e., Venus), it follows that the states that such seemings reports refer to cannot be direct relations to external objects. If not that, then the most likely alternative is that such states are relations to representational contents. Given the assumption that these states just are perceptual experiences, it follows that perceptual experiences are relations to representational contents, not relations to objects instantiating the qualities that appear in them.

27.4 Does having a Perceptual Experience Make one have Justification for a Belief about the External World in Virtue of its Phenomenology?

According to dogmatism *whenever* you have a perceptual experience as of p, you thereby have immediate prima facie justification for believing p. For now let us suppose a weaker thesis is true, namely the thesis that *sometimes* when you have a perceptual experience as of p, you thereby have immediate prima facie justification for believing p. A natural question to ask is: if your perceptual experience as of p immediately prima facie justifies you in believing p, then in virtue of what does it do so? Here are a few possible answers:

Factivism: if your perceptual experience as of p immediately prima facie justifies you in believing p, then it does so in virtue of being a factive mental state (Williamson 2000; McDowell 2011).

Reliabilism: if your perceptual experience as of p immediately prima facie justifies you in believing p, then it does so in virtue of its reliability (Goldman 2008; Lyons 2009).

Functionalism: if your perceptual experience as of p immediately prima facie justifies you in believing p, then it does so in virtue of its functional role in your mental life, e.g. the role it has as an evidence insensitive representation (Brogaard 2016).

None of these answers accords a special role to perceptual consciousness as such. A fourth possible answer does:

Phenomenalism: if your perceptual experience as of p immediately prima facie justifies you in believing p, then it does so in virtue of its phenomenology.

According to phenomenalism there is an explanatory link between the fact that perceptual experience is a distinctive form of consciousness and the fact that perceptual experience is a source of justification: it is a source of justification *because* it is the distinctive form of consciousness that it is (cf. Pryor 2000; Huemer 2001; Smithies 2014).

One motivation for phenomenalism is intuitive. Consider what it is like to have a perceptual experience as of rain, say. The rain seems to be there right before you. Supposing you have no independent evidence that it is not raining and no reason to think your perceptual experience is faulty, what is the reasonable attitude to take toward the claim that it is raining? You might believe it, disbelieve it, or suspend judgment. Disbelieving is irrational and suspending judgment is overly cautious. Believing is the reasonable attitude. If you go out and do not want to get wet you should take an umbrella. In thinking through this scenario and what the reasonable attitude is, all we did was focus on the fact that in it you have a perceptual experience with a certain phenomenology and no defeaters. We did not have to bring in the facts about your environment, the track record of your perceptual capacity, or the causal tendencies of your experience. The phenomenology alone seems to suffice. Hence there is some intuitive motivation for phenomenalism.

A related motivation comes from reflection on two classic thought experiments targeting reliabilism (cf. Smithies 2014).

> *Norman the Clairvoyant* (Bonjour 1980): Norman is a clairvoyant with respect to the whereabouts of the president. He has no normal evidence for or against the existence of this power. One day his clairvoyance gives him the (correct) impression that the president is in New York. He has no normal evidence for or against the claim that the president is in New York. Does Norman have justification for believing that the president is in New York?
>
> *New Evil Demon* (Cohen 1984): Descartes considered the skeptical hypothesis that all of our experiences are the result of the manipulations of an evil deceiver. His aim was to show that experiences do not rule out the possibility of error. But suppose, absent any evidence that it is so, the hypothesis turns out to be true and consider your perceptual experience as of rain. It turns out to be non-veridical, but does it still justify you in believing that it is raining?

The typical response to Norman the Clairvoyant is to say that no, he does not have justification. Reliability is not sufficient. The typical response to New Evil Demon is to say that yes, the perceptual experience still justifies believing that it is raining. Reliability is not necessary. These judgments count against factivism and functionalism as well. The New Evil Demon case counts against factivism because the perceptual experience in the case justifies believing that it is raining even though it is not a fact that it is raining. Both cases count against functionalism. Norman the Clairvoyant counts against functionalism because it is easy to imagine the results of Norman's clairvoyance having the relevant functional role, for example being evidence insensitive, but it would still fail to justify his belief that the president is in New York. The New Evil Demon case counts against functionalism because it is easy to imagine the results of the demon's manipulations lacking the relevant functional role—so, for example, being evidence insensitive—but still they would justify believing that it is raining. Phenomenalism explains both judgments. Norman's impression lacks the kind of presentational phenomenology associated with perceptual experience, and the demon's victim's experience possesses just this kind of phenomenology. Variants on reliabilism, factivism, and functionalism might be designed to *accommodate* the judgments, but phenomenalism seems to provide the simplest, most natural *explanation* of them. So reflection on these cases supports phenomenalism.

A prominent, recent challenge to phenomenalism derives from reflection on the cognitive penetrability of experience. One argument along these lines is Markie's gold prospector argument. It runs as follows:

> Suppose that we are prospecting for gold. You have learned to identify a gold nugget on sight but I have no such knowledge. As the water washes out of my pan, we both

look at a pebble, which is in fact a gold nugget. My desire to discover gold makes it seem to me as if the pebble is gold; your learned identification skills make it seem that way to you. According to [phenomenalism], the belief that it is gold has prima facie justification for both of us. Yet, certainly, my wishful thinking should not gain my perceptual belief the same positive epistemic status of defeasible justification as your learned identification skills. (Markie 2005: 356–7)

The problem here is that because it seems to both the expert and the novice that the pebble is gold, phenomenalism entails that they both have prima facie justification for believing that it is gold. Since the novice possesses no defeater that he has access to, and the novice's belief is based on his experience, the expert and the novice are equally justified in believing that the pebble is gold. This might seem implausible, as the novice's belief is based on wishful thinking and wishful thinking is not a source of justification. So, phenomenalism would seem to make the wrong prediction in this case.

Susanna Siegel (2012) has presented a similar argument. Jill thinks Jack is angry at her. Her belief is unjustified. However, the next day when she encounters Jack, her belief that Jack is angry at her makes her see Jack's neutral facial expression as an angry face. Phenomenalism entails that Jill's experience as of Jack's face expressing anger prima facie justifies her in believing that Jack is angry. Again, this might seem implausible, as Jill's initially unjustified belief causes itself to become justified by its effect on Jill's experience. This looks like circular reasoning, and circular reasoning is not a source of justification. So, phenomenalism would seem to make the wrong prediction in this case too.

Both cases are driven by a form of cognitive penetration (for more on which see e.g. Macpherson 2012). In the first case, wishful thinking makes Peter see the nugget as gold by changing his experience, and his experience then has the phenomenology phenomenalists take to be sufficient to prima facie justify his belief that the nugget is gold. In the second case, Jill's unjustified belief that Jack is angry at her penetrates and thereby changes her perception of his face. Her perception now has the phenomenology phenomenalists take to be sufficient to prima facie justify her belief that Jack is angry at her.

One possible reply here would be to argue against the existence of cognitive penetration. This move is a nonstarter. Although some thinkers have argued that there are early visual processes that are not cognitively penetrable (Fodor 1983; Pylyshyn 1999; Firestone and Scholl 2016), this view does not rule out the possibility that wishful thinking and dogmatic belief might alter the contents of perceptual experience via processes that occur after early visual processes. Further, for philosophical purposes the mere possibility of, not the actual existence of, cognitive penetration might suffice.

Another, more plausible line of response is to question the verdicts about the cases. Markie thinks that the novice gold prospector lacks justification because desires do not justify beliefs. Siegel thinks that Jill lacks justification because beliefs do not justify themselves. But Markie's novice gold prospector does not base his belief that he has found gold on his desire; he bases it on his experience. And Jill does not base her belief that Jack is angry on that very belief; she bases it on her experience. Why not think that this makes all the difference between lacking justification and having justification? The main reason seems to be the idea that taking experiences at face value is on par with reasoning from beliefs or other mental states. If you desire that p, take this to be a reason to think that p, and so believe p, then your belief that p is not justified. If you believe that p without justification, take this belief to be a reason to think that p, and so reaffirm the belief that p, then your belief that p is no more justified than it was initially. But the phenomenalist is likely to deny that taking experiences at face value is on par with reasoning from beliefs or other mental states. Reasoning *transmits* epistemic statuses. Experiences *generate* epistemic statuses.

As we have developed the foregoing reply it requires us to reject our initial, perhaps intuitive, verdicts about Markie's and Siegel's cases. There is another way of developing it, however, that allows one to combine those initial verdicts with phenomenalism. Briefly, the key idea is that the phenomenology of perceptual experience is sufficient to generate epistemic justification, but not all generation is creation *ex nihilo*. So it could be that the phenomenology of Markie's gold prospector's experience and the phenomenology of Jill's experience are of the sort that generates epistemic justification for the propositions in question by creating it in part out of previous supporting justification, which justification, it turns out, Markie's gold prospector and Jill lack. In that case Markie's gold prospector and Jill fail to have justification for their beliefs. We find such an account attractive, but do not have the space to develop it here (A sketch can be found in Chudnoff 2013, and a fuller development in Chudnoff 2020).

Siegel has argued that experiences also transmit epistemic statuses (Siegel 2013). She focuses on reasoning from beliefs and considers the question: what distinguishes beliefs and experiences such that reasoning from a belief transmits epistemic status and taking an experience at face value does not? She argues that there are no features that beliefs have and experiences lack that might be the features in virtue of which reasoning from a belief transmits epistemic statuses and taking an experience at face value does not. Candidates include: being assessable for rationality, being the result of explicit reasoning, being evidence sensitive. We will not review the details of her discussion. Here we would like to make an observation about the form of her overall argument. It goes like this:

(1) Whatever features beliefs have in virtue of which reasoning from them transmits epistemic statuses experiences also have.
(2) So taking an experience at face value also transmits epistemic statuses.

This form of argument, however, is invalid. Consider the property of being a U.S. citizen. There are various features a person might have in virtue of possessing which he or she counts as a U.S. citizen. For example, there is being born in the U.S. or successfully applying for citizenship. Suppose another person has all the same features. It does not follow that that person is also a U.S. citizen. For that person might have all those same features *plus some additional features* that makes him or her not a U.S. citizen. For example, there is being convicted of treason. So it is open to the phenomenalist to argue that even if experiences have whatever features beliefs have in virtue of which reasoning from them transmits epistemic statuses, taking them at face value does not transmit epistemic statuses because experiences have special additional features. And if one is attracted to phenomenalism then the candidate additional features are obvious: those that constitute the distinctive phenomenology of experience.

Suppose one replies: the features we have cited in virtue of which one counts as a U.S. citizen are only partial grounds; for a full ground one needs to add the feature of not being convicted of treason; the form of argument is valid with respect to full grounding. Suppose this is so. It is no help to Siegel's argument because then, at least according to the phenomenalist, the features in virtue of which reasoning from beliefs transmits epistemic statuses would have to include not having a certain kind of phenomenology, in which case step (1) in the argumentative strategy would fail. Siegel could incorporate a denial of phenomenalism into step (1) and avoid this difficulty. But then we would not have an independent argument against phenomenalism.[2]

27.5 ARE PERCEPTUAL EXPERIENCES COMPOSED OF SENSATIONS AND SEEMINGS?

In this section and the next we will consider the detailed elaboration of phenomenal conservatism and phenomenalist versions of dogmatism. Recently a number of writers on these views have promoted the idea that perceptual experience is disunified (Lyons 2005, 2015; Tucker 2010; Bengson et al 2011; Bergmann 2013; Brogaard 2013; Conee 2013; Cullison 2013; Markie 2013; Tooley 2013; Bengson 2015; Reiland 2015b). They distinguish between sensations and seemings and take perceptual experiences to be composed of these two distinct states. That is, they endorse the following:

Composition View: for you to have a perceptual experience as of *p* is for you to have a sensation and for it to seem to you that *p* and for these to be suitably related.

The greatest variation among proponents of this view is in how they conceive of sensations. Sensations might be states with the same kind of content as seemings, whatever that is, or states with nonconceptual content as opposed to the conceptual content of seemings, or states lacking content altogether. We set this issue aside here.

A good way to get a grip on the Composition View is to consider how it treats perceptual experiences in different sensory modalities. In what does the contrast between seeing a texture and feeling the same texture consist? Proponents of the Composition View tend to think of the difference along the following lines. For you to *see* a T-ish texture is (i) for you to have a *visual* sensation and (ii) for it to seem to you that there is something T-ish textured and (iii) for these states to be suitably related. For you to *feel* a T-ish texture is (i) for you to have a *tactile* sensation and (ii) for it to seem to you that there is

---

[2] Thanks to Uriah Kriegel for suggesting we explore this issue.

something T-ish textured, and (iii) for these states to be suitably related. The visual sensation and the tactile sensation are different kinds of mental state. But the seemings are the same kind of mental state. Seemings, on this view, are amodal states.[3]

The Composition View contrasts with what we might call the Identity View:

Identity View: having a perceptual experience as of *p* is the same as having a sensation as of *p*, which is the same as its perceptually seeming to you that *p*.

On this view, seeing a T-ish texture and feeling a T-ish texture are two distinct ways for it to seem to you that there is a T-ish texture. So, on this view seemings are modality-specific; there is no mental state of its seeming to you that there is a T-ish texture that can be factored out as a common component between seeing a T-ish texture and feeling a T-ish texture. The visual seeming and the tactile seeming are two distinct mental states.

Suppose the Composition View were true. Then understanding the relationship between perceptual experience and justification would require facing a significant new question. Take the weakened dogmatist thesis that sometimes when you have a perceptual experience as of *p*, you thereby have immediate prima facie justification for believing *p*. What does the 'thereby' refer back to? If the Identity View is true, then the only option is the perceptual experience. If the Composition View is true, then there are three options: the constituent sensation, the constituent seeming, and the composite perceptual experience. All three positions are occupied in the recent literature on phenomenal dogmatism and phenomenal conservatism (for a representative development of each see Conee 2013; Tucker 2010; Reiland 2015b respectively). In our view, all three face potential difficulties, though we will not pursue them here.

Here we would like to consider the motivation for adopting the Composition View in the first place. The main motivation comes from a series of arguments challenging the Identity View. Three basic patterns dominate the literature. (For further critical discussion of these three patterns of argument and additional references to the relevant literature, see Chudnoff and DiDomenico 2015).

The first is the Speckled Hen (originally introduced for a different purpose by Chisholm 1942, and appealed to by Tucker 2010; Brogaard 2013; Markie, 2013).

Speckled Hen: When you see a hen with 48 speckles you have a visual sensation as of 48 speckles. This is why the phenomenology is slightly different from seeing a hen with 47 or 49 speckles. But when you see a hen with 48 speckles, it does not seem to you that there is a hen with 48 speckles. This is why you cannot form a justified belief that there is a 48-speckled hen just by taking your experience at face value. So sensations are different from seemings.

---

[3] Given that composition theorists think that the recognition of kinds and functions occur at the level of seemings, not sensations, there is a prima facie worry for the view deriving from the fact that agnosias are modality specific. We are not aware of anyone addressing this worry in the literature.

One might deny that there really are phenomenal differences between seeing a hen with 47, 48, or 49 speckles. But we will concede that there are here. For there is another way to resist the argument. And that is to give an alternative explanation of the phenomenal differences. When you see a hen with 48 speckles, say, you might have a visual experience (= sensation = seeming) as of a hen with a speckle there$_1$, there$_2$, there$_3$,..., and there$_{48}$ without this also being a visual experience as of a hen with 48 speckles. The content of the unitary experience would explain both its phenomenal distinctiveness and the inability to form a justified belief that there is a 48-speckled hen just by taking your experience at face value.

The second argument pattern for the Composition view focuses on differences between expert perceivers and novice perceivers (Lyons 2005; Brogaard 2013; Bengson 2015).

Expert vs. Novice: When an expert about seventeenth-century French furniture—or some other natural or artifactual kind—and a novice about seventeenth-century French furniture look at a seventeenth-century French desk, they have visual sensations with the same content. This is why the phenomenology is similar. But while it seems to the expert that there is a seventeenth-century French desk, it does not seem so to the novice. This is why the expert, but not the novice, can form a justified belief that there is a seventeenth-century French desk just by taking his or her experience at face value. So sensations are different from seemings.

One way to resist the argument is to explain the difference between the expert and the novice in terms of overlapping but distinct contents. The idea is that both the expert and the novice have unitary visual experiences with common contents characterizing shape, color, size, ornamentation, basic level categorization, etc. But only the expert's visual experience also has as part of its content that the table is a seventeenth-century French desk. On this view, the expert but not the novice has an experience with a high-level content (Siegel 2005). We will return to the distinction between high-level and low-level content in Section 27.6.

Another way to resist the argument is to say that the expert has a perceptual experience that has a richer *low level* content than the perceptual experience of the novice as a result of perceptual learning (Connolly 2014; Arstila 2015). The expert might, for example, be aware of more details of the table than the novice. This, too, would explain the difference in the phenomenology of the experiences of the expert and the novice as well as the novice's inability to form a justified belief that the table is a seventeenth-century French desk just by taking his experience at face value.

The third argument for the Composition View derives from reflection on cases of blindsight (Tucker 2010; Brogaard 2013; Tooley 2013; Lyons 2015).

Blindsight: If a blindsighter judges there to be an X shape—or some other visual form—in his or her blind spot, then it is because it seems to him or her that there is an X shape there. The seeming explains the judgment. But a blindsighter does not have a visual sensation as of an X shape in his or her blind spot. The absence of a sensation explains the reported lack of visual phenomenology in the blind spot. So sensations are different from seemings.

One way to resist this argument is to argue that the seemings in these cases are epistemic (Chisholm 1957; Jackson 1977; Brogaard 2013, 2015). Seemings are epistemic as opposed to phenomenal if they are belief-like mental states that normally are sensitive to counterevidence by not persisting in the face of it.[4] Suppose you are enjoying a sunset over Biscayne Bay. If you were told that you were a brain in a vat and that no real sunset is taking place, this would not make your seeming recede or become less clear or less lively. This is because your seeming in this case is phenomenal. Compare this to a case where you have been told that a hurricane will hit Miami. It may seem to you that you ought to evacuate but if you are told that the hurricane has changed its direction and is now hitting New York rather than Miami, it no longer will seem to you that you ought to evacuate. In the latter case, your seeming is epistemic.

When a blindsighter detects the shape of a visual stimulus presented to her in her blind field, she has no distinctly visual awareness of the shape of the stimulus. So when she reports on the shape of a stimulus presented to her in her blind field, she cannot make use of any visual phenomenology associated with the shape information. Rather, she must infer from her inclination to guess that the stimulus is X-shaped that it is an X shape. Were she to be presented with a defeater, she would no longer have the inclination to state that the stimulus looks X-shaped. Because she does not have a seeming that is evidence-insensitive, her seeming that the stimulus looks like an X shape is epistemic. Epistemic seemings are belief-like states and not candidates to be constituents of perceptual experiences. So, the argument does not show that sensations are different from seemings of the sort that could be treated as experiential components.

One might worry that the distinction between phenomenal and epistemic seemings is just reintroducing the distinction between seemings and sensations. But this is not the case. Given that epistemic seemings are evidence-sensitive and plausibly thought of in terms of degrees of belief, there is no reason to think that they might be components in a mental state that might count as a perceptual experience as understood by all parties to the present debate.

27.6 What Does Perceptual Experience Reveal?

So far we have taken a relaxed view about what aspects of the world show up in perception. It is common to distinguish low-level properties such as color, shape, and motion from

---

[4] Epistemic seemings may be best captured in terms of degrees of belief. For example, if you say 'Premise 1 seems false' (as opposed to, say, 'Premise 1 *is* false'), you are likely expressing a degree of disbelief in the truth of premise 1.

high-level properties such as the natural kind property of being rain and the artifactual kind property of being a seventeeth-century French desk. We have been writing as if we have perceptual experience of both low-level and high-level properties. And we have been writing as if given such perceptual experiences, they prima facie, immediately justify beliefs about both low-level and high-level properties. But all of this is disputed ground (Peacocke 1992; Tye 1995; Lyons 2005, 2009; Siegel 2005; Fish 2013; Reiland 2014), some of the main areas of which we will discuss in this section.

Whether high-level properties are presented in perceptual experience may be thought to turn in part on what we take to be high-level properties. Uncontroversial high-level properties include natural kind properties (e.g., being an elm), artificial kind properties (e.g., being a cork screw), semantic properties (e.g., the meaning of 'bachelor'), mental state properties (e.g., being sad or trying to do something), aesthetic properties (e.g., being gloomy), moral properties (e.g., being an act of kindness), personal taste properties (e.g., being attractive), and some events (e.g., causing the lights to go on). But rather than simply talking about low-level and high-level properties, one can also talk about some properties being higher level than others. Properties pertaining to faces may be higher level than shape properties but lower level than natural kind properties (e.g., being H_2O). It is questionable that we can settle the dispute about which high-level properties are presented in perception with one easy argument. An argument would likely need to be made for each class of high-level properties (see e.g., Siegel 2005, 2009; Bayne 2009; Block 2014; Scholl and Gao 2013; Audi 2013; Stokes 2014; Chudnoff 2016a; Brogaard 2016; Werner 2016).

Suppose, however, that some of our perceptual experiences represent the instantiation of high-level properties. It is a further thesis to claim that these perceptual experiences also prima facie, immediately justify beliefs about the instantiation of those high-level properties. In one of the few explicit discussions of the topic, Nico Silins (2013) explores the prospects of a principle that bridges the two theses:

Experience to Belief: If you have an experience with the high-level content that *p*, then the experience (at least defeasibly) gives you immediate justification to believe that *p*.

Why think that this principle is true? Silins (2013: 18–19) presents what he calls the 'face value argument' in favor of it:

(1) If your experiences have high-level contents, then you are able to form justified high-level beliefs on their basis without performing any conscious inference, and instead by taking the experiences at face value.
(2) If you are able to form a justified belief on the basis of an experience without conscious inference, and instead by taking the experience at face value, then you have immediate justification from the experience for the belief.
(3) So, if you have experiences with high-level contents, then you have immediate justification from them for high-level beliefs.

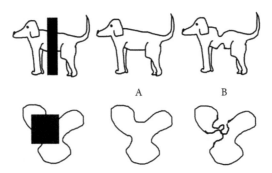

FIGURE 27.2 Amodal completion in two different scenarios. In the cases of both the dog and the blob, we come to believe that the occluded figure is completed as in A rather than B, based on amodal completion. But arguably our belief is justified only in the case of A, because we have justified background beliefs about what dogs look like but not what random blobs look like.

Silins notes a worry. Either taking an experience at face value is compatible with relying on background information or it is not; if it is, then premise (2) is false; if it is not, then premise (1) is controversial. The response he considers is to weaken the conclusion to: 'if experiences have high-level contents, *and* give us immediate justification for some beliefs, then experiences will give us immediate justification for some high-level beliefs' (Silins 2013: 19). So in this paper Silins seems to operate with the assumption that if an experience immediately, prima facie justifies believing some of its content, then it will immediately, prima facie justify believing all of its content, including its high-level content if it has any.[5] One might think that this should be taken as the default view (Huemer 2001; Tucker 2010). But on reflection there are good reasons to think that it is mistaken, and these have nothing to do with high-level content in particular.

Imagine being in real world scenarios corresponding to the leftmost members in the following two sequences of in Figure 27.2.

In the first scenario you see a partially occluded dog. But because of perceptual ('amodal') completion you have a perceptual experience as of a dog that continues behind the bar. Though you do not see the occluded part of the dog, your perceptual experience represents it as continuing behind the bar is a specific way—way A rather than way B. In the second scenario you see a partially occluded blob. But because of perceptual completion you have a perceptual experience as of a blob that continues behind the square. Though you do not see the occluded part of the blob, your perceptual experience represents it as continuing behind the square in a specific way—way A rather than way B.

So far we have made claims about what your perceptual experiences represent. Now let us consider what you have justification for believing. In having the perceptual experience of the occluded dog you also have justification for believing that the dog continues behind the bar in way A rather than way B. This is what you would believe in the scenario,

---

[5] Silins has personally communicated that in his considered judgment the assumption is false, and has pointed out other papers (Silins 2008, 2011) in which he adopts positions incompatible with it.

and it seems perfectly justified. In having the perceptual experience of the occluded blob, however, you do not also have justification for believing that the blob continues behind the square in way A rather than way B. This is probably what you would believe in the scenario, and one might think it seems perfectly excused—for that is how the blob looks—but there is room to doubt that it is a justified belief.

To bring out the contrast between the two cases, consider the attitude of suspending judgment. If you suspended judgment about whether the dog continues in way A rather than way B, this would be unreasonably cautious. Dogs have a familiar nature that makes way A much more likely than way B, so there is no reason not to commit. But if you suspended judgment about whether the blob continues in way A rather than way B, this would be reasonable, and no one could legitimately criticize you for being unreasonably cautious. Unlike dogs, random blobs do not have a familiar nature that makes way A much more likely than way B, so there is some reason not to commit.

If we consider what explains the epistemic difference between the two cases, the following seems like the most plausible story—at least presupposing what we have argued so far.[6] In both cases, your justification depends on background information about the occluded parts of the seen objects. In the case of the dog, you have justified background beliefs.[7] In the case of the blob, you do not have justified background beliefs. What this implies, however, is that although both experiences have contents that represent occluded parts, neither experience prima facie, immediately justifies beliefs about occluded parts. In both cases the prima facie justification is as best mediate, and in the case of the dog, there is justification for the mediating background beliefs, but in the case of the blob, there is no justification for the mediating background beliefs. Notice, further, that this has nothing to do with high-level contents. The properties in question are low-level shape properties.

If the foregoing stands, then there is no unconditional bridge from an experience representing that p to an experience prima facie, immediately justifying the belief that p. The experience must meet some further conditions with respect to the proposition that p.

One natural proposal flows from contrasting the proposition that, say, the dog in Figure 27.2 has a tail with the proposition that it continues behind the bar in way A rather than way B. Plausibly your perceptual experience does prima facie, immediately justify believing that the dog has a tail. Why? Because not only do you represent that the dog has a tail, but you can also see the tail. Your experience has what we might call presentational phenomenology with respect to the proposition that the dog has a tail. Contrast the

---

[6] To see the need for the qualification consider reliabilism. A reliabilist might cite the fact that A-shaped dogs are way more prevalent than B-shaped dogs whereas A-shaped blobs and B-shaped blobs are more or less equally prevalent. Thanks to Uriah Kriegel for drawing our attention to this reliabilist alternative.

[7] On this model, the background information is stored in semantic memory. Another possibility is that it is possessed in virtue of modifications to the perceptual system. These can be seen as two different ways of retaining justification from previous experience over time. We will focus on the first model for simplicity. For a development of the alternative model see (Chudnoff 2020).

occluded part of the dog: you represent it as continuing in way A rather than way B, but, unlike the tail, you cannot see it—it is occluded after all. Your experience lacks presentational phenomenology with respect to the proposition that the dog continues in way A rather than way B. The contrast suggests the following idea: a perceptual experience representing that p can immediately, prima facie justify believing that *p* only if it has presentational phenomenology with respect to the proposition that *p*—that is, only if it is one in which you are, or as in cases of trickery or hallucination at least seem to be, perceptually aware of the bit of the world corresponding to *p*. In order to apply the principle to unclear cases—such as cases of perceptual experience with high-level content—we would need a more articulated understanding of what it is to be, or at least seem to be, perceptually aware of the bit of the world corresponding to *p* over and above just perceptually representing that *p*. For further discussion and elaboration of the sort of view under consideration see Chudnoff (2012, 2013, 2016b).

A second approach to demarcating those contents of perceptual experience that are candidates for immediate, prima facie justification appeals to the notion of evidence insensitivity. There are two ways one might appeal to the notion. Unqualified, evidence insensitivity is a functional property, or a dispositional property that subjects possess with respect to experience. Arguably, however, there is also a phenomenal property corresponding to this dispositional property—this might be compared with the idea that experience has as a phenomenal property, felt objectivity, corresponding to counterfactual dependences capturing its world sensitivity (Siegel 2006; Church 2013; Koksvik 2011). We can call this corresponding phenomenal property felt evidence insensitivity. One way to appeal to the notion of felt evidence insensitivity is to say that an experience immediately, prima facie justifies believing that *p* only if it is felt as evidence insensitive with respect to *p*. Appealing to felt evidence insensitivity might be more attractive than appealing to presentational phenomenology because arguably the resulting view can be more easily generalized beyond perception to cases such as to memory and it can more naturally account for our justification for beliefs about some high-level contents. For further discussion and elaboration of this sort of view and arguments for thinking it is preferable to appealing to presentational phenomenology, see Brogaard (2016).

27.7 Concluding Remarks: Beyond Perceptual Experience

We have worked our way toward the view that perceptual experiences immediately, prima facie justify some beliefs about the external world in virtue of their phenomenology, and we have sketched two different ideas about just what aspects of their phenomenology might be relevant—presentational phenomenology and felt evidence insensitivity. A natural next issue to explore is how far this picture generalizes beyond perceptual experience to other forms of consciousness. We briefly consider two cases—emotions and intuitions.

It is widely accepted that emotions attribute evaluative properties to external objects (see Tappolet 2016 for a recent book-length discussion). For instance, fear of a snake attributes the property of being dangerous to the snake, and anger at a person attributes the property of having done something offensive to the bearer of the emotion. One might consider, then, the view that emotions, in virtue of attributing evaluative properties to external objects can immediately, prima facie justify beliefs about whether the objects have these evaluative properties. Suppose you see a suspicious-looking person and tremble in fear. You have no other reasons to believe the person is dangerous than your perception of the person and your emotional reaction. You nonetheless come to believe that the person is dangerous. Is your belief justified? Generalizing the foregoing discussion of perception, the fact that the emotion is an experience that represents an evaluative property does not itself imply that it also immediately, prima facie justifies believing that it is instantiated. On the view we have considered, there are additional, relevant questions. Does the emotion possess presentational phenomenology with respect to the proposition attributing evaluative properties? Does the emotion possess felt evidence insensitivity with respect to the proposition attributing evaluative properties? See (Brogaard and Chudnoff 2016) for some reasons to think that these questions should receive negative answers.

Perception tells us about features of our surrounding environment. But we also have beliefs about abstract matters—for example beliefs about mathematics, metaphysics, and morality. According to a tradition that traces back at least to Plato, justification for these beliefs derives from a kind of experience, intuition, that is in some ways similar to perception but that reveals truths about abstract, rather than concrete, subject matters. Gödel's is a typical expression of this view:

> The similarity between mathematical intuition and a physical sense is very striking. It is arbitrary to consider 'This is red' an immediate datum, but not so to consider the proposition expressing modus ponens or complete induction (or perhaps some similar propositions from which the latter follows). For the differences, as far as it is relevant here, consists solely in the fact that in the first case a relationship between a concept and a particular object is perceived, while in the second case it is a relationship between concepts.   (Gödel 2001: 359)

Intuition has been an object of intense philosophical debate over the last two decades (for a sampling of the literature, early and late, see DePaul and Ramsey 1998, and Booth and Rowbottom 2014). Though many writers do not follow Gödel in pressing the analogy with perception, a number do, and for them it is incumbent to say just what features of perception intuition is supposed to share in virtue of which it can serve as the basis for our beliefs about abstract matters. The foregoing discussion of perception suggests one approach: intuition must be phenomenally similar to perception though it is directed at different subject matter. Both presentational phenomenology and felt evidence insensitivity are abstract enough features of phenomenology to be present in experiences that are not directed at the sensible features of our surrounding environment (for further elaboration and development of the idea that intuitions possess presentational phenomenology see Chudnoff 2011, 2013; for alternative ways of developing the analogy between intuition and perception see Koksvik 2011; Nagel 2012; and Bengson 2015).

References

Arstila, V. (2015), 'Perceptual Learning Explains Two Candidates for Cognitive Penetration', Erkenntnis, http://doi.org/10.1007/s10670-015-9785-3
Audi, R. (2013), *Moral Perception*. Princeton, NJ: Princeton University Press.
Ayer, A. J. (1963), *The Foundations of Empirical Knowledge*. London: Macmillan.
Bayne, T. (2009), 'Perceptual experience and the reach of phenomenal content'. *Philosophical Quarterly*, 59: 385–404.
Bengson, J. (2015), 'The Intellectual Given', *Mind*, 124/495: 707–60.
Bengson, J., Grube, E., and Korman, D. (2011), 'A New Framework for Conceptualism', *Noûs*, 45/1: 167–89.
Bergmann, M. (2013), 'Phenomenal conservatism and the dilemma for internalism', in C. Tucker (ed.), *Seemings and Justification: New Essays on Dogmatism and Phenomenal Conservatism*. Oxford: Oxford University Press, 154–80.
Block, N. (2014), 'Seeing-As in the Light of Vision Science', *Philosophy and Phenomenological Research*, 89/3: 560–72.
BonJour, L. (1978), 'Can Empirical Knowledge Have a Foundation?' *American Philosophical Quarterly*, 15/1: 1–14.
BonJour, L. (1980), 'Externalist Theories of Empirical Knowledge', *Midwest Studies in Philosophy*, 5/1: 53–73.
BonJour, L. (1999), 'Foundationalism and the external world,' *Philosophical Perspectives*, 13/s13: 229–49.
Booth, A. R. and Rowbottom, D. P. (eds) (2014), *Intuitions*. Oxford: Oxford University Press.
Brewer, B. (2011), *Perception and its Objects*. Oxford: Oxford University Press.
Brogaard, B. (2013), 'Phenomenal Seemings and Sensible Dogmatism', in C. Tucker (ed.), *Seemings and Justification: New Essays on Dogmatism and Phenomenal Conservatism*. New York: Oxford University Press, 270–89.
Brogaard, B. (ed.) (2014), *Does Perception Have Content?*. New York: Oxford University Press.
Brogaard, B. (2015), 'Perceptual Reports', in Mohan Matthen (ed.), *Oxford Handbook of the Philosophy of Perception*. Oxford: Oxford University Press, 237–55.
Brogaard, B. (2016), 'In Defense of Hearing Meanings', *Synthese*, 195/7: 2967–83.
Brogaard, B. (2017), 'Foundationalism' in S. Bernecker and K. Michaelian (eds), *The Routledge Handbook of Philosophy of Memory*. Abingdon: Routledge, 296–309.
Brogaard, B. (2018), Seeing and Saying. New York: Oxford University Press.
Brogaard, B. and Chudnoff, E. (2016), 'Against Emotional Dogmatism', *Philosophical Issues*, 26.
Byrne, A. (2009), 'Experience and Content', *Philosophical Quarterly*, 59: 429–51.
Chalmers, D. (2004), 'The representational character of experience', in B. Leiter (ed.), *The Future for Philosophy*. Oxford: Oxford University Press, 153–81.
Chisholm, R. (1942), 'Discussions: The Problem of the Speckled Hen', *Mind*, LI: 368–73.
Chisholm, R. (1957), *Perceiving: A Philosophical Study*, Ithaca, NY: Cornell University Press.
Chudnoff, E. (2011), 'What Intuitions Are Like', *Philosophy and Phenomenological Research*, 82/3: 625–54.

Chudnoff, E. (2012), 'Presentational Phenomenology', in Miguens and Preyer (eds), *Consciousness and Subjectivity*. Ontos Verlag.
Chudnoff, E. (2013), *Intuition*. Oxford: Oxford University Press.
Chudnoff, E. (2016a), 'Epistemic Elitism and Other Minds', *Philosophy and Phenomenological Research*, DOI: 10.1111/phpr.12308
Chudnoff, E. (2016b), 'Moral Perception: High Level Perception or Low Level Intuition?' in Breyer and Gutland (eds), *Phenomenology of Thinking*. Abingdon: Routledge.
Chudnoff, E. (2018), 'The Epistemic Significance of Perceptual Learning', *Inquiry*, 61/5-6: 520-42.
Chudnoff, E. (2020), 'Experience and Epistemic Structure: Can Cognitive Penetration Result in Epistemic Downgrade?', in Chan and Nes (eds), *Consciousness andInference*. Abingdon: Routledge, 255-75.
Chudnoff, E. and Didomenico, D. (2015), 'The Epistemic Unity of Perception', *Pacific Philosophical Quarterly*, 96/4: 535-49.
Church, J. (2013), *Possibilities of Perception*. Oxford: Oxford University Press.
Cohen, S. (1984), 'Justification and truth.' *Philosophical Studies*, 46/3:279-95.
Conee, E. (2013), 'Seeming Evidence', in C. Tucker (ed.), *Seemings and Justification: New Essays on Dogmatism and Phenomenal Conservatism*. Oxford: Oxford University Press, 52-70.
Connolly, K. (2014), 'Perceptual Learning and the Contents of Perception, 1407-1418', *Erkenntnis*, 79/6:1407-18.
Cullison, A. (2013), 'Seemings and Semantics', in C. Tucker (ed.), *Seemings and Justification: New Essays on Dogmatism and Phenomenal Conservatism*. Oxford: Oxford University Press.
Davidson, D. (1986), 'A Coherence Theory of Truth and Knowledge', in E. LePore (ed.), *Truth and Interpretation, Perspectives on the Philosophy of Donald Davidson*. Oxford: Basil Blackwell.
DePaul, M. R. and Ramsey, W. (eds) (1998), *Rethinking Intuition: The Psychology of Intuition and its Role in Philosophical Inquiry*. Lanham, MD: Rowman & Littlefield Publishers.
Dretske, F. (1995), *Naturalizing the Mind*. Cambridge, MA: MIT Press.
Firestone, C., and Scholl, B. J. (2016), 'Cognition does not affect perception: Evaluating the evidence for "top-down" effects', *Behavioral and Brain Sciences*, 39.
Fish, W. (2009), *Perception, Hallucination, and Illusion*. Oxford: Oxford University Press.
Fish, W. (2013), 'High-level Properties and Visual Experience', *Philosophical Studies*, 162: 43-55.
Fodor, J. (1983), *The Modularity of Mind*. Cambridge, MA: MIT Press.
Glüer, K. (2009), 'In Defence of a Doxastic Account of Experience', *Mind and Language*, 24: 297-327.
Gödel, K. (2001), *Collected Works: Vol 3: Unpublished Essays and Lectures*. Ed. S. Feferman, J. W. Dawson Jr, W. Goldfarb, C. Parsons, and R. Solovay. Oxford: Oxford University Press.
Goldman, A. I. (2008), 'Immediate justification and process reliabilism', in Q. Smith (ed.), *Epistemology: New Essays*. Oxford: Oxford University Press, 63-82.
Hinton, J. M. (1967), 'Experiences', *Philosophical Quarterly*, 17: 1-13.
Huemer, M. (2001), *Skepticism and the Veil of Perception*. Lanham, MD: Rowman and Littlefield.
Huemer, M. (2005), *Ethical Intuitionism*. Basingstoke: Palgrave Macmillan.
Huemer, M. (2007), 'Compassionate Phenomenal Conservatism', *Philosophy and Phenomenological Research*, 74: 30-55.
Jackson, F. (1977), *Perception: A Representative Theory*. Cambridge: Cambridge University Press.

Klein, S. (2014), 'Autonoesis and Belief in a Personal Past: An Evolutionary Theory of Episodic Memory Indices', *Review of Philosophy and Psychology*, 5/3: 427–47.

Koksvik, O. (2011), *Intuition*. Dissertation, Australian National University.

Lyons, J. (2005), 'Perceptual Belief and Nonexperiential Looks', *Philosophical Perspectives*, 19: 237–56.

Lyons, J. (2009), *Perception and Basic Beliefs: Zombies, Modules and the Problem of the External World*. Oxford: Oxford University Press.

Lyons, J. (2015), 'Seemings and justification', *Analysis Reviews*, 75/1: 153–64.

McDowell, J. (1994), *Mind and World*. Cambridge, MA: Harvard University Press.

McDowell, J. (2011), Perception as a Capacity for Knowledge. Milwaukee, WI: Marquette University Press.

Macpherson, F. (2012), 'Cognitive penetration of colour experience: rethinking the issue in light of an indirect mechanism', *Philosophy and Phenomenological Research*, 84/1: 24–62.

Markie, P. (2005), 'The mystery of direct perceptual justification', *Philosophical Studies*, 126: 347–73.

Markie, P. (2013), 'Searching for true dogmatism', in Chris Tucker (ed.), *Seemings and Justification: New Essays on Dogmatism and Phenomenal Conservatism*. New York: Oxford University Press, 248.

Martin, M. G. F. (2002), 'The Transparency of Experience', *Mind and Language*, 17: 376–425.

Nagel, J. (2012), 'Intuitions and Experiments: A Defense of the Case Method in Epistemology', *Philosophy and Phenomenological Research*, 85/3:495–527.

O'Callaghan, C. (2011), 'Against Hearing Meanings', *The Philosophical Quarterly*, 61/245: 783–807.

Pautz, A. (2010), 'Why explain visual experience in terms of content?' in B. Nanay (ed.), *Perceiving the World*. Oxford: Oxford University Press 254—309.

Peacocke, C. (1992), *A Study of Concepts*. Cambridge, MA: MIT Press.

Pryor, J. (2000), 'The skeptic and the dogmatist', *Noûs*, 34: 517–49.

Pryor, J. (2005), 'There is immediate justification', in M. Steup and E. Sosa (eds), *Contemporary Debates in Epistemology*. Malden, MA: Blackwell.

Pylyshyn, Z. W. (1999), 'Is Vision Continuous with Cognition? The Case for Cognitive Impenetrability of Visual Perception', *Behavioral and Brain Sciences*, 22: 341–423.

Reiland, I. (2014), 'On Experiencing High-Level Properties', *American Philosophical Quarterly*, 51: 177–87.

Reiland, I. (2015a), 'On Experiencing Meanings', *The Southern Journal of Philosophy*, 53/4: 481-92.

Reiland, I. (2015b), 'Experience, seemings, and evidence', *Pacific Philosophical Quarterly*, 96/4: 510–34.

Russell, B. (1912), *The Problems of Philosophy*. Home University Library.

Schellenberg, S. (2014), 'The Relational and Representational Character of Perceptual Experience', in B. Brogaard (ed.), *Does Perception Have Content?* Oxford: Oxford University Press, 199-219.

Scholl, B. J. and Gao, T. (2013), 'Perceiving animacy and intentionality: Visual processing or higher-level judgment?' In M. D. Rutherford and V. A. Kuhlmeier (eds), *Social Perception: Detection and Interpretation of Animacy, Agency, and Intention*. Cambridge, MA: MIT Press, 197–230.

Sellars, W. (1956), 'Empiricism and the Philosophy of Mind', in H. Feigl and M. Scriven (eds), *Minnesota Studies in the Philosophy of Science*, vol. I. Minneapolis, MN: University of Minnesota Press, 253–329.

Siegel, S. (2005), 'Which Properties Are Represented in Perception?', in T. Szabo Gendler and J. Hawthorne (eds), *Perceptual Experience*. Oxford: Oxford University Press, 481–503.

Siegel, S. (2006), 'Subject and Object in the Contents of Visual Experience', *Philosophical Review*, 115/3: 355–88.

Siegel, S. (2009), 'The Visual Experience of Causation', *The Philosophical Quarterly*, 59/236: 519–40.

Siegel, S. (2010), *The Contents of Visual Experience*. New York: Oxford University Press.

Siegel, S. (2012), 'Cognitive Penetrability and Perceptual Justification', *Noûs*, 46/2: 1–222.

Siegel, S. (2013), 'The Epistemic Impact of the Etiology of Experience', *Philosophical Studies*, 162/3: 697–722.

Siegel, S. (2017), *The Rationality of Perception*. Oxford: Oxford University Press.

Silins, N. (2008), 'Basic Justification and the Moorean Response to the Skeptic', in *Oxford Studies in Epistemology* Volume 2. Oxford: Oxford University Press.

Silins, N. (2011), Seeing Through the 'Veil of Perception'. *Mind*. 120/478: 329–67.

Silins, N. (2013), 'The Significance of High-Level Content', *Philosophical Studies*, 162/1: 13–33.

Smithies, D. (2014), 'The Phenomenal Basis of Epistemic Justification', in J. Kallestrup and M. Sprevak (eds), *New Waves in Philosophy of Mind*. Basingstoke: Palgrave Macmillan, 98–124.

Snowdon, P. (1980–1), 'Perception, Vision, and Causation', *Proceedings of the Aristotelian Society*, 81: 175–92.

Stokes, D. (2014), 'Cognitive Penetration and the Perception of Art', *Dialectica*, 68/1: 1–34.

Tappolet, C. (2016), *Emotions, Value, and Agency*. Oxford: Oxford University Press.

Tooley, M. (2013), 'Michael Huemer and the Principle of Phenomenal Conservatism', in C. Tucker (ed.), *Seemings and Justification: New Essays on Dogmatism and Phenomenal Conservatism*. New York: Oxford University Press.

Tucker, C. (2010), 'Why Open-Minded People Should Endorse Dogmatism', *Philosophical Perspectives*, 24: 529–45.

Tye, M. (1995), *Ten Problems of Consciousness*. Cambridge, MA: MIT Press.

Werner, P. J. (2016), 'Moral Perception and the Contents of Experience', *Journal of Moral Philosophy*, 13/3: 294–317.

Williamson, T. (2000), *Knowledge and its Limits*. Oxford: Oxford University Press.

CHAPTER 28

CONSCIOUSNESS, INTROSPECTION, AND SUBJECTIVE MEASURES

MAJA SPENER

28.1 Introduction

In recent years, the divide between conscious and unconscious perception has been the focus of a thriving research area in the science of consciousness. Topics include the existence of unconscious, 'subliminal' perception, graded conscious perception, and the threshold between conscious and unconscious perceptual processing. Subjective measures of consciousness play a prominent role in this literature and they are frequently referred to as 'introspective measures'. Subjective measures of consciousness have been the subject of intense criticism. Indeed, as some critics insist, they are in effect rehearsing century-old objections to the use of introspection in the empirical study of consciousness (Irvine 2012: 629).

This chapter discusses the main types of so-called 'subjective measures of consciousness' used in these areas of current-day science of consciousness. I explain the key worry about such measures, namely the problem of a putatively ever-present response bias. I then turn to the question of whether subjective measures of consciousness are introspective. I show that there is no clear answer to this question, as proponents of subjective measures do not employ a worked-out notion of subjective access. In turn, as I explain, this makes the problem of response bias less tractable than it might otherwise be.

28.2 A Methodological Challenge in the Science of Consciousness

The science of consciousness faces the following challenge: getting primary—that is, most immediate or direct—data about consciousness seems to require doing so by relying on individuals' first-person access to their own experience;[1] but scientifically rigorous investigation requires embedding such data-acquisition in the empirical setting of experimental psychology (see, e.g., Overgaard 2006: 629). Currently, there are no so-called *objective measures of consciousness*—no thoroughly third-person observational measures—which are widely agreed to capture conscious aspects of the mind, rather than some behavioural or neural capacity that may be correlated with phenomenal consciousness. More particularly, there are no such measures which provide access to properties of consciousness *qua* conscious properties, or, *qua* conscious contents. We do not have, as some put it, a 'consciousness meter' (Chalmers 1998: 2) which scientists can use to procure directly the needed data about consciousness. Plenty of empirical work employs objective measures of consciousness, for example on different levels of consciousness and on neural correlates of consciousness. Yet, such work invariably depends on assuming bridging hypotheses about the putative objective markers of consciousness (e.g. neural activity held to be associated with consciousness) that provide the link between them and conscious contents (Chalmers 2004; Irvine 2013; Phillips 2015a). Objective measures of consciousness are therefore not only indirect, they are also based on substantial assumptions concerning consciousness itself: certain behavioural or neural properties are assumed to be good markers of conscious content.

As generally acknowledged, people seemingly have immediate access to their own conscious contents from the first-person vantage point, that is, from the subject's perspective. Some scientists therefore believe that the best way to measure conscious content must utilize subjects' apparently direct epistemic access to their experiences (Timmermans and Cleeremans 2016: 3). *Subjective measures of consciousness* thus involve the experimenter eliciting data about consciousness by getting subjects to provide it via reports under experimental conditions. These reports—often referred to as 'subjective reports'—are verbal or non-verbal responses given by subjects who are under explicit instructions to give certain kinds of information in relation to a perceptual task. Subjective reports are taken to be directly about, or significantly reflective of, the subject's experiential situation from their own, first-person perspective.

In relying on subjective reports to provide access to consciousness, subjective measures do not seem open to independent validation in the form of inter-measurement calibration (cf. Spener 2015). The lack of inter-measurement checks is held to be problematic

---

[1] The term 'experience' and its cognates are used here to refer to mental episodes which are conscious.

because there are serious further worries about the reliability of subjective measures, namely that they are reflective of the subject's own views about consciousness, rather than consciousness itself. As a consequence, such measures have faced sharp criticism for apparent failure to comply with sufficiently rigorous scientific standards.

The appearance that subjective measures of consciousness are indispensable, and yet scientifically inadequate, minimally presents a difficult challenge for the science of consciousness. There is debate over whether this challenge constitutes a fundamental and intractable problem for the field. Upbeat voices argue that the problems are significant but not fundamentally unsolvable. Overgaard (2016), for example, considers the challenge a sign of the infancy of the science of consciousness insofar as the latter lacks standardization of its methods. But he is optimistic about finding such standards, in the same way other scientific fields have eventually succeeded in doing so. By contrast, Irvine (2012) holds that subjective measures in the science of consciousness are problematic in a more substantial manner and that these problems are distinctive to the field. She recommends getting rid of subjective measures altogether (Irvine 2012: 630–1, 642). Other sceptical views are more mixed in their message. Schwitzgebel (2011), for example, offers those working in the science of consciousness a choice: either to operationalizse consciousness in terms of some behavioural capacity, or to 'muddle on' with subjective measures (see Spener 2013; Schwitzgebel 2013 for further discussion).

28.3 Subjective and Objective Thresholds of Perception

Developments in the science of consciousness—especially in the debate about subliminal perception—over the last sixty years are a testament to the persisting challenge. Throughout, scientists show recognition of serious problems with subjective measures of consciousness, but the overall trends also indicate a lack of genuinely viable alternatives to them. The problematic situation is manifested by the lack of agreement about how to define and where to locate conscious perception in the first place. Eriksen's (1956, 1960) influential critique of subjective measures of consciousness is a milestone in the debate. Eriksen argued that subjective reports—the key ingredient in subjective measures—are reflective of subjects' response bias and that this undermines their suitability to measure the genuine onset of conscious perception.

Eriksen drew on (then relatively new) work involving the application of signal detection theory (SDT) to cases of perception-based human decision-making (Green and Swets 1966). SDT is a statistical framework which allows one to estimate separately both the sensitivity of a response-making system to detect a stimulus in the presence of noise (its *objective sensitivity* to the stimulus), and the criterion the system uses for deciding when to respond that a signal is present rather than noise (its *decision criterion*).

SDT assumes that in the case of signals under uncertainty, any response by the system is always a product of perceptual sensitivity and a decision criterion.[2]

Perceptual detection invariably involves, and is thus modulated by, a noisy context (the more noise compared to the stimulus signal strength, the less sensitive a detection system is). As soon as noise is present, a system's detection response to a signal involves a decision in the face of some uncertainty about whether the stimulus is present. Such decision-making requires the system to set criteria, where these are, roughly, benchmarks for how strong a signal must be to merit a certain detection response.

These criteria can introduce considerable bias into decision-making, in that they may be asymmetric (e.g., manifest a preference for one response option over others) or not stable (e.g., allow for shifting thresholds for specific response options). The notion of *response bias* 'measures the participant's tilt towards one response or another' (Macmillan and Creelman 1991: 24).[3] For instance, two subjects may differ in their decision criteria under the same stimulus conditions by being liberal and conservative, respectively, in setting their threshold for a positive response to a signal. The first subject might use a criterion that aims to maximize correct positive responses and not be worried about getting a high number of incorrect positive ones in the process. The second subject might be guided in part by minimizing incorrect positive responses. Moreover, a single subject can be easily manipulated to change their own criterion (Green and Swets 1966). Raising the stakes for the subject to get the decision right in various ways—by imposing costs for positive responses when the signal is not present (punishing false alarms)—means that the subject will become more conservative in their decision-making, or less trigger-happy, so to speak. By lowering the stakes and increasing the benefits of right answers (rewarding hits), the subject will become more liberal in responding, trying to maximize rewards.

To get an estimate of perceptual sensitivity per se, one needs to set aside response bias in the response data first. SDT offers a mathematical framework for how to do this, called a 'receiver operating characteristic (ROC) curve analysis', which involves taking account of the relationship between the rate of accurate positive responses (hit rate) and the rate of false positive responses (false alarm rate).[4]

The key lesson from SDT applied to human perception-based decision-making is that one cannot automatically read people's objective perceptual sensitivity to a stimulus off the rate of accurate responses. One first needs to filter out any bias in the responses (via ROC curve analysis). SDT is a model of perceptual sensitivity and decision-making, and it does not itself speak to how consciousness figures in the perceptual process. Eriksen's criticism is that when subjective measures are used to detect the presence or absence of conscious perception, they provide data directly derived from subjects' reports and such data is shown by SDT to be contaminated by response bias. He argued, moreover, that

---

[2] For classic and introductory texts on STD applied to human decision-making, see Green and Swets (1966) and Macmillan and Creelman (1991).

[3] For a discussion of structural biases inherent in different kinds of free choice tasks, e.g., yes/no or same/difference tasks, see Phillips (2015b).

[4] The details do not matter here. See Macmillan and Creelman (1991: 45–70).

at-chance detection performance indicates that the stimulus at that level of intensity is not perceived at all, and that it is above-chance detection performance (measured objectively) that indicates conscious perception of the stimulus.

The first claim—that total lack of ability to detect a stimulus constitutes good evidence that it is not perceptually processed—is widely accepted. The second claim about the onset of consciousness is contentious. Cheesman and Merikle (1984, 1986) reject it, arguing that in addition to the threshold marked by at-chance detection performance (the *objective threshold*), there is an important report-based threshold (the *subjective threshold*), marked by the point of stimulus intensity at which subjects claim not to see the stimulus or to be guessing in relevant tasks. According to them, this 'threshold of claimed awareness' marks the onset of conscious perception because it 'better captures the phenomenological distinction between conscious and unconscious perceptual experiences' (Merikle and Cheesman 1986: 344). On their view, since it can be shown that the subjective threshold is higher along the stimulus intensity dimension than the objective threshold, unconscious perception is perceptual processing *in between* the two thresholds, that is, above the threshold for perceptual processing and below the threshold for conscious perceptual awareness.

It is easy to see that the objective threshold is implicit in the SDT model, mapping onto the estimate for objective perceptual sensitivity. As the model makes clear, though, whatever else subjective thresholds are indicative of, they are also reflective of subjects' response bias. Cheesman and Merikle (1984) note that when one uses subjects' reports about whether they are able to detect a stimulus to measure the boundary between conscious and unconscious perception, one in effect 'allows subjects to set their own thresholds'. Under the same stimulus conditions, two individuals may differ in their subjective thresholds merely because one is cautious and employs conservative decision criterion, resulting in a higher threshold of claimed awareness, and the other is rash and employs a liberal decision criterion, resulting in a lower threshold. To accommodate this worry, Cheesman and Merikle proposed that results concerning the distinction between conscious and unconscious perception that are based on subjective measures, must be confirmed by an additional criterion. Specifically, they propose that there must be evidence that the postulated different perceptual processes have a qualitatively different behavioural effect (Cheesman and Merikle 1986: 363).

28.4 Response Bias and Subjective Report

Response bias is often held to be a methodological affliction of specifically subjective measures of consciousness. This is because they are report-based measures and reports are problematic (see also, e.g., Irvine 2012: 641; Tunney and Shanks 2003: 1061):

[C]ontrary to many researchers' implicit assumptions, (SDT shows) there is no such thing as an unmediated 'subjective report'—ever.   (Snodgrass and Lepisto 2007: 526)

The signal detection theory perspective dictates that there is no such thing as a raw report uncontaminated by decision processes.   (Block 2008: 312)

What exactly is the concern about reports and subjective measures relying on them, which is brought to light by SDT? To assess this, bear in mind two points. First, response bias concerns responses in the context of perceptual detection tasks. When criticizing Marcel's (1980, 1983) results about subliminal perception from masking experiments, for instance, Holender (1986) and Cheesman and Merikle (1984, 1986) pointed out that yes/no tasks have been shown to induce systematic response bias by the subject. Another frequently used task, involving same/difference judgements, is skewed towards the 'same' option in conditions where discrimination performance gets nearer to chance.

Secondly, response bias is not pervasive. A biased response is due to the subject's asymmetric and often unstable decision criteria when choosing an appropriate response to a task at hand. There are, however, genuinely bias-free discrimination tasks, involving n-alternative, typically two-alternative, forced choice tasks (2afc tasks) (see also Phillips 2015b, for discussion). These tasks induce a symmetric criterion in subjects, thus guaranteeing that their performance is not skewed towards one of the options. Responses given in such forced choice tasks, provided the experiment is carefully set up to prevent changes in criteria due to different motivational structures, are therefore non-biased. Nonetheless, these responses are still *mediated* by decision processes of the subject: any response, according to SDT is the product of (perceptual) sensitivity and a decision criterion. But being mediated does not mean being biased.

Thus, if there is bad news for subjective measures of consciousness in particular, it does not simply fall out of the assumption at the heart of SDT, namely that all subjective reports are the products of perceptual sensitivity and decision processes. This assumption does not yet make for a problem of response bias for subjective measures.

In the case of *measures of perceptual sensitivity*, recall, the concern raised by response bias is that one cannot simply read perceptual sensitivity off the average rate of subjects' accurate positive responses to the stimulus. The latter is not automatically an appropriate measurement of the former because it demonstrably includes the effect of subjects' decision criteria. To get an accurate estimate of perceptual sensitivity, this concern can be addressed by either using non-biased tasks (i.e. especially 2afc tasks), or, by taking biased responses and calculating perceptual sensitivity from the relationship between accurate positive responses and false positive responses, using a ROC curve analysis.

When it comes to *measures of consciousness*, if perceptual sensitivity is taken to be a measurement of consciousness (as, e.g., Eriksen proposes), then the concern about response bias is the same as in the above case of measures of perceptual sensitivity, and so is the solution. But, if subjective reports (or, better, thresholds indicated by such reports) are taken to be the appropriate measurement of consciousness, then the problem that the presence of response bias poses is different. It is not that we have any direct evidence of response bias as we do in the perceptual sensitivity case. And, as I pointed out earlier, just because reports are mediated by decision criteria does not on its own provide a reason to think that they are biased. Rather, the evidence is indirect: it is simply implausible that consciousness fluctuates with response thresholds when the latter can be manipulated so easily and by factors that seem unlikely to be causally relevant to perceptual consciousness. So, it seems plausible that reports are contaminated by response bias. This is the problem of response bias for subjective measures of consciousness.

Is this problem intractable? We cannot use the same statistical approach to filter out bias that we use in the case of measuring perceptual sensitivity. The approach must be different: it must focus on making it less plausible that a given set of reports is contaminated by response bias, thereby reducing the implausibility that fluctuations in subjective threshold in a given case mark fluctuations in consciousness. To do so we need to know details about subjective measures: to even begin to distinguish which kinds of fluctuations might be due to consciousness itself and which kind might be due to response biases of various sorts, we need to understand the kinds of subjective access at work in subjective measures. Only once we have an understanding of the nature of subjective access, can we assess the prospects for eliminating or significantly reducing bias in the data provided by subjective reports.

As I argue in the remainder of the chapter, contemporary debate about subjective measures of consciousness does not provide such an understanding. The problem of response bias for subjective measures is therefore currently less tractable than it might be, since we are not in a position to adequately assess whether a given set of response-based data is likely infected by bias. I concentrate on three aspects of the debate in need of clarification. I first soften the ground in Section 28.5, by showing that the distinction between subjective and objective measures is standardly not clearly drawn. In Section 28.6, I discuss subjective measures directly, showing that the notion of subjective access at the heart of them is typically not worked out. I develop this point in Section 28.7, by investigating the role (if any) of introspection in extant subjective measures.

28.5 The Distinction between Objective and Subjective Measures of Consciousness

Although the distinction between objective and subjective measures of consciousness structures the overall area, it is in fact not easy to see what it comes to, based on how it is drawn by participants in the debate. The term 'measures' might refer to methods or to measurements. The latter, in turn, might also be understood in different ways: specific readings obtained on an occasion of measuring versus the general measurement unit.

The objectivity or subjectivity of a given measure thus might depend on aspects of the method of measuring, or on aspects of the measurement. Extant characterizations of the distinction are typically brief and not explicit on this point, the presumption being that the basic idea of the distinction is generally understood. To pick a representative example, Seth et al. (2008) introduce the two types of measures as follows:

> 'Objective measures' assume the ability to choose accurately under forced choice conditions as indicating a conscious mental state. ..... 'Subjective measures' require subjects to report their mental states.   (Seth et al. 2008: 317)

On the objective side, characterizations often emphasize forced choice paradigms in classifying objective measures of consciousness. In the quote above, the focus seems to be on *measurements*, namely that objective measurements of consciousness are measurements of perceptual sensitivity, as defined by SDT. They are response-bias-free measurements of task performance in relation to stimulus intensity. In turn, for a *method* to count as objective, it requires a procedure to filter out any response bias skewing the data ('to eliminate bias' (Lau 2008)). Objective methods thus involve either the use of detection tasks that yield bias-free, accurate responses (as, e.g., 2afc tasks) to determine perceptual sensitivity, or the use of more complex statistical methods, by submitting responses from biased perceptual detection tasks to a ROC curve analysis.

Another frequent suggestion, however, is that the objectivity of measures of consciousness consists mainly in the public observability of the data produced (Timmermans and Cleeremans 2016: 22). Again, the focus seems to be on measurements, namely that an objective measurement is publicly observable. An objective method is then a way of acquiring such publicly observable data. Public observability is typically associated with other general conditions, such as the need for replicability of results, systematic variation, etc. In that way, objective measures are often held to be scientifically valid measures more generally (see discussion in Overgaard 2016: 9).

Note that if the objectivity of a method consists in bias-free measuring, that is, producing a measurement that is not influenced by any response bias, then it seems that in principle—should one be able to eliminate or filter out response-bias in this case—so-called subjective methods might count as objective, too. If the objectivity of a method consists in producing publicly observable data, that is, measurements that are publicly available (replicable, systematically variable, etc.) then this does perhaps rule out subjective methods. On both points, much depends on what the latter exactly are, of course. We will turn to this question in a moment. However, at this point it is already clear that different formulations of the objectivity of measures (freedom from response bias, public observability) draw the line between subjective and objective measures differently.

Let us now turn to the other side of the distinction, subjective measures. The single most mentioned feature in characterizations of subjective measures is that they involve 'subjective reports'. A subjective *method* of consciousness gathers data about consciousness by getting subjects to report something relevant to consciousness. The *measurement* of a subjective measure is report. It is unclear, though, what makes for *subjective* reports. Is it that they (i) are acquired via a specific method, or (ii) have a specific type of content?

Sometimes subjective measures are characterized merely by appeal to the kind of report provided by subjects, that is, in terms of subjective measurement:

> The undeniable merit of subjective measures is their face validity: they are reports about the conscious experience itself, rather than reports about something else, that is the stimulus. (Lau 2008: 253–4)

This will not do, however, at least not without qualification. Distinguish between 'content-subjective-report' and 'content-objective report'. When asked to report on what they perceive, a subject might say:

(1) 'I see that there is a red triangle.'
(2) 'There is a red triangle.'

Sentence (1) has a subjective content in the sense that it is about a mental feature, a seeing, that is, a visual experience as of a red triangle. Sentence (2) has an objective content in the sense that it is about a worldly scene before one. Shea (2012: 310) notes, in ordinary talk (1) and (2) might be used interchangeably. Each might be held expressive of either, a claim about the world, or a claim about one's experience of the world. Shea further points out, experimental psychologists typically take content-objective-reports to be evidence for relevant experiential states of the subject. Presumably, this is because they hold that such reports are expressive of the latter (see also Chirimuuta 2014). In addition, both kinds of report can be made verbally and non-verbally (e.g. button-pressing).

Lau's characterization, then, does not properly capture the distinction between types of measures. Another frequent characterization implies that the subjectivity of subjective measures is a matter of method. The key feature here is that the experimenter instructs subjects in relevant ways to report their mental states.

> In the case of a subjective measure, participants are asked specifically to respond according to their own internal state of awareness. (Tunney and Shanks 2003: 1061)

Thus, the measurements—the reports—are subjective because of how they have been elicited by the experimenter from the subject. This still leaves room for different conceptions. The experimenter might ask subjects to:

  i. report something about their experiences;
  ii. report something about experience by accessing their experience in a specific manner;
  iii. report something, with the experimenter's unstated expectation that in complying with this request subjects access their experiences in a specific manner.

On any of these three conceptions, there is room for taking *prima facie* objective-content-reports to be a species of subjective report. Having been gathered via a subjective method would mean that one can interpret such reports to be expressive of subjective-content-reports as necessary. But the three conceptions potentially offer significantly different answers to what makes reports subjective and hence, to what is characteristic of subjective measures. The first one (i) does not provide much substance to the idea of a subjective measure and it is, at least without further details, consistent with the characterizations of objective measures discussed earlier. In (ii) and (iii), however, the idea is that by eliciting the report in the manner that they do, the experimenter gets the subject to access their experience in a specific way. This access is key to a substantial conception of subjective measures. Let us now turn to the main contemporary types of subjective measures and look at the notion of subjective access they employ.

28.6 Subjective Measures

In the last twenty years, subjective measures of consciousness have seen a revival in the science of consciousness (see, e.g., Jack and Roepstorff 2003, 2004). They rely on gathering data about the presence or absence of consciousness via subjective reports. The latter are typically made in relation to a primary task, involving objectively measurable performances (e.g., perceptual discrimination or identification, or, in the case of artificial grammar learning, judgements of grammaticality). The relationship between accuracy of primary task performance and various aspects of subjective reports forms the basis for conclusions drawn about consciousness (Tunney and Shanks 2003). The main subjective measures of consciousness are Confidence Ratings (CR) and the Perceptual Awareness Scale (PAS), distinguished in terms of the type of subjective report they use.[5] Further distinctions among approaches can be made in terms of the kind of statistical analysis used to evaluate the data obtained via subjective reports. Here, I will focus on the first kind of difference (for discussion of different kinds of data analysis, see, e.g., Fleming and Lau 2014; Norman and Price 2016).

In recent years, proponents of different subjective measures have compared and contrasted the adequacy of these rival methods, but their studies have not yet produced consensus about which subjective measure produces the overall best results (see, e.g., Dienes and Seth 2010; Sandberg et al. 2010, 2013; Overgaard and Sandberg 2012; Wierzchón et al. 2012; Zehetleitner and Rausch 2013).

---

[5] There are other measures, such as Post-Decision Wagering (PDW) and No-Loss Gambling (NG) which are not easily classed as subjective or objective (e.g. Persaud et al. 2007). These are behavioural measures involving betting on something related to stimulus perception. I will concentrate on CR and PAS, since PDW and NG, on the view that they are subjective measures, are confidence-related measures and similar to CR in most respects that are of interest here.

28.6.1 Confidence Ratings

One experimental line of inquiry uses so-called 'confidence ratings' as an index for consciousness. Confidence ratings are subjects' reports about their own confidence concerning some state of affairs obtaining. In consciousness research, they concern subjects' perceptions of a given stimulus, or the accuracy of subjects' responses in a given primary task. The primary tasks—called 'type 1 tasks'—are perceptual discrimination or identification tasks.[6] These form the object of so-called 'type 2 tasks', that is, assessment tasks where the subject has to judge and report on their confidence about how successful they were in a given type 1 task.

Researchers analyze the relationship between performance in type 1 and type 2 tasks and draw conclusions about whether performance on type 1 tasks was influenced by consciously held information available in task 1. In particular, they tend to employ one of two criteria in their data analysis: the non-zero correlation criterion and the guessing criterion (Dienes et al. 1995). The former looks at the relationship between confidence ratings and accurate (type 1) performance: if there is no significant positive relationship between confidence rating and performance, the performance is held to be influenced by unconscious perception. The latter looks at the relationship between low-confidence ratings, where subjects claim to be merely guessing, and accurate (type 1) performance: if accurate type 1 performance is above-chance in the case of low confidence ratings, the performance is held to be influenced by unconscious perception.[7]

Confidence ratings have long been held to be good indicators of conscious episodes. According to Snodgrass et al. (2009: 563), 'confidence ratings are, plausibly, about as basic an indication of subjective experience as there is'. Traditionally, confidence ratings are used as indicators of perceptual experience—that is, of phenomenal consciousness involved in (mainly visual) perception. In their classic paper, Peirce and Jastrow (1885), assume that there is a connection between subjects reporting confidence in their own perceptual discriminations and subjects being consciously aware of the stimulus, supported by their observation that overall high confidence tracks accuracy (for relevant discussion, see Fleming and Lau 2014). The seminal work by Merikle and Cheesman (1986, mentioned in Section 28.3) also uses confidence ratings as their main gauge of the subjective threshold of perceptual awareness.

So, what are confidence ratings? Despite the widespread conviction about their good evidential status with respect to experience, it is unclear exactly what proponents of CR

---

[6] Confidence ratings have more recently been used in research on artificial grammar learning (AGL). The stated aim is to probe the influence of conscious and unconscious knowledge in implicit learning—'the phenomenology of the application of knowledge resulting from implicit learning' (Dienes et al. 2010: 685). It is not straightforward how one should think of the notion of phenomenal consciousness at issue in this research paradigm, in relation to the one associated with sensory perception. I am concentrating on perceptual consciousness here.

[7] For critical discussion see Fleming and Lau (2014), who develop an SDT-based approach to separately estimate so-called metacognitive sensitivity and metacognitive efficiency. As they note (pp. 7–8), the relationship to conscious awareness is unclear.

have in mind by confidence ratings and how they understand the basic relation between such ratings and any target experience. Here is a representative quote introducing confidence ratings:

> A *confidence rating* is a self-report rating of one's confidence in a judgment or decision, usually given retrospectively after the judgement has been made. It involves assessing the validity of an assertion or a prediction .... Confidence judgements are metacognitive, in that they involve 'cognition about one's own cognition' (Metcalfe 2000). They can be seen as belonging to the subcategory of *metacognitive experiences* which reflect 'what the person is aware of and what she or he feels when coming across a task and processing the information related to it' (Efklides 2008, p. 279). (Norman and Price 2016: 159)

Note the following basic features of confidence ratings. First, confidence reports are (verbal or non-verbal) reports that express a subject's confidence judgement. When I say 'I am highly confident that I saw a right-oriented grid', I am reporting my judgement that I am highly confident that I saw a right-oriented grid. The term 'confidence rating' is best reserved for the confidence report, though in the literature it is often used ambiguously for both report and judgement.[8]

Secondly, the confidence judgements are judgements about the subject's own level of confidence concerning a certain state of affairs. In CR, these states of affairs are either the subject's perception of a stimulus, or the accuracy of their performance in a perception-based task. Confidence judgements are *not* the subject's states of confidence concerning these states of affairs themselves. They are the subject's take on their own level of confidence, they represent what the subject thinks their own level of confidence in this case is. Judging that one is highly confident in having made the right choice is not the same as being highly confident that one has made the right choice. Compare: judging that one is in pain, even sincerely, is not the same as being in pain. Just as in the case of pain, it may be hard to imagine that confidence judgements could be mistaken and, if so, such mistakes might only be possible in borderline cases. But none of that can be taken for granted without being spelled out further.

Thirdly, confidence judgements are not directly about the presence or absence of conscious perception. Indeed, according to some proponents, this is one of the best features of CR: confidence ratings are unlike traditional introspective methods in that they do not aim to report experience directly, thereby avoiding the problems that are inherent in such introspective directness (e.g. Tunney and Shanks 2003: 1061). Instead, proponents of CR use terms like 'reflects' or 'indicates' to talk about the relation between confidence ratings

---

[8] The distinction between confidence ratings (reports) and confidence judgements expressed by the reports does not play a significant role in the issues I am raising in this chapter. But the basic distinction between the cognitive upshot of a given kind of subjective access and the report expressing this upshot does matter to various questions about subjective measures not discussed here, e.g., concerns about the suitability of numerical or other kinds of scales to articulate subjective judgements, or about flawed articulation more generally.

(or judgements) and the target phenomenal experience involved in a given primary task. The idea is to 'ask participants to report their phenomenal states by means of confidence ratings' (Tunney and Shanks 2003: 1061), where this is not an instruction to subjects but rather a description of what confidence ratings can be held to be indirectly reporting.

There is a surprising lack of detail on how confidence judgements are revealing of any perceptual consciousness involved in type 1 performances. What is this reflection relation between confidence judgements and relevant phenomenal experiences, such that the former can serve as good evidence for the presence or absence of the latter? One option would be that reflection is a two-step process. The confidence judgement is about a state of confidence and formed on the basis of that state of confidence. In turn, the latter itself is formed in a way that is responsive in part to the presence or absence of relevant phenomenal experience. Thus, the relation that underwrites reflection has two nodes, confidence judgement to state of confidence, state of confidence to relevant phenomenal experience. Another option would be that reflection is a one-step process, in virtue of a relation between confidence judgement and phenomenal experience. The subject's take on their own states of confidence is formed in part directly on the basis of the presence or absence of relevant phenomenal experience. The second option seems more in line with how proponents of CR talk about confidence ratings, but this may be due to the fact that they often conflate confidence judgements with states of confidence.[9]

An added difficulty in reconstructing the overall picture is the frequent reference to feelings of confidence, or feelings of knowing. Confidence ratings are said to either reveal, or be based, on such feelings (e.g. Norman and Price 2016: 165). There does not seem to be any developed story about how these experiences interact with the target experiential episodes involved in type 1 performances of perceptual tasks. *Prima facie*, feelings of confidence or knowledge are phenomenal experiences in their own right and it is not obvious how they relate to perceptual experiences. They also seem distinct from states of confidence, at least according to standard conceptions of those as belief-like propositional attitudes that come in degrees, or beliefs about degreed propositional contents. It is hard to fit feelings of confidence, or knowledge into the narrative above in a way that facilitates the evidential relation confidence judgements supposedly bear to the absence or presence of target phenomenal experiences. Comments such as 'the subjective feeling of knowing that one has perceived a stimulus often accompanies our visual experience and should be considered an important aspect of visual consciousness' (Samaha et al. 2016) are not all that helpful in fleshing out the picture.

The heart of the CR programme seems to rest on a brute intuition about an epistemic connection between confidence ratings and the conscious character of target perceptions: when detection of a stimulus involves conscious perception of the

---

[9] If taken at face value, Tunney and Shanks (2003: 1063) seem to hold that the reflection relation is a two-step affair, the middle step involving a belief that one is correct in one's discrimination. 'When participants are aware of the knowledge used to make a discrimination, they presumably believe themselves to be correct and should respond with high confidence'.

stimulus, high confidence judgements concerning detection are made in response to these conscious episodes.

> These criteria of awareness assume that if participants are aware of the knowledge they use to classify items, they should be more confident in correct than in incorrect decisions. It follows that the information used to make confidence ratings should be the same as that used to classify items. (Tunney 2005: 368)

It is assumed that where confidence judgements track accuracy in type 1 tasks, a subject's take on her own confidence concerning accurate perceptual detection or discrimination of a stimulus flows from the subject's conscious perception of that stimulus, such that we can take the former as an indication of the latter. Not much more is said about this crucial basing relation providing the nexus between confidence judgements and conscious perception.

However, without further articulation of the connection between confidence judgements and target conscious episodes which underlies the use of confidence ratings as measurements for the presence or absence of consciousness, it is hard to see how to make progress with the problem of response bias for subjective measures of consciousness. Recall, response bias is a 'measure of the participant's tilt' towards one of the response options. One of the key insights of SDT is that decisions to respond are made in light of goals (e.g., to maximize correct positive responses, or to avoid punishment for incorrect positive responses, etc.) and that these can have a significant part in shaping the responses. In the case of subjective measures, the approach I suggested we need to take is to identify and understand relevant kinds of 'tilt' subjects might be susceptible to when providing subjective reports. To do so—especially with an eye to perhaps substantially reducing, compensating, or filtering out response bias—we would need to have a clearer picture of what subjects are engaged in, what they are doing, when they subjectively access the relevant data.

Relatedly, it is difficult to see what exactly the subjectivity of CR (as a subjective measure) consists in, since we do not have a filled-out picture of the method of acquisition of the measurement data, that is, of the subjective access used by subjects in providing the ratings. Confidence ratings are subjective reports at least in sense (i) above, in that they are about the subject's mental states—although these are not the target conscious episodes. Confidence ratings are also subjective in sense (iii) above, in that there is the experimenters' background expectation that in producing them subjects access their experiences in a specific manner. But what we need and do not have, is an account of the nature of the subjective access at work in generating the data about conscious experience.

28.6.2 Awareness Ratings

Awareness ratings are the main source of data about conscious perception in a subjective measure called 'perceptual awareness scale' (PAS) (Ramsøy and Overgaard

2004). PAS shares with CR the basic thought that conclusions about consciousness can be drawn based on specific types of relationship between subjective ratings (in this case awareness ratings) and performance in a type 1 task (see Sandberg and Overgaard 2016: 190–2 for a brief overview of statistical analyses of PAS data). Thus, experiments using PAS standardly involve a type 1 perceptual detection task, and a type 2 rating task.

Awareness ratings are reports that are meant to be directly about experience: they result from subjects being asked to 'report on their experiences directly and allowing them to do this on a scale created either by themselves or other participants presented with similar stimuli' (Sandberg et al. 2013: 806). In contrast to CR, the type 2 tasks involved in PAS are not about the performances in type 1 tasks, but instead are directed at any perceptual experiences involved in type 1 tasks.[10]

Again, let us distinguish between report and the judgement expressed by a report, reserving the term 'awareness rating' to refer to awareness reports. Awareness judgements are about the conscious character of the target perceptual episode. The stated aim by proponents of PAS, is for the content of awareness ratings to overlap with the phenomenally conscious content of the perceptual episodes involved in type 1 tasks.[11] PAS seeks to provide an experimental setting 'where reports stand in a "1:1 relationship" with the other relevant inner states' (Sandberg and Overgaard 2016: 182). This means not only that for any awareness judgement, there is a corresponding awareness episode (or lack thereof, in case the awareness judgement is a negative one). The ambition is also that there is a certain descriptive accuracy, so that the content of the awareness judgement (and thus the awareness rating expressing it) adequately captures the phenomenal character of the corresponding episode in relevant respects.

In particular, awareness ratings aim at the key feature of clarity of a given perceptual experience. According to them, conscious perceptual content comes in 'different degrees of clarity' and they base their claim both on empirical work demonstrating preserved residual awareness in blindsight patients (Zeki and ffytche 1998) as well as on simple contemplation of ordinary cases of perceptual experiences. The feature of clarity is thus meant to capture the level or strength of a subject's perceptual awareness of a given stimulus. Low clarity represents partial, weak, or degreed awareness of a stimulus.[12] Ramsøy

---

[10] PAS tends to be used in investigations of visual and auditory perception, but not in investigations of conscious grammar knowledge.

[11] I use 'overlap' to remain neutral on the extent to which phenomenal character can be captured in judgements and, furthermore, be articulated in reports. Thus, ideally, awareness judgements have the same content as the target perceptual episode. Less ideally, some details are lost or added in the process of judging and articulating.

[12] I am emphasizing this because from the point of view of certain debates in philosophy of perception, clarity might be thought to refer to the content of phenomenal character in a different way. An experience might present objects or properties clearly or not very clearly while the overall conscious episode is fully conscious and not faint. For instance, the phenomenal character of a perceptual episode as of a cluttered beach might have a precise content in that one is visually aware of objects on the beach in sharp detail, or it might have a more fuzzy content in that one cannot easily differentiate different object because things look blurry. But either of those visual experiences could still be clear in Ramsøy

and Overgaard take the graded nature of experience to motivate a non-dichotomous, multiple step scale of awareness ratings in experiments designed to test for subliminal perception.

One of the key ideas underpinning PAS is that the multiple-step response scale is developed in co-operation with participants in the experiments, specifically to ensure the right number of steps and an adequate description of the clarity of awareness captured by a given step. Application of PAS therefore begins with a certain amount of training administered to participating subjects, followed by an active development phase. Ramsøy and Overgaard's (2004) instructions for constructing the PAS steps, for instance, ask subjects to report the clarity of their experience by using a scale that is bounded on each side by 'no experience at all' and 'a clear image', but which can otherwise have as many steps as subjects find useful. In addition, every experiment begins with explaining and extensively discussing the meaning of the different scale steps with participants, occasionally even interrupting trials to check with subjects why they used a given scale step in their response. If the experiments and general setup are similar enough, a PAS developed in one investigation may be used in another, or it may be used as a starting point to be tweaked in further experiments.

In part, this aspect of PAS is designed to alleviate concerns about the scientific validity of awareness ratings, particularly concerns about response bias and about the lack of inter-measurement checks (Sandberg and Overgaard 2016). Individual differences and disagreements due to individual bias are claimed to be minimized because experimenters and participants jointly develop the scale, thereby establishing common ground. Furthermore, developing the response scale in this way is meant to facilitate overlap between awareness rating and the phenomenal content of the target perceptual episode—getting as close as possible to a 1:1 relationship between them.

In contrast to CR, PAS also seems to provide a more detailed conception of how awareness judgements epistemically relate to the target conscious perceptions: awareness judgements are directly about perceptual experience and subjects arrive at the former by introspecting the latter. This seems to yield a more precise answer to what the subjectivity of the PAS consists in. Awareness ratings are subjective reports in the sense of (ii) above because they express judgements that are about experience arrived at via introspective access to experience. But as I argue in the next section, this impression is misleading. While proponents of PAS use the term 'introspection' in picking out the type of subjective access at work in their method, they offer little elucidation of what introspection is. Again, without further details about the nature of the subjective access employed in generating the report data—in this case introspective access—we cannot get a precise understanding of the kinds of bias this access is susceptible to. This means that we cannot make progress on the problem of response bias for subjective measures of consciousness. It is, for instance, entirely unclear how the consensus building aspect of PAS is meant to interact with the individual's subjective access exploited in the experiments.

and Overgaard's: they could be fully consciously present. It is just that what is presented might be blurred or not defined.

28.7 Subjective Access and Introspection

Proponents of CR and PAS presuppose considerable familiarity and competence with the kind of first-person access required by their methods. Yet they do not put forward a substantial view of the nature of such access. This combination shows in the sparse instructions given to subjects in experiments, as well as in the lack of elucidation given of access-denoting terms in their discussions within the research community.

On the instruction side, proponents of subjective measures expect experimental subjects to be mostly competent in complying with instructions to select and use the required kind of subjective access.

> (P)articipants usually do what they are asked, so when one asks them about experiences, one should expect that they report their experiences, and when one asks them about their confidence, one should expect that they report their confidence (and not their experience). (Sandberg and Overgaard 2016: 187)

But asking them to do so typically does not involve a lot of detailed direction or guidelines. In standard CR experiments, subjects are simply asked to assess how confident they are in their own type 1 task responses, and they are told to use various kinds of response scales to express their confidence (see, e.g., Tunney 2005; Zehetleitner and Rausch 2013; Norman and Price 2016; Samaha et al. 2016). The practice clearly presupposes that different participants will be making their assessments in the same manner and that the cognitive process involved in each case draws on the presence of the target conscious perception.

In PAS experiments, one might expect that the kind of training involved in preparing subjects for, and guiding them through, developing an awareness scale involves specific explanations and instructions of what to do in order to introspect their experience. However, at least as far as typical published descriptions of PAS procedure are concerned, instructions of this kind, that is, about what to do to introspect, are scant. The procedure takes for granted that subjects know what the basic kind of subjective access is that they need to employ when they are 'asked to report (or guess) all three stimulus properties (shape, color, and position) and then report the clarity of each property using a scale that they developed themselves' (Sandberg and Overgaard 2016: 182). This is not to say that there are no instructions offered—quite the contrary, PAS involves an extended preparatory phase consisting of discussion with participants about the kind of verdicts they might render when they introspect experience (Sandberg and Overgaard 2016: 188). But these instructions and the attending training effort are about getting subjects to understand, and help configure, the steps of the scale used in introspection, and are focused on the content of the different awareness ratings they are making. They do not concern the kind of subjective access itself that is supplying these verdicts.

Yet, invariably, proponents of subjective methods insist that there are different forms of subjective access at work in their respective methods. For instance, the PAS was initially prompted by the thought that, although subjective measures seem to be required for an investigation of conscious perception, confidence ratings cannot automatically be taken to measure conscious awareness because they are not sourced in a sufficiently direct way (Ramsøy and Overgaard 2004). There is broad agreement that PAS involves introspection, whereas CR does not, or at least not in the same, straightforward manner that PAS does, with typically suggestive but not very detailed remarks about the difference (e.g., Overgaard and Sandberg 2012: 1290).

What makes it difficult to understand this difference is that practitioners neither offer a worked-out view about what introspection is, nor do they use consistent terminology (compare e.g., Overgaard and Sandberg 2012, Wierzchón et al.: 2014, and Fleming and Lau 2014). One might be forgiven for suspecting that there is no substantial notion of introspection—or subjective access—in circulation in this area.

Such a suspicion is particularly apt when it comes to CR. There is no consensus in the literature on subjective measures whether confidence judgements are introspective in some significant sense. Some hold confidence judgements (and hence ratings) to be introspective, while others explicitly distinguish them from introspective judgements. Among the former, there is a further difference in how much emphasis they place on such a classification. Many seem to be using 'introspective' interchangeably with 'metacognitive' or even 'subjective', and are best understood as not putting forward a positive view about any special subcategory of metacognition or introspection (e.g., Frith and Lau 2006; Lau 2008). Others, however, seem more committed:

> The central premise here is that confidence ratings reflect subjective experience (or phenomenal consciousness; Block 1995), because they are by definition a variety of introspective reports about our mental processes.   (Norman and Price 2016: 160)

On such a view, the crucial relation which supports the evidential link between confidence ratings and conscious perception is introspective. Next to no detail is offered, though, on what is it about the subject's own assessment of the accuracy of their own type 1 task performance that makes it count as introspective—or, for that matter, even as first-personal. Given that subjects could make such accuracy assessments in all sorts of ways, for example by induction from similar past performance, this is not an idle point.

Proponents of PAS, as noted in the previous section, are clear that the awareness ratings at issue in PAS express awareness judgements that are gotten by introspection.

> When examining conscious experience, the most intuitive thing to ask about is probably just that, conscious experience (i.e. asking participants to introspect on their experience). At least, this is the oldest method, and it is still used very frequently today (in the PAS experiments, for example).
>   (Overgaard and Sandberg 2012: 1291–2)

This is meant to ensure that awareness ratings are directly about experience. Overall, PAS aims to provide an introspective, scaled measure of conscious content that is more directly about experience and more sensitive to its graded nature than CR. However, here too, the notion of introspection itself is not elucidated in serious detail.

Introspection is sometimes held to be *by definition* a process which involves a judgement (or similar) that is about experience—introspection is said to bear 'a necessary link to conscious experience' (Overgaard and Sandberg 2012: 1288). Thus it is the target of introspection—experience—that differentiates introspective from non-introspective types of metacognition, in the first instance. Standard expressions of this view fluctuate between making a claim concerning the proper inputs of introspection (that it must be an experience), and making a claim concerning the proper outputs of introspection (that the content of introspective judgements or episodes must be about an experience). As an example of the latter, Overgaard and Sandberg (2012) insist that 'it should be clear that introspective report by definition is only about what is experienced and not about cognitive processes'. Although the two claims are independent, there seems to be an expectation that they go together. The thought is that introspection takes experiences as input and has as outputs states or episodes the content of which is about experience. When things work well, the content of the output is expected to match the content of the experience in some relevant sense.

Sometimes this characterization of introspection is further filled out by an indication about the specific mental process involved in introspecting. For instance, Ramsøy and Overgaard (2004) gloss introspection as 'a state in which one directs attention towards one's own experiences'. Here it seems introspection is held to be a metacognitive process that essentially involves attention or an observation-like relation to one's own conscious states and episodes (see also Overgaard and Sandberg 2012: 1288). But this initial gloss on introspection as attention to experience is meant to be intuitive and pre-theoretic, not a substantial proposal. It is deliberately permissive with respect to different accounts of the nature of the introspective attitude and its relationship to the conscious states and episodes that form the attentional target of introspection. For instance, the gloss is taken to be neutral on the question of on-line, concurrent processing versus retrospective accounts of introspection. Nor is it meant to determine whether introspectively attending to experience causally affects the latter in some way.

Proponents of CR and PAS sometimes speculate about the underlying cognitive or neural architecture of subjective access. Proposals tend to be based on empirical evidence about dissociations between awareness ratings and confidence ratings, revealed by different sensitivities of the respective awareness and confidence scales in experiments investigating visual perception. A variety of studies have offered evidence for superior sensitivity of PAS, CR, and CR-related measures, respectively (see references at the beginning of section 28.6). As a consequence, there are several empirically motivated proposals for a neurally-based or computational difference between introspective (awareness) measures and confidence measures. These proposals agree that there is such a difference, but they disagree about what the empirical difference consists in, about the details of the neural or computational mechanisms manifesting it, and about the precise empirical evidence for it.

Overgaard and Sandberg (2012), for instance, suggest on the basis of differential sensitivity of PAS and CR, that one might think of introspective judgements as involving a simpler cognitive process than that driving confidence judgements. The latter draw on a more complicated process that includes some introspective processing, but also further processes that yield the kind of metacognitive insight into how accurate one's own discrimination or identification processes are. Zehetleitner and Rausch (2013) argue that the systematic differences in sensitivity between awareness and confidence scales are best explained by taking the judgements involved to be sensitive to different neural events. In turn, they reason that the respective ratings are measures of different cognitive processes, that is, that they track different functions in the cognitive economy. They suggest that awareness ratings track 'the strength or the quality of the internal signals that form part of the sensory data', while confidence ratings track 'those internal signals that are involved in the decision to make a response' (Zehetleitner and Rausch 2013: 1423).[13]

Such views about the underlying neural or cognitive nature of introspective processes are, although motivated by empirical evidence, highly speculative. Their proponents are usually happy to admit as much (Overgaard and Sandberg 2012, Zehetleitner and Rausch 2013; Overgaard and Mogensen 2017 all include serious hedges, for instance). The speculations do seem worthwhile, I suspect, because they appear to forge a path towards obtaining empirically grounded accounts of introspection and metacognition, along the same lines as vision science has done for what we ordinarily might refer to as 'sight'— namely, of visual perception as a form of perception more generally. This is an enticing prospect. However, for all its promise, such a prospect still faces enormous hurdles.

The main hurdle is what I call 'the problem of the starting point'. In short, it is usually not clear what the initial psychological phenomenon is in the first place, with which, or about which we are theorizing. There is no basic, core common-sense take on introspection, or on kinds of first-person access, that constrains the beginning of our enquiries in the same way that common-sense understanding of sight, audition, etc. does. We ordinarily use the term 'introspection' in all sorts of ways and every day talk and practice contains a wide array of ideas of first-person-sourced awareness. The notion of introspection is much more like the common-sense notion of thought, that is, vague, amorphous, and fluid, ranging over active, deliberative inference, quasi-perceptual attention, retrospective episodic memory, passive self-awareness, etc. It does not support the idea that there is a theoretically significant psychological kind or group of mental capacities, or that available empirical evidence gathered in terms of it supports theorizing about neural and cognitive architecture.

As I have shown above, the crucial notions of introspection and subjective access at work in the key assumption characterizing the psychological literature on subjective

---

[13] Along a different dimension of the nature of introspection, Overgaard et al. (2006) take themselves to provide empirical evidence against the view that introspection is always retrospection.

measures, namely that we have certain first-person ways to access aspects of our conscious lives, are never fully articulated but instead merely gestured towards, relying on a common-sense understanding of them. Insofar as the notion of introspection, for instance, is given any elucidation at all, it tends to be dealt with in one or two generic sentences. Fashioning an introspective (or subjective) method out of that gesture means that a fair amount of inchoate common-sense intuition about our first-person access is placed at the heart of it.

Proponents of CR and PAS agree that all subjective methods involve metacognition of some kind, but this does not offer much of a common starting point either.[14] Metacognition is a more general category than introspection, covering any mental state or episode about another mental state, or episode, or process. It is a higher-order state or episode in the sense that it has a first-order, or lower-order mental state, episode, or process as its object.[15] The class of metacognitions is thus large and motley: 'metacognition', as Fleming et al. (2012) put it, is 'an umbrella term'. All sorts of cognitions count as metacognitive cognitions, ranging from person-level judgements that one has a headache, to low-level states of early visual processing to the effect that some visual representation of an edge as oriented to the right is likely to be correct. There is no restriction, that is, on either the metacognitive output or input on that score (i.e., whether they are attributable to an individual or a subsystem), other than that they must be cognitive properties of a given psychological system. Moreover, the broad conception of metacognition does not place constraints on the metacognitive process, that is, on how the output is produced. Thus, early visual automatic processing, conscious deliberation, attention, etc. are all permissible metacognitive processes. There is in principle no restriction to acquiring a metacognitive judgement, say, via testimony by others, or by looking in a mirror and inferring from the expression on one's face.[16]

---

[14] Proponents of PAS sometimes distinguish introspection from metacognition. Since they are also sometimes happy to think of introspection as a subclass of metacognition, I am going to attribute the latter view to them and adjust where necessary, chalking discrepancies up to terminological infelicities on their part.

[15] This is perhaps the most permissive characterization of metacognition, i.e. it is the broadest understanding of metacognition as 'a cognition about cognition' (Fleming et al. 2012: 1280). Insofar as one holds that cognition is a representational phenomenon, metacognition is a system's representation of its own representations. It is not thereby guaranteed that the aspect of cognition represented by the metacognitive output is the causally efficacious input, nor that the aspect of cognition represented concerns the representational content of the represented cognitive state. For a conception of metacognition as meta-representation, see (Shea 2014: 315–16). For other conceptions, see, e.g., Fleming (2017).

[16] Those working on metacognition are, it seems, mainly interested in processes that are in some sense more strictly part of our natural psychological system, and so testimonial relations and other complex inferential methods would not be considered fundamentally metacognitive. But metacognition is normally introduced in terms of a functional characterization, i.e. as serving to control and monitor behaviour, and this does not place much of a constraint on metacognitive process, inputs or outputs. Moreover, the relevant behaviour can be held to include the activity of cognitive processes, or it can be restricted to agent-level behaviour. Depending on the range of behaviours at issue, metacognition may be more or less wide a category. See Fleming et al. (2012) and Fleming and Lau (2014): 7–8 for relevant discussion.

28.8 Conclusion

The discussion in this chapter shows that current-day subjective measures of consciousness do not involve worked-out conceptions of introspection, or of other relevant types of subjective access. We have also seen fairly careless uses of the term 'introspection', even by those who hold that introspective ratings are importantly different from other subjective ratings, where it sometimes covers a specific metacognitive capacity only, and sometimes it is a catch-all term for any capacity underlying a variety of subjective measures. In light of this, we cannot even begin to address the problem of response bias for contemporary subjective measures of consciousness. We do not sufficiently understand the kind of subjective access that is employed in these measures. There is then no hope of trying to figure out whether response bias is inextricably and debilitatingly inherent in the subjective method itself, or whether it can be minimized or filtered out by ingenious experiment or data analysis.

In the introduction, I noted Irvine's (2012: 629) observation that critiques of subjective measures of consciousness are echoing well-known objections to early introspectionist psychology at the turn of the last century, thus indicating a lack of progress in this area of current-day science of consciousness. Indeed, when it comes to the problem of response bias, I think there is not merely stagnation, there is a setback. Early experimentalist psychologists, such as Wilhelm Wundt and Georg Elias Müller, had developed views about the role and nature of subjective access in their introspective methods, quite different from the caricature views attributed to so-called 'introspectionist psychologists' (Spener 2018). The debate about the problem of response bias for subjective measures of consciousness would be much enhanced by revisiting these older views because the latter provide at least a blueprint for how to address this problem by being clear about what subjective access consists in.

References

Block, N. (2008), 'Consciousness and cognitive access', *Proceedings of the Aristotelian Society*, 108: 289–317.
Chalmers, D. (1998), 'On the search for the neural correlate of consciousness', in S. Hameroff, A. Kaszniak, and A. Scott (eds), *Toward a Science of Consciousness II: The Second Tucson Discussions and Debates*. Cambridge, MA: MIT Press.
Chalmers, D. (2004), 'How can we construct a science of consciousness?', in Michael Gazzaniga (ed.), *The Cognitive Neurosciences III*. Cambridge, MA: MIT Press.
Cheesman, J. and Merikle, P. M. (1984), 'Priming with and without awareness', *Perception and Psychophysics*, 36: 387–95.
Cheesman, J. and Merikle, P. M. (1986), 'Distinguishing conscious from unconscious processes', *Canadian Journal of Psychology*, 40.
Chirimuuta, M. (2014), 'Psychophysical methods and the evasion of introspection', *Philosophy of Science*, 81/5: 914–26.

Dienes, Z. and Seth, A. (2010), 'Measuring any conscious content versus measuring the relevant conscious content: Comment on Sandberg et al', *Consciousness and Cognition*, 19/4: 1079–80.

Dienes, Z., Altmann, G. T. M., Kwan, L., and Goode, A. (1995), 'Unconscious knowledge of artificial grammars is applied strategically', *Journal of Experimental Psychology: Learning, Memory, and Cognition*, 25: 1322–38.

Dienes, Z., Scott, R. B., and Seth, A. (2010), 'Subjective measures of implicit knowledge that go beyond confidence: Reply to Overgaard et al.', *Consciousness and Cognition*, 19: 685–6.

Eriksen, C. W. (1956), 'An experimental analysis of subception', *American Journal of Psychology*, 69: 625–34.

Eriksen, C. W. (1960), 'Discrimination and learning without awareness: a methodological survey and evaluation', *Psychological Review*, 67: 279–300.

Fleming, S. M. (2017), 'HMeta-d: Hierarchical Bayesian estimation of metacognitive efficiency from confidence ratings', *Neuroscience of Consciousness*, 2017: 1.

Fleming, S. M. and Lau, H. (2014), 'How to measure metacognition', in *Frontiers in Human Neuroscience*, 8.

Fleming, S. M., Dolan, R. J., and Frith, C. D. (2012), 'Metacognition: computation, biology and function', *Philosophical Transactions of the Royal Society of Biological Sciences*, 367: 1280–6.

Frith, C. D. and Lau, H. (2006), 'The problem of introspection', *Consciousness and Cognition*, 15: 761–4.

Green, D. M. and Swets, J. A. (1966), *Signal Detection Theory and Psychophysics*. New York: Wiley.

Holender, D. (1986), 'Semantic activation without conscious identification in dichotic listening, parafoveal vision, and visual masking: A survey and appraisal', *Behavioral and Brain Sciences*, 9: 1–66.

Irvine, E. (2012), 'Old problems with new measures in the science of consciousness', *British Journal for the Philosophy of Science*, 63: 627–48.

Irvine, E. (2013), 'Measures of consciousness', *Philosophy Compass*, 8/3: 285–97.

Jack, A. and Roepstorff, A. (2003), *Trusting the Subject? The Use of Introspective Evidence in Cognitive Science, Volume 1*. Exeter: Imprint Academic.

Jack, A. and Roepstorff, A. (2004), *Trusting the Subject? Volume 2*. Exeter: Imprint Academic.

Lau, H. (2008), 'Are we studying consciousness yet?' in L. Weiskrantz and M. Davies (eds), *Frontiers of Consciousness*. Oxford: Oxford University Press.

Macmillan, N. A. and Creelman, C. D. (1991), *Detection Theory: A User's Guide*. Cambridge: Cambridge University Press.

Marcel, A. (1980), 'Conscious and preconscious recognition of polysemous words: Locating the selective effect of prior verbal context', in R. S. Nickerson (ed.), *Attention and Performance VIII*. Hillsdale, NJ: Erlbaum, 435–57.

Marcel, A. (1983), 'Conscious and unconscious perception: An approach to the relations between phenomenal experience and perceptual processes', *Cognitive Psychology*, 15: 238–300.

Merikle, P. M. and Cheesman, J. (1986), 'Consciousness is a "subjective" state', *Behavioral and Brain Sciences*, 9: 42–13.

Norman, E. and Price, M. C. (2016), 'Measuring consciousness with confidence ratings', in M. Overgaard (ed.), *Behavioral Methods on Consciousness Research*. Oxford: Oxford University Press, 159–180.

Overgaard, M. (2006), 'Introspection in science', *Consciousness and Cognition*, 15: 629–33.

Overgaard, M. (2016), 'The challenge of measuring consciousness' in M. Overgaard (ed.), *Behavioural Methods in Consciousness Research*. Oxford: Oxford University Press.

Overgaard, M. and Mogensen, J. (2017), 'An integrative view on consciousness and introspection', *Review of Philosophical Psychology*, 8: 129–41.

Overgaard, M. and Sandberg, K. (2012), 'Kinds of access: different methods for report reveal different kinds of metacognitive access', *Philosophical Transactions of the Royal Society of Biological Sciences*, 367: 1287–96.

Overgaard, M., Koivisto, M., Sørensen, T. A., Vangkilde, S., and Revonsuo, A. (2006), 'The electrophysiology of introspection', *Consciousness and Cognition*, 15: 662–72.

Peirce, C. S. and Jastrow, J. (1885), 'On small differences in sensation', *Memoirs of the National Academy of Sciences*, 3: 73–83.

Persaud, N., McLeod, P., and Cowey, A. (2007), 'Post-decision wagering objectively measures awareness', *Nature Neuroscience*, 10: 257–61.

Phillips, I. (2015a), 'No watershed for overflow: Recent work on the richness of consciousness', *Philosophical Psychology*, 29/2: 1–14.

Phillips, I. (2015b), 'Consciousness and criterion', *Philosophy and Phenomenological Research*, 93/2: 419–51.

Ramsøy, T. Z. and Overgaard, M. (2004), 'Introspection and subliminal perception', *Phenomenology and the Cognitive Sciences*, 3/1: 1–23.

Samaha, J., Barrett, J. J., Sheldon, A. D., LaRocque, J. J., and Postle, B. R. (2016), 'Dissociating perceptual confidence from discrimination accuracy reveals no influence of metacognitive awareness on working memory', *Frontiers in Psychology*: 7.

Sandberg, K. and Overgaard, M. (2016), 'Using the perceptual awareness scale (PAS)', in M. Overgaard (ed.), *Behavioral Methods on Consciousness Research*. Oxford: Oxford University Press, 181–95.

Sandberg, K., Timmermans, B., Overgaard, M., and Cleeremans, A. (2010), 'Measuring consciousness: Is one measure better than the other?' *Consciousness and Cognition*, 19/4:1069–78.

Sandberg, K., Bibby, B. M., and Overgaard, M. (2013), 'Measuring and testing awareness of emotional face expressions', *Consciousness and Cognition*, 22/3: 806–9.

Schwitzgebel, E. (2011), *Perplexities of Consciousness*. Cambridge, MA: MIT Press.

Schwitzgebel, E. (2013), 'Reply to Kriegel, Smithies and Spener', *Philosophical Studies*, 165/3: 1195–206.

Seth, A., Dienes, Z., Cleeremans, A., Overgaard, M., and Pessoa, L. (2008), 'Measuring consciousness: relating behavioural and neurophysiological approaches', *Trends in Cognitive Sciences*, 12: 314–21.

Shea, N. (2012), 'Methodological encounter with a phenomenal kind', *Philosophy and Phenomenological Research*, 84/2: 307–44.

Shea, N. (2014), 'Reward prediction error signals are meta-representational', *Noûs*, 48/2: 314–41.

Snodgrass, M. and Lepisto, S. A. (2007), 'Access for what? reflective consciousness', *Behavioral and Brain Sciences*, 30/5: 525–6.

Snodgrass, M., Kalaida, N., and Winder, S. E. (2009), 'Access is mainly a second-order process: SDT models whether phenomenally (first-order) conscious states are accessed by reflectively (second-order) conscious processes', *Consciousness and Cognition*, 18/2: 561–4.

Spener, M. (2013), 'Moderate scepticism about introspection', *Philosophical Studies*, 165/3: 1187–94.

Spener, M. (2015), 'Calibrating introspection', *Philosophical Issues*, 25/1: 300–21.

Spener, M. (2018), 'Introspecting in the Twentieth Century', in A. Kind (ed.) *Philosophy of Mind in the 20th Century*. Abingdon: Routledge.

Timmermans, B. and Cleeremans, A. (2016), 'How can we measure awareness? an overview of current methods', in M. Overgaard (ed.), *Behavioral Methods on Consciousness Research*. Oxford: Oxford University Press.

Tunney, R. J. (2005), 'Sources of confidence judgements in implicit cognition', *Psychonomic Bulletin & Review*, 12/2: 367–73.

Tunney, R. J. and Shanks, D. R. (2003), 'Subjective measures of awareness in implicit cognition', *Memory and Cognition*, 31: 1060–71.

Wierzchón, M., Asanowicz, D., Paulewicz, B., and Cleeremans, A. (2012), 'Subjective measures of consciousness in artificial grammar learning task', *Consciousness and Cognition*, 21/3: 1141–53.

Wierzchón, M., Szczepanowski, R., Anzulewicz, A., and Cleeremans, A. (2014), 'When a (precise) awareness measure became a (sketchy) introspective report', *Consciousness and Cognition*, 26: 1–2.

Zehetleitner, M. and Rausch, M. (2013), 'Being confident without seeing: What subjective measures of visual consciousness are about', *Attention Perception and Psychophysics*, 75/7: 1406–26.

Zeki, S. and ffytche, D. H. (1998), 'The Riddoch syndrome: Insights into the neurobiology of conscious vision', *Brain*, 121: 25–45.

CHAPTER 29

CONSCIOUSNESS AND SELFHOOD

Getting Clearer on For-Me-Ness and Mineness

DAN ZAHAVI

Not that long ago, discussions of selfhood in philosophy of mind tended to focus on diachronic identity and the so-called persistence question. What are the necessary and sufficient conditions that must be met if I am to be identical to a past or future being? Is it the persistence of some psychological relation (beliefs, memories, preferences, etc.), or is my identity through time rather constituted by some brute physical continuity? Important as this question might be, it does, however, not exhaust the topic of selfhood. In recent years, the focus has shifted somewhat from diachronic to synchronic identity and given rise to a lively debate concerning the relationship between phenomenal consciousness and selfhood. Are our conscious experiences self-involving or self-disclosing (in a manner yet to be determined) or was Lichtenberg right in his famous objection to Descartes: Experiences simply take place, and that is all. To say cogito and to affirm the existence of an I is already to say too much (Lichtenberg 2000: 190).

29.1 Denying the Phenomenal Presence of the Experiencer

In *A Treatise of Human Nature* Hume famously wrote:

> For my part, when I enter most intimately into what I call *myself*, I always stumble on some particular perception or other, of heat or cold, light or shade, love or hatred, pain or pleasure. I never can catch *myself* at any time without a perception, and never can observe any thing but the perception (Hume 2007: 165).

This quotation has often been taken as an expression of Hume's commitment to a bundle theory. There is nothing to consciousness apart from a manifold or bundle of changing experiences. There are various experiences and perceptions, but no subject of experience, no experiencer or perceiver. As Jesse Prinz has recently argued, Hume is committed to the thesis that, 'among the various phenomenal qualities that make up an experience, there is none that can be characterized as an experience of the self or subject in addition to qualities found in perceived features of the world, sensations, and emotions' (Prinz 2012: 124). Whether this is a correct interpretation of Hume is debatable,[1] but Prinz's aim is in any case to defend a strong eliminativist position, according to which there is no phenomenal *I*. There might be a phenomenal *me*, that is, the self might figure as the object of a conscious experience, but qua subject of experience, it is experientially invisible. In arguing for this view, Prinz asks us to focus on the actual qualities that make up a concrete experience and then suggests that there are three options: The first possibility is to claim that among these experiential qualities there is a specific item that we can label 'the I'. If we reject this proposal, as we ought to, we are, according to Prinz, left with two further possibilities. We might maintain that there is an I-quale, some kind of mineness of experience, but then argue that it is reducible to other kinds of qualia, that is, that it is nothing over and beyond the qualities of perception, sensation, and emotion. The final possibility, which is the one that Prinz favours, is to opt for eliminativism and simply reject that there is any I-quale at all (Prinz 2012: 123–4). Interestingly, Prinz's eliminativism should not be taken as a defence of metaphysical anti-realism about the self. Prinz is not arguing that consciousness is selfless. Rather consciousness is, as he puts it, 'thoroughly permeated by the self' (Prinz 2012: 149). We always experience the world from a perspective or point of view. Who we are, our goals, interests, and histories, very much filters and constrains what we experience. Thus, the self might be said to be present, not as an item of experience, but as a kind of constraint (Prinz 2012: 149).

By arguing in this manner, Prinz is getting close to what might be considered a more Kantian approach to the self. According to this alternative proposal, each and every experience presupposes by conceptual and metaphysical necessity a subject of experience. Just as there can be no jumping without a jumper, there can be no experiencing without an experiencer. The latter, however, is a condition, rather than a given datum. We can infer that it exists, but it is not itself something experiential. As Kant wrote in *Kritik der reinen Vernunft*: 'I cannot cognize as an object itself that which I must presuppose in order to cognize an object at all' (Kant 1998: A 402). A recent version of this view has

---

[1] It is not obvious that not being able to perceive the self 'without a perception' is equivalent to not being able to perceive the self (Margolis 1988: 32). Indeed, as Strawson has recently argued, far from entailing a denial of the existence of a self or subject of experience, Hume's principal target in the quotation in question is the view that the self or subject is something that can be encountered in separation from the experience, i.e., the view that it is possible to have a naked or bare apprehension of the self. Hume is denying this, just as he more generally speaking is denying that we in experience encounter a simple, unchanging, and persisting subject. But one can deny this, without defending a no-ownership theory, without denying that whenever we observe an ongoing perception, we also observe ourselves, since any perceiving, any experiencing, is necessarily and essentially a subject-involving occurrence (Strawson 2017: 258–9).

been defended by Searle. According to Searle, the self is not a separate and distinct entity but rather a formal feature of the conscious field. Searle claims that we fail to describe the conscious field correctly, if we think of it as a field constituted only by its contents and their arrangements. The contents require a principle of unity, but that principle, namely the self, is not a separate thing or entity. Searle then goes on to say that the postulation of a self is like the postulation of a point of view in visual perception. Just as we cannot make sense of our perceptions unless we suppose that they occur from a point of view, even though the point of view is not itself perceived, we cannot, according to Searle, make sense of our conscious experiences unless we suppose that they occur to a self, even though the self is not consciously experienced. The self is not the object of consciousness, nor is it part of the content of consciousness, indeed we have on Searle's account no experience of the self at all, but since all (non-pathological) consciousness has to be possessed by a self, we can infer that it must exist (Searle 2005: 16–18). One way to understand Searle's argument is consequently to see him distinguishing the question of whether an experience is necessarily had by a self from the question of whether the self necessarily figures in experience. Whereas Searle denies the latter, he affirms the former, thereby taking ownership of experience to be a non-experiential metaphysical relation rather than something phenomenally manifest.

29.2 Highlighting the First-person Perspective

Prinz's and Searle's views might be contrasted with a position that can be called *experiential minimalism*. It is a view I have been defending since the late 1990s (Zahavi 1999, 2000, 2005, 2009, 2011, 2014), but somewhat comparable views can also be found in the writings of, for instance, Galen Strawson (1994, 2009, 2011, 2017), Uriah Kriegel (2009, forthcoming), and Martine Nida-Rümelin (2016).

A guiding idea has been that if we wish to do justice to the subjective character of experiential episodes, we should acknowledge that episodes characterized by a subjective what-it-is-likeness are not merely episodes that happen to take place *in* a subject, regardless of whether the subject is aware of them or not. Rather, the what-it-is-likeness of phenomenal states is properly speaking a what-it-is-like-*for-me*-ness. On this view, experiential processes are characterized by an inherent reflexive (not reflective) or pre-reflective self-consciousness in the weak sense that they are like something *for* the subject, that is, in virtue of their mere existence, they are phenomenally manifest to the subject of those experiences.

One objection that might be made to a proposal like this is the following. To claim that our experiences are first-personally manifest is a fundamental mistake, since there is in fact no for-me-ness, phenomenal consciousness or what-it-is-likeness. Indeed, there is 'nothing that it is like to have qualitative experience' (Garfield 2016: 73). This is not to deny that there is something it is like to experience the blueness of the sky or the sweet scent of a mango, but what should be listed here are exclusively properties of the objects, namely the blueness or the sweet scent. There is nothing in addition that it is like to experience these objects: 'Consciousness is always consciousness *of* something, and when the object is subtracted, nothing remains to be characterized' (Garfield 2016: 75). To say that we are aware of the experience of the object, and not simply of the object, is consequently to confuse the epistemic instrument with the epistemic object (Garfield 2016: 79). As Dretske once put it, mental states are something *with* which we are conscious, rather than something *of* which we are conscious (1995: 100–1). In truth, the only thing that is manifest is the external object and its properties. Another way to make the same point is by saying that whatever we are conscious of is completely objective. The fact that one is aware of it does not add anything. Indeed, as Dretske willingly concedes, on this account, '[e]verything you are aware of would be the same if you were a zombie' (Dretske 2003: 1, cf. Garfield 2016: 76).

One might wonder how an account like this is supposed to deal with qualitative experiences like anguish, nausea, or orgasm, but a more general worry concerns its (in)ability to address the difference between conscious and non-conscious intentional states. If we compare a situation where my visual system contains a non-conscious mango-representation with a situation where I am consciously aware of a mango, the two situations differ. It is hard to see how their difference could be explained simply as a result of a variation in (the amount of) objectual properties. Phenomenality is not merely about *what* is being presented, but also about *how* it is being presented. Whereas there is a phenomenal difference between the manifest gustatory qualities of caviar and liquorice, there is also a phenomenal difference to the taste of liquorice depending upon whether it is perceived, remembered, or imagined. That difference is not a difference in the properties of the object.

Whenever objectual properties appear, they always appear in specific ways (as perceived, remembered, imagined, anticipated, etc.), and they only appear, that is, they only present themselves phenomenally, if the mental state in question is conscious. A non-conscious perception of a mango might establish an informationally rich causal connection between the mango and 'my' visual system, but it does not make the object appear to me, it does not make me aware of what the perception is about.

It could be objected, however, that any reference to the first-personal givenness of experience commits one to the claim that every ordinary intentional experience involves two objects: the external object and the experiencing of the external object, and that this is one object too many (Garfield 2015: 164). If we consider a visual perception of a bottle, Garfield is certainly right in objecting to the claim that there next to the bottle should be another object, the perceptual state, which is either blocking the view or somehow competing for our attention. But as should be clear by now, the claim is not that our access to, say, a tasted mango or a touched bottle is indirect, or that it is mediated, contaminated, or blocked by our awareness of the tasting or touching, since those experiences rather than being objects on a par with the mango or the bottle are precisely what provides us with phenomenal access to the objects in question. Indeed, what the objection overlooks is that part of the motivation for introducing the notion of pre-reflective self-consciousness in the first place was to criticize the idea that the givenness of an experience is always a form of object-givenness. To put it differently, pre-reflective self-consciousness is precisely taken to differ from reflective self-consciousness by being an intrinsic non-objectifying form of self-acquaintance. One that does not contain any subject–object structure, but where the experiential states are rather aware of themselves in a non-dual manner. As Frankfurt once put it,

> What would it be like to be conscious of something without being aware of this consciousness? It would mean having an experience with no awareness whatever of its occurrence. This would be, precisely, a case of unconscious experience. It appears, then, that being conscious is identical with being self-conscious. Consciousness is self-consciousness. The claim that waking consciousness is self-consciousness does not mean that consciousness is invariably dual in the sense that every instance of it involves both a primary awareness and another instance of consciousness which is somehow distinct and separable from the first and which has the first as its object. That would threaten an intolerably infinite proliferation of instances of consciousness. Rather, the self-consciousness in question is a sort of *immanent reflexivity* by virtue of which every instance of being conscious grasps not only that of which it is an awareness but also the awareness of it. It is like a source of light which, in addition to illuminating whatever other things fall within its scope, renders itself visible as well. (Frankfurt 1988: 162)

Some might consider the introduction of a non-objectifying form of self-consciousness an unwarranted ad hoc stipulation, made purely in order to avoid certain troubling objections. It falls outside the scope of the present chapter to offer a more comprehensive account of the different arguments that over time has been offered in support of pre-reflective self-consciousness, but let me mention one influential argument, which is rather transcendental in character.

Most authors are willing to recognize the existence of reflective self-consciousness. This is a form of self-consciousness that involves a subject–object relation between two different mental states, the reflecting and the reflected. Reflective self-consciousness is not simply some form of other-directed mind-reading, however. It does not merely provide the subject of experience with an awareness of somebody's mental episode. To qualify as a form of *self*-consciousness, the identity of the subject and the object must be affirmed. But how is this to be accomplished? How can the identity of the two relata be ascertained without presupposing that which is meant to be explained? If the act of reflection is to recognize or identify something as itself, it needs a prior self-familiarity. As Cramer puts it,

> How should the reflective subject be able to know that it has itself as an object? Obviously only by knowing that it is identical with its object. But it is impossible to ascribe this knowledge to *reflection* and to *ground* it in reflection. The act of reflection presupposes that the self *already knows* itself, in order to know that that which it knows when it takes itself as an object is indeed identical with the one that accomplishes

the act of reflective thinking. The *theory* that tries to make the *origin* of self-awareness comprehensible through reflection ends necessarily in a circle that presupposes the knowledge it wants to explain. (Cramer 1974: 563)

Any attempt to conceive of basic self-consciousness as a form of object cognition, that is, as a subject–object relation, seems bound to fail since it either leads to a regress or presupposes what it is supposed to explain. The solution to this challenge has been to defend the existence of a more primitive form of non-objectifying pre-reflective self-consciousness.[2] In short, if reflective self-consciousness is to be possible, pre-reflective self-consciousness has to be presupposed. As Sartre observed,

Thus reflection has no kind of primacy over the consciousness reflected-on. It is not reflection which reveals the consciousness reflected-on to itself. Quite the contrary, it is the non-reflective consciousness which renders the reflection possible; there is a pre-reflective cogito which is the condition of the Cartesian cogito. (Sartre 2003: 9)

But how do we get from pre-reflective self-consciousness to a sense of self? As Sartre also once wrote, 'pre-reflective consciousness is self-consciousness. It is this same notion of self which must be studied, for it defines the very being of consciousness' (Sartre 2003: 100). Indeed, as he points out in the chapter 'The self and the circuit of selfness' in *Being and Nothingness*, consciousness is by no means impersonal when pre-reflectively lived through. Rather it is characterized by a 'fundamental selfness' (Sartre 2003: 127). As I read Sartre, his proposal is that rather than starting with a preconceived notion of self, we should let our understanding of what it means to be a self arise out of our analysis of self-consciousness. Put concisely, the proposal is to identify the self with the subject of experience, and to conceive of the subject, not as an independent, separable entity, but as the subjectivity of experience, which is then claimed to be something no experience can lack, neither metaphysically nor phenomenologically. To use a formulation of Strawson's, if experience exists, subjectivity exists, and that entails that subject-of-experience-hood exists (Strawson 2009: 419). On this construal, the self is something that is essentially present in each and every experience. It is present, not as a separately existing entity, that is, as something that exists independently of, in separation from, or in opposition to the stream of consciousness. Nor is it given as an additional experiential object or as an extra experiential ingredient, as if there were a distinct self-quale, next to and in addition to the quale of the smell of burnt hay and roasted almonds. No, the claim is that all experiences regardless of their object and regardless of their act-type (or attitudinal character) are necessarily subjective in the sense that they feel like something for

---

[2] This view is not shared by all who defend the existence of a more primitive pre-reflective form of self-consciousness, however. Kriegel has explicitly dismissed the notion of non-objectifying self-consciousness as a somewhat mysterious sui generis intrinsic glow (2009: 102), and has instead proposed and defended a neo-Brentanian self-representationalism, according to which each mental state takes itself as its own peripheral object (Kriegel 2004). For a critical discussion of self-representationalism, see Zahavi 2004, 2014.

someone. In virtue of their inherent reflexive self-consciousness, in virtue of their self-presentational character, they are not anonymous, but imbued with a fundamental subjectivity and first-personal character, and the proposal has been to identify this first-personal presence, this experiential for-me-ness, with what has been called the *minimal self* (Zahavi 2005, 2014). To deny the existence of this for-me-ness, to deny that we have a distinctly different acquaintance with our own experiential life than with the experiential life of others (and vice versa), and that this difference obtains, not only when we introspect or reflect, but already in the very having of the experience, is to fail to recognize an essential aspect of experience.

At this point, however, it might be objected that more caution is needed. Is it really warranted to equate for-me-ness, experiential subjectivity, the first-person perspective, pre-reflective self-consciousness, the minimal self, etc.? As Guillot has recently argued, the indiscriminate use of the notions of *for-me-ness*, *me-ness*, and *mineness* has introduced considerable confusion into the debate, since the three notions are far from being conceptually equivalent and ultimately target three different properties (Guillot 2017: 26).[3]

On Guillot's reading, *for-me-ness* is best understood as a label for the special awareness that the subject has of the experience she is undergoing. On many construals, this special awareness comes about as a result of the experience possessing a special inner awareness, such that in addition to being aware of its ordinary (external) object it also has itself as object of awareness. In short, it is by being aware of itself, that the experience possesses a subjective character that makes it be 'for me' (Guillot 2017: 28–9). *Me-ness*, by contrast, is when the subject of experience rather than simply being aware of the external object (and of the experience of the object) is also aware of herself. Me-ness, in short, is when the subject figures in experience as 'an object of phenomenal awareness' (Guillot 2017: 35), or as Farrell and McClelland (2017: 3) rephrase it in their summary of Guillot's view, as 'a thing-that-appears'. *Mineness*, finally, is when the experience is phenomenally given as mine. On this reading, mineness is the more complex notion, since it not only requires that the subject is aware of her experience, and aware of herself, but also aware of the possessive relation between herself and the experience, that is, aware that she is owning the experience (Guillot 2017: 31, 43).

As Guillot then points out, there is *prima facie* a fairly clear distinction to be drawn between an awareness of an experience, an awareness of an experiencer, and an awareness of the experience as owned by the experiencer, and it is neither obvious that the three notions are co-extensive nor that they stand in relations of mutual entailment (Guillot 2017: 32). Since the experience and the subject of experience are normally taken to be distinct particulars, one cannot without further ado argue that for-me-ness (an awareness of the experience) necessarily entails me-ness (an awareness of the experiencer) (Guillot 2017: 34). One cannot without further ado move from the 'familiar point that a subject is aware of her present experience in a way that others are not' to the claim that 'what makes this "way of being aware" special is that it encompasses... the subject of awareness, the object of her awareness and their relation' (Guillot 2017: 34).

---

[3] I discuss Guillot's position and objections in further detail in Zahavi 2018.

Guillot is surely right in saying that there is a difference between letting the self figure as the dative of experience, that is as the subject of experience, and letting it figure in the accusative as an object of awareness, and that this again is different from being explicitly aware of the possessive relation between the subject and its experience (Guillot 2017: 34–5). But have these differences really been overlooked in the previous debate? One cannot conclude from the fact that certain authors have used, say, the notions of *for-me-ness* and *mineness* interchangeably to the fact that an important conceptual distinction has thereby been overlooked, since it all depends on how the authors in question have been defining the terms.[4] Given how Guillot is defining me-ness and mineness, I, for instance, would dispute that for-me-ness entails either. Being pre-reflectively aware of one's experiences is neither tantamount to being aware of oneself as an object, nor equivalent to being thematically aware of the experiences *as* one's own. In fact, whereas Guillot (2017: 45) claims that for-me-ness, me-ness, and mineness co-occur in the ordinary experience of normal subjects, I would argue that they only co-occur quite rarely.[5]

It is also possible, however, to define mineness differently than Guillot. Consider, for instance, Rowlands' distinction between two ways of understanding *mineness*. In the first case, mineness is an introspectively discerned feature or property of my experiences. On the second reading, which is Rowlands' own, mineness is understood in adverbial terms as the way or mode in which the intentional objects of my experience are presented to me. When I have experiences of objects, I have them *minely*. The objects are given *for-me* (Rowlands 2015: 117). On this latter interpretation, mineness and for-me-ness amount to the same.

The real issue of controversy, however, is arguably different. It concerns the question of how much can be packed into the *for-me-ness* that is arguably present whenever and wherever there is phenomenal consciousness. Does *for-me-ness* entail some sense of self, some form of self-awareness? Guillot denies both. The fact that the experience manifests itself to me does not entail that I am thereby aware of myself in any way. Likewise, the fact that experiences are given first-personally to the subject does not entail that the experiencing subject is thereby self-aware (Guillot 2017: 48–9).

What is overlooked by this objection is the fact that there are many different types of self-awareness or self-consciousness (and I am here using both terms synonymously). Crucial distinctions include the previously mentioned difference between (1) objectifying and non-objectifying forms of self-consciousness, but also (2) the important distinction between egological and non-egological forms of self-consciousness. Given the

---

[4] In my own case, I started out by primarily using the term *mineness* (e.g., Zahavi 2005: 16), but later increasingly opted for the term *for-me-ness* (e.g., Zahavi 2014: 24). The main motivation for this terminological change was that various critics seemed to have taken mineness to refer to a specific I-quale, whereas it was intended to refer to the subjective how of experiencing. The notion of for-me-ness seemed less amenable to that kind of misunderstanding. The difficulty, though, is that the latter notion also runs the risk of being misunderstood, namely as referring to a merely formal, i.e., non-experiential, structure. As a result, I have occasionally used both notions interchangeably.

[5] Farrell and McClelland (2017: 5) are consequently mistaken when they argue that I am committed to a conception of experience according to which all conscious states possess all three features (as they are defined by Guillot).

first distinction, one cannot conclude that the self is not experientially present unless it is given in the accusative, that is, as an object. In fact, as we saw above, there is a long-standing tradition in philosophy which argues that self-consciousness *cannot* primarily be a form of object-consciousness. As for the latter distinction, which can also be found in classical literature on self-consciousness (see, e.g., Thiel 2011), it bears on the question of whether self-consciousness is best understood as consciousness of self or rather simply as the reflexive acquaintance that each conscious episode has to itself. In short, it is perfectly respectable to designate the case where consciousness is aware of itself as a case of self-consciousness.

More generally speaking, what seems to have been somewhat forgotten is the fact that much of the relevant discussion of self-consciousness has taken place in the context of an attempt to understand the difference between conscious and non-conscious mental states. Whereas higher-order representationalists have typically argued that the difference in question rests upon the presence or absence of a relevant meta-mental state, and therefore claimed that it is 'the addition of the relevant meta-intentional self-awareness that transforms a nonconscious mental state into a conscious one' (Van Gulick 2000: 276), defenders of one-level alternatives have argued that conscious mental states possess an inherent pre-reflective self-consciousness. In either case, however, the claim has been that there is a constitutive link between phenomenal consciousness and self-consciousness. One might disagree, but then one should provide arguments that either deny the difference between conscious and non-conscious mental states or offer an alternative account of their difference.

Now, one possible reply would be to argue that even if for-me-ness does in fact entail a kind of self-consciousness, namely a kind of state-self-consciousness, where a mental state is aware of itself (which obviously does not necessarily entail that it is also aware of itself *as* a mental state), it remains the wrong kind of self-consciousness, it is not subject-self-consciousness, it is not a consciousness of self. And as Guillot insists (2017: 34), since the self and the experience are distinct particulars, an awareness of the latter does not automatically involve an awareness of the former. However, this objection lacks purchase against those who opt for a deflationary or thin notion of self, according to which the self, rather than being a distinct entity that has or owns the experience, is itself an experiential dimension. Guillot (2017: 37) has argued that such a move is controversial and in need of independent arguments. That such arguments can be found in the literature, and have been provided by defenders of the thesis that Guillot is criticizing is, however, indisputable (cf. Strawson 2009; Zahavi 2014). As already mentioned, the basic idea is to highlight the irreducible first-personal character of experience, that is, the ineliminable perspectivalness of phenomenal consciousness. Intentional experiences are Janus-faced. They are of something other than the subject and they are like something for the subject. There is a genitive and dative of intentional manifestation. The proposal is to identify the (minimal) self with this dative of manifestation, which does not designate something experientially invisible, but rather the very subjectivity of experience. On this account, the self is an experiential being and is not something that can ever be encountered in separation from the experiences, nor is it something that can be absent whenever experiences are lived through. Of course, some might find this line of reasoning unconvincing, but the proper task would then be to engage with it critically, rather than simply to ignore it. There might be a price to pay for insisting on a very tight constitutive link between self and experience, but the same certainly holds true for any theory that wants to separate the two. There is something counterintuitive to the claim that the subject, self, or I is entirely non-experiential, such that I would remain a self even if I were zombified and ceased having experiences, simply because a brain, a body or a living organism continued to exist. In fact, if self and experience are separated, it is unclear how self-experience would ever be possible, and how a certain object (be it a brain, a body, or a living organism) could ever be singled out and identified as myself. It should not come as a surprise that some Buddhist philosophers after having insisted upon the difference between self and consciousness, and after having defined the self as the possessor or owner of consciousness, argue that there is no such thing and that it can easily be eliminated without loss (Garfield 2015: 106, 129, cf. Siderits et al. 2011).

Let me add, that no proponent of the minimal account of self currently under consideration would present it as an exhaustive account of selfhood. Indeed, the label minimal (or thin) is partially employed in order to highlight how limited the notion is and how much more has to be said in order to account for the full-fledged human self (Zahavi 2014: 50). Consider, by comparison, the relation between the logically and ontogenetically primitive kind of self-consciousness that any phenomenal consciousness arguably entails and the more complex form of self-consciousness that one engages in when one is appraising how one is perceived by others. The former kind of self-consciousness might be necessary for the latter but it is certainly not sufficient. Likewise, although there is certainly more to being a human self than being an experiential self, the claim is that the latter is a necessary precondition, not only for self-conscious thinking and first-person self-reference, but also for mature selfhood (cf. Grünbaum and Zahavi 2013).

To sum up: Whereas distinguishing between for-me-ness, mineness, and me-ness might be helpful as long as the terms are defined in the specific way Guillot does, I am not persuaded by the claim that the for-me-ness that is part and parcel of phenomenal consciousness does not involve any sense of self. Moreover, had it not, I think it would have been a misnomer to label it for-*me*-ness.

29.3 Critiquing the Minimal Self

Over the years, the position just outlined has been subjected to various criticisms. One line of attack has been that the notion of a minimal self is too deflationary and that it is urgent to maintain the distinction between subjectivity and selfhood, since the requirements that must be met in order to qualify as a self are higher than those needed in order to be conscious or sentient. One way to bolster that line of criticism would be by arguing that selfhood is situated within the space of normativity, and that we come to have a perspective and thereby an identity of our own in virtue of our normative commitments and endorsements (see Frankfurt 1988; Rovane 2012). Another recent criticism has been that even though there is indeed something like a minimal self, existing accounts have underestimated the role of sociality, and failed to realize to what extent that self is interpersonally constituted (Ratcliffe 2017). In the following, however, I will focus on criticisms that in various ways engage with the universality question. If it is the case that our experiences are accompanied by a sense of self, is it then something that holds with necessity, such that it characterizes *all* experiences, however primitive or disordered they might be? Is it something that only holds for normal, adult, experiences? Or might it be something that only holds under rather special circumstances, say, when we reflectively scrutinize and appropriate our experiences?

Let me first consider the view of Howell and Thompson, who argue that experiences with for-me-ness are real but exceptional, and who more specifically defend what they call the *Unreflective Naive Transparency thesis*. On their account, our pre-reflective intentional life is so completely world-engaged that it remains entirely oblivious to itself. There is at that stage and on that level no room for any self-consciousness or for-me-ness; rather, experiential ownership is the outcome of a meta-cognitive operation that involves conceptual and linguistic resources. To suggest that experiences are always characterized by for-me-ness is in their view to fall prey to the so-called *refrigerator fallacy*, that is, thinking that the light is always on, simply because it is always on whenever we open the door of the refrigerator (Howell and Thompson 2017: 114; cf. Schear 2009).

Howell and Thompson are not disputing that it is a metaphysical fact and conceptual truth that experiences are owned in the sense of necessarily being someone's experiences. Nor are they disputing that individuals have a privileged access to their own experiential states in the sense that they enjoy a special kind of first-person authority vis-à-vis these states, which they lack when it comes to the experiential states of others. Their target is the claim that the presence of for-me-mess makes a difference to the overall phenomenal character of experience. And in their view, the attempt to define for-me-ness in terms of the distinct first-personal presence of experience (cf. Zahavi 2011: 59) conflates an epistemic point with a phenomenal one (Howell and Thompson 2017: 113). Indeed, they explicitly question whether the epistemic feature 'is phenomenally manifest, or...constitutes a feature of phenomenal character' (Howell and Thompson 2017: 111).

This is a somewhat surprising claim. Is it not rather odd to insist that the difference between my access to my own feeling of nausea (as it is subjectively lived through) and the access I have to your feeling of nausea (as it is displayed in your contorted facial expressions and verbal reports) is a difference with no phenomenal impact? Is there not an experiential, that is phenomenal, difference between being nauseous oneself and observing somebody else's nausea? Given their defence of the unreflective naïve transparency thesis, however, Howell and Thompson would presumably argue that pre-reflectively there is no difference in givenness between the experience that metaphysically belongs to me and the experience that metaphysically belongs to another. There is no such difference in givenness, since the experiences are not given pre-reflectively at all. They do not make any pre-reflective appearance. Creatures who do not possess (or do not yet possess) the cognitive sophistication to reflect upon their experiences will consequently remain oblivious to whatever experiential episodes they undergo, there will be nothing it is like for them to feel, say, nausea. Through reflection, however, and through the imposition of a theoretical framework on the original experience, we can lay claim to and appropriate the experience, and thereby bring it to givenness. As for the sense of self, it is precisely a product of rather than a condition for such appropriation (2017: 123). Howell and Thompson agree, of course, that very few are inclined to deny, upon reflection, that their experiences are theirs, but on their view, there is nothing phenomenal that motivates this appropriation (2017: 114).

For Howell and Thompson, it is consequently not the conscious episodes themselves that provide part of the justification for the subsequent self-ascription of the episodes in question. But if one denies that a reflective self-ascription such as 'I am nauseous' is based on experiential evidence, if one insists that it entirely lacks experiential grounding and is in no way answerable to experiential facts, it is difficult to see how one can then preserve and accommodate something like first-person authority. Ultimately, one must ask whether there is any fact of the matter that can constrain our higher-order beliefs. This seems to be a view Garfield approaches when he claims that it is a myth to think that there is 'a way our inner life is, independent of how we might imagine it' (Garfield 2016: 81).

Were our experience really completely anonymous, impersonal, and invisible when lived through, it is hard to understand how we could even start to target it in reflection, let alone appropriate it as ours, that is, imbue it with first-personal character. This is also why the obvious reply to the *refrigerator objection* is that it leaves it quite mysterious how our reflective gaze or monitoring stance could possibly have that kind of illuminating effect. At one point, Howell and Thompson argue that a mental state cannot be imbued with for-me-ness simply as a result of being the object of a further mental state. Rather, if awareness of awareness is to give rise to for-me-ness, 'the first order state' must already be 'imbued with some phenomenally apparent quality of mine-ness' (Howell and Thompson 2017: 119). I think this is exactly right. Their point is intended as a criticism of self-representationalism,[6] but it also affects their own proposal. If there is no phenomenal for-me-ness on the pre-reflective level, it is quite unclear how such a sense can arise in and through reflection.

Whereas Howell and Thompson want to restrict for-me-ness to experiences that are reflectively grasped, Dainton is more liberal. If I, say, look at a trout in the fishmonger's window, it would not be correct, according to Dainton, to describe my experience in

---

[6] As Garfield has pointed out, one can find an argument purporting to show why self-representationalism cannot escape the regress problem already in the work of the Buddhist philosopher Candrakīrti (570–650 CE). Either the reflexive awareness is awareness of a state that already possesses for-me-ness, and if so, for-me-ness is presupposed. Alternatively, the state is initially non-conscious, but acquires conscious for-me-ness by being self-directed. But if a higher-order state cannot imbue a first-order state with for-me-ness by taking it as an object, it is not clear why a non-conscious state should be able to generate conscious for-me-ness simply by taking itself as an object (Garfield 2015: 143–4). As Henrich once remarked, 'The circularity in the concept of such a self-related knowledge is not removed by attributing to it a quality of immediacy' (Henrich 1971: 13).

impersonal terms as 'trout-like object a few feet away', rather, if the description were to capture the experience, it would have to be something like 'trout-like object being looked at by *me*' (Dainton 2016: 121). But whereas Dainton is prepared to accept that ordinary experiences seem to be bound up with a sense of self, he is critical of the claim that the for-me-ness of experience is a primitive and irreducible feature, and he also challenges the claim that it is something that necessarily characterizes all conscious states (Dainton 2016: 129).[7]

In some places, Dainton suggests that it is the fact that a certain experience is *co-conscious* with my other experiences that clearly and unambiguously makes it belong to me (Dainton 2008: 242). Indeed, as he writes,

> Any sense I have that a typical experience is *experienced by a subject* when it occurs is due to the fact that this experience is co-conscious with certain other experiences, namely those comprising the inner component of the phenomenal background. The inner background largely constitutes *what it feels like to be me*, or so I have just argued. If so, then when the inner background is present, so too am *I*, phenomenologically speaking. Consequently, any experience which is co-conscious with the inner background will seem as though it is occurring to a subject (= me).   (Dainton 2008: 243)

Rather than being due to some irreducible feature, an experience consequently comes to possess ownership by being embedded within, and experienced together with, a multitude of other experiences that make up its inner background. If the background is present, 'so will my sense of (being a) self' (Dainton 2016: 123). In effect, Dainton is consequently offering a reductionist account of selfhood, where the sense of self is 'largely the resultant of the various specific forms of experience which jointly constitute the inner component of the phenomenal background: bodily sense-fields, conscious thinking, emotional feelings, mental images and mental acts of various kinds' (Dainton 2016: 124).

However, Dainton also proposes that the presentational and perspectival character of experience is partially explicable by certain *spatial* aspects of experience (Dainton 2016: 129). The reason that the tree you perceive seems to be presented *to you* is precisely that you yourself seem to have a determinate spatial location. Indeed, as Dainton writes 'The same applies more generally: in any perceiving, experiential contents of whatever type can only seem to be presented to a subject if the subject itself has the impression of being itself spatially related to what it is perceiving. Ordinary human phenomenal fields are thus

---

[7] In his article, Dainton remarks that Zahavi and Kriegel in a paper from 2016 offer some useful clarifications of their position, for instance, by making it clear that for-me-ness is not to be 'associated with a distinctive *quale* of its own, it is not an additional ingredient *in* experience that can occur on its own. Rather, it reflects *how* phenomenal contents are apprehended: whenever I experience something, I always experience it as presented *to me*' (Dainton 2016: 125). This is correct, but the very same clarification can already be found in earlier writings of mine (cf. Zahavi 2005: 124; Gallagher and Zahavi 2008: 50). More generally speaking, I find it regrettable that Guillot, Dainton, and Howell and Thompson, while discussing the Zahavi and Kriegel paper all fail to engage with Zahavi 2014, which the former article draws on, and which anticipates and addresses several of their subsequent criticisms.

centred rather than centreless' (Dainton 2016: 130). The emphasis must be on 'ordinary'. More primitive or exceptional creatures, be it newborn infants or a deaf and blind puppy floating in a well-heated capsule in outer space, would have bodily experiences, but the experiences in question would according to Dainton hardly be centred or presentational in any kind of way (2016: 139).

In addition to rejecting the proposal that the sense of self is a primitive and irreducible feature of experience, Dainton consequently also rejects the claim that it is a necessary a feature of all experiences. Whereas normal adult experience might indeed be centred and owned, there are not only primitive forms of experience, which lacks it, but also pathologically distorted forms of experience (such as can be found in Cotard's syndrome, in advanced stages of Alzheimer or in schizophrenic thought-insertion) where it is absent (2016: 126–7).

I will shortly return to the question of whether pathology provides us with exceptions to the claim that experiences are characterized by for-me-ness, and for now instead focus on the plausibility of Dainton's reductive explanation. Is it plausible to account for the first-personal presentational character of experience by appealing to certain spatial features? This attempt is somewhat reminiscent of the definition of a weak first-person perspective provided by Blanke and Metzinger, which they argue can be understood as 'a purely geometrical feature' of our visuospatial presentation of reality. When we perceive objects, we see objects as being to the right or left, further away or closer by. On this account, the weak first-person perspective is simply the zero-point of projection that functions as the geometrical origin of the 'seeing' organism's embodied perspective (Blanke and Metzinger 2009). The problem with this definition, and also with Dainton's own proposal, is that it does not at all target the relevant subjective or experiential character of the first-person perspective. Not only would a robot (or a non-conscious representational state) presumably also possess the weak first-person perspective in question, although there is nothing it is like for it to undergo such presentations, but consider also something as self-involving and first-personal as emotions. Consider feelings of joy, anger, jealousy, despair, or shame. It is somewhat hard to see how their first-personal character, their for-me-ness, could at all be explained or explicated with reference to the fact that the experiencing subject seems to have a determinate spatial location.

What about the more general ambition of trying to account for the sense of self by appealing to a certain network of experiences? There seem to be two ways to understand the claim. One option is that the inner components of the phenomenal background already possess for-me-ness and that the current experience then acquires for-me-ness by being associated with the background. But this would hardly constitute a reductive explanation. The alternative would be to claim that none of the experiences possesses intrinsic for-me-ness. They are all anonymous. And they then come to acquire for-me-ness by somehow being related to each other. But this proposal seems to run up against the same kind of problem that Cramer was addressing in the quotation given earlier. As Snowdon observes, 'how does the background help me appreciate I am having the experience in question, unless I already appreciate that the background is mine too?' (Snowdon 2016: 155).

29.4 Psychopathology

Whatever qualms one might have about Dainton's reductive explanation, he is certainly right, however, when remarking that the 'the full story concerning the "sense of ownership" is a complex and multifaceted one' (2016: 128). Even if one were to claim that for-me-ness is a feature of all experiential life, it would be implausible to deny that there is no relevant experiential difference between, say, being absorbed in a movie, daydreaming, playing Russian roulette, or being told that one has been sacked. When comparing such experiences, it should be evident to most that they are self-involving and self-conscious in different ways. To deny this is to distort phenomenology. Arguing that our experiential life is as such characterized by for-me-ness is, however, not to deny that we need to recognize a diversity of qualitatively different self-experiences. Indeed, the latter recognition is quite compatible with the view that there is also something that this diversity has in common.

In recent decades, the experiential reality of for-me-ness has become more widely accepted. The main issue of recent controversy concerns its scope and frequency. Whereas quite a few authors are now prepared to defend the view that self-experience is ubiquitous in normal life, the domain of psychopathology has often been considered to offer informative contrast cases. Even if consciousness and self are ordinarily tightly interwoven, their relation cannot be necessary and essential, the argument goes, since pathology offers relevant exceptions, that is, cases of experiences that lack for-me-ness altogether. In the literature, schizophrenic thought-insertion and severe depersonalization are among the most widely discussed cases. Whereas thought-insertion has been claimed to present cases of alienated conscious thoughts that lack mineness (Metzinger 2003: 334, 382, 445–6) or even taken to be thoughts that lack phenomenality and subjectivity altogether (Billon 2011: 306), severe depersonalization in its delusional form (Cotard syndrome) has been claimed to exemplify cases where 'the subjective character seems to recede from all mental states of which the patient is aware' (Billon 2014: 742). Whether these psychopathological phenomena really constitute relevant exceptions, that is, cases of experiences that phenomenologically speaking are nobody's, is, however, open to interpretation. As might be expected, much depends on how robustly one interprets the entailed notions of subjectivity, subjective character, mineness, etc.[8]

Guillot has proposed that her distinction between for-me-ness, me-ness, and mineness can be used to describe the different pathologies more accurately (2017: 26). She has resisted the claim that these pathological experiences are entirely deprived of subjective character. After all, the experiences are for the subjects undergoing them; they are given

---

[8] Whereas Billon initially argued that depersonalization provides evidence for the possibility of phenomenal consciousness without subjective character (Billon 2014), he has in more recent publications revised this interpretation and is now arguing that such experiences 'indicate the existence (and pathological alteration) of a form of self-experience' (Billon 2016: 17). His claim is consequently no longer that they lack basic self-awareness, but rather that their basic self-awareness is impaired (Billon 2016: 14).

to them in ways that are quite unlike how they are available to everybody else. More specifically, she argues that whereas the experiences of Cotard patients exemplify cases where for-me-ness is retained, but me-ness and mineness have been lost, schizophrenic experiences of inserted thoughts exhibit for-me-ness and me-ness, but no mineness (Guillot 2017: 44).

I have already expressed some doubts about the way Guillot defines these terms, but I think her basic intuition is sound (cf. Zahavi 2014: 39–41). The pathological experiences continue to be characterized by a subjective presence and a what-it-is-likeness that make them utterly unlike public objects that in principle are accessible in the same way to a plurality of subjects. Regardless of how alienated or distanced the patient feels vis-à-vis the experiences, the experiences do not manifest themselves entirely in the public domain—whatever the patients might be claiming. This is what most fundamentally make the experiences first-personal, and this is why even these pathological experiences retain their for-me-ness. On my understanding of the concept, this also entails that a certain dimension of self and self-awareness is preserved. But of course, denying that thought-insertion and depersonalization involve a complete effacement of self and self-awareness is not to deny that something is amiss. Parnas and Sass have described and defined schizophrenia as a self-disorder and argued that it involves a fragile and unstable first-person perspective. Unstable in what sense? In the sense that the for-me-ness of the patients has lost some of its normal obviousness, familiarity and unquestionability. It no longer effortlessly leads to or permits reflective self-ascription (Sass and Parnas 2003; Parnas and Sass 2011). James famously argued that our own present thoughts were characterized by a quality of 'warmth and intimacy' (James 1890: 239). This sense of endorsement and self-familiarity seems lost. We are indeed dealing with a kind of self-alienation or alienated self-consciousness, but as these phrasings also make clear, a dimension of self and self-consciousness remains (see also Henriksen, Parnas and Zahavi 2019).

29.5. Conclusion

In this chapter, I have attempted to explain and motivate the view that phenomenal consciousness, self-consciousness, and selfhood are constitutively interlinked. I have considered several recent objections that have been raised against the view. As my discussion has hopefully made clear, even if there might be a price to pay for upholding the essential for-me-ness of experience, its denial also comes with a price.

At the beginning of this chapter, I mentioned that the recent discussion of the relation between consciousness and self could be seen as involving a change of focus from diachronic to synchronic identity. Let me end by briefly acknowledging that the question of diachronicity has not entirely been lost from sight and in fact continues to be a somewhat contentious issue among defenders of a minimalist approach to selfhood. It is one thing to claim that an occurrent experience in virtue of its for-me-ness is self-involving and self-disclosing, but what does this tell us about the existence of an enduring and temporally extended self? Is the for-me-ness something that remains invariant across all other experiential changes? Is the for-me-ness something that remains identical between different experiences? Are two non-overlapping experiences that occur in the same stream of consciousness characterized by the very same for-me-ness? Or is the identity of the experiencer so tightly linked to the identity of the experience that the cessation of the experience entails the cessation of the experiential self? And the arising of a new experience, the birth of a new self? Different proposals currently available cover quite a range of options. Whereas Strawson has argued that each distinct experience has its own experiencer (Strawson 2009: 276), such that one and same human organism over its lifetime might be said to be inhabited by a vast multitude of ontologically distinct short-lived selves, I have previously argued that the experiential self should be identified with the ubiquitous dimension of first-personal character. Although it is not a separately existing entity, it is not reducible to any specific experience, but can be shared by a multitude of changing experiences (Zahavi 2014: 72–7). It falls outside the scope of the present chapter to engage properly with this topic, but it is worth emphasizing that disagreements concerning the duration of the self do not challenge or threaten the fundamental idea: that there is a thin experiential self at any given moment of experience.

References

Billon, A. (2011), 'Does consciousness entail subjectivity? The puzzle of thought insertion', *Philosophical Psychology*, 26/2: 291–314.

Billon, A. (2014), 'Why are we certain that we exist?', *Philosophy and Phenomenological Research*, 91/3: 723–59.

Billon, A. (2016), 'Basic Self-Awareness', *European Journal of Philosophy*, 25/3: 732–63.

Blanke, O. and Metzinger, T. (2009), 'Full-Body Illusions and Minimal Phenomenal Selfhood', *Trends in Cognitive Sciences*, 13/1, 7–13.

Cramer, K. (1974), '"Erlebnis". Thesen zu Hegels Theorie des Selbstbewusstseins mit Rücksicht auf die Aporien eines Grundbegriffs nachhegelscher Philosophie', in H.-G. Gadamer (ed.), *Stuttgarter Hegel-Tage 1970*. Bonn: Hegel-Studien. Beiheft 11, 537–603.

Dainton, B. (2008), *The Phenomenal Self*. Oxford: Oxford University Press.

Dainton, B. (2016), 'I—The Sense of Self', *Aristotelian Society Supplementary Volume*, 90/1, 113–43.

Dretske, F. (1995), *Naturalizing the Mind*. Cambridge, MA: MIT Press.

Dretske, F. (2003), 'How Do You Know You Are Not a Zombie?', in B. Gertler (ed.), *Privileged Access: Philosophical Accounts of Self-Knowledge*. Aldershot: Ashgate, 1–13.

Farrell, J. and T. McClelland (2017), 'Editorial: Consciousness and inner awareness', *Review of Philosophy and Psychology*, 8: 1–22.

Frankfurt, H. (1988), *The Importance of What We Care About: Philosophical Essays*. Cambridge: Cambridge University Press.

Gallagher, S. and Zahavi, D. (2008), *The Phenomenological Mind: An Introduction to Philosophy of Mind and Cognitive Science*. London: Routledge.

Garfield, J. L. (2015), *Engaging Buddhism: Why It Matters to Philosophy*. New York: Oxford University Press.

Garfield, J. L. (2016), 'Illusionism and Givenness', *Journal of Consciousness Studies*, 23/11–12: 73–82.

Grünbaum, T. and Zahavi, D. (2013), 'Varieties of Self-Awareness', in K. W. M. Fulford, M. Davies, R. Gipps, G. Graham, J. Sadler, G. Stanghellini, and T. Thornton (eds.), *The Oxford Handbook of Philosophy and Psychiatry*. Oxford: Oxford University Press, 221–39.

Guillot, M. (2017), '*I Me Mine*: on a Confusion Concerning the Subjective Character of Experience', *Review of Philosophy and Psychology*, 8: 23–53.

Henrich, D. (1971), 'Self-Consciousness, a Critical Introduction to a Theory', *Man and World*, 4: 3–28.

Henriksen, M. G., Parnas, J., and Zahavi, D. (2019), 'Thought insertion and disturbed for-me-ness (minimal selfhood) in schizophrenia', *Consciousness and Cognition*, 74: 102770.

Howell, R. J. and Thompson, B. (2017), 'Phenomenally Mine: In Search of the Subjective Character of Consciousness', *Review of Philosophy and Psychology*, 8: 103–27.

Hume, D. (2007). *A Treatise of Human Nature*. Oxford: Oxford University Press.

James, W. (1890), *The Principles of Psychology* (Vol. I–II). London: Macmillan and Co.

Kant, I. (1998). *The Critique of Pure Reason*. Cambridge: Cambridge University Press.

Kriegel, U. (2004), 'Consciousness and Self-Consciousness', *Monist*, 87/2, 182–205.

Kriegel, U. (2009), *Subjective Consciousness: A Self-Representational Theory*. Oxford: Oxford University Press.

Kriegel, U. (forthcoming), 'The Three Circles of Consciousness', in M. Guillot and M. Garcia-Carpintero (eds), *The Sense of Mineness*. Oxford: Oxford University Press.

Lichtenberg, G. C. (2000), *The Waste Books*, trans. R. J. Hollingdale. New York: The New York Review of Books.

Margolis, J. (1988), 'Minds, Selves, and Persons', *Topoi*, 7/1, 31–45.

Metzinger, T. (2003), *Being No One*. Cambridge, MA: MIT Press.

Nida-Rümelin, M. (2016), 'The experience property frame work: a misleading paradigm', *Synthese*, 195/8: 3361–87.

Parnas, J. and Sass, L. A. (2011), 'The Structure of Self-Consciousness in Schizophrenia', in S. Gallagher (ed.), *The Oxford Handbook of the Self*. Oxford: Oxford University Press, 521–46.

Prinz, J. (2012), 'Waiting for the Self', in J. Liu and J. Perry (eds), *Consciousness and the Self: New Essays*. Cambridge: Cambridge University Press, 123–49.

Ratcliffe, M. (2017), 'Selfhood, Schizophrenia, and the Interpersonal Regulation of Experience', in C. Durt, T. Fuchs, and C. Tewes (eds), *Embodiment, Enaction, and Culture: Investigating the Constitution of the Shared World*. Cambridge, MA: MIT Press, 149–71.

Rovane, C. (2012), 'Does Rationality Enforce Identity?', in A. Coliva (ed.), *The Self and Self Knowledge*. Oxford: Oxford University Press, 17–38.

Rowlands, M. (2015), 'Sartre on pre-reflective consciousness: The adverbial interpretation', in S. Miguens, G. Preyer, and C. B. Morando (eds), *Pre-reflective Consciousness. Sartre and Contemporary Philosophy of Mind*. London: Routledge, 101–19.

Sartre, J.-P. (2003), *Being and Nothingness: An Essay in Phenomenological Ontology*, trans. H. E. Barnes. London and New York: Routledge.

Sass, L. A. and Parnas, J. (2003), 'Schizophrenia, Consciousness, and the Self', *Schizophrenia Bulletin*, 29/3: 427–44.

Schear, J. K. (2009), 'Experience and Self-Consciousness', *Philosophical Studies*, 144/1, 95–105.

Searle, J. R. (2005), 'The Self as a Problem in Philosophy and Neurobiology', in T. E. Feinberg and J. P. Keenan (eds), *The Lost Self: Pathologies of the Brain and Identity*. Oxford: Oxford University Press, 7–19.

Siderits, M., Thompson, E., and Zahavi, D. (eds) (2011), *Self, No Self? Perspectives from Analytical, Phenomenological, and Indian Traditions*. Oxford: Oxford University Press.

Snowdon, P. F. (2016), 'Dainton on Subjects of Experience', *Aristotelian Society Supplementary Volume*, 90/1: 145–59.

Strawson, G. (1994), *Mental Reality*. Cambridge, MA: The MIT Press.

Strawson, G. (2009), *Selves: An Essay in Revisionary Metaphysics*. Oxford: Oxford University Press.

Strawson, G. (2011), 'The Minimal Subject', in S. Gallagher (ed.), *The Oxford Handbook of the Self*. Oxford: Oxford University Press, 253–78.

Strawson, G. (2017), *The Subject of Experience*. Oxford: Oxford University Press.

Thiel, U. (2011), *The Early Modern Subject: Self-Consciousness and Personal Identity from Descartes to Hume*. Oxford: Oxford University Press.

Van Gulick, R. (2000), 'Inward and Upward: Reflection, Introspection, and Self-Awareness', *Philosophical Topics*, 28/2: 275–305.

Zahavi, D. (1999), *Self-Awareness and Alterity: A Phenomenological Investigation*. Evanston, IL: Northwestern University Press.

Zahavi, D. (2000), 'Self and Consciousness', in D. Zahavi (ed.), *Exploring the Self*. Amsterdam: John Benjamins Publishing Company, 55–74.

Zahavi, D. (2004), 'Back to Brentano?', *Journal of Consciousness Studies*, 11/10–11: 66–87.

Zahavi, D. (2005), *Subjectivity and Selfhood: Investigating the First-Person Perspective*. Cambridge, MA: The MIT Press.

Zahavi, D. (2009), 'Is the self a social construct?', *Inquiry*, 52/6: 551–73.

Zahavi, D. (2011), 'The Experiential Self: Objections and Clarifications', in M. Siderits, E. Thompson, and D. Zahavi (eds), *Self, No Self? Perspectives from Analytical, Phenomenological, & Indian Traditions*. Oxford: Oxford University Press, 56–78.

Zahavi, D. (2014), *Self and Other: Exploring Subjectivity, Empathy, and Shame*. Oxford: Oxford University Press.

Zahavi, D. (2018), 'Consciousness, Self-consciousness, Selfhood: a reply to some critics', *Review of Philosophy and Psychology*, 9/3: 703–18.

Zahavi, D. and Kriegel, U. (2016), 'For-Me-Ness: What It Is and What It Is Not', in D. O. Dahlstrom, A. Elpidorou, and W. Hopp (eds), *Philosophy of Mind and Phenomenology: Conceptual and Empirical Approaches*. London: Routledge, 36–53.

CHAPTER 30

CONSCIOUSNESS AND MORALITY

JOSHUA SHEPHERD AND NEIL LEVY

30.1 INTRODUCTION

IT is well known that the nature of consciousness is elusive, and that attempts to understand it generate problems in metaphysics, philosophy of mind, psychology, and neuroscience. Less appreciated are the important—even if still elusive—connections between consciousness and issues in ethics. In this chapter we consider three such connections. First, we consider the relevance of consciousness for questions surrounding an entity's moral status. Second, we consider the relevance of consciousness for questions surrounding moral responsibility for action. Third, we consider the relevance of consciousness for the acquisition of moral knowledge.

This is a disparate set of connections, prompting a question. Is there anything *about consciousness* these connections have in common? One might expect the answer to be no. After all, it is frequently noted that when used without qualification, the term 'consciousness' has multiple potential referents. Perhaps the central notion of consciousness is phenomenal consciousness—the kind of consciousness associated with 'what-it-is-like-ness'. Arguably separate is Ned Block's (1995) notion of access consciousness. As Block has it, access consciousness refers to an explicitly functional, dispositional feature of psychological entities—the availability of information to the psychological mechanisms and systems responsible for things like thinking, reasoning, planning, and action control. Building on access consciousness (and arguably on phenomenal consciousness), a third usage of consciousness refers to *self*-consciousness: that is, roughly, the capacity to think of oneself as oneself, and to think of features of oneself *as* features of oneself. Finally, a fourth usage of consciousness refers to what David Rosenthal has called creature consciousness. As Rosenthal has it, creature consciousness 'consists in a creature's not being unconscious—that is, roughly, its not being asleep or knocked out' (2002: 406).

The distinction between phenomenal, access, creature, and self-consciousness is a start, but it does not exhaust the conceptual space. Various aspects of consciousness may be individually relevant to various moral issues. For example, phenomenal consciousness is a variegated phenomenon, encompassing modalities of perceptual experience, types of cognitive and agentive experience, emotional experience, the experience of pleasure and pain, and so on. Access and self-consciousness often combine to enable a range of sophisticated psychological capacities, including various forms of attention and memory. What is more, our higher psychological capacities depend on background systems that mediate degrees of functioning of these capacities, leading to talk of *modes* or *levels* of consciousness (Bayne et al. 2016). A full assessment of the relevance of consciousness to morality must take account not only of the kinds of consciousness that exist, but of various aspects of these kinds as well.

Given the complexity these various distinctions suggest, one might plausibly expect that the disparate nature of the connections we discuss in this chapter is due to the fact that different senses or aspects of 'consciousness' are at work in each area. As we will see, this is one possibility. But debate in each area has thus far failed to settle just what about consciousness is so intuitively important for moral status, moral responsibility, and moral knowledge. Given this fact, it remains possible that there is some common connection of these different issues in ethics to consciousness. We take up this possibility in this chapter's conclusion.

30.2 Moral Status

Moral status is a property (or set of properties) an entity has in virtue of which it deserves or has the right to certain kinds of treatment. The specific content of these rights may vary depending on one's more specific moral theory, and may vary as well depending on the kind of entity in question. But, at a minimum, moral status is thought to generate prima facie reasons against harming or killing an entity, as well as prima facie reasons against frustrating its interests.

Why think consciousness is relevant to moral status? Consider the fraught set of moral and legal issues concerning patients who apparently lack consciousness. Following traumatic brain injury, stroke, or disease, some patients enter into a coma before awakening into a state in which they are unresponsive to external stimuli. They fail to give any overt sign of responsiveness to their own name or to visual stimuli, despite a lack of impairment in their sensory systems. These patients are said to be in a persistent vegetative state (PVS). Patients may remain in such a state for decades, dependent for their survival on the provision of tube feeding.

Almost everyone (see Gomes et al. 2016), including most medical professionals, hold that these patients lack consciousness (patients who exhibit some, often inconsistent, degree of responsiveness to stimuli are held to be *minimally conscious*, see Giacino et al. 2002). They are also often held to lack an interest in continuing to live. Family members have sometimes petitioned courts to allow the withdrawal of tube feeding, perhaps because they believe that sustaining them in this condition is incompatible with the dignity of a human being (where possessing dignity is an inalienable status, and arguably not one that depends on being conscious at a time—or, indeed, being alive). Courts have sometimes ordered hospitals to withdraw life support in these conditions, indicating that judges often accept that PVS entails a greatly reduced interest in continuing to live.

We might hold that the dramatic reduction in an interest in living is due not to the (putative) lack of consciousness, but instead to the patients' lack of a capacity to engage in worthwhile activities (cf. Sinnott-Armstrong and Miller 2013). However, the excitement produced by recent work indicating that some (almost certainly a very small) proportion of patients who are entirely unresponsive to external stimuli are in fact conscious suggests that the possession of consciousness plays a significant role in explaining our intuitions here. In an important initial study (Owen et al. 2006), fMRI was used to compare the neural correlates of instruction following in (conscious) controls to the brain scans of PVS patients given the same instructions (the instructions given were to imagine playing tennis and to imagine visiting every room in one's house). The brain scans of one patient were indistinguishable from those of healthy controls. Owen et al. interpret this as evidence of consciousness, on the (largely implicit) grounds that consciousness is required for instruction following (see Bayne 2013 for a defence of this claim). Later work by the same team provided stronger evidence for the possession of consciousness by a different PVS patient: this patient used the instruction following paradigm to answer yes/no questions (Monti et al. 2010).[1]

The general reaction to these studies clearly indicated that very many people understood evidence of preserved consciousness in PVS patients as evidence that they possess a higher moral status than we had previously thought. If this intuition is justified—if the possession of consciousness makes a very large difference to the moral status of entities—important conclusions follow, not only with regard to how we ought to treat people who have suffered brain injuries but also for other questions. For instance, the moral status of non-human animals, or of artificial intelligences, might depend on whether they possess consciousness (and perhaps on the degree of consciousness they possess, if consciousness is graded). But is the intuition justified?

This depends in part on the kind or aspect of consciousness at issue. Though there has been little systematic investigation of the question, many people seem to hold that it is the possession of phenomenal consciousness, or perhaps of a capacity for phenomenal consciousness, that underwrites a serious sort of moral status (for some discussion, see Seager 2001; Kahane and Savulescu 2009; Shepherd 2016). Jeff Sebo (2015) offers an articulation of this often-implicit view that he calls sentientism about moral status:

---

[1] One might take issue with this interpretation of the evidence. One of us has expressed doubts that evidence of instruction following is sufficiently strong evidence of the possession of consciousness to outweigh the evidence constituted by PVS patients' overt unresponsiveness (Levy 2014a; Davies and Levy 2016).

(a) If you are sentient, then you have interests (where we can understand interests in terms of present subjective motivational states), (b) if you have interests, then you are capable of being harmed (where we can understand harm in terms of interest-frustration), (c) if you are capable of being harmed, then moral agents have at least a prima facie moral duty not to harm you, and (d) if moral agents have at least a prima facie moral duty not to harm you, then you have at least a prima facie moral right, against these moral agents, not to be harmed. (Sebo 2015: 9)

This articulation is useful, but it raises questions. For example, why think sentience is necessary for the possession of present subjective motivational states? And why think possession of such states is sufficient for the capacity to be harmed as well as the generation of prima facie rights against such harm?

One attractive line of thought appeals to the intrinsic value of at least some phenomenal mental states. Although the notion of intrinsic value remains somewhat controversial, a number of philosophers have argued that at least pleasure is intrinsically valuable, and at least pain intrinsically disvaluable (e.g., Goldstein 1989; Feldman 1997; Rachels 2000; Kahane 2009). For expository purposes, it will be useful to focus on one version of such a view. According to Guy Kahane the kind of value we ought to associate with experiences of suffering (which he takes to be a composite of pain and a kind of experienced attitude of dislike), is *objective* in nature.[2] Its badness is not dependent on any contingent attitudes towards it a subject may have. Rather, the existence of a state of suffering gives one a prima facie moral reason to end that state, whether the sufferer is oneself or someone else.

One of Kahane's arguments for this view involves an appeal to the inconceivability of a kind of hedonic inversion. Kahane has us consider the claim that, on his view of suffering's badness, 'suffering's badness supervenes on the character of an agent's total experiential state' (2009: 333). To deny this would be to allow hedonic inversion: 'that I could be in the same total experiential state I am in when suffering from excruciating pain, yet that this state may not be bad at all, or may even be intensely enjoyable and thus good' (2009: 334). But, as Kahane notes, this 'is not a suggestion we can make sense of' (2009: 334). As Kahane is aware, the truth of his supervenience claim does not establish the further claim that suffering is intrinsically bad *because* of its phenomenal character. But Kahane notes, not unfairly, that this further claim looks to be the best explanation we have got for the truth of the supervenience claim.

We take it, then, that a Kahane-style view—that is, a view that ascribes objective value to at least some phenomenally conscious states—is at least defensible. In order to get from objectivism about the value of (at least some) phenomenal states to a view about moral status, one needs a further step. One needs to claim that the bearers of objective value merit certain types of treatment in virtue of the value they bear. Fortunately, this is a plausible claim. If a psychological subject bears objective value in possessing the capacity to enter into valuable mental states, then it seems that this subject merits certain types of

---

[2] In this connection, see also Charles Siewert's arguments in support of the claim that 'we value our own and others' possession of phenomenal features' (1998: 311).

treatment in virtue of this capacity. Further, it seems that this treatment ought to be sensitive in particular to the properties of the subject that have to do with its capacity to enter into pleasurable states. Prima facie, we ought not frustrate the subject's attempts to enter into such states, and prima facie we ought not cause the subject to move out of these states into non- or disvaluable states.

On this view, then, an entity's moral status is further explicated in terms of that entity's meriting certain kinds of treatment. And this treatment is further explicated in terms of sensitivity to the objective value that the entity bears. It emerges that an entity's moral status is closely related to, and mediated by, the kind and amount of objective value it bears. This raises questions that go beyond the scope of the present chapter. For example, what aspects of phenomenally conscious states constitute objective value? Kahane's view focuses on the disvalue of suffering, which is a composite of pain and dislike directed at the pain. Is it possible to generalize Kahane's arguments beyond suffering? Is there anything more to be said about the phenomenal state of dislike? In virtue of what does it count as dislike? Is it best thought of as a conscious desire, or emotion, or something else? Going beyond Kahane's specific view, how are we to think about the relationship between an entity's conscious mental life and the *degree* of moral status we attribute to it? Answering such questions seems an important task for objectivists about the value of phenomenal consciousness. Even without such answers, however, one might find objectivism an attractive way to make good on the intuition that phenomenal consciousness in some way undergirds moral status.

Attractive, but certainly not irresistible. Indeed, regarding the relationship between phenomenal consciousness and moral status, we are of two minds. One of us has suggested that the intuition that consciousness is necessary for a very serious interest in life is no mistake, but it is *access* consciousness and not phenomenal consciousness that plays this role (Levy and Savulescu 2009; Levy 2014b). In this view, the capacity to have future-oriented desires and plans and to care about how one's life goes is required for the kind of moral status that adult human beings typically possess and many non-humans lack, and this capacity depends on access consciousness. Information must be sufficiently available for rational thought and deliberation in order for a being to be able to have future-oriented desires or to conceive of itself as persisting in time, and this depends on the possession of access consciousness. Further, the states about which we care and which *constitute* one's life going well are themselves (at least) largely informational states, not phenomenal states. Indeed, many of the roles that we might think can be played by phenomenal states alone (responding to the aesthetic qualities of art or of the world; having a sense of satisfaction that one's desires are satisfied; even having *experiences* of satisfaction) may be occupied by informational states rather than phenomenal. On this line of thought, phenomenal consciousness may underwrite an interest in having pleasant experiences and avoiding unpleasant ones, but it will fail to contribute much in the way of moral status. For it will not underwrite an interest in having a life.

Moving beyond discussion of access and phenomenal consciousness, a common assumption in the practical ethics literature is that an interest in having a life, or even significant interests in the future, rest on the possession of self-consciousness. According to Peter Singer, for example:

> Beings that are conscious, but not self-conscious, on the other hand, more nearly approximate the image of receptacles for experiences of pleasure and pain, because their preferences will be of a more immediate sort.... They will not have desires that project their images of their own existence into the future. Their conscious states are not internally linked over time. (Singer 2011: 112)

If this is right, then one might point to self-consciousness as the kind of consciousness that underwrites full moral status. Doing so would have important ramifications for our treatment of many non-human animals, and perhaps for those diagnosed as minimally conscious. For it is not obvious that the minimally conscious retain self-consciousness. One of us has argued, however, that this view of self-consciousness is misguided (Shepherd 2017). Arguably, self-consciousness is not on its own important for moral significance. Instead, its significance emerges along with a suite of psychological capacities that enable high-level cognitive sophistication: features like cognitive and attentional control and the coordination of perception, imagination, memory, and so on. If this is right, a satisfying account of moral status and of the psychological features that mediate its degrees might need to consider the significance of degrees of cognitive sophistication, and perhaps the significance of a closely related notion, namely, that of the levels or modes of consciousness available to a being (for related discussions, see Rowlands 2012; Varner 2012).

30.3 MORAL RESPONSIBILITY

As with moral status, many participants in debates about moral responsibility seem to have implicitly assumed that consciousness is necessary for an agent to be praise- or blameworthy for their actions (Sher 2009). And like the assumption that consciousness is necessary for a serious sort of moral status, this implicit assumption did not receive very much attention until relatively recently. Explicit attention has been motivated by two very different sets of considerations. On the one hand, work in neuroscience and in psychology has been widely interpreted as suggesting that if consciousness is necessary for moral responsibility, agents are never morally responsible for their actions (see Shepherd 2015 for a review of this work). Independently of this work, motivated more by thought experiments and by cases they find in literature, some philosophers have advanced positions according to which consciousness is at most a proxy for the kinds of conditions which are genuinely necessary for moral responsibility.

The most famous experimental results that have been seen as casting doubt on the capacity of actual human agents to satisfy a consciousness condition on moral responsibility stem from the groundbreaking work of Benjamin Libet. In a classic experiment, he had subjects monitor the position of a dot that travelled very rapidly around the circumference of an oscilloscope, and note its position when they felt the 'urge' to move their hand. At the same time, he measured electrical potentials in participants' brains; in particular, the ramping up of the so-called 'readiness potential', which is known to proceed voluntary action. This paradigm allowed him to generate relatively precise timings for the occurrence of the conscious urge to move and the neural activity reliably correlated with actual movement. Libet found that the readiness potential *preceded* participants' reported awareness of the intention to move by around 350 ms. These results have widely, though controversially, been interpreted as demonstrating that the conscious intention to move is epiphenomenal in action initiation. If it is epiphenomenal, it seems unlikely to be able to ground moral responsibility.

Libet's experiments have been widely and devastatingly criticized on multiple grounds (see, especially, Mele 2009). Its methodological flaws aside, it is difficult to see how they might constitute a serious challenge to the claim that consciousness is a necessary condition of moral responsibility. Libet's evidence concerns (at best) consciousness of the proximal intention which actually initiates an action. Morally responsible actions at least typically take time: even spontaneous actions like rushing to push a child out of the way of an oncoming car typically take much longer than 350 ms. They are often the upshot of conscious deliberation, in which the agent is responsive to reasons. Our capacity to weigh reasons for and against our actions may ground our moral responsibility, and this capacity may require consciousness. It is hard to see how a failure to be conscious of one's reasons precisely when one forms an intention to act could make a difference to one's responsibility.

If the gap between brain events that cause our actions and our consciousness of our having committed ourselves to action were much bigger, then our moral responsibility would indeed be threatened. It would be threatened because such a gap would entail that we have greatly impaired reasons-responsiveness: we could not respond to a reason that might present itself after the relevant brain event. Soon et al. (2008) produced evidence that has been interpreted as demonstrating such a gap between intention generation and conscious awareness. In this experiment, subjects chose which of two buttons to press. Patterns of activation in parietal and prefrontal cortex predicted the choice, with around 60 per cent accuracy, an average of 7 seconds prior to the action. The researchers took this to be evidence that the 'subjective experience of freedom is no more than an illusion' (Soon et al. 2008: 543). A little reflection should be sufficient to show that this conclusion rests on a claim that is obviously false: that the agent is unresponsive to reasons that arise once the relevant neural activity has occurred. Were it true that human agents could not respond to reasons which occur less than 7 seconds prior to action, everyday activities like driving a car would be completely impossible. The neural activity in parietal and prefrontal cortex cannot be the correlates of an irrevocable decision. More likely, they are correlates of an inclination (cf. Shepherd 2015).

More persuasive reasons for rejecting the claim that consciousness is required for moral responsibility stem from within moral philosophy. Philosophers like Arpaly (2002) and Smith (2005) have presented thought experiments which they argue show that we do not need to be conscious either of the facts that make our actions morally significant or the moral significance of these facts in order to be morally responsible for our actions. Consider the familiar case of Huck Finn. As the case is commonly understood, Huck helps Jim, a fleeing slave, evade pursuit despite believing that morally he ought to turn Jim in. According to Arpaly, Huck is morally praiseworthy for his action despite failing to be conscious (under an appropriate description) of the facts that make his actions right or (a fortiori) of the fact that they are right. If consciousness of facts about our actions were to be necessary for our being praiseworthy, the only plausible candidates are surely consciousness of the facts that make the action right or consciousness of the fact that it is right; in the absence of consciousness of these facts, we should regard our disposition to attribute praise as a strong reason to think that consciousness of any particular facts is not necessary for moral responsibility, she suggests.

Smith presents a different kind of case, in which an agent is blameworthy despite her failing to be conscious of any relevant facts. In her case, an agent omits to ring a friend to wish her happy birthday because she simply forgets. Clearly, she is not conscious of the fact that it is her friend's birthday, or of the fact that there is some action she ought to perform: she has forgotten the first, and only if she recalls the first can she be aware of the second. Again, there are no mental states to which the agent has (occurrent) access which could plausibly ground the agent's moral responsibility. If she is indeed blameworthy, as Smith suggests (directly blameworthy, that is, and not in virtue of her failure to take steps to ensure that she did not forget her obligation), it appears that moral responsibility does not require consciousness of any particular facts. Like the Huck Finn case, Smith's example is designed to show that access to certain kinds of information is not required for moral responsibility.

This talk of access to information might be taken to suggest that the kind of consciousness at issue in these examples is access consciousness rather than phenomenal consciousness. Certainly in the moral responsibility literature this has often been (implicitly) assumed. But one should be careful here. According to many philosophers, phenomenal consciousness plays cognitively significant roles for psychological subjects, including the role of providing access to information. We discuss ways it has been thought to do so later in this section.

Other kinds of evidence might be seen to support the contention that consciousness—whether access or phenomenal—is not required for moral responsibility. Agents sometimes perform morally significant actions (up to and including killing others) in states in which they appear to lack consciousness (such as somnambulism). Their capacity to perform complex actions in these states, including driving a car over long distances or playing a musical instrument, might suggest that their lack of consciousness does not excuse them: if consciousness is not necessary for the kind of reasons-responsiveness exemplified in successful driving of a car, why should it be necessary for moral responsibility? These cases seem to indicate that not even *creature* consciousness is needed for moral responsibility (Suhler and Churchland 2009).

However, we shall suggest that the conclusion that neither source of evidence—neither the thought experiments cited by philosophers like Arpaly and Smith, nor the evidence showing that agents can exhibit impressive reasons-responsiveness in the absence of creature consciousness—constitutes a persuasive case that consciousness is not needed for moral responsibility. The intuitions generated by both sources of evidence depend for their power on folk conceptions of what consciousness is and what it does. If consciousness plays different roles instead of or as well as the roles ascribed to it folk psychologically, then the intuitions generated by thought experiments and the contemplation of actual cases may be off track. We shall suggest that this is indeed the case: a better understanding of the role consciousness and conscious states play makes it very plausible that they are required for moral responsibility.

Levy (2014a) argues that the impressive degree of reasons-responsiveness exhibited by agents who lack creature consciousness is dependent on the prior acquisition of motor and perceptual routines. The agent has acquired overlearned scripts for responding to the kinds of reasons that typically confront the driver, or the piano player. The acquisition of these scripts themselves seems to require consciousness. There is evidence that acquiring new skills involves large areas of the cortex that are plausibly correlates of consciousness, whereas once these skills are acquired the regions activated by performance shrink significantly (Haier et al. 1992; Raichle et al. 1994). Even implicit learning, such as the unconscious extraction of patterns from data, seems to require consciousness; the subject must be conscious of the stimuli, even though she need not be conscious of the pattern she implicitly learns (Baars 2002). If it is the case that the acquisition of such scripts requires consciousness, it may be that agents are indirectly responsible for actions they cause: responsible in virtue of having (consciously) acquired these scripts.

Consciousness, Levy argues, constitutes or enables a *global (neuronal) workspace* (Baars 1997; Dehaene and Naccache 2001; Dehaene et al. 2011), which is required for the agent to assess actions and their predicted consequences against their own values, plans, and projects. Building on Fischer and Ravizza (1998), a strong case can be mounted for the claim that the lack of a capacity to respond to these reasons appropriately entails a lack of the kind of control required for moral responsibility. Further, because the resulting behaviour is not assessed against the agents' own values and projects, it does not seem to be expressive of their quality of will. It seems to follow that given the truth of either control-based accounts or of quality of will-based accounts of moral responsibility (by far the most popular accounts of moral responsibility in the literature), agents are not responsible for the novel actions they perform in the absence of creature consciousness.

Similar considerations seem to entail that agents are not responsible for their actions in the kinds of cases that feature in the work of Arpaly, Smith, and those who follow or parallel them. Though these agents are conscious, an absence of consciousness of particular facts entails an absence of the capacity to assess the moral significance of the actions against their own values and projects. This, in turn, entails a dramatic reduction of control and of the degree to which the action is expressive of the agent's quality of will, and this in turns seems to constitute strong grounds for excusing them (but cf. Sripada 2015).

On Levy's view, then, it is a necessary condition on (direct) moral responsibility that an agent have control-enabling access to the facts that give her action its moral significance. This view has been influential in the moral responsibility literature. But there may be reasons to explore conceptual space beyond that covered by Levy's view. Levy's consciousness thesis depends on a particular view of consciousness (the global workspace view) that Levy ties explicitly to access consciousness. But, first, a number of other views of consciousness are on offer, generating curiosity regarding the relevance of these views to moral responsibility. Second, most proposed views of consciousness, including the global workspace view, aim to explain—or at least contribute to an explanation of—not just access consciousness, but phenomenal consciousness as well. Third, Levy's consciousness thesis states only a necessary connection. It would thus be consistent with Levy's view if another aspect or kind of consciousness turned out to be important in some way for moral responsibility. Restricting one's attention to access consciousness is fair play, but it seems there is ample motivation for considering the relationship between phenomenal consciousness and moral responsibility.

Interestingly, work on an ancillary issue may here be relevant. Within moral epistemology a number of philosophers have advanced the view that phenomenal consciousness is important for the acquisition of moral knowledge—including, in some cases, knowledge of moral reasons for action. Although these philosophers have not to our knowledge explicitly considered the relevance of their views to moral responsibility, the connection is apparent. With this in mind, we turn to this literature next. Our initial aim will be to understand the proposed relevance of phenomenal consciousness to moral knowledge (which is an interesting issue in its own right). With such an understanding in hand, we return to the issue of moral responsibility.

30.4 Moral Knowledge

To see why phenomenal consciousness is thought to be relevant to moral knowledge, let us consider a recent proposal regarding the way conscious experiences lend epistemic force to the beliefs formed on their basis. According to Susanna Siegel, perceptual experiences are *epistemically charged*, where an experience's charge is a property 'in virtue of which a subject's having the experience by itself redounds on the subject's rational standing' (2015: 291). For Siegel, the perceptual experiences an agent has make a pro tanto contribution to the rational standing of the agent. And the perceptual experiences an agent has make a pro tanto contribution (usually positive, sometimes negative) to beliefs formed on the basis of these experiences.

What is important about phenomenal consciousness here? Siegel gets at this question by way of another—what she calls the grounding question. In virtue of what, Siegel asks, do experiences have any epistemic charge at all (2015: 294)? Her answer involves appeal, initially, to the idea that experiences no less than beliefs can form a part of an epistemic subject's outlook or perspective on the world.

> What might ground the rational standing of belief, and could that factor also ground the rational standing of experience? A natural idea is that what grounds the rational

standing of both states is their role in the mind. Perhaps there is no further feature of belief, or routes to belief, that explains why beliefs can be evaluated as epistemically better or worse. Instead, it is their role as states that contribute to our outlook on the world. (Siegel 2015: 286)

Siegel does not wish to claim that every type of experience contributes to one's outlook. Rather, for Siegel it is perceptual experiences that paradigmatically play this role. And they do so in virtue of a feature of their phenomenal character. Siegel claims that perceptual experiences have a presentational phenomenal character. This is a character that 'purports to characterize how things in the external world are' (2015: 295). The thought appears to be that in possessing this presentational character, one's perceptual experiences strongly suggest that their contents are true. When one perceives a blue sky with a single cloud, one's experience presents the sky as actually blue, and as actually containing one cloud. Confronted with such an experience, one finds it very difficult to avoid believing that the sky is blue, and that there is one cloud in it. Nor, in the usual case, should one make any effort to avoid believing those things—in the normal case we have 'substantial epistemic support' for 'believing our eyes' (2015: 298).[3] Going beyond Siegel, then, but in our view consistent with what she says, we might say that in being presentational, perceptual experience commits the perceiver to the existence of what is presented.

So one aspect of some phenomenally conscious experiences—their presentational character—is argued to play a critical epistemic role. How does this relate to moral knowledge? If one can add to this view a further view about the contents of perceptual experience, one might think that perceptual experience plays critical roles for moral epistemology as well. We have in mind here recent proposals to the effect that 'at least some moral properties can be part of the contents of perceptual experience' (Werner 2016: 298). According to proponents of moral perception, perceptual experience presents us not only with events, objects, and their properties situated in time and space in certain ways. Perceptual experience presents these events and objects as morally good or bad, right or wrong, and it does so, arguably, in a way that underwrites moral judgment, affords non-inferential moral knowledge, and allows for moral improvement (McGrath 2004; Cullison 2010; McBrayer 2010;Audi 2013; Werner 2016).

Preston Werner's argument for moral perception is explicitly phenomenological, involving appeal to contrast cases. Consider Norma, a normal adult, and Pathos, who suffers from an empathic dysfunction. Werner has Norma and Pathos see some young people pouring gasoline on a cat. According to Werner, due to Pathos's empathic dysfunction, his experience will lack a certain strong phenomenological component tracked by features such as skin conductance response, elevated heart rate, and more. Werner argues that there is a phenomenal contrast between Norma's and Pathos's experience, and

---

[3] As Siegel notes, a similar view cast explicitly in terms of prima facie justification is defended at length by so-called phenomenal conservatives (Huemer 2001) or dogmatists (Pryor 2000). Further, John Bengson (2015) has recently offered a proposal regarding the epistemic force of conscious intuitions that appeals to their presentational character.

that 'the best explanation is a difference in the perception of moral properties—Norma's experience represents the cat's burning as *bad*, whereas Pathos's does not' (Werner 2016: 304).

The thesis of moral perception is not without problems. First, as proponents of moral perception recognize, they are committed to a controversial view about the contents of perceptual experience. This is the view that perceptual experience contains high-level content. As Tim Bayne explicates the view,

> We see objects as belonging to various high-level kinds, and this... is part and parcel of perception's phenomenal content. On this view, what it's like to see a tomato, taste a strawberry or hear a trumpet is not limited to the representation of various sensory qualities but also the representation of various 'high-level' properties—being a tomato, a strawberry or a trumpet.   (Bayne 2009: 385)

However, many philosophers argue that perceptual experience presents us only with low-level properties such as color, shape, movement, pitch, volume, and so on (Tye 1995, Lyons 2005). If all perceptual experience presents are low-level properties, then moving beyond these to mental states with contents as of tomatoes et al. will in some sense represent a cognitive, rather than a perceptual, achievement.

A second worry is perhaps more pressing. In an illuminating discussion, Jack McBrayer calls this worry *The Looks Objection*. Here is one way (among others) that McBrayer expresses it.

> What bothers some about the possibility of moral perception seems to be the following: acts that are morally wrong often look just like acts that are morally permissible, where by 'look' we mean something like 'have the very same phenomenology.' When I see one person shoot another in an alley, the act could have been an act of senseless violence (and thus morally wrong) or an act of self-defense (and thus morally permissible). In either case, it would have looked the same to me.   (McBrayer 2010: 318)

In response, McBrayer invokes analogies with other high-level facts. Hot things, for example, do not generate the very same phenomenology across cases. What is needed, McBrayer claims, are looks that normally correlate with the relevant instantiated facts: 'in order to have a perceptual experience as if X is F, things that look like *this* (where the "this" picks out a certain phenomenology) are normally (but not always) F' (2010: 318–19).

It is not clear, however, whether this response adequately addresses the looks objection. It might be true that we perceive some high-level facts in the way McBreyer suggests. But what we want to know is whether we do so with respect to moral facts. Here, the proponent of moral perception must say something about the aspect of perceptual phenomenology that plays the role of McBrayer's 'this'. What kind of phenomenology is at issue, and how ought we to understand it?[4]

---

[4] There are many ways one might seek to do so. Robert Cowan (2015) develops a response to the Looks Objection that emphasizes the influence of a kind of cognitive penetration on the relevant perceptual

One option is to leave moral perception at just this point in favor of a broader thesis. Consider the possibility that, even if perceptual experience alone cannot present the agent with moral properties or afford prima facie justification for beliefs with moral content, non-perceptual forms of conscious experience may do so. In particular, recent writers have emphasized the importance of intuitions—conceived as a type of phenomenally conscious experience[5]—to moral judgment and moral knowledge.

In a recent paper, Elijah Chudnoff (2016) defends a view of conscious moral intuitions that does not rely on a thesis about high-level content in perception. In developing his view, Chudnoff appeals to a distinction between the content of perceptual experience and the object of perceptual awareness. As illustration, Chudnoff asks us to consider hearing a chime indicating that the oven is pre-heated to 450°F. The content of this perceptual experience is as of a chime, and perhaps that the oven is ready. The object of one's perceptual awareness is the chime, but not (directly) the interior of the oven. Now, Chudnoff argues that an experience that p can be the whole basis for knowing that p 'only if it both has p as part of its content and makes one aware of a truth-maker for p' (2016: 212). And he argues further that in cases of purported moral perception that one should ϕ, one's perceptual experience 'can be at most a partial basis for knowing that one should ϕ in that situation' (2016: 212). This is because the truth-maker for p will include objects of which one is not perceptually aware, 'such as that there is a prima facie duty of beneficence that isn't defeated by other features of the situation' (2016: 212).

Motivated by this argument, Chudnoff proposes that conscious experience makes us aware of the truth-makers for moral claims via a kind of collaboration between perception and conscious intuition. Consider a case in which an agent is confronted with a stranger in need of help, and suppose it is true that in this situation, the agent ought to help the stranger. In what Chudnoff calls *low-level intuitions*, an agent can have a perceptual-plus-intuitional experience that she is in a position to help, and that there is a prima facie duty of benevolence. The agent can become 'perceptually aware of a truth-maker for the proposition' that she is in a position to help, 'intuitively aware of a truth-maker for the proposition that there is a prima facie duty of benevolence', and 'perceptually aware of a truth-maker for the proposition that there are no, or at least no apparent, defeaters of the prima facie duty of benevolence' (2016: 216). This is because in low-level intuitions, 'you learn about concrete particulars by subsuming them under general truths' (2016: 216).

Importantly for Chudnoff, one need not possess background knowledge of or prior belief concerning the relevant general truths. The general truths themselves are presented as a part of the content of the intuition. And this feature of moral experience sometimes puts an agent in a position to know previously unknown moral truths, thereby enabling moral improvement.

experiences. Jennifer Church (2013) draws on her general account of the phenomenology of perception to argue that the relevant aspect depends on a kind of imagination.

[5] Intuitions considered in this way are usually thought of as possessing a kind of cognitive phenomenology. For discussion of cognitive phenomenology generally, see the chapters in Bayne and Montague (2011). For discussion of the phenomenology of intuitions more specifically, see Chudnoff (2013).

Chudnoff comments:

> [S]ometimes we see our immediate situation as both illustrating and illuminating moral reality itself. These are the moral perceptions that amount to low-level intuitions. And these are the moral perceptions that enable moral improvement. For when we confront moral reality itself, we can check our prior moral beliefs against how it is now presented to us. (Chudnoff 2016: 217)

Chudnoff's proposal offers us one way to develop a view of the epistemic significance of conscious experience that moves beyond perceptual experience alone.[6] In so doing, it affords a potential way around the looks objection. A proponent of what we might call moral experience, the thesis that at least some moral properties can be part of the contents of phenomenally conscious experience, can accept that there is no stable way morally right or wrongs acts or events perceptually look. Even so, she can maintain that intuition plus perception offers the kind of phenomenological clarity and stability perception alone lacks. Intuition fills a gap by evaluatively presenting the objects given by perception. On the view that emerges, it is not moral perception but evaluative phenomenology more generally that provides a route to moral knowledge.[7]

30.5 Moral Responsibility Redux

Let us return briefly to the relationship between consciousness and moral responsibility. As we saw above, some philosophers have argued that consciousness is not required for responsible behavior, and Levy has argued against these philosophers that a kind of access consciousness is in fact necessary. But we raised the possibility that phenomenal consciousness could be relevant as well. In this connection, the discussion is Section 30.4 reveals two ways one might develop a phenomenal consciousness/moral responsibility connection.

The first is fairly straightforward. If aspects of perceptual and intuitional experience put one in contact with one's reasons for action, then these experiences may play a role similar to the role Levy argues access consciousness plays. Namely, these states may enable reasons-responsive action. Whether this line is ultimately persuasive will depend on the reasons given for favoring phenomenal (as opposed to, or in addition to)

---

[6] For proposals that emphasize the epistemic significance of conscious emotions, see Kauppinen (2013), Cowan (2015).

[7] Such a view is bound to face objections. One obvious worry is this. Why think that phenomenal consciousness does any relevant work here? Arguably, the relevant work is done by the contents of mental states, or by reliable causal relationships between the environment and the subject's relevant perceptual and doxastic states (see, in particular, Lee 2014). We think the worry is worth taking very seriously, but have no space to do that here. For a view on the epistemology of perception that those sympathetic to this worry might like, see Burge (2003). For an alternative view that gives phenomenal consciousness a central role in the immediate justification of beliefs, see Silins (2011).

access consciousness with respect to the function of putting agents in contact with their reasons.

While the first route will likely appeal to so-called reasons-responsive theorists, the second draws on the so-called quality of will views of moral responsibility. In an influential article, Angela Smith argues that 'what makes an attitude "ours" in the sense relevant to questions of responsibility and moral assessment is not that we have voluntarily chosen it or that we have voluntary control over it, but that it reflects our own evaluative judgments or appraisals' (2005: 237). Smith herself does not emphasize phenomenal consciousness (indeed as Levy reads her she is an opponent of the importance of consciousness). Even so, implicit in Smith's case are certain patterns of conscious experiences a subject undergoes—what she notices (and fails to notice), the thoughts, evaluations, and emotions that occur to her as she interacts with others. One attracted to Smith's quality-of-will view might develop a connection with phenomenal consciousness as follows. Recall Siegel's argument that perceptual experiences can themselves redound to one's standing as a rational agent. Analogously, one might argue that an agent's moral experience—the moral properties presented in her perceptual plus intuitional states— redound to the agent's moral standing in such a way as to render her the apt target of morally reactive attitudes. Whether this line is ultimately persuasive will depend in part on the reasons given for taking the tokening of morally salient phenomenal states to redound in just this way.

Certainly the role of phenomenal consciousness in reasons-responsive accounts of responsibility, or in quality of will accounts requires further development to be deemed important to such accounts.[8] But given the evident connections between work on consciousness and moral knowledge and work on consciousness and moral responsibility, it seems developmental efforts in this direction will prove fruitful.

30.6 Conclusion

In conclusion, let us return to a question we broached in this chapter's introduction. We have discussed the potential importance of consciousness for moral status, moral knowledge, and moral responsibility. Is there anything about consciousness these connections share?

As most of the views we have discussed remain under dispute, we take it to be an open possibility that there is not. Nonetheless there is a thread running through this chapter that merits emphasis. In our discussion of moral status we appealed to phenomenal states that possessed intrinsic value, the most obvious of these being painful and pleasurable experiences. In our discussion of moral knowledge we appealed to perceptual/ intuitional/emotional phenomenal states that present aspects of the world as good or

---

[8] In connection with quality of will accounts, see Annas (2008), who develops a connection between patterns of experience and moral excellence in a virtue-theoretic direction.

bad, or as obligating or permitting courses of action. And in our discussion of moral responsibility we (all too briefly) considered views that might appeal to the epistemic and moral qualities of such states to undergird more traditional views of moral responsibility. One thing all of the above discussions share, then, is an appeal to phenomenal states that are broadly evaluative in nature. And this leads to the suggestion that it is evaluative phenomenology that is, in the first instance, intimately connected to morality.

This suggestion might afford insight into why—other than a perhaps unhealthy obsession with tidiness—one might care whether the connections between consciousness and morality share a common feature. If evaluative phenomenology is a key to understanding the relevance of consciousness to morality, then work on evaluative phenomenology emerges as important not only for the philosophy of mind, but for ethics as well. Ethicists may have reason to pay closer attention to phenomenology than they have hitherto done.

In this connection, however, readers will have noticed that an anti-phenomenalist thread runs through this chapter as well. In our discussion of moral status we considered the view that it is access consciousness rather than phenomenal consciousness that undergirds high degrees of moral status. In our discussion of moral responsibility we saw that one influential view in the region is Levy's which explicitly downgrades the importance of phenomenal consciousness in favor of functional aspects of cognition. And in our discussion of moral knowledge we noted problems not only for the thesis of moral perception, but also for views that would give phenomenal consciousness more broadly a central epistemic role.

With respect to the connections between consciousness and morality, there is little philosophical consensus. Even so, relationships between aspects of consciousness and aspects of morality appear to constitute fruitful and important areas for further research.

References

Annas, J. (2008), 'The Phenomenology of Virtue', *Phenomenology and the Cognitive Sciences*, 7/1: 21–34.
Arpaly, N. (2002), *Unprincipled Virtue: An Inquiry Into Moral Agency*. Oxford: Oxford University Press.
Audi, R. (2013), *Moral Perception*. Princeton. NJ: Princeton University Press.
Baars, B. J. (1997), *In the Theater of Consciousness*. New York: Oxford University Press.
Baars, B. J. (2002), 'The Conscious Access Hypothesis: Origins and Recent Evidence', *Trends in Cognitive Science*, 6: 47–52.
Bayne, T. (2009), 'Perception and the Reach of Phenomenal Content', *The Philosophical Quarterly*, 59/236: 385–404.
Bayne, T. (2013), 'Agency as a Marker of Consciousness', in T. Vierkant, J. Kiverstein, and A. Clark (eds), *Decomposing the Will*. Oxford: Oxford University Press.
Bayne, T. and Montague, M. (2011), *Cognitive Phenomenology*. Oxford: Oxford University Press.
Bayne, T., Hohwy, J., and Owen, A. M. (2016), 'Are There Levels of Consciousness?' *Trends in Cognitive Sciences*, 20/6: 405–13.
Bengson, J. (2015), 'The Intellectual Given', *Mind*, 124/495: 707–60.

Block, N. (1995), 'On a Confusion about the Function of Consciousness', *Behavioral and Brain Sciences*, 18: 227–87.
Burge, T. (2003), 'Perceptual Entitlement', *Philosophy and Phenomenological Research*, 67: 503–48.
Chudnoff, E. (2013), *Intuition*. Oxford: Oxford University Press.
Chudnoff, E. (2016), 'Moral Perception: High-level Perception or Low-level Intuition?' in T. Bryer and C. Gutland (eds), *Phenomenology of Thinking*. Abingdon: Routledge.
Church, J. (2013), *The Possibilities of Perception*. Oxford: Oxford University Press.
Cowan, R. (2015), 'Perceptual Intuitionism', *Philosophy and Phenomenological Research*, 90/1: 164–93.
Cullison, A. (2010), 'Moral Perception', *European Journal of Philosophy*, 18/2: 159–75.
Davies, W. and Levy, N. (2016), 'Persistent Vegetative State, Akinetic Mutism and Consciousness', in Walter Sinnott-Armstrong (ed.), *Finding Consciousness: The Neuroscience, Ethics, and Law of Severe Brain Damage*. Oxford: Oxford University Press.
Dehaene, D. and Naccache, L. (2001), 'Towards a Cognitive Neuroscience of Consciousness: Basic Evidence and a Workspace Framework', *Cognition*, 79: 1–37.
Dehaene, S., Changeux, J.-P., and Naccache, L. (2011), 'The Global Neuronal Workspace Model of Conscious Access: From Neuronal Architectures to Clinical Applications', S. Dehaene and Y. Christen (eds), *Characterizing Consciousness: From Cognition to the Clinic?* Berlin: Springer-Verlag, 55–84.
Feldman, F. (1997), 'On the Intrinsic Value of Pleasures', *Ethics*, 107/3: 448–66.
Fischer, J. M. and Ravizza, M. (1998), *Responsibility and Control: An Essay on Moral Responsibility*. Cambridge: Cambridge University Press.
Giacino, J. T., Ashwal, S., Childs, N., Cranford, R., Jennett, B., Katz, D. I., Kelly, J. P., Rosenberg, J. H., Whyte, J. O. H. N., Zafonte, R. D. and Zasler, N. D. (2002), 'The minimally conscious state: definition and diagnostic criteria', *Neurology*, 58/3: 49–353.
Goldstein, I. (1989), 'Pleasure and Pain: Unconditional, Intrinsic Values', *Philosophy and Phenomenological Research*, 50/2: 255–76.
Gomes, A., Parrott, M., and Shepherd, J. (2016), 'More Dead than Dead? Attributing Mentality to Vegetative State Patients', *Philosophical Psychology*, 29/1: 84–95.
Haier, R. J., Siegel, B. V., MacLachlan, A., Soderling, E., Lottenberg, S., and Buchsbaum, M. S. (1992), 'Regional Glucose Metabolic Changes After Learning a Complex Visuospatial/Motor Task: A Positron Emission Tomographic Study', *Brain Research*, 570: 134–43.
Huemer, M. (2001), *Skepticism and the Veil of Perception*. Lanham, MD: Rowman & Littlefield.
Kahane, G. (2009), 'Pain, dislike and experience', *Utilitas*, 21/3: 327–36.
Kahane, G. and Savulescu, J. (2009), 'Brain-Damage and the Moral Significance of Consciousness', *The Journal of Medicine and Philosophy*, 34: 6–26.
Kauppinen, A. (2013), 'A Humean Theory of Moral Intuition', *Canadian Journal of Philosophy*, 43/3: 360–81.
Lee, G. (2014), 'Materialism and The Epistemic Significance of Consciousness', in U. Kriegel (ed.), *Current Controversies in Philosophy of Mind*. Abingdon: Routledge.
Levy, N. (2014a), *Consciousness and Moral Responsibility*. Oxford: Oxford University Press.
Levy, N. (2014b), 'The Value of Consciousness', *Journal of Consciousness Studies*, 21: 127–38.
Levy, N. and Savulescu, J. (2009), 'The Moral Significance of Phenomenal Consciousness', *Progress in Brain Research*, 117: 361–70.
Lyons, J. (2005), 'Perceptual Belief and Nonexperiential Looks', *Philosophical Perspectives*, 19/1: 237–56.

McBrayer, J. P. (2010), 'A Limited Defense of Moral Perception', i *Philosophical Studies*, 149/3: 305-20.
McGrath, S. (2004), 'Moral Knowledge by Perception', *Philosophical Perspectives*, 18/1: 209-28.
Mele, A. R. (2009), *Effective Intentions: The Power of Conscious Will*. Oxford: Oxford University Press.
Monti, M. M., Vanhaudenhuyse, A., Coleman, M. R., Boly, M., Pickard, J. D., Tshibanda, L., Owen, A. M., and Laureys, S. (2010), 'Willful Modulation of Brain Activity in Disorders of Consciousness', *New England Journal of Medicine*, 362: 579-89.
Owen, A. M., Coleman, M. R., Boly, M., Davis, M. H., Laureys, S., and Pickard, J. D. (2006), 'Detecting Awareness in the Vegetative State', *Science*, 5792: 1402.
Pryor, J. (2000), 'The Skeptic and The Dogmatist', *Noûs*, 34/4: 517-49.
Rachels, S. (2000), 'Is Unpleasantness Intrinsic to Unpleasant Experiences?' *Philosophical Studies*, 99/2: 187-210.
Raichle, M. E., Fiez, J. A., Videen, T. O., MacLeod, A. M., Pardo, J. V., Fox, P. T., and Petersen, S. E. (1994), 'Practice-related Changes in Human Brain Functional Anatomy During Nonmotor Learning', *Cerebral Cortex*, 4: 8-26.
Rosenthal, D. (2002), 'Explaining Consciousness', in D. Chalmers (ed.), *Philosophy of Mind: Classical and Contemporary Readings*, Oxford: Oxford University Press.
Rowlands, M. (2012), *Can Animals Be Moral?* Oxford: Oxford University Press.
Seager W. (2001), 'Consciousness, Value and Fuctionalism' *Psyche* 7/so. <http://www.theassc.org/files/assc/2510.pdf>
Sebo, J. (2015), 'Agency and Moral Status', *Journal of Moral Philosophy*, 14/1: 1-22.
Shepherd, J. (2015), 'Scientific Challenges to Free Will and Moral Responsibility', in *Philosophy Compass*, 10/3: 197-207.
Shepherd, J. (2016), 'Moral Conflict in the Minimally Conscious State', in Walter Sinnott-Armstrong (ed.), *Finding Consciousness: The Neuroscience, Ethics, and Law of Severe Brain Damage*. Oxford: Oxford University Press.
Shepherd, J. (2017), 'The Moral Insignificance of Self-Consciousness', *European Journal of Philosophy*, 25/2, 398-415.
Sher, G. (2009), *Who Knew? Responsibility Without Awareness*. New York: Oxford University Press.
Siegel, S. (2015), 'Epistemic Charge', *Proceedings of the Aristotelian Society*, 115/3: 277-306.
Siewert, C. (1998), *The Significance of Consciousness*. Princeton, NJ: Princeton University Press.
Silins, N. (2011), 'Seeing Through the "Veil of Perception"', *Mind*, 120/478: 329-67.
Singer, P. (2011), *Practical Ethics*, 3rd edn. Cambridge: Cambridge University Press.
Sinnott-Armstrong, W. and Miller, F. G. (2013), 'What Makes Killing Wrong?' *Journal of Medical Ethics*, 39: 3-7.
Smith, A. (2005), 'Responsibility for Attitudes: Activity and Passivity in Mental Life', *Ethics*, 115: 236-71.
Soon, C. S., Brass, M., Heinze, H.-J., and Haynes, J.-D. (2008), 'Unconscious Determinants of Free Decisions in the Human Brain', *Nature Neuroscience*, 11: 543-45.
Sripada, C. (2015), 'Acting from The Gut: Responsibility without Awareness', *Journal of Consciousness Studies*, 22/7-8: 37-48.
Suhler, C. L. and Churchland, P. (2009), 'Control: Conscious and Otherwise', *Trends in Cognitive Science*, 13: 341-7.

Tye, M. (1995), *Ten Problems of Consciousness: A Representational Theory of the Phenomenal Mind*. Cambridge, MA: MIT Press.

Varner, G. E. (2012), *Personhood, Ethics, and Animal Cognition: Situating Animals in Hare's Two-Level Utilitarianism*. Oxford: Oxford University Press.

Werner, P. (2016), 'Moral Perception and the Contents of Experience', *Journal of Moral Philosophy*, 13/3: 294–317.

CHAPTER 31

EMBODIED CONSCIOUSNESS

MARK ROWLANDS

31.1 INTRODUCTION: EMBODIMENT AND THE TWO BODIES

LIKE many of the most interesting questions, the question of whether consciousness is embodied can mean so many different things that it is genuinely difficult to know where to start. And when I don't know where to start I generally like to go with bombast, and the sorts of ambitious claims I'm not entirely sure I'll be able to back up. So here we go. I shall argue that the question of whether consciousness is embodied has been vitiated—to the point of making it largely nonsensical—by a failure to ask a more basic, and when you think about it blindingly obvious, question: what is the body? Often, the reason a blindingly obvious question is not asked is because the answer is, similarly, blindingly obvious. This may seem like such a question. We all know what the body is. The body is an organization, of nerve, and sinew, muscle, blood, and bone, etc. The body is what you see when you look in the mirror, see into when you are inserted into an MRI. Except it is not. Or so I shall argue. This is only one version of the body. The body that you see in the mirror, or the parts of this body—the hands, for example, that you see in front of you when, in George Edward Moore style, you prove the existence of the external world—these are only one version of the body. These are only one way the body might be. The body in the mirror, the hands that you hold up in front of you, these are instances of the body as *object*. But the body is more than the body as object. There is also the body as *subject*; the body as *lived*.

You cannot see the lived body by looking in the mirror. The body as lived is that in virtue of which you see the body as object (and many other things also, of course). Furthermore, I shall argue, there is no question concerning whether consciousness is embodied in the lived body. Consciousness *is* the lived body; they are one and the same thing. The body as object, on the other hand, there is not a trace of consciousness in it.

The burden of this chapter is to render defensible these seemingly incredible—at least, I assume they will seem incredible to many—claims. Whether or not this is so, I am not the author of these claims. All these claims have been made by others, most notably others who occupy prominent positions in the phenomenological tradition. Given the oeuvre of this publication—a volume on the philosophy of consciousness rather than German and French phenomenology—I hereby promise to keep issues of textual interpretation to an absolute minimum. But, let me reiterate, I make no claim to originality vis-à-vis these claims, and the relative dearth of explicit discussion of the ideas of Husserl, Sartre, and others should in no way be taken to indicate otherwise. Before we get to the crazy stuff, however, let me begin with a survey of perhaps more familiar terrain.

31.2 Embodiment/embodiment

Even if we forget the lived body for now, and focus on the more traditional understanding of the body as object, the claim that consciousness is embodied could mean several things, all of which have some right to the title of *embodied*. A useful way of at least beginning to organize the possibilities is by availing ourselves of a fourfold distinction that was originally developed in the context of cognition rather than consciousness:

4E Cognition: cognitive processes are *embodied*,[1] *embedded*, *enacted* and/or *extended*.

The claim that cognition is embodied has, accordingly, been understood in two ways, one broader than the other. First, there is the broad sense of embodiment—'embodiment' with a little 'e'. To claim that a cognitive process is embodied is to claim that it is located somewhere on this spectrum of possibilities—that it is embodied, embedded, enacted, or extended, or some combination of these. Each of these 'E's can, in turn, be understood in a variety of ways. The following characterizations are, therefore, rough: merely conveying a sense of the sort of thing (some) people have mind when they talk of one or more of the *Es*.

The idea of *embedding* is a good place to start (Vygotsky 1978; Vygotsky and Luria 1993).[2] A cognitive process is *embedded* if it functions, perhaps has been designed to function, in tandem with a surrounding, environmental scaffolding, such that without the presence of this scaffolding the process will fail to do what it is supposed to do, or be less likely to achieve what it is supposed to achieve, or do what it is supposed to do in a less than maximally efficient way, etc. The external scaffolding carries information pertinent to the cognitive task that the process is designed to accomplish, and a cognizing

---

[1] Or, rather, 'Embodied'. See later in this section.
[2] Although he never employed the terms of 'embedding' or 'scaffolding', the idea of embedding grew out of the work of Vygotsky, and in particular his idea of the *zone of proximal development*. The idea of scaffolding was later taken up by Jerome Bruner, among others.

organism can, by manipulating or exploiting the scaffolding in an appropriate way, avail itself of this information. The net result is that at least some of the difficulty of the cognitive task is offloaded onto the world. The required intra-cranial processing is not as sophisticated as it would have needed to be if there was no environmental scaffolding around. Think of the difference between doing long division in your head or doing it with a pen and paper (Rumelhart et al. 1986), or think how much easier it is to do a jigsaw puzzle when you are allowed to pick up and manipulate the pieces (Kirsh and Maglio 1994). These external structures—written symbols, jigsaw pieces—provide a form of scaffolding that reduces the complexity of the required internal processing. The idea of embedding, in itself, does not challenge the idea that cognition is located inside the skull. It is just that the mind is revealed as being deeply, perhaps essentially, dependent on things outside of it for proper functioning.[3]

Once we have the idea of embedding, the idea of *extended* cognition is easily understood.[4] Take the basic idea of embedding, and convert it from a claim of dependence to a claim of *constitution*. It is not simply that the mind is dependent on external scaffolding. Rather, when an organism, in the performance of a cognitive task, manipulates structures in its environment, in order to avail itself of information they contain, this manipulation is *part* of its cognitive processing. Cognitive processes, in this sense, *extend* out into operations an organism performs on appropriate structures in its environment. These operations are partly constitutive of the cognitive processes rather than being extraneous scaffolding.

A mental process is *enacted* if it involves, or is constituted by, a dynamic, interactive coupling of processes occurring inside the skin or skull of an organism and processes external to said skin or skull. For example, when I see a visual scene, I do not need to construct all the detail of this scene internally, in the form of a mental representation. Rather, I avail myself of the complexity of the scene itself. I can direct my attention, at will, to any part of the scene, and low-level attention-grabbing mechanisms will automatically direct my attention to any changes in the scene. Instead of being grounded in a detailed visual representation, my seeing comprises dynamic, coupled interactions with the external scene itself.[5] Of course, dynamic, coupled interactions with environmental

---

[3] For this reason, those opposed to the general 4E vision of cognition hold up the idea of embedding as a sort of fifth column—which allows one to deflect the force of arguments for embodied, enacted, or extended cognition. Such arguments, they claim, only establish that cognition is embedded, and thus we can hold on to the Cartesian vision of the mind as contained inside the head. To suppose otherwise is to confuse coupling and constitution. See Rupert (2004) and Adams and Aizawa (2008) for versions of this strategy. In my view, this strategy overlooks the fact that even embedding underwrites a profoundly anti-Cartesian conception of cognition. Or, as Georg Theiner once quipped (in conversation), embedding is one for our side, not theirs.

[4] For versions of the extended view, see Donald (1991), Rowlands (1995, 1999), Clark (1997), Clark and Chalmers (1998), Hurley (1998), and Menary (2007, 2012). This peculiarly process-oriented way of expressing the idea of extended cognition is from Rowlands (2010). For opposition to the extended view see Rupert (2004), Adams and Aizawa (2008).

[5] For classic statements of this view, see O'Regan and Noë (2001) and Noë (2004). Note that the absence of a *detailed* representation is not necessarily the absence of a representation.

structures are also central to the idea of extended mental processes. There might be a good explanation of this: the two views are essentially the same. I suspect this is the case.[6]

Consciousness can be embodied with a small 'e' in either one of these three ways. It might be embedded in that it depends on some sort of extrinsic scaffolding to do what it does (whatever that is). It might be enacted in the sense that it depends on tightly coupled, dynamic interactions with the environment. It might be extended in that it is partly constituted by processes performed on the environment by a conscious subject. Consciousness might be 'embodied' be any of these senses, but I do not (here) claim that it is.

Now we have the idea of embodiment with a small 'e', we can think of embodiment with a big 'E' as meaning embodied (i.e. 'Embodied') *as opposed to* embedded, enacted, or extended. This, itself, can be understood in at least two ways. On the one hand, it might mean, as Prinz (2009: 420) puts it, that the process '*depends* on possession and use of a body, not just a brain'. But, of course, much then depends on how we understand 'depends'. Understood as *causal dependence*, the Embodiment thesis turns out to be something like a bodily scaffolding or *embedding* thesis—the scaffolding here *is* the body, or some part or aspect thereof, rather than something outside the body. Understood as a claim of *constitution*, on the other hand, the idea is that processes occurring inside the body, but outside the brain, can be parts or components of mental processes. For example, in processing visual depth information, the (human) brain deploys disparity information from two eyes. Were there fewer than two eyes, or more than two eyes, the processes in the brain that compute depth from disparity would require revision. As Shapiro (2004: 191) puts it: 'Human vision requires a human body.' On the dependence interpretation—which in this case, admittedly, does appear more plausible—the number of, and distance between, the eyes is external (i.e., external to the brain but not, of course, to the bodily) scaffolding that the brain employs to reduce computational demands. On the constitution interpretation, on the other hand, the number of, and distance between, the eyes is part of the computational process whereby the brain processes visual depth information.

There is another way of understanding the idea of Embodiment. As Prinz (2009: 421) puts it: 'Embodied mental capacities are ones that depend on mental representations or processes that relate to the body. Such representations and processes come in two forms: there are representations and processes that represent or respond to the body, such as a perception of bodily movement, and there are representations and processes that affect the body, such as motor commands.' Thus, on this view, a mental process would count as Embodied if it involves, for example, a representation located in the motor cortex, even though the motor cortex is intracranial.

---

[6] Although, see my evil alter ego, Rowlands (2009), for a dissenting view. By the time of Rowlands (2010), my good side had managed to regain control of my body. I suspect my alter ego's point is valid to this extent: whether enactivism and extended mind are the same view all depends on which aspects of enactivism you choose to emphasize.

Embodiment, embeddedness, enactedness, and extendedness are four nominally distinct ideas. The logical relations each view bears to the others, whether one view collapses into another, and so on are crucially dependent on how each view is interpreted. There has, however, been one significant attempt to drive a wedge between at least two of these views. In an influential paper, Andy Clark (2008) argues that Embodiment and extendedness should be kept sharply apart. The basic case for extended mind, Clark thinks, is going to be grounded in functionalism. A mental state or process is defined by *what* it does—its functional role. It does not matter *what* performs the role, *how* it does this, and, crucially for his version of extended cognition, *where* it does this. Following Shapiro, however, Clark also accepts that the principal rationale for thinking of mental processes as Embodied is going to lie in a rejection of functionalism—especially of the liberal sort that is required for extended cognition.[7] Therefore, the considerations that would lead us to an extended view are incompatible with the considerations that would lead us to an Embodied view. The two views must, therefore, be sharply distinguished. Later on, I shall argue against this.

These four positions—Embodiment, embedding, enaction, and extension—were ones initially developed in connection with cognition rather than consciousness. However, they are all on the table as possible ways of understanding the claim that consciousness is embodied—whether with a small 'e' or a big 'E'. The sense of consciousness in question is *phenomenal consciousness*: what it is like to have an experience, or the ways things seem or feel to you when you have an experience. Such consciousness might be embodied (with a small 'e') because is dependent on or constituted by external scaffolding, or because it consists by way of a dynamic transactive coupling between brain and wider environment, or because it consists, in part, of operations performed by a conscious organism on the world around it. Or consciousness might be Embodied—with a big 'E'—in the sense that it depends on, or is partly constituted by, bodily structures that lie outside the brain, or is dependent on, or constituted by, mental representations that relate to the body.

There are further complications. Even if we narrow down the idea of embodiment to one of these claims, there are further decisions to be made. We can understand the claim of embodiment as a necessary or contingent claim. We can understand it as applying to all conscious states or only some conscious states, and so on. We can understand an embodiment as a claim about the existence of a conscious state: some form of embodiment (with a small 'e') is required for a conscious state to exist. Or we can understand it as claim about the character or content of the state: the facts of embodiment play a role in determining the conscious character or content of the state.

Exploration of these possibilities is ongoing in the literature, and it would not be possible to reiterate these explorations in a chapter of this length. Therefore, I am going

---

[7] A form of functionalism is *liberal* if it claims we can characterize these roles in rather broad strokes. For example, if we define a belief as a state that interacts with perception, action, and other mental states to produce behavior then we are embracing a form of liberal functionalism. If we insist on more details—a more fine-grained specification of the functional role—then our functionalism is more *chauvinistic*.

to change tack, and consider a question that, in comparison, has been largely ignored. When we make a claim of embodiment—with either a small 'e' or big 'E'—what, precisely, is the body in which consciousness is supposed to be incarnated?

31.3 Intentionality as Revealing Activity

Consciousness is *often*—some say *always*, and I am inclined to agree, but do not need to make this assumption—intentional. Given that this is so, the argument I am going to develop comes in two stages. First, I shall develop and defend an account of intentionality as *revealing* or *disclosing* activity.[8] Second, I shall examine the notion of the body, and argue that it, too, is revealing or disclosing activity. The body, understood in the way I shall advocate, is intentional directedness towards the world. The 'is', here, should be taken as the 'is' of identity. One further assumption gets us to the claim that consciousness is embodied: intentional directedness is the essence of consciousness. This *intentionalist* or *representationalist* theory of consciousness is not to everyone's tastes. But I happen to believe it is true and will assume, rather than defend, it here. If you do not endorse this assumption, you should take this chapter to be arguing for an identification of the body with intentional directedness—which I take it is radical enough to be going on with.

To make sense of the idea that the body is the same thing as consciousness (or intentional directedness if you prefer), we must distinguish two very different senses of the body. One sense of the body is far more prevalent in philosophical and scientific discussions of embodiment. Curiously, body in the other sense plays a far more prominent role in daily life. Most of the time—unless one is, as we say, pathologically self-conscious—our bodies conform to this second sense of body rather than the one assumed in philosophical and scientific literature.

I shall begin the argument at a place whose relevance to the issue of embodied consciousness is, I shall freely admit, not immediately obvious: Frege's struggles to clarify his notion of *sense* (*Sinn*). As many commentators have noted, there is a pronounced tension in Frege's account. He attributes two distinct roles to *senses* or *thoughts* (*Gedanken*)—where a thought is the sense of a declarative sentence. On the one hand, Frege claims that senses can be objects of mental acts in a way akin—although not

---

[8] I develop this account in much more detail in Rowlands (2010, 2015a, 2015b). Sartre briefly suggests something like this view, early on in *Being and Nothingness* (1943: 23) 'To say that consciousness is consciousness *of* something means that for consciousness there is no being outside of that precise obligation to be a *revealing intuition* of something—i.e. of a transcendent being.' The word 'intuition', in Sartre's hands, is equivalent to 'conscious experience'—although, he would regard the qualifier 'conscious' as redundant—and the notion of *revealing* is, according to Sartre, definitive of any such experience. For conscious experience to be intentional—for consciousness to be consciousness of something—is for it to be a form of *revelation*. This is the idea I am going to develop.

identical—to that in which physical objects can be the objects of mental acts (Harnish 2000). Physical objects can be perceived; senses or thoughts (that is, the sense of a declarative sentence) can be *apprehended*. When we understand a declarative sentence, we do so by apprehending a thought. Moreover, when a thought is apprehended, Frege claims, 'something in consciousness must be *aimed at* the thought' (Frege 1919/1994, 34–5). In one of its guises, therefore, a sense is an intentional object of an act of apprehension.

However, according to Frege, senses also have the role of fixing reference. Although senses can be objects of reference, that is not their only, or even typical, role. In its second guise, the function of sense is to direct the speaker's or hearer's thinking not to the sense itself but to the object picked out by that sense. In this case, senses do not figure as intentional objects of mental acts, but as items *in virtue of which* a mental act can have an intentional object. In their customary role, senses are *determinants* of reference: they are what fix reference rather than objects of apprehension.

The tension between these two conceptions of sense lies in the fact that sense cannot play both roles simultaneously. This inability shows itself in a certain *non-eliminability* that attaches to sense in its reference-determining role. In its first guise, a sense is an object of apprehension: an intentional object of a mental act. But the second characterization of sense tells us that whenever there is an intentional object of a mental act, there is also a sense that fixes reference to this object. If we combine these characterizations, therefore, it seems we must conclude that whenever sense exists as an intentional object of a mental act of apprehension, there must, in that act, be another sense that allows it to exist in this way. (And if this latter sense were also to exist as an intentional object of a mental act, there would have to be yet another sense that allowed it to do so). Sense in its reference-determining guise, therefore, has a non-eliminable status within any intentional act. In any intentional act, there is always a sense that is not, and in that act cannot be, an intentional object.

This idea is not merely an artifact of Frege's theory. One also finds it in early phenomenology, in particular in Husserl's attempts to make sense of what, in the *Logical Investigations*, he called *Auffasungsinn*, and later, in *Ideas*, had evolved into the distinction between *noesis* and *noema*.[9] This ambiguity, and resulting tension, is, in fact, a product of a standard way of thinking about intentionality. According to this, intentionality has a tripartite structure, comprising *act*, *object*, and *mode of presentation*. In this model, mode of presentation functions analogously to Fregean sense, and is ambiguous in exactly the same way.

On the one hand, modes of presentation are often taken to be identical with the *aspects* of objects. If I see a tomato as red and shiny then an act (seeing) is directed towards an object (a tomato) and this object falls under a certain mode of presentation (red and shiny). Mode of presentation in this sense is, or can be, an intentional object of my seeing (thinking, etc.). I can, for example, redirect my attention from the tomato to its red and shiny luster. Thus, understood in this way, a mode of presentation is the sort of thing

---

[9] See Rowlands (2010: ch 7), for discussion.

that can be an object of an intentional act—and will be the object of an intentional act if my attention is suitably engaged.

In this standard model of intentionality, however, a mode of presentation is also assigned another role: that of *connecting* act and object. It does this by specifying certain conditions that something must meet in order to qualify as the intentional object of the act. The intentional object of the act is whatever meets these conditions (if we assume the conditions are uniquely specifying—whatever *objects* meet these conditions if not). For example, on a familiar (but non-obligatory) description-theoretic version of this model, the object of an intentional act is whatever object satisfies a given description. The description provides a set of conditions that the object must meet in order to qualify as the object of the intentional act. In this capacity, the mode of presentation functions to direct an act towards an object, and thus corresponds to Fregean sense in its reference-fixing capacity.

A mode of presentation, therefore, functions in two different ways. On the one hand, there is what we might call an *empirical mode of presentation* (EMOP). An EMOP is the way an object appears to a subject and is, therefore, an actual or potential object of intentional directedness—the sort of thing of which I might become aware if my attention is suitably engaged. On the other hand, there is what we might call a *transcendental mode of presentation* (TMOP).[10] A TMOP is that which connects mental act and intentional object of that act. Since it does this by specifying a set of conditions an item must meet in order to qualify as such an object, this means that TMOP reveals the item as falling under certain aspects. That is, a TMOP—a mode of presentation in its transcendental role—is that aspect of the intentional act in virtue of which an object is presented as falling under a specific EMOP. If I see a tomato as red and shiny, then there is some aspect of my act of seeing in virtue of which I see it in this way. This is the act's TMOP—its transcendental mode of presentation.

A TMOP is defined by what it does. Beyond that, it is difficult to say much about it. Transcendental modes of presentation are *inexpressible*, for the same reason that Frege's notion of sense in its reference-fixing capacity is inexpressible. Consider, for example, a picture of the relation between sense and reference, advanced by John Searle (1958), which invites us to think of sense as a *route* to reference. Searle asks us to think of sense as like a tube through which a ball may pass and drop into a bucket. The bucket is the referent, the pipe is sense, and the ball is the intentional act. The problem, as Michael Dummett (1973) points out, is that this makes sense and reference unduly independent of each other. One might rearrange the pipe so that it drops into a different bucket, for example. Instead of thinking of sense as a route to reference, Dummett advises us to think of sense as a *manner of presenting* a referent. Thus, as Dummett (1973: 227) puts it: 'even when Frege is purporting to give the sense of a word or symbol, what he actually *states* is

---

[10] The terms 'empirical' and 'transcendental', quite obviously, have a Kantian heritage. I am not using the latter term in quite the same way as Kant. Kant tended to think of the transcendental as necessary conditions—'conditions of possibility'—of a given phenomenon. I think of transcendental as sufficient conditions. That is, if a mental act has a certain transcendental mode of presentation, that is sufficient for an object to have, or fall under, a certain empirical mode of presentation.

what its reference is'. Sense, in its reference-fixing capacity, is something that can be *shown* but not *said*. The only way we can indicate sense in its reference-fixing (i.e., transcendental) capacity is by describing the referent in a certain way. By doing this, we *show* what the corresponding, reference-fixing sense is. Similarly, and for precisely the same reason, the only way we can indicate a TMOP is by *showing* it—and we do this by describing the intentional object of the act in terms of its EMOP.

The distinction between EMOPS and TMOPS—inspired by the ambiguity in Frege's concept of sense—supplies us with a general picture of what intentionality is. If we want to understand intentional directedness we will, of course, look in vain to the objects of such directedness—objects *simpliciter*, and the EMOPS under which they fall.[11] Rather, intentional directedness is that in virtue of which objects fall, or are presented, under EMOPS. That is, the intentional directedness of a mental act is that feature of the act in virtue of which an object is revealed or disclosed—presented—as falling under an empirical mode of presentation (or aspect). Intentional directedness is, in this sense, revealing or disclosing activity.[12]

31.4 THE BODY AS OBJECT AND THE BODY AS LIVED

The idea that intentional directedness is revealing or disclosing activity provides the first step in the argument. The second step is to argue that the body is also revealing activity. To make this intelligible, let alone plausible, it is necessary to make a distinction that is familiar to those in the phenomenological tradition but less so to those outside. The distinction is between what Husserl called *Leib* and *Körper*. Sartre, in whose work the distinction receives particularly powerful expression, preferred talking of the body *pour-soi* (for-itself) and the body *en-soi* (in itself). We might call it the distinction between the *body as lived* and the *body as object*.

Sometimes I experience my body as an object. This happens when I look in the mirror. If I look at my hands, I experience them as objects. If I turn my attention to my sore ribs, these ribs (and their soreness) are also objects of my intentional act of attending. In such cases, my body or some part or aspect thereof, is an intentional object—an object of an intentional act such as seeing, attending, or recognizing (or, in other cases, thinking, believing, wishing, etc.). One and the same body can be the object of many intentional acts: the body that I see in a mirror is a body that might be seen by another person. However, most of the time I experience neither my body nor parts of my body

---

[11] EMOPS, remember, are also (actual or potential) objects of consciousness.
[12] More precisely: every instance of intentional directedness is an instance of revealing activity. I need take no stand on the converse dependency. I defend this account in much more detail in Rowlands (2010). See also Rowlands (2015a, 2015b).

as objects of my intentional acts. I am aware of my body, its parts and aspects, in a quite different way.

Suppose I walk into a room, in advance of a meeting that will, almost certainly, prove lengthy. I see the ideal chair—both empty and unobtrusive—tucked away in the corner of the room, where I can remain unnoticed and not be asked any awkward questions. In such circumstances, I may notice little else about this chair—its color, its construction, and so on may all escape my notice. What I do notice are two salient facts: it is empty and it is unobtrusive. The reason I notice these properties of the chair and not others is because I have a goal or desire: I want to find a seat where I can sit, undisturbed, for the length of the meeting. The way I experience the world—at least, this little part of the world that is a chair—is a function of this goal or desire. Equivalently, we can put this in the language of revealing: the chair is *revealed* to me in a certain way *in virtue of* my goal or desire.

However, it is not simply the goal or desire that is relevant to how the chair is revealed to me. Because the chair is empty, it—as James Gibson would have put it—*affords* sitting. That is what I latch onto when I pick out this particular chair: its sit-ability. But that the chair affords sitting depends on my having a body of a certain sort. If I were 12 inches tall, or twelve feet tall, or if had four legs, it would not afford sitting. The chair is revealed to me as being sit-able but this sit-ability of the chair depends on my having a body of a certain sort. Similarly, the weakness in my legs after a long run is why I see the settee as especially inviting. This weakness reveals the settee *as* inviting. And when I see the TV remote as being 'out of reach' this assumes I don't have the extendable arms of the sort possessed by Mr Fantastic of the Fantastic Four. At least part of the way in which we experience the world is a function of our bodies: of its abilities and its limitations, its strengths and its weaknesses.

The lived body is not an intentional object of my awareness. Rather, in such cases, my awareness of my lived body consists in my awareness of *other* things (a chair, for example) *as* being a certain way (in this case, as sit-able). My lived body is that in virtue of which things in the world are revealed as being thus-and-so—that is, a something in virtue of which such things are subsumed under certain modes of presentation rather than others.

This sort of awareness one has of one's lived body is quite distinct from proprioceptive awareness. In proprioception, I am aware of the orientation (and disposition) of my body and its various segments. Proprioception is inwardly directed bodily awareness, and the neurophysiological mechanisms that underwrite it (muscle spindles, intrafusal fibers, sensor nerve fibers, and so on) are well understood. Awareness of the lived body, in contrast, is a form of exteroception rather than proprioception: I am aware of my lived body through, or in virtue of, being aware of other things (i.e., things that are not my body) *as* being a certain way. Or, rather, my awareness of my body consists in my awareness of something else—something that is not my body—as being a certain way.

Put in general terms, the lived body is that in virtue of which the world is revealed or disclosed as being a certain way. But, the intentional directedness of a mental act is that feature of the act in virtue of which an object is subsumed under some given mode of presentation rather than others—and is, thus, disclosed as being one way rather than another. The 'is', in both cases, is the 'is' of identity or constitution rather than the 'is' of predication. Therefore, the lived body must be identified with intentional directedness towards the world. At their core, both intentional directedness and the lived body are revealing or disclosing activity.

One further premise—mentioned earlier—is required to get from this identification of the lived body with intentional directedness to the identification of the lived body with consciousness. This assumption is central to the phenomenological tradition: consciousness *is*—again, an 'is' of identity—intentional directedness. The assumption is also quite popular outside the tradition, particularly amongst the sort of *representationalist* view of consciousness that thinks that phenomenal character is a species of, or is exhausted by, representational content. On this view, what it is like to have or undergo a conscious experience reduces to the representational properties of that experience. If these conditions are met—if intentionality is revealing activity, and the lived body is also revealing activity, and consciousness is essentially intentional—the lived body and consciousness can be counted as one and the same thing: revealing activity.

31.5 Extended Consciousness

Clark (2008) envisages a fairly sharp distinction between the claim that consciousness is embodied and the claim that it is extended—which he regards as distinct and mutually incompatible views. This is because extended views are grounded in a form of functionalism that embodied views are likely to reject. However, in the case of the body as lived, there is no important distinction between the embodiment and extension of consciousness. Consciousness is extended for the same reason it is embodied. Consciousness is revealing activity, and this revealing activity can consist not only in things done by the body but also can stretch beyond the body into the world.

Consider, for example, a blind person's use of a cane (Merleau-Ponty 1962). A blind person uses a cane to navigate his way around the world. There are two stories we can tell of the cane and the body to which it is attached. The first of these treats the body–cane coupling as an *object*, and there is a perfectly legitimate story one can tell about this object. The general contours of the story are familiar. When the cane strikes an object, vibrations will travel up it to the blind person's hand. Tactile and kinesthetic sensors in the hands then transmit messages to the brain. Various events then occur in the person's sensory cortex, and these events are interpreted as the result of ambient objects standing in certain relations to the person's location. There is nothing wrong with this sort of story. But it is limited: it describes the body–cane coupling from the outside, as an object. There is another story, the story of the body–cane coupling as lived.

According to this latter story (Rowlands 2010: 196ff), the operations performed by the body–cane coupling—various probings of the person's immediate environment—reveal or disclose objects. The activities of the body–cane coupling—in conjunction, of course, with the relevant neural machinery—reveal the world as, say, containing an object of such and such dimensions immediately in front of the person, and another object of slightly smaller dimensions to the person's left, and so on. These objects are revealed as falling under certain modes of presentation—being in front of, being on the left-hand side of, being approximately 3 feet wide, and so on.[13]

Intentional directedness is, I have argued, revealing activity. But revealing activity is not confined to processes going on in the brain. Admittedly, not much revealing activity will get done without a brain, but the activity itself often straddles neural processes, wider bodily processes, and operations that an intentional subject performs on the world around it. The blind person's revealing activity straddles processes going on in his brain, the processes that occur in his body as a result of his cane striking ambient objects, the activity of moving the cane to bring it into contact with those objects, and the things that happen in the cane as a result of this.

The body as object is a thing. But revealing activity is a process—a process akin to exploration. And like any such process, revealing activity need have no precise spatial and temporal boundaries. But it is not, in general, brain-bound activity. Thus, as far as the lived body is concerned, there is no important difference between the idea that consciousness is embodied and the idea that it is extended. Intentional directedness is revealing activity and this can straddle bodies and the operations bodies perform on the world around them.

The idea of revealing activity also helps unify extended and enactivist accounts of consciousness. When an enactivist account emphasizes how a subject is able to direct its attention at will to various parts of the visual scene, and thus avail herself of the richness and complexity of that scene (see O'Regan and Noë 2001; Noë 2004), this can be understood in terms of revealing activity. Directing one's attention at will to various part of the visual scene, and indeed having one's attention automatically drawn by low-level visual transient detectors, is part of the activity whereby the world is presented as being a certain way. But the same story of revealing activity is also applicable to extended accounts. Clark and Chalmers (1998) famously describe the case of Otto, a patient with early stage Alzheimer's, who writes down information in a book that he subsequently uses when the situation calls for it. Clark and Chalmers argue that the sentences in Otto's notebook should be numbered among Otto's beliefs (on the grounds that they share the same functional profile as his ordinary, neurally-based, beliefs). I do not think this is quite the right way of thinking about Otto—I would resist their identification of beliefs and sentences.[14] But I do think the process of Otto's remembering can be understood as, in

---

[13] Compare Sartre (1943/57: 426): 'This is why my body always extends across the tool which it utilizes; it is at the end of the cane on which I lean and against the earth; it is at the end of the telescope which shows me the stars; it is on the chair, in the whole house; for it is my adaptation to these tools...the body is perpetually the *surpassed*. The Body as a sensible center of reference is that *beyond* which I am in so far as I am immediately present to the glass or to the table or to the distant tree that I perceive. Perception, in fact, can be accommodated only at the very place where the object is perceived and without distance.'

[14] I would eschew the identification of the sentence with one of Otto's belief, and thus reject a widespread interpretation of what the case of Otto shows. There are many good reasons to resist the identification of

part, constituted by things Otto does to and with his notebook. This is because Otto's manipulation of his notebook can also be understood in terms of revealing activity. When Otto flicks through the pages of his notebook, scanning each page, until he arrives at the relevant sentence, this is also revealing activity—part of the activity whereby the world is revealed as containing a Museum of Modern Art on 53rd Street. When we switch from the body as object to the body as lived—and think of the latter in terms of revealing activity—both extended and enacted accounts of the mental are shown to be versions of the same general idea.

31.6 Embodiment and the Hard Problem of Consciousness

The *hard problem* of consciousness is the problem of understanding how the brain produces or constitutes consciousness (Chalmers 1995). Electro-chemical activity in the brain simply seems to be the wrong sort of thing to produce the glorious, multi-hued, multi-textured phenomenology of consciousness. We know, or strongly suspect, that the brain does it, but we cannot understand how. The whole business seems faintly miraculous (McGinn 1989, 1991).

Some proponents of embodied consciousness think it can solve, or at least make progress in solving, this hard problem. O'Regan and Noë, for example, write: 'Our claim, simply put, is this: there is no explanatory gap because there is nothing answering to the theorist's notion of qualia. That is, we reject the conception of experience that is presupposed by the problem of the explanatory gap' (2001: 962). This claim is, however, contestable. The invocation of qualia is merely one way in which the hard problem may be developed or expressed, but far from the only way (Rowlands 2002). Whether or not attempts to solve the hard problem in embodied terms ultimately prove to be successful, the approach to the problem suggested by the idea of the lived body, and its identification with consciousness, suggests an interesting alternative—one that veers in the direction of a dissolution rather than a solution of the problem.

If we take seriously the idea that the lived body and consciousness are one and the same thing—revealing activity—then the hard problem, as traditionally conceived, may be a problem, and it may be hard, but it has nothing to do with consciousness. The hard problem is set up in a certain way. First there is a given object of consciousness: experience, in all its splendid phenomenology, is something of which I am aware when I turn my attention inwards. Second, there is another object of awareness—neural activity, understood as the sort of thing I might become aware of if I had, say, an fMRI handy. The problem is that these two actual or potential objects of consciousness are so

---

sentence with belief, not least the fact that the intentionality of any sentence is derived not original. In the context of the arguments developed in this chapter, based so heavily on the idea of intentionality, rejection of the identification of sentence and belief is practically obligatory.

seemingly different—disparate—that we cannot understand how the one is produced or constituted by the other.

From the perspective defended in this chapter, the problem of consciousness looks somewhat different—and, in fact, not really a problem at all.[15] The body-as-lived is the same thing as consciousness: both are revealing activity. Therefore, there is no question of having to unite consciousness and the lived body, or understanding how the latter produces the former. Consciousness and the lived body are simply one and the same thing.

The hard problem is typically understood as the problem of understanding how the body-as-object—more precisely, the brain-as-object—produces consciousness, also understood as an object of awareness.[16] The brain is perceived in various ways, for example, in an MRI. Consciousness is also thought of as an intentional object of mental acts—something of which I become aware when I turn my attention inwards. The problem is, then, of understanding how the former can produce or constitute the latter when they seem to be essentially different. The hard problem of consciousness, in other words, is a problem that concerns consciousness as object of awareness—rather than the lived consciousness that is identical with revealing activity.

One further premise is required to yield the conclusion that the hard problem, as traditionally conceived, is not a problem that pertains to consciousness: consciousness exists *only* as lived. Any object of consciousness—whether outer object of inner state or process—is not part of consciousness. This is a prominent theme in the phenomenological tradition, and underwrites, for example, Sartre's seemingly incredible characterization of consciousness as *nothingness*.[17] I have discussed, and provided a partial defense of, this claim elsewhere (Rowlands 2001, 2003, 2015c), and constraints of space do not permit me to reiterate this here.

Assume, for a moment, all this is true. Then there is good news and bad news. The good news: there is no hard problem of consciousness, as standardly conceived. Consciousness exists only as lived revealing activity, and as such is identical with the body as lived. All that other stuff—objects of awareness such as the brain-as-object, experiences and their felt qualities understood as objects of awareness—have nothing whatsoever to do with consciousness. Therefore, there is no hard problem of consciousness.

Unfortunately—and this is the bad news—there may be something equally as bad, or possibly much worse.[18] This would be a problem of understanding how intentional

---

[15] Compare Sartre: 'These difficulties [in understanding the relationship between consciousness and the body] all stem from the fact that I try to unite my consciousness not with *my* body but with the body *of others*. In fact the body that I have just described is not *my* body such as it is *for me*..' (1943/57: 404).

[16] As Sartre puts it: 'The problem of the body and its relations with consciousness is often obscured by the fact that while the body is from the start posited as a certain *thing* having its own laws and capable of being defined from the outside, consciousness is then reached by the type of inner intuition which is peculiar to it' (1943: 401).

[17] Sartre provides a clear statement of the view I have in mind here: 'We cannot continue to confuse the ontological levels... being-for-itself must be wholly body and it must be wholly consciousness: it cannot be *united* with a body. Similarly, being-for-others is wholly body; there are no "psychic phenomena" there to be united with the body' (1943: 404).

[18] See Rowlands (2001, 2003) for a development of this theme.

directedness arises from actual or potential objects of such directedness. If there is such a thing as intentional directedness—if this is real feature of the world—then it seems it must arise from matter. But to understand how this happens would require understanding how something that is not, and cannot be, an actual or potential object of intentional directedness can arise from something that is such an object. From the phenomenological perspective, this is, in effect, a problem of understanding how nothing could come from something. And like the converse problem that troubled the Pre-Socratics, it is unlikely to be the sort of thing that has a solution.[19]

REFERENCES

Adams, F. and Aizawa, K. (2008), *The Bounds of Cognition*. New York: Wiley.
Clark, A. (2007), *Being There: Putting Brain, Body and World Back Together Again*. Cambridge, MA: MIT Press.
Clark, A. (1997), *Being There: Putting Brain, Body and World Together Again*. Cambridge, MA: MIT Press.
Clark, A. (2008), 'Pressing the flesh: a tension in the study of the embodied, embedded mind', *Philosophy and Phenomenological Research*, 76: 37–59.
Clark, A. and Chalmers, D. (1998), 'The extended mind', *Analysis*, 58: 7–19.
Chalmers, D. (1995), 'Facing up to the problem of consciousness', *Journal of Consciousness Studies*, 2: 200–19.
Donald, M. (1991), *Origins of the Modern Mind*. Cambridge, MA: Harvard University Press.
Dretske, F. (1988), *Explaining Behavior*. Cambridge, MA: MIT Press.
Dummett, M. (1973), *Frege's Philosophy of Language*. London: Duckworth.
Frege, G. (1919/1994), 'The thought: a logical inquiry', in R. Harnish (ed.), *Basic Topics in the Philosophy of Language*. Englewood Cliffs, NJ: Prentice Hall.
Harnish, R. (2000), 'Grasping modes of presentation: Frege vs. Fodor and Schweizer', *Acta Analytica*, 15, 19–46.
Hurley, S. (1998), *Consciousness in Action*. (Cambridge, MA: Harvard University Press.
Kirsh, D. and Maglio, P. (1994), 'On distinguishing epistemic from pragmatic action', *Cognitive Science*, 18, 513–49.
McGinn, C. (1989), 'Can we solve the mind-body problem?' *Mind*, 98: 349–66.
McGinn, C. (1991), *The Problem of Consciousness*. Oxford: Blackwell.
Menary, R. (2007), *Cognitive Integration: Attacking the Bounds of Cognition*. Basingstoke: Palgrave-Macmillan.
Menary, R. (ed.), (2012), *The Extended Mind*. Cambridge, MA: MIT Press.
Merleau-Ponty, M. (1962), *The Phenomenology of Perception*. London: Routledge.
Noë, A. (2004), *Action in Perception*. Cambridge, MA: MIT Press.
O'Regan, K. and Noë, A. (2001), 'A sensorimotor account of vision and visual consciousness', *Behavioral and Brain Sciences*, 23: 939–73.
Prinz, J. (2009), 'Is conscious embodied?' In P. Robbins and. M. Aydede (eds), *Cambridge Handbook of Situated Cognition*. Cambridge: Cambridge University Press.

---

[19] I would like to thank Uriah Kriegel and two unnamed referees for Oxford University Press for very helpful comments on earlier versions of this chapter.

Rowlands, M. (1995), 'Against methodological solipsism: the ecological approach', *Philosophical Psychology*, 8: 5–24.

Rowlands, M. (1999), *The Body in Mind: Understanding Cognitive Processes*. Cambridge: Cambridge University Press.

Rowlands, M. (2001), *The Nature of Consciousness*. Cambridge: Cambridge University Press.

Rowlands, M. (2002), 'Two dogmas of consciousness', *Is the Visual World a Grand Illusion?* Special edition of *Journal of Consciousness Studies* 9, ed., A. Noë, 158–80.

Rowlands, M. (2003), 'Consciousness: the transcendentalist manifesto', *Phenomenology and the Cognitive Sciences*, 2: 205–221.

Rowlands, M. (2009), 'Enactivism and the extended mind', *Topoi*, 28: 53–62.

Rowlands, M. (2010), *The New Science of the Mind: From Extended Mind to Embodied Phenomenology*, Cambridge, MA: MIT Press.

Rowlands, M. (2015a), 'Bringing philosophy back: 4e Cognition and the argument from phenomenology' in D. Dahlstrom, A. Elpidorou, and W. Hopp (eds), *Philosophy of Mind and Phenomenology*, New York: Routledge, 310–26.

Rowlands, M. (2015b), 'Consciousness unbound', *Journal of Consciousness Studies*, 22: 34–51, special edition, *Consciousness Unbound*, ed. M. Silberstein and T. Chemero.

Rowlands, M. (2015c), 'Sartre on pre-reflective consciousness: the adverbial interpretation', in S. Migunes, G. Preyer, and C. Morando (eds), *Pre-Reflective Consciousness: Sartre and Contemporary Philosophy of Mind*. New York: Routledge 2015.

Rumelhart, D., McClelland, J., and the PDP Research Group (1986), *Parallel Distributed Processing* 3 vols. Cambridge, MA: MIT Press.

Rupert, R. (2004), 'Challenges to the hypothesis of extended cognition', *Journal of Philosophy*, 101: 389–428.

Sartre, J.-P. (1943/57), *Being and Nothingness*, trans. Hazel Barnes. London: Methuen.

Searle, J. (1958), 'Proper names', *Mind*, 67: 166–73.

Shapiro, L. (2004), *The Mind Incarnate*. Cambridge, MA: MIT Press.

Vygotsky, L. S. (1978), *Mind in Society: The Development of Higher Psychological Processes*, ed. M. Cole, V. John-Steiner, S. Scribner, and E. Souberman. Cambridge, MA: Harvard University Press.

Vygotsky, L. S. and Luria, A. R. (1993), *Studies on the History of Behavior: Ape, Primitive, and Child*, ed. J. Knox and V. Golod. New York: Psychology Press.

Index

A

access 11, 33–4, 44, 46, 91, 112, 117, 147–8, 154–7, 205, 210, 212, 239, 241, 245, 271, 280–2, 285, 312, 317, 348, 352–9, 362–8, 403, 406, 408, 414–18, 423, 433, 440, 443, 450, 453–5, 520–2, 525–8, 533, 550–1, 578, 580, 610–11, 616–33, 638, 645, 651, 654–5, 658, 661–3, 667–9
acquaintance 3, 20, 154, 300, 307, 309, 324–5, 352, 355, 402–3, 412, 414, 479–80, 487, 639, 641, 643
agency 4, 85–8, 93–5, 98–100, 122, 163–4, 168–72, 177–87, 326, 525–7, 541, 551, 556–7, 559, 608–9, 655, 659–63, 669, 671 *see also* phenomenology, agentive
Alter, T. 29, 34, 283, 303, 321, 324, 485, 489, 495
Aristotle 400, 439, 455, 467, 480
Armstrong, D.M. 16, 34, 47, 61, 336–7, 345–6, 371, 383–6, 405, 408, 422, 434, 442–3, 445, 455, 462, 479
attention 12, 40, 53–5, 74, 84, 114–16, 151, 179, 208, 213, 236–8, 242–5, 252–3, 355–6, 367, 418, 427, 499–516, 520–22, 525–35, 543, 547, 553, 628–30, 638, 655, 659, 675, 679–81, 684–6
attitudes 89, 116–18, 120, 146, 150, 154, 157, 162–3, 182, 213, 216, 273, 350, 444, 468–9, 561–4, 572–4, 579, 584, 603, 622, 628, 657, 668, 671
Audi, R. 601, 606, 664, 669
awareness 12, 88, 142, 147–8, 165, 167, 178–9, 182, 199, 236–41, 246, 252–3, 314–23, 443–7, 450–54, 459, 465–79, 502, 506–7, 511–12, 516, 531, 539, 591–2, 623–9, 660, 682, 685–6
  bodily 79, 82–8, 91–8
  inner 443, 450, 472–80, 641, 651

introspective 28, 45–6, 94, 522–5, 646
perceptual 27, 39–40, 45–7, 58, 66–71, 75–9, 111, 195–6, 238–9, 450, 600, 614, 618–20, 666
self- 14, 86, 154, 439–42, 447, 638–43, 646, 649–50

B

Baars, B. 233, 254, 500, 516, 649, 662
Balog, K. 281, 299, 360–1, 369
Bayne, T. 4, 33, 35, 50, 56–7, 61–2, 69, 74, 76, 80–1, 85, 98, 109, 119, 149, 155, 157–8, 160–3, 166–7, 174, 177–8, 184–5, 209–10, 212–13, 217, 220, 227–8, 408, 436, 541, 554, 583–5, 601, 606, 655–6, 665–6, 669
behaviorism 2, 13, 348–9, 362–3, 368–70
Bengson, J. 590, 597, 599, 606, 664, 669
Berkeley, G. 50, 62, 70, 267, 275, 328, 333–7, 341–2, 345–6, 435
Bermúdez, J.L. 88–9, 92, 95–6, 98, 100, 174, 184
binding 75–6, 80–1, 168–9, 224–6, 431, 474–5, 477, 518–19
blindsight 12, 104, 123, 155, 243, 247, 257, 259, 276, 323, 456, 506–7, 599–600, 624
Block, N.J. 10, 13, 21, 26, 33–4, 48, 57, 62, 64, 103, 119, 139–40, 147, 155, 160, 239, 245, 254, 256, 258, 351, 364–5, 369, 388, 403, 411, 413, 421, 427, 430–1, 434–6, 441, 446, 452–3, 455–8, 462, 467, 479, 481, 520, 526, 529, 532–3, 535–6, 550–1, 554, 563, 573, 581, 601, 606, 615, 627, 631, 654, 670
BonJour, L. 570, 581, 588–90, 594, 606
Bourget, D. 12, 433, 561–2, 564–6, 569, 571, 573, 575–82, 584
Braddon-Mitchell, D. 144, 146, 160, 384–6, 439, 455, 491, 495

Brentano, F. 164, 184, 212, 228, 467, 469, 480–1, 523, 536, 640, 653
Brewer, B. 60, 62, 409, 415–16, 434, 592, 606
Briscoe, R. 50, 54, 62, 179, 184, 242, 254, 545, 549, 552–3, 555
Brogaard, B. 12, 550, 555, 586, 589, 592–3, 597–601, 604–6, 608
Brown, R. 240–1, 254, 448, 451, 455–6
Burge, T. 58, 62, 71, 80, 162, 238, 254, 416–17, 435, 583, 667, 670
Byrne, A. 45, 48, 56–7, 62, 65, 129, 140, 408, 414, 422–3, 427, 431, 435, 440, 448, 455, 522–3, 536, 564, 573, 582, 589, 604

C

Campbell, J. 60, 62, 412, 415, 427, 435, 503, 516
Campbell, C.A. 182, 184, 540, 555
Campbell, K. 302, 324, 346, 371, 386
Carnap, R. 408–9, 417, 494–5
Carruthers, G. 94, 99, 165, 168–9, 184
Carruthers, P. 47, 64, 102, 120, 143–5, 147–9, 151, 154, 157–8, 160–1, 165, 354, 369, 442–3, 446, 455, 462, 479–80, 522–3, 536, 543, 555
Caston, V. 439, 455, 467, 480
categorical (basis/nature/properties) 154, 297, 302–6, 311–23, 327, 331–45, 532, 568
causal closure 15–17, 304, 310–11, 380
Chalmers, D.J. 10, 13, 26, 34, 48, 50, 60–2, 76, 80, 157, 161, 182, 209–10, 220, 228, 235, 254, 263, 266, 272, 275, 281, 283, 286, 288–90, 299, 302–3, 305, 307–8, 313–14, 317, 322–4, 329, 346, 351, 354, 369, 372–3, 386–8, 391–6, 403–4, 408, 427–9, 432–3, 435, 438, 441, 455, 484, 494–5, 538, 555, 563, 568, 570, 575, 582, 592, 606, 611, 631, 675, 684–5, 687
Churchland, P.S. 305, 324, 661, 671
Clark, A. 71–2, 76, 80, 179, 185, 444, 455, 545–7, 551, 555, 675, 677, 683–4, 687
Cleeremans, A. 249, 254, 366, 370, 611, 617, 633–4
cognitive closure 488, 495
Coleman, S. 6, 29, 34, 265, 292, 303–4, 307, 310–2, 314, 316–24, 462, 473, 475, 479–80
conceivability 34, 290, 307–10, 388–9, 404, 427

argument 302–3, 307–8, 322, 340, 388–92, 396–8, 485–8, 491
of zombies 28, 298, 322, 387–9, 394, 452–3
concepts 18–20, 25–7, 30–3, 71, 112–14, 118–21, 123, 140, 149, 159, 181, 209–10, 296–300, 308–9, 348, 350, 352–8, 362, 367–8, 384, 387, 389–93, 396–402, 409–11, 439, 443–4, 446, 456, 471, 487, 507, 521–5, 528, 536, 551, 556, 558, 577, 646, 650
of consciousness *see* consciousness, concept of
phenomenal 19–20, 24–35, 65, 140, 157, 281–2, 290, 299–300, 360, 389–91, 401–4, 581
conceptual analysis 34, 383, 386, 403, 473, 494–5, 583
consciousness
  animal 98, 153, 236, 244–7, 304–5, 310–14, 323, 446–7, 455, 480, 557, 659
  concept(ion) of 11, 103, 145, 362, 366–9, 457, 464, 481, 554
  evolution of 235, 362, 365, 369, 422–3, 443
  function of 13, 241, 251–4, 259, 368–9
  hard problem of 157, 327, 361, 368, 405, 423, 438–9, 452–4, 482–5, 488, 491–4, 685–6
  neural correlate(s) of 5–7, 12, 104, 227, 233–76, 339, 366–7, 426, 455–6, 536–7, 611, 631, 656, 660
  phenomenal 12, 33–4, 64, 103–4, 108, 110, 146–9, 155–7, 162, 211–13, 216, 239, 254, 270, 272, 326, 348, 351–2, 359–71, 375, 385, 388–90, 394–7, 423, 441–2, 455, 458, 460, 480–1, 520–1, 528–35, 560–5, 571–3, 577, 579, 581, 620, 624, 627, 637, 642–4, 649–50, 654–8, 661–4, 667–70
  philosophy of 1, 12, 315, 333, 345, 674, 678
  science of 1–5, 11–13, 27–8, 35, 99–101, 164–5, 171, 233–62, 267, 272–5, 280–5, 290, 302, 305–6, 348–52, 361–8, 423–5, 452, 454–5, 539, 545–6, 553–4, 610–2, 619, 629–31
  self- 88, 98, 456, 481, 637–45, 649–55, 659, 671
  unity of 4, 76, 80–1, 208–29, 327
co-consciousness 74–9, 180, 192–3, 196, 203–4, 213, 309, 647

content 14, 26, 46, 50–2, 54, 58, 60–5, 76, 82, 90, 95–6, 112, 129, 138–9, 143, 145, 147–8, 150, 152–7, 161–3, 180–2, 188–207, 212, 215, 219, 225, 234, 237–8, 241, 243–4, 314–15, 317, 319–20, 323, 334, 336, 339, 345, 354, 361, 370, 403, 406–9, 415, 417–18, 421, 430, 435–6, 440, 444, 449, 456, 461–76, 479, 502–3, 505, 508, 512, 521–3, 530, 532, 535, 546–7, 550–3, 555–6, 561–4, 567–80, 582–4, 587, 592, 597, 599, 601–4, 608–9, 611, 618–19, 622, 624–8, 630, 632, 637, 647, 665–7, 677, 683
   non-conceptual 96, 113–14, 121, 443, 597
   perceptual 50, 52, 62, 64–5, 68, 72, 76, 90, 129, 155, 187, 202, 204, 370, 539, 547–53, 555, 595, 607, 609, 624, 664–6
   phenomenal 50, 58, 61–3, 150, 152, 192, 212, 564, 572–5, 578, 625, 647, 665 see also intentionality, phenomenal
contrast, phenomenal 51–6, 63, 99, 150–2, 161–2, 210, 221, 576, 583, 664
Crane, T. 41, 46, 62, 573, 582
Crick, F. 233, 235, 237–8, 255

D

Dainton, B. 189–205, 210, 213, 228, 309, 325, 646–9, 651, 653
Damasio, A. 102, 120, 451, 455
Davies, M. 60, 62, 144, 161
Davidson, D. 16, 34, 588, 617
Dehaene, S. 187, 233, 237, 240, 242, 251–2, 254–5, 259, 364–5, 369, 452, 455, 662, 670
Dennett, D.C. 20, 34, 104, 120, 191, 196, 206, 239, 254, 348, 351–62, 365–6, 369, 455, 541, 555
Descartes 15–16, 85, 99, 102, 120, 126–8, 140, 351, 483, 495, 524–5, 568, 590–2, 594, 635, 640, 653, 675
dispositions/dispositional 6, 148, 157, 181, 301–4, 312–13, 316, 318, 322, 327, 331–2, 336–7, 347, 359, 363, 427, 431, 438, 443–4, 472, 520, 525, 526, 532, 567, 573–9, 604, 654, 661, 682
Dokic, J. 70, 80, 84, 90–4, 97, 99, 118, 120
Dretske, F.I. 44–7, 62, 104, 111, 134, 152, 405, 408, 422–3, 433, 435, 439, 441, 447–8, 455, 465, 480, 566, 573, 582, 592, 607, 638, 651, 687

dualism 6–12, 16, 18–24, 30–4, 262–3, 266–74, 277–305, 311, 318, 321, 325, 333, 336–9, 342–5, 378–9, 382, 387, 403, 430, 433, 455, 486–7
   interactionist 7, 9, 15
   naturalistic 7–9, 266–8, 272, 278, 284, 289
   property 7, 9, 277–8, 538, 554, 568
   substance 7, 9, 277

E

eliminativism 5–12, 266–7, 348–69, 486–7
embodiment 12, 85–6, 138, 342, 551, 558, 648, 652, 673–8, 683–8
emergence 29, 77, 210, 222–3, 235, 241, 256, 266–7, 317, 324
emergentism 303, 306–7, 310–13, 317–18, 324, 388
emotion 4, 17, 53, 67, 74, 81, 93, 102–23, 126, 151, 171–3, 180, 225, 255, 272, 323, 455, 520, 560, 584–5, 604–6, 609, 633, 636, 647–8, 655, 658, 667–8
epiphenomenalism 7, 9, 15–17, 27–30, 35, 187, 268, 294–300, 326, 378, 538–9, 545–8, 554, 660
explanation, reductive 35, 403, 433–4, 438–9, 449, 453, 484–5, 492, 648–9 see also reduction
explanatory gap 13, 16–26, 30, 32, 34–5, 157, 160, 162, 284, 286, 299–300, 308, 361, 381, 386–90, 397–404, 438, 452–5, 685
externalism 64, 377, 422–34, 436, 583, 606

F

Feigl, H. 16, 35, 301, 317, 325–6
Fish, W. 57, 62, 592, 601, 607
Flohr, H. 237, 255, 451, 455
fMRI 236, 240, 244–6, 251, 270, 280, 555, 557, 656, 685
Fodor, J. 144, 152, 154, 159, 161, 439, 456, 489, 495, 566–8, 582, 595, 607, 687
for-me-ness 218, 222, 239, 439, 457, 472, 635, 637, 641–51, 653 see also mineness
Frankish, K. 351, 354, 359–62, 369
Frith, C.D. 98, 167, 175, 185, 247, 255, 627, 632
functionalism 5, 140, 155, 322, 371–2, 384–5, 491, 593–4, 677, 683
functional role 10–11, 155, 173, 319, 384, 402, 563, 566–71, 580, 582, 593–4

G

Gallagher, S. 175, 185, 647, 651
Gennaro, R.J. 439, 443, 448, 456, 462, 471–3, 476, 480
Gertler, B. 6, 281, 296, 300, 459, 473, 480
Giustina, A. 212, 228
global workspace 147, 233–4, 239–42, 246, 249–50, 253–4, 452, 471, 662–3, 670
Goff, P. 6, 26, 29, 35, 152, 158, 161, 301–4, 307, 309–10, 313–14, 316, 322, 325
Goldman, A. 47, 63, 89, 100, 150, 154, 161, 280, 300, 445, 456, 592, 607
Goodale, M. 33, 35, 70, 78, 81, 179, 186, 233, 238, 250, 257, 539, 545–50, 552, 554–8
Graham, G. 150, 152, 161, 570, 582–3
Graziano, M. 362, 369, 509, 517–18
grounding 2, 4–5, 8, 10, 12–13, 152–3, 211–14, 223, 227–8, 266, 303, 307, 310, 312, 325, 328, 332, 394, 418, 430, 433, 565, 597, 663
Grush, R. 194, 206, 545, 556

H

Haggard, P. 83, 94, 109, 168, 175, 184–5, 187, 468, 480, 540, 543–5, 556
hard problem *see* consciousness, hard problem of
Harman, G. 40–1, 44, 63, 114, 120, 262, 272, 275, 450, 456, 566, 573, 582
Heil, J. 145, 149, 161, 302, 325–6
higher-order theory 7, 102, 120, 160, 240–1, 254, 257–8, 324, 438–57, 459–64, 472, 481, 643
Hill, C.S. 12, 212, 228, 529, 535–6
Hohwy, J. 234, 256, 264, 276, 669
Horgan, T.M. 150, 152, 157–8, 161, 172–3, 176–7, 181–2, 185, 408, 427–8, 432, 562–4, 575–6, 579–80, 582–4
Howell, R. 29, 35, 281, 300, 303, 325, 645–7, 652
Huemer, M. 269, 276, 293, 300, 590, 593, 602, 607, 609, 664, 670
Hume, D. 27, 39, 42, 50, 52, 63, 125, 128–31, 140–1, 164, 176, 185, 187, 189–90, 206, 309, 318, 325, 345–6, 392, 395, 435, 635–6, 652–3, 670
Hurley, S.L. 196, 206, 212–13, 228, 675, 687
Husserl, E. 206, 467, 674, 679, 681

I

idealism 7–10, 64, 265, 267–8, 328–47, 377
identity theory 293, 371, 383–4, 386
    see also physicalism, reductive
ignorance 7, 36, 290, 309, 323, 326, 346, 483–93
illusionism 348, 352, 354, 359–62, 368–70, 430, 434, 652
imagination 31, 36, 65, 68, 89, 91, 101, 109, 124–41, 271, 274, 316, 410, 659, 666
intentionalism 44–5, 50, 52, 61–2, 65, 67, 121–2, 155, 159, 435, 583–5, 678
intentionality 12, 14, 103, 105, 107, 109, 111, 117–18, 138, 152–3, 155–7, 161–3, 188, 435, 444, 459–60, 467, 480, 560–75, 578–81, 584–5, 608, 679–83, 685 *see also* content
    phenomenal 152, 161–3, 185, 435–6, 562–5, 571–2, 575–84 *see also* content, phenomenal
internalism 377, 413–14, 416, 425, 427–33, 606
introspection 2, 4, 12, 27–9, 32–4, 41, 44–9, 62, 79, 108, 145, 154, 157, 160, 162–3, 172–3, 182, 185, 195–6, 199–200, 202, 205, 210–11, 214, 219, 255, 258, 271, 274, 280–1, 285, 290, 292–3, 304, 351–8, 360–1, 363, 366, 383, 445–6, 470, 473, 480, 506, 520–5, 543–4, 561–2, 578, 580, 584, 590–1, 610, 616, 621, 625–34, 642
Irvine, E. 7, 266, 364, 366–9, 610–12, 614, 631–2

J

Jackson, F.C. 7, 20, 24, 26, 34–5, 41, 63, 72, 76, 80, 114, 120, 144, 146, 157, 160–1, 206, 264, 286–7, 300, 302, 318, 320–1, 325–6, 372–3, 376, 378–9, 384–6, 388, 391, 403, 412, 431, 435, 439, 455, 483–4, 491, 495, 538, 557, 575, 583, 600, 607
James, W. 83, 100, 102, 104–5, 111, 115–16, 120–2, 164, 173, 185, 190–1, 196–200, 206, 307, 315, 317–19, 325, 374, 386, 499, 517, 650, 652

K

Kant, I. 69, 71, 208, 212, 316, 328–42, 346, 583, 636, 652, 680
Kim, J. 294, 296, 300
Kind, A. 4, 43, 63, 91, 100–1, 124, 126, 129, 137, 141, 354, 369, 573, 583

Kirk, R. 148, 162, 318, 321–2, 322, 373, 386
Koch, C. 190, 204, 233, 235, 237–8, 241–2, 244–5, 252, 255–6, 259, 503, 506, 517–8, 536–7
Koksvik, O. 53, 63, 150, 152, 162, 210, 222, 228, 576, 583, 604, 606, 608
Koriat, A. 94, 100, 169, 179
Kriegel, U. 47–8, 50, 61, 63, 65–3, 68, 80, 131, 136–8, 141–2, 149–50, 152, 158, 162, 172–3, 176, 181, 185, 218, 228–9, 262, 274, 276, 315, 323, 325, 428, 430–1, 433, 435, 439, 447, 449, 456–7, 459, 462, 465–7, 471–7, 480–1, 495, 536, 561–2, 564, 566, 570, 574–5, 577, 580–4, 633, 637, 640, 670
Kripke, S. 35, 152, 162, 286, 300, 378, 386, 389, 393, 395, 404, 570, 575, 583

L

Lamme, V.A.F. 233, 239, 256, 259, 365, 370, 452, 456, 522, 536–7
Langton, R. 316, 325, 332, 346
Lau, H.C. 6, 167, 181, 185–6, 233, 236–7, 241–2, 244, 247–50, 252, 254, 256–8, 261–2, 276, 366, 370, 451, 456, 617–20, 627, 630, 632
Lee, G. 33, 35, 191, 194–7, 204–6, 667, 670
Leibniz, G.W. 212–14, 223–8, 261, 264, 267, 328, 333–7, 345–6, 386, 400, 402–3, 411, 567–8
Levine, J. 7, 10, 13, 17, 21, 26, 35, 151, 154, 157–8, 284, 286, 300, 354, 370, 381, 386–8, 390, 400–2, 404, 427, 434, 462, 467, 473, 475–6, 480
Levy, N. 12, 177, 184, 654, 656, 658, 662–3, 667–8, 670
Lewis, D.K. 16, 20, 35, 144, 162, 321–2, 325–6, 336–7, 346, 371, 386, 408–9, 417, 420, 435, 439, 456, 487, 490–2, 495, 570
Libet, B. 93, 100, 164–7, 171, 178, 184–5, 468, 480, 539–45, 554, 556–9, 659–60
Loar, B. 152, 162, 390, 404, 564, 575, 577, 583
Locke, J. 47, 63, 189–90, 200, 206, 316, 432, 439, 483, 495
Lockwood, M. 29, 35, 276, 301, 318, 323, 326
Logue, H. 416, 427, 435

Lycan, W.G. 45, 47, 63, 102, 104, 121, 180, 186, 240, 257, 378, 386, 442–5, 456, 459, 462, 480, 562, 564, 583
Lyons, J. 590, 593, 597, 599, 601, 608, 665, 670
Lyons, W. 108, 121, 145, 162

M

McClelland, T. 7, 57, 62–3, 158, 162, 316, 318–19, 326, 465, 473, 480–1, 641–2, 651
McDowell, J. 86, 89, 100, 589, 593, 608
McGinn, C. 17, 35, 60, 63129, 132–3, 138–9, 141, 316, 326, 482–3, 488, 495–6, 685, 687
McLaughlin, B. 306, 311, 326, 410, 429, 436
Mach, E. 315, 317–18, 326, 349, 370
Marcel, A. 103, 116, 121, 175, 178, 186, 615, 632
Martin, M. 45, 60, 63, 70, 80, 88, 96, 100, 114, 121, 592, 608
Masrour, F. 4, 57, 63, 212–13, 223, 227–8, 429, 436, 564, 583
materialism 13, 34–6, 65, 262, 266–74, 299, 302, 324, 326–7, 347, 371, 383, 386–404, 487–8, 538, 554 *see also* physicalism
  eliminative *see* eliminativism
Matthen, M. 71, 81, 84, 90–1, 100
Mehta, N. 45, 60–1, 64, 473, 481
Mele, A.R. 165–6, 186, 542, 544, 557, 660, 671
memory 11–2, 68, 94, 128–31, 136, 138, 141, 149, 191, 207, 236–9, 244–5, 249, 252, 255, 257, 259, 285, 351, 356–9, 369–70, 511, 517, 519–37, 536, 538, 603–4, 606, 608, 629, 633, 655, 659
Mendelovici, A. 12, 109, 113, 115, 121, 408, 428, 430, 433, 436, 560–7, 571, 573–85
Merleau-Ponty, M. 164, 176, 467, 683, 687
metacognition 83, 89, 94–5, 94–5, 98–9, 169–71, 174, 181, 184, 186, 243, 254–5, 257, 259, 276, 451, 456, 620, 627–33
Metzinger, T. 95, 100, 648–9, 651–2
Millikan, R.G. 111, 121, 152, 439, 456, 566, 584
Milner, D. 33, 35, 179, 186, 233, 238, 250, 257, 539, 545–6, 549–53, 555–9
mineness 101, 169, 175–81, 183, 481, 635–6, 641–2, 644, 649–50, 652 *see also* for-me-ness
misrepresentation 98, 148, 361, 413, 427, 447–51, 453, 463, 465, 476, 479–81, 584

Mole, C. 12, 179, 186, 499, 503, 513, 518, 545, 551, 558
monism 7–10, 15, 292, 314, 325, 328, 333, 335, 338
  Russellian 6, 28–30, 34–5, 267–8, 299, 301–4, 310–14, 324–5, 327, 333, 342, 496 *see also* panprotopsychism, panpsychism
  neutral 7–10, 27, 265, 313, 315, 317, 324, 327
Montague, M. 103, 109, 121, 149, 157, 160, 162, 564, 584
Moore, G.E. 40, 64, 151, 162, 379, 609, 673
Mylopoulos, M. 4, 88–9, 100, 168, 174, 177, 179, 181, 186–7
mysterianism 488–9, 495

N

Nagel, T. 17, 35, 103, 121, 140, 146, 162, 306, 317, 326, 374, 386, 441–2, 456, 483, 496, 538, 558, 560, 584
Nanay, B. 53, 57–8, 64, 91, 101, 179, 186
naturalism 305, 460, 468–9, 474, 478, 538, 566, 571
naturalization/naturalizing 62, 153, 186, 228, 346, 459–61, 466, 468–9, 472, 474, 476, 478–9, 566, 584
neuroscience 1–2, 5, 12, 102, 164, 171, 233–5, 242, 244, 250, 273, 280, 288–90, 302, 309, 311, 356, 358, 361, 371, 374–5, 385, 423, 425, 427–8, 452, 539, 546, 654, 659
Nida-Rümelin, M. 26, 35, 355, 370, 637, 652
Noë, A. 84, 91, 101, 234, 258, 502, 518, 675, 684–5, 687–8

O

O'Regan, J.K. 454, 456, 502, 518, 537, 675, 684–5, 687
O'Shaughnessy, B. 70, 81, 85, 101, 133, 141, 176, 186, 545, 558
Owen, A.M. 244, 255, 656, 669, 671
ownership 82–90, 95–101, 175, 186, 636–7, 644–5, 647, 649

P

panprotopsychism 303, 306, 311–24
panpsychism 28–9, 34, 265, 302–27, 374–5, 386
Papineau, D. 6, 18, 23, 31–2, 35, 295, 300, 311, 317, 400–1, 404, 410–12, 418–20, 436
pathologies 82, 87–8, 95, 97, 526, 648–50, 652, 678

Pautz, A. 7, 56, 60, 64, 153, 163, 408, 411, 419, 421, 425, 427–9, 431–2, 434, 436, 464, 570, 577, 584, 592, 608
Peacocke, C. 77, 81, 95, 101, 119, 121, 154, 163, 212, 228, 406, 410, 412–13, 418, 431, 436, 545, 558, 601, 608
Pelczar, M. 7, 193–4, 202, 205–6, 265, 276, 337, 347
perception 4, 17, 39, 42, 47–51, 61–82, 90, 97, 99–102, 108, 111–17, 120–2, 125, 128–43, 146, 152, 154–5, 166, 168–9, 175–6, 179–80, 183–4, 186–7, 190–8, 201–3, 205–6, 225, 233–60, 324, 344–7, 349, 360–1, 367, 369–70, 384, 415–16, 421–2, 434–8, 442–3, 446, 450–7, 462–3, 469, 475, 481, 500–4, 508–10, 516–18, 524–5, 528–31, 533–7, 543, 546–7, 550, 554–63, 567, 581, 586–633, 635–8, 655, 659, 662–72, 676–7, 684
  unconscious 48, 64, 253, 555, 610–15, 620–1, 625, 632–3, 638
Pereboom, D. 301, 316, 327, 361, 370
phenomenal contrast *see* contrast, phenomenal
phenomenology 4, 17, 23, 31–2, 34, 41–2, 51–7, 63–4, 66, 68, 70, 76–80, 82–98, 101, 103–18, 121, 125–7, 129–31, 133, 135–41, 146, 149–58, 161–88, 191, 193–4, 197, 199–201, 203–5, 208, 221, 238, 330–1, 334, 344, 362, 373, 383–4, 407, 412, 415, 420, 431, 439, 445, 456, 463–4, 467, 470, 472–4, 476–7, 479, 481, 520–1, 523, 529, 535, 548, 572–3, 576, 581, 583–6, 590, 593–600, 603–7, 614, 620, 640, 647, 649, 651–3, 664–7, 669, 674, 681, 683, 685
  agentive 85, 95, 161, 164–83, 185
    see also agency
  cognitive 5, 109, 119, 121, 127, 146, 149–58, 161–3, 581, 583, 585, 666
  presentational 407, 594, 603–7
Phillips, I. 48, 64, 190–3, 196–7, 201–2, 206–7, 239, 252, 258, 364, 370, 611, 613, 615, 633
physicalism 5–10, 12, 15–19, 22–33, 35, 264, 277–82, 286–98, 300–5, 308–9, 312–28, 332–3, 336–45, 371–85, 387, 404, 419, 436, 452, 454, 496, 568, 577 *see also* materialism
  a priori 7–10, 286, 318, 321, 371–80, 383–5
  a posteriori 7–10, 25–30, 35, 286, 373, 377–83, 387
  eliminativist *see* eliminativism

grounding 8, 430
nonreductive 8–10, 16, 300, 319
reductive 8–10, 434, 452, 454
Pitt, D. 12, 109, 145, 150–1, 154, 163, 251, 258, 563–4, 575–6, 580, 584
presence 635, 641, 645, 650
bodily 82–93, 98–100
perceptual 91, 101, 409–11, 414, 419
Price, H.H. 337, 347, 412, 420, 436
Price, R. 52–3, 56, 64, 114
Prinz, J. 50, 52–3, 56–7, 64, 67, 81, 111, 121, 145, 149, 151, 154, 157, 163, 173, 186, 361, 370, 500, 518, 525, 532, 536, 546, 550, 558, 636–7, 652, 676, 687
Pryor, J. 433, 436, 590, 593, 618, 664, 671
psychology 1–5, 12–13, 17, 31, 63–4, 103, 108, 121, 132, 146, 164, 166, 171, 185, 238 254, 280, 325, 352, 362–3, 370, 375–6, 451, 454, 500, 519, 523, 536, 539, 546, 607, 631, 654, 659
experimental 75, 439, 500, 503, 611, 618, 631
folk 161, 350, 355, 439, 441, 456, 544–5, 662
introspectionist 4, 145, 160, 162, 363, 631, 634
Putnam, H. 16, 35, 43, 64, 376, 386, 389, 393, 395, 404, 569–70, 572, 584

Q

qualia 13, 41–2, 45, 62, 65, 77–8, 120, 139, 153, 327–8, 340, 351–60, 369–70, 406, 409, 413–14, 422, 424, 431–2, 435, 453–4, 521, 583, 636, 685
Quine, W.V.O. 152, 163, 268, 276, 349, 370, 494, 496

R

Ratcliffe, M. 83, 101, 107, 121, 645, 652
reduction 11, 83, 86–90, 93, 96, 147, 162, 171–4, 192, 200, 202, 225, 279, 310, 313–14, 318–20, 328, 331–2, 334, 341, 386, 405, 422–34, 438, 454, 535, 566, 636, 647, 651, 683 see also explanation, reductive
reflexivity 439, 441–2, 461, 470, 474, 523–4, 637, 639, 641, 643, 646 see also self-representationalism
representation 7, 39, 44, 50–1, 62, 65, 90, 98, 100, 111, 114, 117, 147–9, 159, 166, 170, 173, 188, 193–5, 198, 201–2, 206, 210, 218, 238–41, 250–2, 254–5, 259, 334, 361–2, 368, 383, 395–6, 401, 405, 408–9, 413–14, 419–21, 423, 426–36, 438–9, 441–54, 456–7, 460, 467–81, 501, 508–9, 517–18, 520–1, 525–33, 535, 537, 549–53, 558, 561–3, 567–73, 575, 578–80, 582–4, 592–3, 630, 638, 665, 675–7
representationalism 35, 65, 67, 90, 186, 194–5, 384, 386, 405–10, 413–36, 443, 456, 460, 462–4, 487, 562–5, 567, 573, 580–5, 640, 678, 683
higher-order see higher-order theory
self- see self-representationalism
report 2, 33, 87–8, 90, 92, 95, 103–4, 131, 165–7, 170, 173, 178, 235–6, 238–43, 245–7, 249, 254, 257, 259, 280, 351, 353, 358, 362, 364–8, 383, 409, 440, 473, 506, 530, 540, 542–4, 546, 550–2, 558, 592, 600, 606, 611–28, 633–4, 645, 660
revelation 25–32, 72–3, 76–9, 116, 382, 586, 600, 605, 678–86
Robinson, H. 41, 64, 302, 327, 335, 345, 347
Roelofs, L. 211, 213, 228, 304, 309, 320, 327
Rosenthal, D. 47, 64, 102, 104, 122, 148, 163, 187, 218, 228, 233, 235, 237, 240–2, 244, 252, 257–9, 315, 319, 323, 327, 438–9, 442–51, 456–7, 459, 462–5, 468–9, 475, 481, 522–3, 537, 654, 671
Rowlands, M. 12, 642, 652, 659, 671, 673, 675–6, 678–9, 681, 683, 685–6, 688
Russell, B. 41, 64, 125, 132, 136, 141, 276, 292, 297, 300–2, 313, 315–19, 327, 342, 347, 406, 410, 412–14, 432–3, 436, 483, 488–9, 496, 591, 608 see also monism, Russellian
Ryle, G. 143, 363, 370

S

Sartre, J.-P. 125, 132–8, 141, 164, 186, 439, 456, 467, 480, 640, 652, 674, 678, 681, 684, 686, 688
Schellenberg, S. 61, 64–5, 592, 608
Scholl, B. 457, 535–6, 595, 601, 607–8
Schwenkler, J. 179, 184, 242, 254, 545, 549, 552–3, 555
Schwitzgebel, E. 154, 163, 354, 360, 370, 503, 518, 612
Seager, W.E. 304, 307, 310, 327, 441, 457, 459, 481, 562, 573, 584, 656, 671
Searle, J.R. 158–9, 163, 351, 370, 564, 570, 574, 584, 637, 652, 680, 688
Sebastián, M.A. 451, 457, 465, 475–6, 481

seemings 359, 361, 409–11, 414, 419, 586, 590, 592, 597–600, 606–8
Sellars, W. 317, 327, 588–9, 608
self 12, 67, 71, 83–4, 98, 173, 176–7, 182, 185, 444, 635–7, 639–53
self-consciousness *see* consciousness, self-
self-knowledge 12, 65, 99–100, 154, 163, 481, 536, 651
self-representationalism 7, 63, 218, 446, 449, 457–62, 465–71, 474–81 *see also* reflexivity
sensation 36, 52, 64, 67, 74, 78, 83–5, 88–92, 95–8, 114, 116, 126, 132, 142, 146, 151, 153–4, 181, 280, 294–6, 326, 330–3, 336–44, 357–8, 383–4, 412, 414, 435–6, 444, 448, 560, 586, 597–600, 633, 636
Shea, N. 33, 35, 618, 630, 633
Shepherd, J. 4, 12, 164–6, 173–5, 177, 179–80, 187, 548, 552–3, 559, 654, 656, 659–60, 670–1
Shoemaker, S. 47, 65, 235, 259, 427, 436
Siegel, S. 50–6, 64–5, 68–9, 77, 81, 150, 163, 179, 187, 535, 537, 589, 592, 595–7, 599, 601, 604, 609, 663–4, 668, 671
Siewert, C.P. 54, 65, 145, 151, 154, 163, 440, 457, 459, 469, 481, 564, 575–6, 584, 657, 671
Silins, N. 56, 65, 601–2, 609, 667, 671
Sligte, I. 239, 259, 365, 370, 522, 537
Smart, J.J.C. 16, 36, 273, 276, 299–300, 371, 383–4, 386, 487
Smith, A. 660–2, 668, 671
Smith, A.D. 46, 65, 71, 81, 416, 436
Smithies, D. 149, 163, 499, 518, 564, 573, 584–5, 593–4, 609, 633
Sober, E. 274, 276, 293, 300
Soteriou, M. 156, 163, 192–3, 207
Speaks, J. 44, 57, 60, 65, 69, 79, 81, 408, 414, 418, 421, 430, 436
Sperling, G. 364, 521, 529–33, 537
Stoljar, D. 7, 29, 36, 47, 65, 279, 292, 300, 316, 321, 327, 441–2, 457, 485–90, 492, 496
Strawson, G. 29, 36, 68, 81, 142, 151–2, 163, 182, 187, 191–2, 207, 301–2, 306, 318, 323, 327, 345, 347, 351, 370, 473, 481, 570, 574, 576, 585, 636–7, 640, 643, 651, 653

Strawson, P.F. 52, 65, 70–1, 78, 81
supervenience 8, 10, 27, 62, 266–7, 328–33, 337, 340–3, 379, 387–91, 394–6, 577–8, 657

T

Tappolet, C. 107, 113, 118, 122, 605, 619
Titchener, E. 4, 145, 363, 370, 547
transitivity principle 438–42, 446–54, 459–60, 464–8, 472–4, 478
transparency (of experience) 39–49, 63–5, 114–17, 121, 180, 197, 480, 536, 583, 645
Treisman, A.M. 76, 81, 500–2, 506, 517–19
Tye, M. 20, 36, 40–5, 48, 60–1, 65, 74, 79, 81, 113–15, 122, 141, 156–7, 163, 193–4, 197, 207, 210, 212–13, 217, 220, 229, 252, 259, 354, 370, 384, 386, 405, 408, 417, 422–5, 427, 433, 437, 448, 457, 573, 585, 592, 601, 619, 665, 672

V

Van Gulick, R. 448, 457, 462, 465, 471–6, 481, 643, 653
de Vignemont, F. 4, 79, 80, 89, 91–3, 95, 98–100

W

Wallhagen, M. 179, 187, 545, 551, 559
Watson, J.B. 2, 13, 363, 370
Watzl, S. 197, 207, 213, 229, 508, 518
Wegner, D.M. 166, 169, 171, 187, 539, 559
Weisberg, J. 7, 449, 451, 457, 462–3, 471–2, 475, 477, 481
Weiskrantz, L. 104, 123, 243, 247, 260, 370, 632
Wittgenstein, L. 100, 125, 132, 134, 140–1, 271, 353, 358, 363, 370, 485, 496, 583
Wu, W. 88, 95, 101, 179, 187, 242, 250, 260, 519, 545, 550–1, 558–9
Wundt, W. 509, 519, 631

Z

Zahavi, D. 12, 218, 229, 439, 447, 457, 467, 473, 481, 637, 640–5, 647, 650–3
Zeki, S. 550, 559, 624, 634
zombies 23, 25, 28–9, 119, 186–7, 286–93, 298, 308–10, 322–3, 325, 373, 379, 386–9, 391, 394–5, 452–4, 484–5, 493, 555, 558–9, 608, 638, 651

The manufacturer's authorised representative in the EU for product safety is
Oxford University Press España S.A. of el Parque Empresarial San Fernando de
Henares, Avenida de Castilla, 2 – 28830 Madrid (www.oup.es/en or product.
safety@oup.com). OUP España S.A. also acts as importer into Spain of products
made by the manufacturer.

www.ingramcontent.com/pod-product-compliance
Lightning Source LLC
Chambersburg PA
CBHW052348290825
31867CB00028B/1263